Commercial Injunctions

(formerly Mareva Injunctions and Anton Piller Relief)

Commercial Injunctions

(formerly Mareva Injunctions and Anton Piller Relief)

Fifth Edition

Steven Gee Q.C., M.A. (OXON.)
of the Middle Temple,
and of the New York Bar,
sometime of Brasenose College,
Oxford University, and standing junior
counsel to the Department of
Trade and Industry (ECGD)

Foreword to the Fifth Edition by
The Right Honourable Lord Hoffmann

Appendix A on New York Law and Federal Practice by
Jonathan Greenblatt,
Litigation Partner with
Shearman & Sterling, and
A.Benjamin Spencer,
a former Litigation Associate with Shearman &
Sterling and currently Assistant Professor of Law at the Univer-
sity of Richmond School of Law.

LONDON
Sweet & Maxwell
2004

© Steven Gee 2004

ISBN 978-0-421-83040-0

Published by
Sweet & Maxwell Limited of
100 Avenue Road, London NW3 3PF

Typeset by LBJ Typesetting Ltd of Kingsclere

Reprinted and bound in Great Britain by William Clowes Ltd, Beccles, Suffolk

Steven Gee has asserted his right under the Copyright, Designs and Patents
Act 1988 to be identified as the author of this work

A CIP catalogue record for this book is available from the British Library

ISBN 978-0-421-83040-0

9 780421 830400

Contents

"..Our law (like all others) consists of two parts, viz., of body and soul, the letter of the law is the body of the law, and the sense and reason of it is the soul *'quià ratio legis est anima legis'*. And the law may be resembled to a nut, which has a shell and a kernel within, the letter of the law represents the shell, and the sense of it the kernel. So you will receive no benefit by the law if you rely only upon the letter. . . ."

(Serjeant Plowden on the report of *Eyston v Studd* 2 Plowden's Reports 465).

Preface

The Preface to Meagher Gummow and Lehane's awesome 4th edition on *Equity* says that "those who assert that law and equity are fused should explain what they mean, how it happened and what follows from it". The injunction has come a long way from its equitable origins. Change in one part of the law naturally produces change elsewhere. It is like a living body. The study of the ways of the old Chancery courts is like embryology. It accounts for birth but excludes the changes which have led to the mature organism.

First, there have been the developments through the Common Law Procedure Act 1854, which extended the injunction to the common law courts, and then the Judicature Acts, to a remedy available from a single High Court, administering a single system of justice. In consequence the injunction has not been confined to situations where it had previously been granted before the Judicature Acts, but has had a new place carved out for it in an evolving single set of rules. There has been the challenge of integrating it with substantive rights. In commercial law examples are its availability to protect property rights, to enforce contractual rights, to assist in restitution of unjust enrichment, and its operation on transactions involving banks. No account of a substantive right is complete without the remedies which may be granted in support of it. The availability of an injunction is part of what defines the right itself.

Secondly, there has been the emergence of the Mareva injunction, and the developments in orders providing information so that claims can be brought and orders enforced, the jurisdictions to grant Norwich Pharmacal relief, orders ancillary to injunctions, and Anton Piller relief. If claims cannot be brought for lack of evidence or judgments are ineffective, there is no point in having access to the courts. This has also affected the positions of parties who control relevant information or assets. It has been a revolution in commercial litigation which has produced change elsewhere. There is now a complex code, mainly statutory, which has borrowed from these jurisdictions, for freezing assets in contemplation of confiscation of them as the proceeds of crime.

Thirdly, for cases not governed by the Brussels Convention or the Judgments Regulation, there is the anti-suit injunction. At its heart is the question of when is it acceptable for a court to take it into its own hands to order a person not to proceed before a foreign tribunal, notwithstanding civilised standards of respect for the sovereignty of other countries, and comity between nations. Like the Mareva jurisdiction, the anti-suit injunction cannot adequately be described in the terms used in *The Siskina*, of merely a remedy for the enforcement of, and ancillary to, a substantive right.

Fourthly, there has been the free standing interim relief jurisdictions, originally under the Brussels Convention, but now extended to support any court or arbitration tribunal anywhere in the world. These apply when the merits of the underlying case are not to be decided in England. They recognise that interim remedies should not be unavailable in England simply because the merits are to be decided elsewhere. If assets can be frozen in England or through English court orders, this can promote the doing of justice elsewhere in the world, in courts or tribunals which otherwise would be without the means to achieve a fair result.

This book is about the injunction as a living, integral part of commercial law and litigation.

It is dedicated to my family, to my parents, Dr and Mrs Sidney Gee who made it all possible, to my wife Meryll, and to my children, Alexander and Harry, who have had long days without me and who have in a magical way contributed to this endeavour.

Steven Gee Q.C.
June 2004

Acknowledgments

I would like to acknowledge the help and support provided by Philip Riches in gathering materials for this book. The Hon. Mr Justice Lawrence Collins commented on chapters 6 (Jurisdiction) and 14 (Anti-Suit Injunctions), and Professor Charles Debattista[1], Professor of Commercial Law at Southampton University, commented on chapter 15 (letters of credit, and performance bonds and guarantees).

I would also like to thank all those who gave me materials including David Malkoff and Aviva Zetler of S.Friedman & Co (Israel), Anthony Dessain of Bedell Christin (Jersey), Angus Foster and Ingrid Pierce of Walkers (Cayman Islands), and Andrew Jones QC and Colin McKie of Maples and Calder (Cayman Islands).

In addition I would like to thank Kathryn Swift (out of house editor), and those at Sweet and Maxwell: Catherine Redmond (senior editor) who took over from Kate Auer, Johanna Whelehan (in house editor) and the entire production and marketing team.

See also *www.commercialinjunctions.com*.

The Appendix on New York Law and Federal practice.

Jonathan Greenblatt[2] is a senior litigation partner of Shearman Sterling based in Washington and New York. He acted for the the Bank of China in a series of actions around the world to recover more than $43 million that had been diverted from China's foreign exchange reserves in a massive bank fraud, and is an expert in on lender liability, international arbitration, international insolvency and litigation practice. Benjamin Spencer[3] was at the London School of Economics and at Harvard University, on the Harvard Law Review, is a former Litigation Associate at Shearman Sterling. They have together written the appendix on New York Law and Federal practice.

The federal courts have the equity jurisdiction that was exercised by the English Court of Chancery at the time the Constitution was adopted and the Judiciary Act of 1789 was enacted, and in *Grupo Mexicano De Desarrollo S.A. v Alliance Bond Fund Inc*,[4] the Supreme Court, by a majority of 5 to 4, declined the invitation to introduce Mareva relief as an existing head of Federal equity jurisdiction. The appendix is an invaluable guide to what is available in the US to achieving freezing relief.

---

[1] (http://www.iml.soton.ac.uk/staff/cdebattista.html).
[2] (http://www.shearman.com/lawyers/partners/greenblatt.html).
[3] He is currently an Assistant Professor of Law at the University of Richmond School of Law.
[4] 527 U.S. 308.

Foreword to the Fifth Edition
by The Right Honourable
Lord Hoffmann

With this edition, the book and its subject have reached an age of sober maturity. The respectability of the subject is shown by the change of name from Mareva Injunctions and Anton Piller orders to Commercial Injunctions. The heroic days, in which Mr Laddie—not yet Laddie J. or even Laddie Q.C.—could invent a new remedy in an afternoon and have it named after the case in which it was first granted, are over. The commercial injunctions are now sanctioned by statute and regulated by the Civil Procedure Rules. A substantial jurisprudence has been built up around them both in England and the rest of the common law world.

Likewise, the book is now an established authority, regularly cited in England and abroad. As I pointed out in the foreword to the fourth edition, it owes its success to the energy and enthusiasm of the author, who seldom leaves any knotty point unconsidered or relevant authority uncited. The new edition shows that he has not been content to rest upon his laurels. One of the dangers of successful legal text books which pass through several editions is that the structure laid out in the beginning becomes choked with additions and footnotes which detract from the clarity of exposition. No such complaint can be made about this edition, in which many parts have been entirely recast to reflect developments in the law. It is therefore a pleasure for me to have another opportunity to commend it to the profession.

Lord Hoffmann

August 2004

Foreword to the Fourth Edition by The Right Honourable Lord Hoffmann

My first impression of Steven Gee was disconcerting. He was appearing as junior to Mr Nicholas Phillips QC in a case in the Court of Appeal about the sale of a ship. I was on the other side. The issue was whether the judge of the Commercial Court had jurisdiction to make an interlocutory order authorising a Queen's Bench Master to sign a notice of readiness (in Chinese, as it happened) on behalf of my clients. I was trying to persuade the court that this was going too far. But my argument was undermined when Mr Phillips produced a judgment of Sir George Jessel MR, which he said had been discovered by the researches of his junior, stating the jurisdiction in the widest possible terms. After that, there was no stopping the judges of the Court of Appeal. Mr Phillips despatched my appeal to the House of Lords with ease and fluency to the forensic boundary.

In retrospect, the episode was curiously prophetic. It revealed in our author all the qualities which show themselves in this book: energy, boundless enthusiasm for research and an eager interest in the inter-locutory process. The result is a work which deals comprehensively with a subject which did not exist before the mid-1970s and which probably represents the most remarkable example of judicial creativity in this century.

It is perhaps worth reflecting upon why the *Mareva* and *Anton Piller* jurisdictions sprang up as they did. English legal procedure was devised to enable disputes to be decided. The centrepiece of the system was the trial, that climactic and theatrical event for which all previous inter-locutory process was a preparation. In the 1960s, however, it became apparent that civil law remedies were inadequate to deal with cases in which there was often no serious dispute: the problem was simply the enforcement of the law against a party who was determined to evade it. An early symptom was the fashion for squatting in temporarily unoccupied houses which made it necessary to introduce a new summary procedure for eviction. The *Anton Piller* order was devised on behalf of the sound recording industry to provide a remedy against sellers of counterfeit and bootleg records. The *Mareva* was a response to the use of the one-ship company registered in Liberia with directors in Sark and a bank account in Zurich. The *Norwich Pharmacal* order could be used to try to penetrate the veil of secrecy behind which financial transactions had taken place. These developments created a new form of litigation. Instead of the interlocutory process being ancillary to a trial, it became in many cases an end it itself. Often it was extremely unlikely that the matter would come to trial at all. If the interlocutory orders were successful in securing the goods or freezing the assets, the defendant submitted to judgment and that was an end of the matter. The judge granting the orders, usually *ex parte*, acted more in the role of a *juge d'instruction*, controlling a privatised police inquiry, than the referee of traditional English justice. This represents a radical change of role and it is therefore not surprising that judges over the past 25 years have been feeling their way to an adequate system of rules and guidelines.

All the more necessary, therefore, to have a book such as this to keep one aware of the latest developments. Practitioners can turn to this book confident that few, if any, of the questions which may perplex them are not discussed and that all relevant authorities in the common law world have been mentioned. It is a remarkable achievement worthy of a remarkable new jurisdiction.

Lord Hoffmann

January 1998

Foreword to the Third Edition by The Right Honourable Lord Justice Saville

Mareva injunctions are based upon a simple notion; that justice requires the courts to take appropriate steps in appropriate cases to try and ensure that judgments are not rendered valueless by an unjustifiable dissipation of assets.

Anton Piller orders are based upon an equally simple notion; that justice also requires that our legal processes should not be subverted by the wilful destruction of evidence.

The difficulty lies in reconciling these simple notions with other aspects of justice.

Chief among these is what is commonly regarded as one of the most basic rules of justice of all; that courts or other decision making tribunals should give all the parties concerned a fair opportunity to present their respective cases and to answer those of their opponents, before making orders affecting the rights and obligations of those parties.

By their nature Mareva injunctions and Anton Piller orders might seem on the face of it to breach this basic rule, since their very effectiveness depends upon the court making orders imposing obligations on parties who have not been given that opportunity.

To my mind, however, such a view would be incorrect. *Audi alterem partem* is in truth not a basic rule of justice but a basic rule for the doing of justice. It is the means to that end, not an end in itself. Thus if the application of this basic rule will result in injustice, then it must give way to the extent necessary to do justice. Mareva injunctions and Anton Piller orders are examples of this happening in practice.

These principles are easy to state in the abstract. It is their application through the common law to the endless variety of situations that arise in the conduct of human affairs which has produced over the last twenty years a very substantial body indeed of case law on the subject. The law on Mareva injunctions and Anton Piller orders is now complex, with highly developed safeguards and other detailed checks and balances designed (as the result of experience) to try and ensure that by departing from the basic rule, justice rather than injustice is done.

In his Foreword to the previous edition, the Master of the Rolls described this book as a godsend to the prudent practitioner. I would say the same about this new edition. Steven Gee, despite the drawback of once working as my pupil, combines in a unique way his great practical experience as an advocate, with both the most meticulous research and the ability to express complicated matters in a simple, clear way. In my view this book is itself a major and essential contribution to our jurisprudence on the subject.

Mark Saville

London

April 1995

Table of Cases

Table of United States Cases

Table of Statutes

Table of Statutory Instruments

Table of Civil Procedure Rules

Chapter 1

The Evolution of Injunctions and Anton Piller relief

(1) What is an "injunction"?

Justice Story in his *Commentaries on Equity Jurisprudence* described a **1.001**
"writ of injunction" as a judicial process whereby a party is required to do
a particular thing, "according to the exigency of the writ".[1] The writs of
injunction were issued only[2] by the order and under the seal of courts of
equity. They might be issued before a decree as a restraint upon a party,
this was called a "remedial writ", or after decree, as a "judicial writ",
which was in the nature of an execution,[3] *e.g.* a writ commanding a party
to give up possession of land which was the subject of the decree. Of
remedial writs of injunction Eden writing in 1821 stated that[4] ". . . it
would indeed be difficult to enumerate" all the instances in which those
writs could be obtained, there were an "endless variety of cases".

These writs were not adapted to every case in which the court could
grant a remedy. Therefore the court of equity also granted orders in the
nature of writs of injunction. Breach of an order was a contempt of court
for which there could be imprisonment. Although these orders were not
enforced by means of a writ of injunction, the writs and the orders were
indiscriminately called "injunctions".[5]

Story classified the jurisdiction of a court of equity under three categories,[6] namely the "exclusive" jurisdiction, the "concurrent" jurisdiction
and the "auxiliary" jurisdiction.

---

[1] *Commentaries on Equity Jurisprudence* (13th ed., 1886) Vol. II, p. 178; see also *Kerr on Injunctions* (1st ed., 1867), p.11. The courts of common law were empowered by s.79 of the Common Law Procedure Act 1854 to grant injunctions in particular cases (see para.1.003) and there was also statutory power for them to grant injunctions in patent cases under 15 & 16 Vict. c.83.
[2] *Commentaries on Equity Jurisprudence* (13th ed., 1886) Vol. II, pp.183–184.
[3] *Eden on Injunctions* (1821) ch. I, pp.1–2.
[4] *ibid.*, ch. I, p.2.
[5] *ibid.*, ch. 14, p.290.
[6] R. P. Meagher, J. D. Heydon and M. J. Leeming, *Meagher, Gummow and Lehane's Equity: Doctrines and Remedies* (4th ed., 2002) pp.10–11.

1.002   The "exclusive" jurisdiction was where the claimant could not sue in any court other than a court of equity.[7] The "concurrent" jurisdiction included cases in which a claimant could sue either in a court of equity or in another court—a court of law or an ecclesiastical court, and could obtain from either court equivalent relief. An example was an action for an account.[8] It also included, as a second branch, cases in which the relief which could be obtained from the court of equity was altogether different from that which could be obtained from another court. For example, a court of equity could order specific performance of a contract and regularly did so for contracts relating to land, whereas the remedy for breach of contract in a common law court was damages. The "auxiliary" jurisdiction concerned cases in which the claimant sued on a right recognised by a court of law and the court of equity acted in aid of or in support of that right, *e.g.* to grant discovery, to prevent a multiplicity of suits or to prevent irreparable injury pending determination of the legal right, *e.g* by *quia timet* injunction.

Story's classification has been adopted by judges and writers but also has been vigorously criticised.[9] Another classification was that made by Lord Redesdale in his treatise on *Pleading*.[10] These classifications are helpful as a framework for seeing what cases were decided in equity, how they were decided and why, and thus as a route to understanding what equity was. In the case of injunctions, as Story himself pointed out,[11] they were available in each class. Thus restraining a breach of trust was in the "exclusive jurisdiction", restraining a breach of contract was within the second branch of the "concurrent" jurisdiction, and restraining enforcement of a judgment obtained in a common law court or an injunction granted *quia timet* was within the "auxiliary jurisdiction". This is unsurprising because an injunction is a remedy.

1.003   The classifications looked at the case law of equity as it stood in the 19th century and provided what was a logical framework for explaining the broad purposes which then informed the exercise of jurisdiction by the courts of equity. With the passing of the Judicature Acts came a single High Court which provided a final result for each case. The former limitations of the courts of common law and the Chancery courts, gave way to a single court, administering 'one stop' justice. It was a consequence of the change that the new court had to act by reference to a single set of governing principles. Instead of the jurist having to search for the law in what could be done in two different courts, judgments laid down a single

---

[7] For example, for breach of trust or in respect of an exclusively equitable right.
[8] An action of account lay at common law, but the procedure in Chancery was so superior that by the 18th century the common law action fell into disuse: *Tito v Wadell* [1977] Ch. 106 at 250; *Attorney-General v Dublin Corporation* (1827) 1 Bli N.S. P.C. 312 at 337, *per* Lord Redesdale; R. P. Meagher, J. D. Heydon and M. J. Leeming, *Meagher, Gummow and Lehane's Equity: Doctrines and Remedies* (4th ed., 2002) pp.869 et seq.
[9] R. P. Meagher, J. D. Heydon and M. J. Leeming, *Meagher, Gummow and Lehane's Equity: Doctrines and Remedies* (4th ed., 2002), p.11.
[10] Considered in *Kerr on Injunctions* (1st ed., 1867), pp.7–8.
[11] *Commentaries on Equity Jurisprudence* (13th ed., 1886) Vol. II, p.182.

set of coherent principles which would determine the result, albeit that those principles might be derived from precedents from two different sources. In the 21st century, the lawyer can usefully be aware of these classifications for understanding the precedents of the Chancery courts. But if the jurist continues to use them in analysing cases he runs the risk of being criticised for putting past authorities on a pedestal, and masking the rational integrity of the law.[12]

In the development of equity by the Chancery courts, there was a tension between two principles. First, courts of equity operated by reference to established principles, rules and precedent. The court did not exercise an unbounded power of freeing itself from all regard to former rules and precedents. Equity was not an arbitrary power exercised according to the will of the individual Chancellor, and therefore uncertain like the length of "the Chancellor's foot".[13]

Secondly, equity was not a static set of rules applied to an enumerated **1.004** list of circumstances. The cases in which the jurisdiction had been exercised were merely examples and not definitive. There was not to be a too strict adherence to forms and rules. As society changed so new cases arose and new solutions had to be found.[14]

There was no jurisdiction in the courts of common law to grant injunctions. The remedy granted by those courts was damages. This changed but only as a result of statute. Section 79 of the Common Law Procedure Act 1854 authorised the granting of an injunction in all cases of breach of contract or other injury where the party injured was entitled to maintain and had brought an action. This jurisdiction was not subject to any limits to be imported from the Court of Chancery, and so went wider than what would be done by that court.[15] Under s.82 of the 1854 Act, the injunction could be granted *ex parte* at any time after the commencement of the action. However, the statutory jurisdiction depended upon there being an existing power to award damages at common law. So the common law courts could not grant injunctions to enforce rights only recognised in equity, and did not have any jurisdiction to restrain threatened or apprehended wrongs when there had been no past wrong. This was because there was no existing cause of action for damages. In contrast the Court of Chancery could intervene to protect an equitable or legal right when there was the threat of infringement, by granting an injunction based on the fear that the right would be infringed—an injunction granted *quia timet*.

That jurisdiction depended upon there being evidence that a wrongful act would be committed in the future. The threat of future injury,

---

[12] See the opinion expressed by Professor Peter Birks Q.C. in (2004) 120 L.Q.R. 344, in his review of R. P. Meagher, J. D. Heydon, M. J. Leeming, *Meager, Gummow and Lehane's Equity: Doctrines and Remedies* (4th ed., 2002).
[13] *Grupo Mexicano De Desarrollo SA v Alliance Bond Fund Inc.* 527 U.S. 308 at 332–333 (1999) quoting from Story's *Commentaries on Equity Jurisprudence* about the rebuke of Seldon.
[14] *Kerr on Injunctions* (1st ed., 1867), pp.4–5.
[15] *Quartz Hill Consolidated Gold Mining Company v Beall* (1882) 20 Ch.D. 501 at 509–510.

unaccompanied by a past wrong, was the most frequent cause of bills in equity seeking injunctions.[16] The *quia timet* jurisdiction did not depend on proving a certainty of a future wrong. But, even in a case where there had been a past wrong, there still had to be at least some real threat that a future wrong would be committed.[17]

1.005   In cases where the old Court of Chancery was asked to grant an injunction in support of a contractual right, but not specific performance of the contract, the existence of that contractual right had to be tried out in a common law court. In equity an injunction could be granted pending the trial in the common law court, or a perpetual injunction could be granted after the contractual right had been established at trial in a common law court. After Sir John Rolt's Act (25 & 26 Vict. c.42) the Court of Chancery had jurisdiction itself to try out the merits of the underlying action.[18]

Following the Judicature Act 1873, the procedure changed and writs of injunction were not to be issued.[19] An injunction was to be by judgment or order. The 1873 Act transferred all the jurisdiction of the Court of Chancery to the High Court of Justice and provided in s.25(8) for a further jurisdiction to grant injunctions. Under the section, an injunction could be granted by an interlocutory order of the court in all cases in which it shall appear to the court to be "just or convenient" that such an order be made. This was re-enacted in s.45 of the Supreme Court of Judicature (Consolidation) Act 1925, which was replaced by s.37 of the Supreme Court Act 1981.

Although that statutory jurisdiction is wide it is not an unlimited jurisdiction to be exercised according to the will of the court. It can only be exercised when the claimant has a legal or equitable right,[20] or, in the case of an anti-suit injunction, when there is actual or threatened conduct of a defendant, which is or would be unconscionable.[21] Thus the new statutory jurisdiction did not supersede and render the old equitable principles and precedents irrelevant. But neither did they dictate solutions to new problems.

---

[16] *Frearson v Loe* (1878) 9 Ch.D. 48 at 65, *per* Sir George Jessel M.R.

[17] *Proctor v Bailey* (1889) 42 Ch.D. 390 at 398.

[18] *J.C. Williamson Ltd v Lukey and Mulholland* (1931) 45 C.L.R. 282 at 298–299, *per* Dixon J.

[19] *Kerr on Injunctions* (6th ed., 1927), p.1.

[20] *Bremer Vulkan Schiffbau v South India Shipping Corporation Ltd* [1981] A.C. 909 at 979–980; *Mercedes Benz AG v Leiduck* [1996] A.C. 284; *Pickering v Liverpool, Daily Post and Echo Newspapers Plc* [1991] 2 A.C. 370 at 420–421; *Cardile v LED Builders Pty Ltd* (1999) 198 C.L.R. 381 at 395–396; *Siskina v Distos Compania Naviera SA (The Siskina)* [1979] A.C. 210 at 256E–F; *North London Railway Co. v Great Northern Railway Co.* (1883) 11 Q.B.D. 30 limiting the dicta of Sir George Jessel M.R. in *Beddow v Beddow* (1878) Ch.D. 89 and *Malmesbury Railway Co. v Budd* (1876) 2 Ch.D. 113.

[21] *South Carolina Insurance Co. v Assurantie Maatschappij "De Zeven Provincien" NV* [1987] A.C. 24 at 39G–40H; *Pickering v Liverpool Daily Post* [1991] 2 A.C. 370 at 420–421; *Siskina v Distos Compania Naviera SA (The Siskina)* [1979] A.C. 210; *Cardile v LED Builders Pty Ltd* (1999) 198 C.L.R. 380 at 395–396.

Before the Judicature Acts the Court of Chancery would not restrain a **1.006** libel[22] because (1) it granted injunctions to protect property rights and libel did not come within this;[23] (2) the court could not know what would be regarded as libellous before there had been a verdict of a jury. After the Judicature Acts it became established that the court had jurisdiction to restrain a libel[24] or a malicious falsehood.[25] The Common Law Procedure Act had enabled the common law courts to do so when there had already been an actionable publication, and it was logical to recognise the power of the High Court to do so *quia timet*.

The Civil Procedure Rules (CPR) include a "glossary" which is referred to in CPR r.2.2(1). This is a "guide" to meanings and does not give an expression ". . . any meaning in the Rules which they do not have in the law generally". In the glossary "Injunction" is given the meaning, "A court order prohibiting a person from doing something or requiring a person to do something". This is a description often used by writers, but it is not a definition. An order for costs against a party orders him to pay those costs but would not be classified by a lawyer as an injunction. The same is true of many court orders,[26] *e.g.* an order for specific restitution of chattels.[27] Legal usage alone controls what is an injunction.[28]

The word can also be used in a statute for a remedy to be granted by the court under that statute. When it is, the grounds for granting or refusing it will be governed by the statute. Those grounds may, or may not,[29] be related to those which are relevant to the discretionary remedy granted by a court of equity. Section 187B of the Town and Country Planning Act 1990 empowered the court to grant an "injunction" to restrain a breach of planning control. This provided a remedy in a public law context which fell to be exercised bearing in mind the legislative purpose.[30] But the House of Lords considered that the use of the word "injunction" by the

---

[22] *Prudential Assurance Company v Knott* (1875) 10 L.R. Ch.App. 142.

[23] *ibid.* at 145, *per* Lord Cairns L.C.

[24] *Bonnard v Perryman* [1891] 2 Ch. 269; *Quartz Hill Consolidated Gold Mining Company v Beall* (1882) 20 Ch.D. 501; *Sim v H.J. Heinz Co. Ltd* [1959] 1 W.L.R. 313.

[25] *Thorley's Cattle Food v Massam* (1877) 6 Ch.D. 582.

[26] *Cardile v LED Builders Pty Ltd* (1999) 198 C.L.R. 380 at 412, *per* Kirby J.

[27] Compare *Doulton Potteries Ltd v Bronotte* [1971] 1 N.S.W.L.R. 591, holding that such an order was not an "injunction" within r.8A of the Fourth Schedule to the Equity Act 1901 of NSW.

[28] *CSR Ltd v Cigna Insurance Australia Ltd* (1997) 189 C.L.R. 345 at 390; *ISC Technologies Ltd v W. K. Radcliffe*, unreported, December 7, 1990 (Millett J.) at 10–12, when deciding that neither an order for an account and payment nor an order to restore a fund was an injunction within the meaning of the relevant rule of court; *Cardile v LED Builders Pty Ltd* (1999) 198 C.L.R. 380 at 395; R. P. Meagher J. D. Heydon and M. J. Leeming, *Meagher, Gummow and Lehane's Equity: Doctrines and Remedies* (4th ed., 2002), p.703.

[29] *Bristol City Council v Lovell* [1998] 1 W.L.R. 446 at 452–454, *per* Lord Hoffmann. Another example is s.380(3) of the Financial Services and Markets Act 2000 which creates a statutory Mareva jurisdiction available to the FSA or the Secretary of State against a person who has contravened, or been knowingly concerned in the contravention of, a "relevant requirement": *Financial Services Authority v Fitt* Unreported 23/4/2004 Ch.D. (Lewison J.).

[30] *South Bucks District Council v Porter* [2003] 2 A.C. 558.

legislature in its context showed that there was to be imported from s.37(1) of the Supreme Court Act 1981 the concepts which apply generally to injunctions. Thus the statutory remedy was one in respect of which the court would take into account the relative hardship which would be caused to the defendant by the granting of the injunction.[31] The legislature had borrowed from equity.

(2) Equitable or legal rights, a "cause of action" and injunctions

1.007   The need for a legal or equitable right which was to be enforced or protected before an injunction could be granted is illustrated by the cases about intervening by injunction in arbitration proceedings. The court could not intervene to prevent an arbitration when there was a perfectly valid arbitration agreement and the question was whether a dispute had arisen under the clause[32] because there was no legal or equitable right not to be proceeded against under the clause.[33] But the court could intervene when the arbitration agreement itself was impeached as void or voidable *ab initio* because then the injunction held the position pending the outcome of the action in which the agreement was impeached.[34]

The contrast can also be seen in two first instance decisions of Hoffmann J. In *Kingdom of Spain v Christie, Manson & Woods Ltd*,[35] the Spanish Government alleged that the *La Marquesa de Santa Cruz* by Goya had been exported from Spain using forged export authorities and licences. The plaintiff had no title to the painting and the second defendant had not been responsible for the exportation of the painting in breach of the regulatory provisions of Spanish law designed to protect the cultural heritage of Spain. The plaintiff sought only declaratory relief about the forgeries. An

---

[31] *ibid.*, at [28], [63], [65] and [98].

[32] *Bremer Vulkan Schiffbau v South India Shipping Corporation Ltd* [1981] A.C. 909 at 981; *R. v National Joint Council for the Craft of Dental Technicians (Disputes Committee) Ex p. Neate* [1953] 1 Q.B. 704; *North London Railway Co. v Great Northern Railway Co.* (1883) 11 Q.B.D. 30.

[33] *London and Blackwall Railway Co. v Cross* (1886) 31 Ch.D. 354 at 368 (injunction refused against arbitration claimant, who (1) had no title to sue, and (2) had brought arbitration proceedings in name of another without authority). *Otaki Borough Council v Sinmac Construction Ltd* [1980] 2 N.Z.L.R. 178 (no injunction to restrain pursuit of arbitration because no legal or equitable right of the plaintiff infringed).

[34] *Kitts v Moore* [1895] 1 Q.B. 253; *Compagnie Nouvelle France Navigation SA v Compagnie Navale Afrique Du Nord (The Oranie and The Tunisie)* [1966] 1 Lloyd's Rep. 477 (alleged that the charterparties were not the effective bargains—injunction refused because of (1) insufficient evidence in support of the impeachment and (2) delay, because the application was not made until one week before the hearing of the arbitration). After *Bremer Vulkan Schiffbau v South India Shipping Corporation Ltd* [1981] A.C. 909 at 981, *The Ithaka* (1939) 64 Ll.L.Rep. 141 (injunction refused when agreement being impeached for duress in Turkey) must also be regarded as falling within this category.

[35] [1986] 1 W.L.R. 1120.

application to strike out the statement of claim failed. The reason was that although lacking any claim based on ownership the plaintiff did have an arguable claim that the forgeries affected the credibility of genuine export documents issued by the Spanish Government. An analogy was drawn to the case where a Hungarian refugee had put into circulation documents which purported to be Hungarian currency although not imitating the real currency. The refugees' notes threatened the value of the real currency and this was treated as sufficient interest as to amount to an equitable right which could be protected by injunction.[36]

In contrast in *Associated Newspapers Group plc v Insert Media Ltd*,[37] the defendants put advertising leaflets in newspapers published by the plaintiff. The newspapers were no longer owned by the plaintiff when the insertions were made, but the plaintiff claimed that selling the papers with the inserts passed them off as part of the plaintiff's product and had obtained an interlocutory injunction on this ground. The plaintiff then sought leave to amend to plead as alternative causes of action that the insertions and marketing were actionable as (1) deliberate acts which caused them damage in their business, or (2) because they were unfair trade practices, or (3) s.37(1) of the Supreme Court Act 1981 enabled an injunction to be granted regardless of the existence of a cause of action. All three grounds were held to be unarguable as sufficient in themselves to enable an injunction to be granted, and leave to amend was refused. Put another way to ground an injunction there must be a cause of action known to the law, "passing off" was such a cause of action but neither (1) nor (2) amounted to a cause of action.[38]

The language of "cause of action" is casting into convenient terminology   **1.008** the legal conclusion about whether a remedy could be granted on particular facts. As Lord Nicholls in his dissenting opinion in *Mercedes Benz AG v Leiduck*[39] said:

"To a large extent any discussion of this question [*i.e.* whether there was a "cause of action"] is doomed to be circular.[40] A cause of action is no more than a lawyer's label for a type of facts which will attract a remedy from the court. If the court will give a remedy, ex hypothesi there is a cause of action."

---

[36] *Emperor of Austria v Day* (1861) 3 De G.F.&J. 217—it may be that the reasoning in the case was based on the proposition, subsequently established to be incorrect, that the deliberate infliction of damage on someone in itself gave that person a cause of action.

[37] [1988] 1 W.L.R. 509.

[38] See also *White v Mellin* [1895] A.C. 154 where an injunction was refused when it was not proved that the intended trade libel was false, there was no evidence that any injury had been caused or would be caused, and so on both grounds there was no threat to carry out what would be an actionable wrong.

[39] [1996] A.C. 284 at 310.

[40] See also *Australian Broadcasting Corporation v Lenah Game Meats Pty Ltd* (2001) 208 C.L.R. 199 at 241, para.91.

What can be said that where there is a right which the law protects, the court can grant a remedy (*ubi jus ibi remedium*); what cannot be said is that because the claimant points to a remedy, therefore he has a right.[41]

What in the past had been regarded as a rule can now be seen not to be of universal application. The Mareva jurisdiction is an exception. Another is the anti-suit jurisdiction in which conduct which is unconscionable can be restrained.

In Australia, the Mareva jurisdiction is not placed on the jurisdiction to grant injunctions. It is part of a jurisdiction not based on statute but which is part of the inherent jurisdiction—that a court can act by injunction so as to protect the integrity of its own process or in support of the due administration of justice.[42] In Australia this has been used to justify granting an injunction against the Registrar General preventing him from registering a document when the consequence of registration would be to undermine the plaintiff's substantive claim,[43] *e.g.* where registration of a mortgage would defeat a prior equitable interest in the land. It is also the basis of the Mareva jurisdiction against non-parties[44] and can provide the justification for an anti-suit injunction, independently of the jurisdiction of the old Court of Chancery to restrain proceedings based on the conduct of the defendant being "unconscionable" or the "unconscientious" exercise of legal rights.[45]

1.009   In England this principle of inherent jurisdiction is one of the justifications for the jurisdiction to grant Anton Piller relief. The jurisdiction to grant anti-suit injunctions[46] is founded on s.37(1) of the Supreme Court Act 1981.[47] However, there are cases in which the remedy is available because of the need to protect the integrity of the English's court's own proceedings and the due administration of justice. It may also be the justification for a claimant obtaining an injunction against a bank preventing it from paying on a letter of credit or performance bond when there is a clear case of fraud—the bank is a third party caught up in the dispute between the claimant and the fraudster and the injunction is granted to prevent the fraudster defeating the ends of justice by obtaining the money and then absconding.

Outside of anti-suit injunctions the mere fact that the defendant has behaved unconscionably cannot be said to give rise to a legal or equitable right or in itself justify the granting of an injunction. In *Australian*

---

[41] *Day v Brownrigg* (1878) 10 Ch.D. 294, where no injunction could be granted for changing the name of the house to "Ashford Lodge", which was that of the neighbour's house, because no right had been infringed; *Cowley (Earl) v Cowley (Countess)* [1901] A.C. 450 in which the Earl failed to obtain an injunction to stop his former wife calling herself Countess Cowley after her remarriage.

[42] *Cardile v LED Builders Pty Ltd* (1999) 198 C.L.R. 381.

[43] *Williams v Marac Australia* (1986) 5 N.S.W.L.R. 529.

[44] *Cardile v LED Builders Pty Ltd* (1999) 198 C.L.R. 381.

[45] *CSR Ltd v Cigna Insurance Australia Ltd* (1997) 189 C.L.R. 345 at 391–392.

[46] *The Eras EIL Actions* [1995] 1 Lloyd's Rep. 64 at 70–74.

[47] See *Glencore International AG v Metro Trading International Inc.* [2002] 2 All E.R. (Comm) 1 at [70].

Broadcasting Corporation v Lenah Game Meats Pty Ltd[48] the appellant wished to broadcast a film which had been given to it, which had been made through trespassing on the respondent's premises and filming using hidden cameras. The trespass was a criminal offence. The film was of the slaughtering process used by the respondent. The majority held that no injunction could be granted because there was no underlying right to be protected. To reach this conclusion it was necessary to rule out each of the potential rights or causes of action put forward. Thus, the process was not confidential information, protected as a trade secret or as a "private act" of an individual which should be protected from disclosure to avoid humiliation[49] or as personal information which is protected by a duty of confidence.[50] Nor could the remedy for trespass against the trespasser be extended to include the right to delivery-up of the film. The fact that the trespass was itself criminal did not confer on the respondent any legal right in the film or to prevent its broadcast. Nor was the fact that the trespassers had behaved unconscionably sufficient to confer a relevant right on the respondent—it did not make the information confidential.

In *Campbell v MGN Limited*,[51] Naomi Campbell, a famous fashion **1.010** model, had given wide publicity to statements that she had not taken drugs. In fact this publicity was untrue, and by making false statements to the public had exposed herself to the defendant newspaper correcting the record. The defendant had also published certain details of where and how she was being treated, and a photograph of her coming out of Narcotics Anonymous in the King's Road in Chelsea. The information had come to the newspaper from someone in her entourage, or another participant who had attended Narcotics Anonymous. It had been obtained in breach of confidence. But the information was also highly personal in that it went to her dignity as a individual. An obligation of confidence may arise out of a confidential relationship. This does not depend upon contract. The information has to be private and disclosed to another in confidence.[52] But

---

[48] (2001) 208 C.L.R. 199. See also *Tillery Valley Foods v Channel Four Television* [2004] EWHC 1075 (Ch) (injunction refused to restrain broadcast of investigatory report prepared by a journalist, who had posed as a factory worker, on allegedly unhygienic food production practices of the claimant which supplied food to the NHS. It was a defamation case "in disguise" because the information about food production practices lacked the necessary ingredient that they were confidential).

[49] *Hellewell v Chief Constable of Derbyshire* [1995] 1 W.L.R. 804 at 807 (giving the example of a "private act" photographed using a telephoto lens); *Australian Broadcasting Corporation v Lenah Game Meats Pty Ltd* (2001) 208 C.L.R. 199 at para.50 (gratuitously humiliating photograph taken in circumstances attracting the application of the law of confidential information); *P v D* [2000] 2 N.Z.L.R. 591 (fact that P, who was a public figure, had been treated at psychiatric hospital); *A v B plc* [2003] Q.B. 195 at p.206 (bugging someone's home): these are examples of circumstances where something which is normally done only in private or information going to personal dignity is also protected by the law of abuse of confidence.

[50] *Campbell MGN Limited* [2004] 2 W.L.R. 1232.

[51] [2004] 2 W.L.R. 1232.

[52] *Coco v A N Clak (Engineers) Limited* [1969] RPC 41 at pp.47–48.

whether information is protected by a duty of confidence does not depend upon there being some communication made where the recipient has received the information in confidence. There does not have to be some initial confidential relationship[53] The nature of the information itself may be such that anyone coming across it is bound to respect its confidentiality.

The photograph, and the details about Naomi Campbell's attempts to rid herself of addiction, did not have to be published by the newspaper in order to correct her incorrect statements to the public. The House of Lords decided that in determining the scope of protection to be accorded to her it was necessary to take into account the values which underlay Art.8 of the ECHR (respect for family life), and Art.10 (right to freedom of expression). This was so although these articles themselves only directly applied to the rights of individuals against public authorities. But the values underlying the existence of these rights were also relevant to the appropriate formulation of the scope of the duty of confidence owed by a private person. The Convention affected the rights between private persons,[54] what can be called "horizontal rights" as contrasted with rights between persons and public authorities. The photograph and details were highly personal and went to her personal dignity in a major way. In a split decision the majority decided that she was entitled to confidence in the photograph and the details of her treatment and efforts to rid herself of drug addiction.

1.011   Because the court is itself a public authority, an application for an injunction which would prevent publication by the media engages Art.10 ECHR. In the case of an application for an interim injunction it is also subject to the threshold requirement in s.12(3) of the Human Rights Act 1998. In *A v B plc,*[55] the claimant was a premier division footballer who was married and had had short term sexual relations with two other women, one of whom was a lap dancer in a bar, who had sold their stories to the press. His application for an injunction to restrain publication of the stories of these relationships failed because the freedom of the press prevailed over such privacy as the footballer was entitled to expect to be accorded to his short term extra marital affairs.

The developments of the law of confidence and the enactment of the Human Rights Act 1998 have resulted in an area where analysis based on *The Siskina* and whether there is a cause of action, would be wholly out of place. Instead, once the claimant shows some legitimate expectation of privacy the court engages in a value judgment weighing up the facts, more akin to the exercise of a discretion than to whether there is a cause of action.[56] The Human Rights Act 1998 affects how the court itself must

---

[53] *Attorney-General v Guardian Newspapers Limited (No. 2)* [1990] 1 A.C. 109 at p.281; *Campbell v MGN Limited* [2004] 2 W.L.R. 1232 at paras 14,44–48,92,134.
[54] See also "Injunctions and the Human Rights Act 1998: Jurisdiction and Discretion" (2002) 21 C.J.Q. 29 (Linda Clake).
[55] [2003] Q.B. 195.
[56] [2003] Q.B. 195 at para.12.

conduct itself in relation to granting relief against companies, individuals, or the media, and what rights there are both against public authorities, and between private persons. This can find expression through the exercise of discretion of whether to grant an injunction or as to whether the claimant has a cause of action,[57] or both.

In the area of public law and judicial review the injunction is a remedy available according to whether the applicant has *locus standi* to enforce the public law right or duty. For example, in *Gouriet v Union of Post Office Workers*,[58] the plaintiff had no standing to enforce the criminal law; it was the Attorney-General who could enforce the criminal law in the public interest and not a private citizen.

In *Broadmoor Special Hospital Authority v Robinson*[59] the majority of the   **1.012**
Court of Appeal held that where a public authority was given a statutory responsibility then in the absence of contrary words or implication into the statute it has standing to apply for an injunction restraining interference with performance of that responsibility. This is a different area from that of private rights. It is also an area where the courts should tread with caution. The crucial question is not about the availability of the injunction as a remedy; there is the earlier question of what are the underlying legal rights and liberties of those involved. Lord Woolf M.R. sought in his judgment to justify *Chief Constable of Kent v V*[60] as a case in which the court intervened to enable the police to perform a public responsibility. But as the House of Lords subsequently held[61] there is no common law right to take or confiscate people's property and there was no scope to extend the common law given the statutory intervention that there has been in this field. The Attorney–General, or a local authority under s.222 of the Local Government Act 1972, can seek an injunction enforcing the criminal law by restraining a breach of it, the court cannot grant to them an injunction which goes beyond enforcement of the criminal provisions.[62] The statements made by Lord Woolf M.R. in his judgment about the availability of an injunction by way of remedy are no replacement for analysis of the underlying legal rights and liberties of the persons who would be affected by the granting of an injunction; this is so both in the field of private and public law.

---

[57] "Injunctions and the Human Rights Act 1998: Jurisdiction and Discretion (2002) 21 C.J.Q. 29 (Linda Clake).
[58] [1978] A.C. 435.
[59] [2000] Q.B. 775.
[60] [1983] Q.B. 34; see also Chapter 25, Para. 25.001.
[61] *Attorney-General v Blake* [2001] 1 A.C. 268.
[62] *Worcestershire CC v Tongue* [2004] 2 W.L.R. 1193 (where the court declined to grant an injunction permitting the local authority to go on to land belonging to the defendant in order to remove cattle kept there, when the criminal legislation did not authorise removal or confiscation).

(3) Emergence of the "Mareva" jurisdiction

1.013 The Court of Chancery did not grant an injunction to restrain a man who was alleged to be a debtor of the claimant from parting with or dealing with his own property as he pleased[63]—a person who claimed to be a creditor could not file a bill in Chancery and obtain an injunction on the ground that he was "about to be defrauded by reason of [the defendant company] making away with [its] assets".[64]

Following the Judicature Act 1873, there were repeated judicial statements that before judgment the High Court had no power to restrain a man from removing his property out of the jurisdiction or otherwise dealing with it.[65]

But even before 1975 the absence of a way to prevent foreign defendants from removing their assets from the jurisdiction so as to render useless any judgment which the plaintiff might obtain was beginning to come under review.

1.014 The final report of the Committee on the Supreme Court Practice and Procedure (Cmd 8878, 1953) proposed that the writ of *ne exeat regno* (under which a defendant is arrested to prevent him leaving the jurisdiction) should become available post-judgment to prevent a judgment debtor from leaving the jurisdiction so as to evade his judgment creditor. This proposal was not acted upon. In *Felton v Callis*,[66] Megarry J. held that the writ was not available for the purpose of preserving assets within the jurisdiction, but indicated that it would be appropriate to consider changing the law in this area. Subsequently, the Committee on the Enforcement of Judgment Debts (Cmnd 3909, 1969) recommended reform of the law.

The Mareva injunction first emerged in *Nippon Yusen Kaisha v Karageorgis*,[67] when the late Mr Geoffrey Brice, Q.C. persuaded the Court of Appeal to make such an order *ex parte*. The case was followed in *Mareva Compania Naviera SA v International Bulkcarriers Ltd*,[68] the case from which the Mareva injunction derived its name. In both cases the "assets" which were made the subject of the injunction were bank accounts; the defendants were resident out of the jurisdiction and the applications were

---

[63] *Mills v Northern Railway of Buenos Aires Co.* (1870) 5 Ch.App. 621 at 627–628, *per* Lord Hatherley L.C.; W. Joyce, *The Law and Practice of Injunctions in Equity and at Common Law* (1872), Vol. 2, p.923.
[64] *Mills v Northern Railway of Buenos Aires Co.* (1870) 5 Ch.App. 621 at 628, *per* Lord Hatherley L.C. Likewise in *Grupo Mexicano De Desarrollo SA v Alliance Bond Fund Inc.* 527 U.S. 308 at 318–321 (1999), the Supreme Court held that a creditor could only obtain such relief after he had obtained judgment.
[65] *Robinson v Pickering* (1881) 16 Ch.D. at 661 and 663; *Newton v Newton* (1885) 11 P.D. 11; *Lister & Co. v Stubbs* (1890) 45 Ch.D. 1 at 14; *Burmester v Burmester* [1913] P. 76; *Jagger v Jagger* [1926] P. 93 at 96 and 101; *Scott v Scott* [1951] P. 193.
[66] [1969] 1 Q.B. 200.
[67] [1975] 1 W.L.R. 1093.
[68] [1975] 2 Lloyd's Rep. 509.

made and granted *ex parte*. The Court of Appeal based the jurisdiction to grant the relief sought on s.45 of the Supreme Court of Judicature (Consolidation) Act 1925, which provided as follows: "A mandamus or an injunction may be granted or a receiver appointed by an interlocutory order of the court in all cases in which it shall appear to the court to be just or convenient."

The jurisdiction to grant such relief was affirmed by the Court of Appeal in the case of *MBPXL Corporation v International Banking Corporation Ltd*,[69] although it was described as "exceptional". Subsequently, the existence of the jurisdiction was challenged on an *inter partes* basis in *Rasu Maritima SA v Perusahaan Pertambangan*.[70] The Court of Appeal held that the order could in principle be granted, and that to obtain such relief, the plaintiff need not show that he could obtain summary judgment, but merely that he had a "good arguable case".

1.015 In the course of his judgment Lord Denning M.R. reviewed the history of pre-trial attachment and the cases decided before the emergence of the Mareva jurisdiction. He referred to the process of foreign attachment available in London and on the continent of Europe, and the modern procedure of *saisie conservatoire* (see Appendix 1, below). The *Lister v Stubbs*[71] line of authority was distinguished on the basis that it did not apply to foreign defendants who were abroad but who had assets within the jurisdiction which were liable to be removed at short notice. Lord Denning M.R. also found an historical antecedent in a process called "foreign attachment".

(4) Foreign attachment

1.016 This was available as part of the custom of the City of London as far back as the late 15th century.

If a citizen of London issued a plaint of debt in the Court of the Mayor and Aldermen of London, and the defendant was not to be found within the jurisdiction of the court, the plaintiff was able to make an application to attach any effects of the defendant, whether money or goods or debts in the hands of third parties, to be found within the jurisdiction of the court. If a certain procedure was followed, after the defendant had failed to appear, his goods were appraised and goods to the value of the amount demanded were delivered to the plaintiff. The plaintiff had to give security that he would make restitution if the defendant appeared before the court within a year and a day, and proved that he owed nothing to the plaintiff at the time when the plaint was made, or that he owed only part of the

---

[69] Court of Appeal (Civil Division) Transcript No.411 of 1975 (August 28, 1975).
[70] [1978] Q.B. 644.
[71] (1890) 45 Ch.D. 1.

debt. The debt had to be owed in London, and the defendant had to be "foreign" in the sense of being "not civic", *i.e.* out of the jurisdiction of the London court. He need not have been abroad.

By the middle of the 19th century, the process of foreign attachment was riddled with fictions. The absence of notice to the defendant was contrary to modern notions of natural justice, and the procedure raised difficulties as to the jurisdiction of the London court over defendants abroad. The procedure fell into disuse, although it thrived in the United States. There the Supreme Court has limited its use for the purpose of founding jurisdiction for the court to determine the merits of the case.

(5) Gradual extension of the Mareva injunction to English defendants

1.017   For some time there was considerable doubt whether Mareva relief could be obtained against English defendants resident within the jurisdiction. In *Van Weelde v Homeric Marine Services*,[72] Lloyd J. held that there was a settled practice against doing so, referring to the earlier unreported case of *Adler Cosmetica v Minnahurst Ltd* in which he had refused such relief, and the Court of Appeal had upheld his judgment (*inter alia*) on that point.

In *Chartered Bank v Daklouche*,[73] the Court of Appeal held that the temporary presence of a defendant within the jurisdiction would not prevent the court from granting Mareva relief, and this was approved in dicta in *Third Chandris Shipping Corporation v Unimarine SA*.[74] But in *Bank Leumi (UK) Ltd v Ricky George Sportain (UK) Ltd*,[75] Ormrod L.J., with whom Brandon L.J. agreed, stated that a Mareva injunction could not be obtained against a defendant within the jurisdiction.

In *Siskina v Distos Compania Naviera SA (The Siskina)*,[76] the Mareva jurisdiction was considered for the first time by the House of Lords. There were two points in the case. First, could jurisdiction over the defendant be obtained pursuant to RSC Ord.11 enabling service of the writ upon the defendant out of the jurisdiction? Secondly, did the court have power to grant a Mareva injunction? Argument stopped after the first point had been argued and the decision of the House of Lords was that the plaintiffs in that case could not bring their claim within the former RSC Ord.11, r.1(1)(i) then in force, and that consequently there was no jurisdiction to entertain the claim on the merits or to maintain an interlocutory injunction in relation to that claim. The House of Lords did not decide whether or not there was jurisdiction to grant a Mareva injunction.

---

[72] [1979] 2 Lloyd's Rep. 117.
[73] [1980] 1 W.L.R. 107.
[74] [1979] Q.B. 645.
[75] Court of Appeal (Civ Div) Transcript No.753 of 1979 (November 1, 1979).
[76] [1979] A.C. 210.

Lord Hailsham pointed out that the distinction between English and foreign-based defendants was unjustifiable. He observed that either the position of a plaintiff making a claim against an English-based defendant would have to be altered, or the principle of the Mareva cases would have to be modified. Subsequently, in *Barclay-Johnson v Yuill*.[77] Sir Robert Megarry VC granted a Mareva injunction in respect of the assets of an English defendant temporarily absent abroad, but ordinarily resident within the jurisdiction.

The Mareva jurisdiction was further extended by the Court of Appeal in **1.018** *Rahman (Prince Abdul) bin Turki al Sudairy v Abu-Taha*.[78] In that case, the Court of Appeal granted a Mareva injunction in terms which prohibited the dissipation of the defendant's assets within the jurisdiction, as well as their removal from the jurisdiction.

(6) Section 37(3) of the Supreme Court Act 1981 and public policy

In England, the jurisdiction of the courts to grant Mareva injunctions has **1.019** been put beyond doubt by s.37(3) of the Supreme Court Act 1981, which provides as follows:

> "The power of the High Court under subsection (1) to grant an interlocutory injunction restraining a party to any proceedings from removing from the jurisdiction of the High Court, or otherwise dealing with, assets located within that jurisdiction shall be exercisable in cases where that party is, as well as in cases where he is not, domiciled, resident or present within that jurisdiction."

Section 37(1) of the Supreme Court Act 1981 replaced s.45 of the Supreme Court of Judicature (Consolidation) Act 1925, which had provided as follows:

> "The High Court may by order (whether interlocutory or final) grant an injunction or appoint a receiver in all cases in which it appears to the court to be just and convenient to do so."

The effect of s.37(3) is that in England the jurisdiction is statutory and the order is "an injunction".

The Court of Appeal cases, which put the jurisdiction to grant the remedy on s.45, ran counter to the practice of the old Court of Chancery, the restrictive interpretation which had been put by authority upon s.45

---

[77] [1980] 1 W.L.R. 1259.
[78] [1980] 1 W.L.R. 409.

and its predecessor, and repeated statements of principle made in the case law after the Judicature Act 1873. *Meagher, Gummow and Lehane's Equity: Doctrines and Remedies* states that "In truth, there is no jurisdiction at all to grant a Mareva Injunction."[79]

1.020   The desire of some people not to pay their debts and to deal with their assets so as to prevent enforcement is not new. The statute 13 Eliz I c.5 was directed to schemes made to transfer away assets with intent to defeat creditors. The statute[80] was drafted in a "torrential"[81] style indicative of the numerous ways in which debtors deliberately avoided paying their debts several hundred years ago. These included voluntarily giving away assets to friends and relatives whilst leaving debts unpaid, and thus failing to be just before they were generous.[82]

So why did the old Court of Chancery not invent Mareva relief? The reason was one of policy. A man's assets were his own. A debt gave the creditor no legal or equitable right to those assets. For the court to assume a power to interfere with a defendant's right to deal with his property because of an alleged debt would be "a fearful authority for [the] Court to assume".[83] It would be capable of great abuse by would be creditors because defendants could find themselves unfairly placed under great financial pressure. It might interfere with a defendant carrying on his business or destroy it altogether. Third parties could find themselves let down. There were also cases in which a creditor could stipulate for security to be given before he gave credit. If he did not, he had agreed to be unsecured and could not complain of the consequences.

The Mareva cases thought this view too narrow. The law on fraudulent conveyances required proof of an intent to defraud creditors. The means available to dispose of assets and thereby to defeat claims had become much more extensive and more difficult to undo. They included transferring large amounts by electronic transfer from one country to another, switching assets between offshore companies, and hiding assets in offshore trusts. Leaving creditors to obtain judgment first and then to discover and unravel what had happened to assets, perhaps through a series of different jurisdictions and entities, was impractical and unfair. The question was one of policy and who should first determine it—the courts or the legislature? In the United States the question has been left to the legislature.[84] In England the courts, presided over by Lord Denning M.R., took the first step, and this has been confirmed by the legislature. The statement in

---

[79] 4th ed., 2002, p.798, para.21–435, which was relied on in *Miller Brewing Co. v Mersey Docks and Harbour Company* [2004] F.S.R. 5 at 81, paras 84–85 for distinguishing the practice for protecting innocent third parties on freezing injunctions, see Chapter 11.

[80] Reproduced in *Re Eichholz* [1959] Ch. 708 at 721–722.

[81] *i.e.* a drafting style trying to cover expressly every conceivable case, see *Norwich Union v BRB* [1987] 2 E.G.L.R. 137 at 138, *per* Hoffmann J.

[82] *Freeman v Pope* (1870) L.R. 5 Ch.App. 538 at 540, *per* Lord Hatherley L.C.

[83] *Mills v Northern Railway of Buenos Aires Co.* (1870) 5 Ch.App. 621 at 628, *per* Lord Hatherley L.C.

[84] *Grupo Mexicano De Desarrollo. SA v Alliance Bond Fund Inc.* 527 U.S. 308 (1999).

Meagher, Gummow and Lehane's Equity: Doctrines and Remedies belongs to legal history.[85]

In the Bahamas the legislature in s.21(1) of the Supreme Court Act 1996   **1.021**
adopted the same language as the former s.45 of the Supreme Court of Judicature (Consolidation) Act 1925 but not the equivalent of s.37(3) of the Supreme Court Act 1981. It was argued that this had the consequence that there was no Mareva jurisdiction. The Privy Council rejected that, deciding that since the Mareva jurisdiction had already been established in England based on s.45 prior to the enactment of the 1981 Act, s.21(1) in the Bahamas was to be interpreted as including Mareva jurisdiction.[86]

(7) "Mareva orders" in Australia

Section 23 of the Federal Court of Australia Act 1976, provides that: **1.022**

> "The Court has power, in relation to matters in which it has jurisdiction, to make orders of such kinds, including interlocutory orders, and to issue, or direct the issue of, writs of such kinds, as the Court thinks appropriate."

The power conferred by the section is limited by the words "in relation to matters in which it has jurisdiction . . .".[87] One view was that s.23 was limited by the same constraints as applied to s.45 of the Supreme Court of Judicature (Consolidation) Act 1925, the language being somewhat similar. However it has been decided by the courts that it is wide enough to enable the Federal Court to grant an order freezing or preserving the assets of a defendant—in other words to grant what in England was a Mareva injunction against a defendant to a substantive claim being advanced in the Federal Court proceedings.[88]

The order is also justified as an order to prevent conduct which may frustrate possible future process of the court to enforce a judgment.[89] This does not impose a requirement that the defendant subjectively intends to deal with his assets so as to prevent enforcement of a judgment which may

---

[85] Contrast *Miller Brewing Co. v Mersey Docks and Harbour Company* [2004] F.S.R. 5 at 81, paras 84–85.
[86] *Jeanette Walsh v Deloitte & Touche Inc.* [2002] 4 L.R.C. 345 at [9]; see also *Meespierson (Bahamas) Ltd v Grupo Torras SA* [2000] 1 L.R.C. 627, Bahamas Court of Appeal.
[87] *Cardile v LED Builders Pty Ltd* (1999) 198 C.L.R. 380 at 400–401; *Jackson v Sterling Industries Ltd* (1987) 162 C.L.R. 612 at 625, *per* Deane J.; *Patrick Stevedores Operations No.2 Pty Ltd v Maritime Union of Australia* (1998) 195 C.L.R. 1 at 32.
[88] *Cardile v LED Builders Pty Ltd* (1999) 198 C.L.R.380; *Hiero Pty Ltd v Somers* (1983) 47 A.L.R. 605.
[89] *Jackson v Sterling Industries Ltd* (1987) 162 C.L.R. 612 at 617–618, *per* Wilson and Dawson JJ. and at 623, *per* Deane J.; *Patrick Stevedores Operations No.2 Pty Ltd v Maritime Union of Australia* (1998) 195 C.L.R. 1 at 32; *Cardile v LED Builders Pty Ltd* (1999) 198 C.L.R. 380 at 400–401.

be granted in the future.[90] For the Federal Court this jurisdiction is implied under the statute which created it. For a superior court of unlimited jurisdiction the power can exist as part of its "inherent jurisdiction" to protect its own process.[91]

The High Court of Australia has said that the order should be called a "Mareva order" rather than a "Mareva injunction".[92] This was to avoid confusion that might otherwise arise that this type of order was justified as an "injunction" which could have been granted by a court of equity prior to the Judicature Act, or as an "injunction" granted under a supposed[93] unlimited jurisdiction conferred on the courts by s.25(8) of the Judicature Act 1873 or s.45 of the Supreme Court of Judicature (Consolidation) Act 1925. Kirby J. preferred the term "asset preservation order".[94]

1.023   The High Court has also recognised the jurisdiction to grant Mareva orders against third parties or "non-parties",[95] meaning persons other than a defendant to the substantive claim. There is jurisdiction to make Mareva orders in the Australian Capital Territory,[96] New South Wales,[97] the Northern Territory,[98] Queensland,[99] South Australia,[1] Tasmania,[2] Victoria[3] and Western Australia.[4]

In Australia, prior to *Cardile v LED Builders Pty Ltd*, whilst accepting that there is a general rule that Mareva relief could not be granted before the claimant had an *existing* cause of action the courts had already recognised that the requirement should be approached flexibly[5] and that Mareva relief could be granted in cases[6] not falling within the general rule. In England, for cases against third parties or non-parties there is no requirement of an existing cause of action against such parties as long as

---

[90] *Hayden v Teplitzky* (1997) 154 A.L.R. 497; *Glenwood Management Group Pty Ltd v Mayo* [1991] 2 V.R. 49; *Beach Petroleum NL v Johnson* (1992) 9 A.C.S.R. 404 at 405–406; *Northcorp Ltd v Allman Properties (Australia) Pty Ltd* [1994] 2 Qd Rep. 405, Queensland Court of Appeal.

[91] *Wheeler v Selborn Pty Ltd* [1984] 1 N.S.W.L.R. 555; *Pelechowski v The Registrar, Court of Appeal (NSW)* (1999) 198 C.L.R. 435 at 451.

[92] *Cardile v LED Builders Pty Ltd* (1999) 198 C.L.R. 380 at 401, *per* Gaudron, McHugh, Gummow and Callinan JJ.

[93] *Cardile v LED Builders Pty Ltd* (1999) 198 C.L.R. 380 at 397.

[94] *ibid.*, at 412.

[95] *ibid.*, at 412–413, *per Kirby J.*

[96] *Basiric v Topic* (1981) 58 F.L.R. 262.

[97] *Riley McKay Pty Ltd v McKay* [1982] 1 N.S.W.L.R. 264; *Jackson v Sterling Industries* (1987) 162 C.L.R. 612 at 617.

[98] Supreme Court Act 1979, s.69.

[99] *Bank of New Zealand v Jones* [1982] Qd R. 466.

[1] *Devlin v Collins* (1984) 37 S.A.S.R. 98.

[2] Supreme Court Civil Procedure Act 1932, s.11(12).

[3] Supreme Court Act 1986, s.37(3); *Brereton v Milstein* [1988] V.R. 508 at 514.

[4] *Sanko Steamship Co. Ltd v DC Commodities* [1980] W.A.R. 51.

[5] *Patterson v BTR Engineering (Aust) Ltd* (1989) 18 N.S.W.L.R. 319 at 329C–330A.

[6] *Construction Engineering (Aust) Pty Ltd v Tambel* [1984] 1 N.S.W.L.R. 274 (relief granted notwithstanding *Scott v Avery* clause); *Deputy Commissioner of Taxation v Sharp* (1988) 82 A.C.T.R. 1 (existing debt but not immediately payable); *Vereker v Choi* (1985) 4 N.S.W.L.R. 277 at 284, in which relief was granted against the defendant's wife against whom there was no cause of action.

there is an existing cause of action against somebody in respect of which the Mareva relief can be justified.[7]

What about the position in Australia, after *Cardile v LED Builders Pty Ltd*, about obtaining immediate relief against a defendant against whom there is no existing cause of action? Does the *Siskina* rule still apply in Australia subject to certain limited "exceptions"[8] or is there jurisdiction regardless, with the point going only to discretion? In the case of the Federal Court, s.23 of the Federal Court of Australia Act 1976 only sanctions the granting of Mareva relief if it is "in relation to matters in which it has jurisdiction". This wording would require there to be a "matter in which [the court] has jurisdiction" before an injunction could be granted under the section. However the finding of jurisdiction in the Federal Court to grant relief to prevent conduct which may frustrate the future process of the court to enforce a judgment or to prevent conduct which may interfere with the due administration of justice imports no requirement that there be an existing cause of action.

The English requirement is based on *The Siskina* and Lord Diplock's **1.024** analysis of the remedy as an interlocutory injunction granted under what was s.45 of the Supreme Court of Judicature (Consolidation) Act 1925. Under that analysis the injunction could only be granted in proceedings against the defendant based on a cause of action—the remedy was only ancillary to that cause of action. That analysis has been rejected as the source for jurisdiction in *Cardile*,[9] and logically its constraints do not apply to preventing abuse of the process of the court or interfering with the due administration of justice. It is no less a frustration of possible future process of the court or an interference with the due administration of justice whether a man disposes of his assets to defeat a future judgment moments before his debt becomes due or moments afterwards.[10] Furthermore the rationale based on interference with the due administration of justice applies with equal force against a prospective defendant against whom there is no existing cause of action, as it applies to a third party or non-party who likewise is not the defendant to a substantive claim. Whilst *Cardile* was about the source of the jurisdiction against third parties, its logic casts away the constraints of *The Siskina* rule for the Federal Court.

---

[7] *Yukong Line Ltd v Rendsburg Investments Corporation* [2001] 2 Lloyd's Rep. 113; *TSB Bank International v Chabra* [1992] 1 W.L.R. 231 at 241–242; *C Inc. v L* [2001] 2 Lloyd's Rep. 459 at 474–475, applying *Cardile v LED Builders Pty Ltd* (1999) 198 C.L.R. 380.

[8] F. Kunc and S. Hepburn, "Mareva Orders" in *The Principles of Equity* (P. Parkinson ed., 2nd ed., 2003), p.704.

[9] *Cardile v LED Builders Pty Ltd* (1999) 198 C.L.R. 380 at 397, 400–401 and 423–424.

[10] Contrast *Official Receiver for the State of Israel v Raveh* (2001) 159 F.L.R. 471, which is discussed below. There could have been Mareva relief once the Israeli judgment was being registered but not before, because there had to be a cause of action sued upon before the Australian court.

(8) Free-standing Mareva relief: *The Siskina*, s.25 of the Civil Jurisdiction and Judgments Act 1925 and later developments

1.025 The initial cases were of Mareva injunctions granted in proceedings in England in which the plaintiff was claiming substantive relief. The jurisdiction could also be exercised by the High Court in aid of arbitration proceedings in England pursuant to what was s.12(6)(f) and (h) of the Arbitration Act 1950. But could relief be given when the only factor connecting the case with England was the presence of assets within the jurisdiction of the court?

In *Siskina v Distos Compania Naviera SA (The Siskina)*,[11] cargo interests had a claim against a Panamanian company. The dispute had no connection with England. The defendant's only ship had sunk and there were insurance proceeds in England to which the defendant was entitled. The cargo interests sought leave to serve the writ on the defendant under what was then RSC Ord. 11, r.1(1)(i). The House of Lords held that there was no jurisdiction to commence substantive proceedings in England, that the writ and all subsequent proceedings in the action had to be set aside and consequently there could be no Mareva injunction. A Mareva injunction was merely an interlocutory injunction and such an injunction could only be granted as "ancillary and incidental to the pre-existing cause of action".

Three consequences arose from the decision in *The Siskina*:

(1) The former RSC Ord. 11, r.1(1)(i) was not interpreted allowing the English court to assume jurisdiction on the merits of a claim provided that the plaintiff could point to assets of an intended defendant which could be used to satisfy a judgment and which might be disposed of by a defendant unless an injunction was granted. The English court would not assert a substantive jurisdiction over a defendant just because he had assets within the jurisdiction. This remains the current position. The contrary proposition would have had the unsatisfactory consequence that the court would find itself asserting jurisdiction over a foreigner to decide the merits of substantive proceedings which had nothing to do with England.

(2) There was no jurisdiction to grant Mareva relief unless and until the plaintiff had an accrued right of action. This was decided by the Court of Appeal in *Veracruz Transportation Inc. v VC Shipping Co. Inc. and Den Norske Bank A/S (The Veracruz)*. This remains the law in England[12] and in the Bahamas,[13] although it is not the position in

---

[11] [1979] A.C. 210.

[12] *Re Q's Estate* [1999] 1 Lloyd's Rep. 931 at 938–939; *Petroleum Investment Company Ltd v Kantupan Holdings Company Ltd* [2002] 1 All E.R. (Comm) 124 at [54].

[13] *Meespierson (Bahamas) Ltd v Grupo Torras SA* [2000] 1 L.R.C. 627.

Australia and has been criticised. A person may be in great need of such a time prior to the cause of action vesting. For example, a debt may be due in a few days' time and the debtor may be on the point of removing assets from the jurisdiction.

(3) There was no jurisdiction to preserve assets within the jurisdiction of the court which would be needed to satisfy a claim against the defendant if it eventually succeeded regardless of where the merits of the substantive claim were to be decided. In short, the statutory power to grant injunctions under s.45 of the Supreme Court of Judicature (Consolidation) Act 1925 did not empower the court to grant free-standing interlocutory relief brought in proceedings claiming only that type of relief.

Strictly speaking, *The Siskina* concerned the jurisdiction to decide the **1.026** merits of substantive proceedings because of the presence of assets of the defendant in England. But the decision appeared to confine the availability of Mareva relief to substantive proceedings brought in England. The majority of the Privy Council in *Mercedes Benz AG v Leiduck*[14] left it open whether there could be free-standing proceedings claiming Mareva or other interlocutory relief, deciding the case against the applicant on the ground that there was no provision permitting service out of the jurisdiction.[15]

The position in relation to free-standing interlocutory relief has been eroded by a succession of developments.

First, s.25 of the Civil Jurisdiction and Judgments Act 1982 conferred a statutory jurisdiction to grant interim relief including Mareva relief in aid of proceedings brought or to be brought in a contracting state to the Brussels Convention 1968 subsequently widened to include contracting states to the Lugano Convention, which were within Art.1 of the Convention. Such a jurisdiction was consistent with Art.24 of the Brussels Convention, which provided:

> "Application may be made to the courts of a contracting state for such provisional, including protective, measures as may be available under the law of that State, even if, under this Convention, the courts of another contracting state have jurisdiction as to the substance of the matter."

Secondly, in *Channel Tunnel Group Ltd v Balfour Beatty Construction* **1.027** *Ltd*,[16] the House of Lords recognised that the court had jurisdiction to grant interlocutory relief in substantive proceedings brought in England even though those proceedings had to be stayed in order for the claim to be decided in arbitration abroad.

---

[14] [1996] A.C. 284.
[15] [1996] A.C. 284 at 304F–G.
[16] [1993] A.C. 334.

Thirdly, s.44 of the Arbitration Act 1996 enables the court to grant free-standing Mareva relief in relation to arbitral proceedings wherever the seat of the arbitration is or even if no seat has been designated or determined, whereas the jurisdiction to act in aid of arbitration proceedings under s.12(6)(f) and (h) of the Arbitration Act 1950 only applied to arbitrations within the jurisdiction.

Fourthly, the Civil Jurisdiction and Judgments Act 1982 (Interim Relief) Order 1997[17] empowers the High Court to grant interim relief under s.25(1) of the Civil Jurisdiction and Judgments Act 1982 in relation to "proceedings" regardless of where they are commenced or whether their "subject-matter" comes within Art.1 of the Brussels Convention. Further-more, earlier difficulties with regard to service out of the jurisdiction of the originating process commencing free-standing proceedings for interim relief under s.25 were done away with because of the coming into force of the former RSC Ord.11, r.8A, and now CPR r.6.20(4) which permits service out of the jurisdiction of a claim made "for an interim remedy under section 25 (1) of the 1982 Act".

1.028   These developments recognise that justice may require assets to be preserved by an order made in one jurisdiction whilst the merits of a substantive claim are determined in another. They allow a distinction to be drawn between proceedings which have as their purpose the preservation of assets and proceedings on the merits of a substantive claim, and this distinction often has to be made. For asset preservation it may be appropriate to apply to the court where the assets are located so that an order can be obtained which is effective against the asset holder, or to the court which has jurisdiction over the place where the defendant is physically to be found so that it can enforce its orders directly against him. It may well be appropriate in such a case to ask that court for a worldwide order because that court is best placed to enforce the order if the defendant were to disobey it.[18] Commonly the appropriate forum for seeking freezing relief is different from the appropriate forum for the resolution of the substantive issues.[19]

In *Official Receiver for the State of Israel v Raveh*[20] the plaintiff had brought proceedings in Israel based on a claim for debt and obtained the equivalent of a worldwide freezing order. There were proceedings in Western Australia which could result in substantial sums coming to the defendant. The plaintiff intended to obtain a judgment in the Israeli proceedings and then register it in Western Australia. In the meantime

---

[17] SI 1997/392.
[18] *Jeanette Walsh v Deloitte & Touche Inc.* [2002] L.R.C. 545 at [21–24]; *Crédit Suisse Fides Trust SA v Cuoghi* [1998] Q.B. 818.
[19] *Jeanette Walsh v Deloitte & Touche Inc.* [2002] L.R.C. 545 at [22].
[20] (2001) 159 F.L.R. 471. In contrast the position in Israel is that a temporary attachment order can be requested when proceedings on the merits are outside Israel, and Israel is not an appropriate forum for the merits, but there are assets in Israel: *RCA 102/88 Maadenei Avaz Hakesef v Cent Or SARL* PD 42(3) 201 (attachment in support of London Arbitration).

Mareva relief from the Australian court was sought over the proceeds of the pending proceedings. Thus the cause of action was an existing cause of action which was sued on in Israel and the plaintiff was seeking the equivalent of s.25 relief from the Australian court over assets situated there. No objection was taken based on a lack of a mechanism for the service of proceedings on a defendant, which was the basis of *Mercedes Benz AG v Leiduck*. The principle in *Channel Tunnel Group Ltd v Balfour Beatty Construction Ltd* did not arise because the plaintiff had not sued in Australia based on the underlying debt. The judge held that Mareva relief was not available for the reason that the cause of action was not before the Australian court because it was the subject of the Israeli litigation nor would it be in due course, because the Australian court would be enforcing a judgment which had been registered and not the underlying cause of action. In consequence, the principle as stated in *Cardile* did not apply because it did not apply to foreign proceedings but only "to operate upon a defendant who seeks to evade or acts in a way calculated to defeat the enforcement in [the Australian] Court of a substantive right pursued by the plaintiff in [that] Court".

The judgment which would be defeated was the judgment to be enforced **1.029** by the Australian court which would be the judgment obtained in Israel registered under the statutory enforcement regime. If it would be an abuse of the process of the Australian court if the defendant dissipated assets with the effect of defeating eventual enforcement by the Australian court of a judgment of an Australian court, why was it not equally an abuse of that process to defeat enforcement by the Australian court of the registered judgment? It would be more satisfactory to say that there was no jurisdiction to act in support of the proceedings in Israel because this was a matter of policy for the Australian legislature which had not enacted any equivalent to s.25.

(9) The change of terminology—freezing injunction, freezing order, asset preservation order and Mareva order

The CPR brought with it in April 1999 a change of terminology for the **1.030** Mareva injunction. It is now a type of "freezing injunction"[21] because it is an "injunction" which freezes assets. Under CPR r.25.1(1)(f) a "freezing injunction" is described as an order:

"(i) restraining a party from removing from the jurisdiction assets located there; or

(ii) restraining a party from dealing with any assets whether located within the jurisdiction or not."

---

[21] CPR r.25.1(1)(f).

CPR r.25.1(1)(f) followed a wording appropriate for Mareva relief, and had the aim of putting into plain language a concept which already had a name used worldwide. The terms "freezing injunction" or "freezing order" should not be allowed to obscure the history and the true nature of relief granted under the Mareva jurisdiction:[22]

(1) The words "freezing injunction" or "freezing order" suggest that particular assets are frozen by an order granted under the Mareva jurisdiction. This is not so. A Mareva injunction imposes a restraint on the conduct of the person enjoined and does not operate *in rem* on an asset. Because of the financial limit and the liberties in a Mareva injunction, the order has an ambulatory effect on assets, which potentially come in or outside the scope of its restraint according to how the person enjoined organises his affairs.

(2) A "freezing injunction" could also be granted outside the scope of the court's Mareva jurisdiction. For example, an order in these terms could be granted against a trustee requiring him not to dispose of trust property, or as an injunction granted in aid of a proprietary claim, or in aid of a claim under s.423 of the Insolvency Act 1986[23] or as an injunction granted in aid of an order appointing a receiver by way of equitable execution or granting a charging order, or granting relief over assets *quia timet*. The words of the order described in CPR r.25.1(1)(f) are not restricted to assets belonging beneficially to the party restrained, nor to cases in which the claimant claims no right to or interest in the assets sought to be preserved. The substantive rules applicable to each of these various jurisdictions of the court are different.

(3) CPR r.25.1(1)(f) has in both (i) and (ii) the words "restraining a party". The Mareva jurisdiction also enables an order to be made against a non-party. In *C Inc v L*,[24] a judgment had been obtained against the defendant and the claimant sought appointment in England of a receiver over the defendant's right against her husband to an indemnity in respect of the judgment. The right of indemnity was an asset of the defendant's wife. The injunction was sought to preserve the husband's own assets so that they would be available to satisfy the obligation to indemnify, and thus the judgment obtained against the wife. No substantive claim based on the indemnity was being made or to be made against the husband

---

[22] Compare *Société Eram Shipping Co. Ltd v Compagnie Internationale de Navigation* [2004] 1 A.C. 260 at [112]—Lord Millett's criticism of CPR Pt 72, the terms of which obscure the proprietary nature of execution by third party debt order (formerly a garnishee order).

[23] *Gill v Flightwise Travel Service Ltd* [2003] EWHC 3082 at [26], Ch.D. ("The expression 'freezing order', in the absence of a good reason to the contrary, is to be given its natural meaning. [The] orders purported to freeze property in the hands of the appellants.")

[24] [2001] 2 Lloyd's Rep. 459, following *Cardile v LED Builders Pty Ltd* (1999) 198 C.L.R. 380.

in the English proceedings. So the description of a "freezing injunction" used in the CPR is not apt to cover Mareva injunctions against non-parties.

(4) In Australia the use of the word "injunction" is criticised on historical grounds[25]—Mareva relief was not available as an "injunction" (or at all), and because there Mareva relief is viewed as an order granted to prevent conduct which might frustrate possible future process of the court to enforce a judgment.[26] In England the case law since 1975 has justified the relief as an "injunction" albeit a special type of injunction with its own set of rules.

After CPR r.25.1(1)(f), the injunction continues to be referred to by the House of Lords,[27] and by writers,[28] as the Mareva injunction, words readily understandable to lawyers, including those in other common law jurisdictions, the public and the international community. It is often appropriate, for clarity, to use the words "Mareva Injunction"rather than the more general expression of "freezing injunction". **1.031**

(10) The appointment of a receiver

In *Hart v Emelkirk*,[29] Goulding J. made an order appointing a receiver in a pre-judgment case in respect of certain assets. The plaintiff claimed no proprietary right in the assets and was not entitled to have them used in any particular way. The appointment was made simply on the basis that it was "just and convenient" to do so and that s.37(1) of the Supreme Court Act 1981 conferred jurisdiction to enable the appointment to be made. It is now established that a receiver may be appointed over property irrespective of whether the plaintiff's claim involves some substantive claim over or in respect of that property and may be appointed either before or after judgment. The emergence of the Mareva jurisdiction has also led to more flexibility in relation to the appointment of receivers by way of equitable execution. This is a procedure for a remedy to assist in the enforcement of an existing judgment and is a long-established jurisdiction in equity. **1.032**

---

[25] *Cardile v LED Builders Pty Ltd* (1999) 198 C.L.R. 380.
[26] *Jackson v Sterling Industries Ltd* (1987) 162 C.L.R. 612 at 617–618, *per* Wilson and Dawson JJ. and at 623, *per* Deane J.; *Patrick Stevedores Operations No.2 Pty Ltd v Maritime Union of Australia* (1998) 195 C.L.R. 1 at 32; *Cardile v LED Builders Pty Ltd* (1999) 198 C.L.R. 380 at 400–401.
[27] *Société Eram Shipping Co. Ltd v Compagnie Internationale de Navigation* [2003] 1 A.C. 260 at [23], *per* Lord Bingham, with whose reasons Lord Nicholls agreed at [31], and, *per* Lord Hoffmann at [56]; *R. (on the application of McCann) v Crown* Court *at Manchester* [2003] 1 A.C. 787 at [25] (Lord Steyn whose reasons were also adopted by Lord Hobhouse and Lord Scott).
[28] *e.g.* Dicey and Morris on the *Conflict of Laws*, 13th ed., 2000, ch. 8, including para.8–006, which makes the point that it should be distinguished from tracing cases.
[29] [1983] 1 W.L.R. 1289.

An injunction operates in *personam* against the person who is restrained by it. But sometimes the assets can be defined, *e.g.* the proceeds of a transfer, but it remains unclear who has them. An injunction can be granted against the person who is thought to control them but this may not be effective when steps are being taken to render people judgment proof and when offshore companies or trusts are being used. In those circumstances the court may be driven to the conclusion that there is a risk that injunctions against named persons may not be sufficient to preserve the assets. The appointment of a receiver over those assets may be the most effective way of piercing the corporate veil.[30]

(11) Ancillary orders

1.033   The courts have found in s.37 of the Supreme Court Act 1981 a statutory basis for the jurisdiction to make a wide variety of different types of order in aid of freezing relief. A defendant may be required to give information to the claimant about specified assets, to assist the plaintiff in ensuring that the Mareva relief will be effective in safeguarding the relevant assets. That information may have to be provided on affidavit or by discovery of documents, and the defendant may be ordered to attend the court for cross-examination concerning the information provided. The defendant may be ordered to provide the plaintiff with authority to ask banks about assets, and he may in an extreme case be ordered to surrender his passport so that he cannot leave the country.

(12) Mareva relief granted worldwide

1.034   The courts departed from the original rule that Mareva relief would be granted only in respect of assets situated within the jurisdiction. In this they followed the initiative taken in certain Australian courts and took into account the provisions for international reciprocity in granting interim relief in aid of substantive proceedings abroad and in recognising orders made by way of interim relief by foreign courts. This change in practice has given rise to the need to consider the extent to which third parties, including banks, are bound to respect a Mareva order in so far as it applies to assets abroad, and what wording should be incorporated governing the position of third parties holding assets abroad.[31] This step was the natural

---

[30] *International Credit and Investment Company (Overseas) Ltd v Adham*, unreported, November 20, 1996 (Robert Walker J.) referring to *Re a Company* [1985] B.C.L.C. 332 and *Jones v Lipman* [1962] 1 W.L.R. 832.

[31] *Bank of China v NBM LLC* [2002] 1 W.L.R. 844; *Baltic Shipping Co. v Translink Shipping* [1995] 1 Lloyd's Rep. 673; *Babanaft International Co. SA v Bassatne* [1990] Ch. 13.

consequence of the Mareva injunction being an injunction granted against a person to preserve assets to meet a judgment. The principle applied regardless of where assets were located.

(13) Carrying on business and making payments out of assets subject to Mareva relief

As a consequence of the emergence of the Mareva jurisdiction the courts **1.035** have laid down the principles which are to be applied in deciding whether or not assets are to be released from a Mareva injunction to be used for a particular purpose.

(14) Effects on third parties

The granting of Mareva relief is liable to have an impact on third parties **1.036** who deal with the defendant or are involved in dealing with assets falling within the scope of the order. The courts have evolved rules of practice concerning undertakings to be provided by the claimant in favour of third parties and the drafting of the terms of the order. They have also laid down principles as to the effect of Mareva relief on third parties and the extent to which their interests are to be taken into account when a court decides whether to grant or continue Mareva relief.

(15) Criminal law

The Mareva jurisdiction has provided the context for the evolution of rules **1.037** concerning the freezing of alleged proceeds of crime at common law. Statutory provisions are in force providing for the making of restraint orders in connection with the prosecution of drug offences and other crimes.

(16) Other jurisdictions

The Mareva jurisdiction is applied in numerous jurisdictions around the **1.038** world, including Australia,[32] Bermuda, the Bahamas, the Cayman Islands,

---

[32] R. P. Meagher, J. D. Heydon and M. J. Leeming, *Meagher, Gummow and Lehane's Equity: Doctrines and Remedies* (4th ed., 2002) paras 21–430 *et seq.*; I. C. F. Spry, *The Principles of Equitable Remedies: Specific Performance, Injunctions, Rectification and Equitable Damages* (6th ed., 2001), ch. 4; F. Kunc and S. Hepburn, "Mareva Orders" in *The Principles of Equity* (P. Parkinson ed., 2nd ed., 2003), p.704.

Canada,[33] Hong Kong, Singapore, Malaysia, New Zealand, Gibraltar, Jersey, the Turks and Caicos Islands, the Isle of Man, New Zealand[34] and the Republic of Ireland.[35] In Canada,[36] the fact that assets are to be transferred from one province to another does not in itself make it appropriate for Mareva relief to be granted. This is because the provinces are part of a federal system.

In Jersey, the Court of Appeal in *Sovalub Ltd v Match Investments Ltd*[37] decided that as a matter of Jersey law there could be free-standing proceedings in Jersey brought for the purpose of obtaining Mareva relief against a defendant who was being sued in foreign proceedings. Such proceedings can be brought in England under s.25 of the Civil Jurisdiction and Judgments Act 1982, which by virtue of SI 1997/302 applies to any proceedings commenced or to be commenced anywhere, or in aid of any arbitral proceedings under s.44 of the Arbitration Act 1996. The Royal Court also decided in *Krohn GmbH v Varna Shipyards*[38] that proceedings claiming only Mareva relief could be served out of the jurisdiction under r.7(b) of the Service of Process (Jersey) Rules 1994, which corresponds to what is now CPR r.6.20(2).[39] This contrasts with the majority decision in *Mercedes-Benz v Leiduck*. In England, there are now specific rules of court directed to enabling there to be permission to serve free-standing proceedings seeking Mareva relief under statute to be served out of the jurisdiction.

In Scotland there is a procedure of arrestment which is "a form of attachment brought by the arrester in an action for the payment of money which prevents a third party who holds moveable property or money due to the respondent from parting with it pending the disposal of the action".[40] But this is very different from the Mareva jurisdiction and there is no equivalent to the English jurisdiction to grant ancillary orders.[41]

---

[33] See Robert Sharpe in *Injunctions and Specific Performance* (1999, Looseleaf ed., Canada Law Book Inc.).

[34] Described in *Equity and Trust in New Zealand* (ed. A. Butler, 2003), Chapter 23.

[35] T. B. Courtney, *Mareva Injunctions and Related Interlocutory Orders* (1998).

[36] *Aetna Financial Services Ltd v Feigelman* [1985] 1 S.C.R. 2; *Gudaitis v Abacus Systems Inc.* (1995) 35 C.P.C. (3rd) 266; which are discussed by Robert Sharpe in *Injunctions and Specific Performance* (3rd ed., 1999, looseleaf), para.2.830.

[37] Unreported, December 13, 1996.

[38] Unreported, July 24, 1997.

[39] Followed in *Yachia v Levi*, unreported, March 26, 1998. See also P. Matthews, "No Black Holes , Please , We're Jersey" *Jersey Law Review* (June 1997), "*Sovalub* and Black Holes— A Postscript" *Jersey Law Review* (February 1998), "*Sovalub* Strikes Again" *Jersey Law Review* (October 1998) and "*Sovalub* Again" *Jersey Law Review* (October 1999), and W. Bailhache, "The Concept of Black Holes—*Krohn* Revisited" *Jersey Law Review* (February 1999). Cf. *Bass v Bass* [2001] C.I.L.R. 317 (where the Grand Court of the Cayman Islands declined to follow *Solvalub Ltd v Match Investments Ltd* and held there was no free-standing interim injunction jurisdiction).

[40] R. Aird, "The Scottish Arrestment and the English Freezing Order" (2002) 51 I.C.L.Q. 155 at 157.

[41] See R. Aird, "The Scottish Arrestment and the English Freezing Order" (2002) 51 I.C.L.Q. 155 for a description of the differences.

(17) The Anton Piller jurisdiction—search orders

The granting of Anton Piller orders dates from 1974, the first reported case **1.039**
in which one was granted being *EMI Ltd v Pandit*.[42] The jurisdiction to
grant the relief was first upheld by the Court of Appeal in *Anton Piller KG
v Manufacturing Processes*,[43] in which the procedure was distinguished
from that of granting search warrants.

The jurisdiction to grant the relief was found in the inherent jurisdiction
of the court. The reasoning was that the court had jurisdiction to make an
order *inter partes* requiring a party to permit another to come on to his
property to carry out an inspection. However, there were cases where, if
the application was made *inter partes*, the defendant might in the meantime
take steps which would render useless any order eventually made. The
merit of an order made *ex parte* would be that the defendant would be
bound to obey it or be in contempt of court. Such an order would prevent
the ordinary process of the court being rendered useless.

The jurisdiction can also be justified as being an exercise of the power to
grant injunctions under s.37(1) of the Supreme Court Act 1981.

The defendant is made subject to a mandatory order of the court to give **1.040**
permission to a limited number of persons, including the claimant's
solicitors and a supervising solicitor appointed by the court, to enter the
relevant premises within certain hours to search for evidence, property or
other material falling within the categories defined in the order and to
remove the material found there so that it can be safeguarded. It is of the
essence of the procedure that the application is made without notice, and
the hearing is conducted in chambers in the Queen's Bench Division, or in
camera in the Chancery Division. In the Court of Appeal, an application
will usually be heard in *camera*, but may occasionally be made in open
court if the identity of the respondents to the application can be satisfactorily concealed from the public.

In 1992, a committee appointed by the Judges' Council reported about
the practical operation of the jurisdiction, and in 1994 a standard form
order was provided for by a Practice Direction, which was updated in 1996
and again in Form SO in 2002. The jurisdiction has now been put on a
statutory basis by s.7 of the Civil Procedure Act 1997.

Often application is made so as to safeguard vital evidence which is
needed to prove the claimant's claim, but the procedure can be invoked to
obtain information necessary to safeguard the claimant's rights, or to locate
assets upon which a judgment might be enforced, or to preserve property
which otherwise might be dissipated or destroyed.

Because the application for the relief is made without notice, the **1.041**
emergence of the jurisdiction has focused special attention on the duty of
the applicant to make full disclosure to the court, and the practice and

---

[42] [1976] Ch. 75.
[43] [1975] 1 W.L.R. 302.

procedure to be followed on an application to discharge the order. When the defendant is served with a search order, after a short period allowed to him for taking legal advice, he becomes under an immediate obligation to comply with the order, otherwise he will be in contempt of court, and liable to be penalised even if subsequently he succeeds in having the order set aside.

The claimant is required to give undertakings to the court as to how the order is to be executed, and breach of these undertakings constitutes a contempt of court. The claimant's solicitors have an onerous personal responsibility when they take on the conduct of an application for Anton Piller relief and execution of the order. Failure to adhere to the requisite professional standards is liable to result in criticism from the court, penal orders in relation to costs and possibly a disciplinary complaint either to the court or under the Solicitors Act 1974.

Any order made must preserve to a defendant the right to invoke privilege against self-incrimination if this is available to him. If the privilege applies, then a defendant is entitled not only to decline to produce incriminating materials, but to decline to permit persons to enter premises to search for them. The position remains unaltered by s.7 of the Civil Procedure Act 1997.

1.042   There are statutory exceptions to the privilege, the most important in practice being s.72 of the Supreme Court Act 1981 (which applies to claims for infringement or apprehended infringement of intellectual property rights or for passing off) and s.31 of the Theft Act 1968, which also applies to the Theft Act 1978, but does not remove privilege when the defendant may be prosecuted for conspiracy (*e.g.* when funds have been stolen and there is a real risk of a prosecution for conspiracy to defraud).

The jurisdiction to grant Anton Piller relief is widely recognised in common law jurisdictions throughout the world, including Australia, New Zealand, Hong Kong, Singapore, Canada and South Africa.

(18) Security for costs under CPR r.25.13 and the court's case management powers under CPR Pt 3

1.043   The jurisdiction of the court to grant security for costs is set out in CPR r.25.13(2) which includes the jurisdiction under s.726(1) of the Companies Act 1985. This jurisdiction now includes a Mareva-type jurisdiction to order security when the claimant has taken steps in relation to his assets that would make it difficult to enforce an order for costs against him. This looks at what steps he has already taken which may have this consequence. There is no requirement in CPR r.25.13(2)(g) of the steps having been taken with nefarious intent.

There is also a separate jurisdiction to make orders under CPR Pt 3 which concerns the court's powers of case management. This is a very wide jurisdiction. It could extend to making an order against the claimant granting a stay of the proceedings until he gave security such as security for costs or security for payment of an existing unperformed court order for costs. It could also be used against a defendant by requiring him to make a payment into court.

However, under this jurisdiction, there has to have been regular flouting of court orders or lack of good faith[44] and the order must be a proportionate response to the conduct which has led to it being made. Furthermore the power must not be used if the claim or defence would stifled. In relation to a defendant it would require extreme circumstances to justify an order that he make a payment into court because of his previous misconduct in relation to his conduct of the proceedings. Whether being contemplated against a claimant or a defendant the court has to bear in mind that party's right under Art.6(1) of the European Convention on Human Rights to a fair trial, and the requirement that he have access to justice.

Under CPR r.52.3(7) conditions may be imposed on the granting of **1.044** permission to appeal, and under CPR r.52.9(1)(c) the Court of Appeal has jurisdiction to impose conditions on the prosecution of an appeal when there is a "compelling reason" to do so. This can include where the appellant has not satisfied a judgment or costs order made in the court below, there are good reasons for believing that it will continue not to comply with the order of the court, and the evidence does not show that it is not possible for the appellant to comply, or that the appeal will be stifled.[45]

---

[44] *Olatawura v Abiloye* [2003] 1 W.L.R. 275; *Ali v Hudson* [2003] EWCA Civ 1793 at [39–45]; *CIBC Mellon Trust v Mora Hotel Corporation NV* [2003] 1 All E.R. 564.
[45] *Hammond Suddard Solicitors v Agrichem International Holdings Ltd* [2001] EWCA Civ 2065; *CIBC Mellon Trust Co. v Stolzenberg* [2004] EWCA Civ 117 (Sir Swinton Thomas: ordering security for costs for an appeal including for past costs unpaid when there had been a previous history of flouting court orders); *Contract Facilities Limited v The Estate of Rees (Deceased)* [2003] EWCA Civ 1105 (where there was a non-party funding the litigation and the pending appeal, costs orders had not been satisfied by the impecunious claimant, and the Court of Appeal exercised its case management powers in CPR 3.1 to order that the appeal be struck out unless certain costs orders were satisfied and a sum was paid into court as security for an interim costs order.

Chapter 2

General principles and enforcement of contracts

(1) Introduction

An injunction is a discretionary remedy, granted or refused in accordance **2.001** with principles elucidated by the courts. For the remedy to be available there must be proceedings about to be commenced or commenced before the court, which have been served on the defendant, or there must be procedural machinery under which the proceedings can be served on the defendant, which the claimant is about to utilise, so that the court has territorial jurisdiction over the defendant in respect of those proceedings under its own domestic rules.[1] Equity acts *in personam* so that provided that there are such proceedings the court can grant an injunction against the defendant.[2] However, if the object of the proceedings is to obtain an injunction in relation to actions abroad the court may as a matter of discretion abstain from granting relief altogether[3] or only grant it pending application to the local court for relief.

An injunction may be sought as a remedy in an infinite variety of situations and it must be recognised that any attempt to state principles must accomodate this. In a case concerning trespass on to land, or infringement of a right to light, or a patent, the court is concerned with the protection of a property right, which, if not protected by an adequate remedy, becomes diminished. It is the policy of the law that certain rights,

---

[1] *Siskina v Distos Compania Naviera SA (The Siskina)* [1979] A.C. 210 and *Mercedes Benz AG v Leiduck* [1996] A.C. 284 were cases in which there was no territorial jurisdiction in the sense of there being machinery enabling the proceedings to be served on the defendant. Even where this is possible the foreign aspects may make it inappropriate to grant an injunction.

[2] *Penn v Lord Baltimore* (1750) 1 Ves.Sen. 444; *National Australia Bank Ltd v Dessau* [1988] V.R. 521 at 522; *Australian Competition and Consumer Commission v Purple Harmony Plates Pty Ltd (No. 3)* (2003) 196 A.L.R. 576 at paras 43–45 (the court can act *in personam* in respect of property abroad or ordering someone amenable to the jurisdiction to do some act, or refrain from doing acts, abroad). On the potential relevance of an inability to enforce an injunction effectively against a foreigner, see Chapter 6, para.6.080.

[3] *White Sea and Onega Shipping Co. Ltd v International Transport Workers' Federation (The Amur-2528 and the Pyalma)* [2001] 1 Lloyd's Rep. 421 (no injunction granted in respect of blacking discharge of ships in Denmark); see also Chapter 6, paras 6.006–6.009 and Chapter 22.

because of their nature, should not in general be bargained away, by the court refusing an injunction, and leaving the claimant to his remedy in damages. In a case concerning an application for a mandatory interim injunction before trial in a commercial dispute, the concern of the court is to arrive at an order which carries with it the least overall risk of injustice at the end of the day.[4] The principles to be applied cannot be divorced from the nature of the rights claimed, the stage of the proceedings in which the application is made, and the purpose for which an injunction is being sought, and the foreseeable effects of granting or refusing it.

(2) The terminology

2.002   Injunctions can be mandatory, prohibitory or negative in form. The former requires some positive act to be done by the person enjoined, *e.g.* to pull down a building or to provide information. The latter restrains the commission of an act; it can be complied with through the defendant doing nothing.

Under CPR r.25.1(1)(a) reference is made to the power of the court to grant an "interim injunction". This expression in the CPR covers all injunctions which are not granted as final relief. The word "interim" is used to show that the injunction is only temporary. It is to be contrasted with a final injunction which is an injunction given as part of final relief in the action usually after a successful application for summary judgment, or at trial, after judgment. An "interlocutory" injunction (literally an injunction granted between hearings) is an injunction which is temporary and to expire on a particular date when a further hearing is due to take place or on further order of the court. It may be expressed to be until further order. An interim or interlocutory injunction can be granted after the trial in the action, *e.g.* an injunction granted as an aid to execution. A "perpetual" injunction is a final injunction granted without limit of time.

An injunction granted on a without notice application is an injunction granted when no prior notice has been given to the respondent and the respondent is unrepresented before the judge. Prior to the CPR, *ex parte* injunctions included both those where no notice had been given and those in which informal notice had been given to the defendant, which were called *ex parte* on notice. There were also opposed *ex parte* applications in which the defendant had been given informal notice (often very short notice indeed) and was represented before the judge. The corresponding terminology to be used after the CPR would be "without notice", "on informal notice" and an "opposed without notice application". All such applications require full disclosure and fair presentation.

---

[4] *Zockoll Group Ltd v Mercury Communications Ltd* [1998] F.S.R. 354; *Films Rover Ltd v Cannon Film Sales Ltd* [1987] 1 W.L.R. 670; *R. v Secretary of State for Transport Ex p. Factortame (No. 2)* [1991] 1 A.C. 603 at 683; *Nottingham Building Society v Eurodynamic Systems* [1993] F.S.R. 468.

A *quia timet* ("since he fears") injunction is an injunction granted for the **2.003** purpose of preventing what would be an actionable wrong if it was committed. Either the defendant has threatened a wrongful act or there is a real risk that unless an injunction is granted an actionable wrong will be committed. A Mareva injunction is not a *quia timet* injunction because it does not restrain what would be an actionable wrong.

"Balance of convenience" is normally used today as referring to the exercise of discretion to be made by the court in deciding whether to grant an interim injunction, but in the times[5] of Lord Cairns L.C. and later,[6] it has been used to describe the considerations which apply to the granting of final relief.[7]

(3) Relationship between specific performance and injunctions, and the specific enforcement of a negative contractual promise by injunction

(i) An interim injunction granted in anticipation of a decree of specific performance or an interim or final injunction granted ancillary to the decree

An interim injunction can be granted for the purpose of holding the **2.004** position,[8] or preparing it by mandatory injunction,[9] to enable there to be an eventual order for specific performance. In *Smith v Peters*[10] there was a contract to sell a public house and fixtures and fittings at a "fair valuation" to be made by a named valuer. At that time it was thought that if the valuer did not fix the price the court would not enforce the contract.[11] Sir George

---

[5] *Doherty v Allman* (1878) 3 App.Cas. 709 at 720 (perpetual injunction granted at trial); *Jenkins v Jackson* (1888) 40 Ch.D. 71.

[6] *Kerr on Injunctions* (6th ed., 1927), p.32.

[7] *Texaco Ltd v Mulberry Filling Station* [1972] 1 W.L.R. 814 at 830.

[8] *Preston v Luck* (1884) 27 Ch.D. 497 (interim injunction preserving a patent pending the hearing of buyer's claim for specific performance); *Hart v Herwig* (1873) L.R. 8 Ch.App. 860 (interim injunction preserving a ship within the jurisdiction pending buyer's claim for specific performance). *London and County Banking Company v Lewis* (1882) 21 Ch.D. 490 (equitable mortgagee entitled to injunction against third party volunteers to restrain dealings by them with the legal estate in the mortgaged property pending conveyance of it to the mortgagee through enforcement by the court of the mortgage).

[9] *Astro Exito Navegacion SA v Chase Manhattan Bank (The Messiniaki Tolmi)* [1983] 2 A.C. 787 affirming [1982] Q.B. 1248, discussed in Chapter 7, paras 7.012–7.013; *Sky Petroleum Ltd v VIP Petroleum Ltd* [1974] 1 W.L.R. 576 (interim mandatory injunction to deliver fuel to plaintiff's filling stations under contract for supply non-specific/unascertained goods because of risk of destruction of plaintiff's business).

[10] (1875) L.R. 20 Eq. 511.

[11] *Vickers v Vickers* (1867) L.R. 4 Eq. 529, which was eventually overruled in *Sudbrook Trading Estate Ltd v Eggleton* [1983] 1 A.C. 444. Under the analysis in *Sudbrook*, the contract in *Smith v Peters* could have been enforced by specific performance by taking a fair and reasonable price for the fixtures and fittings with every reasonable allowance being made against the seller who was impeding the entry of the agreed valuer in breach of contract.

Jessel M.R. granted a mandatory injunction requiring the seller to permit the valuer to enter the premises to carry out the valuation, preparatory to a decree of specific performance. The jurisdictions under CPR r.25.1(c) can also be used in relation to the property which is the subject of a claim for specific performance.[12] An injunction can also be granted at trial ancillary to a decree for specific performance,[13] or as itself compelling specific performance by the defendant, either when the contract has been performed by the claimant, or when that performance is executory.[14]

(ii) The enforcement of a negative engagement by injunction when specific performance of the entire contract is not available

2.005 There are also situations in which the court cannot or would not grant specific performance of a contract, but will grant an injunction to enforce a particular negative promise made in the agreement. The leading case is *Lumley v Wagner*[15] where there was a contract for the defendant to sing for two days per week over a period of three months for the plaintiff at Her Majesty's Theatre, Drury Lane, and a covenant not to sing for anyone else during that period. Lord St Leonards L.C. granted an injunction enforcing the negative covenant not to sing for anyone else. The positive contract was not appropriate for a decree of specific performance; it was a contract for personal services and involved not the mere achieving of a specified result,[16] which could be checked by the court, but the achieving of whole performances. So the fact that a negative engagement forms part of a contract which would not be specifically enforced does not have the consequence that an injunction will be refused.[17] On the contrary the assumption is that the defendant will be held to his bargain and an injunction will be granted. In *James Jones & Sons Ltd v Earl of Tankerville*,[18] Parker J. considered that specific performance could be granted in the sense of compelling execution of a document which was irrevocable and entitled the plaintiff to enter the land to cut the timber. This analysis

---

[12] *Strelley v Pearson* (1880) 15 Ch.D. 113.

[13] *Benke v Bede Shipping* [1927] 1 K.B. 649 (injunction restraing defendant from parting with ship to anyone other than the plaintiff, granted ancillary to specific performance of contract of sale of a ship which was "peculiar and [of] practically unique value to the plaintiff".)

[14] *James Jones & Sons Ltd v Earl of Tankerville* [1909] 2 Ch. 440.

[15] (1852) 1 De G.M. & G. 604.

[16] *Cooperative Insurance Society Ltd v Argyll Stores (Holdings) Ltd* [1998] A.C. 1 at 13; likewise in *Ryan v Mutual Tontine Westminster Chambers Association* [1893] 1 Ch. 116 the covenant was not just to employ a porter, but was a covenant to employ a porter *"who should perform the specified duties"* (*per* Lopes L.J. at 125) and therefore was a covenant for the provision of continuous services which the court would not supervise through contempt proceedings.

[17] *Donnell v Bennett* (1883) 22 Ch.D. 835 (injunction granted to restrain the defendant from obtaining supplies of fish from another source); *Dietrichsen v Cabburn* (1846) 2 Ph. 52 (injunction granted to enforce a negative promise given by the defendant, who had discovered a medicine, from supplying or selling it to anyone other than the plaintiff who had been appointed wholesale distribution agent for the medicine by the plaintiff).

[18] [1909] 2 Ch. 440.

looked to enforcement of a promise to produce a legally enforceable document entitling the grantee to entry, as opposed to whether all the terms of that document were themselves capable of specific performance. It was compellable as a promise to produce a particular "result",[19] in contract to a promise to perform various activities.

In this class of case the court is considering whether to enforce a negative covenant notwithstanding that specific performance of the contract is not available. There is the consideration that *pacta sunt servanda* and contracts should be kept, but there is also the consideration whether it is just to enforce only the negative covenant leaving the rest of the contract to be dealt with by an award of damages. It is here that the unavailability of specific performance may become of critical importance.

The law sets its face against forcing people who do not desire to maintain a close personal relationship, which involves mutual trust and confidence,[20] to do so. The court will not grant an injunction which would in effect put the defendant in a position where he would in practice be compelled to continue with such a contract.[21] Contracts of employment fall within this category. The decision of the Court of Appeal in *Hill v C. A. Parsons & Co.*[22] must be regarded as a case decided on highly exceptional facts, where both employer and employee were happy for the relationship to continue and damages would have been a wholly inadequate remedy. The court will not indirectly by an injunction compel something which it would not compel directly or which in practice would compel such performance or be tantamount to doing so.[23] Under this principle the court will also decline to grant an injunction against a third party for inducing breach of contract when the practical effect of doing so would be to force the employer and employee back together;[24] this is on the basis that the court will not compel indirectly that which it would not compel directly.

---

[19] See *Cooperative Insurance Society Ltd v Argyll Stores (Holdings) Ltd* [1998] A.C. 1 at 13.

[20] *Chappell v Times Newspapers* [1975] 1 W.L.R. 482 at 503 and 506; *Page One Records Ltd v Britton* [1968] 1 W.L.R. 157 (no injunction granted to restrain The Trogs pop group from engaging another manager or using a different music publisher because the effect would be tantamount to enforcing the group to continue with the existing managers and publishers); *Warren v Mendy* [1989] 1 W.L.R. 853 (boxer and manager not kept together).

[21] *Warren v Mendy* [1989] 1 W.L.R. 853 at 860–866 criticising the actual result in *Warner Brothers v Nelson* [1937] 1 K.B. 209 on the ground that Branson J. was mistaken in thinking that Miss Bette Davis would have foregone screen and stage for up to three years in that time of her "youth and soaring talent".

[22] [1972] Ch. 305.

[23] *Warren v Mendy* [1989] 1 W.L.R. 853 at 860–866; *Ehrman v Bartholomew* [1898] 1 Ch. 671; *William Robinson & Co. Ltd v Heuer* [1898] 2 Ch. 451; *Atlas Steels Pty Ltd v Atlas Steels Ltd* (1948) 49 S.R. (N.S.W.) 157 at 164–165; *Whitwood Chemical Company v Hardman* [1891] 2 Ch. 416 (where there was no negative covenant and a positive engagement of the employee to give "the whole of his time"; if an injunction could be granted against any activity inconsistent with the positive covenant this would in practice compel specific performance of the employment contract).

[24] *Warren v Mendy* [1989] 1 W.L.R. 853 at 866–867, pointing out that an injunction against a particular third party employer could still leave the employee free to approach other potential employers; everything turns on the practical effect of granting the relevant injunction.

2.006   The court will grant an injunction which although it is an inducement to perform the contract of employment, does not indirectly compel its performance.[25] Where the contract is not a contract of employment but is a commercial contract for services such as a sole distribution agreement, likewise, provided the injunction does not indirectly compel performance, the court may still grant an injunction to enforce a negative stipulation even though it could not, and would not, specifically enforce the contract itself. A sole distribution agreement for a particular territory contains a negative engagement not to appoint any other agent for that territory. Can such a negative engagement be enforced by injunction under the principle in *Lumley v Wagner*? The answer is that it depends on the particular circumstances. The court will not specifically enforce a sole distribution agreement because of the difficulty of supervising such a contract and because of the undesirability of yoking together a supplier and a distributor in a close relationship for services requiring mutual trust and confidence. It follows from this that the court will not grant an injunction the practical effect of which would be to require the supplier to continue to work with the sole distributor. In *Atlas Steels Pty Ltd v Atlas Steels Ltd*[26] the court refused an injunction where, if an injunction had been granted, the only alternative to going on with the contract would have been to cease doing business altogether in a vast territory where that business was already established and was very active. On the other side of the line is *Evans Marshall & Co. v Bertola SA*[27] where an interim injunction was granted restraining breach of the negative engagements on the theory that this could induce the supplier to perform but would not compel him to do so.

(iii) He who seeks equity must do equity and whether an existing or potential breach of contract will bar relief

2.007   The very factors that make specific performance not a just remedy may also make it inappropriate to grant any injunction. For example, a claimant in an action for specific performance, or for a *quia timet* injunction preventing the other party from purporting to terminate the contract,[28] who is not

---

[25] *Evans Marshall & Co. v Bertola SA* [1973] 1 W.L.R. 349 at 379; *Warren v Mendy* [1989] 1 W.L.R. 853 at 860–866 (boxer and manager) criticising the result in *Warner Brothers v Nelson* [1937] 1 K.B. 209 (film producer and actress); *Marco Productions Ltd v Pagola* [1945] K.B. 111; *Atlas Steels Pty Ltd v Atlas Steels Ltd* (1948) 49 S.R. (N.S.W.) 157 at 165–166 (the third group of cases).

[26] (1948) 49 S.R. (N.S.W.) 157.

[27] [1973] 1 W.L.R. 349; similarly see *Decro-Wall SA v Practitioners in Marketing Ltd* [1971] 1 W.L.R. 361 at 378H where the suppliers would have inflicted on the distributor a ruinous blow which would have broken up their business, and *Thomas Borthwick & Sons (Australasia) Limited v South Otago Freezing Co. Ltd* [1978] 1 N.Z.L.R. 538 , where the New Zealand Court of Appeal upheld an injunction to enforce an express covenant (clause 10) not to handle stock for anyone other than the plaintiff which was part of a 20-year-contract for the defendant to buy in stock, process and sell it to the plaintiff.

[28] *Chappell v Times Newspapers* [1975] 1 W.L.R. 482. So also when enforcement would cause undue hardship to the defendant, even when this has arisen from events after the contract was concluded for which the claimant is not responsible: *Patel v Ali* [1984] Ch. 283 at 287.

willing to assure the court that he is ready willing and able to perform his part of the agreement in its essential[29] respects, will not obtain specific performance. He who seeks equity must do equity.

The same principle may debar a party who is already seriously in breach of contract from obtaining specific performance[30] or an injunction.[31] Not every breach has this effect; all depends on the circumstances and how much the breach deprives the other party of the essence of what he contracted to receive.[32] This is so when the term of which enforcement is sought is conditional on some other term which the claimant has not performed, but is also so independently of this.

(iv) Mutuality

A further example of a discretionary factor relevant both to specific **2.008** performance and an injunction to enforce a negative promise, is when, at the time of considering whether to grant the relief,[33] the contract has not yet been performed by the claimant and so is executory, and the court would not compel by specific performance those outstanding obligations of the claimant. In such circumstances the fact that no specific performance is available[34] to compel performance of the claimant's obligations, and the defendant would be left to damages in the event of breach, can be a factor leading[35] to the conclusion that no injunction should be granted to enforce

---

[29] *Mehmet v Benson* (1965) 113 C.L.R. 295 at 307–309.

[30] *Australian Hardwoods Pty Ltd v Commissioner for Railways* [1961] 1 W.L.R. 425 at 432–433.

[31] *Measures Bothers Ltd v Measures* [1910] 2 Ch. 248; *Telegraph Despatch and Intelligence Company v McLean* (1873) 8 Ch.App. 658 (injunction refused because of plaintiff's breach of the contract); *Besant v Wood* (1879) 12 Ch.D. 605 at 627–628 (minor breach unconnected with the promise sought to be enforced will not bar the granting of specific performance or injunction).

[32] See also 'Unclean hands', para.2.034, below. Where there is some defect in the property to be transferred but the defendant would get substantially what he had contracted for, there can be an order for specific performance but allowing compensation to the defendant for that defect: *Re Contract between Fawcett and Holmes* (1889) 42 Ch.D. 150; *Shepherd v Croft* [1911] 1 Ch. 521.

[33] In *Price v Strange* [1978] Ch. 337 the Court of Appeal disapproved of Sir Edward Fry's statement in *Fry on Specific Performance* (6th ed., 1921) at p. 219 that the question of "mutuality" was to be considered at the time of conclusion of the contract. The question is one of remedy and whether it is just at the time of considering granting a remedy to require the defendant to perform his obligation but leaving him with no assurance that the plaintiff will in fact perform his.

[34] As in *Blackett v Bates* (1865) L.R. 1 Ch.App. 117, where the plaintiff would otherwise have been granted the lease at once, in return for the plaintiff providing steam engines to enable the defendant to use the railway line.

[35] *Price v Strange* [1978] Ch. 337 at 353E–354E; *Rainbow Estates Ltd v Tokenhold Ltd* [1998] Ch. 64 at 69C–D; J. C. Williamson *Ltd v Lukey and Mulholland* (1931) 45 C.L.R. 282 at 299–300, *per* Dixon J. who draws attention to the possibility that the injunction is granted subject to a condition that it will be dissolved if the plaintiff broke his promises. The problem is that if performance of the contract is ongoing and complicated (as it was on the facts of that case which concerned selling ice creams and confectionary in a theatre) this might be a cumbersome and impractical solution; *Page One Records Ltd v Britton* [1968] 1 W.L.R. 157 at 165; *Johnson v Shrewsbury and Birmingham Railway Company* (1853) 3 De G.M. & G. 914 at 927; *Warren v Mendy* [1989] 1 W.L.R. 853 at 866 (indicating that want of "mutuality" is not an absolute bar but a matter going to discretion).

the negative engagement of the defendant. The more of the contract that has been performed by the claimant before the time of considering whether to grant the injunction, the less one-sided it would be to grant it, and the more the court will consider it just to grant it.[36] In *Lumley v Wagner* this point did not arise because the only obligation of the plaintiff was to pay money and so this could be enforced.

(v) Injunction when the negative undertaking is not express

2.009   In the judgment in *Lumley v Wagner*,[37] emphasis was placed by Lord St Leonards L.C. on the fact that there was an express negative covenant in the contract which was not simply the correlative of the positive engagement. Thus the opera singer might consistently with the positive engagement have sung at other times. It was thought at one time[38] that there was a need for an express covenant; but this would have been a triumph of form over substance and equity looks only to the substance.[39] The result has been that there are cases in which there was only a positive covenant in form but an injunction has been granted. In *Metropolitan Electric Supply Co. v Ginder*,[40] the promise was to take the whole of the electricity required for the Red Lion public house in Holborn from the plaintiff and an injunction was granted to prevent the defendant from taking electricity from anyone else. In that case there was no promise to take any quantity of electricity at all; although formulated as a positive engagement the substance of it was negative—not to take electricity for the public house from anyone else.[41] In *National Provincial Bank v Marshall*,[42] there was a bond promising to pay £1,000 "liquidated" damages in certain circumstances and this was interpreted as a contract not to do what was specified as triggering this obligation to pay. Liquidated damages were payable for a breach of contract, and an injunction was granted to restrain the breach.

---

[36] See the reporter's note to *Hills v Croll* (1845) 2 Ph. 60 at 63–64 quoted with approval in *Price v Strange* [1978] Ch. 337 at 353–354.

[37] (1852) 1 De G.M. & G. 604

[38] *Whitwood Chemical Company v Hardman* [1891] 2 Ch. 416; *Mortimer v Beckett* [1920] 1 Ch. 571 at 581. (It is suggested that the agreement by using the word "sole" did import a negative promise not to have anyone else to arrange boxing matches for the defendant—compare *Atlas Steels Pty Ltd v Atlas Steels Ltd* (1948) 49 S.R. (N.S.W.) 157 at 161 and *W. T. Lamb & Sons v Goring Brick Company Ltd* [1932] 1 K.B. 710, but it was one which would not be enforced by injunction because it would have yoked together the boxer and his manager in a contract for personal services, see [1920] 1 Ch. 571 at 581, *Page One Records Ltd v Britton* [1968] 1 W.L.R. 157, and *Warren v Mendy* [1989] 1 W.L.R. 853.)

[39] *Wolverhampton and Walsall Railway Company v London and North Western Railway Co.* (1873) L.R. 16 Eq. 433 at 440 (defendant lessee of a railway line not using the line as it promised to do, and an injunction granted from using other lines); *J. C. Williamson Ltd v Lukey and Mulholland* (1931) 45 C.L.R. 282 at 299, *per* Dixon J. ("It appears to be of little importance now whether the duty is imposed by a term of the contract expressed in negative or affirmative language").

[40] [1901] 2 Ch. 799.

[41] See also *Manchester Ship Canal v Manchester Racecourse Co.* [1901] 2 Ch. 37 (right of first refusal enforced by injunction).

[42] (1888) 40 Ch.D. 112.

There does not have to be an express negative covenant provided that a negative engagement can be found in the contract, the significance of the presence of an express negative covenant being that it makes clear what is the scope of the negative engagement, and possibly it makes the case for enforcement by injunction stronger because the parties expressly bargained on the basis of that engagement and so it is more difficult for the defendant to make out a sufficient case of hardship to result in the court declining to grant the injunction.[43]

(vi) Lord Cairns's dictum in Doherty v Allman

Turning to the consideration that contracts should be kept, this is a strong **2.010** reason for enforcing an express or implied negative engagement. In *Doherty v Allman*,[44] Lord Cairns L.C. said obiter in a famous dictum that where there is a negative covenant "a Court of Equity would have no discretion to exercise", it would grant an injunction by way of "specific performance . . . of that negative bargain". This dictum has been followed from time to time. But it goes too far.

First, an injunction to enforce a contractual bargain is itself a discretionary remedy. Lord Cairns L.C.'s dictum does not oust the discretion.[45] For example, a negative covenant may not be enforced because of laches or acquiescence[46] or circumstances which have supervened since the contract was concluded.[47]

Secondly, there could be circumstances which would make it positively unjust or inconvenient to enforce that bargain. The words of Lord Cairns L.C. should not be taken as overruling the words of s.37(1) of the Supreme Court Act 1981.

Thirdly, the position stated by Lord Cairns L.C. is in marked contrast **2.011** with the well-established situation, in the context of anti-suit injunctions,[48] that the contractual promise will be enforced in the absence of "strong reason" not to do so. It also contrasts with the position that in strong cases a court will exercise a discretion to give permission for service of a claim form out of the jurisdiction when the claimant is seeking to bring

---

[43] *Thomas Borthwick & Sons (Australasia) Limited v South Otago Freezing Co. Ltd* [1978] 1 N.Z.L.R. 538 at p.545 line 52–p.547 line 54.
[44] (1878) 3 App.Cas. 709 at 720.
[45] *Insurance Co v Lloyd's Syndicate* [1995] 1 Ll. Rep. 272 at pp.276–277; *Thomas Borthwick & Sons (Australasia) Limited v South Otago Freezing Co. Ltd* [1978] 1 N.Z.L.R. 538 at p.545 lines 33–51 *per* Cooke J. delivering the judgment of the New Zealand Court of Appeal, referring to Lord Blackburn's '. . . more guarded observations . . .' in *Doherty v Allman* (1878) 3 App. Cas. 709 at p.730. *Elliston v Reacher* [1908] 2 Ch. 374 at 395. *Ernst & Young v Kiwi Property Holdings Ltd* [2003] 3 N.Z.L.R. 103 at paras 55–57.
[46] *Shaw v Applegate* [1977] 1 W.L.R. 970.
[47] *ibid.*, 980.
[48] See Chapter 14, para.14.014; *Donohue v Armco* [2002] 1 Lloyd's Rep. 425; for the principle on stays based on an exclusive jurisdiction clause, see *Aratra Potato Co. Ltd. v Egyptian Navigation Co. (The El Amria)* [1981] 2 Lloyd's Rep. 119; *The Eleftheria* [1970] p.94.

proceedings in breach of a foreign jurisdiction clause.[49] There is a strong policy of enforcing contracts, but the need to do substantive justice is even stronger.

Fourthly, *Doherty v Allman* was a case where a final injunction was granted at trial and not a case concerning interim injunctions, and in that area other considerations can arise.[50] This is not to say that because the matter arises on an interlocutory application the covenant will not be enforced and the covenantor will be given a "holiday"[51] from observing the covenant up until trial. It was also a case which did not involve a negative covenant.[52]

Fifthly, if what is sought is a mandatory injunction, again other considerations can arise,[53] including hardship to the defendant. In that category of case Megarry J. looked to producing "a fair result"; but this is the ultimate objective in every injunction case, including that of enforcing a negative covenant by a negative injunction.

2.012   It is suggested that the correct analysis is that there is a strong policy for enforcing bargains and that this goes to the extent of enforcing a negative covenant. There is a strong presumption that the covenant will be enforced. But the matter remains discretionary. For example, if the consequence of the injunction would be to leave the defendant at the claimant's mercy with the claimant seeking to obtain an extortionate sum in return for release from the covenant, then the court should consider awarding damages under Lord Cairns' Act instead of granting an injunction, and can assess the damages on the basis of a fair price to pay in return for being released from the promise.[54] Damages would not be assessed at a ransom price. It is no part of the function of equity in the enforcement of a contractual bargain, to put the claimant in a position of unfair bargaining power from which he can make an extortionate demand.[55]

It is suggested that the true rule is that when seeking an injunction to restrain breach of a negative covenant, the claimant does not have to prove that if there is breach he will suffer loss,[56] or that damages would be an inadequate remedy. Where the defendant's positive obligations under a

---

[49] *Evans Marshall & Co. v Bertola SA* [1973] 1 W.L.R. 349 at 375.
[50] *Texaco Ltd v Mulberry Filling Station* [1972] 1 W.L.R. 814 at 830; *Hampstead & Suburban Properties Ltd v Diomedous* [1969] 1 Ch. 248.
[51] *Hampstead & Suburban Properties Ltd v Diomedous* [1969] 1 Ch. 248 at 259.
[52] *ibid.*, at 259.
[53] *Shephard Homes Ltd v Sandham* [1971] Ch. 340 at 350–351; *Sharp v Harrison* [1922] 1 Ch. 502; *Charrington v Simons & Co. Ltd* [1970] 1 W.L.R. 725 at 730.
[54] *Jaggard v Sawyer* [1995] 1 W.L.R. 269 approving *Wrotham Park Estate Co. Ltd v Parkside Homes Ltd* [1974] 1 W.L.R. 798 at 815; *Tito v Waddell (No. 2)* [1977] Ch. 106 at 335.
[55] *Cooperative Insurance Society Ltd v Argyll Stores (Holdings) Ltd* [1998] A.C. 1 at 15; *Isenberg v East India House Estate Co.* (1863) 2 De G.J. & S. 263 at 273, *per* Lord Westbury L.C.; *Jaggard v Sawyer* [1995] 1 W.L.R. 269 at 287.
[56] *Insurance Co v Lloyd's Syndicate* [1995] 1 Ll. Rep. 272 at pp.276–277; *Marco Productions Ltd v Pagola* [1945] K.B. 111 (dancers and entertainers restrained from appearing in any other entertainment when this was likely to prove an inducement to appear in *Jack and the Beanstalk* as contracted). *Elliston v Reacher* [1908] 2 Ch. 374 at p.395 (enforcement of a restictive covenant about the user of land).

contract are executory, this is because such an injunction could act as an inducement to the defendant to perform the rest of the contract even though they are not susceptible to a decree for specific performance. Therefore the injunction furthers the legitimate interests of the claimant based on the contract. But where the defendant proves hardship, and that damages would be an adequate remedy to the claimant, an injunction may be refused.[57] Unreasonable or heavy-handed conduct in breach of a negative covenant can be a strong factor reinforcing the case for an injunction.[58]

The position is to be distinguished from that where the claimant has a proprietary right, such as a right to light, which is valuable because it has to be bought out before a development can proceed. No man has the right to expropriate his neighbour's property to enable him to carry out a development. In those circumstances the claimant's property has a special value because of its location and the defendant must buy out his neighbour before he can proceed.[59]

(4) *American Cyanamid* and the balance of convenience for interim injunctions

(i) *The principles in American Cyanamid*

Prior to *American Cyanamid Co. v Ethicon Ltd*,[60] there were cases stating **2.013** in different terms the relevance of showing a case of a certain quality to obtain an interim injunction and what the threshold was.[61] One line of authority required the plaintiff to show a "real probability of the plaintiff succeeding" at trial.[62] In *American Cyanamid*, the plaintiff owned a patent for surgical sutures. The defendant was about to launch its own sutures on

---

[57] *Insurance Co v Lloyd's Syndicate* [1995] 1 Ll. Rep. 272 at p.277 RHC; *Donnell v Bennett* (1883) 22 Ch.D. 835 at 837–838. See also British *Glass Manufacturers Confederation v Sheffield University* [2003] EWHC 3108; [2004] 09 E.G. 146 (injunction refused to restrain replacement of buildings demised under 1,000-year lease, when the replacement would improve the property); *Thomas Borthwick & Sons (Australasia) Ltd v South Otago Freezing Co. Ltd* [1978] 1 N.Z.L.R. 538 at p.545 line 52; p.547 line 54.

[58] *James Jones & Sons Ltd v Earl of Tankerville* [1909] 2 Ch. 440 at 446, where the contractual rights had not only been infringed "but [had] been deliberately and wantonly disregarded with every circumstance of indignity and violence . . .".

[59] *Cooper v Laidler* [1903] 2 Ch. 337 (ancient rights of light for a cottage which blocked a new development protected by injunction and the plaintiff not left to damages).

[60] [1975] A.C. 396.

[61] See *Series 5 Software Ltd v Clarke* [1996] 1 All E.R. 853 at 856–861.

[62] *Zaidener v Barrisdale Engineers Ltd* [1968] R.P.C. 488 at 495, *per* Diplock L.J.; *Beecham Group Ltd v Bristol Laboratories Pty Ltd* (1968) 118 C.L.R. 618 (proof of a "probality" of success; but it is suggested that "probability" did not mean more probable than not, but meant taking into account the strength of the case to see whether in the circumstances it justified granting the relief sought—see also R. P. Meagher, J. D. Heydoa and M. J. Leeming, *Meagher, Gummow and Lehane's Equity: Doctrines and Remedies* (4th ed., 2002), para.21–350).

the British market, and challenged the validity of the patent and whether, if valid, it applied to the defendant's product. At first instance the judge had held that on the evidence available at the interlocutory hearing the plaintiff was likely to succeed at trial and granted an injunction. The Court of Appeal considered that on the evidence there was not a "prima facie case" of infringement. The question before the House of Lords was whether there was a rule of law that an interlocutory injunction could only be granted if the court was satisfied on a balance of probabilities that on the evidence then before the court the plaintiff's right would be infringed. The House held that there was no such rule. Unless the evidence "fails to disclose that the plaintiff has any real prospect of succeeding in his claim for a permanent injunction at the trial",[63] in other words once the claimant has shown "a serious issue to be tried"[64] on whether he is entitled to an injunction, the court should consider three questions.

The first question is whether if the claimant were correct at trial, an award of damages would be an adequate remedy. If damages in the measure awarded at common law would be an adequate remedy, and the defendant would be in a financial position to pay them,[65] then, however strong the claimant's case appeared to be, no injunction should "normally" be granted.

The second question is whether if the injunction was granted and the defendant was successful at trial damages under the cross-undertaking would be an adequate remedy. If damages in a measure which would be recoverable under the cross-undertaking would be an adequate remedy and the claimant would be in a financial position to pay them (or provide security for them) then there would be "no reason on this ground" to refuse an interim injunction.

2.014　　The third question which is balance of convenience only arises when there is doubt as to the adequacy of the remedy of damages available to either party or to both. The extent to which there is doubt to which damages would be an inadequate remedy for either party comes in again in assessing the relative balance of convenience. In *American Cyanamid* preserving the "status quo" was of particular relevance. This is the position as it stands immediately before the claim form is issued, or, if there has been an unreasonable delay before the application for an injunction, the position immediately before the issuing of that application.[66] In *American Cyanamid* the relevance was because, if an injunction was refused, the plaintiff's monopoly would have been at an end, and the opportunity for the plaintiff to build up lasting goodwill from that period of monopoly would have been taken away irreversibly.

There can be no exhaustive list of the factors which can play a part in assessing the balance of convenience. The fundamental objective of the

---

[63] [1975] A.C. 396 at 408.
[64] *Eng Mee Yong v Letchumann* [1980] A.C. 331 at 337C–D.
[65] [1975] A.C. 396 at 408.
[66] *Garden Cottage Foods Ltd v Milk Marketing Board* [1984] A.C. 130 at 140.

court, when weighing up all the factors, is to take the course which involves the least risk of injustice at the end of the day, if the court's decision to grant or refuse an injunction should turn out to have been "wrong" by reference to the final result at trial. So the court considers (1) the risk of injustice to the defendant if it were to grant an injunction to the claimant who at trial is, or if there was a trial would be, unable to establish his right to an injunction; and (2) the risk of injustice to the claimant if it were to refuse to grant an injunction against the defendant when at trial the claimant is able to establish his entitlement to an injunction, or if there was a trial would be able to establish such an entitlement.[67] Where the factors are evenly balanced it may be a counsel of prudence to preserve the status quo.[68]

There can also be special factors such as matters of public policy or public interest,[69] or the effect of granting or refusing the injunction on non-parties.[70]

The *American Cyanamid* case is an important statement of the principles **2.015** to be applied in deciding applications for interim injunctions. But it has to be seen in the context of the facts of the case before the House of Lords. The claim was to enforce a proprietary right to a monopoly. Patents were enforced by injunction by the old Court of Chancery because if inventions were to be encouraged and the purposes of the patent legislation were to be achieved the monopoly granted had to be an effective one, enforced by the court. Notoriously damages are not an adequate remedy for the patentee because they would be difficult to assess and because the monopoly can generate a goodwill which persists for some considerable time after expiry of the patent. It was a case in which if the strength of the merits were to be assessed at the interlocutory application, the result would be a complicated mini trial of some considerable length.[71] What the case clearly established was that there is "normally"[72] no need on applications for an interim injunction to embark on a mini trial[73] on witness statements or affidavits to assess the quality of the claimant's case or the defendant's defences, or to assess the rival merits on a disputed, complicated question

---

[67] *Films Rover Ltd v Cannon Film Sales Ltd* [1987] 1 W.L.R. 670 at 680; *R. v Secretary of State for Transport Ex. p. Factortame (No. 2)* [1991] 1 A.C. 603 at 683.

[68] *American Cyanamid Co. v Ethicon Ltd* [1975] A.C. 396 at 408.

[69] *Attorney-General v Guardian Newspapers* [1987] 1 W.L.R. 1248 (mass publication would be liable to damage the morale of the security service and public confidence in it); *Miller v Jackson* [1977] Q.B. 966 (cricket not stopped by injunction) contrast *Kennaway v Thompson* [1981] Q.B. 88; *Brown v Healthlands NHS Trust* [1996] 1 All E.R. 133 (restrictive covenant not enforced by injunction when land to be used for a statutory purpose and there was in place a statutory scheme for compensation).

[70] For example, *Garden Cottage Foods Ltd v Milk Marketing Board* [1984] A.C. 130 at 143 (the effect on the four distributors to whom the Milk Marketing Board had already made commitments). *Ernst & Young v Kiwi Property Holdings Ltd* [2003] 3 N.Z.L.R. 103 (where on the particular facts the consideration that the defendant would probably be put in breach of contract with a third party did not prevent the court from granting the injunction).

[71] *Series 5 Software Ltd v Clarke* [1996] 1 All E.R. 853 at 863.

[72] Emphasised in *Series 5 Software Ltd v Clarke* [1996] 1 All E.R. 853 at 863.

[73] *Series 5 Software Ltd v Clarke* [1996] 1 All E.R. 853 at 864g–h.

of law.[74] This would be wasteful of the parties' resources and those of the court. It would also be inconsistent with the objective of the court not to pronounce an opinion on the substantive merits of the case until trial. This objective encourages judges not to decide important applications on an assessment of the apparent merits based on evidence which is incomplete, and without the benefit of cross-examination, full disclosure of documents and detailed argument. These features made it fair and sensible to avoid assessment of the merits in *American Cyanamid*, and the approach adopted by the Court of Appeal, impracticable.

American Cyanamid principles are usually the correct approach in a case of enforcement of a covenant in restraint of trade,[75] and in a passing-off action.[76]

However, the principles are "guidelines", and not a "straitjacket", where the function of the court is to hold the position as justly as possible pending final determination of a triable issue at trial.[77]

(ii) Where the apparent strength of the merits is important to the exercise of discretion

2.016 There are cases in which it is still necessary to have regard to the apparent merits and where the principles in *American Cyanamid* cannot or should not be applied:

(1) One of those cases is where there never will be a trial, and the result of the application for an interim injunction will in effect conclude the litigation. In *Cayne v Global Natural Resources Plc*,[78] an injunction was refused when, if it had been granted, there would have been no prospect of a trial, and the granting of the injunction would in effect have summarily decided the litigation in favour of the plaintiff. The same was so in *Lansing Linde Ltd v Kerr*,[79] where because of congestion in the courts the trial could not take place until towards the end of a post-employment covenant of 12 months. The Court of Appeal took into account the merits of whether the covenant was invalid as being in unreasonable restraint of trade and refused the injunction. In labour disputes the decision about an

---

[74] [1975] A.C. 396 at 407 (it is no part of the court's function to decide "difficult questions of law which call for detailed argument and mature consideration"); *Series 5 Software Ltd v Clarke* [1996] 1 All E.R. 853 at 865f–g; *Associated British Ports v TGWU* [1989] 1 W.L.R. 939 at 979, *per* Lord Goff (mere fact the point of law takes a little longer to understand that some other points of law does not make it inappropriate to decide on an application for an interim injunction).

[75] *Lawrence David Ltd v Ashton* [1991] 1 All E.R. 385; contrast the particular facts in *Lansing Linde Ltd v Kerr* [1991] 1 W.L.R. 251.

[76] *County Sound Plc v Ocean Sound Plc* [1991] F.S.R. 367.

[77] *Cambridge Nutrition Ltd v BBC* [1990] 3 All E.R. 523 at 534.

[78] [1984] 1 All E.R. 225.

[79] [1991] 1 W.L.R. 251.

interim injunction will often be the end of the litigation. In those circumstances the grant or refusal of the injunction is likely to result in loss to the losing party which will be complete and cannot be compensated for in damages. In those circumstances the likelihood of success if there were a trial is a matter to be taken into account.[80] A further example is where the court has to reach a decision on whether a solicitor should be allowed to act for a client on a case or a transaction such as a take-over bid,[81] which is imminent and there is not time to have a trial.

(2) *American Cyanamid* principles cannot be applied where there is a rule of law which requires the merits to be taken into account to a particular standard before an injunction can be granted. An example of this is s.12(3) of the Human Rights Act 1998, which relates to restraints on publications[82] and protects freedom of speech. This requires the merits of the claimant's claim to be looked at to see whether the statutory threshold has been reached.[83]

(3) *American Cyanamid* principles are not to be applied where the merits of the case are clear,[84] *e.g.* where the defendant has no reasonably arguable case that he has a defence,[85] or where the claimant has been unable to show a serious issue to be tried as to whether he is entitled to an injunction. For example, the claimant may not have a cause of action.[86] A corollary of this where a defendant is seeking to vary a proprietary freezing injunction to enable him to use funds to pay legal costs, he has to show at least an arguable case that he is entitled to use the assets for this purpose.[87]

There can be circumstances in which the claimant cannot show a serious case to be tried against a respondent on the evidence presently available but it seems likely that further critical evidence will shortly be available, which may put a different complexion on matters. This may happen in a case in which a serious case to be tried is made out against one of the defendants but not against another defendant who is closely connected. In such circumstances

---

[80] *N. W. L. Ltd v Woods* [1979] 1 W.L.R. 1294 at 1306–1307.

[81] *Marks and Spencer Plc v Freshfields Bruckhaus Deringer* [2004] EWHC 1337 at para.23 (permission to appeal was refused by the Court of Appeal).

[82] *Douglas v Hello! Ltd* [2001] Q.B. 967.

[83] *Cream Holdings Ltd v Banerjee* [2003] Ch. 650 gives the legislative history to this provision, and spells out the test as being a real prospect of success convincingly established.

[84] *Series 5 Software Ltd v Clarke* [1996] 1 All E.R. 853.

[85] *Patel v W. H. Smith (Eziot) Ltd* [1987] 1 W.L.R. 853, where the plaintiff was entitled to restrain a trespass on to his land regardless of whether the trespass harmed him, because the defendant had no arguable case that he was entitled to go on to the land; *Hampstead & Suburban Properties Ltd v Diomedous* [1969] 1 Ch. 248 (defendant in clear breach of covenant); *Manchester Corporation v Connolly* [1970] Ch. 420 at 427.

[86] See Chapter 1, paras 1.006–1.009

[87] See Chapter 20, para.20.057. *The Ostrich Farming Corporation Ltd v Ketchell*, CA, unreported, December 10, 1997, at p. 7 of the transcript, *per* Millett L.J.

the guidelines in *American Cyanamid* should not result in the refusal of an interim injunction against the connected defendant pending clarification of the position through the emergence of further evidence.[88]

(4) *American Cyanamid* principles do not apply to the jurisdiction to restrain by injunction the presentation of a winding-up petition or its advertisement. The basis for such an application is that it would be an abuse of the process of the court to allow such a petition to proceed, and that the court should grant an injunction under its inherent jurisdiction to prevent an abuse of its process.[89] The risk of the petition being allowed to proceed is that, even though it is doomed to failure, it will irretrievably damage the company.[90] One ground on which such an injunction can be granted is when the threat is of a creditor's petition but there is no underlying debt, or the alleged debt is disputed bona fide and on substantial grounds[91] and the dispute should be resolved through ordinary civil proceedings[92] and not by the Companies Court. Although the form of the application is for an interim injunction the substance is to strike out the petition or apprehended petition, on the ground of abuse of the process. The claimant must prove the threatened abuse. This is why in this category of case, failure to prove that the petition is doomed removes the platform for obtaining the injunction.[93]

(5) *American Cyanamid* principles do not appear to apply to public law injunctions where the applicant is the Attorney-General or a local authority or some public authority seeking to enforce the law for the public good.[94] Here, if the injunction is "wrongly granted", there will be no cross-undertaking in damages and no redress for the defendant.

(6) *American Cyanamid* principles do not apply to a Mareva injunction sought before trial. The threshold to be met is that of a "good

---

[88] *Roseneath Holdings Limited v Grieve* [2004] 2 N.Z.L.R. 168 at paras 41–44 (where an injunction was granted against the registered transferee of a mortgage in contemplation that material would become available to show that the transferee had acted dishonestly so as to defeat the rights of the purchasers of a property). In New Zealand there has been emphasis on an analysis based on the 'overall justice' of the case, following *Klissers Farmhouse Bakeries Ltd v Harvest Bakeries Limited* [1985] 2 N.Z.L.R. 129 at p.142 *per* Cooke J. delivering the judgment of the Court of Appeal, and see *Equity and Trusts in New Zealand* (2003) (edited by A.Butler) in section 22.3.

[89] *Bryanston Finance Ltd v De Vries No. 2* [1976] Ch. 63; *Charles Forte Investments Ltd v Amanda* [1964] Ch. 240; *Mann v Goldstein* [1968] 1 W.L.R. 1091 at 1093–1094; *James Dolman & Company Ltd v Pedley* [2003] EWCA Civ 1686 at [10].

[90] *James Dolman & Company Ltd v Pedley* [2003] EWCA Civ 1686 at [5] citing *Re a Company No. 006685 of 1996* [1997] B.C.C. 830 at 832.

[91] *James Dolman & Company Ltd v Pedley* [2003] EWCA Civ 1686.

[92] *Stonegate Securities v Gregory* [1980] Ch. 576; *Celtech International Ltd v Dalkia Utilities Services Plc* [2004] EWHC 193, Ch; *Re a Company No. 006685 of 1996* [1997] B.C.C. 830 at 832.

[93] *Re a Company (No. 160 of 2004)* [2004] EWHC 380, February 20, 2004).

[94] See Chapter 11, para.11.002.

arguable" case,[95] as opposed to a serious issue to be tried. Therefore there is a difference between the "good arguable" case threshold which applies to an application for a pre-judgment freezing order based on pure Mareva principles, where no proprietary claim is made, and the serious issue to be tried threshold which applies to freezing orders based on a proprietary claim.

(7) For the principles applicable to restraining a bank from making payment under an irrevocable letter of credit or performance guarantee—see Chapter 15, below.

(8) The principles do not apply to an interim injunction to restrain an alleged libel or malicious falsehood when the defendant intends to justify, because that would be an excessive restraint on freedom of speech.[96]

(iii) The losses to be taken into account for the purpose of deciding whether damages would be an adequate remedy for the claimant

Sometimes damages are not an adequate remedy for the claimant because **2.017** of the great difficulties which will be involved in assessing them. For example, the nature of the case may involve assessing imponderables about what hypothetically would have happened in a business over a period of years.[97] Another factor which may make damages inadequate as a remedy is when to refuse an injunction would lead to the destruction of the claimant's business.[98]

Another is when the defendant has no assets or has no assets against which a judgment could be readily enforced; this can in itself be a strong factor in favour of granting an injunction to enforce the claimant's asserted rights, including enforcement of a contractual promise.[99] In patent actions, one way of dealing with this is for the defendant to undertake to the court to set aside and place into a separate bank account to stand as security for the claimant a sum of money covering every sale which the claimant contends infringes his patent, and on the basis of this undertaking the court can then decline to grant the interim injunction.[1]

---

[95] See Chapter 12, paras 12.023–12.026.
[96] *Bonnard v Perryman* [1891] 2 Ch. 269; *Quartz Hill Consolidated Gold Mining Company v Beall* (1882) 20 Ch.D. 501; *Sim v H. J. Heinz Co. Ltd* [1959] 1 W.L.R. 313.
[97] *Evans Marshall & Co. v Bertola SA* [1973] 1 W.L.R. 349 at 379–380. *Anvil Jewellery Ltd v Riva Ridge Holdings Ltd* [1987] 1 N.Z.L.R. 35 (damages are not an adequate remedy when the defendant will not be able to pay them).
[98] *J. Lyons & Sons v Wilkins* [1896] 1 Ch. 811 at 827; *Garden Cottage Foods Ltd v Milk Marketing Board* [1984] A.C. 130 at 153B–D. Correspondingly when the effect of granting an injunction would be to prevent the defendant from earning his living this will come into balance of convenience as a factor against granting an injunction: *Series 5 Software Ltd v Clarke* [1996] 1 All E.R. 853 at 868e–f; *Potters-Ballotini Ltd v Weston-Baker* [1977] R.P.C. 202.
[99] *Evans Marshall & Co. v Bertola SA* [1973] 1 W.L.R. 349 at 380H–381E.
[1] *Vernon & Co. (Pulp Products) Ltd v Universal Containers Ltd* [1980] F.S.R. 179; *Brupat Ltd v Sandford Marine Products Ltd* [1983] R.P.C. 61.

In *Bath and North East Somerset District Council v Mowlem Plc*,[2] the claimant authority owned the hot springs at Bath and was developing the site as a heritage site and public amenity, and the defendant was a building contractor in possession of the site, resisting an application for an interim injunction restraining it from refusing access to the site by another contractor appointed by the claimant to carry out certain works. There was an issue about whether the claimant was entitled under the contract to appoint the other contractor to perform the particular works. The defendant contended that a liquidated damages clause in the contract meant that the claimant had an adequate remedy in damages because that is what the claimant had agreed to receive. This argument was rejected. The liquidated damages clause was a contractual mechanism for dealing with the assessment of monetary damages; it did not mean that whatever losses were caused to the claimant by a breach of contract unrestrained by injunction these would all in fact be covered by this machinery. Those losses would potentially be in fact far greater than the liquidated damages amount, and would include matters for which it would be difficult if not impossible to put a figure, and matters for which money could not compensate the claimant as a local authority advancing public purposes, such as all the losses to the public of the advantages of earlier completion of the works to the heritage site.

(iv) Enforcement of proprietary rights by interim or final injunction when substantial damages may not be recoverable

2.018   An injunction can be granted purely to protect a proprietary right of the claimant even though the infringement of that right would not give rise to substantial damages. An example of this is actions to restrain a trespass.[3] On the other hand the court will not restrain by injunction every trivial interference with a proprietary right, or where the application is a heavy-handed, capricious, or otherwise unreasonable.[4]

Just because no damages can be recovered for one reason or another, it does not follow that no injunction will be granted to protect the proprietary right. In *Smithkline Beecham Plc v Apotex Europe Plc*[5] a claim

---

[2] [2004] EWCA Civ 115. A distinction is to be drawn between a sum which is payable as an alternative mode of performance by the defendant, and a liquidated damages clause. The latter does not bar specific performance but only regulates damages if specific performance is not insisted upon: *Long v Bowring* (1864) 33 Beav. 585 at 588; *Tay Ah Poon v Chionh Hai Guan* [1997] 2 S.L.R. 363. The same principle applies to granting an injunction to enforce the contract.

[3] *Jaggard v Sawyer* [1995] 1 W.L.R. 269; *Patel v W. H. Smith (Eziot) Ltd* [1987] 1 W.L.R. 853 at 858–859; *Woolerton and Wilson Ltd v Richard Costain Ltd* [1970] 1 W.L.R. 411; *John Trenberth Ltd v National Westminster Bank* (1979) 39 P. & C.R. 104 at 108.

[4] *Llandudno Urban Council v Woods* [1899] 2 Ch. 705 (application refused to stop a clergymen preaching on the seashore); *Behrens v Richards* [1905] 2 Ch. 614 at 622, *per* Buckley J., later Lord Wrenbury, the court would not restrain "nurserymaids from wheeling their perambulators on the sands or children from playing on the rocks ...".

[5] [2003] F.S.R. 31.

in a patent was sued upon which had been upheld in earlier proceedings between different parties in which other claims had been held invalid. The defendant argued that the claimant could not obtain damages for the infringement because of a statutory bar which might apply if some of the claims made by the patent were invalid. The potential statutory bar to damages would not invalidate the proprietary right claimed which could be enforced by injunction.

On the other hand, there are cases where on the particular facts the reasons which result in no substantial damages being recoverable for infringement of the proprietary right also lead to the conclusion that no injunction should be granted. This is because it is not the purpose of the proprietary right to secure to the claimant the advantage which he seeks to secure by the injunction. In *Polaroid Corporation v Eastman Kodak Company*,[6] the plaintiff could not bring into account on the interim injunction application the damage likely to be caused to its "peel apart" camera business if an injunction was not granted to restrain infringement to its "integral" camera patents. This was because, on the facts, it was no part of the purpose of the patents protecting the "integral" camera monopoly to give the plaintiff a monopoly protecting its "peel apart" process;[7] the proprietary right only protected the market in "integral" cameras. In contrast in *Smithkline Beecham Plc v Apotex Europe Plc*[8] the valid claim in the patent applied to one form of chemical and another form was so close to it that it was to be contemplated that damages for infringement of the patent would take into account the claimant's losses covering both forms. With patent infringement, the losses to be considered are the losses of the claimant patentee and not those of other companies albeit part of the same group of companies;[9] this is because the purpose of the patent is to secure the monopoly for the patentee.

(v) Relevance of conduct of the claimant or defendant, including delay

American Cyanamid also does not affect the relevance of the claimant's and defendant's conduct to the exercise of discretion. Delay, laches, acquiescence, breach of contract or wilful breach of contract[10] by the claimant can all be relevant to whether an interim injunction is to be granted. When there has been delay and the application is made without notice because of urgency, then this in itself may result in the application being refused.[11]

2.019

---

[6] [1977] R.P.C. 379.
[7] See also *Bath and North East Somerset District Council v Mowlem Plc* [2004] EWCA Civ 115 at [17].
[8] [2003] EWCA Civ 137 at [31].
[9] *Peaudouce SA v Kimberly-Clark Ltd* [1996] F.S.R. 680, where losses to other group companies would not have been losses of the plaintiffs and therefore did not enter into account in deciding whether to grant an interim injunction.
[10] Likewise such conduct by the applicant for relief from forfeiture is a ground going to refusal to allow the relief as a matter of discretion: *Shiloh Spinners v Harding* [1973] A.C. 691 at 725C–F, and *Hill v Barclay* (1811) 18 Ves. Jun. 56 at 63.
[11] *Bates v Lord Hailsham of St Marylebone* [1972] 1 W.L.R. 1373 at 1379F–1380C.

Delay in the claimant applying for an interim injunction is relevant because it is liable to affect the practical doing of justice on the application. It raises questions about whether the claimant really needs an injunction pending trial,[12] the quality of the claimant's case and whether the delay has affected the defendant. There have been patent cases in which an interim injunction has been refused solely on the ground of serious delay,[13] on the basis that the claimant still has open to him his remedies at trial. It is suggested that as a general principle on an application for an interim injunction the applicant should apply promptly,[14] and the court should consider delay as a discretionary matter which needs to be looked at taking into account the prejudice, if any caused to the defendant by that delay,[15] and all the other circumstances of the case. If the applicant has taken up time making reasonable enquiries prior to launching his application this is not to be taken against him.[16]

(vi) The certainty principle and an interim injunction

2.020   An injunction, whether interim or final, must be expressed in clear and precise terms so that a defendant knows exactly what he must not do or what he must do.[17]

With an interim injunction, the claimant's rights have not yet been defined at trial. One way of dealing with this is to grant an interim injunction which is free-standing in the sense that it defines precisely what can and cannot be done, and is not linked to what are the claimant's claimed rights.[18] The problem with this is that where the claimant is suing on a broad right such as a copyright or a patent, it can be difficult to foresee all the ways in which the defendant may subsequently go about infringing that right, and granting interim relief in such specific terms could or would deprive the claimant of effective interim protection. With a patent there is no difficulty in granting a final injunction in terms which

---

[12] *Meespierson NV v Industrial and Commercial Bank of Vietnam* [1998] 2 S.L.R. 632 (failure to apply promptly was an indication that there was no real risk of dissipation and that the purpose of applying for a Mareva injunction was that, if granted, it would interfere with the bank's business in Singapore thereby putting pressure on the bank to put up security); *Carlton and United Breweries (NSW) Pty Ltd v Bond Brewing New South Wales Ltd* (1987) 76 A.L.R. 633 at [15] (delay in seeking an interim injunction is an "important discretionary consideration"); *Dubai Bank Ltd v Galadari* [1990] 1 Lloyd's Rep. 120 at p.133 RHC (freezing relief refused when the defendants had already had several years in which to dissipate assets); *Bank of Nova Scotia v Emerald Seas Ltd* [1984] C.I.L.R. 180 at pp.189–190 (delay indicative that Mareva relief not necessary).

[13] *Bovill v Crate* (1865) L.R. 1 Eq. 388; *Aluminium Co. v Domeiere* (1898) 15 R.P.C. 32; *Gillette Safety Razor Co. v A. W. Gamage Ltd* (1907) 24 R.P.C. 1; *Versil Ltd v Cork Insulation and Asbestos Co. Ltd* [1966] R.P.C. 76.

[14] *North British Rubber Co. v Gormully and Jeffery Co.* (1894) 11 R.P.C. 17 at 20.

[15] *Monsanto Co. v Stauffer Chemical Co. (N.Z.)* [1984] F.S.R. 559 at 572.

[16] *Bradford & Bingley Plc v Holden* [2002] EWHC 2445.

[17] See Chapter 4, paras 4.001–4.003.

[18] *Staver Co. Inc. v Digitext Display Ltd* [1985] F.S.R. 512; *Video Arts Ltd v Paget Inc. Ltd* [1986] F.S.R. 623.

restrain the defendant from infringing the patent[19] and, in principle, there should not be a difficulty with an interim injunction restraining acts which would infringe the claimant's claimed patent right.

It may be possible to grant effective relief in sufficiently precise terms to be enforceable by contempt proceedings, by restraining the defendant from acting in any way inconsistently with the rights asserted by the claimant in the proceedings.[20]

This is a broader restraint but gives rise to the possibility that if contempt proceedings are brought the court will find itself in the course of the motion trying out substantive issues in the underlying action.[21] Although the court will do this on a motion for contempt because it is necessary to uphold the rule of law and ensure that court orders are obeyed, it is suggested that it is preferable, if possible, to avoid this by formulating an interim injunction in terms which are independent of the width of the underlying rights claimed in the action. **2.021**

In a patent action where the claimant is in the process of amending the claims of the patent upon which he sues[22] the court will not grant an interim injunction.[23] This is because the monopoly claimed by the patentee has not yet been defined. It would be unfair and oppressive to grant an injunction leaving its ambit to be defined through contempt proceedings.

(vii) The 'Springboard' Principle

A defendant may have obtained confidential information which he was not entitled to use. An example is a former employee who has copied a confidential list of customers of his previous employer whilst in his employ and who has subsequently left the employment and used the list to acquire customers of his former employer. The former employee, assuming that there is no restrictive covenant, is entitled to compete with the former employer using his skills, including specialist skills learnt in his former employment. But he must not use a list of customers as opposed to names that he may have carried away in his head.[24] In the absence of any express terms, there is an implied term that after his employment has ceased the **2.022**

---

[19] *Coflexip SA v Stolt Comex Seaway MS Ltd* [2001] 1 All E.R. 952 disapproving [1999] 2 All E.R. 593 at [22].

[20] *Spectravest Inc. v Aperknit Ltd* [1988] F.S.R. 161 (injunction interpreted as restraining the defendant from infringing what the plaintiff claimed to be its copyright or from passing off).

[21] *Spectravest Inc. v Aperknit Ltd* [1988] F.S.R. 161; *Chanel Ltd FGM Cosmetics* [1981] F.S.R. 471; *Director General of Fair Trading v Tobyward Ltd* [1989] 1 W.L.R. 517 at p.522H–p.524A; *Schindler Lifts Australia Pty Ltd v Debelak* (1989) 89 A.L.R. 275 at paras 230–231.

[22] The claimant can still seek an injunction in respect of a claim which he is not amending and which is prima facie valid: *Hoffman-La Roche & Co. AG v Inter-Continental Pharmaceuticals Ltd* [1965] R.P.C. 226.

[23] *Mölnlycke AB v Proctor & Gamble* [1990] R.P.C. 487.

[24] *Universal Thermosensors Limited v Hibben* [1992] 1 W.L.R. 840 at pp.855–856; *Roger Bullivant Ltd v Ellis* [1987] F.S.R. 172; *Robb v Green* [1895] 2 Q.B. 1; *Louis v Smellie* (1895) 73 L.T. 226.

employee must still not use trade secrets or information entitled to the same degree of confidentiality as a trade secret, of the former employer, whether obtained through copying documents, taking documents away, committing the information to memory or otherwise.[25]

The former employer can claim damages for breach of the confidentiality in misusing the information. This may be assessed on the basis of loss of profits sustained through lost business with the former employer having the burden of proving what he has lost through the misuse.[26] An alternative basis is to award damages based on the value of the information misused, looking at the benefit derived from the information by the wrongdoer, applying the 'user principle'.[27] This is a form of restitution of unjust enrichment based on the defendant paying for the advantage secured by him from his misuse of the information . The same measure is available under Lord Cairns's Act.[28]

An injunction can be granted to restrain future misuse. There is also a remedy available by way of injunction which prevents the defendant enjoying an advantage over the claimant through having previously misused the information.

The latter is granted on the 'springboard' principle, which prevents the defendant using the position already acquired through misuse as a 'springboard' for further competition with the claimant. Its purpose is to put the parties back into the position they would have been had there not been the past misuse[29] through putting the defendant at a special disability for a period to ensure that the defendant does not obtain an unfair start over the claimant.[30] It lasts no longer than is required to prevent the defendant having the unfair advantage.[31] The principle applies to enable the 'springboard' injunction to be granted even after all the information has entered the public domain.[32] Damages may, depending on the particular facts, be a wholly inadequate remedy because no-one can know what would have

---

[25] *Faccenda Chicken Limited v Fowler* [1987] Ch 117; *FSS Travel & Leisure Systems Ltd v Johnson* [1998] I.R.L.R. 382; *AT Poeton (Gloucester Plating) Ltd v Horton* [2000] I.C.R. 1208; *Intelsec Systems Ltd v Grech Cini* [2000] 1 W.L.R. 1190. This is narrower than the information which is confidential, although not a trade secret, and which the employee must not divulge during his employment, but can use after it has ended: *Printers & Finishers Ltd v Holloway* [1965] 1 W.L.R. 1; *Dranez Anstalt v Hayek* [2002] 1 B.C.L.C. 693.
[26] *Universal Thermosensors Limited v Hibben* [1992] 1 W.L.R. 840 at pp.850–851.
[27] *Universal Thermosensors Limited v Hibben* [1992] 1 W.L.R. 840 at p.856 referring to *Stoke-on-Trent City Council v W & J Wass Ltd* [1988] 1 W.L.R. 1406 at 1416–1418.
[28] Para. 2.040.
[29] *Universal Thermosensors Limited v Hibben* [1992] 1 W.L.R. 840 at pp.853–855, (where on the facts the defendants would have acquired the information through undertaking their own researches, would have competed for the customers anyway, and so no 'springboard' injunction was available); *Bradford & Bingley Plc v Holden* [2002] EWHC 2445.
[30] *Terrapin Limited v Builders' Supply Co (Hayes) Ltd* [1960] R.P.C. 128 at p.130; *Seager v Copydex Limited* [1967] 1 W.L.R. 923 at p.931.
[31] *Roger Bullivant Limited v Ellis* [1987] F.S.R. 172.
[32] *Cranleigh Precision Engineering Limited v Bryant* [1965] 1 W.L.R. 1293.

happened to the claimant's business had the confidential information not been misused.[33]

For the principle to be applicable there must have been particular information which can be clearly identified which the defendant could not lawfully have used[34] and which has been wrongfully misused. The principle has also been applied in the case of patent infringement to prevent the infringer getting a head start on the patentee through granting an injunction which applies even after expiry of the patent.[35]

(viii) Appeals against the exercise of discretion

The discretion whether to grant or refuse an interim injunction is that of **2.023** the first instance judge, and will not be interfered with by an appellate court, unless the judge took into account something he should not have taken into account, failed to take into account something which he should have taken into account, was wrong in law, misunderstood the evidence, or was plainly wrong, or if there has been further evidence which shows that the judge proceeded on a mistaken view of the facts, or there has been, since the decision at first instance, a material change of circumstances.[36]

(ix) Granting the whole relief claimed on an application for an interim injunction

There is no rule of practice that the court will not on an interlocutory **2.024** application give the claimant by interim injunction effectively the whole of the relief that he seeks in the action.[37] But the court is more reluctant to grant an order without a trial when the practical result is to give the claimant all that he is claiming in the action[38] and in consequence of this the likelihood is that there will not be a trial; this is because such an order intrudes upon according due process to the defendant. In *Locabail International Finance Ltd v Agroexport*,[39] the application was for a mandatory order that the defendant pay a sum of money to a non-party, this

---

[33] *Bradford & Bingley Plc v Holden* [2002] EWHC 2445; damages were the appropriate remedy in *Universal Thermosensors Limited v Hibben* [1992] 1 W.L.R. 840 at pp.853–855 and *Lock Plc v Beswick* [1989] 1 W.L.R. 1268 at p.1276A–D.

[34] *Lock Plc v Beswick* [1989] 1 W.L.R. 1268 at p.1274.

[35] *Dyson Appliances Ltd v Hoover Ltd (No.2)* [2001] R.P.C. 27.

[36] *Hadmore Productions Ltd v Hamilton* [1983] 1 A.C. 191 at 220A–F; *Garden Cottage Foods Ltd v Milk Marketing Board* [1984] A.C. 130 at 137; *G v G (Minors: Custody Appeal)* [1985] 1 W.L.R. 647 at pp.651–653 (holding that the applicable test is not that of whether a reasonable judge could have reached the decision which was made at first instance); *Dupont Steels Ltd v Sirs* [1980] 1 W.L.R. 142 at 171G–H, *per* Lord Scarman.

[37] *Manchester Corporation v Connolly* [1970] Ch. 420 at 425H–426B (where there was no defence to the claim); cf. *Dodd v Amalgamated Marine Workers' Union* (1923) L.J. Ch. 65 at 66 which should be regarded as incorrect. See also *Meagher, Gummow and Lehane's Equity: Doctrines and Remedies*, n.61, above, at para.21–440.

[38] *Films Rover Ltd v Cannon Film Sales Ltd* [1987] 1 W.L.R. 670 at 680.

[39] [1986] 1 W.L.R. 657 at 664.

constituted "a major part of the relief claimed in the action" and it was said that "Such an application should be approached with caution and the relief only granted in a clear case".

(5) Interim mandatory injunctions

(i) *The general principles*

2.025   The distinction between an interim negative injunction and an interim mandatory injunction turns on whether the injunction can be complied with by the defendant doing nothing. Therefore it is a distinction based on the form of the order. What a defendant may be compelled to do under an injunction may range from the insignificant and trivial, to pulling down a building or handing over his home. A negative injunction likewise can range from the trivial to being restrained in personal liberty or a defendant entering his own home. A negative injunction may be said to preserve the *status quo* but then there are cases in which the purpose of an interim mandatory injunction is to restore the position to what it was before the allegedly wrongful act was committed and so preserve the *status quo* as it then existed, and where the court is ready to order this because the inconvenience to the defendant is slight, and there is no great hardship involved.[40] A distinction based on form and not substance is unlikely to reveal any fundamental differences in the principles which apply. Arguments about whether the relief is positive or negative do not advance the debate; they "are barren".[41] What one can say is that mandatory injunctions are in their nature liable to be more intrusive, result in greater risk in contempt proceedings, result in greater waste of time and money if they are "wrong" and have to be undone, and are more likely to affect the status quo. They are also often difficult to formulate with precision[42] so as to meet the need for certainty in a court order granting such an injunction.[43] It is these practical matters which create a greater reluctance for the court to interfere by interim mandatory order. But each case depends on its own circumstances. The principles stated in the cases[44] reflect these considerations. In summary:

---

[40] *Oggi Advertising Ltd v McKenzie* [1999] 1 N.Z.L.R. 631 (granting an interim mandatory injunction for the assignment of a domain name based on alleged passing off); *The Principles of Equitable Remedies* by I.C.F. Spry (6th ed: 2001) at pp.546–549.

[41] *Films Rover Ltd v Cannon Film Sales Ltd* [1987] 1 W.L.R. 670 at 680.

[42] *ibid.*

[43] *Redland Bricks Ltd v Morris* [1970] A.C. 652 at 666–667; see Chapter 4, paras 4.001–4.003.

[44] *Zockoll Group Ltd v Mercury Communications Ltd* [1998] F.S.R. 354 at 364–366 where the cases are also considered; *Films Rover Ltd v Cannon Film Sales Ltd* [1987] 1 W.L.R. 670; *R. v Secretary of State for Transport Ex p. Factortame (No. 2)* [1991] 1 A.C. 603 at 683; *Nottingham Building Society v Eurodynamic Systems* [1993] F.S.R. 468; *Businessworld Computers Pty Ltd v Australian Telecommunications Commission* (1988) 82 A.L.R. 499 at paras 8–15 *per* Gummow J. (rejecting as a minimum threshold for the granting of a

(1) The general principle is to take the course which involves the least risk of injustice if it turns out to be "wrong".

(2) The court should keep in mind that ordering a positive step to be taken may involve an increased risk of injustice for the defendant if the decision turns out to be "wrong".

(3) It is legitimate to consider whether the court does feel a "high degree of assurance"[45] that the claimant will succeed at trial. This is because the greater the degree of assurance, the less the risk of injustice if the injunction is granted.

(4) Even where the court does not feel this high level of assurance there are still exceptional[46] cases in which it is correct to grant an interim mandatory injunction because that course involves the least risk of injustice.

Thus on an application for an interim mandatory injunction the court does pay attention to the relative strength of the apparent merits in exercising its discretion, and in this respect *American Cyanamid* principles do not apply.[47]

Where a defendant has with knowledge of an impending application to **2.026** the court deliberately acted so as to alter the position pending the decision of the court, the court will take this into account and may order the defendant by interim order to undo what he has done.[48]

(ii) Enforcement of a positive contractual promise by interim mandatory injunction

There is no difficulty in principle with granting an interim mandatory **2.027** injunction to hold the position pending trial of proceedings in which specific performance is sought and in which that remedy may be granted. There are also cases in which an interim mandatory injunction can be granted so as best to preserve the position pending trial of the action, even though at the trial, the court would not grant specific performance of the contract.

The position is different from enforcement of a negative engagement under the theory of *Lumley v Wagner* because affirmative conduct of the defendant is required. It is suggested that:

---

mandatory interim injunction the need for a "high degree of assurance" that the plaintiff would succeed at the trial).

[45] *Shepherd Homes Ltd v Sandham* [1971] Ch. 340 at 351, *per* Megarry J.

[46] *Films Rover Ltd v Cannon Film Sales Ltd* [1987] 1 W.L.R. 670 at 680.

[47] *Locabail International Finance Ltd v Agroexport* [1986] 1 W.L.R. 657 at 664.

[48] *Daniel v Ferguson* [1891] 2 Ch. 27; *Von Joel v Hornsey* [1895] 2 Ch. 774 (defendant evaded service of the writ and continued building work in the meantime); *Colls v Home and Colonial Stores Ltd* [1904] A.C. 179 at 193, *per* Lord Macnaghten ("if [the defendant] has endeavoured to steal a march upon the plaintiff or to evade the jurisdiction of the Court . . .").

(1) With an interim order the "object [is to make] whatever order will be likely best to enable the trial judge to do justice between the parties, whichever way the decision goes at trial . . .".[49] If on the hearing of an application for interim relief, it appears that some simple mandatory order against the defendant would enable the contract to be performed up until trial, this may be the best way of preserving the position so that, whichever way the case is eventually decided, the least injustice will be done. For example, a defendant may be compelled to provide telecommunications services to a claimant, who in turn is required to furnish security for payment for those services, which is calculated by reference to the defendant's highest reasonably arguable case on quantum.[50] With a sub-distribution agreement concerning a particular film the delivery of the film to the sub-distributor can be compelled by injunction so that he can get on with the distribution of it.[51]

(2) Absence of "mutuality" is a consideration going to discretion whether to enforce a contract by specific performance or injunction, but it does not bar the remedy. In *James Jones & Sons Ltd v Earl of Tankerville*[52] the substance of the agreement was for entering on to land to cut timber. The plaintiff's promised activities were not themselves appropriate for a decree of specific performance. However, the defendant's promise was capable of being specifically enforced. A negative injunction was granted to restrain the defendant from preventing the plaintiff having access to the land, because the defendant had acted in a high-handed way and should be held to his bargain. If it had been necessary for the plaintiff to be given a key to have access to the land, then the court could, and it is suggested, would, have granted an injunction which included a mandatory order for supply of the key.

(6) Continuous supervision by the court

2.028   The court will not grant a decree of specific performance or grant a mandatory injunction when enforcement of the order would potentially involve numerous applications to the court in the form of contempt proceedings about whether or not the order was being carried out by the defendant. This is because it is not just or desirable for such a method of enforcement to be employed. It is capable of being heavy-handed, wasteful

---

[49] *Polaroid Corporation v Eastman Kodak Company* [1977] R.P.C. 379 at 395, lines 15–20, *per* Buckley L.J.
[50] *Business Online Group Plc v MCI Worldcom Ltd* [2001] EWCA Civ 1399.
[51] *Films Rover Ltd v Cannon Film Sales Ltd* [1987] 1 W.L.R. 670 (mandatory order to deliver films under a sub-distribution agreement).
[52] [1909] 2 Ch. 440.

of costs and time, and it puts the litigating parties through a further period of having to deal with each other before the litigation is at an end. For these reasons the courts have declined to grant decrees of specific performance or mandatory injunctions requiring "continuous supervision". For example, for this reason the court will not specifically enforce a covenant to carry on a business[53] and in *Ryan v Mutual Tontine Westminster Chambers Association*[54] the court decided not to order the landlord to employ a porter to provide various services because the court would not supervise whether the appointee performed those various duties properly, and damages were the appropriate remedy.

(7) *Quia timet* injunctions

A *quia timet* (since he fears) injunction is an injunction granted where no **2.029** actionable wrong has been committed, to prevent the occurrence of an actionable wrong, or to prevent repetition of an actionable wrong.[55] Before the Judicature Acts it was the sole preserve of the old High Court of Chancery to grant such an injunction where there had been no prior wrong.[56] Sir George Jessel M.R. said no jurisdiction of the old Court of Chancery was more valuable and no subject more frequently the cause for bills for injunction than to restrain threatened injury[57] But the jurisdiction involves proof that unless the court intervenes by injunction there is a real risk that an actionable wrong will be committed;[58] that an injunction would do no harm is not a justification for granting it. Usually this will be by evidence that the defendant has threatened[59] to do the particular wrongful act: "no-one can obtain a *quia timet* order by merely saying 'Timeo'".[60]

---

[53] *Cooperative Insurance Society Ltd v Argyll Stores (Holdings) Ltd* [1998] A.C. 1; *Dickson Property Management Services Pty Ltd v Centro Property Management (Vic) Pty Ltd* (2001) 180 A.L.R. 485 (injunction refused to enforce cleaning contract for a shopping centre which had over two years to run).

[54] [1893] 1 Ch. 116 (where the appointed porter to a block of flats in fact acted as the chef to a local hotel or restaurant and at a "luncheon club"); contrast *Posner v Scott-Lewis* [1987] Ch. 25 at 33–37 (covenant to employ resident porter specifically enforced when capable of definition and not involving superintendence to an unacceptable degree), and see *Rainbow Estates LTd v Tokenhold LTd* [1998] Ch. 64 at 70G.

[55] *Proctor v Bayley* (1889) 42 Ch.D. 390 at 398.

[56] See Chapter 1, para.1.01.

[57] *Frearson v Loe* (1878) 9 Ch.D. 48 at 65.

[58] *Coflexip SA v Stolt Comex Seaway MS Ltd* [1999] 2 All E.R. 593 at [7–10] making a general point about injunctions, not affected by [2001] 1 All E.R. 952 disapproving [22] and [23] which concerned the form of injunction in patent proceedings; *Gill v Flightwise Travel Service Ltd* [2003] EWHC 3082 at [32], Ch.

[59] *Coflexip SA v Stolt Comex Seaway MS Ltd* [1999] 2 All E.R. 593 at [7–10] cites case law about insufficient evidence to justify granting an injunction because either there is no evidence of a threat or the threat has long since passed.

[60] Literally "I fear". *Attorney-General for the Dominion of Canada v Ritchie Contracting and Supply Co. Ltd* [1919] A.C. 999 at 1005. *Drury v Secretary of State for the Environment, Food and Rural Affairs* [2004] EWCA Civ at paras 40–41.

The jurisdiction to act *quia timet* is considered in Chapter 12.

There is no fixed or "absolute"[61] standard for measuring the degree of apprehension of a wrong which must be shown in order to justify *quia timet* relief. The more grave the likely consequences, the more the court will be reluctant to consider the application as "premature".[62] But there must be at least some real risk of an actionable wrong.[63] If the court decides to grant a final injunction the width of that injunction is a matter for the court's discretion and can be tailored according to the circumstances.[64]

2.030   If the defendant is willing to do what he reasonably can to avoid the wrong the court may decide that it would not be appropriate to grant the injunction.[65]

Where there is a real risk of trespassers relocating either on another part of the same site, or some other site of the claimant, an application can be made for a *quia timet* injunction. But depending on the circumstances an injunction may not be an effective remedy to clear land of a group of trespassers, and to prevent them relocating to the claimant's land. Where only one site is involved the court can simply grant a possession order in respect of part or the entirety of that site.[66] In the case of other sites of the claimant the court will wish to be satisfied ". . . that there is a real danger of actual violation of all the areas in question by those actually trespasssing on at least one of the areas when the proceedings are instituted.[67] This adopts of test for *quia timet* injunctive relief, and grants the possession order as the effective remedy; it is a possession order granted in respect of the other sites, *quia timet*.

(8) Relevance of whether damages are "an adequate remedy" and matters going to discretion

(i) Damages "an adequate remedy"

2.031   With an application for an interim injunction, except where there is no defence, a relevant question is whether damages are an adequate remedy for either party and the extent to which any loss is likely to be irreparable.

---

[61] *Hooper v Rogers* [1975] Ch. 43 at 50. See the cases cited by I.C.F. Spry, *The Principles of Equitable Remedies: Specific Performance, Injunctions*, (6th ed., 2001), pp. 377–382 and 469.

[62] *Hooper v Rogers* [1975] Ch. 43 at 50. The application was considered premature in *Attorney-General v Nottingham Corporation* [1904] 1 Ch. 673 because there was insufficient evidence to show that when the smallpox hospital was erected near to homes this would constitute an actionable nuisance.

[63] *Fletcher v Bealey* (1885) 28 Ch.D. 688.

[64] *Microsoft Corporation v Plato Technology Ltd*, CA, unreported, July 15, 1999 (where the final relief in a trade mark and passing off action was limited by the words "which [the defendant] knows or ought upon reasonable enquiry to know are Infringing Products".

[65] *Bridlington Relay Ltd v Yorkshire Electricity Board* [1965] Ch. 436.

[66] *University of Essex v Djemal* [1980] 1 W.L.R. 1301.

[67] *Ministry of Argiculture, Fisheries & Food v Hayman* 59 P. & C.R. at p.50, *per* Saville J., approved in *Drury v Secretary of State for the Environment, Food and Rural Affairs* [2004] EWCA Civ 200.

In specific performance whether damages are likely to be an adequate remedy is a vital consideration.[68] It is because damages are usually an adequate remedy for loss of a chattel that equity will normally not intervene by injunction or specific performance to enforce a contract for the sale of chattels or to compel delivery-up of goods. In contrast where a claimant is entitled to a security interest over a fund which has been dissipated the court may compel by specific performance of the promise to hold apart that fund, reconstitution of that fund so that the claimant has the benefit of the security for which he has contracted.[69]

With final injunctions sometimes whether damages are an adequate remedy is an important consideration. In other cases it hardly appears as a factor.

In *Redland Bricks Ltd v Morris*,[70] the plaintiff's land had slipped because **2.032** of loss of support caused by excavations by the defendant on its land. The question arose as to whether the defendant should be compelled by injunction to carry out works which might cost £35,000 when the value of an acre of the plaintiff's land was between £1,500 and £1,600. The judge had ordered work to stop the effects of the loss of support. The defendant had acted wrongly but not wantonly or in a high-handed way. The injunction was to compel works to prevent landslip which if and when it occurred would then be actionable, but not before, and which would only be actionable for the damage which then occurred.[71] It was because of this special feature of the cause of action for damage caused by loss of support, that the injunction sought was by way of mandatory *quia timet* injunction. Damages were an inadequate remedy in the sense that the consequence of the excavations was to threaten to deprive the plaintiff of the use of his land, and no-one could tell how much or how little damage might happen in the future. The House of Lords discharged the injunction holding that the granting of a mandatory injunction, unlike the case of a negative injunction, can never be as of course, and that the fact that damages was an inadequate remedy was only a factor to be taken into account in the exercise of the discretion.

---

[68] *Beswick v Beswick* [1968] A.C. 58 at 102 ("Equity will grant specific performance when damages are inadequate to meet the justice of the case"); *Ryan v Mutual Tontine Westminster Chambers Association* [1893] 1 Ch. 116 at 125 ("the Court will not compel specific performance when there is another adequate remedy"); *Evans Marshall & Co. Ltd v Bertola SA* [1973] 1 W.L.R. 349 at 379 ("Is it just, in all the circumstances, that a plaintiff should be confined to his remedy in damages?").

[69] *Lexington Insurance Company v Flashpoint Ltd* [2002] WL 15044, January 19, 2001, Comm Ct (ordering specific performance on a summary judgment application ordering reconstitution of a fund which had been dissipated by the fundholder who had promised the claimant to hold the fund separate and subject to a floating charge, which could become a fixed charge at any time, in favour of the claimant).

[70] [1970] A.C. 652.

[71] *Darley Main Colliery Co. v Mitchell* (1886) 11 App.Cas. 127; *Redland Bricks Ltd v Morris* [1970] A. C. 652 at 664. This is a peculiarity of the nature of the cause of action for loss of support where the occurrence of damage is itself the cause of action, and the cause of action is limited to the damage which has already occurred: see *Homburg Houtimport BV v Agrosin Private Ltd (The Starsin)* [2003] 2 W.L.R. 711.

On the other hand, there are cases where a negative injunction is sought based on a proprietary right where the granting of an injunction is the ordinary remedy and its availability does not depend upon any showing that damages would be an inadequate remedy. An illustration of this is cases of preservation of trust funds, continuous private nuisance to the claimant's property, which will be restrained by injunction unless there are "special circumstances . . . including . . . that damages would be an adequate remedy . . .",[72] and cases of trespass to land. Unless an injunction were to be granted, the claimant's proprietary rights would themselves be diminished.[73] Another example is enforcement of a negative covenant in a contract by injunction, where there is no affirmative burden on the claimant to show that breach of the covenant will cause him loss, or that damages are an inadequate remedy.[74]

(ii) Discretionary factors

2.033   An injunction is an equitable remedy and the court can refuse the remedy on discretionary grounds.

(iii) Laches

2.034   Laches is an equitable doctrine which gives rise to a bar to equitable relief. Where it arises the bar is personal to the claimant and does not affect successors in title to land.[75] It is concerned with delay and its consequences, and whether it would be "practically unjust"[76] to give the remedy sought. It applies both to an application for a final injunction and an interlocutory application, and regardless of whether the underlying right sought to be enforced is legal or equitable in origin.[77] At trial where the claimant establishes a proprietary right for which the ordinary remedy is an injunction, delay alone may be irrelevant.[78]

(iv) Unclean hands

2.035   There can be circumstances in which the applicant for an injunction comes with "unclean hands"[79] and should as a matter of discretion be debarred from relief.

---

[72] *Pride of Derby and Derbyshire Angling Association v British Celanese Ltd* [1953] Ch. 149 at 181.

[73] *Patel v W. H. Smith (Eziot) Ltd* [1987] 1 W.L.R. 853.

[74] See para.2.012, above.

[75] *Nwakobi v Nzekwu* [1964] 1 W.L.R. 1019 at 1024.

[76] *Lindsay Petroleum Co. v Hurd* (1874) L.R. 5 P.C. 221 at 239–240; *Erlanger v New Sobrero Phosphate Co.* (1878) 3 App.Cas. 1218 at 1279, *per* Lord Blackburn; *Nelson v Rye* [1996] 1 W.L.R. 1378 at 1392.

[77] *Habib Bank Ltd v Habib Bank AG* [1981] 1 W.L.R. 1265 at 1285.

[78] For example, a claim asserting a proprietary right in land for an injunction to restrain a trespass should not be affected by delay alone.

[79] See the discussion in *Meagher, Gummow and Lehane's Equity: Doctrines and Remedies*, n.61, above, paras 3–130 and 3–135; Spry on *Equitable Remedies*, n.142, above, pp. 409–414.

There is a relationship between the equitable doctrine of the bar for "unclean hands" and the general public policy defence of illegality.

When the issue is whether illegality bars the claim to a proprietary right as a matter of public policy, the same principles apply whether the label is *ex turpi causa non oritur actio*, or the equitable bar of "unclean hands".

In *Tinsley v Milligan*,[80] Miss Milligan (M) claimed a half share in a **2.036** lodging house which was in the sole name of Miss Tinsley(T). M did not need to prove why the lodging house had been put into the sole name of T in order to prove her cause of action resting as it did on a resulting trust based on the money she had contributed to the purchase price of the lodging house. Therefore the fact that the purpose of putting the house in the sole name of T was to enable M to make fraudulent claims on the Department of Social Security, from which both T and M benefited, did not have to be proved by M to make good her equitable proprietary claim to a half share in the house.[81] The consequence was that M was still entitled to her share in the house even though it was an equitable right.[82] Public policy and illegality operate according to the same principles whether the property right claimed is legal or equitable.

In intellectual property cases where the claimant has acted in a way which is misleading for the purchasing public, the question can arise as to whether he should be barred from equitable relief. In *Ford v Foster*[83] the plaintiff claimed infringement of his trade mark, but had misrepresented to the public that he was the proprietor of a patent for a shirt sold under the trade mark. The Court of Appeal granted an injunction pointing out that the misrepresentation to the public was not by virtue of the trade mark itself, that it would not bar establishment in the courts of common law of the right to the trade mark, and that it should not affect the ancillary relief by injunction granted in equity. In contrast in *Kettles and Gas Appliances Ltd v Anthony Hordern and Sons Ltd*[84] the plaintiff was marketing its kettles with the words "Patented. Copyrighted". This was done with the intention of preventing others from manufacturing kettles of the same design through misleading the public about the intellectual property rights. No injunction to restrain passing off was granted because the plaintiff was guilty of a fraud on the public. Likewise no injunction was granted for trade mark infringement in *Newman v Pinto*[85] where the plaintiff's trade in marketing cigars was assisted through fraudulent misrepresentations on the

---

[80] [1994] 1 A.C. 340.
[81] In *Gascoigne v Gascoigne* [1918] 1 K. B. 223 the plaintiff husband failed because he had to rely on his own fraudulent scheme to rebut the presumption of advancement and therefore had to rely on his own fraudulent conduct as part of his cause of action—see also the other cases cited by Lord Browne-Wilkinson in *Tinsley v Milligan* [1994] 1 A.C. 340 at 374G–H.
[82] *Griffiths v Griffiths* [1973] 1 W.L.R. 1454 at 1456–1457 was correctly decided because the husband in that case did not have to found on his own fraud so as to make good his claim likewise, *Singh v Singh* [1985] Fam. L.R. 97.
[83] (1872) L.R. 7 Ch.App. 611.
[84] (1934) 35 S.R. (N.S.W.) 108.
[85] (1887) 4 R.P.C. 508; see also *Leather Cloth Co. Ltd v American Leather Cloth Co. Ltd* (1863) 4 De G. J. & S. 137.

labels placed on the cigar boxes. In *Chocosuisse Union Des Fabricants Suisse de Chocolat v Cadbury Ltd*,[86] Laddie J. considered that the test of whether to refuse an injunction in the action for passing off chocolate as "Swiss chocolate" depended on whether the plaintiff's conduct was such that it would be "unconscionable" to grant the relief.

Fraud on the public is a ground upon which all relief of any kind can be refused in respect of a transaction, on the grounds of public policy.[87] Attempted fraud on the court in support of a claim to equitable relief can result in the court refusing the claimant any equitable relief.[88] In any case in which relief is sought by injunction the relief is discretionary and the court may on the ground of the deliberate prosecution of a false case refuse all injunctive relief. Once it is accepted that there are cases in which fraud in the prosecution of a case is so serious that as a matter of public policy the court will grant the claimant no relief, then it would not be acceptable to confine this to cases in which equitable or discretionary relief is sought. The application of the principle depends upon the engagement of public policy, and cannot be dependent upon the classification of the cause of action or the remedy, as being "equitable" or "discretionary".

2.037   There can also be cases where a claimant is left to a claim for damages and refused an injunction because of his misconduct, which falls short of disentitling him to any relief.

In *Armstrong v Sheppard & Short Ltd*[89] the applicant had both misled the defendant and attempted to mislead the court in the course of the proceedings and was refused an injunction at trial requiring the removal of a sewer and manhole. Whether to grant an injunction or leave the plaintiff to his claim in damages for a trivial injury was a matter of discretion. The court was entitled in exercising that discretion to take into account the plaintiff's misconduct because it related directly to how he had gone about maintaining the claim and whether he deserved to obtain an injunction.

The claimant's conduct may also be a factor which together with other factors can lead to a refusal of relief.[90]

---

[86] [1998] R.P.C. 117, affirmed [1999] R.P.C. 826.
[87] *Scott v Brown Doerring McNab & Co.* [1892] 2 Q.B. 724.
[88] *Willis v Willis* [1986] 1 E.G.L.R. 62 (claim for proprietary estoppel rejected because the claimant had fraudulently relied in the proceedings upon a letter evidencing expenditure which had not been incurred), followed in *Gonthier v Orange Contract Scaffolding Limited* [2003] EWCA Civ 873 (claim for proprietary estoppel rejected because the claimants had concocted documents falsely exaggerating the quantum of expenditure incurred).
[89] [1959] 2 Q.B. 384 at 397. In *Mayo Associates SA v Anagram (Bermuda) Ltd* [1995] J.L.R. 190 the plaintiff's private detective planted a listening device in the defendant's offices during execution of an Anton Piller order and the plaintiff was not straightforward with the court about what had happened. This misconduct resulted in the Jersey Court of Appeal discharging Mareva relief granted in the same proceedings. Circulation of documents obtained under the Anton Piller order to investors in the plaintiff in breach of the implied undertaking only to use the documents for the purpose of the proceedings would not have justified on its own discharge of the Mareva relief.
[90] *D v L* [2004] E.M.L.R. 1 (threatening letters in a claim for an injunction to prevent tapes of private conversations being published in breach of confidence); *Hubbard v Vosper* [1972] 2 Q.B. 84 at 99–101 (protecting secrets by deplorable means and therefore interim injunction against breach of copyright refused).

As a general principle it is not enough that the court disapproves of the applicant's conduct; there must be an immediate and necessary relationship between the improper conduct and the relief sought[91] and the refusal of the injunction must be a proportionate response of the court to the applicant's misconduct. In short, it must be both directly relevant to the discretion to be exercised about what remedy to grant and sufficiently important to affect how in the circumstances of the case the discretion is exercised. In *Duchess of Argyll v Duke of Argyll*,[92] the Duchess was not barred from obtaining an injunction to restrain publication of marital confidences by her own previous conduct because that conduct did not justify the threatened breach of confidence.

Cases in which there is an existing breach of contract by an applicant for 2.038 equitable relief to enforce that contract are considered at para.2.007 above and can also be regarded as raising the question whether the applicant has come with "clean hands";[93] whichever terminology is used, the principles to be applied are the same.

(v) Acquiescence

The word "acquiescence" can be used in a number of different ways.[94] For 2.039 example, it can be used to describe a defence to a legal or equitable right, or as interchangeable with estoppel, laches, or simply consent. Consent to acts done in breach of contract may give rise to a waiver or estoppel, or may result in the claimant being refused an injunction and left to claim damages either for breach of contract or under Lord Cairns' Act.[95]

(9) Damages under Lord Cairns' Act

By s.2 of the Chancery Amendment Act 1858, which is known as Lord 2.040 Cairns's Act, the old Court of Chancery was empowered to award damages in addition to or in substitution for specific performance or an injunction. The power became an established part of English law, independently of the repeal of the original Act.[96] It is now to be found in s.50 of the Supreme Court Act 1981. The main purpose of the Act was to enable the old Court of Chancery when refusing to grant specific performance or an injunction to assess damages itself and not to send a plaintiff to the common law

---

[91] *Moody v Cox and Hatt* [1917] 2 Ch. 71 at 87–88; *Sterling Winthrop Pty Ltd v Boots Company (Australia)* (1995) 33 I.P.R. 302 at 305.
[92] [1967] Ch. 302 at 332.
[93] *Besant v Wood* (1879) 12 Ch.D. 605 at 626–628, *per* Sir George Jessel M.R.
[94] *Goldsworthy v Brickell* [1987] Ch. 378 at 410; *Meagher, Gummow and Lehane's Equity: Doctrines and Remedies*, at n.61, above, at para.36–090
[95] *Shaw v Applegate* [1977] 1 W.L.R. 970 at 978–979 and 981.
[96] *Leeds Industrial Cooperative Society v Slack* [1924] A.C. 851; *Attorney-General v Blake* [2001] 1 A.C. 268 at 281A–B; *Johnson v Agnew* [1980] A.C. 367 at 400B–C.

courts for the assessment of damages.[97] Given this procedural purpose it follows that a court of equity does not adopt some measure of damages different from what would be adopted at common law.[98]

However, the Act went beyond this. The common law courts could not award damages until the wrong had occurred and the plaintiff had a completed cause of action. The damages at common law were limited to the loss suffered up until the commencement of the action.[99] In Chancery a bill for an injunction could be brought *quia timet* in respect of future wrongs or against the repetition of a wrong. The power to award damages instead of granting an injunction enabled the court to compensate the applicant for the refusal to grant the relief, which gave him the equivalent in money to what he had lost by not having the injunction.[1] The Act empowered the courts of equity to award damages now for these threatened wrongs which were not actionable at common law.[2] Another situation covered by the Act is for breach of a restrictive covenant to which the defendant is not a contracting party but which is binding on him in equity.[3] Another potential situation is where an arbitration clause or exclusive jurisdiction clause binds the defendant because he is seeking to assert rights which are subject to the clause even though he is not a contracting party; there is jurisdiction to grant an anti-suit injunction,[4] and it follows that there is also jurisdiction to award damages. Another is when the court has jurisdiction to entertain an action for specific performance and there is a threatened breach of contract but no actual breach has occurred and the time for performance of the relevant contractual obligation has not yet arrived.[5]

The jurisdiction applies whether the underlying complaint is for breach of contract, or commission of a tort, or other "wrongful act". It depends upon there being at the date of commencement of the proceedings "jurisdiction to entertain an application . . ." for an injunction or specific performance,[6] regardless of whether it would have been wise to exercise the jurisdiction.[7] Whether the jurisdiction is to be exercised depends on

---

[97] *Jaggard v Sawyer* [1995] 1 W.L.R. 269 at 284, proposition (2); *Ferguson v Wilson* (1866) L.R. 2 Ch.App. 77 at 88; *Attorney-General v Blake* [2001] 1 A.C. 268 at 281B–C (referring to the practice before enactment of sending suitors to the common law courts for damages, see *Todd v Gee* (1810) 17 Ves. 273).

[98] *Johnson v Agnew* [1980] A.C. 367 at 400.

[99] *Attorney-General v Blake* [2001] 1 A.C. 268 at 281C–D referring to *Battishill v Reed* (1856) 18 C.B. 696.

[1] *Leeds Industrial Co-operative Society Limited v Slack* [1924] A.C. 851 at 859; *Attorney-General v Blake* [2001] 1 A.C. 268 at 281D–E.

[2] *Leeds Industrial Cooperative Society v Slack* [1924] A.C. 851; *Johnson v Agnew* [1980] A.C. 367 at 400B–C.

[3] *Johnson v Agnew* [1980] A.C. 367 at 400C.

[4] See Chapter 14, para.14.008.

[5] See Chapter 12, para.12.003–4.

[6] *Jaggard v Sawyer* [1995] 1 W.L.R. 269 at 284; *Lavery v Pursell* (1888) 39 Ch.D. 508 at 518–519 (the doctrine of part performance in equity did not enable there to be damages under the Act).

[7] *Hooper v Rogers* [1975] Ch. 43 at 48; *City of London Brewery Co. v Tennant* (1873) L.R. 9 Ch.App. 212.

circumstances up until the date of the hearing at which the question of remedy is decided. It is not necessary to include a claim to damages in the claim form,[8] or the particulars of claim.[9] The jurisdiction can be used so as to award damages in addition to granting specific performance, *e.g.* when there has been loss caused by delay[10] or where the defendant's ordered performance is in breach of contract and damages make good that loss.[11] There can also be a limited injunction and damages granted in respect of that part of the injunctive relief which is refused.[12]

In *Johnson v Agnew*,[13] the House of Lords decided that in an action for specific performance, after a decree for specific performance, the seller can still apply to the court to put an end to the contract and award him damages, which would be assessed on a compensatory basis using common law principles. The contract is not merged in the decree for specific performance, and the seller retained the right under that contract to accept the repudiation as terminating that contract and to sue for damages. In that case the seller had reasonably pressed for the contract to be completed by the defaulting purchaser, and damages were to be assessed as at the date the seller aborted the contract. The termination of the contract also leaves intact rights and obligations which flow from performance of the contract prior to its termination, including any accrued cause of action for breach.[14] Whether the court will permit the seller to terminate the contract after a decree of specific performance will be determined according to equitable principles.[15]

2.041

Where damages are awarded under Lord Cairns's Act for future wrongs instead of an injunction then no injunction will be granted; this does not license the wrongs but under the doctrine of *res judicata* it prevents the claimant obtaining any further remedy for them.[16] In *Seagar v Copydex Ltd (No.2)*[17] the defendant had misused confidential information belonging to the claimant, who has been refused an injunction to restrain that use, and awarded damages on the basis of the full market value of the confidential information taken by the defendant. The defendant was in consequence left with the benefit of the information as if it had been purchased by it.[18]

Where damages are awarded they are compensatory; but this can include assessing a fair price which the defendant would have had to pay in order

---

[8] CPR r.16.2(5).
[9] *Betts v Neilson* (1868) L.R. 3 Ch.App. 429 at 444 ("though not specifically prayed for by the bill"); *Jaggard v Sawyer* [1995] 1 W.L.R. 269 at 285.
[10] *Ford-Hunt v Singh* [1973] 1 W.L.R. 738 (damages for loss caused by delay after the decree).
[11] *Grant v Dawkins* [1973] 1 W.L.R. 1406 (damages for cost of discharging mortgages on property when the contract was to sell free from incumbrances).
[12] *Chiron Corporation v Organon Teknika Ltd (No. 10)* [1995] F.S.R. 325.
[13] [1980] A.C. 367.
[14] *Johnson v Agnew* [1980] A.C. 367 at 396–398 approving *McDonald v Dennys Lascelles Ltd* (1933) 48 C.L.R. 457 at 476–477, *per* Dixon J.
[15] *Johnson v Agnew* [1980] A.C. 367 at 399E–H.
[16] *Jaggard v Sawyer* [1995] 1 W.L.R. 269 at 280–281 and 285–286.
[17] [1969] 1 W.L.R. 809.
[18] *ibid.* at p.813F–H.

to get the claimant to release his right to object to the defendant's conduct.[19] The practical effect of this reasoning can be to award damages taking into account the benefit obtained by the respondent through the refusal of the injunction. Damages can also be awarded on this basis to compensate a claimant for past wrongs and this is so even if an injunction is granted to restrain future breaches.[20]

2.042   In *Cardwell v Walker*,[21] the defendant had threatened to interfere wrongly with an easement which enabled the claimants to have uninterrupted supplies of electricity to their bungalows. Neuberger J. set aside an award of damages under the Act for the past threat, on the grounds that there had been no application for *quia timet* relief in respect of it, no *quia timet* relief could now be granted in respect of it, and there could be no award of damages under the Act. It is considered that this decision was incorrect, because it looked at the availability of an injunction at the time of the hearing, as opposed to whether an injunction could have been granted had it been applied for in time in respect of the past conduct.[22] If an injunction to restain that threat had been applied for in time, it could have been granted. It is considered that damages could have been awarded for the diminished enjoyment of the bungalows arising from that threat hanging over the properties.

This is a discretionary jurisdiction. Because damages can be awarded instead of an injunction the question arose as to in what circumstances a court would decline to grant an injunction based on damages being an available remedy. The jurisdiction does not operate so as to enable defendants freely to expropriate to themselves the rights of a claimant; the court does not simply allow a wrong to continue because the defendant is willing to pay damages.[23] Prima facie once there is an infringement of a claimant's property rights he is entitled to an injunction.[24] An injunction will be granted even if the defendant is in some sense carrying out activities which benefit the public.[25]

In *Shelfer v City of London Electric Lighting Co.*,[26] A. L. Smith L.J. stated as a "good working rule" that damages may be given instead of an injunction when:

---

[19] *Attorney-General v Blake* [2001] 1 A.C. 268 at 283–284 and 298 disapproving *Surrey County Council v Brodero Homes Ltd* [1993] 1 W.L.R. 1361; *Jaggard v Sawyer* [1995] 1 W.L.R. 269 approving *Wrotham Park Estate Co. Ltd v Parkside Homes Ltd* [1974] 1 W.L.R. 798 at 815; *Bracewell v Appleby* [1975] Ch. 408; *Tito v Waddell (No. 2)* [1977] Ch. 106 at 335.

[20] *Enterprise Hendrix LLC v PPX Enterprises Inc.* [2003] 1 All E.R. (Comm) 830.

[21] [2003] EWHC 3117 at paras. 66–72; [2004] 4 E.G.C.S. 108.

[22] *Enterprise Hendrix LLC v PPX Enterprises Inc* [2003] E.M.L.R. 25, p.515, at para.35.

[23] *Shiloh Spinners v Harding* [1973] A.C. 691 at 723G–H (in relation to relief from forfeiture of land for breach of a covenant): "equity expects men to carry out their bargains and will not let them buy their way out by an uncovenanted payment . . .".

[23] *Jaggard v Sawyer* [1995] 1 W.L.R. 269 at 284; *Nelson v Nicholson*, CA, unreported, December 1, 2000 (mandatory injunction granted requiring the defendant to stop a trespass on to the claimant's land).

[25] *Oxy Electric Ltd v Zainuddin* [1991] 1 W.L.R. 115 at 121A–D referring to *Shelfer v City of London Electric Lighting Co.* [1895] 1 Ch. 287 at 315–316, *per* Lindley L.J.

[26] [1895] 1 Ch. 287 at 322–323.

"(1) the injury to the [claimant's] legal rights is small, (2) And is one capable of being estimated in money, (3) And the case is one which can be adequately compensated by a small money payment, (4) And the case is one in which it would be oppressive to the defendant to grant an injunction . . .".

The later cases turn on the application of this approach to particular facts.[27] The test is one of "oppression" of the defendant and not mere balance of convenience. This takes into account the reasonableness or high-handednessof the defendant's conduct and the practical consequences for the defendant if the injunction were to be granted.[28]

(10) Stay of an injunction

The court may stay an injunction whether interim or final in the exercise of **2.043** its discretion. Examples are where an immediate injunction against the defendant would be oppressive or where the court considers that the defendant should be given a period in which to rectify matters before an injunction comes into effect,[29] or where the public interest[30] or the interests of third parties[31] make it inappropriate for there to be an immediate injunction.

(11) Contracts for building works or works of repair

Ordinarily specific performance will not be ordered of a contract for **2.044** building works[32] because damages are an adequate remedy. A distinction is to be drawn between specific performance of a contract requiring building

---

[27] The cases are reviewed in *Jaggard v Sawyer* [1995] 1 W.L.R. 269.
[28] *Shaw v Applegate* [1977] 1 W.L.R. 970 (injunction refused when the effect of granting it would have been to compel the defendant to stop an established business); *Leader v Moody* (1875) L.R. 20 Eq. 145 (after Her Majesty's Theatre in the Haymarket had been rebuilt , it was let to sub-lessees for three months to hold religious meetings. Nominal damages awarded instead of an injunction to enforce a covenant that the premises were not be used except as a theatre, because the theatre was not in use, the plaintiff would suffer no loss from the breach, the breach was only temporary, and the defendant sub-lessees would suffer great hardship).
[29] *Pride of Derby and Derbyshire Angling Association v British Celanese Ltd* [1953] Ch. 149; *Miller v Jackson* [1977] Q.B. 966 at 987 (the dissenting judgment of Geoffrey Lane L.J. who would have given the cricket club a year to find a different pitch).
[30] *Miller v Jackson* [1977] Q.B. 966 at 982 and 988; *Hopkinson v St James and Pall Mall Electric Light Co. Ltd* (1893) 10 R.P.C. 46 at 62.
[31] *World Wide Fund for Nature (formerly world Wildlife Fund) v THQ/Jakks Pacific LLC (World Wrestling Federation intervening)* [2004] F.S.R. 10 at 161, at paras 56–61 and 71–73 and the dissenting judgment's statement of the principle at paras 44–45; *Miller v Jackson* [1977] Q.B. 966 at 988; *Galaxia Maritime SA v Mineralimportexport* [1982] 1 W.L.R. 539 (refusal of injunction on this ground) discussed in Chapter 20, para.20–081.
[32] *Wolverhampton Corporation v Emmons* [1901] 1 K.B. 515 at 524; *Ryan v Mutual Tontine Westminster Chambers Association* [1893] 1 Ch. 116 at 128.

works and that which requires a particular end result which can only be achieved by building. The latter is more amenable to a decree of specific performance then the former, because it only involves checking the end result. For this reason,[33] where damages are an inadequate remedy, the courts have sometimes ordered specific performance of a building contract[34] or of a covenant to repair.[35] This depends upon there being sufficient certainty and precision about what has to be built to enable a mandatory order to be drafted, which can then subsequently become an appropriate order to enforce by contempt proceedings.[36]

(12) Charterparties, contracts for the sale or hiring of a chattel and contracts for services

(i) Contracts for the sale of a chattel

2.045   As a general proposition the court will leave a buyer to an action for damages when a contract for the sale of a chattel is not performed by the seller. This is because damages are an adequate remedy.[37] However, where damages would not be an adequate remedy and the goods are specific or ascertained the court can grant specific performance under s.52 of the Sale of Goods Act 1979, which reflects a part of the court's jurisdiction to order specific performance or an injunction. Its constraints do not oust the general power of the court to grant specific performance or to enforce a contract by injunction; so a mandatory injunction may be granted requiring a seller to perform a contract for the supply of unascertained goods.[38]

---

[33] *Cooperative Insurance Society Ltd v Argyll Stores (Holdings) Ltd* [1998] A.C. 1 at 13; *Shiloh Spinners v Harding* [1973] A.C. 691 at 724D–E.

[34] *Wolverhampton Corporation v Emmons* [1901] 1 K.B. 515. *Rainbow Estates Ltd v Tokenhold Ltd* [1998] Ch. 64 at 69–70; *Ryan v Mutual Tontine Westminster Chambers Association* [1893] 1 Ch. 116 at 128 distinguishing the cases where the court has declined to intervene because the court would not supervise the works: *Blackett v Bates* (1865) L.R. 1 Ch.App. 124, *Powell Duffryn Steam Coal Company v Taff Vale Railway Company* (1874) L.R. 9 Ch. App. 331.

[35] *Rainbow Estates Ltd v Tokenhold Ltd* [1998] Ch. 64. *Jeune v Queen's Cross Properties* [1974] Ch. 97.

[36] See Chapter 4, para 4.001–4.003.

[37] *Re Clarke* (1887) 36 Ch.D. 348 at 352, *per* Cotton L.J.; *Fothergill v Rowland* (1873) L.R. 17 Eq. 132 (contract for supply of coal to be mined at a colliery not specifically enforced and the plaintiff left to his remedy in damages). In contrast a contract for the sale of land will normally be specifically enforced because every piece of land is different and cannot be replaced, and in most cases damages would be "a wholly inadequate and unjust remedy": *Sudbrook Trading Estate Ltd v Eggleton* [1983] 1 A.C. 444 at 478G; *Patel v Ali* [1984] Ch. 283 at 286G–H (where specific performance was refused on the grounds of hardship to the defendant caused by supervening events post-contract for which the plaintiff was not responsible).

[38] *Sky Petroleum Ltd v VIP Petroleum Ltd* [1974] 1 W.L.R. 576 (interim mandatory injunction to deliver fuel to plaintiff's filling stations under contract for supply non-specific/ unascertained goods because of risk of destruction of plaintiff's business. See also the discussion by Trietel in "Specific Performance in the Sale of Goods" [1966] J.B.L. 211 at 222–229.

There are also further policy reasons for not specifically enforcing contracts for the sale of chattels, where legal ownership has not passed to the buyer. First, the courts should not alter the effect of the insolvency laws based merely on contractual rights by ordering a chattel to be delivered up which is owned by a bankrupt, or an insolvent company.[39] Secondly, it would be highly inconvenient in trade if, as a result of a contract of sale of a chattel, the buyer acquired some equitable interest in the chattel or the bulk from which it was to be delivered, which could prevail over the rights of those in possession of the goods, such as a bank to which a bill of lading had been pledged.[40]

Since 1995 it has been possible to acquire under a contract of sale a legal proprietary interest in an undivided bulk.[41] Furthermore s.52 when interpreted together with the meaning of "specific goods" in s.61(1) applies to a contract for the sale of an undivided share out of a bulk "specified as a fraction or percentage, of goods identified and agreed on". In *Re Wait*[42] the buyer had agreed to buy 500 tons out of 1,000 tons to be shipped on the "Challenger"; under ss.20A and 20B ownership could pass to a proprietary interest in the cargo once shipped. Where such a legal interest has vested in the buyer his proprietary interest will not be defeated by supervening insolvency of the seller, or by third parties who deal with the seller except in accordance with exceptions to the *nemo dat quod non habet* rule (*e.g* a dealing by a seller in possession of the goods).

The court may intervene by specific performance and by injunction to   **2.046** prevent a shipowner breaking a contract of sale of a ship. It is essential for the purchaser to show that damages would be an inadequate remedy.[43] This may be because the ship is of unique value to the claimant, or because the defendant would not be good for damages or that an award of damages could not be enforced.[44] The same jurisdiction applies to irreplaceable machinery needed for a business.[45] Mere disruption and inconvenience are

---

[39] *Re Wait* [1927] 1 Ch. 606. In *Lutscher v Comptoir D'Escompte De Paris* (1876) 1 Q.B.D. 709 the plaintiff had been promised the bill of lading as security for a loan by the owner who had become insolvent and the court held on demurrer that the contract for pledge of the particular bill could be specifically enforced. One view of this case is that as soon as the owner obtained the bill of lading he held it as agent for the plaintiff, to whom he had promised it, and therefore the plaintiff had a completed legal pledge.

[40] *Re Wait* [1927] 1 Ch. 606.

[41] Sale of Goods Act 1979, ss.20A and 20B.

[42] [1927] 1 Ch. 606.

[43] *C. N. Marine Inc. v Stena Line A/B (The Stena Nautica) No. 2* [1982] 2 Lloyd's Rep. 336 at 341–342 (Parker J.), 347 RHC and 348 RHC; *Eximenco Handels AG v Partrederiet Oro Chief (The Oro Chief)* [1983] 2 Lloyd's Rep. 509 at 520–521 (which also looks as a matter of discretion at which of two competing purchasers would have obtained the order for specific performance); *Hart v Herwig* (1873) L.R. 8 Ch.App. 860.

[44] *Astro Exito Navegacion SA v Chase Manhattan Bank (The Messiniaki Tolmi)* [1983] 2 A.C. 787 affirming [1982] Q.B. 1248.

[45] *Société des Industries Metallurgiques SA v The Bronx Engineering Co. Ltd* [1975] 1 Lloyd's Rep. 465.

not enough.[46] The court will not in its discretion grant specific perfor-mance for goods available in ordinary commerce,[47] even where property in the goods has passed to the buyer. Specific performance or an injunction requiring delivery-up can be granted for special goods that could not be replaced from elsewhere[48] and where damages would not be an adequate remedy.

(ii) Order for delivery-up of a chattel under s.3(2)(a) of the Torts (Interference with Goods) Act 1977 or an interim order under s.4 and CPR r.25.1(1)(e)

2.047   The same is the position in tort where the court will not ordinarily make an order for specific delivery-up (and consequential damages) under s.3(2)(a) of the Torts (Interference with Goods) Act 1977 in respect of goods in the possession or control of the defendant, which are ordinary articles of commerce.[49]

Likewise with the jurisdiction under s.4 of that Act, and CPR r.25.1(1)(e), to grant an interim order for the delivery-up of goods.

In *Howard E. Perry & Co. Ltd v British Railways Board*[50] the plaintiff was deprived of its steel during industrial action by railwaymen in support of a strike of steel workers. The defendant board refused to allow the plaintiff to collect its own steel from the defendant's depot. The steel could not be kept for a long period without the risk of its becoming impossible to work through it hardening. The risk was of destruction or severe damage to the plaintiff's business and damages were not an adequate remedy. Sir Robert Megarry V.-C. made an interim order under s.4 requiring the defendant to permit the plaintiff to collect its steel.

2.048   Although these jurisdictions are statutory and not part of the jurisdiction to grant an "injunction" under s.37(1) of the Supreme Court Act 1981,[51] the same principles apply in exercising the discretions under the statute as are applied by the court in deciding whether to grant the equivalent order by way of specific performance or injunction.

---

[46] *C.N. Marine Inc v Stena Line A/B (The Stena Nautica) No. 2* [1982] 2 Lloyd's Rep. 336 at 342 RHC.

[47] *Cohen v Roche* [1927] 1 K.B. 169 (eight Hepplewhite chairs which were ordinary furniture); *Whiteley Ltd v Hilt* [1918] 2 K.B. 808 at 819 (a piano).

[48] *Phillips v Lamdin* [1949] 2 K.B. 33 at 41–42 (order against the vendor for an Adam door to be brought back and reinstalled, which had been removed by him from premises which were the subject of a contract for a lease). *Falke v Gray* (1859) 4 Drew 651 (holding that specific performance could be granted for items of unusual beauty, rarity and distinction but refusing it on the facts because the seller had mistakenly agreed to sell the objects for an inadequate price); Trietel, "Specific Performance in the Sale of Goods" [1966] J.B.L. 211.

[49] *Howard E. Perry & Co. Ltd v British Railways Board* [1980] 1 W.L.R. 1375 at 1382G to 1383F; *Whiteley Ltd v Hilt* [1918] 2 K.B. 808 at 819 (a piano); *General and Finance Facilities Ltd v Cooks Cars (Romford) Ltd* [1963] 1 W.L.R. 644 at 649–650.

[50] [1980] 1 W.L.R. 1375.

[51] See Chapter 1, para.1.001

(iii) Charterparties

There are different types of charterparty. A bare boat charterparty is a **2.049** hiring of the physical vessel itself, without any crew. It is common in financing transactions which relate to the sale of a vessel. With ordinary chattels when there is a threatened breach of a contract of hire by the owners of them the court will ordinarily leave the innocent party to a claim in damages. In *North v Great Northern Railway*,[52] the plaintiff was granted an injunction to restrain the owner of 54 coal wagons taking them back and selling them, when this would destroy the plaintiff's business, replacements were not available, and therefore damages were not an adequate remedy.

Where a ship has been chartered by time charter or voyage charter the contract will not be capable of specific performance because it is a complicated contract for provision of services. The court will not supervise such a contract, and there is too much risk of repeated disputes about the performance of the contract which would have to be resolved through applications to the court and the heavy-handed machinery of contempt proceedings.[53]

But such a contract contains an implied negative engagement not to use the vessel for another engagement inconsistent with the charter, and the court can, on the principle in *Lumley v Wagner*[54] as reformulated in *Wolverhampton and Walsall Railway Company v London and North Western Railway Co.*,[55] grant an injunction restraining such use, when damages would be an inadequate remedy.[56] Since the contract is not capable of specific performance the court will not grant an injunction which although negative in form is directed to compelling performance of the contract, such as an injunction restraining the defendant owner from withdrawing his ship from performance of the charterparty.[57]

Where the owner of a chattel enters into a contract of hire or to make it **2.050** available to another, those contractual responsibilities will not be binding on a third party transferee of the chattel, even if the transferee had notice of the contract on acquisition of the chattel. This is the result of the doctrine of privity of contract. There is no proprietary right in the chattel vested in the promisee.[58] If the third party in acquiring the chattel induced breach of contract by the transferor[59] then he can be liable in tort and

---

[52] (1860) 2 Giff. 64.
[53] *Cooperative Insurance Society Ltd v Argyll Stores (Holdings) Ltd* [1998] A.C. 1; *Ryan v Mutual Tontine Westminster Chambers Association* [1893] 1 Ch. 116.
[54] (1852) 1 De G.M. & G. 604.
[55] (1873) L.R. 16 Eq. 433 at 440.
[56] *Associated Portland Cement Manufacturers v Teigland Shipping A/S (The Oakworth)* [1975] 1 Lloyd's Rep. 581 at 583 LHC (defendant would not have been good for damages); *Sevin v Deslandes* (1860) 30 L.J. (Ch.) 457; *De Mattos v Gibson* (1859) 4 D. & J. 276; *Lord Strathcona Steamship Company v Dominion Coal* [1926] A.C. 108.
[57] cf. *Gatoil Anstalt v Omenial Ltd* [1983] 1 Ll.Rep. 492.
[58] *Port Line Ltd v Ben Line Steamers Ltd* [1958] 2 Q.B. 146 (time charterer had no rights against the purchaser of the ship to require the use of the ship for the time charter).
[59] In *The Lord Strathcona* [1925] P 143 the owners were free to sell the ship although contractually bound to perform the timecharter because the owners were too poor to perform the charterparty.

could be required by injunction to make available the chattel to the seller so that he in turn can perform the contract.[60] In *Law Debenture Trust Corporation v Ural Caspian Oil Company*,[61] a purchaser (C) had acquired certain shares from a seller (B) who had acted in breach of his contract with the plaintiff (A) not to part with the shares. The purchaser (C) had then transferred on the shares to the defendant (D), who was sued by A for inducing breach of the contract. Hoffmann L.J. (at first instance) had considered that because an injunction could have been granted at the suit of A against C requiring reconveyance of the shares to B,[62] the transfer from C to D interfered with the right to an injunction and therefore was actionable by A as against D. This was reversed by the Court of Appeal. There was no injunction prohibiting transfer from C, who had become the owner of the shares, to D. D was not inducing breach of any contract by C. The contractual right of A against B was not binding on D and D had not interfered with it. An injunction against C prohibiting conveyance on to D would have been a remedy against C but its availability against C as a remedy did not affect the position of D. It is an illustration of how important it is to obtain an injunction to preserve assets because once they have been transferred away the claimant's rights may be irreversibly prejudiced. This is a classic reason for the court granting an injunction restraining dealings with an asset, for example an injunction to prevent a transfer when the claimant's rights in the asset would not avail against a bona fide purchaser for value, or Mareva relief to prevent unjustifiable dissipation of assets.

There can also be circumstances in which a chattel has been mortgaged, the mortgagor in possession has entered into a contract of hire and a question arises as to whether the mortgagee's rights enable it to prevent performance of the contract of hire.[63]

In time charterparties it is common for there to be a clause allowing the owner to withdraw the ship in the event of non-payment of the hire by a particular time. There is no jurisdiction in the court to grant "relief from forfeiture" against such a provision.[64] In a commercial contract freely negotiated between the parties the policy of the law is to enforce the contract according to its terms;[65] if the charterers had wanted an "anti-

---

[60] *Esso Petroleum Co Limited v Kingswood Motors* [1974] Q.B. 142 (mandatory injunction requiring conveyance of land back to the transferor so that the transferor would perform the solus tie agreement entered into with the plaintiff); there has to be a causal connection between the transferee's conduct and the inducement of the breach of contract, see *Law Debenture Trust Corporation v Ural Caspian Oil Company* [1995] Ch 152 reversing [1993] 1 W.L.R. 138; *Chitty on Contracts (29th ed. 2004) paras 18–134.*

[61] [1995] Ch 152 reversing [1993] 1 W.L.R. 138.

[62] *Esso Petroleum Co Ltd v Kingswood Motors* [1974] Q.B. 142.

[63] *The Myrto* [1977] 2 Ll. Rep. 243 at pp.253–254 lists the earlier authorities on ships, including *The Manor* [1907] P 339 and *The Lord Strathcona* [1925] P 143.

[64] *Scandanavian Trading Tanker Co. AB v Flota Petrolera Ecuatoriana (The Scaptrade)* [1983] 2 A.C. 694.

[65] *Steedman v Drinkle* [1916] 1 A.C. 275 at 279; *Union Eagle Ltd v Golden Achievement Ltd* [1997] A.C. 514.

technicality" clause,[66] it was up to them to negotiate one. When time is of the essence in a contract for sale then if the purchaser is late, he has repudiated the contract and equity will not grant relief from forfeiture,[67] or specific performance, or an injunction to preserve the asset.

Relief from forfeiture by equity can be exercised in relation to provisions **2.051** requiring payment of what would be a penalty or forfeiture of property where the "primary object of the bargain" was to achieve a particular result and the penalty or the forfeiture was only by way of security for the attainment of that result.[68] In the commercial field it is often essential for businessmen to know where they stand and to conduct their affairs with confidence on the basis of accrued rights. Furthermore it is open to them to shape the rights which would arise on a particular eventuality by negotiating their arrangements accordingly. These considerations may make the equitable jurisdiction inapplicable. Equity does not exercise any general jurisdiction to relieve against the consequences of commercial bargains.

---

[66] For example, see cl. 33 in *Santiren Shipping Ltd v Unimarine SA (The Chrysovalandou Dyo)* [1981] 1 Lloyd's Rep. 159 at 162.
[67] *Steedman v Drinkle* [1916] 1 A.C. 275 at 279; in *Union Eagle Ltd v Golden Achievement Ltd* [1997] A.C. 514 a purchaser, who was 10 minutes late for completion of a flat in Hong Kong when time was of the essence, was in repudiatory breach of contract and could not obtain relief from forfeiture.
[68] *Shiloh Spinners v Harding* [1973] A.C. 691 at 723F–H.

Chapter 3

Common types of commercial injunctions—Mareva relief

(1) Nature of Mareva relief

A Mareva injunction is an interlocutory order[1] of the court granted either **3.001** before judgment, or in aid of execution of a judgment, which restrains the party enjoined from disposing of or dealing with his own assets. The assets covered by the order may be specified, but more usually are assets falling within one or more categories of asset set out in the order. The assets may be situated within or outside the jurisdiction.

Section 37(1) of the Supreme Court Act 1981 is in wide terms and there is nothing in its language to stop it being used to require the defendant to constitute a fund which would stand as security.[2] However, a Mareva injunction does not confer on the claimant a pre-trial attachment or any form of security.[3] This is because this is not the purpose of the jurisdiction. It is also not the effect of the words used in the order.[4] Mareva relief does not confer on the claimant any proprietary rights or security over assets which fall within its ambit. Even where there is a proprietary claim against the defendant a court may decide to grant relief restricted to constituting a fund which is to be frozen but which the order does not require to be provided as security for the claim.[5]

The jurisdiction is not to be used for the purpose of putting pressure on the defendant to secure the claim.[6] A distinction is to be drawn between

---

[1] "Interlocutory" includes the period after final judgment is given on the substantive claim: *Smith v Cowell* (1880) 6 Q.B.D. 75 and *Orwell Steel v Asphalt Ltd* [1984] 1 W.L.R. 1097.

[2] Compare s.37(2) of the Matrimonial Causes Act 1973 which is discussed in Chapter 7, paras 7.018–23 and *Re Mordant; Mordant v Hills* [1996] 1 F.L.R. 334.

[3] *Cretanor Maritime Co. Ltd v Irish Marine Management Ltd* [1978] 1 W.L.R. 966; *Flightline Ltd v Edwards* [2003] 1 W.L.R. 1200; *Bank Mellat v Kazmi* [1989] Q.B. 541; *Re Multi Guarantee Co. Ltd* [1987] B.C.L.C. 257. *Kastner v Jason* [2004] EWHC 592 (Ch) at para.31.

[4] See further Chapter 23.

[5] *Millenium Federation Pty Ltd v Bigjig Pty* [2000] 1 Qd Rep. 275.

[6] *Derby & Co. Ltd v Weldon (Nos 3 and 4)* [1990] Ch. 65 at 76F; *K/S A/S Admiral Shipping v Portlink Ferries* [1984] 2 Lloyd's Rep. 166. *Choy Chee Kee Collin v Public Utilities Board* [1997] 1 S.L.R. 604 at paras 23–25 (which contemplates that an injunction will be discharged if the ulterior purpose of the applicant is to put pressure on the defendant to

what is the purpose of the court in granting an injunction, and what may be a consequence of the injunction being grant. It is no purpose of the court granting Mareva relief to put pressure on the defendant to grant security for the claim, or to facilitate the claimant in obtaining a favourable settlement, but it may be that a result of the injunction will be that the defendant chooses to provide security so as to get the injunction discharged, or even to settle the case. The fact that an injunction may have such a consequence does not mean that the court in granting it, or the claimant in seeking it, has this as an unarticulated and illegitimate aim. Nor does it follow necessarily that because the defendant may be disadvantaged in this foreseeable, and undesirable way as a consequence of the granting of the relief, it is unfair to grant it.[7] It has been suggested that an arbitrary penalty could be imposed on a claimant who acts improperly,[8] but this is not within the scope of the cross-undertaking in damages[9] and may well be unfair to the claimant and give a windfall to the defendant. What does follow from there being a real risk of an undesirable consequence is that if the relief is to be granted there should be clear justification for it such as to make the overall decision appropriate, and the court should discourage any attempt by the claimant to make the relief more onerous for the defendant than is necessary to achieve its legitimate objective of preventing unjustified dissipation of assets. The purpose of the jurisdiction includes both preventing a defendant from taking action "designed to ensure"[10] that an existing or future judgment or order of the court is rendered less effective than would otherwise be the case, and any conduct which may have this effect regardless of whether it is so intended. Thus, the circumstances in which Mareva relief may be appropriate include but are not limited to those

---

provide security; see also *Meespierson NV v Industrial and Commercial Bank of Vietnam* [1998] 2 S.L.R. 632. It is considered that the issue is whether there is a real risk of dissipation of assets which needs to be guarded against and which in the circumstances justifies the granting of the injunction. The fact that the defendant may put up security so as to discharge the injunction is provided for in the example order, and is a possible consequence of the injunction which the applicant would have in mind). *Cf. Mooney v Orr* [1995] 3 W.W.R 116 at 131, discussed in J. Epp, "World-wide Mareva Injunctions in Common Law Canada" (1996) 59 M.L.R. 460.

[7] In "Freezing Injunctions as Security" [2000] C.F.I.L.R. 101 (Peter Devonshire) it is argued that Mareva relief can result in putting the claimant in a position to exert pressure on the defendant to obtain a favourable settlement or security for the claim; but the court has to balance the potential competing injustices which may flow from granting or refusing the relief.

[8] See the suggestion made in "Freezing Injunctions as Security" [2000] C.F.I.L.R. 101 at p.122.

[9] *Harris v Digital Pulse Pty Ltd* [2003] NSWCA 10 (February 7, 2003) at paras 340–342, and see Chapter 11 under "Causation, Measure of Damages and Remoteness in an inquiry as to damages".

[10] *Derby & Co. Ltd v Weldon (Nos 3 and 4)* [1990] Ch. 65, at 76E, *per* Lord Donaldson M.R. The words "designed to" might have been thought to require proof of an intent to defeat enforcement of a judgment, but Lord Donaldson M.R. explained his observation in *R. v Home Secretary Ex. p. Muboyayi* [1992] Q.B. 244 at 257H, saying "designed to" did not mean "intended" but rather "having the consequence that"; see further *Ketchum plc v Group Public Relations Ltd* [1997] 1 W.L.R. 4 at 13; *Mediterranean Feeders LP v Bernd Meyering Schiffahrts*, Court of Appeal Transcript No.966 of 1997 (June 5, 1997).

where there is reason to believe that the defendant intends to cheat[11] the claimant of the fruits of a judgment; there is no necessity to prove "nefarious intent" on the part of the defendant.

The practice in England is to provide for a maximum limit in the order. **3.002** This is because where there is a claim or judgment against a defendant the order should only interfere with how he can use his assets in so far those assets need to be preserved for the claim or judgment. If an injunction is expressed to apply to assets only so far as their value does not exceed a stipulated sum, then if the value does exceed that sum, the injunction allows the enjoined party to deal with his assets to the extent of the excess value.

In *Cretanor Maritime Co. Ltd v Irish Marine Ltd*,[12] Buckley L.J. said that in relation to a body of unspecified assets the injunction "must be capable of having an ambulatory effect" so as to apply to assets from time to time coming within its ambit. Buckley L.J. distinguished Mareva relief from an attachment:[13]

"...[I]t is, I think, manifest that a *Mareva* injunction cannot operate as an attachment. 'Attachment' must, I apprehend, mean a seizure of assets under some writ or like command or order of a competent authority, normally with a view to their being either realised to meet an established claim or held as a pledge or security for the discharge of some claim either already established or yet to be established. An attachment must fasten on particular assets..."

A Mareva injunction, however, even if it relates only to a particularised asset ... is relief *in personam* ... All that the injunction achieves is in truth to prohibit the owner from doing certain things in relation to the asset. It is consequently, in my judgment, not strictly accurate to refer to a Mareva injunction as a pre-trial attachment."

The number of applications for Mareva injunctions has steadily increased **3.003** since the emergence of the jurisdiction in 1975 and they are now often granted. However, the relief is not to be granted except when the court is satisfied that it would be just and convenient in all the circumstances of the case to grant the relief sought. In practice two particular factors which should be considered are whether:

(1) the claimant has a good arguable case against the defendant;

(2) there is a real risk that judgment will go unsatisfied by reason of the disposal by the defendant of his assets, unless he is restrained by court order from disposing of them.

The drastic nature of Mareva relief has led to its being described somewhat graphically as "one of the law's two 'nuclear' weapons", the other being the Anton Piller order.[14]

---

[11] *PCW (Underwriting Agencies) v Dixon* [1983] 2 Lloyd's Rep. 197 at 201–202, *per* Lloyd J.
[12] [1978] 1 W.L.R. 966.
[13] *ibid.*, at 974.
[14] *per* Donaldson L.J. in *Bank Mellat v Nikpour* [1985] F.S.R. 87 at 92.

A third party with knowledge of the injunction must not deliberately aid and abet a breach by the defendant of its terms. The third party is not himself enjoined by the injunction, but the court will not "allow its process to be set at naught and treated with contempt".[15] Thus, for example, a bank with knowledge of a Mareva injunction must not honour cheques drawn on an account when payment of them would be inconsistent with the order.[16]

3.004   A third party can also be in contempt of court for participating in acts which are contrary to the terms of the order, even though the party enjoined has not learned of the granting of the injunction.[17] The court order takes effect as soon as it is pronounced. Although the defendant would not be in contempt of court if he acted inconsistently with its terms before he knew the order has been made, nevertheless the third party would be guilty of contempt if he deliberately caused the court order "to be set at naught".

Although the third party has not aided and abetted the defendant acting in breach of the injunction, the third party can be in contempt because his conduct is an interference with the administration of justice in that it defeats the purpose of the court in making the order.[18] This should not be confused with the purpose of the claimant in seeking the order.[19] The purpose of the court in granting a Mareva injunction is to preserve the relevant assets. A third party who interferes with those assets knowing of the order is prima facie defeating the purpose of the court order.

The injunction can be said to operate as if it had an effect on an asset *in rem*, in that the defendant is precluded from dealing with the assets, and third parties with knowledge of the order must not aid and abet a breach or defeat the purpose of the order.

3.005   Since the Mareva injunction gives the claimant no proprietary rights over the defendant's assets, a bona fide purchaser or assignee for value or chargee of the assets without notice of the injunction will obtain good title or good security. Similarly, anyone with an existing charge over the assets is entitled to enforce it.[20]

In principle, judgment creditors of the defendant who is subject to a Mareva injunction can execute their judgments against any of his assets.

---

[15] *Seaward v Paterson* [1897] 1 Ch. 545 at 555, *per* Lindley L.J. See also *Lord Wellesley v Earl of Mornington* (1848) 11 Beav 180: *Acrow (Automation) Ltd v Rex Chainbelt Inc.* [1971] 1 W.L.R 1676; and *Z Ltd v A-Z and AA-LL* [1982]1 Q.B. 558; see for contempt of court Chapter 19.

[16] *Z Ltd v A-Z and AA-LL* [1982] Q.B. 558.

[17] For example, a bank with knowledge of the order paying a cheque drawn by the defendant before the injunction was made: see *Z Ltd v A-Z and AA-LL* [1982] Q.B. 558.

[18] *Attorney-General v Punch* [2003] 1 A.C. 1046.

[19] *ibid.*, at [39–40], *per* Lord Nicholls.

[20] In *Boeing Capital Corporation v Wells Fargo Bank Northwest* [2003] EWHC 1364, Comm Ct the claimant had judgment for delivery-up on its security claim on a Boeing 737, but was not allowed to enforce the order for delivery-up of the aeroplane until after first obtaining a variation to the Mareva injunction obtained by a third party. See further Chapter 19, para.19.032.

This is the consequence of the principle that the Mareva creates no security and the principle that prior to insolvency of a defendant a judgment creditor can enforce his judgment as soon as he obtains it.

Execution by a third party under a court order would not normally, in itself, amount to a breach of the terms of the injunction. This is because the dealing with the assets is by order of the court and not by an act of the defendant and because the restraint is a personal restraint on the defendant and does not operate directly against the assets: see further *Re Noel Ling Ex p. Enrobook Pty Ltd.*[21] See also the dicta of Robert Goff J. in *Iraqi Ministry of Defence v Arcepey Shipping (The Angel Bell)*,[22] and of Parker J. in A v B (*X intervening*),[23] which appear to suggest that a judgment creditor does not need to seek a variation of the Mareva injunction before executing the judgment on the assets.

However a third party can be in contempt of court even though he has not aided and abetted a breach of the court order. This is under the principle that a third party must not deliberately frustrate the purpose of the order.[24] The purpose of the order is the court's purpose in making the order. That purpose is normally to be defined from the terms of the order. Thus the purpose of the Mareva is to preserve the assets which are caught by the injunction subject to the financial limit and the permitted uses authorised under the order. **3.006**

There can be circumstances when even though a judgment has been obtained by a third party the court will refuse to allow the frozen assets to be taken in satisfaction of that judgment. That the judgment debtor is insolvent would be a powerful reason for refusing to make a final third party debt order.[25] Likewise, if winding-up proceedings or bankruptcy proceedings are about to be commenced or it is clear that the judgment debtor is insolvent, the court should preserve the frozen assets for the benefit of creditors generally pending the commencement of the insolvency proceedings and not permit the judgment creditor to obtain priority over other creditors.

Another example is where a parent company had lent its subsidiary money to be used as trading capital and there was a trading claim against the subsidiary. It was unfair to allow that fund to be used to repay the parent before the trading claim had been resolved and satisfied,[26] or to pay the subsidiary's legal costs incurred in resisting the trading claim when the parent could pay those costs and was to be expected to pay those costs if the fund could not be used.[27] If the parent, or the subsidiary's solicitors,

---

[21] (1996) 142 A.L.R. 87 at 92–93, Federal Court of Australia.
[22] [1981] Q.B. 65 at 72.
[23] [1983] 2 Lloyd's Rep. 532 at 534. See also para. 20.070 below.
[24] *Attorney-General v Punch* [2003] 1 A.C. 1046 at [4]; see Chapter 19, paras 19.028–34.
[25] *Roberts Petroleum v Bernard Kenny Ltd* [1983] 2 A.C. 192.
[26] *Atlas Maritime v Avalon Maritime Ltd No.1* [1991] 1 Lloyd's Rep. 563; contrast *Hurrell v Fitness Holdings Europe*, unreported, March 15, 2002 in which repayment to parent company of loan in the ordinary course of business was permitted.
[27] *Atlas Maritime v Avalon Maritime Ltd No.3* [1991] 1 W.L.R. 917.

had obtained judgment against the subsidiary then this would have been merely a formal step which would not have affected the underlying justice of the case. It would still have been unfair to allow the fund to be used to pay the judgment and the court would have refused to vary the injunction to allow the fund to be so used.

3.007   Thus it does not necessarily follow that because the third party has a judgment the court will authorise execution of that judgment on the assets. Often it would be just to allow enforcement of the judgment. However, there are cases in which it would not be. If the third party is aware of this possibility and goes ahead regardless to take the assets, then he could be held to be in contempt of court. For this reason a judgment creditor who wishes to enforce his judgment against funds frozen by a Mareva injunction should apply for a variation of the injunction permitting him to do so.[28] This is because once he knows of the injunction he knows that the purpose of the court was to preserve the assets. The court, by granting a variation permitting the judgment to be enforced against the frozen assets, recognises that the purpose of the original order must be qualified so as to give way to the judgment. If a judgment creditor obtains an interim third party debt order in respect of a bank account which is subject to a Mareva injunction then, unless the injunction is varied, the third party can object to a final order being made. In practice the court may adjourn the application for a final order until an application has been successfully made for a variation to the Mareva permitting the assets to be used to satisfy a third party debt order, or the application for a variation and a final order can be heard together.

The court has jurisdiction to grant Mareva relief pending presentation of a winding-up petition[29] or bankruptcy proceedings. Once a liquidator or trustee in bankruptcy has been appointed, assets should be transferred to the liquidator or trustee. A claimant who has a claim against a bankrupt has no right to prevent the trustee in bankruptcy from taking over the defendant's assets, and an injunction preventing the trustee from taking over the assets will not be granted or maintained.[30] Similarly, once administrative receivers have been appointed under a debenture granted by a corporate defendant, the injunction should be varied to enable the assets caught by the debenture to be made over to them.[31] Mareva relief can,

---

[28] See *Boeing Capital Corporation v Wells Fargo Bank Northwest* [2003] EWHC 1364, at [14], Comm Ct, mortgagee of a Boeing 737 required to obtain a variation to a Mareva injunction before enforcing his judgment for delivery-up.

[29] *United Bank v Claybridge Shipping SA* (1980) 14 *Lloyd's Maritime Law Newsletter* (May 15, 1980); 16 *Lloyd's Maritime Law Newsletter* (June 12, 1980) cited in *Deutsche Schachtbau- und Tiefbohrgesellschaft mbH v Shell International Petroleum Co. Ltd* [1990] 1 A.C. 295 at 326; *Re Claybridge Shipping SA*, Court of Appeal (Civ Div) Transcript No.143 of 1981 (March 9, 1981), subsequently reported at [1997] 1 B.C.L.C. 813.

[30] *Peasegood v Peasegood*, Court of Appeal (Civ Div) Transcript No.629 of 1994 (April 14, 1994).

[31] *Capital Cameras Ltd v Harold Lines Ltd* [1991] 1 W.L.R 54 applying *Cretanor Maritime Co. Ltd v Irish Marine Management Ltd (The Cretan Harmony)* [1978] 1 W.L.R 966; *Deputy Commissioner of Taxation v Advanced Communications Technologies (Australia) Pty Ltd* [2003] V.S.C. 67 (March 5, 2003) (Mareva relief discharged when an administrator, and receivers and managers, had control of the assets).

however, be maintained in force even after a winding-up order[32] or a bankruptcy order has been made,[33] provided that its purpose is to preserve the assets held by or for the defendant, for the creditors as a whole. In *Mercantile Group (Europe) AG v Aiyela*,[34] an injunction was granted against the wife of the bankrupt defendant, on the grounds that the injunction against the wife was ancillary to protecting the substantive rights of the plaintiff against the bankrupt husband.

(2) "Disposing of or dealing with his assets"

The *Practice Direction—Interim Injunctions* which supplements CPR Pt 25 **3.008** has annexed to it an "example of a Freezing Injunction"[35] and provides that the example "may be modified as appropriate in any particular case". Standard forms were issued in 1994[36] and 1996.[37] The CPR example order for a freezing injunction, which is labelled F.I., is dated September 2002. That form has different provisions for injunctions limited to assets in England and Wales and for worldwide orders.

The example order was drafted after the decision of the Court of Appeal in *Federal Bank of the Middle East Ltd v Hadkinson*.[38] In that case the claimant bank had obtained a worldwide freezing order against Mr Hadkinson and certain companies with which he was connected. The order prohibited them from disposing of or dealing with or diminishing the value of any of "their assets and/or funds", whether in their name or not and whether solely or jointly owned, up to a particular value. It ordered disclosure of all of "their assets and/or funds;". After the injunction had been granted, Mr Hadkinson transferred money from an account held in his own name to an account in the name of his wife. He claimed that the money transferred was not beneficially owned by him but was owned by third party investors who had entrusted him with that money. The claimant bank raised the contempt issue against Mr Hadkinson on its application against him for an order that he should not be allowed to take any further step in the proceedings until he had complied with the disclosure order and had purged his contempt.[39] The issue was whether Mr

---

[32] *Re Claybridge Shipping SA*, Court of Appeal [1997] 1 B.C.L.C. 813.
[33] *Mercantile Group (Europe) AG v Aiyela* [1993] F.S.R 745 at 757–758, *per* Hobhouse J. citing *Re Claybridge Shipping SA*, [1997] 1 B.C.L.C. 813. The judgment of Hobhouse J. was affirmed at [1994] Q.B. 366. *Lawindi v Elkateb* [2001] N.S.W.S.C. 865 (October 3, 2001) at para.15–21 citing this text.
[34] [1994] Q.B. 36.
[35] Paragraph 6.1 of the Practice Direction.
[36] [1994] 1 W.L.R 1233.
[37] [1996] 1 W.L.R 1552.
[38] [2000] 1 W.L.R 1695.
[39] The court will only refuse to hear a party in contempt "when the contempt itself impedes the course of justice and there is no other effective means of securing compliance. . .", *per* Denning L.J. in *Hadkinson v Hadkinson* [1952] P. 285 at 298; *X Ltd v Morgan, Grampian (Publishers) Ltd* [1991] 1 A.C. 1 at 46 and 50–51.

Hadkinson was in contempt of court in making the transfers, assuming, without deciding, that the money did belong beneficially to others and not to him. This assumption in his favour was made because of the procedure which had been adopted at first instance.

On this assumption the money neither belonged to Mr Hadkinson nor could be taken in execution of any judgment obtained by the bank against Mr Hadkinson or the defendant companies. However, the claimant bank contended that since the account, from which the transfers were made, was in the name of Mr Hadkinson and he had had control over that account, the account came within the words "their assets and/or funds". This was rejected by the Court of Appeal—the words meant that the assets or funds had to be owned beneficially by Mr Hadkinson or one of the companies. The order did not apply to assets held by a defendant as a trustee.[40]

3.009   The case was unusual. The fact that formal contempt proceedings were not brought by the bank against Mr Hadkinson and the summary procedure adopted by it for making its application to prevent him being heard, led to the first instance judge declining, rightly in the opinion of the Court of Appeal, to decide whether a transfer of £4,235,000 was from his own money. This led to the first instance judge adopting the assumption that he was a trustee, and considering the construction of the order on that assumption. If formal contempt proceedings had been brought the court would then have heard evidence about whether he was a trustee. This would have included evidence, which, if not satisfactorily explained by Mr Hadkinson, was likely to have lead to the conclusion that the transfers were not of trust money:

(1) the transfers were from bank accounts in his own name and not accounts which named him as a trustee;

(2) the transfers were to his wife and referred to his children, and thus appeared to be transfers which his wife was to hold for the benefit of their children; and

(3) the transfers were not to any of the "investors" who were said by him to be beneficially entitled to the money.

The example freezing injunction issued in September 2002, refers in para.5 to "his assets" meaning the respondent's assets, and applies to all the respondent's assets "whether or not they are in his own name and whether they are solely or jointly owned".[41] This follows the previous practice in the standard forms in the *Practice Direction (Mareva and Anton Piller Orders: Forms)*.[42] These had required the defendant not to remove

---

[40] Following *Westpac Banking Corporation v Gill (No.1)* (1987) 2 P.R.N.Z. 52, cited in P. Devonshire "Mareva Injunctions and Third Parties: Exposing the Subtext" (1999) 62 M.L.R. 539.

[41] Para.6.

[42] [1996] 1 W.L.R. 1552, superseding the forms at [1994] 4 All E.R. 52.

"assets" from the jurisdiction or ". . .in any way [to] dispose of or deal with or diminish the value of any of his assets . . . whether in his name or not and whether solely or jointly owned. . ."

The example order goes on to provide in the second and third sentences of para.6 that:

". . . For the purpose of this order the Respondent's assets include any asset which he has the power, directly or indirectly, to dispose of or deal with as if it were his own. The Respondent is to be regarded as having such power if a third party holds or controls the asset in accordance with his direct or indirect instructions."

These provisions would apply when the third party controls assets, **3.010** which might not be in his own name,[43] but in fact acts in accordance with instructions given by the respondent and the respondent is able to have the benefit of the assets "as if [they] were his own". A trustee holds property so that the real benefit of the property accrues not to the trustee but to the beneficiaries or other objects of the trust.[44] So if money is held by a trustee for the benefit of the respondent that money would be frozen. Also it is common for a defendant to control offshore companies and their subsidiaries, and to use the assets of those companies as if they were the defendant's own. Such a situation would come within para.6 of the standard form order.

In contrast if Mr Hadkinson had been a trustee of the money for investors he would not have had power "to dispose of or deal with [it] as if it were his own" within para.6, and the inclusion of para.6 in the order in that case would not have reversed the result.

The example order follows the practice that a Mareva injunction is usually to be expressed in terms which enjoin the defendant from "disposing of" or "dealing with" his assets except in certain defined circumstances, *e.g.* payment of living expenses.

The purpose of Mareva relief before judgment is to prevent unjustifia- **3.011** ble[45] dissipations of or dealings with assets which are liable to result in a judgment being unsatisfied. The procedural means to achieve this is the granting of an injunction, subject to defined exceptions and usually a financial limit, which is an injunction restraining disposals of or dealings with assets.

---

[43] It is considered that in this context, where the order is intended to bite regardless of whether the Respondent has a proprietary right in the asset, the word "controls" does not require the assets to be in the possession or name of the third party, and it includes the situation in which the third party has neither, but has a legal right to tell someone who holds the asset what to do with it; see also *Aqua-Leisure Industries Inc. v Aqua Splash Ltd* [2003] 1 H.K.L.R.D. 142 at para.24 referring to *Dollfus Mieg et Compagnie SA v Bank of England* [1950] Ch. 333 at 359.

[44] See the definition of a trust given by Professors Sheridan and Keeton cited in *Snell's Equity* (13th ed., 2000), p.110.

[45] See Chapter 10 below.

In considering what is or is not a contempt of court it is important to know (i) what constitutes "disposing of an asset" or "dealing with it" within the meaning of the injunction; and (ii) what constitute the defendant"s "assets".

(i) "Disposing of or dealing with"

3.012   In *Z Ltd v A-Z* and *AA-LL* Lord Denning M.R. said that if an asset is covered by the terms of a Mareva injunction a third party who holds the asset and knows of the injunction must "do what he reasonably can to preserve the asset. He must not assist in any way in the disposal of it. He must hold it pending further order. . .".[46]

It might have been the case that the courts interpreted the terms of a Mareva injunction which precluded "disposing of" or "dealing with" assets abroad as having the effect of preventing the defendant from removing chattels from a bailee, or receiving a debt which was due to be paid to him. For debts, this appears to have been what was envisaged by Lord Denning M.R. in *Z Ltd v A-Z* and *AA-LL* when he referred to a bank "freezing" a bank account. Such an approach would have the merit of making clear to third parties where they stood as a result of the injunction. It would also tend to promote the efficacy of the injunction because third party debtors or bailees would retain the relevant asset in the same form, pending further order of the court.

However, in *The Law Society v Shanks*,[47] the defendant was an individual who was subject to a Mareva injunction which restrained him "by himself, his servants, or agents or otherwise . . . from disposing, pledging or transferring or dealing with any assets" of his within the jurisdiction including any gratuity to be received from the Ministry of Defence, which had been the employer of the defendant. The Ministry did not pay the defendant either the gratuity or his pension. Sir John Donaldson M.R., with whom the other members of the court agreed, refused to follow the observations of Lord Denning M.R. in two passages[48] of his judgment in *Z Ltd v A-Z and AA-LL* saying that:

". . . I know of no authority other than this particular passage [*i.e.* the passage at 574E] for the proposition that [the injunction] prevents anybody handing the asset over to the owner of the asset, in this case the defendant. That does not amount to a dissipation or a disposal of any kind whatsoever. In special circumstances, where it is known that

---

[46] [1982] Q.B. 558 at 574.
[47] [1988] 1 F.L.R. 504.
[48] [1982] Q.B. 558 at 572 and 574E; these passages were relied upon in *Gangway Ltd v Caledonian Park Investments* (Jersey) Ltd [2001] 2 Lloyd's Rep. 715 at 717 (referring to the report in [1982] 1 Lloyd's Rep. 240 at 244) but *The Law Society v Shanks* was not cited and it is considered that the view expressed that the bank as a non-party had to apply for a variation to enable it to exercise its own rights of security was wrong, see Chapter 20, para.20–014.

the sole purpose of requiring the asset to be handed over to the defendant is to facilitate a dissipation of that asset, different considerations may arise . . . That would be a very peculiar case indeed.

. . . [W]hilst [the two passages] are entitled to the greatest possible respect as coming from Lord Denning, they do not in my judgment represent a general statement of the law which is applicable in any ordinary case."

The court was concerned in that case with the fact that the injunction **3.013** contained no provision for payment by the defendant of his living expenses, and that even had provision been made, the injunction, as interpreted by the Ministry in reliance on the observations of Lord Denning M.R., was to be taken as preventing payment to the defendant within the jurisdiction of money due to him.

In *Bank Mellat v Kazmi*,[49] the defendant had been convicted of defrauding the plaintiffs who had obtained judgment against him. A question arose as to the effect of a Mareva injunction which restrained the defendant from "disposing [of], pledging, transferring or otherwise dealing with any assets he may have within the jurisdiction of this court", and whether that injunction ought to be varied. The defendant had made a claim for supplementary benefit and an adjudication officer had determined that he was entitled to receive a substantial sum from the Secretary of State for Social Services who had thereby become a debtor of the defendant. The plaintiff judgment creditors wanted the money to be paid into one of the defendant's bank accounts, but the defendant wanted it to be paid to him directly. The Secretary of State sought to intervene in the proceedings and asked for directions as to what he should do. Nourse L.J., with whom the other members of the court agreed, after citing from the judgment of Sir John Donaldson M.R. in *The Law Society v Shanks* said[50] that:

". . . Mere notice of the existence of a Mareva injunction cannot render it a contempt of court for a third party to make over an asset direct. Otherwise it might be impossible, for example, for a debtor with notice to pay over to the defendant even the most trivial sum without seeking the directions of the court. A distinction must be drawn between notice of the injunction on the one hand and notice of a probability that the asset will be disposed of or dealt with in breach of the order on the other. It is only in the latter case that the third party can be in contempt of court. No general test can be propounded for the latter class of case, although the facts here suggest that it may not be quite as peculiar as Sir John Donaldson M.R. thought."

Accordingly, it appears that although a Mareva injunction is expressed as **3.014** restraining any "dealing with" an asset, the court will not interpret this as preventing any conduct of the defendant which merely results in the same

---

[49] [1989] Q.B. 541.
[50] [1988] 1 F.L.R. 504 at 547.

asset, or in the case of a debt the financial proceeds of the debt, being held by the defendant himself. The injunction in the example order will restrain the defendant from disposing of the asset or the financial proceeds of the debt. Consequently, if a claimant wishes to prevent the defendant from receiving payment of a debt due or accruing due to him from a third party, it is necessary to make an application for special wording to be inserted in the injunction. Those words would expressly prohibit the defendant from (1) giving directions for accepting, or (2) receiving payment of the relevant debt due or to become due from the third party.[51] Sometimes an injunction will be granted restraining the defendant from changing the location of an asset[52] so as to avoid the defendant moving assets out of the hands of non-parties, and then disposing of them in breach of the injunction. On the basis of the approach adopted by the Court of Appeal in these two cases it would appear that the effect of a Mareva injunction in the example order is simply to prevent dissipation or disposals of assets[53] and that the defendant remains free to receive assets.

The defendant is at liberty to pay money into a bank account which is in credit because this is not a disposal or dissipation of the asset,[54] but merely the equivalent of the deposit of an asset for safe keeping. Crediting money or a cheque to an overdrawn bank account would be a disposal of an asset,[55] and a breach of the injunction.

The position which has been reached is not entirely satisfactory. A defendant subject to Mareva relief should not be left with the right to require substantial sums to be paid to him in cash by his debtors. A third party should not be placed in the position where there is doubt whether he is obliged to pay the defendant or can properly do so. Wherever possible, the order should provide for what the defendant can or cannot receive so that the order will operate smoothly and effectively.

(ii) "His assets"

3.015   The purpose of the injunction is to preserve assets so that the claimant's claim can be satisfied. "Assets" are property of a person or company which may be made liable for debts. It might therefore be thought that the order should be construed so as to cover anything against which a judgment

---

[51] This was done by the plaintiffs in *Deutsche Schachtbau-und Tiefbohrgesellschaft GmbH v R'as Al-Khaimah National Oil Co.* [1990] 1 A.C. 295, HL, in a separate application to Bingham J. on July 24, 1986.

[52] *Mane Market v Temple* [1998] S.A.S.C. 6986.

[53] An analogy can be drawn with the ambit of s.127 of the Insolvency Act 1986 which contains a provision formerly contained in s.227 of the Companies Act 1948 and s.522 of the Companies Act 1985. Under s.127 a bank which pays a cheque is acting as an agent for its client. If the money were simply paid to the company itself there would be no disposal of the asset by the company within s.127—see *Hellicourt (Contracts) Ltd v Bank of Ireland* [2001] Lloyd's Rep. (Bank.) 6 and *Re Gray's Inn Construction* [1980] 1 W.L.R 711. Contrast the effect of a criminal restraint order; see Chapter 25.

[54] *cp. Re Barn Crown Ltd* [1995] 1 W.L.R. 147.

[55] *cp. Re Gray's Inn Construction Co. Ltd* [1980] 1 W.L.R. 711 at 715–716.

could be enforced, or anything which might be taken and applied towards satisfying a judgment through bankruptcy or winding-up proceedings or otherwise. But if contempt proceedings are brought, it will be incumbent on the claimant to show that what was done was in breach of the terms of the order. If there is genuine ambiguity as to how the order is to be interpreted and therefore as to whether it has been broken, the ambiguity will preclude a finding of contempt.[56]

The purpose of the example orders is to inform the defendant in clear English what he must not do. The need for transparency is a requirement of fairness towards the defendant and anyone else who might be affected by the order. The technical rules as to what property or rights can be taken through bankruptcy or winding-up proceedings cannot be allowed to affect how the words of the order should have been interpreted, on an objective basis, by the recipient. The order should not give rise to difficult points of construction and should enable someone looking at the order to know with certainty what can or cannot be done consistently with the order.[57]

In *R & I Bank of Western Australia Ltd v Anchorage Investments*,[58] an injunction was granted in respect of "assets" of the defendants. One of the defendants and his wife were within the class of beneficiaries of a discretionary trust. That defendant had control over the trust because of his right to appoint the trustee and because the trustee at the time of the granting of the injunction was a company over which he had control. A few days after the injunction had been granted, documents were executed which had the effect of excluding the defendant and his wife from the class of beneficiaries and removing the defendant from control of the trust. Contempt proceedings failed because it was not clear that the defendant had dealt with his "assets" within the meaning of the order. It was at least arguable that he had merely divested himself of *power* to control the trust and not any *property* of his own. Paragraph 6 of the example order issued in September 2002 would have caught this because the defendant had had control of the trust and its assets, and could have used them for his own benefit.

In *SA Development Ltd v Fair Fashion Co. and Wing Hang Bank Ltd*,[59] **3.016** the plaintiff had obtained judgment in the High Court on two dishonoured cheques. There was Mareva relief restraining the defendant from disposing of or otherwise dealing with its assets save in so far as they exceeded a specified amount. The plaintiff sought to enforce its judgment by obtaining

---

[56] *Federal Bank of the Middle East Ltd v Hadkinson* [2000] 1 W.L.R. 1695 at 1705D–1706G; *R & I Bank of Western Australia Ltd v Anchorage Investments* (1992) 10 WAR 59 (Southern Australia); *Iberian Trust Ltd v Founders Trust and Investment Co. Ltd* [1932] 2 K.B. 87 at 95; *R. v City of London Magistrates' Court Exp. Green* [1997] 3 All E.R. 551 at 558g. If the injunction is clear, the fact that the defendant misconstrued it does not provide any answer to the charge of contempt. If he acted on legal advice, this may go in mitigation of the penalty: *Spectavest Inc v Aperknit Ltd* [1988] F.S.R 161; *Z Bank v DI* [1994] 1 Lloyd's Rep. 656 at 660.

[57] *Potters-Ballotini Ltd v Weston-Baker* [1977] R.P.C 202 at 206.

[58] (1992) 10 W.A.R 59.

[59] [1997] H.K.L.R.D. 167, Litton V.-P., Godfrey and Liu JJ.A.

a charging order on land owned by the defendant. But the property had been mortgaged to a bank. Under the mortgage, in the event of default by the mortgagor, the mortgagee had the right to go into possession of the property.[60] The defendant had defaulted under the mortgage and voluntarily delivered up possession of the property to the bank, who sold it at public auction. It was argued that the defendant had been in contempt of the Mareva injunction in that he had voluntarily given up possession to the mortgagee bank and that the officers of the bank were also guilty of contempt. The Court of Appeal held that the plaintiff should not have leave to pursue contempt proceedings because the bank had a legal right to possession and the defendant had simply recognised that right. The defendant had not disposed of his assets,[61] he had merely recognised the bank's pre-existing rights as mortgagees, which included property rights over the land.

The exercise or enforcement by a creditor of his rights, including rights to enforce his security or to obtain execution, so long as there is no dealing by the person restrained with his assets, will not be a breach of the Mareva.[62] The position is different when a receiver has been appointed by the court over certain assets.

The claimant should draft his application for an injunction in terms which are sufficiently clear to catch each type of transaction he wishes to prevent.[63] If he does this, it will be up to the defendant to apply to the court for permission to carry out the transaction. If the claimant cannot show a means of reaching the underlying property by execution or through insolvency proceedings or otherwise, then the Mareva injunction should not be allowed to prevent the transaction from proceeding. If, on the other hand, the claimant shows a means of reaching the underlying assets, then Mareva relief may be available.[64]

(3) When the defendant has a claim against a third party

3.017   A claimant who has obtained Mareva relief against a defendant who also happens to be a party to some other proceedings before the court is not regarded as having sufficient direct interest in the other proceedings to entitle him to intervene in those proceedings.[65] The claimant may be liable

---

[60] The mortgagee is entitled to *possession* at any time after execution of the mortgage except as varied by contract or statute: *National Westminster Bank v Skelton* [1993] 1 W.L.R. 72.

[61] Applying *Capital Cameras v Harold Lines* [1993] 1 W.L.R. 54 at 56D–F; see also *Re R (Restraint Order)* [1990] 2 Q.B. 307 at 314.

[62] *Re Ling, Ex p. Enrobook Pty Ltd* (1996) 142 A.L.R. 87 at 92–93, Federal Court of Australia. See also *Re Ousley Ex p. FCT* (1994) 48 F.C.R 131 at 138–139, Federal Court of Australia.

[63] The standard form wording may need to be modified.

[64] *Cardile v LED Builders Pty Ltd* (1999) 198 C.L.R 380.

[65] *Woodstock Shipping Co. v Kyma Compania Naviera SA (The Wave)* [1981] 1 Lloyd's Rep. 521.

to be affected financially by the result of the other proceedings. Thus, *e.g.* the other proceedings may involve a chose in action which represents all or a substantial part of the assets of the defendant. It would, though, be impracticable to allow a claimant to intervene in proceedings when he has no direct interest in the subject-matter as such, but only a commercial interest in the outcome of the litigation. The fact that a Mareva injunction is obtained, applying to the chose in action which is the subject of the other proceedings, does not confer on the claimant a direct interest in the subject-matter of those proceedings.[66] This is the case even though an adverse result in the other proceedings is liable to leave the Mareva injunction without subject-matter—the chose in action having been nullified by an adverse judgment.

The position is different once the claimant becomes a judgment creditor. He may then be able to obtain a garnishee order nisi if the subject of the other proceedings is an alleged debt.[67] Alternatively, he may apply to the court to appoint a receiver by way of equitable execution to pursue the other proceedings in the name of the judgment debtor.[68] As a further option, it may be possible for the claimant to commence winding-up or bankruptcy proceedings against the defendant. A liquidator or trustee in bankruptcy would then have the opportunity of taking over the conduct of the other proceedings.

A Mareva injunction in standard form precludes a defendant from settling other proceedings in which he is a claimant if the chose in action is an asset falling within the ambit of the injunction. This is because the chose in action is liable to be destroyed or altered by the settlement. In such circumstances the defendant should seek a variation of the Mareva injunction under the principles established in *Iraqi Ministry of Defence v Arcepey Shipping Ltd (The Angel Bell)*,[69] before concluding the settlement.

In *Normid Housing Association Ltd v Ralphs and Mansell*,[70] the plaintiffs **3.018** had a substantial claim against the defendant architects for negligence and breach of contract in the design of certain works. The defendants had professional indemnity cover and the insurers had made a comparatively small offer to settle the claims against them by the defendant architects. The plaintiffs desired to prevent the defendants from compromising the claim with the insurers and obtained an injunction restraining them from doing so. The plaintiffs originally sought to uphold the injunction on the basis that they had a legal or equitable interest in the insurance claim by reason of the Third Parties (Rights Against Insurers) Act 1930. However, this Act has the effect of transferring an insurance claim to a third party only in the events[71] set out in s.1 of the Act—*e.g.* if an individual assured

---

[66] *Sanders Lead Inc. v Entores Ltd* [1984] 1 W.L.R. 452. CA.
[67] See *Sanders Lead Inc v Entores Ltd. above*, per Kerr L.J. at 461.
[68] See, *e.g. Allied Irish Bank v Ashford Hotels Ltd* [1997] 3 All E.R. 309.
[69] [1981] Q.B. 65.
[70] [1989] 2 Lloyd's Rep. 265.
[71] See generally *Firma C-Trade SA v Newcastle Protection and Indemnity Association* [1991] 2 A.C. 1.

becomes bankrupt or makes a composition or arrangement with his creditors or if a winding-up order is made. None of those events had occurred. Section 3 of the Act afforded protection to third parties against settlements made after the commencement of bankruptcy or winding up, but not against settlements concluded beforehand. Accordingly, the Court of Appeal declined to uphold the injunction by reference to the Act.[72] The plaintiffs then sought to uphold the injunction by reference to Mareva principles, arguing that the claim of the architects against the insurers was an asset and that the defendants should be precluded from dealing with that asset. The insurers and the architects submitted that the pending claim against the insurers was not an asset for Mareva purposes. The Court of Appeal found it unnecessary to deal with this submission.[73] But Mareva injunctions are commonly granted in respect of choses in action as such,[74] and in the context of the appointment of receivers, it is well established that a receiver may be appointed over a claim or potential claim against a third party.[75] The court did, however, decide that the compromise of the claim by the architects would be a transaction entered into "in the ordinary course of business" in the sense that it was not suggested that the proposed settlement was in any way collusive, nor were the defendants "putting their assets or seeking to put their assets beyond the [claimants'] reach".[76] Otherwise the case might have been brought within the category where the defendant is destroying or damaging his assets for the ulterior purpose of putting pressure on the claimant or denying him any fruits of success, or where the defendant is simply not acting rationally.[77] Accordingly, no Mareva injunction should be granted to prevent the compromise. The same principle applies to a mortgagee or chargee of an asset who wishes to realise his security; he is entitled to exercise his own rights bona fide in the ordinary course of business provided that he is not acting collusively with the defendant so as to achieve what would amount to an unjustifiable dissipation of assets by the defendant.[78]

3.019   The insurers also sought to suggest that there should not be an injunction because if a settlement was entered into by the architects for the purpose of prejudicing the interests of the plaintiffs, it could be impugned under s.423 of the Insolvency Act 1986. The Court of Appeal did not deal with this argument, which goes to the manner in which the discretion was to be exercised. But the consideration that if a settlement were to proceed the claimant may subsequently be able to have it set aside under s.423

---

[72] *ibid.*, at pp 267–274. See also *Re Greenfield*, ChD, unreported, January 19, 1998.
[73] *Normid Housing Association Ltd v Ralphs and Mansell (No.2)* [1989] 2 Lloyd's Rep. 274 at 275.
[74] An obvious example is a bank account.
[75] *Bourne v Colodense* [1985] I.C.R. 291; *Maclaine Watson & Co. v International Tin Council* [1988] Ch. 1 at 21; and see also [1989] Ch. 253 at 271; *Allied Irish Bank v Ashford Hotels Ltd* [1997] 3 All E.R. 309.
[76] [1989] 2 Lloyd's Rep. 265 at 276, *per* Lloyd L.J.; and see *Re Greenfield*, n.68 above.
[77] *Standard Bank v Walker* [1992] 1 W.L.R. 561.
[78] *Gangway Ltd v Caledonian Park Investments (Jersey) Ltd* [2001] 2 Lloyd's Rep. 715.

cannot in itself preclude the granting of Mareva relief. If there are substantial grounds for believing that the intended settlement is not bona fide, then it is likely to be appropriate to prevent its being concluded. Prevention may well be better than a possible future cure.

Accordingly, as a general rule, Mareva relief granted to a claimant who is not a judgment creditor will be varied so as to leave the defendant free to deal with claims against third parties, including the prosecution of litigation and the negotiation and conclusion of any settlement. Exceptionally, relief may be available pre-judgment if the circumstances indicate that, *e.g.* the defendant is seeking to rush through a highly disadvantageous settlement in the hope of spiriting away the proceeds. The fact that relief may be available under ss423–425 of the Insolvency Act 1986 is no more than a factor which may fall to be taken into account in the exercise of the discretion of the court. Indeed, if the relevant third party is outside the jurisdiction, any subsequent claim under those sections to impeach a settlement may be difficult to prosecute or enforce.[79] The same is in principle true of an application by a claimant before judgment to have a receiver appointed over the claim, with authority to negotiate a settlement, prosecute litigation and collect any proceeds. The appointment of a receiver would be appropriate only in circumstances which justified the granting of relief by way of Mareva injunction, and as a matter of discretion should not be granted where the grant of an injunction would itself not be just and convenient. However, if the claimant is a judgment creditor, then he will be entitled to look to the claim for the purpose of satisfying the judgment.

(4) Courts in which Mareva injunctions can be obtained

Mareva injunctions can be obtained in any of the three Divisions of the High Court, although in view of the special statutory powers to grant relief in certain matrimonial actions derived from s.37 of the Matrimonial Causes Act 1973, they are less frequently sought in the Family Division than in the Queen's Bench and Chancery Divisions. 3.020

Section 37 of the Supreme Court Act 1981 empowers the High Court to grant Mareva relief in cases in which there is a substantive claim before it. It is essential for the claimant to be able to serve the claim form commencing the proceedings on the defendant. If the defendant cannot be served in England and Wales, then the claimant must be able to serve the defendant out of the jurisdiction. This can be done without permission if CPR r.6.19 applies. But otherwise the claimant must be able to apply for

---

[79] In *Normid Housing Association Ltd v Ralphs and Mansell (No.2)* [1989] 2 Lloyd's Rep. 274 it would appear that, although the insurers were foreign, there was no reason to suppose that there would be any special difficulties in making a claim under s.423.

permission to serve the claim out of the jurisdiction, *e.g.* under CPR r.6.20.[80] Mareva relief can also be obtained in free-standing proceedings brought for that purpose under s.44 of the Arbitration Act 1996 in support of arbitral proceedings wherever the seat of the arbitration may be and in free-standing proceedings seeking relief under s.25 of the Civil Jurisdiction and Judgments Act 1982.[81] The jurisdiction under s.37 also extends to proceedings commenced to enforce a substantive right which is justiciable in an inferior court in England and Wales, at least when that right can also be enforced by the High Court, but not where the inferior court is intended by Parliament to be the only court to which recourse is to be had for the purpose of enforcing the right.[82]

In Canada it has been held that the courts have an inherent jurisdiction to act in aid of proceedings in inferior courts and that this is a source for Mareva relief.[83] However, in England there is no "inherent jurisdiction" for the granting of Mareva relief.

3.021   It used to be possible to obtain Mareva relief in the county court if the claimant's claim fell within the county court limits.[84] By s.3 of the Courts and Legal Services Act 1990 a new section 38 was inserted into the County Courts Act 1984. Under this the jurisdiction of the county courts to grant injunctions no longer depends upon the existence of a money claim which falls within the county court limits,[85] and a jurisdiction corresponding to the jurisdiction of the High Court was conferred on the county courts. Under s.38(3)(b) of the 1984 Act the county court does not have the power to make orders prescribed by regulations made by the Lord Chancellor. The relevant regulations are the County Court Remedies Regulations 1991.[86] Under these regulations, "prescribed relief is defined in terms which cover both Anton Piller relief under reg.2(a) and Mareva relief under reg.2(b).

Under reg.3(2)(b) a patents county court is able to grant Mareva and Anton Piller relief when it is acting within its "special jurisdiction" conferred on it pursuant to s.287 of the Copyright, Designs and Patents Act 1988.[87] A county court is also able to grant such relief when the judge sitting is a High Court judge or a judge of the Court of Appeal.

Mareva relief may be granted by a nominated[88] judge in proceedings in the Central London County Court Mercantile List,[89] which is the list established at the Central London County Court under CPR Pt 59.[90]

---

[80] See Chapter 6, para.6.079, below.
[81] See Chapter 6, paras 6.043–6.059.
[82] *Department of Social Security v Butler* [1995] 1 W.L.R. 1528.
[83] *Adler Coleman Clearing Corporation v Roddy DiPrima Ltd* (1996) 28 B.C.L.R. 181 applying *BMWE v Canadian Pacific Ltd* [1996] 2 S.C.R. 495.
[84] For examples, see *Naz v Kaleem* [1980] C.L.Y. 409 and *Vanse v Bray* [1987] C.L.Y. 2997.
[85] For the historical background, *see Joyce v Liverpool City Council* [1996] Q.B. 252 at 264–267, *per* Sir Thomas Bingham M.R.
[86] SI 1991/1222 as amended by SI 1995/206.
[87] *McDonald v Graham* [1994] R.F.C. 407 at 435.
[88] The nomination is made by the Senior Presiding Judge appointed under s.72 (2) of the Courts and Legal Services Act 1990.
[89] For the relevant practice, see Appendix 3 below.
[90] SI 1991/1222, reg.3(3)(d).

Proceedings under the Arbitration Act 1996, including those pursuant to s.44 of the 1996 Act, may be commenced in the Central London County Court Business List,[91] and in such proceedings the power of the county court is the same as it has in substantive proceedings before that court,[92] *i.e.* power to grant Mareva relief but not to grant Anton Piller relief.

A county court can still grant Mareva relief in aid of enforcement of a **3.022** county court judgment or order, when exercising jurisdiction under Pt V of the Matrimonial and Family Proceedings Act 1984, or for the purpose of making an order for the preservation, custody or detention of property which is or may form the subject-matter of the proceedings.[93] Thus a distinction is drawn between granting relief based on a proprietary claim before the court, which may be granted in the county court, and Mareva relief, which the county court cannot grant.

Particular care must be exercised in considering whether to seek Mareva relief where the claim is relatively small. Thus in *Sions v Ruscoe-Price*,[94] the judge had refused Mareva relief on the ground (among others) that the sum involved was only £2,000. The Court of Appeal upheld the decision of the judge, Woolf L.J. observing that in general it was inappropriate for Mareva relief to be granted in respect of a relatively small sum, particularly in view of the costs which might be involved. Staughton L.J. emphasised that Mareva relief should not be granted as a matter of routine in every case of an unpaid debt; the risk of removal or dissipation of assets must be viewed in the context of the importance of the case and the sum involved. Accordingly, Mareva relief should not be granted in relation to a relatively small claim unless the court is satisfied that in all the circumstances the possible adverse consequences of the relief sought are in proportion to the objective sought to be achieved.[95]

(5) Mareva injunctions are available before and after judgment

The nature of Mareva relief is such that the majority of applications are **3.023** made at a very early stage, usually before the claim form has been issued. However, if it emerges during the course of a case that the defendant may be about to remove his English assets from the jurisdiction, the claimant can make an application for Mareva relief at that time. Furthermore, the court has jurisdiction to extend a Mareva injunction which has been granted initially "to judgment or further order", to cover the period

---

[91] Arbitration Act 1996, s.105; High Court and County Courts (Allocation of Arbitration Proceedings) Order 1996 (SI 1996/3215), reg.5(1).

[92] See s.44(1).

[93] SI 1992/1222, reg.3(3)(a), (b) and (c).

[94] Court of Appeal (Civ Div) Transcript No.1027 of 1988 (November 30, 1988) followed in *American Express Bank Ltd v Cheung Kam Fung Betty*, Hong Kong Court of Appeal No.101 of 2000 (March 28, 2000).

[95] See also *First Farm Inc. v Bob's Backhoe Services Inc.* (1993) 108 D.L.R (4th) 551.

between judgment and satisfaction of the judgment. A Mareva injunction may be granted to a judgment creditor in aid of execution of his judgment even if he did not apply for or obtain a Mareva injunction originally.[96] The injunction is granted in the action in which the claimant has obtained judgment.[97] Assets acquired by the defendant after judgment and before satisfaction will fall within the scope of any Mareva injunction extended or granted in aid of execution.[98] This is because a Mareva injunction which refers to unspecified assets has "an ambulatory effect so as to apply to all assets of the defendant which at any time while the injunction remains on foot may be within the ambit of the assets covered by the injunction".[99]

If a claimant has become a judgment creditor, this is important to the exercise of discretion by the court on an application by the defendant to have the injunction varied to enable assets to be dealt with or disposed of for a particular purpose. Thus, before judgment a claimant who appears to have a clear right to be paid by the defendant still cannot insist on his claim being paid or secured either in priority to or pro rata with other claims made against the defendant. In *K/S A/S Admiral Shipping v Portlink Ferries Ltd*,[1] the plaintiffs had a good arguable claim against the defendants; it appeared that the business of the defendants had been sold to a third party and that the assets of the defendants would probably only suffice to pay ordinary trade creditors, leaving the plaintiffs, if and when they established their claim, with nothing. The plaintiffs could not apply to wind up the defendants because the claim was a disputed one for unliquidated damages, and the statutory provisions in relation to setting aside preferences were unlikely to be applicable in due course, in particular because of the statutory time limit of six months.[2] The plaintiffs sought an order which would permit the defendants to pay their trade creditors, but require sums to be set aside which would be available to be paid towards discharging the plaintiffs' claim, if and when this was established. The Court of Appeal held that the injunction should be varied to enable trade creditors to be paid, without any provision to establish a fund to meet the plaintiffs' claim.

---

[96] *Stewart Chartering v C. & O. Managements SA (The Venus Destiny)* [1980] 1 W.L.R 460; *Hill Samuel & Co. Ltd v Littaur* (1985) 135 N.L.J. 57; *Orwell Steel (Erection and Fabrication) Ltd v Asphalt and Tarmac (UK) Ltd* [1984] 1 W.L.R .1097; *Deutsche Schachtbau-und Tiefbohrgesellschaft MBH v Shell International Petroleum Co. Ltd* [1990] 1 A.C. 295 at 317; *Jet West Ltd v Haddican* [1992] 1 W.L.R 487 at 490E.

[97] An application may be made before or after the trial: *Smith v Cowell* (1880) 6 Q.B.D. 75. In *Zeeland Navigation Co. Ltd v Banque Worms*, Comm Ct, unreported, December 13, 1995, Waller J., it was held that the court had *jurisdiction* post-judgment to grant an injunction restraining a party to the action from raising matters in a foreign action between the parties when those matters were *res judicata* or the subject of an issue estoppel by reason of the English judgment. For the position at the trial, see Chapter 8, para. 8.002 below.

[98] See *TDK Tape Distributor (UK) Ltd v Videochoice Ltd* [1986] 1 W.L.R. 141.

[99] *Cretanor Maritime v Irish Marine Management Ltd* [1978] 1 W.L.R 966 at 973, *per* Buckley L.J..

[1] [1984] 2 Lloyd's Rep. 166.

[2] The provisions now applicable are to be found in ss.239, 240 and 241 of the Insolvency Act 1986.

It would be wrong for the Mareva jurisdiction to be used to produce a "quasi-winding-up" of the defendants in advance of judgment being obtained.[3]

However, once the claimant has obtained judgment the position is different.[4] He may then be able to make an individual defendant bankrupt or have a corporate defendant wound up. Furthermore, he will be in a position to enforce the judgment by executing it on assets of the defendant. In these circumstances the injunction is granted or continued in aid of execution or, as may be the case, bankruptcy or winding-up proceedings. It will not be a good answer to execution for a defendant to say that he wishes to use the asset in question to pay another creditor. Nor in principle should it be a good reason for a judgment debtor to seek a variation to a Mareva injunction which has been granted in aid of execution. Thus, in *Deutsche Schachtbau-und Tiefbohrgesellschaft GmbH v R'as Al-Khaimah National Oil Company (No.1)*,[5] the Court of Appeal upheld Mareva relief granted in aid of enforcement of an arbitration award against a foreign company. Judgment had been obtained but was not yet enforceable under the rules of court, and it was contemplated that garnishee proceedings would be taken in relation to the relevant asset, which was a debt due or accruing due from a third party. Sir John Donaldson M.R., with whom the other members of the court agreed, observed that the injunction was not, strictly speaking, an injunction which fell into the Mareva category, but was an injunction granted as protection for a judgment creditor, under a jurisdiction recognised[6] before the emergence of the Mareva jurisdiction. "The purpose of the injunction was . . . to maintain the status quo during the period covered by the stay of execution and not to preserve assets against the probability that DST might at some later date be able to establish its claim—the ordinary Mareva situation." In the House of Lords the appeal against the injunction was dealt with at the same time as the appeal against the garnishee order, which was set aside on the grounds that if upheld it would place the garnishee at risk of having to pay the same debt twice, and thus would be inequitable. In those circumstances the injunction had to be set aside on precisely the same ground, namely that it would be inequitable to the third party debtor.

The purpose for which the injunction has been granted or is being maintained is an essential consideration in the exercise of a discretion as to whether that injunction should be varied or discharged so as to release assets to be dealt with by the enjoined party.

3.024

---

[3] Applying *Iraqi Ministry of Defence v Arcepey Shipping (The Angel Bell)* [1981] Q.B. 65. See also *Investors and Pensions Advisory Service Ltd v Gray* (1989) 139 N.L.J. 1415 at 1415–1416.

[4] *Soinco SACI v Novokuznetsk Aluminium Plant* [1998] Q.B. 406.

[5] [1990] 1 A.C. 295.

[6] For example, in *Bullus v Bullus* (1910) 102 L.T. 399. See also, *Mercantile Group (Europe AG) v Aiyela* [1994] Q.B. 366 at 376. *per* Hoffmann L.J., and *Goldtron Ltd v Most Investment Ltd* [2002] J.L.R. 424 at [25–30] (injunction sought in aid of contemplated enforcement of an arbitration award).

3.025   Pre-judgment, the claimant, who seeks a money judgment, has no legal interest in the assets of the defendant. The defendant is not entitled to dispose of assets in fraud of his creditors.[7] But leaving this aside, the defendant can spend his money as he pleases, unless the court intervenes by granting Mareva relief, which it does in order to preserve assets for enforcement of an eventual judgment. In that situation the function of the injunction is to prevent inappropriate dissipation of assets.[8] The defendant is allowed to use his money for meeting living expenses, carrying on his business and paying his debts because there is nothing inappropriate in his doing so.

Post-judgment, the claimant still has no legal interest in the assets of the defendant.[9] However, unless the court grants a stay of execution pending appeal, he can take steps to enforce his judgment against those assets.

Accordingly post-judgment, it is relevant to consider the position as to whether there is to be a stay of execution and whether, even if there were not a stay, enforcement of the judgment can be had against the assets in question. In *Lloyds Bank plc v Croad*.[10] Evans L.J. pointed out that "there is in practice a considerable overlap between the circumstances in which a stay may be ordered and what I might call the general Mareva jurisdiction of the court [which] may be exercised to safeguard a creditor, including a judgment creditor. . .". Whether a stay will be granted pending appeal involves the exercise of a discretion which, on the one hand, recognises that the claimant has a judgment which prima facie he should be able to enforce[11] and, on the other hand, seeks to avoid a position in which a defendant succeeds on appeal, but in the meantime has been irretrievably prejudiced, *e.g.* if he has been ruined by being made bankrupt.[12] An appeal in itself does not operate as a stay on any order of the court of first instance and a stay must be sought either from that court or the Court of Appeal.[13] The general principle is that solid grounds must be shown if a stay is to be granted and the normal rule is that a stay is not granted.[14] In *One Life Ltd v Roy*,[15] the judge at first instance (Carnwath J.) gave judgment in favour of the plaintiff on tracing claims[16] and declared that the

---

[7] See s.423 of the Insolvency Act 1986 and paras 12.017 and 13.018–29, below.
[8] See further paras 12.037–8, below.
[9] *Mercedes Benz AG v Leiduck* [1996] A.C. 284 at 306C–E, *per* Lord Nicholls.
[10] Court of Appeal (Civ Div) Transcript No.1661 of 1996 (November 28, 1996); *Combi (Singapore) Pte Ltd v Sriram and Sun Ltd*, Court of Appeal Transcript No.1414 of 1997 (July 23, 1997). *Goldtron Ltd v Most Investment Ltd* [2002] J.L.R. 424 at [25–30] (which treats an injunction granted in aid of possible enforcement of an arbitration award as involving similar considerations as apply to an application for an injunction in aid of a judgment, which is itself subject to appeal).
[11] See also *Soinco SACI v Novokuznetsk Aluminium Plant* [1998] Q.B. 406 at p.421E–F
[12] *Linotype-Hell Finance Ltd v Baker* [1992] 4 All E.R. 887; *Winchester Cigarette Machinery Ltd v Payne (No.2)*, The Times, December 15, 1993; *Combi (Singapore) Pte Ltd v Sriram and Sun Ltd*, Court of Appeal Transcript No.1414 of 1997 (July 23, 1997).
[13] CPR 52.7.
[14] *Leicester Circuits Limited v Coates Brothers plc* [2002] EWCA Civ 474 at para.13.
[15] Court of Appeal (Civ Div) Transcript No.128 of 1997 (January 30, 1997). See also para.20.068 below.
[16] [1996] 2 B.C.L.C. 608.

assets belonged to the plaintiff. The judge deleted a provision from the injunction allowing for the defendant to be able to use the money for living expenses, and this was upheld by the Court of Appeal. This was because on the facts there was no good reason for the defendant to be allowed to go on using as living expenses what had been decided to be the plaintiffs money.

If there is no stay pending appeal, the purpose of the injunction is as an aid to enforcement of the judgment, by preventing dissipation of assets available for execution or which can be taken to satisfy the judgment[17] (*e.g.* through the appointment of a receiver). **3.026**

Whether an injunction is granted after judgment to aid execution or to assist the judgment creditor to be paid his judgment debt is discretionary. The court will not grant such relief because it may be helpful to the judgment creditor regardless of the other consequences for the debtor and third parties of granting the relief. Whilst there is a public interest in debtors paying their creditors, it does not follow that the court will grant an injunction to secure this end when it would be liable to have other consequences which would be undesirable.

In *Camdex International Ltd v Bank of Zambia (No.2)*,[18] the defendant judgment debtor was the Central Bank of Zambia.[19] It had arranged to have high denomination bank notes printed in England, which it planned to have issued in Zambia. The Central Bank had debts which were far in excess of its assets and the unissued bank notes had no value as such. As Phillips L.J. said: "The reality is that these bank notes have no value whatsoever. They are a worthless and potentially embarrassing quantity of scrap paper . . .".[20] But if the Central Bank was prevented by the post-judgment injunction from taking the unissued bank notes to Zambia, this would have caused very considerable hardship in Zambia. The Court of Appeal held that the injunction should be varied so as to enable the bank notes to be dealt with by the bank. The injunction would otherwise operate not to facilitate execution but in order to put pressure on the Central Bank to pay the plaintiff in priority to other creditors.[21]

---

[17] If the asset cannot be taken in execution of the judgment, then an injunction over that asset cannot be justified on this basis: *Hitachi Leasing (Singapore) Pty v Vincent Ambrose* [2001] 2 S.L.R. 525 (where the defendant's flat could not be made subject to execution, and in the absence of any evidence of an intended disposal the court declined to grant an injunction in respect of proceeds of sale of the flat); *National Australia Bank Limited v Blacker* (2001) 179 A.L.R. 97 at paras 40–41 (citing the text, and granting a post judgment injunction in aid of execution of a judgment which had not been stayed pending appeal. over particular sums to be received by the defendants, but the injunction was qualified so as to allow living expenses and legal costs at first instance and costs on appeal. The defendants had not undertaken not to oppose recovery procedures in respect of the judgment.)

[18] [1997] 1 W.L.R. 632.

[19] Sovereign immunity had been waived.

[20] [1997] 1 W.L.R 632 at 639.

[21] The Court of Appeal indicated that there might be an application for a stay of execution granted in respect of the judgment so as to prevent there being execution on the unissued bank notes: [1997] 1 W.L.R. 632 at 637B.

3.027   In *Kensington International Ltd v Republic of Congo*[22] the claimant was an assignee which had obtained summary judgment against the Republic. It sought an injunction to enforce a negative pledge agreement, and an undertaking to pay creditors *pari passu*. The court declined to grant this relief holding that the claimant should be left to its ordinary remedies as a judgment creditor. The relief, if granted, would be liable to disrupt arrangements which the Republic was making to pay creditors and would potentially interfere with commercial arrangements entered into by third parties including transactions which had no connection with England.

In *Deutsche Schachtbau-und Tiefbohrgesellschaft Gmbh v R'as Al-Kaimah National Oil Co*,[23] there was a risk that if the garnishee order was made absolute, Shell International (the garnishee) would be forced to pay its debt twice. This made it inequitable to grant a garnishee order. It also made it inequitable for the debt to be affected by Mareva relief post-judgment in aid of execution.

If an injunction is granted in contemplation of the presentation of a winding-up petition, it will be appropriate only to permit those dispositions of the assets of the company which are validated by the court under s.127 of the Insolvency Act 1986.[24] If, however, the judgment creditor has deliberately refrained from petitioning for the winding up of a company which is continuing to trade, then it may be inequitable for the court not to permit the judgment debtor to continue its business and pay its trade creditors notwithstanding the existence of the judgment.

(6) Mareva injunction in respect of land

3.028   If Mareva relief has been granted in an action pre-judgment, the order is not one made "for the purpose of enforcing a judgment" within the meaning of s 6(1) of the Land Charges Act 1972. The claimant may not obtain a final judgment to enforce.[25] Accordingly, the claimant is not entitled to register a land charge, or, in the case of registered land, a caution.[26] Once the claimant obtains and seeks to enforce a judgment the position is different.[27]

The position in relation to Mareva relief is to be contrasted with the position when a receiver is appointed over land. In those circumstances a land charge or a caution may be registered.[28]

---

[22] [2003] EWCA Civ 709 at para [7], referring to the first instance proceedings.
[23] [1990] A.C. 295, applied in *Soinco SACI v Novokuznetsk Aluminium Plant (No.2)* [1998] 2 Lloyd's Rep. 346.
[24] This course was adopted by the Court of Appeal in *United Bank Ltd v Claybridge SA* (1980) 14 *Lloyd's Maritime Law Newsletter* (May 15, 1980); 16 *Lloyd's Maritime Law Newsletter* (June 12, 1980); [1997] 1 B.C.L.C. 813; the relevant statutory provision in force when the case was decided on March 9, 1981, was s.227 of the Companies Act 1948.
[25] *Stockler v Fourways Estates Ltd* [1984] 1 W.L.R. 25.
[26] *Kastner v Jason* [2004] EWHC 592 (Ch) at para.34 referring to *Elias v Mitchell* [1972] Ch. 652 at p.659.
[27] *Re Overseas Aviation Engineering GB Ltd* [1963] Ch. 24.
[28] *Clayhope Properties v Evans* [1986] 1 W.L.R. 1223.

(7) Types of claim for which Mareva relief is available

A Mareva injunction is designed to protect the claimant against the 3.029
dissipation of assets against which he might otherwise execute judgment
whether immediately or in the future. It follows that Mareva relief is
suitable only when the claimant's claim is one which would result in his
being able to enforce judgment against the defendant's assets. If there is a
claim to the assets themselves, the jurisdiction is not "Mareva" jurisdiction
but an injunction granted in support of a proprietary interest and the court
is more ready to make orders requiring the defendant to state where the
assets are located and preserving those assets.[29] The purpose of the
injunction based on a proprietary claim is to preserve those assets so that
they can be made over to the claimant as his property if this is the case.
This is different from the Mareva jurisdiction where the purpose is to
prevent unjustifiable disposals of the defendant's assets. When there is a
proprietary claim the court may order a fund to be set aside by the
defendant which is not subject to the usual liberties inserted into Mareva
relief and which will await determination of the claim;[30] such an order
does not create any security over the fund created in favour of the
claimant.[31]

A claimant who seeks purely declaratory relief may not have an existing
cause of action and so be unable to invoke the court's jurisdiction to grant
him Mareva relief.[32]

However, there are no constraints on the nature of the claimant's cause
of action or on the types of monetary relief which he may seek: his claim
may be for payment of a debt, or damages, or an account, or even for
statutory compensation. Mareva injunctions have been granted in actions
for damages for nuisance, actions brought by husbands or wives for
maintenance, and in actions for damages for personal injuries: *Allen v
Jambo Holdings*.[33] A Mareva injunction has been granted in an action by a
former employee for damages for wrongful dismissal: see *Quinn v Marsta
Cession Services Ltd*.[34]

---

[29] *Bankers Trust Co. v Shapira* [1980] 1 W.L.R. 1274; *A v C (No.1)* [1981] Q.B. 956;
Mediterranea Raffineria Siciliana Petroli SpA v Mabanaft GmbH Court of Appeal (Civ Div)
Transcript No.816 of 1978 (December 1, 1978); *London and County Securities Ltd v
Caplan*, unreported (May 26, 1978), Templeman J. referred to in *Bankers Trust & Co. v
Shapira* (above); *A v C (No.1)*, above; *Polly Peck International plc v Nadir (No.2)* [1992] 4
All E.R. 769 at 784; *Purple Star Shipping Ltd v Fortune Shipping Ltd*, Comm Ct,
unreported, December 13, 2001 (Moore-Bick J.)—injunction granted in aid of proprietary
claim when inadequate evidence to show cogent case of likelihood of dissipation of assets
Hampshire Cosmetic Laboratories Ltd v Mutschmann. [1999] C.I.L.R. 21 at 34 (worldwide
relief more readily granted in support of a proprietary claim than in support of a claim to a
money judgment).

[30] *Polly Peck International plc v Nadir (No.2)* [1992] 4 All E.R. 769 at 784

[31] *Millenium Federation Pty Ltd v Bigjig Pty* [2000] 1 Qd Rep. 275; see Chapter 23,
para.23.009.

[32] See *The Steamship Mutual Underwriting Association (Bermuda) Ltd v Thakur Shipping Co.
Ltd* [1986] 2 Lloyd's Rep. 439 and paras 12.001–4 and 12.007–8 below.

[33] [1980] 1 W.L.R. 1252.

[34] (1981) 133 D.L.R. (3d) 109, High Court of Ontario.

3.030   The Financial Services Act 1986 provided for the bringing of proceedings for the benefit of persons who have suffered loss as a result of infringements of the Act. In proceedings brought by the Securities and Investment Board acting in pursuance of powers delegated to it by the Secretary of State for the benefit of such persons, Mareva relief has been granted to the Board in respect of the total losses suffered by those affected.[35] Thus, in principle, Mareva relief can be obtained in respect of a statutory cause of action put forward by the claimant for the benefit of others, and the injunction will be granted by reference to final relief which the claimant claims in the action, *e.g* a claim for a restitution order under s.382 of the Financial Services and Markets Act 2000. A claimant who puts forward a claim based on ss.423, 424 and 425 of the Insolvency Act 1986 for the benefit[36] of the "victims" of a transaction defrauding creditors will obtain Mareva relief which is not confined to such losses as he personally may have suffered by reason of the transaction sought to be impugned. The Mareva relief to be granted will be related to the nature of the final relief likely to be obtained by way of an order made under s.423 of the 1986 Act.

In *Department of Social Security v Butler*,[37] the Child Support Agency had made a maintenance assessment against the defendant for the support of his child. He was in arrears. The statutory regime under the statute set out detailed provisions for the collection of maintenance and the enforcement of liability orders. However, there was no provision for the enforcement of a maintenance assessment through the High Court and the Court of Appeal held that by implication any jurisdiction of the High Court that there might otherwise be was therefore excluded by the Act. Accordingly, no Mareva relief could be granted under s.37 of the Supreme Court Act 1981, because the High Court had no jurisdiction to enforce the maintenance assessment—there was no cause of action capable of enforcement in the High Court.

Mareva relief is available in respect of an order for costs to be taxed even though the costs have not yet been taxed,[38] and in respect of damages or other sums which are liable to be the subject-matter of an order to pay based on an undertaking which has been given to the court.[39]

---

[35] *Re DPR Futures Ltd* [1989] 1 W.L.R. 778 at 782; *Securities and Investment Board v Pantell SA* [1990] Ch. 426.

[36] Every application for an order under s.423 is required by s.424(2) to be treated as made "on behalf of every victim of the transaction." Accordingly, the order to be made under s.423 will take into account the interests of all the "victims" and not merely the limited personal interest of an applicant who is a "victim."

[37] [1995] 1 W.L.R. 1528.

[38] *Jet West Ltd v Haddican* [1992] 1 W.L.R. 487; *Faith Panton Property Plan Ltd v Hodgetts* [1981] 1 W.L.R. 927.

[39] *Commodity Ocean Transport Corpn v Basford Unicorn* [1987] 2 Lloyd's Rep. 197 at 200. (See also *Yandil Holdings Pty Ltd v Insurance Company of North America* (1986) 7 N.S.W.L.R. 571, Supreme Court of New South Wales, in relation to a personal undertaking given by an individual in respect of costs which had resulted in an order for costs being made against that person.)

There is jurisdiction for the court to freeze assets of an insurance **3.031** company on an application made by the Secretary of State under the Insurance Companies Act 1982. This jurisdiction includes freezing the assets of an insurer with its head office in another state, on an application made by the Secretary of State after receipt of a duly formulated request by the supervisory authority in the company's home state.[40]

(8) Claims against the Crown

In proceedings against the Crown, the court cannot issue an injunction of **3.032** any description by reason of the Crown Proceedings Act 1947, s.21(1), proviso (a). The court cannot grant an injunction against an officer of the Crown if the effect would be to give relief against the Crown which could not have been obtained against the Crown directly: Crown Proceedings Act 1947, s.21(2).[41] An injunction cannot be granted against the Crown, or its ministers in their official capacity, except to enforce European Community legislation and in judicial review proceedings.[42] Under CPR 25.1 (1)(b) the court now has a new jurisdiction to grant an interim declaration. This is a declaration which is to regulate the position until the merits are decided at the trial. This power may be useful in proceedings against the Crown to set out what the court would have ordered by way of interlocutory injunction, or by way of advisory jurisdiction,[43] setting out the opinion of the court about what ought to happen pending determination of a case.[44]

If a defendant subject to Mareva relief is entitled to receive money from the Crown, then in principle the Crown could intervene in the proceedings in appropriate circumstances to seek directions, and the court would have jurisdiction to give directions concerning payment of the money by the Crown.[45] An order made in such circumstances directing the Crown to pay the money into a designated bank account or into court is not "execution or attachment or process in the nature thereof . . . for enforcing payment by the Crown of . . . money"[46] because the Crown is ready, willing and

---

[40] *Re the Secretary of State for Trade and Industry and Prevision Sanitaria National, PSN Mutua De Seguros Y Reaseguros A Prima Fija*, August 27, 1997, Neuberger J.

[41] *M v Home Office* [1994] 1 A.C. 377.

[42] *M v Home Office* [1994] 1 A.C. 377; *R. v Secretary of State for Transport Ex p. Factortame* [1990] 2 A.C. 85; *R. v Secretary of State for Transport Ex p. Factortame (No.2)* [1991] 2 A.C. 603; s.21 Crown Proceedings Act 1947.

[43] *Re S (Hospital Patient: Court's Jurisdiction)* [1996] Fam. 1 affirming [1995] Fam. 26 (Hale J).

[44] *Governor and Company of the Bank of Scotland v A Ltd* [2001] 1 W.L.R. 751 at paras 45–47 (where the bank has obtained an injunction against itself from making payment at first instance, a procedure which is unknown to the law). An interim declaration would have set out the court's guidance as to what should happen pending decision of the parties' substantive rights. The jurisdiction is discussed in The Declaratory Judgment by Lord Woolf and J.Woolf (3rd ed. 2002) paras 3.094–3.099.

[45] *Bank Mellat v Kazmi* [1989] Q.B. 541.

[46] Crown Proceedings Act 1947, s.25(4).

able to pay the money, and is simply seeking a direction as to how the money is to be paid.[47] Accordingly, such a direction is not precluded by s.25(4) of the Crown Proceedings Act 1947.

(9) Claims against foreign states: State Immunity Act 1978

3.033   Section 13(2) of the State Immunity Act 1978 provides as follows:

> "Subject to subsections (3) and (4) below:
>
> (a) relief shall not be given against a state by way of injunction or order for specific performance for the recovery of land or other property; and
>
> (b) the property of a state shall not be subject to any process for the enforcement of a judgment or arbitration award or as an action *in rem* for its arrest, detention or sale."

Under the State Immunity Act 1978 there are a number of different types of proceedings to which states are not immune from suit. This is because states enjoy only restrictive immunity. Nevertheless, s.13(2)(a) contains a bar against the granting of an injunction against a state except where the state concerned has given written consent. Under s.14(1) and (4) of the 1978 Act a state includes the sovereign or other head of state in his or her public capacity, the government of the state, any department of the government, and the state's central bank (reversing the effect of the decisions in *Trendtex v Central Bank of Nigeria*[48] and *Hispano Americana Mercantile SA v Central Bank of Nigeria*[49]) or monetary authority. However, other state-owned or controlled entities are not immune from the granting of Mareva relief and whether an injunction is to be granted is a matter of discretion; see *Et Esefka International v Central Bank of Nigeria*,[50] the 1978 Act did not apply in that case and the court refused to grant an injunction as a matter of discretion. These entities may have immunity from suit in relation to proceedings relating to acts done by them "in the exercise of sovereign authority": s.14(2). In view of the wording of s.13(2)(a) the courts may not grant a Mareva injunction even against assets of a state which are in use or intended for use for "commercial purposes" and even after a judgment has been given against the state; unless the state has given written consent within s.13(3). For this purpose "a provision merely submitting to the jurisdiction" of the court is not sufficient: s.13(3) (see also on the need for the written consent to be clear on its face: *Arab Bank v International Tin Council*).[51]

---

[47] *Bank Mellat v Kazmi* [1989] Q.B. 541.
[48] [1977] Q.B. 529.
[49] [1979] 2 Lloyd's Rep. 277.
[50] [1979] 1 Lloyd's Rep. 445.
[51] (1986) 77 Int.L.R. 1.

In *A Company Ltd v Republic of X*,[52] a claim was brought on an ordinary **3.034** commercial transaction entered into by a state which included a provision that:

"SOVEREIGN IMMUNITY

> The Ministry of Finance hereby waives whatever defence it may have of sovereign immunity for itself or its property (present or subsequently acquired)."

Saville J. held that this clause enabled Mareva relief to be granted,[53] but that the injunction should exclude from its ambit property covered by the Diplomatic Privileges Act 1964, because a mere contract could not bind a state in respect of such property.[54] If a question of the immunity of a state from the court's power to grant injunctions is raised, such a question goes to the jurisdiction of the court and must be resolved as quickly as possible.[55]

If a state intervenes in an action to seek a variation of a Mareva **3.035** injunction so as to take outside its ambit any property which is asserted to belong to the state, then the mandatory terms of s.13(2)(a) which go to the jurisdiction of the court make it inappropriate for the court to postpone determination of any issue as to whether the assets are the property of the state: *A Company Ltd v Republic of X*.[56] Such a delay might otherwise have been appropriate: *SCF Finance v* Masri.[57] In view of the terms of the section the court should not be willing to risk interfering with the state's enjoyment of its property simply by continuing an injunction granted against a third party.

If the property is immune from execution by virtue of state immunity, it is pointless to grant Mareva relief in respect of that property, even if the state concerned has given a written consent which would remove the bar to injunctive relief in s.13(2)(a) of the Act. Mareva relief should be limited to property which in due course the plaintiff can require by one means or another to have applied so as to satisfy a judgment against the state.

---

[52] [1990] 2 Lloyd's Rep. 520.
[53] The approach of Saville J. on interpretation giving the words an unrestricted interpretation was followed on a different clause in *Sabah Shipyard (Pakistan) Ltd v Islamic Republic of Pakistan* [2003] 2 Lloyd's Rep. 571.
[54] Criticised by Dr F.A. Mann in (1991) 107 L.Q.R. 362.
[55] *A Company Ltd v Republic of X* [1990] 2 Lloyd's Rep. 520 at 524–535, referring to *J.H. Rayner (Mincing Lane) Ltd v Department of Trade and Industry* [1989] Ch. 72 at 194–195, 252, affirmed [1990] 2 A.C. 418.
[56] [1990] 2 Lloyd's Rep. 520 at 524–525.
[57] [1985] 1 W.L.R. 876.

(10) Types of asset which can be subject to a Mareva injunction

3.036   It appears clear that Mareva injunctions are available to prevent the disposal or removal from the jurisdiction of any type of asset, ranging from cash, goods, ships and aircraft to industrial machinery: *Rasu Maritima v Perusahaan Pertambangan*,[58] the goodwill of a company: *Darashah v UFAC (UK) Ltd*,[59] choses in action such as insurance policies: *TDK Tape Distributor (UK) Ltd v Videochoice Ltd*,[60] and the proceeds of sale of a flat: *Barclay-Johnson v Yuill*,[61] or other interests and estates in land.

(i) Mareva injunctions over ships and aircraft

3.037   The circumstances in which an action *in rem* can be brought against an aircraft are narrowly circumscribed: Supreme Court Act 1981, ss.20(2) and 21. A claimant may obtain a Mareva injunction in respect of a ship even in circumstances in which he could not arrest it: *The Rena K*.[62] The courts have been willing to grant Mareva relief in respect of aircraft: see, *e.g. Allen v Jambo Holdings*.[63] Section 89 of the Civil Aviation Act 1982 excludes the availability of Mareva relief (or any relief involving seizure) in connection with certain patent claims in respect of aircraft and spare parts. This gives effect to Art.27 of the Chicago Convention 1944.

There is also jurisdiction under s.16 of the Merchant Shipping Act 1995 (Sch.1, para.6) to prohibit any dealing with a British ship or in any share in the ship on the application of any interested person. But a mere creditor is not an "interested person" within the section. The applicant must have a substantive claim to an interest in the ship or the shares in the ship: *NCNB Texas National Bank v Evensong Co. Ltd (The Mikado)*.[64]

(ii) Bills of exchange

3.038   A bill of exchange can be the subject of a Mareva injunction restraining a party from dealing with the bill. The court will usually grant a claimant summary judgment on a bill of exchange. Furthermore, the court will refuse a counterclaiming defendant a stay of execution, save in exceptional circumstances: *Nova (Jersey) Knit Ltd v Kammgarn Spinneret GmbH*.[65] The

---

[58] [1978] Q.B. 644.
[59] *The Times*, March 30, 1982.
[60] [1986] 1 W.L.R. 141.
[61] [1980] 1 W.L.R. 1259.
[62] [1979] 1 Q.B. 377, esp. at 409.
[63] [1980] 1 W.L.R. 1252.
[64] [1992] 1 Lloyd's Rep. 163. See also *Hughes v Clewley* [1994] J.L.R. 227 (interested person included plaintiff vendor who had claimed to avoid contract of sale for misrepresentation).
[65] [1977] 1 W.L.R. 713.

reason is that the bill is to be treated as the equivalent of cash. Nevertheless, the court may grant an injunction restraining dealings with the proceeds of a bill of exchange or a judgment founded on a bill of exchange even at the suit of the party liable on the bill: *Montecchi v Shimco (UK) Ltd*.[66] Similarly, if there is an agreement that payment will be made by direct debit, this is equivalent to an undertaking to pay cash without set-off, but the court may grant Mareva relief over the proceeds in respect of a counterclaim.[67]

(iii) Judgment debts

A Mareva injunction is capable of applying to a judgment debt owed by a third party to the defendant. However, if the injunction is to be limited to assets within the jurisdiction, it is undesirable that the wording of the order should leave it to the defendant to decide for himself whether the relevant judgment debt is properly to be regarded, for the purposes of the injunction, as located within the jurisdiction. The defendant should know precisely what he is prohibited from doing from the face of the order. It is considered that an English judgment debt is to be regarded as located within the jurisdiction for the purposes of a Mareva injunction (see *Attorney-General v Bouwens*),[68] and that an injunction limited to assets within the jurisdiction should be formulated so as to include expressly within its ambit any relevant English judgment debt. If a judgment debt is made subject to Mareva relief, it does not preclude enforcement of the judgment, provided that the result of enforcement will be simply to provide proceeds which are also subject to the injunction. Although the effect of successful enforcement would be to discharge the judgment debt, overall the value of the defendant's assets held subject to the injunction is unaffected.[69]

3.039

(iv) Claims under letters of credit, performance bonds and bank guarantees payable on demand

There are particular problems concerning injunctions which affect letters of credit and other banking instruments which are considered in Chapter 15.

3.040

(v) Documentary collections

In *Lewis & Peat (Produce) Ltd v Almatu Properties*,[70] a bank was making a collection against shipping documents on instructions from a foreign bank, which in turn had received the documents from its customer. The claimant

3.041

---

[66] [1979] 1 W.L.R. 1180.
[67] *Esso Petroleum v Milton* [1997] 1 W.L.R. 938.
[68] (1838) 4 M.&N. 171 at 191.
[69] See paras 3.012–14 above.
[70] [1993] 2 Bank L.R. 45; *The Times*, May 14, 1992; see further N. Thodos, "Mareva Injunctions, Attachment and the Independence Principle: Balancing the Interests" (1995) 6 J.B.F.L.P. 101.

had a judgment against the customer and wished to obtain Mareva relief in respect of the proceeds of the collection. Since the proceeds of collection were simply a debt owed by the collecting bank to the foreign bank, the judgment debtor did not have any right as against the collecting bank. No Mareva relief could be granted against the collecting bank in aid of enforcement of the judgment against the foreign bank's customer. The Court of Appeal also held that it was wrong in principle to interfere, by Mareva relief, with the documentary collections being carried out in the ordinary course of banking business. In principle this is because a documentary collection involves making credits and debits between the banks involved as principals, the instructing bank in turn having a debtor/creditor relationship with its customer. If Mareva relief is to be obtained, it should ordinarily be sought at the court for the place where the customer has his account, and the relief should be in respect of that account.

(11) Effect of statutes which preclude any assignment or charge on certain assets

3.042   There are statutory provisions which prevent certain assets being assigned or being made the subject of a charge. Mareva relief does not as such effect an assignment of or a charge on an asset covered by the scope of the injunction. Such statutory provisions can, though, be relevant to whether Mareva relief is to be granted because the purpose for which relief is sought must be considered. If the claimant would not be able to obtain execution on the relevant asset even if he obtains a judgment, then it would be wrong in principle to grant Mareva relief pre-judgment or post-judgment in relation to that asset for the purpose of safeguarding the asset in anticipation of possible execution proceedings.[71] Furthermore, even if it may eventually be possible to reach an asset by execution, or through bankruptcy or winding-up proceedings, there will still be the question whether it is just and equitable that the asset should be the subject of a restraint in the meantime.

(12) Joint ownership of assets

3.043   In *Z Ltd v A-Z and AA-LL*.[72] Kerr L.J. said that in cases in which a Mareva injunction is granted over a joint bank account, the order should include a specific reference to the account. However, the practice grew up of

---

[71] For example, see the position under s.203 of the Army Act 1955, and the decision in *Walker v Walker* [1983] Fam. 68 and *Bank Mellat v Kazmi* [1989] Q.B. 541.
[72] [1982] 1 Q.B. 558 at 591.

drafting Mareva injunctions in wide terms so as to cover "moneys held to the account of the defendant whether in his own name or jointly with some other party" and injunctions were commonly granted in this or in a similar form. This practice was adopted in the standard forms provided by the 1996 Practice Direction,[73] and is adopted in paragraph 5 of the example order for a freezing injunction. Otherwise a person could make himself Mareva-proof by putting his assets into the joint names of himself and his wife, or into a company controlled by him.

If the claimant has a proprietary claim to trace into the assets which are in joint names, no difficulty arises. That claim will be against both of the persons in whose names the assets are held.

But it may be that the claimant has no proprietary claim and seeks relief in anticipation of obtaining a money judgment, which he hopes to enforce against the jointly held assets. A situation often encountered in practice is a joint bank account held in the names of a husband and wife, or of a partnership. In such circumstances the claimant needs to show a real prospect that if he obtains judgment he will be able to enforce it against the joint bank account.

In the case of a joint bank account in the names of A and B where both are contracting parties with the bank and either of them can draw cheques on the account, either can demand payment by the bank from the account. However, even when a demand is made, the credit balance is due to A and B jointly and not one or other of them alone. Because of this it has been held that a garnishee order cannot be made over the account in order to enforce payment of a judgment debt owed by one of them.[74] **3.044**

There is no justification for taking one man's property to pay another's debt.[75] So in principle the Mareva injunction should only apply so as to preserve the rights of the defendant and not to diminish or take away the rights of the other co-owner. In principle a judgment creditor ought to be able to step into the shoes of a judgment debtor and use such rights as the judgment debtor has in respect of the jointly owned asset in order to pay the judgment debt.

If assets are held in the name of the judgment debtor and another who is merely a trustee or nominee for the judgment debtor, then the judgment debtor can force payment of his judgment out of those assets. It may well be that this could be achieved by means of the appointment of a receiver by way of equitable execution under s.37 of the Supreme Court Act 1981 who is authorised to get in the assets.[76] Similarly if, as between A and B, A had a beneficial entitlement to a particular part of or share in jointly held assets, it may be that a receiver could be appointed to realise that part or share.

---

[73] [1996] 1 W.L.R. 1552.
[74] *Hirschorn v Evans* [1938] 2 K.B. 801; *MacDonald v Tacquah Gold Mines Co* (1884) 13 Q.B.D. 535; *Beasley v Roney* [1891] 1 Q.B. 509 at 512. Criticism of the current state of the law is to be found in D. Capper, "Garnishee Orders: The Untouchability of Joint Accounts" (1997) 48 N.I.L.Q. 162.
[75] *Harrods Ltd v Tester* (1937) 157 L.T. 7.
[76] See further Chapter 16.

3.045   Also, if assets are held jointly by A and B, then if the judgment is against both of them one would expect there to be a mechanism for enforcing that judgment against the jointly owned assets. Thus it is to be expected that a judgment against a partnership for a debt would be enforceable against a partnership bank account. This might be achieved by appointing a receiver by way of equitable execution over the bank account.

If assets are owned beneficially jointly by a judgment debtor and another, then one would expect it to be possible for the judgment creditor to be able to require the judgment debtor to sever his joint ownership[77] and become the absolute owner of a half share in the assets, which would then be available to meet the judgment. Again, this might be achievable through the appointment of a receiver.

It is also possible to envisage circumstances in which an account is jointly owned by a husband and wife and the arrangement is that either can have recourse to an account for family expenses. If there is a claim against the husband, provision ought to be made for the family to have living expenses and prima facie any injunction ought to allow the existing arrangement to continue, on the ground that drawings for family expenses pursuant to the arrangement would be pursuant to the arrangement between them and would not be an unjustified dissipation of assets. The effect of a freezing injunction on a joint account, and whether the wife can draw on the account, is discussed in Chapter 19, para.19.035.

3.046   In the case of joint interests in land, there is a trust for sale with each party having an interest in the proceeds of sale. Such an interest may be the subject of a Mareva injunction and, after judgment, the subject-matter of a charging order: *Harman v Glencross*.[78] Joint ownership of an asset is to be distinguished from the position where an asset is in joint names, but there is good reason for supposing that the asset is in fact owned beneficially by the defendant to the substantive claim. In these circumstances the court may grant Mareva relief against both parties in whose names the asset is held.[79] If the position is that the claimant is entitled to seek to set aside a transaction under which a third party acquired a joint interest in an asset together with the defendant (*e.g.* an interest acquired by a spouse), then again in principle the court may grant Mareva relief against both the defendant and the third party.

---

[77] Such a severance would put an end to any possibility of the other obtaining sole ownership of the whole by reason of survivorship—see further D. Capper, "Survivorship Rights in Joint Deposit Accounts" (1996) 47 N.I.L.Q. 281. If an account is in fact owned beneficially by one spouse who has put it into the joint names of himself and the other, then it may be, depending on the facts, that the other would take by way of survivorship if the beneficial owner had died: *Re Figgis* [1969] 1 Ch. 123. But this is irrelevant to the question whether a judgment creditor should be able to enforce a judgment against the account when the beneficial owner is still alive.

[78] [1986] Fam. 81.

[79] *SCF v Masri* [1985] 1 W.L.R. 876 and see paras 13.033–17 below.

Chapter 4

Forms of order

(1) The certainty principle

There is a general principle that an order must be expressed in unam- **4.001**
biguous language so that the defendant knows exactly what is forbidden or
required by the order.[1] Contempt proceedings will not succeed when the
order is unclear or ambiguous.[2]

The principle applies to all injunctions. This is a matter of fairness to the
person enjoined. It goes not only to the drafting of an injunction when in
principle the decision has been made to grant it, but also to the decision
itself on whether to grant an injunction or specific performance.[3] The
degree of certainty required should be considered with the possibility of
contempt proceedings in mind and whether the injunction would be
enforceable in such proceedings. An injunction should not be granted in
terms which leave it to be argued out in contempt proceedings what it does
and does not require.[4]

---

[1] *Redland Bricks v Morris* [1970] A.C. 652 at 666; *Potters-Ballotini Ltd v Weston-Baker* [1977]
R.P.C. 202 at 206 (confidential information); *Kennard v Cory Brothers and Co. Ltd* [1922] 1
Ch. 265 at 274, [1922] 2 Ch. 1 at 21, "the exact thing to be done is specified . . ."; *A Co. v
B Co.* [2002] 3 H.K.L.R.D. 11 at para.30 (*Norwich Pharmacal* relief) *Greetings Oxford
Koala Hotel Pty Ltd v Oxford Square Investments Pty Ltd* (1989) 18 N.S.W.L.R. 33.
[2] *Federal Bank of the Middle East v Hadkinson* [2000] 1 W.L.R. 1695 at 1705C–D; *Iberian
Trust Ltd v Founders Trust and Investment Co. Ltd* [1932] 2 K.B. 87 at 95; *R. v City of
London Magistrates' Court Ex p. Green* [1997] 3 All E.R. 551 at 558; *R & I Bank of Western
Australia Ltd v Anchorage Investments* (1992) 10 W.A.R. 59.
[3] *Co-operative Insurance v Argyll Stores Ltd* [1998] A.C. 1 at 13–14.
[4] *Electronic Applications (Commercial) Ltd v Toubkin* [1962] R.P.C. 225; *Staver Company
Inc. v Digitext Disply Ltd* [1985] F.S.R. 512; *P. A. Thomas & Co. v Mould* [1968] 2 Q.B.
913 at 922–923 (confidential information not specified); *Liverpool Household Stores
Association v Smith* (1887) 37 Ch.D. 170 (difficulty in spelling out what would be libellous);
Coflexip SA v Stolt Comex Seaway MS Ltd [1999] 2 All E.R. 593 at [21] making a general
point about injunctions, not affected by [2001] 1 All E.R. 952 disapproving [22] and [23]
which concerned the form of injunction in patent proceedings. *Director General of Fair
Trading v Tobyward Ltd* [1989] 1 W.L.R. 517 at p.522H–p.524A *per* Hoffmann J. (not
limiting injunction to reproducing the particular infringing advertisements, and including
advertisements 'in similar terms or likely to convey a similar impression' in respect of any of
the particular misleading claims); *Schindler Lifts Australia Pty Ltd v Debelak* (1989) 89
A.L.R. 275 at paras 230–231 (declining to grant a permanent injunction because it was not
satisfactory simply to grant injunction in general terms by reference to legal obligations
leaving the question of breach to be tried out in contempt proceedings).

It is also necessary to bear in mind the potential for the injunction to affect third parties because of the principle that they must not aid or abet a breach, or deliberately frustrate the purpose of the order. This is particularly important when the order is likely to affect third parties. It is therefore desirable that the order should so far as possible be free-standing and comprehensible without having to refer to material not found on the face of the order. Particular emphasis is placed on precision when the injunction is mandatory because the defendant does not have the option of refraining from acting near the fringes of the injunction but is obliged to act. CPR Pt 25, Practice Direction, para.5.3 provides that

> "Any order for an injunction must set out clearly what the Respondent must do or not do."

4.002   There is also the principle that an injunction should not be expressed in wider terms than the claimant's right. The claimant should not get more than to what he us entitled as a matter of law. So, *e.g.* an injunction may be granted to restrain threatened breach of a contract which remains in force but not if the contract has already been terminated.[5] With contracts, it is no part of the specific performance jurisdiction of the court to extend the burden of a contractual obligation over "the very minimum of that which is expressed in the terms creating the obligation. . .".[6] The same is true of the principles for assessing damages for breach of contract.[7] The principle allows destruction of items which infringed intellectual property rights which were valid and in force at the time the infringing items were created.[8] An injunction can also be granted to prevent the infliction by the defendant of further actionable loss on the claimant arising from an earlier tort.[9]

The principle is not absolute and may have to give way to the practical doing of justice.[10]

---

[5] *Medina Housing Association v Case* [2003] 1 All E.R. 1084 at [7].

[6] *Wilson v Northampton and Banbury Junction Railway Company* (1874) L.R. 9 Ch. App. 279 at 285, a case refusing specific performance of a promise to construct a railway station because the covenant said nothing about the design.

[7] *Laverack v Woods of Colchester* [1967] 1 Q.B. 278 at 294, the general rule is that the contract breaker is not as a general rule liable for what he is not obliged to do. In *The Mihalis Angelos* [1971] 1 Q.B. 164, where although the charterers had repudiated the charterparty by purporting to exercise the cancelling clause prematurely the charterparty was worthless to the owners because it was subject to the cancelling clause and would have been cancelled had the charterparty continued.

[8] *Crossley v Derby Gas Light Co.* (1834) 4 L.T. 25.

[9] In *Dyson v Hoover* [2001] R.P.C. 27 and 544 the judge considered that the court could grant an injunction to restrain conduct post expiry of a patent on the basis that such conduct would be building on goodwill obtained by the defendant through infringement of the patent prior to expiry. The final injunction was to restrain acts not in themselves actionable as an infringement of the patent, but which, if committed by the defendant, would be taking advantage of an earlier actionable wrong to the prejudice of the claimant. The argument is that such conduct by the defendant can be restrained under s.37(1) because it would otherwise aggravate the actionable damage caused by the earlier tort.

[10] *Hubbard v Pitt* [1976] Q.B. 142 at 190.

This principle is more readily applicable to a final injunction after a trial because by then those rights will have become defined. With an interlocutory injunction sought prior to trial the court has to look at what width of rights is arguable and formulate any injunction by reference to what the rights of the claimant may ultimately be found to be. The quest for precision and clarity may well come into tension with this principle and a pragmatic solution may have to be found which will enable the order to work effectively, but at the same time not impose too wide a restraint.[11]

However, there is also the principle that relief granted by injunction **4.003** should be effective. Whilst the substantive right is relevant to the drafting of the relief, that relief should also be drafted so as to provide the claimant with an effective remedy. There may need to be an additional envelope of restraint. An example is having an exclusion zone so that the defendant does not harass the claimant. There is no substantive right to prevent the defendant entering the zone, but if on the facts of the case it is reasonably necessary to provide for a zone for the injunction to achieve its purpose, to prevent harassment, then an injunction will be formulated accordingly.[12]

The cases provide examples of the application of these principles. It is often not possible to specify in minute detail the scope of the injunction,[13] and so some leeway is allowed in using a generality in the order. But the extent to which this may properly be done is a matter of degree and depends on the circumstances. An interlocutory injunction restraining the use of confidential information, without specifying what that information is, will not be granted because it is insufficiently precise.[14] An interlocutory injunction which prohibits infringement of the copyright in certain materials without more particularity of what constitutes an infringement may be expressed too generally.[15] On the other hand a limiting definition in the injunction may properly use the concept of whether an activity would be actionable at the suit of the claimant so as to avoid having a scope of injunction which gives the claimant relief expressed in too wide terms.[16] After the trial of a patent action an injunction will be granted so as to restrain infringement of the patent because by then the monopoly has been construed by the court in the context of what the defendant has done or wishes to do.[17] But even with final relief the width of any injunction is a matter of discretion for the court which will exercise it according to the

---

[11] *Attorney-General v Punch* [2003] 1 A.C. 1046 at [61–63] and [82–84], *per* Lord Hoffmann on the proviso which enabled a third party publisher to obtain consent from the Attorney-General to a publication; *Burris v Azadani* [1995] 1 W.L.R. 1372 at 1377; *Khorasandjian v Bush* [1993] Q.B. 727 at 732–733.

[12] *Burris v Azadani* [1995] 1 W.L.R. 1372 at 1377.

[13] See *Spectravest Inc. v Aperknit Ltd* (1988) 14 F.S.R. 161 at 174, referring the difficulties in envisaging what forms might be taken by further infringements of copyright.

[14] *Potters-Ballotini Ltd v Weston Baker* [1977] R.P.C. 202 at 206.

[15] *Staver Company Inc. v Digitext Disply Ltd* [1985] F.S.R. 512. *Schindler Lifts Australia Pty Ltd v Debelak* (1989) 89 A.L.R. 275 at paras 230–231 (declining to grant a permanent injunction in general terms to protect confidential information).

[16] *Thompson-Scwab v Costaki* [1956] 1 W.L.R. 335 at 340.

[17] *Coflexip SA v Stolt Comex Seaway MS Ltd* [2001] 1 All E.R. 952.

particular circumstances[18] and what degree of protection for the claimant is appropriate and proportionate.

(2) The form of the freezing injunction

4.004 When the Mareva jurisdiction was beginning to develop, the form of injunction adopted usually had no financial limit. In addition, some of the early injunctions merely prohibited the defendant from removing his assets from the jurisdiction, thus leaving it open for him to pay off debts within the jurisdiction, or otherwise deal with his assets. This wording stemmed from the fact that at that time there was still doubt about the scope of the jurisdiction because of what had been repeatedly laid down in the case law before 1975.[19] The temptation was to regard the Mareva jurisdiction as a limited inroad into this case law.

(3) Example form—prohibition on dealings with assets

4.005 The example order prohibiting disposal of assets in England and Wales[20] is expressed as an order to the defendant not to "remove from England and Wales or in any way dispose of or deal with or diminish the value of any of his assets which are in England and Wales . . .". The words "remove," "dispose of," "deal with," and "diminish the value of" are alternatives, each of which is forbidden by an order made in this form. If a third party holds a chattel for the defendant, the mere receipt of that chattel by the defendant is not a breach of the order because it is not a disposal of the asset, nor does it diminish the value of the asset, nor is it a dealing with the asset for the purposes of the order.[21] For there to be a dealing with the asset by the defendant, there must be some positive act by him. Transfer of custody or possession of an asset by the defendant to a third party without transfer of title could amount to a dealing within the meaning of the order. Forfeiture of a lease by a third party landlord does not involve any act by the defendant or on his behalf and is not a dealing by him with his assets.[22]

---

[18] *Microsoft Corporation v Plato Technology Ltd*, CA, unreported, July 15, 1999 (where the final relief in a trade mark and passing off action was limited by the words "which [the defendant] knows or ought upon reasonable enquiry to know are Infringing Products".

[19] *Mills v Northern Railway of Buenos Aires Co.* (1870) 5 Ch. App. 621 at 627–628, *per* Lord Hatherley L.C.; W. Joyce, *The Law and Practice of Injunctions in Equity and at Common Law* (1872), Vol. 2, p.923; *Robinson v Pickering* (1881) 16 Ch.D. at 661 and 663; *Newton v Newton* (1885) 11 P.D. 11; *Lister & Co. v Stubbs* (1890) 45 Ch.D. 1 at 14; *Burmester v Burmester* [1913] P. 76; *Jagger v Jagger* [1926] P. 93 at 96, and 101; *Scott v Scott* [1951] P. 193.

[20] CPR Pt 25, Practice Direction, para.6.1 and annexure form F.I.

[21] *Bank Mellat v Kazmi* [1989] Q.B. 541 at 547; *The Law Society v Shanks* [1988] 1 F.L.R. 504.

[22] *Re R (Restraint Order)* [1990] 2 Q.B. 307 at 314.

The example order applies expressly to the defendant's assets "whether or not they are in his own name . . .". So if assets belonging to the defendant are held by a nominee, they are subject to an order. Assets of the defendant which are the subject of a bailment are caught by the order.

The example order applies to assets "whether they are solely or jointly owned . . .". The wording of the example order contrasts with the view of Kerr L.J. in *Z Ltd v A-Z and AA-LL*[23] that it would only be justifiable to grant Mareva relief in respect of joint accounts "in rare cases". The rejection of the view of Kerr L.J. is because very substantial assets may be owned jointly by a husband and wife and to exempt those assets from a Mareva could result in injustice to the claimant.

So under the example order if a defendant has a joint account with his wife, the injunction applies to the joint account. The wife has her own right to draw on that account and such a drawing will not be a breach of the injunction because it is not an act of the defendant. However, since the purpose of the order is to preserve the assets of the defendant unless the wife applies to the court to authorise drawings, she could find herself in a difficulty because of the principle that a third party should not deliberately frustrate the purpose of the court in making the order.[24] If the order allows the defendant to draw living expenses, then drawing within the limit will in any event not be contrary to the purpose of the injunction. However, the wife can always apply to the court to enable her to continue to use the joint account for ordinary living expenses or for other expenditure and she will be permitted to do so provided that her use of the account is not inconsistent with the purpose of the Mareva relief. If she is entitled to a share in the account, she can also ask that her share of the account be made over to her free from the injunction. **4.006**

If the claimant is aware of the existence of particular assets (such as bank accounts) the order should refer to them with as much particularity as possible. The defendant is then left with a more difficult task, if the assets are dealt with, in seeking to defend or mitigate in contempt proceedings. Also, a third party served with notice of the order is able more readily to identify the particular assets and thus ensure that he does not aid or abet any breach of the order. This could well be relevant to whether the third party has committed contempt of court by aiding and abetting a breach of the order consisting of a disposal by the defendant of those assets. It would also be relevant to whether a third party could be held in contempt for deliberately frustrating the purpose of the order.[25]

It was said by Kerr L.J. in *Z Ltd v A-Z and AA-LL*, above, that a Mareva injunction should not apply to shares or title deeds which a bank may hold as security, or articles in a safe deposit which a bank may hold in the name of a defendant. The justification for the view was that it would be too great a burden on banks to have to assess the value of unspecified assets with

---

[23] [1982] Q.B. 558 at 591.
[24] *Attorney-General v Punch* [2003] 1 A.C. 1046 at [4].
[25] *ibid.*, at [39–40], *per* Lord Nicholls.

reference to the maximum sum specified in the injunction. But this would create a black hole—assets which could not be preserved by Mareva relief. The current practice is not to exclude such assets from the term of the without notice order. If a bank considers itself to be in an embarrassing position, then it may apply to the court for specific directions.

4.007   It appears that a freezing injunction in the example form of order is interpreted by the court as prohibiting only *disposal* of chattels, and therefore it would seem that a bank is bound to release share certificates, title deeds or articles in a safe deposit to its customer, unless the bank knows that this is a step taken as a preliminary to commission of a breach of the injunction. A bank on which notice of a Mareva injunction is served must not aid and abet breach of the injunction and must not deliberately frustrate the purpose of the injunction, but is not under a duty to act carefully so as to prevent a breach taking place.

(4) Variation by consent

4.008   Paragraph 11(3) of the example form provides that:

> "The Respondent may agree with the Applicant's legal representatives that the [spending limits for living expenses] should be increased or that this order should be varied in any other respect, but any agreement must be in writing."

The purpose of this is to enable a variation to be agreed without there having to be an application to the court. It provides a quick and inexpensive way for the defendant or third parties to obtain a variation without in any way affecting their entitlement to apply to the court.[26]

(5) "Maximum sum" orders

4.009   It is not a precondition to the granting of Mareva relief that the claimant can show that he has a good arguable case in support of a claim for a "certain or approximate sum".[27] In most cases, however, the court will insert a maximum sum to avoid any unnecessary interference with the defendant's freedom to use his own assets, and it is now very rare for a Mareva injunction to be granted without a financial limit.[28] The reason is

---

[26] *cp. Attorney-General v Punch* [2003] 1 A.C. 1046 at [84].

[27] *McDonald v Graham* ob1994] R.P.C. 407 at 438; *Darashah v UFAC (UK) Ltd, The Times,* March 30, 1982.

[28] *McDonald v Graham* [1994] R.P.C. 407 at 437–439 and 439–440 (where a financial limit would have been of only academic importance and would have unnecessarily complicated the order); *Macy's Candies Ltd v Chan Man Hong* [1997] H.K.L.R. 554; *Ng Chun-fai v Tamco Electrical & Electronics (Hong Kong) Ltd* [1994] H.K.L.R. 289.

that the claimant's claim is for a limited amount only and it would be unjustified to freeze assets in excess of that amount. This is because the purpose behind the order is simply to preserve sufficient assets to satisfy the judgment.[29] It has been suggested that when the defendant's assets do not consist entirely of cash the maximum sum infringes the principle that the injunction should be certain.[30] But the alternative would be not to include the limit and this would infringe the principle that the claimant should not have an order which goes beyond what is necessary to safeguard his legitimate interests.[31] The balance has been struck by including the limit in the *ex parte* order and continuing the order in that form unless and until application is made for a more precise order. Once a claimant is informed of what assets are covered by the injunction under the disclosure order he can consider applying for a variation which will adapt the order according to the particular assets of the defendant.[32]

The practice of inserting a financial limit for a Mareva injunction can be contrasted with a freezing injunction granted over assets to which a proprietary claim is made. Normally the whole of the property claimed will be preserved by the injunction and a financial limit will not be appropriate. There can be an injunction preserving certain assets held by the defendant, or in a fund to be constituted by the defendant,[33] regardless of whether they represent property of the claimant, to be available to answer for a future money judgment on a claim which has a proprietary base (*e.g.* misapplication of the claimant's assets). In such a case a financial limit will be part of the order, and the assets will not be constituted by the order as security for the claim.

In determining the limit for Mareva relief, the court will consider for how much the claimant has a good arguable case. If the claimant has alternative claims, the court will assess the maximum sum by reference to the claim for the highest amount in respect of which the claimant has a good arguable case.[35] Prima facie the court by granting the injunction is seeking to preserve the position and fairness requires that the limit is assessed on the basis of the highest amount for which the claimant has a good arguable case. This is similar to the practice for assessing the amount of security in an Admiralty action *in rem*.[36] The court will not fix a limit so

[29] T. Willoughby and S. Connal, "The Mareva Injunction: A Cruel Tyranny?" (1997) 8 E.I.P.R. 479 at 481.
[30] *Abella v Abella* [1987] 2 Qd R. 1 at 4.
[31] *Gill v Flightwise Travel Service Ltd* [2003] E.W.H.C. 3082, Ch.D, at [29].
[32] See *A v C* [1981] Q.B. 956 at 959.
[33] *Millenium Federation Pty Ltd v Bigjig Pty* [2000] 1 Qd Rep. 275.
[34] *Millenium Federation Pty Ltd v Bigjig Pty* [2000] 1 Qd Rep. 275 ($200,000 to be placed in an account and preserved); *Polly Peck International plc v Nadir (No.2)* [1992] 4 All E.R. 769 (the injunction in relation to £8.9 million).
[35] *Mayor and Burgesses of the London Borough of Lambeth v Clarke*, Court of Appeal (Civ Div) Transcript No.1563 of 1993 (December 22, 1993; and see *Business Online Group v MCI Worldcom Ltd* [2001] EWCA Civ 1399 in which security was required from the claimant as the price for an injunction requiring the defendant not to cut off its service and security was calculated on the "highest arguable figure".
[36] *The Moschanthy* [1971] 1 Lloyd's Rep. 37; *The Bazias 3* [1993] Q.B. 673.

as to preserve a cushion for the defendant to discharge other indebtedness and have sufficient at the likely date of judgment to pay the claim in its entirety.[37]

4.010   When the claimant sues for damages there can be uncertainties as to what will happen in the future and how this will affect the calculation of damages. Provided that there is an existing cause of action for damages, there is jurisdiction to grant Mareva relief.[38] The quantum of the injunction will be a matter for the exercise of discretion by the court. It can be that the quantum should subsequently be reduced because of events which occur after the injunction was granted and which are likely to result in any eventual award of damages being less than what was originally contemplated.[39]

At one time doubts were expressed as to whether it would be appropriate to include an element for the plaintiff's costs (on the grounds that this would be tantamount to ordering a defendant to put up security for costs), but in practice nowadays an element for recoverable costs is usually included: *Charles Church Developments plc v Cronin*.[40] Usually the addition made is comparatively modest.

The example form order prohibiting disposal of assets in England and Wales provides that the restraint applies "up to the value of £   ".[41]

4.011   This operates as an exception to the order permitting a defendant to do acts which would otherwise be a breach of the order. The defendant must be within the exception at the time of doing the acts and the limit in the order applies at that time. The limit applies to the defendant's assets within England and Wales at that time, including assets which have become subject to the order as a result of having been brought within England and Wales subsequent to the order.[42]

In contempt proceedings, if the defendant wishes to justify what appears to be a clear breach of the order by reference to the limit, he will have to provide evidence showing that his conduct was allowed because of the limit: *Canadian Imperial Bank of Commerce v Bhattessa*.[43] The reason for this is pragmatic. In practice the defendant will usually have the necessary information available to him to show what the position was whereas the claimant will not. Unless the defendant had to adduce evidence about his other assets he could not be made to disclose the position because of the privilege against self-incrimination and it would be difficult if not impossible for the claimant to prove the contempt up to the criminal standard.

---

[37] *K/S A/S Admiral Shipping v Portlink Ferries Ltd* [1984] 2 Lloyd's Rep. 166.
[38] See paras 12.001–4, below.
[39] *A/S D/S Svendborg v Wansa* [1997] 2 Lloyd's Rep. 183 at 189–190.
[40] [1990] F.S.R. 1 at 10.
[41] Paragraph 5.
[42] *Cretanor Maritime Co. Ltd v Irish Marine Management Ltd (The Cretan Harmony)* [1978] 1 W.L.R. 966 at 973; *TDK Tape Distributors (UK) Ltd v Videochoice Ltd* [1986] 1 W.L.R. 141 at 145; *Soinco SACI v Novokuznetsk Aluminium Plant* [1998] Q.B. 406 at 422A–E.
[43] Court of Appeal (Civ Div) Transcript No.694 of 1993 (April 21, 1993), approving *The Times*, September 10, 1991; *Great Future International Ltd v Sealand Housing Corporation* [2004] EWHC 124, ChD, at [19–24].

This would be a substantial inroad into the effectiveness of Mareva injunctions and the due administration of justice in cases in which they are granted. The Court of Appeal regarded the limit as an exception to the order and regarded the defendant as having to show that he came within the exception.

Canadian Imperial Bank of Commerce v Bhattessa was decided before the Human Rights Act 1998 was enacted. This provides in Art.6(2):

> "2. Everyone charged with a criminal offence shall be presumed innocent until proved guilty according to law."

Contempt proceedings are within the meaning of "a criminal offence" within the Article because if the defendant is held in contempt he can be punished for that contempt by a fine or being imprisoned. The meaning of Art.6(2) is autonomous and does not depend upon how the contempt proceedings would be classified under English domestic law.

The article does not prohibit merely a shifting in evidential burden[44] and not the persuasive burden. This is because the placing of an evidential burden on the defendant does no more than require him to raise an issue and once an issue is raised the legal burden remains on the prosecutor who has the burden of disproving the issue.   **4.012**

Applying this approach the first question is whether the necessary ingredients of the contempt consist only of dealing with assets caught by the injunction otherwise than for an authorised purpose, or whether those ingredients also include a requirement that the dealing brings the value of the assets remaining below the limit. It is suggested that this is a necessary ingredient because the restraint in the example order is itself expressed subject to whether the dealing has this effect,[45] and unless this ingredient is present there is no breach of the order.

The second question is whether the principle merely raises an evidential burden sufficient to raise an issue, or whether it casts a legal burden on the defendant to prove the existence of other assets of sufficient value. It is thought that the principle does no more than cast an evidential burden on the defendant. Once the prosecutor has adduced evidence apparently disclosing a clear breach of the injunction, it is for the defendant to adduce the necessary evidence to raise the issue, and it is then up to the prosecutor to knock it down and disprove the issue to the criminal standard. If this is correct there is no infringement of Art.6(2).

The third question is whether this principle could be an infringement of Art.6(1) of the European Convention, the right to a fair trial. Part of the protection afforded by that Article is the right not to be convicted on   **4.013**

---

[44] *R. v Lambert* [2002] 2 A.C. 545; *Attorney-General's Reference No.4 of 2002* [2003] EWCA Crim 762.
[45] *Great Future International Ltd v Sealand Housing Corporation* [2004] EWHC 124 at [75], ChD, rejecting the submission that as long as there were sufficient assets before the dealing it did not matter whether the result of the dealing was to bring the value of the remaining assets below the limit.

statements obtained from the defendant under compulsion.[46] The principle may be said to take away this right if in effect on the facts of a particular case it forces the defendant to speak in order to raise the necessary issue.

There is a distinction under Art.6(1) between compelling the defendant to make statements himself which go into evidence, and requiring him to furnish documents or other material which already exist and which have not been created by the defendant as a result of the compulsion.[47] The latter is not within the protection of Art.6(1). Accordingly Art.6(1) can only be engaged if on the particular facts the defendant is compelled to furnish evidence created as a result of the compulsion.

The rights under Art.6(1) are not absolute—the right to remain silent may be qualified in appropriate circumstances.[48] Likewise Art.6(2), when it does apply, does not prohibit all reversals of the burdens of proof. Whether an inroad on the right to silence or a reversal of the burden is permissible, consistently with the European Convention, depends on the reasonableness of the rule and whether it is proportionate. In the present circumstances:

(1) when the defendant has a defence that he had assets in excess of the limit it would normally be extremely easy for him to produce the evidence;

(2) a defendant who has dealt with assets covered by an injunction will know that unless the dealing is authorised by the court or he retains assets up to the limit he is acting in breach of the court order;

(3) although matters of contempt can be serious they are not of similar gravity to offences to the most serious criminal offences;

(4) if there was not this principle it would be very difficult to punish breaches of Mareva injunctions and this would undermine the effect of Mareva injunctions and thus the due administration of justice in cases in which they have been granted;

(5) the principle does not apply unless what is shown by the prosecutor discloses, in the absence of explanation, what would appear to be a clear breach of the injunction;

4.014   It is suggested that Art.6(2) is not engaged. But if the principle did place a legal burden on the defendant, the balancing question would then arise— whether the principle is reasonable and proportionate and is justified by the public interest. On this it is suggested that (1) a rule placing an evidential burden on the defendant would have sufficed on the facts of

---

[46] *Saunders v United Kingdom* (1996) 23 E.H.R.R. 313 at para.68; *Brown v Stott* [2003] 1 A.C. 681; *R. v Hertfordshire County Council Ex p. Green Environmental Industries Ltd* [2000] 2 A.C. 412 at 422.
[47] *R. v Kearns* [2002] EWCA Crim 748 at [53(4)].
[48] *Brown v Stott* [2003] 1 A.C. 681; *R. v Kearns* [2002] EWCA Crim 748.

Canadian Imperial Bank of Commerce v Bhattessa, (2) would be sufficient in other cases to secure the public interest, and (3) the principle should be reformulated as one raising an evidential burden alone,[49] so as to make it consistent with Art.6(2).

As for Art.6(1) even if on the facts it were engaged, it is suggested that the court ought to find that the principle is a reasonable and proportionate one which strikes a fair balance between the rights of the individual and the public interest.

The words in the example order for an injunction limited to assets in England and Wales read: **4.015**

> "5. . . . the Respondent must not remove from England and Wales or in any way dispose of, deal with or diminish the value of any of his assets which are in England and Wales up to the value of £   ".

These words are intended to preserve the full value of assets within the jurisdiction up to the value stipulated in the order. This is implicit in the wording and the purpose of the order. The purpose is to ensure that after a dealing permitted by the exception there will remain available within the jurisdiction assets of the defendant which have an aggregate value of not less than the limit after taking into account all encumbrances on those assets. It could be made express by providing that in calculating the value of an asset then if that asset is pledged, charged, mortgaged, or subject to any other encumbrance which diminishes its value, the value is to be calculated after making an appropriate allowance for the relevant encumbrance. A pledge, mortgage or charge would constitute an encumbrance.[50] In the case of a defendant company which has granted a floating charge over its assets, there is to be taken into account the amount secured by the charge when calculating the value of assets covered by the floating charge for the purpose of operating the exception. This is because a floating charge constitutes an immediate equitable charge upon assets covered by it, subject to a power of the charger, while the charge continues to float, to deal with assets as permitted by the charge.[51] Crystallisation of the charge puts an end to that power. It does not create an encumbrance. The encumbrance was created by the instrument granting the floating charge.

The example form prohibiting disposal of assets worldwide includes the following wording:

> "5. . . .the Respondent must not—

---

[49] See also Chapter 19, para.19.060; *Great Future International Ltd v Sealand Housing Corporation* [2004] EWHC 124 at [19–24], Ch.D.

[50] An equitable charge gives security to the chargee and the Mareva relief will be varied so as to allow the chargee to enforce his rights: *Pharaoh's Plywood Co. Ltd v Allied Wood Product*, Court of Appeal (Civ Div) Transcript No.217 of 1980 (January 18, 1980).

[51] *Cretanor Maritime Co. Ltd v Irish Marine Management Ltd (The Cretan Harmony)* [1978] 1 W.L.R. 966.

    (1) remove from England and Wales any of his assets which are in England and Wales up to the value of £   ; or

    (2) in any way dispose of, deal with or diminish the value of any of his assets whether they are in or outside England and Wales up to the same value."

This wording operates so that if there are assets of sufficient value in England and Wales, the injunction applies to affect dealings with those assets alone, leaving the defendant free to deal with his other assets so long as the value of the assets in England and Wales does not fall below the specified limit.

(6) Unlimited orders

4.016 Unlimited orders are rarely justifiable in ordinary Mareva cases.[52] But in tracing cases, *e.g.* where the claimant is seeking to trace into the defendant's bank accounts the proceeds of an alleged fraud, it may be appropriate for the court to place no financial limit on the injunction, either because the full quantum of the claimant's claim is unascertainable, or because it is just and equitable that all assets should be preserved until investigations have been carried out with a view to ascertaining which are arguably subject to a trust and which are not. Similar considerations may apply where the claimant is claiming for the breach of intellectual property rights (*e.g.* breach of copyright, infringement of trade marks or patents), where the extent of the claimant's claim is impossible to predict and the number of infringing copies in circulation is unknown.

(7) Orders limited to specific assets

4.017 It is possible to obtain orders which relate not to the defendant's assets generally, but are limited to specific assets. These are particularly appropriate where the claimant knows that the defendant has one asset, which is worth as much as, or more than, the claimant's claim. If the injunction can be confined to a particular asset, this has the advantage of limiting the exposure of the claimant to claims under his cross-undertaking in damages. It is possible for the court to confine the scope of a Mareva injunction to specific assets after it has been granted in wider terms, if sufficient information about the defendant's assets has been revealed pursuant to an order for discovery, or voluntarily.

(8) Ancillary orders

4.018 The Mareva injunction may be granted in an order which includes ancillary orders to assist the efficacy of the injunction, *e.g.* orders for the disclosure of assets, search orders relating to documents or articles which require

---

[52] *Macy's Candies Ltd v Chan Man Hona* [1997] H.K.L.R.D. 554.

preservation, orders under the Bankers' Books (Evidence) Act 1879, or even orders restraining the defendant personally from leaving the jurisdiction.

(9) Mandatory Mareva relief

In *Derby v Weldon (No. 6)*,[53] certain assets had been deposited by Swiss **4.019** banks on behalf of account holders in banks outside Switzerland. The Court of Appeal held that it had power to order that assets should be moved from one jurisdiction to another, although it declined to exercise the power on the facts of the case.[54] The court's jurisdiction to grant such an order arose from its jurisdiction over the defendant and was not limited to a territorial jurisdiction to be exercised by reference to the location of assets.

The court can also in an appropriate case require assets to be transferred into a blocked account: 3 *Style Ltd v Goss*,[55] or paid into court: *United Norwest Co-operatives Ltd v Johnstone (No. 2)*,[56] referred to in *Themehelp Ltd v West*.[57]

---

[53] [1990] 1 W.L.R. 1139.
[54] See also *Federal Commissioner of Taxation v Karageorge* (1996) A.T.C. 114; 34 A.T.R. 196; *Equipment Finance Ltd v C. Keeton Ltd* (1999) 13 P.R.N.Z. 319 (mandatory injunction requiring return of a container, unopened, to New Zealand, which was in transit to Panama).
[55] Court of Appeal (Civ Div) Transcript No.395 of 1990 (April 11, 1990).
[56] Court of Appeal (Civ Div) Transcript No.1482 of 1994 (December 6, 1994); see also para. 22.037 below.
[57] [1996] Q.B. 84 at 103F.

Chapter 5

Proceedings relating to assets

(1) Admiralty actions *in rem*

The right to proceed against a vessel or aircraft *in rem* is governed by ss20– **5.001**
24 of the Supreme Court Act 1981, which provide a statutory code.[1] An
action *in rem* is sometimes described as an action against the *res*, but this is
a fiction. The owners of the *res* are the defendants to the action *in rem*.[2]
Unless they submit to the jurisdiction of the English court, a judgment can
only be enforced against the *res* and they will be bound by the judgment
but only to the extent of their interest in the *res*. If and when the owners
submit to the jurisdiction of the court in the action, including if they take a
step to defend the action on the merits, the action continues in addition in
personam against the owners.[3] If process was served on the *res*, the action
continues both[4] *in rem* and in *personam*, but if the process has not been
served on the *res*, then the action is only *in personam*.[5]

Certain claims which can be enforced by action *in rem* (*e.g.* salvage and
collision claims) give rise to a maritime lien. A maritime lien is available
against the vessel even though ownership of the vessel has been transferred
to a bona fide purchaser for value (*The Ripon City*)[6] and even though this
has occurred prior to the commencement of the action. Under English law
the right to a maritime lien is a matter of procedure and is to be
determined according to the *lex fori: Bankers Trust Ltd v Todd Shipyards*.[7]
In the case of other rights to proceed *in rem* against a vessel, the admiralty
jurisdiction is invoked when the writ is issued (*Re Aro Co.*)[8] and the right to
arrest the vessel continues notwithstanding a change in ownership of the
res after the issue of the writ: *The Monica S.*[9] If the claimant has a statutory
right of action *in rem* not amounting to a maritime lien and the ship is sold

---

[1] For the rules on entertaining jurisdiction when the defendant shipowner is domiciled in a
foreign state—see *Dicey and Morris on The Conflict of Laws* (13th ed., 1999), Ch. 13.
[2] *Republic of India v India Steamship Co. Ltd (No.2)* [1998] A.C. 878.
[3] *The Gemma* [1899] P. 285; *The August 8* [1983] 2 A.C. 450.
[4] *The Nordglint* [1988] Q.B. 183; *The Maciej Rataj* [1992] 2 Lloyd's Rep. 552.
[5] *The Tuyuti* [1984] Q.B. 838.
[6] [1897] P. 226 at 241.
[7] [1981] A.C. 221.
[8] [1980] Ch. 196.
[9] [1986] P. 741.

after the accrual of the cause of action but before the issue of proceedings he cannot proceed *in rem* against the ship.[10] The right to arrest is available both before or after judgment. The vessel may be arrested before judgment in order to obtain further security provided that this is not oppressive or vexatious.[11] The warrant of arrest is granted on an application for arrest supported by a declaration in the form set out in the Admiralty Practice Direction.[12] The measure of priority afforded by the right *in rem* depends on the nature of the cause of action. Thus, *e.g.* a claim in respect of salvage takes priority over a mortgage.

The practice of the Admiralty Court is not to determine priorities until after the vessel has been sold. If security is not provided, the court will usually order a sale *pendente lite: The Myrto*.[13] The court has the power to release a vessel from arrest.[14] However, in principle, if a person is entitled to bring an action *in rem* and arrest a ship, then the fact that it may do him no good because the ship is heavily mortgaged will not result in the ship being released.[15] Security for the claim is assessed on the basis of the claimant's reasonably arguable best case, interest and costs.[16] Usually, a vessel is released from arrest by agreement of the parties upon provision of security acceptable to the claimant.[17]

In an admiralty action *in rem*, the shipowners can give security to the full value of the ship and thereby obtain release of the ship when its value is less than that of the claim.[18]

5.002   In Mareva cases, the limit of the injunction will be assessed on the basis of the amount for which the claimant has a good arguable case together with an allowance for interest and costs: *Mayor and Burgesses of the London Borough of Lambeth v Clarke*.[19] Likewise, if the defendant wishes to substitute security for assets caught by the Mareva injunction, then in principle he is free to do so, by providing security in an amount equivalent to the value of the assets released. If the assets are earning interest (*e.g.* bank accounts), then it is to be expected that the substitute security will include an appropriate uplift to put the claimant in the same position as if interest had continued to accrue on assets caught by the injunction.

In an action *in rem* the claimant can re-arrest the ship before judgment for increased security provided that it is not oppressive or unfair—*e.g.*

---

[10] *The Heinrich Bjorn* (1886) 11 App.Cas. 270.
[11] CPR r.61.6(2)(b).
[12] CPR r.61.5.
[13] [1977] 2 Lloyd's Rep. 243.
[14] CPR r.61.8(4)(b); as for "inherent jurisdiction", see *The APJ Shalini* [1991] 2 Lloyd's Rep. 62 at 66.
[15] *The APJ Shalini* [1991] 2 Lloyd's Rep. 62; *The World Star* [1986] 2 Lloyd's Rep. 274; *cf. The Marco Reefer* (1981) 50 *Lloyd's Maritime Law Newsletter* (August 19, 1981)
[16] *The Bazias 3* [1993] Q.B. 673 at 682 applying *The Moschanthy* [1971] 1 Lloyd's Rep. 37. [1971] 1 Lloyd's Rep. 37 at 44; *Gulf Azov v Idisi* [2001] 1 Lloyd's Rep. 727 at 736; *The Clarabelle* [2002] 2 Lloyd's Rep. 479.
[17] CPR r.61.8(4)
[18] CPR r.61.5(3) and see *The Charlotte* [1920] P. 78.
[19] Court of Appeal (Civ Div) Transcript No.1563 of 1993 (December 22, 1993).

when the security given has been adversely affected by the defendant's acts.[20] This is because where an action *in rem* can be brought it is an incident of the action that the claimant ought to be entitled to full security on the basis of the claimant's best arguable case.

There is no such presumption in proceedings which are not *in rem*. However, the limit to a Mareva injunction can be raised or a new injunction granted before judgment when it is just to do so. If an earlier injunction has been varied or discharged by agreement, it is material to take into account the terms of that agreement, including whether it was part of the contract that no new Mareva relief would be sought by the claimant against the defendant pending judgment. Such a promise, if given, will provide a strong reason for the matter not being reopened. But it is not conclusive. The question is whether it is just in all the circumstances which have arisen that the new relief should be granted to the claimant. Even if such a promise has been given strong reason might be shown by the claimant for not giving effect to that promise. If such a promise has not been given then whether it is just to grant the new relief still depends on the particular circumstances.

A claimant can usually issue a warrant of arrest as of right under CPR **5.003** r.61.5 and so he has no obligation to make full disclosure of relevant facts.[21] There are circumstances listed in CPR r.61.5 when the ship cannot be arrested as of right. The claimant who arrests a vessel does not provide a cross-undertaking in damages: *The Bazias* 3.[22] But he may be made liable for damages in tort for wrongful arrest if he acts maliciously or with gross negligence: *The Walter D Wallett*;[23] *The Kommunar (No.3)*.[24]

(2) Third party debt orders—garnishment

Third party debt order is the name given by CPR Pt 72 to what previously **5.004** was a garnishee order made under RSC Ord. 49, r.1 and the Supreme Court Act 1981, ss.40 and 139, for execution of a judgment for a liquidated sum, upon debts[25] due or accruing due[26] National Savings and deposit and

---

[20] *The Clarabelle* [2002] 2 Lloyd's Rep. 479 (re-arrest allowed following error in fixing quantum by the registrar); *The Arctic Star, The Times* February 5, 1985 (re-arrest allowed following impairment of security by defendant's act); *The Ruta* [2000] 1 W.L.R. 2068 at 2077–2079 (guarantee given by club which had gone into liquidation—claimant would have been entitled to re-arrest); *The Hero* (1865) 13 W.R. 927 (re-arrest allowed following clerical error in calculating security).

[21] *The Varna* [1993] 2 Lloyd's Rep. 253.

[22] [1993] Q.B. 673.

[23] [1893] P. 202.

[24] [1997] 1 Lloyd's Rep. 22 at 28–32; *Gulf Azov v Idisi* [2001] 1 Lloyd's Rep. 727 at 736–737.

[25] There must be an existing debt capable of enforcement by the court in a civil suit: *Camdex International Ltd v Bank of Zambia (No.2)* [1997] C.L.C. 714.

[26] This includes *debitum in praesenti, solvendum in futuro*, but not a debt which does not yet exist *Dunlop & Ranken Ltd v Hendall Steel: Structures Ltd* [1957] 1 W.L.R. 1102 at 1107.

withdrawable share accounts, including assets expressed in foreign currency: *Choice Investments Ltd v Jeromnimon.*[27] The procedure is only available after judgment (even an order for costs to be taxed will not suffice). The procedure is to apply without notice for an interim third party debt order. The application notice must be in the form and set out the information required by the Practice Direction[28] which includes a requirement of some real evidence, and not merely speculation,[29] that the third party is indebted to the judgment debtor. The application is dealt with initially by a judge without a hearing.[30] Under CPR r.72.4(2)(b), the interim order will include a direction to the third party that he must not make any payment which reduces the amount he owes the judgment debtor to less than the amount specified in the order. The interim order attaches the debt pending decision of the court whether to make a final third party debt order.

With one possible exception of little practical importance, debts situated abroad are outside of the limits of the procedure.[31] This is as a matter of the territorial jurisdiction of the court and not merely discretion[32]—the English court only has jurisdiction over assets within its territorial jurisdiction because of its duty to respect the sovereignty of foreign states and their courts over persons and assets within their territorial jurisdictions. The exception is that an order may be made relating to a chose in action sited abroad if it appears that by the law of that place the English order would be recognised as discharging *pro tanto* the amount of the debt owed by the third party to the judgment debtor.[33] An example might be when the debt is governed by English law.[34]

The interim order becomes binding on the debt when it is served on the third party.[35] If the order is made final, the third party is bound to pay the debt to the judgment creditor instead of the judgment debtor.

5.005   The procedure is a mode of execution which operates *in rem* against the debt by attaching the debt to answer the judgment debt. The plain English of the rule is deceptive in obscuring that the procedure operates on the debt itself and not merely by *in personam* orders made against the judgment debtor and the third party.[36]

---

[27] [1981] Q.B. 149.

[28] CPR r.72, Practice Direction, para.1.2.

[29] CPR r.72, Practice Direction, para.1.3.

[30] CPR r.72.4(1).

[31] *Société Eram Shipping Co. Ltd v Compagnie Internationale de Navigation* [2004] 1 A.C. 260; *Richardson v Richardson* [1927] P. 228; *Brooks Associates Inc. v Basu* [1983] Q.B. 220 at 222–223.

[32] Dicta in *SCF v Masri (No.2)* [1987] Q.B. 1002 in which the matter was said to be a question of discretion were disapproved of by the House of Lords in *Société Eram Shipping Co. Ltd v Compagnie Internationale de Navigation* [2004] 1 A.C. 260.

[33] *Société Eram Shipping Co. Ltd v Compagnie Internationale de Navigation* [2004] 1 A.C. 260 at [26].

[34] *Kuwait Oil Tanker Co. SAK v Qabazard* [2004] 1 A.C. 300 at [13], *per* Lord Hoffmann, "the discharge [given by the rules of court] cannot affect a debt which . . . is neither situate in England nor governed by English law . . .".

[35] CPR r.72.4(4).

[36] *Société Eram Shipping Co. Ltd v Compagnie Internationale de Navigation* [2004] 1 A.C. 260 at [112], *per* Lord Millett.

The making of a third party debt order is a matter of discretion exercised upon the same principles as those which apply to charging orders. Thus, the order will be made unless there are special factors making it inequitable to grant it: *Roberts Petroleum Ltd v Bernard Kenney Ltd*.[37] This is a discretion to be exercised judicially—so, *e.g.* the fact that the bank account had been used by a state to deposit funds obtained by it under a grant from the European Community made for specified purposes, did not result in the refusal of a garnishee order.[38] Subject to exercise by the court of the hardship jurisdiction in CPR r.72.7, the mere fact that a judgment debtor wishes to use the asset to satisfy other debts is insufficient; but, if the judgment debtor is bankrupt or insolvent, the asset will be released for distribution *pro rata* among the creditors. To found jurisdiction to make a third party debt order, it is sufficient if the third party has agreed to submit to the jurisdiction or is within the jurisdiction when the application for an interim order is made.[39]

If the third party would in fact be subjected to a real risk of having to pay twice, then the order will not be made final even though it relates to a debt situated within the jurisdiction. Thus, in *Deutsche Schachtbau-und Tiefbohrgesellschaft GmbH v Shell International Co. Ltd*,[40] the judgment creditors were refused a garnishee order when the intended garnishees had been successfully sued by the judgment debtors for the debt in foreign court proceedings. Although the relevant foreign court had no jurisdiction over the matter under English rules of conflicts of law, nevertheless there was on the facts a "real or substantial risk"[41] of the foreign judgment being successfully enforced against the intended garnishees, and it would therefore have been inequitable to the intended garnishees to grant a garnishee order.

A third party debt order is a form of execution. It applies only to the **5.006** debt owed to the judgment debtor and it is an essential aspect of the procedure that the effect of payment to the judgment creditor of the debt under a final order would be to give the third party an effective discharge.[42] It does not operate as an assignment or transfer of the debt to the judgment creditor,[43] nor does it transfer security for the debt.[44] The judgment creditor is spoken of as having a lien or charge over the debt because he can enforce the debt as against the third party and payments made by the third party to the judgment debtor after service on the third party of the

---

[37] [1983] 1 A.C. 192.
[38] *Philipp Brothers v Republic of Sierra Leone* [1995] 1 Lloyd's Rep. 289, affirming *A Co. v Republic of X* [1994] 1 Lloyd's Rep. 111.
[39] *SCF v Masri (No.2)* [1987] Q.B. 1002.
[40] [1990] 1 A.C. 295; followed in *Soinco SACI v Novokuznetsk Aluminium Plant* [1998] 2 Lloyd's Rep. 346.
[41] *Deutsche Schachtbau-und Tiefbohrgesellschaft GmbH v Shell International Co. Ltd* [1990] 1 A.C. 295 at 353C–D, *per* Lord Goff.
[42] *Société Eram Shipping Co. Ltd v Compagnie Internationale de Navigation* [2003] 1 A.C. 260.
[43] *Re Combined Weighing and Advertising Machine Company* (1889) 43 Ch.D. 99 at 104.
[44] *Chatterton v Watney* (1881) 17 Ch.D. 259 at 262.

interim order will not reduce the debt which the judgment creditor can enforce. In cases where the debt is situated in a state which is a party to the Brussels or Lugano Conventions or the Jurisdiction Regulations it is the court having jurisdiction at the place where the debt is situated which has exclusive jurisdiction over enforcement of a judgment against that debt.[45]

A number of aspects of the law on third party debt orders are relevant to the Mareva jurisdiction:

(1) The court will not make orders over assets or against persons when this would be inconsistent with respecting the sovereignty of a foreign state over assets and persons within its own territorial jurisdiction.[46] This has the consequence that for third party debt orders the court will, subject to the one exception, not make an order over a debt situated abroad. The same principle applies to injunctions granted pre-judgment or in aid of execution. So the proviso which is to be inserted in a freezing order[47] is based on the same principle.

(2) This principle also limits the exercise of the court's jurisdiction to make ancillary orders against third parties. The sovereignty principle applies whether the underlying claim includes a proprietary claim or whether the relief sought is Mareva relief.

(3) Mareva relief depends on there being a way in which the claimant can one way or another require his claim to be satisfied out of the relevant assets. One route to consider may be third party debt procedure, but it may be that on the particular facts this procedure will not carry the claimant through to the underlying assets. For example, the asset may be a debt situated abroad, in which case the procedure will be through registration or enforcement of an English judgment abroad. Another situation is when the asset is not a debt due or accruing due. The asset may still be amenable to execution with the assistance of the appointment of a receiver, or it may be reachable through bankruptcy or winding up proceedings.

(4) The presumption is that a court will assist a judgment creditor to get paid, but third party debt relief is discretionary and this is not the only factor. Other relevant factors include the impact of a final order on non-parties, *e.g.* if the effect would be to prefer the judgment creditor over other creditors, or a real risk of a third party debtor having to pay twice. The injunction jurisdiction is a means to an end—factors which affect whether the end can be achieved also affect the granting of an injunction.

---

[45] *Kuwait Oil Tanker Co. SAK v Qabazard* [2004] 1 A.C. 300.
[46] *Société Eram Shipping Co. Ltd v Compagnie Internationale de Navigation* [2004] 1 A.C. 260 *Mackinnon v Donaldson Lufkin & Jenrette Securities Corporation* [1986] Ch. 482; *Babanaft International Co. SA v Bassatne* [1990] Ch. 13 at 44.
[47] *Bank of China v NBM LLC* [2002] 1 W.L.R. 844; *Baltic Shipping v Translink Shipping Ltd* [1995] 1 Lloyd's Rep. 673.

(3) Charging orders

A charging order provides a means by which judgment for a liquidated sum 5.007 may be executed upon an interest in land, funds in court, shares or an interest in a partnership. The procedure is very similar to that for third party debt orders. A charging order is available only after judgment.

If there is a dispute as to the beneficial ownership of the property over which the order absolute is sought, the court can direct that the issue of beneficial ownership be tried.[48]

If the order is made final, the claimant acquires a judicial charge over the asset as from the date of the interim order. The charge is realised by fresh proceedings for the sale of the asset and distribution of the proceeds.

(4) Appointment of a receiver

The court has power to appoint a receiver over any type of asset 5.008 (including, *e.g.* a claim for unliquidated damages) and even over assets situated outside the jurisdiction. The court may appoint a receiver over an asset at any stage of proceedings whether before or after judgment; the statutory power to do so by interlocutory order whenever it is just and convenient is contained in the same section as that conferring jurisdiction to grant Mareva injunctions: Supreme Court Act 1981, s.37, preserving the jurisdiction previously exercised under the Supreme Court of Judicature (Consolidation) Act 1925, s.45.

The order does not confer on the claimant any priority not enjoyed previously. The appointment of the receiver is often made for the purpose of protecting some interest or rights of the claimant in or concerning the underlying assets. The development of the Mareva jurisdiction from s.45 of the Supreme Court of Judicature (Consolidation) Act 1925 opened the way for the courts to appoint a receiver even where the claimant is not asserting rights relating to the underlying assets. Since the Supreme Court Act 1981, the courts have appointed receivers on an interlocutory basis even though the claimant does not claim any right to or in respect of the underlying assets.

(5) Summary of comparison

(1) A Mareva injunction can be obtained both before and after judg- 5.009 ment in the action. When it is obtained after judgment, it is granted as an aid to execution. A warrant of arrest *in rem* and an order

---

[48] CPR r.73.8(2)(c) and (d); *Rosseel NV v Oriental Commercial* [1991] E.G.C.S. 94; Court of Appeal (Civ Div) Transcript No.906 of 1991 (October 8, 1991).

appointing a receiver are likewise obtainable before or after judgment. Charging orders and third party debt orders, however, can be obtained only after judgment and are modes of execution.

(2) There are no restrictive rules relating to the nature of the cause of action in respect of which Mareva relief can be granted, although the claimant will not be entitled to Mareva relief if he cannot demonstrate some route by which his claim may be satisfied out of the defendant's assets. A warrant of arrest *in rem*, can be obtained only in an admiralty action *in rem*.

(3) A Mareva injunction may be granted and a receiver may be appointed in relation to assets of the defendant, wherever situated. A warrant of arrest is limited to an asset within the jurisdiction. A third party debt order may be made only against a third party who is within the jurisdiction at the time of application for the interim order or who has voluntarily submitted to the jurisdiction. With one possible exception, it is limited to debts located within the jurisdiction. In principle the sovereignty principle applies to charging orders so that, *e.g.* a charging order cannot be made on the shares of a foreign company.

(4) A Mareva injunction does not affect the defendant's proprietary interest in his assets. The claimant gains no priority over any other creditor of the defendant and no proprietary interest in or charge over the assets which are subject to the injunction. He will obtain security only if the defendant puts up security to achieve the release of the injunction. The issue of a writ *in rem* may lead in due course to the claimant obtaining security, *e.g.* by the arrest of the vessel followed by provision of security for the release of the vessel, or by the sale of the vessel *pendente lite*. Charging orders, when made final, give the claimant security. A third party debt order entitles the judgment creditor to enforce and receive payment of the debt. But it does not transfer or assign the attached debt to the judgment creditor.[49]

(5) The court may decide to vary or discharge a Mareva injunction for reasons of commercial convenience, or to enable the defendant to pay debts or even to meet moral obligations. See generally, *Iraqi Ministry of Defence v Arcepey Shipping (The Angel Bell)*.[50] The court will ensure that third parties are not unduly burdened by the granting of Mareva relief. See *e.g.* *Galaxia Maritime SA v Mineralimport/export*.[51]

This is not the position with a warrant of arrest. Indeed the arrest will be maintained notwithstanding the fact that the vessel was sold

[49] *Re Combined Weighing and Advertising Machine Company* (1890) 43 Ch.D. 99.
[50] [1981] Q.B. 65.
[51] [1982] 1 W.L.R. 539.

to a bona fide purchaser after the writ was issued but before it was served: *The Andria (now renamed The Vasso)*;[52] *The Monica S.*[53] Accordingly, a third party with no knowledge of the dispute in relation to which the vessel was arrested may find himself in the unfortunate position of having to provide security to obtain the release of his ship. The risk of arrest, however, has been treated by the courts as one of the normal incidents of the ownership of vessels and the purchaser of a vessel should be prepared to put up security if the arrest causes him substantial financial or commercial hardship. See *The Helene Roth.*[54]

If the claimant seeks the appointment of a receiver as a means of facilitating the operation of a Mareva injunction, in circumstances where the claimant claims no proprietary interest in the assets, third party rights are taken into consideration by the court in accordance with the normal principles affecting the grant or variation of Mareva relief.

(6) Third parties with notice of the Mareva injunction may not aid or assist the defendant to break the order. The same principle applies to an order appointing a receiver and a warrant of arrest.

(7) A Mareva injunction does not produce the effect that an asset is attached or seized by an officer of the court. The defendant remains in possession or with a legal right of control, albeit that he is restrained from exercising his rights to deal with the asset unless the court permits him to do so.

(8) A Mareva injunction or an order appointing a receiver can be made over almost any type of asset. Warrants of arrest, charging orders and third party debt orders apply to special types of asset only.

(9) A Mareva injunction does not result in possession of an asset being transferred. If this is to be achieved, it must be done under an ancillary order. An order appointing a receiver has the objective of putting the receiver into possession of the asset and may give him powers of management. Such an order may be made over an asset abroad, but before it has effect on third parties, the order must be recognised and given effect to by the foreign court at the place where the asset is situated.

(10) An admiralty action *in rem* is an action based on a substantive legal right in which the *res* can be arrested and sold. Mareva relief is relief granted *in personam* for the purpose of preserving assets as an interim measure.

---

[52] [1984] Q.B. 477.
[53] [1986] P. 741.
[54] [1980] Q.B. 273.

Chapter 6

The jurisdiction to grant injunctions and Anton Piller relief

When substantive proceedings on the merits of a cause of action are **6.001** properly before the English court no difficulty arises about granting injunctive relief, whether based on a proprietary claim or Mareva relief or otherwise, against a defendant.

But cases have arisen in which injunctive relief is sought in England when proceedings on the merits will have to be brought abroad. Can the English court grant injunctive relief? The problem of the scope of the jurisdiction to grant relief against foreigners is one which has come time and again before the English courts.

In *Siskina (Cargo Owners) v Distos SA (The Siskina)*[1] the cargo interests claimed damages from the defendant Panamanian shipowning company for failure to carry the cargo to Jeddah, and wrongly discharging the cargo in Cyprus. The bills of lading conferred exclusive jurisdiction on the court in Genoa. Following the discharge in Cyprus the ship set sail and sank. There were insurance proceeds payable in London to the company these apparently being the only substantial asset of the company. Could Mareva relief be granted over the insurance proceeds in London by the English court? In those days there was no equivalent to s.25 of the Civil Jurisdiction and Judgments Act 1982. So the attempt was made to bring the substantive damages claim in England with leave to serve the proceedings out of the jurisdiction based on what was then RSC Ord.11, r.1(1)(i). Because there was no proprietary claim by the cargo interests to the insurance proceeds the action did not come within the rule and this attempt failed.

It is conceivable that on the facts of *The Siskina* relief could have been **6.002** sought from the Companies Court with presentation of a winding-up petition against the Panamanian company and an application for appointment of a provisional liquidator or an injunction safeguarding the assets of the company pending winding-up. It is true that the plaintiffs did not have a judgment. But it was not necessary for them to obtain a judgment in order to have standing to present a petition to wind up the company.[2] The

---

[1] [1979] A.C. 210.
[2] *Re A Company* [1973] 1 W.L.R. 1566 at 1571, *per* Megarry J., disapproving of the statement to the contrary in *Buckley on the Companies Acts* (13th ed., 1948)—a claim for unliquidated damages was sufficient to make each of the plaintiffs a "prospective creditor . . ." within the meaning of s.224(1)(c) of the Companies Act 1948.

rule that a winding-up order would not be made founded on a disputed debt was a rule of practice which was not absolute.[3] On the evidence the only business of the company had effectively come to an end with the sinking of the ship. Given the conduct of those running the company there was every prospect that the assets of the company were about to be dealt with leaving the company as an insolvent shell. It could have been argued that it was just and equitable to wind up the company, or that it appeared to be insolvent. But this was not how the case was run, and the result of the House of Lords' decision was to emphasise the lack of a procedural platform which would enable the English court to serve proceedings out of the jurisdiction which had as their purpose the freezing of assets situated within the court's territorial jurisdiction.

In *Mercedes Benz AG v Leiduck*,[4] the plaintiff ("Mercedes") had lent US$20 million to a company incorporated in Monaco. The company had provided a promissory note to Mercedes and Mr Leiduck had added his guarantee through an *aval* endorsed on the note. Mercedes alleged that the money advanced under the loan had been misappropriated, and brought substantive proceedings in Monaco against Mr Leiduck.

Mercedes wished to obtain Mareva relief in Hong Kong against Mr Leiduck. In Hong Kong there was no equivalent to s.25 of the Civil Jurisdiction and Judgments Act 1982. Mercedes in fact purported to bring substantive claims in Hong Kong against Mr Leiduck, but in the appeal to the Privy Council there was no attempt to contend that any of the relief claimed in the writ against Mr Leiduck (which did not include any claim for an injunction)[5] fell within RSC Ord.11.[6] However, Mercedes argued that had they sought to proceed with a writ claiming a Mareva injunction they could have obtained leave to serve it out of the jurisdiction upon Mr Leiduck. They also argued that the court had power to grant a Mareva injunction against Mr Leiduck in proceedings limited to a claim for Mareva relief.

6.003   The majority of the Privy Council held that there would have been no power to allow service of proceedings claiming only Mareva relief on Mr Leiduck out of the jurisdiction, even if there had been a writ formulated in this way, and that therefore the proceedings were incapable of cure by amendment and must be set aside.[7] Mercedes argued their case on RSC

---

[3] *Re Russian and English Bank* [1932] 1 Ch. 663 (a foreign company, where the alleged creditor would otherwise be without remedy, and an immediate winding-up order was made leaving the validity of the debt to be dealt with by the liquidator); the authorities after *The Siskina* decision are: *Re Claybridge Shipping Co. SA* [1981] Com. L.R. 107, Court of Appeal (Civ Div) Transcript No.143 of 1981 (March 9, 1981) now reported at [1997] 1 B.C.L.C. 572; *Alipour v Ary* [1997] 1 W.L.R. 534 at 546A–B

[4] [1996] A.C. 284; see also L. Collins, "*The Siskina* Again: An Opportunity Missed" (1996) 112 L.Q.R. 8; D. Capper, "The Trans-jurisdictional Effects of Mareva Injunctions" (1996) 15 C.J.Q. 211 at 228–232; and S. Gee, "*Mercedes* and Mareva" (1995) 139 S.J. 1076.

[5] [1996] A.C. 284 at 297D.

[6] *ibid.*, at 296B–H.

[7] *ibid.*, at 304F–G.

Ord.11 under two heads of the rule—RSC Ord.11, r.1(1)(b)[8] and (m).[9] As for (m), the rule required that the intending plaintiff had a judgment which he wished to enforce. Mercedes did not have any judgment, so there was nothing to enforce and the rule did not apply.

As for (b), this was in the same terms as the former RSC Ord.11, r.1(1)(i) considered in *The Siskina*.[10] The majority held that this rule did not apply to Mareva relief because the injunction was not relief based on a substantive[11] right asserted by the intending plaintiff in the intended proceedings—". . . it merely ensures that once the mechanisms of enforcement are set in motion, there is something physically available on which they can work".[12] This should be contrasted with where an injunction is sought restraining a defendant dealing with assets over which the plaintiff claims a substantive right. In such a case (*e.g.* a tracing claim) the trial or other resolution of the case will decide whether the plaintiff has the claimed right, and the injunction is sought in support of that right. The majority[13] decided that an application for a Mareva injunction alone was not an action or matter which would itself decide upon and give effect to rights—there was not a 'cause of action'.[14]

The majority also criticised the reasoning in *X v Y*[15] in which service out of the jurisdiction of proceedings for an injunction under s.25 of the Civil Jurisdiction and Judgments Act 1982 had been upheld under RSC Ord.11, r.1(1)(b). They further commented adversely on part of the judgment of Staughton L.J. in *Republic of Haiti v Duvalier*[16] in which the Court of Appeal had held that a claim to interim relief under s.25 could be served out of the jurisdiction under RSC Ord.11, r.1(2) on a person domiciled in a Convention territory. Thus the majority threw great doubt on the scope of the Rules of Court which might be used for authorising service out of the jurisdiction of proceedings seeking interim relief under s.25 of the 1982 Act.

In commencing his dissenting advice, Lord Nicholls said: **6.004**

---

[8] "An injunction is sought ordering the defendant to do or to refrain from doing anything within the jurisdiction . . ."

[9] "The claim is brought to enforce any judgment or arbitral award."

[10] See Chapter 1, paras 1.022–6, above. The unsuccessful argument in *The Siskina* was that the claim to a Mareva injunction came within what was then r.1(1)(i) and that this enabled a writ to be issued and served claiming monetary relief against the one-ship company. The argument in *Mercedes* was that a claim to a Mareva injunction could be brought as the sole claim in an action for which leave could be granted for service out of the jurisdiction under the sub-rule.

[11] [996] A.C. 284 at 302A–F.

[12] *ibid.*, at 302C.

[13] Lord Nicholls in his dissenting advice considered that a Mareva injunction is an "injunction" within (b) and would have held that it was possible to have free-standing proceedings seeking Mareva relief alone.

[14] This argument is circular because a "cause of action" is something on which the plaintiff can bring an action, so whether there is a "cause of action" depended on whether Mercedes could have brought an action claiming Mareva relief alone: see, *per* Lord Nicholls at [1996] A.C. 284 at 310E–F.

[15] [1990] 1 Q.B. 220 (Anthony Diamond, Q.C.).

[16] *ibid.*, at 211.

... [Mr Leiduck's] argument comes to this: his assets are in Hong Kong, so the Monaco court cannot reach them; he is in Monaco, so the Hong Kong court cannot reach him. That cannot be right. That is not acceptable today. A person operating internationally cannot so easily defeat the judicial process. There is not a black hole into which a defendant can escape out of sight and become unreachable."[17]

The position in England and Wales has now been altered by:

(1) the coming into force of the Civil Jurisdiction and Judgments Act (Interim Relief) Order 1997;[18]

(2) amendment of the Rules of Court to introduce provisions enabling service out of the jurisdiction,[19] now to be found in CPR r.6.20(4); and

(3) the coming into force of s.44 of the Arbitration Act 1996.[20]

In summary, the position is as follows:

(1) Section 37(1) of the Supreme Court Act 1981 enables interlocutory relief, including Mareva or Anton Piller relief, to be granted in an English action in which substantive relief is claimed based on a cause of action.

(2) Even if an English action, in which the claimant claims substantive relief, is stayed the court is not bound to discharge or set aside interlocutory relief granted in the action.

(3) In respect of arbitration proceedings whether or not the seat of the arbitration is in England and Wales, Mareva or Anton Piller relief may be granted under s.44 of the Arbitration Act 1996.[21]

(4) An arbitration claim form seeking relief under s.44 may be served out of the jurisdiction with permission of the court (CPR r.62.5(1)(b)).

(5) An injunction or search order or other interim remedy may be granted under s.25 of the Civil Jurisdiction and Judgments Act 1982 in English proceedings brought for the sole purpose of seeking interim relief in relation to proceedings anywhere else in the world.

---

[17] [1996] A.C. 284 at 305B–C; for a summary of the position in England and Wales as it stood after the Privy Council decision, see L. Collins, (1996) 112 L.Q.R. 8 at 11–12: "It is no credit to a developed legal system that [the position] should be so complex and uncertain".

[18] SI 1997/302.

[19] Originally by RSC Ord.11, r.8A (giving leave to serve out of the jurisdiction proceedings seeking relief under s.25), and RSC Ord.29, r.8A (governing the procedure for applications under s.25).

[20] Section 44 applies to arbitral proceedings commenced on or after January 31, 1997.

[21] See para.6.020 below. For arbitral proceedings commenced before January 31, 1997 Mareva or Anton Piller relief may be granted under s.12(6) of the Arbitration Act 1950.

(6) Relief may be granted in contemplation of or in aid of winding-up or bankruptcy proceedings in England and Wales.

(7) If a claimant has obtained an English judgment or arbitration award or a foreign judgment or award which is valid and which is enforceable in England, freezing relief or a search order may be granted in contemplation of or in aid of such enforcement.

(8) If the intended application falls within none of the above categories, there is no jurisdiction to grant relief.

(1) Action on the merits before the English court

(i) *Jurisdiction to grant relief before proceedings are commenced or at any time afterwards in those proceedings*

In a case in which leave is required to serve the substantive proceedings out **6.005** of the jurisdiction, s.24(1)(a) of the Civil Jurisdiction and Judgments Act 1982 confers on the court jurisdiction to grant interim relief when the question of jurisdiction on the merits is in issue in the proceedings. Thus, Mareva relief is commonly granted without notice in an action against a defendant who is to be served out of the jurisdiction under the provisions of CPR Pt 6, and it is clear that the court has jurisdiction to grant Anton Piller relief against such a defendant.

Under CPR r.25.2(1) and (2), where the case is one of urgency, or it is otherwise necessary to do so in the interests of justice, an application for the grant of an injunction may be made before proceedings are commenced. Normally the applicant has to undertake to issue the claim form immediately and the claim form is served with the injunction.[22] This procedure is often used on Mareva and Anton Piller applications.[23]

(ii) *Granting Anton Piller relief in respect of premises abroad or against foreigners*

Can Anton Piller relief be granted in respect of premises outside England **6.006** and Wales? Section 7(3) of the Civil Procedure Act 1997 provides that an order under that section can provide for someone to be permitted ". . . to enter premises in England and Wales". This follows the legislative principle of only prescribing conduct within the territorial jurisdiction of the legislature.[24]

---

[22] CPR Pt 25, Practice Direction, para.4.4.
[23] Anton Piller relief can be regarded as an injunction granted under s.37 of the Supreme Court Act 1981. Alternatively, the rule is applied by analogy to such an application under the "inherent jurisdiction", see para.1.036, above.
[24] *Société Eram Shipping Co. Ltd v Compagnie Internationale de Navigation* [2004] 1 A.C. 260 at [78–80].

However, s.7 is an enabling section and the debates show that it was not intended to derogate from other powers which the court has. Prior to s.7, the court regarded itself as having the power to grant Anton Piller relief against a defendant *in personam*,[25] *i.e.* jurisdiction was exercisable by ordering the individual or entity sued to permit entry, and during the parliamentary debate assurances were given that the section would not cut down the court's jurisdiction.[26]

The principle of respecting the sovereignty of foreign states to control conduct of foreigners within their own borders has the consequence that a court will normally not make an order against a non-party foreigner for production of documents which are abroad, even though the foreigner has a presence within the jurisdiction and can be served with process here. The court exercise restraint in making orders regulating the conduct of foreigners abroad.[27] It is not an absolute rule but may be relaxed in cases of necessity. The principle concerns not whether the foreigner can be served with process, but the limits of the court's subject-matter jurisdiction.

6.007   There are exceptions. When the court properly has before it substantive proceedings on the merits against a person it can make orders against that person in respect of those proceedings including, *e.g.* an order for the transfer of land abroad, or an order for discovery.

Anton Piller relief is far more intrusive on the soil of a foreign sovereign state than an injunction and is more of an invasion of that state's sovereignty. It includes the attendance of a supervising solicitor, who is fulfilling a role on behalf of the court, not dissimilar from that which in other jurisdictions would be performed by a bailiff or court official. It is very likely to affect foreign non-parties caught up in the execution of the order. Although not a search warrant, it is very like one. It is much more than just the enforcement of an *in personam* order against a defendant.

Because Anton Piller relief is so intrusive to the foreign state's sovereignty and because of the advantages of a local court managing the procedure, normally, if such relief is to be granted at all in respect of premises abroad, it should be granted by the local court having jurisdiction over the premises in question.

6.008   The current practice is that the court should only grant Anton Piller relief against a foreigner on terms that it be suspended to give a foreign defendant the opportunity to challenge the jurisdiction of the court to entertain the proceedings on the merits. In *Altertext v Advanced Data Communications Ltd*[28] Scott J. declined as a matter of discretion to grant Anton Piller relief against a foreigner in respect of premises abroad when

---

[25] *Cook v Galliher* [1979] Ch. 439.
[26] See further Chapter 17.
[27] *Société Eram Shipping Co. Ltd v Compagnie Internationale de Navigation* [2004]; 1 A.C. 260; *Mackinnon v Donaldson Lufkin & Jenrette Securities Corporation* [1986] Ch. 482.
[28] [1985] 1 W.L.R. 457 at 463, in which Scott J. considered the decision of Goulding J. in *Protector Alarms Ltd v Maxim Alarms Ltd* [1978] F.S.R. 442.

there might well be a challenge to the jurisdiction of the court. In *Grupo Torras v Sheikh Al-Sabah*[29] Steyn L.J. said that:

". . . the reason why an Anton Piller was not appropriate in the *Altertext* case is comity and the constraints of public international law. The principle is that a state should generally refrain from demanding obedience to its sovereign authority by a foreigner in respect of his conduct outside of the jurisdiction: *Mackinnon v Donaldson, Lufkin & Jenrette Securities Corporation* [1986] Ch. 482 at p.493. An Anton Piller order is in the nature of a search and seize order, or a civil search warrant, and it may well be an affront to the dignity of the country concerned to execute it within its jurisdiction. By contrast a worldwide Mareva, in its current usual form, limits the risk of interference with foreign sovereignty because the injunction operates *in personam* against the defendant and because it restricts the effect of the injunction to persons subject to the jurisdiction of the English Court."

In deciding whether or not to make an immediately effective Anton **6.009** Piller order against a foreigner who is to be served under the provisions of CPR Pt 6, the factors to be taken into account include the following:

(1) "The moment a person is properly served under . . . [CPR Pt 6] that person, so far as the jurisdiction is concerned, is precisely in the same position as a person in this country."[30] This principle has been regarded as applying at a time when the relevant person has not yet been served but permission to serve him has been granted.[31] The fact that the relevant person may apply to the court to set aside the permission does not impeach the jurisdiction of the court in the interim.[32] However, if there are substantial doubts as to the granting of permission, this is plainly a factor to be taken into account in relation to whether or not Anton Piller relief should be granted.

(2) If the premises in question are in England, then prima facie the English court should deal with the application on its merits.

(3) If the premises in question are abroad (as was the case in *Altertext Inc. v Advanced Data Communications Ltd*[33]) then the court exercising jurisdiction at that location is normally to be the appropriate court to which an application should be made. In *Denilauler v SNC Couchet Frères*,[34] the European Court of Justice said of the Brussels Convention[35]:

---

[29] Court of Appeal (Civ Div) Transcript No.159 of 1994 (February 16, 1994) at pp. 11–12 of the transcript.
[30] *Re Liddell's Settlement Trusts* [1936] Ch. 365 at 374, *per* Romer L.J.
[31] *Republic of Haiti v Duvalier* [1990] 1 Q.B. 202 at 216, a case in which the *ex parte* relief granted against the defendants included mandatory disclosure orders (see at 208–210 and para.(4) of the order made by Knox J. on June 3, 1988).
[32] Civil Jurisdiction and Judgments Act 1982, s.24; see Appendix 2.
[33] [1985] 1 W.L.R. 457.
[34] [1980] E.C.R. 1555.
[35] *ibid.*, at 1570.

The courts of the place or, in any event, of the contracting state, where the assets subject to the measures sought are located, are those best able to assess the circumstances which may lead to the grant or refusal of the measures sought or to the laying down of procedures and conditions which the plaintiff must observe in order to guarantee the provisional and protective character of the measures ordered. The Convention has taken account of these requirements by providing in Article 24 that application may be made to the courts of a contracting state for such provisional, including protective, measures as may be available under the law of that state, even if, under the Convention, the courts of another contracting state have jurisdiction as to the substance of the matter.

This is particularly true of complex relief such as Anton Piller relief, which is liable to give rise to local difficulties including questions of local custom and practice, as well as those of language.

(4) Since an Anton Piller order is granted without notice it will not be capable of recognition and enforcement by the courts of another Member State under Council Regulation 44/2001, even if made in proceedings falling within Art.1 of the Regulation, *i.e.* proceedings in civil and commercial matters.[36] This is because it is only after the defendant has had an opportunity to resist an order that it is capable of qualifying for enforcement and recognition. In the context of premises situated in a Member State, it is to be expected that an application for *ex parte* Anton Piller relief would ordinarily have to be made to the courts of that state pursuant to Art.31 of the Regulation (Art.24 of the Brussels or Lugano Convention). For premises situated in a non-Member State, in principle it is similarly to be expected that the application will ordinarily be made to the courts of that state.

(5) If the premises in question are abroad, the circumstances of the case may exceptionally make it of urgent necessity for the English court to deal with the application for relief. In the analogous context of Mareva relief, the English courts may, in the exercise of their discretion, grant a Mareva injunction over assets abroad even though the courts having jurisdiction at the place where the assets are located might themselves have dealt with the application. Thus in *Republic of Haiti v Duvalier*,[37] the Court of Appeal upheld Mareva relief which had been granted over assets abroad despite the principle that, in general, the courts having jurisdiction at the

---

[36] *EMI Records Ltd v Modern Music Karl-Ulrich Walterbach GmbH* [1992] Q.B. 115; *Denilauler v SNC Couchet Frères* [1980] E.C.R. 1553; *Babanaft Co. SA v Bassatne* [1990] Ch. 13 at 31–32, *per* Kerr L.J.
[37] [1990] 1 Q.B. 202 at 216.

location of the assets are those "best able to assess the circumstances". The reason was that in that case it was not known at the time of the *ex parte* application in what jurisdiction or jurisdictions the assets might be found. It is thought that in certain highly exceptional circumstances it might be appropriate for the English court to grant *ex parte* Anton Piller relief in respect of premises abroad. To justify the granting of such relief the English court ought to satisfy itself that it is the appropriate tribunal to deal with the application notwithstanding the considerations set out in (3) above, which have particular force in the context of the granting of mandatory relief which has as its objective the entry and search of premises. If relief is granted, then it should be directed solely to the defendant and expressed not to have an effect on third parties. This is because the English court's sole justification for granting such relief is that it has jurisdiction over the defendant in respect of the claim on the merits. In addition, plainly the English court should neither authorise nor require to be carried out acts which may be illegal at the location in question. It is thought that any Anton Piller relief granted should contain a specific provision to this effect, and should be granted only on the claimant's undertaking to comply with the law in force at the relevant location.

(iii) When the English court becomes "seised" with proceedings in which interim relief has been granted

Does the granting of a Mareva injunction or other interim relief by the **6.010** court in England affect when it becomes "seised" with an action for the purposes of applying Art.27 of Council Regulation 44/2001[38] or Art.21 of the Brussels (which still applies to Denmark) or the Lugano Convention? Often proceedings can be brought in more than one contracting state. Article 27 adopts a rigid rule that whichever court becomes "the court first seised" is the court which will determine the merits of the substantive dispute between the parties. The question has to be decided according to the rules of the national law of each of the courts which are said to have become "first seised" and considering which first became definitively pending.[39] In England the court becomes "seised" of proceedings for the purposes of Art.27 when the claim form or other originating process is served on the defendant: *Dresser UK Ltd v Falcongate Freight Management Ltd.*[40] It makes no difference that at an earlier stage the English court has granted a Mareva injunction or other interim relief against the defendant: *Neste Chemicals SA v DK Line SA (The Sargasso).*[41] When the court grants

---

[38] Of December 22, 2000 on jurisdiction and the recognition and enforcement of judgments in civil and commercial matters (O.J. No.L012, January 16, 2001, pp.1–23).
[39] *Zelger v Salinitri (No.2)* [1984] E.C.R. 2397; *Gabisch Maschinenfabrik KG v Palumbo* [1987] E.C.R. 4861 at 4875; *Grupo Torras SA v Al-Sabah* [1996] 1 Lloyd's Rep. 7.
[40] [1992] Q.B. 502.
[41] [1994] 2 Lloyd's Rep. 6.

"provisional measures" it is exercising its jurisdiction to do so, which is separate and distinct from its jurisdiction over the substantive merits of the case.[42] When it grants interim relief under s.25 of the Civil Jurisdiction and Judgments Act 1982 it is doing so in free-standing proceedings in which it has no jurisdiction over the substantive merits of the claimant's claim: *Channel Tunnel Group Ltd v Balfour Beatty Construction Ltd.*[43] Thus the granting of Mareva or Anton Piller relief does not affect the rule that the English court does not become "seised" with the merits of the claim within Art.27 until the claim form is served.

(iv) Compliance with disclosure orders pending application to set aside the interim relief

6.011   In *Grupo Torras v Sheikh Al-Sabah,*[44] it was argued that in a case where a challenge to the jurisdiction of the court was pending, no order for disclosure of information about assets should be made save exceptionally. The Court of Appeal rejected the suggested principle and distinguished *Altertext* on the grounds that it related to Anton Piller orders which were described as draconian and invasive in their effect, and at the extremity of the court's jurisdiction. In a case which is otherwise suitable for worldwide Mareva relief together with a disclosure order, it is not normally right to decline to grant the relief pending resolution of a challenge to the jurisdiction, because of the risk of rendering the relief useless.[45] Similarly in *Federal Republic of Nigeria v Union Bank of Nigeria*[46] Laddie J. declined to stay disclosure orders made in a very substantial fraud claim.

In *Motorola Credit Corporation v Cem Cegiz Uzan*[47] the claim was for more than US$2 billion and the defendants, who were alleged to have obtained funds by fraud from the claimant, had a pending application to the Commercial Court to have discharged worldwide freezing relief which had been granted against them. They contended that pending that application, the disclosure orders, including the requirement to provide affidavits, should be stayed. If a stay was not granted the effect would be that the disclosure orders would have to be complied with before the defendants were heard on their application to set them aside. It is, of course, possible for a court to order that a mandatory interim order for disclosure of information is to have effect before a defendant can be heard on a discharge application. This is so with Anton Piller relief. It gives the claimant the information before the defendant is heard on whether the

---

[42] *Neste Chemicals SA v DK Line SA (The Sargasso)* [1994] 2 Lloyd's Rep. 6 at 11.
[43] [1993] A.C. 334 at 365.
[44] Court of Appeal (Civ Div) Transcript No.159 of 1994 (February 16, 1994).
[45] The court has power to grant relief pending a challenge to its jurisdiction and can maintain relief in place pending an appeal concerning its jurisdiction; see the Civil Jurisdiction and Judgments Act 1982, s.24.
[46] Unreported, October 18, 2001; Transcript No. WL 1422955.
[47] [2002] 2 All E.R. (Comm) 945; [2002] EWCA Civ 989. D2 and D3 succeeded on the discharge applications see [2004] 1 W.L.R. 113.

claimant should have it. But this involves an infringement of the principle *audi alterem partem* which is one of basic justice. This is because once the disclosure is given it cannot be reversed.

The answer is that although this principle is very important it is not absolute. The fundamental principle is that whichever course is adopted by the court it should carry the lower risk of injustice if it should turn out to be wrong.[48] The granting of a stay in that case would have rendered the freezing relief potentially toothless, the risk being particularly high given the finding in the United States after a six-day hearing with witnesses that "every preliminary indication is that the defendants . . . engaged in repeated acts of fraud . . .". Putting the information into an envelope to await the outcome of the discharge application would still have run this risk.

In these circumstances the majority of the Court of Appeal followed the **6.012** approach taken in *Grupo Torras v Sheikh Al-Sabah*, above, and declined to interfere with the judge's exercise of discretion. Sedley L.J. held that the judge had asked himself the wrong question—namely whether, accepting that there was freezing relief in place it was right to uncouple the disclosure order from the freezing relief? This placed the burden of persuasion on the defendants, when the right question was whether the claimant could justify the immediate disclosure orders given the imminence of the discharge applications. However, given the decision of the majority he did not answer that question.

(v) Reciprocal recognition and enforcement a provisional or interim order made by the courts of Member States

The recognition and enforcement provisions in Chap. III of Regulation **6.013** 44/2001 and Title III to the Brussels Convention are important for the purposes of the recognition and enforcement of (1) English orders by another Member State and (2) orders made in another Member State by the English courts.

In relation to (1) this may be of crucial importance to whether an English order will prove to be effective and could be important to the exercise of discretion on whether to make an order. As for (2), a judgment made in another Member State is to be recognised and enforced in England subject to the provisions of Chap. III and this is capable of applying to a provisional or interim order made in another Member State.

(vi) Obtaining an English order to be enforced in another Member State

Orders made without notice for Mareva or Anton Piller relief or any other **6.014** type of relief are outside Chap. III of Regulation 44/2001 and Title III of the Brussels Convention (which applies to Denmark) and the Lugano

---

[48] *Films Rover Ltd v Cannon Film Sales Ltd* [1987] 1 W.L.R. 670 at 680.

Convention. Furthermore, they are not brought within by serving the order obtained *ex parte* on the defendant and giving him an opportunity to discharge it.[49]

If the claimant wishes to obtain an order in England which will be enforced in another Member State, he should serve the defendant with the claim form and should serve him with a notice of application seeking the interim relief, and sufficient time should be allowed to the defendant to enable him to contest the application for relief. If this is done, then any order made on the hearing of the application, including a provisional or interim order (*e.g.* an order freezing assets), will fall within Art.32 of Regulation 44/2001 and is capable of being recognised and enforced. This is because there is no requirement that a judgment or order be "final and conclusive".

This is impractical for enforcement of an Anton Piller order because it is of the essence of the procedure that the relief is sought without notice. But the procedure can be used after the granting of an *ex parte* Mareva injunction in order to seek a new injunction *inter partes*, albeit an injunction substantially in similar terms to the original injunction. Article 34(2) of Regulation 44/2001 provides that:

"ARTICLE 34

A judgment shall not be recognised:
. . .
    2. where it was given in default of appearance, if the defendant was not served with the document which instituted the proceedings or with an equivalent document in sufficient time and in such a way as to enable him to arrange for his defence, unless the defendant failed to commence proceedings to challenge the judgment when it was possible for him to do so;
. . ."

This ensures that a judgment or order[50] is not recognised or enforced in a Member State if the defendant has not been served with the relevant documents and has had an opportunity of defending himself before the English court.[51] But there is nothing to prevent there being a new injunction in the same terms as the earlier injunction, which can be recognised and enforced.

---

[49] *EMI Records v Modern Music GmbH* [1992] Q.B. 115 at 121 rejecting the submission that an order made *ex parte is* capable of becoming a registrable order *ex post facto*, see also *Minalmet GmbH v Brandeis Ltd* [1992] E.C.R. 1–5661. *TSN Kunststoffrecycling GmbH v Jurgens* [2002] 1 W.L.R. 2459 (Art.27(2) of the Brussels Convention was a limited exception to freedom of movement of judgments between contracting states and did not apply when the defendant had had in fact sufficient time to defend himself in advance of and against a default judgment being entered against him).
[50] See Regulation 44/2001, Art.32.
[51] *Hendrikman v Magenta Druck* [1997] Q.B. 426, ECJ.

In practice, when the application comes back *inter partes* before the **6.015** court, a defendant may say that he wishes to take a number of points on the application and he wants further time to put in evidence. In such circumstances the court can and usually will give directions and grant a temporary injunction *inter partes*, pending further hearing of the application. Is such an injunction capable of recognition and enforcement under Chap. III? Such an injunction is not an *ex parte* order; nor is it an order made "in default of appearance": the defendant was represented in court. Also, the claim form and the application notice have been served on him. Thus no difficulty arises under the commencing words of Art.34(2) which concern an order made "in default of appearance". The mere fact that the order is in its nature provisional or interim and so liable to be varied or discharged does not have the consequence that it should not be recognised or enforced in the meantime. This is so on the words of the Regulation and because the defendant has had the opportunity to present his case on whether the order should be made, albeit as a temporary order liable to be discharged or varied after further evidence or argument.

If the defendant does not appear before the court on the application, provided that he was given sufficient time to be represented there and to argue about whether a temporary order ought to be made, then an order made on the application should be capable of recognition and be enforceable. This is so even though the defendant is given an opportunity under the order to apply for its discharge or variation.

(vii) Enforcement in England of an interim order made in another Member State

This is likely to be required when the defendant is physically present, or he **6.016** has assets, within the jurisdiction. Under Regulation 44/2001:

"ARTICLE 33

1. A judgment given in a Member State shall be recognised in the other Member States without any special procedure being required.
. . ."

This applies regardless of whether the defendant is domiciled in a Member State. It includes orders which are interim or provisional and regardless of whether they require payment of money. Such orders including injunctions are treated in the same way as other judgments or orders including a final money judgment.[52] A foreign order is not be

---

[52] See *Dicey and Morris on Conflict of Laws* (13th ed., 1999) Vol. 1, r.48, p.542 and following for a full account of recognition and enforcement.

recognised if such recognition would be "manifestly contrary to [English] public policy",[53] which is to be interpreted narrowly, or it comes within Art.34(2) (see above), or it is "irreconcilable" with an English decision or earlier decision made by the courts of another Member State:

"ARTICLE 34

A judgment shall not be recognised:
. . .
3. if it is irreconcilable with a judgment given in a dispute between the same parties in the Member State in which recognition is sought;
4. if it is irreconcilable with an earlier judgment given in another Member State or in a third State involving the same cause of action and between the same parties, provided that the earlier judgment fulfils the conditions necessary for its recognition in the Member State addressed."

6.017   What is meant by "irreconcilable"? In *Italian Leather SpA v WECO Polstermöbel GmbH & Co*[54] the claimant supplier sought an injunction in Germany against the defendant distributor from marketing goods under a particular brand name. This was refused by the German court but subsequently was granted by the Italian court which had jurisdiction over the substantive dispute under a jurisdiction clause in the distribution agreement. The claimant sought from the German court an order for enforcement of the Italian interim order. The judgments of the Italian court and the German court on the applications for interim relief were "irreconcilable" within Art.27(3) of the Brussels Convention (now Art.34(3) of Regulation 44/2001) because their "legal consequences" were "mutually exclusive".[55] The German court had decided that the distributor was to be free to use the brand name and the Italian court had decided the opposite. In consequence it was mandatory under that article for the German court to refuse to recognise or enforce the Italian interim order. *Italian Leather SpA* concerned identical applications which were made in Germany and then Italy with opposite outcomes.

6.018   Article 51 of Regulation 44/2001 provides:

"No security, bond or deposit, however described, shall be required of a party who in one Member State applies for enforcement of a judgment given in another Member State on the ground that he is a foreign national or that he is not domiciled or resident in the State in which enforcement is sought."

---

[53] Regulation 44/2001, Art.34(1)
[54] [2002] E.C.R. I–04995.
[55] See also *Hoffmann v Krieg* [1988] E.C.R. 645.

Under Art.38 of Regulation 44/2001 it is mandatory for the foreign order to be enforced in England provided that the requirements of the Convention are met. The intention is that the foreign order should have exactly the same effect in England as it does in the Member State whose courts made the order. Therefore there is no route for the English court to impose on the applicant a requirement to furnish a cross-undertaking in damages. That is a matter to be dealt with by the foreign court when deciding what interim order to make. The principle is that the purpose of the English order is to give full effect to the foreign order, and Art.36 prohibits any review of it as to its substance.

(2) If an action on the merits is stayed

Once there is an action on the merits before the English court, there is **6.019** jurisdiction to make orders under s.37 of the Supreme Court Act 1981. This jurisdiction exists regardless of whether the action is stayed. This is so even though it is mandatory to stay the action under s.9 of the Arbitration Act 1996.

(i) Supreme Court Act 1981, s.37

In *Channel Tunnel Group Ltd v Balfour Beatty Construction Ltd*,[56] the **6.020** claimant sought an injunction restraining the defendant builders from suspending work on the Channel Tunnel. Under the building contract any disputes had first to be submitted to a panel of three experts. There was then provision for arbitration, with the seat of the arbitration to be in Brussels.

The House of Lords held that the action should be stayed so that the parties could proceed through their agreed dispute resolution procedure. It was held that a stay could be granted under the inherent jurisdiction to enable the dispute to go to the panel of experts,[57] but that also s.1 of the Arbitration Act 1975 applied.[58]

The plaintiffs sought interim relief preventing suspension of the work under s.12(6) of the Arbitration Act 1950. However, that section did not apply to a foreign arbitration.[59]

---

[56] [1993] A.C. 334.
[57] Under the dispute resolution clause the panel were to act as experts and not arbitrators.
[58] If the case had fallen to be decided under the Arbitration Act 1996, then similarly to the position under s.1 of the 1975 Act, an application could have been made under s.9(2) of the 1996 Act for a stay ". . . notwithstanding that the matter is to be referred to arbitration only after the exhaustion of other dispute resolution procedures".
[59] Section 44 of the Arbitration Act 1996, which includes the power to grant injunctions, applies in relation to arbitral proceedings regardless of whether the seat of the arbitration is abroad or has been designated or determined: see s.2(3) of the 1996 Act. So if the case had arisen under the 1996 Act there would have been power to grant the injunction sought under s.44.

6.021   Nevertheless, the House of Lords held that there was still power to grant an injunction in the English action notwithstanding the stay, and that there was no inconsistency between granting the stay and the application for the injunction. This was because the injunction would simply be a holding order to govern the interim position pending resolution of the merits by the arbitrators.

However, as a matter of discretion, it was not appropriate to grant the relief sought. One of the matters relevant on discretion was that it was the courts having jurisdiction at the seat of the arbitration which were the natural forum for deciding whether interim relief should be granted. The onus was on the plaintiff to prove that for whatever reason it was appropriate for the English court to grant interim relief rather than leaving the matter to the local court.[60]

Accordingly, in an action brought on the merits in England, there is jurisdiction to continue or grant freezing relief or other interlocutory relief such as the appointment of a receiver,[61] although the merits of the underlying cause of action are to be resolved in a foreign court or by arbitration. This is not novel. Even prior to the Judicature Acts, the High Court of Chancery exercised a jurisdiction consisting of granting interim relief whilst the substantive merits of a dispute were to be resolved in another forum, including in a foreign court.[62]

6.022   The court has jurisdiction to try the merits, but by virtue of the stay (whether discretionary or mandatory) declines to do so. The granting of interim relief does not involve adjudicating on the merits of the substantive claim. The relief is granted pending resolution of the merits by the foreign court or arbitration tribunal. Thus the relief is not inconsistent with the "merits" being decided in due course by the foreign court or arbitrators, and is not inconsistent with the granting of the stay.[63]

---

[60] "If the appellants had wished to say that the Belgian court would have been unable or unwilling to grant relief, and that the English court is the only avenue of recourse, it was for them to prove it . . .", *per* Lord Mustill [1993] A.C. 334 at 368D, cp. s.2(3) of the Arbitration Act 1996 which would produce the same result under that Act.

[61] *Law v Garrett (1878)* 8 Ch.D. 26 at 38; *Pini v Roncoroni* [1892] 1 Ch. 633 (receivers and managers appointed over partnership business with otherwise a stay of proceedings for the dispute to go to arbitration); *Companie du Sénégal v Woods* (1883) 53 L.J. (Ch) 166 (receiver appointed and action stayed); *Machin v Bennett* [1900] W.N. 146 (action stayed without prejudice to future application for appointment of a receiver).

[62] *Department of Social Security v Butler* [1995] 1 W.L.R. 1528; *Daniell's Practice of the High Court of Chancery* (5th ed., 1871), Vol. II, pp. 1572–1574; *Transatlantic Company v Pietroni* (1860) Johns 604. The pre-Judicature Act jurisdiction in Chancery is also referred to by Saville L.J. in *Balkanbank v Taher (No.2)* [1995] 1 W.L.R. 1067 at 1075F—G: "One of the chief features of equity was that it did provide 'ancillary relief' jurisdiction in respect of actions where the 'merits' jurisdiction lay in the common law courts."

[63] There is a distinction between preserving assets for enforcement of an award or judgment, and resolution of the substantive merits of the claim: *The Rena K* [1979] Q.B. 377; *Law v Garrett* (1878) 8 Ch.D. 26 at 38; *Marazura Navegacion SA v Oceanus Mutual* [1977] 1 Lloyd's Rep. 283; *Sanko Steamship v DC Commodities* [1980] W.A.R. 51 (Western Australia); *Petromin SA v Secnar Marine Ltd* [1995] 1 Lloyd's Rep. 603 at 613; *Banque Cantonale v Waterlily* [1997] 2 Lloyd's Rep. 347 at 357.

Where a stay is granted, the fact that the merits are to be resolved by a foreign court[64] or a foreign arbitration tribunal[65] is a relevant matter to be taken into account in exercising the discretion. The discretion becomes similar to that to be exercised in a case under s.25 of the Civil Jurisdiction and Judgments Act 1982 in that the English court is not the court deciding the merits and is acting in a supportive way to that court. Freezing relief can still be maintained on a worldwide basis[66] notwithstanding the stay.

Under s.34 of the Civil Jurisdiction and Judgments Act 1982, a judgment in a foreign court which is enforceable and capable of recognition in England precludes the claimant from suing in England on the underlying cause of action. However, the fact that a foreign judgment would result in the English action becoming moribund does not prevent the court from granting interlocutory relief in the English action in the meantime.[67]

Attempts were made to obtain leave to serve out of the jurisdiction **6.023** under the former RSC Ord.11 for the purpose of seeking interlocutory relief in England, albeit that the merits of the underlying cause of action should be tried out by a foreign court.[68] It was suggested in those cases that leave could be granted under RSC Ord.11 and then the action could be stayed. Those attempts were unsuccessful. With the expansion in the availability of s.25 of the Civil Jurisdiction and Judgments Act 1982 there was no reason to use CPR 6.20 as a platform to enable interim relief to be granted in cases in which the merits should be tried out abroad.

Cases in which there is an arbitration clause are different in that a defendant has a choice whether to seek a stay and the application for a stay can only be made after the defendant has acknowledged service.[69] Accordingly, when there is an arbitration clause, this does not prevent the claimant obtaining permission to serve out of the jurisdiction and freezing relief in the action.[70]

(ii) Attaching terms to a stay

In a case in which it is mandatory by statute to grant a stay the court **6.024** cannot attach conditions to the stay in the absence of statutory provisions allowing it to do so.[71] This is because the stay cannot be refused or lifted if the defendant does not comply with the terms. Where a statute compels a

---

[64] *Phonogram Ltd v Def American Inc.*, *The Times*, October 7, 1994, considering *Channel Tunnel Group Ltd v Balfour Beatty Construction Ltd*, above; *Telesystem International Wireless Incorporated v CVC/Opportunity Equity Partners L.D.* [2002] C.I.L.R. Note 22.
[65] In effect the English court would be exercising a jurisdiction similar to that under s.44 of the Arbitration Act 1996.
[66] *Jeanette Walsh v Deloitte & Touche Inc.*, [2002] L.R.C. 545 at [22] (Privy Council) referring to *Crédit Suisse Fides Trust SA v Cuoghi* [1998] Q.B. 818.
[67] *House of Spring Garden v Waite* [1984] F.S.R. 277.
[68] *Baidini v Baidini* [1987] F.L.R. 463; *A/S D/S Svendborg v Maxim Brand*, Court of Appeal (Civ Div) Transcript No.39 of 1989 (January 23, 1989).
[69] Arbitration Act 1996, s.9(3).
[70] See also *Channel Tunnel Group Ltd v Balfour Beatty* [1993] A.C. 334 at 363A–D.
[71] *The Rena K* [1979] Q.B. 377 at 400; *The World Star* [1986] 2 Lloyd's Rep. 274.

particular solution there is no room for any inherent jurisdiction to attach terms.[72] In a case in which it is discretionary whether to grant a stay, the court can attach conditions to the stay. Also, in both cases, there remains the jurisdiction under s.37.

If a stay is to be granted on discretionary grounds (*e.g.* because of the existence of a foreign jurisdiction clause or on the grounds of *forum non conveniens*), then the stay may be granted subject to conditions and it may be that the court would grant the stay only if it is satisfied that the claimant's position in relation to the Mareva or other interim relief will be adequately protected. In the context of granting a stay on the grounds of *forum non conveniens*, in *Spiliada Maritime Corporation v Consulex*,[73] Lord Goff referred to the analogous situation in which security had been obtained for the plaintiff by commencing proceedings on the merits in England, *e.g.* by means of threatening or effecting the arrest of a vessel in admiralty proceedings *in rem*,[74] and said that:

> "It would not, I think, normally be wrong to allow a plaintiff to keep the benefit of security obtained by commencing proceedings, while at the same time granting a stay of proceedings in this country to enable the action to proceed in the appropriate forum. Such a conclusion is, I understand, consistent with the manner in which the process of *saise conservatoire* is applied in civil law countries; and cf s.26 of the Civil Jurisdiction and Judgments Act 1982, now happily in force."

6.025   Section 26 of the Civil Jurisdiction and Judgments Act 1982, as amended by the Arbitration Act 1996, and s.11 of the Arbitration Act 1996 (which replaced part of what was s.26) enables the court, notwithstanding that an admiralty action *in rem* is stayed or dismissed so that the claim can be adjudicated upon either in arbitration or by a court outside the jurisdiction, to retain the *res* as security, or to order that the stay or dismissal is conditional upon the provision of security.[75] Even before s.26 came into force, in cases where a stay was being granted as a matter of *discretion* (*e.g.* because of the existence of a foreign jurisdiction clause), the court could and usually did make the granting of the stay in an admiralty action *in rem*

---

[72] *Crawford v Financial Services Institutions Ltd* [2003] 1 W.L.R. 2147.

[73] [1987] A.C. 460 at 483.

[74] Usually this will result in the provision of a guarantee either to forestall such an arrest or to procure release of the vessel. If security is not provided by way of a guarantee, nevertheless, by invoking the admiralty jurisdiction of the court by commencing an action *in rem*, the claimant does obtain the status of secured creditor, at least for certain purposes: *Re Aro Co. Ltd* [1980] Ch. 196 at 209, in which leave was granted to the claimant to continue with admiralty proceedings *in rem* against a ship and *in personam* against the owner of the ship, which was a company in compulsory liquidation, under the statutory provision now contained in s.130(2) of the Insolvency Act 1986.

[75] For the difficulties under the law as it stood in relation to retaining security in an action *in rem* which was subject to a mandatory stay under s.1 of the Arbitration Act 1975, prior to s.26 of the Civil Jurisdiction and Judgments Act 1982 coming into force, see *The Rena K* [1979] Q.B. 377 at 396–401; *The Bazias 3* [1993] Q.B. 673 at 680–682.

conditional upon the provision of alternative security.[76] If the dismissal or the stay of the action *in rem* is mandatory,[77] then under these sections the court will retain the res under arrest by refusing to release it until security is provided.[78]

(3) Arbitration applications: Arbitration Act 1996, s.44

Section 44 of the Arbitration Act 1996 confers power on the court to make **6.026** orders in support of arbitral proceedings. That section replaces what was s.12(6) of the Arbitration Act 1950, making a number of changes to the old law.

If the arbitral proceedings were commenced before January 31, 1997, then s.12(6) and the "old law" continue to apply.[79] But if the arbitral proceedings were not commenced before that date, the new law including s.44 applies.

(i) The "old law"—Arbitration Act 1950, s.12(6); arbitral proceedings commenced before January 31, 1997

A Mareva injunction may be granted by the High Court on the application **6.027** of a party to an arbitration which is taking place[80] within the jurisdiction and which was commenced before January 31, 1997. The power is derived from a combination of s.37(3) of the Supreme Court Act 1981 and s.12(6) of the Arbitration Act 1950. Section 12(6) provides as follows:

> "The High Court shall have, for the purpose of and in relation to a reference, the same power of making orders in respect of:
> . . .
> (e) the preservation, interim custody or sale of any goods which are the subject matter of the reference;
> (f) securing the amount in the reference;
> (h) interim injunctions or the appointment of a receiver; as it has for the purpose of and in relation to an action or matter in the High Court."

---

[76] *The Rena K* [1979] Q.B. 377 at 398; and *The El Amria* [1981] 2 Lloyd's Rep. 119 at 123–124 and 128.

[77] For example, under Art.23 or 27 of Regulation 44/2001 or under s.9 of the Arbitration Act 1996.

[78] *The Bazias 3* [1993] Q.B. 673 at 682; CPR r.61.8(4).

[79] Arbitration Act 1996 (Commencement No.1) Order 1996 (SI 1996/3146), art.4 and Sch.2, para.2(c); the "old law" is defined in Sch.2, para.1(c). The "old law" also applies to arbitration applications commenced or made before January 31, 1997.

[80] Section 12(6) of the Arbitration Act 1950 did not apply to foreign arbitrations: *Channel Tunnel Group Ltd v Balfour Beatty Construction Ltd* [1993] A.C. 334 at 360.

There is jurisdiction under CPR r.62.16[81] to grant permission to serve out of the jurisdiction an arbitration claim form seeking relief under s.12(6) of the 1950 Act and any order made on the application. RSC Ord.73, r.29 only authorised the granting of leave to serve another party to the arbitration. It did not authorise leave being given to serve a third party outside the jurisdiction.[82] So, *e.g.* if it was sought to obtain an injunction against a third party in connection with matters which were the subject of an arbitration, RSC Ord.73, r.29 did not authorise service out of the jurisdiction of proceedings against the third party. The reasoning in *Unicargo v Flotec Maritime S de RL and Cienvik Shipping Co.* applies equally to CPR r.62.16. That rule is concerned with an application for relief against another party to the arbitration proceedings, either within the jurisdiction or of which the curial law is English law. That other party will be a party to the arbitration agreement and therefore will have consented to arbitration proceedings within the jurisdiction, or agreed to English law as the curial law. His agreement makes it appropriate prima facie for the English court to entertain the application against him, and is relevant to the exercise of discretion under CPR r.62.16(1) as to whether permission should be granted, because the arbitration agreement precludes the claimant from pursuing his substantive claim elsewhere.[83] To assert jurisdiction to control by injunction the conduct of a foreigner, which is not a party to the arbitration agreement or the arbitration, outside the territorial jurisdiction of the court is to assert an exorbitant jurisdiction inconsistent with respect for the sovereignty of foreign states.[84]

6.028   A Mareva injunction obtained in aid of arbitration proceedings is usually granted until a specified period after the final award is made. The successful claimant can then make an application for the extension of the injunction. The court may grant a Mareva injunction in aid of the enforcement and subsequent execution of an English arbitration award in exactly the same way as for a judgment; the only difference is that an English arbitration award must be converted into a judgment before it can be executed, and for this reason it may take longer to enforce an arbitration award than a judgment in an action. The successful party has two courses; he can bring an action in the High Court founded on the award (which proceeds in the normal way), or he can apply to the court for an order for summary relief under s.26 of the Arbitration Act 1950. The latter course is speedy and cost-effective, but is unsuitable for cases in which proceedings to set aside are pending, or where the respondent is seeking to object to the validity of the award.[85]

---

[81] Formerly RSC Ord. 73, r.29, which had replaced RSC Ord.73, r.7(1).
[82] *Unicargo v Flotec Maritime S de RL and Cienvik Shipping Co.* [1996] 2 Lloyd's Rep. 395; see also *Tate & Lyle v Cia Usina Bulhoes and Cargill Inc.* [1997] 1 Lloyd's Rep. 355 at 357, per Hobhouse L.J. (*obiter*).
[83] *Mayer Newman and Co. Ltd v Al Ferro Commodities Corporation SA* [1990] 2 Lloyd's Rep. 290 at 293.
[84] *Société Eram Shipping Co. Ltd v Compagnie International de Navigation* [2004] 1 A.C. 260.
[85] *Middlemiss & Gould v Hartlepool Corporation* [1972] 1 W.L.R. 1643.

Where the claimant has been unsuccessful in the arbitration but still wishes to appeal to the High Court, it is thought that the court still has jurisdiction to continue relief under s.12(6) of the Arbitration Act 1950 pending the outcome of the appeal. Thus, in the High Court there is jurisdiction to grant or continue a Mareva injunction pending the outcome of an appeal to the Court of Appeal.[86] A Mareva injunction is an "interim injunction",[87] and it is considered that the granting of the relief is made "in relation to a reference", namely the reference in which the arbitration award has been made, which is subject to challenge on appeal and may be varied or set aside.

If the respondent to an arbitration has unsuccessfully defended the arbitration, then Mareva relief can be granted or continued by the court in aid of proceedings to enforce the award. If the unsuccessful respondent seeks leave to appeal, the court has power to impose conditions on the granting of leave to appeal, and in suitable cases leave can be granted on terms that the amount in dispute is paid into court or otherwise secured.

Similarly, if the unsuccessful party to an award seeks to have it set aside **6.029** for misconduct, the court is empowered under s.23(3) of the Arbitration Act 1950 to order that the amount of the award be paid into court or otherwise secured pending the determination of the application. This applies only where the challenger wishes to have the award set aside, and not where he merely seeks to have it remitted.

Scott v Avery arbitration clauses are commonly found in certain standard form contracts. There are two distinct types, namely:

(1) a clause providing that no action shall be brought until an arbitration has been conducted and an award made; and

(2) a clause providing that the only obligation of the defendant shall be to pay such sum as the arbitrator shall award.

Scott v Avery clauses have long been accepted as valid and effective. A *Scott v Avery* clause postpones accrual to the claimant of a cause of action which can be pursued in court proceedings. If a claimant brings court proceedings by writ before obtaining an arbitration award, then he has no cause of action.

In Australia it had been decided by the Supreme Court of New South **6.030** Wales[88] that Mareva relief could be granted, notwithstanding that the plaintiff had no existing cause of action, because of the clause. In England,

---

[86] *Erinford Properties Ltd v Cheshire County Council* [1974] Ch. 261 at 262–267; *Orion Property Trust Ltd v Du Cane Court Ltd* [1962] 1 W.L.R. 1085. There is also jurisdiction in the court of first instance to grant a stay pending appeal of an injunction granted as final relief: *El Du Pont de Nemours & Co. v Enka BV* [1988] R.F.C. 497, which is similar in that the court was granting interim relief after trial to preserve the position pending appeal.

[87] *Orwell Steel (Erection and Fabrication) v Asphalt and Tarmac (UK)* [1984] 1 W.L.R. 1097; *Siskina v Distos SA (The Siskina)* [1979] 2 A.C. 210.

[88] *Construction Engineering (Australia) Pty Ltd v Tamber* [1984] 1 N.S.W.L.R. 274.

under s.12(6) of the Arbitration Act 1950 or s.44(1) of the Arbitration Act 1996, the court has power to grant a Mareva injunction in relation to a claim advanced in arbitration under a *Scott v Avery* clause. Depending on its precise wording, the clause may also have the effect of precluding either party from bringing any foreign legal proceedings at all, including proceedings seeking security, in relation to the claim pending the making of the award, as in *Mantovani v Carapelli*,[89] distinguishing *Marazura Navegacion SA v Oceanus Mutual*.[90]

In *Mantovani v Carapelli*, damages were awarded when proceedings were brought in Italy for the purpose of obtaining security for a claim which had to be pursued in arbitration in London. In that case there was a clause in the contract (cl. 26(b) of GAFTA Form No.119) which prohibited the bringing of "any action or other legal proceedings against [the other party] in respect of any [dispute arising out of or under the contract] . . .". The Court of Appeal held that the proceedings in Italy were brought in breach of the clause and that this was so even though the only purpose of the proceedings was to obtain security.

Would such a clause preclude proceedings for relief brought in England under s.12(6) of the Arbitration Act 1950 or s.44 of the Arbitration Act 1996? The Court of Appeal in *Mantovani v Carapelli* thought not.[91] Such proceedings would be merely ancillary to the London arbitration. In the case of s.12(6), the jurisdiction conferred on the court is "for the purpose of and in relation to a reference . . ." and is therefore no more than an integral part of what has been agreed to in the arbitration clause.[92] This is so even though the proceedings in court under s.12(6) have to be commenced by an arbitration claim form. The same is true of an application under s.44 of the Arbitration Act 1996 because the power to grant relief is "for the purposes of and in relation to the arbitral proceedings . . .".[93] Accordingly under such a clause the application to the English court is justified by the terms of the agreement to arbitrate.

6.031   Section 44(1) confers power on the court to make orders about the matters listed in s.44(2) (including power to grant Mareva or Anton Piller relief), "Unless otherwise agreed by the parties . . .". A clause such as that considered in *Mantovani v Carapelli* does not have the effect of contractually excluding the power to make orders ancillary to the reference under s.44(1); it merely confines the dispute to resolution by arbitration in London, which includes the jurisdiction of the court to make orders in support of the arbitral proceedings in London unless that jurisdiction has itself been excluded by agreement.

Consistently with such a clause the claimant could apply in London for Mareva relief and if that is granted in respect of assets in Italy then the

---

[89] [1980] 1 Lloyd's Rep. 375.
[90] [1977] 1 Lloyd's Rep. 283.
[91] [1980] 1 Lloyd's Rep. 375 at 382.
[92] *Comdel Commodities Ltd v Siporex Trade SA* [1997] 1 Lloyd's Rep. 424 at 428–429.
[93] s.44(1).

order could be enforced in Italy under Chap.III of Regulation 44/2001. The application in London can be made *ex parte* for an injunction which is to last until after the hearing of an *inter partes* application for an injunction, which if granted would be enforceable in Italy under Regulation 44/2001.[94]

If, after *ex parte* relief was obtained in England, an application were made in Italy for the purpose of obtaining preservative relief from the Italian court which went no further than the *ex parte* English order, would this be in breach of the contractual clause?

The Italian proceedings would be separate proceedings from the arbitral   **6.032** proceedings in London and from the proceedings in England for the injunction brought under s.44 of the 1996 Act. Accordingly, it could be said that bringing the Italian proceedings would be a breach of the clause because they are proceedings other than the arbitration proceedings. This is so even though they are proceedings brought solely to obtain security and not for the purpose of resolving the substantive merits.[95] However, on the facts the purpose of the Italian proceedings would be solely to obtain a holding order in Italy which in substance does no more than give effect to the *ex parte* relief obtained in England. *Mantovani v Carapelli* can be distinguished because there was not (and could not have been)[96] any injunction granted in England under s.12(6) of the Arbitration Act 1950 restraining dealings with the assets in Italy. On such facts there would not have been a breach of the clause because the Italian court order would have done no more than to give effect to the English court order. Similarly, no breach occurs if the sole purpose of interim relief granted abroad was to enforce an interim order made by the arbitrators (*e.g.* under s.38(4) of the 1996 Act).

In *Alfred C. Toepfer International GmbH v Société Cargill France*,[97] the construction adopted in *Mantovani v Carapelli* was criticised on the ground that it was not satisfactory as a matter of implication to apply the barring provision to ancillary proceedings outside the jurisdiction but not to those within the jurisdiction. The court decided that the barring provision did not bar proceedings in England to enforce the barring provision itself so whether it barred English ancillary proceedings did not arise and was not decided. The thrust of the criticism was that the barring provision applied either to all ancillary proceedings or none. The clause in *Mantovani v Carapelli* was agreed against the background of the regime of the Arbitration Act 1950 and that the powers of the court under s.12(6) could not be excluded by contrary agreement. It was also most unlikely that commercial parties would have agreed to exclude all the ancillary powers of the English

---

[94] The *ex parte* injunction would not be: *EMI Records Ltd v Modern Music Karl-Ulrich Walterbach GmbH* [1992] Q.B. 115.

[95] *Mantovani v Carapelli*, above; but see *Alfred C. Toepfer International GmbH v Société Cargill France* [1998] 1 Lloyd's. Rep. 379.

[96] See Chapter One above.

[97] [1998] 1 Lloyd's Rep. 379 at 385.

court, leaving such matters to be dealt with by the arbitrators in so far as they were able to do so, or not at all. For example, the arbitrators could not compel the attendance of a witness or grant an injunction affecting non-parties.

In *Re Q's Estate*[98] there was an English arbitration agreement which conferred on the arbitrators "exclusive jurisdiction" over "any disputes", but no clause like cl.26(b) which barred the bringing of any action or "other legal proceedings". The argument was that the arbitration clause barred application to the English court for interim measures under s.44 of the Arbitration Act 1996. The opening words of the section are "Unless otherwise agreed . . .", and it was contended that the arbitration clause was a contrary agreement within the opening words and s.4(2) of that Act. Rix J. decided that the arbitration clause applied to substantive disputes only and not to applications for ancillary relief made to the English court,[99] and doubted whether the arbitration clause barred an application for ancillary relief to a foreign court. For an arbitration agreement to bar any application anywhere for any interim measures or ancillary relief the case law shows that it is to be expected that specific words will be used,[1] and this will be part of the background against which contractual provisions governed by English law will fall to be interpreted.

6.033   Even if a clause did seek to preclude the bringing of proceedings for a Mareva injunction under s.12(6), the court would still have jurisdiction to grant an injunction, albeit that the existence of the clause would be a factor to take into account on discretion.[2]

Anton Piller relief is also capable of coming within s.12(6) of the Arbitration Act 1950. Section 12(6)(b) of the 1950 Act, which allowed the court to make orders concerning discovery and interrogatories in respect of an arbitration, was repealed by s.103 of the Courts and Legal Services Act 1990. The arbitrator has no power, however, to make an Anton Piller order; this can be done only by the court. Relief can be granted by virtue of s.12(6)(h) on the grounds that the order is an interim injunction[3] which in High Court proceedings is justified by s.37 of the Supreme Court Act 1981. Depending on its purpose, the relief may also be justifiable under s.12(6)(e) on the grounds that its purpose is to preserve or to provide for interim custody of "any goods which are the subject matter of the reference";[4] or

---

[98] [1999] 1 Lloyd's Rep. 931.
[99] Following *Mantovani v Carapelli*, above, and applying the approach in *Petromin SA v Secnav Marine Ltd* [1995] 1 Lloyd's Rep. 603 at 613 and *Ultisol Transport Contractors Ltd v Bouyguyes Offshore SA* [1996] 2 Lloyd's Rep. 140 at 144–145. See also *Mike Trading and Transport Ltd v R. Pagnan & Fratelli (The Lisboa)* [1980] 2 Lloyd's Rep. 546 where the court declined to grant an anti-suit injunction based on an English exclusive jurisdiction clause to prevent the plaintiff in English proceedings retaining security obtained in Venice.
[1] *Re Q* [1999] 1 Lloyd's Rep. 931 at 938.
[2] *cp.* the position on security for costs sought under s.12(6)(a) of the Arbitration Act 1950. *Coppée-Lavalin SA/NV v Ken Ren Chemicals and Fertilizers Ltd* [1995] A.C. 38.
[3] *Distributori Automatici v Holford Trading Co.* [1985] 1 W.L.R. 1066 at 1 073; *Rank Film Ltd v Video Information Centre* [1982] A.C. 380 at 417, *per* Templeman L.J.; *Third Chandris v Unimarine SA* [1979] Q.B. 645 at 699, *per* Lord Denning M.R.
[4] Corresponding to the former RSC Ord. 29, r.2(1) which was relied on by Lord Denning M.R. in *Anton Piller KG v Manufacturing Processes Ltd* [1976] Ch. 55 at 60H.

under s.12(6)(j) on the ground that the purpose is to find out about the location of assets so as to secure "the amount in dispute . . .".

(ii) The new law—Arbitration Act 1996, s.44; arbitral proceedings commenced on or after January 31, 1997 or not, yet commenced

Section 44 of the Arbitration Act 1996[5] confers on the court the power to **6.034** make orders about the matters listed in subs.(2) "[u]nless otherwise agreed by the parties . . .". Thus the parties to an arbitration agreement can exclude or curtail the jurisdiction of the court to make orders under the section. To be effective they must do so in writing.[6] Those powers include the granting of Mareva relief under s.44(2)(e).[7] The reason is the principle in s.1(b) of the Arbitration Act 1996. This states that the provisions of Pt I of the Act are founded on the principle that "the parties should be free to agree how their disputes are resolved, subject only to such safeguards as are necessary in the public interest." This power can be exercised before any award is made or in support of a final award pending satisfaction of it. Under s.70(7), the court may make an order for security for any money payable under an award pending determination of a challenge under s.67 (jurisdiction of the tribunal), s.68 (serious irregularity) or s.69 (appeal on a point of law). As a matter of discretion the court will not normally order security for a challenge to jurisdiction made on substantial grounds.[8]

Assuming that the powers under s.44 have not been excluded or curtailed by agreement, then in principle the court also has jurisdiction conferred on it by s.44 to grant Anton Piller relief. Section 44(2)(b) allows orders for "the purposes of or in relation to the arbitral proceedings" concerning "the preservation of evidence." Anton Piller relief may have this purpose.[9] The court has equivalent jurisdiction for making orders for the purpose of preserving evidence as it does in High Court proceedings and this includes an equivalent power to make orders for that purpose as is conferred on it by s.7 of the Civil Procedure Act 1997[10] or under its inherent jurisdiction.

---

[5] See Appendix 2 below. Section 44 is based in part on s.12(6)(d)–(h) of the Arbitration Act 1950, and Art.9 of the Model Law produced in 1985 by the United Nations Commission on International Trade Law ("It is not incompatible with an arbitration agreement for a party to request, before or during arbitral proceedings , from a court an interim measure of protection and for the court to grant such measure.").

[6] Arbitration Act 1996, s.5.

[7] *i.e.* "the granting of an interim injunction or the appointment of a receiver".

[8] *Paterson Farms Inc v C&M Farming Limited* [2004] 1 Lloyd's Rep. 614.

[9] Civil Procedure Act 1997, s.7(1)(a).

[10] Section 7 was enacted and came into force after s.44 of the Arbitration Act 1996. However, the purpose of s.44 is to equip the court with the same powers as it has for the relevant purpose in legal proceedings. This was to avoid there being a procedural gap because of the nature of arbitration proceedings for matters covered by s.44(2). Given that this is the purpose of the section and that the power conferred on the court is defined by reference to the power which "it has" for legal proceedings, s.44 is to be read as giving to the court the equivalent power to that which "it has" from time to time in relation to High Court proceedings.

Section 44(2)(c) is concerned with "orders relating to property which is the subject of the proceedings or as to which any question arises in the proceedings . . .". Those orders are made under the equivalent power to that which the court has "for the purposes of and in relation to legal proceedings". The wording of s.44(2)(c) followed[11] the wording of RSC Ord.29, r.2(1), which applied to High Court proceedings. These powers are now to be found listed in CPR r.25.1. Under the subsection, the court can order that property which is the subject of the proceedings (*i.e.* property claimed in the proceedings) or as to which any question arises in the proceedings[12] is to be delivered up, to be preserved or held in safe custody.

6.035   An order made under s.44(2)(c) can "authorise any person to enter any premises in the possession or control of a party to the arbitration". This does not enable an order to be made against a third party who is not a party to the arbitration. But it enables the court to confer authority on a person to enter the relevant premises; it is not merely a provision enabling the court to make an order requiring someone to permit entry.[13]

Section 44(2)(e) allows the granting of an interim injunction. Anton Piller relief can be granted pursuant to this subsection in the same way as relief can be granted in High Court proceedings under s.37 of the Supreme Court Act 1981.

Under s.44(3) and (4) of the Act:

"(3) If the case is one of urgency, the court may, on the application of a party or proposed party to the arbitral proceedings, make such orders as it thinks necessary for the purpose of preserving evidence or assets.

(4) If the case is not one of urgency, the court shall act only on the application of a party to the arbitral proceedings (upon notice to the other parties and to the tribunal) made with the permission of the tribunal or the agreement in writing of the other parties."

In High Court proceedings the ordinary rule is that the court must hear both parties before making any order affecting them. This is a basic rule of natural justice. However, that rule is about how justice is to be done—it is a means to an end and not the end itself; thus "it must give way to the extent necessary to do justice".[14] It is this which lies at the heart of subss. (3) and (4).

6.036   RSC Ord.29, r.1(2) allowed an application for an injunction to be made *ex parte* where ". . . the case is one of urgency", and RSC Ord.29, r.1(3) allowed such an application to be made before the issue of the writ or

---

[11] Taking photographs was capable of being authorised under RSC Ord.29, r.2(1): *Lewis v Earl of Londesborough* [1893] 2 Q.B. 191.

[12] For example, whether, in the case of a document, it is a genuine document or a forgery, when this is an important issue in the proceedings: *Re Saxton* [1962] 1 W.L.R. 859.

[13] Contrast s.7 of the Civil Procedure Act 1997, and para.6 of the standard form search order provided for by CPR Pt 25, Practice Direction, para.8.6.

[14] See the Foreword to the third edition of this book written by Saville L.J., who was responsible for drafting the Arbitration Act 1996.

other originating process. CPR Pt 25, Practice Direction, para.4.1 deals with urgent applications for relief under the CPR. In practice, applications for Mareva relief are often, but not invariably, made without notice[15] because of the risk that if there were prior notice, the defendant would take action which would render any subsequent order useless. Anton Piller applications are almost invariably made without notice for this reason and, unless this can be justified on the facts of the case, should not be granted. A case is one of "urgency" within s.44(3) and (4) if:

(1) the application is for an order for the purpose of preserving evidence or assets;[16] and either

(2) it is on the facts justifiable to apply *ex parte*; or

(3) (exceptionally)[17] it is not justifiable to apply *ex parte*, but there will be some delay before the arbitration tribunal is appointed and the application should be dealt with without delay. In such circumstances the applicant cannot be expected to obtain the permission of the tribunal to make the application and the case will still be one of "urgency", albeit that the application should be made *inter partes*.

The applicant makes the application by arbitration claim form and should make an affidavit complying with the CPR Pt 25 Practice Direction. This must state why (if it be the case) the application is made without notice, why it was not possible to obtain permission from the tribunal in advance, and why the tribunal (or anyone else given powers by the parties) has no power to make an order or is unable to act effectively.

Leaving aside cases of urgency, an application under s.44 can only be made either with the permission of the tribunal or with written consent of the other parties.[18] There is no appeal against the giving or refusing of permission.

The tribunal will decide whether to give permission after hearing from **6.037** both parties. In deciding whether to give permission the tribunal should look to achieving the "fair resolution of [the dispute] . . . without unnecessary delay or expense". The tribunal should consider its own powers to make orders, *e.g.* power under s.38(4) to preserve property

---

[15] CPR Pt 25, Practice Direction para.3.4 requires evidence to be placed before the court justifying the application being made without notice—see also *Thane Investments Ltd v Tomlinson*, CA, unreported, July 29, 2003. Not all Mareva applications are suitable for relief being granted without notice.

[16] This includes obtaining information from a defendant for the purpose of enabling assets to be preserved.

[17] *Hiscox Underwriting Limited v Dickson Manchester & Co Limited* [2004] 1 All E.R. (Comm) 753 (where an interim injunction was granted against the defendant requiring access to information, when the tribunal had not been appointed until the day when the court gave judgment on the application, there was an urgent need for mandatory relief, and there was the risk of serious irreparable harm). If the application is made *inter partes*, then often it will have been possible to get permission from the tribunal in advance.

[18] Arbitration Act 1996, s.44(5).

which is the subject of the proceedings or as to which any question arises. If the tribunal can make an effective order which in its view is sufficient, then permission to apply under s.44 should be refused.

Proceedings under s.44 will involve expense and could distract the parties from getting on with the arbitration. The applicant for permission has an onus to satisfy the tribunal that, notwithstanding this, permission should be given. But if, *e.g.* there is a real risk that the respondent will dissipate his assets and an award will not be satisfied, this could render the whole arbitration process useless. If there is temporary Mareva relief granted *ex parte* already in place, the tribunal may wish to know, before deciding whether to give permission for an application to be made to continue the relief, whether the respondent is prepared to offer security or some suitable undertaking.

The tribunal should give a prompt ruling on the application for permission and should avoid having a drawn-out and costly hearing for this purpose. The tribunal can give a limited permission, *e.g.* permission to apply for Mareva relief not exceeding a particular limit or restricted to particular assets.

6.038   Cases of "urgency" within s.44(3) are a limited exception to s.44(5), which requires permission of the tribunal or written consent from the other parties. The 1996 Act allows the court to grant a temporary order without the permission of the tribunal being given in advance because requiring permission in advance would give the respondent an opportunity to take steps to render any order useless or because delay would have this effect. But once it becomes practical to obtain permission this should be sought promptly. The applicant must seek permission if the relief is to continue in force.

If an order is made *ex parte*, the court may provide in the order that it shall cease to have effect in whole or in part if the arbitration tribunal so orders.[19]

Section 44 applies to arbitral proceedings regardless of whether the seat of the arbitration is in England and Wales. But if the court is asked to exercise its powers under the section in relation to a foreign arbitration this is relevant to discretion. There has to be some good reason for the court intervening in what otherwise may be a matter which should be dealt with by the foreign court.[20]

6.039   An application under s.44 is an "arbitration claim".[21] Such an application can be served out of the jurisdiction with permission of the court and there is jurisdiction to grant such permission under CPR r.62.5(1)(b). But does this rule, like the former RSC Ord.73, r.7,[22] only enable

---

[19] *ibid.*, s.44(6).
[20] Arbitration Act 1996, s.2(3), which is in line with the approach of the House of Lords in the *Channel Tunnel* case: [1993] A.C. 334 at 368.
[21] CPR r.62.2(1).
[22] *Tate & Lyle v Cia Usina Bulhoes and Cargill Inc.* [1997] 1 Lloyd's Rep. 355; *Unicargo v Flotec Maritime* [1996] 2 Lloyd's Rep 395.

permission to be granted for service on a party or anticipated party to arbitral proceedings?

It is possible to envisage situations in which s.44 could be used as the source of jurisdiction to make orders against a third party who is not a party to arbitral proceedings or to the arbitration agreement. For example, under s.44(2)(e), Mareva relief may be sought against an intended respondent to an arbitration in circumstances where there is reason to believe that a third party holds assets for the respondent and in which if there were an action it would be desirable to join the third party as a co-defendant and grant an injunction against the third party.[23] In such circumstances s.44(2)(e), which gives the court the same power to grant an interim injunction for the purposes of and in relation to arbitral proceedings as the court has "for the purposes of and in relation to legal proceedings", gives the court power to grant an injunction against a third party when this is ancillary to Mareva relief granted against the respondent.

Similarly, it is possible to envisage an order being made by the court against a third party under s.44(2)(c) for the inspection of property physically held by that third party.[24]

What about the scope of CPR r.62.5 which allows service out of the **6.040** jurisdiction of a claim for an order under s.44? It should also be borne in mind that s.44 applies to foreign arbitral proceedings and it must have been contemplated that service could be authorised on a foreigner who was a party to a foreign arbitration. Such a person has not consented to English arbitration. Nor has he agreed to the English court exercising jurisdiction over him. If such a person can be served out of the jurisdiction under the rule, then the basis of the new rule does not rest on there having been consent[25] by the foreigner to the English court exercising jurisdiction over him. This rule is in different terms from what was formerly RSC Ord.73, r.7, and is sufficiently widely drafted to include any application under s.44. The position of a party who is added solely for the purpose of making an effective interim order under s.44, is to be distinguished from proceedings against the third party which make a substantive claim against the third party.[26] There are no limiting words to CPR r.62.5(1)(b) and it is in the nature of applications for an interim injunction that relief may have to be

---

[23] See *C Inc. v L* [2001] 2 Lloyd's Rep. 459; *Cardile v LED Builders Pty Ltd.* (1999) 198 C.L.R. 380 at 405–406; *TSB Private Bank v Chabra* [1992] 1 W.L.R. 231; *Mercantile Group (Europe) AG v Aiyela* [1994] Q.B. 366 affirming [1993] F.S.R. 745; *Aiglan Ltd v Gau Shan Co. Ltd* [1993] 1 Lloyd's Rep. 164. The principle is discussed by Peter Devonshire in "The Implications of Third Parties Holding Assets Subject to a Mareva Injunction" [1996] L.M.C.L.Q. 268 at 274–277.
[24] See *Unicargo v Flotec Maritime S de RL and Cienvik Shipping Co. Ltd* [1996] 2 Lloyd's Rep. 395 at 404, *per* Clarke J. concerning the equivalent provision to s.44(2)(c) in s.12(6) of the Arbitration Act 1950, and what was formerly RSC Ord.29, r.7A(2).
[25] Contrast the rationale of the old RSC Ord. 73, r.7, which rested on consent: *Unicargo v Flotec Maritime S de RL* [1996] 2 Lloyd's Rep. 395 at 405, *per* Clarke J.
[26] *Vale do Rio v Shanghai Bao Steel* [2000] 2 Lloyd's Rep. 1 (where the claim for a declaration against the third party brokers was for substantive relief about whether they had brought into being a binding contract, was not within the arbitration exception to the Lugano Convention, and jurisdiction was governed by that Convention).

granted against a non-party.[27] accordingly it is suggested that, unlike the former RSC Ord.73, r.7, CPR r.62.5 allows the court to grant permission to serve out of the jurisdiction an application for an injunction under s.44(2)(e) against a non-party.

However, it does not follow that the English court would make an order against a foreigner, who is not a party to the arbitral proceedings, in relation to his conduct outside of the jurisdiction. Such a situation would fall within the area in which out of respect to the sovereignty of foreign states the English court shows restraint, and it would require a case justified by very strong and urgent reasons for such relief to be granted.[28]

Section 44(7) provides that an appeal can only be brought with the leave of the court of first instance.

(iii) Article 24 of the Brussels and Lugano Conventions and Article 31 of Council Regulation 44/2001

6.041   Article 24 of the Conventions and Art.31 of Regulation 44/2001 authorises provisional measures. If a court has jurisdiction over the substantive claims under a Convention or the Regulation this carries with it jurisdiction under the Convention to grant provisional measures.[29] If the substantive claims are to be determined in arbitration, then no court is seised with the substantive claims and so this aspect of the article will not apply.[30] If the subject-matter of the claims falls outside the Conventions or the Regulations then these articles do not apply.[31] However, where the subject-matter of the substantive rights does come within the scope of the Convention or Regulation (*e.g.* a claim for breach of contract), then the fact that it is to be resolved in arbitration does not have the consequence that these articles do not apply. They apply because the provisional measures are granted in relation to the substantive rights and those are in principle within the scope of the Convention albeit that matters concerning arbitration proceedings are excluded.

For Art.24 (and Art.31 of the Regulation) to apply there must still be a real connecting link between the provisional measures and the territorial jurisdiction of the national court.[32]

The power of the court under s.44 of the Arbitration Act 1996 is subject to the constraint in s.2(3)(b) that where the arbitration proceedings are to be held abroad the court may refuse to grant relief when it would be inappropriate to do so. Where Art.24 of the Conventions or Art.31 of the Regulation applies the connecting link requirement must also be satisfied.

---

[27] See Chapter 13.
[28] *Société Eram Shipping Co. Ltd v Compagnie Internationale de Navigation* [2004] 1 A.C. 260, and see also *Tate & Lyle v Cia Usina Bulhoes and Cargill Inc.* [1997] 1 Lloyd's Rep. 355, where Hobhouse L.J. refused to grant such relief.
[29] *Van Uden Maritime BV v Firma Deco-Line* [1998] ECR–I 7091.
[30] *ibid.*
[31] *De Cavel v De Cavel* [1979] E.C.R. 1055 at para.9.
[32] [1998] ECR–I 7091.

What are provisional measures? This has an autonomous meaning **6.042** independent of the classification of the measures under national law. They are to be distinguished from final relief or resolution of the substance of the case. In the case of an interim payment, to be a provisional measure it must in principle not involve determination of the merits and be reversible. So with an interim payment this could only be a provisional or protective measure if the defendant was sure to get his money back if he won on the substantive dispute.[33]

(d) Jurisdiction of the arbitration tribunal to grant an injunction or appoint a receiver.

Only the court can grant an injunction or appoint a receiver in the sense of **6.043** making an order the breach, or the frustration, of which would be a contempt of court. The tribunal has only limited power to make effective its own directions. Depending upon whether the parties have agreed otherwise, the scope of the directions which may be made by the tribunal is narrower than the powers which may be exercised by the court.

A direction made by arbitrators is binding on the parties, but will not be binding on persons who are not parties to the arbitration. However a direction may have an effect on third parties. A party is contractually bound to the other party to the reference to comply with a lawful direction or provisional award made by the tribunal under the terms of reference.[34] Therefore it is considered that the court could enforce that contractual obligation as between the parties, and in a suitable case do so by way of injunction. If a third party with knowledge of the direction were knowingly to procure or facilitate breach of the direction this would be actionable in tort, and the court might grant a mandatory injunction against the third party requiring him to undo what had been done.[35] The fact that a direction had been made to preserve assets, and broken by a party acting together with a third party who knew of the facts, could also be very relevant to any proceedings to undo the breach through proceedings against the third party under s.423 of the Insolvency Act 1986.

Under s.38(1) of the Arbitration Act 1996 the parties are "free to agree **6.044** on the powers exercisable by the tribunal for the purposes of and in relation to the proceedings." Unless otherwise agreed the tribunal has power to give directions as set out in s.38(4), which includes for the "custody, preservation or detention of the property by the tribunal, an

---

[33] *Van Uden Maritime BV v Firma Deco-Line* [1998] E.C.R.–I 7091 at paras 46 and 47; *Wermuth v Wermuth* [2003] 1 W.L.R. 942 (on Art.12 of Council Regulation 1347/2000 on divorce, judicial separation and nullity, generally known as Brussels II).

[34] It is considered that the reasoning in *Bremer Oeltransport v G.m.b.H v Drewry* [1933] 1 K.B. 753 about the effect of a submission to arbitration would apply also to an interim direction or provisional award made pursuant to that submission.

[35] *Esso Petroleum Co Limited v Kingswood Motors (Addlestone) Limited* [1974] Q.B. 142 at pp.155–157; *Law Debenture Trust Corporation v Ural Caspian Oil Corporation Limited* [1995] Ch. 152 at p. 166 B–D, and p.172.

expert or a party", about "any property which is the subject of the proceedings or as to which any question arises in the proceedings"; this mirrors the limitation now to be found in CPR25.1(2) about "relevant property" for the purposes of the interim remedies which may be granted by the court in court proceedings under CPR25.1(c) and (g). There is the added limitation in the case of the powers under s.38(4) that the property must be ". . . owned by or in the possession of one of the parties to the proceedings. . .".

The report in February 1996 on the Arbitration Bill by Departmental Advisory Committee on Arbitration Law chaired by Saville L.J. at paragraph 201 stated:

". . . the July 1995 draft would arguably (and inadvertently) have allowed the arbitrators to order *ex parte Mareva* or even *Anton Piller* relief. These draconian powers are best left to be applied by the Courts, and the provisions of the Bill with respect to such powers have been adjusted accordingly."

It follows that, in the absence of agreement, which may be express or implied,[36] under s.38 an arbitration tribunal does not have the power to make a interim direction in the nature of a Mareva injunction, or an anti-suit injunction. However the parties are free under s.38(1) to confer on the tribunal jurisdiction to grant Mareva type or anti-suit directions based on claims pending before it.

6.045   There is an essential difference between making a final award on the merits and making a provisional[37] award on the merits which will be subject to revision in a final award. In the absence of agreement between the parties it is no part of the arbitration tribunal's function to make temporary or provisional financial arrangements between the parties.[38] Under s.39(1) the parties are free to confer power for a tribunal to grant "on a provisional basis" any relief which it could grant by way of relief in a final award. This is an opt in provision. Therefore, unless the parties agree to confer such a power on the tribunal, it will not have jurisdiction to make a provisional award.

Section 48 of the Act deals with "remedies" which the tribunal can grant. From its position in the Act it concerns remedies in a final award in respect of the merits. Unless otherwise agreed these include an award

---

[36] *Kastner v Jason* [2004] EWHC 592 (Ch) (where it was held on the facts that the submission to arbitration before the Beth Din impliedly conferred the power on the tribunal to make an interim Mareva direction).

[37] see the judgment of Lawrence Collins J. in *Wermuth v Wermuth* [2003] 1 W.L.R. 942 for a discussion of what is meant by 'provisional' in the context of the European Conventions on Jurisdiction.

[38] *The Kostas Melas* [1981] 1 Lloyd's Rep. 18 at p.26; The report on the Arbitration Bill by Departmental Advisory Committee on Arbitration Law, paras 201 and 231.

equivalent to what a court can order by way of an injunction,[39] and specific performance.[40] It is considered that s.45 (5) is concerned with remedies in respect of a substantive claim which itself is before the arbitration tribunal in the arbitral proceedings, when making a final award.[41] It looks to the substantive claim on the merits, and confers on the tribunal a jurisdiction to make a final award in terms equivalent to a final injunction which could be granted by a court in relation to that same substantive claim if it had been the subject of court proceedings.[42]

Therefore it is considered that if there is a proprietary claim pending **6.046** before it, the tribunal can by its final award make an order governing what is to happen to that property, and where the parties have opted in under s.39, a provisional award may be made in respect of that property. In addition under s.38(4) an interim direction may be made in respect of that property as long as it is owned by or in the possession of a party to the reference. Section 38(4) allows the tribunal to require the property to be transferred into its custody and it seems that this could include requiring a ship to be registered in the name of the tribunal, or cash to be paid into a bank account in the name of the tribunal.

Where the parties have agreed to confer power on the tribunal to make provisional awards under s.39(1), it is necessary to look at those substantive claims which are then pending before the tribunal. If such a claim at the final award stage could attract a particular remedy, then, subject to the parties having conferred power on the tribunal pursuant to s.39(1) to make a provisional award, an order can be made granting that same remedy on a provisional basis.

Mareva relief is separate and "wholly disconnected"[43] from the merits of a case. Whether granted before judgment on the merits or in aid of execution, it is necessarily in the nature of interim relief to preserve the position pending enforcement. For this reason if a power was to be conferred by the Act on a tribunal to grant Mareva type relief one would expect to find it in s.38(4). Furthermore an injunction in aid of enforcement of an award would be based on a contractual right to satisfaction of that award. That right arises from an express or implied agreement in the

---

[39] s.48(5)(a), which was by way of clarification of the law: The report on the Arbitration Bill by Departmental Advisory Committee on Arbitration Law, para.234. The dictum of Tucker L.J. in *Chandris v Isbrandtsen-Moller Co Inc* [1951] 1 K.B. 240 at p.262 was to the effect that the tribunal could not itself 'grant an injunction'. The court could grant an injunction in effect specifically enforcing a final award which was in sufficiently certain terms to be enforced in this way: *Birtley and District Co-Operative Society Limited v Windy Nook and District Industrial Co-Operative Society Limited* [1960] 2 Q.B. 1 at p.19.

[40] s.48(5)(b) (other than a contract relating to land).

[41] *Kastner v Jason* [2004] EWHC 592 (Ch) at para.26.

[42] cf. *Kastner v Jason* [2004] EWHC 592 (Ch) at para.27, which looked at the procedural limitations which applied to particular judges as opposed to what remedy could be granted by a court in respect of the substantive claim. It is considered that, in its context, the purpose of s.45 (5) is that the equivalent final relief to that set out in the sub-section ought to be available to a claimant whether his claim is decided in court or arbitration proceedings.

[43] *Mercedes Benz AG v Leiduck* [1996] A.C. 284 at p.303 E.

original submission to arbitration.[44] Such a right does not exist, and cannot be sued upon, until the relevant award has been made.

6.047   Where there is a substantive claim before the tribunal in respect of which a court could grant an injunction by way of final relief, then the tribunal can grant an equivalent remedy by way of final award.

Under s.38 the parties are free to confer on the tribunal the power to give an interim direction in the nature of Mareva relief. It has been suggested that the parties can confer on the tribunal power to grant freezing relief in support of a final award under s.48(1).[45] But since relief in aid of enforcement is itself in the nature of interim relief, and is disconnected from the merits on which the final award is based, it is considered that the better view is that the parties are free to do this under s.38.[46]

Under s.44(4) the tribunal has an essential role in deciding whether to permit a party to apply to the court for an order in support of the proceedings, which includes an interim injunction or appointment of a receiver, and if the tribunal does give permission then the court will take into account the terms of the permission and any reasons given in deciding whether to grant the order.[47]

(4) Civil Jurisdiction and Judgments Act 1982, s.25(1)

(i) Scope of the section

6.048   Section 25 of the Civil Jurisdiction and Judgments Act 1982 empowers the English court to grant interim relief in proceedings in England in which there is no claim to substantive relief on the merits of a case, based on a cause of action. The proceedings authorised by the statute are free-standing proceedings brought solely for the purpose of obtaining the interim relief. The merits will not be decided in England and Wales. The English court is able to grant relief which is ancillary to and in aid of proceedings on the merits elsewhere.

Had there not been statutory intervention the court would not have had jurisdiction to entertain free-standing proceedings for interim relief. This is because the jurisdiction of the court to grant interim injunctions under s.37(1) of the Supreme Court Act 1981 is a jurisdiction to do so as an interim measure in proceedings before the English court claiming substantive relief.[48]

---

[44] *Bremer Oeltransport v G.m.b.H v Drewry* [1933] 1 K.B. 753 at p.764.

[45] *Kastner v Jason* [2004] EWHC 592 (Ch) at para.27.

[46] Since the parties can do this under s.38(1) for interim Mareva relief to be granted before any final award, one would expect that they can also do this for relief to be granted in support of a final award.

[47] The court exercises its own discretion, but is acting in a role which is in support of the arbitration proceedings, and takes into account what the tribunal has said: see also *Willesford v Watson* (1873) 8 Ch. App. 473 at p.480 per Lord Selbourne L.C.

[48] *The Siskina* [1979] A.C. 210 at 256; *Crédit Suisse Fides Trust SA v Cuoghi* [1998] Q.B. 818 at 825 and 831; *Department of Social Security v Butler* [1995] 1 W.L.R. 1528 at 1536.

Article 24 of the Brussels Convention allowed[49] contracting states to assume jurisdiction for the granting of provisional measures in support of substantive proceedings which were pending in another contracting state. Art.24 corresponds to Art.31 of Council Regulation 44/2001. Section 25(1) allows interim relief to be granted by the English court in relation to proceedings commenced or to be commenced anywhere in the world and regardless of whether the subject-matter of those proceedings comes within Art.1 of the Brussels Convention.[50]

(ii) Service out of the jurisdiction

In *Republic of Haiti v Duvalier,*[51] the plaintiffs alleged that the former **6.049** President of Haiti (Jean-Claude Duvalier) had embezzled US$120 million, and commenced proceedings against him in the Tribunal de Grande Instance at Grasse. Orders were obtained in England against a firm of solicitors in London requiring them to give information about what had happened to funds, and worldwide relief was granted under s.25 of the 1982 Act. The Court of Appeal held that the proceedings seeking interim relief could be served on the defendants without leave under RSC Ord.11, r.1(2), which applies to "a claim" against defendants domiciled in a Convention territory. Staughton L.J. considered that it was irrelevant to whether the rule applied, whether an application for interim relief was "a cause of action". It was ". . . merely a matter of semantics".[52]

The Republic sought to uphold jurisdiction based upon what was then RSC Ord.11, r.1(1)(i), and is now CPR r.6.20(2). The Court of Appeal expressed no opinion on this point. But it could only have been justified if the claim by the Republic in England was a proprietary claim based on a substantive cause of action. The substantive proceedings were already in being in France, and the court in Grasse was already seised with them. It was also in issue whether applying the relevant foreign law the claim was a proprietary one.

What about RSC Ord.11, r.1(2)? The English court did not have before it any claim for substantive relief. This is because an application for interim relief is not a claim for substantive relief on the merits. Section 25 does not transform an application for interim relief into a claim on the merits, it merely provides a jurisdiction which was previously lacking for the High

---

49 *Crédit Suisse Fides Trust v Cuoghi* [1998] Q.B. 818 at 825D–E *per* Millett L.J.; *The Siskina* [1979] A.C. 210 at 259; *Dicey and Morris on the Conflict of Laws* (13th ed., 1999), Vol. 1, p.190, para.8–020. Contrast *Republic of Haiti v Duvalier* [1990] 1 Q.B. 202 at 212, *per* Staughton L.J., who thought that under the Convention the United Kingdom had an obligation to create a jurisdiction for granting interim relief in support of the courts of other contracting states.
50 This is the combined effect of s.25(1) and the Civil Jurisdiction and Judgments Act 1982 (Interim Relief) Order 1997 (SI 1997/302), which came into force on April 1, 1997.
51 [1990] 1 Q.B. 212.
52 [1990] 1 Q.B. 202 at 211D–E. This observation was criticised by the Privy Council in *Mercedes Benz AG v Leiduck* [1996] A.C. 284 at 302, whilst recognising that the case may have been rightly decided.

Court to grant free-standing interim relief in support of substantive proceedings elsewhere. The scope of the rule remained limited by the requirement that the injunction had to be based on a substantive claim to that relief.

6.050   In *X v Y*,[53] the judge decided that an application for interim relief under s.25 could be served out of the jurisdiction on defendants not domiciled in a Convention territory, with leave of the court under RSC Ord.11, r.1(1)(b). The reasoning was that the rule had a different scope from what was previously RSC Ord.11, r.1(1)(i), which was the rule considered in *The Siskina*. This was criticised by the majority of the Privy Council in *Mercedes Benz AG v Leiduck*[54] and *X v Y* should be regarded as wrongly decided.

The rules of court were subsequently changed so that an application for interim relief under s.25 had to be made by originating summons,[55] and leave granted for service of the summons out of the jurisdiction under RSC Ord.11, r.8A. The affidavit in support had to state that "the plaintiff has a good claim to interim relief".[56] In view of the *Mercedes* case the only safe way to proceed on an application for interim relief against a foreigner was to seek leave to serve out of the jurisdiction under that rule.

CPR r.6.19 (service out of the jurisdiction without permission) does not apply to a claim for interim relief; this is because such a claim is for a provisional or protective measure under Art.31 of Regulation 44/2001 and not for a substantive claim in relation to which jurisdiction is governed by ss1–7 of Chap.2 to the Regulation. For this reason the decision in *Republic of Haiti v Duvalier*[57] that the former RSC Ord.11, r.1(2) enabled service out of the jurisdiction was wrong. It only applied to substantive claims within the scope of the jurisdiction rules in ss1–6 of Title II of the Brussels Convention, and not to a protective measure granted in aid of substantive proceedings on the merits in France, a measure which was not inconsistent with the rules on jurisdiction in the Brussels Convention because of Art.24.

6.051   Under CPR r.6.20(4) permission may be given to serve a claim form out of the jurisdiction which seeks an interim remedy under s.25, and it is thought that permission must be sought under this rule for any claims for relief under s.25 which are to be served out of the jurisdiction. Under CPR r.25.4(1)(a) and (2), except in the Commercial Court,[58] the application is to be made in accordance with the general rules for applications in CPR Pt 23, *i.e.* by application notice. CPR r.6.19 and r.6.20 are to be read as applicable to application notices.[59]

---

[53] [1990] 1 Q.B. 220.
[54] [1996] A.C. 284 at 304; see also *Department of Social Security v Butler* [1995] 1 W.L.R. 1528 at 1535H, *per* Evans L.J.
[55] RSC Ord.29, r.8A.
[56] RSC Ord.11, r.8A(2)(b). This is to be contrasted with RSC Ord.11, r.4(1)(b) which applies to RSC Ord.11, r.1(1) and requires the deponent to state that ". . . the plaintiff has a good cause of action", referring to a substantive claim.
[57] [1990] 1 Q.B. 202 at 212G.
[58] See *Admiralty and Commercial Courts Guide*, para.F15.15 which requires the application to be made by a Pt 8 claim form. (The *Admiralty and Commerical Courts Guide* (6th ed., February 2002) is available by following the link at *www.courtservice.gov.uk/cms/ commercial court.htm.)*
[59] CPR r.6.18(h) and (l); *C Inc. v L* [2001] 2 Lloyd's Rep. 459 at [89–94].

Section 25 enables interim relief to be granted in certain circumstances against persons who are not parties to the substantive proceedings. It is thought that leave could have been granted under the former RSC Ord.11, r.8A for an originating summons to be served on such a person out of the jurisdiction.[60] CPR r.6.20(4) seems wide enough to include relief sought against such persons.

(iii) "Interim relief" under s.25(1)

The definition of "interim relief" in s.25(7) provides that the term: 6.052

> "means interim relief of any kind which [the High Court] has power to grant in proceedings relating to matters within its jurisdiction, other than—
>
> (a) a warrant for the arrest of property; or
> (b) provision for obtaining evidence."

Section 25(7)(a) excludes arresting a ship in an admiralty action in *rem* from the jurisdiction conferred on the court by s.25(1). Admiralty arrests are the subject-matter of s.26 of the Act and s.11 of the Arbitration Act 1996. Section 25(7)(b) excludes measures directed to "obtaining evidence" for the substantive hearing of the case. This is because there is a separate regime for "obtaining" evidence for use in a foreign court. That regime is statutory and is founded on the Evidence (Proceedings in Other Jurisdictions) Act 1975. For foreign arbitrations s.44(2)(a) of the Arbitration Act 1996 enables the court to make orders about the taking of the evidence of witnesses but the exercise of those powers depends on whether it is appropriate.[61]

Although s.25(7)(b) excludes measures directed to obtaining evidence, it   6.053 does not exclude interim relief designed to give the applicant information, *e.g.* about the location of assets. In *Republic of Haiti v Duvalier; Re an application by Mr Turner and Mr Matlin*,[62] the Court of Appeal upheld a mandatory order requiring the defendants "acting by Messrs Turner and Matlin, to disclose" to the plaintiffs' solicitors certain information relating to assets held by the defendants, so that orders could be obtained freezing those assets. The objection was raised that the information required was "evidence" falling within s.25(7)(b) of the Act. But this was rejected

---

[60] This was similar to the position under RSC Ord.73, r.8 for applications under s.44 of the Arbitration Act 1996 affecting persons who are not parties to the reference: see para.6.040, above.

[61] Arbitration Act 1996, s.2(3), and see *Commerce and Industry Insurance Co. v Certain Underwriters at Lloyd's of London* [2002] 1 W.L.R. 1323.

[62] Court of Appeal (Civ Div) Transcript No.490 of 1988 (June 7, 1988). The hearing was held *in camera* on June 7, 1988 before Lord Donaldson M.R., Woolf L.J. and Sir John Megaw, and the judgment was subsequently released. It is referred to by Staughton L.J. in the subsequent appeal in the case by Jean-Claude Duvalier, his wife and his mother: [1990] 1 Q.B. 202 at 209.

because the information was required for the purpose of seeking to freeze dealings with assets, and not as evidence to be used for the purpose of the substantive hearing. If the information obtained did reveal large, unexplained cash balances or other valuable assets it seems likely that this would have been relevant to the prosecution of the case on the merits, which had been commenced before the Tribunal de Grande Instance at Grasse.[63] While s.25(7)(b) precludes an application under s.25(1) for the purpose of *obtaining* evidence for the prosecution of the claim on the merits, it does not preclude the making of an order for the purpose of preserving assets, even if a consequence of compliance with the order may be to provide the applicant with information and material of assistance to him in the prosecution of the substantive claim.

A purpose of interim relief may be to preserve evidence: see s.7(1)(a) of the Civil Procedure Act 1997 and s.44(2)(b) of the Arbitration Act 1996, both of which use the word "preserve". Preservation involves safeguarding material which may be used as evidence in due course. Section 25(7)(b) does not preclude the making of orders under s.25(1) for preserving material. Nor would it exclude the granting of Anton Piller relief for this purpose. Just as s.44(2)(b) enables Anton Piller relief to be granted so as to preserve evidence for an arbitration, whether English or foreign, so s.25(1) enables such relief to be granted for the purpose of preserving material which may be used in evidence in foreign proceedings.

It was also argued by Messrs Turner and Matlin that s.25(1) included within "interim relief" only orders which related to assets or other subject-matter within the territorial jurisdiction of the court. In relation to this submission, Lord Donaldson M.R., with whom the other members of the Court of Appeal agreed, said:

> "What [s.25(7)] is saying is not that the court can make no orders relating to the subject matter outside the geographical limits of this country, but that it cannot make orders which it could not make in support of proceedings properly begun in the English courts.
>
> If there were some unusual form of ancillary relief available in the French courts, as indeed there is of course in the United States courts in the form of pre-trial examination of witnesses, the English courts, in accordance with subsection (7), have no power to grant that relief. They can only do in support of foreign proceedings what they can do in support of their own proceedings."[64]

6.054   The relief which can be granted under s.25 is not limited to what relief could be granted by the foreign court having jurisdiction on the merits.[65] So in *Motorola Credit Corporation v Cem Cengiz Uzan*[66] although the New

---

[63] The defendants disputed the jurisdiction of the French court to entertain the claim on the merits and at the time of the English proceedings that dispute had not been resolved.

[64] See also: *Alltrans Inc. v Interdom Holdings* [1991] 4 All E.R. 458 at 468j; *Crédit Suisse Fides Trust SA v Cuoghi* [1998] Q.B. 818 at 827E–F.

[65] *Motorola Credit Corporation v Cem Cengiz Uzan (No.2)* [2004] 1 W.L.R. 113 at [118].

[66] [2004] 1 W.L.R. 113.

York court, which had jurisdiction on the merits, could not grant Mareva relief worldwide, the section still empowered the English court to do so in a supportive role.

(iv) Inexpediency, "real connecting link" with the territorial jurisdiction of the court, and worldwide relief

Under s.25(2) of the 1982 Act, the court may decide to refuse relief if the **6.055** fact that the court has no jurisdiction "in relation to the subject matter of the proceedings" (*i.e.* the substantive merits of the case) makes it "inexpedient" for the court to grant it. This goes to the exercise of discretion. There is a similar provision in s.2(3) of the Arbitration Act 1996 in relation to applications under s.44 of that Act in support of arbitral proceedings if the fact that the seat of the arbitration is outside of England and Wales or Northern Ireland or is likely, when designated or determined, to be so makes it "inappropriate" to grant relief. Both provisions indicate that the fact that the merits are to be determined abroad may in itself make it "inexpedient" or "inappropriate" for the English court to be granting interim relief. The application should be made abroad.

An example of this was the *Channel Tunnel* case.[67] Similarly in *Tate & Lyle v Cia Usina Bulhoes and Cargill Inc.*,[68] the applicant (Tate & Lyle) had a claim against the respondent (Bulhoes) in arbitration in London for non-delivery of sugar. The applicant alleged that it became the owner of certain sugar as soon as it had been produced by the respondent and that the respondent had wrongly sold on the relevant sugar to Cargill Inc. Tate & Lyle sought an order freezing the proceeds of the sale from Bulhoes to Cargill Inc. Clarke J. had held that there was no jurisdiction under what was RSC Ord.73, r.7[69] to grant leave to serve the proceedings on Cargill out of the jurisdiction and set aside the injunction so far as it related to Cargill. Hobhouse L.J. dismissed an application for an injunction against Cargill to be granted pending appeal. Cargill was not within the jurisdiction and could not be served within the jurisdiction. Tate & Lyle had no substantive claim against Cargill which was to be determined in England. The injunction sought would concern conduct by a foreigner abroad in respect of a fund abroad. Any application against Cargill ought to be made abroad.[70]

An order for provisional measures made by a court without jurisdiction over the substantive claim on the merits is only authorised by Art.24 of the Brussels and Lugano Conventions, or Art.31 of Regulation 44/2001, provided that there is a real connection between the provisional measures

---

[67] [1993] A.C. 334 at 368.
[68] [1997] 1 Lloyd's Rep. 355.
[69] Now RSC Ord. 73, r.29.
[70] See also in relation to an application under s.25(1): *Qingdao Ocean Shipping Co. v Grace Shipping* [1995] 2 Lloyd's Rep. 15, where relief was refused as inexpedient when it was sought against parties domiciled in Germany in respect of German assets.

and the territorial jurisdiction of that court. In *Van Uden Maritime BV v Firma Deco-Line* the European Court of Justice said:[71]

> ". . . the granting of provisional or protective measures on the basis of Art.24 is conditional on, *inter alia*, the existence of a real connecting link between the subject-matter of the measures sought and the territorial jurisdiction of the contracting state of the court before which those measures are sought."

6.056   This is an extra requirement imposed directly on the court by Art.31 of the Regulation and which must be met in cases governed by that regulation or the Conventions. It was not expressed as a requirement in *Motorola Credit Corporation v Cem Cengiz Uzan*[72] because s.25 was invoked in support of the Federal Court in New York and so that was not a case governed by the Conventions or the Regulation, and the Court of Appeal ruled that its discretion was not "governed or informed" by the Conventions.[73]

In the *Republic of Haiti* case, the key to the whereabouts of the assets lay with solicitors in London—they had the relevant information—and that was why it was appropriate to grant the interim relief in England. If there were tracing claims in the substantive proceedings, and the assets had passed through a bank in London, this could make it not "inexpedient" to grant interim relief designed to locate those assets or their proceeds and to freeze them. The decision went to the very edge of what was permissible consistently with the principle that the court exercises restraint in regulating the conduct of foreigners abroad.[74] As for the real connecting link requirement, this was argued[75] and in his judgment Staughton L.J. saw "considerable force" in the point that the proper court was the court having jurisdiction over the substantive merits or the court(s) having jurisdiction where the assets were located.[76] The relief granted, which was under appeal, temporarily met this requirement until the disclosure exercise was complete and the Republic had been given an adequate opportunity to freeze assets located in other jurisdictions.[77] The reasoning in the case was limited to justifying the relief for this limited period.

When there are no connecting factors with England making it appropriate for the English court to grant interim relief, then as a matter of discretion the court will not do so.[78]

---

[71] [1998] E.C.R.–I 7091 at para.40.
[72] [2003] EWCA Civ, 752 at [114] and [115].
[73] *ibid.*, at [65].
[74] See Lawrence Collins in *Essays on Internationl Litigation and the Conflict of Laws* in 1994 cited by Potter L.J. in *Motorola Credit Corporation v Cem Cengiz Uzan (No.2)* [2004] 1 W.L.R. 113 at [68].
[75] [1990] 1 Q.B. 202 at 204G and 216–217.
[76] *ibid.*, at 216–217.
[77] *ibid.*, at 216D–E.
[78] *Qingdao Ocean Shipping Co. v Grace Shipping* [1995] 2 Lloyd's Rep. 15 at 24 and 29.

Once there is good reason for granting a measure of interim relief in 6.057
England, this may make it desirable for the English court shaping its orders
to avoid the applicant having to go to other courts for further interim
measures. As a general principle it is desirable to avoid having fragmented
litigation in several jurisdictions. Fragmentation is liable to cause extra
expense and delay. One court is more likely to produce a consistent set of
measures to be carried out in an orderly way.

Under s.25 the court does not have a practice of necessarily confining
any relief under s.25 to assets within England and Wales. In the *Republic of
Haiti* case the Court of Appeal upheld relief granted worldwide, describing
the relief as "A most unusual measure". In *Rosseel NV v Oriental
Commercial Shipping (UK) Ltd*[79] the Court of Appeal declined to grant
worldwide relief in proceedings against a defendant resident in England to
enforce a New York arbitration award, and the judgment in that case was
applied in *S & T Bautrading v Nordling*[80] in which the Court of Appeal
declined to grant worldwide relief in support of substantive proceedings in
Germany. These decisions appeared to give rise to a rule of practice that,
save in exceptional circumstances, the English court would not grant extra-
territorial relief in support of foreign proceedings. However, that was
swept away in *Crédit Suisse Fides Trust v Cuoghi*.[81]

In that case Mr Cuoghi was domiciled in England. Proceedings were
brought against him in Switzerland alleging that he was an accomplice in
fraudulent misappropriations. Mr Cuoghi argued that because the Swiss
court did not have the power to order a non-resident to disclose assets
located outside Switzerland the relief sought from the English court was
relief which the Swiss court had no power to grant and therefore should
not be granted.[82] This argument was rejected because the English court had
the power to grant such relief in respect of assets within its territorial
jurisdiction and therefore could supplement the lack of territorial jurisdiction of the Swiss court.[83]

Mr Cuoghi also relied on the earlier decisions in support of an argument 6.058
that the Mareva relief should be confined to his assets in England and
Wales. The Court of Appeal rejected this argument and restated the law on
the basis of the terms of s.25(2), namely the correct question was whether
the fact that the substantive proceedings were taking place in Switzerland
made it "inexpedient" to grant interim relief. Since Mr Cuoghi lived in
England and the Swiss court could not itself grant the relief sought, it was
not inexpedient for the English court to make orders designed to preserve
assets. There was no reason why an English court should not restrain a
person properly before it from disposing of assets abroad. The English
court could assert jurisdiction *in personam* against Mr Cuoghi. Viewed as

---

[79] [1990] 1 W.L.R. 1387.
[80] [1997] 3 All E.R. 718.
[81] [1998] Q.B. 818. Reviewed by D. Capper (1998) 17 C.J.Q. 35.
[82] [1998] Q.B. 818 at 826G.
[83] *Refco Inc. v Eastern Trading* [1999] 1 Lloyd's Rep. 159.

such, the relief did not involve any unacceptable intrusion on another country's sovereignty.[84]

Particular matters which were mentioned by Lord Bingham of Cornhill C.J. as potentially making it "inexpedient" to grant interim relief could be:

(1) relief which would obstruct or hamper case management by the court seised with the substantive proceedings ("the primary court");

(2) relief which could give rise to overlapping, inconsistent or conflicting orders with those of other courts;[85]

(3) if the primary court has jurisdiction to grant the relief and has declined to do so.

In *Crédit Suisse Fides Trust v Cuoghi*, the defendant lived in England and this in itself provided an acceptable foundation for the court to grant relief. This case was decided before the European Court of Justice's decision in *Van Uden*. On the facts the "real connecting link" requirement was met because the defendant was domiciled in England and had assets here, and it was appropriate to grant relief in a worldwide form so as to have a single court managing the provisional measures granted against an individual in England. In *Jeanette Walsh v Deloitte & Touche Inc.*,[86] the Privy Council upheld worldwide relief in proceedings in the Bahamas which were stayed to enable the merits to be determined in Ontario, where no worldwide order had been sought. The defendant lived in the Bahamas and was subject to the coercive powers of the court there and so it was the sensible place in which to obtain the worldwide relief. The Privy Council approved of the reasoning in *Crédit Suisse Fides Trust v Cuoghi*.

6.059 In *Refco Inc. v Eastern Trading*[87] application was made for relief in support of the Federal court in Chicago. This was before the decision of the Supreme Court in *Grupo Mexicano De Desarrollo SA v Alliance Bond Fund Inc.*.[88] The defendants were resident outside of the jurisdiction, but there was a substantial asset within the jurisdiction. At that time it was thought that the Federal court had jurisdiction to grant the relief but applied a much more stringent test than the English court as to whether it should be granted.[89] Rix J. declined to decide the application for relief applying English Mareva principles—the application should first be made to the Chicago court and ruled on there. When Refco refused to make that application Rix J. dismissed its application in England. The Court of

---

[84] See also the analysis by Steyn L.J. in *Grupo Torras SA v Sheik Fahad Al-Sabah*, Court of Appeal Transcript No.159 of 1994 (February 16, 1994).

[85] See also *Motorola Credit Corporation v Cem Cengiz Uzan (No.2)* [2004] 1 W.L.R. 113 at [120], application for relief which would conflict with an order of the court where assets were located.

[86] [2002] L.R.C. 545.

[87] [1999] 1 Lloyd's Rep. 159.

[88] 527 U.S. 308 (1999).

[89] [1999] 1 Lloyd's Rep. 159 at 165–166.

Appeal upheld his decision ruling that there was insufficient evidence of risk of dissipation of assets. There was disagreement about whether if the Chicago court had power to grant the relief but would apply a higher standard of proof than the English court the English court should offer the English test to the claimant. Millett L.J. considered that this was not within the policy of s.25 as had Rix J. This is because s.25 should not be used by a claimant to shop for a forum when the appropriate court to which the application for interim relief should be made was the court seised with the substantive merits. *Crédit Suisse Fides Trust v Cuoghi* was distinguished by Millett L.J. as being a case in which the English court had supplemented a lack of territorial jurisdiction of the Swiss court.[90] Morritt and Potter L.JJ. thought on the facts that it might still be expedient to grant the relief because of the apparent lack of concern of the Federal judge as to whether the relief was granted.

It is thought that in a case in which interim relief has not been granted by the court having jurisdiction over the substance of the case, the first question is why no such relief is available. Once that question has been answered, the second question is whether this should affect the exercise of discretion by the English court. Thus if the primary court will not grant relief because the assets are situated outside of its territorial jurisdiction, this may provide a good reason for the English court acting in support of the primary court. On the other hand, if the reason is because the primary court applies a higher threshold test for the strength of the case that has to be shown to justify such relief, then the English court should take into account that it is undesirable for the claimant to be encouraged to shop for another forum. This is particularly so if the parties have agreed to the jurisdiction of the primary court. The point is one of policy for the English court in operating the section and should not be affected by what may be the personal views of the foreign judge assigned to the case.

In *Motorola Credit Corporation v Cem Cengiz Uzan (No.2)*,[91] there were **6.060** four defendants. This case was decided after the Supreme Court decision and so the issue which was the subject of disagreement between the judges in *Refco* did not arise. The Federal court in New York had no jurisdiction to grant the relief because of the lack of territorial jurisdiction to restrain dealings with assets located abroad. Accordingly the only court to which application could be made would be the English court, and the absence of jurisdiction in the Federal court did not, in itself, make it inexpedient to grant relief sought in England.[92] However, D2 and D3 had no connection with the jurisdiction and no assets in the jurisdiction. There was every prospect that they would disobey any order made by the English court and no mode of enforcement of any order available to the English court. The Turkish court had granted anti-suit injunctions against the claimant both in

[90] [1999] 1 Lloyd's Rep. at 174–175; see also *The State of Brunei Darussalam v Prince Jefri Bolkiah, The Times*, September 5, 2000 (Jacob J.).
[91] [2004] 1 W.L.R. 113.
[92] *Motorola Credit Corporation v Cem Cengiz Uzan (No.2)* [2004] 1 W.L.R. 113 at [119].

relation to the substantive claims being prosecuted in New York and the proceedings in England. The Court of Appeal held that the position of each defendant must be looked at separately to see whether it was expedient to grant the relief against that particular defendant.[93] It was not expedient to grant relief against D2 and D3 because of the absence of connection with the jurisdiction and the absence of a mode of enforcement of the order.[94] The orders of the Turkish court were also relevant because the English court was being asked to grant orders concerning assets in Turkey, which would conflict with them. D1 had substantial assets in England and visited England from time to time and D4 was resident and had substantial assets in the jurisdiction. The claim was for a substantial international fraud. The Court of Appeal upheld worldwide relief on the grounds that it could be enforced against them and it was expedient to grant the relief.

The Court of Appeal also held that it was not an abuse of the process for D4 to argue about whether a good arguable case had been established when this point had already been decided against her by the Federal court in the context of her challenge to the jurisdiction. A reasoned judgment of the foreign court on the strength of case is part of the evidence but it did not preclude the defendant from asking the English court to look at the strength of the case in the context of the application for interim relief.

6.061   The purpose of Mareva relief granted in support of foreign proceedings under s.25 is to preserve assets for the eventual enforcement of a judgment should the claimant obtain judgment in the foreign proceedings. The rationale for this is to assist in the eventual enforcement of a foreign judgment. But if such a judgment would not be valid and enforceable in England, the English court should decline to grant Mareva relief in support of the foreign jurisdiction.[95] This is because as far as the English court is concerned any judgment eventually given by the foreign court would itself be invalid, and there would be nothing to enforce. Relief can be granted to a claimant if he shows a good arguable case that an eventual judgment would be enforceable in England.

Section 25(1) of the 1982 Act is not directed to a situation in which the English court is being asked to enforce an order for protective measures made by the court having jurisdiction over the claim on the merits. The court having jurisdiction on the merits of the substantive claim has jurisdiction to make an order for provisional measures in relation to assets located in another contracting state.[96] Such an order, even though only provisional, is to be enforced by the courts of other Member States under Regulation 44/2001.[97]

---

[93] *ibid.*, at [116] and [122].

[94] Applying *Derby & Co. v Weldon Nos 3 and 4* [1990] Ch. 65 at 81, and *Locabail International Finance Ltd v Agroexport* [1986] 1 W.L.R. 657 at 665.

[95] *Motorola Credit Corporation v Cem Cengiz Uzan (No.2)* [2004] 1 W.L.R. 113 at [129–137].

[96] *Van Uden Maritime BV v Firma Deco-Line* [1998] ECR–I 7091; see also L.Collins, "The Territorial Reach of Mareva Injunctions" (1989) 105 L.Q.R. 262 at 290–292.

[97] Chapter III of Regulation 44/2001; for the Brussels Convention, see Arts 1, 25, 26–28 and 31, and the comments of Professor Jenard on Title III to the Convention in O.J. No. C59 1979, at p. 42 and following, and also *Babanaft Co. SA v Bassatne* [1990] Ch. 13 at 31.

Provided that the real connection requirement is met, and the order has been made in accordance with the applicable provisions of Chap. III, it will be capable of recognition and enforcement by the courts of other contracting states.[98]

In exercising its discretion under s.25(1), the High Court is entitled to **6.062** proceed upon the basis that preservative relief granted by it, which is within Art.31 of the Regulation or Art.24 of the Conventions,[99] which satisfies the real connection requirement, which is not *ex parte*,[1] and which complies with Chap. III, will be recognised and enforced by the courts of other Member States.[2] This is a factor to be taken into account in relation to the exercise of the discretion under s.25(1) and whether it would be "inexpedient" within s.25(2) to grant relief in the circumstances of the particular case in question.

The jurisdiction under s.25(1) can be exercised post-judgment. Thus, in the context of Mareva relief in relation to proceedings in England, it is established that there is jurisdiction to grant or continue the relief after judgment, and s.25(7) imports the equivalent jurisdiction where substantive proceedings which come within s.25(1) have been commenced. Furthermore, the fact that the judgment is to be enforced by the courts of another contracting state does not preclude the granting of Mareva or Anton Piller relief designed to assist in the enforcement process. Article 31 of the Regulation justifies the High Court in exercising the jurisdiction conferred on it by s.25(1), and Art.22(5) of the Convention does not affect the granting of such relief because it is concerned with execution of a judgment and not provisional measures.[3]

In *Ryan v Friction Dynamics*,[4] Neuberger J. stated the following as **6.063** general principles[5] applicable to s.25:

"In my judgment, in light of the guidance from the authorities and sensible practice, the following general principles apply when the court is asked to exercise its jurisdiction under section 25.

---

[98] *Babanaft Co. SA v Bassatne* [1990] Ch. 13 at 31–32.
[99] These have an autonomous scope which is independent of how relief is classified under national law. Thus in *Mietz v Intership Yachting Sneek BV* [1999] ECR I–2277 the relief was not preservative, did not come within Art.24 and consequently was not within Title III of the Brussels Convention; see also *Reichert v Dresdner Bank (No.2)* [1992] ECR I–2149.
[1] *EMI Records Ltd v Modern Music Karl-Ulrich Walterbach GmbH* [1992] Q.B. 115.
[2] See generally L. Collins, "The Territorial Reach of Mareva Injunctions" (1989) 105 L.Q.R. 262.
[3] *Babanaft Co. SA v Bassatne* (above); *Kuwait Oil Tanker Co. SAK v Qabazard* [2004] 1 A.C. 300.
[4] [2001] C.P. Rep. 75; *The Times*, June 14, 2000.
[5] In *Indosuez International Finance BV v National Reserve Bank* [2002] EWHC 774, Comm Ct, Morison J. said: "Helpful though his analysis is, I have to say that there is a danger in a judge formulating general principles when its discretionary powers are being invoked. The danger is that in a subsequent cases the advocates will concentrate on looking at each of the principles as though each was a requirement that needed to be fulfilled. Further, some of the principles are couched in such wide terms as to amount to no discernible principle at all."

1. The court should always exercise caution before granting any freezing order. The decision and observation of the US Supreme Court in the *Grupo Mexicano* case emphasises the potentially draconian nature of a freezing order in personam, but, before the court has ruled definitively on the parties' rights, it can be said that such an order is obviously potentially harsh, even when it is made on a proprietary basis.

2. As Millett L.J. indicated in *Cuoghi*, particular caution is appropriate where a freezing order is sought under section 25. The fact that the primary forum for the litigation is abroad means that this court is likely to be even less fully appraised of all the facts than in a case where it is exercising primary jurisdiction. See also the observations in *Refco v Eastern Trading Co.* [1999] 1 Lloyd's Rep. 159 of Rix J. at p.164.

3. However, factors such as comity and the need to stop international fraud mean that this court should not be timid about granting an injunction under section 25, if satisfied that good grounds exist. It should be remembered, as pointed out in *Cuoghi*, that section 25(2) indicates that an order should be made unless it is "inexpedient" to do so.

4. Just as when exercising its primary jurisdiction to grant a freezing order, the court should not make such an order under section 25 unless the basic requirements are satisfied, namely that the claimant has a good arguable case and there is a real risk of dissipation. See *Refco* at p.164, *per* Rix J., and at p.171, *per* Morritt L.J.

5. Where a foreign court has refused to grant a freezing order then this court should be slow to grant a freezing order. However, as is clear from the majority view in *Refco*, it may be appropriate nonetheless for this court to grant a freezing order under s.25: see, *per* Morritt L.J. at 173 and Potter L.J. at 174.

6. The fact that there is a worldwide freezing order granted by the principal foreign court does not prevent this court from granting a freezing order, at least in relation to British assets and/or against defendants resident and domiciled within the jurisdiction. As Mr Smith points out, to hold otherwise would be inconsistent with the practice of this court. Worldwide freezing orders are frequently granted by this court, as the primary court, on terms which specifically envisage that the claimant will apply for freezing orders in the courts of the Channel Islands, or the Isle of Man, or Gibraltar in respect of assets within their jurisdiction. Further, to hold otherwise would involve implying an absolute fetter on a statutory jurisdiction which on its face appears to be intended to give a wide and flexible discretion.

7. However, before such an overlapping freezing order is made under s.25 the court should expect to be given cogent reasons to justify it. Overlapping orders mean overlapping applications, which in turn result in substantial increased costs and court time. In this connection the present application, which was merely to discharge or vary a s.25 order, took well over a day and the claimants' schedule of costs in

relation to these two applications alone throws up a figure of over £75,000.

Furthermore, overlapping injunctions in different jurisdictions can lead to a risk of double jeopardy for defendants and the opportunity for forum shopping by a claimant. In *Re BCCI SA* [1994] 1 W.L.R. 708, at 713, Dillon L.J. said that a freezing order in this country should not be "enforced oppressively by a multiplicity of applications in different countries throughout the world". If anything, there is an even stronger case for discouraging a multiplicity of applications for overlapping freezing orders against the same defendants in respect of the same assets in different jurisdictions. No doubt Lord Bingham had that in mind in *Cuoghi*.

8. Where it is appropriate to grant a freezing order under s.25 in respect of British assets, and the order overlaps with a worldwide or similar freezing order of the foreign court with primary jurisdiction, it is sensible to have some indication as to which court is to have the primary role for enforcing the overlapping injunctions. This would at least substantially reduce the risk of double jeopardy and forum shopping. In general, I would have thought that, save where there is good reason to the contrary, it should be the foreign court to which such applications should normally be made.

9. Where an overlapping order is made under s.25, it is in general desirable that it should track the terms of the order made by the foreign court. Any inconsistency could lead to uncertainty and extra complications for a defendant, which would be unfair. Worse, it could in some cases lead to a position where a defendant finds itself bound to be in breach of one order or the other. I derive support for this view from a decision of Jacob J., *The State of Brunei Darussalam v Prince Jefri Bolkiah* (unreported) 20th March 2000 . . . I should add that, of course, there may be good reasons in a particular case why an order made under s.25 should be in different terms from the order made by the primary court."

In *The State of Brunei Darussalam v Prince Jefri Bolkiah*[6] an English **6.064** injunction limited to assets in England and Wales was granted in support of proceedings in Brunei in which worldwide relief had been granted. The Brunei court had granted a liberty to pay living expenses and legal fees out of the assets caught by the injunction regardless of whether such assets were the subject of a proprietary claim when the defendant had not shown that he had no assets of his own from which such payments could be made. This was not the order which would have been made by an English court when dealing with a proprietary claim.[7] Since the English court's role was

---

[6] *The Times*, September 5, 2000 (Jacob J.).
[7] *Fitzgerald v Williams* [1996] Q.B. 657; *Ostrich Farm Corporation Ltd v Ketchell*, unreported, December 10, 1997, CA.

to grant relief ancillary to and supportive of the primary court's relief, the English order followed what had been decided in Brunei.[8]

(v) Counterclaims

6.065　Under the Rules of the Supreme Court, except in pending proceedings, an application for relief under s.25 had to be made by originating summons.[9] RSC Ord.28, r.7(4) had the effect that it was no longer possible to make a counterclaim in interim relief proceedings brought under the section. This was because there was no longer[10] any procedural machinery enabling a counterclaim to be made,[11] and procedural machinery could not be supplied under the inherent jurisdiction of the court.[12] The rationale for allowing counterclaims is so that all matters in dispute between the parties can be brought before a single court, and thus avoid multiplicity of proceedings. In *Balkanbank v Taher (No.2)*[13] the counterclaim arose out of the granting of the relief under s.25 and was closely connected with matters to be dealt with in connection with enforcement of the cross-undertaking in damages. However, an application under s.25 is not the bringing of substantive proceedings on the merits, but only an application for interim measures. It is likely that it was for this reason that the rule was changed in the RSC, after the decision in *Balkanbank v Taher*. Under the RSC as changed such a counterclaim would have had to have been brought by a separate action. This was also the position for proceedings brought under s.44 of the Arbitration Act 1996 commenced by an arbitration application. There was no machinery under the RSC for making a counterclaim in proceedings commenced by arbitration application.[14]

Under the CPR the position is different. The *Admiralty and Commercial Courts Guide*[15] requires that an application to the Commercial Court for relief under s.25 must be made by a claim form under Pt 8 of the CPR. The Guide appears to contemplate that the position for other courts may be

---

[8] See the same approach applied in the Isle of Man granting an application for a variation to a injunction granted there to bring it in line with a variation already made to an injunction granted in England: *Kobuleti Shipping Co Limited v Dilworth* [2000] M.L.B., 33, pp.60–61.

[9] RSC Ord.5, r.3.

[10] Previously RSC Ord.28, r.7 applied and a counterclaim could be made: *Balkanbank v Taher (No.2)* [1995] 1 W.L.R. 1067; *Balkanbank v Taher (No.3)*, The Times, April 14, 1995.

[11] *The Gniezno* [1968] P. 418.

[12] The court also has inherent jurisdiction under s.49(2) of the Supreme Court Act 1981 to provide procedure when the procedural machinery under the rules of court is inadequate: *Toke v Andrews* (1882) 8 Q.B.D. 428, or inconvenient: *Renton Gibbs & Co. Ltd v Neville & Co* [1990] 2 Q.B. 181. But inherent jurisdiction did not apply to cases covered by RSC Ord.28, r.7(4), which was introduced on April 1, 1997 for the very purpose of removing the procedural machinery for making a counterclaim in an application for interim relief under s.25(1) of the Civil Jurisdiction and Judgments Act 1982. This was because "inherent jurisdiction" could not be used to override a change in the rules made for the purpose of preventing counterclaims in such applications—see further 'M. Dockray, "The Inherent Jurisdiction to Regulate Civil Proceedings" (1997) 113 L.Q.R. 120 at 128.

[13] [1995] 1 W.L.R. 1067.

[14] See also RSC Ord.73, r.7(4).

[15] Paragraph F15.15.

different because of CPR r.25.4. CPR r.25.4(1) and (2) provides for the application of "the general rules about applications contained in Part 23". However, it is thought that a claim form under Pt 8 is the correct procedure in other courts as well. This is because of CPR Pt 8, Practice Direction 8.[16] Prior to April 26, 1999, the application had to be made by originating summons, and therefore under that Practice Direction a claim form under Pt 8 has to be used. CPR r.25.4 does not govern the issue of the claim form. The claim form must include an address for service within the jurisdiction.[17] Under CPR r.8.7 where Pt 8 procedure is used, Pt 20 procedure applies except that a party may not make a Pt 20 claim (which includes a counterclaim) without the court's permission. Accordingly there is under CPR a procedural mechanism for making a counterclaim but only with permission of the court. Service of the Pt 20 claim form is dealt with at the same time as the court grants permission to make the Pt 20 claim.[18] Since the claimant has an address for service within the jurisdiction, the court can direct that he can be served with the counterclaim within the jurisdiction.

An application for relief under s.44 of the Arbitration Act 1996 comes **6.066** within Section I of CPR Pt 62 and must be made by arbitration claim form.[19] There is no special provision in Pt 62 which provides for counterclaims. CPR r.62.3(1) provides for the issue of the arbitration claim form "in accordance with Part 8 procedure". This must include an address for service within the jurisdiction. No defence is provided for in the procedure under CPR Pt 62 and therefore CPR r.20.4(2)(a) will not apply.

It seems that CPR r.20.4(2)(b) applies and that a counterclaim can be made with the court's permission.

Whether the court will grant permission for a counterclaim is dealt with in CPR r.20.9.

If the claimant is domiciled in a Member State then the defendant can **6.067** only bring substantive proceedings against him in the cases set out in Chap. II of Regulation 44/2001. Article 6(3) of the Regulation allows a counterclaim "arising from the same contract or facts on which the original claim was based . . .". A defendant to proceedings which are free-standing proceedings for "provisional measures" against him cannot use this article to justify bringing a counterclaim against a claimant who is domiciled in a Member State. This is because the "original claim" must be a claim based on the substance of the matter and does not include free-standing proceedings for provisional relief.[20]

---

[16] Under CPR Pt 8, Practice Direction 8b, supplementing CPR Pt 8 and Schedule 1 and Schedule 2 to the CPR, Section A, para.A.1(3).

[17] CPR r.6.5(2), Form N 208.

[18] CPR r.20.8(3). CPR r.6.20(3A) is permissive, is appropriate for what was formerly third party proceedings, and does not require a counterclaim against a claimant who is out of the jurisdiction to be served out of the jurisdiction.

[19] CPR r.8.1.

[20] See also Art.31 of Regulation 44/2001.

(vi) Section 25(1) and proceedings on the merits which have been or are to be commenced in any other part of the United Kingdom

6.068   Section 25(1) of the 1982 Act enables the High Court to grant "interim relief" when proceedings on the merits have been or are to be commenced in any part of the United Kingdom outside England and Wales, *e.g.* in Scotland. Mareva injunctions and Anton Piller orders are "provisional measures" within s.18(5)(d) of the Civil Jurisdiction and Judgments Act 1982 and accordingly do not qualify for enforcement by other courts in the United Kingdom under s.18 of the Act.

Section 25 applies, however, to the High Court in Northern Ireland, and a similar jurisdiction has been conferred on the Court of Session in Scotland under s.27 of the Act. Accordingly, if, *e.g.*, the High Court in England grants Mareva relief in relation to assets located in Scotland or Northern Ireland, in proceedings on the merits commenced or to be commenced in England, the Court of Session or the High Court in Northern Ireland (as the case might be) could itself entertain an application for and grant relief under s.27(1) or s.25(1) of the Act respectively. The granting of Mareva relief in England would not be a precondition to the exercise of the jurisdiction. Similarly, the granting of provisional measures by the Court of Session or the High Court in Northern Ireland is not a precondition to the exercise of jurisdiction by the High Court in England under s.25(1).

(vii) Particular problems in preparing applications under s.25.

6.069   Because applications under s.25 involve substantive proceedings to be tried abroad, and not in England, and liasing with foreign lawyers, they present special problems to English lawyers responsible for preparing them who may find themselves acting in a supportive role. The English lawyers have a personal duty to ensure that matters are dealt with promptly, accurately and with proper disclosure being made to the English court.[21]

(5) Winding-up or bankruptcy proceedings[22]

6.070   In *United Bank v Claybridge, SA*,[23] Robert Goff J. had granted a Mareva injunction against a Panamanian company which was chartering in vessels and sub-chartering them. In the Commercial Court the injunction was

---

[21] *Lennox Lewis v Eliades, The Times*, February 28, 2002.
[22] This head of jurisdiction is discussed by P. St J. Smart, "Safeguarding Assets in International Litigation: The Insolvency Option" (1996) 112 L.Q.J.R. 397. See also Chapter, below.
[23] (1980) 14 *Lloyd's Maritime Law Newsletter* (May 15, 1980); 16 *Lloyd's Maritime Law Newsletter* (June 12, 1980); [1997] 1 B.C.L.C. 572 (March 9, 1981), also in *The Times*, March 13, 1981, [1981] Com. L.R. 107, and Court of Appeal (Civ Div) Transcript No.143 of 1981 (March 9, 1981).

qualified so as to enable the defendant company to pay trading debts and expenses.[24] But the plaintiffs appealed to the Court of Appeal against an order enabling the defendant to pay out certain moneys and in the course of the appeal, Templeman L.J. suggested that the plaintiffs should petition for the winding-up of the company. In contemplation of the commencement of winding-up proceedings, the injunction was modified so as to restrain the defendant from making any payment except those validated by the Companies Court under s.227 of the Companies Act 1948, which is now s.127 of the Insolvency Act 1986.

In the *United Bank* case there were substantive proceedings on the merits of the plaintiffs' claims pending before the Commercial Court. The existence of such substantive proceedings is not, however, a precondition for the exercise of the jurisdiction. Section 37(1) of the Supreme Court Act 1981 confers on the High Court a jurisdiction which can be exercised in the context of winding-up proceedings. Section 37(1) applies to the winding-up jurisdiction of the court and, in principle, Mareva or Anton Piller relief can be granted in aid of or ancillary to the exercise of that jurisdiction.[25] If assets of the company are in jeopardy, then the court may appoint[26] a provisional liquidator under s.135 of the Insolvency Act 1986 and this may be done *ex parte* on sufficient cause being shown. Ordinarily in such a case the applicant will be required to give an undertaking in damages, although this requirement is dispensed with where the application is made by the Secretary for Trade and Industry for the purpose of enforcing the law and in pursuance of his public duty.[27] In such cases, the application should set out why the case cannot be dealt with by the applicant seeking undertakings or by the granting of an injunction.[28]

---

[24] Applying *Iraqi Ministry of Defence v Arcepey Shipping Co. SA (The Angel Bell)* [1981] Q.B. 65.

[25] *Re Cayman Capital Trust Company* [1988–1989] C.I.L.R. 444 (in winding up proceedings, mareva injunctions were granted against a director/contributory and his wife, based on the possibility that the liquidator might bring a misfeasance summons in respect of missing funds of the company); see also *Deutsche Schachtbau-und Tiefbohrgesellschaft GmbH v Shell International Co. Ltd* [1990] 1 A.C. 295 at 361, *per* Lord Goff where the possibility of granting an injunction in aid of winding-up proceedings was addressed but the injunction was refused on discretionary grounds; cp. *Walter Developments Pty v Roberts* (1995) 16 A.C.S.R. 280 at 282–283, Supreme Court of Western Australia, in which the applicant was a shareholder seeking to have a company wound up on the "just and equitable" ground. On the facts in that case there was no real risk of dissipation of assets (see at 282 (line 46)–283 (line 10)) and so the Mareva jurisdiction did not arise—see also *Bond Brewing Holdings Ltd v National Australia Bank* [1991] 1 V.L.R. 580, and (1990) 169 C.L.R. 271, in which likewise the application was not for Mareva relief.

[26] *Re Highfield Commodities Ltd* [1985] 1 W.L.R. 149 at 158–159; *Re Union Accident Insurance Co. Ltd* [1972] 1 All E.R. 1105.

[27] *Re Highfield Commodities* [1985] 1 W.L.R. 149; *Re City Vintners* [2002] F.S.R. 33. This is by analogy to the principle applicable to interlocutory injunctions discussed in *F. Hoffman-La Roche & Co. AG v Secretary of State* [1975] A.C. 295; see also *Belize Alliance of Conservation Non-Governmental Organisations v The Department of Environment and Belize Electricity Company*, Privy Council Appeal No.47 of 2003.

[28] *Re City Vintners* [2002] F.S.R. 33.

The jurisdiction to entertain winding-up or bankruptcy proceedings falling within the scope of Council Regulation 1346/2000[29] is governed by that Regulation.

6.071　　In other cases, winding-up proceedings may be successfully brought in England against a foreign company under Pt V of the Insolvency Act 1986.[30] An "unregistered company"[31] can be wound up if it has been dissolved,[32] or has ceased to carry on business, or is only carrying on business for the purpose of winding up its affairs, or if the company is unable to pay its debts, or if it is "just and equitable" that the company be wound up.[33] However, although the statutory jurisdiction is expressed in wide terms, the exercise of the jurisdiction is discretionary and it is relevant to see what is the justification for winding up a foreign company without a place of business within the jurisdiction.

The courts have exercised the discretion taking into account that it may be inappropriate for the English court to exercise jurisdiction over a foreign company and persons abroad.[34] The discretion has been exercised in favour of exercising the jurisdiction when there are assets within the jurisdiction belonging to the company which could be fairly distributed to creditors through English winding-up proceedings and which could not be distributed through proceedings in the country of incorporation,[35] or even when such a company does not have assets within the jurisdiction,[36] provided that the affairs of the company in question have a sufficient connection with England,[37] and there is a reasonable possibility of benefit for the creditors from the winding up.[38] In *Re Real Estate Development Ltd*[39] it was held that three requirements were to be satisfied: (i) there must be sufficient connection with the jurisdiction; (ii) there must be a reasonable possibility that the winding-up order would benefit those applying for it; and (iii) the court had to be able to exercise jurisdiction over one or more persons interested in the distribution of the company's assets.

It is the usual practice of the Companies Court to dismiss petitions to wind up based on a disputed debt. This is because normally it is just to leave the petitioner to take proceedings to establish his claim before

---

[29] Of May 29, 2000 on insolvency proceedings (O.J. No. L160, June 30, 2000, pp.1–18).

[30] *Re Compania Merabello San Nicholas SA* [1973] Ch. 75; *Re Allobrogia Steamship Corporation* [1979] 1 Lloyd's Rep. 190; *Re Eloc Electro-Optiek and Communicate BV* [1982] Ch. 43; *Re a Company (No.00359 of 1988)* [1988] Ch. 210; *Re a Company (No.003102 of 1991) Ex p. Nyckeln Finance Co. Ltd* [1991] B.C.L.C. 539.

[31] Defined in s.220 of the Insolvency Act 1986.

[32] Insolvency Act 1986, ss221(5)(a) and 225.

[33] *ibid.*, s.221.

[34] *Banco Nacional de Cuba v Cosmos Trading* [2000] 1 B.C.L.C. 813.

[35] *Banque des Marchands de Moscou v Kindersley* [1951] Ch. 112; *Re Azoff-Don Commercial Bank* [1954] Ch. 315.

[36] *Re Latreefers Inc.* [2001] 2 B.C.L.C. 116.

[37] For this requirement on a petition to wind up a foreign company in the public interest, see *Re Titan International Inc.* [1998] 1 B.C.L.C. 102.

[38] *Re a Company (No.00359 of 1987)* [1988] Ch. 210 at 225–226; *Banco Nacional de Cuba v Cosmos Trading* [2000] 1 B.C.L.C. 813.

[39] [1991] B.C.L.C. 210, approved in *Re Latreefers Inc.* [2001] 2 B.C.L.C. 116

entertaining insolvency proceedings. However this is not invariably the case and, at its highest, this is a rule of practice.[40] The court may decide to allow the petition to proceed notwithstanding that there is a dispute about the debt or on a contributory's petition where there is a dispute as to the contributory's status.[41] In particular this is so where the effect of dismissing the petition would be to deprive the petitioner of a remedy which he ought to have or where the dismissal could cause or would be likely to cause serious injustice (*e.g.* allowing the company to spirit away its assets whereas if the petition is allowed to proceed the assets could be preserved either by injunction or by the appointment of a provisional liquidator).[42]

The petition may be presented and proceeded with, regardless of the fact that the claim on which the petition is based could not have been made the subject of a substantive action on the merits for which permission to serve proceedings out of the jurisdiction could have been obtained. **6.072**

A Mareva injunction does not improve the petitioner's position as regards other creditors in a liquidation. When a receiver has been appointed under a debenture, those with established claims are entitled to a variation of the injunction which will enable the receiver to satisfy their claims; see *Cretanor Maritime Co. Ltd v Irish Marine Management Ltd (The Cretan Harmony)*.[43]

Except for bankruptcy proceedings falling within the scope of Council Regulation 1346/2000,[44] the circumstances in which a bankruptcy petition may be presented against a debtor are set out in s.265 of the Insolvency Act 1986. The presence of assets within the jurisdiction is never in itself sufficient to establish jurisdiction. A petition may be presented in respect of an individual if, on the day the petition was presented, the debtor was domiciled in England or was personally present in England or, even though he is neither domiciled in England and Wales nor personally present in England and Wales on the day of presentation of the petition, if, in the period of three years ending with the day the petition is presented, he was ordinarily resident or has had a place of residence in England and Wales or has carried on business in England and Wales (either personally, in partnership with others, or by means of an agent or manager). The debtor may have carried on business himself, or by a firm or partnership of which he is or was a member, or by an agent or manager acting for him or for the firm or partnership. Again, there is no requirement that the debt on which the petition is founded could have been made the subject of substantive proceedings for which leave to serve out of the jurisdiction could have been obtained. Under s.286 of the Insolvency Act 1986, the court has

---

[40] *R. W. H. Enterprises Ltd v Portedge Ltd* [1998] B.C.C. 556; *Re Claybridge Shipping Co. SA* [1997] 1 B.C.L.C. 572

[41] *Alipour v Ary* [1997] 1 W.L.R. 534, applying *Re Claybridge Shipping Co. SA* [1981] Com. L.R. 107, now reported at [1997] 1 B.C.L.C. 572.

[42] If the company is obviously insolvent and there is a strong risk of dissipation of its assets, a provisional liquidator might well be appointed.

[43] [1978] 1 W.L.R. 966.

[44] May 29, 2000 on insolvency proceedings.

jurisdiction to appoint an interim receiver "if it is shown to be necessary for the protection of the debtor's property" and such an appointment may be made at any time after presentation of the petition. Section 37(1) of the Supreme Court Act 1981 applies to the jurisdiction of the court in bankruptcy and Mareva and Anton Piller relief may be granted in aid of or ancillary to the exercise of that jurisdiction by the court. If Mareva relief were to be granted in relation to bankruptcy proceedings, then it would not be appropriate for the injunction to have an unqualified exception to allow the payment of debts of the debtor, but would ordinarily allow payments sanctioned by the court under s.284(1) of the Insolvency Act 1986.

6.073   In cases governed by Regulation 1346/2000 the jurisdiction of the courts of Member States to entertain insolvency proceedings is governed by the Regulation. Under Art.38 of Regulation 1346/2000 preservative measures may be granted by the court of another Member State. Under that Article, "a temporary administrator" may be appointed in order to ensure the preservation of the assets of the company or debtor for the period between "the request for the opening of the insolvency proceedings and the judgment opening the proceedings". This enables a provisional liquidator or an interim receiver to be appointed.

(6) Mareva or Anton Piller relief granted in aid of enforcement of an English judgment, or an enforceable foreign judgment or an enforceable arbitration award whether made in England or abroad

6.074   It is well established that Mareva or Anton Piller relief can be granted post-judgment in an action in England. This jurisdiction is ancillary to enforcement of the judgment.[45] The relief can also be granted in proceedings taken to enforce a foreign judgment in England or to enforce an arbitration award.

In the case of a claimant who has obtained a foreign judgment which he wishes to register in England, the procedure is set out in CPR Pt 74. Such a claimant is not entitled to seek to enforce the foreign judgment for a period of time after a registration order has been made (CPR r.74.9). Once the claimant has obtained a foreign judgment, he is entitled to commence substantive proceedings in England for the registration of that judgment, and upon completion of those proceedings he will have a final judgment which can be enforced in England. In principle therefore, the claimant is entitled to apply for Mareva relief in connection with those substantive proceedings immediately prior to or upon commencement of those proceedings. Thus, Mareva relief is available in cases in which the foreign

---

[45] See Chapter 3, paras 3.023–7 below.

judgment is to be enforced within the jurisdiction by registration. In New Zealand it has been decided that this is the case in relation to provisions corresponding to the Foreign Judgments (Reciprocal Enforcement) Act 1933: *Hunt v BP Exploration Company (Libya) Ltd.*[46] In that case the original *ex parte* injunction (granted on *ex parte* registration of the judgment) was maintained even though the overseas judgment was subject to an appeal and an application to set aside the registration of the judgment had been adjourned pending the outcome of the appeal (pursuant to the provision corresponding to s.5(1) of the Foreign Judgments (Reciprocal Enforcement) Act 1933). In *Deutsche Schachtbau-und Tiefbohrgesellschaft GmbH v R'as Al-Khaimah National Oil Company (No.2),*[47] the Court of Appeal upheld an injunction granted by Bingham J. in proceedings to enforce a foreign arbitration award by registration. In that case Bingham J. had made an order *ex parte* pursuant to what was then RSC Ord.73, r.10 and s.3(1)(a) of the Arbitration Act 1975 granting leave to the plaintiffs to enforce the arbitration award as a judgment. Under the former RSC Ord.73, r.10(6), the award was not immediately enforceable in the same manner as a judgment or order, but the injunction was granted for the purpose of preserving assets pending the award becoming enforceable and execution being sought. In the interim period, it was regarded by Sir John Donaldson M.R. (with whom the other members of the court agreed) as "at least doubtful" whether the injunction was to be regarded as a Mareva injunction or an injunction granted to a judgment creditor in aid of execution, albeit that by reason of the former RSC Ord.73, r.10(6) the right to levy execution was "subject to a suspension", and that the order made *ex parte*, granting leave to enforce, might subsequently be set aside.

Proceedings to enforce an arbitration award, other than by action on the award, are governed by CPR Pt 62 and there is jurisdiction under CPR r.62.16 to permit service out of the jurisdiction of proceedings to enforce the award.

Under CPR r.6.20(9) the court has jurisdiction to grant permission to serve out of the jurisdiction proceedings in which the claim is brought to enforce any judgment or arbitral award.[48] CPR r.6.19 enables service out of the jurisdiction to be effected without leave, on a defendant domiciled in any part of the United Kingdom or "Regulation State" or any other "Convention territory" (as defined in CPR r.6.18), of proceedings to enforce a judgment under the provisions of the Regulation,[49] or of the Conventions, or a judgment under s.18 of the Civil Jurisdiction and Judgments Act 1982 (judgments and arbitration awards from another part of the United Kingdom). **6.075**

---

[46] [1980] 1 N.Z.L.R. 104.
[47] [1990] 1 A.C. 295 at 306 *et seq.*
[48] The judgment or arbitral award must already exist: *Mercedes Benz AG v Leiduck* [1996] A.C. 284.
[49] Council Regulation 44/2001 of December 22, 2000 on jurisdiction and the recognition and enforcement of judgments in civil and commercial matters (O.J. No. LO12, January 16, 2001, pp.1–23).

If a judgment or award cannot be enforced by registration, it may still be open to the party seeking to enforce to bring an action at common law on the judgment or the award, and Mareva and Anton Piller relief may be granted in those proceedings.[50]

The fact that proceedings to enforce the relevant judgment against the assets in question have been commenced or are to be commenced before the courts of another "Regulation State"[51] or "Convention territory" (see CPR r.6.18) does not preclude the High Court from granting Mareva or Anton Piller relief in aid of the enforcement proceedings to be brought abroad—Art.22.5 of the Regulation and Art.16(5) of the Conventions do not prevent the High Court from granting provisional measures. The exclusive jurisdiction under these Articles applies only to proceedings for the enforcement of the judgment against an asset as opposed to "provisional measures" which come within Art.31 of the Regulation or Art.24 of the Conventions.[52]

(7) An application for relief against a non-party, when proceedings on the merits are being brought in England

6.076 What is the position if the non-party is outside of the jurisdiction? The questions which arise are:

(1) Does the non-party have to be served with process out of the jurisdiction?

(2) Does the court have power to permit service of the process out of the jurisdiction?

(3) Should the court exercise jurisdiction over him?

(i) Does the non-party have to be served with process out of the jurisdiction?

6.077 CPR Pt 6 includes powers for service by an alternative method[53] or dispensing with service altogether.[54] Under the former RSC, when service of process could not be had legitimately under the rules, the court would not use substituted service under RSC Ord.65, r.4(1) to bypass RSC Ord.11, r.1(1).[55] The principle is that dispensing with service or ordering

---

[50] *NEC Corporation v Steintoon* (1986) 52 O.R. 201 (Ontario).
[51] *i.e* a Member State.
[52] *Babanaft & Co. SA v Bassatne* [1990] Ch. 13; *Kuwait Oil Tanker Co. SAK v Qabazard* [2004] 1 A.C. 300.
[53] CPR r.6.8—previously substituted service.
[54] CPR r.6.9.
[55] *Myerson v Martin* [1979] 1 W.L.R. 1390.

service by an alternative method is not to be used when the real problem is one of exercising territorial jurisdiction over the respondent.

(ii) Does the court have power to permit service of the process out of the jurisdiction?

Where a claim on the merits was to be made on a foreigner, the former **6.078** RSC Ord.11 provided a complete code as to when the writ or other origination process could be served out of the jurisdiction, and there was no power to bypass the need to fit the intended action within one or more of the sub-rules permitting service out of the jurisdiction. The failure to bring the case within what was then RSC Ord.11, r.1(1)(i) is what led to the plaintiffs losing in *The Siskina*. The reasoning in *The Siskina* was that the rule only applied to claims for an injunction based on a cause of action.

When relief is sought against a non-party there are already proceedings on the merits on foot before the English court or there must be some method immediately available of commencing and serving proceedings on the merits. The problem is different from that in *The Siskina* where unless the action could be brought within the rule, there was no way in which the writ could be served out of the jurisdiction, and the court had no power to entertain the substantive proceedings to which the Mareva relief was ancillary.

The problem is also very different from when an application is being made for an injunction against the defendant who has already submitted to the jurisdiction in respect of the claim or is amenable to be served with a claim on the merits. In such a case, provided that the injunction is concerned with the substantive claim or the proceedings in which that claim is made, the jurisdiction over the defendant flows from the personal jurisdiction being exercised over him in respect of the underlying substantive claim. Under the former rules of court, RSC Ord.11, r.9(4) enabled the court to permit service out of the jurisdiction of a summons or notice of motion seeking the injunction.[56] CPR r.6.30(2) is directed to the case where the claimant needs to obtain permission to serve the claim form out of the jurisdiction on the defendant—in such a case, if the claimant wishes to make an application against the defendant in those proceedings by application notice, he must also seek permission to serve the application notice out of the jurisdiction.

What is the position about seeking Mareva relief against a non-party in **6.079** proceedings which have been properly served or can be properly served on the defendant? In *National Justice Co. Naviera v Prudential Assurance Co. Ltd*[57] the question arose about the defendant making a claim against a non-

---

[56] *National Justice Co. Naviera v Prudential Assurance Co. Ltd (No.2)* [2000] 1 W.L.R. 603; *Mansour v Mansour* [1989] 1 F.L.R. 418—in contempt proceedings the court has a power to dispense with service of the claim form or application notice under RSC Ord.52, r.4(3). That rule is expressed to be without prejudice to its powers under CPR Pt 6.

[57] [2000] 1 W.L.R. 603.

party for costs under s.51 of the Supreme Court Act 1981. RSC Ord.11 remained in force and the Court of Appeal held that the application for costs could be made by summons served on the non-party out of the jurisdiction under RSC Ord.11, r.9(4).

CPR r.6.20 is very different from what was RSC Ord.11, r.1(1). It includes matters which previously were dealt with in other rules. Thus CPR r.6.20(17) enables a claim for costs against a non-party to be served out of the jurisdiction, whereas previously this was covered by RSC Ord.11, r.9(4) and CPR r.6.20(4) enables a claim for an interim remedy under s.25(1) of the Civil Jurisdiction and Judgments Act 1982 to be served abroad, whereas previously this was dealt with in RSC Ord.11, r.8A. CPR r.6.20 and r.6.21[58] are not restricted so as only to include within their scope claims for substantive relief.

By CPR r.6.18(h) "claim form" in CPR r.6.20 is defined to include an "application notice", and by r.6.18(i) "claim" includes "application". Accordingly CPR r.6.20 applies directly to applications which must be made by application notice in pending proceedings.

6.080   In *C Inc. v L*,[59] the claimant had obtained a default judgment against Mrs L and wanted to obtain Mareva relief against her husband in respect of his own assets. Mr L was resident in Guernsey. This was on the ground that he was liable to indemnify Mrs L against her liability on the judgment. The claimant did not intend to bring any substantive claim against Mr L in England.

The case was argued[60] on the basis that the injunction was not being sought under s.25 in aid of execution proceedings to be brought in Guernsey, but as interlocutory relief to be granted post-judgment against a non-party in the English proceedings. The claimant applied for a receiver to be appointed by the English court over the right of indemnity by way of equitable execution and for Mareva relief against Mr L so that his assets could be used to pay the receiver.

Although called "equitable execution" the relief sought was equitable relief in aid of execution and not execution itself.[61] The right of indemnity was situated outside of the jurisdiction. The correct analysis would appear to be that the English court would not itself execute the default judgment on the asset in Guernsey and that the relief sought had to be justified as preservative relief sought in aid of anticipated execution, *i.e.* pending enforcement of the judgment on Mrs L's asset in Guernsey.[62] Such relief could have been granted under s.25, and CPR r.6.20(4) enabled permission

---

[58] This contrasts with the former RSC Ord.11, r.4(1)—see *Mercedes Benz v Leiduck* [1996] A.C. 284 at 302.

[59] [2001] 2 Lloyd's Rep. 459.

[60] [2001] 2 Lloyd's Rep. at 467 at [35].

[61] *Re Shephard Atkins v Shephard* (1889) 43 Ch.D. 131 at 136 and 137.

[62] *Société Eram Shipping Co. Ltd v Compagnie Internationale de Navigation* [2004] 1 A.C. 260; *Kuwait Oil Tanker Co. SAK v Qabazard* [2004] 1 A.C. 300; *Mackinnon v Donaldson Lufkin & Jenrette Securities Corporation* [1986] Ch.482; *Babanaft International Co. SA v Bassatne* [1990] Ch.13 at 44.

to be granted for service on the husband of a claim form, or application notice issued in the pending proceedings, for interim relief to be granted in support of the Guernsey proceedings. However, this was not the way in which the case was argued or decided.[63]

In a case in which there is only a substantive claim against the defendant, **6.081** the relief is sought against the non-party ancillary to the cause of action against the defendant. In those circumstances the application for the injunction against the non-party still had to fit within CPR r.6.20. The decision in *C Inc v L* was that the effect of CPR r.6.18(h) and (i) when read with CPR r.6.20(3), the "necessary or proper party . . ." provision, enabled an application notice to be served on Mr L out of the jurisdiction, which included both the application for the appointment of a receiver and the application for Mareva relief against him. The court also granted Mareva relief against him.

The application for the appointment of the receiver concerned both the wife and Mr L. It was the same question as against both of them and service on him of the application seeking the appointment of the receiver would seem justified based on CPR r.6.20(3). As a matter of fairness it was appropriate to give the opportunity to the husband to contest the application for the appointment of the receiver. He was a "proper party" to that application. However, the application for the Mareva injunction against him went beyond the application for the appointment of the receiver. Even if the receiver were appointed, the order would not require the husband to do anything, and the receiver would have had to apply to the Guernsey court to enforce the indemnity.[64] Normally the English court would only grant relief which became effective against the foreigner once application had been successfully made to the relevant foreign court for the English order to be recognised and enforced against the foreigner.[65] It was one matter to appoint the receiver, and another to grant Mareva relief against the husband. When considered separately it is thought that it was a matter for the Guernsey court to hear the claim on the indemnity against the husband and so the appropriate head of CPR r.6.20 was sub-paragraph (4) and not sub-paragraph (3).

In a case in which no judgment has been obtained against a defendant the English court can still grant relief against a non-party foreigner under s.25 in support of proceedings to be brought against him abroad to preserve assets. So, *e.g.* if the local court had a jurisdiction to proceed against the non-party, then the English court could grant relief under s.25 in anticipation of those proceedings.

---

[63] The case was decided before the decisions of the House of Lords in *Société Eram Shipping Co. Ltd v Compagnie Internationale de Navigation* [2003] 1 A.C. 260 and *Kuwait Oil Tanker Co. SAK v Qabazard* [2004] 1 A.C. 300.
[64] *Re Maudsley Sons & Field* [1900] 1 Ch.602 at 611–612.
[65] *Bank of China v NBM LLC* [2002] 1 W.L.R. 844; *Société Eram Shipping Co. Ltd. v Compagnie Internationale de Navigation* [2004] 1 A.C. 260.

6.082   An application for Mareva relief is not a claim for substantive relief and so lies outside the mandatory rules on jurisdiction in Regulation 44/2001 or the Brussels or Lugano Conventions.[66]

(iii) Should the court exercise jurisdiction over the non-party?

6.083   In *C Inc. v L* the asset was located out of the jurisdiction and Mr L was out of the jurisdiction, and he was a non-party—he had not submitted to the jurisdiction of the English court nor was he a party to a substantive claim. There was also the possibility for the receiver to execute on the right of indemnity through the local court to whose jurisdiction Mr L was amenable. This could have been done through enforcing the default judgment in Guernsey. Furthermore the position could have been pre-served by the English court under s.25(1) with relief granted subject to a proviso about its effect on the husband. In these circumstances it is thought that the court should not have entertained the application except as an application against the husband under s.25.[67]

(8) An application for relief which falls into none of the above categories

6.084   Section 37 of the Supreme Court Act 1981 enables the relief to be granted in substantive proceedings in England brought against a defendant on the merits. But if the defendant cannot be served within the jurisdiction it is essential that there is a rule of court under which he can be served with the claim out of the jurisdiction. If this cannot be done, then s.37 does not enable the relief to be granted.[68]

   Section 25 of the Civil Jurisdiction and Judgments Act 1982 confers a jurisdiction on the court to grant interim relief in English proceedings brought solely for that purpose, the interim relief being granted in support of foreign proceedings either commenced or to be commenced. Mareva relief can be granted in those English proceedings for the purpose of preserving assets, so that assets will be available to satisfy a judgment obtained in the foreign proceedings, which will be enforceable in England. There is a similar jurisdiction under s.44 of the Arbitration Act 1996 for relief to be granted in support of arbitral proceedings, including arbitral proceedings abroad. Both s.25 proceedings and s.44 proceedings are the

[66] *National Justice Co. Naviera v Prudential Assurance Co. Ltd (No.2)* [2000] 1 W.L.R. 603; *C Inc. v L* [2001] 2 Lloyd's Rep. 459.
[67] *Société Eram Shipping Co. Ltd v Compagnie Internationale de Navigation* [2004] 1 A.C. 260.
[68] *Mercedes Benz v Leiduck* [1996] A.C. 284 applying *The Siskina* [1979] A.C. 210; *Donohue v Armco* [2002] 1 Lloyd's Rep. 425 at [19] and [21] (application for an anti-suit injunction failed because the respondents were not amenable to the jurisdiction).

subject of rules enabling service of the proceedings, to be made with permission outside of the jurisdiction.

There was a gap as regards substantive proceedings which are to be brought in England and where the only basis for serving an intended defendant was under the former RSC Ord.11, r.1(1)(c), *i.e.* that one defendant has been duly served (the primary defendant) and that another defendant is a proper or necessary party to the claim against the primary defendant. If the primary defendant had not yet been served, there was no jurisdiction under the former RSC Ord.11, r.1(1)(c) for the court to give leave for service out of the jurisdiction on the secondary defendant. The fact that service would be possible in due course after the primary defendant had been served was viewed as insufficient to enable any interim relief to be granted under s.37 against the secondary defendant.[69] The position has been remedied in CPR r.6.20(3) which enables permission to be granted regardless of whether the claim form has yet been served on the primary defendant.

(9) The exercise of discretion against a "lawless and truculent" foreigner

In proceedings in which the court has jurisdiction to grant relief against a foreigner, an injunction can be granted, even before issue of the claim form and can be granted against a foreigner who is to be served out of the jurisdiction. In exercising the discretion to grant an injunction when the defendant is subject to the coercive power of the court, the court does not contemplate that its order will not be obeyed;[70] ". . . there is not one law for the law abiding and another for the lawless and truculent".[71] Where (1) the court does not have coercive power over the foreigner (2) an injunction would be without teeth (3) the defendant is a foreigner abroad owing no allegiance to England, and (4) the foreigner is "lawless and truculent", then the absence of an effective mode of enforcement becomes a relevant factor to be taken into account.[72]

6.085

---

[69] *Kuwait Oil Tanker Co. SAK v Al Bader* [1997] 2 All E.R. 855 at 859; *Qingdao Ocean Shipping Co. v Grace Shipping* [1995] 2 Lloyd's Rep. 15 at 27 (*per* Rix J., saying that he did not know of "a doctrine of contingent jurisdiction").

[70] *Republic of Haiti v Duvalier* [1990] 1 Q.B. 202 at 216 following *Re Liddell's Settlement Trusts* [1936] Ch. 365 at 374, *per* Romer L.J.; *Castanho v Brown & Root UK* [1981] A.C. 557 at 574; and *South Bucks District Council v Porter* [2003] 2 A.C. 558 at [32].

[71] *South Bucks District Council v Porter* [2003] 2 A.C. 558 at [32].

[72] See for an anti-suit injunction against a foreigner: *Donohue v Armco* [2002] 1 Lloyd's Rep. 425 at [19], proposition (3), and *Royal Exchange Assurance v Compania Naviera Santi SA (The Tropaioforos No.2)* [1962] 1 Lloyd's Rep. 410, which are discussed in Chapter 14, para.14.005; and for freezing injunctions granted under s.25 of the Civil Jurisdiction and Judgments Act 1982 against foreigners, see *Motorola Credit Corporation v Cem Cengiz Uzan (No.2)* [2004] W.L.R. 113 at [125] and para.6.055 above.

Chapter 7

Preservation of assets: other types of relief

The use of the Mareva injunction has become so widespread that it is now **7.001** regarded as probably the foremost type of interlocutory relief for the preservation of assets. The courts do, however, have other procedures available, and the power to grant other forms of interlocutory relief in circumstances in which Mareva relief is inappropriate, or liable to be ineffective.

(1) Buyer's claim on contracts for the sale of a ship

A recurring problem in practice has been that of a purchaser who believes **7.002** that a vessel which is about to be delivered under a concluded sale agreement (usually on the Norwegian Sale Form) suffers from defects. If the vessel is indeed defective when delivered, the buyer may have a claim for damages under the sale agreement. This depends on the terms of the agreement; although terms as to fitness for purpose and merchantable quality implied by ss13 and 14 of the Sale of Goods Act 1979 can be implied in a ship sale contract, such sales are nowadays more often concluded on an "as is" basis. Accordingly, if the buyer has a claim at all, it is more likely to arise in respect of a breach of an express term of the sale agreement. For example, in *Ninemia Maritime Corporation v Trave Schiffahrtsgesellschaft GmbH (The Niedersachsen),*[1] the claim was in respect of, *inter alia*, the alleged breach of the term providing for the vessel to be delivered "free of average damage affecting class".

A buyer who has reason to believe that he would have a good claim for damages if he took delivery of the vessel will often have in mind the following considerations.

(1) The buyer, for commercial reasons, wishes to take delivery of the vessel.

---

[1] [1983] 1 W.L.R. 1412.

(2) The buyer does not wish to be left with an unsecured claim for damages against the seller. The seller is often a company which is selling its only known asset.

(3) The proceeds of sale may be payable to a bank which holds a mortgage over the vessel, and has first claim over the sale proceeds.

(4) The provisions of the sale agreement usually entitle the seller:

(a) to serve a notice making time of delivery of the essence, and
(b) to forfeit the buyer's deposit and cancel the contract if the buyer fails to comply with such a notice.

(5) The buyer may not be entitled to reject the vessel, even if he wishes to do so.

(6) The buyer may not even have reliable detailed information about the suspected defects, upon which to consider the position and decide what prospects he has of legitimately rejecting the vessel, or to assess the quantum of his prospective liability in damages if he makes the wrong decision.

7.003   Buyers have attempted to deal with these considerations by proceeding to take delivery of the vessel and applying for a Mareva injunction over the sale proceeds within the jurisdiction either before or after delivery. In *Ateni Maritime Corporation v Great Marine Ltd (The Great Marine No.1)*[2] the sellers argued that because of the Mareva relief the price had not been paid under the contract, and they were entitled to cancel. This argument was rejected on the ground that payment of the price is effectively made under the contract even though the proceeds are then immediately frozen in the hands of the seller.

The courts have shown a marked reluctance to assist buyers with Mareva relief. In relation to an application before delivery of the vessel is accepted by the buyer, two major objections have arisen. First, it is often the case that the buyer will not acquire a right of action in damages until he has accepted delivery. Secondly, it is said that the buyer should not be allowed to use the Mareva injunction procedure to set a "trap" for the unwary seller, who gives up the vessel, only to find the sale proceeds immediately frozen in his hands.[3]

The first objection is based on the rule that Mareva relief is not available unless and until the claimant has an accrued cause of action. The courts have consistently refused to grant Mareva injunctions to assist a claimant who has strong grounds for believing that the potential defendant

[2] [1990] 2 Lloyd's Rep. 245.
[3] *Z Ltd v A-Z and AA-LL* [1982] Q.B. 558 at 585, *per* Kerr L.J. *Ninemia Maritime Corporation v Trave Schiffahrtsgesellschaft GmbH (The Niedersachsen)* [1983] 1 W.L.R. 1412 at 1419, *per* Kerr L.J. citing with approval a passage from Mustill J. whose judgment is reported at [1983] 2 Lloyd's Rep. 600.

will break his contract or commit a tort. In *Siporex Trade SA v Comdel Commodities Ltd*,[4] Bingham J. refused to grant a Mareva injunction to a plaintiff who had not yet acquired a cause of action. However, upon the plaintiff acquiring a cause of action by making a payment to the defendant, Bingham J. subsequently granted an injunction restraining the defendant from dealing with (*inter alia*) the fund resulting from the payment.

If the claimant does not yet have a cause of action against the defendant, **7.004** then he is not claiming any final relief to which a Mareva injunction can be ancillary, and there is no jurisdiction to grant the Mareva relief.[5] In cases outside of the *quia timet* jurisdiction, the refusal to grant relief in respect of a cause of action which a claimant expects to acquire in the near future is both inconvenient and liable to cause injustice. The claimant will have to make an immediate, urgent application to the judge upon acquiring the cause of action. In the meantime, the intended defendant may remove assets from the jurisdiction or deal with those assets. If the assets have yet to be acquired by the intended defendant, he may nevertheless enter into a valid equitable assignment, which will bind the assets when they are acquired and defeat the Mareva when it is eventually granted: *Pharaoh's Plywood Co. Ltd v Allied Wood Products*.[6]

In Australia the courts have declined to impose a rigid requirement that the plaintiff must have an existing maintainable cause of action (see para.1.020–1 above). Furthermore, such a requirement is in contrast to the result sought to be achieved by the court on the exercise of the *quia timet* jurisdiction, where injunctive relief is granted to prevent the commission of future wrongs. That jurisdiction enables the court to grant final relief in the form of a negative or a mandatory injunction,[7] and s.37 of the Supreme Court Act 1981 gives jurisdiction to the court to grant (*inter alia*) an interlocutory injunction *quia timet*. Mareva relief is necessarily only by way of interlocutory injunction whether granted before or after judgment and so is to be distinguished from the *quia timet* jurisdiction. Under the *quia timet* jurisdiction the claimant has an existing right which the defendant is threatening to infringe. Despite the distinctions to be drawn between the granting of relief *quia timet* and an application for Mareva relief in anticipation of acquiring a cause of action, there is a similarity. In each case the objective of the claimant is to prevent or forestall injustice through future conduct of the defendant.

In *A v B*,[8] the plaintiffs sought an injunction to freeze sums in a joint account prior to taking delivery of a vessel. An injunction was granted, to take effect if and when delivery of the vessel took place, and to be served

---

[4] [1986] 1 Lloyd's Rep. 428.
[5] *Veracruz Transportation Inc. v VC Shipping Co. Inc. (The Veracruz 1)* [1992] 1 Lloyd's Rep. 353; *Zucker v Tyndall Holdings Plc* [1992] 1 W.L.R. 1127; *Re Q's Estate* [1999] 1 Lloyd's Rep. 931 at 938; *Steamship Mutual Underwriting Assn (Bermuda) v Thakur Shipping* [1986] 2 Lloyd's Rep. 439.
[6] Court of Appeal (Civ Div) Transcript No.217 of 1980 (January 18, 1980).
[7] *Hooper v Rogers* [1975] Ch. 43; *Morris v Redland Bricks* [1970] A.C. 652.
[8] [1989] 2 Lloyd's Rep. 423.

on the defendants before delivery of the vessel. In granting this order Saville J. sought to avoid the inconvenience to the plaintiff of being required to make the application *ex parte* to the judge only after delivery. However, this practice has now been overruled by the Court of Appeal.[9] The best that can now be done is for matters to be explained to the judge in advance, the judge to give an indication that he is willing to grant relief once the cause of action arises, and then for this indication to be followed by the making of a court order immediately after the cause of action vests.[10]

7.005   The second objection raises the question whether the court should be willing to grant a Mareva injunction unless the buyer is prepared to disclose its existence to the seller before delivery of the vessel. If the court insists on such disclosure, the buyer will run the risk that the seller may refuse to complete the transaction unless the injunction is discharged. If, however, the buyer waits until after taking delivery of the vessel before seeking Mareva relief, the sale proceeds may be paid away before the injunction can be made effective. Furthermore, there is the consideration that it would not in principle be proper for the injunction to be kept secret in circumstances where the buyer is encouraging the seller to complete, in the expectation that he will obtain free use of the purchase money. In effect, the buyer would himself not be acting consistently with good faith in his dealings with the seller. In *Negocios Del Mar SA v Doric Shipping SA*,[11] the buyers obtained a Mareva injunction *ex parte* from Mocatta J. without disclosing their plan to keep the injunction secret pending completion. The injunction was discharged by the judge *inter partes* in view of the non-disclosure, and because he felt that the buyers had acted unfairly to the sellers in not disclosing to them the existence of the injunction before completion. Mocatta J. refused to give "the blessing of this court to what happened at the Eastcheap Branch of Lloyds Bank whilst a copy of [the] order was being . . . shown to the National Bank of Greece at Bevis Marks". The Court of Appeal upheld the judge's discretion on the same grounds, Shaw L.J. observing that:

". . . discretionary relief which is designed to prevent injustice is not to be sought by or accorded to a party whose conduct appears to have been governed by the principle of catch as catch can."

---

[9] *Veracruz Transportation Inc. v VC Shipping Co. Inc. (The Veracruz)* [1992] 1 Lloyd's Rep. 353; see para.12.002, below.

[10] *Re Q's Estate* [1999] 1 Lloyd's Rep. 931. The plaintiffs did not argue that they were entitled to a solicitor's lien under their retainer. This was governed by English law and contained a London arbitration clause. Arguably it entitled them to an equitable lien on the proceeds of the case on which they had acted for their client, which could have been protected *quia timet* by injunction in anticipation of those proceeds going into the bank account of their client in Jersey.

[11] [1979] 1 Lloyd's Rep. 331.

In *Z Ltd v A-Z and AA-LL* Kerr L.J. observed[12] that even disclosure of 7.006
the intention to use the injunction "as a means of setting a trap for the
payee" should not suffice to justify the grant of the injunction in such
cases. If the payer, "appreciating the implications", is willing to make the
payment, then "the courts should not assist him to safeguard the payment
in advance by means of a Mareva injunction. However, this is a special
type of situation, and, like all others in this field, [is] ultimately a matter for
the discretion of the judge". Nevertheless, the court may still grant Mareva
relief *ex parte*[13] on the basis that it will be disclosed to the seller only after
delivery of the vessel. Thus, in *Ateni Maritime Corporation v Great Marine
Ltd*,[14] Phillips J. in chambers made an order *ex parte* which contained an
undertaking by the plaintiffs to give notice of the order "immediately after
(but not before) the completion of the Ship Sale Agreement and delivery of
the vessel".

Even leaving aside these difficulties there are further considerations
which may render Mareva relief unsatisfactory to the buyer:

(1) If the vessel is mortgaged (and most trading vessels are) the
mortgagees would be entitled to receive the sale proceeds towards
discharge of their mortgage. The mortgagees' prior claim over the
sale proceeds cannot be defeated by a Mareva injunction.

(2) Even if the vessel is not mortgaged, the proceeds of the sale may be
whittled away by *Angel Bell* orders enabling the seller to meet legal
fees or other debts and expenses.

(3) The seller may assign his right to receive the sale proceeds to a third
party before the Mareva injunction is granted. A bona fide assignee
would be entitled to have the injunction discharged.

(2) Possible alternative remedies available to buyers

If the vessel does suffer from defects on delivery in breach of the sale 7.007
agreement, then at common law the buyer has a right to abate the price
under the principles established by *Mondel v Steel*[15] (see further, *Modern*

---

[12] [1982] Q.B. 552 at 585. See also the observations of Mustill J. in *Ninemia Maritime
Corporation v Trave Schiffahrtsgesellschaft GmbH (The Niedersachsen)* [1983] 2 Lloyd's
Rep. 600 at 612, cited with approval by the Court of Appeal, reported in [1983] 1 W.L.R.
1412 at 1419 (where it was said "there is something unattractive about the idea" of the
buyer ostensibly paying the full price to obtain the vessel while "preparing . . . behind the
seller's back to deprive him of part of the price").
[13] In *The P* [1992] 1 Lloyd's Rep. 470 at 474, Evans J. held that the application in that case
should not have been made *ex parte* because the parties were already locked in dispute and
were communicating through solicitors.
[14] Unreported, May 25, 1989. The order is referred to in *Ateni Maritime Corporation v Great
Marine Ltd (The Great Marine No.1)* [1990] 2 Lloyd's Rep. 245 at 247.
[15] (1841) 8 M.&W. 858.

Engineering v Gilbert-Ash[16]). If the buyer tenders what he considers to be an appropriately abated price, first the seller is unlikely to give delivery of the vessel and, secondly, the buyer may not have sufficient details of the defects to assess accurately the quantum of the abatement. Accordingly, the buyer runs the risk that the seller will cancel the agreement and forfeit the deposit. But if the buyer could have proceedings heard and determined before delivery of the vessel, it would be possible to obtain an appropriate declaration as to the extent of the abatement which could legitimately be made. Has the court jurisdiction to preserve the position by interim order pending resolution of the claim to abatement of the price?

This is a different approach from that which buyers have adopted in the Mareva cases. Thus, instead of seeking to freeze the seller's assets in respect of a claim for damages, the buyer is seeking to claim that the seller has the legal right to be paid only an amount lower than the price set out in the sale agreement. The buyer is thus seeking an order preserving the position pending the quantification of the seller's claim for the price, that quantum being a matter of dispute.

The court could make an order directing that part of the purchase price is to be paid to a receiver appointed by the court, or into a joint bank account or into court pending resolution of the dispute.[17] The buyer, by complying with the order and paying the balance of the price under the court order would then place the seller under a contractual duty to give delivery of the vessel. If the seller refuses to give delivery, this would constitute a breach of contract on his part. Consequently he would not be entitled to forfeit the deposit, and would be at risk that the buyer might accept his conduct as a repudiation of the contract.

7.008   The order falls within s.44(2)(e) of the Arbitration Act 1996, which corresponds to what was s.12(6)(h) of the 1950 Act. This section justifies the granting of interim injunctions including Mareva relief in relation to arbitration proceedings which have been or are to be commenced.[18] In *Seven Seas Properties Ltd v Al-Essa*,[19] the plaintiffs obtained an order against the defendant for specific performance of a contract of sale of leasehold property. The order contained a provision for retention by the buyers of a substantial sum out of the purchase money payable under the contract. This part of the order was upheld by Hoffmann J. on the grounds that it could be justified by reference to the Mareva jurisdiction of the court, and it would be "excessively formalistic" to require two separate orders, one for specific performance and the other by way of a Mareva injunction. Such an injunction could have ordered the defendants to permit

---

[16] [1974] A.C. 689.
[17] See the discussion in Chapter 23 below.
[18] *The Rena K* [1979] Q.B. 377 at 408; *Third Chandris v Unimarine SA* [1979] Q.B. 645 at 663. The section does not apply to a claim for final relief, nor to a claim for an injunction which is not "for the purpose of or in relation to" arbitration proceedings commenced or about to be commenced, *i.e.* an injunction which is not in aid of a claim made or to be made in arbitration: *Sokana v Freyre & Co.* [1994] 2 Lloyd's Rep. 57.
[19] [1988] 1 W.L.R. 1272.

the plaintiffs to retain a certain amount of the purchase money pending further order of the court, and could have restrained the defendants from receiving that sum from the plaintiffs. Thus the direction to pay part of the purchase money into court is Mareva-type relief which puts aside a fund which will either go to the respondent as part of the purchase price or be returned to the claimant as damages. Another possible analysis is that the order is made "in relation to" the vessel which is part of the subject-matter of the proceedings. This is because the order concerns the terms under which delivery of the vessel is to be made. It would fall within s.44(2)(c) of the Arbitration Act 1996 which applies to "orders, relating to property which is the subject of the proceedings . . .".

Where there is no arbitration clause, and the case is appropriate for specific performance, then if there is a question of damage the court can grant an interim injunction preserving the vessel with the purchase price being paid into court pending trial of the action for specific performance.[20] A final order for specific performance would then contain an adjustment to the payment of the price to allow for the damage. Another way of looking at the matter is that there could be damages awarded additional to or in substitution for specific performance under Lord Cairns's Act, and a Mareva injunction could be granted immediately in support of such an award, consistently with the *Siskina* rule,[21] even though there was no existing cause of action for breach of contract.[22] If the vessel is defective then the decree for specific performance can order delivery of the defective vessel and damages under Lord Cairns's Act for the defects. If the court would as a matter of discretion refuse specific performance, it can still award damages under the Act.[23]

In a case where there was an arbitration clause, and specific performance **7.009** was appropriate, if the sellers declined to give delivery of the vessel, the buyer, in return for payment being made as directed by the court, could seek from the court interim orders in the nature of interim specific performance under s.44(2)(e) of the Arbitration Act 1996.[24]

(3) Disappearing assets

A Mareva injunction will be of no value to the claimant if it is in respect of **7.010** an asset of the defendant which is liable to perish or disappear before judgment can be obtained (*e.g.* a chose in action liable to become time-barred). Section 37(1) of the Supreme Court Act 1981 provides that the

---

[20] *Hart v Herwig* (1873) L.R. 8 Ch. App. 860.
[21] see Chapter 12, para.12.001.
[22] see Chapter 2, para.2.039.
[23] *Jaggard v Sawyer* [1995] 1 W.L.R. 269; *Wroth v Tyler* [1974] Ch. 30.
[24] *Astro Exito Navegacion SA v Southland Enterprise Co. Ltd (The Messiniaki Tolmi) (No.2)* [1983] 2 A.C. 787 affirming [1982] Q.B. 1248. See further Chapter 2, para.2.004.

court has power to appoint receivers by interlocutory or final order "in all cases in which it appears to the court to be just and convenient to do so". Prior to the emergence of the Mareva jurisdiction, unless the plaintiff asserted a right in the underlying assets or to be paid from a fund,[25] courts would not appoint a receiver over assets of the defendant unless the plaintiff had obtained judgment.

However, this approach was based on the reasoning which precluded the granting of Mareva injunctions.[26] It is now clear from the decision of the Court of Appeal in *Derby & Co. Ltd v Weldon (Nos 3 and 4)*[27] that s.37(1) of the Supreme Court Act 1981 enables the court to appoint a receiver before judgment when it is just and right to do so. The remedy of appointing a receiver is likely to be particularly appropriate when the asset in question needs to be managed, preserved or exploited. For example, if the asset consists of the controlling shareholding in a company which in turn holds assets, then a Mareva injunction in respect of the shares will not be effective in itself to prevent the defendant from dissipating the assets of the company. One approach to this problem is for the court to grant Mareva relief directly against the company. But that would not enable the company's assets to be managed.

7.011   Another approach would be for the court to appoint a receiver by way of interlocutory relief over the shares.[28] This would also be appropriate when the asset consists of a claim against a third party, and active steps need to be taken to preserve the claim and, in due course, obtain the proceeds. For example, a receiver could be appointed over the claim to take steps to protect it against the expiry of applicable time limits.[29] In *Standard Bank v Walker*,[30] the defendant was restrained by injunction from exercising votes otherwise than in favour of certain reconstruction proposals. This was because, if the reconstruction was not approved, the shares in question would become valueless, whereas otherwise they would have "some hope value". Irrespective of the motive of the defendant, the court has jurisdiction to restrain him from destroying his property when the effect of so doing would be to deplete the limited assets available to satisfy the plaintiff's claim, and he is not acting in the ordinary course of his business: *Normid Housing Association Ltd v Ralphs and Mansell (No.2)*.[31] Thus, *e.g.* the defendant could be restrained from setting light to his stock or giving it away. Similarly, if it was necessary for the defendant to give notice of a claim so as to preserve the possibility of claiming on an insurance policy, a

---

[25] *Cummins v Perkins* [1899] 1 Ch. 16.
[26] See *Kerr on Injunctions* (6th ed., 1927), pp.613–614.
[27] [1990] Ch. 65 (see also Chapter 16, para.16.004 below).
[28] This was done in Hong Kong in *Asean Resources Ltd v Ka Wah International Merchant Finance Ltd* (1987) 8 I.P.R. 241.
[29] For example, giving timeous notice to an insurer so that the claim is not barred under the terms of the insurance policy—see the facts in *The Vainqueur Jose* [1979] 1 Lloyd's Rep. 557.
[30] [1992] 1 W.L.R. 561.
[31] [1989] 2 Lloyd's Rep. 274 at 276.

mandatory injunction requiring him to take the necessary steps could be granted. It is thought that in such a case the court could compel disclosure of the insurance policy to the claimant so that he could check that the order sought would be adequate to protect the claim.

(4) Interim specific performance and mandatory injunctions

There are circumstances in which merely negative relief by way of a **7.012** Mareva injunction will be inappropriate because it is insufficient for the claimant's purposes, and where it is necessary to seek mandatory relief which requires the defendant to take active steps to preserve or maintain assets intact pending trial. The court has powers which can be used to make interim orders to preserve the position so that in due course, if appropriate, an effective order for specific performance of a contract can be granted. It may be necessary to grant mandatory relief simply to enable a plaintiff to preserve the possibility of specific performance.

In *Astro Exito Navegacion SA v Chase Manhattan Bank (The Messiniaki Tolmi)*,[32] the plaintiffs had agreed to sell a vessel to the defendants and deliver her at Kaohsiung Harbour, Taiwan. Payment was to be made under a letter of credit. The defendants made a late amendment to the letter of credit (accepted under protest by the plaintiffs), requiring the notice of readiness (which was one of the documents to be tendered under the letter of credit) to be signed and accepted by the buyers' agents. The defendants refused to accept the notice of readiness and the plaintiffs brought proceedings for specific performance which were then stayed, pending arbitration, on the defendants' application. However, Parker J. ordered the defendants to sign the notice of readiness before the letter of credit expired, so that the money payable under the letter of credit could be released into a joint account until further order. The court also made provision in the order for a Master of the Supreme Court to sign the notice of readiness if the buyers' agents did not.[33] This in fact happened. The bank refused to pay under the letter of credit. The House of Lords held that the judge had jurisdiction to make the interlocutory order, which he did under ss45 and 47 of the Supreme Court of Judicature (Consolidation) Act 1925, the predecessor of the 1981 Act, and that, in view of the fact that he thought, rightly, that there was a strong case for ordering specific performance in favour of the sellers, he was entitled in his discretion to make an order in those terms. In principle, the court would also be able to appoint a receiver in pursuance of bringing about the position whereby a final decree of specific performance could in due course be granted at trial.

---

[32] [1983] 2 A.C. 787, HL.
[33] Under s.47 of the Supreme Court of Judicature (Consolidation) Act 1925, now s.39 of the Supreme Court Act 1981.

The jurisdiction of the court to grant immediate specific performance by interlocutory order, subject to suitable undertakings should it subsequently appear that the order was unjustified, is particularly useful where the claimant is caught in time difficulties, *e.g.* if a letter of credit is about to expire. Although it is a strong step to exercise this jurisdiction, refusal to entertain such applications could have the effect of causing serious injustice.

7.013   In *Continental Grain Company v Islamic Republic of Iran*[34] the plaintiff had agreed to sell soya bean oil to a company which had agreed to sell it on to the second defendant (an Iranian State company). The first defendant was the owner of the vessel carrying the oil to Iran. The plaintiff held the bill of lading covering that cargo. The second defendant had not paid for, but was nevertheless claiming that it owned, that cargo. The risk was that if the vessel continued to Iran, the second defendant would take the cargo and not pay for it. The plaintiff was granted an interlocutory mandatory injunction requiring the first defendant to divert its ship. This was on the grounds that (1) the first defendant owed the plaintiff a contractual duty under the bill of lading, and a duty as a bailee for reward, to look after the cargo for the plaintiff; and (2) if the ship was not diverted, the first defendant would arguably be in breach of these duties. Accordingly this case is an example of an interim mandatory injunction granted *quia timet*, to enforce specifically those duties.

It has been said that the court will be required to be satisfied that if a mandatory injunction is granted it will be capable of enforcement.[35] However, the apprehension that a defendant may not obey an injunction has also been said to be not a good justification for refusing to grant it simply on the ground that it might be a mere *brutum fulmen*.[36]

(5) Assets subject to a trust

7.014   A court has never hesitated to use the strongest powers to protect and preserve a trust fund in interlocutory proceedings.

There are many reported cases in which relief has been granted by the courts in favour of a plaintiff claiming a proprietary interest in the assets which he seeks to preserve. Such cases range from the more straightforward tracing cases (*e.g.* where the claimant has sold goods to the defendant subject to a retention of title clause and the defendant fails to pay him) to cases involving allegations of fraud. The court has a broad equitable jurisdiction to preserve trust assets, regardless of whether or not they are within the jurisdiction, and regardless of whether the trust arises from an

---

[34] [1983] 2 Lloyd's Rep. 620.
[35] *Locabail International Finance v Agroexport (The Sea Hawk)* [1986] 1 W.L.R. 657.
[36] *Castanho v Brown & Root (UK) Ltd* [1981] A.C. 557 at 574; see further para.6.080 above.

express declaration or from operation of law by way of constructive trust.[37]
A parallel jurisdiction exists in such cases under CPR r.25.1(1)(c), (l) and
(m). In such cases the court may grant an interlocutory order appointing a
receiver over foreign assets: *Re Maudslay Sons and Field*;[38] *Duder v
Amsterdamsch Trustees*.[39]

The word "fraud" is used in different senses. It can cover a case in which
money has been dishonestly misappropriated in which the owner had no
intention to transfer ownership of it. It can cover a voidable contract
induced by fraudulent misrepresentation under which money is paid by the
innocent party. In the former it is not difficult to see that the principle is
that theft of the money does not in itself vest in the thief good title as
against the victim. This is because the thief has knowledge of the theft and
a constructive trust arises in favour of the victim.[40] Likewise with a void
transaction—there is nothing to avoid and the constructive trust arises
when the asset is transferred.[41]

As for a contract which is voidable, both legal and equitable ownership **7.015**
in the assets transferred under the contract, has passed with the consent of
the victim, and if the victim elects to affirm the transaction, no constructive
or resulting trust can exist because it would be inconsistent with the
contract which has been affirmed by the victim. There cannot be a
proprietary right unless and until the contract has been avoided.[42]

In a case involving fraudulent misrepresentation, the claimant has to be
able to give *restitutio in integrem* if he is to be able to rescind but the court
is all the more ready to achieve substantive justice through directing an
account which give the fraudster a fair financial allowance for what cannot
be restored to him *in specie*.[43] There are still limits such as when what has
been transferred by the fraudster were shares which no longer exist[44] or

---

[37] *London and Counties Securities v Caplan*, unreported, 26 May 1978, referred to at [1981]
Q.B. 958; *Mediterrania Raffineria Siciliana Petroli SpA v Mabanaft GmbH*, Court of Appeal
(Civ Div) Transcript No.816 of 1978 (December 1, 1978); *Bankers Trust v Shapira* [1980] 1
W.L.R. 1274; *A v C (No.1)* [1981] Q.B. 956; *Bekhor v Bilton* [1981] Q.B. 923 (especially at
937–939); and *PCW (Underwriting Agencies) Ltd v Dixon* [1983] 2 Lloyd's Rep. 197, and
para.3.029, above.
[38] [1900] 1 Ch. 602.
[39] [1902] 2 Ch. 132.
[40] *Westdeutsche Landesbank v Islington London Borough Council* [1996] A.C. 669 at 716;
Papamichael v National Westminster Bank [2003] 1 Lloyd's Rep. 341 at 373–375.
[41] *Jyske Bank (Gibraltar) v Heinl* [1999] Lloyd's Rep. (Bank.) 511.
[42] *Halifax Building Society v Thomas* [1996] Ch. 217 (defrauded building society affirmed
mortgage transaction and so could not claim surplus from sale of the property after it had
been repaid what was due to it under the mortgage); *Box v Barclay's Bank Plc* [1998]
Lloyd's Rep. (Bank) 185; *El Ajou v Dollar Land Holdings Plc* [1993] 3 All E.R. 717; *Lonrho
v Fayed (No.2)* [1992] 1 W.L.R. 1.
[43] *O'Sullivan v Management Agency* [1985] Q.B. 428 at 451–454 which cites many of the
relevant authorities; *Spence v Crawford* [1939] 3 All E.R. 271.
[44] *Smith New Court Securites Ltd v Scrimgeour Vickers (Asset Management) Ltd* [1994] 1
W.L.R. 1271 at 1280D–G (if money has been received by the claimant under the contract
he does not have to restore the very bank notes he has received, and where shares in a
publicly quoted company have been received one would expect rescission to be available
provided the same generic shares were tendered back. It is suggested that on the facts

have been altered in kind.[45] Rescission can also be barred by laches, delay, acquiescence or the intervention of rights of third parties.

If the contract has been successfully avoided, the claimant becomes entitled to a restitutionary tracing[46] claim, with the other party holding what he has received on trust.

7.016   It is suggested that where a voidable contract is avoided for fraud, the particular property of which the claimant has been defrauded, and which is then held by or on behalf of the fraudster or under his control or by a volunteer with notice of the fraud,[47] is held on trust for him. It is the notification of the avoidance for fraud which constitutes the fraudster trustee of that property.[48] The tracing remedy is available to a defrauded party to enable him to obtain restitution of what has once again become his property.

Where rescission is available the court can also order that the defendant indemnify the claimant against liabilities contracted by him as part of or in direct consequence of the transaction which has been avoided.[49]

Because the proprietary right only arises once the contract has been avoided it will be necessary to avoid the contract before an injunction can be granted in aid of the tracing claim. This is because until then the claimant has no "cause of action" on the proprietary claim.[50]

The victim of deceit has a claim for damages but it does not necessarily follow that, because he has been dishonestly deceived, he will have a proprietary claim. The deceiver may not have procured the victim to part with assets, but merely caused him loss. In *Daraydan Holdings Limited v Solland International Limited*,[51] an agent retained by his principal to secure contracts for the refurbishment of properties had obtained secret commissions from those providing the services to his principal and together with them had fraudulently deceived his principal, who was held entitled to a

---

rescission was not available because the sale of the Ferranti shares after discovery of the fraud amounted to affirmation of the contract); *Western Bank of Scotland v Addie* (1867) 1 Sc. & Div. 145 at 160.

[45] *Armstrong v Jackson* [1917] 2 K.B. 822 (where rescission could be made because the shares were the same); *Western Bank of Scotland v Addie* (1867) 1 Sc. & Div. 145 at 160.

[46] *El Ajou v Dollar Holdings* [1993] 3 All E.R. 717 at 734d, *per* Millett J. (not affected on this point by the appeal [1994] 2 All E.R. 685), citing *Daly v Sydney Stock Exchange Ltd* (1986) 160 C.L.R. 371 at 387–390, *per* Brennan J.; *Bristol and West Building Society v Mothew* [1998] Ch. 1 at 22–23, *per* Millett L.J. *Westdeutsche Landesbank v Islington London Borough Council* [1996] A.C. 669 rejected the theory that a payer of money under a void contract retained equitable title to the money, and at 708–709 rejected the idea that a resulting trust could be a proprietary remedy available when value had been transferred under a mistake or for no consideration and so the suggestion in *El Ajou v Dollar Holdings* that the trust was a resulting trust cannot be supported.

[47] There might be the possibility of a "retrospective" proprietary right acquired on rescission mentioned by Millett J. in *El Ajou v Dollar Holdings* [1993] 3 All E.R. 717 at 734 and considered in Bristol and *West Building Society v Mothew* [1998] Ch. 1 at 22–23. See also the judgment of Brennan J. in *Daly v Sydney Stock Exchange Ltd* (1986) 160 C.L.R. 371.

[48] See further G. Jones, *Goff and Jones: The Law of Restitution* (6th ed., 2002), paras 2–015–2–018.

[49] *Adam v Newbiggin* (1883) 13 App.Cas. 308.

[50] see chap. 10 under "The Siskina rule".

[51] [2004] EWHC 622 (Ch).

proprietary remedy in respect of the commissions.[52] This was a bribery case, and in such cases the agent or fiduciary has received property which as between himself and his principal belongs to the principal. However it is consistent with good sense and justice that if a person has been tricked out of his own property by deceit then, subject to affirmation by the victim of a contract under which the property has been transferred, he has a property based claim for restitution and can claim back his property, or assets representing that property. The argument against the availability of this relief is that the creditors of the fraudster will not have a claim against those assets on insolvency. But this is so of assets stolen otherwise than by fraudulent misrepresentation, and it is difficult to see why the victim who has lost his assets through deceit should not also have a proprietary claim.

A defendant is required to use his own assets or assets not arguably 7.017 subject to a tracing claim before there is any question of using assets subject to a proprietary claim to pay the defendant's expenses.[53] Once the defendant has proved that he has no assets not subject to a tracing claim from which to pay the expense then the court has what may be a difficult[54] decision to make, balancing the risks of injustice to the defendant of freezing those assets with the risk of injustice to the claimant if what turns out to be his assets are used to pay the defendant's legal or other expenses.

In a trust case, therefore, it is possible to obtain orders preserving assets situated abroad and ancillary orders for discovery of their whereabouts (see *e.g. Cook Industries v Galliher*[55]—inspection of the contents of an apartment in Paris); furthermore, third parties (*e.g.* banks) may be required to provide information concerning the whereabouts of such assets and their proceeds.[56]

(6) Family law relief

In the Family Division of the High Court, special jurisdiction is available 7.018 under s.37(2) of the Matrimonial Causes Act 1973. This consists of (1) a jurisdiction to grant freezing orders; and (2) a jurisdiction to set aside a "disposition", which does not include any provision contained in a will or a codicil.[57] These are separate jurisdictions in the sense that a court may

---

[52] Following *Attorney-General v Reid* [1994] 1 A.C. 1.
[53] *PCW (Underwriting Agencies) Ltd v Dixon (PS)* [1983] 2 All E.R. 158 at 697; *Ostrich Farm Corporation v Ketchell* December 10, 1997, CA, unreported. *Fitzgerald v Williams* [1996] Q.B. 657; *Sundt Wrigley & Co. v Wrigley* Court of Appeal (Civ Div) Transcript No.685 of 1993 (June 23, 1993); *The State of Brunei Darussalam v Prince Jefri Bolkiah, The Times,* September 5, 2000 (Jacob J.).
[54] *Fitzgerald v Williams* [1996] Q.B. 657; *Sundt Wrigley & Co. v Wrigley* Court of Appeal (Civ Div) Transcript No.685 of 1993 (June 23, 1993).
[55] [1979] Ch. 439.
[56] See *Bankers Trust v Shapira* [1980] 1 W.L.R. 1274 and *A v C (No.1)* [1981] Q.B. 956.
[57] Matrimonial Causes Act 1973, s.37(6).

have discharged an injunction but will still set aside a subsequent disposition.[58]

Section 37(2) provides as follows:

"Where proceedings for financial relief are brought by one person against another, the court may, on the application of the first-mentioned person:

(a) if it is satisfied that the other party to the proceedings is, with the intention of defeating the claim for financial relief, about to make any disposition or to transfer out of the jurisdiction or otherwise deal with any property, make such order as it thinks fit for restraining the other party from so doing or otherwise for protecting the claim;

(b) if it is satisfied that the other party has, with that intention, made a reviewable disposition and that if the disposition were set aside financial relief or different financial relief would be granted to the applicant, make an order setting aside the disposition;

(c) if it is satisfied in a case where an order has been obtained under any of the provisions mentioned in subsection (1) above by the applicant against the other party, that the other party has, with that intention, made a reviewable disposition, make an order setting aside the disposition;

and an application for the purpose of paragraph (b) above shall be made in the proceedings for the financial relief in question."

"Financial relief" is defined in s.37(1) as an order for maintenance of or for the provision of money for the benefit of children, under ss22, 23, 24, 27, 31 (except subs.(6)) or 35 of the 1973 Act.

7.019   The application must be made by a spouse or ex-spouse in proceedings for financial relief as defined by s.37(1).

The rights of a bona fide purchaser for value without notice remain unaltered (s.37(4)), so that an order will not be made if it would affect the equitable rights of a mortgagee who is a purchaser for value without notice. The word "value" includes a transaction at an undervalue in favour of a third party, but then there would be the questions of bona fides whatever it was concluded and without notice.[59] Notice includes actual or constructive notice and would include a third party put on reasonable inquiry.[60]

The statutory jurisdiction under s.37(2) and its predecessors, s.32(1) of the Matrimonial Causes Act 1965 and s.16(1) of the Matrimonial Proceedings and Property Act 1970, rendered obsolete a number of decisions to the effect that an injunction would not be granted to restrain the disposal

---

[58] *Sherry v Sherry* [1991] 1 F.L.R. 307.
[59] *Trowbridge v Trowbridge* [2003] 2 F.L.R. 231 at [63].
[60] *Kemmis v Kemmis* [1988] 1 W.L.R. 1307; *Trowbridge v Trowbridge* [2003] 2 F.L.R. 231.

of property by a spouse against whom no maintenance order had yet been made, or whose payments under such an order had not fallen into arrears: *Burmester v Burmester*,[61] *Fanshawe v Fanshawe*,[62] and *Scott v Scott*.[63] This line of authorities is likewise no obstacle to ordinary Mareva relief in a family law case.

Section 37(2)(a) of the 1973 Act confers a jurisdiction on the court to **7.020** restrain a party from making a disposition or transfer if the court is satisfied that such disposition or transfer would be made with "the intention of defeating the claim for financial relief." If the intention to defeat the claim is a "substantial" part of a person's overall purpose in carrying out a disposition, transfer or other dealing, then this satisfies the section.[64] The test is a subjective one.[65] By s.37(5) there is a statutory presumption of intention for cases within that subsection but subject to this, the issue of intention is to be decided on the balance of probabilities. It does not apply when a husband does not intend to do anything in respect of his pension rights.[66]

Under s.37(3) power is conferred on the court to give effect to the order setting aside a disposition by requiring payments to be made or the disposal of property. In *Padley v Padley*[67] the sister of the husband had received the proceeds of the sale as agent for the husband and accounted to him for them. She was on notice there was something "fishy" but had not acted dishonestly and had only acted as the agent for the husband. It was held that no order could be made for payment by the sister because she had only acted as an agent for the husband, and had had no interest herself in the property or the proceeds.

A transaction bringing a periodic tenancy to an end by giving notice to quit is not a "reviewable disposition".[68] The tenancy has come to an end by effluxion of time. The notice to quit destroyed the periodic tenancy but did not dispose of it within s.37(2)(b). A transfer which enhances the net asset value of the spouse by transferring assets into her company is not a reviewable disposition;[69] this is because the section is concerned about dispositions from the spouse and not dispositions to the spouse. A transfer of assets to a close relative or a company owned by the spouse, which still leaves the beneficial ownership of the asset in the spouse, does not have to be set aside under s.37(2) because the court can still make effective orders against those assets.[70]

---

[61] [1913] P. 76.
[62] [1927] P. 233.
[63] [1951] P. 193.
[64] *Kemmis v Kemmis* [1988] 1 W.L.R. 1307 at 1331A.
[65] *Kemmis v Kemmis* [1988] 1 W.L.R. 1307 at 1315; *Trowbridge v Trowbridge* [2003] 2 F.L.R. 231 at [57].
[66] *F v F* [2003] 1 F.L.R. 376.
[67] Court of Appeal, unreported, June 12, 2000.
[68] *Newlon Housing Trust v Alsulaimen* [1999] 1 A.C. 313; *Bater v London Borough of Greenwich* [1999] 2 F.L.R. 993; *Harrow London Borough Council v Johnstone* [1997] 1 W.L.R. 459 at 471, *per* Lord Hoffmann.
[69] *McGladdery v McGladdery* [1999] 2 F.L.R. 1102.
[70] *Purba v Purba* [2000] 1 F.L.R. 444; *W v H* [2001] 1 All E.R. 300.

7.021 Lord Hoffmann has drawn attention to the fact that the court has power under the section to restrain by injunction not only any intended disposition, but also any transfer out of the jurisdiction or any dealing with any property: the jurisdiction to intervene by injunction is not dependent on showing that what is intended would amount to a "disposition"[71] (see further s.37(4)).

It is possible to imagine circumstances in which a party to proceedings for financial relief (A) had some valuable right exercisable as against another (B), but made an arrangement with (B) allowing it to lapse in return for some benefit being conferred on a third party (C). Such an arrangement or transaction would fall within the mischief at which the section was directed if it were carried out with the requisite intention. This is because it would defeat the claim. It would also do so whilst securing some benefit for A or for someone he wanted to benefit. It would be odd if the question of the court's jurisdiction with regard to restoring the position to what it was before the arrangement or transaction depended, not on the substance of what was achieved, but the form of the particular transaction (*e.g.* whether the arrangement consisted of allowing a right to lapse or an assignment of the right to C, followed by C making a further arrangement with B). If this were the case, depending on the facts, (A) could design a transaction which would defeat the claim for relief and be incapable of being set aside under the section.

Under the section there is jurisdiction to freeze the relevant assets. So, *e.g.* an order can be made which will have the effect of stopping a party from even moving a particular painting from one house to another. The purpose of the court would be to ensure that the asset remains preserved, and any future order of the court in relation to it will be readily enforceable. Otherwise it might be hidden or taken abroad out of the jurisdiction of the court by the person intending to defeat the claim. If it were hidden or taken abroad, this would not in itself constitute a reviewable disposition, but it could result in the frustration of enforcement of future orders of the court. The width of the provisions relating to the *quia timet* jurisdiction is because Parliament has conferred on the court power to freeze the assets with a view to future orders of the court being enforced effectively.

7.022 The section empowers the court to order a party to give security for the claim. This is because of the words "or otherwise" in s.37(2)(a).[72]

The court retains an inherent jurisdiction in family matters to make Mareva orders in support of financial and proprietary remedies which may be awarded in the future whether or not falling within s.37 of the 1973

---

[71] *Newlon Housing Trust v Alsulaimen* [1999] 1 A.C. 313 at 318–319.
[72] *Re Mordant; Mordant v Hills* [1996] 1 F.L.R. 334.

Act: see *Shipman v Shipman*;[73] *Roche v Roche*.[74] There is no requirement of intent as a precondition for the granting of Mareva relief.

Section 37(2) is capable of applying to property[75] wherever situated,[76] as is now the case in relation to the granting of Mareva relief.[77]

Mareva relief can be granted on a worldwide basis in matrimonial **7.023** proceedings when there is an issue as to whether the court will take jurisdiction over the proceedings: s.24 of the Civil Jurisdiction and Judgments Act 1982. Such relief should not, however, extend to all the assets of the respondent and should be subject to a proviso as to the effect of the order on third parties who are outside the jurisdiction: *Ghoth v Ghoth*.[78]

(7) Insolvency Act 1986, s.423[79]

Unlike s.37(2) of the Matrimonial Causes Act 1973, s.423 of the **7.024** Insolvency Act 1986 does not provide for restraining a transaction before it has been entered into by the parties. The statute itself only applies once a transaction has been entered into for one of the purposes set out in s.423(3), namely putting assets beyond the reach of a person who is making or may at some time make a claim, or of otherwise prejudicing the interests of such a person. It appears that s.423 is capable of applying to assets or property wherever situated. Thus, s.436 of the 1986 Act defines "property" to include "money, goods, things in action, land and every description of property wherever situated" and s.425 of the 1986 Act must be read with this definition of property incorporated into it.[80] Furthermore, the jurisdiction of the courts under s.423 is to be exercised *in personam* against those who entered into the impugned transaction, and

---

[73] [1991] 1 F.L.R. 250.
[74] (1981) 11 Fam. Law 243. See also: *Harrow London Borough Council v Johnstone* [1997] 1 W.L.R. 459 at 466H–467A; *Khreino v Khreino (No.2)* [2000] 1 F.C.R. 80 at 84; *H. C. Mathews v I. V. Mathews and C. E. Coutanche* [2001] J.L.R. 671 at [23–32] in which the Jersey Court of Appeal held that a different approach applies in family cases for ancillary relief from that in commercial cases, and which does not have the Mareva threshold test of real risk of dissipation, because the claimant spouse is in substance claiming a share of the assets held by the other spouse. The correct approach in family law ancillary relief cases between spouses is to make such order as is just holding the balance bearing in mind that the underlying claim is to a share in assets to be covered by the injunction.
[75] See *Crittenden v Crittenden* [1990] 2 F.L.R. 361.
[76] *Hamlin v Hamlin* [1986] Fam. 11.
[77] *Babanaft International Co. SA v Bassatne* [1990] Ch. 13; *Derby & Co. Ltd v Weldon* [1990] Ch. 48; *Republic of Haiti v Duvalier* [1990] 1 Q.B. 202; *Derby & Co. Ltd v Weldon (Nos 3 and 4)* [1990] Ch. 65.
[78] [1992] 2 All E.R. 920.
[79] See Chapter 12, para.12.017 and Chapter 13, paras 13.018–29 below.
[80] *Attorney-General v Corporation of Worcester* (1846) 15 L.J. Ch. 398 at 399, *per* Lord Cottenham L.C.; *Phoenix General Insurance Co. of Greece v Administratia Asigurarilor de Stat* [1988] Q.B. 216 at 267–268. Sections 423, 425 and 436 are reproduced in Appendix 2, below.

any relevant third parties, and in principle it is to be expected that a jurisdiction which is *in personam* will not be restricted, in the absence of express provision to the contrary, to property or other assets within the territorial jurisdiction of the court.[81]

A cause of action vests under s.423 in a "victim" immediately a "transaction" is entered into, and "transaction" is defined in s.436 as including an "agreement or arrangement". Accordingly, as soon as even an informal "arrangement" is made, although it is not legally binding, the court would have jurisdiction under s.423(2) of the 1986 Act to make such order as it thought fit for protecting the interests of persons "who are victims". Section 423(5) defines "a victim" in terms which include a person who is "capable of being prejudiced" by the arrangement. Although s.423 does not have an express provision for restraining dispositions or transfers before they occur, nevertheless it is sufficiently wide to catch an intended disposition or transfer as soon as an arrangement is made for it to occur.

The court has jurisdiction *quia timet* to restrain a disposition or transfer before it is carried out. Thus, it is clear that under the section the court would have the power to undo a transaction the moment it was carried out and, in principle, it cannot be correct that the court must wait until the damage is done before it can act pursuant to the statute.

7.025   The jurisdiction under s.423 applies only in respect of transactions entered into for a purpose specified in s.423(3) and thus, in this respect, it is narrower than the Mareva jurisdiction. But it is likely to be of particular relevance when the claimant wishes to seek to restrain dealings with assets held in the names of third parties or claimed by third parties who are closely connected with the defendant, and who have apparently received the assets from the defendant in circumstances giving rise to a strong inference that the assets were transferred to the third party for the purpose of prejudicing creditors.[82]

(8) Stay of execution by writ of *fieri facias* under RSC Ord.47, r.1(1)(a)

7.026   It may be that a claimant company has a claim against a defendant who in turn has a claim against another company, which is in the same group of companies as the claimant company. In such circumstances, the claimant company might be entitled to seek a Mareva injunction over the chose in action against the third party. However, the courts have recognised that in such a situation it may be appropriate to allow the third party company a stay of execution on a judgment obtained by the defendant against a third

---

[81] Compare the analogous position under s.37 of the Matrimonial Causes Act 1973: *Hamlin v Hamlin* [1986] Fam. 11 at 18 and 22–23.
[82] See paras 13.018–29.

party, pending the outcome of the claimant's claim.[83] A stay of execution has the advantage that the claimant's group of companies does not have to pay money to the defendant in satisfaction of the stayed judgment. Even if the money has to be paid into court as the price of a stay, the claimant has greater control over the future disposal of the fund than would be the case with a Mareva injunction (which is liable to be discharged or varied under the *Angel Bell* principle). Thus the stay of execution granted to the third party judgment debtor enables the third party, acting in the interests of the claimant, to prevent the defendant from executing the judgment, obtaining thereby, and thereafter dissipating, the fruits of that judgment. The jurisdiction is separate and distinct from the power to grant a stay of execution pending appeal.[84]

The discretion will be exercised only when the court is satisfied that **7.027** there are "special circumstances" which render it "inexpedient" to enforce the judgment. These circumstances may be found to exist if there is a risk that unless the stay is granted the defendant may obtain the fruits of the judgment and dispose of them, with the result that in due course the claimant may obtain and be left with an unsatisfied judgment. In exercising the discretion in such circumstances, the factors to be taken into account include the following:[85]

(1) Ordinarily the third party judgment debtor will be required as a term of any stay to pay money into court[86] or otherwise give security for the judgment debt. Unless this is done, a stay of execution may result in the defendant being deprived in due course of the fruits of the judgment. If there is any substantial risk of this, it would be a powerful (if not conclusive) factor against the jurisdiction being exercised.[87]

(2) The jurisdiction is exceptional, and it is not sufficient for a third party judgment debtor merely to identify a claim by the claimant against the defendant and to offer to give security for the judgment debt.[88]

(3) The onus of satisfying the court that the jurisdiction should be exercised in any particular case lies on the applicant third party, who accordingly has the burden of proving the facts on the basis of which the jurisdiction is to be exercised.[89]

[83] *Burnett v Francis Industries plc* [1987] 1 W.L.R. 802; *Canada Enterprises v McNab Distilleries Ltd* [1987] 1 W.L.R. 813; *Orri v Moundreas* [1981] Com.L.Rep. 168.
[84] *Ellis v Scott* [1964] 1 W.L.R. 976 on what was RSC Ord.42, r.19.
[85] In *Burnett v Francis Industries plc* [1987] 1 W.L.R. 802 at 811, Bingham L.J. listed a number of matters which call for consideration by the judge. The factors listed here include those matters.
[86] There was an offer to pay money into court in *Burnett v Francis Industries plc* [1987] 1 W.L.R. 802 at 810 and in *Canada Enterprises v McNab Distilleries Ltd* [1987] 1 W.L.R. 813 at 814.
[87] [1987] 1 W.L.R. 802 at 811 (see the seventh matter listed by Bingham L.J.).
[88] [1987] 1 W.L.R. 802 at 809.
[89] This follows from the wording of RSC Ord.47, r.1(1)(a).

(4) The claim of the claimant must be one of substance on the merits. The stronger the claim the greater the risk of prejudice if a stay is not granted.[90]

(5) The court is entitled to have regard to whether there are co-defendants to the claim. In considering the relevance of there being co-defendants, the court should take into account whether the claimant's claim could fail against them and yet succeed against the relevant defendant, and the financial standing of the co-defendants.[91]

(6) The extent of any stay which may be ordered must be limited by the quantum of the claimant's claim against the defendant. The size of the claim is, in any event, relevant.[92]

(7) The discretion is to be exercised taking into account the closeness of the connection between the claimant and the third party, notwith-standing that this connection lies behind the corporate veil of the third party.[93] The relevant question is whether in the circumstances of the case, including that connection and its extent, justice demands that the stay be imposed.

(8) It is not necessary to show a connection between the transaction or circumstances giving rise to the claimant's claim against the defen-dant and the transaction or circumstances which gave rise to the judgment.[94] If there is a connection, however, then the nature of that connection is likely to be a material consideration in deciding what the justice of the case demands.[95]

(9) The nature of the claim which gave rise to the judgment debt may be relevant. Thus, if it is a claim on a bill of exchange or for freight, it would follow that the application for a stay would rarely, if ever, succeed.

(10) The court should take into account the likely delay before the claimant's claim will be adjudicated upon and determined.

(11) The court should take into account the extent of any prejudice which may be suffered by the defendant as a result of a stay of execution.

(12) The court should take into account the extent of any prejudice which may be suffered by the claimant unless a stay is granted.

---

[90] [1987] 1 W.L.R. 802 at 811.
[91] *ibid.*, at 810.
[92] *ibid.*, at 811.
[93] *ibid.*
[94] See the citation from the judgment of Mustill J. in *Orri v Moundreas* set out in [1987] 1 W.L.R. 802 at 808–809.
[95] [1987] 1 W.L.R. 802 at 811.

Chapter 8

The without notice application

(1) The application

The initial application for a freezing injunction is usually made without **8.001**
notice to the defendant because knowledge by the defendant that the
application is pending may defeat the very object which the claimant is
trying to achieve. An application for a search order is invariably made on
an application made without notice.

It is a basic principle of fairness that an order should not be made against
a party without giving him an opportunity to be heard.[1] But there is an
exception to that general principle when it appears likely that:

(1) if notice of an application were to be given, the defendant or others
would take action which would defeat its purpose before the order
could be made; and

(2) any damage which may be caused by the order could be compensated under the cross-undertaking; or the risk of uncompensatable
loss is outweighed by the risk of injustice to the plaintiff if the order
is not made without notice: *Re First Express Ltd.*[2]

This exception applies in many freezing injunction cases.[3] But when, on the
facts, it does not apply, the general principle applies; an application for a
search order is inappropriate and an application for freezing relief should
be made *inter partes*.[4] Under CPR Pt 25, Practice Direction, para.2.1 the

---

[1] In principle Art.6(1) of the European Convention on Human Rights does not have the
effect of prohibiting interim relief granted without notice, subject to safeguards which
ensure that it is only temporary, and can be reconsidered at an early stage: *R. (M) v
Secretary of State for Constitutional Affairs* [2004] 2 All E.R. 531.

[2] [1991] B.C.C. 782 at 785, *per* Hoffmann J.

[3] Because of the risk that the defendant may dissipate assets before the order can be made;
see *TRP Ltd v Thorley* Court of Appeal (Civ Div) Transcript No.862 of 1993 (July 13,
1993), *per* Sir Thomas Bingham M.R.; *Lee Kuan Yew v Tang Liang Hong (No.1)* [1997] 2
S.L.R. 819 at para.4.6. In *Oaktree Financial Services Limited v Higham*, May 11, 2004
(Chancery Division), although the solicitors for the claimant had written to the defendant
warning of the possibility of a freezing injunction, the merits were so strong and the risk of
prejudice from delay so great, Laddie J. granted a without notice application.

[4] *Thane Investments Ltd v Tomlinson* [2003] EWCA Civ. 1272; *The P* [1992] 1 Lloyd's Rep.
470 at 474, *per* Evans J. where the parties were already in dispute and were corresponding
through solicitors; *Williamson v Crosthwaite*, Court of Appeal (Civ Div) Transcript No.314
of 1993 (February 25, 1993) where the person intended to be restrained did not have
possession or control of the relevant funds.

normal procedure on seeking an interim injunction is for the application notice and supporting evidence to be served on the respondent in advance. If an application is to be made without notice the evidence must set out why notice was not given.[5]

8.002   In *Lunn v All Star Video Ltd*,[6] an application was made *ex parte* to the trial judge during the trial. The judge granted relief, but it was set aside on appeal. The Court of Appeal strongly disapproved of what had been done. In effect, counsel for the applicant had made a speech to the trial judge in the absence of the other party and his representatives. There was an obvious risk of unfairness. The application could have been made to the trial judge at the trial when the other party was present in court, albeit without prior notice if it was genuinely urgent. It is in general highly undesirable that the trial judge should be faced with such an application, because it may mean reaching and expressing premature conclusions, albeit expressed provisionally, before hearing all the evidence and argument on the evidence. The judge should be seen to be keeping an open mind so that all the evidence, when given, is taken into account in a fair and balanced way. Also, such premature expressions of opinion may in themselves affect individual witnesses and interfere with the giving of their evidence at the trial, and affect the conduct of the trial by the representatives of the parties. These considerations show that the court should be reluctant to entertain an application at the trial unless there is a good reason for its not having been made earlier. The trial judge could deal with such an application *ex parte* after he has announced the result of the trial.[7] If an attempt is made to apply *ex parte* to another judge during the trial, this may give rise to a highly unsatisfactory situation. It will be difficult to give the second judge an accurate picture of what is happening at the trial and this may give rise to material non-disclosure. The usual procedure is to make the application *inter partes* to the trial judge. If it is essential, this can be done at short notice to the defendant's counsel and the judge can be invited to make an immediate order to preserve the status quo whilst the matter is argued.[8]

The application for a search order or freezing injunction must be made to a judge. In the Queen's Bench Division (including the Commercial Court) the application for a freezing injunction is made to a judge in chambers. In the Chancery Division it is made on motion to the judge in open court, although the court may sit *in camera*.

CPR Pt 5, Practice Direction—Interim Injunctions lays down the procedure to be followed for an urgent application to be made without notice. Applications for search orders and freezing injunctions must be supported by affidavit evidence whereas applications for other interim injunctions are

---

[5] *Thane Investments Ltd v Tomlinson*, CA, unreported, July 29, 2003, referring to CPR Pt 25, Practice Direction—Interim Injunctions, para.3.4.
[6] *The Times*, March 25, 1993.
[7] *Gas & Fuel Corporation Superannuation Fund v Saunders* (1994) 123 A.L.R. 323.
[8] *Mooney v Orr* (1994) 100 B.C.L.R. (2d) 335 at 339–342.

to be supported by a witness statement, or a statement of case or application, verified by a statement of truth.[9] In this context a "freezing injunction" includes any order which purports to freeze property whether that order is made under the Mareva jurisdiction or otherwise.[10] Under CPR Pt 25, Practice Direction, para.3.3 the evidence must include both the evidence in support of the application and the disclosure to be given pursuant to the duty to disclose all material matters to the court on the without notice application.

The Practice Direction distinguishes between applications made without **8.003** notice after issue of a claim form and those before issue. There are extra requirements where the application is to be made before issue of the claim form. For those made after issue, the application notice, evidence in support and a draft order should be filed with the court two hours before the hearing wherever possible,[11] and by para.4.3(3) "except in cases where secrecy is essential, the applicant should take steps to notify the respondent informally of the application". Thus the application should be made *ex parte* on notice, except when secrecy is necessary. Extra requirements are imposed by the Practice Direction for applications made before issue of the claim form.[12] These include providing for provision of an undertaking immediately to issue a claim form, and directing service of the claim form with the order.[13]

A telephone application for an injunction can only be made when the applicant is represented by counsel or solicitors.[14] The judge will usually require a draft order to be faxed to him. The papers will have to be filed with the court on the same or the next working day after the application.

The Practice Direction in para.5.1 makes provision for certain matters to be provided for in the order such as the undertaking in damages covering loss sustained by the respondent or any person served with or notified of the order,[15] and an undertaking by the applicant to serve on the respondent the order, the evidence in support and the application notice.[16]

The Committee on Anton Piller Orders chaired by Staughton L.J., which **8.004** was appointed by the Judges' Council, described it as of "paramount importance"[17] that the judge hearing the *ex parte* application for Anton Piller relief should have ample time beforehand to read the papers, which should therefore be lodged either the night before the application or at

[9] Paragraphs 3.1 and 3.2.
[10] *Gill v Flightwise Travel Service Ltd* [2003] EWHC 3082, ChD (order made against non-parties based on the allegation that they held assets which belonged beneficially to the judgment debtor or which could be reached under s.423 of the Insolvency Act 1986).
[11] See also *Memory Corporation v Sidhu (No.2)* [2000] 1 W.L.R. 1443 at 1460B–C.
[12] Paragraph 4.4.
[13] For the practice in the Family Division see *Re S (A Child) (Family Division: Without Notice Orders)* [2001] 1 All E.R. 362.
[14] Paragraph 4.5(5).
[15] Paragraph 5.1(1).
[16] Paragraph 5.1(2); *Re S (a Child) (Family Division: Without Notice Orders)* [2001] 1 All E.R. 362.
[17] Staughton Committee Report, para.3.6.

least two hours before the time fixed for a hearing. In the Chancery Division, applications for a search order are usually heard in camera: *Columbia Picture Industries v Robinson*.[18] First, the applicant in a case which is suitable for the granting of Anton Piller relief will wish to avoid alerting the defendant to what is happening. This is because the defendant may take avoiding action which would leave the claimant without any benefit from an order. Secondly, following a recommendation made in the report of the Staughton Committee,[19] the example order requires the claimant to undertake not to inform third parties about the proceedings until after the return date. This is to avoid causing unnecessary damage to the defendant by undermining business confidence as a result of publicity based on allegations which may be ill-founded, and by the fact that the court has made an order. The hearing of an application in camera likewise reduces the risk of such damage. An application for a search order in an intellectual property case should be made in the Chancery Division.[20]

In family proceedings the ordinary practice, in contrast to that in the other Divisions, is that no undertaking as to damages will be required.[21] However, there are circumstances in which an undertaking is required, most usually in matters concerning property and in which a third party is involved who is not one of the parties to the marriage.[22] In *W v H*[23] an undertaking was required when the wife sought an injunction in respect of property acquired by a company when the company produced documents showing that it had acquired them as a purchaser for value.

Although a search order may be granted in matrimonial proceedings,[24] it is seldom appropriate,[25] and it will be granted only on strong evidence[26] and then usually as a last resort when it is thought that a spouse has failed to make truthful disclosure of his or her assets.[27]

8.005   Where an application for freezing relief is made against a bank, building society or similar institution whose business depends on public confidence, the court should consider hearing the application in camera[28] because of the risk of irreparable damage to the business by incorrect allegations and publicity based on court proceedings at which the defendant has not yet been heard. The court should consider this of its own motion on without notice application.

On the without notice hearing, the judge's attention should be drawn to the requirements of CPR Pt 25, Practice Direction—Interim Injunctions

---

[18] [1987] Ch. 88 at 71.
[19] At para.4.16.
[20] CPR Pt 25, Practice Direction—Interim Injunctions, para.8.5.
[21] *W v H* [2001] 1 All E.R. 300; *Practice Direction (Injunction: Undertaking as to Damages)* [1974] 1 W.L.R. 576.
[22] *W v H* [2001] 1 All E.R. 300.
[23] [2001] 1 All E.R. 300.
[24] *Emanuel v Emanuel* [1982] 1 W.L.R. 669.
[25] *Araghchinchi v Araghchinchi* [1997] 2 F.L.R. 142; *Burgess v Burgess* [1996] 2 F.L.R. 34 at 41.
[26] *Francis v Francis*, Court of Appeal (Civ Div) Transcript No.197 of 1986.
[27] See Staughton Committee Report, para.1.9.
[28] *Polly Peck International plc v Nadir*, *The Times*, November 11, 1991.

and so far as there is any divergence between the procedure adopted by the applicant and the procedure laid down in the Practice Direction. This includes differences between the form of order proposed and the example order. These should be specifically drawn to the attention of the judge.[29] The application should be made to that part of the High Court to which the business has been assigned by statute or otherwise. For example, an application in a copyright case should be made to a Chancery judge. Since the High Court is a single court, making application to the wrong part of it will not result in the judge not having jurisdiction; but to apply to the wrong court, and not explain the position to the judge, is irregular and might result in the order being set aside.[30]

It is the duty of solicitors and counsel on making an application for relief on an application made without notice, particularly in connection with freezing injunctions and search orders, to make a full note and to provide it as soon as possible to the respondent, whether or not he has asked for it,[31] or any other person affected by the relief, so that they can know what happened and on what basis the relief was granted.[32]

In practice, the procedure envisaged in the Practice Direction is often **8.006** not followed, particularly in the case of freezing injunctions, which, by their very nature, tend to arise as matters of urgency. It is not unusual for the affidavit to be placed before the judge in draft form, with an undertaking to swear it forthwith being given in the court and embodied in the order. In cases of extreme urgency, where there is no time even to draft the affidavit, the grounds on which freezing relief is sought may be explained orally by the claimant's counsel, but this procedure should only be adopted if there is no alternative. If it is accepted, a very careful note should be kept of what was said to the judge, so that the affidavit which is compiled and sworn after the hearing is accurate.[33] The decision whether to make an application on the basis of a draft affidavit or limited information, or to wait until a more orderly procedure can be adopted or more information obtained, can be difficult. The longer the time before making the application, the greater the risk that the defendant will remove the assets. On the other hand, a badly prepared or over-hasty application can have serious consequences for the claimant, the injunction may be refused, or the application may be adjourned for additional information to be gathered and placed before the court, or the application may be granted

---

[29] *Memory Corporation v Sidhu (No.2)* [2000] 1 W.L.R. 1443; *The Budget Shop Ltd v Bug. Com Ltd* [2001] F.S.R. 383.

[30] *Elvee v Taylor* [2002] F.S.R. 738; *Apac Rowena Ltd v Norpol Packaging* [1991] 4 All E.R. 516.

[31] *Thane Investments Ltd v Tomlinson, The Times*, December 6, 2002, not affected by the successful appeal where the point was accepted by counsel: [2003] EWCA Civ. 1272 at para.19.

[32] *Interoute Telecommunications (UK) Ltd v Fashion Gossip Ltd, The Times*, November 10, 1999; *Gill v Flightwise Travel Service Ltd* [2003] EWHC 3082 at [21–22]. This rule does not apply in the Family Division—*W v H* [2001] 1 All E.R. 300; *Kelly v BBC* [2001] Fam. 59; *Re S (A Child) (Family Division: Without Notice Orders)* [2001] 1 All E.R. 362.

[33] *Gill v Flightwise Travel Service Ltd* [2003] EWHC 3082 at [27].

and the injunction subsequently discharged because the duty of full disclosure has not been complied with. Even before CPR a plaintiff who had successfully obtained a Mareva injunction or Anton Piller relief could have his costs of doing so disallowed if the court took the view that he made insufficient inquiries before embarking on the application.[34]

Freezing relief must be sought with reasonable promptness, once all the facts and matters on which the application is to be founded are known to the claimant. The failure to make the application until several weeks may suggest to the court that the motive in seeking the relief is not to protect the claimant's position, but instead to put pressure on the defendant. This may lead to a refusal to grant the injunction. This should not be the case, however, if the delay arose because the claimant was investigating matters relevant to the application, with a view to ensuring that he had sufficient information to support his case and that he had complied with his duty to make full disclosure of all relevant facts and matters. This is of particular relevance in cases in which the claimant is a large organisation and several people are involved as sources of information.

(2) Documentation

8.007   It is of the utmost importance that as far as is possible the documents should be in good order for the judge.

(3) Dishonestly or illegally obtained evidence

8.008   Illegally obtained evidence is in general still admissible evidence in civil proceedings.[35] However (1) the fact that evidence has been obtained illegally or improperly may, but not invariably,[36] be information known to or reasonably available to the applicant, which is material to the without notice application. This could be because it goes to the reliability or weight of the evidence, or the probity of the applicant or his sources,[37] and (2) there will be no litigation or legal professional privilege protecting material which has been obtained by crime, dishonesty[38] or "iniquity".[39] The

---

[34] *Systematica Ltd v London Computer Centre Ltd* [1983] F.S.R. 313 in which Whitford J. so held in relation to an Anton Piller order. The reasoning applies equally to Mareva cases.
[35] *Kuruma v The Queen* [1955] A.C. 197; *R. v Khan* [1997] A.C. 558.
[36] *Memory Corporation v Sidhu (No.2)* [2000] 1 W.L.R. 1443 at 1458.
[37] In *St Merryn Meat Ltd v Hawkins*, unreported, June 29, 2001, ChD, evidence obtained illegally by phone tapping was used on an without notice application and thereafter the claimant lied about how the evidence had been obtained. The injunction was discharged for deliberate non-disclosure and the relief was not regranted.
[38] *Barclays Bank v Eustice* [1995] 1 W.L.R. 1238; *Gamlen Chemical Co. (UK) Ltd v Rochem Ltd*, Court of Appeal (Civ Div) Transcript No.777 of 1979 (December 7, 1979).
[39] *Barclays Bank v Eustice* [1995] 1 W.L.R. 1238.

principle does not apply to mere civil wrongs such as trespass or conversion.[40] This is because the gravity of the wrongdoing must be such as to bring the case outside the purpose of,[41] or outweigh, the public interest underlying litigation or legal professional privilege. In *Dubai Aluminium v Al Alawi*[42] there was a strong case that the plaintiff's inquiry agents had obtained information, including information about bank accounts, by fraud or impersonation, and, applying this principle, it was held that there was no privilege attaching to documents which were generated by or resulted from this, including reports by the agents on their inquiries.

In July 1997 the following advice was issued by the Bar Council in relation to settling documents for applications:[43]

"THE DATA PROTECTION ACT 1984 AND THE BAR

The Professional Standards Committee's attention has been drawn to a case in which a barrister was instructed to settle pleadings and an affidavit in support of a Mareva injunction. With the instructions were an enquiry agent's report, the content of which included information about the defendant's assets, notably two bank accounts. The information became stale and Counsel advised that it should be updated. It was produced before three High Court judges without any adverse comment being made from the Bench. However, such information may have been obtained contrary to the Data Protection Act 1984. The Office of the Data Protection Registrar wishes to investigate the conduct of the barrister.

Section 5(6) of the Act makes it an offence for a person to procure the disclosure of personal data in contravention of Section 5(2) and (3) 'knowing or *having reason to believe* that the disclosure constitutes such a contravention . . .'. There is a real risk that the words 'having reason to believe' may be construed as a purely objective evaluation of the relevant material regardless of the actual belief of the barrister concerned.

The Bar Council is taking Counsel's advice on the provisions of the Act and proposes to consult the Office of the Data Protection Registrar in order to provide definitive guidance on barristers' duties and responsibilities under the Act. We aim to do this as a matter of urgency. In the meantime, I should be grateful if you could ensure that members of your chambers, Circuit or Association have their attention

---

[40] *Crescent Farm (Sidcup) Sports Ltd v Sterling Offices Ltd* [1972] Ch. 553 at 565.
[41] Hence the distinction between consulting a lawyer about (1) how to carry out a fraud –no privilege; and (2) how to defend a fraud case –privilege attaches: *O'Rourke v Darbishire* [1920] A.C. 581 at 613.
[42] [1999] 1 W.L.R. 1964.
[43] Referred to in *Dubai Aluminium v Al Alawi* [1999] 1 W.L.R. 1964 at 1969, and *Memory Corporation v Sidhu (No.2)* [2000] 1 W.L.R. 1443 at 1457.

drawn to this problem. In particular, if they receive instructions which include material which should normally only be held by a registered data user (for example details provided by an enquiry agent about bank balances) counsel should consider the effect of the 1984 Act when advising. Failure to do this could unwittingly procure a breach of the Act and expose Counsel to investigation or prosecution. Counsel should also consider the provisions of the Act when advising that enquiry agents should be instructed and, in particular, as to the scope of their enquiries.

This advice applies to barristers in all fields and is likely particularly to affect family practitioners.

Fuller guidance will be drafted in the near future but in the meantime it is most important that members of the Bar should be aware of this warning."

8.009   In September 2003 the Bar Council issued the following advice:

"Guidance on Illegally Obtained Evidence in Civil and Family Proceedings

1. It is increasingly common for counsel to have to advise in cases where evidence has, or may have been, obtained illegally.

2. Whilst it will be for counsel to decide, in each particular case, whether or not the evidence falls into the category of illegally obtained evidence, this note is designed to assist in any situation in which it appears that the evidence has, indeed, been so obtained.

3. It goes without saying that it would be serious professional misconduct for counsel to advise or otherwise participate in the obtaining of information illegally. Attention is drawn, in particular, to section 55(1) of the Data Protection Act 1998 which provides that a person must not:—

'. . . *knowingly or recklessly, without the consent of the data controller—*
(a) obtain or disclose personal data or the information contained in personal data;
or
(b) procure the disclosure to another person of the information contained in personal data.'

Subsection (3) renders such conduct a criminal offence.

4. Subsection (2)(a), however, provides as follows:—

'*Subsection (1) does not apply to a person who shows—*

(a) *that the obtaining, disclosing or procuring—*
(i) *was necessary for the purpose of preventing or detecting crime, or*
(ii) *was required or authorised by or under any enactment, by any rule of law or by order of a court.'*

5. The disclosure requirement of CPR Rule 31.6 is plainly a 'rule of law' within the meaning of section 55(2)(a)(ii).

6. It follows, therefore, that there is an important distinction between the obtaining of such data in the first place, which amounts to a criminal offence, and the disclosure of such material thereafter in legal proceedings which is likely to be lawful provided that the disclosure was compulsory.

7. In *Dubai Aluminium v Al Alawi [1999] 1 W.L.R. 1964*, Rix J. ruled that legal professional privilege did not apply in relation to any relevant documents unlawfully obtained. It follows that all such data obtained, the source of the data and the letters of instruction to the person who obtained them, will have to be disclosed to the other side in any case in which data has already been so obtained. This will be the case whether or not so doing will assist the client or prejudice him and his sources, by revealing unlawful activity.

8. The following principles therefore apply:—

(a) Counsel must never advise that evidence be obtained illegally.

(b) If evidence has already been so obtained, counsel must advise the client of his disclosure obligations, including the ramifications of the decision in *Dubai Aluminium*.

(c) If the client is in breach of the consequent disclosure obligations, counsel will almost invariably have to withdraw from the case.

(d) If the client complies with the disclosure obligations, counsel is entitled to utilise the evidence in the proceedings in the ordinary way.

(e) Counsel must not advise that any further action be taken that could fall foul of section 55. In other words, no advice can be given to update the information or clarify it in any way.

(f) There may be doubt, for whatever reason, as to whether use of the evidence is permissible or whether disclosure is required. Equally, some further apparently unlawful step may appear necessary. Clearly, no such step can be taken without the prior informed permission of the court. In each such case, counsel should consider a 'without notice' application to the judge for authorisation pursuant to section 55(2)(a)(ii).

9. There are other situations, apart from those involving disclosure or deployment in court, in which counsel may wish to make use of such documents in the litigation. One possible example would be putting such a document to a prospective witness for comment. Again, if there is any doubt as to whether such use is required or authorised pursuant to a rule of law, counsel should consider an application to the judge as in 8(f) above.

September 2003"

(4) Guidance by the Bar Council on duties under the data protection legislation

8.010   Applications for relief to be granted without notice are usually prepared on one or more computers and are the subject of communications made by e-mail. To what extent can third parties compel disclosure of such communications? Often a question of legal professional or litigation privilege will arise which would protect the material from disclosure but this is not always the case.

In September 2003 the Bar Council issued the following guidance,[44] which relates to material held by barristers on a computer, including e-mails:

"THE DATA PROTECTION ACT 1998: BARRISTERS' DUTIES RE DATA SUBJECT RIGHTS

A. Concepts and definitions

1. *Data*. In section 1 'data' has a definition with four limbs:—

1. Information being processed by means of automatic equipment, which must mean what in common parlance we call a computer. 'Processing' includes recording, holding, organising, adapting, altering etc etc. So as soon as any information is on a barrister's computer it will almost certainly be processed. Therefore, this limb seems to cover all information in a barrister's computer, but nothing else.

2. Information 'recorded with the intention that it should be processed'. This expression does not very naturally describe any activity which a barrister normally carries out. It might apply to the above example of abnormal use, namely a barrister assembling information for a directory of experts.

---

[44] Available at *www.barcouncil.org.uk* (following the links Rules & Guidance, Practice Administrator & IT and Data Protection). The footnotes have been added to the Bar Council Guidance by the author.

3. Information recorded as part of a 'relevant filing system', which is defined as a set of information structured by reference to individuals or criteria. Barristers do not normally operate filing systems, so this limb is likely to have limited application to barristers.

4. Health, educational and public records—irrelevant to barristers.

Therefore, for most practical purposes the only 'data' within the Act which barristers have is information on their computers.

2. *Personal data*[45] is defined as data relating to an identifiable living individual. In the circumstances in which a barrister has data, often it will be personal: the individual may be the client, the opposing party, witnesses, and so on. But data relating to companies and statutory bodies is not 'personal data'. Nor is data relating to deceased persons. Therefore, some pieces of barrister paperwork will not contain any personal data.

3. *Data controller* means a person who

determines the purposes for which and the manner in which any personal data are, or are to be, processed.

A barrister is clearly the data controller of the data in his personal computer or on the section of a networked chambers system in which he carries out word processing activities.

4. *Processing* covers not only recording data and carrying out operations on data, such as organisation, alteration and use, but also the mere act of "holding" data, and even erasing and destroying data.

5. In a recent case a client requested under the 1998 Act copies of a barrister's brief and notebooks. Such hard copy documents are not 'data' and are wholly outside the Act.[46]

B. Duties in connection with data subject rights

Data subjects' right of access: section 7

6. By section 7 the Act creates a right of individuals to be given by a data controller copies of information held on him. There is also a more limited right to be informed whether personal data on the data subject

---

[45] This must be information which has the individual as its focus and not merely information which features that individual: *Durant v Financial Services Authority (Disclosure of Information)* [2003] EWCA Civ 1746, *The Times*, January 2, 2004; *Johnson v Medical Defence Union Ltd* [2004] EWHC 347 (Ch).

[46] *Johnson v Medical Defence Union Ltd* [2004] EWHC 347 (Ch) at paras 22–29 (manual search of papers not required under the Act).

is being processed, and, if so, to give a description. This is a right only of natural persons: companies and public bodies have no such right of access.

7. The requisite formalities of a request are that it be in writing, and that any fee required by the barrister is paid. Statutory instruments fix the maximum fee which can be required as £10 per request (SI 2000/191 reg.3).

8. A data controller is under a duty to comply with a request promptly (section 7(8)). If that provision applied to all barristers' documents, it would be deeply worrying. It could, for example, entitle the opposing party to see a barristers' opinions. However, that result is in general avoided by the following provisions.

9. By section 37 effect is given to miscellaneous exemptions in Schedule 7. By paragraph 10 of Schedule 7:—

> 10. *Personal data are exempt from the subject information provisions if the data consist of information in respect of which a claim to legal professional privilege . . . could be maintained in legal proceedings*

10. By section 27(2) 'the subject information provisions' is defined to mean inter alia section 7.

11. Paragraph 10 of Schedule 7 is not wholly free from problems. For the concept of legal professional privilege in English law is one which attaches to communications and documents, rather than 'information.' To take an obvious example, the whole of a barrister's Opinion is subject to privilege, even if the first dozen pages merely contain a summary of facts which are within the knowledge of both parties. However, I would suggest that barristers may at present conduct themselves on the basis that any English court will construe paragraph 10 of Schedule 7 so as to exempt all documents to which legal professional privilege attaches from section 7.

12. Therefore, no individual has any right of access to any document held by a barrister subject to legal professional privilege. This ought to encompass not only advices, but also drafts of pleadings. Even if in the event the solicitor uses the draft unaltered, this ought not to detract from the privileged nature of the draft.

13. It was held under similar provisions of the 1984 Act that legal professional privilege did not apply to information obtained contrary to the Act: see *Dubai Aluminium Co. Ltd v Sayed Reyadh Abdulla S Nasser Al Alwani* "The Times" January 6th, 1999. This would apply to information unlawfully obtained by private investigators.

14. If for any reason reliance on legal professional privilege fails, a barrister could have a second possible line of defence under section 7(4) in respect of advices and drafts if he can show:—

1. That the data contains information on some other individual, in addition to the data subject making the request. This will very often be the case with a barrister's documents.

2. That it is not reasonable to comply with the request without the consent of all such other individuals. (One may assume that this consent will normally be lacking, since if all concerned consent to disclosure of the barrister's advice or draft, the request for the copy of the document is unlikely to have had to be made to the barrister in the first place.) In considering reasonableness, regard shall be had, inter alia, to any duty of confidentiality owed to the other person. Thus a barrister's duty of confidentiality to his own client would be relevant.

Request from opposing party

15. Therefore, a barrister ought to refuse any request from an opposing party for copies of any advice or draft which the barrister has produced. The barrister should for the same reason refuse any request for a copy of instructions or privileged enclosures, such as witness statements or experts reports, which the barrister may have received in electronic form, or may have scanned into his computer.

16. But the position may not be so clear if a barrister had on disc all the contemporaneous documents in a complicated case. There would probably be no privilege attaching to them. Complying with a request from a vexatious opposing party for all such documents could be onerous, and the fee of £10 wholly inadequate to cover the work involved in responding. The task of separating the words which constituted personal data from all the other words would be even more onerous. If the documents were supplied in electronic form to save the cost of printing out thousands of pages, the opposing party would secure for himself the benefit of the work involved in scanning all the documents into a computer, without having contributed to the cost.

17. Other unsatisfactory scenarios can also be envisaged. One party may pay for a transcript of a hearing, and may receive it in electronic form. The other party may have chosen not to pay for the transcript. Can this other party then on payment of just £10 secure for himself a copy of the transcript costing £1,000 per day?

Request from own client

18. What if the person requesting a copy of the documents is the barrister's own lay client? There would probably be a duty under section 7 to comply with such a request, since privilege would not shield the documents from being seen by the client. But in any event

such a request should be complied with, whether or not the 1998 Act creates a duty to do so. The PCC had taken the view prior to the enactment of the 1998 Act that such requests for copies of documents created at the instruction of, and delivered to, the lay client's solicitor ought in any event to be complied with (irrespective of whether the drafts were written out by hand, typed on an old-fashioned typewriter or produced on a computer). Such requests are occasionally made where a lay client has parted company with his solicitor, and cannot get access to documents owing to a lien.

19. There is no obligation, of course, to supply copies of the barrister's notebooks or own notes. The brief or instructions will normally have already been returned to the solicitor before any subject request is made; if it, or some of its enclosures, have not, then, if in hard copy form, they will be outside the Act. But it would seem that the barrister should, upon request, supply to the lay client any parts of the enclosures or instructions which are in electronic form.

Skeleton arguments

20. The final version of a skeleton argument may be in a category of its own. For this is normally a document which the barrister issues as his own document, rather than a draft which he presents to the solicitor. So legal professional privilege would seem not to attach. Therefore, if a barrister were to receive a data subject request as to a skeleton argument it would seem that it ought to be complied with, provided the request was made in proper form.

. . .

Data subject's right to prevent processing: section 10

26. Under section 10 an individual is entitled by notice in writing to a data controller to require the data controller to cease processing personal data of which he is the subject. Potentially this right could be used vexatiously to interfere with the work of the Bar. The most obvious example of such vexatious use would be a litigant calling on the barrister for the opposing party to stop using his computer to produce drafts for the case!

27. Happily, there appear to be sufficient safeguards to prevent such abuse occurring. A requirement under section 10 must be made, *on the ground that, for specified reasons—*

(a) the processing of those data or their processing for that purpose or in that manner is causing or is likely to cause substantial damage or substantial distress to him or to another, and

(b) that damage or distress is or would be unwarranted.

No doubt a litigant might argue that the skeleton argument of the barrister for the other side would cause him substantial distress. But it would be far harder for the litigant to argue that such distress is unwarranted, if it is an inevitable incident of the court proceedings.

28. The data controller who receives such a notice of requirement must respond within 21 days. The notice of response may either state that he will comply with the notice or state reasons for regarding it as unjustified. One assumes that any barrister who receives such a notice will take the latter course. In that event nothing more would happen unless the litigant exercised his right under section 10(4) to invite a court to order the data controller to comply with the requirement notice. It seems likely that a court would regard such a notice directed against a barrister as unwarranted.

September 2003"

Data protection issues can arise on a without notice application which **8.011** involves using "personal data" of a defendant, which is private information which focuses on that individual,[47] held on a computer system of which the applicant is a "data controller". Section 35 of the Data Protection Act 1998 provides:

> 35.—(1) Personal data are exempt from the non-disclosure provisions where the disclosure is required by or under any enactment, by any rule of law or by the order of a court.
>
> (2) Personal data are exempt from the non-disclosure provisions where the disclosure is necessary—
>
> (a) for the purpose of, or in connection with, any legal proceedings (including prospective legal proceedings), or
> (b) for the purpose of obtaining legal advice,
>
> or is otherwise necessary for the purposes of establishing, exercising or defending legal rights.

The "non-disclosure provisions" are defined in s.27 of 1998 Act, and in relation to the first principle which requires that personal data must be "processed" fairly and lawfully, one or more of the provisions of Sch.2 to the 1998 Act must apply, if the personal data is to be used. It is considered that Sch.2:

> (1) allows disclosure to the court in fulfilment of the duty of disclosure;[48] and

---

[47] *Durant v Financial Services Authority* [2003] EWCA Civ 1746; *Johnson v Medical Defence Union* [2004] EWHC 347, ChD.
[48] See the Data Protection Act 1998, Sch.2, paras 3 and 5(a).

(2) depending on the facts, it can also apply so as to allow the use of the information so as to advance the case of the applicant on the application.[49]

(5) The lawyers' duties to the court—the fair presentation of the application

8.012　There is no clear distinction to be made between the duty to make full disclosure of material facts and matters and the duty of fair and accurate presentation of the application to the court. The application in all its aspects must be made fairly, accurately, without misrepresentation, or non-disclosure of anything which may be material whether of fact, law, practice or expectations.[50] Part of that presentation is the responsibility of the lawyers, for whose conduct the client is responsible.[51] On the other hand the fact that the breach of duty has been committed by the lawyer without the privity or fault of his client, and the lawyer has not acted deliberately to mislead the court, is material in considering the consequences.[52] Those consequences should not be disproportionate to the wrongdoing.

Part of fair presentation concerns the drafting of the draft order and what is said or not said about it to the judge hearing the without notice application. An advocate has a personal obligation owed to the court to be satisfied that the draft order is an appropriate one to place before the court: *Z Ltd v A-Z and AA-LL*.[53] Any difference between the draft order and the appropriate example order should be drawn to the attention of the judge on the hearing of the application, who has to authorise the departure from that form.[54]

In *Memory Corporation v Sidhu (No.2)*[55] the applicant's lawyers laid before the court a draft order which was inconsistent with what the Court of Appeal had said in an earlier case[56] about the effects of the privilege against self-incrimination and how that privilege must be respected. An order requiring a respondent to deposit materials with a supervising solicitor regardless of whether the privilege applied could not properly be made because once the materials had been handed over there was no guarantee that they would not come into the hands of a prosecutor. What

---

[49] See *ibid.*, Sch.2, para.6(1), which requires a balancing exercise to be undertaken balancing the "legitimate interests" of the applicant and the "prejudice to the rights and freedoms or legitimate interests of the data subject".

[50] *Memory Corporation v Sidhu (No.2)* [2000] 1 W.L.R. 1443 at 1459–1460.

[51] *Hytec Information Systems v Coventry City Council* [1997] 1 W.L.R. 1666 at 1675, applied in *Memory Corporation v Sidhu (No.2)* [2000] 1 W.L.R. 1443 at 1455.

[52] *Memory Corporation v Sidhu (No.2)* [2000] 1 W.L.R. 1443 at 1455.

[53] [1982] Q.B. 558 at 578.

[54] *Admiralty and Commercial Courts Guide*, para.F15.5.

[55] [2000] 1 W.L.R. 1443.

[56] *Den Norske Bank ASA v Antonatos* [1999] Q.B. 271 at 290.

had been said in the earlier case was material. Furthermore the applicant's counsel had misdescribed the draft order as being in the standard form when it was not. The relief was not discharged by the judge and his decision was upheld by the Court of Appeal. This was because the lawyers had not intentionally misled the court, the error had been rectified within three days, it had not affected whether relief should have been granted as opposed to the form of the relief and because it was a professional error by counsel in a fraud case in which it was undesirable that, if the defendant had been fraudulent, he should escape from paying.

Once an advocate finds his conduct under justifiable scrutiny and criticism and his integrity called into question by the other side, consideration should be given to immediate withdrawal from the case. His role has been changed. He has to make a full explanation to the court, which must be done in writing and at the earliest possible opportunity.[57] Part of the seriousness with which the Court of Appeal viewed counsel's conduct in *Memory Corporation v Sidhu (No.2)* was because counsel sought to explain what had happened as part of his oral submissions made long after the relevant events, whereas he should have given a full written explanation and apology to the court promptly after the matter had arisen. **8.013**

The applicant should prepare a draft order which follows as far as appropriate the relevant example order given by CPR Pt 25, Practice Direction—Interim Injunctions. This is not to say that the forms must be followed slavishly. On the contrary, each order should be shaped for the particular case, but the starting point is the example both for the drafting and for the explanation of the draft to the court. It is good practice to draft an order for an interim remedy so that it includes a proviso which permits acts which would otherwise be a breach of the order to be done with the prior written consent of the claimant's solicitors. This enables the parties to agree to variations or the discharge of the order without the necessity of coming back to the court.[58]

In the case of an application for a search order where no supervising solicitor is to be used, the judge must give reasons in the order.[59] If a mandatory order is to be made requiring the respondent to deliver up materials forthwith upon being served with the order, there should be a provision providing the respondent with a reasonable opportunity to take legal advice before having to comply with the order, and it is usually sensible for the order to provide for a supervising solicitor.[60]

It is usual for the judge to be given a chronology and a *dramatis personae*. In the Commercial Court, in applications of any weight the applicant should provide a skeleton argument,[61] and the use of skeleton **8.014**

---

[57] *Memory Corporation v Sidhu (No.2)* [2000] 1 W.L.R. 1443 at 1459C–H.
[58] *Admiralty and Commercial Court Guide*, para.F15.7.
[59] CPR Pt 25, Practice Direction—Interim Injunctions, para.8.2.
[60] *Adam Phones v Goldschmidt* [1999] 4 All E.R. 486 (claimant required to pay the costs of a successful contempt motion brought by it when the contempt was not intentional, was technical, and where these safeguards were missing from the mandatory order which was served on a Saturday morning).
[61] *Admiralty and Commercial Courts Guide*, para.F15.3(b).

arguments has been encouraged in the Queen's Bench Division generally: *ALG Incorporated v Uganda Airlines Corporation.*[62]

The applicant must also be prepared to furnish a bond by an insurance company or make a payment into court, or make a deposit subject to the control of the court, to support the cross-undertaking in damages. Paragraph F15.4 of the Commercial Court Guide provides:

> "(a) Where the applicant for an interim remedy is not able to show sufficient assets within the jurisdiction of the Court to provide substance to the undertakings given, particularly the undertaking in damages, he may be required to reinforce his undertakings by providing security.
>
> (b) Security will be ordered in such form as the judge decides is appropriate but may, for example, take the form of a payment into court, a bond issued by an insurance company or a first demand guarantee or standby credit issued by a first-class bank.
>
> (c) In an appropriate case the judge may order a payment to be made to the applicant's solicitors to be held by them as officers of the court pending further order. Sometimes the undertaking of a parent company may be acceptable."

Any difficulty that there may be in honouring an award made on the cross-undertaking must be addressed in the affidavit in support of the application.

(6) Sources of information and belief

8.015   CPR Pt 32, Practice Direction—Written Evidence provides:

> "4.2 An affidavit must indicate:
>
> (1) which of the statements in it are made from the deponent's own knowledge and which are matters of information or belief, and
> (2) the source for any matters of information or belief."

For a witness statement, para.18.2 of the Practice Direction states:

> "18.2 A witness statement must indicate:
>
> (1) which of the statements in it are made from the witness's own knowledge and which are matters of information or belief, and
>
> (2) the source for any matters of information or belief."

---

[62] *The Times*, July 31, 1992.

Under s.1(1) of the Civil Evidence Act 1995 in civil proceedings evidence is not to be excluded on the ground that it is hearsay. Under the former RSC Ord.41, r.5(2), an affidavit sworn for the purpose of being used in interlocutory proceedings[63] could contain statements of information or belief with the sources and grounds thereof. Although in practice affidavits which were defective in this respect were often used, it was of particular importance that the requirements of the former RSC Ord.41, r.5 were complied with on applications for Mareva or Anton Piller relief. Under CPR an application for a freezing injunction or a search order must be supported by evidence given by affidavit.[64] Paragraph 4.2 of the Practice Direction has the same function as the former RSC Ord.41, r.5(2). On an without notice application the claimant has a duty of full disclosure and this extends to all matters which the court would wish to take into account in the weighing operation which it has to undertake in deciding whether or not to grant the order. The extent to which matters deposed to are within the deponent's own knowledge may be material. So in relation to matters outside his own knowledge, the relevant source of information or ground for his belief could be material. If a source or ground for belief is not identified then, subject to contrary indication appearing from the evidence, the court might be left with the incorrect impression that the matters deposed to are within the personal knowledge of the deponent. If a witness statement states that the information has been obtained from someone else but does not condescend into any detail about the source, then the court may either give the evidence no weight at all or very little weight.[65]

The purpose of the requirement is to enable the court to evaluate the **8.016** quality of the evidence and decide what weight to give it.[66] There was some uncertainty under the former rule of court as to whether an affidavit could contain "second-hand hearsay", namely hearsay based on a source which in turn relies on hearsay. In *Deutsche Rückversicherung AG v Walbrook Insurance Co.*,[67] Phillips J. declined to follow *Savings & Investment Bank Ltd v Gasco Investments (Netherlands) BV*,[68] and held that an affidavit could contain any material whatever its source provided that the source and grounds of belief were identified. This was the better view of the rule. The coming into force of s.1(1) of the Civil Evidence Act 1995, removed any rationale for previous doubts. Paragraph 4.2 of the Practice Direction caters for any degree of hearsay but requires the affidavit to disclose the provenance of the evidence. Under the former rule it was possible to give

---

[63] In the context of the rule, interlocutory proceedings in general included proceedings other than the trial of the action or final determination of the proceedings in the case of an originating summons or other process: *Savings Bank v Gasco BV (No.2)* [1988] Ch. 422.

[64] CPR Pt 25, Practice Direction—Interim Injunctions, para.3.1; *Thane Investments Ltd v Tomlinson* [2003] EWCA Civ 1272.

[65] *Parker v CS Structured Credit Fund Ltd* [2003] 1 W.L.R. 1680 at [14–15].

[66] Compare *Lyell v Kennedy* (1883) L.R. 9 App. Cas. 81 at 92. *cf. Zambia Steel v Clark & Eaton* [1986] 2 Lloyd's Rep. 225 at 233, *per* Ralph Gibson L.J.: "The purpose of the rule is to force responsibility for the truth of the assertion of fact upon an identified source."

[67] [1995] 1 W.L.R. 1017.

[68] [1984] 1 W.L.R. 271.

the "source" of information or the "grounds" for belief without necessarily naming a particular individual.[69]

A broad general reference to "documents in my possession" or "inquiries I have made" is not sufficient. In *Deputy Commissioner of Taxation v Ahern (No.2)*[70] a Mareva injunction had been granted to the Deputy Commissioner of Taxation on the basis of evidence which included an affidavit by an employee of the Commissioner which set out the ambit of inquiries made by him and his conclusions. The deponent did not exhibit the documents seen by him nor did he list them, nor did he state what their contents were, nor did he seek to relate his conclusions to specific documents which he had seen or particular information which he had received. In these circumstances, on appeal, the injunction was set aside, the court observing that to uphold the injunction would be "to sanction trial by the averment of officials" and that:

> "In circumstances of great urgency a court may accept a general statement of sources as sufficient compliance with the rule, although this will more readily happen in the case of an interim rather than an interlocutory injunction. The question as to what is a sufficient disclosure of sources must be decided according to the exigencies of each particular case, and the court's discretion is not to be fettered. In the present case there were no apparent circumstances of urgency justifying the absence of disclosure of sources, and the bulk of the material may fairly be described as oppressive and embarrassing."

Under the former rule it might have been suggested that if material was placed before the court which did not sufficiently identify the sources of information and grounds of belief, then this material would not fall within the rule and that in consequence it was wholly inadmissible on the application.[71] However, it is considered that the correct analysis even under the former rule was that the material was still admissible, and the failure to indicate the sources of information and grounds of belief was only an irregularity. The court was still able to act on the defective material, and the claimant could subsequently be required to rectify the position by incorporating the missing information in a further affidavit to be prepared as soon as possible.

8.017   Paragraphs 4.2 and 18.2 of the Practice Direction—Interim Injunction are provisions under s.2(2)(b) of the Civil Evidence Act 1995 and so non-compliance does not render the evidence inadmissible on the ground that it is hearsay.[72] These paragraphs taken with para.3.1 of the Practice Direction should not be interpreted as laying down a precondition to the evidence

---

[69] *Zambia Steel v Clark & Eaton* [1986] 2 Lloyd's Rep. 225 at 233, *per* Ralph Gibson L.J.
[70] [1988] 2 Qd R. 158 (Queensland, Australia). The Queensland Rules of Court contained in Ord.41, r.3 a provision similar to the former RSC Ord.41, r.5(2).
[71] *Re J.L. Young Manufacturing Co. Ltd* [1990] 2 Ch. 753 at 754 and 755.
[72] Civil Evidence Act 1995, s.2(4).

being admissible on the application. This approach leaves the procedure for granting interlocutory injunctions unfettered by any absolute rule.[73]

Where the evidence lies within the personal knowledge of a party and is contentious it is appropriate that the affidavit is made by that person and not deposed to by a solicitor acting on information and belief based on what he has been told by his client. For example, a defendant to allegations of dishonesty who seeks to persuade the court not to continue freezing relief based on his account of contentious matters should make the affidavit personally.[74] The reason is that the individual should be prepared to take personal responsibility for its accuracy. This goes to the weight which should be given to the evidence.

(7) Applications in the course of proceedings, including after judgment, against non-parties

Where an injunction is sought in the course of ongoing proceedings, 8.018 without notice against a non-party, then the applicant must prepare the documentation so as to show exactly what case is being pursued against the non-party, on what grounds and on the basis of what material. This includes an affidavit which sets out all the evidence relied upon in support of the application for an injunction against that non-party and a note of the without notice hearing. It is not for the non-party to show why an injunction is not to be granted against him; the burden is upon the applicant and the non-party is entitled to see all the material relied upon as against him.[75]

Grounds for seeking an injunction against a non-party are considered in Chapter 13. Often the grounds rely in part on the evidence and case made against a defendant. Accordingly where an injunction is sought against a non-party, after judgment has been obtained against a defendant at trial, and in reliance upon material used at the trial, the affidavit will have to set out that material[76] and the relevant documents will have to be served upon the non-party,[77] so that can see exactly what is relied upon against him.

---

[73] *Deutsche Rückversicherung v Walbrook Insurance Co. Ltd* [1995] 1 W.L.R. 1017.
[74] *Bracken Partners Ltd v Gutteridge*, Ch.D., unreported, December 17, 2001 *A Co. v B Co.* [2002] 3 H.K.L.R.D. II at para.29 (affidavits on application for Norwich Pharmacal).
[75] *Gill v Flightwise Travel Service Ltd* [2003] EWHC 3082, Ch.D. *Thane Investments Limited v Tomlinson* [2003] EWCA Civ 1272 at paras 22–23.
[76] In *Gill v Flightwise Travel Service Ltd* [2003] EWHC 3082 at [34–35] this should have included verbatim transcripts of parts of the evidence, the judgment and facts which were in the judge's mind as a result of what had happened at the trial, which were relevant to risk of dissipation.
[77] In *Gill v Flightwise Travel Service Ltd* [2003] EWHC 3082 at [33] and [35], these should have included the trial bundle.

(8) Appeals

8.019   Appeals are discussed in Chapter 23. The overlap between the jurisdiction to grant a stay of execution to a defendant pending appeal and the Mareva jurisdiction post-judgment is discussed in Chapter 3, paras 3.025–6.

Chapter 9

The duty to make full and frank disclosure and fair presentation

(1) General principles

Any applicant to the court for relief without notice must act in the utmost **9.001** good faith and disclose[1] to the court all matters which are material to be taken into account by the court in deciding whether or not to grant relief without notice, and if so on what terms.[2] This is a general principle which applies to all applications for relief to be granted on an application made without notice.[3] It applies not just to disclosure of facts but to absolutely anything which the judge should consider. It is part of the duty of an applicant for without notice relief to present the application fairly.[4] Incorrect submissions or arguments, including erroneous legal submissions, will not amount to non-disclosure or material misrepresentation provided that such errors do not deprive the court of knowledge of any material circumstance.[5] This is on the basis that the applicant has acted fairly and is entitled to advance his arguments as he wishes provided that the court receives a fair presentation of the case.

This rule applies with special force[6] to applications for Mareva or Anton Piller relief, which by their nature are particularly liable to cause substantial

---

[1] The applicant must also refrain from making misrepresentations. The same principles apply to material misrepresentations as apply to material non-disclosure. Both involve misleading the court in a material respect: *Thomas A. Edison Ltd v Bullock* (1912) 15 C.L.R. 679 at 682, *per* Isaacs J.

[2] *R. v Kensington Income Tax Commissioners Ex p. Princess Edmond de Polignac* [1917] 1 K.B. 486 at 504–506, 509, and 514–515; *Dormeuil Freres SA v Nicolian Ltd* [1988] 1 W.L.R. 1362 at 1368.

[3] *MRG (Japan) Ltd v Engelhard Metals Japan Ltd* [2003] EWHC 3418 at [23]; *Network Telecom (Europe) Ltd v Telephone Systems International* [2004] 1 All E.R. (Comm) 418; *Dalglish v Jarvie* (1850) 2 Mac. & G. 231; and see generally *Kerr on Injunctions* (6th ed., 1927), pp.323, 637 and 661, *Seton's Judgments and Orders* (7th ed. pp.516–517 and the cases there cited; *Spry on Equitable Remedies* (4th ed., 1990), pp.485–490.

[4] *Memory Corporation v Sidhu (No.2)* [2000] 1 W.L.R. 1443; *The Gadget Shop Ltd v Bug.Com Ltd* [2001] F.S.R. 383 at [48]; *Re S (A Child) (Family Division: Without Notice Orders)* [2001] 1 All E.R. 362.

[5] *Hispanica de Petroleos v Vencedora Oceanica Navigation (The Kapetan Markos)* [1986] 1 Lloyd's Rep. 211.

[6] In *A/A D/S Svendborg v Maxim Brand*, Court of Appeal (Civ Div) Transcript No.39 of 1989 (January 23, 1989), Kerr L.J. said in relation to a case concerning an application to

prejudice to a defendant or other parties. Thus Donaldson L.J. in *Bank Mellat v Nikpour* said:[7]

> "The rule requiring full disclosure seems to me to be one of the most fundamental importance, particularly in the context of the Draconian remedy of the Mareva Injunction. It is in effect, together with the Anton Piller order, one of the law's two 'nuclear' weapons. If access to such a weapon is obtained without the fullest and frankest disclosure, I have no doubt at all that it should be revoked."

9.002   Therefore, the applicant is permitted to apply without notice only on the basis that he has complied with this duty, which has been described as being governed by the same principles which require an applicant for insurance to act in the utmost degree of good faith.[8] The duty extends to placing before the court all matters which are relevant to the court's assessment of the application,[9] and it is no answer to a complaint of non-disclosure that if the relevant matters had been placed before the court, the decision would have been the same.[10] The test as to materiality is an objective one, and it is not for the applicant or his advisers to decide the

---

discharge leave to serve out of the jurisdiction granted under RSC Ord.11 as well as Mareva relief that "in principle the same duty of disclosure arises in relation to Order 11. But in practice such oversights are more likely to be penalised only in the form of costs, since it would not be right to drive the plaintiffs to an inappropriate jurisdiction or to bar a bona fide claim from a proper one. To that extent the practice may be different in relation to Order 11 from cases involving injunctions." *Pacific Bank NA v Bell*, Court of Appeal (Civ Div) Transcript No.143 of 1991 (February 27, 1991); *Payabi v Armstel Skipping Corporation (The Jay Bola)* [1992] Q.B. 907 at 918B–D, *per* Hobhouse J.; *Arab Business Consortium International Finance and Investment Co. v Banque Franco-Tunisienne* [1996] 1 Lloyd's Rep. 485 at 490, *per* Waller J. "it does of course make a difference what form of *ex parte* application the Court is dealing with . . ." (on appeal: [1997] 1 Lloyd's Rep 531); *Nicekind Holdings v Yim Wai Ning* [2001] H.K.C.A. 106, *per* Stock J.A. citing the text; *MRG (Japan) Ltd v Engelhard Metals Japan Ltd* [2003] EWHC 3418 at [25–32], Comm Ct on an application for permission to serve out of the jurisdiction under CPR r.6.21 it is not necessary to set out all matters which go to the strength of the merits as opposed to matters which might have gone to the granting of the permission.

[7] [1985] F.S.R. 87 at 92.
[8] *Dalglish v Jarvie* (1850) 2 Mac & G 231 at 243, *per* Rolfe B.
[9] *R. v Kensington Income Tax Commissioners Ex p. Princess Edmond de Polignac* [1917] 1 K.B. 486 at 505, *per* Lord Cozens-Hardy M.R. citing the judgment of Rolfe B. in *Dalglish v Jarvie* (above). *Brink's Mat Ltd v Elcombe* [1988] 1 W.L.R. 1350 at 1356, *per* Ralph Gibson L.J.: "The material facts are those which it is material for the judge to know in dealing with the application as made'. In *Siporex Trade SA v Comdel Commodities Ltd* [1986] 2 Lloyd's Rep. 428 at 437, Bingham J. said that the applicant "must disclose all the facts which reasonably could or would be taken into account by the Judge in deciding whether to grant the application". See also *Boyce v Gill* (1891) 64 L.T. 824, at 825: "the court should be in a position to weigh all matters which might influence it so as to decide whether . . . an injunction should be granted".
[10] *Behbehani v Salem* [1989] 1 W.L.R. 723 at 729, *per* Woolf L.J.; *Eastglen International Corporation v Monpare SA* (1987) 137 N.L.J. 56; *Sal Oppenheim JR Cie KGaa v Rotherwood (UK) Ltd*, Court of Appeal (Civ Div) Transcript No.386 of 1996 (April 19, 1996).

question;[11] hence it is no excuse for the applicant subsequently to say that he was genuinely unaware, or did not believe, that the facts were relevant or important.[12] All matters which are relevant to the "weighing operation" that the court has to make in deciding whether or not to grant the order must be disclosed.[13] This includes disclosure to the court of matters which are or may be adverse to the applicant. In CPR Pt 25, Practice Direction—Interim Injunctions, para.3.3 provides:

> "The evidence must set out the facts on which the applicant relies for the claim being made against the respondent, including all material facts of which the court should be made aware."

The duty to disclose applies to matters known to the applicant or his agents, or matters which they would have known, had they made all the inquiries which should reasonably have been made prior to the application.[14] The applicant has a duty to make sure as far as he can that the full story is before the court; this includes asking witnesses to produce all the relevant documents which they have, so as to ensure that the court is not misled.[15] It has been held that even if the applicant has forgotten the matters in question, nevertheless this does not justify failure to disclose them.[16] But it would be a relevant factor to be taken into account by the

---

[11] *Brink's Mat Ltd v Elcombe* [1988] 1 W.L.R. 1350 at 1356, *per* Ralph Gibson L.J., citing *R. v Kensington Income Tax Commissioners Ex p. Princess Edmond de Polignac* [1917] 1 K.B. 486 at 504; *MRG (Japan) Ltd v Engelhard Metals Japan Ltd* [2003] EWHC 3418 at [24]; *Dalglish v Jarvie* (1850) 2 Mac & G 231 at 238 and *Thermax Ltd v Schott Industrial Glass Ltd* [1981] F.S.R. 289 at 295.

[12] *Brink's Mat Ltd v Elcombe* [1988] 1 W.L.R. 1350 was a case in which the non-disclosure was "innocent in the sense that the plaintiffs did not intentionally omit information which they thought to be material" (see the passage in the judgment of Ralph Gibson L.J., which is not in the report, but which is cited by Woolf L.J. in *Behbehani v Salem* [1989] 1 W.L.R. 723 at 728). Also see *Martigny Investments SA v Elmbranch*, Court of Appeal (Civ Div) Transcript No.276 of 1985 (June 12, 1985); *Siporex Trade SA v Comdel Commodities Ltd* [1986] 2 Lloyd's Rep. 428 at 437; *Thomas A. Edison Ltd v Bullock* (1912) 15 C.L.R. 679 at 681–682.

[13] *Thermax Ltd v Schott Industrial Glass Ltd* [1981] F.S.R. 289 at 298, *per* Browne-Wilkinson J. The text was cited with approval in *New Asia Energy Ltd v Concord Oil (Hong Kong) Ltd* [1999] H.K.C.A. 548 (November 3, 1999).

[14] *Brink's Mat Ltd v Elcombe* [1988] 1 W.L.R. 1350 at 1356–1357; *Kuwait Oil Tanker Company SAK v Al Bader (No.1)*, Court of Appeal (Civ Div) Transcript No.1549 of 1995 (November 27, 1995). The extent of the necessary inquiries depends on all the circumstances of the case, including the nature of the case raised by the applicant, the order sought and its likely effects on the defendant and the degree of legitimate urgency, and the time available for the making of inquiries. See also *Bank Mellat v Nikpour* [1985] F.S.R. 87. For an *ex parte* injunction case in which urgency justified not waiting for the outcome of an indirect approach which had been made to a defendant, see *Semple v The London and Birmingham Railway Co.* (1838) 1 Ra.Ca. 480 (Lord Cottenham L.C.).

[15] *Abbasford Ltd v Poly Focus (Europe) Ltd*, Court of Appeal (Civ Div) Transcript No.1044 of 1989 (November 2, 1989).

[16] *Clifton v Robinson* (1853) 15 Beav. 355; *Thomas A. Edison Ltd v Bullock* (1912) 15 C.L.R. 679 at 682. This is regarded as an "unnecessarily harsh view" in *Spry on Equitable Remedies* (4th ed., 1990), p.486. However, it is in line with the requirement that the applicant make all proper inquiries that the standard of the applicant's duty is one of due

court in deciding what should be the consequences of the non-disclosure.[17]

9.003 It may well not be a sufficient answer to an allegation of non-disclosure for an applicant to say that the relevant information giving rise to the defence was contained in an exhibit, though not referred to in the body of the affidavit in the context of a possible defence. Exhibits to such affidavits are often voluminous. Because without notice applications are frequently dealt with comparatively shortly and the judge may not have had the opportunity of considering the papers in detail before the hearing, the applicant has the responsibility of ensuring that all relevant points are presented clearly and distinctly.[18] Thus, in *Siporex Trade SA v Comdel Commodities Ltd*, Bingham J. said[19] that the applicant must "identify the crucial points for and against the application, and not rely on the mere exhibiting of numerous documents".[20] Any contractual provision (*e.g.* an exclusion clause) which is relevant to the court's consideration of the application should be referred to and preferably set out in the body of the affidavit.[21] It will not usually be sufficient simply to exhibit the entire contract. In *National Bank of Sharjah v Dellborg*,[22] Lloyd L.J. said:

> "If the facts are not fairly stated in the affidavit, it will not assist the plaintiff to be able to point to some exhibit from which the fact might be extracted. If they are fairly stated then it should not avail the defendant to show that some document, relevant on discovery, has been omitted . . ."

It is of the utmost importance that the applicant carefully considers the nature of the cause of action and the facts on which it is based before

---

care. Furthermore, if the court considers that the applicant has not been guilty of culpable conduct this can be adequately dealt with in the context of what consequences should flow from the non-disclosure in question.

[17] *Brink's Mat Ltd v Elcombe* [1987] 1 W.L.R. 1350 at 1357, principle (6) stated by Ralph Gibson L.J., see paras 9.017–18, below.

[18] *O'Regan v Iambic Productions* (1989) 139 N.L.J. 1378; Sir Peter Pain said: "It is clearly the duty of Counsel and of the solicitor to point out to the Judge any points which are to their client's disadvantage, which the Judge should take into account in considering whether or not to grant the injunction. It is difficult for a Judge upon an *ex parte* application at short notice to grasp all the relevant points." Sir Peter Pain went on to say that the judge's attention should have been drawn to particular matters there in question. See also *Art Corporation v Schuppan, The Times*, January 20, 1994; *Bakmawar Sdn Bhd v Malayan Banking Bhd* [1992] 1 M.L.J. 67.

[19] [1986] 2 Lloyd's Rep. 428 at 437.

[20] See also *ALG Incorporated v Uganda Airlines Corporation, The Times*, July 31, 1992.

[21] *Bakarim v Victoria P. Shipping* [1980] 2 Lloyd's Rep. 193 at 199. In *Knauf UK GmbH v British Gypsum Ltd* [2002] 1 W.L.R. 907, the *ex parte* application was for an order for service by an alternative method. The purpose was to accelerate the date of service of the claim form and therefore the date when the English court would become first seized. Arguably an exclusive jurisdiction clause providing for German jurisdiction had been agreed. This was material and non-disclosure of it led to the *ex parte* order being set aside.

[22] [1993] 2 Bank L.R. 109; *The Times*, December 24, 1992. See also *Goldtron Ltd v Most Investment Ltd* [2002] J.L.R. 424 at [16] and *Intergraph Corporation v Solid Systems* [1993] F.S.R. 617 at 625.

formulating the application. A thorough check should be made to ensure that all defences actually raised by the defendant are identified and fairly summarised in the affidavit.[23]

Furthermore, on the hearing of the without notice application it is the duty of counsel to ensure that defences[24] and evidence in support of them are specifically drawn to the attention of the judge. Merely mentioning the existence of such material without showing it to the judge may in itself be misleading, or give the case a different flavour. Counsel has a personal duty to the court to ensure that the judge sees all the relevant material.[25]

It is usual for a skeleton argument to be used on an application of any **9.004** complexity.[26] If a skeleton argument is used, it will be one of the primary documents used by the judge in hearing the application and it is very important that it is an entirely fair document. It must not, by failing to mention matters, divert the judge's attention away from material which he should have in mind if he is to have a fair view of the case.

The applicant must identify any defences, which, although not yet taken, would have been available to be taken by the defendant had he been present at the application,[27] provided that:

(1) the defence is one which can reasonably be expected to be raised in due course by the defendant;[28]

(2) the defence is not one which can be dismissed as without substance or importance[29] (*e.g.* an argument based on a misconceived interpretation of a statutory provision).

---

[23] *Dubai Bank v Galadari* [1990] 1 Lloyd's Rep. 120 at 133 ("there can scarcely be any more important topic for disclosure . . .", *per* Staughton L.J.); *Practice Direction (Judge in Chambers: Procedure)* [1983] 1 W.L.R. 433, Part B, para.3(2)(d) (no longer in force); *Third Chandris Corp v Unimarine SA* [1979] Q.B. 645 at 668; *Bank Mellat v Nikpour* [1985] F.S.R. 87 at 89; *Harbottle v Pooley* [1869] 30 L.T. 436; *Escott v Thomas* [1934] N.Z.L.R. 175.

[24] *United People's Organisation (Worldwide) Inc v Rakino Farms Limited (No. 1)* [1964] N.Z.L.R. 737.

[25] *Art Corporation v Schuppan. The Times,* January 20, 1994; *Brown v Bennett (No.2)* [2002] 1 W.L.R. 713; *O'Regan v Iambic Productions* (1989) 139 N.L.J. 1378; *Admiralty and Commercial Courts Guide,* para.F2.5 *Bakmawar Sdn Bhd v Malayan Banking Bhd* [1992] 1 M.L.J. 67; *Intergraph Corporation v Solid Systems* [1993] F.S.R. 617.

[26] *Admiralty and Commercial Courts Guide,* para.F15.3(b).

[27] *Lloyd's Bowmaker Ltd v Britannia Arrow* [1988] 1 W.L.R. 1337 at 1341 and 1343, where Glidewell L.J. says that the authorities cited support the proposition that the applicant "must disclose any defence he has reason to anticipate may be advanced". In advance of commencement of legal proceedings a defendant may not be in a position, or have yet sought, to set out all the defences which may arise. The ambit of the duty of disclosure is not limited to the defence (if any) which may have been indicated by the defendant up to the time of the without notice application. In *Town & Country Sport Resorts v Partnership Pacific Ltd* (1988) 49 A.T.P.R. 783 at 786, the full court of the Federal Court of Australia expressly referred to the duty of the applicant "to place before the court all relevant matters including such matters which would have been raised by the [defendant] in his defence if he had been present".

[28] *The Electric Furnace Co. v Selas Corporation of America* [1987] R.F.C. 23; *Practice Direction* [1983] 1 W.L.R. 433 at para.3(2)(d) (no longer in force).

[29] *Weston v Arnold* (1873) L.R. 8 Ch. App. 1084 at 1090, *per* Sir W.M. James L.J.; *The Electric Furnace Co. v Selas Corporation of America* (above) at 29, *per* Slade L.J. citing with approval *BP Exploration Co. (Libya) Ltd v Hunt* [1976] 3 All E.R. 879 at 893, *per* Kerr J.

This is simply an aspect of the applicant's duty to give a fair account of the case for and against the defendant, identifying the crucial points for and against the granting of the application. Thus, if there is an obvious answer to the claim, such as a defence under the Limitation Act or a contractual time-bar, the applicant must refer to it even if the defendant has not explicitly raised it.

9.005   Similarly, if there is a point on what quantum may be recoverable this should be clearly stated. For example, if there is an application for Mareva relief on a claim against shipowners which prima facie is subject to a limit applicable under the Convention on Limitation of Liability for Maritime Claims 1976, then if it is contended that the limit is inapplicable the judge should be told the amount of the limit as calculated for the particular ship, what is the basis for arguing that the limit is inapplicable, and what can be said against that contention.

The applicant should make adequate inquiries about the standing of the defendant and his business and should disclose the results.[30]

It is often a difficult exercise to settle a suitable affidavit which achieves the right balance between full and fair disclosure and a far too detailed description of the facts, with perhaps too much generosity towards the defendant. The duty of disclosure does not require the applicant to describe his case or the factual background in minute detail, nor does it require him to search for possible but unlikely defences.

9.006   A matter which must be carefully considered is whether the applicant is likely to be good for any damages which he may be required to pay on the cross-undertaking as to damages.[31] Such an undertaking is almost invariably required to be given on an application for an injunction or search order, and will be dispensed with only in special circumstances (*e.g.* a claim by the Crown to enforce the law, see para.11.002 below). In general it is strongly advisable for this matter to be expressly dealt with on the application, giving particulars of the applicant's solvency and worth. If nothing is said and an order is made, then the court will be proceeding on the basis that there is no reason to doubt that the person giving the cross-undertaking will be good for the damages. If facts are disclosed which raise doubts as to the likely worth of the cross-undertaking, should it be called upon, the

---

[30] *Naf Naf SA v Dickens (London) Ltd* [1993] F.R.S. 424; *Thermax Ltd v Schott Industrial Glass Ltd* [1981] F.R.S. 289 at 297.
[31] *Czarnikow-Rionda Sugar Trading v Standard Bank London Ltd* [1999] 2 Lloyd's Rep. 187 at 207; *Swedac Ltd v Magnet & Southerns plc* [1989] F.R.S. 243 at 251; *Manor Electronics Ltd v Dickson* [1988] R.F.C. 618; *Anchor Glass Company Ltd v O'Connor* Court of Appeal (Civ Div) Transcript No.715 of 1996 (June 13, 1996); *Automatic Parking Coupons Limited v Time Ticket International* (1996) 10 P.R.N.Z. 538 (injunction discharged because of failure to give financial information about applicant which on the facts was regarded as failure to comply with a fundamental requirement under the New Zealand rules of court); *Capitanescu v Universal Weld Overlays Inc.* [1997] 3 W.W.R. 714 (individual plaintiffs had given an undertaking, so the fact that the corporate plaintiff was a shell company was not material).

court may nevertheless, in the exercise of its discretion, decide to grant the application if there are circumstances which make it just to do so.[32]

Thus in *Block v Nicholson*,[33] the plaintiff failed to disclose to the court on an *ex parte* application for Mareva relief that he had been arrested and charged with fraud prior to the application. This was a matter which was plainly relevant to whether, on an *ex parte* application, the court could safely accept the plaintiff's undertaking in damages. Accordingly, the judge discharged the relief granted on the grounds of non-disclosure, and his decision was upheld by the Court of Appeal. Similarly, in *Manor Electronics v Dickson*,[34] Scott J. set aside an Anton Piller order which had been obtained without disclosure of facts concerning the plaintiff's financial status, saying that if no reference is made on the *ex parte* application to the plaintiff's worth, then an assumption is made by the court that the plaintiff's financial status is "adequate for the purpose of the cross-undertaking".[35]

In formulating an application it is appropriate to include all matters which could reasonably be regarded as capable of being relevant to the assessment of the application, including what undertakings should be sought from the applicant and the precise terms of any order which might be made. Consideration should be given as to whether non-parties are liable to be affected by the order sought and all relevant information should be given to the court to enable it to assess what undertakings should be sought from the applicant at the ex parte stage. This has a particular importance because the court has no power to order a party to give an undertaking, or to modify the wording of an undertaking which has been given; or to require a bond or other security in support of an undertaking, without the consent of the party who gives the undertaking.[36] Accordingly, if a non-party appears before the court subsequently, complaining that inadequate protection is given to him by the *ex parte* order, the court may find that meanwhile the *ex parte* relief is no longer required (*e.g.* the Anton Piller order has been executed, or the Mareva relief has been discharged). In such circumstances the court will not be in a position to extract a suitable undertaking because continuation of the relief, for which an undertaking would have been required, will not be sought.[37]

---

[32] *Allen v Jambo Holdings* [1980] 1 W.L.R. 1252, *Szentessy v Woo Ran* (1985) 64 A.C.T.R. 98, Supreme Court of the Australian Capital Territory; *Smith v Tenneco Energy Queensland Pty Ltd* [1996] A.L.M.D. (Advance), July 2, 1996, No.2097 and para.11.003 below.

[33] Court of Appeal (Civ Div) Transcript No.409 of 1986 (April 17, 1986).

[34] [1988] R.F.C. 618.

[35] *ibid.*, at 623.

[36] *Commodity Ocean Transport Corpn v Basford Unicorn* [1987] 2 Lloyd's Rep. 197 at 200; *Remm Construction (SA) Pty Ltd v Allco Newsteel Pty* (1991) 56 S.A.S.R. 515 (South Australia).

[37] *Commodity Ocean Transport Corpn v Basford Unicorn* (above); *Remm Construction (SA) Pty Ltd v Allco Newsteel Pty* (above).

9.007   Accordingly, it is right and proper that the court, on the without notice application, should insist on full disclosure of the position in relation to non-parties so that adequate undertakings and security can be required to protect third parties as the price of relief at that stage.[38]

If the claimant is engaged in open negotiations with the defendant, that is relevant to the exercise of the court's discretion as going to the question whether the claimant needs urgent without notice relief. If the defendant is willing to attend an open meeting to discuss the claim, this may indicate a measure of responsibility in relation to his legal obligations which might cast doubt on whether the case was suitable for Mareva relief. In considering what matters should be disclosed to the court, the applicant should bear in mind that he must include any facts which are relevant to the exercise of the discretion, regardless of whether they would also be relevant to the merits of the claim. For example, matters relating to whether there has been delay in making the application can be material.[39]

In a case based on allegations of fraud it will be material that the applicant has known of the alleged fraud for some time,[40] or that the defendant has admitted the diversion of funds but says it was done with consent. Non-disclosure of matters which, if they had been disclosed, would have given ". . . a seriously different flavour to the case' resulted in the discharge of all *ex parte* relief in *Dubai Bank v Galadari*, even though the plaintiff maintained that there was a strong prima facie case of fraud.

9.008   If assets of a defendant have already been frozen in a foreign jurisdiction, this is relevant to an application for a freezing injunction because it is material to consideration of whether the applicant should have further relief and the limit in any injunction granted. In the case of an application under s.25(1) of the Civil Jurisdiction and Judgments Act 1982 it is necessary to consider disclosing matters which could be relevant to whether it is "inexpedient"[41] for the court to grant interim relief in aid of a foreign court.[42]

If the applicant wishes to obtain relief in respect of money paid by him to the defendant by way of the purchase price of a ship, it is somewhat unattractive for the applicant to have paid over the full purchase money in return for delivery of the ship and then to seek, behind the seller's back, Mareva relief blocking use of the funds. If this is to be done, then it must

---

[38] In relation to undertakings which have been thought appropriate to protect the position of third parties, see generally *Allied Irish Bank v Ashford Hotels Ltd* [1997] 3 All E.R. 309 at 316–317; *Z Ltd v A-Z and AA-LL* [1982] Q.B. 558; *Clipper Maritime v Mineral Import/Export* [1981] 1 W.L.R. 1262 and *Searose v Seatrain UK Ltd* [1981] 1 W.L.R. 894. It is also necessary to consider whether proper disclosure is being made to enable the court to decide whether the circumstances are such that it would be unjust to grant an injunction at all because of the likely prejudice to third parties, *e.g.* as in *Galaxia Maritime SA v Mineralimportexport* [1982] 1 W.L.R. 539.

[39] *Kuwait Oil Tanker Co. SAK v Al Bader (No.1)*, Court of Appeal (Civ Div) Transcript No.1549 of 1995 (November 27, 1995).

[40] *Dubai Bank v Galadari* [1990] 1 Lloyd's Rep. 120 at 133.

[41] See further Chapter 5 above.

[42] Cited with approval in *Armco Inc v NPV Ltd* [1998] H.K.C.F.I. 632.

be disclosed on the *ex parte* application.[43] The court should be informed if the applicant intends to lead the defendant to act in a particular way without disclosing the intended application when, had the defendant known of it, he might well have acted differently.

The duty to make full disclosure of material facts does not prevent the claimant from making adverse comment about the defendant's defences, provided that he does not mislead the court; indeed if he can show that the defences are spurious, this may assist him. When settling the affidavit, however, care must be taken not to seek to draw too strong an adverse inference from the fact that thin defences have been raised; it is one thing to say that the applicant believes that he has a strong case because the defences raised are thin, and that summary judgment may be given, but it is quite another to suggest that the defendant has not raised them bona fide and that they have been raised at the last minute as a means of putting off the day of payment. Allegations of the latter kind should be made only if there is a proper basis. If an applicant wishes to include in the application matters which are discreditable to the defendant, he must take care to ensure that they are presented fairly: the applicant cannot seek to "pile on the prejudice" but only tell "half of the story".[44]

It is the responsibility of the claimant's legal advisers to ensure that a **9.009** without notice application is not made to a court other than that to which the proceedings are assigned under a statute or under the CPR.[45]

An applicant for *inter partes* relief does not have a duty to make full disclosure of material facts, but is under an obligation not knowingly to mislead the court. The reason for the duty to make full disclosure on a without notice application is that the applicant is himself asking the court to undertake the hazardous course of granting relief against a party in his absence and without the opportunity of presenting his case. This consideration does not apply on a with notice application, namely on an application made after adequate prior notice has been given to the defendant in accordance with the CPR by due service on him of an application notice, where the defendant has chosen not to appear.[46] If an application is made on informal notice to the defendant (*i.e. ex parte* on notice) and the defendant does not appear, the rule requiring full disclosure still applies. Even if the defendant is represented, this is not equivalent to the standard of representation which would be achieved had there been a full and proper opportunity to prepare for the application, and it is considered that the requirement for compliance remains in place. If there is "innocent" non-disclosure on such an application which could and ought to have been corrected by the defendant or his representatives, this is a material factor for the court in considering the consequences of the non-disclosure.

---

[43] *The P* [1992] 1 Lloyd's Rep. 470 at 473, citing the earlier authorities. *Ateni Maritime Corporation v Great Marine (The Great Marine No.1)* [1990] 2 Lloyd's Rep. 245 at 250. See further paras 6.050–59, above.

[44] *Lloyd's Bowmaker v Britannia Arrow* [1988] 1 W.L.R. 1337 at 1348, *per* Dillon L.J.

[45] *Apac Rowena Ltd v Norpol Packaging* [1991] 4 All E.R. 516; *Elvee v Taylor* [2002] F.S.R 738.

[46] *Maclaren v Stainton* (1852) 15 Beav. 279 at 290.

(2) Wasted costs—claims against the other side's lawyers

9.010   In the context of compliance with orders for disclosure a solicitor has a personal responsibility to ensure that the party for whom he is acting makes proper disclosure of documents pursuant to the order,[47] and similarly in principle those acting for the applicant have a personal responsibility to take all reasonable steps to ensure that there is full and frank disclosure to the court on the application.[48] Thus, if the applicant's solicitor causes the application to proceed when he knows such matters are not being disclosed, he will render himself liable to compensate the defendant in respect of the loss which would be covered by the cross-undertaking.[49] This may be dealt with by the court, under its inherent jurisdiction to order solicitors to pay compensation to the other party on the grounds of serious neglect or dereliction of duty, on an application made against the solicitor as an officer of the court.[50] The solicitor will not be made liable personally under the inherent jurisdiction of the court if there has been a mere slip or accidental oversight. But that jurisdiction can be exercised when the conduct of the solicitor is "inexcusable and such as to merit reproof".[51] "A simple mistake or oversight or a mere error of judgment will not, of itself, be sufficiently serious. . . . the test [is] whether the conduct amounted to a serious dereliction of duty".[52] The solicitor is responsible for misconduct of his assistant or clerk to whom the work has been delegated.[53]

---

[47] *Myers v Elman* [1940] A.C. 282; *Rockwell Machine Tool Co. Ltd v EP Barrus (Concessionaires) Ltd* [1968] 2 All E.R. 98; *Woods v Martins Bank Ltd* [1959] 1 Q.B. 55 at 60; *El Du Pont de Nemours & Co. v Commissioner of Patents* (1987) 83 A.L.R. 499, Federal Court of Australia: General Division; *Practice Note* [1944] W.N. 49.

[48] In *O'Regan v Iambic Productions* (1989) 139 N.L.J. 1378 at 1379, Sir Peter Pain said: "I find [the solicitor's] attitude very disappointing coming from a solicitor. I could understand a litigant in person not familiar with the procedure adopting [that attitude] . . . but [the person in question] is a solicitor and an officer of the court. If the Anton Piller jurisdiction is to work at all, the court must rely on its officers to be very careful and lean over backwards to make sure there is full disclosure, especially if it is to the client's disadvantage . . . The point is that it is the duty of the solicitor to apprise the court of the facts so that the court can make up its own mind." Counsel also has a personal duty to ensure that there is full disclosure at the hearing of the application: *Art Corporation v Schuppan, The Times*, January 21, 1994.

[49] In *Schmitten v Faulks* [1893] W.N. 64, the applicant's solicitor had not disclosed to the court on the *ex parte* application that he himself had commenced bankruptcy proceedings against his client. Although the non-disclosure was not committed in bad faith in the sense that the solicitor erroneously believed that the matter did not have to be disclosed because the solicitor had control over the bankruptcy proceedings, nevertheless, on an application brought by the defendant against the solicitor, Chitty J. ordered that the solicitor should pay the loss caused by the *ex parte* injunction, the cross-undertaking of the plaintiff being of no value.

[50] *Udall v Capri Lighting Ltd* [1988] Q.B. 907; *R & T Thew Ltd v Reeves (No.2)* [1982] Q.B. 1283; *Myers v Elman* [1940] A.C. 282; *Harley v McDonald* [2001] 2 A.C. 678.

[51] *Udall v Capri Lighting Ltd* [1988] Q.B. 907 at 917. Reliance on advice from counsel does not necessarily exonerate the solicitor. Although it will be a factor to be taken into account, the solicitor may still be ordered to pay compensation where that advice was obviously wrong: *Davy-Chiesman v Davy-Chiesman* [1984] Fam. 48.

[52] *Harley v McDonald* [2001] 2 A.C. 678, at [53].

[53] *Myers v Elman* [1940] A.C. 282 at 291, 302, 307, 321 and 335.

There is also a separate jurisdiction under s.51 of the Supreme Court Act **9.011** 1981 for the court to order a legal or other representative, including a barrister,[54] to bear "wasted costs". The jurisdiction, which is discretionary, arises when there has been ". . . any improper, unreasonable or negligent act or omission" on the part of a representative or an employee. This includes ". . . failure to act with the competence reasonably to be expected of ordinary members of the profession".[55] This jurisdiction applies not just against the other side's lawyers—it applies to any representative including the applicant's own lawyer. So the scope of the wording takes account of all the potential situations in which it might be used, including where the client proceeds against his own lawyer for negligently causing him loss. There has to be causation between the conduct complained of and the particular costs which have been wasted.[56] This jurisdiction can be used against a legal representative of the other side in respect of the wasted costs caused by non-disclosure which occurred by reason of his negligence or that of his employee. The jurisdiction over counsel and solicitors depends upon there being a breach of duty owed to the court by the lawyer.[57] It should only be used in respect of matters which are suitable for summary determination.[58] It is not restricted to conduct in court but also includes conduct immediately relevant to representing someone before the court, *e.g.* preparing an application for *ex parte* relief.

In the case of applications against the other side's lawyers the jurisdiction is affected by the important policy consideration that it is in the public interest that lawyers are able to act freely independently and effectively on behalf of a client without fear of being sued by the other side. The integrity of the judicial process depends on this.[59] Thus, if the allegation is that they have run a hopeless case it is not enough to show negligence, there must be some serious breach of duty owed to the court involving what amounts to causing or assisting in an abuse of the process of the court.[60] A failure which significantly affects the fairness of the presentation of the without notice application itself interferes with the judicial process. On the other hand the possibility of applications against the other side's lawyers threatens to chill their independence.[61] Unless fully justified as based on serious dereliction of duty to the court, they should be firmly discouraged.[62] It is considered that on such an application there has to be

---

[54] *Medcalf v Mardell* [2003] 1 A.C. 120.
[55] *Ridehalgh v Horsefield* [1994] Ch. 205 at 233C.
[56] *ibid.*, at 237E–F.
[57] *Medcalf v Mardell* [2003] 1 A.C. 120; *Persaud v Persaud* [2003] P.N.L.R. 519; *Dempsey v Johnstone* [2003] EWCA 1134.
[58] *Manzanilla Ltd v Corton Property & Investments Ltd, The Times*, August 4, 1997; *Turner Page Music v Torres Design Associates Ltd, The Times*, August 3, 1998; *Harley v McDonald* [2001] 2 A.C. 678 at [50].
[59] *Medcalf v Mardell* [2003] 1 A.C. 120 at [51–56], *per* Lord Hobhouse; *Brown v Bennett No.2* [2002] 1 W.L.R. 713 at 66.
[60] *Persaud v Persaud* [2003] P.N.L.R. 519.
[61] *Harley v McDonald* [2001] 2 A.C. 678 at [49].
[62] *Medcalf v Mardell* [2003] 1 A.C. 120.

clear proof[63] of a seriously culpable breach of duty to the court before the court should consider making such an order. When the lawyer cannot produce the materials which might justify his conduct because of privilege which his client declines to waive, a wasted costs order should not be made because it cannot be made consistently with due process being accorded to the lawyer.[64]

9.012   In *Brown v Bennett (No.2)*[65] an application was made against both counsel and solicitors for the other side for wasted costs on the ground that there was non-disclosure of certain letters at an *ex parte* application. The court allowed the application to proceed to the next stage against the counsel involved, as well as the solicitors, holding that the letters were material and that whether counsel had in fact seen the documents before the *ex parte* application was not privileged information, and therefore it could be fully investigated at the next stage of the application. The decision, which did not determine the outcome of the application, was made before the judgment of the Court of Appeal in *Medcalf v Mardell* was reversed. Even if a lawyer had a material document in his possession which should have been disclosed to the judge it does not follow that an order should be made against him in respect of wasted costs. Mere inadvertence or carelessness would not be enough.

The judge also mooted the possibility that where more than one lawyer was involved and someone must have been responsible an order might be made against all as a "group".[66] It is a serious matter for a lawyer to be proceeded against under this jurisdiction and neither the words of the statute, nor the obligation of the court to the lawyer to act fairly and in accordance with due process,[67] are consistent with this suggestion.

(3) Disclosure of confidential information

9.013   The general rule in litigation[68] is that the court can act only on information or evidence which can be revealed to the defendant, albeit at a later stage, so that the defendant can have an opportunity of applying to discharge the relief granted *ex parte*.[69] This is a requirement made necessary by the rule

---

[63] The standard is on the balance of probabilities but taking into account the inherent unlikelihood of the allegation: *Re H (Minors)* [1996] A.C. 563.
[64] *Medcalf v Mardell* [2003] 1 A.C. 120.
[65] [2002] 1 W.L.R. 713.
[66] *ibid.*, at [182].
[67] *Medcalf v Mardell* [2003] 1 A.C. 120 at [42]; European Convention on Human Rights, Art.6(1).
[68] The position is different in non-adversarial litigation (*e.g.* an application for directions by a trustee) and in certain procedures designed to enable investigations to proceed: *Re Murjani* [1996] 1 W.L.R. 1498 at 1507–1509.
[69] *WEA Records v Visions Channel 4 Ltd* [1983] 1 W.L.R. 721 at 724; *The Coca Cola Company and Schweppes Ltd v Gilbey* [1996] F.S.R. 23 at 27–28; *Kelly v BBC* [2001] Fam. 59; *Re S (A Child) (Family Division: Without Notice Orders)* [2001] 1 All E.R. 362.

of natural justice that the court must listen to both sides, and by Art.6 of the European Convention on Human Rights.[70] It is not an absolute rule and must give way in compelling circumstances when, on the facts, it conflicts with a higher public policy, *e.g.* the interests of a child in adoption proceedings,[71] or when the requirement of disclosure would be inconsistent with a statutory procedure for investigation which disclosure would prejudice.[72]

One of the matters which can be material on an application for Mareva or Anton Piller relief is whether the applicant intends to commence, or has commenced, proceedings abroad connected with his claim, particularly proceedings in which relief may be sought or has been sought to assist in the prosecution or enforcement of the claim.[73] If the intention is to launch proceedings, the applicant often commences the overseas proceedings at the same time as the English proceedings; there will then be no difficulty in referring to the intended foreign application in the affidavit made in support of the *ex parte* application, or recording the information relied on in the application.[74]

It may be, however, that intended foreign proceedings cannot be **9.014** commenced immediately and that the applicant has good grounds for concealing his intentions from the defendant for the time being. In these circumstances the applicant cannot justify failure to disclose his intentions to the court on the grounds that the defendant might, on obtaining this information, take steps designed to frustrate an order made by the foreign court.[75] The appropriate procedure is to inform the court of the applicant's intentions on the *ex parte* application. This can be done orally, with the information being set out in a separate document prepared by the applicant, with the intention of serving it on the defendant following commencement of the foreign proceedings. This procedure results in full disclosure to the court on the *ex parte* application and does not involve disclosing the information prematurely to the defendant.[76] On the other hand, it will not infringe the principle that the defendant is entitled, albeit

---

[70] *Kelly v BBC* [2001] Fam. 59.
[71] *Re D (Minors) (Adoption Reports: Confidentiality)* [1996] A.C. 593; *Kelly v BBC* [2001] Fam. 59.
[72] *Re Murjani (A Bankrupt)* [1996] 1 W.L.R. 1498.
[73] *Behbehani v Salem* [1989] 1 W.L.R 723 at 730–734, 736–737; *Kuwait Oil Tanker SAK v Al Bader (No.1)*, Court of Appeal (Civil Division) Transcript No.1549 of 1995 (November 27, 1995).
[74] The applicant "must, for the protection and information of the defendant, summarise his case and the evidence in support of it by an affidavit or affidavits sworn before or immediately after the application": *Siporex Trade SA v Comdel Commodities Ltd* [1986] 2 Lloyd's Rep. 428 at 437. Thus, if further information is placed before the court beyond what is contained in the affidavit placed before the court on the *ex parte* application, this should be recorded in a further affidavit to be made following the application, and an undertaking should be proffered to the court that this will be done.
[75] *Behbehani v Salem* [1989] 1 W.L.R 723 esp. at 732 and 737.
[76] Orders are frequently made under which the court requires the existence of the proceedings not to be revealed to the defendant for a relatively short period while the claimant takes steps to execute the *ex parte* relief which has been granted, *e.g. Republic of Haiti v Duvalier* [1990] 1 Q.B. 202 at 208–209.

at a later stage, to full information about what has occurred before the court on the *ex parte* application. Once the defendant applies to have the order set aside, however, he must be told of all that took place on the *ex parte* application.

(4) Effects of non-disclosure or material misrepresentation

9.015   On without notice applications not involving a freezing injunction or a search order, where there has been non-disclosure, and it is proportionate to do so,[77] courts have simply set aside the *ex parte* relief, leaving the applicant to make fresh application.[78] In those circumstances the court has considered that the applicant has been deprived of any advantage obtained by the granting of the *ex parte* relief.

The position is different in relation to injunction and search order cases, because the applicant has in effect struck prematurely and the defendant's position might have been adversely affected by the granting of *ex parte* relief. Thus, *e.g.* in relation to freezing relief the defendant might have disposed of assets but for the granting of the relief.[79] Furthermore, the position is not as simple as in cases where the consequences of setting aside *ex parte* relief and leaving the applicant free to renew his application merely results in delay for the applicant and consequences in costs. In the context of freezing relief the question would be whether the applicant could make an immediate application for relief in the same terms. If he could, the consequences in costs would not be likely to be very severe[80] and he would in effect have had the benefit of a continuous period from the time of the original without notice application when an appropriate injunction was in place. On the other hand, if he was precluded from making an immediate application, the result could be very severe. The defendant would have a period during which he would be free to deal with and dispose of his assets. In relation to a search order, damages on the cross-undertaking could be substantial if the order is set aside.[81]

In practice the courts have adopted an approach which enables all relevant factors to be taken into account while maintaining, as a matter of policy, a sufficiently penal approach[82] that would-be applicants for *ex parte*

---

[77] *MRG (Japan) Ltd v Engelhard Metals Japan Ltd* [2004] 1 Lloyd's Rep. 731 (the court would have refused to set aside permission to serve out of the jurisdiction when this was disproportionate).

[78] *R. v Kensington Income Tax Commissioners, Ex p. Princess Edmond de Polignac* [1917] 1 K.B. 486 at 506, *per* Lord Cozens-Hardy M.R.; *Fitch v Rochfort* (1849) 18 L.J. Ch. 458 at 460 (*per* Lord Cottenham L.C., during argument).

[79] *Bank Mellat v Nikpour* [1985] F.S.R. 87 at 91.

[80] The defendant would be entitled to damages on the cross-undertaking for any loss suffered in the interim, but this might well not be substantial.

[81] A common effect of a search order is to close down or seriously damage the defendant's business: *Columbia Pictures Inc. v Robinson* [1987] Ch. at 73.

[82] *Brink's Mat Ltd v Elcombe* [1988] 1 W.L.R. 1350 at 1359, *per* Slade L.J.

relief are deterred from making less than full and frank disclosure to the court of all relevant matters.[83] The purpose of the penal aspect is to uphold the integrity of the judicial process on without notice applications.[84]

The applicable principles have been stated in the context of Mareva **9.016** relief by Ralph Gibson L.J. in *Brink's Mat Ltd v Elcombe*:[85]

> (1) The duty of the applicant is to make "a full and fair disclosure of all the material facts": see *Rex v Kensington Income Tax Commissioners, ex p Princess Edmond de Polignac* [1917] 1 K.B. 486, 514, *per* Scrutton L.J.
>
> (2) The material facts are those which it is material for the judge to know in dealing with the application as made: materiality is to be decided by the court and not by the assessment of the applicant or his legal advisers: see *Rex v Kensington Income Tax Commissioners, per* Lord Cozens-Hardy M.R., at p.504, citing *Dalglish v Jarvie* (1850) 2 Mac & G 231, 238, and Browne-Wilkinson J. in *Thermax Ltd v Schott Industrial Glass Ltd* [1981] F.S.R. 289, 295.
>
> (3) The applicant must make proper inquiries before making the application: see *Bank Mellat v Nikpour* [1985] F.S.R. 87. The duty of disclosure therefore applies not only to material facts known to the applicant but also to any additional facts which he would have known if he had made such enquiries.
>
> (4) The extent of the inquiries which will be held to be proper, and therefore necessary, must depend on all the circumstances of the case including (a) the nature of the case which the applicant is making when he makes the application; and (b) the order for which application is made and the probable effect of the order on the defendant: see, for example, the examination by Scott J. of the possible effect of an *Anton Piller* order in *Columbia Picture Industries Inc v Robinson* [1987] Ch. 38; and (c) the degree of legitimate urgency and the time available for the making of inquiries: see *per* Slade L.J. in *Bank Mellat v Nikpour* [1985] F.S.R. 87, 92–93.
>
> (5) If material non-disclosure is established the court will be 'astute to ensure that a plaintiff who obtains [an *ex parte* injunction] without full disclosure . . . is deprived of any advantage he may have derived by the breach of duty': see *per* Donaldson L.J. in *Bank Mellat v Nikpour*, at p.91, citing Warrington L.J. in the *Kensington Income Tax Commissioners'* case [1917] 1 K.B. 486, 509.
>
> (6) Whether the fact not disclosed is of sufficient materiality to justify or require immediate discharge of the order without examination of the merits depends on the importance of the fact to the issues

[83] *Brink's Mat Ltd v Elcombe* [1988] 1 W.L.R. 1350 at 1358, *per* Balcombe L.J. and 1359, *per* Slade L.J.; *Behbehani v Salem* [1989] 1 W.L.R. 723 at 726–729, *per* Woolf L.J.
[84] *Kuwait Oil Tanker Company SAK v Al Bader (No.1)*, Court of Appeal (Civ Div) Transcript No.1549 of 1995 (November 27, 1995).
[85] [1988] 1 W.L.R. 1350 at 1356.

which were to be decided by the judge on the application. The answer to the question whether the non-disclosure was innocent, in the sense that the fact was not known to the applicant or that its relevance was not perceived, is an important consideration but not decisive by reason of the duty on the applicant to make all proper inquiries and to give careful consideration to the case being presented.

(7) Finally, it 'is not for every omission that the injunction will be automatically discharged. A *locus penitentiae* may sometimes be afforded', *per* Lord Denning M.R. in *Bank Mellat v Nikpour* [1985] F.S.R. 87, 90. The court has a discretion,[86] notwithstanding proof of material non- disclosure which justifies or requires the immediate discharge of the *ex parte* order, nevertheless to continue the order, or to make a new order on terms.[87]

> 'when the whole of the facts, including that of the original non-disclosure, are before [the court, it] may well grant . . . a second injunction if the original non-disclosure was innocent and if an injunction could properly be granted even had the facts been disclosed': *per* Glidewell L.J. in *Lloyd's Bowmaker Ltd v Britannia Arrow Holdings Plc* [1988] 1 W.L.R. 1337 at pp 1343H–1344A.

The same principles apply to a search order. Often an application to discharge the order for non-disclosure will not be made until after the order has been fully executed, in which case it may be appropriate for the application not to be dealt with until the trial. In such circumstances the court is not confronted with the same problem as arises when the question is whether freezing relief should be set aside, with the consequence that an otherwise meritorious claimant may not be able to enforce his claim. The consequences of setting aside a search order will be reflected in terms of costs and damages on the cross-undertaking. The likely severity of the consequences to a claimant of setting aside an order for non-disclosure is a factor to which the court should have regard in deciding whether in any particular case the order should be set aside.[88]

9.017   If the non-disclosure is such that the court, on reviewing the matter *inter partes*, is of the opinion that the *ex parte* relief was inappropriate and should not have been granted, then plainly the court will discharge the order.[89] But the "acid test" for whether or not the order will be discharged is not whether or not the original judge who granted the order *ex parte* would have been likely to have arrived at a different decision if the material matters had been before him.[90] It has been said that in considering

---

[86] See also *Dubai Bank v Galadari* [1990] 1 Lloyd's Rep. 120 at 127.
[87] Approved by the Privy Council in *Jeanette Walsh v Deloitte & Touche Inc.* [2002] L.R.C. 545.
[88] *Arab Business Consortium International v Banque Franco-Tunisienne* [1996] 1 Lloyd's Rep. 485 at 491–492 (leave to appeal refused: [1997] 1 Lloyd's Rep. 531).
[89] *Ali and Fahd Shobokshi Group v Moneim* [1989] 1 W.L.R. 710.
[90] *Behbehani v Salem* [1989] 1 W.L.R. 723 at 729, *per* Woolf L.J.; *Sal Oppenheim JR & Cie KGaa v Rotherwood (UK) Ltd*, Court of Appeal (Civil Division) Transcript No.386 of 1996 (April 19, 1996). See also *Boyce v Gill* (1891) 64 L.T. 824 at 825: "what the court would have done if all the facts had been known, I cannot say".

whether to discharge for non-disclosure the answer to the question is not "a matter of great significance unless the facts which were not disclosed would have resulted in a refusal of the order".[91]

Whether or not the relevant non-disclosure was "innocent", in the sense that there was no intention to omit or withhold information which was thought to be material,[92] is an important factor to be taken into account by the court.[93] The court should assess the degree and extent of culpability.

If there has been non-disclosure which was otherwise than "innocent", then it would only be in the most exceptional circumstances that the court would decline to discharge the order.[94] This was the position in *Eastglen International Corporation v Monpare SA*.[95] The original solicitor who had acted for the plaintiff, who was a non-resident foreigner, had sworn an affidavit which clearly omitted a most material fact. When the defendant applied to discharge the injunction, the plaintiffs changed solicitors. The new solicitors discontinued the first action and started a fresh application in new proceedings for Mareva relief supported by an affidavit which made clear the failure to disclose in the original action. Gatehouse J. discharged the order for non-disclosure, but his decision was reversed by the Court of Appeal on the grounds that the fault was wholly that of the first solicitor, and not that of the client.

Where the non-disclosure was "innocent" in the sense used above, the court will take into account the degree of culpability of the applicant and his advisers.[96] Hence it is considered that if the court concludes on the evidence that the applicant had genuinely forgotten the relevant information, this would be a factor[97] against setting aside the order.

9.018

---

[91] *Behbehani v Salem* [1989] 1 W.L.R. 723 at 729.

[92] *ibid.*, at 728.

[93] *Ali and Fahd Shobokshi v Moneim* [1989] 1 W.L.R. 710 at 719–720; *Brink's Mat Ltd v Elcombe* [1989] 1 W.L.R. 1350, at 1358 and 1360; *Behbehani v Salem* [1989] 1 W.L.R. 723 at 728.

[94] *Arab Business Consortium International v Banque Franco-Tunisienne* [1996] 1 Lloyd's Rep. 485 at 490; (upheld on appeal at [1997] 1 Lloyd's Rep. 531); *St Merryn Meat Ltd v Hawkins* [2001] C.P. Rep. 116 at 59–65.

[95] (1987) 137 N.L.J. 56. This case is highly exceptional, see *Lloyd's Bowmaker Ltd v Britannia Arrow* [1988] 1 W.L.R. 1337 at 1347; *Behbehani v Salem* [1989] 1 W.L.R. 723 at 729.

[96] *Behbehani v Salem* [1989] 1 W.L.R. 723 at 729; *Dubai Bank v Galadari* [1990] 1 Lloyd's Rep. 120 at 126. The court is reluctant to allow the client to suffer for the fault of the adviser: *PT Bank Pembangunan Indonesia (Persero) v Tan Eddy Tansil* [1997] 1 H.K.L.R.D. 57 (defendant in prison was out of time under an "unless order" because of the fault of his lawyer) citing *Doyle v Olby (Ironmongers) Ltd* [1969] 1 Q.B. 158 at 166C, *per* Lord Denning M.R. Contrast *Hytec Ltd v Coventry City Council* [1997] 1 W.L.R. 1666 at 1675C, where the defendant was itself "the author of its own misfortune" (at 1679C).

[97] See the facts in *Clifton v Robinson* (1853) 16 Beav. 355, where Sir John Romilly M.R. declined as a matter of policy to give effect to this excuse, saying that otherwise it would be relied upon "in every instance". The court would be astute to ensure that if the excuse was put forward, all relevant particulars were made out, and if necessary the court could order cross-examination of the deponent to the relevant affidavit which set out the excuse. See also *Spry on Equitable Remedies* (4th ed., 1990), p.486.

It will be relevant to take into account whether the non- disclosure was of matters which were important[98] or only of peripheral importance on the application.

The discretion to maintain the order, or to allow a new application for relief in the same terms, is to be exercised "sparingly".[99] On the other hand, where there is a clear prima facie case of a substantial fraud, innocent albeit careless non-disclosure may not result in the discharge of the *ex parte* relief. Whilst a penal jurisdiction is necessary in order to deter non- disclosure, when there is non-deliberate material non- disclosure which is not of central importance in a serious fraud case, courts have, in the exercise of their discretion, often been willing to continue the relief on the ground that the need to do substantive justice outweighs that consideration.[1] In such cases once the first instance judge has exercised his discretion the Court of Appeal will only interfere with it when it was not legitimately open to the judge to take that view.[2] There are still occasions on which the breach of the disclosure duty is so serious that the court will refuse freezing relief to the claimant even though this may result in an alleged fraudster against whom a prima facie case has been made out, not being held to account.[3]

9.019   In *Yardley v Higson*[4] an *ex parte* injunction had been granted in a passing-off action for a period of three weeks. At the end of the period the plaintiffs applied to renew their injunction and brought to the attention of the court that there had been non-disclosure of material matters at the *ex parte application*. The judge granted a modified injunction on the *inter partes* application and his decision was upheld by the Court of Appeal. This case and the subsequent decision of the Court of Appeal in *Eastglen International Corporation v Monpare SA*,[5] in which an application for an injunction was also granted notwithstanding earlier non-disclosure, show how important it may be, on an application to renew an injunction, that a

---

[98] *Gulf Interstate Oil Corporation LLC v ANT Trade & Transport Ltd (The Giovanna)* [1999] 1 Lloyd's Rep. 867—non-disclosure of problems about title to sue and of an offer of security made in without prejudice negotiations.

[99] *Brink's Mat Ltd v Elcombe* [1988] 1 W.L.R. 1350 at 1358, *per* Balcombe L.J., followed in *Goldtron Ltd v Most Investment Ltd* [2002] J.L.R. 424 at [21–24] (injunction discharged and then re-granted when there had been innocent non-disclosure of possible grounds for challenging the foreign arbitration award which the plaintiff was seeking to enforce). *Tay Long Kee Impex Pte Ltd v Tan Beng Huwah (t/a Sin Kwang Wah)* [2000] 2 S.L.R. 750 at para.38 (where an application for a second interlocutory injunction was refused where there had been culpable non-disclosure and the plaintiff had not diligently pursued the case to trial).

[1] *Marc Rich & Co. Holding GmbH v Krasner* [1999] EWCA Civ 581; *Kuwait Oil Tanker Company SAK v Al Bader (No.1)*, Court of Appeal (Civ Div) Transcript No.1549 of 1995 (November 27, 1995); *Fitzgerald v Williams* [1996] Q.B. 657 at 667–669 reversing the first instance judge.

[2] *Dubai Bank v Galadari* [1990] 1 Lloyd's Rep. 120; *Kuwait Oil Tanker Company SAK v Al Bader (No.1)* Court of Appeal (Civ Div) Transcript No.1549 of 1995 (November 27, 1995).

[3] *The Arena Corporation Ltd v Shroeder* [2003] EWHC 1089 at [233–234], Ch.D.

[4] [1984] F.S.R. 304. This was heard after *Bank Mellat v Nikpour* [1985] F.S.R. 87 had been decided.

[5] (1987) 137 N.L.J 56.

claimant who has been guilty of non-disclosure at the without notice stage puts the non-disclosure fully and frankly to the court at the *inter partes* application. In both these cases the plaintiff adopted this course.

The principle should not be carried to extreme lengths, and it is important that the court should consider the practical realities of the case, and not allow the principle to be used as a refuge of last resort[6] for litigants when the substantial merits of the case and the balance of convenience strongly favour maintaining the relief which has been granted, and when the likely consequences of setting aside the order could be very severe for the claimant. Such litigants should not be encouraged "to search ingeniously for facts" which might be viewed as relevant, in order to mount an application to discharge the order for non-disclosure.[7]

In the case of a search order which has been set aside on an interlocutory application the question may arise as to whether the claimant should nevertheless be able to use the material obtained, *e.g.* in order to make an application for an interlocutory injunction. In general a consequence of a search order being set aside will be that the claimant will be obliged to return all the documents, items and other material obtained under the order to the defendant and the claimant will be precluded from utilising any information acquired under and by virtue of the order. However, the court retains a discretion to allow the material or part of it to be used, although this discretion is not to be exercised save for good reason, particularly if the relevant non-disclosure was serious and substantial.[8] **9.020**

In a case in which there is both non-disclosure and other failings in breach of the duty to present the application fairly the court will look at all the failings together when considering whether to discharge the relief.[9]

(5) Effect of new developments after the *ex parte* application, including fresh information

The duty of the applicant for *ex parte* relief to act with the utmost good faith towards the court does not cease with the granting of the application. The court is exercising a jurisdiction which is obviously very hazardous and **9.021**

---

[6] *Brink's Mat Ltd v Elcombe* [1988] 1 W.L.P. 1350 at 1359, *per* Slade L.J.; *Dormeuil Frères SA v Nicolian Ltd* [1988] 1 W.L.R. 1362 at 1369; *Swedac Ltd v Magnet & Southerns plc* [1989] F.S.R. 243 at 250; *Knauf UK GmbH v British Gypsum Ltd* [2002] 1 W.L.R. 907 [71] referring to a *tabulum de naufragio*—a piece of wood grasped in a shipwreck; in *Armco Inc v NPV Ltd* [1998] H.K.C.F.I. 632 there is a review of the results in the case law. These show a strong tendency to discharge the *ex parte* relief where there has been material non-disclosure, tempered by a reluctance to refuse fresh relief where this is needed to hold the position pending trial.

[7] *Citibank NA v Express Ship Management Services Ltd* [1987] H.K.L.R. 1184, Court of Appeal of Hong Kong.

[8] *Naf Naf SA v Dickens (London) Ltd* [1993] F.S.R. 424; Staughton L.J. in *Dubai Bank v Galadari* [1990] 1 Lloyd's Rep. 120 at 135 commenting upon *Guess? Inc. v Lee* [1987] F.S.R. 125 at 132. In *Dubai Bank v Galadari* the judge exempted from documents to be returned documents exhibited to affidavits, and this was upheld on appeal on the basis that the judge was exercising his discretion. Exhibiting documents does not preclude return of them. See also Chapter 17, para.17.049 below.

[9] *The Gadget Shop Ltd v Bug.Com Ltd* [2001] F.S.R. 383.

liable to cause serious prejudice to the defendant or third parties.[10] The granting of *ex parte* relief is an exception to the general rule that no order is to be made to the prejudice of a party unless he has had the opportunity of being heard in his defence. Furthermore, with Anton Piller orders, there will almost invariably be a period between the granting of the order and the time when the claimant is ready to execute it at the premises concerned. With Mareva relief there may similarly be a not insubstantial period between the making of the order and the time the defendant is notified of it. During this time the claimant is giving notice of the order to banks and other non-parties, and possibly obtaining information from them under the order in respect of the defendant's assets.[11]

Thus, when the court grants *ex parte* relief of this nature, it is in effect entrusting the applicant with its order, at least for the period immediately following the application, on the basis that the applicant will be using the order to forward the interests of justice. It is not for the applicant to act as judge in his own cause and decide what effect, if any, new developments are to have on the *ex parte* relief. Thus the general principle on the *ex parte* application is that an applicant may not select the material to be placed before the court.[12] This applies with equal force in relation to new developments in the case, at least while the defendant is under a continuing disability in relation to protecting his own interests.[13]

Thus in *Commercial Bank of the Near East plc v A*,[14] Saville J. considered the position in relation to Mareva relief when, following the application, the plaintiffs had obtained leave to register cautions over property belonging to the defendants in Greece. Although the case was not one in which the court had been misled or incomplete information had been given on the initial *ex parte* application, Saville J. held that "while the proceedings remain on an *ex parte* basis", the applicant has a duty to the court to bring to its attention any subsequent material changes in the situation, *i.e.* any new or altered facts or matters which, had they existed at the time of the application, should have been disclosed to the court.[15]

---

[10] Mareva relief often prevents a defendant from dealing with his assets at all, except for very limited purposes, and is liable to damage his standing with third parties who are notified of the order. It is also liable to cause serious complications for third parties concerned with assets covered by the order. As for the possible consequences of Anton Piller relief, see the observations of Scott J. in *Columbia Pictures v Robinson* [1987] Ch. 38 at 69–74.

[11] Thus in *Republic of Haiti v Duvalier* [1990] 1 Q.B. 202 at 208–209, the defendants were not notified of the existence of the *ex parte* relief until a week after it had originally been granted. In the interim parties required to give information about the defendants' assets to the plaintiffs had already taken the case to the Court of Appeal: Court of Appeal (Civil Division) (June 7, 1988).

[12] See para.9.002, above.

[13] The position is not at all analogous to that following placement of a contract of insurance where the insurer has taken the risk of new developments.

[14] [1989] 2 Lloyd's Rep. 319.

[15] See also *Knox D'Arcy Ltd v Jamieson* Court of Appeal, (Civil Division) Transcript No.137 of 1996 (February 19, 1996) where there was a failure to return to court to correct *ex parte* material before the order was served. This is a breach of the duty owed to the court, but on

In *O'Regan v Iambic Productions*,[16] the applicant, who had been granted   **9.022**
Anton Piller relief, received a letter from the defendant offering to allow
the plaintiff access to premises to search for certain items. Other items
were returned to the plaintiff with an explanation that there had been an
unsuccessful attempt to return the items a short time earlier. The applicant
then executed the Anton Piller order without having first informed the
court of the new developments. Sir Peter Pain held that the applicant and
the solicitor involved were in breach of their duties to the court in failing
to return to the court before executing the order, and he followed the
approach which had been adopted by Saville J. Similarly, if it comes to
light that certain evidence placed before the court on the *ex parte*
application was false, misleading or incomplete, then the applicant has a
duty to inform the court of the position as soon as possible.[17] If a claimant
has obtained *ex parte* relief on a basis which he knows he can no longer
support, he should apply to the court either to discharge the order, or to
continue the order on a new basis.

It may be that certain material has been placed before the court which
the claimant discovers to be misleading, but there is other material in the
affidavit evidence from which he feels he can still draw a sufficiently
adverse conclusion to enable him to maintain the order. In those circumstances, the correct approach is to tell the court and the defendant why the
material in question has been discovered to be misleading, and to disclaim
any further reliance on it, leaving the court to consider the merits of
continuing the injunction on the basis of the material remaining. A variant
of this situation is where fresh information obtained by the claimant is
given to his legal advisers in circumstances which would attract a claim for
privilege, or (perhaps less frequently) where a third party claims the fresh
information is confidential and prohibits its disclosure or use in the
litigation, so the claimant may not wish to state what it is unless the court
orders him to do so. It is impossible to lay down any specific rules which
the practitioner should observe in those circumstances, as the proper

---

the facts was an omission which did not amount to a contempt of court; *John Siddall
Holdings v Simmonds*, unreported, July 14, 1997, Lloyd J. (detailed response to plaintiff's
allegations received after *ex parte* application and before execution of Anton Piller order
should have been disclosed immediately to the court).
[16] (1989) 139 N.L.J. 1378.
[17] This was common ground between the parties in argument before Saville J. in *Commercial
Bank of the Near East plc v A* (above). See also *Myers v Elman* [1940] A.C. 282 at 293–294.
In *Network Telecom (Europe) Ltd v Telephone Systems International* [2004] 1 All E.R.
(Comm) 418 (a case about setting aside permission to serve out of the jurisdiction) at [65–
72], Burton J. approved the above text, and the analogy drawn with *Myers v Elman*, and
said "... there can be no distinction, as a matter of principle, between subsequent
developments, which falsify or cast doubt on the information as known at the time of the
application, and information coming to hand which shows that the earlier information was
either false or incomplete". *C Corporation v P* [1994–1995] C.I.L.R. 189 at pp.199–200
(plaintiff discovered after the *ex parte* application that affidavit had been deliberately
misleading, and then failed to investigate the matter and place the results before the court.
This was held to be a breach of its duty owed to the court, and resulted in discharge of the
ex parte order).

course of action will depend on the facts in each case. However, one possible approach would be for the claimant to swear an affidavit, identifying the material in question and stating that since the *ex parte* hearing he has obtained further information, under circumstances attracting a claim for privilege or confidentiality, which shows the material to be false or misleading and consequently he disclaims all further reliance upon it. The claimant then applies to the court to reconsider the order.

9.023　In *Commercial Bank of the Near East plc v A* (above), Saville J. said that the duty continued while the proceedings remained on an *ex parte* basis. The circumstances in question there, however, were also known to the defendants, so that once the defendants had been fully apprised of what had occurred on the *ex parte* application, they would themselves have been in a position to apply to the court to discharge or vary the order in the light of the change of circumstances. A situation could also arise where new information becomes available only to the applicant, or there is a new development known only to the applicant, after the defendant has been fully apprised of what had occurred *ex parte* and:

(1) the defendant does not know or have full information of the new development or fresh information; and

(2) the new development or fresh information means either that the information given to the court on the *ex parte* application was misleading, or that the basis on which the relief has been granted *ex parte* could no longer be supported or has been substantially impugned.

If the applicant still has the benefit of the *ex parte* relief, in such circumstances the applicant should either consent to the discharge of the order, or disclose to the court the new position, so that the court can consider what to do in the changed circumstances of the case.

9.024　In relation to the claimant's financial position, if this deteriorates after the application relevant materially to the worth of the undertaking in damages given by the claimant to the court, the deterioration must be disclosed to the respondent so that he can consider applying for the discharge of the relief.[18]

(6) The timing of the application to discharge Anton Piller or Mareva relief for material non-disclosure

9.025　If an application to discharge Anton Piller relief for material non-disclosure is made after the order has been fully executed, the only real question between the parties may be whether or not the order should be discharged

---

[18] *Staines v Walsh* [2003] EWHC 1486, Ch.D.

so as to give rise to a possible claim on the cross-undertaking as to damages. Thus, if the material obtained by the claimant under the order would in any event be covered by the defendant's obligations as to disclosure, the defendant will not be in a position to contend that it is necessary for the court to entertain an immediate application to discharge the order so that the relevant material can be retrieved from the claimant.

In *Dormeuil Frères SA v Nicolian Ltd*,[19] the court was concerned with an application to discharge Anton Piller relief which had already been fully executed, and with the exact terms of an interim injunction, it being common ground that an injunction should be made until the trial. The application to discharge the Anton Piller relief for non-disclosure gave rise to questions which called for detailed consideration of the voluminous evidence and which would be best determined at the trial of the action in the light of cross-examination of the witnesses. In these circumstances Sir Nicolas Browne-Wilkinson V.-C. decided that there was no urgency to determine the application and that it should therefore be adjourned to be dealt with at the trial. However, in doing so, the Vice-Chancellor observed that in his judgment:

"save in exceptional cases, it is not the correct procedure to apply to discharge an *ex parte* injunction on the grounds of lack of full disclosure at the interlocutory stage of the proceedings. The purpose of interlocutory proceedings is to regulate the future of the case until trial. Where an Anton Piller order has been made *ex parte*, in the vast majority of cases, the order has been executed before the *inter partes* hearing. Setting aside the *Anton Piller* order cannot undo what has already been done . . . The sole relevance of the question 'Should the *ex parte* order be set aside?' is, so far as I can see, to determine the question whether the plaintiff is liable on the cross-undertaking in damages given on the *ex parte* hearing. That is not an urgent matter. It is normally much better dealt with at the trial by the trial judge who knows all the circumstances of the case and is able, after cross-examination, to test the veracity of the witnesses (at 1369–1370)."

The Vice-Chancellor also said that similar considerations applied in the case of Mareva relief.

These observations need to be viewed in the factual context of that case because there are circumstances in which an application should be dealt with at the interlocutory stage. Often Anton Piller relief is granted in conjunction with Mareva or other injunctive relief, and the non-disclosure question will go to the issue whether or not the relief should continue in place until trial. In these circumstances plainly the non-disclosure question must be addressed at the interlocutory stage, and ordinarily is to be

---

[19] [1988] 1 W.L.R. 1362.

resolved at that time.[20] In *Lloyd's Bowmaker v Britannia Arrow Holdings plc*,[21] such an interlocutory application was made successfully two years after the grant of the *ex parte* Mareva relief.

9.026   Similarly, if the execution of the Anton Piller relief has not been completed, the court will entertain the application to discharge the order on the grounds of non-disclosure, because then the relevant consequences are not confined to the liability of the claimant on the cross-undertaking as to damages.[22]

Even if the Anton Piller relief has been fully executed and the non-disclosure question does not go to whether or not interlocutory relief is to be continued until trial, it is still a matter of discretion for the court to decide whether or not to deal with the non-disclosure at the interlocutory stage.[23] In *Dormeuil Frères SA v Nicolian Ltd* there were good grounds for postponing consideration of the issue until trial. But this is not always the case. It is clear that in appropriate cases the court will discharge Anton Piller relief which has been fully executed and will do so even on an interlocutory application.[24] Thus, *e.g.*, a defendant may wish to seek to remove the stigma which has arisen from the granting of the *ex parte* Anton Piller relief, and the court may consider that it is in the interests of justice that the defendant is afforded the opportunity to do so as soon as possible.[25] If the issue which arises is clear and can be dealt with conveniently at an interlocutory stage, then the court ought in general to entertain the application. In New Zealand it has been said that the fact that an application to discharge an order which has been fully executed is made on the grounds of non-disclosure in itself provides a good reason for

---

[20] *Dubai Bank v Galadari* [1990] 1 Lloyd's Rep. 120 at 126; *Ali and Fahd Shobokshi Group v Moneim* [1989] 1 W.L.R. 710 at 721–722 citing *Bank Mellat v Nikpour* [1985] F.S.R. 87, and see generally the cases cited above on the effects of material non-disclosure or misrepresentation, and *Arab Monetary Fund v Hashim* [1989] 1 W.L.R. 565 at 569–570 distinguishing *Dormeuil Frères SA v Nicolian Ltd* (above).

[21] [1988] 1 W.L.R. 1337.

[22] *Arab Monetary Fund v Hashim* [1989] 1 W.L.R. 565 at 569–570; *The Gadget Shop Ltd v Bug.Com Ltd* [2001] F.S.R. 383, where the supervising solicitor still held certain materials pending the determination of the discharge application.

[23] Applied in *Pulse Microsystems Ltd v Safesoft Systems Inc.* [1996] 6 W.W.R. 1 at 14, Manitoba Court of Appeal in which an executed order was set aside on appeal when there had been serious non-disclosure ("The newly-disclosed facts leave [Ormrod L.J.'s] three essential preconditions in tatters . . .") and the defendants were not "fly by night operators".

[24] *Booker McConnell plc v Plasgow* [1985] R.F.C. 425 at 434–435 and 442–443; *Randolph M. Fields v Alison Watts* (1985) 129 S.J. 67 (a case against certain members of the Bar); *Jeffrey Rogers Ltd v Vinola* [1985] F.S.R. 184; see also "Piller Problems" (1990) 106 L.Q.R. 601 at 619; *Pulse Microsystems Ltd v Safesoft Systems Inc.*, cited above.

[25] *Booker McConnell plc v Plasgow* (above) involved as defendants two public companies and *Randolph M. Fields v Alison Watts* (above) concerned defendants who were barristers and barristers' clerks, and who were therefore unlikely to destroy or conceal documents, so that it was unnecessary and inappropriate to make an Anton Piller order.

dealing with the application at an interlocutory stage.[26] There is an element of public policy in entertaining such applications at the interlocutory stage in that it helps deter future applicants for Anton Piller relief from failing to make full disclosure of material facts to the court. Furthermore, it would be inappropriate to allow an applicant who has obtained the relief through deliberate or culpable misconduct to retain the benefits of that misconduct.

If leave to serve a foreign defendant out of the jurisdiction is set aside, then any Mareva or Anton Piller relief will be set aside at the same time.[27] Similarly, if an action is struck out under an interlocutory order, any Mareva or Anton Piller relief granted in that action will be set aside.[28] The observations of the Vice-Chancellor in *Dormeuil Frères SA v Nicolian Ltd* are not directed to either of those situations.

Accordingly, it is considered that while it may be appropriate to adjourn **9.027** an application to discharge fully executed Anton Piller relief on the grounds of non- disclosure until the trial, this is not a general rule of practice, and whether or not it is done must depend on the circumstances of the particular case. The relevant factors to be taken into account will include the following:

(1) Whether the defendant is likely to suffer continuing prejudice to his reputation or commercial standing by reason of the Anton Piller order, or there is some other good reason to deal with the application promptly.

(2) Whether the issue involves questions of the credibility of witnesses or otherwise is likely to require cross-examination of witnesses so that it should be dealt with at the trial.[29]

(3) Whether the issue will involve a detailed review of voluminous evidence.

(4) Whether the issue can conveniently be dealt with at an interlocutory hearing and will not be likely to lead to unnecessary costs.

(5) Whether the issue arises in connection with another application before the court, such as an application to set aside leave granted to serve a defendant with proceedings out of the jurisdiction or an application to discharge injunctive relief.

---

[26] *DB Baverstock Lord v Haycock* [1986] 1 N.Z.L.R. 342 at 345 (if the order has been obtained *mala fide*, or by material non-disclosure or if there are 'special circumstances' which clearly demonstrate the need for immediate relief by way of discharge), cited as the applicable principle in *Fujitsu General New Zealand v Melco New Zealand Ltd* (2002) 16 P.R.N.Z. 395; [2002] N.Z.C.A. 91 (May 8, 2002) at para.7; *Anvil Jewellery Ltd v River Ridge Holdings Ltd* [1987] 1 N.Z.L.R. 35 at 43.

[27] *Siskina v Distos SA (The Siskina)* [1979] A.C. 210 is an illustration.

[28] *Swedac Ltd v Magnet & Southerns plc* [1989] F.S.R. 243 at 253.

[29] *Tate Access Inc. v Boswell* [1991] Ch. 512 at 532–534; In *OMV Supply & Trading AG v Nicholas Clarke*, Ch.D., unreported, January 14, 1999 there was a prima facie case of dishonesty, and allegations of non-disclosure which included hotly disputed matters which could only be resolved at trial; *Crown Resources AG v Vinogradsky*, QBD, unreported, June 15, 2001.

If a claimant has obtained injunctive relief *ex parte* which has since been discharged or expired, and the defendant wishes to claim damages on the cross-undertaking, it is still open to the defendant to apply to the court either to assess damages summarily or to order an inquiry as to damages on the grounds that the *ex parte* order was obtained by non-disclosure.

(7) Giving notice and particulars of the allegation of non-disclosure

9.028   A party seeking to have without notice relief discharged for non-disclosure must give adequate notice that this ground is relied upon together with sufficient particulars enabling the other party to understand the case to be advanced.[30] An allegation of non-disclosure is potentially serious both for the other party and his legal advisers and the party complaining of non-disclosure must give sufficient notice of his complaint so that there can be a fair hearing, and it should be made without unnecessary delay.[31] Usually the application to discharge for non-disclosure ought to be resolved at the same time as the application by the claimant to continue the relief.[32]

---

[30] *Bracken Partners Ltd v Gutteridge*, Ch.D., unreported, December 17, 2001.
[31] *OMV Supply & Trading AG v Nicholas Clarke*, Ch.D., unreported, January 14, 1999.
[32] *Network Multimedia Television v Jobserve*, Ch.D., unreported, December 15, 2000.

Chapter 10

The "without prejudice" rule

(1) The "without prejudice" rule and injunctions

Applications for injunctions are often concerned with the "without preju- **10.001**
dice" rule. For example, it may affect what has to be disclosed on the *ex
parte* application,[1] what evidence can be used on the application, there may
be a waiver arising out of the way an injunction application is pursued
which results in "without prejudice" materials coming into evidence at the
trial,[2] there may be a question of whether the rule is inapplicable because
of "unambiguous impropriety" in the events leading up to or after the
application,[3] and it may be relevant on costs.

(2) General principles

Public policy encourages settlement of disputes. Litigation is better avoided **10.002**
by compromise where that can be achieved. In order to settle the parties
should be free to discuss their disputes freely—fully and frankly with all
their cards on the table,[4] without fear that what they say may subsequently
used against them in litigation.[5] In consequence the rule[6] is that what has
passed in the course of negotiations cannot be used in evidence. Although
disclosure of documents is not limited to those which can be adduced in
evidence the effect of the rule may result in disclosure not being ordered of
documents covered by the rule. The rule avoids the obligation to give
disclosure to a third party in related litigation. In *Rush & Tomkins v*

---

[1] *Gulf Interstate Oil Corporation LLC v ANT Trade & Transport Ltd (The Giovanna)* [1999]
1 Lloyd's Rep. 867—Mareva relief discharged for non-disclosure of "without prejudice"
materials.
[2] *Somatra Ltd v Sinclair Roche & Temperley* [2000] 2 Lloyd's Rep. 673—"without prejudice"
waived by putting materials into evidence on the ex parte application.
[3] *Dora v Simper*, CA, unreported, March 15, 1999—threat to transfer assets to avoid
enforcement of a judgment held to be "unambiguous impropriety".
[4] *Scott Paper Co. v Drayton Paper Works* (1927) 44 R.P.C. 151 at 156.
[5] *Cutts v Head* [1984] Ch. 290 at 306.
[6] The history is considered by Professor David Vaver in [1974] U. Br. Col. L.R. 152, which
was referred to in *Unilever Plc v Proctor & Gamble* [2000] 1 W.L.R. 2436 at 2445H.

Greater London Council,[7] a party was refused discovery of "without prejudice" correspondence which passed in negotiations which the other party had had with another. Although the documents were relevant, public policy required negotiations with someone else to be protected, because otherwise this would inhibit settlement negotiations.

The rule is also partly based on upholding contracts. The effect of the contract is to exclude from evidence material which is relevant and which might otherwise affect the result of a case. A contract between the parties to exclude evidence for the purpose of the court deciding on their legal rights is binding and will be enforced by the court.[8] So in principle where parties agree that evidence shall not be adduced the court gives effect to the agreement and will not allow the evidence to be adduced. In the two-party situation the negotiations have taken place on an agreement or tacit understanding that they are not to be used against either party. Refusing to allow the negotiations to be admitted into evidence, or to order disclosure of documents[9] falling within the umbrella of the rule, or to take them into account on costs[10] upholds and enforces the arrangement. But this is not the whole basis for the rule as is shown by the three-party situation and by the principle that an "opening shot" communication is protected.[11] In some cases both of these justifications are present and in some, one or the other.[12] If an injunction is sought to restrain the use of "without prejudice" communications abroad the basis is contractual and the claim is to enforce the contract.[13]

Negotiations have to start somewhere, and the rule applies to an "opening shot" which is a claim or denial of liability, combined with an offer to negotiate about it. Thus it applies to an offer to accept a sum in settlement of an as yet unquantified claim.[14] It does not apply to a letter which contains only an assertion of rights. The *obiter dictum* in *Re Daintrey*[15] that "some person [has to be] in dispute or negotiation with another" for the rule to apply, is too narrow. What matters is whether a

---

[7] [1989] A.C. 1280.

[8] *Bache & Co. (London) Ltd v Banque Vernes et Commerciale de Paris SA* [1973] 2 Lloyd's Rep. 437 (conclusive evidence clause) followed in *Harbottle Ltd v National Westminster Bank* [1978] Q.B. 146 at 156H–157A; *Toepfer v Continental Grain* [1974] 1 Lloyd's Rep. 10 (certificate of inspector was conclusive under the contract of sale).

[9] *Rabin v Mendoza & Co.* [1954] 1 W.L.R. 271, approved in *Rush & Tomkins v Greater London Council* [1989] A.C. 1280 at 1303–1304.

[10] *Cutts v Head* [1984] Ch. 290 at 306E–F; *The Prudential Insurance Company of America v The Prudential Assurance Company Ltd* [2004] E.T.M.R. 29; [2003] EWCA 1154.

[11] *Standrin v Yenton Minster Homes Ltd, The Times*, July 22, 1991; *South Shropshire District Council v Amos* [1986] 1 W.L.R. 1271 at 1275 overruling *Norwich Union Life Insurance Society v Tony Waller Ltd* (1984) 270 E.G. 42; *Buckingham County Council v Moran* [1990] Ch. 623 at 634–635 overruling Hoffmann J. but not on the principle.

[12] *Muller v Lindsley and Mortimer* [1996] 1 P.N.L.R. 74 at 77.

[13] *The Prudential Insurance Company of America v The Prudential Assurance Company Ltd* [2004] E.T.M.R. 29; [2003] EWCA 1154; *David Instance v Denny Brothers* [2000] F.S.R. 869.

[14] *Standrin v Yenton Minster Homes Ltd* (above) at 9G–H of the transcript referring to *Shropshire District Council v Amos* [1986] 1 W.L.R. 1271.

[15] [1892] 2 Q.B. at 119.

purpose of the communication was to engage in settlement discussions to resolve an actual dispute or one in reasonable contemplation,[16] and therefore whether it was "a negotiating document".[17] In deciding whether that was a purpose of the communication, context is everything. It includes a communication for the purpose of settling part of a dispute, or agreeing particular matters which would otherwise be part of the dispute, such as figures and values.[18] It does not include what only amounts to a statement of legal rights without any suggestion of willingness to engage in settlement negotiations.[19]

Because the consequences of the rule include the exclusion of evidence **10.003** and not having to disclose documents, it is often spoken of as a "privilege". But this should not obscure the substantive principles which apply. It can only be waived through agreement of both the parties to the negotiations,[20] and possession of a "without prejudice" document does not entitle a person to use it in evidence—indeed it will be usual for both parties to have access to the "without prejudice" correspondence. Where the rule applies it prohibits proof of the protected material, including evidence from an independent witness who fortuitously overheard a conversation or read a document protected by the rule.[21]

A letter can be written "without prejudice save as to costs" in which case it will be protected by the rule except for the purpose of deciding costs.[22] A "without prejudice" letter cannot be taken into account on costs except with the agreement of both parties.[23]

The rule also covers what is produced pursuant to an agreement between the negotiating parties so that it can be used to forward the negotiations. Thus in *Rabin v Mendoza & Co.*[24] a survey report was produced as a result of an agreement in negotiations to do this so as to enable a quote for insurance to be obtained to be used in settlement negotiations. This was within the protection of the rule. In contrast in *Field v Commissioner for Railways*[25] a plaintiff, pursuant to "without prejudice" negotiations, agreed to be examined by a surgeon retained by the defendant and in the course of

---

[16] *Lukes v Ripley No.2* (1994) 35 N.S.W.L.R. 283. Contrast *BNP Paribas v Mezzotero*, (EAT) Employment Appeal Tribunal March 30, 2004 where the employee had already activated a grievance procedure because of alleged discrimination against her following her return to work following maternity leave and had a meeting to seek to resolve her grievances which included the alleged discrimination: the decision that no dispute was "extant" and therefore the privilege could not apply would appear to be wrong.

[17] *Buckingham County Council v Moran* [1990] Ch. 623 at 623, *per* Hoffmann J. approved at 635A–B.

[18] *Lukes v Ripley No.2* (1994) 35 N.S.W.L.R. 283.

[19] *Buckingham County Council v Moran* [1990] Ch. 623 at 634–635; *Kooltrade Ltd v XTS Ltd* [2001] F.S.R. 158 is an example of this.

[20] *Walker v Wilshier* (1880) 23 Q.B.D. 335 at 337, *per* Lord Esher M.R.; *Rush & Tomkins v Greater London Council* [1989] A.C. 1280.

[21] *Theodoropoulas v Theodoropoulas* [1964] P. 311 at 314.

[22] *Cutts v Head* [1984] Ch. 290; the position is governed by CPR Pt 36.

[23] *Walker v Wilshier* (1880) 23 Q.B.D. 335 at 337, *per* Lord Esher M.R.; *Cutts v Head* [1984] Ch. 290; *Calderbank v* Calderbank [1976] Fam. 93; *Stotesbury v Turner* [1943] 1 K.B. 370.

[24] [1954] 1 W.L.R. 271.

[25] (1957) 99 C.L.R. 285.

the examination told him what had happened in the accident. What was said was outside the rule because it was not what had been agreed to be produced for the purpose of the negotiations. It was not "part of the negotiations for the settlement of the action [or] what was reasonably incidental thereto".

10.004   The rule applies to settlement negotiations even though "without prejudice" is not used on the correspondence.[26] Thus even if the words are not used if the parties are seeking genuinely to settle their dispute the rule will apply.[27] If a letter is sent "without prejudice" shortly after an earlier letter which did not have that label it can have the effect of being a postscript to the first letter and adding "without prejudice" to it.[28] This shows that whether a purpose of a letter was to achieve settlement does not depend solely upon looking at the face of the letter. Everything relevant to that issue is to be taken into account , including the context in which the letter was sent, and any postscript to it added shortly afterwards. Once negotiations have started on a "without prejudice" basis the assumption is that this basis continues to apply to the subsequent negotiations unless and until it is made clear that the correspondence is to be open.[29]

The rule is not limited to where the parties discuss the legal issues and does not depend upon their having done so—there are many "without prejudice" negotiations which do not address the legal issues or indeed any issues at all relating to the underlying dispute.[30] If an offer is intended to be made "openly" outside of the umbrella of the rule, then the rule will not apply.[31] An example of this is a letter before action setting out the claim. In a sense it seeks to achieve resolution of the claim but it is sent as an open letter. Also the use of "without prejudice" does not necessarily have the consequence that the rule applies. Those words have various different meanings in different contexts.[32]

Where the rule applies to exclude the evidence, there is no discretion in the court to admit it.[33] Often issues about whether the evidence is to be excluded is decided by a judge other than the trial judge, so as to exclude

---

[26] *Chocoladefabriken Lindt & Sprungi v Nestlé Co.* [1978] R.P.C. 287.
[27] *Rush & Tomkins v Greater London Council* [1989] A.C. 1280 at 1299; *Scott Paper Co. v Drayton Paper Works Ltd* [1927] R.P.C. 151 at 157; *Dixons Stores Group v Thames Television* [1993] 1 All E.R. 349 at 351; *Foster v Friedland*, Court of Appeal (Civ Div) Transcript No.1052 of 1992 (November 10, 1992) at p.5 of the transcript; *Sampson v John Boddy Timber Ltd* [1995] N.L.J. Rep. 851; *Rodgers v Rodgers* (1964) 114 C.L.R. 608 at 614.
[28] *Peacock v Harper* (1877) 23 W.R. 109; see also *Oliver v Nautilus Steam Shipping* [1903] 2 K.B. 639 (second payment was accepted "without prejudice" and this basis was held also to relate back to the first payment).
[29] *Cheddar Valley Engineering Ltd v Chaddlewood Homes Ltd* [1992] 1 W.L.R. 820; *Dixons Stores Group v Thames Television plc* [1993] 1 All E.R. 349 at 351.
[30] *Foster v Friedland*, Court of Appeal (Civ Div) Transcript No.1052 of 1992 (November 10, 1992) at p.6 of the transcript.
[31] *Foster v Friedland*, Court of Appeal (Civ Div) Transcript No.1052 of 1992 (November 10, 1992) at p.7 of the transcript; *Re Legal Costs Negotiators Ltd*, unreported, June 3, 1998, ChD.
[32] *Peterborough City Council v Mancetter Developments Ltd* [1996] E.G.C.S. 50.
[33] *Chocoladefabriken Lindt & Sprungi v Nestlé Co.* [1978] R.P.C. 287 at 289.

any concern that it might be taken into account unconsciously by the trial judge even though it was inadmissible. This is good practice because then parties are not inhibited in engaging in settlement discussions by the thought that the admissibility of their discussions may be decided by a trial judge. However, there are occasions when the point is of such minor importance in the context of the dispute that it can be dealt with by the trial judge.[34] Where "without prejudice" material is seen by a judge deciding the case on the merits and this has happened by accident or otherwise, without the consent of both parties the question may arise as to whether he has to recuse himself.[35] "Without prejudice" material should not be placed before a trial judge without the prior consent of the other party.[36] If that consent cannot be obtained, then directions should be obtained as to how the matter is to continue.

(3) Exceptions to the rule

The rule must be broad so that litigants and their lawyers can safely rely **10.005** upon it without their communications being used against them and without the risk that what happened in "without prejudice" negotiations may itself become the subject of a dispute. Negotiations are often conducted with the involvement of lawyers and, unless the rule is broad, the advocate could find himself transformed into a witness.

Nevertheless there are limits to the rule. Just as the rule is the product of case law, so are its limits. Often the decisions have been interlocutory. This is an area where judicial observations need to be looked at with care and seen in the context of arriving at a decision on the particular facts which takes into account competing public policy considerations.

In *Unilever Plc v Proctor & Gamble*,[37] the Court of Appeal decided[38] that **10.006** settlement negotiations could not be used for the purpose of bringing proceedings claiming an injunction and damages based on s.70 of the Patents Act 1977, for threatening the plaintiff with proceedings for infringement of a patent. The negotiations were protected by the rule. Robert Walker L.J. summarised certain of the ". . . numerous occasions on which, despite the existence of without prejudice negotiations, the without prejudice rule does not prevent the admission into evidence of what one or both of the parties said or wrote" and said that:

"[the] following are among the most important instances.

---

[34] *Redifusion Simulation Ltd v Link Miles Ltd* [1992] F.S.R. 195.
[35] *Berg v IML London Ltd* [2002] 1 W.L.R. 3271.
[36] *Berg v IML London Ltd* [2002] 1 W.L.R. 3271; *Sampson v John Boddy Timber Ltd* [1995] N.L.J. Rep. 851.
[37] [2000] 1 W.L.R. 2436 at 2444–2445.
[38] Overruling *Kurtz v Spence* (1888) 5 R.P.C. 161.

(1) As Hoffmann L.J. noted in [*Muller v Lindsley and Mortimer* [1996] 1 P.N.L.R. 74], when the issue is whether without prejudice communications have resulted in a concluded compromise agreement, those communications are admissible. *Tomlin v Standard Telephones and Cables* [1969] 1 W.L.R. 1378 is an example.

(2) Evidence of the negotiations is also admissible to show that an agreement apparently concluded between the parties during the negotiations should be set aside on the ground of misrepresentation, fraud or undue influence. *Underwood v Cox* (1912) 4 D.L.R. 66, a decision from Ontario, is a striking illustration of this.

(3) Even if there is no concluded compromise, a clear statement which is made by one party to negotiations, and on which the other party is intended to act and does in fact act, may be admissible as giving rise to an estoppel. That was the view of Neuberger J. in *Hodgkinson & Corby v Wards Mobility Services* [1997] F.S.R. 178, 191, and his view on that point was not disapproved by this court on appeal.

(4) Apart from any concluded contract or estoppel, one party may be allowed to give evidence of what the other said or wrote in without prejudice negotiations if the exclusion of the evidence would act as a cloak for perjury, blackmail or other 'unambiguous impropriety' (the expression used by Hoffmann L.J. in *Foster v Friedland*, 10 November 1992, [Court of Appeal (Civ Div) Transcript No.1052 of 1992]). Examples . . . are two first-instances decisions, *Finch v Wilson* (8 May 1987) and *Hawick Jersey International v Caplan* (*The Times* 11 March 1988). But this court has, in *Foster v Friedland* and *Fazil-Alizadeh v Nikbin*, [Court of Appeal (Civil Division) Transcript No.205 of 1993], warned that the exception should be applied only in the clearest cases of abuse of a privileged occasion.

(5) Evidence of negotiations may be given (for instance, on an application to strike out proceedings for want of prosecution) in order to explain delay or apparent acquiescence. Lindley L.J. in *Walker v Wilsher* (1889) 23 QBD 335, 338, noted this exception but regarded it as limited to 'the fact that such letters have been written and the dates at which they were written'. But occasionally fuller evidence is needed in order to give the court a fair picture of the rights and wrongs of the delay.

(6) In *Muller* (which was a decision on discovery, not admissibility) one of the issues between the claimant and the defendants, his former solicitors, was whether the claimant had acted reasonably to mitigate his loss in his conduct and conclusion of negotiations for the compromise of proceedings brought by him against a software company and its other shareholders. Hoffmann L.J. treated that issue as one unconnected with the truth or falsity of anything stated in the negotiations, and as therefore falling outside the principle of public policy protecting without prejudice communications. The other members of the court agreed but would also have based their decision on waiver.

(7) The exception (or apparent exception) for an offer expressly made 'without prejudice except as to costs' was clearly recognised by this court in *Cutts v Head*, and by the House of Lords in *Rush & Tomkins*, as based on an express or implied agreement between the parties. It stands apart from the principle of public policy (a point emphasised by the importance which the new Civil Procedure Rules, Part 44.3(4), attach to the conduct of the parties in deciding questions of costs). There seems to be no reason in principle why parties to without prejudice negotiations should not expressly or impliedly agree to vary the application of the public policy rule in other respects, either by extending or by limiting its reach. In *Cutts v Head* Fox L.J. said (at p.316) 'what meaning is given to the words "without prejudice" is a matter of interpretation which is capable of variation according to use in the profession. It seems to me that, no issue of public policy being involved, it would be wrong to say that the words were given a meaning in 1889 which is immutable ever after'.

(8) In matrimonial cases there has developed what is now a distinct privilege extending to communications received in confidence with a view to matrimonial conciliation: see *Re D* [1993] 2 All E.R. 693, 697, where Sir Thomas Bingham M.R. thought it not . . . fruitful to debate the relationship of this privilege with the more familiar head of 'without prejudice' privilege. That its underlying rationale is similar, and that it developed by way of analogy with 'without prejudice' privilege, seems clear. But both Lord Hailsham and Lord Simon in *D v National Society for the Prevention of Cruelty to Children* [1977] 1 All ER 589 at 602, 610 [1978] A.C. 171 at 226, 236 regarded it as having developed into a new category of privilege based on the public interest in the stability of marriage."

(4) Protection of admissions only or does the rule go further? Does the rule render issues non-justiciable?

Muller v Lindsley and Mortimer[39] concerned a claim against solicitors for **10.007** negligence. Their client had settled earlier proceedings against a third party and now wished to recover damages against the solicitors pleading that the recovery in the former proceedings was reasonable mitigation of his loss. The solicitors pleaded that the settlement was not reasonable mitigation and sought disclosure of the "without prejudice" communications which had resulted in the settlement. Hoffmann L.J. allowed the appeal on the ground that the rule based on the public policy justification, which was the only justification capable of applying on the facts because the solicitors were not parties to the settlement negotiations, only applied to admissions

---

[39] [1996] 1 P.N.L.R. 74 followed in *Murrell v Healy* [2001] 4 All E.R. 345 at [16] and [17].

whereas what was sought was disclosure of facts relevant to whether Mr Muller had acted reasonably. The other judges agreed with him. They also relied upon there being an implied waiver by the client in bringing the proceedings against the solicitors, a ground for the decision which has subsequently been described as not revealing any general statement of principle on waiver,[40] and which is inconsistent with the rule that waiver must be by both parties to the negotiations.[41]

The reasoning based on drawing a distinction between allowing the privilege to protect admissions but not for proof of facts has been criticised by commentators.[42] In *Unilever Plc v Proctor & Gamble* it was questioned whether the rule applied only to exclude admissions.[43] But it cannot be cast away as an aberrant comment made in the course of an interlocutory judgment. The same description of the scope of the rule was given by the High Court of Australia, presided over by Sir Owen Dixon C.J., in *Field v Commissioner for Railways*,[44] a case not drawn to the attention of the court in *Unilever Plc*.[45] The analysis of Hoffmann L.J., like that of the High Court of Australia, was confined expressly to where the sole justification for the rule was public policy, unenlarged by any tacit agreement between the negotiating parties. Dean Wigmore in his seminal work on *Evidence*[46] described the rule as based on the law concerning admissions.[47] It must be accepted that Hoffmann L.J.'s description of the rule is a classic statement of the principle, even though the rule can also sometimes apply where the material is not to be used as an admission.

As for *Unilever Plc v Proctor & Gamble* the decision in that case was that no evidence could be given of the conversations said to contain the threat which was actionable under the statute. The effect of the decision was to apply a rule of evidence so as to make it impossible to prove the alleged threat. This engrafted on to s.70 of the Patents Act 1977 a substantive exception to the statutory cause of action. Although this was achieved through a rule of evidence, this disguised a public policy exception to the statutory cause of action. This should not be allowed to obscure that the primary purpose of the rule is to preclude the proof of admissions, albeit that the same public policy may, as shown by the decision in *Unilever Plc*, be sufficiently strong to alter the substantive rules governing the parties' underlying rights and liabilities.

---

[40] *Paragon Finance v Freshfields* [1999] 1 W.L.R. 1183 at 1191.
[41] See para.10.003 above.
[42] C. Hollander, *Documentary Evidence* (8th ed., 2003), pp.242–243; *Phipson on Evidence* (15th ed., 2001), para.21–15.
[43] [2000] 1 W.L.R. at 2446B.
[44] (1955) 99 C.L.R. 285 at 291–292.
[45] See [2000] 1 W.L.R. 2436 at 2436–2437.
[46] *Wigmore on Evidence* (1972 rev. by Professor Chadbourn), Vol.4, paras 1060–1062, especially para.1061(c).
[47] This is illustrated by the mischief of treating proposals as admissions described in *Jones v Foxall* (1852) 15 Beav. 388 at 396–397 which is referred to in *Cutts v Head* [1984] Ch. 290 at 306–307.

Muller v Lindsley and Mortimer was a three-party situation. Whilst one **10.008** purpose to which negotiations might otherwise be put by a third party is as an admission, this is not the only way in which they might be used. For example, if the rule did not apply, the fact that a person had negotiated in a particular way or sought particular terms might be used as a matter going to his credit as a witness. It might be thought that public policy ought to protect the negotiations against use by the third party whether the proposed use is as an admission or to discredit a negotiating party as a witness. Another example is the *Unilever Plc* case where the proposed use was to bring an action under the Patents Act. The negotiations were to be used not as an admission but because of the fact that a threat was made. If settlement negotiations are to be encouraged, the rule must have a broad effect.[48] This is an area in which the making of fine distinctions would undermine the purpose of the rule.[49]

If the "without prejudice" rule had applied in *Muller v Lindsley and Mortimer* it would also have prevented evidence being called by anyone of what had happened in the negotiations. Mr Muller could not have been cross-examined on it. The effect would have been dramatic. It would have prevented the trial judge hearing any evidence on, and therefore considering, what had happened in the negotiations. The settlement figure would be known, but there would be no way in which the issue of whether that figure had been arrived at reasonably could be investigated at the trial. The choice was between the issue not being justiciable[50] because the trial judge could not investigate the mitigation issue, or ordering the discovery. It is one matter to exclude evidence or disclosure of documents, it is another to render claims or defences non-justiciable. It was better not to apply a rule of exclusion based on the "without prejudice" rule than to deny the doing of justice to the solicitors, by refusing to allow them any effective means of running their defence and proving unreasonableness. It is thought that the decision in *Muller v Lindsley and Mortimer* was correct—it would have been unjustifiable to render the issue of mitigation non-justiciable at the trial based on the public policy of encouraging settlement negotiations. Once this conclusion had been reached it followed that the discovery had to be given.

Put another way the case did not come within the classic statement of the principle and public policy did not require a contrary result. One is left with the impression that had the other judges not mistakenly considered waiver to apply, and if there had been the argument presented that the admission analysis could be too narrow because of the public policy which ought now to be applied in cases different on the facts from those in *Muller*

---

[48] *Houghton v Houghton* (1852) Beav. 278.
[49] See the House of Lords's lack of enthusiasm for extending *Waldridge v Kennison* (1794) 1 Esp. 143 in *Rush & Tomkins v Greater London Council* [1989] A.C. 1280 at 1300.
[50] See the judgment of Swinton Thomas L.J. In *Gnitrow Ltd v Cape* [2000] 3 All E.R. 763, disclosure of an agreement reached "without prejudice" was ordered because its contents affected the amount the claimant could recover against a third party.

v Lindsley and Mortimer, the court would have emphasised this aspect. It is unsurprising that such an argument was not advanced in *Muller v Lindsley and Mortimer*—the unsuccessful respondent was arguing why the public policy applied to the facts in that case, and not whether public policy required an enlarged scope of protection in other cases.

10.009   Another situation in which the "without prejudice" rule does not render an issue non-justiciable is when it is alleged that the negotiations have themselves led to a binding contract of settlement. For the limited purpose of ascertaining whether a contract has been arrived at in the course of those negotiations, they can be examined, and in proceedings to determine whether there is a binding contract made in the negotiations, they must be disclosed. In *Tomlin v Standard Telephones*,[51] this was put on the basis that "without prejudice" was itself impliedly subject to an exception if the proposal was accepted. This rationalises the position based on the interpretation of the implied contractual understanding between the parties when they negotiate. But it is also a consequence which flows from the purpose of the rule. The encouragement of settlement includes encouragement of making a binding contract of settlement. It is just, and consistent with and forwarding the purpose of the rule, that the court should be able to enforce such a contract. The parties expect this. The issue of whether such a contract has been concluded in the course of the negotiations is justiciable. For the purpose of resolving that issue, but not otherwise, those negotiations are subject to scrutiny by the court. As Dankwerts L.J. said ". . . it would be impossible to decide whether there was a concluded agreement or not unless one looked at the correspondence".[52] The exception does not extend to negotiations subsequently about whether to compromise a "dispute" about whether a settlement agreement has been concluded. The purpose of the rule applies to them, the issue about whether there was a contract remains justiciable, and the consequence is that they are protected. Also the communications, notwithstanding that a settlement has been reached, remain protected by the rule for other purposes such as disclosure to third parties.[53]

The general principle is that the rule is only one of admissibility of evidence and it does not render claims or defences non-justiciable, or alter the parties' substantive rights and liabilities. It leaves unaffected any underlying substantive legal rights arising from the negotiations. Therefore "without prejudice" negotiations can, *e.g.*, be proved (1) in support of an allegation that they gave rise to an estoppel,[54] or (2) in support of a defence that a settlement agreement was induced by misrepresentation, duress, or undue influence in the course of the negotiations,[55] or (3) to show

---

[51] [1969] 1 W.L.R. 1378, applying *Walker v Wilshier* (1883) 23 Q.B.D. 335 at 337; see also *Quad Consulting Pty Ltd v David R. Bleakley & Associates Pty Ltd* (1991) 27 F.C.R. 86 at 90–91.
[52] [1969] 1 W.L.R. 1378 at 1382G–H.
[53] *Rush & Tomkins v Greater London Council* [1989] A.C. 1280.
[54] *Hodgkinson & Corby v Wards Mobility Services* [1997] F.S.R. 178 at 191.
[55] *Underwood v Cox* (1912) 4 D.L.R. 66.

severance of a joint tenancy in the course of the negotiations,[56] or (4) to show that notice of the exercise of an option was given in the negotiations[57] or (5) to show actionable discrimination in a meeting dismissing an employee.[58] These can be seen as the use of the negotiations otherwise than for the purpose of proof of an admission. The fact of what happened in the negotiations is itself relied upon as having given rise to or affected the parties' substantive legal rights.

(5) Public policy and the insolvency legislation

Re Daintrey Ex p. Holt[59] concerned a circular sent to a creditor who was **10.010** suing for the debt. It offered to compromise the debt but also said that the debtor could not pay his debts and would suspend payment unless the compromise was accepted. This was said to be a clear act of bankruptcy and not to be within the "without prejudice" rule because that rule did not apply to a document which may prejudice the recipient. This statement has been described as obscure.[60] However the decision can be rationalised on the basis that the purpose of the bankruptcy legislation in enabling a creditor to petition based on an act of bankruptcy is to protect all creditors by ensuring payment to them *pari passu*, and that the public policy of ensuring that one creditor does not receive a preference and that all are treated equally outweighs the public policy underlying the rule. The appellant creditor had decided not to accept the offer made in the circular. If the rule had prevented him from proving the act of bankruptcy he would not have been in a position to have the debtor declared bankrupt—at least immediately. In the meantime other creditors might have been prepared to accept less than they were owed and there was a danger that the appellant's position would be prejudiced by reduction in the assets of the debtor. A later bankruptcy with less assets available for distribution would have prejudiced his position. It would have done so in a way inconsistent with the public policy underlying the legislation. The rule, had it applied, would not have meant that no act of bankruptcy had occurred but would have barred proof of it. Hence the statement "the writer is not entitled to make [the reservation of "without prejudice"] in respect of a document which, from its character, may prejudice the person to whom it is addressed, if he should reject the offer . . .". Another way of putting the point was that the statute gave the creditor a legal right to petition based on the act of bankruptcy and the rule of evidence did not take away that right by rendering it non-justiciable.

---

[56] *McDowell v Hirschfield Lipson & Rumney* [1991] 2 F.L.R. 126.
[57] *Tenstat Pty Ltd v Permanent Trustee Aust Ltd* (1992) 28 N.S.W.L.R. 625.
[58] *BNP Paribas v Mezzotero* (EAT) Employment Appeal Tribunal, March 30, 2004.
[59] [1893] 2 Q.B. 116.
[60] By Professor David Vaver in [1974] U.Br.Col. L.R. 152, a comment mentioned in *Unilever Plc v Proctor & Gamble* [2000] 1 W.L.R. 2436 at 2447–2448.

(6) "Unambiguous impropriety"

10.011 Here the person who would seek to set up the rule is seeking to conceal his own "unambiguous impropriety". The party seeking to unmask that conduct must prove it to a high standard of proof and must exclude any ambiguity on the point. The conduct must also go beyond the type of colourful or exaggerated language which might be expected in settlement negotiations. The "impropriety" must be of sufficient gravity and of such a nature that it is to be regarded as outside the scope of a genuine bona fide attempt to compromise.

In *Foster v Friedland*[61] the defendant denied that an oral binding contract had been entered into by him and in "without prejudice" negotiations accepted that he was bound "in honour" to acquire the relevant shares at the agreed price. He wanted time to make arrangements to avoid having to make an offer to all the other shareholders in accordance with the City Takeover Code. It was argued that this was the making of an improper threat and so outside the scope of the rule. Nothing short of "unambiguous impropriety" would do. Within the exception are the cases of a defendant who threatened to give perjured evidence, bribe other witnesses and leave the country rather than pay damages,[62] and a plaintiff's representatives, recorded on tape, who admitted that the claim was bogus and intended to put pressure on the defendant to negotiate through blackmail.[63] In *Dora v Simper*[64] the Court of Appeal held that an unequivocal threat improperly to transfer assets so as to defeat any judgment disclosed "unambiguous impropriety". The fact that the threat had been made was what was relevant and the conduct in making it was seriously improper and outside of genuine settlement negotiations. If the evidence only reaches the level of permitting an inference that a claimant is putting forward an untruthful case this is not unambiguous and so not within the exception.[65] The putting forward of an implausible or even a case inconsistent with that pursued openly is not within the exception.[66]

In *Merrill Lynch v Mohamed Raffa*[67] the defendant had in the course of "without prejudice" negotiation admitted to his involvement in a fraud and it was held that if he sought to run his case on the basis that he was not involved, then this would result in the rule not applying. The ground was said to be "unambiguous impropriety". The problem with this is that the admission made is exactly what the rule is there to encourage—a frank putting of cards on the table. The fact that an admission is made would be

---

[61] Court of Appeal (Civ Div) Transcript No.1052 of 1992 (November 10, 1992).
[62] *Greenwood v Fitts* [1961] 29 D.L.R. (2nd) 260 at 268–269.
[63] *Hawick Jersey International Ltd v Caplan, The Times*, March 11, 1988.
[64] *The Times*, May 26, 1999 (judgment delivered March 15, 1999).
[65] *Fazi-Alizadeh v Nikbin*, CA, Unreported, February 25, 1993.
[66] *W. H. Smith v Peter Colman* [2001] F.S.R. 91.
[67] May 11, 2000, Comm Ct.

prejudicial if it were admissible. It was made to encourage settlement. The conduct in making the admission was entirely proper. What about the exception that the rule cannot be used to shut out evidence when otherwise there is a danger that the court might otherwise be misled? The problem with this is that the principle applies when the conduct of the case suggests that there has been no communication of a particular type when that communication has in fact been made "without prejudice". The label cannot be used to prevent the court being informed that there was in fact such a communication. For example, if a person who had received a generous "without prejudice" offer to settle were subsequently to argue on costs that there had been no attempt to settle the litigation, the exception would apply. It is an entirely different matter to say that a defendant is bound by his admissions made "without prejudice" and that the rule is swept aside if he seeks to act inconsistently with them. This is what the rule does permit the negotiating party to do—he is not bound by his admissions.[68]

In *Savings & Investment Bank v Fincken*[69] a claimant was given at first **10.012** instance permission to amend to plead an alleged admission made in "without prejudice" communications, the judge saying that the exception applied when there was an "unambiguous" admission of facts "without prejudice" followed by "an equally unambiguous denial of those facts by the same party". The only evidence before the courts in these two cases was that the alleged admission had been made. But even so there may be many reasons for an admission being made at one moment only subsequently to be withdrawn, which have nothing to do with perjury. If litigants are to be threatened with the risk that admissions in "without prejudice" discussions will come into the open arena if they subsequently seek to resile from them this would undermine the aim of the public policy.[70] The decision was subsequently reversed by the Court of Appeal which held that inconsistency between a pleaded case and an admission did not prove future perjury,[71] and that there had to be actual abuse of the privileged occasion for the "unambiguous impropriety" exception to apply. The decision of the judge had been wrong because although the making of the admission was not denied it did not follow that the defendant was going to commit perjury at the trial. The argument of the claimant had been been founded on the honesty and accuracy of the admission made

---

[68] *Wigmore on Evidence* (1972 rev. by Professor Chadbourn), Vol. 4, paras 1060–1062.
[69] [2004] 1 W.L.R. 667.
[70] See also *Kristansson v R. Verney & Co. Ltd*, CA (Civ Div), June 18, 1998. Contrast *BNP Paribas v Mezzotero* (EAT) Employment Appeal Tribunal, March 30, 2004, where the employer claimed the protection of the privilege for the actual meeting at which the employee was dismissed, and Cox J. at paras 35–38 looked to the difficulty in proving the underlying complaint if evidence of the meeting was excluded, as justifying there being no without prejudice privilege. It is considered that this justification for the decision was incorrect, but that the case was correctly decided on the ground that the conduct of the employer at the meeting was itself actionable discrimination, and the privilege did not prevent the employee suing the employer for this.
[71] *The Times*, November 25, 2003.

during the settlement discussions, so the claimant was not asserting any abuse of the privileged occasion.

It was also argued unsuccessfully before the Court of Appeal that the admission was inconsistent with a previous sworn statement made by the defendant in the proceedings, it indicated that the previous statement had been made dishonestly, and that for this reason the "without prejudice" rule was to be displaced. This argument involved the assumption that the defendant had been dishonest in making the previous sworn statement. If so, the defendant would have been guilty of contempt of court. Yet there had been no attempt by the claimant to bring any formal proceedings against the defendant making such a charge and to give the defendant an opportunity to defend himself in such proceedings. The court should not entertain a charge of perjury against a party except where there is a formal charge made against him and proceedings are conducted to establish that charge which comply with Art.6 of the European Convention on Human Rights and which are fair to a defendant facing such a serious allegation. There is machinery for this to be done in contempt proceedings. Guilt of such a serious allegation is not to be presumed; on the contrary the defendant is to be presumed innocent until guilt is established in proper proceedings brought for this purpose. If the admission is covered by the "without prejudice" rule, then that rule would also exclude from use at the trial all discussion of the admission at the contempt proceedings; that discussion would be excluded from being admissible in evidence at the trial of the claim by the same public policy as excludes proof of the admission itself made in the settlement discussions. It is considered that the argument unsuccessfully made before the Court of Appeal was misconceived because it involved as its starting point the assumption that the defendant was guilty of a serious contempt of court in making the previous statement when no charge had been made and no guilt established. It also confused admission into evidence of the admission for the purpose of proving such a charge, in the context of proceedings which were almost criminal in their nature, and its admission into evidence at the trial of the civil claim. These were different issues. In relation to the latter, public policy required that the admission made in the settlement discussions be excluded from the trial of the claim.

10.013   In *Berry Trade Ltd v Moussavi*[72] there were long wide-ranging and unrecorded settlement discussions which the claimant said gave rise to admissions. They should come into evidence because of the risk of perjury. The Court of Appeal disagreed. Nothing short of "unambiguous impropriety" would do. The risk of perjury is not enough. There should not be a trial of an issue on whether there would be perjury because this would be undesirable satellite litigation and would tend to undermine the purpose of the "without prejudice" rule because it would chill the willingness of litigants to entertain such discussions. It is thought that this

---

[72] [2003] EWCA Civ 715.

judgment correctly identifies what is needed so as to achieve the aim of the public policy. To use "unambiguous impropriety" as a label to fasten admissions made "without prejudice" on litigants would be to reintroduce the very mischief which the rule seeks to avoid.

Both *Merrill Lynch v Mohamed Raffa*[73] and *Savings & Investment Bank v Fincken*[74] at first instance were referred to, but the Court of Appeal on that occasion found it unnecessary to overrule them. This was because in neither case was there evidence denying the alleged "unambiguous impropriety", whereas in *Berry Trade Ltd v Moussavi* there was an issue about whether the alleged admissions had been made. The subsequent decision of the Court of Appeal in *Savings & Investment Bank v Fincken*[75] reversing the decision at first instance also shows that *Merrill Lynch v Mohamed Raffa* was wrongly decided.

(7) Misleading the court with a contention or seeking to draw an inference which is inconsistent with the existence of the "without prejudice" communications

The rule also must give way to the principle that the rule cannot be used to shut out the material when otherwise there is a danger that the court might be misled about its existence. This exception is not concerned with letting in admissions or alleged admissions made in "without prejudice" correspondence. It is the primary object of the rule to prevent the use of admissions made in settlement discussions. This purpose of the rule stated by Hoffmann L.J. in *Muller v Lindsley and Mortimer* remains relevant to understanding its limits and the exceptions to it.   10.014

This exception is concerned with whether the existence of the "without prejudice" communication can be proved so as to disprove an allegation or an inference that no such communication has been made whether "without prejudice" or otherwise. It is the fact of that communication which is relevant and not that it contains any admission.

In *McFadden v Snow*[76] evidence was given by a party that no reply had been received to a letter. This was said to amount to an admission by silence. The court allowed a "without prejudice" letter to be admitted to disprove the allegation stating that "The privilege which may arise from the cloak of 'without prejudice' must not be abused for the purpose of misleading the court." The existence and content of the "without prejudice" letter was itself inconsistent with the allegation. In *Pitts v Adney*[77]

---

[73] May 11, 2000, Comm Ct.
[74] [2003] EWHC 719, ChD.
[75] [2004] 1 W.L.R. 667.
[76] (1951) 69 W.N. (N.S.W.) 8.
[77] [1961] N.S.W.L.R. 535; see also *J. A. McBeath Nominees Pty Ltd v Jenkins Development Corporation Pty Ltd* [1992] 2 Qd R. 121; *Cedenco Foods Ltd v State Insurance Ltd* [1996] 3 N.Z.L.R. 205 at 213–214.

possession of premises was sought against a tenant. It was material whether the tenant was willing to purchase the property at the price required by the landlord. In fact the tenant had made a "without prejudice" offer to purchase the premises at that price with interest. This was placed before the magistrate who rescinded his earlier order for possession. The landlord appealed on the ground that the evidence should have been rejected because of the rule. The appeal was dismissed. If the landlord had sought to gain any advantage "from an inference that there had been no such communication . . ." the evidence would have been admissible because the rule, being based on public policy, "cannot be permitted to put a party into the position of being able to cause a court to be deceived as to the facts by shutting out evidence which would rebut inferences upon which that party seeks to rely . . .". The exception does not apply to let in admissions, nor does it depend upon proof of any intent to mislead the court or of deliberate wrongdoing[78] or of "unambiguous impropriety".

10.015   The exception exists so as to ensure that the court is not misled about the very existence of the "without prejudice" material. This exception is based on the need for integrity of the judicial process and the due administration of justice. It is one matter to shut out evidence of what may otherwise be an admission, it is another for the rule to be used so that the court proceeds on a mistaken view of whether there has been any communication. This is objectionable whatever the motives of the person seeking to set up the exclusionary rule and regardless of whether subjectively that person appreciates that it is wrong for the case to proceed with the material excluded. It follows that whether the rule applies to protect the material may depend vitally upon how a party seeking to insist upon it conducts his case and what inferences the court is invited to make.

In *Knightstone Housing Association v Crawford*[79] an employee claimed that the employers had made up their minds against offering her a part-time job or job-share arrangements from the moment she returned from maternity leave. The employer had in fact put forward a proposal in "without prejudice" negotiations with the employee. The employee was conducting her case on a basis inconsistent with the very existence of the "without prejudice" proposal. The negotiations including the proposal were ruled admissible because of the way she had chosen to run her case. It should be observed that the employer was not seeking to adduce the evidence as an admission, but in order to counter a case which impliedly asserted that no such proposal had been made by the employer. Although the decision has been criticised,[80] it is considered that the case was correctly decided and for the right reason. In contrast, in *Independent Research Services v Catterall*,[81] the employee had claimed that the relationship of trust and confidence had broken down between employer and

---

[78] Contrast C. Hollander and T. Adam, *Documentary Evidence* (7th ed., 2000), para.11–12.
[79] Employment Appeal Tribunal, October 27, 1999 (Holland J.).
[80] *Documentary Evidence*, above, para.11–12.
[81] [1993] I.C.R. 1.

employee. During his employment he had written a "without prejudice" letter offering to remain with the company as a full-time employee. The argument was that the rule did not apply because the letter showed a fact namely that the employee was happy at a particular moment of time. But many admissions are of facts and the letter contained what was to be relied upon as an admission, namely a statement that the employee was prepared to continue in the employment. In those circumstances it was decided that the letter was protected by the rule because for the rule not to apply there had to be "unambiguous impropriety". It is thought that the decision was right because the purpose for which the letter was to be relied upon by the employer was to prove the admission.

In *Gulf Interstate Oil Corporation LLC v ANT Trade & Transport Ltd (The Giovanna)*[82] an application was made for Mareva relief based on an affidavit which gave the impression that the defendants had abandoned their responsibilities and that therefore there was a real risk of dissipation of assets. There had been "without prejudice" negotiations in which an offer of security had been made by the defendants and their protection and indemnity club. This had not proceeded because the plaintiff cargo interests were unable to warrant their title to the cargo. The plaintiff's silence, on the *ex parte* application, about the offer of security made "without prejudice" enabled it to advance the case on the *inter partes* application, that there was a real risk of dissipation of assets. The judge considered that the offer should have been disclosed to the court on the *ex parte* application and thought that an analogy could be drawn with the case where correspondence can be looked at on a strike-out application. It is considered that the material was not excluded by the "without prejudice" rule. This is because it was not relevant on the *ex parte* application as an admission by the defendant. Its relevance was that the defendant had not been silent in the face of the claim, but had made a perfectly reasonable offer of security, conduct which directly undermined the plaintiff's case that there was a real risk of dissipation. What mattered was the fact that such an offer had been made. The affidavit, used on behalf of the plaintiff, had given an impression inconsistent with the very existence of the "without prejudice" material.

A problem could arise about admitting into evidence material on this **10.016** ground when the material might also be used against a party as an admission. In *UYB Ltd v British Railways Board*,[83] a draft "without prejudice" report was sought to be introduced into evidence to counter the allegation that the true extent of the claim was not known to the other party until a later date. The appellants argued that it should have been admitted so as to prevent the court being misled. The Court of Appeal disagreed, commenting, "That [argument] at first sight may seem a powerful [one] but the difficulty is that it may often be possible to dress up

---

[82] [1999] 1 Lloyd's Rep. 867.
[83] *The Times*, November 15, 2000, at paras 39–45 of the transcript.

an argument that something said in without prejudice negotiations could demonstrate that what is being said at a trial is untrue, and thus caution must be exercised." If a party puts forward a case which is incorrect about the very existence of the communication, the material is admissible, but only for the limited purpose of rebutting that case. It cannot be used for the different purpose of relying on an admission. It may be possible to deal with this position by obtaining a ruling from a judge other than the trial judge on whether the material comes within the exception. If it does, the party putting forward the case which exposes him to its admission in evidence can consider whether he wishes to persist in that case. If he does, then the material comes into evidence.

(8) Applications to strike out for want of prosecution

10.017   The existence, dates and contents of correspondence "without prejudice" can be referred to on an application to strike out for want of prosecution. This is not inconsistent with the public policy underlying the rule.[84] First, the material is not being relied upon for any admissions it contains[85] but for the fact that such communications took place.[86] Secondly, if the existence of such material could not be referred to, the court might infer that all that had happened was silence and therefore proceed on a mistaken view of the facts because of the holding back of the existence of such material. Thirdly, the fact that the material is used on the strike-out application does not make it admissible at a trial. It remains protected by the rule.[87]

If the offer of security made in *Gulf Interstate Oil Corporation LLC v ANT Trade & Transport Ltd (The Giovanna)* had been disclosed on the *ex parte* application. It would still have remained protected against use at the trial. This is because it was not covered by the exclusionary rule for the purpose of the *ex parte* application, and therefore no question of waiver could have arisen.

There is no general exception enabling "without prejudice" communications to be referred to in interlocutory applications—*e.g.*, an application for security for costs[88]

(9) Non-disclosure on the *ex parte* application

10.018   The purpose of the rule requiring full disclosure on an *ex parte* application is to overcome the problem that the respondent is not there and so cannot take points in his favour. If the "without prejudice" rule applied to exclude

[84] *Family Housing Association v Hyde & Partners* [1993] 1 W.L.R. 354.
[85] *Somatra Ltd v Sinclair Roche & Temperley* [2000] 2 Lloyd's Rep. 673 at [31–34] makes this distinction which explains why the use of the materials of a strike-out application does not result in there being available at the trial.
[86] *Walker v Wilshier* (1889) Q.B.D. 335 at 338.
[87] *Family Housing Association v Hyde & Partners* [1993] 1 W.L.R. 354.
[88] *Kristansson v R. Verney & Co. Ltd*, CA (Civ Div), June 18, 1998; *Simaan General Contracting Co. v Pilkington Glass Ltd* [1987] 1 W.L.R. 516.

material, then it would not have been available to the respondent had he been represented at the *ex parte* application and so it is not material which has to be disclosed on the *ex parte* application pursuant to the duty of full disclosure.[89] In *Gulf Interstate Oil Corporation LLC v ANT Trade & Transport Ltd (The Giovanna)*[90] the offer of security was not within the umbrella of the rule and thus had to be disclosed on the *ex parte* application. This case is to be accommodated within existing principles governing the rule and does not support any wider proposition that "without prejudice" privilege is overridden by the exigencies of *ex parte* applications.[91] In *Harmony Precious Metals Services SAS v BCPMS (Europe) Ltd*[92] the defendant had written an e-mail offering to settle a claim based on breach of trust. The court rejected the submission that this should have been disclosed on the *ex parte* application because it was contrary to the defendant's interests for this to be put before the court. In that case the e-mail could not properly be used as evidence of an admission—this was covered by the exclusionary rule. It also did not materially affect the case put forward on risk of dissipation of assets and so the fact that it had been made was not material and it was not potentially misleading not to disclose it.

(10) Waiver of privilege through deployment on the *ex parte* application

In *Somatra Ltd v Sinclair Roche & Temperley*[93] the claimant brought a **10.019** negligence action against its former solicitors. The managing partner of the solicitors had tried to settle the proceedings and unbeknown to him these discussions had been taped by the former client using video and audio equipment. The solicitors sued for their fees and obtained *ex parte* Mareva relief against their former client. On the *ex parte* application material was put before the court which in fact consisted of settlement discussions, but which the deponent may or may not have thought was "without prejudice". This material went well beyond what would have been necessary had the consideration been disclosure of material facts and went to the strength of the solicitors' case against their client for fees and their client's case against them for negligence. The tapes indicated that the material was inaccurate. It was accepted by the solicitors that the client could use the tapes for the purpose of an application to discharge the Mareva relief but they contended that the "without prejudice" rule excluded the use of the tapes at the trial of the action. The Court of Appeal decided that the

[89] *Somatra Ltd v Sinclair Roche & Temperley* [2000] 2 Lloyd's Rep. 673 at [16].
[90] [1999] 1 Lloyd's Rep. 867.
[91] See also *Somatra Ltd v Sinclair Roche & Temperley* [2000] 2 Lloyd's Rep. 673 at [16].
[92] [2002] EWHC 1687, TCC.
[93] [2000] 2 Lloyd's Rep. 673.

material had been deployed by the solicitors on the Mareva application on the merits of the cause of action and that once the material had been used in this way there was a waiver of the privilege which the client could accept. It made no difference that the deployment had occurred on an interlocutory application.[94] It extended to evidence of the whole of the discussions.[95]

The case is different from the principle applicable to strike out applications because the materials deployed by the solicitors on the *ex parte* application were not simply deployed to prove the fact of the communications but went to the underlying merits of the dispute—whether an apology offered by the solicitors should be taken as an admission of fault. Accordingly the materials in fact used were covered by the protection of the "without prejudice rule", were relevant only as admissions and there was no duty to refer to them on the *ex parte* application.[96] The use of the materials on the issue of whether an admission had been made by the solicitors deployed them on the merits and therefore resulted in the waiver. This was so regardless of whether the solicitor who had deposed to the affidavit used on the *ex parte* application had appreciated that the materials to which he had referred were settlement negotiations or had mistakenly thought that they were open communications. The principle was that it would be unjust to allow a party to rely on the material for its benefit on the merits in one part of the litigation without allowing the other party to do so too in another.[97] It is thought that this decision is correct and that on the facts the use of the material on the *ex parte* application on the merits broke the "without prejudice" arrangement between the parties and thereby enabled the other side to use the material on the merits. It was also relevant that a cross-undertaking in damages had been given and the question of whether this was to be enforced would depend on the merits at the trial. It would be unjust to allow the applicant to use the material to obtain the injunction but not to allow the client to use the materials, including the tapes, to show that the injunction had been wrongly granted.[98]

---

[94] Following *Derby & Co. Ltd v Weldon (No.10)* [1991] 1 W.L.R. 660 at 667–668.
[95] *Great Atlantic Insurance Co. v Home Insurance Co.* [1981] 1 W.L.R. 529.
[96] *Somatra Ltd v Sinclair Roche & Temperley* [2000] 2 Lloyd's Rep. 673 at [16].
[97] *ibid.*, at [39].
[98] *ibid.*, at [49].

Chapter 11

The undertaking in damages

(1) Provision of the undertaking

The practice of the court is to require the applicant for an injunction or a **11.001** search order to give the court an undertaking to abide by any order for damages which may be made if the defendant suffers loss as a result of the order, and the court is of the opinion that the applicant should compensate him.[1] The undertaking is given to the court,[2] and not to the defendant, and any breach is a contempt of court.[3] The court obtains the undertaking from the applicant as part of the price of the *ex parte* relief.[4] Unless the undertaking is provided, the defendant will not be able to obtain compensation for loss caused by the court order,[5] unless he can show a cause of action for damage, *e.g.* on the ground that the order was obtained by the applicant maliciously and without reasonable cause, or in abuse of the process of the court,[6] or in breach of contract.[7]

In *Smith v Day*,[8] Sir George Jessel M.R. said that the undertaking in damages had been invented by Knight-Brace L.J. when he was Vice-Chancellor, and had originally been inserted only in *ex parte* orders for injunctions. This was repeated by Lord Diplock in *F. Hoffman-La Roche v Secretary of State*.[9] It appears, however, that the practice of requiring an undertaking in damages or making express provision in an order for a

---

[1] *Smith v Day* (1882) 21 Ch.D. 421; *Attorney-General v Albany Hotel Co.* [1896] 2 Ch. 696; *F. Hoffman-La Roche & Co. AG v Secretary of State* [1975] A.C. 295; *Air Express Ltd v Ansett Transport Industries (Operations) Pty Ltd* (1981) 146 C.L.R. 249 esp. at 260–261 and 311.

[2] *Cheltenham & Gloucester Building Society v Ricketts* [1993] 1 W.L.R. 1545 at 1551E; *F. Hoffman-La Roche & Co. AG v Secretary of State* [1975] A.C. 295 at 361.

[3] A breach would occur once the court had made an order requiring the claimant to pay a particular sum and the claimant failed to comply with the order.

[4] *Tucker v New Brunswick Trading Co.* (1890) 44 Ch.D. 249; *Commodity Ocean Transport v Basford Unicorn* [1987] 2 Lloyd's Rep. 197 at 200; *Fletcher Sutcliffe Wild Ltd v Burch* [1982] F.S.R. 64 at 69.

[5] *Bond Brewing Holdings Ltd v National Australia Bank Ltd (No.2)* [1991] 1 V.L.R. 580, Supreme Court of Victoria; Full Court; *Chisholm v Rieff* (1953) 2 F.L.R. 211, Supreme Court of the Northern Territory of Australia.

[6] *Digital Equipment Corporation v Darkcrest Ltd* [1984] Ch. 512; *Metall and Rohstoff AG v Donaldson Lufkin & Jenrette Inc.* [1990] 1 Q.B. 391 at 469.

[7] *Mantovani v Carapelli* [1980] 1 Lloyd's Rep. 375.

[8] (1882) 21 Ch.D. 421 at 424.

[9] [1975] A.C. 295 at 360.

defendant to be protected from loss caused by the making of an interlocutory injunction which is subsequently found to be unjustified pre-dates 1841, when Knight-Bruce L.J. became Vice-Chancellor, and therefore was not originated by him.[10] The practice has been adopted in common law jurisdictions throughout the world.

11.002   The court will not require an undertaking from the Crown a local authority, public body or office holder when bringing proceedings to enforce the law,[11] as opposed to bringing proceedings for their own financial benefit.[12] In cases at neither end of the spectrum the court may require a cross-undertaking.[13] Accordingly no cross-undertaking has to be provided on an application by the Secretary of State for the appointment of a provisional liquidator even when made *ex parte* and when the likely consequence is the immediate cessation of the company's business.[14] Also, in proceedings in the Family Division, the general practice is that no cross-undertaking is to be required,[15] but if the matter concerns a claim for property against a third party who has given value for it, and so is a contested action over property, then a cross-undertaking will be required.

When Mareva relief is sought after judgment pending enforcement of the judgment an undertaking in damages should be required.[16] This is because notwithstanding the obtaining of judgment the injunction may still have been wrongly obtained or there may be loss caused either to the judgment debtor or non-parties for which the claimant should be responsible.

---

[10] *Chisholm v Rieff* (1953) 2 F.L.R. 211 at 214, Supreme Court of the Northern Territory of Australia; *Southern Tableland v Schomberg* (1986) 11 A.C.L.R. 337 at 340, Supreme Court of New South Wales; *Bond Braving Holdings Ltd v National Australia Bank Ltd* [1991] 1 V.L.R. 580 at 599, *per* Brooking J. referring to the early 19th century case law.

[11] *F. Hoffman-La Roche & Co. AG v Secretary of State* (above); *R v Secretary of State for Transport, Ex p. Factortame (No.2)* [1991] A.C. 603 at 672; *Kirklees Metropolitan BC v Wickes Building Supplies Ltd* [1993] A.C. 227 (local authority instituting proceedings under s.222 of the Local Government Act 1972); *Belize Alliance of Conservation Non-Governmental Organisations v The Department of Environment and Belize Electricity Company* [2003] 1 W.L.R. 2839 at [36], PC; *Coventry City Council v Finnie, The Times*, May 2, 1996 (a local authority case); *Securities and Investment Board v Lloyd-Wright* [1993] 4 All E.R. 210 (remedy conferred by statute not for applicant's benefit but for the benefit of the public at large or a section of it); *Re City Vintners Ltd* unreported, December 10, 2001, Ch.D. (Secretary of State applying to wind up a company in the public interest).

[12] *Commonwealth v John Fairfax & Sons Ltd* (1980) 147 C.L.R. 39 at 59; *Australian Competition and Consumer Commission v Giraffe World Australia Pty Ltd* (1998) 84 F.C.R. 512.

[13] *Customs and Excise v Anchor Foods* [1999] 1 W.L.R. 1139 at 1150E–1152E (claim to enforce customs duties where, if an injunction was granted, absence of a cross-undertaking would be oppressive for the defendant).

[14] *Re Highfield Commodities Ltd* [1985] 1 W.L.R. 149; *Re City Vintners Ltd*, unreported, December 10, 2001, Ch.D. which considers specifically the position on an *ex parte* application. The judge on the *ex parte* application should have his attention drawn to the fact that no cross-undertaking is being offered and it should be explained why it is thought that the position cannot be held by asking for undertakings from the company or by the granting of an injunction.

[15] *W v H* [2001] 1 All E.R. 300; *Kelly v BBC* [2001] Fam. 59; *Re S (A Child) (Family Division: Without Notice Orders)* [2001] 1 All E.R. 362.

[16] *Cardile v LED Builders Pty Ltd* (1999) 198 C.L.R. 380 at 401.

If an applicant may not be good for damages on the undertaking, this is a **11.003**
material fact which must be disclosed to the court on the *ex parte*
application.[17] The point should be dealt with in the affidavit evidence used
on the *ex parte* application, otherwise the court proceeds on the assumption that adequate assets are and will remain available within the jurisdiction to support the undertakings proffered to the court. Where a freezing
order is in force there is a continuing obligation on the party who has
obtained it to inform the respondent if there is any material deterioration
in his financial position such that he might not be good for an award of
damages on the undertaking.[18]

Even though the applicant is impecunious, the court may, in rare cases
where the merits are strongly in favour of the applicant, in its discretion,
still decide to grant the relief sought, accepting that the risk that the
undertaking may not be honoured if called upon should not prevent the
injunction being granted.[19] In *RBG Resources v Rastogi*[20] the provisional
liquidators of a company were pursuing strongly arguable claims for
dishonesty[21] against former directors and persons previously involved in
the running of the business of the company. Freezing relief had been
granted, and the liquidators offered an undertaking in damages limited to
the net value of the realisable assets of the company. This was accepted
by the court because they could not be expected to risk their own assets.[22]
The company ought to have the freezing relief even if at the end of the
day it did not have any assets from which to honour any award on the
cross-undertaking. The alternative was that a legal remedy might be
denied to the company because of the consequences of the alleged
dishonesty.

---

[17] *Czarnikow-Rionda Sugar Trading v Standard Bank London Ltd* [1999] 2 Lloyd's Rep. 187 at
207; *Swedac Ltd v Magnet & Southerns plc* [1989] F.S.R. 243 at 251; *Manor Electronics
Ltd v Dickson* [1988] R.F.C. 618; *Anchor Glass Company Ltd v O'Connor*, Court of Appeal
(Civ Div) Transcript No.715 of 1996 (June 13, 1996); *Capitanescu v Universal Weld
Overlays Inc.* [1997] 3 W.W.R. 714 (individual plaintiffs had given an undertaking, so the
fact that the corporate plaintiff was a shell company was not material); *Admiralty and
Commercial Courts Guide*, para.F15.4 and para.9.006 above.
[18] *Staines v Walsh* [2003] E.W.H.C. 1486 at [36], Ch.D.
[19] *Allen v Jambo Holdings* [1980] 1 W.L.R. 1252 (a legal aid case) considered in *Belize
Alliance of Conservation Non-Governmental Organisations v The Department of Environment and Belize Electricity Company* [2003] 1 W.L.R. 2839 at [39], PC; *Fleming
Fabrications Ltd v Albion Cylinders* [1989] R.P.C. 47; *Smith v Tenneco Energy Queensland
Pty Ltd* [1996] A.L.M.D. (Advance) July 2, 1996, No.2097 Fed. Court of Australia). In
Szentessy v Woo Ran (1985) 64 A.C.T.R. 98 at 104, Supreme Court of the Australian
Capital Territory, the court dispensed with the undertaking, but this was in altogether
exceptional circumstances.
[20] [2002] H.C. 3002, May 31, 2002, Ch.D.
[21] This is described in *Shierson v Rastogi* [2003] 1 W.L.R. 586 in which the Court of Appeal
upheld an order for examination made under s.236 of the Insolvency Act 1986 against two
directors who were also defendants in the Chancery Proceedings.
[22] *Re DPR Futures Ltd* [1989] 1 W.L.R. 778 at 786D.

(2) Fortification of the undertaking

11.004   The court may require the undertaking to be fortified[23]—by the provision of either an unlimited undertaking given by someone other than the applicant, or a limited undertaking (*e.g.* by a bank), the limit being in the discretion of the court. Usually that limit will be fixed by reference to a reasonable estimate of what losses might be suffered by reason of the order by the party or parties covered by the undertaking.[24] The applicant is required to give an undertaking which is not subject to a financial limit.[25]

The form, which is given by CPR Pt 25, Practice Direction—Interim Injunctions as an example of a freezing order, provides in Undertaking (2) (see Schedule B, Undertakings Given to the Court by the Applicant):

"[(2) The Applicant will—

(a) on or before [*date*] cause a written guarantee in the sum of £ to be issued from a bank with a place of business within England or Wales, in respect of any order the court may make pursuant to paragraph (1) above; and

(b) immediately upon issue of the guarantee, cause a copy of it to be served on the Respondent.]"

This reflects the practice set out in the former *Practice Direction (Mareva and Anton Piller Orders: New Forms):*[26]

"(A) *On an application for either a Mareva or an Anton Piller order . . .*
2. An applicant should be required, in an appropriate case, to support his cross-undertaking in damages by a payment into court or the provision of a bond by an insurance company. Alternatively, the judge may order a payment by way of such security to the applicant's solicitor to be held by the solicitor as an officer of the court pending further order."

---

[23] *Tarasov v Nassif*, Court of Appeal (Civ Div) Transcript No.876 of 1994 (June 29, 1994); *Admiralty and Commercial Courts Guide*, para.F15.4; *Baxter v Claydon* [1952] W.N. 376; *Harman Pictures NV v Osborne* [1967] 1 W.L.R. 723 at 739; *Commodity Ocean Transport v Basford Unicorn* [1987] 2 Lloyd's Rep 197 at 198; *Re DPR Futures Ltd* [1989] 1 W.L.R. 778; *Select Personnel Pty Ltd v Morgan & Banks Pty Ltd* (1988) 12 I.P.R. 167, Supreme Court of New South Wales; *First Netcom Pty Ltd v Telstra* (2001) 179 A.L.R. 725.
[24] *Re DPR Futures Ltd* [1989] 1 W.L.R. 778 at 786.
[25] *O'Mahony v Morgan* [1996] 1 I.L.R.M. 161 at 170, Supreme Court.
[26] [1994] 1 All E.R. 52. The standard forms were superseded by those attached to *Practice Direction* [1996] 1 W.L.R. 1552, which in turn have been replaced by the example orders annexed to the Practice Directions—Interim Injunctions Supplementing CPR Pt 25, see Appendix 3, below.

The practice is also described in para. F15.4 of the *Admiralty and* **11.005**
Commercial Courts Guide which states:

"FORTIFICATION OF UNDERTAKINGS

F15.4 (a) Where the applicant for an interim remedy is not able to
show sufficient assets within the jurisdiction of the Court to provide
substance to the undertakings given, particularly the undertaking in
damages, he may be required to reinforce his undertakings by providing security.
(b) Security will be ordered in such form as the judge decides is
appropriate but may, for example, take the form of a payment into
court, a bond issued by an insurance company or a first demand
guarantee or standby credit issued by a first-class bank.
(c) In an appropriate case the judge may order a payment to be
made to the applicant's solicitors to be held by them as officers of the
court pending further order. Sometimes the undertaking of a parent
company may be acceptable."

Whether fortification of a cross-undertaking is appropriate, and if so for
how much, is a matter of discretion for the court. It is relevant whether or
not there are assets within the territorial jurisdiction of the court which
would be readily available to satisfy any liability under it.[27] The relevance
of the applicant being resident in the jurisdiction is that this may indicate
that his assets are likely to be within the jurisdiction. On an *inter partes*
hearing, if the court considers that the unsecured cross-undertaking is not
satisfactory, then it should go on to consider what security should be
provided as a condition of maintaining the injunction. Immediate discharge
without providing the applicant with the option to put up adequate
security may be set aside on appeal.[28] If security is not provided after it has
been ordered, this in itself justifies discharge of the injunction.[29]

(3) Undertakings in favour of other defendants

The established practice of the court prior to introduction of the CPR was **11.006**
to require an undertaking in damages in favour of all the defendants in the
action even though only one or some of them may be enjoined by the

---

[27] *Tarasov v Nassif Court* of Appeal (Civ Div) Transcript No.876 of 1994 (June 29, 1994); see
also *Mattos Junior v Macdaniels Ltd*, unreported, November 22, 2002, Ch.D. where there
were charging orders over land within the jurisdiction, and consequently no fortification
was ordered.
[28] *Southway Group Ltd v Wolff, The Times*, May 21, 1991, in which the judge failed to
address the point on providing security although it was raised in argument.
[29] *Macdonald v Pottersfield Ltd (No.2)* [2002] E.W.H.C. 1778 Ch.D.

relevant injunction.[30] The defendants covered by the undertaking were those persons who were defendants to the action at the time of the undertaking being given to the court.[31] Thus a defendant may suffer loss as a result of an injunction against another defendant, and in such circumstances the court has jurisdiction, under the cross-undertaking in damages in the usual form, to require the claimant to pay compensation to that defendant. But if the loss is suffered by a non-party the standard form of undertaking in favour of the defendants will not cover the loss.[32]

The practice that the undertaking also applies to defendants not enjoined by the injunction is appropriate because (1) it may not be clear which of the defendants are liable to suffer loss as a result of the injunction, particularly in complicated cases; and (2) the undertaking confers a jurisdiction on the court to achieve a just result in the working out of the order at the end of the day, and it is fair that the court should have jurisdiction to produce a just result for all the parties before it.

Paragraph 5.1 of the Practice Direction—Interim Injunctions provides that:

> "5.1 Any order for an injunction, unless the court orders otherwise, must contain:
>
> (1) an undertaking by the applicant to the court to pay any damages which the respondent(s) (or any other party served with or notified of the order) sustain which the court considers the applicant should pay,"

The word "respondent" refers to the person enjoined by the order. This is clear from the standard forms annexed to the Practice Direction by para.6.

11.007   What is meant by "any other party"?

In *The Gadget Shop Ltd v. Bug.Com Ltd*[33] the judge questioned whether this paragraph applies to non-parties or is confined to persons who are named parties to the proceedings. The suggestion was that it may not be enough that a person is served with or notified of the order he must also be a party in a technical sense to the proceedings, such as a defendant.

Such a limitation to the meaning might be taken as departing from the long-established practice of extending the cross-undertaking to all defendants regardless of whether they are enjoined. Also it would fail to give

---

[30] *Dubai Bank Ltd v Galadari (No.2), The Times*, October 11, 1989; *Tucker v New Brunswick Trading Co.* (1890) 44 Ch.D. 249.

[31] *Berkeley Administration Inc. v McClelland (No.2)* [1996] I.L.P.r.772 at 792–793.

[32] *R. v Medicines Control Agency & Primecrown Ltd* [1999] R.P.C. 705; *United Norwest Co-Operatives Ltd v Johnstone*, unreported, December 4, 2000 (Mackinnon J.) at pp. 38–39 of the transcript (the relevant loss was that of a non-party and had not been sustained by the defendant).

[33] [2001] F.S.R. 383 at [93].

effect to the reasons underlying the established practice of the court in protecting innocent third parties affected by interlocutory injunctions (see below). On the wider meaning, sooner or later any defendant who is affected by an injunction will be served with the order or notified of its existence, and this will bring that defendant within the ambit of the paragraph. The wording does not limit the losses covered by the undertaking to those sustained after he has been served with or notified of the injunction. It is implausible that this paragraph intended to make any change to the established practice of extending the cross-undertaking to all defendants whether or not enjoined. It is desirable that the formulation of the undertaking in the order should be clear on this point.

The paragraph also omits to state expressly that the undertaking is restricted to losses caused by the order, but this is implied given the function of the undertaking.

(4) Undertakings in favour of innocent third parties affected by the injunction

Under para.(7) of the undertakings set out in the example order for a **11.008** freezing injunction—

"(7) The Applicant will pay the reasonable costs of anyone other than the Respondent which have been incurred as a result of this order including the costs of finding out whether that person holds any of the Respondent's assets and if the court later finds that this order has caused such person loss, and decides that such person should be compensated for that loss, the Applicant will comply with any order the court may make."

The words from "and if the court later finds. . ." are a cross-undertaking in damages covering losses caused by the order to anyone other than a defendant. The words "such person. . ." refer back to "anyone other than the Respondent . . .". This is an added protection for third parties which was included in the standard form Mareva orders attached to the Practice Direction in 1994, remained in the same words in the standard forms introduced in 1996,[34] and now with immaterial changes is in the example order. Under the previous practice an undertaking was expressed to be for losses sustained by any of the defendants by reason of the order. If this

---

[34] See also *Allied Irish Bank v Ashford Hotels Ltd* [1997] 3 All E.R. 309 at 316–317.

undertaking is given to the court,[35] then the court has jurisdiction under the cross-undertaking in para.(1) in respect of loss to the respondent, and, under this additional undertaking, to award compensation to anyone in respect of loss caused to them by the order. This practice is adopted for Mareva relief and also in cases in which the claim is proprietary and relief is being sought over bank accounts or funds or other assets held by third parties.

There is a question as to whether the applicant should consider asking the court to accept a qualified undertaking in relation to banks or other asset holders so that a bank or asset holder following service of the order upon it will have a limited time in which to decide whether voluntarily to accept a duty of care to the applicant to preserve assets under its control caught by the order or forego the right to charge for its services under this undertaking. The position on this is considered in Chapter 20, paras 20.015–6.

11.009   What is the position for other injunctions? In *Miller Brewing Co. v Mersey Docks and Harbour Company*,[36] an injunction had been granted based on alleged trade mark infringement. The claimant sought delivery-up and destruction of the infringing goods. A company which had possession of the goods incurred charges because the injunction had had the effect of impounding the goods in their hands. The company had been notified of the injunction.[37] The company sought extension of a cross-undertaking to them with retrospective effect to cover the 17 months from when the injunction had been granted. The court declined to do this, holding that the application was made too late, after the injunction had ceased to have any value.

The judge said that Mareva relief was different from what he described as "more classic interlocutory injunctions", and that there was no comparable practice protecting third parties for those other types of injunction.

In the Mareva jurisdiction it has long been the practice to make specific provision for protection of persons served with or notified of the order, such as banks, port authorities or others, regardless of whether they were named as parties to the action. Normally they would not be named as a party to the action, but they had to ensure that they did nothing to aid and abet a breach of the order, and were affected by it. A bank would incur expense in searching to ascertain whether there was an account caught by the order and taking steps to freeze the account. A port authority would lose revenue from a berth occupied by a ship which could not sail because of an injunction over its cargo or its bunkers. Protection for banks and others notified of the order (usually they would first be informed by telex or telephone, and then served with a copy of the order) became the

---

[35] It is a matter of discretion for the judge on the *ex parte* application whether or not to dispense with it or accept some other form of undertaking: *Practice Direction (Mareva and Anton Piller Orders: New Farms)* [1994] 4 All E.R. 52 at 53, para.(2), no longer in force.
[36] [2004] F.S.R. 5 at 81.
[37] See *ibid.*, at [18–21].

standard practice of the court.[38] Such persons were often called "third parties". They were parties affected by the injunction,[39] although not named as parties to the action. In *Clipper Maritime Co. v Mineralimportex-port*[40] in a classic statement of principle addressed to the commercial community at large, Robert Goff J. referred to imposing undertakings to protect "the interests of innocent third parties . . ." such as clearing banks and port authorities.

In *Allied Irish Bank v Ashford Hotels Ltd*[41] Phillips L.J., with whom the **11.010** other members of the Court of Appeal agreed, said:

"Once the cross-undertaking for the benefit of third parties became a recognised feature of the court's jurisdiction in the context of Mareva relief, it necessarily followed that the court could make use of it when granting other discretionary relief, at least where that relief was empowered under the same statutory provision."

Where there is a risk that an injunction of whatever type is going to cause loss to a party not before the court, then fairness requires that the court considers whether and if so how to safeguard the position for that party. Just as under the practice established prior to CPR, the court protected the position of defendants regardless of whether they had been enjoined,[42] so it should protect the position of non-parties who are likely to be affected by the order the court makes. Those served with the order or notified of it are liable to be affected by it. The court avoids putting innocent non-parties to the trouble, expense and hazards of applying to the court, when fairness requires that their position be protected, at least to the extent of the court putting in place a mechanism conferring jurisdiction to achieve a just result. This is and has been for some considerable time standard practice both with Mareva relief[43] and also for injunctions freezing assets which were not based on the Mareva jurisdiction, such as a proprietary injunction sought in support of a claim to trace into funds in a bank account. It is the practice in cases concerning breach of confidence, following the practice for freezing injunctions.[44] The underlying principle is that of the need for protection of the legitimate interests of innocent third parties caught up in the dispute of others.[45]

---

[38] *Rahman (Prince Abdul)v Abu-Taha* [1980] 1 W.L.R. 1268 at 1273G; *Searose Ltd v Seatrain* [1981] 1 W.L.R. 894 at 896.

[39] See *Clipper Maritime Co. Ltd v Mineralimportexport* [1981] 1 W.L.R. 1262; *Project Development Co. Ltd v KMK Securities* [1982] 1 W.L.R. 1470 at 1471; *Capital Cameras v Harold Lines Ltd* [1991] 1 W.L.R. at 57H;

[40] [1981] 1 W.L.R. 1262 at 1264.

[41] [1997] 3 All E.R. 309 at 317.

[42] *Dubai Bank Ltd v Galadari (No.2)*, *The Times*, October 11, 1989; *Tucker v New Brunswick Trading Co.* (1890) 44 Ch.D. 249.

[43] *Project Development v KMK Securities* [1982] 1 W.L.R. 1470 at 1471C.

[44] *Imutran Ltd v Uncaged Campaigns Ltd* [2002] F.S.R. 20 at [45].

[45] See the citations in *Guinness Peat Aviation (Belgium) NV v Hispania Lineas Aereas SA* [1992] 1 Lloyd's Rep. 190 at 195.

The facts of *Miller Brewing Co. v Mersey Docks and Harbour Company*[46] brought the case directly within the statement of principle made by Robert Goff J. in *Clipper Maritime Co. v Mineralimportexport.* In that case it was a port authority caught up in the consequences of an injunction over goods which *(inter alia)* would cause it to incur costs. In *Miller Brewing Co.* the injunction prevented the goods being moved from the docks and therefore imposed on the company the need to incur storage charges.

The effects of the injunction did not depend upon the cause of action. Fairness to innocent "third parties" or "non-parties" affected by the injunction cannot be governed by the cause of action. It is considered that the opinion expressed in *Miller Brewing Co.* that a different practice applied according to the cause of action was wrong.

11.011   The position under para.5.1(1) of the Practice Direction depends upon the meaning of "any other party served with or notified of the order . . .". These words when read in the context of the established practice for freezing injunctions and the reasons for it, do not limit that paragraph to persons who are technically parties to the action.[47] However, even if this limit applied, para.5.1 applies to "Any order for an injunction . . ." and is thus setting out a basic bare minimum for all injunctions regardless of whether on the facts there is a likelihood of an innocent non-party sustaining loss by reason of the order. Accordingly it does not exclude the established practice of the court in such cases.

An injunction obtained against a company which is the parent company of a group may well be liable to cause loss to other companies in the group. The subsidiaries may have a claim in tort for their losses even though they were not defendants to the claimant's claim against their parent company: *Balkanbank v Taher (No.3)*.[48] But in the absence of an undertaking in damages in favour of third parties, the subsidiaries should apply to the court for the injunction to be discharged unless an undertaking to cover losses sustained by the subsidiaries is given. Otherwise the losses of the subsidiaries will not in themselves be covered by an undertaking covering losses sustained by the parent,[49] and any claim by the parent based on the cross-undertaking would have to be by reference to its position as a shareholder. When the subsidiaries have no cause of action for their loss and it is not recoverable by them under an undertaking given to them, the parent company can claim on the cross-undertaking for its own loss even though it consists in loss in value of its shareholdings.[50] If the subsidiaries

---

[46] [2004] F.S.R. 5 at 81.
[47] *Imutran Ltd v Uncaged Campaigns Ltd* [2002] F.S.R. 20 at [45] (the RSPCA were not named as a party to the proceedings and intervened to obtain a variation); contrast *The Gadget Shop Ltd v Bug.Com Ltd* [2001] F.S.R. 383 at [93].
[48] *The Times*, April 14, 1995.
[49] *R. v Medicines Control Agency & Primecrown Ltd* [1999] R.P.C. 705.
[50] *Johnson v Gore Wood & Co.* [2002] 1 A.C. 1 at 35H; *George Fischer v Multi-Construction* [1995] B.C.L.C. 260, following *Lee v Sheard* [1956] 1 Q.B. 192 and distinguishing *Prudential Assurance v Newman Industries (No.2)* [1982] Ch. 204 at 223 on the ground

do have a cause of action or an undertaking in their favour, then the parent cannot recover for losses suffered by it as a shareholder which merely reflect losses for which the subsidiaries could claim.[51] The subsidiaries should also consider applying for a bond or other security to be required, in support of an undertaking covering their losses, as a condition of continuing the injunction. It is for the applicant to decide whether or not to provide the undertaking, bond or other security required by the court. Provision of one is the voluntary act of the applicant.[52]

If a party not included in the scope of an undertaking wishes to be so **11.012** included, he must apply to the court for the relief which has been granted to be discharged unless the applicant provides a widened undertaking. In such circumstances the applicant may choose not to provide a widened undertaking even though the court seeks it from him, and in consequence the relief granted is discharged. If the relief granted has already lapsed or been discharged or has ceased to be of any value to the claimant, or if, in the case of Anton Piller relief, it has already been fully executed, then the court will not be in a position to stipulate for a widened undertaking, or a bond or other security in support of an undertaking, as the price for continuing the relief which has been granted.[53]

The applicant may be willing to furnish an undertaking or security in support in favour of the party applying, but wish to restrict its scope to loss suffered by that party from the date of that application, as opposed to the date of the original application. If application is made whilst the injunction is still in force[54] for the continuation of the injunction to be made dependent upon the furnishing of a cross-undertaking, then the court can order this as the price for continuation of the injunction and it will be a matter for the claimant to choose whether to furnish the undertaking as the price for the continuance. In principle the court can ask for whatever

---

that it was a case concerning the application of the rule in *Foss v Harbottle* (1843) 2 Hare 461; *Gerber Garment Technology Inc. v Lectra Systems Ltd* [1997] R.F.C. 443; *Berkeley Administration Inc. v McClelland (No.2)* [1996] I.L.P.r.772 at 793 *Ng Thiam Kiat v Universal Westech (S) Pte Ltd* [1997] 3 S.L.R. 419 (individuals who were restrained could claim on the cross-undertaking for losses sustained by them as shareholders in a company which they controlled and through which they carried on business, when the injunction prevented them using the company to do acts restraining by the injunction).

[51] *Johnson v Gore Wood & Co.* [2002] 1 A.C. 1 at 35E–36E in which Lord Bingham referred to the earlier authorities; *Shaker v Al Bedrawi* [2003] 2 Ch. 350 at [1] and [2].

[52] *Cheltenham & Gloucester Building Society v Ricketts* [1993] 1 W.L.R. 1545 at 1551D; *Attorney-General v Albany Hotel Company* [1896] 2 Ch. 696 at 700, *per* North J.; *Commodity Ocean Transport v Basford* [1987] 2 Lloyd's Rep. 197; *F. Hoffman-La Roche & Co. AG v Secretary of State* [1975] A.C. 295 at 361.

[53] *Deutsche Schachtbau-und Tiefbohrgesellschaft GmbH v Ra's Al-Khaimah National Oil Company* [1990] 1 A.C. 295 at 362, *per* Lord Goff; *Commodity Ocean Transport v Basford* (above). *Remm Construction (SA) Pty Ltd v Allco Newsteel Pty* (1991) 56 S.A.S.R. 515 (South Australia); *First Netcom Pty Ltd v Telstra* (2001) 179 A.L.R. 725; Contrast *Marc Rich v Oroleum International* noted in 197 Lloyd's Maritime Law Newsletter (May 21, 1987), a decision from Singapore.

[54] In *Commodity Ocean Transport v Basford* [1987] 2 Lloyd's Rep. 197 the application was too late because the injunction had already been discharged. See also *Miller Brewing Co. v Mersey Docks and Harbour Company* [2004] F.S.R. 5 at [91–98]—the injunction had become of "no value" because of the order made for delivery-up.

undertaking it considers is just, including an undertaking which if given would extend to costs already incurred or losses already sustained.[55] It will be a matter for the discretion of the court to decide whether or not to accept the restricted undertaking as the price for continuance of the relief. In principle, provided that the third party has applied promptly, the undertaking ought not to be so restricted. The general principle is that innocent third parties caught up in the granting of Mareva relief ought not to be left to suffer loss caused by the order, but ought to be protected from that loss.[56] This should be regarded as by way of an adjustment of the original order in the light of further information, which, had it been available to the court originally, would have resulted in the court's stipulating for an undertaking in damages to cover the third party at the *ex parte* application.

(5) Inadvertent omission of an undertaking in damages

11.013   Whenever the court grants an injunction, unless the contrary is expressly said, the applicant will be taken to have given the usual undertakings in damages by implication.[57] It is the responsibility of the applicant to provide a draft order to the court. That order must contain undertakings in damages in favour of the respondents and "any other party" served with or notified of the order.[58] The same is true of the undertakings in the example orders referred to in para.6 of the Practice Direction, unless the court has otherwise directed, having had its attention clearly drawn to the relevant point. This is because those examples are the starting point of any *ex parte* application for a freezing injunction or search order and the applicant has a duty to the court to explain to the judge any differences between his draft and those forms.

If, through inadvertence or otherwise, the undertakings are not included, the order can be corrected either under CPR r.40.12[59] or under the inherent jurisdiction of the court. In cases where the cross-undertaking in favour of the party enjoined has been omitted, or where an undertaking has been given orally, it is obvious that it must be written in because that is what everyone intended and understood at the *ex parte* application.

The application should be made to the court of first instance and not to the Court of Appeal.[60] Alternatively, the defendant or non-party can invite

---

[55] *Guinness Peat Aviation (Belgium) NV v Hispania Lineas Aereas SA* [1992] 1 Lloyd's Rep. 190 at 196 LHC (the undertaking which would have been required would have covered losses from when the order had first affected the charterer which was on the previous day; this case is discussed in Chapter 20, para.20.024.); *First Netcom Pty Ltd v Telstra* (2001) 179 A.L.R. 725.

[56] *Project Development Co. Ltd SA v KMK Securities Ltd* [1982] 1 W.L.R. 1470.

[57] *Spanish General Agency Corporation v Spanish Corporation* (1890) 63 L.T. 161; *Colledge v Crossley, The Times*, March 18, 1975; *Kerridge v Foley* (1968) 70 S.R. (NSW) 251.

[58] CPR Pt 25, Practice Direction—Interim Injunctions, para.5.1 (1)

[59] *Colledge v Crossley* (above).

[60] *Tucker v New Brunswick Trading Co* (1890) 44 Ch.D. 249.

the court to proceed as if the undertaking in damages had been set out in the order.[61]

Is the jurisdiction to amend the order limited to such cases? It is **11.014** suggested that the jurisdiction arises whenever through a breach of duty to the court by the applicant an undertaking which otherwise would have been required has been omitted from the order.

This is because:

(1) The applicant is responsible for ensuring the integrity of the judicial process on the *ex parte* application and in consequence owes duties to the court. The applicant, by applying *ex parte*, agrees to perform those duties owed to the court.

(2) These duties require scrupulously fair presentation of the application in all its aspects,[62] including presentation so as to obtain affirmative informed decisions by the court on that application in relation to the provision of undertakings to protect the respondent and anyone else who may be affected by the order. The applicant's duty includes drawing the judge's attention to any practice of the court relevant to undertakings,[63] disclosing facts which are material to what undertakings should be required, and ensuring that everything material to the draft order laid before the court is drawn specifically to the attention of the judge.

(3) The applicant's agreement to perform his duties owed to the court on the *ex parte* application implicitly includes agreement that any undertaking, which is omitted from the order as a result of his breach of duty to the court, is to be treated as given by him. Alternatively the duty of utmost good faith, which applies to the applicant on the *ex parte* application, precludes him from denying that the omitted undertaking was provided by him.

If the position has gone wrong at the *ex parte* application and the correct undertakings have not been given then it is also the responsibility of the applicant and his legal representatives to point this out to the court on the *inter partes* hearing and to have the position corrected. In *Frigo v Culhaci*,[64] counsel for the plaintiff had omitted to ensure that an undertaking in damages was included in the original *ex parte* order or the order made *inter partes*. The Court of Appeal of New South Wales[65] said:

"The onus was on the plaintiff through his counsel to ensure that the undertaking was offered . . .

---

[61] *Oberrheinische Metallwerke GmbH v Cocks* [1906] W.N. 127.
[62] *Memory Corporation v Sidhu (No.2)* [2000] 1 W.L.R. 1443; *The Budget Shop Ltd v Bug.Com Ltd* [2001] F.S.R. 383 at [48]; *Re S (A Child) (Family Division: Without Notice Orders)* [2001] 1 All E.R. 362.
[63] *Frigo v Culhaci* [1998] N.S.W.S.C. 393, Court of Appeal of NSW.
[64] [1998] N.S.W.S.C. 393, Court of Appeal of NSW.
[65] Mason P., Sheller J.A. and Sheppard A.J.A.

We regret to add that the failure to have drawn this matter to the attention of a busy judge who may have been inexperienced in matters of equitable jurisdiction represented a serious breach of counsel's obligations to the Court. See generally Ipp, "Lawyers' Duties to the Court" (1998) 114 LQR 63 . . .

It was quite wrong for counsel for the plaintiff to take the stance that an undertaking as to damages would be offered if and when but only if and when it was sought. He should have reminded the judge of this invariable incident of an interlocutory injunction of this nature at the time when the injunction was sought *ex parte*. [The judge] should have refused to continue the interim injunction beyond [the return date] unless and until such undertaking were proffered. And counsel for the plaintiff should have reminded the judge about this if it were thought, as has been submitted before us, that his omission to engraft this condition was an oversight. See *National Australia Bank Ltd v Bond Brewing Holdings Ltd* [1991] 1 V.R. 386 at 560.

The absence of an undertaking as to damages is a severe detriment to a defendant who, if the proceedings fail, will be left without remedy against the plaintiff with respect to any loss flowing from obedience to the injunction. Before us, counsel for the plaintiff offered the undertaking *nunc pro tunc*.[66] In the circumstances of the case, where the omissions to give the undertaking at the outset and on [the *inter partes* hearing] were not an oversight, we would dissolve the injunction on this ground alone."

11.015   In *Tucker v New Brunswick Trading Co.*,[67] an injunction had been granted on an application made *inter partes* against a company. There were other defendants. Counsel on behalf of one of them (D1) asked for the usual undertaking in damages and the plaintiff's counsel agreed to give it, but no request was made on behalf of the other defendant (D2). The Court of Appeal ordered variation of the order as drawn up so as to record a cross-undertaking in respect of loss suffered by the company or D1, but not D2. This was on the principle that an undertaking can only be given voluntarily. That case depended upon the practice then followed in providing undertakings. The scope of an undertaking depends upon what would reasonably have been understood by the court which heard the application. The then prevailing practice provided the context for understanding the words used by counsel. If the same case happened today, the assumption would be that, unless counsel clearly excluded the undertaking set out in para.5.1 of the Practice Direction, this was impliedly being offered by the claimant. The conversation would be treated as merely confirming the application of that undertaking to D1, and not excluding the undertaking required from the applicant under para.5.1, which would cover D2. The order could therefore be amended under the slip rule.

---

[66] *i.e.* by backdating the undertaking.
[67] (1890) 44 Ch.D. 249.

In *Miller Brewing Co. v Mersey Docks and Harbour Company*,[68] the applicant had slipped up both on the *ex parte* application and when the matter came back before the court *inter partes*, because the judge was not referred to either the established practice of the court concerning injunctions affecting third parties and its likely application on the facts, or para.5.1 of the Practice Direction and its potential application, or asked to consider the position of the company holding the goods. If this had been done, an undertaking should have been required which covered the company. It was an understandable error but it should not have been allowed to prejudice the position of the non-party. It is considered that the case was wrongly decided and that the court should have proceeded to deal with the application by first correcting the error in the original *ex parte* order, and the order continuing it, by inserting into them an undertaking in the form of the undertaking which would have been required had the proper procedure been followed and the applicant had performed the duties owed to the court. The applicant should not have been permitted to obtain any advantage from the omission of the undertaking which ought to have been given and would have been required had the applicant's duties to the court been duly performed.

If a defendant offers an undertaking to the court to stand in the place of **11.016** an injunction, the defendant would be wise to ensure that the applicant expressly provides an undertaking in damages in respect of loss caused by the provision of the defendant's undertaking. In the Chancery Division the practice in this situation is to include an undertaking in damages unless the contrary is expressly stated.[69] This came about as a result of a direction by the judges of the Chancery Division following the decision of the Court of Appeal in *Howard v Press Printers Ltd*.[70] In that case the court refused to include an undertaking in damages when this had not been expressly given by the plaintiff in return for the defendant's undertaking. In the *Chancery Guide* the current practice is described as follows:

"IMPLIED CROSS-UNDERTAKINGS IN DAMAGES WHERE UNDERTAKINGS ARE GIVEN TO THE COURT

5.22 Often the party against whom an injunction is sought gives to the court an undertaking which avoids the need for the court to grant the injunction. In these cases, there is an implied undertaking in damages by the party applying for the injunction in favour of the other. The position is less clear where the party applying for the injunction also gives an undertaking to the court. The parties should consider and, if necessary, raise with the Judge whether the party in whose favour the

---

[68] [2004] F.S.R. 5 at 81.
[69] *Practice Note* [1904] W.N. 203 at 208.
[70] (1904) 91 L.T. 718.

undertaking is given must give a cross-undertaking in damages in those circumstances."

(6) Effect of the undertaking in damages

11.017   The undertaking in damages is given to the court,[71] not directly to the party or parties identified in it. That party is not entitled to sue on the undertaking by way of a claim in contract.[72] Nor will that party or any other party be able to sue in tort for damages caused by the court order, unless the order was obtained maliciously, or in abuse of the process of the court.[73] Thus to make good an action in tort, the party injured would need to sue for malicious prosecution *(Speed Seal Products Ltd v Paddington)*[74] or perhaps for the tort of abuse of the process of the court.[75] But a party covered by the undertaking will have the right, at the appropriate stage, to ask the court[76] to enforce the undertaking against the claimant, and the court can do so, either assessing the damages summarily[77] or, more usually, by directing that the claimant pay the damages awarded on an inquiry as to damages.

Thus the initial question is whether the injunction was "wrongly granted".[78] If the claimant fails at trial then normally it would follow that the injunction was wrongly granted. But this is not always so. In *Yukong Line Ltd v Rendsburg Investments Corporation*[79] the claimant failed on their substantive claims at trial against an individual but were able to justify the freezing relief granted against him personally in respect of his own assets on the ground that he could have assets of the judgment debtor which could not be specifically identified, and the freezing order against him was ancillary to the claim to enforce the judgment against the company.

---

[71] *Cheltenham & Gloucester Building Society v Ricketts* [1993] 1 W.L.R. 1545 at 551E.
[72] *Fletcher Sutcliffe Wild Ltd v Burch* [1982] F.S.R. 64; *Cheltenham & Gloucester Building Society v Ricketts* [1993] 1 W.L.R. 1545 at 1551E ("The undertaking . . . does not found any cause of action . . .") and 155B; *Bond Brewing Holdings Ltd v National Australia Bank Ltd (No.2)* [1991] 1 V.L.R. 580, Supreme Court of Victoria, Full Court, contrasting where an undertaking is given to the court as part of a bargain between the parties; see further *Hinde v Hinde* [1953] 1 W.L.R. 175 at 185.
[73] *Digital Equipment Corporation v Darkcrest Ltd* [1984] Ch. 512.
[74] [1985] 1 W.L.R. 1327 at 1333–1334.
[75] *Metall & Rohstoff AG v Donaldson Lufkin & Jenrette Inc.* [1990] 1 Q.B. 391; *Speed Seal Products Ltd v Paddington* [1985] 1 W.L.R. 1327; *Grainger v Hill* (1838) 4 Bing NC 212.
[76] If the undertaking has been given to a county court, application should be made to that court even though the damages claimed exceed the county court limit: *Shanks v Law Society*, Court of Appeal (Civ Div) Transcript No.444 of 1994 (January 27, 1994). In the case of the High Court, application should usually be made in the proceedings in which the undertaking was given, to the part of the High Court seised with those proceedings; see further *Re Hailstone* (1910) 102 L.T. 877.
[77] As in *Columbia Picture Industries Inc. v Robinson* [1987] Ch. 38.
[78] *Yukong Line Ltd v Rendsburg Investments Corporation* [2001] 2 Lloyd's Rep. 113 at [32].
[79] [2001] 2 Lloyd's Rep. 113.

Whether or not the injunction had been wrongly granted[80] is to be decided by the court and should be dealt with before any inquiry as to damages is directed. Such an inquiry should be concerned only with the quantum of damages to be awarded to the defendant pursuant to the jurisdiction conferred on the court by the undertaking. The inquiry should not be concerned with whether or not the injunction was justified.[81] Nor in principle should it be concerned with whether the court, in the exercise of its discretion should decline to award damages either wholly or in part. Thus, once an inquiry has been directed it should be concerned only with matters of causation and the quantification of damages.

In *Cheltenham & Gloucester Building Society v Ricketts*[82] an injunction **11.018** granted in a fraud action had been discharged before the trial, on the ground that the evidence before the court did not make out a sufficient case, and the judge had decided that there should be an inquiry as to damages. The Court of Appeal set aside the order on the basis that it was premature to exercise the discretion on the facts of that case before the trial. The building society had alleged that it had been induced to lend money by the deceit of the defendants. If the allegation of fraud were made out at trial, this would be most material to the proper exercise of the discretion.

If an interlocutory injunction is discharged before trial, the court has a number of courses available:

(1) it can enforce the undertaking by awarding damages assessed summarily;[83] and payable forthwith;

(2) it can exercise its discretion to enforce the undertaking and order an inquiry as to damages;[84]

---

[80] Just because the claimant recovers less on his claim than the maximum sum limit on Mareva relief, it does not follow that the relief was wrongly granted: *Elaine Kinhult-Ng v Tay* [1998] W.A.S.C. 235. Where the claimant used a standard form for Mareva annexed to a practice direction which was in force at the time, and was entitled to Mareva relief, then it was erroneous for the court to hold that it was "wrongly granted" because the order could be ambiguous to a layman: *Coutts & Co. v Vickers*, CA (Civ Div), unreported, January 27, 1998. In *Hughes v Clewley* [1996] J.L.R. 24, the plaintiff succeeded in deceit but failed to obtain relief carrying into effect rescission of the contract of sale of a ship because an escort agency called "Villas Rouge" was being conducted on board by the defendant. The court (1) declined to discharge the injunction which had been granted under what was then s.30 of the Merchant Shipping Act 1894 to protect the plaintiff's interest in the ship, because the plaintiff had not carried on the immoral business; and (2) refused to award damages to the defendant.

[81] *Norwest Holst Civil Engineering Ltd v Polysius Ltd*, The Times, July 23, 1987, disapproving an observation to the contrary made in *Barclays Bank Ltd v Rosenberg*, The Times, May 9, 1985; *Cheltenham & Gloucester Building Society v Ricketts* [1993] 1 W.L.R. 1545 at 1552B–C.

[82] [1993] 1 W.L.R. 1545.

[83] *Practice Direction (Mareva and Anton Piller Orders: New Forms)* [1994] 4 All E.R. 52 (no longer in force) at 54, para. (4) required consideration of this when an Anton Piller order or Mareva injunction was discharged on the return date.

[84] As in *Norwest Holst Civil Engineering Ltd v Polysius Ltd*, The Times, July 23, 1987, in which, regardless of the merits of the substantive claim, the obtaining of Mareva relief had been misconceived. Accordingly, the discretion could be exercised at that stage without risk of injustice.

(3) it can determine forthwith that the undertaking is not to be enforced;

(4) it can adjourn the application for an inquiry to the trial or further order;[85]

(5) it can adjourn the application to a hearing on the question of discretion whether to enforce the undertaking and, if so, assessment of damages.[86]

In Seton's *Chancery Forms*, the draft order directing an inquiry contains provision for the plaintiff to recover the costs of the inquiry, but this is not the modern practice. Costs of the inquiry remain in the discretion of the court and the claimant may choose to protect his position on costs by making a payment into court or under CPR Pt 36.

11.019   Difficulties have often arisen as to whether an order directing an inquiry means that the undertaking is to be enforced by the court in the exercise of its discretion. If the judge making the order makes it clear that the discretion remains to be exercised in the future, then the order will not be treated as having determined it: *Zygal Dynamics v McNulty* (above). So also if counsel for the claimant expressly reserves the point and the order is made on the footing of this reservation.[87] If the judge orders an inquiry, having in principle decided that damages are to be paid, then if the claimant wishes to contend that the undertaking should not be enforced as a matter of discretion this should be done by way of appeal against the order directing an inquiry: *Cheltenham & Gloucester Building Society v Ricketts*[88] (leave to appeal out of time was granted).

A consent order directing an inquiry as to damages sustained by the defendant "which the plaintiff ought to pay", when no argument was addressed to the court on whether the undertaking ought to be enforced, was construed as not precluding the plaintiff from subsequently contending that as a matter of discretion the undertaking should not be enforced.[89]

In *Hodgkinson & Corby Ltd v Wards Mobility Services Ltd*,[90] at the trial the plaintiff's claim was dismissed with costs and the judge ordered an

---

[85] As in *Cheltenham & Gloucester Building Society v Ricketts* [1993] 1 W.L.R. 1545. *Fujitsu General New Zealand v Melco New Zealand Ltd* [2002] N.Z.C.A. 91 (May 8, 2002) concerned an application for discharge of the Anton Piller order for the sole purpose of obtaining damages on the cross-undertaking and was adjourned to be dealt with at the trial, see also Chapter 23, para.23.026.

[86] *Zygal Dynamics v McNulty*, Court of Appeal (Civ Div) Transcript No.571 of 1989 (June 20, 1989); *Cheltenham & Gloucester Building Society v Ricketts* [1993] 1 W.L.R. 1545 at 1557H.

[87] See *Financiera Avenida v Shiblaq, The Times*, January 14, 1991.

[88] [1993] 1 W.L.R. 1545.

[89] *Balkanbank v Taher* [1995] 1 W.L.R. 1056. (The injunction had been granted under s.25(1) of the Civil Jurisdiction and Judgments Act 1982 and the consent order in England was made after the trial in Ireland.) The court accepted that the order took effect in the same way as if it had been made after argument, but held that in the circumstances there could not be imputed to the parties, by virtue of their consent to the order, an agreement that any issue on discretion was decided in favour of the defendants.

[90] [1997] F.S.R. 178.

inquiry as to "what damages (if any) the defendant has sustained by reason of" an interlocutory injunction. The plaintiff wished to contend that the defendant had suffered no loss because it could not have done what was restrained by the injunction without infringing copyright. There had been no claim by the plaintiff at the trial for infringement of copyright.[91] The judge proceeded on the basis that the order made by the trial judge was an exercise of discretion by the court to enforce the undertaking leaving quantum to be resolved.[92]

If an inquiry is ordered at the conclusion of the trial, then if there is an appeal which includes challenging the basis on which the inquiry was directed, the court may stay the inquiry pending the appeal so as to avoid wasting costs. If the court of first instance decides that an interim injunction was wrongly granted and there should be an inquiry on the cross-undertaking as to damages, the order will not normally[93] be stayed pending appeal. However where the inquiry would be very expensive and the appeal would be short it may be appropriate to grant a stay pending appeal, or stay the inquiry after certain procedural steps have been completed, *e.g.* after pleadings have been exchanged. **11.020**

In *Smith v Day*,[94] Sir George Jessel M.R. expressed the view that no inquiry as to damages would be directed if the court had made an error in law in granting the original relief, Cotton L.J. dissenting. It was subsequently established that an inquiry would be directed whenever an injunction was found not to have been justified, and even if the plaintiff could not be said to have been at fault in any respect in obtaining or maintaining the interlocutory relief.[95] Thus, *e.g.* if the claimant fails on a point of law, the defendant will be entitled to an inquiry as to damages.

The ordinary practice on interlocutory injunctions is not to order an inquiry into damages on the cross-undertaking unless and until the claimant has failed on the merits of the action: *Ushers Brewery Ltd v King (P.S.) & Co. (Finance) Ltd*.[96] However, in a case involving a Mareva injunction, a defendant may obtain an inquiry into damages once it is apparent that the injunction was obtained wrongly or without jurisdiction. Thus in cases involving non- disclosure the courts have ordered inquiries as to damages once it is clear that the injunction should not have been granted[97] and even though the plaintiff had obtained a substantial judgment

---

[91] The claims had been for passing off and trade mark infringement.
[92] [1997] F.S.R. 178 at 197–198.
[93] *Smithkline Beecham Plc v Apotex Europe Ltd* [2003] EWHC 3185, (2004) 27(3) I.P.D. 27029 at paras 5–8; *Leicester Circuits Limited v Coates Brothers plc* [2002] EWCA Civ 474 at para.13; see also para.3.025 above.
[94] (1882) Ch.D. 421.
[95] *Griffith v Blake* (1884) 27 Ch.D. 474; *Re Hailstone* (1910) 102 L.T. 877 at 880, 881; *Vieweger Construction Co. Ltd v Rush & Tompkins* (1964) 48 D.L.R. (2d) 509 at 518–519, Supreme Court of Canada; *Nelson Burns & Co. v Grantham Industries* (1987) 19 C.P.R. (3d) 71, Ontario Court of Appeal; *Bond Brewing Holdings Ltd v National Australia Bank Ltd (No.2)* [1991] 1 V.L.R. 580.
[96] [1972] Ch. 148.
[97] *Barclays Bank Ltd v Rosenberg, Financial Times*, June 12, 1985; *Barclays Bank plc v Illingworth*, Court of Appeal (Civ Div) Transcript No.304 of 1985 (May 10, 1985).

against the defendant or might do so. The position is the same for other injunctions.

11.021 Once it is clear in a Mareva case that there was not a sufficient risk of dissipation of assets, the court may enforce the undertaking and direct an inquiry even though the merits of the claim have not yet been decided: *Norwest Holst v Polysius*.[98]

In considering whether to enforce the undertaking in damages, two of the important factors are whether the claimant has succeeded on the merits of his claim, and whether there was a real risk of dissipation of assets. If the discretion is being exercised after judgment, then if the claimant has succeeded in his claim and there was a real risk of dissipation, then ordinarily the court will not enforce the undertaking: *Armhouse Lee Ltd v Anthony Chappell*,[99] where the defendant unsuccessfully sought enforcement because part of the evidence used on the *ex parte* application had been perjured, although the plaintiff and its advisers did not know this and had not been at fault in using it on the hearing of the application.

On an application for an inquiry the applicant should adduce some evidence[1] to show an arguable case that he has sustained loss falling within the undertaking. The court will not order an inquiry if it would be pointless to do so because the intended claim is obviously bad or because any recoverable loss is trivial.[2] On the other hand, at the discretion stage the court should not hear protracted argument on whether the suggested loss will be recoverable.[3]

11.022 Once an inquiry has been ordered before the trial, it is usually just and convenient to hold it at the same time as the claim is tried.[4] If the claimant has already obtained judgment, the defendant may be able to obtain a stay

---

[98] *The Times*, July 23, 1987; see also *Canadian Pacific (Bermuda) Ltd v Nederkorn Pte Ltd* [1999] 2 S.L.R. 18 (plaintiff succeeded against the first respondent on appeal but order for inquiry on the cross-undertaking upheld because the plaintiff had obtained Mareva relief based on an untrue allegation of misappropriation of joint venture assets); *Jau-Wau Stewart v E, Excel Ltd* HKCFI (October 10, 2001)(where the plaintiff had failed to uphold *inter partes* leave to serve out of the jurisdiction and worldwide relief, and an inquiry was directed because trial in the appropriate forum would not alter the fact that the injunction had been "wrongly granted", or the exercise of discretion on whether to enforce the undertaking). In *Heng Holdings SEA (Pte) Ltd v Tomongo Shipping Co. Ltd* [1997] 3 S.L.R. 547 the cross-undertaking was enforced after the plaintiff had won on its substantive claim because it had failed to demonstrate a real risk of dissipation of assets and therefore the injunction, which the court classified as a Mareva injunction, had been wrongly granted. On the facts it is considered that the injunction should have been regarded as part of the *quia timet* relief sought in the action based on the contractual right to an indemnity—see Chapter 12, para.12.008. Therefore the fact that the plaintiff had succeeded on its claim to *quia timet* relief should have been regarded as a strong, albeit not conclusive, factor against enforcing the undertaking.

[99] Court of Appeal (Civ Div) Transcript No.1507 of 1994 (December 1, 1994).

[1] *Yukong Line Ltd v Rendsburg Investments Corporation* [2001] 2 Lloyd's Rep. 113 at [35]— "some credible evidence that he has suffered loss as the result of the making of the order". In *Smith v Day* (1882) 21 Ch.D. 421 at 428 and 430, the suggested loss was too remote.

[2] Particularly if there has been delay in making the application: *Ex p. Hall* (1883) 23 Ch.D. 644 at 651.

[3] See generally *Williams and Humbert Ltd v WDH Trademarks* [1986] A.C. 368 at 441.

[4] *Barclays Bank plc v Illingworth*, Court of Appeal (Civ Div) Transcript No.304 of 1985 (May 10, 1985), *per* Kerr L.J. (*obiter*).

of execution on the judgment pending the outcome of the inquiry as to damages. If an inquiry is ordered and the claimant has not yet obtained judgment, then ordinarily the inquiry will be heard at the same time as the trial of the action, and judgment will be given for the balance between the amount due on the claim in the action (if it succeeds) and the amount found to be due in the inquiry.

If the inquiry is not heard at the trial, then there can be a stay of execution on the judgment given on the claim pending the outcome of the inquiry.[5] The court can grant Mareva relief in support of a claim for loss which falls within the undertaking.[6]

(7) "Special circumstances" justifying the refusal of an inquiry as to damages

Once it is established that the injunction was wrongly granted, even though without fault on his part,[7] the court will ordinarily order an inquiry as to damages.   **11.023**

In *Graham v Campbell*,[8] James L.J., delivering the judgment of the Court of Appeal, said that the undertaking ought to be given effect to by the court except "under special circumstances". The court, in deciding whether to enforce the undertaking, has a discretion. The discretion is to be exercised by reference to all the circumstances of the case, bearing in mind that since the injunction should not have been obtained, prima facie the claimant ought to bear the loss: *Financiera Avenida v Shiblaq*.[9]

The mere fact that the defendant has broken his contract with the claimant or has been guilty of tortious conduct,[10] even deliberate tortious conduct,[11] or outrageous and dishonest conduct,[12] has not resulted in a refusal by the court to enforce the undertaking. There is, however, a discretion to refuse to enforce the undertaking and each case must be decided on its particular facts.[13] It has been exercised in Canada to refuse an inquiry in a case when the claimant was acting in the public interest and the defendant's conduct leading to the institution of the proceedings was

---

[5] *Keller v Cowen* [2001] EWCA Civ 1704 at [24].
[6] *First Netcom Pty Ltd v Telstra* (2001) 179 A.L.R. 725.
[7] *Hunt v Hunt* (1884) 54 L.J. (NS) 289.
[8] (1877) 7 Ch.D. 490 at 494.
[9] *The Times*, January 14, 1991, CA (Civ Div). The very fact that a claimant has lost argues strongly in favour of enforcement: *Tribune Investment Trust Inc. v Soosan Trading Co. Ltd* [2000] 3 S.L.R. 405.
[10] *Nelson Burns & Co. v Grantham Industries* (1987) 19 C.P.R. (3d) 71, Ontario Court of Appeal.
[11] *Columbia Picture Industries v Robinson* [1987] Ch. 37.
[12] *Universal Thermosensors Ltd v Hibben* [1992] 1 W.L.R. 840 at 858.
[13] *Cheltenham & Gloucester Building Society v Ricketts* [1993] 1 W.L.R. 1545 at 1557A–F. See further A. Zuckerman, "The Undertaking in Damages" [1994] Camb. L.J. 546.

viewed with disfavour.[14] If the defendant has provoked the bringing of the proceedings[15] or brought them on himself,[16] it may be inequitable to enforce the undertaking.

11.024   In *F. Hoffmann-La Roche & Co. AG v Secretary of State*,[17] Lord Diplock said that the discretion not to enforce the undertaking could be exercised if the court considered that the conduct of the defendant in relation to the obtaining, continuing or enforcement of the injunction makes it inequitable to do so. Unnecessary delay in making an application to the court to enforce the undertaking can result in the court's declining to enforce it.[18] This is irrespective of prejudice being caused; *Barratt Manchester Ltd v Bolton Metropolitan Borough Council*.[19]

The court will take into account all the circumstances of the case, including the duration of the delay, any explanation for it, whether it has caused prejudice to the other party, whether any prejudice can adequately be dealt with by an award of costs, and whether the claim for loss is substantial and reasonably arguable.

If there is delay in prosecuting an inquiry, the court can decide to dismiss the inquiry. It is not necessary for there to be prejudice caused by the delay.[20] It is for the court to decide in pursuance of its "broad equitable jurisdiction"[21] whether to enforce it or to release it, and it can be released even after an inquiry has been ordered. The question is whether the party claiming in the inquiry has conducted itself so unreasonably that the inquiry should be struck out.[22]

11.025   There is jurisdiction in the court to enforce the undertaking even after the action had been discontinued[23] or dismissed.[24] If the action has been discontinued, it does not necessarily follow that the undertaking will be enforced. The party who has discontinued may be able to show that in the

---

[14] *Attorney-General for Ontario v Harry* (1982) 35 O.R. (2d) 248, Ontario Supreme Court. See also *Municipality of Metropolitan Toronto v NB Theatrical Agencies Inc.* (1991) 76 D.L.R. (4th) 522, appeal dismissed at (1994) 117 D.L.R. (4th) 228 and *Great House at Sonning v Berkshire*, unreported, December 18, 1996 (Sir John Wood) in which the defendant local authority was refused an inquiry because it had acted high-handedly and unreasonably.

[15] *Modern Transport Co. Ltd v Duneric Steamship Co.* [1917] 1 K.B. 370 at 380.

[16] *Goldman Sachs International Ltd v Lyons, The Times*, February 28, 1995.

[17] [1975] A.C. 295 at 360.

[18] *Ex Hall* (1883) 23 Ch.D. 644; *Cornhill Insurance plc v Barclay*, Court of Appeal (Civ Div) Transcript No.948 of 1992 (October 6, 1992), *per* Stuart Smith L.J.: "If the application is not made at the time of discharge or promptly thereafter to the judge who discharged the injunction, the court will have a discretion to refuse to make the order."

[19] [1998] 1 W.L.R. 1003 at 1009G.

[20] *Barratt Manchester Ltd v Bolton Metropolitan Borough Council* [1998] 1 W.L.R. 1003; *Smith v Wilmslow Motors*, Court of Appeal (Civ Div) (June 21, 1999).

[21] *C. T. Bowring v Corsi and partners* [1994] 2 Lloyd's Rep. 567 at 582; *Barratt Manchester Ltd v Bolton Metropolitan Borough Council* [1998] 1 W.L.R. 1003 at 1009.

[22] *Smith v Wilmslow Motors*, CA (Civ Div), unreported, June 21, 1999.

[23] *Newcomen v Coulson* (1877) 7 Ch.D. 764; *Daniell's Chancery Practice* (7th ed., 1901), p.1365.

[24] *Newby v Harrison* (1861) 2 De G.F. &J. 889. The jurisdiction arises from the undertaking and is independent of the jurisdiction of the court to make orders in the action, and so is unaffected by the ending of the action.

circumstances the discontinuance should not be regarded as recognition of defeat.[25] If there has been a compromise agreement in respect of the continuance of the injunction, it is a matter of interpretation of that agreement whether the parties have agreed that no claim is to be made to enforce the cross-undertaking. Where the agreement is silent on this it is a question of inferring whether the parties intended that the respondent abandoned the right to make such a claim.[26]

Once there has been judgment at the trial on the merits, that judgment will have the effect of producing a *res judicata*. Unless and until that judgment is set aside on appeal or through action for fraud, it is binding on the parties and precludes the losing party from disputing the merits. So for example once there has been a final judgment finding the defendant liable for infringement of a patent, and ordering an inquiry as to damages, even if the patent is revoked in subsequent proceedings the defendant is estopped from disputing that he infringed a valid patent held by the claimant.[27] Similarly with a final judgment dismissing a claim, there is an estoppel preventing the claimant from reopening liability. This estoppel would operate both on the question of whether an inquiry as to damages on the undertaking should be directed, and the assessment of quantum at the inquiry. The trial on the merits may also result in points being barred to a party at the inquiry because of issue estoppel or abuse of the process of the court.[28]

(8) Causation, measure of damages and remoteness in an inquiry as to damages

In *F. Hoffmann-La Roche & Co. AG v Secretary of State*,[29] Lord Diplock 11.026 said that if an inquiry as to damages is ordered, the:

---

[25] *Goldman Sachs International Ltd v Lyons, The Times*, February 28, 1995, where the injunction had been properly obtained and the plaintiff discontinued because there was no prospect of making any worthwhile recovery, and the undertaking was not enforced because the defendant had brought the injunction upon himself. Similarly where the claimant does not maintain his substantive claim at trial, this in itself is not conclusive that there must be an inquiry: *Waterlow Publishers Ltd v Rose* [1995] F.S.R. 207 at 223.

[26] *Cornhill Insurance Plc v Barclay*, Court of Appeal (Civil Division) Transcript No.948 of 1992 (October 6, 1992) (where the parties came to an agreement for the discharge of the Mareva relief, which halted the pending discharge application before the judge, and it was held that the defendants had by implication abandoned all their rights in connection with their discharge application, which had itself been compromised); *Heng Holdings SEA (Pte) Ltd v Tomongo Shipping Co. Ltd* [1997] 3 S.L.R. 547 at paras 35–44 (where before the compromise the enjoined party had applied to the judge to hear further argument on whether to dismiss its application for discharge, time was then running for appeal when the agreement was concluded, the compromise was silent about an appeal, and held not to be a bar. It compromised only the position on the injunction, and not the possible appeal against the refusal to discharge the injunction).

[27] *Coflexip SA v Stolt Offshore MS Ltd* [2004] F.S.R. 7, p.118; *Poulton v Adjustable Cover and Boiler Block Co* (1908) 25 R.P.C. 529.

[28] See para.11.031 below.

[29] [1975] A.C. 295 at 361.

"principles to be applied are fixed and clear. The assessment is made upon the same basis as that upon which damages for breach of contract would be assessed if the undertaking had been a contract between the plaintiff and the defendant that the plaintiff would *not* prevent the defendant from doing that which he was restrained from doing by the terms of the injunction."

If an injunction is excessively wide and if the effect was to restrain the defendant from pursuing activities which he ought to have been at liberty to pursue, and loss has resulted, damages can be recovered.[30] Thus, *e.g.* if a Mareva injunction was subject to a limit which was excessive and loss was caused because the injunction was excessively onerous, damages may be recoverable.[31]

The defendant is entitled to recover only compensation for loss caused by the making of the order. If a cross-undertaking is given in respect of a mandatory order for an item to be delivered up, then the claimant is liable for loss caused to the defendant from being deprived of the item, and the defendant is not entitled to claim an account in respect of the benefit derived by the claimant from having the item.[32] A defendant who is deprived of the use of a trading vessel by an injunction will be prima facie entitled to the market rate of hire less any earnings in fact obtained.[33]

11.027   It is not sufficient that the order provided the factual context within which the loss occurred.[34] Thus if the loss would have been suffered because of the bringing of the proceedings, regardless of the granting of the order, then this is not covered by the undertaking.[35] Also, if the loss would have been suffered in any event because of an injunction properly obtained in the proceedings against other defendants, this will not be recoverable: *Tharros Shipping Co. Ltd v Bias Shipping*.[36] The burden of proof is on the defendant to prove that the loss was suffered as the result of the order. For this purpose, to show that the loss would not have been suffered "but for"

---

[30] *Universal Thermosensors Ltd v Hibben* [1992] 1 W.L.R. 840 at 858; *Jet West Ltd v Haddican* [1992] 1 W.L.R. 487 at 491E; *A. T. Poeton (Gloucester Plating Ltd) v Horton* [2001] F.S.R. 169 (at first instance).

[31] *Atlas Maritime Co. SA v Avalon Maritime Ltd (No.3)* [1994] 1 W.L.R. 917 at 920E.

[32] *Dr Rentschler Biotechnologie GmbH v Biogen Inc.*, Comm Ct, unreported, November 28, 1996 (Tuckey J.).

[33] *Gatoil Anstalt v Omenial Ltd* [1983] 1 Lloyd's Rep. 492, applying the approach of Lord Diplock in *F. Hoffmann-La Roche & Co. AG v Secretary of State* [1975] A.C. 295 at 361.

[34] *Schlesinger v Bedford* (1893) 9 T.L.R. 370.

[35] *Air Express Ltd v Ansett Transport Industries* (1981) 146 C.L.R. 249, High Court of Australia, esp. at 262–268, 312–313, 323–324; *International Pediatric Products Ltd v Lambert* (1967) 66 D.L.R. (2d) 157 (loss caused by threats to sue customers); *United Norwest Co-Operatives Ltd v Johnstone*, unreported, December 4, 2000 (Mackinnon J.) at pp.39–41 of the transcript (defendant unable to show any particular loss caused by the orders, as opposed to the bringing of the proceedings alleging dishonesty).

[36] [1994] 1 Lloyd's Rep. 577.

the injunction may well not be sufficient,[37] but it is sufficient if the injunction was an effective cause of the loss.[38] However, once the defendant shows that he has suffered loss which was prima facie caused by the order, then the evidential burden of any contention that the relevant loss would have been suffered regardless of the making or continuance of the order will pass to the claimant.[39]

A Mareva injunction prevents a defendant from dealing with his assets, and this inability to use assets may be the cause of loss.[40] The injunction may, however, cause loss in other ways, *e.g.* because of its effect on third parties in their business dealings with the defendant. Such loss may be the subject of an award of damages. Thus in *Financiera Avenida v Shiblaq*[41] the defendant had to resign as a broker because of the injunction, and was awarded damages for loss of his position. A claimant can expect a Mareva injunction to come to the attention of third parties, *e.g.* as a result of service of the order by the claimant, or because the defendant has had to inform others (*e.g.* his bankers) about it. Loss of profits or extra expenses may be caused because a bank withdraws the line of credit on which a company was relying in order to fund the carrying on of its business.[42] A company's business may be destroyed in which case the damages are to be measured by what it was worth as a going concern—by investigating what price would have been paid for the company as a going concern.[43] This will include a value for goodwill.[44]

In the case of an appointment of a receiver and manager, the damage: **11.028**

"to be apprehended by the making of an order is not so much that the receiver and manager may so exercise his powers as to occasion loss in

---

[37] In *Tharros Shipping v Bias Shipping* [1994] 1 Lloyd's Rep. 577 at 581–582, Waller J. used the expression "the" cause. He questioned whether, in *Financiera Avenida v Shiblaq, The Times*, November 21, 1988; Lexis Transcript, October 21, 1988, there were "any other possible causes which displaced that cause . . .". See also *Galoo Ltd v Bright Grahame Murray* [1994] 1 W.L.R. 1360 at 1369–1375, which stresses the application of "the court's common sense". The purpose of the undertaking is not to protect against losses caused by the litigation, but losses caused by the injunction which is the subject of the undertaking, and it is the injunction which must be "the" cause of the loss in the sense that it has been the dominant or an effective cause, even though there may have been other contributory factors.

[38] *Bonz Group (Pty) Ltd v Bonz Group (NZ) Ltd* [2000] N.Z.C.A. 44 (March 9, 2000), where the decision of the defendant to stop her business was because of (1) the interim injunction, and (2) the need to prepare for a complicated trial on the merits. Since the existence of the interim injunction was "a significant determinant of that decision", causation was established for the loss flowing from cessation of the business, for the purpose of awarding damages on the undertaking.

[39] *Financiera Avenida SA v Shiblaq, The Times*, November 21, 1988 (Saville J.); *Tharros Shipping Co. Ltd v Bias Shipping* [1994] 1 Lloyd's Rep. 577.

[40] Lord Diplock appears to contemplate this form of causation in *Hoffman-La Roche* [1975] A.C. 295 at 361F.

[41] *The Times*, January 14, 1991.

[42] *Keller v Cowen* [2001] EWCA Civ 1704 at [26–29], in which it was held that these losses were also not too remote.

[43] *Johnson Control Systems Ltd v Techni-Track Europa* [2003] EWCA Civ 1126.

[44] *Bonz Group (Pty) Ltd v Bonz Group (NZ) Ltd* [2000] N.Z.C.A. 44 at paras 15–23 (March 9, 2000) referring to the decision at first instance which was upheld on appeal.

the business to which he has been appointed. It consists of the consequences flowing from the fact of appointment and of the defendant's loss of its title to control its assets and affairs . . .">[45]

It is for the defendant to plead and prove its loss.[46] The purpose of the inquiry is compensatory. Where the applicant makes a huge claim which it fails to prove, and does not plead an alternative case, it will not recover anything.[47]

The defendant must have taken all reasonable steps to avoid altogether or mitigate his loss. This will include taking steps to apply for a variation of the injunction in appropriate circumstances, *e.g.* to enable business debts to be paid and to allow a business to continue to be conducted.[48] The damages to be awarded are not to be artificially restricted to losses suffered during the period for which the order was in force. The losses to be taken into account will include losses suffered as a result of the order, even though they were not in fact suffered or incurred until after the order had been discharged.[49]

The principles of remoteness of damage apply.[50] Accordingly, the claimant will not be held liable for loss which is too remote, taking into account what losses could reasonably have been contemplated by him as not unlikely to result from the order at the time he furnished the relevant undertaking,[51] or at any renewal of the undertaking voluntarily entered into by him. The undertaking applies to loss suffered by reason of the making of the order, and does not restrict recoverable loss to what was foreseeable. As a matter of fairness, however, the court will usually only award damages for loss which was reasonably foreseeable at the time the undertaking was provided, and which would be recoverable in an assessment of damages for breach of contract: *Smith v Day*.[52] *Schlesinger v Bedford*.[53]

---

[45] *National Australia Bank Ltd v Bond Brewing Holdings Ltd* (1990) 169 C.L.R. 271 at 277, High Court of Australia.

[46] *Barratt Manchester Ltd v Bolton Metropolitan Borough Council* [1998] 1 W.L.R. 1003 at 1008G.

[47] *Tyco European Metal Framing Ltd v New Systems Ltd*, unreported, December 21, 2001, Ch.D.

[48] *Re DPR Futures Ltd* [1989] 1 W.L.R. 778 at 786–787.

[49] *Algonquin Mercantile Group v Dart Industries* (1996) 12 C.P.R. (3d) 289, Federal Court of Canada.

[50] *Smith v Day* (1882) 21 Ch.D. 421; *Air Express Ltd v Ansett Transport Industries* (1981) 146 C.L.R. 249.

[51] *Chen v Lord Energy Ltd* (2002) 5 H.K.C.F.A.R. 297 at para.42, *per* Lord Hoffmann (where delay in completion had resulted in a loss of a resale, and, because of the nature of the property market in Hong Kong, it was foreseeable that delay could result in this type of loss).

[52] (1882) 21 Ch.D. 421; see also *Abbey National plc v Robert McCann*, CA (NI), unreported, June 11, 1997, *per* Carswell L.J. in relation to an *ex parte* injunction, and *Bonz Group (Pty) Ltd v Bonz Group (NZ) Ltd* [2000] N.Z.C.A 44 at paras 5 and 6, in which it was decided that although the injunction had been drafted with the objective that the defendant would stay in business it was foreseeable that in fact it would cause her to cease her business.

[53] (1893) 9 T.L.R. 370.

Thus in Australia the view has been expressed[54] that it would seldom be **11.029**
just and equitable that the unsuccessful claimant ". . . should bear the
burden of damages which were not foreseeable from circumstances known
to him at the time". This approach leaves it open to a defendant to draw to
the attention of the claimant an unusual type of loss which may well be
sustained by reason of the order, and to seek his confirmation that he will
accept responsibility for that type of loss on the undertaking. If the
claimant declines to give such confirmation, it is open to the defendant to
apply to the court to discharge the injunction unless the confirmation is
forthcoming.

If a claimant has obtained an injunction fraudulently or maliciously, the
court should hold him responsible for all loss directly caused by the
injunction regardless of its foreseeability—compare the position in an
action for deceit.[55] In such circumstances it is just that the claimant should
bear all the loss, and the court can be expected to form the opinion
required by the undertaking that the claimant should pay damages in
respect of all the loss.

The defendant will not be able to recover compensation for the loss of a
business which it was illegal for him to conduct, *e.g.* a business selling
videotapes or computer software in breach of copyright.[56] But if the order
effectively causes a legitimate business to cease, the court can award
damages for the loss of that business, which would take into account loss
of goodwill.

It has been said that the court can award exemplary damages.[57] **11.030**
However, the wording of the undertaking obliges the claimant to pay
damages only in respect of losses suffered by reason of the order, and
therefore is restricted to damages awarded to compensate the defendant
for those losses.[58] In principle, the court could award aggravated damages
when the effect of making and implementing the order has been made
more severe for the defendant by the high-handedness or misconduct of
the claimant or his agents, but only as compensation to the defendant.

The Staughton Committee on Anton Piller orders recommended that if
an Anton Piller order was discharged on the return date a defendant should
have "a summary remedy in damages . . .", and that the defendant's

---

[54] *Air Express Ltd v Ansett Transport Industries (Operations) Pty Ltd* (1979) 146 C.L.R. 249 at 269; *Cheltenham & Gloucester Building Society v Ricketts* [1993] 1 W.L.R. 1545 at 1552. In *R. v Medicines Control Agency & Primecrown Ltd* [1999] R.P.C. 705 it was pointed out that contractual principles may not necessarily be applicable.
[55] *Doyle v Olby Ltd* [1969] 2 Q.B. 158 at 167; *Smith New Court Ltd v Scrimgeour Vickers* [1997] A.C. 254 at 265B–C.
[56] *Columbia Picture Industries v Robinson* [1987] Ch. 37.
[57] *ibid.*, at 87; *Smith v Day* (1882) 21 Ch.D. 421 at 427–428, *per* Brett L.J.
[58] *Harris v Digital Pulse Pty Ltd* [2003] N.S.W.C.A. 10 (February 7, 2003) at paras 340–342. Hobhouse L.J., *in Berkeley Administration Inc. v McClelland* [1995] I.L.P.r.201 at 217–218, considered that exemplary damages could not be awarded. See also *Universal Thermosensors Ltd v Hibben* [1992] 1 W.L.R. 840 at 858B, and the Report of the Staughton Committee on Anton Piller orders at para.3.13 (Lord Chancellor's Department, 1992). The claimant has only undertaken to pay compensation.

". . .damages should be assessed forthwith".[59] The *Practice Direction (Mareva and Anton Piller Orders: New Forms)*[60] in para.(4) made it mandatory for a judge to consider, when an Anton Piller order or Mareva injunction is discharged on the return date, whether damages should be assessed at once and immediate payment directed. The Practice Direction provided a summary procedure for the exercise of a power to award general damages in respect of such loss, *i.e.* damages without pleading or proving special damage.

The award in *Columbia Pictures Industries Inc. v Robinson* was an award of general damages both for the damage to the defendants' business interests and for the shock, distress and outrage caused to the defendants through the carrying out of the order.[61] An Anton Piller order or a Mareva injunction granted *ex parte* against a defendant who is a trader or businessman can be expected to damage his credit before he can defend himself. In this area the court can and will, in appropriate cases, award general damages, including compensation for damage to a trader's credit and commercial reputation caused by the *ex parte* order by way of summary order.[62]

11.031   If the court has decided as a matter of discretion to enforce the undertaking, then the inquiry which has been ordered is concerned with quantum alone. The claimant will find himself unable to take a point going to quantum if it would be an abuse of the process of the court to allow him to raise it at that stage. This can arise when it could and should have been raised earlier by the claimant and, if it had been, it would have been resolved[63] or if the claimant were now allowed to take it the defendant would sustain some substantial prejudice.[64]

In *Hodgkinson & Corby Ltd v Wards Mobility Services Ltd*,[65] the plaintiff could not take its point on copyright in the inquiry because the point could and should have been taken, if it was going to be taken, at the trial on the substantive merits. It would have been an abuse to allow the plaintiff to

---

[59] Report, para.3.13
[60] [1994] 4 All E.R. 52 and subsequently [1996] 1 W.L.R. 1552, which are now replaced by the Practice Direction—Interim injunctions supplementing CPR Pt 25.
[61] See also *Bonz Group (Pty) Ltd v Bonz Group (NZ) Ltd* [2000] N.Z.C.A. 44 at para.24 where a modest award was made for the emotional distress caused by an Anton Piller order executed at the defendant's home. A search order is particularly likely to cause emotional distress, especially when the search is of a home, and so damages can readily be awarded for this. Emotional distress will usually be too remote in respect of an injunction which only restricts use of assets: *Teo Siew Har v Lee Kuan Yew* [1999] 4 S.L.R. 560.
[62] See also *The Quartz Hill Consolidated Gold Mining Company v Eyre* (1883) 11 Q.B.D. 674, on the availability of general damages at common law for malicious presentation of a winding-up petition.
[63] See *Barrow v Bankside Agency Ltd* [1996] 1 W.L.R. 257 at 263D and 268F–H. This will often be fatal to an argument founded on the omission to take a point which could have gone to discretion to order an inquiry. This is because on the facts it cannot be shown that the point would have been dealt with at that stage.
[64] *Berkeley Administration Inc. v McClelland (No.2)* [1996] I.L.P.r.772 at 795–796 and 796–797; see also *Barrow v Bankside Agency Ltd* [1996] 1 W.L.R. 257 at 268F–H.
[65] [1997] F.S.R. 178.

defend itself on quantum by reference to a point which, had it been raised previously, would already have been disposed of at the trial.[66]

An argument on abuse was also raised by the defendant by reference to the failure of the plaintiff to take the point at the time the trial judge was asked to and did exercise his discretion to enforce the undertaking. The court rejected this argument, apparently on the ground that in the circumstances it would not be fair to shut out the plaintiff from taking the point in view of the absence of any real prejudice resulting from the failure to take the point at the conclusion of the trial. This part of the decision could also have been put on another ground. It would not have been right for the trial judge to allow the plaintiff to justify the interlocutory injunction by reference to a cause of action upon which the plaintiff had not relied in the action. Thus even had it been raised as an argument going to discretion, it would have been unnecessary to decide it.

Once it is apparent that the defendant may be entitled to recover **11.032** damages on the undertaking, the court could grant Mareva relief against the claimant in respect of the undertaking.[67] The position is analogous to that where there is an untaxed order for costs.[68] Thus if the court is satisfied that damages will or may be awarded either summarily or on an inquiry as to damages, then in principle Mareva relief is available in respect of the claim. If, on the other hand, it is not clear that an injunction was wrongly granted, then it might well be premature to grant Mareva relief in respect of a possible claim which might be entertained in due course under the undertaking in damages should it later appear that the injunction was unjustified.

When damages are awarded under the undertaking, an order is made by the court directing the claimant to pay those damages. In principle the court can award interest on those damages under s.35A of the Supreme Court Act 1981. In Canada interest has been ordered on damages awarded on the undertaking.[69]

(9) The recovery by a defendant or non-party of legal costs caused by the order

The statutory jurisdiction of the court over costs of and incidental to **11.033** proceedings is under s.51 of the Supreme Court Act 1981. The CPR regulate the position in CPR Pt 44.

[66] Applying *Henderson v Henderson* (1843) 3 Hare 100. Cp. *Alliance Paper Group plc v John Prestwich* (1997) *The Times*, December 11, 1997 in which there had been a trial, but it had been limited to certain matters which had not included deciding liability for damages for breach of contract. The plaintiff was not precluded from advancing claims for damages for breaches of contract which had not been covered by the judgment at the trial.

[67] *Commodity Ocean Transport v Basford Corporation* [1987] 2 Lloyd's Rep. 197 at 200; *First Netcom Pty Ltd v Telstra* (2001) 179 A.L.R. 725.

[68] *Faith Panton Property Plan v Hodgetts* [1981] 1 W.L.R. 927.

[69] *Algonquin Mercantile Group v Dart Industries* (1996) 12 C.P.R. (3d) 289.

Outside of the costs jurisdiction conferred by statute there are situations in which a person can claim costs under a substantive cause of action. One example is where there is an express indemnity given in respect of those costs. In the case of a contractual indemnity taxation of costs is upon the basis set out in the contract.[70] Another is where a person has settled a claim brought against him by a purchaser of defective goods and seeks to recover both the costs he has paid and those he has incurred from the person who sold the goods to him on the grounds that he incurred them as a result of the seller's breach of contract.[71]

There has been a series of cases in which, where the claim is for damages, the claimant has only recovered an order for costs to˙ be taxed on the standard basis. The person entitled to damages cannot recover the extra amounts of costs incurred or paid by him over and above what he is awarded in the taxation. In *Berry v British Transport Commission*[72] the plaintiff, who had pulled the communication cord in a train, brought an action for malicious prosecution against the defendant. She sought as damages the costs she had incurred in defending the criminal proceedings before the magistrates and then on appeal. She was able to recover those costs because they had been incurred in criminal proceedings. She would not have been able to recover them had they been costs in civil proceedings because the only remedy given for costs in civil proceedings is the award of costs to be made under the statutory jurisdiction.[73]

11.034   There have subsequently been a series of cases decided under the rules of court which applied prior to CPR. The effect of those cases is that the "standard basis" for the assessment of costs is regarded as giving a reasonable indemnity to a party entitled to damages.[74] It puts the burden on the party claiming the costs to show that they were reasonably incurred. Thus in those cases the sole remedy was to obtain an order for costs to be taxed on the standard basis, this in substance being what the claimant would be entitled to on an award of damages. Under CPR r.44.4 (2) costs awarded on the standard basis must also be "proportionate to the matters in issue".

Where an injunction has been "wrongly granted" then normally the defendant will be awarded his costs arising out of the injunction and this will be the only remedy to which he will be entitled. Whilst one can accept that incurring legal costs could give rise to a "loss" within the scope of the undertaking,[75] normally the sole remedy for costs is an award of costs in

---

[70] *Gomba Holdings (UK) Ltd v Minories Finance Ltd* [1993] Ch. 171.
[71] *Hammond v Bussey* (1888) 20 Q.B.D. 79; *Butterworth v Kingsway Motors* [1954] 1 W.L.R. 1286.
[72] [1962] 2 Q.B. 306, considered in *Union Discount Co. Ltd v Zoller* [2002] 1 W.L.R. 1517.
[73] *Cockburn v Edwards* (1881) 18 Ch.D. 449 at 462 and 463; *Standard Bank v Bank of Tokyo* [1995] 2 Lloyd's Rep. 169 at 187.
[74] *British Racing Drivers' Club v Hextall Erskine & Co.* [1996] 3 All E.R. 667; *Penn v Bristol & West Building Society* [1997] 1 W.L.R. 1356; *Seavision Investment SA v Evenett (The Tiburon)* [1992] 2 Lloyd's Rep. 26; *Lonrho v Fayed (No.5)* [1993] 1 W.L.R. 1492.
[75] *Stonehocker v King*, Ontario CA C24769 (October 2, 1998).

the proceedings under s.51 Supreme Court Act 1981. This is because that remedy usually gives a complete remedy and there is no room for any further remedy to be granted under the undertaking. Taxation on the standard basis gives him what he would be otherwise entitled to under the cross-undertaking. This view of the matter is also supported by the case law on cross-undertakings.[76] In relation to legal costs incurred in foreign legal proceedings as the result of the injunction, such as the costs of discontinuance caused by an anti-suit injunction, then in principle this would be a head of loss recoverable under the cross-undertaking. If they had been caused by a breach of contract they would be recoverable,[77] and there is equally no policy reason precluding recovery under the cross-undertaking.

In *FSL Services Ltd v Macdonald*[78] the claimant had discontinued its claim and an order for an inquiry as to damages had been made. The defendants sought to recover in that inquiry costs which had been awarded against them in respect of their own unsuccessful opposition to the freezing order at two applications to discharge the relief. The defendants contended that they had failed on those applications because of fraudulent evidence served by the claimants. The claimants sought to strike out the inquiry on the ground that the alleged losses were irrecoverable in law. The Court of Appeal held that there was jurisdiction to terminate an inquiry summarily but declined to order this on the ground that it was unclear whether the costs were irrecoverable particularly given the allegation of fraud which had been made.

In this case the problem for the defendants was that costs orders already **11.035** been made against them covering the costs which they wished to recover using the mechanism of the inquiry. It is considered that unless and until they were set aside, either on appeal, or by an action in fraud, they were binding decisions of the court as to how the costs ought to be borne as between the parties and they were binding. The court had already decided that the defendants should not recover their costs and ought to pay the costs of the claimants. In these circumstances the cross-undertaking could not properly be used for a court of co-ordinate jurisdiction to reverse those costs orders on a basis less than an action for fraud.[79]

---

[76] In *Harrison v McSheehan* [1885] W.N. 207, there was a consent order for an inquiry into what damages had been caused to a plaintiff by certain acts of a defendant. The court refused to include in those damages the difference between the costs recoverable under a court order and the costs incurred as between solicitor and client, Pearson J. observing that this was "contrary to the practice of the court". Contrast *Stonehocker v King*, Ontario CA C24769 (October 2, 1998) holding that the undertaking was sufficient to include costs, awarding costs under the undertaking and disapproving of *Israel Discount Bank of Canada v Genova* (1992) 13 C.P.C. (3d) 112.

[77] *Union Discount Co. Ltd v Zoller* [2002] 1 W.L.R. 1517.

[78] [2001] EWCA Civ 1008.

[79] *Commissioners of Customs & Excise v Anchor Foods No.2, The Times*, September 28, 1999; *McGowan v Chadwick* [2002] EWCA Civ 1758 at [95–101] (there could not be a claim for legal costs as damages for breach of duty when the court had declined to award them under

As for costs incurred by non-parties in order to comply with the order, prior to the change to the taxation rules to provide for costs on the "standard basis", these used to be taxed on an "indemnity basis" but with the burden of proof to show reasonableness on the non-party.[80] These included the costs of applying to the court. The standard undertaking in Schedule B, undertaking (7) of the example freezing injunction is "to pay the reasonable costs . . . incurred as a result of this order . . ." The burden of proof is upon the non-party to prove reasonableness and the standard basis as set out in CPR r.44.4 (2) is usually the appropriate basis for the taxation.[81] Section 51 enables the court to make an order for costs in respect of an application by a non-party and in those circumstances the undertaking in favour of non-parties adds nothing. If the court decides that the non-party should not get the costs under s.51 the same reasons produce the same result under the jurisdiction conferred by the undertaking.[82]

(10) Security for costs of application to set aside a freezing injunction

11.036   In *Ali and Fahd Shobokshi Group Ltd v Moneim*[83] an application was made to Hoffmann J. for security for costs prior to the hearing of a motion[84] by the plaintiffs to renew Mareva relief which had been granted *ex parte*. The judge made an order for security in an amount which took "into account the possibility that the defendant may be given an order for costs on an indemnity basis". In so doing the judge declined to go into the merits of the pending motion because there was no evidence before the court that, if ordered to provide security for costs, the plaintiffs would be unable to comply. Hoffmann J. made the timely provision of the security a condition for the continuance of the Mareva relief, saying that:

> "I will deal firstly with the point of principle, whether it would be right that the continuance of the Mareva should be conditional not only on the cross-undertaking in damages but also as to there being security for costs. The normal way in which security for costs is required to be provided by a foreign plaintiff is pursuant to an

---

its costs jurisdiction); *Abdul-Haq Al-Ani v Shubber*, *The Times*, April 28, 1999 where one judge had sought to undo the order of another, when the slip rule did not apply, and when the earlier order had been made in the exercise of the first judge's discretion. The correct course was to appeal; *Markos v Goodfellow* [2002] EWCA Civ 1542 (misuse of the slip rule).

[80] *Project Development Co. Ltd SA v KMK Securities Ltd* [1992] 1 W.L.R. 1470 at 1473.

[81] See the reasoning in *British Racing Drivers' Club v Hextall Erskine & Co.* [1996] 3 All E.R. 667.

[82] *Imutran Ltd v Uncaged Campaigns Ltd* [2002] F.S.R. 20 at [45].

[83] [1989] 1 W.L.R. 710.

[84] By Mervyn Davies J., reported at [1989] 1 W.L.R. 710.

application under Order 23. If the court decides that security is appropriate it will order that in default of security, proceedings shall be stayed. Such an order would not be sufficient to do justice in this case because it would leave the plaintiff in possession of its Mareva without the defendant having any assurance that if he successfully moves to discharge it, the costs of his doing so would be covered. Accordingly it would seem to me appropriate in such a case for the court to use its general discretion which derives from s37 of the Supreme Court Act 1981 to ensure that the continuance of the Mareva will not cause injustice to the defendant. In principle therefore I see no reason why the Mareva should not be made conditional not only on the cross-undertaking for damages but also for costs.

[Counsel for the defendant] submits that in this case it would be inappropriate to make such an order at this stage of the proceedings. He points out that an application in ordinary form under Order 23 was made on 27 October and is due to come on with other motions on 20 February. This he says would be the appropriate time for the whole question of security for costs to be considered. The court would then be seised of the merits of the action as emerge from the interlocutory evidence and the merits are matters which the court can take into account in exercising its discretion whether to grant an order for security for costs. If I were to make such an order today I would be deprived of an opportunity to consider the merits.

Now I accept that there are occasions when the courts do take the merits into account. The reason why they do so is because it could be unjust to deprive a meritorious plaintiff of the opportunity to litigate in this country by making his action subject to providing security for costs which in practice he could not provide. That would amount to a summary denial of justice. In this case however there is no suggestion that the plaintiff would be unable to provide the amount of security for which the defendant asks. No doubt it is always inconvenient to have to put up security, but there is no question of the plaintiff being deprived of the opportunity to present his case. On the other hand, if no security is given at this stage there must be a real possibility that the plaintiff, if defeated on the motions later this month, would be tempted to abandon the proceedings here and leave the defendant with an unsatisfied claim for costs.

It seems to me therefore that without investigating the merits further than to acknowledge the possibility that the motions could go either way, the balance of convenience is strongly in favour of giving the defendant reasonable security in respect of his costs as a condition of continuing the Mareva."

In principle the court has *jurisdiction* to order that an injunction, or **11.037** other discretionary remedy, is to be granted or continued only if provision is made for security for costs for the defendant, regardless of whether security for costs would otherwise be available under statute or the rules of court. However, as a matter of *discretion* it is normally to be expected that the court will usually only order security for costs as a condition of granting or continuing discretionary relief, if security for costs could be ordered under CPR Pt 25. This is because if the case falls outside of the ambit of Pt II of CPR Pt 25, this is as a result of policy. For example, there is a policy not to have machinery to order security for costs against a claimant who is an individual resident within the jurisdiction—see CPR r.25.13(2)(a); this is so that such an individual has free access to the court. The same policy about the availability of security for costs is also relevant to whether security for costs should be ordered as a condition of continuance of the discretionary relief. In *Ali and Fahd Shobokshi Group Ltd v Moneim* (above) the plaintiff was a foreign plaintiff who fell within the jurisdiction to order security under what was the former RSC Ord.23. The exercise of the discretion to order security for costs as a condition of the continuance of the injunction in that case was therefore not in conflict with the policy underlying the rules of court governing the availability of security for costs. The question was only one of timing; whether some effective order for provision for security for costs should as a matter of fairness be made before the discharge application was heard and determined.

(11) Security for costs and the inquiry

11.038   A defendant who sought to enforce an undertaking in damages was not a "plaintiff" or "in the position of a plaintiff" within the former RSC Ord.23, r.1(3), and the proceedings to enforce the undertaking were not "an action or other proceeding" within the meaning of the former RSC Ord.23, r.1(1). There was no jurisdiction[85] under that rule, or under s.726 of the Companies Act 1985, to make an order for security for costs against the defendant. This was so whether or not the court has yet exercised its discretion to enforce the undertaking.

Before the former RSC Ord.23, r.1 was made, the court's jurisdiction to order security for costs was derived from its inherent jurisdiction to regulate its proceedings. RSC Ord.23, r.1 was based on the practice of the court in the exercise of that inherent jurisdiction and replaced it by a code which it has been said "must be regarded as . . . complete and exhaustive . . ."[86] The position is the same now under CPR r.25.12 and r.25.13. These only apply to a claimant. The costs of the defendant in prosecuting the inquiry are the costs of working out the consequences of the order granting or continuing the injunction and the claimant's costs of defending the inquiry are not covered by CPR r.25.12—they are not the defendant's "costs of the proceedings".

---

[85] *C.T. Bowring v Corsi and Partners* [1994] 2 Lloyd's Rep. 567.
[86] *ibid.*, at 580, *per* Millet L.J.

Nevertheless, it may be that a defendant is advancing unreasonable claims in circumstances where serious difficulties in enforcing any eventual order for costs are likely. The claimant is then placed in a position of choosing to pay an unreasonable amount by way of settlement, rather than litigate and risk a large costs bill with no prospect of recovering any fruits from an eventual costs order. If this is the case, proceedings to enforce the undertaking may well put unfair and oppressive pressure on the plaintiff.[87]

The members of the Court of Appeal in *C.T. Bowring v Corsi and* **11.039** *Partners* expressed different views as to what could be done in such circumstances. Dillon L.J. considered that the defendant had an immunity from providing security for costs, which continued so as to cover proceedings to enforce and recover damages on the undertaking. However, it is considered that as a matter of *jurisdiction*:

(1) the court has power to release the undertaking or to stop an inquiry and could in an appropriate case do so summarily[88] at any time, either unconditionally or unless the defendant provides security for costs;

(2) the court has a discretion whether to enforce the undertaking, and could decide to do so subject to the provision of security for costs in respect of the ensuing inquiry.

In *C. T. Bowring v Corsi and Partners* Millett L.J. considered that security for costs could be required only in the exceptional circumstances that the claimant can satisfy the court that there is an abuse of the process of the court in the sense that the defendant is pursuing claims which are not genuine so as to put unfair pressure on the claimant and to extract an excessive offer of settlement, or at least where the court "is left in real doubt that the claim is genuine . . .".[89] Sir Michael Kerr agreed that there was jurisdiction in such a case, but expressed the view that the powers to require security for costs were "somewhat wider" than suggested by the expression "abuse of the process of the court". This was in the context of his view that the jurisdiction over the undertaking is a "broad equitable jurisdiction", a view subsequently cited by Millett L.J.[90]

In principle, although there is jurisdiction at any time to release the **11.040** cross-undertaking in damages unless the defendant provides security for costs, it would be appropriate to hear the application to enforce the undertaking before contemplating exercising that power. If, in principle,

---

[87] Contrast *Pearson v Naydler* [1977] 1 W.L.R. 899 for the rationale for requiring security for costs under s.726 of the Companies Act 1985.

[88] *FSL Services Ltd v Macdonald* [2001] EWCA Civ 1008 (see above).

[89] See also *Abraham v Thompson* [1997] 4 All E.R. 362 at 369, *per* Potter L.J. The mere funding of the claim by a third party would not in itself justify granting security for costs but could result in a costs order being made in due course against the third party under s.51 of the Supreme Court Act 1981.

[90] *Barratt Manchester Ltd v Bolton Metropolitan Borough Council* [1998] 1 W.L.R. 1003 at 1009H.

the claimant should pay damages, then it would not ordinarily be just to require security for costs as a condition for enforcement of the undertaking, if this would be likely to prevent enforcement of the undertaking. The discretion is different from that conferred on the court by CPR r.25.12 or s.726 of the Companies Act 1985. The purpose of an inquiry as to damages is purely remedial, namely to restore the defendant to the position he would have been in had the injunction not been granted. The inquiry is merely part of the process of working out the consequences of the order obtained by the claimant, a process which was voluntarily agreed to by the claimant when he furnished his undertaking. This is to be contrasted with the situation where the party against whom security is sought has voluntarily brought the action or counterclaim in order to advance a substantive claim against the party seeking security for costs.

(12) Counterclaims

11.041 In an inquiry as to damages, there is commonly an issue on causation of loss. It may be that the claimant (the defendant in the action) has another way of putting his claim, founded on a substantive cause of action for breach of contract[91] or in tort[92] or otherwise, in which he does not have to prove that the injunction itself was "the" cause of the loss. In such circumstances the issues on the alternative claim may substantially overlap with the issues in the inquiry; indeed they may overlap to such an extent that the claimant in the inquiry can be said to be seeking alternative relief in the event of a particular outcome on issues in the inquiry which have been raised by the defence in the inquiry.

The inquiry is part of the proceedings in the action commenced by the claimant. That action is still "extant";[93] it is still "a cause or matter pending before . . ." the court within the meaning of s.49 of the Supreme Court Act 1981. This is so even though judgment may have been given in the action on the claimant's claim,[94] provided that there has not been both final judgment and satisfaction of that judgment.[95]

In an action based on a substantive cause of action, the defendant can bring the alternative claim against the claimant by way of counterclaim and ask to have it heard at the same time as the inquiry.[96]

---

[91] For example, for breach of a joint venture agreement or other contract between the claimant and defendant in the transaction, on which the claimant has sued.

[92] For example, for maliciously bringing the proceedings and obtaining the injunction; see *Metall und Rohstoff AG v Donaldson Lufkin* [1990] 1 Q.B. 391 at 469.

[93] *CSI International Co. Ltd v Archway Personnel (Middle East) Ltd* [1980] 1 W.L.R. 1069 at 1075, *per* Lord Roskill.

[94] *Salt v Cooper* (1880) 16 Ch.D. 544 at 551; *Hart v Hart* (1881) 18 Ch.D. 670; *Re Clagett, Fordham v Clagett* (1882) 20 Ch.D. 637 at 653.

[95] *CSI International Co. Ltd v Archway Personnel (Middle East) Ltd* [1980] 1 W.L.R. 1069; *Rahman v Sterling Credit Ltd* [2001] 1 W.L.R. 496 (order for possession obtained but not enforced so action still extant); *Laib v Aravindan* [2003] EWHC 2521; *The Times*, November 13, 2003 (property sold by bank under its security and bank repaid but no judgment in the action commenced by the bank, so action still extant).

[96] See Chapter 6, paras 6.060–2 above.

If the claimant is domiciled within a state which is a a Member State **11.042** under Regulation 44/2001,[97] then a counterclaim can be brought in England only if permitted by that Regulation. A tort claim in which the injunction is said to have caused loss would appear to come within Art.5(3) of the Regulation, because the application for and the obtaining of the injunction was "where the harmful event occurred . . .". Article 6(3) allows a counterclaim to be brought if it arises ". . . from the same contract or facts on which the original claim was based, in the court in which the original claim is pending".

By the stage of enforcement of the undertaking, the claimant's claim may have been dismissed so that Article 6(3) would then no longer apply. To avoid this loss of jurisdiction to entertain the counterclaim, a defendant who contemplates seeking an inquiry as to damages after judgment could plead the counterclaim while "the original claim is pending", in contemplation of proceeding with the counterclaim at the same time as an inquiry as to damages, if one is ordered.

In the case of a foreign claimant in an action, whose position is not regulated by Regulation 44/2001 or the Brussels Convention, and who is making a substantive claim against the defendant, the counterclaim can be brought without seeking leave to serve it out of the jurisdiction under CPR r.6.20 and regardless of whether it would fall within that rule.[98]

While security for costs of the counterclaim could be sought under CPR **11.043** r.25.12, or under s.726 of the Companies Act 1985, if the issues substantially overlapped with the issues in an inquiry as to damages which has been ordered, then security should ordinarily be ordered only in respect of the extra costs involved in the counterclaim. This is because the defendant will usually be free to proceed with the inquiry without providing any security for costs, and jurisdiction under CPR Pt 25 or s.726 of the Companies Act 1985 should not be used for securing the claimant for costs attributable to issues in the inquiry. If those costs will be incurred regardless of whether or not the counterclaim is stayed, then providing security for those costs should not be made a precondition of the counterclaim proceeding. This is because it is not the prosecution of the counterclaim as such which threatens to leave the claiamant with an unsatisfied order for costs.

---

[97] Of December 22, 2000 on jurisdiction and the recognition and enforcement of judgments in civil and commercial matters (O.J. No.L012, January 16, 2001, pp.1–23)
[98] *Balkanbank v Taher (No.2)* [1995] 1 W.L.R. 1067; *Metal Scrap Trade Corporation v Kate Shipping* [1990] 1 W.L.R. 115; *Republic of Liberia v Gulf Oceanic Inc.* [1985] 1 Lloyd's Rep. 539; *Balkanbank v Taher (No.3)*, The Times, April 14, 1995 in which subsidiaries of a defendant were joined as defendants pursuant to the former RSC Ord. 15, r.6(2)(b)(ii) so that they also could sue a foreign plaintiff by way of counterclaim for damages in tort. Clarke J. followed the reasoning of Griffiths L.J. in *Union Bank of the Middle East Ltd v Clapham*, The Times, July 20, 1981 and held that the subsidiaries had an arguable case in tort for loss caused by the proceedings brought against the parent company.

(13) The giving of a cross-undertaking after judgment

11.044 If a claimant succeeds at trial on a claim which results in the granting of a final injunction, no cross-undertaking in damages is required. This is because the claimant has succeeded and the final injunction is relief to which he has been adjudged entitled.[99] The injunction goes no wider than to protect the substantive rights of the claimant. If the defendant wishes to appeal against the granting of an injunction without a cross-undertaking, the judge or the Court of Appeal can grant a stay of the injunction pending the hearing of the appeal. As the price for not granting a stay pending appeal, terms can be imposed requiring the claimant to give a cross-undertaking, failing which the injunction will be stayed.[1]

If Mareva relief is sought post-judgment, the purpose is to preserve assets so that the judgment can be satisfied. If such an injunction is sought *ex parte*, or whilst there is the possibility that it may be said that the injunction was wrongly granted, a cross-undertaking must be given.[2] If the relief is granted *inter partes*, after the judgment debtor has had an opportunity to dispute the granting of the injunction if he wishes, then if there is no prospect of an issue about the injunction being "wrongly granted" or improperly used, it may be appropriate to dispense with the cross-undertaking in favour of the judgment debtor. This is because the judgment debtor has brought about the position by defaulting on the judgment. It is still necessary to require the judgment creditor to give the cross-undertaking covering non-parties.

In *Allied Irish Bank v Ashford Hotels Ltd*,[3] there was an order appointing the judgment creditor's solicitor as receiver over a contractual claim against third parties. This claim was being resolved in New York in an action commenced by the third parties against the judgment debtor. The third parties asked that there be an order that the receiver be discharged unless the judgment creditor gave a cross-undertaking in damages. The Court of Appeal held that there was jurisdiction to require a cross-undertaking in damages from a judgment creditor as the price for not discharging an order appointing a receiver by way of equitable execution. However, on the particular facts as a matter of discretion they declined to make such an order, because the third parties had chosen to litigate in New York and should bear the consequences of that decision.[4]

---

[99] *Fenner v Wilson* [1893] 2 Ch. 656.
[1] *Minnesota Mining and Manufacturing v Johnson & Johnson Ltd* [1976] R.F.C. 671.
[2] *Cardile v LED Builders Pty Ltd* (1999) 198 C.L.R. 380 at 401. This is also the reason for a cross-undertaking being necessary when a receiver is appointed *ex parte* by way of equitable execution: *Evans v Lloyd* [1889] W.N. 171, or when an injunction is granted *ex parte* so as to hold the position because property is said to be in jeopardy: *Lloyd's Bank v Medway Upper Navigation Company* [1905] 2 K.B. 359 at 360.
[3] [1997] 3 All E.R. 309.
[4] *ibid.*, at 318–319.

(14) The giving of an undertaking in damages by the claimant as the price for keeping alive a weak claim, the existence of which threatens to cause the defendant loss

In *Blue Town Investments Ltd v Higgs and Hill Plc*[5] the plaintiff brought an **11.045** action for a final injunction requiring the defendant to refrain from continuing with a development on land adjoining that of the plaintiff, and pulling down what had been constructed, on the ground that it interfered with the plaintiff's right to light. The plaintiff's case for an injunction was weak because of the plaintiff's previous acquiescence in the development and delay in seeking relief. The plaintiff did not seek an interim injunction. The defendant applied to strike out the action as vexatious. If the action was permitted to proceed the defendant would have to decide whether to halt the development rather than incur costs of development which would be wasted if the plaintiff succeeded. Sir Nicolas Browne-Wilkinson V.-C. would only allow the action to proceed if the plaintiff applied for an interim injunction supported by the usual cross-undertaking in damages.[6] The cross-undertaking machinery can be a useful tool in cases in which the claimant brings a weak case, when the existence of the claim, threatens to cause loss to the other party. This may be because the existence of the claim interferes with a defendant's own use of his property or the conduct of his business. In such circumstances the court can strike out the claim under CPR r.3.4(2)(b) as abusive, unless the claimant provides a cross-undertaking in damages. This can also be achieved under CPR r.3.1(2)(m).

---

[5] [1990] 1 W.L.R. 696.
[6] See also *Oxy Electric Ltd v Zainuddin* [1991] 1 W.L.R. 115 in which Hoffmann J. considered that there was a seriously arguable case for an injunction at trial and so declined to make such an order.

Chapter 12

The granting of Mareva relief

(1) Need for an underlying "actual or potential action"

(i) *The* Siskina *rule*

In *Siskina v Distos SA (The Siskina)*,[1] Lord Diplock said[2] that s.45(1) of the **12.001**
Supreme Court of Judicature (Consolidation) Act 1925, from which the
power of the court to grant Mareva injunctions was derived, "presupposes
the existence of an action, actual or potential, claiming substantive relief
which the High Court has jurisdiction to grant and to which the interlocutory orders referred to are but ancillary".

The English authorities show that there is a rule that Mareva relief will
be granted only in support of an *existing* cause of action.[3]

In *Chief Constable of Kent v V*,[4] Lord Denning M.R. said that under s.37
(1) of the Supreme Court Act 1981, it was not essential for an injunction to
be ancillary to an action claiming a legal or equitable right. His opinion
was not, however, adopted by Donaldson L.J., and Slade L.J. dissented.
The view of Lord Denning M.R. has subsequently been disapproved.[5]

In Australia, the courts recognised that the requirement should be **12.002**
approached flexibly[6] and that Mareva relief could be available in cases not
falling within the general rule.

---

[1] [1979] A.C. 210.
[2] *ibid.*, at 254.
[3] *Veracruz Transportation Inc. v VC Shipping Co. Inc.* [1992] 1 Lloyd's Rep. 353; *Re Premier Electronics (GB) Ltd* [2002] 2 B.C.L.C. 634 (minority shareholders who were petitioners under s.459 of the Companies Act 1985 had no cause of action against the directors in respect of wrongs done to the company); *Department of Social Security v Butter* [1995] 1 W.L.R. 1528 at 1536H, 1540C–F, 1541H–1542A; *Steamship Mutual Underwriting Associa-tion (Bermuda) v Thakur Shipping* [1986] 2 Lloyd's Rep. 439; *Siporex Trade SA v Comdel Commodities* [1986] 2 Lloyd's Rep. 428 at 436–437; *Ninemia Maritime Corporation v Trave Schiffahrtsgesellschqft GmbH (The Niedersachsen)* [1983] 2 Lloyd's Rep. 600 at 602. See also paras 7.003–4, above on buyer's claims on contracts for the sale of a ship.
[4] [1983] Q.B. 34.
[5] *P v Liverpool Post* [1991] 2 A.C. 370 at 420–421, House of Lords; see also *Chief Constable of Leicestershire v M* [1989] 1 W.L.R. 20 at 22, *per* Hoffmann J.; *South Carolina Co. v Assurantie NV* [1987] A.C. 24 at 39–40, *per* Lord Brandon.
[6] *Patterson v BTR Engineering (Aust) Ltd* (1989) 18 N.S.W.L.R. 319 at 329C–330B, referred to by Lord Nicholls in his dissenting advice in *Mercedes Benz AG v Leiduck* [1996] A.C. 284 at 312A–E; see also paras 1.020–1.

In *Construction Engineering (Australia) Pty Ltd v Tamber*,[7] the Supreme Court of New South Wales granted Mareva relief in substantive proceedings where the claim was subject to an arbitration clause in the *Scott v Avery* form. In *Vereker v Choi*[8] (see also para.13.004, below), the court granted an injunction against the wife of the defendant although there was no cause of action against her, justifying the injunction on the grounds that the case should be regarded as an exception to the general rule.[9] The question whether Mareva relief was so limited was raised but not decided by the Court of Appeal of New South Wales in *Riley McKay Pty Ltd v McKay*.[10] In *Deputy Commissioner of Taxation v Sharp*,[11] the plaintiff had issued tax assessments to the defendant, who owed an existing debt which was not immediately payable. This was held to be sufficient to justify the granting of Mareva relief. The logic of the decision in *Cardile v LED Builders Pty Ltd*[12] is that not even the general rule applies. This is because the justification for the jurisdiction does not depend on the injunction jurisdiction, but on the inherent jurisdiction of the court to prevent abuse of its process.[13]

In *A v B*,[14] Saville J. accepted an argument *ex parte* that an injunction could be granted in a conditional form, worded so that nothing would come into effect until the plaintiff had acquired his cause of action. The plaintiff had entered into a contract to purchase a ship from the defendant and feared that the vessel would be defective on delivery. There was no right to sue for damages until delivery. But, in *Veracruz Transportation Inc. v VC Shipping Co. Inc. (The Veracruz 1)*,[15] the Court of Appeal held that no such jurisdiction exists. Mareva relief can be granted only as ancillary to an existing cause of action.[16] Mareva relief can be granted against a party against whom the claimant has no direct cause of action, when the claimant has an existing cause of action against a defendant, and the injunction sought is ancillary to and in aid of the eventual enforcement of the claimant's asserted rights against the defendant.[17]

---

[7] [1984] 1 N.S.W.L.R. 274.

[8] [1985] 4 N.S.W.L.R. 277.

[9] See also the remarks of Rogers J. in his contribution to Hetherington's *Mareva Injunctions* (1983) at p.29. The general rule was also recognised in *Bank of Queensland Ltd v Grant* [1984] 1 N.S.W.L.R. 409 and *Hortico (Australia) v Energy Equipment Co.* [1985] 1 N.S.W.L.R. 545 at 557.

[10] [1982] 1 N.S.W.L.R. 264 at 277.

[11] (1988) 82 A.C.T.R. 1 (Australian Capital Territory).

[12] (1999) 198 C.L.R. 380.

[13] See Chapter 1, paras 1.020–1.

[14] [1989] 2 Lloyd's Rep. 423.

[15] [1992] 1 Lloyd's Rep. 353, criticised in L. Collins, "The Legacy of The Siskina" (1992) 108 L.Q.R. 175 and in [1993] *Lloyd's Maritime and Commercial Law Quarterly* 309.

[16] *Siporex Trade SA v Comdel Commodities Ltd* [1986] 2 Lloyd's Rep. 428 at 436; *Zucker v Tyndall Holdings plc* [1992] 1 W.L.R. 1127; *Newport Association Football Club Ltd v Football Association of Wales Ltd* [1995] 2 All E.R. 87 (interlocutory injunction granted in an action claiming a declaration that decisions were in unreasonable restraint of trade).

[17] *Yukong Line Ltd v Rendsburg Investments Corporation* [2001] 2 Lloyd's Rep. 113; *C Inc. v L* [2001] 2 Lloyd's Rep. 459 at 474–475, following *Cardile v LED Builders Pty Ltd* (1999)

An action for specific performance may be commenced before the **12.003** contractual date for performance: *Hasham v Zenab*.[18] Until that date, the proceedings for specific performance seek merely declaratory relief. In *Zucker v Tyndall Holdings plc*,[19] the plaintiff had brought proceedings in Switzerland claiming payment in cash under a contract governed by Swiss law with the payment date in the future.[20] The plaintiff's expert evidence on Swiss law was to the effect that the claim was for an immediate right to payment albeit satisfaction of the right would be in three months, time.[21] The plaintiff had also commenced proceedings in England seeking various declarations and specific performance. The Court of Appeal refused Mareva relief on the ground that there was no existing cause of action for invasion actual or threatened, of a legal or equitable right. Neill and Staughton L.JJ. held that there was no jurisdiction to grant Mareva relief for the threatened breach of a term not presently performable.[22] So a debt which exists as a chose in action but where performance is to be in the future (*debitum in praesenti solvendum in futuro*) would not suffice, and there was no jurisdiction to grant Mareva relief in support of that debt. Dillon L.J. held that[23] the plaintiff's right to payment of money depended entirely on Swiss law and that until the Swiss court had made its determination there was no jurisdiction to grant Mareva relief.

In *Zucker v Tyndall Holdings plc* the plaintiff did not argue that there was an existing "cause of action" for damages under Lord Cairns's Act to be awarded instead of specific performance in the English action. This appears to have been because it was no part of the purpose of the English action for specific performance to obtain an order for the payment claimed in Switzerland;[24] it was an action brought so that Mareva relief could be granted in support of the Swiss jurisdiction[25] and the claim being made before the Swiss court for the payment of money under the contract.

198 C.L.R. 380; *Mercantile Group (Europe) A.C. v Aiyela* [1994] Q.B. 366, affirming [1993] F.S.R. 745 (injunction against a wife ancillary to right of plaintiff as a judgment creditor of the husband, who was bankrupt); *TSB Private Bank International SA v Chabra* [1992] 1 W.L.R. 231 (injunction against company when there was evidence that assets held by the company "may . . . be assets . . ." of the first defendant against whom the plaintiff had a claim under a guarantee).
[18] [1960] A.C. 316.
[19] [1992] 1 W.L.R. 1127.
[20] The contract was for transfer of shares but in the events which had occurred the plaintiff alleged that under Swiss law he could obtain an order for payment of money in the place of transfer of the shares.
[21] [1992] 1 W.L.R. 1127 at 1133E–H.
[22] [1992] 1 W.L.R. 1127 at 1135–1136.
[23] The passage at 1137D–E is referring to fixing a fair price when valuation machinery has broken down; see *Sudbrook Trading Estate Ltd v Eggleton* [1983] 1 A.C. 444.
[24] See [1992] 1 W.L.R. at 1137E. *per* Dillon L.J.: "the English court has no jurisdiction to award [the money payment] . . . nor is it asked to . . .".
[25] See Chapter 6, paras 6.020–21 and *Channel Tunnel Group Ltd v Balfour Beatty Construction Ltd* [1993] A.C. 334.

12.004   If at the date of issue of the claim form there is jurisdiction to entertain a claim for specific performance, then even though the time for payment has not yet arrived under the contract, or has not been fixed through service of a notice,[26] it is thought that Mareva relief could still be granted in support of an award of damages under Lord Cairns's Act.[27] The right to such damages in the action does not depend upon there being an existing breach of contract,[28] or an existing contractual right to immediate payment. Nor is the jurisdiction to make the award in the proceedings dependent upon there being loss sustained at the date of issue of the proceedings.[29] The proceedings in which such an award can be made are legitimately before the court and are not premature, and therefore s.37(1) applies to those proceedings and gives jurisdiction for a Mareva injunction to be granted ancillary to the jurisdiction to award damages under Lord Cairns's Act. If Mareva relief were granted which preserved assets of the defendant pending trial those would be available to satisfy an award of damages made at trial under the Act.

If Mareva relief is granted, the practice of the court is to make allowance for interest and costs in calculating the sum in respect of which the injunction is to be granted.[30] Although the claimant has no "cause of action" for interest or costs, these form part of the final relief sought in the action, and, provided the action can be brought, there is no difficulty in principle in granting Mareva relief based on s.37(1) by reference to the final relief sought.[31] This jurisdiction is distinct from the jurisdiction to order security for costs; the jurisdictions have different justifications and the freezing injunction does not create security. The financial limit marks the point above which dissipations whatever their nature are to be permitted. Once it has been decided that the case is a suitable one for Mareva relief, then in fixing the financial limit it is normally "just" to take into account that the final relief is likely to include costs and to allow an amount for this. The extent of the allowance to be made is a matter for the discretion of the court. Usually it is comparatively modest.

---

[26] For example, as in *Marks v Lilley* [1959] 1 W.L.R. 749, which was cited in *Zucker v Tyndall Holdings plc* [1992] 1 W.L.R. 1127 at 1128.

[27] See Chapter 2, paras 2.039–40.

[28] *Oakacre Ltd v Claire Cleaners (Holdings) Ltd* [1982] Ch. 197 (damages under the Act awarded even though the writ for specific performance was issued four days before completion date).

[29] *Chapman, Morsons & Co. v Guardians of the Auckland Union* (1889) 23 Q.B.D. 294. *Attorney-General v Blake* [2002] 1 A.C. 268 at 281 C–E (the same reasoning would apply to awarding damages instead of specific performance as applies to an award of damages instead of an injunction).

[30] *Charles Church Developments plc v Cronin* [1990] F.S.R. 1 at 10; *Fenn Kar Bik Lily v Goh Kim Lay* [1994] H.K.C.F.I. 241.

[31] "to cover any judgment or award which they may reasonably expect to obtain in respect of damages, interest and their own costs . . .", *per* Lord Donaldson M.R. in *Atlas Maritime SA v Avalon (No.3)* [1991] 1 W.L.R. 917 at 920D–E; see also *Jet West Ltd v Haddican* [1992] 1 W.L.R. 498 at 491. But it should not include the costs that the other party may incur in defending the claim: *Atlas Maritime SA v Avalon (No.3)* [1991] 1 W.L.R. 917 at 925G–H.

(ii) Quia timet *relief*

Quia timet[32] relief was available only from the former Court of Chancery 12.005
and became part of the jurisdiction conferred on the High Court by the
Judicature Acts and then s.45 of the Supreme Court of Judicature
(Consolidation) Act 1925 and s.37(1) of the Supreme Court Act 1981. It is
relief granted where there is a threat of an infringement of a right of the
claimant. There is as yet no cause of action in respect of infringement. The
purpose of granting the relief is to prevent the occurrence of an infringement of the claimant's right, *e.g.* a breach of contract, an infringement of a
patent, or a threatened misapplication of funds in respect of which the
claimant has a right. The claimant's right has to be an existing right albeit it
can be one which is only contingent[33] and it had to be a legal or equitable
right recognised by the Court of Chancery as grounding relief.

(iii) Quia Timet *relief in support of a right to an indemnity*

Within this head of jurisdiction is a case in which a person (A) has an 12.006
existing right to be held harmless by another (B) against a potential liability
of (A) to another (C). (A) can obtain equitable relief *quia timet* against (B)
for the purpose of ensuring that (A) never comes under any personal
liability to C.[34] At common law A could sue B for damages for breach of
contract but could only do so when he could prove actual loss.[35]

In Mareva cases the claimant has no right to the assets of the defendant.
The purpose of the injunction is not to prevent conduct which, if it
occurred, would constitute an infringement of a substantive right of the
claimant. In *Mercedes Benz AG v Leiduck*,[36] the Privy Council rejected the
argument that Mareva relief could be regarded as analogous to *quia timet*
relief:

> "With a Mareva injunction the right to the injunction and the ultimate
> right to damages or whatever else is claimed in the action are wholly
> disconnected . . . the threatened dispersal of assets is not a wrongful
> act . . . for subject to any special rules relating to insolvency, a person
> can do what he likes with his own . . .""

---

[32] "Since he fears."
[33] *Flight v Cook* (1755) 2 Ves. Sen. 619, where the plaintiff had a contingent right to be paid
out of certain designated assets.
[34] *Papamichaels v National Westminster Bank* [2002] 1 Lloyd's Rep. 332; *Rowland v Gulfpac
Ltd* [1999] Lloyd's Rep.(Bank.) 86; *McIntosh v Dalwood (No.4)* (1930) 30 S.R. (N.S.W.)
415; *Re Anderson-Berry* [1928] Ch. 290 at 307–308, *per* Sargent L.J., referring to *Ascherson
v Tredegar Dry Dock and Wharf Co.* [1909] 2 Ch. 40; *Firma C-Trade SA v Newcastle
Protection and Indemnity Association (The Fanti and the Padre Island)* [1991] 2 A.C. 1 at
28, 35–36 and 39–41; *Heng Holdings SEA (Pte) Ltd v Tomongo Shipping Co. Ltd* [1997] 3
S.L.R. 547.
[35] *Collinge v Heywood* (1839) 9 Ad. & K. 633, which is explained in *Firma C-Trade SA v
Newcastle Protection and Indemnity Association (The Fanti and the Padre Island)* [1991] 2
A.C. 1 at 35–36 and 39–41.
[36] [1996] A.C. 284 at 303B–G.

The Mareva injunction was outside the *quia timet* jurisdiction exercised by the Court of Chancery. That jurisdiction only applied to restrain conduct which, if it took place, would arguably be an actual infringement of a legal or equitable right. Mareva relief was also unrelated to the jurisdiction conferred on courts of common law by ss.79–81 of the Common Law Procedure Act 1854.

12.007   In *Rowland v Gulfpac Ltd*,[37] the directors of an English company sued that company claiming that they were entitled to an indemnity under their contracts of employment against any liability which it might be found that the directors were under in proceedings brought against them in Idaho by an American company, which was the parent company of the English company. The directors also sought an indemnity in respect of the costs of defending themselves in Idaho—covering both costs incurred and future costs. Rix J. held that as a matter of construction there was not a good arguable case that the particular contractual indemnity covered the Idaho action, but if it had been otherwise, he would have granted an injunction restraining A from disposing of its assets. As a matter of principle equity can grant relief by injunction *quia timet* if there is "a sufficiently clear right to an indemnity . . . together with a clear indication that the indemnifier is going to ignore his obligations". This is so even though there is no accrued cause of action for damages for breach of contract, and even though there has been no breach of the obligation to indemnify.

In *Steamship Mutual Underwriting Assn (Bermuda) v Thakur Shipping*[38] a P and I Club had provided a guarantee so as to avoid arrest of a ship of one of its members. It seems that there was an accrued cause of action for the arrest claim against the member in respect of which the club had given its guarantee, but the club would not become liable under the guarantee until the claim had been prosecuted to judgment against the member, and the member had not paid. A counter-undertaking was given by the member to the club, who believed that the member was moving assets and would default on it. The Court of Appeal declined to grant Mareva relief because as yet there was no accrued cause of action available to the club against its member for payment under the counter-undertaking. Sir John Donaldson M.R. said:

"What [the plaintiff] really wants is security for a future cause of action . . . a cause of action which will give rise to entitlement to monetary relief. I think that that would be contrary to a long line of authority which says that s 37 is to be used in support of an existing legal or equitable right . . . if we extended it to this case, even assuming we have jurisdiction to do so, it would be difficult to see what possible limits there could be to the Mareva jurisdiction."

---

[37] [1999] Lloyd's Rep. (Bank.) 86.
[38] [1986] 2 Lloyd's Rep. 439. A similar statement was made by Mustill J. in *Ninemia Maritime Corporation v Trave Schiffahrtsgesellschaft GmbH (The Niedersachsen)* [1983] 2 Lloyd's Rep. 600 at 602.

It seems that no argument was addressed to the court about the **12.008**
availability of relief to the club against its member *quia timet*. The report
does not set out the terms of the counter-undertaking, but it seems that it
provided that if the club had to pay under the guarantee the member
would pay the club. Such a term was still consistent with the arrangement
between the member and the club being a contract of indemnity with the
member being responsible to indemnify the club against its liability under
the guarantee. Under the contract the cause of action for damages at
common law would not arise until the club could show actual loss.[39]
However, in equity, as a general rule, an indemnity required that the party
to be indemnified should never be required to pay[40] and it is this which
gave rise to the jurisdiction of equity to intervene *quia timet*. It would only
have been if there was a term of the contract between the member and the
club that the club had to pay first and then be reimbursed that the equity
would not intervene.[41] This jurisdiction does not depend upon the guarantor having an existing liability under the guarantee[42]—so, *e.g.* in *Re
Anderson Berry*[43] there was only a threat that the surety would become
liable under its bond if and in the event that the administrator acted
improperly. Nor does it depend upon the liability which is the subject of
the guarantee being an existing and quantified liability which has already
accrued[44]—in *Re Anderson Berry* the administrator was threatening acts
which if committed would render the surety liable. The member was
threatening acts the result of which would leave the club exposed to having
to pay a liability without being reimbursed when, as between them, the
member was responsible for holding the club indemnified. The *quia timet*
jurisdiction against the principal debtor does not depend upon the guarantor having a vested cause of action against the debtor for the debt—its
purpose is to prevent the guarantor from having to pay anything under his
guarantee. It does not follow from the fact that no debt was yet due to the
club that the court was without the power to act *quia timet* to preserve
assets of the member for the purpose of ensuring that the club would be
held harmless and would not have to bear the liability.[45]

[39] *Collinge v Heywood* (1839) 9 Ad. & E. 633.
[40] *Re Richardson* [1911] 2 K.B. 705 at 716.
[41] *Firma C-Trade SA v Newcastle Protection and Indemnity Association* [1991] 2 A.C. 1 at 35D–36C.
[42] *Thomas v Nottingham Incorporated Football Club* [1972] Ch. 596—it did not matter whether in the case of a demand guarantee a demand for payment had been made. See also *Stimpson v Smith* [1999] Ch. 340 and *Papamichaels v National Westminster Bank* [2002] 1 Lloyd's Rep. 332.
[43] [1928] Ch. 290.
[44] *Papamichaels v National Westminster Bank* [2002] 1 Lloyd's Rep. 332 at [53–72]; *Rowland v Gulfpac Ltd* [1999] 1 Lloyd's Rep. (Bank.) 86 at 98. Contrast *Snell's Equity* (13th ed., para.29–11, relying on *Morrison v Barking Chemicals Co. Ltd* [1919] 2 Ch. 325 which was not followed in *Thomas v Nottingham Incorporated Football Club* [1972] Ch. 596.
[45] *Papamichaels v National Westminster Bank* [2002] 1 Lloyd's Rep. 332 at [63–66]; *Rowland v Gulfpac Ltd* [1999] 1 Lloyd's Rep.(Bank.) 86; it is considered that in *Heng Holdings SEA (Pte) Ltd v Tomongo Shipping Co. Ltd* [1997] 3 S.L.R. 547, the injunction ancillary to the

(iv) The differences between an injunction to enforce a solicitor's "lien" on proceeds of litigation and Mareva relief

12.009   A solicitor has a "lien" on any fund recovered as the fruits of his exertions and this right is protected both at common law and in equity. The use of the word "lien" has been criticised[46] because the right does not depend on possession of the fruits, and the right is in the nature of an equitable interest in the fund. There is also a statutory jurisdiction entitling a solicitor to obtain a declaration of charge on property recovered or preserved.[47]

In *Re Q's Estate*[48] the daughter of a wealthy man brought proceedings against other members of her family in a foreign country challenging the dispositions made by his will which had omitted her. Her challenge was successful in that the beneficiaries agreed to settle her claim for a very large sum of money. The lawyers had acted on a contingency fee retainer and sought to freeze the proceeds of the settlement pending payment of the fee. Rix J. held that there was no jurisdiction to grant Mareva relief to the plaintiff lawyers against the daughter because they had no vested cause of action. There was no cause of action for the fee until the proceeds of the settlement agreement were paid over to the daughter.

12.010   The plaintiffs did not argue that they were entitled to an attorney's or solicitor's "lien" under their retainer. The principles which apply to this lien are:

(1) It is based on the consideration that where an "attorney"[49] who has expended effort, and often also his own money, has produced the fruits of litigation, he should have an interest in those proceeds for his fees and disbursements.[50] The same principle applies to receivers, provisional liquidators and liquidators who by their own efforts secure proceeds from litigation. The principle appears to apply to any "attorney" who is lawfully employed by the client to conduct litigation on his behalf. It does not apply to barristers because they have no right to sue for their fees and the client, who is entitled to the proceeds, has no liability to the barrister.

---

claim to enforce the indemnity by requiring security, was incorrectly classified as being a Mareva injunction when it was an injunction to preserve assets which could be used to provide the promised security, and thus part of the *quia timet* relief. Since the plaintiff had won on its claim on the indemnity to *quia timet* relief this should in itself have been a strong factor against enforcing the undertaking in damages, see also para.11.021 above.

[46] *Re Fuld No.4* [1968] P. 727 at 735–736; *ex p. Patience; Makinson v The Minister* (1940) 40 S.R. (N.S.W.) 96.

[47] Solicitors Act 1974, s.73.

[48] [1999] 1 Lloyd's Rep. 931.

[49] *Read v Dupper* (1795) 6 T.R. 361.

[50] *Firth v Centrelink* (2002) 55 N.S.W.L.R. 451; *Firth v Centrelink No.2* (2002) 55 N.S.W.L.R. 494; *Twigg v Kung* (2002) 55 N.S.W.L.R. 485.

(2) A "solicitor's lien" applies to proceeds whether obtained under a judgment or a compromise.[51]

(3) It gives rise to a form of equitable interest in the proceeds of the litigation, including any order for costs, analogous to what is created by an assignment for value of future property.[52]

(4) It takes effect as soon as the proceeds come into existence.

(5) A person who, with notice of the assertion of the lien, pays out the proceeds, is liable to pay again.

(6) In a bankruptcy the lien entitles the solicitor to claim against the proceeds in priority to the unsecured creditors.[53]

(7) It applies regardless of whether the solicitor is continuing to act for the client when those proceeds actually come into existence.[54] The later solicitor who in fact effects the final recovery has priority over the earlier solicitor.[55]

(8) It gives the solicitor no greater right to the proceeds of the litigation than his client could have assigned to him.[56]

The retainer in *Re Q's Estate* was governed by English law and contained **12.011** a London arbitration clause. Arguably it entitled the lawyers to the "lien" for their contingency fees as soon as the proceeds came into existence and regardless of the fact that the lawyers did not have the proceeds in their possession. Such a right could have been protected by relief granted *quia timet*, in appropriate circumstances, in anticipation of the proceeds of their exertions coming into existence and going into the bank account of their client in Jersey. This is because the misapplication of the proceeds by the client would itself have been an interference with the lawyers' property right in the fund. The plaintiffs failed to show a real risk of dissipation of assets by the daughter[57] and this finding would have been relevant,

---

[51] *Ross v Buxton* (1889) 42 Ch.D. 190 at 198–199; *Ex p. Patience: Makinson v The Minister* (1940) 40 S.R. (N.S.W) 96 at 100, *Firth v Centrelink* (2002) 55 N.S.W.L.R. 451 at paras 34 and 35; *Halvanon Insurance Co. Ltd v Central Reinsurance Corporation* [1988] 1 W.L.R. 1122 at 1129G–1130B.

[52] In *Ex p. Patience; Makinson v The Minister* (1940) 40 S.R. (N.S.W.) 96 at 100, Jordan C.J. said that the solicitor's right to have his costs paid out of the money was "analogous to the right which would be created by an equitable assignment of a corresponding part of the money by the client to the solicitor".

[53] *Re Born* [1900] 2 Ch. 433; *Re Meter Cabs Ltd* [1911] 2 Ch. 557.

[54] *Re Wadsworth* (1886) 34 Ch.D. 155; *Knight v Gardner* [1892] 2 Ch. 368.

[55] *Re Wadsworth* (1886) 34 Ch.D. 155; *Wimborne v Fine* [1952] Ch. 869; *Halvanon Insurance Co. Ltd v Central Reinsurance Corporation* [1988] 1 W.L.R. 1122 at 1130B–C.

[56] *Halvanon Insurance Co. Ltd v Central Reinsurance Corporation* [1988] 1 W.L.R. 1122 at 1130F–1131B.

[57] See [1999] 1 Lloyd's Rep. at 932 LHC. Where there is a proprietary claim based on an equitable interest which may be extinguished through dealings with the asset the court can intervene by injunction against anyone holding the assets who is threatening to deal with them: *London and County Banking Company v Lewis* (1882) 21 Ch.D. 490 (equitable mortgagee entitled to injunction against third party volunteers, who had refused to give an appropriate undertaking, to restrain dealings with the mortgaged property pending conveyance of it to the mortgagee through enforcement by the court of the mortgage).

conclusive, when considering under the *quia timet* jurisdiction whether the plaintiffs had proved a real threat that the proceeds would be misapplied.

Notice could also have been given to the bank of the claim to the lien so that when the bank did receive the proceeds they would not have been able to pay them away without being potentially liable to pay again.

(v) *The* Siskina *rule: proprietary claims right to be paid out of a "fund" or for a fund to be preserved*

12.012   The *Siskina* rule that before there can be a Mareva injunction there must be an accrued cause of action does not apply to a freezing injunction granted in support of a proprietary claim. This is because equity can intervene by injunction granted *quia timet* in relation to property not yet in existence when there was a present threat to make away with it as soon as it came into existence.

Another possible way of putting the point in *Re Q's Estate* was that the retainer was to be interpreted as requiring the contingency fee to be paid out the fund which would come into existence when there was completion. Normally a contingency fee arrangement would require the fee to be paid out of the proceeds with the client being entitled to the balance. Provided that there was a legal obligation owed to the creditor to pay him from the fund, this would give rise to an equitable charge on the fund.[58]

Another is that under the retainer the client had agreed not to spend the proceeds before she had paid the lawyers. The negative promise is sufficient justification for equity to intervene to protect that fund,[59] even though there was no equitable charge on it.[60] A contractual or other legal obligation not to deal with a fund except in a particular way can be enforced by injunction.

These rights to equitable intervention enabled the court to grant relief *quia timet.*

12.013   The right to safeguard the fund so as to be paid out of it would also have been sufficient to enable the court to make an order under what was then RSC Ord. 29, r.2(3) and is now CPR r.25.1(1)(l) once the fund came into existence, even though it gave rise to no security interest. In *Myers v Design Inc. (International)*[61] a creditor sought to invoke this power in order to obtain an immediate payment into court of the amount of the debt. The application was unsuccessful in that case because there was only a disputed

---

[58] *Flightline v Edwards* [2003] 1 W.L.R. 1200 at [43–47]; *Palmer v Carey* [1926] A.C. 703 at 706–707; *Swiss Bank Corporation v Lloyd's Bank Ltd* [1982] A.C. 584 at 613. See also para. 23.006 below.

[59] *Cummins v Perkins* [1899] 1 Ch. 16; *Kearns v Leaf* (1864) 1 M. & M. 681. In *Bradley Resources Corporation v Kelvin Energy Ltd* (1985) 18 D.L.R. (4th) 468 there was a statutory right of a shareholder to be paid for his minority shareholding, and the injunction can be regarded as granted to preserve the company's assets as a fund from which, under the statute, the shareholder was entitled to be paid.

[60] *Flightline v Edwards* [2003] 1 W.L.R. 1200 at [47].

[61] [2003] 1 W.L.R. 1642.

debt and no relevant "fund" out of which the claimant was entitled to be paid or in respect of which the claimant had a right, and thus no "fund" to be preserved.

(vi) The Siskina *rule: preservation of "corporeal" property under s.33(1) of the Supreme Court Act 1981*

Under s.33(1) of the Supreme Court Act 1981:   12.014

"33. POWERS OF HIGH COURT EXERCISABLE BEFORE COMMENCEMENT OF ACTION

(1) On the application of any person in accordance with rules of court, the High Court shall, in such circumstances as may be specified in the rules, have power to make an order providing for any one or more of the following matters, that is to say—the inspection, photographing, preservation, custody and detention of property which appears to the court to be property which may become the subject-matter of subsequent proceedings in the High Court, or as to which any question may arise in any such proceedings; and the taking of samples of any such property as is mentioned in paragraph (a), and the carrying out of any experiment on or with any such property."

Section 35 has supplementary provisions which include in s.35(5) that "'property' includes any land, chattel, or any other corporeal property of any description". So it must have a body.

CPR r.25.1(1) (i) lists:

"(i) an order under section 33 of the Supreme Court Act 1981 or section 52 of the County Courts Act 1984 (order for disclosure of documents or inspection of property before a claim has been made);".

Under CPR r.25.2(4):

"(4) In particular, the court need not direct that a claim be commenced where the application is made under section 33 of the Supreme Court Act 1981 or section 52 of the County Courts Act 1984 . . ."

The jurisdiction is also referred to in CPR r.25.4(1)(b) which provides   12.015
for the general rules about applications in CPR Pt 23 to apply to an application made seeking to invoke it, and in CPR 25.5 which includes:

"(1) This rule applies where a person makes an application under—

(a) section 33(1) of the Supreme Court Act 1981 or section 52(1) of the County Courts Act 1984 (inspection etc. of property before commencement);

(2) The evidence in support of such an application must show, if practicable by reference to any statement of case prepared in relation to the proceedings or anticipated proceedings, that the property—

(a) is or may become the subject matter of such proceedings; or
(b) is relevant to the issues that will arise in relation to such proceedings."

The words "property which may become the subject-matter of subsequent proceedings" in s.33(1) and the words "property . . . may become the subject matter of such proceedings" in CPR r.25.5 appear to be wide enough to justify an order being made now when there is a threat to make off with what will be the applicant's tangible property as soon as it comes into existence. If there will be a proprietary claim in respect of future property, then proceedings can be brought under s.33(1) to preserve that property in contemplation of subsequent substantive proceedings in the High Court. Section 44(1) and (2) of the Arbitration Act 1996 enable the equivalent order to be made "for the purposes of and in relation to arbitral proceedings . . .". Therefore the same power is exercisable by the court under s.44(1) of the Arbitration Act 1996 to make an order now in relation to property which "may become the subject of", or "as to which any question may arise", in subsequent arbitral proceedings.

12.016   The *Siskina* rule does not apply to a claim in respect of "corporeal" property within the scope of s.33. This is because the jurisdiction applies pre-action. Section 33(1) provides a free-standing jurisdiction to make an order now, providing for the preservation custody or detention of tangible property which may become the subject-matter of future proceedings or as to which any question may arise in any such proceedings. This applies to future proceedings asserting a proprietary claim in the High Court, or, by virtue of s.44(1) of the Arbitration Act 1996, to future arbitral proceedings.

What about a case in which a valuable painting is about to be received by the intended defendant and it is feared that soon after he receives it he will make away with it? Does the applicant have to wait until the defendant has received the painting before the proceedings under s.33 can be brought and an order obtained? As long as the evidence is that the painting will be the subject-matter of the future substantive proceedings if they are commenced, or will be relevant to the issues in those proceedings, if they are commenced, this is enough to bring the position within the section. It is thought that an order can be made which will apply to the painting as soon as it is received by the respondent.

(vii) Insolvency Act 1986, ss.423–425

12.017   These provisions relate to transactions defrauding creditors.[62] If there has already been a transfer of assets falling within the statutory provisions,

---

[62] See Chapter 13, paras 13.018–29, below.

orders can be made for the purpose of preserving those assets pending the resolution of an action seeking relief in respect of them.[63] The applicant has a cause of action under the statute for substantive relief in respect of the fund constituting those assets.

The court can also intervene to prevent a disposal which, if it were made, would fall within these provisions. This is because a creditor or a person who may in the future have a claim against the defendant has a right not to be made a victim of a transaction which would fall within the sections. Relief can be granted *quia timet* to an applicant to prevent his becoming a "victim" of an intended transaction provided that it can be proved that there is a threat to enter into such a transaction with the requisite intent, *i.e.* for a purpose within s.423(3).[64]

Thus, there could be a case in which an applicant for relief (A) will be owed money in a few days' time by B, who is intending to take his assets out of the jurisdiction and dissipate them. In such a case there could be no Mareva injunction granted in England under s.37 of the Supreme Court Act 1981 because of the *Siskina* rule.[65] However, if A could prove that B was threatening to dispose of his assets for the dominant purpose of ensuring that A was never paid, then A could seek *quia timet* relief to stop a transaction being entered into by B for the purpose of defrauding his creditors. If B could not be served within the jurisdiction but the assets were in England and Wales, such a claim would come within CPR 6.20(2), r.1(1) (b) because the injunction would be sought on the basis of a substantive right conferred on the applicant by the statute.

---

[63] See *Re Mouat* [1899] 1 Ch. 831 and *Beyfus v Bullock* (1868) L.R. 7 Eq. 391 decided under the statute 13 Eliz c.5 which was the statutory predecessor to s.172 of the Law of Property Act 1925, and ss.423–425 of the Insolvency Act 1986. See also *Aiglon v Gau Shau* [1993] 1 Lloyd's Rep. 164 in which Mareva relief was granted against the transferee; *Cardile v LED Builders Pty Ltd* (1999) 198 C.L.R. 380 at paras 55 and 65–68; *Aetna Financial Services Ltd v Feigelman* [1985] 1 S.C.R. 2 at para.9, *per* Estey J. referring to *Campbell v Campbell* (1881) 29 Gr. 252 at 254–255 and *Toronto Carpet Co. v Wright* (1912) 3 D.L.R. 725; *Reiser (Robert) and Co. Inc. v Nadorfe Food Processing Equipment Ltd* (1977) 81 D.L.R. (3rd) 278; *City of Toronto v McIntosh* (1977) 16 O.R. (2d) 257; *Kuan Han Pty Ltd v Oceanview Group Holdings Pty Ltd* [2003] F.C.A. 1063 (September 12, 2003) (claim based on s.37A of the Conveyancing Act 1919 (NSW) which corresponds to what was s.172 of the Law of Property Act 1925).

[64] See Chapter 13, paras 13.019–13.021. It is considered that the court could restrain such a transfer *quia timet* if there was a clear threat of such a transfer to a transferee against whom no effective relief could be obtained in respect of the assets if transferred. The dictum in *Campbell v Campbell* (1881) 29 Gr. 252 at 254–255 quoted by Estey J. in *Aetna Financial Services Ltd v Feigelman* [1985] 1 S.C.R. 2 at para.9 that the court would not intervene before transfer assumes that an injunction granted after transfer in respect of the asset will be effective to preserve the position. It was because the intended disposal was for the purpose of reorganisation of the US company in Chapter 11 proceedings and not for a purpose within s.423(3) that this argument failed in *Rowland v Gulfpac Ltd* [1999] Lloyd's Rep.(Bank.) 86.

[65] See the concern of Lord Nicholls in *Mercedes Benz A.C. v Leiduck* [1996] A.C. 284 at 312B–E.

(viii) Commencement of proceedings

12.018 The court can grant an "interim remedy" which includes[66] an injunction, freezing injunction or search order, at any time including before proceedings are started or after judgment.[67] The court can grant the remedy before proceedings are started only if "the matter is urgent"[68] or "it is otherwise necessary to do so in the interests of justice".[69] Unless the court otherwise orders a defendant may not apply for an interim remedy until after he has filed an acknowledgment of service or a defence.[70] The purpose of this is to ensure that the defendant has submitted to the jurisdiction of the court before any remedy is granted to him, or irrevocable arrangements are made for this to be done.

(ix) Civil Jurisdiction and Judgments Act 1982, s.25

12.019 Under s.25, interim relief can be granted where proceedings have been or are to be commenced abroad. Under CPR r.25.2(1)(a) there is jurisdiction to grant an injunction before proceedings are started. Under s.25 and CPR r.25.4(1)(a), there is not a precondition that the foreign proceedings have in fact been started. However. there must be an intention to commence the foreign proceedings, because the purpose of the relief is to operate in support of the foreign proceedings.

The purpose of Mareva relief granted under s.25 is to preserve assets in contemplation of an eventual judgment in the foreign proceedings which can be enforced against the assets. What preconditions have to be met in order to launch the relevant proceedings abroad is a matter for the foreign court, applying whatever law it considers is appropriate.

(x) When there is a risk of dissipation if a disputed debt is paid and there are potentially serious consequences for the paying party if the disputed debt is not paid immediately

12.020 A situation which can arise where the *Siskina* rule creates a difficulty is where a paying party disputes that he owes money under a contract, which includes provision for payment of interest at an enhanced rate if amounts are not paid when due, and the only reason that the paying party is not paying and awaiting a refund once the dispute is eventually determined is the risk of dissipation of assets by the receiving party. The contractual provision for the elevated interest rate may well not be invalid as a penalty,[71] because it reflects the increased risk to the creditor of a debt

---

[66] CPR r.25.1(1).
[67] CPR r.25.2(1).
[68] CPR r.25.2(2)(b)(i).
[69] CPR r.25.2(2)(b)(ii), *e.g.* to avoid tipping off the intended respondent.
[70] CPR r.25.2(2)(c).
[71] *Lordsvale Finance Plc v Bank of Zambia* [1996] Q.B. 752.

which has not been paid when it is due. When the paying party is justifiably concerned at the risk of dissipation of assets by the recipient, how does he protect himself against this without making himself liable for further interest running at the elevated contractual rate? A similar difficulty arises if there is a cancelling clause which entitles the receiving party to cancel a contract unless the correct payment is made on time, and the amount of that payment is in dispute.

The problem can arise at any time pending final determination of whether he owes the money.

CPR r.25.1(1)(l) does not apply because there is no specified fund over which there is a dispute.[72] It is difficult to see how CPR r.25.1 (1)(c) could apply because of the definition of "relevant property" in CPR r.25.1(2) and because the dispute is only about the amount of the debt.

If he chooses to pay voluntarily, it could be a payment made under a mistake of fact or of law, if he is right in the underlying dispute. This could be so if as a matter of fact the paying party would not have made the payment had he known the true position about the recipient's entitlement to the payment;[73] the eventual result in the underlying dispute would then retrospectively show that a mistake had been made by him. But he has paid deliberately, knowing of the dispute, weighing up what he should do, and having done so to stop the accrual of contractual interest, or of the right to cancel, in case he is wrong in the underlying dispute. It would be difficult for him, immediately following his payment, to justify an interim freezing injunction on the proceeds based on his payment having been made by mistake. Much better to have an interim order made in advance of payment which enables him to pay without being exposed to the risk of dissipation, and which protects everyone's legitimate entitlements and expectations. **12.021**

A possible solution is that the court may appoint a receiver[74] under s.37(1) of the Supreme Court Act 1981 to receive that part of the debt which is in dispute and give good discharge for it, with the beneficial entitlements to the fund so created being ascertained according to the result in the substantive proceedings. If the order provides for this to be the result of the paying party constituting the fund in the hands of the receiver, then when he does so he is making payment under a declaration of trust, the terms of which are in the order. The fund so created would be held according to the beneficial interests stipulated in the order. Those interests would depend upon whether the disputed amount is due. This circumvents the *Siskina* rule because the fund would then be a trust fund, and not the defendant's money subject to a claim to freeze it made under the Mareva jurisdiction. In effect the court would have intervened prior to payment being made to stop the continuing accrual of interest or the right to cancel once the paying party has made over a fund of which the receiving party

---

[72] See para.12.93, above.
[73] See the majority in *Kleinwort Benson Ltd v Lincoln City Council* [1999] 2 A.C. 349.
[74] See Chapter 16.

would have immediate beneficial ownership if he is correct in the underlying dispute, but not otherwise.

12.022   Whether the court would make such an order would depend upon the particular circumstances including whether the real risk of dissipation had only become apparent to the paying party after he had concluded the relevant contract or whether this was a known risk at that time. In principle the court could also achieve the same interim holding order by granting a mandatory injunction requiring the defendant to direct the paying party to make payment under the contract through payment pursuant to the order into court or into an account in joint names of solicitors, and with the order providing what are to be the beneficial interests in the fund so created by the parties.[75]

(2) Good arguable case

12.023   It was established early in the emergence of the Mareva jurisdiction that the plaintiff did not need to show that his case against the defendant was so strong that he was likely to obtain summary judgment.[76] The test is whether the claimant has a "good arguable case".[77] In *Rasu Maritima v Perusahaan Pertambangan*, Lord Denning M.R. observed[78] that this test applied in the context of granting leave to serve out of the jurisdiction, and was "in conformity with" the test for granting injunctions laid down by the House of Lords in *American Cyanamid Co. v Ethicon Ltd*.[79]

In *Derby & Co. Ltd v Weldon*, Parker L.J. said[80] that the court must not try to resolve conflicts of evidence on affidavit, or to decide difficult questions of law which call for detailed argument and mature consideration.[81] Thus, cases concerning Mareva injunctions fall to be dealt with in accordance with the *approach* laid down in the *American Cyanamid* case, but with the special feature that the minimum test to be satisfied is that of a "good arguable case" as compared with the test ordinarily applicable to injunction cases, namely that there is a serious question to be tried. "A

---

[75] See the discussion in Chapter 23, para.23.009.
[76] *Rasu Maritima SA v Perusahaan Pertambangan* [1978] Q.B. 644.
[77] *Ninemia Maritime Corporation v Trave GmbH (The Niedersachsen)* [1983] 1 W.L.R. 1412 at 1415–1417. In *Aetna Financial Services Ltd v Feigelman* [1985] 1 S.C.R. 2 at para.30, Estey J., delivering the judgment of the Supreme Court of Canada, put the requirement as showing a "strong prima facie case" following *Chitel v Rothbart* (1982), 39 O.R. (2d) 513 at 522 and this test is used generally in Canada as opposed to a "good arguable case".
[78] [1978] Q.B. 644 at p 661.
[79] [1975] A.C. 396.
[80] [1990] Ch. 48 at 57–58; May L.J. agreed with these views at 56 and Nicholls J. at 64.
[81] Citing from the speech of Lord Diplock in *American Cyanamid* [1975], A.C. 396 at 407–408. See also *Allied Trust Bank v Shukri Financial Times*, November 14, 1989, and *Frogmore Estates plc v Berger* (1989) 139 N.L.J. 1560 at 1561.

stronger case must be shown than would justify relief of a less stringent kind."[82]

In *Ninemia Maritime Corporation v Trave Schiffahrtsgesellschaft GmbH (The Niedersachsen)*,[83] Mustill J. described a good arguable case as "one which is more than barely capable of serious argument, but not necessarily one which the judge considers would have a better than 50 per cent chance of success".[84]

This conclusion had been reached earlier by Mustill J. in relation to the meaning of "good arguable case" on an application for leave to serve a writ out of the jurisdiction under the former RSC Ord.11, r.1, in which there was a dispute on the facts. In *Orri v Moundreas*,[85] Mustill J. had said:

12.024

> "The judge is not required to apply the standard of proof which must be attained at the trial . . . Since this standard is one of the balance of probabilities it must follow that the plaintiff does not fail under Order 11 just because he cannot demonstrate a better than even chance that the qualifying condition is satisfied.
>
> This still leaves open the question how far short of an even chance the prospects are allowed to fall before the court should refuse leave under Order 11. Here the words 'strong' and 'good' do become material. It is not enough to show an arguable case, namely, one which a competent advocate can get on its feet. Something markedly better than that is required, even if it cannot be said with confidence that the plaintiff is more likely to be right than wrong."

In Mareva cases the all-important question is whether, in the circumstances of the case, it is "just and convenient"[86] to grant the injunction. A requirement that the court must form the provisional view that the claimant will probably succeed at trial would be plainly inconsistent with an approach which enables the court to achieve "its great object viz abstaining from expressing any opinion upon the merits of the case until the hearing".[87] Nevertheless, the court will take into account the *apparent* strength or weakness of the respective cases in order to decide whether the

---

[82] *Lewis v Freighthire Ltd*, Court of Appeal (Civ Div) Transcript No.519 of 1996 (February 1, 1996), *per* Millett L.J., *cf.* the view of Rogers A.J.A in Patterson v BTR Engineering (Aust) Ltd (1989) 18 N.S.W.L.R. 319 at 330E–331C, who considered that strength of case and risk of dissipation should be looked at together without pre-set minimum criteria for each, and the similar view of Huddart J. in *Mooney v Orr* (1994) 100 B.C.L.R. (2d) 335 at 348–349 (British Columbia).

[83] [1983] 2 Lloyd's Rep. 600 at 605.

[84] Followed in *Nycal (UK) Ltd v Lacey* [1994] C.L.C. 12 at 20. This test was applied in relation to a disputed question of law by Bingham J. in *Siporex Trade SA v Comdel Commodities* [1986] 2 Lloyd's Rep. 428 at 438–439; see also on a disputed question of law *Page v Combined Shipping Co.* [1997] 3 All E.R. 656 and *Donelly v Karess Properties Ltd* [1998] C.I.L.R. Notes–13.

[85] [1981] Com. L.R. 168.

[86] Supreme Court Act 1981 s.37(1).

[87] *Derby & Co. Ltd v Weldon* [1990] Ch. 48 at 57.

claimant's case, on the merits, is sufficiently strong to reach the threshold,[88] and this will include assessing the apparent plausibility of statements in affidavits.[89] The test is not a particularly onerous one, however.

12.025   Although a good arguable case remains the minimum requirement, the judge's view of the merits of the claimant's case and his chances of ultimate success are obviously important factors in the exercise of his discretion. Sufficient of the facts giving rise to the claim must be set out in the affidavit to enable the judge to make a realistic assessment of the merits. On an *ex parte* application the claimant must place before the court the results of inquiries conducted by him or on his behalf into the claim and into defences or partial defences which may be raised by the defendant, even though the legal burden of proof in relation to those possible defences lies upon the defendant. The claimant must disclose all defences to the claim which the defendant has already raised, or which are open to him, though he need not indulge in speculation.[90]

The fact that the claimant has a claim which is unanswerable or virtually incapable of being defended may be a powerful factor in favour of granting the Mareva injunction, though it cannot be decisive in itself.[91] But the court may infer the necessary risk of the judgment going unsatisfied from the behaviour of the defendant if he kept promising to honour a bill of exchange but persistently defaulted with implausible excuses, or if the defendant, after a lengthy silence, or after admitting liability, raised extremely thin defences once the matter became the subject of litigation.

The claimant may have an independent right to proceed on his claim against some other party as well as against the defendant in question. If so, that is likely to be a material matter to be taken into account by the court in the exercise of its discretion, and will fall to be dealt with as one of the circumstances of the particular case.[92]

12.026   A situation which may cause problems is where the claimant's claim may be met by a time-bar defence, which in turn may be defeated if the claimant obtains leave to prosecute the claim out of time (*e.g.* under s.12 of the Arbitration Act 1996). In such circumstances the court should take into account the merits of the claimant's application for leave to prosecute out

---

[88] In *Allied Trust Bank v Shukri, Financial Times*, November 14, 1989, Lloyd L.J. reiterated the observations of Parker L.J. that the time taken in arguing a Mareva case should be "measured in hours, not days . . ." and that appeals should be "rare", and in general confined to matters of principle. See also *Frogmore Estates plc v Berger* (1989) 139 N.L.J. 1560 at 1561 and *Bakarim v Victoria P. Shipping Co.* [1980] 2 Lloyd's Rep. 192 at 198.

[89] *Silvera v Faleh Al-Rashidi*, Court of Appeal (Civ Div) Transcript No.1039 of 1993 (August 17, 1993); *Eng Mee Yong v Letchumanan* [1980] A.C. 331 at 341. On an application for summary judgment in deciding whether there is "no real prospect" of success under CPR r.24.2(a), the court likewise looks at the credibility of affidavit evidence, see *National Westminster Bank v Daniel* [1993] 1 W.L.R. 1453. This text was cited with approval in *Jau-Hwa Stewart v E.Excel Ltd* [2001] HKCFI 866 (August 30, 2001) at paras 64–65.

[90] See further paras 9.004–5, above.

[91] See para.12.041, below.

[92] See, *e.g. A v C (No.1)* [1981] Q.B. 956 at 961.

of time,[93] together with all the other relevant factors, and grant a freezing injunction, if appropriate, pending the determination of the claimant's application for an extension of time. If that application is successful, and a freezing injunction would still be appropriate, the court could then extend the order. If the application for an extension of time fails, the claimant will almost certainly have to bear the costs of the initial application for the injunction, but his exposure to liability under the cross-undertaking in damages would have been of relatively short duration, and his position would have been adequately safeguarded pending the determination of the application for the extension of time.

(3) Counterclaims and the obtaining of Mareva relief

(i) Jurisdiction

The jurisdiction of the court to entertain counterclaims is derived from **12.027** s.49(2) of the Supreme Court Act 1981, which preserves the court's earlier jurisdiction under ss36 and 39 of the Supreme Court of Judicature (Consolidation) Act 1925: *Balkanbank v Taher (No.2)*.[94] The rules of court provide procedural machinery for the exercise of that jurisdiction. Under s.39(1) of the 1925 Act, the defendant could be granted relief against the plaintiff which "the defendant has properly claimed by his pleading . . ." To grant Mareva relief in respect of the counterclaim, the court must have jurisdiction to entertain the counterclaim. Since the claimant has brought proceedings against the defendant, there is a right to counterclaim to which the provisions about service of the claim form out of the jurisdiction in CPR Pt 6 do not apply.[95] The claimant, by bringing the proceedings, has brought himself within the jurisdiction for the purposes of those proceedings.

If the claimant has already obtained judgment in the proceedings but that judgment has not yet been satisfied then, with the court's permission the defendant can still make a counterclaim.[96] This is because the proceedings are still extant.

If the claimant has already served his particulars of claim, the defendant is entitled to serve a counterclaim, together with his defence without

---

[93] For example, see *Comdel Commodities Ltd v Siporex Trade SA* [1997] 1 Lloyd's Rep. 424 at 431–432 in which there was an appeal pending against an order dismissing the claim for want of prosecution.

[94] [1995] 1 W.L.R. 1067.

[95] *Balkanbank v Taher (No.2)* [1995] 1 W.L.R. 1067 at 1071–1074, where the earlier authorities were reviewed; the claimant has had to give an address for service within the jurisdiction under CPR r.6.5.

[96] CPR r.20.4(2)(b); *Rahman v Sterling Credit Ltd* [2001] 1 W.L.R. 496 distinguishing *CSI International Co. Ltd v Archway Personnel (Middle East) Ltd* [1980] 1 W.L.R. 1069, in which the judgment had been satisfied and no counterclaim could be made because the proceedings were no longer extant.

obtaining the court's permission.[97] Also Mareva relief can be granted in respect of the counterclaim before it is made but on an undertaking to commence it: this applies CPR r.25.2(3) to the counterclaim and is also in line with what the position was under the former rules of court.[98]

The question might arise whether the counterclaim could still be made if the claimant then sought to discontinue as of right under CPR r.38.2 before service of the defence and counterclaim. CPR r.38.5 provides that:

"When discontinuance takes effect where permission of the court is not needed

38.5 (1) Discontinuance against any defendant takes effect on the date when notice of discontinuance is served on him under rule 38.3(1).

(2) Subject to rule 38.4, the proceedings are brought to an end as against him on that date.

(3) However, this does not affect proceedings to deal with any question of costs."

This prevents the defence being served, but does it prevent service of a pleading setting out the counterclaim?

12.028   If the Mareva relief has already been obtained prior to the discontinuance, then the better view is that the counterclaim has already been made even though the formal pleading has not been served.[99] Furthermore if the injunction has already been granted and there is also the potential issue of costs, the proceedings are still extant; the "cause or matter"[1] is still pending before the court notwithstanding the claimant's discontinuance. CPR r.38.5(2) does not affect this because it means that the proceedings *against* the defendant are at an end except for costs. Therefore under CPR r.20.4(2)(b) the court can grant permission to make the counterclaim by serving a formal pleading, and make directions for service of particulars of counterclaim as a free-standing pleading.[2]

Another answer is that CPR r.38.4(1) enables an application to be made within a time limit of 28 days after service of a notice of discontinuance, to

---

[97] CPR r.20.4(2)(b).

[98] *Ernst & Young v Butte Mining plc* [1996] 1 W.L.R. 1605 at 1614B–1615G; *Fakih Brothers v A. P. Moller (Copenhagen) Ltd* [1994] 1 Lloyd's Rep. 103; see also *M v Home Office* [1994] 1 A.C. 377 at 423 (an interim injunction can be granted before an application for leave to apply for judicial review).

[99] *Fakih Brothers v A. P. Moller (Copenhagen) Ltd* [1994] 1 Lloyd's Rep. 103 at 110 and *Ernst & Young v Butte Mining plc* [1996] 1 W.L.R. 1605 at 1615D–G.

[1] See s.39(1) of the 1925 Act.

[2] CPR r.20.4(2)(b) and CPR Pt 20, Practice Direction, para.6.1 envisage that the counterclaim does not have to be served with the defence and this distinguishes *The Gnieszno* [1968] P. 418 in which no counterclaim could be made because no pleading which made the counterclaim could be served under the rules of court then in force because no defence could be served.

strike out the notice and, if granted, this would be an answer to the problem.[3]

It is suggested that in order to avoid these questions arising, if an injunction is to be sought in relation to a proposed counterclaim then the defendant should at the time of the application apply also for the court's permission to make the counterclaim under CPR r.20.4(2), and for directions providing for service of particulars of counterclaim. Then if the claimant does subsequently discontinue as of right the defendant can serve particulars of counterclaim as a free-standing document.

If a claim has been discontinued as of right or pursuant to permission **12.029** before any application for an injunction has been made, then the question is whether the proceedings are still extant. If they are then CPR r.20.4(2)(b) is still available, but the fact that there is no substantive claim against the defendant is very relevant to how the discretion is to be exercised.

(ii) Mareva relief in counterclaim cases

In most cases where the counterclaim arises only if the claim fails (*e.g.* if **12.030** each party alleges that the other wrongfully terminated a contract), the court will assess the merits of the claim in the usual way. It may grant a Mareva injunction for the full amount of the claim (*e.g.* as in *Avant Petroleum Inc v Gatoil Overseas Inc.*[4] Alternatively, the court may be willing to grant a Mareva injunction only on terms that the claimant makes available a fund within the jurisdiction upon which the defendant could execute a judgment should he succeed on the counterclaim. In cases in which both the claim and the counterclaim could succeed, the court has to go through the more complex exercise of reviewing the relative merits of each claim, and assessing how much (if anything) the applicant is likely to recover at the end of the case. The court might decide to limit the amount of the injunction to the sum by which the claim exceeds the counterclaim (or vice versa if the defendant is seeking the injunction). There are, though, cases where the claim and counterclaim effectively cancel each other out. This was the position in *Barry (JD) Pty Ltd v M&E Construction Ply Ltd.*[5] One of the factors which the court must take into account is the likelihood that the claim or counterclaim will be extinguished.

A further variant arises in cases in which the claimant is to obtain summary judgment against the defendant on the claim, leaving the defendant seeking Mareva relief on the counterclaim: *e.g.* if the claimant's

---

[3] Notice of discontinuance was struck out as an abuse of the process in *Fakih Brothers v A. P. Moller (Copenhagen) Ltd*, above, where had it been necessary to apply for leave to discontinue terms would have been imposed and the discontinuance without leave was an attempt to avoid imposition of the terms; see also *Ernst & Young v Butte Mining plc* [1996] 1 W.L.R. 1605 at 1615D–G, where on the facts the notice of discontinuance was set aside as an abuse of the process (see at 1622D–K).

[4] [1980] 2 Lloyd's Rep. 236.

[5] [1978] V.R. 185 at 187.

claim is on a bill of exchange and the defendant has a good counterclaim (*e.g.* for damages under the sale contract in respect of which the bill of exchange was given). Can the defendant obtain a Mareva injunction on the counterclaim? The position appears to be as follows:

(1) The existence of the claimant's claim is an important factor to be taken into account in deciding whether to grant Mareva relief and, if so, upon what terms.

(2) The court may grant an immediate Mareva injunction against the claimant restraining him from disposing of the claim (*e.g.* by assigning the claim or its proceeds or negotiating the bill of exchange on which the claim is based). This would not be inconsistent with the principle that the claimant's claim is one on which he is entitled to payment free of any claim of set-off or stay of execution. Thus if the claimant had already obtained judgment on the claim, the defendant could obtain Mareva relief to restrain the plaintiff from dealing with the proceeds of the judgment: *Montecchi v Shimco (UK)*;[6] *Intraco Ltd v Notis Shipping Corporation*.[7] This is because an injunction restraining the claimant from disposing of the fruits of his judgment is not the same as taking action (*e.g.* by staying execution) which would prevent the claimant from obtaining the cash. Accordingly, if the claimant has not yet obtained judgment, an injunction restraining him from disposing of the claim is not the same as preventing him from prosecuting his claim to judgment and obtaining cash under that judgment.

(3) As a matter of discretion, the court may not be prepared to grant the defendant Mareva relief in respect of the counterclaim unless he undertakes to secure the claimant's claims together with interest and costs (*e.g.* by providing a bank guarantee or making a payment into court).

(4) If the counterclaim exceeds the claimant's claim, the court may grant the defendant Mareva relief over the claimant's claim together with further Mareva relief over other assets of the claimant, in respect of the amount by which the counterclaim exceeds the claimant's claim. Again, the granting of such relief may be made conditional upon the claimant's claim being secured.

12.031   If the claimant succeeds in obtaining a Mareva injunction on a claim and there is a counterclaim, the question may arise as to whether the claimant can also obtain security for costs in respect of the defendant's counterclaim. If the Mareva injunction has succeeded in trapping substantial assets of the defendant within the jurisdiction, then no order will be made

---

[6] [1979] 1 W.L.R. 1180 at 1183–1184.
[7] [1981] 2 Lloyd's Rep. 256 at 258.

in favour of the claimant for security for costs to be provided on the counterclaim. This may also be the position if the Mareva injunction has meanwhile been varied, with the defendant providing the claimant with partial security for the claim: *Hitachi Shipbuilding & Engineering Co. Ltd v Viafel Compania Naviera SA.*[8]

(4) A real risk that a judgment or award may go unsatisfied

(i) Test is of objective risk of dissipation

The early authorities in which the principles governing the exercise of the 12.032
Mareva jurisdiction were first laid down tended to suggest that the applicant would have to satisfy the court that the defendant would remove his assets from the jurisdiction *for the purpose* of defeating any judgment which the plaintiff might obtain against him. This was interpreted in at least one case as meaning that it was necessary to show "nefarious intent".[9] This would have been an extremely difficult test to satisfy, because it is far from easy to prove the defendant's subjective state of mind in relation to future dealings with his assets.

In *Ninemia Maritime Corporation v Trave Schiffahrtsgesellschaft GmbH (The Niedersachsen)*,[10] Mustill J. at first instance set out a series of citations[11] from Mareva cases[12] directed to the risk the applicant had to show, and invited the Court of Appeal, if the case should go further, to give guidance. In the Court of Appeal, the applicable test was formulated as:

> ". . . whether, on the assumption that the plaintiffs have shown 'a good arguable case', the court concludes, on the whole of the evidence then before it, that the refusal of a Mareva injunction would involve a real risk that a judgment or award in favour of the plaintiff's would remain unsatisfied."[13]

---

[8] [1981] 2 Lloyd's Rep. 498 at 508–509.
[9] *Home Insurance Co. v Administration Asigurarilor de Stat* (unreported) referred to by Kerr L.J. at [1983] 1 W.L.R. 1412 at 1422.
[10] [1983] 1 W.L.R. 1412, CA (affirming Mustill L.J., reported at [1983] 2 Lloyd's Rep. 600 at 601–602).
[11] [1983] 2 Lloyd's Rep. 600 at 605–606.
[12] *Mareva Compania Naviera SA v International Bulkcarriers Ltd* [1975] 2 Lloyd's Rep. 509; *Rasu Maritima SA v Perusahaan* [1978] Q.B. 644; *Iraqi Ministry of Defence v Arcepey Shipping* [1981] Q.B. 65; *Third Chandris Shipping Corporation v Unimarine SA* [1979] Q.B. 645 at 669 (*per* Lord Denning M.R.) and 672 (*per* Lawton L.J.); *Montecchi v Shimco (UK) Ltd* [1979] 1 W.L.R. 1180 at 1183–1184; *Barclay-Johnson v Yuill* [1980] 1 W.L.R. 1259; *Rahman v Abu-Taha* [1980] 1 W.L.R. 1268; *Z Ltd v A-Z and AA-LL* [1982] QB 558 at 571 (Lord Denning M.R.) and 585–586 (*per* Kerr L.J.).
[13] [1983] 1 W.L.R. 1412 at 1422.

12.033   It is now clear that to justify Mareva relief, there is no requirement for an applicant to show that the defendant intends to deal with his assets with the *purpose* of ensuring that any judgment will not be met.[14] The test is an objective one of assessment of the risk that a judgment may not be satisfied. This approach has also been adopted in Australia.[15]

In Canada, the Court of Appeal in Ontario referred in *Chitel v Rothbart*[16] to the judgment of Lord Denning M.R. in *Third Chandris Shipping Corporation v Unimarine*[17] and said:

"Turning finally to item (iv) of Lord Denning's guidelines—the risk of removal of these assets before judgment—once again the material must he persuasive to the court. The applicant must persuade the court by his material that the defendant is removing or there is a real risk that he is about to remove his assets from the jurisdiction to avoid the possibility of a judgment, or that the defendant is otherwise dissipating or disposing of his assets, in a manner clearly distinct from his usual or ordinary course of business or living, so as to render the possibility of future tracing of the assets remote, if not impossible in fact or in law."

---

[14] *Ketchum International plc v Group Public Relations* [1997] 1 W.L.R. 4 at 13A–D, referring to *Ninemia Maritime Corporation v Trave Schiffahrtsgesellschaft GmbH* [1983] 1 W.L.R. 1412 at 1422 and *R. v Secretary of State for the Home Department Ex P. Muboyayi* [1992] Q.B. 244 at 257H, which explained the dictum of Lord Donaldson M.R. in *Derby & Co. Ltd v Weldon (Nos 3 and 4)* [1990] Ch. 65 at 76 ("the fundamental principle . . . is that . . . no court should permit, a defendant to take action designed to ensure that subsequent orders of the court are rendered less effective than would otherwise be the case") so that "designed" did not mean "intended". The dictum of Kerr L.J. in *Z Ltd v A-X and AA-LL* [1982] Q.B. 558 at 585, which also used the phrase "designed to ensure", has similarly to be reinterpreted. *Patterson v BTR Engineering (Aust) Ltd* (1989) 18 N.S.W.L.R. 319 at 321–322, *per* Gleeson C.J.: *Glenwood Management Group Pty Ltd v Mayo* [1991] 2 V.R. 49 at 53, *per* Young C.J.; *Dixon & Webster v Liddy* [2002] S.A.D.C. 143 (November 12, 2002) at para.60. See also Chapter 20, paras 20.053–4 (variations allowing payment out of assets within the jurisdiction when there may be assets available outside the jurisdiction). For criticism of the objective approach, see T. Willoughby and S. Connal. "The Mareva Injunction: A Cruel Tyranny" (1997) 8 E.I.P.R. 479 at 481.

[15] *Hayden v Teplitzky* (1997) 154 A.L.R. 497; *National Australia Rank Ltd v Bond Brewing Holdings Ltd* (1990) 169 C.L.R. 271 at 277, High Court of Australia; *Jackson v Sterling Industries Ltd* (1987) 162 C.L.R. 612 at 623, High Court of Australia; *Beach Petroleum v Johnson* (1992) 9 A.C.S.R. 404, Federal Court of Australia; *Patterson v BTR Engineering (Aust) Ltd* (1989) 18 N.S.W.L.R. 319 at 321–322; *Hortico (Australia) Pty Ltd v Energy Equipment Co. (Australia) Pty Ltd* (1985) 1 N.S.W.L.R. 545 at 557–558; *Ausbro Ferex Pty Ltd v Mare* (1986) 4 N.S.W.L.R. 419 at 423–424.

[16] (1982) 39 O.R. (2d) 513 at 532–533. See also: *Gudaitis v Abacus Systems Inc.* (1995) 35 C.P.C. (3rd) 266; *Di Menza v Richardson Greenshields of Canada Ltd* (1989) 74 O.R. (2d) 172; *Price v CIBC* (1987) 19 C.P.C. (2d) 13, New Brunswick Court of Appeal. The Canadian case law is discussed by Robert Sharpe in *Injunctions and Specific Performance* (1999, looseleaf edition, published by Canada Law Book Inc.) at para.2.880. Some Canadian judgments suggest that the plaintiff must, show that the defendant intends to frustrate enforcement of a judgment (*R. v Consolidated Fastfrate Transport Inc.* (1995) 125 D.L.R. (4th) 1 at 14–15, the majority basing themselves on passages in *Aetna Financial Services Ltd v Feigelman* [1985] 1 S.C.R. 2, in which the Supreme Court of Canada had upheld the Mareva jurisdiction). This would place an evidential burden on the plaintiff which would seldom be met and which would in practice emasculate the jurisdiction. Others follow the objective test.

[17] [1979] Q.B. 645 at 669.

In *O'Mahony v Horgan*,[18] the Irish Supreme Court set aside a Mareva **12.034**
injunction on appeal in a case in which the claim was brought by a
liquidator of a company against the directors for £11.5 million and the
relevant asset was an amount of £71,000 payable to one of the directors,
who was a farmer, under an insurance policy in respect of a fire which
destroyed a shed. Hamilton C.J. relied (*inter alia*) on a dictum of Kerr L.J.
in *Z Ltd v A-Z and AA-LL*, to the effect that it was a necessary precondition
to Mareva relief that there were reasons to believe that the defendant "may
well take steps designed to ensure that [assets] are no longer available or
traceable when judgment is given against him", and treated that dictum as
authority for the proposition that the applicant had to show that the
apprehended dissipation of assets would be made for the purpose and with
the intention of evading any decree that might be made.[19] However, that
dictum must now be treated as explained by the later cases as not requiring
proof of subjective intention. O'Flaherty J. (with whom Blayney J. agreed)
refused the relief on the ground that the £71,000 was so little in
comparison to the amounts claimed that it was not appropriate to freeze it.
He also said[20] that "the Mareva remedy is to protect assets which may be
dissipated . . ." and that "the case in regard to assets has not been made
out even to a *prima facie* extent . . .".[21] These observations are consistent
with the objective test. The decision in *Felixstowe Dock & Railway Co. v
United States Lines Inc.*[22] illustrates that the court is not concerned with
motive or purpose as opposed to effect. The defendant was an insolvent
company incorporated in the United States and the subject of proceedings
in New York under Chapter 11 of the United States Federal Bankruptcy
Code. If the English assets of the defendant were repatriated to New York,
the consequence would have been to prejudice the English claimants (who
intended to apply for summary judgment on their claims) because they
would have been unlikely to obtain payment even pro rata with the
creditors in the United States. Although the purpose of the intended
transfer was to advance the commercial interests of the defendant,
nevertheless Mareva relief was granted because, in the circumstances of the
case, the balance of convenience strongly favoured the assets remaining in
England, where in due course they could be the subject of ancillary
winding-up proceedings as a result of which they would be fairly distributed among the relevant creditors. Hirst J. declined to treat the

---

[18] [1996] I.L.R.M. 161.
[19] [1996] I.L.R.M. 161 at 168. See also *Deutsche Bank Aktiengesellschaft v Murtagh* [1995] 1
I.L.R.M. 381; *Countyglen plc v Carway* [1995] 1 I.L.R.M. 481 and *Fleming v Ranks
(Ireland) Ltd* [1983] I.L.R.M. 541.
[20] [1996] I.L.R.M. 161 at 170.
[21] The judgment at first instance is quoted at p.165 of the report and proceeded on whether
there was a likelihood that the money would be spent. But it would not be the purpose of a
Mareva injunction to prevent expenditure of the insurance proceeds on a replacement shed
or in the ordinary course of business. So the judge at first instance asked himself the wrong
question, namely whether the money would still be there by the time of judgment as
opposed to whether there was a real risk of inappropriate dissipation of assets. This point is
made by Hamilton C.J. at p.169.
[22] [1989] Q.B. 360.

existence of the Chapter 11 proceedings in New York and the wish of the defendants to make the English assets available to be dealt with under its provisions, as a paramount or overriding factor, inconsistent with the granting of Mareva relief.[23]

In *Customs and Excise Commissioners v Anchor Foods Ltd*[24] the Customs sought payment of alleged arrears of customs duties which were being challenged by the defendant, which wished to make a transfer of its business to a new company, which was not at arm's length from the defendant, at a valuation approved by a firm of accountants. The Customs challenged that valuation and obtained Mareva relief. The possibility of the transfer being challenged subsequently under ss238 and 423 of the Insolvency Act did not give Customs complete protection and there was the risk that if the transfer proceeded the defendant's assets would be diminished because the accountants had under valued the business.

12.035   In *Derby & Co. Ltd v Weldon*,[25] it was submitted that in regard to Mareva relief in respect of assets situated outside the jurisdiction there was a requirement that the applicant produce evidence of "previous malpractice or nefarious intent". This was not, however, accepted by the court, even in the context of the wide relief (described by May L.J. as "draconian") sought in that case.

A defendant may be openly arranging to leave the jurisdiction with his family and assets pursuant to a plan made long ago. This may provide the basis for granting Mareva relief,[26] because the court is concerned with the effect of the defendant's conduct as opposed to the motives underlying it. An exercise of discretion refusing relief because the motives for the move may be innocent is liable to be set aside on appeal: *Ulfcar International AS v Miles*.[27]

In *Stronghold Insurance Co. Ltd v Overseas Union Insurance*,[28] the defendant was a financially solid company carrying on business in

---

[23] See also *Rowland v Gulfpac Ltd* [1999] Lloyd's Rep. (Bank.) 86, where Rix J. (*obiter*) would have granted Mareva relief against an English subsidiary company, restraining it from transferring assets to its American parent company to he used in a reorganisation under Chapter 11.

[24] [1999] 1 W.L.R. 1139.

[25] [1990] Ch. 48.

[26] *Ulfcar International AS v Miles*, Court of Appeal (Civ Div) Transcript No.808 of 1991 (August 29, 1991), where the defendant had openly moved abroad with his wife and daughter; *Glenwood Management v Mayo* [1991] 2 V.R. 49 (Victoria); *Lee Kuan Yew v Tang Liang Hong (No.1)* [1997] 2 S.L.R. 819 at para.23; contrast *Di Menza v Richardson Greenshields of Canada Ltd* (1989) 74 O.R. (2d) 172 where relief was refused when a family had moved abroad before the stock market crash which had given rise to the claim, and a judgment would be enforceable where they had moved.

[27] Court of Appeal (Civ Div) Transcript No.808 of 1991 (August 29, 1991).

[28] [1996] L.R.L.R. 13. In *Aetna Financial Services Ltd v Feigelman* [1985] 1 S.C.R. 2 the Supreme Court of Canada declined to grant relief against a company operating in various provinces, and transferring assets across provincial borders because in Canada there is a federal system and judgments can readily be enforced in other provinces. But there can still be circumstances in which the relief will be granted because of the cost and delay of enforcing across provincial borders: *Gateway Village Investments Ltd v Sybra Food Services Ltd* (1987) 12 B.C.L.R. (2nd) 234. In Australia Mareva relief will not be granted because of

Singapore, where any London arbitration award would be readily enforceable. The defendant's London operation had been transferred to Singapore and the run-off of the London business was being conducted from Singapore. It was not disputed that the defendants wished to transfer out of the jurisdictioin all funds collected from London brokers. Potter J. upheld Mareva relief on the ground that the effect of the funds being transferred to Singapore would be to leave the claimant having to go to the extra expense of enforcing an award for a relatively small amount in Singapore and having increased delay in payment. The money collected from brokers in London on the run-off ought to remain available in London to meet claims.

It may be that the defendant would in the ordinary course expect to **12.036** receive payment of a debt out of the jurisdiction from his debtor within the jurisdiction. The fact that such remittance would not be *designed* to prejudice enforcement in due course of a future judgment does not preclude the granting of Mareva relief. Nor does the fact that such a remittance would be an ordinary commercial transaction confer immunity. In such circumstances Mareva relief can be granted, and the claimant would be prudent[29] to seek an order which expressly restrains the defendant from taking steps to obtain or accept payment of the debt, except payment into a designated account.

(ii) Unjustifiable disposals[30]

It is not every risk of a judgment being unsatisfied which can justify Mareva **12.037** relief:

(1) A defendant may be faced with insolvency if the claimant's claim succeeds. However, regardless of whether this is so, in the meantime[31] the defendant is entitled to carry on business,[32] and it would be contrary to principle for Mareva relief to be granted for the purpose either of preventing the defendant from doing so, or

---

threatened transfer of assets from one State or Territory to another: *Brew v Crouch* [1998] S.A.S.C. 6633 (April 23, 1998); *Parsram v Australian Foods* [2001] N.S.W.S.C. 436 (May 15, 2001) at para.13.

[29] In view of *Bank Mellat v Kazmi* [1989] Q.B. 541; see generally paras 3.013–4, above.

[30] See also Chapter 20, paras 20.042–8, where unjustifiable disposals are discussed in the context of variations to an injunction.

[31] Once judgment has been obtained the position is different: see Chapter 3, paras 3.023–7, above.

[32] *Normid Housing Association Ltd v Ralphs and Mansell (No.2)* [1989] 1 Lloyd's Rep. 275; *Avant Petroleum Inc. v Gatoil Overseas Inc.* [1986] 2 Lloyd's Rep. 236; *Iraqi Ministry of Defence v Arcepey Shipping* [1981] Q.B. 65; *J. P. Morgan Multi-Strategy Fund LP v Macro Fund Ltd* [2002] C.I.L.R. 569 at paras 8–15 (investment funds not restrained from redeeming shares in the ordinary course of business because this was not the type of dealing which was to be restrained by Mareva relief); *Hortico (Australia) Pty Ltd v Energy Equipment Co. (Australia) Pty Ltd* (1985) 1 N.S.W.L.R. 545 at 558; *Gold Leaf Investments Inc. v Uniform International* Court of Appeal (Civ Div) Transcript No.582 of 1990 (June 7, 1990); *Marine Atlantic Inc v Blyth* (1994) 113 D.L.R. (4th) 501, Federal Court of Canada.

preserving some assets for the claimant in case he succeeds at trial;[33] thus relief was refused in *Kruger (Service) Gibraltar v In-Town Developments Ltd*[34] in which the defendant was a subsidiary of a large group of companies, which was used as single purpose vehicle for the particular transaction and the applicant knew at the time of concluding the transaction of its lack of assets.

Because Mareva relief pre-judgment is not granted for the purpose of interfering with ordinary business transactions it follows that even if there is some element of speculative risk in such a transaction the court will still not interfere with it.[35]

(2) An individual is entitled to pay his ordinary[36] living expenses. Mareva relief will not be granted so as to prevent him using his assets to pay such expenses.[37]

(3) A defendant may have some pre-existing legal or moral obligation to a third party which it is appropriate for him to satisfy (*e.g.* repay a loan). Mareva relief should not be granted for the purpose of preventing the defendant from honouring the obligation even though in consequence the risk of an eventual judgment going unsatisfied is substantially increased.[38]

(4) In *O'Mahony v Horgan*[39] the defendant farmer might have used the insurance proceeds to build a new shed or pay expenses of running the farm. Mareva relief would not be granted to prevent this.

---

[33] *K/S A/S Admiral Shipping v Portlink Ferries* [1984] 2 Lloyd's Rep. 166; *Hurrell v Fitness Holdings Europe*, unreported, March 15, 2002 (repayment to parent company of loan in the ordinary course of business); *Bond Brewing Holdings Ltd v National Australia Bank Ltd* [1991] 1 V.L.R. 386, Supreme Court of Victoria, Full Court; *J.P. Morgan Multi-Strategy Fund LP v Macro Fund Ltd* [2002] C.I.L.R. 569 at para.12; *Marine Atlantic Inc. v Blyth* (1993) 113 D.L.R. (4th) 501. *Tranquil Holdings Ltd v Hudson* (1987) 2 P.R.N.Z. 551.

[34] Civil Appeal No.18 of 1999 (Gibraltar).

[35] *Deputy Commissioner of Taxation v Ngu* (1996) 32 A.T.R. 125 at 127, Supreme Court of New South Wales, Commercial Division, *per* Bainton J.: ". . . I can see no justification for sterilising . . . [a] taxpayer's funds preventing him from carrying out a development which may, to some extent, be speculative on the basis that tax may, or will, become payable . . . and the money . . . [will] be locked up in some commercial development . . .'; *Halifax Plc v Chandler* [2001] EWCA Civ 1750 at [18] (the defendant obtained permission to use assets to prosecute an action against a third party which involved risk).

[36] *i.e.* "ordinary, recurrent expenses in maintaining the subject of the injunction in the style of life to which he is reasonably accustomed": *TDK Tape Distributor v Videochoice Ltd* [1986] 1 W.L.R. 141 at 146. An over-extravagant lifestyle may itself justify the granting of Mareva relief: *3 Style Ltd v Cross*, Court of Appeal (Civ Div) Transcript No.395 of 1990 (April 11, 1990); *Ng Chun-fai v Tamco Electrical & Electronics (Hong Kong) Ltd* [1994] 1 H.K.L.R. 289. See also para.20.066, below.

[37] *Law Society v Shanks* [1988] F.L.R. 504; *PCW (Underwriting Agendas) Ltd v Dixon* [1983] 2 Lloyd's Rep. 197; *Mayo Associates SA v Anagram (Bermuda) Ltd* [1995] J.L.R. 190 at 204; *Baptiste Builders Supply Ltd v F. W. Smith* [1995] J.L.R. Notes-16a

[38] *Iraqi Ministry of Defence v Arcepey Shipping* (above); *J. P. Morgan Multi-Strategy Fund LP v Macro Fund Ltd* [2002] C.I.L.R. 569 at para.12.

[39] [1996] I.L.R.M. 161, see also para.12.034, above.

In assessing the risk of dissipation the court is concerned with the risk of dissipation which, if it were to take place, would be "unjustifiable",[40] not the overall risk of whether the asset will be preserved intact until judgment in the action, including the risk of proper expenditure. What is "unjustifiable" depends upon the purpose of the injunction. **12.038** What is justifiable before judgment may become unjustifiable once there is a judgment and the judgment creditor is entitled to be paid.[41]

(iii) Solid evidence of risk of dissipation by the defendant

The claimant must adduce "solid evidence" to support his assertion that **12.039** there is a real risk that the judgment or award will go unsatisfied.[42] Since each case depends on its own facts it is impossible to lay down any general guidelines on satisfying this evidential burden, but some of the factors which may be relevant are as follows:[43]

(1) The nature of the assets which are to be the subject of the proposed injunction, and the ease or difficulty with which they could be disposed of or dissipated.[44] The claimant may find it easier to establish the risk of dissipation of a bank account, or of moveable chattels,[45] than the risk that the defendant will dispose of real estate, *e.g.* his house or office. Nevertheless, in appropriate cases Mareva injunctions can be, and have been, granted where the defendant's

---

[40] *Ketchum plc v Group Public Relations Ltd* [1997] 1 W.L.R. 4 at 10F–G, *per* Stuart-Smith L.J. In *Mediterranean Feeders LP v Bernd Meyering Schiffahrts*, Court of Appeal (Civ Div) Transcript No.966 of 1997 (June 5, 1997), Evans L.J. said (at 9C–D of the transcript) in relation to a German shipowning partnership which had lost its ship and expected to receive insurance money that ". . . there must be a risk that it will be used otherwise than for normal and proper commercial purposes"; see also *Marine Atlantic Inc. v Blyth* (1993) 113 D.L.R. (4th) 501.
[41] See Chapter 3, paras 3.023–4, above.
[42] *Ninemia Maritime Corporation v Trave Schiffahrtsgesellschaft GmbH (The Niedersachsen)* [1983] 2 Lloyd's Rep. 600 at 606–607, *per* Mustill J. *Choy Chee Kee Collin v Public Utilities Board* [1997] 1 S.L.R. 604 at paras 19–22; *Lee Kuan Yew v Tang Liang Hong (No.1)* [1997] 2 S.L.R. 819 at para.7; *Meespierson NV v Industrial and Commercial Bank of Vietnam* [1998] 2 S.L.R. 632 at para.16.
[43] In *O'Regan v Iambic Productions* (1989) 139 N.L.J. 1378 at 1379, Sir Peter Pain approved these factors as a "very useful check list . . . as to the sort of factors about which the court should have information before it decides to grant an application for a Mareva injunction". See also *Guan Chong Cocoa Manufacturer Sdn Bhd v Pratiwi Shipping SA* [2003] 1 S.L.R. 157 at para.20 referring to these factors.
[44] See *CBS United Kingdom Limited v Lambert* [1983] Ch.37 and paras 22.035–7 below; discussing an order for delivery up of valuables or cash. The fact that a defendant's house is not in his own name can be relevant as indicating that if a judgment is obtained there may well be difficulties in enforcing it: *Pearce v Waterhouse* [1986] V.R. 603 (Victoria).
[45] But if the chattels are ordinarily moved from country to country in the usual course of the defendant's business, the relief may well be refused on the grounds that it would interfere with the business or tend unfairly to put pressure on the defendant to settle the claim: *Gold Leaf Investments Inc. v Uniform International* Court of Appeal (Civ Div) Transcript No.582 of 1990 (June 7, 1990) (injunction refused in respect of *grand prix* racing cars). *Rocket Cargo (NZ) Ltd v Chipperfield Enterprises Ltd* (1988) 2 P.R.N.Z. 566 (injunction refused in respect of removal of ill circus animals from New Zealand to Indonesia).

only known asset within the jurisdiction is his house (*e.g.* if he has put it up for sale[46] and has evinced an intention to go and live abroad).

(2) The nature and financial standing of the defendant's business:[47] see Lord Denning's remarks about certain types of offshore company in *Third Chandris Shipping Corporation v Unimarine*,[48] and Lawton L.J.,[49] and *Siporex Trade SA v Comdel Commodities Ltd*.[50] Contrast, however, *The Niedersachsen*:[51] even a "one-ship" company incorporated in Panama or Liberia may be a subsidiary of a substantial company incorporated elsewhere, and would be likely to honour its debts.

(3) The length of time the defendant has been in business. Stronger evidence of potential dissipation will be needed where the defendant is a long-established company with a reasonable market reputation[52] than where little or nothing is known or can be ascertained about it.

(4) The domicile or residence of the defendant. At one time, Mareva injunctions were granted to prevent only foreign defendants from removing their assets from the jurisdiction to defeat a judgment or arbitration award. While the jurisdiction has widened to include domestic defendants, the court will be less ready to infer that a defendant who is based in England, and has a home or established business here, will remove or dissipate his assets. On the other hand, if the defendant company, though English, is controlled by an offshore company of the kind described by Lord Denning in *Third Chandris Shipping Corporation v Unimarine*, the inference that there

---

[46] *GE Capital Australia v Davis* [2001] N.S.W.S.C. 933 at para.7 (house put up for sale after defendants' companies had gone into liquidation leaving a substantial claim on the guarantees and no defence put forward). The fact that a defendant puts property up for sale or has ceased to carry on business may, depending on the circumstances and whether there is an explanation for this, be a good indication of a risk of dissipation of assets: *Guan Chong Cocoa Manufacturer Sdn Bhd v Pratiwi Shipping SA* [2003] 1 S.L.R. 157 at para.19. *Earthquake & War Damage Commission v Aperteryx Insurance Co Ltd* (1989) 1 P.R.N.Z. 710 (injunction granted when the defendant intended to close its office in New Zealand).
[47] An injunction was readily granted against a prostitute who had allegedly received cash loans obtained by fraud from a divorced man: *Leslie Mitchell v Poolperm Saengjan* [1994] N.T.S.C. 34 (March 23, 1994). See also *Goldtron Ltd v Most Investment Ltd* [2002] J.L.R. 424 at para.32(e) (injunction granted in support of contemplated enforcement of an arbitration award against a foreign company with no published accounts and no information about its business or financial position). *Raukura Moana Fisheries Limited v The Ships Irina Zharkikh and Ksenia Zharkikh* [2001] 2 N.Z.L.R. 801 at paras 98 and 123, referred to in A. Butler (General editor) *Equity and Trusts in New Zealand* (2003) at para. 25.5.3.(partial disclosure about assets and absence of evidence about shipowners led to adverse inference of risk of dissipation).
[48] [1979] Q.B. 645.
[49] *ibid.* at 672.
[50] [1986] 2 Lloyd's Rep. at 439.
[51] [1983] 1 W.L.R. 1412.
[52] *Hadid v Lenfest Communications Inc.* (1996) 67 F.C.R. 446, Federal Court of Australia.

is a real risk that a judgment or award may go unsatisfied may be more readily drawn.

(5) If the defendant is a foreign company, partnership, or trader, the country in which it has been registered or has its main business address, and the availability or non-availability of any machinery for reciprocal enforcement of English judgments or arbitration awards in that country.[53] If such machinery does exist, the length of time it would take to implement it may be an important factor.[54]

(6) The defendant's past or existing credit record. A history of default in honouring other debts may be a powerful factor in the claimant's favour—on the other hand, persistent default in honouring debts, if it occurs in a period shortly before the claimant commences his action, may signify nothing more than the fact that the defendant has fallen upon hard times and has cash-flow difficulties, or is about to become insolvent. The possibility of insolvency does not justify the granting of Mareva relief.[55] As a factor it may weigh against it, on the grounds that an injunction would be oppressive because it might deprive the defendant of a last opportunity to put his business affairs in good order again.[56] The fact that a Mareva injunction has been granted over the defendant's assets may well discourage a bank or other company from lending him money or otherwise coming to his aid.

(7) Any intention expressed by the defendant about future dealings with his English assets,[57] or assets outside the jurisdiction.[58]

(8) Connections between a defendant company and other companies which have defaulted on arbitration awards or judgments. If the defendant company is the subsidiary of a foreign company which has allowed other subsidiaries to default on awards or judgments, or go into liquidation owing large sums of money to trade creditors, this may be a powerful factor in favour of granting an injunction.

(9) The defendant's behaviour in response to the claimant's claims: a pattern of evasiveness, or unwillingness to participate in the litigation or arbitration, or raising thin defences after admitting liability, or total silence, may be factors which assist the claimant.

---

[53] *Reches Pty v Tadiran Ltd* (1998) 155 A.L.R. 478 (no Mareva relief granted to prevent a substantial defendant removing its only asset from Australia when nothing to suggest it would default and reciprocal enforcement of judgments available).

[54] *Montecchi v Shimco (UK) Ltd* [1979] 1 W.L.R. 1180, *per* Bridge L.J. at 1183–1184; *Third Chandris Shipping Corporation v Unimarine* [1979] Q.B. 645 at 672; *The "Niedersachsen"* (above).

[55] *Midas Merchant Bank v Bello* [2002] EWCA Civ 1496; *Brigitte Lipman v AG Lifestyle Mangement Pty Ltd* [2001] N.S.W.I.R. Comm 115 at para.24; *Woodside Hospital Consulting Pty v Stockleton Nominees* [1998] V.S.C. 121 at paras 26–33.

[56] *Pressurefast Ltd v Hall and Brushett Ltd*, Court of Appeal (Civ Div) Transcript No.336 of 1993 (March 9, 1993).

[57] *Ulfcar International AS v Miles* Court of Appeal (Civ Div) Transcript No.808 of 1991 (August 29, 1991); *Glenwood Management v Mayo* [1991] 2 V.R. 49 (Victoria).

[58] These words have been added to take into account the fact that Mareva relief can be granted in respect of assets abroad as well as assets within the jurisdiction.

12.040   Mere unsupported statements to the effect that the deponent to an affidavit fears that assets may be dissipated do not comply with the requirements of CPR Pt 32. Practice Direction, para.4.2, can be of no evidential weight[59] and do not satisfy the requirement of evidence of risk of dissipation.[60]

Good grounds for alleging that the defendant has been dishonest is relevant. Dishonesty is not essential to the exercise of the jurisdiction and there is no need to show an intention to dissipate assets.[61] But if there is a good arguable case in support of an allegation that the defendant has acted fraudulently or dishonestly[62] (*e.g.* being implicated in an ingenious scheme for the misappropriation of funds belonging to the claimant[63]), or with an unacceptably low standard of commercial morality giving rise to a feeling

---

[59] *Third Chandris Shipping Corporation v Unimarine SA* [1979] Q.B. 645 at 672, *per* Lawton L.J.; *Ninemia Maritime Corporation v Trave Schiffahrtsgesellschaft GmbH (The Niedersachsen)* [1983] 1 W.L.R. 1412 at 1419 ("bare assertions . . . are clearly not enough"); *O'Regan v Iambic Productions* (1989) 139 N.L.J 1378 at 1379, *per* Peter Pain: "unsupported statements and expressions of fear, carry very little, if any, weight. The court needs to act on objective facts"; *First Farm Inc. v Bob's Backhoe Services Inc.* (1993) 108 D.L.R. (4th) 551.

[60] *Thane Investments Ltd v Tomlinson* [2003] ELCA Civ 1272 referring to CPR Pt 25 Practice Direction—Interim Injunctions, para.3.3.

[61] *The Niedersachsen, above; National Australia Bank Ltd v Bond Brewing Holdings Ltd* (1990) 169 C.L.R. 271 at 277, High Court of Australia.

[62] *United Bank Ltd v Hussain*, CA, February 25, 2000; *Harmony Precious Metals Services SAS v BCPMS (Europe) Ltd* [2002] EWHC 1687, TCC (total denial of any liability made dishonestly); *Mayor and Burgers of Lambeth v Clarke*, Court of Appeal (Civ Div) Transcript No.1563 of 1993 (December 22, 1993); *Patterson v BTR Engineering (Aust) Ltd* (1989) 18 N.S.W.L.R. 319; *Pearce v Waterhouse* [1986] V.R. 603; *Norwich Union Fire Insurance Society v Eden*, Court of Appeal (Civ Div) Transcript No.516 of 1996 (January 25, 1996); *Grupo Torras SA v Sheik Fahad Al-Sabah*, court of Appeal (Civ Div) Transcript No.462 of 1997 (March 21, 1997) in which the relevant defendant had personally received a large sum derived from allegedly misappropriated funds; *Mitchell v Saengjan* (1994) 117 F.L.R. 273, Supreme Court of Northwest Territory, in which a prostitute was alleged to have defrauded her lover; *Deputy Commissioner for Taxation v Robertson* [2000] W.A.S.C. 42 (evidence of previous history of dishonesty); *Snap-On UK Holdings Ltd v S. Winkles*, unreported November 26, 2002 (Judge Rich, Q.C.)(defendant had submitted to judgment for full amount of a claim based on dishonesty); *Hurrell v Fitness Holdings Europe Ltd*, unreported, March 15, 2002 (Cooke J.) at p.29 of the transcript (a risk of dissipation can be shown from the defendant's dishonest conduct): *Jarvis Field Press v Chelton* [2003] EWHC 2674, ChD (the fact that other proceedings seeking substantial amount had been brought against the defendant, led to successful application for freezing relief, when that relief had not been sought initially on a claim based on dishonesty); *Armco Inc v NPV Ltd* [1998] H.K.C.F.I. 632 (evidence of funds siphoned off in an attempt to defraud the plaintiff); *CAC Brake Co. Ltd Zhuhai v Bene Manufacturing Co. Ltd*, Hong Kong Court of Appeal 1998 No.94 (April 30, 1998) (citing this text and granting Mareva relief on appeal when the defendants were sued for fraud). In *Mediterranean Feeders LP v Bernd Meyering Schiffahrts*, Court of Appeal (Civ Div) Transcript No.966 of 1997 (June 5, 1997), in which it was alleged that a partner had acted irresponsibly in his capacity as ship's master on the ill-fated voyage (including signing a ship's protest which was materially untruthful), but this was considered to be irrelevant to what decisions the partners (including the master) might make about what to do with the insurance money.

[63] *Patterson v BTR Engineering (Aust) Ltd* (1989) 18 N.S.W.L.R. 319. *663309 Ontario Inc v Bauman* (2000) 190 D.L.R. (4th) 491 at paras 40–41 (on the facts the injunction was refused because although the defendant had apparently defrauded the revenue he had not done so for any personal gain, and he had not defrauded the plaintiff).

of uneasiness about the defendant,[64] then it is often[65] unnecessary for there to be any further specific evidence on risk of dissipation for the court to be entitled to take the view that there is a sufficient risk to justify granting Mareva relief. Once the risk of dissipation is shown, the limit of the Mareva relief will take into account claims for which the claimant has a good arguable case, including those which do not involve such an allegation.[66] The fact that a defendant is experienced in intricate, sophisticated, international transactions involving movements of large sums of money may also indicate that there is a real risk of dissipation.[67] Past convictions may also be taken into account.[68] The fact that the defendant has provided evidence about his assets and affairs which is mutually inconsistent may permit the inference that he is not being straightforward with the court and that there is a real risk of dissipation of his assets.[69]

The claim in the proceedings may be very large, so large that there may **12.041** well be a temptation for the defendant to dissipate his assets. But the courts still require some evidence of a risk of unjustified dissipation by the particular defendant.[70]

The risk of dissipation has to be shown by reference to the person or persons who have control over whether the relevant funds are dissipated.[71] Thus, if an individual who is alleged to have been dishonest does not

---

[64] *Thane Investments Limited v Tomlinson* [2003] EWCA Civ 1272 at para.28 emphasising that it is necessary in each case to consider whether the particular dishonesty alleged against the respondent justifies the inference of risk of dissipation.

[65] *Standard Chartered Securities v Lai Arthur* [1993] H.K.C. 375; *Armco Inc v NPV Ltd* [1998] H.K.C.F.I. 632 (prominent figure who had apparently siphoned off assets fraudulently); *Chapper v Chapper*, Court of Appeal (Civ Div) Transcript No.1475 of 1995 (November 8, 1995), where the defendant had "deliberately chosen not to answer the allegations except in a very limited way".

[66] *Mayor and Burgers of Lambeth v Clarke* Court of Appeal (Civ Div) Transcript No.1563 of 1993 (December 22, 1993).

[67] *Grupo Torras SA v Sheik Fahad Al-Sabah*, Court of Appeal (Civ Div) Transcript No.462 of 1997 (March 21, 1997).

[68] *Pearce v Waterhouse* [1986] V.R. 603 (breach of exchange control); *Glenwood Management v Mayo* [1991] 2 V.R. 49 (convictions for using false pretences).

[69] *Snap-On UK Holdings Ltd v S. Winkles*, unreported, November 26, 2002 (Judge Rich, Q.C.) (defendant had also submitted to judgment for full amount of a claim based on dishonesty).

[70] *Mediterranean Feeders LP v Bernd Meyering Schiffahrts*, Court of Appeal (Civ Div) Transcript No.966 of 1997 (June 5, 1997); see also *O'Mahony v Morgan* [1996] I.L.R.M. 161.

[71] In *Mediterranean Feeders IP v Bernd Meyering Schiffahrts*, Court of Appeal (Civ Div) Transcript No.966 of 1997 (June 5, 1997), the allegedly irresponsible master was not the only partner in the defendant and it was relevant to consider how the partnership would spend the insurance money (transcript at p.9E); this is why Mareva relief is discharged once a trustee in bankruptcy, an administrative receiver or a liquidator has been appointed and taken control of the assets—see Chapter 3, para.3.007, above. See also *Flightwise Travel Service Ltd v Gill* [2003] EWHC 3082 at [53–55], *The Times*, December 5, 2003 (no freezing injunction in support of claim under s.423 of the Insolvency Act 1986 against third party when risk of dissipation not shown against the third party); *Thane Investment Ltd v Tomlinson* [2003] EWCA Civ 1272 at para.28; *Westpac Banking Corporation v Hilliard* [2001] V.S.C. 187 at paras 47–49 (no risk of dissipation shown against third party).

control the assets sought to be frozen, then the evidence of dishonesty will not advance the case on risk of dissipation.[72]

There is no requirement that there must be a "more than usual likelihood" of a defendant dissipating his assets.[73] The court is not concerned with the probabilities of what will happen but whether there is evidence establishing a real[74] risk that assets may be dissipated.

(5) No need to produce evidence that assets are within the jurisdiction

12.042   The original basis upon which Mareva relief was granted was to restrain a foreigner from removing his assets from the jurisdiction, and the plaintiff was required to produce clear evidence[75] that assets within the jurisdiction were liable to be removed. However, in *Third Chandris Shipping Corporation v Unimarine SA*,[76] it was held that this requirement had been put too high, and that evidence of a bank account in overdraft, situated within the jurisdiction, could suffice. It was the practice that the Mareva jurisdiction was available only to prevent threatened dissipation of assets within the jurisdiction.[77] But it is now clearly established that Mareva relief can be granted, whether before or after judgment, in relation to assets of the defendant wherever situated.[78] This presupposes that the defendant can be served with the process of the court. In the case of proceedings on the merits which are not to take place in England, s.25(1) of the Civil Jurisdiction and Judgments Act 1982 enables Mareva relief to be granted which applies to assets wherever situated.[79]

A claimant often will not know the exact location and extent of the defendant's assets. For this reason, a strict requirement that there must be evidence of a certain quality about the existence of assets and their location would unnecessarily restrict availability of the relief.

---

[72] *Hurrell v Fitness Holdings Europe*, March 15, 2002, QBD, at p.30 of the transcript. *Petromar Energy Resources Pte LTd v Glencore International AG* [1999] 2 S.L.R. 609 (close commercial relationship of the defendant with an alleged fraudster does not make out a case for Mareva or Anton Piller relief).

[73] *Patterson v BTR Engineering (Aunt) Ltd* (1989) 18 NSWLR 319; *Leslie Mitchell v Poolperm Saengjan* [1994] N.T.S.C. 34 at para.43 (March 23, 1994); *Victoria University of Technology v Wilson* [2003] V.S.C. 299 (June 30, 2003) at paras 36 and 38.

[74] As opposed to a fanciful or insignificant risk: *Commissioner of State Taxation (WA) v Mechold Pty Ltd* (1995) 95 A.T.C. 4053 at 4056.

[75] *MBPXL Corporation v International Ranking Corporation Ltd* Court of Appeal (Civ Div) Transcript No.411 of 1975 (August 28, 1975).

[76] [1979] Q.B. 645.

[77] *Ashtiani v Kashi* [1987] Q.B. 888; *Intraco Ltd v Notis* [1981] 2 Lloyd's Rep. 256.

[78] *Babanaft Co. SA v Bassatne* [1990] Ch. 13; *Republic of Haiti v Duvalier* [1990] 1 Q.B. 202; *Derby & Co. Ltd v Weldon* [1990] Ch. 48; *Derby & Co. Ltd v Weldon (Nos 3 and 4)* [1990] Ch. 65. See also: L. Collins, "The Territorial Reach of Mareva Injunctions" (1989) 105 L.Q.R. 262.

[79] *Crédit Suisse Fides Trust SA v Cuoghi* [1997] 3 W.L.R. 871; *Republic of Haiti v Duvalier*, above; see further Chapter 6, paras 6.043 above.

In *Noble Resources Ltd v Greenwood (The Vasso)*,[80] a ship sank with her   **12.043** cargo. The cargo interests and their underwriters considered bringing a claim against the shipowners, who were a "one-ship" company. But the cargo interests refused to apply for Mareva relief against the shipowners, and sought to claim on their cargo insurance. Could the underwriters avoid or reduce their liability because the assured had not taken reasonable measures for minimising the loss? Hobhouse J. held that no criticism could be made of the cargo interests because it was an essential part of an application for an injunction restraining a defendant from removing assets from the jurisdiction that an affidavit was sworn to the effect that the defendant probably[81] had assets within the jurisdiction, and giving "the actual source of information".[82]

This overstated the requirements. The cargo interests could have sought Mareva relief in relation to the hull proceeds wherever situated, together with a disclosure order. It was unnecessary to show that the shipowners had assets within the jurisdiction either at the commencement of the proceedings or at the date of the application.[83] Once there was the real prospect that there were assets somewhere, the purpose of the application was to prevent those assets being unjustifiably dissipated with the consequence that a judgment would not be satisfied. The location of the assets did not affect that purpose, and therefore the foundation upon which the initial application for the relief would have rested.

When Mareva relief first emerged, the purpose of the remedy used to be to prevent assets located within the jurisdiction being removed from the jurisdiction by a foreign defendant.[84] In that context it was necessary to show by evidence[85] that there were assets within the jurisdiction which were liable to be removed. However, the Mareva jurisdiction can now be seen as a jurisdiction to prevent unjustifiable dissipations of assets leaving an eventual judgment unsatisfied. The focus is on the unjustified dissipation of assets and this does not depend on their location. With the recognition that because the remedy operates *in personam* it can apply to assets outside of the jurisdiction, it is no longer a fatal objection that the applicant does

---

[80] [1993] 2 Lloyd's Rep. 309.
[81] [1993] 2 Lloyd's Rep at 312. Contrast *Third Chandris Corporation v Unimarine SA* [1979] Q.B. 645 at 668.
[82] [1993] 2 Lloyd's Rep. at 312. However, an "intermediate" source can be given; see *Deutsche Ruckversicherung AG v Walbrook Insurance* [1994] 4 All E.R. 181 (and now CPR Pt 32, Practice Direction—Written Evidence, para.4.2), and the cargo interests had information about assets from such a source.
[83] *Derby & Co. Ltd v Weldon (Nos 3 and 4)* [1990] Ch. 65 at 77–80; *Planet International Ltd v Garcia* [1989] 2 Qd R. 427 *(Queensland)*; *DFC of Taxation v Hickey* (1996) 33 A.T.R. 453; *Commissioner of State Taxation (WA) v Mechold Pty Ltd* (1995) 95 A.T.C. 4053 at 4057.
[84] See Chapter 1, above.
[85] In *MBPXL Corporation v International Banking Corporation Ltd* Court of Appeal (Civ Div) Transcript No.411 of 1975 (August 28, 1975), Mareva relief was refused because of lack of evidence that there were assets within the jurisdiction. In *BNZ v Hawkins* (1989) 1 P.R.N.Z. 451, a requirement of assets within the jurisdiction was specified but this was overtaken by the emergence in New Zealand of an extra territorial jurisdiction.

not know enough about the defendant's financial affairs to be able to adduce evidence of location of assets.[86] This is particularly so when it is borne in mind that the relief often has to be sought urgently without much time for detailed inquiries. In a case where a ship has been lost and Mareva relief is sought against hull insurance proceeds, where those proceeds are to be collected is often a matter of little importance, except to the enforcement of the injunction.

12.044   The position is different when there is no real evidence of the defendant having assets. In such a case, even after judgment there should not be an injunction.[87] This is because the injunction will serve no purpose and is likely to cause substantial hardship to the defendant.[88]

(6) Relief affecting assets abroad

12.045   The jurisdiction to grant Mareva relief is an *in personam* jurisdiction against the defendant. But an injunction may have an impact on third parties. This aspect must be addressed when the court considers granting relief over assets abroad, and the practice has been adopted of inserting a proviso in the order which is intended to circumscribe its effect on third parties who are outside the jurisdiction. The proviso in the former standard form order given by the *Practice Direction (Mareva and Anton Piller Orders: Forms)*[89] was modelled on that in *Derby & Co. Ltd v Weldon (Nos 3 and 4)*[90] and read:

> "2) *Effect of this order outside England and Wales.* The terms of this order do not affect or concern anyone outside the jurisdiction of this court until it is declared enforceable or is enforced by a court in the relevant country and then they are to affect him only to the extent they have been declared enforceable or have been enforced UNLESS such person is (a) a person to whom this order is addressed or an officer or an agent appointed by power of attorney of such a person; or (b) a person who is subject to the jurisdiction of this Court and (i) has been given written notice of this order at his residence or place of business within the jurisdiction of this Court and (ii) is able to prevent acts or omissions outside the jurisdiction of this Court which constitute or assist in a breach of the terms of this order."

This provision is now redrafted in para.19 of the example order, which reads as follows:

---

[86] *Commissions of State Taxation (WA) v Mechold Pty Ltd* (1995) 95 A.T.C. 4053 at 4058, Supreme Court of Western Australia.

[87] *Hill Samuel Brink Ltd v Nicholas Soutos*, unreported, October 23, 1996, Comm Ct (Langley J).

[88] T. Willoughby and S. Connal, "The Mareva Injunction: A Cruel Tyranny?" (1997) E.I.P.R. 479 at 480.

[89] [1996] 1 W.L.R. 1552.

[90] [1990] Ch. 65. See also *Securities and Investment Board v Pantell SA* [1990] Ch. 426.

19. Persons outside England and Wales

(1) Except as provided in paragraph (2) below, the terms of this order do not affect or concern anyone outside the jurisdiction of this court.
(2) The terms of this order will affect the following persons in a country or state outside the jurisdiction of this court—

  (a) the Respondent or his officer or agent appointed by power of attorney;
  (b) any person who—

     (i) is subject to the jurisdiction of this court;
     (ii) has been given written notice of this order at his residence or place of business within the jurisdiction of this court; and
     (iii) is able to prevent acts or omissions outside the jurisdiction of this court which constitute or assist in a breach of the terms of this order; and

  (c) any other person, only to the extent that this order is declared enforceable by or is enforced by a court in that country or state."

The practice is for this to be further relaxed in favour of third parties or **12.046** non-parties complying with what they reasonably believe to be their obligations under foreign law or foreign court orders. This is addressed in para.20 of the example order:

20. Assets located outside England and Wales

Nothing in this order shall, in respect of assets located outside England and Wales, prevent any third party from complying with—

(1) what it reasonably believes to be its obligations, contractual or otherwise, under the laws and obligations of the country or state in which those assets are situated or under the proper law of any contract between itself and the Respondent; and
(2) any orders of the courts of that country or state, provided that reasonable notice of any application for such an order is given to the Applicant's solicitors.

The rights and liabilities of banks or other institutions or persons holding assets abroad would ordinarily fall to be determined by the court having jurisdiction at the location of those assets, and third parties should not find themselves exposed to liability when complying with their responsibilities to their customer under the law which would be applied by the local court.[91] The proviso is also an aspect of the principle that a state should generally refrain from demanding obedience to its sovereign authority by a foreigner in respect of his conduct outside of the jurisdiction.[92] Mere presence within the jurisdiction and thus amenability to the coercive orders of the English court does not affect the need to avoid asserting an altogether exorbitant jurisdiction to regulate matters abroad which should be dealt with by the local court. Furthermore provided that third parties act reasonably they should not be regarded as acting in contempt of court. The position of third parties in relation to extra-territorial Mareva relief is considered at paras 19.041–6, below.

12.047   Although Neill L.J., in *Derby & Co. Ltd v Weldon (Nos 3 and 4)*, envisaged that it would be unusual to grant Mareva relief in respect of foreign assets, the Court of Appeal has declined to impose any restrictions on availability, *e.g.* that the claimant has to have a case of a special strength or that the defendant has to be shown to be intent on transferring and hiding assets so as to defeat enforcement of a possible future judgment.

In cases before judgment, the defendant may be ordered to disclose information, including documents, relating to the whereabouts and details of his assets by way of ancillary order made in aid of the Mareva relief. After judgment, disclosure of such information may also be ordered to be provided by a judgment debtor under CPR Pt 71.[93] Ordinarily Mareva relief and disclosure orders in relation to assets abroad will be granted only if the claimant gives undertakings to the court restricting his ability to commence foreign proceedings and to use information derived from the disclosure order: *Re Bank of Credit and Commerce International SA.*[94] These undertakings give the court sufficient control of matters to prevent the claimant acting oppressively by forcing the defendant "to face litigation, brought by financially more powerful parties, in overseas courts throughout the world".[95]

12.048   The granting of Mareva relief over assets abroad is likely to involve substantial costs for the parties and may lead to protracted interlocutory proceedings in England or abroad, possibly involving third parties, who are not within the jurisdiction of the court. It is also liable to deflect the efforts of the parties from the resolution of the substantive merits of the litigation. Furthermore, it is undesirable that litigation should be made more complex and onerous than is necessary for doing justice between the parties, and the defendant to a disputed claim is not to be treated as if he were a judgment debtor. These considerations are particularly important when the court is considering the granting of Mareva relief over assets abroad, and underlie

---

[91] *Bank of China v NBM LLC* [2002] 1 W.L.R. 844; *Baltic Shipping Co. v Translink Shipping Ltd* [995] 1 Lloyd's Rep. 673.

[92] *Mackinnon v Donaldson, Lufkin & Jenrette Securities Corporation* [1986] Ch. 482 at 493; *Société Eram Shipping Co. Ltd v Compagnie Internationale de Navigation* [2004] 1 A.C. 260.

[93] Chapter 22, para.22.033, below.

[94] [1994] 1 W.L.R. 708.

[95] *Derby & Co. Ltd v Weldon* [1990] Ch. 48 at 60, *per* Nicholls L.J.

why such relief is regarded as "exceptional"[96] and why it should only be granted on cogent evidence.[97]

If it appears that the assets within the jurisdiction are likely to suffice for the purposes of enforcing an eventual judgment, the court will not as a matter of discretion grant relief over assets abroad.[98] If, on the other hand, the assets within the jurisdiction may well not suffice, then the court will consider granting extra-territorial relief. In *Motorola Credit Corporation v Uzan (No.2)*[99] it was argued unsuccessfully that because defendants had disclosed assets having a value in excess of the limit in the freezing injunction, no cross-examination on assets should have been ordered. The disclosed assets were not effectively frozen and it was most unlikely that a judgment would be satisfied out of such assets. The claimant was entitled to find out whether there were other assets which were more accessible for the purpose of satisfying a judgment and therefore the order for cross-examination was "just and convenient".[1]

The court is reluctant to grant worldwide relief against a defendant who **12.049** carries on business in the ordinary course on a worldwide basis (*e.g.* an international airline, insurance company or bank). This is because such relief would inevitably cause problems for the defendant in carrying on its business. If an application for worldwide relief is made against such a defendant, the applicant must show why it is appropriate to grant the relief notwithstanding the likely interference to the defendant's business: *ALG Incorporated v Uganda Airlines Corp.*[2]

If Mareva relief restricted to assets within the jurisdiction is granted, it will apply to any assets which are subsequently acquired by the defendant within the jurisdiction or brought into the jurisdiction by him.[3]

In cases in which the claimant makes a proprietary claim to an asset outside the jurisdiction, the court may grant interlocutory relief, independently of the Mareva jurisdiction, in respect of assets abroad. Thus in an action in which the claimant is seeking to trace property which in equity belongs to him, the courts are anxious "to see that the stable door is locked before the horse has gone".[4] In the context of such claims, the courts have

---

[96] *Derby & Co. Ltd v Weldon* [1990] Ch. 48 at 55C; *Federal Commissioner of Taxation v Karageorge* (1996) 34 A.T.R. 196, at 202 (lines 5–25) Supreme Court of New South Wales.
[97] *Grupo Torras SA v Sheik Fahad Al-Sabah*, Court of Appeal (Civ Div) Transcript No.159 of 1994 (February 16, 1994), *per* Steyn L.J.
[98] *Derby & Co. Ltd v Weldon (Nos 3 and 4)* [1990] Ch. 65 at 79, *per* Lord Donaldson M.R.; *DFC of Taxation v Hickey* (1996) 33 A.T.R. 453 (also refusing to allow cross-examination about assets because on the evidence sufficient assets within the jurisdiction were the subject of effective Mareva relief) a case distinguished on the facts in *Motorola Credit Corporation v Uzan No.2* [2004] 1 W.L.R. 113 at [143–147].
[99] [2004] 1 W.L.R. 113.
[1] Supreme Court Act 1981, s.37(1) and *Yukong Lines Ltd v Rendsburg Investments Corporation of Liberia* [1996] 2 Lloyd's Rep. 604.
[2] *The Times*, July 31, 1992.
[3] See para.3.023 above.
[4] *Mediterranea Raffineria Siciliana Petroli SpA v Mabanaft GmbH*, Court of Appeal (Civ Div) Transcript No.816 of 1978 (December 1, 1978), *per* Templeman L.J.; *A v C* [1981] Q.B. 956 at 958–959; *Bankers Trust v Shapira* [1980] 1 W.L.R. 1274 at 1280–1281.

granted interlocutory relief by injunction or the appointment of a receiver over assets abroad in support of the claimant's claim against the defendant in respect of the asset itself. With the recognition that Mareva relief can be granted over assets abroad, in cases where the risk of dissipation is established, it is no longer necessary for a court considering an application for interlocutory relief over assets abroad to consider in detail the strength of the claimant's claim on the merits to proprietary relief.[5] Nevertheless, where it is clear that the claimant has an apparently well-founded proprietary claim, this is an important factor in favour of granting an injunction or appointing a receiver over assets abroad.

(7) Justice and convenience

12.050 For relief to be granted, it must be "just and convenient" to do so within s.37(1) of the Supreme Court Act 1981. *In Films Rover Ltd v Cannon Film Sales Ltd*,[6] Hoffmann J. pointed out that with any interlocutory injunction there is a risk that the court may make the "wrong" decision. Thus an injunction may be granted and ultimately turn out to be unjustified, or the court may refuse an injunction which is subsequently shown to have been essential if the claimant's rights were to be preserved. In the context of Mareva relief, the court has to hear in mind that there is a discretion to be exercised in all the circumstances of the case.[7]

Those circumstances may themselves make it inappropriate to grant Mareva relief even though the claimant shows a good arguable case and a risk that, without the injunction, judgment may go unsatisfied. An example is where, if an injunction were granted, it would interfere in an unacceptable way with third parties (see Chapter 20, para.20.081). Another is where an injunction might itself destroy the defendant's business. A bank depends on business confidence to continue in business. Mareva relief may destroy that confidence at a stroke, leaving the defendant deprived of its business,[8] but with the prospect of uncertain and expensive litigation on the cross-undertaking, with losses which of their nature are difficult to quantify and prove. The cross-undertaking in damages provides, in such a case, no adequate safeguard against the possibility that the injunction was wrongly granted. This is the more so since a Mareva injunction may have the effect of depriving the defendant of the resources necessary to prosecute, in due course, a claim on the cross-undertaking. The same is true of other businesses liable to be destroyed if confidence is undermined

---

[5] *Republic of Haiti v Duvalier* [1990] 1 Q.B. 202.
[6] [1987] 1 W.L.R. 670 at 680D–C.
[7] The approach in *American Cyanamid Co. v Ethicon Ltd* [1975] A.C. 396 does not apply to the granting of Mareva relief: *Polly Peck International plc v Nadir (No.2)* [1992] 4 All E.R. 769 at 786.
[8] *Polly Peck International plc v Nadir (No.2)* [1992] 4 All ER 769 at 784c–e, 786d.

or credit is withdrawn. Similarly, if, on the facts, Mareva relief is likely to result in denying the defendant the possibility of finding employment, or preventing him from continuing his business or trade, or starting afresh, this is an important factor to be taken into account in deciding whether to grant the relief.[9]

The court should be satisfied before granting the relief that the likely **12.051** effect of the injunction will be to promote the doing of justice overall, and not to work unfairly or oppressively. This means taking into account the interests of both parties and the likely effects of an injunction on the defendant. The same principle applies whether the relief sought is merely negative in form, restraining the defendant from acting in a particular way, or the relief includes mandatory orders.[10]

Concerns have been raised that some Mareva cases may get out of hand, with costs being incurred which are out of proportion to the end sought to be achieved and there being delay to the resolution of the merits of the case because of interlocutory applications.[11] Mareva relief is not available when the claim in the action is too small to justify the procedure.[12] Also, if Mareva relief is sought in relation to assets whose value is trivial compared with what is claimed in the action, this can be a good reason in itself for refusing to grant an injunction.[13]

[9] *Pressurefast Ltd v Hall and Brushett Ltd* Court of Appeal (Civ Div) Transcript No.336 of 1993 (March 9, 1993), where the likely interference with the lives and businesses of the defendants amounted to hardship which went beyond what was appropriate for the legitimate protection of the plaintiff; the defendants had limited means and were unemployed, and the injunction would probably have prevented them from earning their livelihood.

[10] *Films Rover International Ltd v Cannon Film Sales Ltd* [1987] 1 W.L.R. 670 at 680–681; *Nottingham Building Society v Eurodynamics Systems plc* [1993] F.S.R. 468 at 474; *Newport Association Football Club v Football Association of Wales* [1995] 2 All E.R. 87.

[11] In the annual statement made by the judge in charge of the Commercial Court List on July 31, 1992, Evans J. referred to cases in which the "pursuit of assets acquires its own momentum and the Mareva tail begins to wag the dog, meaning the action itself . . . The plaintiffs need to obtain a judgment seems to be overlooked—perhaps deliberately . . .".

[12] Chapter 3, para.3.001, above.

[13] *Rasu Maritima SA v Perusahaan Pertambangan Minyak Dan Gas Bumi Negara (Pertamina)* [1978] Q.B. 644 at 663C–D, *per* Lord Denning M.R.; *O'Mahony v Horgan* [1996] I.L.R.M. 161 at 170.

Chapter 13

Mareva relief against assets in the name of or claimed by a third party

(1) An injunction is granted against a party to the action

The usual rule is that an injunction will be granted only against a party to **13.001** an action. As Lord Eldon L.C. said in *Iveson v Harris*,[1] "you cannot have an injunction except against a party to the suit".[2] In consequence, an injunction should be addressed to a party to an action or to someone who is about to be joined as a party.

Furthermore, an injunction should be addressed to the named party restraining him "by himself, his servants or agents or otherwise howsoever", or equivalent wording which makes it clear that the injunction does not enjoin the party's servants or agents, but has effect against the named party and restrains him from doing the prohibited acts, whether by his own act or by that of others acting as his servants or agents.[3] This rule of practice applies to the drafting of freezing injunctions. The example order is addressed to the named respondent and includes:[4]

"INTERPRETATION OF THIS ORDER

14. A Respondent who is an individual who is ordered not to do something must not do it himself or in any other way. He must not do it through others acting on his behalf or on his instructions or with his encouragement.
15. A Respondent which is not an individual which is ordered not to do something must not do it itself or by its directors, officers, partners, employees or agents or in any other way."

---

[1] (1802) 7 Ves. 251.
[2] See also *Bridges v Brydges* [1909] P. 187; *Royal Bank of Canada v Canstar Sports Group Inc.* [1989] 1 W.W.R. 662, Manitoba Court of Appeal; *Elliott v Klinger* [1967] 1 W.L.R. 1165.
[3] *Marengo v Daily Sketch* [1948] 1 All E.R. 406 at 407; *Z Ltd v A–Z* [1982] Q.B. 558 at 572C; *cf. Greenpeace Canada v Macmillan Bloedel* [1996] 2 S.C.R. 1048, Supreme Court of Canada.
[4] See also *Abella v Anderson* [1987] 2 Qd R. 1, Supreme Court of Queensland.

Occasionally, the courts grant injunctions against persons who are not parties to the proceedings. Thus an injunction was granted against a person threatening to aid and abet a contempt of court,[5] and against trustees of a will who held a legacy for a man who had absconded from the jurisdiction having appointed an agent to receive the legacy.[6]

13.002   However, once an injunction is to be granted against a person who is not a party, the practice is to join that person as a party to the proceedings.[7] In *SCF Finance Co. v Masri*,[8] *ex parte* relief was granted against a defendant's accounts at three named London banks. Subsequently the plaintiffs became aware of certain matters which showed that the defendant might be using the bank accounts of his wife for his business. As a result, she was added as a defendant and the injunction was extended to include accounts held by or on behalf of the husband in the name of the wife. This practice applies to non-parties who are to be enjoined under the Mareva jurisdiction against third parties.[9]

The example order states

> "[*For injunction limited to assets in England and Wales*]
> 5. Until the return date or further order of the court, the Respondent must not remove from England and Wales or in any way dispose of, deal with or diminish the value of any of his assets which are in England and Wales up to the value of £   ."

This is limited to assets beneficially owned by the respondent and not to assets which he holds as a trustee.[10] If certain assets are thought to be in the name of a trustee or bare nominee, those assets should be specifically designated in the order. In *SCF v Masri*[11] the Commercial Court made an order which applied to assets "held by or on behalf of the defendant jointly with any other persons or by nominees or otherwise howsoever." The example order provides:

> "6. Paragraph 5 applies to all the Respondent's assets whether or not they are in his own name and whether they are solely or jointly owned. For the purpose of this order the Respondent's assets include any asset which he has the power, directly or indirectly, to dispose of or deal with as if it were his own. The Respondent is to be regarded as having

---

[5] *Hubbard v Woodfield* (1913) 57 S.J. 729, see also *Halsbury's Laws of England* (4th ed.) Vol. 24, para.1045.

[6] *Bullus v Bullus* (1910) 102 L.T. 399. *Kerr on Injunctions* (6th ed., 1927), p.614.

[7] *C Inc. PLC v L* [2001] 2 Lloyd's Rep. 459.

[8] [1985] 1 W.L.R. 876.

[9] *Yukong Line Ltd v Rendsburg Investments Corporation* [2001] 2 Lloyd's Rep. 113; *C Inc. v L* [2001] 2 Lloyd's Rep. 459, following *Cardile v LED Builders Pty Ltd* (1999) 198 C.L.R. 380; *Mercantile Group (Europe) A.C. v Aiyela* [1994] Q.B. 366, affirming [1993] F.S.R. 745; *TSB Private Bank International SA v Chabra* [1992] 1 W.L.R. 231.

[10] *Federal Bank of the Middle East Ltd v Hadkinson* [2000] 1 W.L.R. 1695.

[11] [1985] 1 W.L.R. 876 at 878 where the relevant extract from the order of Webster J. is set out.

such power if a third party holds or controls the asset in accordance with his direct or indirect instructions."

(2) Mareva relief against non-parties

In *SCF v Masri* the question was whether it was right in principle for the **13.003** court to grant or continue Mareva relief in respect of assets which were in the name of and claimed by a third party, in that case the wife of the defendant to the substantive claim. The husband had used a cheque to complete a substantial exchange transaction. The cheque was drawn on a bank account in the name of his wife and had been pre-signed in blank by his wife in her maiden name. An injunction had been granted in respect of bank accounts in the wife's name and she applied to have it discharged. She raised a preliminary point to the effect that when there is an issue as to whether or not particular assets truly belong to the defendant to the substantive claim or to the third party, the court should always discharge or vary the Mareva relief to enable the third party to deal with the assets. The Court of Appeal rejected the contention and summarised the applicable principles as follows:[12]

"(i) Where a plaintiff invites the court to include within the scope of a Mareva injunction assets which appear on their face to belong to a third party, the court should not accede to the invitation without good reason for supposing that the assets are in truth the assets of the defendants.

(ii) Where the defendant asserts that the assets belong to a third party, the court is not obliged to accept that assertion without inquiry, but may do so depending on the circumstances. The same applies where it is the third party who makes the assertion, on an application to intervene.

(iii) In deciding whether to accept the assertion of a defendant or a third party, without further inquiry, the court will be guided by what is just and convenient, not only between the plaintiff and the defendant, but also between the plaintiff, the defendant and the third party.

(iv) Where the court decides not to accept the assertion without further inquiry, it may order an issue to be tried between the plaintiff and the third party in advance of the main action, or it may order that the issue await the outcome of the main action, again depending in each case on what is just and convenient."

The Court of Appeal also found that the judge had been "plainly right" to hold that he could not decide the matter without further inquiry.[13]

---

12 [1985] 1 W.L.R. 876 at 884.
13 For subsequent proceedings in the action see *SCF v Masri (No.2) and (No.3)* [1987] Q.B. 1002 and 1028.

13.004   If the court directs the trial of an issue as to the rights of the third party over the assets, but considers that the issue should await the outcome of the main action, the issue can be tried at the same time as an application for execution of the judgment. In the case of assets which can be made the subject of a charging order, the issue whether the assets belong beneficially to the third party can be directed in the proceedings to make absolute the charging order nisi: *Rosseel NV v Oriental Commercial*.[14]

In England it is an established principle that Mareva relief will be granted only in relation to an accrued cause of action against the defendant.[15] The granting of Mareva relief against an alleged nominee, who is said to hold or control assets for the defendant to the substantive claim, but against whom there is no substantive claim, might be viewed as an infringement of the principle. Thus in *Vereker v Choi*[16] the Supreme Court of New South Wales granted Mareva relief against a wife on the basis that the facts in the case justified Mareva relief as "an exception to the general rule", namely that "it was necessary for an applicant for a Mareva injunction to establish the existence of [an existing] cause of action".[17]

The position is not to be so analysed, however.[18] The cause of action lies against the defendant to the substantive proceedings. Mareva relief can properly be granted enjoining that defendant from dealing with his assets. Whether particular assets are properly to be regarded as assets of the defendant to the substantive claim is a separate question. That question must be resolved before it can be unequivocally stated that the assets in question fall within the Mareva relief granted against the defendant to the substantive claim, and so it is inappropriate to limit the injunction to the defendant to the substantive claim. Thus, first, until the matter is resolved, third parties such as banks will not know what acts are prohibited by the injunction. Secondly, the defendant to the substantive claim and the claimant to the asset will be in the same position. Thirdly, whether the assets in question are to be maintained intact should not be left to the interpretation of the injunction by the defendant and third parties. Fourthly, if the assets are to be maintained intact under an injunction it is appropriate that a third party claimant to the assets should have the benefit of an undertaking in damages and any bond or security required in support, and should be made a party to an issue of ownership of the assets.

---

[14] Court of Appeal (Civ Div) Transcript No.906 of 1991 (October 8, 1991).
[15] *Veracruz Transportation Inc. v VC Shipping* [1992] 1 Lloyd's Rep. 353; *Siporex Trade SA v Comdel Commodities* [1986] 2 Lloyd's Rep. 428; *Steamship Mutual Underwriting Association (Bermuda) v Thakur Shipping* [1986] 2 Lloyd's Rep. 439. This is a legacy of the decision of the House of Lords in *Siskina v Distos Compania Naviera SA* (*The Siskina*). [1979] A.C. 210. See also Chapter 12, paras 12.001–4.
[16] (1985) 4 N.S.W.L.R. 277.
[17] (1985) 4 N.S.W.L.R. 277 at 283 citing the judge's own previous decision in *Bank of Queensland Ltd v Grant* [1984] 1 N.S.W.L.R. 409.
[18] See n.20, below and P. Devonshire, "The Implications of Third Parties Holding Assets Subject to a Mareva Injunction" [1996] L.C.M.L.Q. 268 at 273–277.

These considerations show that the injunction against the third party is **13.005** in effect ancillary relief granted by the court in aid of and as part of the Mareva relief against the defendant to the substantive claim. In effect, it is relief granted in respect of the substantive claim against that defendant, albeit that the injunction has had to be directed to the third party, because of the rule of practice that an injunction enjoins only the person or persons to whom it is directed. Accordingly, the granting of Mareva relief against a third party, pending resolution of an issue as to the scope and effect of Mareva relief granted against the defendant to the substantive claim, is to be distinguished from the case in which an applicant is seeking Mareva relief without any existing cause of action at all, and, perhaps, without even an existing chose in action against the prospective respondent or respondents.

The jurisdiction is in extremely wide terms. It is not limited to cases in which the non-party may hold assets of the defendant or has become mixed up in the affairs of the defendant or where there may be a remedy to set aside a fraudulent gift. The High Court of Australia has said that such an order may be appropriate when:

"(i) the third party holds, is using, or has exercised or is exercising a power of disposition over, or is otherwise in possession of,[19] assets, including 'claims and expectancies', of the judgment debtor or potential judgment debtor; or

(ii) some process, ultimately enforceable by the courts, is or may be available to the judgment creditor as a consequence of a judgment against the actual or potential judgment debtor, pursuant to which, whether by appointment of a liquidator, trustee in bankruptcy, receiver or otherwise, the third party may be obliged to disgorge property or otherwise contribute to the funds or property of the judgment debtor to help satisfy the judgment against the judgment debtor."[20]

In Australia the jurisdiction against third parties is part of the jurisdiction **13.006** to protect the due administration of justice. This has been used to justify granting an injunction against the Registrar General, when there is no cause of action against him, preventing him from registering a document when the consequence of registration would be to undermine the plaintiff's substantive claim,[21] *e.g.* where registration of a mortgage would defeat a prior equitable interest in the land. The same scope of the jurisdiction has

---

[19] For example, *Basiric v Topic* (1981) 37 A.C.T.R. 1 (Mareva relief granted against the defendants to an action, and against a third party who had received a transfer of land from the defendants but appeared to have no substantial assets or income of his own).
[20] *Cardile v LED Builders Pty Ltd* (1999) 198 C.L.R. 380 at 405–406.
[21] *Williams v Marac Australia* (1986) 5 N.S.W.L.R. 529.

been recognised in England, but is based on s.37(1) of the Supreme Court Act 1981.[22]

(3) Application of the jurisdiction against non-parties

(i) The claimant must show "good reason to suppose"[23] as against the non-party that the assets of or held by the non-party would be susceptible to a procedure which would lead to satisfaction of a judgment; the width of the injunction against the non-party depends upon what it is that there is "good reason to suppose"

13.007　In *SCF v Masri*, the Court of Appeal did not elaborate on the general principle that Mareva relief should not be granted in relation to assets which appear on their face to belong to a third party "without good reason" for supposing that the assets "are in truth assets of the defendants", but held that it was satisfied on the facts of that case.

In contrast, in *Allied Arab Bank v Hajjar*,[24] the wife of one of the defendants, who was being sued on his personal guarantee by the plaintiff bank for a substantial sum, had two bank accounts against which the defendant husband had authority to draw. Hirst J. refused to direct trial of an issue as to whether money in those two accounts was owned by the husband, and his decision was upheld by the Court of Appeal. Thus the existence of material on which an issue could be raised, as to whether the accounts belonged beneficially to the husband, was insufficient to justify extending the Mareva injunction to include the bank accounts in the name of the wife.[25] There had to be "good reason to suppose" that the bank accounts were owned beneficially by the husband before such a course could be taken.[26]

---

[22] See *C Inc. v L* [2001] 2 Lloyd's Rep. 459 ; *TSB Private Bank v Chabra* [1992] 1 W.L.R. 231; *Mercantile Group (Europe) AG v Aiyela* [1994] Q.B. 366 affirming [1993] F.S.R. 745; *Aiglan Ltd v Gau Shan Co. Ltd* [1993] 1 Lloyd's Rep. 164. The jurisdiction is discussed by Peter Devonshire in "The Implications of Third Parties Holding Assets Subject to a Mareva Injunction" [1996] L.M.C.L.Q. 268 at 274–277 "Mareva Injunctions and Third Parties: Exposing the Subtext" (1999) 62 M.L.R. 539 at 540–541; and "Freezing Orders, Disappearing Assets and the Problem of Enjoining Non Parties" (2002) 118 L.Q.R. 124.

[23] This is the same as a "good arguable case", and for the purpose of evaluating this, there is to be taken into account the credibility of statements made on affidavit: *Silvera v Faleh Al-Rashidi*, Court of Appeal (Civ Div) Transcript No.1039 of 1993 (August 17, 1993); *Hill Samuel Bank Ltd v Nicholas Soutos*, unreported, October 23, 1996 Comm Ct (Langley J.), where the plaintiff failed to show a good "arguable case that the [third party's] accounts contain or are assets of [the judgment debtor] . . ." and the injunction was set aside. See also *DCT v Ousley* (1992) 23 A.T.R. 176 at 183, in which the defendants failed to put in evidence dealing with the applicant's evidence and this gave rise to an adverse inference—see at 184.

[24] [1988] Q.B. 787.

[25] See also *Bank of Montreal v Page Properties Ltd* (1981) 32 O.R. (2d) 9.

[26] This formulation was taken from *SCF v Masri* [1985] 1 W.L.R. 876 in which the evidence had shown "good reason to suppose" that the wife's accounts belonged beneficially to the husband.

It is sufficient to show that:

(1) the defendant to the substantive claim has caused assets to be held by or vested in a third party who is effectively acting as a nominee for the defendant.[27] The nominee is simply holding assets which fall within the scope of "his assets," *i.e.* assets owned beneficially by the defendant; or

(2) the non-party is a debtor or "banker"[28] or has some form of liability[29] to the defendant which is or will be enforceable. The assets to be frozen are those of the non-party[30] to answer for the non-party's liability to the defendant; or

(3) although the defendant to the substantive claim has no legal or equitable right to the assets in question, the defendant has some right in respect of, control over, or other right of access to the assets.[31] If a defendant has set up a network of trusts and companies to hold assets over which he has control, and he has apparently done this to make himself judgment-proof, this would be an appropriate case for the granting of Mareva relief against the relevant non-party. If the defendant is a shareholder in a private company and were left free to deprive the company of assets to which it may be entitled, this could affect the value of his shareholding and so an injunction can be granted against non-parties to preserve those assets.[32]

Cases can involve more than one category and whether there is "good reason" does not involve subjecting a case to a category by category analysis. The court is not required to decide "the ultimate rights of the parties" in the underlying assets which are to be preserved.[33] For the position under the Drug Trafficking Act 1994 and the Criminal Justice Act 1988, see Chapter 25. **3.008**

---

[27] This appears to have been the position in relation to the eighth and ninth respondents in *Jackson v NIM* (1986) 66 A.L.R. 657 at 673. This point was not affected by the subsequent appeal to the Court of Appeal and then the High Court of Australia *sub nom. Jackson v Sterling Industries* (1987) 69 A.L.R. 92, and (1987) 162 C.L.R. 612; see para.6 of the example order. See also *Teo Siew Har v Lee Kuan Yew* [1999] 4 S.L.R. 560 (arguable case that third party holding assets belonging to defendant to the claim); *Lee Kuan Yew v Tang Liang Hong (No.1)* [1997] 2 S.L.R. 819; P. Devonshire, "Mareva Injunctions and Third Parties: Exposing the Subtext" (1999) 62 M.L.R. 539 at 540–541.
[28] As was the wife in *SCF v Masri* (above): see *SCF v Masri (No.3)* [1987] Q.B. 1028.
[29] *C Inc. v L* [2001] 2 Lloyd's Rep. 459—liability of the husband to indemnify the wife against the judgment.
[30] *Yukong Line Ltd v Rendsburg Investments Corporation* [2001] 2 Lloyd's Rep. 113 at [45].
[31] *Winter v Marac Australia* (1986) 6 N.S.W.L.R. 11.
[32] *Caboche v Southern Equities Corporation* [2001] S.A.S.C. 55 at para.23; *TSB Private Bank v Chabra* [1992] 1 W.L.R. 231; *P v P* [2002] J.L.R. Note 18 principle (d).
[33] *Caboche v Southern Equities Corporation* [2001] S.A.S.C. 55 at para.25; this is a flexible jurisdiction which does not require detailed investigation at the injunction stage of the underlying rights, which otherwise would itself lead to delay and opportunity for evasion: P. Devonshire, "Freezing Orders, Disappearing Assets and the Problem of Enjoining Non Parties" (2002) 118 L.Q.R. 124 at 142.

An example of a case falling within all three categories is *TSB Private Bank v Chabra*.[34] The defendant and his wife had left the jurisdiction. The substantive claim was against him. An injunction was granted *ex parte* against him in respect of his assets including his shareholding in a company. Subsequently an *ex parte* injunction was granted against the company, against which the plaintiff had no cause of action, restraining the company from dealing with its assets, including the proceeds of a hotel and restaurant business. The evidence showed a good arguable case that some of the company's assets were assets of Mr Chabra, and an injunction was granted against the company *inter partes* restraining it from dealing with assets held by it, including its own assets, pending establishment of which, if any, of the assets vested in the company ". . . are available to satisfy any judgment obtained against Mr Chabra".[35]

In *DCT v Winter*,[36] summary judgment had been obtained by the Deputy Commissioner of Taxation against the same Mr Winter as featured in *Winter v Marac Australia*. His sister, mother and companies which he controlled were co-defendants, and it appeared well arguable that Mr Winter had used the various co-defendants to hold assets so that they would not be available to pay his debts. Mareva relief was continued against the co-defendants in contemplation of bankruptcy proceedings against Mr Winter.

13.009   In *Mercantile Group AG v Aiyela*[37] judgment had been obtained against Mr Aiyela. There was evidence that Mr Aiyela was hiding assets so as to evade satisfaction of the judgment. Funds were transferred from Nigeria to a bank account in the name of Mrs Aiyela. An injunction was granted restraining her from dealing with any bank account over which she held a mandate or which was in her name at a particular branch. There was an issue about what interest Mr Aiyela had in the funds in his wife's bank accounts but those funds could be frozen pending decision on whether they could be compulsorily applied in satisfaction of the judgment. The Mareva injunction was incidental to and in aid of the enforcement of the right to have the judgment against Mr Aiyela satisfied.

In *Yukong Line Ltd v Rendsburg Investments Corporation*,[38] after Mr Yamvrias had successfully defended the action brought against him an order was made ordering Rendsburg by Mr Yamvrias to pay money into court and continuing Mareva relief against him personally. The mandatory order had only been directed against Rendsburg.[39] Indeed the making of an order direct against Mr Yamvrias personally would have been problematic because the judgment debtor was the company and it had not been shown

---

[34] [1992] 1 W.L.R. 231.
[35] [1992] 1 W.L.R. at 242F–G; see also *Yukong Line Ltd v Rendsburg Investments Corporation* [2001] 2 Lloyd's Rep. 113 at [44].
[36] (1987) 19 A.T.R. 827, Supreme Court of New South Wales.
[37] [1994] Q.B. 366 approving [1993] F.S.R. 745 (Hobhouse J.).
[38] [2001] 2 Lloyd's Rep. 113.
[39] *Yukong Line Ltd v Rendsburg Investments Corporation* [1998] EWCA Civ 2795 (June 23, 1998).

why Mr Yamvrias and his assets should have to satisfy the judgment against Rendsburg.[40] Was the Mareva relief "wrongly granted" for the purpose of considering whether to enforce the cross-undertaking in damages in favour of Mr Yamvrias? The Court of Appeal held that it was not because funds had been transferred out of Rendsburg and there was an inference that Mr Yamvrias held or controlled the proceeds of those funds. Since there was no evidence of what had happened to the funds a Mareva covering all of Mr Yamvrias's assets could properly be made.

In *Re A Company*,[41] the plaintiffs (which were companies in liquidation) **13.010** brought an action against the defendant alleging deceit, and for breach of trust and fiduciary duty. The evidence disclosed "an elaborate and most ingenious scheme brought into operation at the instance of the . . . defendant, whereby his personal assets were organised in such a way that they were held by foreign and English corporations and trusts in a manner that effectively conceals his true beneficial interest in English assets". There was strong evidence that the defendant had deliberately set up this network of companies and trusts to defeat the defendant's creditors and those with claims against him. In these circumstances the Court of Appeal upheld orders requiring disclosure of information of "an unusually extensive and detailed character" and imposing injunctions restraining the defendant from disposing of his shares in companies or his rights under the trusts, and from causing the companies or trusts to dispose of those assets. The court did so on the ground that it would use its powers "to pierce the corporate veil if it is necessary to achieve justice irrespective of the legal efficacy of the corporate structure under consideration".[42]

At that time the courts were restricting Mareva relief to assets within the jurisdiction, and accordingly the relief was directed to restraining dealings with assets within the jurisdiction, although they were held by a foreign company or trust. As for the possibility that non-parties might be entitled to, or claim, an interest in the relevant assets, Cumming-Bruce L.J. said:

"If there are other genuine interests vested in third parties beneficially, the first defendant can state the facts in his answer to the interrogatories, and the notice of the injunctions can be served on the parties

---

[40] See the concerns expressed about Toulson J.'s mandatory order being an illegitimate short cut—[1998] EWCA Civ 2471 and [1998] EWCA Civ 2795 (June 23, 1998), which were referred to in [2001] 2 Lloyd's Rep. 113 at [18]. The unhappy wording of the mandatory injunction reflected the fact that an order for payment of money in respect of Rendsburg's liability to Yukong could only be made at that stage against the judgment debtor.
[41] [1985] B.C.L.C. 333. Also reported as *X Bank v G, The Times*, April 13, 1985; followed in *International Credit and Investment Company (Overseas) Ltd v Adham* [1998] B.C.C. 134 (Robert Walker J.), a claim for huge amounts based on allegations of dishonesty found proved at trial in the Cayman Islands, in which a receiver was appointed in respect of assets covered by Mareva relief. See also *Bank Bumiputra Malaysia Bhd v Lorrain Osman* [1985] 2 M.L.J. 236 (Malaysia).
[42] Applied in relation to criminal restraint orders in *Re H (Restraint Order: Realisable Property)* [1996] 2 All E.R. 391 at 401–402 which was followed in *Crown Prosecution Service v Compton* [2002] EWCA Civ 1720 at [44] and [48].

alleged to be beneficially interested, and their objection can be made to the court and its validity upheld. When there is such massive evidence of nominees, and puppet directors dancing to the first defendant's tune, it is for him to state on oath his belief, if he holds it, that one or more persons implicated in the silken skein of his spider's web has a genuine beneficial interest."

13.011   The expression "piercing the corporate veil" can be used to describe different situations,[43] and it is helpful to the analysis to be clear in what sense or senses it is being used. Thus:

(1) One situation is where a company or trust is used to hold assets which are controlled by and held for the benefit of the defendant. In that situation the analysis is that the assets are owned beneficially by the defendant and can be frozen based on the substantive claim against him.

(2) Another analysis is that although the assets belong beneficially to another person the defendant has rights the value of which depends upon the preservation of those assets, there is a legal route by which those assets can be required to satisfy a judgment and therefore an injunction can be granted to preserve those assets.

(3) Another is that the underlying cause of action is also available against that person because of "piercing the veil",[44] with the consequence that his assets can be frozen.

(4) Another is when a transfer of an asset is regarded as "a sham" transaction in the sense that ". . . the outward and visible form does not coincide with the inward and substantial truth".[45] The asset is treated as that of the transferor.

These categories are not mutually exclusive and the granting of an injunction or appointment of a receiver can be made without carrying out a category by category analysis.

---

[43] *The Tjaskemolen* [1997] 2 Lloyd's Rep. 465 at 471 LHC; *Crown Prosecution Service v Compton* [2002] EWCA Civ 1720 at [55].

[44] For example, *Trustor AB v Smallbone No.2* [2001] 1 W.L.R. 1176 (where a transfer had been made to a company, and both that company and the individual who controlled it, were held liable as constructive trustees for knowing receipt of trust money); *Creasey v Breechwood Motors* [1992] B.C.C. 638 (transferee of business liable for claim of dismissed employee of transferor when the transfer carried out in the knowledge of the existence of the claim and without making any provision for it); *Gilford Motor Co. Ltd v Horne* [1933] Ch. 935 (injunction also granted against the company); *Jones v Lipman* [1962] 1 W.L.R. 832 (specific performance of the contract entered into by the individual ordered against both him and his company).

[45] *Miles v Bull* [1969] 1 Q.B. 258 at 264D–E; *Snook v London & West Riding Investments Ltd* [1967] 2 Q.B. 786 at 802; *The Tjaskemolen* [1997] 2 Lloyd's Rep.465 at 474 (concealed retention of beneficial ownership); *Garnac Grain Co. Inc v Faure Fairclough* [1966] 1 Q.B. at 684 (not a sham unless it was proved that ". . . the ostensible contract should not give rise to legally enforceable rights or liabilities"); *Haryanto v E. D. & F. Mann* [1986] 2 Lloyd's Rep. 44 (need to prove different transactions to displace the apparent contracts).

In *Cardile v LED Builders Pty Ltd*[46] the plaintiff had successfully sued the   **13.012**
defendant for copyright infringement and an account of profits was to be
taken. The proceedings had been commenced in 1993. In 1994 and 1996,
before judgment on liability, substantial dividends had been declared by the
defendant company (Eagle Homes Pty Ltd) in favour of its shareholders
(Mr and Mrs C). Another company (Ultra Modern Pty Ltd) was incorporated in 1995. Its parent company was owned and controlled by Mr and
Mrs C. Shortly after its incorporation Ultra became the registered proprietor of the business name "Eagle Homes." Both Eagle and Ultra used the
business name "Eagle Homes".

The plaintiff contended that the payment of dividends were transactions
entered into by Eagle for the purpose of defrauding creditors which were
voidable under s.37A of the Conveyancing Act 1919 (NSW). The plaintiff
applied for Mareva relief against Eagle, Mr and Mrs C and Ultra and this
was granted on appeal.

The Federal Court had held that it was not necessary to show that Eagle
had some proprietary right in assets held by the third parties. The court
had rejected the argument that the Mareva jurisdiction could only be
exercised against assets of Eagle or to which Eagle had an existing right. It
sufficed that the plaintiff ". . . although having no vested or accrued cause
of action against the third party, may become entitled to have recourse to
the third party or his assets to meet his debt, and there is a danger that the
third party will send his assets abroad or otherwise dispose of them".[47]

The High Court of Australia upheld the jurisdiction to grant relief   **13.013**
against persons who were not parties to the plaintiff's substantive claim. It
was not necessary to show that the non-parties held assets to which the
defendant was entitled. It also held that on the facts the relief granted by
the Federal Court was too wide. In relation to the dividends declared and
paid by Eagle to its shareholders, relief was granted against them for the
amount of the dividends received on the ground that this was arguably a
fraudulent conveyance which could be avoided. Relief was also granted
against Ultra but only so as to prevent Ultra destroying the goodwill
attached to the "Eagle Homes" name.[48]

The test is not higher than "good reason to suppose". In *Uttamchandai v
Central Bank of India*,[49] the defendant bank refused payment of a credit
balance on the basis that there were strong grounds for believing that
another customer of the bank had an equitable interest in the account; that
other customer owed substantial sums to the bank, which sought to justify

---

[46] (1999) 198 C.L.R. 380 on appeal from *LED Builders Pty Ltd v Eagle Homes Pty Ltd* (1997) 148 A.L.R. 247. Federal Court of Australia. Beaumont, Branson and Tamberlin JJ. See also P. Devonshire, "Mareva Injunctions and Third Parties: Exposing the Subtext" (1999) 62 M.L.R. 539 at 558–562.
[47] *Coxton Pty Ltd v Milne* NSW, CA, unreported, December 20, 1985, CA, *per* Hope J.A.
[48] The goodwill attaching to the name was enjoyed by both Eagle and Ultra and the relief was apparently granted on the basis that Ultra was arguably bound not to destroy Eagle's goodwill.
[49] (1989) 139 N.L.J. 222.

the non-payment on the grounds that it could exercise a right of set-off. The Court of Appeal held that the defence of equitable set-off was not available where it was not clear beyond argument that the third party was entitled to the money due on the account. This is because set-off is a substantive right. But in such circumstances, provided that there is good reason to believe that the third party was so entitled, Mareva relief over the proceeds of the account could be granted. As with bills of exchange and letters of credit and direct debit arrangements (see para.3.038 and paras 15.031–3 above), the fact that there is no set-off available does not preclude the granting of relief in respect of the proceeds. The difference in the test is because Mareva relief is temporary relief granted to hold the position pending the establishment and working out of the legal rights, whereas allowing the set-off would have decided what the legal rights were.

(ii) It is necessary to show that the assets will be amenable to compulsory application in satisfaction of the judgment

13.014   In *Coxton Pty Ltd v Milne*,[50] a decision of the Court of Appeal of New South Wales, Hope J.A., in a judgment with which Glass J.A. and Priestly J. agreed, specified a number of conditions which, if met, would make it appropriate to grant Mareva relief against a third party in respect of whom no principle relief was claimed, as follows:

> "Without attempting to define or to limit the extent of the exception, the necessary circumstances will exist when [1] the affairs of a defendant sued by a creditor for an alleged debt and of the third party against whom the injunction is sought are intermingled, [2] the alleged debtor and the disposition of his assets are effectively controlled, *de jure or de facto*, by the third party, [3] the debtor's assets will be insufficient to meet the debt, [4] the creditor, although having no vested or accrued cause of action against the third party, may become entitled to have recourse to the third party or his assets to meet his debt, and [5] there is a danger that the third party will send his assets abroad or otherwise dispose of them."

(The numbers in square brackets have been inserted into the text for the purpose of identifying separately each of the five factual requirements.)

Condition [4] was further explained by Hope J.A. in *Winter v Marac Australia* (above):[51] it is not sufficient for the plaintiff to satisfy the court that the defendant to the substantive claim could persuade the third party

---

[50] Unreported, December 20, 1985 referred to in *Sterling v NIM* (1986) 66 A.L.R. 657 at 673; *Winter v Marac Australia* (1986) 6 N.S.W.L.R. 11 at 12; and *DCT v Winter* (1988) 19 A.T.R. 827 at 829–830.
[51] (1986) 6 N.S.W.L.R. 11 at 12–13.

to accede to any request by him in relation to the assets in question. Thus:
"It must be shown that the person against whom judgment may be obtained has some right in respect of or control over or other access direct or indirect, to the relevant assets so that they or the proceeds of their sale or other disposition could be required to be applied in discharge of the judgment debt."[52]

It is clearly not a sufficient basis for the granting of Mareva relief against **13.015** a wife that a substantive claim is made against her husband and the wife owns property which she could be persuaded by the husband to use to satisfy a judgment against him.[53] Facts must be proved establishing that the assets in the hands of the wife could be required to be applied directly or indirectly in satisfaction of the judgment debt.[54]

(iii) There is no requirement of an existing cause of action against the non-party

There is no requirement that there be an existing cause of action available **13.016** against the party,[55] whether by the claimant, the defendant or anyone else.

(iv) The court can direct an issue between the claimant and the non-party.

When the facts are such that Mareva relief should be granted against assets **13.017** in the name of a non-party (*e.g.* the wife of a defendant), an issue can be directed between the claimant and the non-party as to what assets can be made compulsorily available to satisfy a judgment against the defendant. This will be dealt with in the existing action in which the Mareva relief has been granted and not in separate proceedings.[56] The court will direct pleadings in the issue and give directions for disclosure.

---

[52] Applied in *DCT (NSW) v Winter* (1988) 19 A.T.R. 827 and *DCT v Ousley* (1992) 23 A.T.R. 176 at 183.
[53] *Allied Arab Bank v Hajja. The Times*, January 18, 1998; *Winter v Marac Australia* (1986) 6 N.S.W.L.R. 11 at 12–13.
[54] *Gibb Australia v Cremor* (1992) 106 F.L.R. 453. These can include facts which enable a claim to be made against the wife under statutory provisions to set aside one or more prior transfers of assets to the wife by her husband.
[55] *Cardile v LED Builders Pty Ltd* (1999) 198 C.L.R. 380 at 405–406 and 427; *Aiglon Ltd v Gau Shan Co. Ltd* [1993] 1 Lloyd's. Rep. 164 at 170 (the possibility of a claim under s.238 of the Insolvency Act 1986 by a future liquidator or administrator to set aside a transaction at an undervalue); *Mercantile Group v Aiyela* [1993] F.S.R. 745, affirmed [1994] Q.B. 366; *Yukong Line Ltd v Rendsburg Investments Corporation* [2001] 2 Lloyd's Rep. 113; P. Devonshire, "Freezing Orders, Disappearing Assets and the Problem of Enjoining Non Parties" (2002) 118 L.Q.R. 124 at 130–136.
[56] *McIntyre v Pettit* (1988) 90 F.L.R. 196, Supreme Court of New South Wales, implementing the procedure envisaged in *SCF v Masri* (above).

(4) Claims involving setting aside under statutory provisions prior transfers of assets[57]

(i) The scope of the sections

13.018   Section 172 of the Law of Property Act 1925 re-enacted a provision in the Law of Property (Amendment) Act 1924, Sch.3, Pt II, para.31, and replaced in different terms ss1 and 5 contained in the Statute of Elizabeth I (13 Eliz. I c.5). That section made provision that every conveyance of property made "with intent to defraud creditors" should be voidable at the instance of "any person thereby prejudiced." Section 172 has been repealed,[58] and it is replaced by s.423 of the Insolvency Act 1986 which was introduced following the Cork Report.[59] In the case of individuals who have been adjudged bankrupt, provisions for dealing with transactions at an undervalue and transactions entered into by way of preference are set out in ss339 and 340 of the Insolvency Act 1986. The corresponding provisions for a company subject to an administration order or liquidation are set out in ss238 and 239 of the Act. In cases falling within their ambit, ss339 and 340 enable the trustee of the bankrupt's estate, and ss238 and 239 enable the liquidator or administrator of the company, to apply to the court for relief to reverse the effect of transactions entered into at an undervalue or preferences. Sections 423, 424 and 425 of the Act:

(1) apply to transactions entered into at an undervalue (defined in s.423(1)) for the purpose of "putting assets beyond the reach of a person who is making, or may at some time make, a claim against him" or "of otherwise prejudicing the interests of such a person in relation to the claim which he is making, or may make";

(2) confer a direct cause of action on a claimant regardless of whether or not he has obtained judgment, and regardless of whether, in the case of an individual, the defendant has been adjudged bankrupt, and, in the case of a company, the defendant has been put into liquidation or made the subject of an administration order. If a corporate transferor is in liquidation or subject to an administration order, or an individual transferor has been adjudged bankrupt, the victim needs the leave of the court. There is no requirement that the transaction must have occurred within a specified period prior to insolvency proceedings;[60]

(3) allow transactions to be impeached which have been entered into before proceedings were commenced by the claimant on his claim against the defendant;

---

[57] See also Chapter 7, paras 7.024–5 and para.12.017, above.
[58] By s.235(3) and Sch.10, Pt IV of the Insolvency Act 1985.
[59] 1982, Cmnd 8558, paras 1210–1220 and 1283–1284.
[60] Insolvency Act 1986, s.424(1)(a).

(4) allow transactions to be impeached which have been entered into by the defendant before the claimant acquired a cause of action against the defendant, provided that, as a result of the transaction, the claimant either has been prejudiced by it or may be prejudiced by it,[61] and thus has become, in the words of the statute, "a victim".

Section 423(3) of the Act imposes a requirement[62] as to the purpose of **13.019** the person entering into the transaction, which is additional to the requirement in s.423(1) that the transaction is one "entered into at an undervalue".

The fact that a transaction has had the result of prejudicing creditors does not necessarily mean that the person entered into it for the purpose set out in s.423(3). Result cannot be equated with purpose.[63] What a person's purpose was in entering into a transaction depends on his subjective[64] intention, and is a question of fact.[65] In deciding what a person subjectively intended, the court is entitled to take into account the likely natural consequences of a transaction.[66] Does a person have the purpose set out in s.423(3) of the Act when this is not his only purpose? It suffices if it was a "substantial" purpose and not merely a collateral effect of the transaction[67]—it is not necessary to show that it was the "dominant"[68] or "predominant"[69] purpose. So the fact that the transferor wanted to benefit the transferee out of natural love and affection will not prevent the section applying—even if this was his principal motive. Also it suffices if the purpose was to put the assets out of reach of a person who might in the future make a claim against him.[70]

A claimant can seek relief based on the sections even though the **13.020** transaction sought to be impugned was not entered into for the purpose of defeating enforcement of his particular claim or potential claim, provided that in consequence of the transaction he is a victim.

It is not a requirement of s.423(3) that the purpose of the transaction was dishonest. If the effect of the transaction falls within s.423(3) and the

---

[61] In *Pinewood Joinery v Starelm Properties* [1994] 2 B.C.L.C. 412, the property transferred for £1 was mortgaged for far more than its value, and there was no evidence of "hope value." In consequence the applicants failed to show prejudice—they were no worse off than they had been before the transaction.

[62] *Pagemanor v Ryan*, unreported, October 2, 2002, CA.

[63] *Roycott Spa Leasing Ltd v Lovett* [1995] B.C.C. 502.

[64] *Trowbridge v Trowbridge* [2003] 2 F.L.R. 231.

[65] *Edgington v Fitzmaurice* (1885) 29 Ch.D. 459 at 483, *per* Bowen L.J.: "the state of a man's mind is as much a fact as the state of his digestion . . .".

[66] *Kemmis v Kemmis* [1988] 1 W.L.R. 1307 at 1326G–H.

[67] *IRC v Hashmi* [2002] 2 B.C.L.C. 489; *Kubianghi v Ekpenyong* [2002] 2 B.C.L.C. 597; *Re Brabon Treharne v Brabon* [2001] 1 B.C.L.C. 11; *Roycott Spa Ltd v Lovett* [1995] B.C.C. 502; *Pinewood Joinery v Starelm Properties* [1994] 2 B.C.L.C. 412 at 418–419; see also, on s.37(1) of the Matrimonial Causes Act 1973, the same test applies—*Kemmis v Kemmis* [1988] 1 W.L.R. 1307 at 1331A–B, *per* Nourse L.J.; *Trowbridge v Trowbridge* [2003] 2 F.L.R. 231.

[68] As previously suggested in *Chogan v Saggar* [1992] B.C.C. 306 (on appeal reported at [1994] B.C.L.C. 706).

[69] As previously suggested in *Moon v Franklin, The Independent*, June 2, 1990.

[70] *Midland Bank v Wyatt* [1995] 1 F.L.R. 696.

person entering into the transaction intended this, then it matters not that he acted on advice from solicitors and counsel.[71] A person who in the course of settlement negotiations threatens to dispose of assets so as to defeat a possible judgment is threatening improper conduct of sufficient seriousness that it may result in an exception to the protection of "without prejudice" privilege.[72]

The sections apply to transactions by way of gift and transactions at an undervalue.[73] The test as to whether it is at an "undervalue" is the same as applies under s.238(4) of the Act:[74]

> "It requires a comparison to be made between the value obtained by [the debtor] for the transaction and the value of consideration provided by the debtor. Both considerations must be measurable in money or money's worth and both must be considered from the [debtor's] point of view."[75]

13.021   Under that section what consideration is obtained by the debtor for the transaction is a question of substance and the answer is not dictated by the form.[76] In *Phillips v Brewin Dolphin Bell*,[77] the transaction of selling a business consisted of a number of stages, which included providing the transferor with the benefit of a rental agreement from a third party— the benefit of the rental agreement formed part of the consideration for the transfer of the business. In *National Westminster Bank v Jones* the transferors were shareholders in the transferee company—the increase in value of their shares in the transferee was not part of the value obtained by them for the transfers, and so did not come into the calculation of the value of the consideration received for the transfers. The defendant may, as a result of a transaction, put a third party in a position from which he could demand a ransom to restore the status quo. For example, the defendant may have transferred one out of a set of valuable antiques, thereby destroying the value of the set unless the individual item is restored. The court would take this into account in deciding whether the transaction was at an undervalue.[78] In *Pagemanor Ltd v Ryan*[79] there was in

---

[71] *Arbuthnot Leasing International Ltd v Havelet Leasing Ltd (No.2)* [1992] 1 W.L.R. 455; see also *Barclays Bank plc v Eustice* [1995] 1 W.L.R. 1238 at 1250–1252. For the same position in Australia under s.121 of the Bankruptcy Act (Cth) 1966: *Re World Expro Park Pty Ltd* (1994) 12 A.C.S.R. 759. Under s.172 of the Law of Property Act 1925 it had been necessary to prove dishonesty or sharp practice: *Lloyd's Bank v Marcan* [1973] 1 W.L.R. 1387 at 1391c and 1392 c–d.
[72] *Dora v Simper*, unreported, March 15, 1999, CA.
[73] Insolvency Act 1986, s.423(1).
[74] *Trowbridge v Trowbridge* [2003] 2 F.L.R. 231 at [62]; *National Bank of Kuwait v Menzies* [1994] 2 B.C.L.C. 306; *Re MC Bacon Ltd* [1990] B.C.L.C. 324 (a case under s.238).
[75] *Re M. C. Bacon Ltd* [1990] B.C.L.C. 324 at 340, approved in *Phillips v Brewin Dolphin Bell* [2001] 1 W.L.R. 143 and followed in *National Westminster Bank v Jones* [2001] 1 B.C.L.C. 98.
[76] *Phillips v Brewin Dolphin Bell* [2001] 1 W.L.R. 143.
[77] [2001] 1 W.L.R. 143.
[78] *Agricultural Mortgage Corp plc v Woodward* [1995] 1 B.C.L.C. 1 (wife put in a "ransom" position because she could deny to the mortgagee vacant possession of the mortgaged property); *Barclays Bank v Eustice* [1995] 1 W.L.R. 1238 at 1246.
[79] Unreported, October 2, 2002, CA.

existence a pre-existing contract for the sale of a house by the first and second defendants to the third and fourth defendants concluded seven years before the transaction which the claimant sought to challenge under the section. The value of what the first and second defendants were giving up had to be assessed immediately prior to the later transaction, and taking into account the encumbrances on the house and their obligations in respect of the house at that time. Since the earlier contract remained in force at that point of time, and was only varied through conclusion of the second transaction, the obligations imposed by that contract on the first and second defendants had to be taken into account in assessing whether the second transaction was at an undervalue from their point of view.

The sections enable direct claims to be made against third parties who have benefited from an impugned transaction (s.425(1)(a) and (d)). An application for relief by a victim is treated as made on behalf of every victim of the transaction. It is a form of class action. A consequence of this is that the relief sought is not restricted to the prejudice suffered by the applicant, and accordingly Mareva relief would be granted by reference to the cumulative prejudice caused or liable to be caused by the impugned transaction to all the victims.[80]

The jurisdiction under s.423(2) of the Insolvency Act 1986 is exercisable **13.022** where "a person has entered into . . . a transaction" at an undervalue. Once such a transaction has been entered into by a person, for the purpose of putting assets beyond the reach of a person who is making or may make a claim against him, or otherwise prejudicing the interests of a claimant or a person who may make a claim, then the court, which includes any part of the High Court,[81] has jurisdiction to make "such order as it thinks fit . . ." to restore the position to what it was before the transaction and[82] to protect the interests of victims. That jurisdiction, like the jurisdiction under ss238[83] and 340[84] of the Insolvency Act 1986, can be exercised by the court against foreigners in the course of English insolvency proceedings, in which case the insolvency rules will apply about service out of the jurisdiction: *Re Paramount Airways Ltd (In Administration)*.[85] But the jurisdiction applies regardless of whether there are insolvency proceedings,[86] *e.g.* the question

---

[80] *Dora v Simper* [2000] 2 B.C.L.C. 561.
[81] *TSB v Katz The Times*, May 2, 1994 (Arden J.); see also the Insolvency Act 1986, s.423(4).
[82] The word "and" between s.423(2)(a) and (b) must be read conjunctively so that the order must be designed to do both: *Chogan v Saggar* [1994] 1 B.C.L.C. 706. Where a trustee has disposed of trust property at an undervalue with the statutory purpose, then if in the absence of the transfer, the trust property could have been required to be made available in one way or another to satisfy the claim (*e.g.* because the claim is against the trustee who is in turn entitled to an indemnity from the trust property) the section will apply: *Beckenham M.C. Limited v Centralex Ltd* [2004] EWHC 1287 (Ch) at [23–32] (trustee transferred trust property for no consideration to avoid payment of management charges incurred by the trustee in respect of the trust property, and if the transfer had not taken place, a charging order could have been made under s.2(1)(b)(i) of the Charging Orders Act 1979 on the trust property).
[83] Transactions at an undervalue entered into by a company.
[84] Transactions at an undervalue entered into by an individual.
[85] [1993] Ch. 223.
[86] *Re Banco Nacional de Cuba* [2001] 1 W.L.R. 2039; *Jyske Bank (Gibraltar) Ltd v Spjeldnaes* [1999] 2 B.C.L.C. 101.

may arise in connection with the enforcement of a judgment, in which case service out of the jurisdiction will depend on CPR Pt 6. A claim under s.423 does not come within CPR r.6.19(2),[87] which concerns a claim under an enactment which must on its face contemplate claims being made under it against a foreigner outside the jurisdiction. If the property transferred is located within the jurisdiction then CPR r.6.20(10) will apply.[88]

Although s.423 itself applies to transactions regardless of where they take place and to persons regardless of whether they are foreigners, the court in deciding whether to grant permission for service out of the jurisdiction of a claim or in the exercise of discretion whether to grant relief under the section, will take into account the absence of connections with the territorial jurisdiction of the court. If a transaction has been entered into abroad between foreigners the absence of a sufficient connection with the jurisdiction may make it appropriate for the court to refuse permission to serve proceedings out of the jurisdiction impugning that transaction, or to decline to grant any substantive relief under the section.[89]

13.023   The interests of a bona fide transferee for value without notice "of the relevant circumstances . . ."[90] are protected, so that no order should be made which disadvantages any such transferee (*e.g.* if a transfer is made to a wife who mortgages the property to a building society, provided the building society has acted bona fide and without notice, its rights as mortgagee will be preserved). Subject to this, the court will, though, seek to protect the interest of victims (*e.g.* by charging the property, subject to the building society's mortgage, in favour of the victims as security for their claims).

It may be that the transferee has spent the proceeds of a transaction. The court has power to order him to pay the victims an amount reflecting the benefits obtained by him from the transaction: s.425(1)(d). This is a personal claim against the transferee and can itself be the subject of Mareva relief.[91] If assets are transferred from one company to another and then on a series of transfers, and this is arranged by an individual who controls or is in a position to instruct the various recipients what to do, an order can be made directly against the individual who caused the transfers to be made, even though he personally did not receive any property.[92] This interpretation would further the purpose of the statutory provisions, which is to give adequate protection to "victims" of such transactions. It is also just that those who knowingly participate in a wrongful venture with a common

---

[87] *Re Banco Nacional de Cuba* [2001] 1 W.L.R. 2039 not following *Jyske Bank (Gibraltar) Ltd v Spjeldnaes* [1999] 2 B.C.L.C. 101.

[88] *Re Banco Nacional de Cuba* [2001] 1 W.L.R. 2039.

[89] *Re Banco Nacional de Cuba* [2001] 1 W.L.R. 2039 at [41] and [42]; see also the discussion in Chapter 6, paras 6.006–9; *cf. Jyske Bank (Gibraltar) Ltd v Spjeldnaes* [1999] 2 B.C.L.C. 101.

[90] Defined in s.425(3) as those ". . . by virtue of which an order may be made under section 423(2)".

[91] *Shaw v Narain* [1992] 2 N.Z.L.R. 544.

[92] See the opening words of s.425(2). The orders contemplated in s.425(1) are said to be "without prejudice to the generality of section 423 . . .".

design should be responsible to those who are wronged. In such circumstances the victims would have a direct claim against the individual who caused the transfers to be made with the intention of defrauding creditors, as set out in s.423(3).

In *Aiglon Ltd v Gau Shan*[93] Hirst J. granted Mareva relief against a transferee of assets where there was a strong prima facie case of a transfer coming within s.423. In that case:

(1) there was a direct claim under s.425(1)(d) against the transferee;

(2) the transferee might well have held assets for the transferor, so that the injunction could be extended to the transferee as ancillary to the plaintiff's rights against the transferor; and

(3) there was the potential for winding up the transferor, and then an administrator or liquidator could seek an order under s.238 setting aside the transfer.

If there is only the possibility of a future claim against the transferee, by **13.024** an administrator or liquidator, once appointed, taking steps to set aside the transaction, there is no present right of action against the transferee. The claimant does not have any existing cause of action in tort against the transferee on the grounds that the performed transfer has prevented a subsequent Mareva injunction from being effective in respect of the transferred asset as against the transferor: *Law Debenture Trust Corporation plc v Ural Caspian Oil Corporation*.[94] Nor does the transferor have any legal right against the transferee which could be preserved by Mareva relief. The transferor is bound by the transfer and has no right to reopen or avoid it. Avoidance of the transfer will be available only in the future.

Nevertheless, there is still jurisdiction to grant Mareva relief against the transferee, provided the claimant has a subsisting cause of action against the transferor.[95] This is because the assets held by the transferee may be made available for satisfaction of the claimant's claim in consequence of the claimant obtaining judgment in the action and then bringing winding-up or bankruptcy proceedings against the transferor whilst the judgment remains unsatisfied. Although this procedure lies in the future, there is an existing substantive right of the claimant which is being relied upon in the proceedings, and the Mareva jurisdiction enables assets to be preserved so that a future judgment in that action can be satisfied.[96] Thus the statutory provisions,[97] which enable the court to undo transactions on the application of an administrator or liquidator of a company or the trustee in

---

[93] [1993] 1 Lloyd's Rep. 164.
[94] [1995] Ch. 152 discussed in para.2.048 above.
[95] *Aiglon Ltd v Gau Shan* supports this view at 170. *Westpac Banking Corporation v Hilliard* [2001] V.S.C. 187 at paras 41–43 and 46 following *Cardile v LED Builders Pty Ltd* (1999) 198 C.L.R. 380 at 405.
[96] See *Coxton Pty Ltd v Milne*, discussed at para.13.014, above; *Gibb Australia v Cremor* (1992) 106 F.L.R. 453, Federal Court of Australia.
[97] Insolvency Act 1986, ss238–241 and 339–342. These cover transactions entered into at an undervalue and preferences, but there is a limited time laid down by ss.240 and 341 within which to impugn the transaction.

bankruptcy of an individual, supply procedures which can enable the claimant to obtain satisfaction of his judgment in the action. In principle Mareva relief can be granted with these procedures in mind because the relief can preserve assets to satisfy the judgment.

13.025   In England the jurisdiction is derived solely from s.37 of the Supreme Court Act 1981, and this has the consequence that in England Mareva relief can only be sought against a defendant based on an existing substantive cause of action.[98] In such circumstances the claimant could have a receiver appointed by interlocutory order to get in a debt due to the defendant.[99] The granting of a Mareva injunction against the defendant and the third party debtor as opposed to having a receiver appointed to get in the debt merely goes to procedural mechanics. Is it sufficient to show a potential future claim which might be made by or in the name of the defendant against the third parties, *e.g.* to avoid transactions at an undervalue once a corporate defendant goes into liquidation? The High Court of Australia in *Cardile v LED Builders Pty Ltd*[1] considered that this would be sufficient, and rejected any requirement that there had to be a subsisting cause of action or right to relief as against the non-party—it sufficed that there could in the future be a route leading to effective relief.[2] In that case the plaintiff had an accrued cause of action against Mr and Mrs Cardile to bring proceedings based on the statute in respect of the declaration and payment to them by the corporate defendant of the dividends, and on the plaintiff's undertaking to commence such proceedings, an injunction was granted in support of that right.

The Siskina requirement of an existing cause of action is only a requirement that the claimant has a cause of action against the defendant. The Mareva relief is granted in aid of that cause of action. The purpose of the Mareva jurisdiction is to safeguard assets which could be required to meet a money judgment, and in particular to prevent unjustifiable dissipations of assets which could be required for the purpose of satisfying the judgment. The plaintiff had a cause of action for copyright infringement and the benefit of a judgment on liability. Therefore there was jurisdiction to restrain dealings with assets which could be required in order to satisfy a judgment against Eagle.

13.026   *Cardile* was followed in England in *C Inc. v L*,[3] albeit on facts on which the right of the defendant against the non-party was an existing right to an indemnity against a judgment which the claimant had obtained against the defendant. The principle stated in *Cardile* was also that adopted by the Court of Appeal in *Yukong Line Ltd v Rendsburg Investments Corporation.*[4] In that case the plaintiff had obtained judgment against a company but

---

[98] See Chapter 12, paras 12.001–4 above.
[99] See Chapter 16, para.16.021 below.
[1] (1999) 198 C.L.R. 380.
[2] *Ibid.*, at 405–406 and 427.
[3] [2001] 2 Lloyd's Rep. 459 at [75–79].
[4] [2001] 2 Lloyd's Rep. 113 at [38–47].

failed on the merits against the individual who was found by the trial judge to be in control of that company. Mareva relief was granted against that individual. An order was made by the judge ordering the company by the individual to pay a sum of money into court.[5] The Court of Appeal at an earlier hearing had held that the individual was not in breach of that order because the words of the order only required the company to pay the money into court.[6] It was held that the freezing injunction was not "wrongly granted" because it was ancillary to enforcement of the judgment against the company—the evidence indicated that the individual had had money from the company and was still controlling assets of the company.[7]

In practice in Mareva cases an applicant may seek to rely on ss.423–425 as well as the other provisions, enabling a transfer to be avoided.[8] If this is done, the claimant, as a victim, will have a direct substantive claim against the transferee under ss.423–425. If the claimant can make out on the evidence a case that the transaction was entered into with the relevant intention, this will be an important factor in deciding whether to grant an injunction against the third party. It will also be relevant to look at whether there is a real risk that unless an injunction is granted against the third party the third party may deal with assets with the effect of defeating that claim.[9]

Without proof of the intention the case is less persuasive and may result in the court as a matter of discretion declining to grant an injunction.[10] The burden of proof in a case founded on s.423 is upon the applicant seeking relief, even if this is in the context of proceedings where an interim charging order has been made and the question is whether it should be made final.[11]

In *DCT v Ahern*,[12] summary judgment had been obtained against the first **13.027** defendant, and the plaintiff sought Mareva relief against the third and fourth defendants which were companies incorporated and resident outside the jurisdiction of the court. These companies were alleged to have assets within the jurisdiction, but otherwise had no connection with it. The plaintiff originally sought leave to serve a writ out of the jurisdiction on

---

[5] The order is set out in *Yukong Line Ltd v Rendsburg Investments Corporation* [2001] 2 Lloyd's Rep. 113 at [14].
[6] Described in *Yukong Line Ltd v Rendsburg Investments Corporation* [2001] 2 Lloyd's Rep. 113 at [41].
[7] [2001] 2 Lloyd's Rep. 113 at [45].
[8] *Kuan Han Pty Ltd v Oceanview Group Holdings Pty Ltd* [2003] F.C.A. 1063 (September 12, 2003) (claim based on s.37A of the Conveyancing Act 1919 (NSW) which corresponds to what was s.172 of the Law of Property Act 1925); this was done in *Mercantile Group v Aiyela* [1993] F.S.R. 745, although that was not the basis on which the judge made the order, or the Court of Appeal at [1994] Q.B. 366, upheld it—see *Yukong Line Ltd v Rendsburg Investments Corporation* [2001] 2 Lloyd's Rep. 113 at [46].
[9] *Flightwise Travel Service Ltd v Gill* [2003] EWHC 3082 at [53], Ch.D.
[10] Relief limited to the assets transferred is not Mareva relief but relief granted to preserve the subject-matter of the claim against the third party. See also Chapter 12, para.12.009; *Re Mouat* [1899] 1 Ch. 831 at 833; *Bank of Queensland v Grant* [1984] 1 N.S.W.L.R. 409.
[11] *Habib Bank Ltd v Ahmed* [2003] EWHC 1697.
[12] [1986] 2 Qd R. 342, Supreme Court of Queensland.

these companies in respect of the Mareva relief, but without alleging a cause of action directly against either company. This was refused on the grounds that, under the Queensland rules of court, leave could be granted only for a claim based on a cause of action, and since the claim for Mareva relief was not an assertion of a cause of action, then, following *Siskina v Distos SA*,[13] no leave could be granted. But the plaintiff also put forward a claim based on s.228 of the Property Law 1974 of Queensland which provided:

> "Save as provided in this section, every alienation of property . . . with intent to defraud creditors shall be voidable at the instance of any person thereby prejudiced."

(The same wording as what was s.172(1) of the Law of Property Act 1925.)

The court granted leave to serve out of the jurisdiction a writ against the companies seeking to set aside prior transfers of the relevant assets from the first defendant, based on this section, and granted Mareva relief, in respect of that claim, against the two companies. Similarly in *FCT v Goldspink*,[14] the court granted Mareva relief against the wife of a judgment debtor in contemplation of proceedings to set aside prior transfers by the husband to the wife which were said to be voidable dispositions under the relevant statutory provisions.

13.028 Once the claimant is in a position to commence proceedings against a third party to set aside a transfer, Mareva relief may more readily be granted against the third party[15] in support of the cause of action conferred by statute. Anton Piller relief can also be granted in these circumstances[16] against the transferor and the third party.

If the defendant is already subject to Mareva relief and wishes to have the injunction varied to enable a transfer to proceed, the court is not obliged to refuse the application simply because there is the possibility that, once the claimant has obtained judgment, he will take steps to have the transfer impeached on the grounds that it was carried out at an undervalue or constituted a preference falling within the statutory provisions.[17]

---

[13] [1979] A.C. 210.

[14] (1985) 17 A.T.R. 290 at 297–298, Supreme Court of New South Wales.

[15] An injunction limited to the property transferred or its proceeds (see Insolvency Act 1986, s.425(1)(b)) is available under the jurisdiction to grant relief over the subject-matter of the proceedings, and is relief *quia timet* in support of a legal right of the claimant in respect of that property: *Re Mouat* [1899] 1 Ch. 831 at 833; *First Industry Corporation v Goh* [2002] W.A.S.C. 111 (May 14, 2002) (where Mareva relief against the third party was refused because of lack of risk of dissipation but an injunction was granted to preserve the property transferred). An injunction can be granted over the asset in the hands of the transferee because if it were disposed of to a bona fide purchaser for value without notice the claimant would have no remedy against the asset (Insolvency Act 1985, s.425(2)). If an injunction is sought in respect of assets belonging to the third party which are not the subject of a claim under the statute or their proceeds, then the relief sought is Mareva relief and a real risk of dissipation by the third party must be shown.

[16] *Cook Industries v Galliher* [1979] Ch. 439.

[17] *Iraqi Ministry of Defence v Arcepey Shipping Co. (The Angel Bell)* [1981] Q.B. 65 at 72.

Whether the intended transfer is to be allowed is a matter of discretion for the court.

(ii) No "privilege": fraud, dishonesty and iniquity

A transferor may have sought advice in relation to the structuring of a **13.029** transfer of assets to a third party. Such documents may be very relevant to the intention behind the transfer and what has been done with those assets. If the advice was from legal advisers, the documents would ordinarily be privileged from production, being the subject of legal professional privilege. However, no one is entitled to maintain confidentiality in communications with a lawyer for advice on how to commit or further a crime, a fraud or acts of dishonesty.[18] This is so regardless of whether the lawyer is privy to the purpose or not.[19] If the court considers on a prima facie[20] view that legal advice was sought for a transaction entered into for the purpose of defrauding creditors within ss423–425, then this purpose is regarded as sufficiently "iniquitous" to have the consequence that the documents relating to the obtaining of that advice will not be privileged.[21] Privilege will not be upheld when advice has been sought in connection with setting up and carrying out a fraudulent or dishonest scheme, *e.g.* misappropriating assets and hiding them through a series of transfers. Privilege in a witness statement taken by a solicitor for possible use in legal or arbitration proceedings extends to the identity of the witness and the contents of the statement even if they indicate the commission of a crime or a past fraud.[22]

(5) Service out of the jurisdiction of proceedings against a non-party in respect of assets in the name of and held by the third party

For the purposes of service out of the jurisdiction, a distinction needs to **13.030** be drawn between three categories of case as follows.

(1) Cases in which a direct substantive cause of action is asserted in England against the third party, *e.g.* in respect of assets within the jurisdiction which are the subject of a claim to relief under ss423, 424 and 425 of the Insolvency Act 1986, or in respect of which the claimant asserts a tracing claim.

---

[18] *Derby & Co. Ltd v Weldon (No.7)* [1990] 1 W.L.R. 1156; *Crescent Farm (Sidcup) Sports v Sterling Offices* [1972] Ch. 553; *Gamlen Chemical Co. (UK) v Rochem (No.2)* (1980) 124 S.J. 276.
[19] *Barclays Bank v Eustice* [1995] 1 W.L.R. 1238 at 1252C–E.
[20] *O'Rourke v Derbyshire* [1920] A.C. 581 at 604 and 633.
[21] *Barclays Bank v Eustice* [1995] 1 W.L.R. 1238.
[22] *China National Petroleum Corporation v Fenwick Elliott* [2002] EWHC 60 at paras [44–46], Ch.D.

(2) Cases in which a cause of action is asserted only against a defendant to a substantive claim on the merits in proceedings in England, and the claim against the non-party is only for relief which is only ancillary to the substantive claim.

(3) Cases in which a cause of action is asserted only against a defendant to a substantive claim on the merits otherwise than in England, who is subject to interim relief granted against that defendant under the provisions of s.25 of the Civil Jurisdiction and Judgments Act 1982, and the claim against the third party is for relief which is only ancillary to Mareva relief granted against the defendant to the substantive claim.

Category (1)

13.031 The claimant is asserting a substantive claim against the non-party and may proceed with it against a defendant who has to be served outside of the jurisdiction if he can satisfy one of the requirements of CPR r.6.19 or 6.20. If the claim is a proprietary claim in respect of assets within the jurisdiction, then in principle the substantive claim will fall within CPR r.6.20(2); the injunction is claimed as part of the substantive relief consequential on a cause of action, and thus satisfies the test which was appropriate under the former RSC Ord.11, r.1(1)(i) considered by the House of Lords in *Siskina v Distos SA*.[23]

In a case against a foreign non-party who is domiciled in a Member State under Council Regulation 44/2001 (The Judgments Regulation),[24] if the defendant can be sued in England on the substantive claim against him, substantive proceedings may be possible against the third party under Art.6(1) of the Judgments Regulation: *Aiglon v Gau Shan*[25] (the claim against L'Aiglon SA).

Category (2)

13.032 As to obtaining an injunction against a non-party who is outside of the jurisdiction,[26] see Chapter 6, above at para.6.071–8.

Once a judgment has been obtained against the defendant the involvement of the non-party will be in the proceedings to execute or enforce the judgment. Article 22(5) of the Judgments Regulation covers proceedings to enforce that judgment when the judgment is to be enforced inside the jurisdiction.[27] In such proceedings there may well be issues concerning

---

[23] [1979] A.C. 210. Also see *Mercedes Benz AG v Leiduck* [1996] A.C. 284; *DCT v Ahern* [1986] 2 Qd R. 342, Supreme Court of Queensland.
[24] O.J. No.L012, January 16, 2001, pp.1–23.
[25] [1993] 1 Lloyd's Rep. 164.
[26] *C Inc. v L* [2001] 2 Lloyd's Rep. 459.
[27] *Société Eram Shipping Co. Ltd v Compagnie Internationale de Navigation* [2004] 1 A.C. 260; *Kuwait Oil Tanker Co. SAK v Qabazard* [2004] 1 A.C. 300.

third parties' rights in assets which have to be resolved. Proceedings under Article 22(5) can be served without permission under CPR r.6.19. In cases not governed by CPR r.6.19, the non-party can be served with proceedings in relation to the enforcement of a judgment or arbitral award under CPR r.6.20(9).

In cases in which the judgment is to be enforced by a foreign court an injunction can be granted by the English court in support of the enforcement proceedings abroad pursuant to s.25 of the Civil Jurisdiction and Judgments Act 1925.

Category (3)

An application for interim relief under s.25(1) of the Civil Jurisdiction and Judgments Act 1982 can be served out of the jurisdiction with permission granted under CPR 6.20(4). That rule is wide enough to allow permission to be granted to enable interim relief proceedings on a defendant to the foreign proceedings on the merits and upon a person who is not a party to the substantive proceedings but who is to be made subject to an order made by way of interim relief.[28] As a matter of discretion it may be "inexpedient" to grant interim relief in such circumstances.[29] **13.033**

(6) Cases in which the non-party does not claim to own the assets outright

It may be that the non-party does not claim that he owns the assets outright, only that he has an existing right to possess or to sell them: *e.g.* because he has a charge or lien over them. Mortgagees and debenture-holders are among the most common types of third party affected by Mareva injunctions falling within this category; frequently they are also banks. A Mareva injunction will not normally be allowed to interfere with the exercise by a mortgagee of his powers of sale.[30] Similarly, if the assets are clearly subject to a pre-existing lien or other charge, the court will usually exclude them from the terms of the Mareva injunction, or the third party will be granted a specific variation enabling him to exercise his rights in respect of those assets.[31] **13.034**

An equitable charge or assignment can be created by contract, and will be effective to create priority even though, in the case of a debt, it has not

---

[28] See Chapter 6, paras 6.073–77, above.
[29] See Chapter 6, paras 6.050–59, above.
[30] For an example of a case where an injunction specifically aimed at preventing the sale of two mortgaged vessels was discharged, see *The Arietta and Julia* [1985] 2 W.L.R. Rep. 50.
[31] *Capital Cameras Ltd v Harold Lines Ltd* [1991] 1 W.L.R. 54; *Cretanor Maritime Co. Ltd v Irish Marine Management Ltd* [1978] 1 W.L.R. 966; *Pharoah's Plywood Co. Ltd v Allied Wood Products*, Court of Appeal (Civ Div) Transcript No. 217 of 1980 (January 18, 1980). See also Chapter 4, para.4.015.

yet been notified to the debtor.[32] If there is a bona fide commercial agreement which regulates how particular assets are to be dealt with, then ordinarily Mareva relief will be varied to enable that agreement to be performed. In *SSAB Oxelosund AB v Xendrai Trading Pte Ltd*,[33] there was a binding commercial agreement regulating the distribution of proceeds of a hull insurance policy, and the court declined to grant an injunction interfering with performance of this agreement. The Mareva injunction should not interfere with carrying out bona fide transactions agreed at arm's length with a third party in the ordinary course of business.

---

[32] *Pharoah's Plywood Co. Ltd v Allied Wood Products*, Court of Appeal (Civ Div) Transcript No.217 of 1980 (January 18, 1980); *Holt v Heatherfield Trust Ltd* [1942] 2 K.B. 1 at 14.
[33] [1992] 1 S.L.R. 600 (Singapore).

Chapter 14

Anti-suit injunctions

(1) The "anti-suit injunction"

An anti-suit injunction is an injunction against a person enjoining him from **14.001** commencing or continuing with proceedings in a court abroad. In England the jurisdiction is found in s.37(1) of the Supreme Court Act 1981.[1] It is not directed at the foreign court,[2] it does not call into question the jurisdiction of the foreign court, and it is granted under the *in personam* jurisdiction of a court of equity.[3] That the injunction is only directed at the conduct of the defendant and does not call into question the jurisdiction of the foreign court has been called the "English Artifice".[4] This is because, although the injunction is based on the conduct of the defendant, (1) depending on the grounds on which it is sought, it requires investigation of whether the foreign court is a *forum conveniens*, and (2) if granted, it affects the exercise of jurisdiction by the foreign court. Because the injunction acting on a party before the foreign court affects the assumption or exercise of jurisdiction by a foreign court the European Court held in *Turner v Grovit*[5] that the anti-suit injunction was inconsistent with the Brussels Convention in that it interfered with the court first seized deciding whether it had jurisdiction under the Convention, and when one looks at the substance of granting an effective anti-suit injunction it is equivalent to restraining the foreign proceedings themselves.[6]

---

[1] *South Carolina Insurance Co. v Assurantie Maatschappij "De Zeven Provincien" NV* [1987] A.C. 24 at 39G–40H.
[2] *Turner v Grovit* [2002] 1 W.L.R. 107 at [23].
[3] *Société Nationale Industrielle Aerospatiale v Lee Kui Jak* [1987] A.C. 871 at 892; *Turner v Grovit* [2002] 1 W.L.R. 107 at [23]; *Donohue v Armco* [2002] 1 Lloyd's Rep. 425 at [19]; *Barclays Bank v Homan* [1993] B.C.L.C. 680 at p.700.
[4] C. Ambrose, "Can Anti-Suit Injunctions Survive European Community Law?" (2003) 52 I.C.L.Q. 401 at 407–410.
[5] ECJ judgment April 27, 2004, agreeing with the Opinion of A–G Colomer.
[6] *Laker Airways Ltd v Pan American* Airways, 559 F.Supp. 1124 at p.1128 (US Dist Ct. DC, 1983) *per* Judge Harold Greene (". . . a direct interference with proceedings in this Court."); *Stonington Partners Inc v Lernout & Hauspie Speech Products N.V.* 310 F.3d 118 (3d Cir.2002); *Compagnie des Bauxites de Guinea v Insurance Co of North America*, 651 F.2d 877 at p.887 (3d Cir. 1981).

14.002   The Courts of Appeals for each of the District of Columbia, the First,[7] Second, Third[8] and Sixth Circuits follow a restrictive approach[9] to the granting of anti-suit injunctions, in which the general rule is to permit parallel proceedings to go on abroad without interference by injunction at least until final judgment is achieved which can be pleaded as *res judicata* in the other jurisdiction.[10] These courts emphasise that the injunction should be used sparingly, with great restraint, recognising the need to uphold respect and comity for foreign states and their courts, but recognise that it may be granted if the parties before the US court and the foreign court are the same and the issues are the same or substantially identical, in (1) the protection of the jurisdiction of the court or (2) the protection or the advancement of important national policies. The First Circuit Court of Appeals has declined to view it as essential to cross one of these two thresholds before an anti-suit injunction could be granted, and to that extent has endorsed a less restrictive approach than the other Circuits.[11] The Fifth, Seventh and Ninth Circuits adopt a "lax" or "liberal" approach.[12] Those courts place greater emphasis on the desirability of avoiding the same actions going on both in the United States and abroad and the need to avoid the risk of conflicting decisions.

The resolution on anti-suit injunctions adopted in 2003[13] by the Institut de Droit International recognised that they have a limited place and considered that there should be restraint because of the needs of comity, and that injunctions ought not to be granted outside of (1) enforcing contractual jurisdiction clauses or arbitration agreements, (2) where a

---

[7] *Quaak v Klynveld Peat Marwick Goerdeler Bedrijfsrevisoren* 361 F.3d 11 (1st Cir. 2004), upholding an anti-suit injunction restraining an application by the defendant in Belgium for an order which would have placed penalties upon the plaintiffs if they sought to take any step to obtain the disclosure ordered by the US District Court; this came within both (1) the protection of the jurisdiction of the US District Court and (2) the protection or the advancement of important national policies.

[8] *Stonington Partners Inc v Lernout & Hauspie Speech Products N.V.* 310 F.3d 118 (3d Cir. 2002) in which the case was remitted to first instance to reconsider the question of an anti-suit injunction which was sought to prevent a creditor achieving in insolvency proceedings in Belgium a higher priority than would be accorded to it in chapter 11 proceedings in the US; *General Electric Co. v Deutz AG* 270 F.3d 144 at p.161 (3d Cir. 2001).

[9] *Gau Shan Co. v Bankers Trust Co.*, 956 F.2d 1349, 1354–58 (6th Cir. 1992); *China Trade & Dev. Corp. v M.V. Choong Yong*, 837 F.2d 33 at pp.36–37 (2d Cir. 1987); *Paramedics Electromedicina Commercial, Ltda v GE Medical Systems Information Technologies Inc* 2004 US App. Lexis 10 235 (2d Cir. 2004) and *Laker Airways Limited v Sabena*, 731 F.2d 909 at pp.937–45 (D.C. Cir. 1984).

[10] *Laker Airways Limited v Sabena, Belgian World Airlines*, 731 F.2d 909 at pp.926–927 (D.C. Cir. 1984).

[11] *Quaak v Klynveld Peat Marwick Goerdeler Bedrijfsrevisoren* 361 F.3d 11 (1st Cir. 2004).

[12] *Kaepa Inc v Achilles Corporation* 76 F.3d 624 (5th Cir. 1996); *Allendale Mutual Insurance Co. v Bull Data Systems., Inc.*, 10 F.3d 425, 431–32 (7th Cir. 1993) (restraining a French company suing in France on an insurance taken out to cover the contents of a French warehouse, because of doubts on whether the commercial court at Lille would be capable of fairly disposing of the insurer's defence based on arson); *Seattle Totems Hockey Club, Inc. v Nat'l Hockey League*, 652 F.2d 852, 855–56 (9th Cir. 1981).

[13] "Le recours à la doctrine du forum non conveniens et aux "anti-suit injunctions" principes directeurs." Session de Bruges, 2003; Rapporteur: Sir Lawrence Collins, Co-Rapporteur: M. Georges Droz (text available at *http://www.idi-iil.org/*).

plaintiff has acted oppressively or unreasonably in a foreign jurisdiction, or (3) in the protection of a court's own jurisdiction in matters such as insolvency or administration of estates. Whilst there is a spectrum of different views in the United States, in Europe, and elsewhere, about the proper use of the jurisdiction, the intrusion on to the sovereignty of other nations and the rights of their citizens, which is involved in granting an anti-suit injunction restraining proceedings in a foreign court, means that "comity" takes on a sense in this context which goes well beyond mere courtesy, mutual respect, and even the desirability of co-operation between states.

In Australia, besides the jurisdiction derived from the Court of Chancery, there is also an inherent jurisdiction of the court to act so as to prevent abuse of its process or to protect the integrity of those processes.[14] Criticism has been made in the High Court of Australia of the English case law not recognising the existence of this inherent jurisdiction of the court.[15] The law on anti-suit injunctions has proceeded in different directions in England, Canada[16] and Australia.[17]

In *British Airways Board v Laker Airways Ltd*,[18] Lord Diplock put the anti-suit jurisdiction as being based on a right not to be sued in the foreign court, and included within that cases in which the English court gives anticipatory effect to a defence to the foreign action. But he also endorsed the opinion expressed by Lord Scarman in *Castanho v Brown & Root (UK) Ltd*[19] that:

> "the width and flexibility of equity are not to be undermined by categorisation. Caution in the exercise of the jurisdiction is certainly needed; but the way in which the judges have expressed themselves from 1821[20] onwards amply supports the view . . . that the injunction can be granted against a party properly before the court, where it is appropriate to avoid injustice."

14.003 Where an anti-suit injunction is granted restraining pursuit of foreign proceedings brought against the applicant, then if the injunction is broken contempt proceedings can be brought against the contemnor; this is

---

[14] *CSR Ltd v Cigna Insurance Australia Ltd* (1997) 189 C.L.R. 345 at 390–392; *Australian Broadcasting Corporation v Lenah Game Meats Pty Ltd* (2001) 208 C.L.R. 199 at paras 93–95.
[15] *Australian Broadcasting Corporation v Lenah Game Meats Pty Ltd* (2001) 208 C.L.R. 199 at paras 93–95.
[16] *Amchem Products Inc. v British Columbia (Workers' Compensation Board)* [1993] 1 S.C.R. 897 (presumption in favour of anti-suit injunction if the foreign court is not the *forum conveniens*).
[17] *CSR Ltd v Cigna Insurance Australia Ltd* (1997) 189 C.L.R. 345 (lack of any "single forum" anti-suit jurisdiction), and limiting the anti-suit jurisdiction to where the injunction protects the jurisdiction of the Australian court and where it is needed to protect a contractual right or to prevent oppressive or vexatious conduct.
[18] [1985] A.C. 58 at 81.
[19] [1981] A.C. 557 at 573.
[20] *Bushby v Munday* (1821) 5 Madd. 297.

discussed in Chapter 19. In addition any foreign judgment obtained through contempt would not be recognised or enforced in England on the grounds of English public policy; this is so under the Judgments Regulation,[21] and the same would be so in other cases.

(2) The revolutions in the case law associated with the adoption of *forum non conveniens*

14.004 The case law has undergone two swings of the pendulum. First there was the period up until the doctrine of *forum non conveniens* became incorporated into English law. During that period the test for obtaining an anti-suit injunction outside of enforcement of a substantive right (*e.g.* a contract) was whether the foreign proceedings were vexatious.[22] This was a high test seldom satisfied.[23] For this purpose the applicant "had to show that the plaintiff in the foreign court could not obtain an advantage from the foreign procedure which he could not obtain in the English court".[24]

After the incorporation of *forum non conveniens*, the House of Lords in *Castanho v Brown & Root (UK) Ltd*[25] had apparently thought that the question whether an anti-suit injunction was to be granted was governed by the same legal principles as whether a stay was to be granted, although this may have been because this was the assumption made in argument before them.[26] This led to a second period in which stay principles were applied and the question was viewed as one turning on whether England was the more appropriate forum.[27] In *South Carolina Insurance Co. v Assurantie Maatschappij "De Zeven Provincien" NV*, Lord Brandon gave two categories of case which qualify for an injunction to be granted by the English court. The first is when there is a threatened invasion of a legal or equitable right.[28] The second is when conduct is threatened which would be "unconscionable".[29] The anti-suit injunction based on *forum non conveniens* was considered by him to be an exception to these categories.[30]

---

[21] Council Regulation 44/2001 (O.J. January 16, 2001, pp.1–23). See *Philip Alexander Securities and Futures Ltd v Bamberger* [1997] I.L.Pr. 73; *Through Transport Mutual Insurance Association (Eurasia) Ltd v New India Assurance Co. Ltd* [2004] 1 Lloyd's Rep. 206 at [42].

[22] *Hyman v Helm* (1882) 24 Ch.D. 531; *Vardopulo v Vardopulo* (1909) 25 T.L.R. 518; *Cohen v Rothfield* [1919] 1 K.B. 410; *Kerr on Injunctions* (6th ed., 1927), pp. 596–600.

[23] *Orr-Lewis v Orr-Lewis* [1949] P. 347.

[24] *Bank of Tokyo Ltd v Karoon* [1987] A.C. at 60D–F, *per* Robert Goff L.J.; *Armstrong v Armstrong* [1892] P. 98 at 101.

[25] [1981] A.C. 557 at 574.

[26] *Société Nationale Industrielle Aerospatiale v Lee Kui Jak* [1987] A.C. 871 at 896.

[27] *Smith Kline & French v Bloch* [1983] 1 W.L.R. 730 at 737–738; *British Airways Board v Laker* [1985] A.C. 58 at 80; *South Carolina Insurance Co. v Assurantie Maatschappij "De Zeven Provincien" NV* [1987] A.C. 24 at 40E–H, *per* Lord Brandon.

[28] *South Carolina Insurance Co. v Assurantie Maatschappij "De Zeven Provincien" NV* [1987] A.C. 24 at 40C–D.

[29] *South Carolina Insurance Co. v Assurantie Maatschappij "De Zeven Provincien" NV* [1987] A.C. 24 at 40D; *British Airways Board v Laker* [1985] A.C. 58 at 81.

[30] [1987] A.C. at 40F–H.

This second period was brought to an end by the decision of the Privy Council in *Société Nationale Industrielle Aerospatiale v Lee Kui Jak*,[31] in which it was held that there was no jurisdiction to grant an anti-suit injunction based solely on the court's view about *forum non conveniens.*

The reason is that the injunction jurisdiction is essentially different from the stay jurisdiction. The stay is a self-denying restraint by the English court in exercising its jurisdiction. The injunction, although granted against the individual and not the foreign court, has the effect of preventing the foreign proceedings from going ahead. Prima facie it is for the foreign court to decide whether it is going to proceed and the assumption must be that justice will be equally available and will be done in the foreign court. The principles of comity,[32] and restraint in interfering in the conduct abroad of foreigners,[33] inhibit the exercise of the jurisdiction to grant an anti-suit injunction. It is for these reasons that the jurisdiction to grant an anti-suit injunction should only be granted with caution.[34] An argument which shows only that there could be differences in view between the English court and the foreign court about where is the natural forum and where a case could more appropriately be tried, cannot justify the granting of an anti-suit injunction.[35] The English court will not arrogate to itself the right to decide this through granting an anti-suit injunction.[36] In cases in which there is a non-exclusive jurisdiction clause, if it is to be interpreted as not only making the English jurisdiction an appropriate forum but also so as to enable the English court to decide where the underlying case on the merits ought to be tried then there would be no impermissible arrogation.[37]

14.005 (margin)

(3) The principles which apply to anti-suit injunctions

The general principles are:

14.006 (margin)

(1) Rigid categorisation has no place in this field. One reason is that equity does not stand still and new solutions have to be found to

---

[31] [1987] A.C. 871.
[32] *Turner v Grovit* [2002] 1 W.L.R. 107 at [25]; *Airbus Industrie GIE v Patel* [1999] 1 A.C. 119 at 133.
[33] *Société Eram Shipping Co. Ltd v Compagnie Internationale de Navigation* [2004] 1 A.C. 260; *Mackinnon v Donaldson Lufkin & Jenrette Securities Corporation* [1986] Ch. 482.
[34] *Aggeliki Charis Compania Maritima SA v Pagnan SpA (The Angelic Grace)* [1995] 1 Lloyd's Rep. 87 at 96 LHC, a consideration which does not normally apply to enforcement of a clear covenant not to sue in the foreign court. See also A. Briggs, "Anti-suit Injunctions in a Complex World" in *Lex Mercatoria* (F. Rose ed., 2000), Chapter 12.
[35] *Société Nationale Industrielle Aerospatiale v Lee Kui Jak* [1987] A.C. 871 at 895.
[36] *Royal Bank of Canada v Cooperatieve Centrale Raiffeisen-Boerenleenbank BA* [2004] 1 Lloyd's Rep. 471; *E.I. Du Pont de Nemours v Endo Laboratories Inc.* [1988] 2 Lloyd's Rep. 240 at 244 RHC.
[37] See paras 14.015–8, below.

new problems. Another is that broad statements of general principle will be too general and may omit essential qualifications.

(2) The idea that the remedy can be granted when a person has a right not to be sued in the foreign jurisdiction includes cases where there is an exclusive jurisdiction clause or arbitration clause, or where the English court gives effect to an anticipatory defence[38] available against the claim made in the foreign forum. But that idea cannot explain all the cases, and it has, on occasions, led to parties contending for the existence of a "right" which is difficult to formulate in argument and which, on analysis, evaporates.[39] "Under English law, a person has no right not to be sued in a particular forum, domestic or foreign, unless there is some specific factor which gives him that right."[40] One type of English anti-suit injunction which is firmly based on a threatened abuse of the process of the English court is the jurisdiction to restrain presentation or advertisement of a winding-up petition.[41]

(3) The word "unconscionable" used by Lord Diplock in *British Airways Board v Laker Airways Ltd*[42] and by Lord Brandon in *South Carolina Insurance Co. v Assurantie Maatschappij "De Zeven Provincien" NV*[43] to describe conduct which may be enjoined emphasises that:

(a) it is not necessary to show that the foreign proceedings are vexatious,

(b) an opinion formed by the English court about *forum non conveniens* is not enough to justify granting the injunction,[44] and

(c) the jurisdiction is not to be fettered by classification. This is not an area in which the narrow formulation of the injunction jurisdiction stated by Lord Diplock in *Siskina v Distos Compania Naviera SA (The Siskina)*[45] has left a legacy.[46]

(4) If the question is which court should hear and determine the underlying substantive dispute, an alternative forum case, then whether the English court is the more appropriate forum is a starting point or threshold question. If the foreign court applies the

---

[38] *British Airways Board v Laker Airways Ltd* [1985] A.C. 58 at 81.
[39] An example was that of the unsuccessful argument advanced by the respondents and rejected in *South Carolina Insurance Co. v Assurantie Maatschappij "De Zeven Provincien" NV* [1987] A.C. 24 at 40H–41C.
[40] *Turner v Grovit* [2002] 1 W.L.R. 107 at [25].
[41] *Bryanston Finance Ltd v De Vries No.2* [1976] Ch. 63; *Charles Forte Investments Ltd v Amanda* [1964] Ch. 240; *Mann v Goldstein* [1968] 1 W.L.R. 1091 at 1093–1094.
[42] [1985] A.C. 58 at 81.
[43] [1987] A.C. 24 at 40D.
[44] *E. I. Du Pont de Nemours v Endo Laboratories Inc.* [1988] 2 Lloyd's Rep. 240.
[45] [1979] A.C. 210 at 256.
[46] *Castanho v Brown & Root (UK) Ltd* [1981] A.C. at 573C–F; *British Airways Board v Laker Airways Ltd* [1985] A.C. 58 at 81.

principle of *forum non conveniens* normally the English court should respect its decision. If the threshold question is answered in favour of England then the court considers whether "the ends of justice" require the granting of the injunction.[47] The court also takes into account whether the respondent to the application would be deprived ". . . of advantages in the foreign forum of which it would be unjust to deprive him".[48]

(5) It follows that in an alternative forum case, the court will usually not grant an anti-suit injunction preventing what may constitute a decision being reached by the foreign court which should be respected by the English court.[49] However, there are still occasions outside of the enforcement of a contractual promise, where an injunction will be granted without waiting for a decision of the foreign court, *e.g.* where the appropriate forum is overwhelmingly the English court, the English proceedings were started first and an anti-suit injunction was being sought in the foreign proceedings against English jurisdiction.[50]

(6) There is also a role for the injunction in protecting the integrity of the judicial process in England, the due administration of justice, and protecting "the ends of justice".[51] It can be the vehicle by which English public policy of sufficient importance is advanced.

(7) An anti-suit injunction, although granted against the party and not the foreign court, has a direct effect on proceedings before the foreign court and may be regarded by it as an inappropriate intrusion into the sovereignty of the foreign state.[52] Comity and judicial restraint in exercising jurisdiction over foreigners over their

---

[47] *Airbus Industrie GIE v Patel* [1999] 1 A.C. 119 at 139 citing *Amchem Products Inc. v British Columbia (Workers' Compensation Board)* [1993] 1 S.C.R. 897 at 931–932, *per* Sopinka J.

[48] *Société Nationale Industrielle Aerospatiale v Lee Kui Jak* [1987] A.C. 871 at 896, cited with approval in *Donohue v Armco* [2002] 1 Lloyd's Rep. 425 at [19].

[49] *Barclays Bank v Homan* [1993] B.C.L.C. 680 at 701; *Pan American World Airways v Andrews* 1992 S.L.T. 268 (application dismissed as premature where if proceedings were launched abroad before a court in the United States that court could decide the *forum non conveniens* issue); see also *Deaville v Aeroflot Russian International Airlines* [1997] 2 Lloyd's Rep. 67 at 74–75.

[50] *General Star International Indemnity Ltd v Sterling Cooke Browne Reinsurance Brokers Ltd,* January 17, 2003, Comm Ct; see also *Glencore International AG v Metro Trading International Inc.* [2002] 2 All E.R. (Comm) 1 and *Tonicstar Ltd v American Assurance Co* [2004] EWHC 1234 (Comm) (where the dispute arose in connection with a reinsurance placed on the Lloyd's market on a Lloyd's slip policy which contained an arbitration clause which did not provide for where the seat of the arbitration was. Injunction granted against pursuit of proceedings in New York to compel arbitration when the English court was the natural forum for compelling arbitration and it was vexatious to pre-empt this through the New York proceedings).

[51] *Société Nationale Industrielle Aerospatiale v Lee Kui Jak* [1987] A.C. 871 at 892; *Donohue v Armco* [2002] 1 Lloyd's Rep. 425 at [19].

[52] "Restraint of Foreign Proceedings—The View from the Other Side of the Fence" [1997] C.J.Q. 283; *Re the Enforcement of an English Anti-suit Injunction* [1997] I.L.Pr. 320 and see 14.001 above.

conduct abroad, requires the English court, in cases outside of the enforcement of clear contractual promises,[53] to exercise caution.

(8) An injunction will only be granted against a person who is "amenable to the jurisdiction of the court"[54] in the sense of the court having territorial jurisdiction over him either because of his presence within the jurisdiction or through service out of the jurisdiction.[55] In *Donohue v Armco*,[56] the persons who were not parties to the contract containing the exclusive jurisdiction clause had no basis for serving the respondents to the injunction application with a claim form out of the jurisdiction. They could not use the proceedings in England brought by Mr Donohue "as a Trojan horse" so as to sue the respondents when they had no basis under CPR r.6.20 for obtaining permission to effect service out of the jurisdiction.

(9) The injunction must be "an effective remedy".[57] In *The Tropaioforos No.2*[58] the defendant was acting in breach of a contract to be bound and the consequence was that he was bound under that contract by a final judgment reached at trial against another insurer that he had connived in the scuttling of the vessel. The defendant was not present within the jurisdiction and there was the risk that the injunction would be a *brutum fulmen*[59] at least in the immediate future. This did not prevent the court from granting the injunction. In *The Tropaioforos No.2*, (1) the defendant had submitted to the jurisdiction of the English court for the purpose of resolving the substantive dispute; (2) the defendant had concluded an agreement governed by English law which was being enforced against him by the other insurers; and (3) there was the possibility that an anti-suit injunction might be effective, either because it might be obeyed, or because the foreign court might be minded to take it into account, or the English court could enforce it at some time in the future. This was sufficient to justify granting it.

---

[53] *Aggeliki Charis Compania Maritima SA v Pagnan SpA (The Angelic Grace)* [1995] 1 Lloyd's Rep. 87 at 96; *National Westminster Bank v Utrecht America Finance Company* [2001] 3 All E.R. 733 at [35].

[54] *Donohue v Armco* [2002] 1 Lloyd's Rep. 425 at [19] and [21]; *Glencore International AG v Metro Trading International Inc.* [2002] 2 All E.R. (Comm) 1 at [42].

[55] The discussion in *The Tropaioforos No.2* [1962] 1 Lloyd's Rep. 410 at 415–420 puts together the questions of (1) whether the defendant is amenable to the jurisdiction; (2) whether the English court should exercise restraint out of comity and because the injunction concerned the conduct of a foreigner abroad; and (3) whether an injunction, if granted, would be useless. In that case the defendant was clearly amenable to the jurisdiction for the purpose of enforcing the agreement to be bound which was "an English agreement governed by English law" (see [1962] 1 Lloyd's Rep. at 413).

[56] [2002] 1 Lloyd's Rep. 425 at [21].

[57] *Donohue v Armco* [2002] 1 Lloyd's Rep. 425 at [19]; see also Chapter 6, para.6.080. The factor of whether the relief, if granted, is going to be effective is important for freezing injunctions granted under s.25 of the Civil Jurisdiction and Judgments Act 1982, see *Motorola Credit Corporation v Cem Cengiz Uzan* [2003] EWCA Civ 752 at [125].

[58] [1962] 1 Lloyd's Rep. 410.

[59] An ineffective or useless thunderbolt.

Besides contempt proceedings there is also the prospect of indirect enforcement of the injunction by the English court refusing, on grounds of English public policy, to recognise or enforce any judgment obtained abroad in breach of the injunction.[60]

(4) Enforcement of a contractual right not to be sued in the foreign forum

(i) Enforcement of the promise: the general principle

An exclusive jurisdiction clause which confers jurisdiction on the English 14.007 court exclusively contains within it a negative covenant that a party will not sue abroad. The same is true of an English arbitration clause. Both can be enforced by injunction restraining foreign proceedings.[61]

A contractual provision promising not to sue abroad will "ordinarily"[62] be enforced by injunction unless "strong reason" is shown for not doing so.[63] It does not matter that the promise is not given in the form of a jurisdiction clause but is a promise not to bring an action in the foreign court.[64]

The cases on the granting of a stay to enforce an exclusive jurisdiction clause likewise place great weight on the importance of holding parties bound to their contract and are valuable as a source of factors which may serve to override this consideration.[65] The case law on stays and anti-suit injunctions has many cases in which the result has been to enforce the exclusive jurisdiction clause.[66] Where the English court is enforcing a

---

[60] *Through Transport Mutual Insurance Association (Eurasia) Ltd v New India Assurance Co. Ltd* [2004] 1 Lloyd's Rep. 206 at [42].

[61] The same principles apply whether the anti-suit injunction is sought to enforce an arbitration clause or an exclusive jurisdiction clause: *American International Specialty Lines Insurance Co. v Abbott Laboratories* [2003] 1 Lloyd's Rep. 267 at 275 proposition 6; the jurisdiction to enforce the arbitration clause by injunction is based on s.37 of the Supreme Court Act 1981: *Welex AG v Rosa Maritime Ltd* [2003] 2 Lloyd's Rep. 509 at [40] (a final anti-suit injunction is not made under s.44 of the Arbitration Act 1996, but under s.37(1) of the Supreme Court Act 1981, and there is no restriction in the Arbitration Act 1996 on the right of appeal to the Court of Appeal against the granting or refusal of a final injunction).

[62] The word "ordinarily" was used by Lord Bingham in *Donohue v Armco* [2002] 1 Lloyd's Rep. 425 at [24] because the jurisdiction is discretionary and is affected by matters going to discretion such as delay.

[63] *Donohue v Armco* [2002] 1 Lloyd's Rep. 425 at [24] and [45]; Art.6 of the European Convention on Human Rights as enacted by the Human Rights Act 1998 does not require that a claimant should be free to choose where he can sue: *O.T. Africa Line Ltd v Hijazy* [2001] 1 Lloyd's Rep. 76.

[64] *National Westminster Bank v Utrecht America Finance Company* [2001] 3 All E.R. 733 at [35].

[65] *Donohue v Armco* [2002] 1 Lloyd's Rep. 425 at [23–29]; where the stay case law was examined for assistance in deciding that on the facts strong reason for not giving effect to the exclusive jurisdiction clause was shown.

[66] A selection of cases were listed by Lord Bingham in *Donohue v Armco* [2002] 1 Lloyd's Rep. 425 at [25].

promise not to sue in the foreign court there is no reason for diffidence, the exercise of caution on the grounds of comity, or, in general, adopting an approach of waiting to see what the foreign court decides to do.[67]

14.008   If the clause is valid under the proper law which applies to this question under English conflicts of law rules then the fact that the foreign tribunal will not recognise it as valid or give effect to it because of its own local public policy will often not prevent an English court enforcing it through anti-suit injunction.[68]

In *Akai Pty Limited v People's Insurance Co. Limited*[69] the defendant insurer had insured the claimant by a contract which had been placed with the defendant in Singapore and which contained an express choice of English law clause and a jurisdiction clause that ". . . Any dispute arising from this policy shall be referred to the Courts of England." Under English law this clause was an exclusive jurisdiction clause.[70] The claimant, which was incorporated in New South Wales, had brought proceedings in England to protect the time limit and also brought proceedings in New South Wales, where the insured had sought a stay based on the clause and on grounds of *forum non conveniens*. The High Court of Australia,[71] based on ss8 and 52 of the Insurance Contracts Act 1984 enacted in Australia, held by a majority of 3–2 that (1) the choice of English law clause was invalidated by the statute, (2) the forum selection clause was also void because the English court would apply English and not New South Wales law as the governing law,[72] and (3) a stay was to be refused. The Austalian statute provided the insured with the protection of an Australian proper law notwithstanding the contrary agreement; the statutory anti-evasion provision had the effect in New South Wales of striking down the English jurisdiction clause. The decision of the High Court of Australia that the clauses were void did not give rise to an issue estoppel in England because the insurer had not submitted to the jurisdiction of the Australian court. Subsequently the insurer was granted an anti-suit injunction by the English court restraining further pursuit by the insured of the proceedings brought by it in New South Wales, the judge holding that the public policy furthered by the Australian statute

---

[67] *Aggeliki Charis Compania Maritima SA v Pagnan SpA (The Angelic Grace)* [1995] 1 Lloyd's Rep. 87 at 96; *National Westminster Bank v Utrecht America Finance Company* [2001] 3 All E.R. 733 at [35]; these cases disapprove of the approach of waiting for the foreign court to pronounce on the contract which was supported by *The Golden Anne* [1984] 2 Lloyd's Rep. 489 and *Sokana v Freyre & Co.* [1994] 2 Lloyd's Rep. 57 at 66 RHC.

[68] *Youell v Kara Mara Shipping* [2000] 1 Lloyd's Rep. 102 at [60]; *Akai v People's Insurance Co.* [1998] 1 Lloyd's Rep. 90 at 99–100; *XL Insurance v Owens Corning* [2001] 1 All E.R. (Comm) 530 (where the putative proper law of the apparent arbitration agreement was English and an injunction was granted when there was a possibility that the Delaware court would apply the Federal Arbitration Act in a way which would result in the apparent agreement being invalid).

[69] [1998] 1 Lloyd's Rep. 90.

[70] See *A/S D/S Svedborg v Wansa* [1997] 2 Lloyd's Rep. 183 at p.186 and para.14.015 below.

[71] *Akai Pty Limited v People's Insurance Co. Limited* (1996) 188 CLR 418.

[72] Applying similar reasoning to that applied by the House of Lords in *The Hollandia* [1983] 1 A.C. 565 in holding that the foreign jurisdiction clause in that case was struck down by article III rule 8 of the Hague-Visby Rules.

was an Australian public policy and not an English one, and therefore did not stand in the way of the granting of an anti-suit injunction by way of enforcement of the English jurisdiction clause. The judge looked at whether if the proceedings had been brought in England, the English courts would have applied the Australian statute notwithstanding the choice of law clause. Because the English court would not have applied the Australian statute to the claim the judge considered that the public policy to be enforced by the English court was that of upholding the contractual bargain.

The problem with an approach to the granting of anti-suit injunctions   **14.009** which would ignore entirely the public policies of foreign jurisdictions in favour of upholding contractual bargains is that it goes too far.In *Akai Pty Limited v People's Insurance Co. Ltd* the facts were of an insured seeking out and contracting in an arm's length commercial transaction with an insurer who did not carry on business in Australia and who had not entered into this transaction in Australia. Therefore the enforcement of the bargain by anti-suit injunction was justifiable.

However, just as in England exclusive jurisdiction clauses may be invalidated by the legislature for reasons of domestic policy,[73] it is to be expected that in foreign states legislation may in certain circumstances invalidate clauses which if upheld would result in evasion of an important domestic policy such as providing protection for consumers using the services of a particular industry in that state. That policy may be a domestic policy which applies to activities carried on within a state's own borders by persons who have no connection with England. In those circumstances respect for the sovereignty of the foreign state, the absence of connection of the parties with England, the authority of a foreign state to regulate activities within its own borders, and the legitimacy of the state adopting such a policy, *e.g.* a policy adopted to regulate how and on what terms business can be transacted, should argue strongly against the granting of an anti-suit injunction.[74] It is not simply a question of what English public policy provides but the legitimacy of a friendly foreign state adopting its own public policy for matters within its own borders, and whether the English court should by way of anti-suit injunction prevent implementation by the courts of that foreign state of that policy.

(ii) Enforcement against a person claiming the benefit of the contract

The English court will also enforce an English jurisdiction clause or   **14.010** arbitration clause against an assignee[75] of rights under the contract, or anyone asserting that he has the benefit of the contract, and who seeks to

---

[73] Arts 8 to 13 of the Council Regulation (EC) No. 44 /2001 contain entrenched provisions enabling insureds to have access to the courts of member states notwithstanding certain agreements to the contrary.

[74] See also paras 6.006–6.009.

[75] *Schiffahrtsgesellschaft Detlev Von Appen GmbH v Voest Alpine Intertrading GmbH* [1997] 2 Lloyd's Rep. 279 at 285–286; *The Jordan Nicolev* [1990] 2 Lloyd's Rep. 11 at 15; *The League* [1984] 2 Lloyd's Rep. 259; *Aspel v Seymour* [1929] W.N. 152; *Shayler v Woolf* [1946] Ch. 320.

enforce those rights inconsistently with the clause.[76] He cannot claim the benefit of the contract without complying with the clause which forms a part of it and which is relevant to the exercise of those rights. The applicant has an equitable right against the respondent which can be enforced by injunction. The same position applies where there is a claim for damages against the assignor which can be set off against the assignee albeit that the assignee is not personally liable for those damages.[77] The equitable principle which applies is that he who claims to enjoy rights cannot do so without honouring the conditions which are both relevant to and attached to the exercise of those rights.[78]

In this situation it is considered that the claimant could seek damages under Lord Cairns's Act against the defendant even though the defendant is not a contracting party to the clause, being damages awarded to the claimant in substitution for or in addition to an injunction.[79]

Whether the claim in the foreign court is to be regarded as coming within the clause depends on (1) interpretation of the clause, which depends on the proper law, and (2) how the claim in the foreign court is itself to be regarded. On issue (2) this is a question of looking at the substance of the claim in the foreign court; the English court will look at the substance of the matter regardless of how the foreign court would itself characterise the position.[80]

(iii) The Judgments Regulation: English court is court second seised and there is a jurisdiction clause conferring jurisdiction on the English court

14.011   Under the Judgments Regulation when the English court is second seised, it is not able consistently with Arts 27–30 to rule that the court first seised has no jurisdiction. In *Continental Bank v Aeakos SA*,[81] the Court of Appeal had decided that Art.17 of the Brussels Convention, which concerns jurisdiction clauses, took precedence over Art.21. This had been criticised[82] and the decision, and the cases which follow it,[83] cannot stand with the

---

[76] *Youell v Kara Mara Shipping* [2002] 1 Lloyd's Rep. 102; *Schiffahrtsgesellschaft Detlev Von Appen GmbH v Voest Alpine Intertrading GmbH* [1997] 2 Lloyd's Rep. 279; *Through Transport Mutual Insurance Association (Eurasia) Ltd v New India Assurance Co. Ltd* [2004] 1 Lloyd's Rep. 206.

[77] *Young v Kitchen* (1878) 3 Ex D. 127; *Barker v Stickney* [1919] 1 K.B. 121.

[78] *Rhone v Stephens* [1994] 2 A.C. 310 at 322, explaining *Halsall v Brizell* [1957] Ch. 169 and disapproving of the wider principle of benefit and burden contended for based on *Tito v Waddell (No.2)* [1977] Ch. 106 at 301 and following; *Schiffahrtsgesellschaft Detlev Von Appen GmbH v Voest Alpine Intertrading GmbH* [1997] 2 Lloyd's Rep. 279 at 291.

[79] See Chapter 2, paras 2.039–40.

[80] *Through Transport Mutual Insurance Association (Eurasia) Ltd v New India Assurance Co. Ltd* [2004] 1 Lloyd's Rep. 206.

[81] [1994] 1 W.L.R. 588.

[82] A. Briggs, "Anti-European Teeth for Choice of Court Clauses" (1994) L.C.M.L.Q. 158.

[83] *Evialis SA v SIAT* [2003] 2 Lloyd's Rep. 377 at [90–96]; *O. T. Africa Line Ltd v Hijazy* [2001] 1 Lloyd's Rep. 76 at [40] and [53].

decision of the European Court of Justice in *Erich Gasser GmbH v Misat Srl*[84] and *Turner v Grovit*.[85]

In *Erich Gasser GmbH v Misat Srl* the question was whether if there was an exclusive jurisdiction agreement in favour of a court which was second seized under the Brussels Convention, that court could proceed with determining the merits before the court first seized had pronounced on its jurisdiction. The European Court decided that the court second seized could not so proceed and that it had to stay its proceedings pending the decision by the court first seized. Before that court the defendant might not wish to rely on the jurisdiction agreement or there might be a dispute as to its validity and effect which has to be resolved by that court.

In *Turner v Grovit*, Mr Turner had successfully sued a company in the Chequepoint Group for damages for unfair dismissal before an Employment Tribunal in London. Subsequently another company in the same group sued Mr Turner for substantial damages in respect of alleged misconduct. The Court of Appeal granted an anti-suit injunction restraining pursuit by the company of the Spanish proceedings on the ground that those were brought in bad faith to vex Mr Turner. The European Court, which followed the same approach as had been adopted by the Advocate General,[86] decided that the anti-suit injunction was inconsistent with the Brussels Convention. This was because under the Convention there is a principle of mutual trust which applies between the courts of different states, with limited exceptions no court can review another court's jurisdiction, and although the injunction is against the party and not the foreign court, which is indirectly affected, and the injunction might be regarded as procedural, nevertheless it impaired the effectiveness of the Convention. Furthermore if allowed, the procedure might result in anti-suit injunctions granted by courts indirectly against each other.

The decision in *Turner v Grovit* did not concern an injunction based on a jurisdiction agreement. But in principle its reasoning, taken together with that in *Erich Gasser GmbH v Misat Srl*, would also prohibit anti-suit injunctions granted by the court second seized based on a jurisdiction clause. This is not because the same cause of action is before the two courts; the causes of action are different, one being the substantive cause of action and the other being the cause of action supporting the claim for the injunction. It is because the claim for the injunction restraining pursuit of the foreign proceedings is itself inconsistent with the proper working of the Regulation as declared by the European Court. *Continental Bank v Aeakos S.A.*, and the cases following it, must be regarded as wrongly decided.

The English court, as the court second seized, must wait to see whether the court first seized is prepared to recognise and uphold the exclusive jurisdiction clause.

---

[84] [2004] 1 Lloyd's Rep. 222.
[85] European Court, April 27, 2004.
[86] *Turner* [2004] 1 Lloyd's Rep. 216.

14.012   Before these decisions of the European Court, it had been decided that where the English court is first seized then it can grant an anti-suit injunction in relation to proceedings before the courts of another member state.[87] However, the reasoning in *Turner v Grovit* that the injunction is an attack on the jurisdiction should lead to the conclusion that in this situation as well no injunction can be granted.

Although *Erich Gasser GmbH v Misat Srl* and *Turner v Grovit* concerned the Brussels Convention in principle the same applies to proceedings governed by the Judgments Regulations.

The English court can grant an anti-suit injunction in relation to proceedings on the merits before a court of another Member State for the purpose of enforcing an English arbitration clause[88] because the claim to enforce the arbitration clause is itself outside the scope of the Regulation. Proceedings to enforce an arbitration clause by anti-suit injunction fall within the arbitration exception in Art.1(4) of the Brussels Convention and the equivalent exclusion in Art.1(2)(d) of the Council Regulation.[89] The clause can be enforced by injunction against a defendant domiciled in a member state restraining proceedings in a court of a member state. Service of the claim form out of the jurisdiction is regulated by CPR r.6.20.

(iv) Service out of the jurisdiction of the claim to enforce a jurisdiction or arbitration clause

14.013   Article 23 of the Judgments Regulation is as follows:

> "1. If the parties, one or more of whom is domiciled in a Member State, have agreed that a court or the courts of a Member State are to have jurisdiction to settle any disputes which have arisen or which may arise in connection with a particular legal relationship, that court or those courts shall have jurisdiction. Such jurisdiction shall be exclusive unless the parties have agreed otherwise. Such an agreement conferring jurisdiction shall be either:
>
> (a) in writing or evidenced in writing; or
> (b) in a form which accords with practices which the parties have established between themselves; or

---

[87] *Banque Cantonale v Waterlily* [1997] 2 Lloyd's Rep. 347.
[88] *Aggeliki Charis Compania Maritima SA v Pagnan SpA (The Angelic Grace)* [1995] 1 Lloyd's Rep. 87.
[89] *Navigation Maritime Bulgare v Rustal Trading Ltd (The Ivan Zagubanski)* [2002] 1 Lloyd's Rep. 106; *Through Transport Mutual Insurance Association (Eurasia) Ltd v New India Assurance Co. Ltd* [2004] 1 Lloyd's Rep. 206. See also *Marc Rich & Co. v Societa Italiana Impianti PA* [1991] E.C.R. I–3855, *Philip Alexander Securities and Futures Ltd v Bamburger* [1997] I.L.Pr. 73 (affirmed on other grounds [1997] I.L.Pr. 104), *cf. The Heidberg* [1994] 1 Lloyd's Rep. 287 in which a French judgment pronouncing against the validity of an arbitration clause was recognised—*sed quare*. For a full account of the case law see *Dicey and Morris on Conflict of Laws* (13th ed., 2000), rule 48; see also C. Ambrose, "Can Anti-Suit Injunctions Survive European Community Law?" (2003) 52 I.C.L.Q. 401 at 419–421.

(c) in international trade or commerce, in a form which accords with a usage of which the parties are or ought to have been aware and which in such trade or commerce is widely known to, and regularly observed by, parties to contracts of the type involved in the particular trade or commerce concerned.

2. Any communication by electronic means which provides a durable record of the agreement shall be equivalent to 'writing'.

3. Where such an agreement is concluded by parties, none of whom is domiciled in a Member State, the courts of other Member States shall have no jurisdiction over their disputes unless the court or courts chosen have declined jurisdiction.

4. The court or courts of a Member State on which a trust instrument has conferred jurisdiction shall have exclusive jurisdiction in any proceedings brought against a settlor, trustee or beneficiary, if relations between these persons or their rights or obligations under the trust are involved.

5. Agreements or provisions of a trust instrument conferring jurisdiction shall have no legal force if they are contrary to Articles 13, 17 or 21, or if the courts whose jurisdiction they purport to exclude have exclusive jurisdiction by virtue of Article 22."

This Article provides for conferment of jurisdiction by reason of a jurisdiction agreement, which is to be exclusive jurisdiction unless the parties have agreed to the contrary. It applies where one or more parties to the proceedings are domiciled in a Member State, and except where there is agreement "otherwise", in which case the clause will be non-exclusive, the jurisdiction clause excludes the jurisdiction of the courts of all other Member States. In cases falling within the scope of CPR r.6.19, service out of the jurisdiction without permission can be made in a case based on an English court jurisdiction agreement within Art.23. Article 5(a) also applies because the obligation is only to bring proceedings in England, and the claim to enforce is a matter "relating to a contract".

Do the opening words of Art.23 cover the case of enforcement of an English exclusive jurisdiction clause against an assignee or other person claiming the benefit of a contract governed by English law? Article 23 respects the "autonomy of the parties to a contract"[90] to select a forum to determine their disputes. If that "autonomy" is to be meaningful the clause must bind assignees and successors, otherwise a party might by assignment circumvent the clause. Under English law, the assignee or transferee by seeking to take the benefit of and enforce rights under the contract has "agreed" to the exclusive jurisdiction clause, and thus the first sentence of Art.23 is satisfied. The effect of the assignment or transfer "is to create contractual rights and liabilities directly between the parties. . .".[91]

---

[90] Recitals (11) and (14) of the Judgments Regulation.
[91] *DR Insurance Co. v Central National Insurance Co.* [1996] 1 Lloyd's Rep. 74 at 78, cited with approval in *Schiffahrtsgesellschaft Detlev Von Appen GmbH v Voest Alpine Intertrading GmbH* [1997] 2 Lloyd's Rep. 279 at 287.

If the defendant to the anti-suit proceedings is domiciled in the United Kingdom then Art.2 of the Judgments Regulation will apply. A claim may also fall within the scope of Art.6 of the Judgments Regulation which concerns special jurisdiction.[92] If the proposed defendant to the anti-suit proceedings is domiciled in another Member State, then the proceedings for the anti-suit injunction can only be brought against him in England based on a head of jurisdiction authorised by the Judgments Regulation, unless it can be said that the basis for the anti-suit injunction does not rest on a substantive claim in a civil or commercial matter.

14.014   In cases outside of the Judgments Regulation, including cases to enforce an English arbitration clause, permission to serve the claim form out of the jurisdiction must be obtained under the sub-paragraphs of CPR r.6.20. Cases to enforce an English arbitration clause can be within CPR r.6.20(5) as being a claim "in respect of a contract" falling within one or more of the heads of that rule. Does this apply even if the respondent is not a party to the contract containing the clause, but is only claiming the benefit of it abroad? The former RSC Ord.11, r.1(1)(d) applied where the claim was brought "to enforce . . . or otherwise affect a contract", and this was sufficient to cover such cases.[93] The claim for an anti-suit injunction against a person claiming the benefit of the contract abroad, is a claim "in respect of" that contract because it is enforcing a term of that contract against that person, and therefore is connected with that contract.

(v) Interim injunction to enforce the contractual promise

14.015   If the application is for an interim injunction and the applicant can show no more than an arguable case that there is a promise not to sue in the foreign forum then the injunction will usually be refused.[94] It has been said that on an interlocutory application to enforce an alleged promise the applicant must show "to a high degree of probability that its case is right";[95] this reflects the fact that if there is not confidence that such an enforceable promise presently exists the principles of comity and restraint in interfering with foreign proceedings would weigh heavily against the granting of relief. In *Settlement Corporation v Hochsfield*[96] the existence of an enforceable promise was in issue and it was convenient for all the issues to be decided in France and so an interlocutory injunction was refused.

---

[92] *The Eras EIL Actions* [1995] 1 Lloyd's Rep. 64 at 77 (Brussels Convention).
[93] *Schiffahrtsgesellschaft Detlev Von Appen GmbH v Voest Alpine Intertrading GmbH* [1997] 2 Lloyd's Rep. 279; *Youell v Kara Mara Shipping* [2000] 1 Lloyd's Rep.102.
[94] *National Westminster Bank v Utrecht America Finance Company* [2001] 3 All E.R. 733 at [37]; *American International Specialty Lines Insurance Co. v Abbott Laboratories* [2003] 1 Lloyd's Rep. 267 at 275 proposition 7; *cf. Society of Lloyd's v Crotty* [2003] EWHC 2178 where the defendants were not represented and the court was invited to and did proceed on a test of "good arguable" case.
[95] *American International Specialty Lines Insurance Co. v Abbott Laboratories* [2003] 1 Lloyd's Rep. 267 at 275 proposition 8.
[96] [1966] Ch. 10.

Repudiation of a contract containing an arbitration or jurisdiction clause does not affect the enforceability of the clause, and so does not affect the existence and continued validity of that clause.[97] Likewise with such a clause in a contract of insurance which a party claims to have avoided for non-disclosure.[98] It is different if the validity of the clause itself is in issue,[99] or if the arbitration agreement or jurisdiction agreement has itself been repudiated.[1] Once there is a final judgment deciding that such a promise has been given, and is valid and enforceable, the English court will enforce that promise unless strong reason is shown for not doing so.[2]

(vi) Strong reason for not enforcing the promise

Where the result of giving effect to the clause would be to expose parties,   **14.016** including non-parties involved in litigation abroad,[3] to the risk of inconsistent findings and results because of different jurisdictions determining different matters this can be a powerful reason for overriding the clause.[4] The "ends of justice" would normally[5] favour a single forum for resolution of all the various claims so as to avoid inconsistent results, unnecessary costs and delay and the problems of having to call the same witnesses before more than one court. If foreigners, who are not bound by an exclusive jurisdiction clause have perfectly properly founded jurisdiction abroad, in circumstances where those proceedings are to continue,[6] then the ends of justice may well not require an anti-suit injunction to be granted to enforce an exclusive jurisdiction clause against other persons in respect of related disputes—the strong effect of the exclusive jurisdiction clause will have been countered. On the facts in *Donohue v Armco*, where a conspiracy to act dishonestly was alleged against four individuals, it was not in the interests of justice for different courts, perhaps on different evidence to have to weigh up the motives and honesty of the four individuals with the possibility of conflicting findings and inconsistent results. The same principle would apply where a claim was made against

---

[97] *Heyman v Darwins Ltd* [1942] A.C. 356.
[98] *Mackender v Feldia AG* [1967] 2 Q.B. 590.
[99] *Crédit Suisse First Boston (Europe) Ltd v Seagate Trading Co. Ltd* [1999] 1 Lloyd's Rep. 784 at 794–798; *Harbour Insurance (UK) Ltd v Kansa General International Insurance Co. Ltd* [1993] Q.B. 701 at 712 and 724–725.
[1] *Downing v Al Tameer Establishment* [2002] 2 All E.R. (Comm) 545 at [25].
[2] *National Westminster Bank v Utrecht America Finance Company* [2001] 3 All E.R. 733 at [34] and [38].
[3] *Bouygues Offshore SA v Caspian Shipping Co.* [1998] 2 Lloyd's Rep. 461 at [27], approved in *Donohue v Armco* [2002] 1 Lloyd's Rep. 425 at [27].
[4] *Donohue v Armco* [2002] 1 Lloyd's Rep. 425 at [27]; *Aratra Potato Co. Ltd v Egyptian Navigation Co. (The El Amria)* [1981] 2 Lloyd's Rep. 119
[5] Sometimes this is simply not a practical option open to the court see *Crédit Suisse First Boston (Europe) Ltd v MLC Bermuda Ltd* [1999] 1 Lloyd's Rep. 767 which is considered in *Donohue v Armco* [2002] 1 Lloyd's Rep. 425 at [28].
[6] In *Ultisol Transport Contractors Ltd v Bouygues Offshore SA* [1996] 2 Lloyd's Rep. 140 the argument put forward by the respondent on multiplicity of proceedings failed because there was a way open to the respondent which could overcome the problem.

two defendants which ought to succeed against at least one of them and the consequence of having two courts would be the risk of the claimant failing against each.[7] The court will not grant an anti-suit injunction based on an arbitration clause or exclusive jurisdiction clause so as to prevent a person arresting a vessel abroad in an action *in rem* for the sole purpose of obtaining security for a claim which appears to have merit and is to be advanced in the English arbitration or action.[8] There is also the question whether proceedings confined to obtaining security would in any case be a breach of the particular clause.[9] The loss of security in the proceedings abroad is capable of providing a strong reason for not enforcing the clause by an injunction, but this depends on the circumstances.[10]

(vii) Exclusive and non-exclusive jurisdiction clauses

14.017 The word "exclusive" does not have to be used to make the effect of a clause an agreement to submit disputes only to the English court.[11] If parties have agreed to submit "disputes" to be determined by the English court it is a question of interpretation whether this applies to all disputes or whether it only goes so far as requiring a party sued in England on such a dispute to submit to the jurisdiction of the English court.[12]

An "exclusive" jurisdiction clause contains mutual promises that the dispute will only be resolved in the designated forum. If a party commences proceedings in another forum this will in itself be a breach of

---

[7] *Aratra Potato Co. Ltd v Egyptian Navigation Co. (The El Amria)* [1981] 2 Lloyd's Rep. 119; see also *Sokana v Freyre & Co.* [1994] 2 Lloyd's Rep. 57 at 66–67 (multiplicity of litigation to be avoided).

[8] *Mike Trading and Transport Ltd v R. Pagnan & Fratelli (The Lisboa)* [1980] 2 Lloyd's Rep. 546; *Donohue v Armco* [2002] 1 Lloyd's Rep. 425 at [24] and [26] also support this view. The English court will usually not release the vessel from arrest or stay its proceedings based on a foreign exclusive jurisdiction clause where the effect would be to force the claimant to litigate without security in the foreign jurisdiction: see *Aratra Potato Co. Ltd v Egyptian Navigation Co. (The El Amria)* [1981] 2 Lloyd's Rep. 119 and *The Eleftheria* [1970] P. 94 at 99–100.

[9] See Chapter 6 paras 6.030–2 above; *Re Q's Estate* [1999] 1 Lloyd's Rep. 931; *Marazura Navegacion SA v Oceanus Mutual* [1977] 1 Lloyd's Rep. 283; *Mantovani v Carapelli* [1980] 1 Lloyd's Rep. 375; *Ultisol Transport Contractors Ltd v Bouyguyes Offshore SA* [1996] 2 Lloyd's Rep. 140 at 144–145; *Petromin SA v Secnar Marine Ltd* [1995] 1 Lloyd's Rep. 603; *Alfred C. Toepfer International GmbH v Société Cargill France* [1998] 1 Lloyd's Rep. 379.

[10] *Welex AG v Rosa Maritime Ltd* [2003] 2 Lloyd's Rep. 509 at [49] (injunction granted given the behaviour of the respondent who had brought the problem on himself through his own unreasonable conduct).

[11] *Sohio Supply Co. v Gatoil (USA) Inc.* [1989] 1 Lloyd's Rep. 588 at 591–592; *A/S D/S Svendborg v Wansa (trading as Melbourne Enterprises)* [1997] 2 Lloyd's Rep. 183 at 186; *British Aerospace Plc v Dee Howard Co.* [1993] 1 Lloyd's Rep. 368; *Berisford Plc v New Hampshire Insurance* [1990] 2 Q.B. 631 at 636–638; *Continental Bank v Aeakos SA* [1994] 1 W.L.R. 588 at 593–594; *Austrian Lloyd Steamship Co. v Gresham Life Assurance Society* [1903] 1 K.B. 249.

[12] See *Sabah Shipyard (Pakistan) Ltd v Islamic Republic of Pakistan* [2003] 2 Lloyd's Rep. 571 at [28–34]; *Crédit Suisse First Boston (Europe) Ltd v MLC Bermuda Ltd* [1999] 1 Lloyd's Rep. 767 at 775–776 (where the clause was interpreted as an English exclusive jurisdiction clause subject to the bank's entitlement to sue elsewhere).

contract. A "non-exclusive" jurisdiction clause contains a facility enabling proceedings to be brought in the designated jurisdiction. This facility will then be a ground for jurisdiction in the designated forum which will co-exist with the jurisdictions of other courts to entertain the claim.[13]

If the clause is a "non-exclusive" jurisdiction clause there is still a broad spectrum of meanings that are covered by this label. The court has to interpret the clause to establish exactly what is its meaning.

It may be interpreted as being contrary to the terms of the clause to   **14.018** commence proceedings in any other jurisdiction unless there is some exceptional reason for doing so, in which case if there is no such reason the foreign proceedings will have been commenced and continued in breach of contract and possibly also vexatiously and oppressively. In *Sabah Shipyard (Pakistan) Ltd v Islamic Republic of Pakistan*[14] the jurisdiction clause was a non-exclusive jurisdiction clause providing for English jurisdiction. The *spirit* of the clause precluded the bringing of parallel proceedings in another jurisdiction unless there were "exceptional circumstances". This is because the parties could be taken to have contemplated any dispute being resolved on the merits in a single forum which would be the agreed forum absent some exceptional circumstance. In that case the commencement of the proceedings abroad was a pre-emptive strike designed to prevent the operation of the agreed jurisdiction clause, the continuation of the foreign proceedings was held to be vexatious and oppressive and an anti-suit injunction was granted.

There was also a further ground for the decision. The foreign proceedings brought in Pakistan sought an injunction to restrain any demand by Sabah against the Government of Pakistan under the contract of guarantee. Therefore the prosecution of the foreign proceedings themselves sought to prevent Sabah from bring proceedings in England under the jurisdiction clause. At the time of concluding the contract the parties had addressed their minds to jurisdiction. The choice of England was a selection of a neutral forum. The Court of Appeal held that the pursuit of proceedings in Pakistan seeking to prevent the yard from commencing proceedings before the English court was itself a breach of contract.[15] This was because there was to be implied a negative engagement not to interfere with the yard obtaining a binding final decision in England. The continuation of the proceedings in Pakistan was itself in breach of this implied negative promise and could be restrained.[16] This implied promise did not convert the clause into an "exclusive jurisdiction" clause, because there could be proceedings abroad which did not infringe that promise, *e.g.* proceedings brought before the other party had chosen to have the matter resolved in

---

[13] *Insured Financial Structures Ltd v Elektrocieplownia Tychy SA* [2003] Q.B. 1260.
[14] [2003] 2 Lloyd's Rep. 571.
[15] See [2003] 2 Lloyd's Rep. 571 at [37]; *Royal Bank of Canada v Cooperatieve Centrale Raiffeisen-Boerenleenbank BA* [2004] 1 Lloyd's Rep. 471 at [31] and [47].
[16] See [2003] 2 Lloyd's Rep. 571 at [52] which treats the injunction restraining continuation of the proceedings in Pakistan as enforcement of the agreement.

England or proceedings to obtain security for the claim. The case therefore was one in which the foreign proceedings were brought in breach of the promise to be implied in that case into the "non-exclusive" jurisdiction clause,[17] and therefore within the principle that strong reasons had to be shown for not enforcing the clause.

14.019   In *Evialis SA v SIAT*[18] the particular clause was governed by Italian law and interpreted as a non-exclusive jurisdiction clause which did not have this effect; that clause permitted the bringing of foreign proceedings seeking a declaration of non-liability. In *Royal Bank of Canada v Cooperatieve Centrale Raiffeisen-Boerenleenbank BA*[19] the clause was a non-exclusive clause in favour of England, and it expressly provided that nothing in the agreement was to preclude either party from bringing proceedings in any other jurisdiction. An injunction was sought to prevent a party from proceeding to final judgment in New York in advance of trial of the case in England. The express wording precluded implication of a negative promise not to prevent the other party from obtaining final resolution of the merits in England before determination abroad. It also precluded the suggestion that the parties had agreed to the English court deciding where their substantive dispute ought to be resolved on the merits. The case therefore had to be determined as an alternative forum case applying the principles in *Société Nationale Industrielle Aerospatiale v Lee Kui Jak*.

It is suggested that the first question with a non-exclusive clause is to consider, as a matter of interpretation of the contract, whether there is an express or implied negative promise and if so what is its scope. This is to be resolved applying the proper law. For example, the negative promise may be that the other party will do nothing to prevent the other party from using the facility and having a binding final determination of the dispute in the named jurisdiction.

14.020   If there is no promise precluding the pursuit of the proceedings abroad the second question is what is and what is not within the "spirit" of the clause. This again involves interpreting the particular clause and considering how far the parties intended to go in selecting England as the non-exclusive jurisdiction. If there is an express contractual provision permitting the foreign proceedings as in *Royal Bank of Canada v Cooperatieve Centrale Raiffeisen-Boerenleenbank BA*[20] then the matter is to be determined on alternative forum principles. If the clause is silent, and the proceedings abroad are not specifically authorised by the contract, either expressly or impliedly, then the burden of showing vexation or oppression will be "lightened" by the presence of the clause.[21] This is because the

---

[17] *Royal Bank of Canada v Cooperatieve Centrale Raiffeisen-Boerenleenbank BA* [2004] 1 Lloyd's Rep. 471 at [31] "a plain breach"; *Evialis SA v SIAT* [2003] 2 Lloyd's Rep. 377 at [101].

[18] [2003] 2 Lloyd's Rep. 377.

[19] [2004] 1 Lloyd's Rep. 471.

[20] *ibid.*

[21] *Royal Bank of Canada v Cooperatieve Centrale Raiffeisen-Boerenleenbank BA* [2004] 1 Lloyd's Rep. 471 at [40].

parties will be taken to have agreed both that England is an appropriate jurisdiction, and that the English court can properly decide where the substantive dispute itself ought to be tried. Putting it in a negative way, in such circumstances the English court cannot be regarded as "arrogating" to itself the decision where the dispute is to be tried and this creates "a radical difference to the situation referred to by Lord Goff . . ."[22] in *Société Nationale Industrielle Aerospatiale v Lee Kui Jak*.

Where there is a jurisdiction clause in favour of England, whether **14.021** exclusive or non-exclusive, and a party is seeking to resist the English court assuming jurisdiction over the substantive proceedings, or a stay of the English proceedings, in breach of that agreement, strong grounds will be needed for the court not to hold him to his promise.[23] This is so even when England has been selected as a "neutral forum" unconnected with the parties.[24] This principle applies so that the bargain is enforced notwithstanding matters which would have been foreseeable by the parties at the time of conclusion of the contract and which would otherwise have pointed away from the contractual forum. The principle is that such matters are covered by the parties' agreement to English jurisdiction and a party is not to be allowed to throw over his agreement by relying on such matters as grounds for not giving effect to the clause. So, for example, the fact that England is not where witnesses are based, when that was a foreseeable circumstance at the time of the contract, will not prevent the court holding the parties to their bargain.[25] But matters which would not have been foreseeable at that time are given their full impact on the discretion on the basis that they could not have been taken into account when that bargain was concluded.[26] The same principle applies where the jurisdiction clause is in favour of a foreign court and the English court is being asked to assume jurisdiction notwithstanding that agreement.[27]

A "service of suit" clause allows the party to serve proceedings on the other commencing proceedings in that jurisdiction. It is not an exclusive jurisdiction clause and either party may sue the other wherever it has the

---

[22] *Pathé Screen Entertainment Ltd v Homemade Films (Distributors) Ltd*, unreported, July 11, 1989, Comm Ct, at 52, *per* Hobhouse J., supported by Waller J. in *Amoco v TGTL*, unreported, June 26, 1996, Comm Ct, cited with approval in *Royal Bank of Canada v Cooperatieve Centrale Raiffeisen-Boerenleenbank BA* [2004] 1 Lloyd's Rep. 471 at [15], [18] and [40].

[23] *BAS Capital Funding Corp v Medfinco Ltd* [2004] 1 Lloyd's Rep. 652 at paras 189–193 (Lawrence Collins J.), referring to *Egon Oldendorff v Liberia Corporation* [1995] 2 Lloyd's Rep. 64 at p.72 and *Akai Ply Ltd v People's Insurance Co Ltd* [1998] 1 Lloyd's Rep. 90 at p.105.

[24] *Attock Cement Co v Roumanian Bank for Foreign Trade* [1989] 1 W.L.R. 1147 at p.1161; *BAS Capital Funding Corp v Medfinco Ltd* [2003] EWHC 1798 at para.189.

[25] *BAS Capital Funding Corp v Medfinco Ltd* [2004] 1 Lloyd's Rep. 652 at para.191; *British Aerospace v Dee Howard* [1993] 1 Lloyd's Rep. 368 at p.376.

[26] *BAS Capital Funding Corp v Medfinco Ltd* [2004] 1 Lloyd's Rep. 652; *Crédit Suisse First Boston (Europe) Ltd v MLC Bermuda Ltd* [1999] 1 Lloyd's Rep. 767 at p.781; *Sinochem International Oil (London) Co Ltd v Mobil Sales and Supply Corporation* [2000] 1 Lloyd's Rep. 670 at pp.679–680.

[27] *Akai Pty Ltd v People's Insurance Co Ltd* [1998] 1 Lloyd's Rep. 90 at p.104; *Import Export Metro Ltd v Compania Sud Americana De Vapores SA* [2003] 1 Lloyd's Rep. 405 at para.14.

right to do so;[28] it is a form of non-exclusive jurisdiction clause. It does not lie easily in a party's mouth to assert that the jurisdiction which is named in a non-exclusive jurisdiction clause[29] or the service of suit clause, is inconvenient or an inappropriate forum unless there is some factor which was unforeseeable when the clause was agreed between the parties. The English court will usually not grant permission for proceedings to be served out of the jurisdiction which duplicate proceedings brought abroad under a foreign court service of suit clause,[30] and will normally respect the decision of that foreign court as to where the merits should be tried.

(viii) The right to damages for breach of an arbitration or exclusive jurisdiction clause

14.022 Breach of an exclusive jurisdiction clause[31] or an arbitration clause[32] gives rise to a right to claim damages. Damages are seldom an adequate remedy. This is why the legislature originally enacted in the Common Law Procedure Acts the procedure of seeking a stay of court proceedings so that a case could be referred to arbitration.[33] It is because damages are an inadequate remedy that the clause will be enforced by injunction.[34]

The right to claim damages for breach of contract is relevant to discretion.[35] If there is a real risk of the foreign forum getting to a result different from that which would be reached by the agreed forum and there is the prospect that the applicant would then claim damages in the agreed forum for this, this would itself be a strong factor in favour of enforcement of the clause.[36] In *Donohue v Armco*, the proceedings against the applicant in New York included "RICO" claims and a potential liability for triple damages. In the event the respondent gave an undertaking not to enforce any multiple or punitive damages award and based on this the injunction was refused. The analysis of what damages may be recoverable for the breach may be affected by there being a *res judicata* or issue estoppel[37] arising from the decision of the foreign forum if the applicant has submitted to its jurisdiction.

---

[28] *Ace Insurance v Zurich Insurance* [2001] 1 Lloyd's Rep. 618 at [59]; *American International Specialty Lines Insurance Co. v Abbott Laboratories* [2003] 1 Lloyd's Rep. 267 at 276.
[29] *British Aerospace Plc v Dee Howard Co.* [1993] 1 Lloyd's Rep. 368 at 376.
[30] *Ace Insurance v Zurich Insurance* [2001] 1 Lloyd's Rep. 618 at [62]; *Excess Insurance Co. Ltd v Allendale Mutual Insurance Co.*, March 8, 1995, referred to in *Ace Insurance v Zurich Insurance* [2001] 1 Lloyd's Rep. 618 at [59].
[31] *Union Discount Co. Ltd v Zoller* [2002] 1 W.L.R. 1517.
[32] *Mantovani v Carapelli* [1980] 1 Lloyd's Rep. 375; *Schiffahrtsgesellschaft Detlev Von Appen GmbH v Voest Alpine Intertrading GmbH* [1997] 2 Lloyd's Rep. 279 at 285; *Doleman & Sons v Ossett Corporation* [1912] 3 K.B. 257 at 267–268. See also paras 6.030–2, para.14.014 and para.23.010.
[33] *Doleman & Sons v Ossett Corporation* [1912] 3 K.B. 257 at 267–268.
[34] *Bankers Trust Co. v P. T. Jakarta International Hotels* [1999] 1 Lloyd's Rep. 910 at 915.
[35] *Donohue v Armco* [2002] 1 Lloyd's Rep. 425 at [48]; *Tracomin SA v Sudan Oil Seeds* [1983] 1 W.L.R. 1026 at 1036–1037.
[36] *Tracomin SA v Sudan Oil Seeds* [1983] 1 W.L.R. 1026 at 1036–1037.
[37] *The Sennar No.2* [1985] 1 W.L.R. 490 where the decision of the Dutch court produced an issue estoppel on the effect of a contract.

(ix) Delay

Whether an injunction is to be granted will also be affected by discretion- **14.023**
ary factors including delay.[38] In *Industrial Maritime Carriers (Bahamas) Inc.
v Sinoca International Inc. (The Eastern Trader)*,[39] although the applicant
was disputing the jurisdiction of the foreign court, that court had already
given judgment against the applicant and an interlocutory injunction
against reliance upon that judgment was refused *(inter alia)* because such an
injunction was even more intrusive on the sovereignty of the foreign state
that an injunction restraining further proceedings.

(5) To restrain reliance on or enforcement of a foreign judgment obtained by fraud

In *Ellerman Lines Ltd v Read*[40] the defendant had obtained a judgment in **14.024**
Turkey both in breach of contract and through fraud committed on that
court. The English court had jurisdiction to grant an injunction restraining
the defendant from enforcing the judgment on both grounds. This is a case
in which the applicant had a substantive right to impeach the foreign
judgment. The same grounds could have been relied upon successfully in
advance of any judgment being obtained, because the conduct of the
defendant itself was actionable and the defendant could be restrained from
pursuit of the Turkish proceedings because (1) this would be in breach of
the English arbitration agreement, or (2) this would be part of obtaining an
advantage through the fraud.

---

[38] *Aggeliki Charis Compania Maritima SA v Pagnan SpA (The Angelic Grace)* [1995] 1 Lloyd's
Rep. 87 at 96 ("provided that it is sought promptly and before the foreign proceedings are
too far advanced"); *Donohue v Armco* [2002] 1 Lloyd's Rep. 425 at [19] ("a party may lose
his claim to equitable relief through dilatoriness or other unconscionable conduct");
Schiffahrtsgesellschaft Detlev Von Appen GmbH v Voest Alpine Intertrading GmbH [1997] 2
Lloyd's Rep. 279 at 288 (short culpable delay did not result in refusal of injunction, and the
judge's exercise of discretion was upheld on appeal); *Through Transport Mutual Insurance
Association (Eurasia) Ltd v New India Assurance Co. Ltd* [2004] 1 Lloyd's Rep. 206
(injunction granted when applicant had not applied promptly for an interim injunction, and
had unsuccessfully challenged the jurisdiction of the foreign court); *Advent Capital Plc v
GN Ellinas Importers-Exporters Ltd* [2003] EWHC 3330 (injunction granted based on an
exclusive jurisdiction clause, notwithstanding some delay); *Akai Pty Limited v People's
Insurance Co. Limited* [1998] 1 Lloyd's Rep. 90 at pp. 107–108 (injunction must be applied
for promptly, but granted despite delay and an indemnity granted to the respondent against
the extra costs incurred by it in Singapore because of that delay); *Mike Trading and
Transport Ltd v R. Pagnan & Fratelli (The Lisboa)* [1980] 2 Lloyd's Rep. 546 at 551 LHC;
A/S D/S Svendborg v Wansa (trading as Melbourne Enterprises) [1996] 2 Lloyd's Rep. 559 at
570 LHC; *Toepfer International GmbH v Molino Boschi SRL* [1996] 1 Lloyd's Rep. 510 at
515–516 in which the delay was fatal; *Bankers Trust Co. v P. T. Jakarta International Hotels*
[1999] 1 Lloyd's Rep. 910 at 915.
[39] [1996] 2 Lloyd's Rep. 585.
[40] [1928] 2 K.B. 144.

(6) To enforce the *res judicata* or issue estoppel effect of an English judgment

14.025 The English court may grant an injunction to prevent a party bound by the *res judicata* or issue estoppel effect of an English judgment relitigating the underlying dispute or issue abroad. This extends to litigating abroad matters which could and should have been litigated as part of the original action.[41] Granting an anti-suit injunction for this purpose both forwards an important English public policy of preventing collateral attack[42] on a final judgment by a disappointed litigant, and gives effect to a substantive right not to be sued which has been created by the relevant judgment. This is very different from an alternative forum case where the English court has not yet rendered a judgment on the merits.[43] On the other hand in *E. D. & F. Man (Sugar) Ltd v Haryanto (No.2)*[44] the public policy was not so strong as to justify an injunction against a party relying in any court worldwide upon a foreign judgment which was inconsistent with an English one. The granting of a declaration established the position in English law, whereas a worldwide injunction would have been an illegitimate intrusion on the processes of courts throughout the world.

The application can be made by application notice issued in the original proceedings. This is because the purpose of the anti-suit injunction is in effect to uphold and enforce the judgment given in the action. Proceedings to do this are within the scope of the original action for which both parties have submitted to the English jurisdiction.[45] A Mareva injunction in aid of execution would be a matter within the scope of the proceedings in which a final judgment had been obtained and this can be sought by application in those proceedings. It is not necessary to bring separate proceedings for the purpose of enforcing the judgment or obtaining relief in aid of execution. Likewise where the purpose of the injunction is to prevent litigation abroad of a point covered by that judgment.

(7) To protect assets abroad which are covered by English bankruptcy, administration or winding-up proceedings

14.026 The court will restrain proceedings abroad when the purpose of doing so is to protect the jurisdiction being exercised by the English court over an administration of assets, a bankruptcy or winding-up proceedings. One way

---

[41] *Zeeland Navigation Company v Banque Worms, The Times,* December 26, 1995; the judgment delivered at the trial is reported at [1995] 1 Lloyd's Rep. 251.
[42] See the dicta of Hoffmann J. in *Arab Monetary Fund v Hashim, Financial Times,* July 23, 1992.
[43] *Bank of Tokyo Ltd v Karoon* [1987] A.C. 45 at 58E–G.
[44] [1991] 1 Lloyd's Rep. 161 followed in *Akai Pty Limited v People's Insurance Co. Limited* [1998] 1 Lloyd's Rep. 90 at 108.
[45] *Glencore International AG v Metro Trading International Inc.* [2002] 2 All E.R. (Comm) 1 at [52–53].

of looking at this is that the purpose of the injunction is to protect the integrity and effectiveness of the English proceedings in achieving their aim.[46] Another way of putting the point in the context of bankruptcy and winding up is that there is an English public policy of treating creditors equally and distributing proceeds *pari passu* and the foreign proceedings seeking to seize foreign assets are inconsistent with and an attempted evasion of an important English public policy.[47] There is underlying this type of case the idea of protecting the integrity of the English proceedings, an idea which in Australia provides a source of the jurisdiction to grant an anti-suit injunction.[48]

In *Barclays Bank v Homan*[49] a different point arose. The question was whether the bank had obtained a preference from the company prior to the commencement of the administration proceedings in respect of the company, or the proceedings under Chap.11 of the US Bankruptcy Code. The bank was an English company which had lent money in London under a contract governed by English law to an English customer. The repayment to it, which was alleged to be a preference, was made in London but out of the proceeds of an asset located in America. There were the administration proceedings in London and the Chap. 11 proceedings in the US District Court for the Southern District of New York. Should the English court grant an anti-suit injunction to prevent the preference issue being raised in New York against the bank? If decided against the bank the issue would result in extra assets being available to the company in administration. There was no contract requiring the issue to be decided in England. Whether an injunction was to be granted depended on the principles applicable when deciding if the English court ought to grant an injunction which would have the effect of preventing a foreign court from deciding the merits of a dispute in an alternative forum case. Even a difference of view as to which was the more appropriate court to decide the issue could not justify the English court arrogating to itself the sole jurisdiction to do so. There was also the problem that the issue had not been raised in London by the administrators and the court considered that the bank had no right to raise it through a claim for a negative declaration.

---

[46] *Bank of Tokyo Ltd v Karoon* [1987] A.C. 45 at 60, *per* Robert Goff L.J. citing *Graham v Maxwell* (1849) 1 Mac. & G. 71 (after a decree of administration of an estate), *Re Distin* (1871) 24 L.T. 157 (after a petition in bankruptcy) *Re North Carolina Estate Co. Ltd* (1889) 5 T.L.R. 328 (after commencement of winding-up proceedings), see also principle 5 of the resolution on anti-suit injunctions adopted in 2003 by the Institut de Droit International referred to in para.14.001 above.

[47] *Bank of Tokyo Ltd v Karoon* [1987] A.C. 45 at 58G–H referring to the judgment of Judge Wilkey in *Laker Airways Ltd v Sabena, Belgian World Airlines*, 731 F.2d 909 at 926–927 (1984), *Barclays Bank v Homan* [1993] B.C.L.C. 680 at 686e–f, *per* Hoffmann J. ("evading the *pari passu* distribution policy of English insolvency law by proceedings to seize the company's assets in a foreign country").

[48] *CSR Ltd v Cigna Insurance Australia Ltd* (1997) 189 C.L.R. 345 at 390–392.

[49] [1993] B.C.L.C. 680.

(8) Alternative forum cases: to prevent the substantive merits of a claim being decided abroad when those merits ought to be decided in England

(i) *The principles*

14.027   *Société Nationale Industrielle Aerospatiale v Lee Kui Jak*[50] was an alternative forum case. Under the law prior to incorporation of the principle of *forum non conveniens* the court would not act unless the foreign proceedings were vexatious or oppressive. The fact that proceedings were brought abroad by a party which mirrored the issues to be determined in pending English proceedings was not sufficient. This was because there was no presumption that the parties would not get justice abroad and as a matter of comity and restraint the court would not restrain the foreign proceedings. In *Vardopulo v Vardopulo*[51] a wife sought judicial separation from her husband and was met with a petition for divorce in the French court. She was not granted an injunction, the Court of Appeal was not moved by the consideration that she could not afford to be represented in France as well as England—she would still get justice in France. The result was that where there were proceedings both in England and abroad there would be a race to get to judgment first and thereby produce a *res judicata* effect in the slower forum.[52]

Under the principles stated in *Société Nationale Industrielle Aerospatiale v Lee Kui Jak*, the fact that the English court considers England to be the more appropriate forum or even the natural forum, is not enough to justify the granting of an injunction but it is an important threshold question.[53] It is important both to evaluation of whether the respondent's conduct is unconscionable, and whether as a matter of discretion the injunction should be granted. Even if answered in the affirmative there will still have to be facts which make it unconscionable for the respondent to continue with the foreign proceedings, something which makes it positively unjust for those proceedings to continue. There are also to be taken into account matters which make it just for the foreign proceedings to continue such as where the plaintiff in those proceedings has arrested a ship and has security for his claim.[54] Each case depends on its own particular circumstances and there is no definition of what would be vexatious, or oppressive.[55] With a

---

[50] [1987] A.C. 871.
[51] (1909) 25 T.L.R. 518 following *Hyman v Helm* (1882) 24 Ch.D. 531.
[52] This is why in *Orr-Lewis v Orr-Lewis* [1949] P. 347 the judge criticised the wife for making the application instead of pressing on to trial.
[53] *Turner v Grovit* [2002] 1 W.L.R. 107 at [25].
[54] *Ascot Commodities NV v Northern Pacific Shipping (The Irini A)* [1999] 1 Lloyd's Rep. 196 at 200; In *The Hartlepool* (1950) 84 Ll.L.Rep.145, an injunction was granted where security had not been obtained in the foreign proceedings.
[55] *Royal Bank of Canada v Cooperatieve Centrale Raiffeisen-Boerenleenbank BA* [2004] 1 Ll.Rep. 471 Civ 07 at [38] referring to Bowen L.J. in *McHenry v Lewis* (1882) 22 Ch.D. 397 at 407–408 "[vexation and oppression] must vary with the circumstances of each case".

"non-exclusive" jurisdiction clause, depending upon the interpretation of the particular clause, there may be a lessening of the burden in showing that foreign proceedings are vexatious or oppressive.[56]

In *Aerospatiale* it was unjust for the Texan proceedings brought against **14.028** the manufacturers because of their position in obtaining an indemnity or contribution from those responsible for maintaining the helicopter, who were subject to the jurisdiction in Brunei but contesting it in Texas. This provided the crucial factor justifying the granting of the injunction restraining continuation of the proceedings in Texas.[57] This included the possibility of multiplicity of proceedings and inconsistent results in different jurisdictions if the Texan proceedings were allowed to continue. It was a similar factor to that which in *Donohue v Armco*[58] led to refusal to enforce the exclusive jurisdiction clause.

In *Glencore International AG v Metro Trading International Inc*,[59] an injunction was granted against the foreign shipowners who had brought proceedings before a US District Court when there were already advanced, complex English proceedings involving numerous parties including those shipowners, and two phases of that litigation had already been adjudicated upon by the Commercial Court. The Court of Appeal considered that the US proceedings threatened to compromise, as between the parties to that litigation, the overall binding effect of what had happened and would happen in the litigation before the English court, including the abandonment of issues or "ducking" of issues which could have been raised. It was unconscionable for the shipowners to do this when they had submitted to the merits jurisdiction of the English court and actively participated in the English proceedings.

In the United States there are very different approaches between the Federal Circuit Courts of Appeal adopted to the jurisdiction. In some courts a "stricter standard"[60] is applied which only permits an injunction to protect its own jurisdiction or to enforce its own public policies. In others a "laxer" standard is applied allowing an injunction if foreign proceedings are vexatious, oppressive or otherwise inequitable, albeit allowing the effect of comity to be taken into account. These approaches reflect underlying differences in the balancing of (1) the need to do substantive justice between the litigants and (2) of "comity" between nations and their courts in the sense of a court's respect for the international rules which ought to govern it so as to avoid trespassing on another state's sovereignty and the independence of its courts.

---

[56] See para.14.015–14.018, above.
[57] [1987] A.C. 871 at 900–902.
[58] [2002] 1 Lloyd's Rep. 425 at [27].
[59] [2002] 2 All E.R. (Comm) 1.
[60] See para.14.001, above; *Airbus Industrie GIE v Patel* [1999] 1 A.C. 119 at 136–137, *per* Lord Goff, referring to an article by Lawrence Collins "International Jurisdiction and Forum-Shopping: An Overview", *Current Legal Issues in International Litigation* (published by the Faculty of Law of the National University of Singapore) 3 at 6–8.

14.029   In alternative forum cases the purpose of the injunction is to require the merits of the underlying case to be decided in England. In *Airbus Industrie GIE v Patel*[61] the applicants sought to restrain proceedings brought against them in Texas. They said that they should be sued in Bangalore where the aeroplane had crashed when coming into land. They had obtained an anti-suit injunction from the court in Bangalore restraining the respondents from suing the applicants except in India and a declaration that the defendants were not entitled to proceed against Airbus Industrie except in India. The applicants established territorial jurisdiction over the respondents by serving an originating summons on the defendants seeking to enforce the Bangalore injunction and seeking an anti-suit injunction from the English court. The Bangalore injunction was not enforceable in England, and the court would not grant an injunction under its own anti-suit jurisdiction to restrain the proceedings in Texas. The alternative forum jurisdiction applies to protecting proceedings on the merits in the English court but not to intervening in support of the merits jurisdiction of a foreign court. The reason is comity, and judicial restraint in granting injunctions affecting the conduct of foreigners abroad or intruding on another state's sovereignty. The application had to be in support of a legitimate domestic interest.

In *Turner v Grovit*,[62-63] Lord Hobhouse said that the applicant for the injunction must have "a legitimate interest"[64] and that leaving aside where the applicant is relying on a contractual right, where there could be an injunction granted regardless of whether there were English proceedings on the underlying merits, there had to be in existence proceedings in this country to be protected by the restraining order. This statement has been criticised[65] as introducing an additional and unwelcome limitation which prevents an anti-suit injunction being granted in protection of an English forum on grounds of unconscionability, or plainly vexatious or abusive conduct, before proceedings on the merits have been commenced in England. In *Airbus Industrie G.I.E. v Patel*,[66] the absence of proceedings on the merits in England was fatal to the application because the English court would not grant an anti-suit injunction to protect on these grounds the merits jurisdiction of a foreign court, in that case the Indian court. It also follows that section 25 of the Civil Jurisdiction and Judgments Act will not be used to grant an anti-suit injunction on these grounds to support a foreign court's jurisdiction over the merits. But it does not follow that

---

[61] [1999] 1 A.C. 119.
[62-63] [2002] 1 W.L.R. 107 at para.27.
[64] Terminology originally used by Hobhouse L.J. in his judgment in the Court of Appeal in *Airbus Industrie G.I.E. v Patel* [1997] 2 Ll.Rep.8 at 16, which was subsequently reversed in the House of Lords, and which had focused on the legitimacy of the plaintiff's expectations, rather than the question treated by the House of Lords as critical, whether the English court should be involved as decision maker as to which of two foreign jurisdictions should decide the underlying merits.
[65] Briggs in [2002] B.Y.I.L. at 442.
[66] [1999] 1 A.C. 119.

where proceedings on the merits can be brought in England the English court will not grant an anti-suit injunction based on vexation or oppression in the respondent prosecuting proceedings abroad rather than in England. In *Aerospatiale* Lord Goff did not say that the English court had in fact to be already seized with the merits before granting an injunction on this ground.

(ii) The position under the Brussels Convention and the Judgments Regulation

In *Turner v Grovit*, the House of Lords referred to the European Court of **14.030** Justice the question whether an anti-suit injunction could be granted by the English court to restrain a defendant from commencing or continuing with proceedings in another Convention country when the defendant was "acting in bad faith with the intent and purpose of frustrating or obstructing proceedings properly before the English courts". When referring this question, the House of Lords expressed the opinion that since the jurisdiction to grant an anti-suit injunction is not concerned with the jurisdiction of the foreign court but with the improper conduct of the defendant in bringing and continuing with the foreign proceedings the Convention does not exclude the anti-suit jurisdiction.[67] In proceedings governed by the Brussels Convention where there are proceedings in the courts of another Member State, the Convention itself is inconsistent with applying a doctrine of *forum non conveniens*. Jurisdiction over the substantive case is decided by what are for the main part rigid rules,[68] which are simple and apply automatically.[69] Problems which would result from allowing a jurisdiction to grant anti-suit injunctions in respect of proceedings before the court of another Member State would have been that this would have been inconsistent with each court being equal to each other court and the principle of reciprocal trust between courts which underlies the Convention, and it would have given rise to the possibility of clashes between courts of different states such as that which took place in the *Laker Airways* litigation[70] between the English courts and those in the United States. The European Court of Justice decision in *Turner v Grovit*[71] has decided that it is inconsistent with the Convention to grant anti-suit relief restraining proceedings commenced before the courts of another Member State in respect of matters falling within the scope of the

---

[67] *Turner v Grovit* [2002] 1 W.L.R. 107 at [25] and [26], referring to the Brussels Convention; the same is true of the Judgments Regulation.
[68] *Airbus Industrie GIE v Patel* [1999] 1 A.C. 119 at 131–132.
[69] Case C–111/01 *Gantner Electronic GmbH v Basch Exploitatie Maatschappij BV* at para. 30.
[70] See *British Airways Board v Laker Airways* [1984] Q.B. 142 at 185–186, *Laker Airways v Sabena Belgian Airlines*, 731 F.2d 909 at 937 (1984), Court of Appeals for the DC circuit, *Airbus Industrie GIE v Patel* [1999] 1 A.C. 119 at 136–137, and for a full account, see L. Collins, *Essays in International Litigation and the Conflict of Laws* (1994), pp. 110–117.
[71] April 27, 2004; see paras 14.011–14.012 above.

Convention, and by parity of reasoning this must also apply to the Judgments Regulation.

(iii) Personal jurisdiction over the defendant and service out of the jurisdiction

14.031 Where proceedings on the merits are before the English court, then in an alternative forum case the injunction is in support of the English court's jurisdiction over the merits and that jurisdiction in itself enables the injunction to be granted. The respondent is amenable to the English jurisdiction to grant the injunction because of his submission to the jurisdiction of the English court over the merits[72] and there is no need to obtain permission to serve out of the jurisdiction a claim form or an application notice: the application notice can be issued and served within the jurisdiction as an application made in the pending proceedings. In the *Eras EIL Actions*[73] the applicant sought anti-suit injunctions against parties to the litigation with whom they had no direct *lis*. The court held that such relief could be sought by interlocutory application made in the various proceedings because the respondents had submitted to the jurisdiction for determination of their cases and this submission extended to the English court making orders for the purpose of protecting the English jurisdiction[74] in the litigation as a whole. This was put as being an exercise of the inherent jurisdiction of the English court to prevent abuse of its proceedings. This is the same idea as that adopted by the High Court of Australia[75] as the source of the jurisdiction in alternative forum cases. Once the jurisdiction is seen in this way it is logical that there is no need for some further submission to the jurisdiction on which to base the granting of the injunction.

Furthermore if the English court has jurisdiction over the merits against a party and this is invoked by the applicant then this in itself should suffice to make that party amenable to the English jurisdiction for the purpose of

---

[72] *Glencore International AG v Metro Trading International Inc.* [2002] 2 All E.R. (Comm) 1 at [52–53]; *Al-Bassam v Al-Bassam* [2003] EWHC 2278 at [19], Ch.D. (respondent to the injunction application had counterclaimed in the English proceedings on matters overlapping with those in the foreign proceedings), not affected by the successful appeal [2004] EWCA Civ 857, in which the Court of Appeal disapproved of the grant of an injunction restraining pursuit of the proceedings in Saudi Arabia based on the fear that there might not be a fair trial there, but granted a temporary, interim injunction so that the claimant would not be distracted by the Saudi proceedings from pursuit of preliminary issues in the English proceedings.

[73] [1995] 1 Lloyd's Rep. 64, also reported as *Société Commerciale de Réassurance v Eras International* [1995] 2 All E.R. 278.

[74] *Airbus Industrie GIE v Patel* [1999] 1 A.C. 119 at 136, *per* Lord Goff referring to the judgment of Judge Wilkey in *Laker Airways Ltd v Sabena, Belgian World Airlines* 731 F.2d 909 at 926–927 (1984); *Bank of Tokyo Ltd v Karoon* [1987] A.C. 45 at 57–58, *per* Robert Goff L.J. referring to that judgment.

[75] *CSR Ltd v Cigna Insurance Australia Ltd* (1997) 189 C.L.R. 345 at 390–392; *Australian Broadcasting Corporation v Lenah Game Meats Pty Ltd* (2001) 208 C.L.R.199 at [93–95].

granting an anti-suit injunction in an alternative forum case.[76] The injunction is granted ancillary to the exercise of jurisdiction over the merits and is not dependent on there being some formal act of submission to the jurisdiction by the respondent. This is the position for Mareva relief and it should also apply to injunctions in alternative forum cases. In the *Eras EIL Actions* the court did grant an injunction against syndicate 109 which was not yet a party to the litigation but which was amenable to the jurisdiction of the English court over the merits. This injunction could be justified as an injunction granted in anticipation of that syndicate being made a party to proceedings being brought in England against it based on the underlying merits of the dispute.[77]

That the anti-suit injunction is granted so as to protect the English **14.032** jurisdiction does not have the consequence that the applicant is without any legal or equitable right not to be sued in the foreign jurisdiction. The cases show that the Chancery Court did exercise a jurisdiction to restrain proceedings abroad which were vexatious or oppressive[78] and therefore in the eyes of English law there was and is a "right" to be protected from such proceedings.[79] In the *Eras EIL Actions* the court viewed such a right to be protected from vexatious or oppressive proceedings as one on which proceedings on the merits could be based under the Brussels and Lugano Conventions.[80] If the foreign proceedings are before the courts of another Member State under the Judgments Regulation, or the Brussels or Lugano Conventions, then the decision of the European Court of Justice in *Turner v Grovit* precludes the granting of anti-suit relief.[81]

CPR r.6.20 is unlike[82] the former RSC Ord.11, r.1(1), which only applied to substantive claims against the intended defendant,[83] but under CPR r.6.20 there is no separate head devoted to enabling service out of the jurisdiction of a claim form or application notice seeking an anti-suit injunction to restrain foreign proceedings. CPR r.6.20(1) would apply to enable service out of the jurisdiction against any person domiciled within the jurisdiction. CPR r.6.20(2) is restricted to restraining acts within the jurisdiction and so would not apply.[84]

---

[76] In *Amoco (UK) Exploration Co. v British American Offshore Ltd* [1999] 2 Lloyd's Rep. 772 the court had no merits jurisdiction over Rowan, and hence the failure of the applicant to obtain leave to serve the originating summons out of the jurisdiction seeking the anti-suit relief against Rowan was fatal to the application seeking an injunction against it.
[77] *Turner v Grovit* [2002] 1 W.L.R. 107 at [27].
[78] *Bushby v Munday* (1821) 5 Madd. 297; *Lord Portarlington v Soulby* (1834) 3 My & K. 104; *Carron Iron Co. v MacLaren* (1855) 5 H.L. Cas. 416.
[79] *Youell v Kara Mara Shipping* [2000] 2 Lloyd's Rep. 102 at [45].
[80] [1995] 1 Lloyd's Rep. 64 at 74–79.
[81] See paras 14.009–14.010 and 14.027 above.
[82] *C Inc. PLC v L* [2001] 2 Lloyd's Rep. 459.
[83] *Mercedes Benz AG v Leiduck* [1996] A.C. 284; *Amoco (UK) Exploration Co. v British American Offshore Ltd* [1999] 2 Lloyd's Rep. 772.
[84] *Amoco (UK) Exploration Co. v British American Offshore Ltd* [1999] 2 Lloyd's Rep. 772 at 778.

(9) Single forum cases

14.033   These are cases in which the foreign court is the only forum in which the applicant can be sued. An example is where the applicant is being sued in the United States under American anti-trust legislation. If the conduct complained of has taken place in England, the applicant is an English company and there is no basis for the United States court taking jurisdiction over a foreigner in respect of conduct abroad then a single forum anti-suit injunction can be granted. This is different from the principle of *forum non conveniens* because what is in issue in single forum cases is not where the proposed litigation should take place but whether it should take place at all. The question is whether through the mechanism of the anti-suit injunction the proposed defendant to the threatened substantive claim should gain immunity from suit in the foreign jurisdiction and in consequence immunity from any liability.

In *British Airways Board v Laker Airways Ltd*[85] it was held that because British Airways were parties to the applicable agreement between the United Kingdom and the United States regulating transatlantic air traffic therefore they had accepted that they were bound by the domestic law of both countries and could not complain about the bringing of the anti-trust proceedings against them in the United States.[86]

14.034   In *Midland Bank v Laker Airways*[87] an injunction was granted on the application of the Midland Bank because Laker Airways were seeking to complain in the United States of dealings of an English company in the course of carrying on its business in England which were subject to English law. It was an exorbitant exercise of jurisdiction by the United States to entertain a civil suit in respect of conduct by a foreigner abroad and to subject it to determination by American domestic law. It was unconscionable for Laker Airways to subject the bank to such proceedings and potential liability. It was also contrary to the entitlement of the bank in England to carry on its business in England in accordance with the norms dictated by English law and without being answerable in the courts of a foreign state which would apply foreign law.

An English court does not use its anti-suit jurisdiction in a single forum case to restrain proceedings abroad which relate to matters in which the English court had no legitimate interest even though the court had exercised what appeared to be a plainly exorbitant jurisdiction.[88] In *Midland Bank v Laker Airways* it was the English court which had

[85] [1985] A.C. 58 at 81.
[86] *Airbus Industrie GIE v Patel* [1999] 1 A.C. 119 at 137.
[87] [1986] Q.B. 689. Contrast the approach of the majority of the High Court of Australia with the dissenting judgment of Brennan C.J. in *CSR Limited v Cigna Insurance Australia Limited* (1997) 189 C.L.R. 345. The majority considered that the pleaded claim by CSR to treble damages before the US District Court based on conduct outside of the US, was not a ground on which anti-suit relief could properly be given.
[88] *Airbus Industrie GIE v Patel* [1999] 1 A.C. 119 at 138.

jurisdiction over the activities of the English bank in England. In *Airbus Industrie GIE v Patel* the jurisdiction dispute was between India and Texas, and the English court was a bystander which happened to have coercive power over the defendants who wished to sue in Texas but no legitimate interest in determining that dispute.

(10) A right not to be sued in the foreign court through the English court giving effect to a defence or absence of a legitimate cause of action

In a clear case where the plaintiff in the foreign court has no cause of **14.035** action or there is a clear defence to the claim the English court can intervene to restrain him from pursuing the foreign proceedings on the grounds that continuing those proceedings is vexatious, oppressive or unconscionable.[89] This is giving anticipatory effect to a defence.[90]

(11) Restraint of proceedings abroad relating to obtaining documents or dispositions of witnesses

In *South Carolina Insurance Co. v Assurantie Maatschappij "De Zeven* **14.036** *Provincien" NV*,[91] by the time the proceedings reached the House of Lords the object of the proceedings in the United States brought under 28 USC s.1782 was confined to obtaining documents from non-parties to the English proceedings. The conduct of South Carolina in seeking to obtain the documents was not regarded as "unconscionable". It did not interfere with the conduct of the proceedings in England, it was made before the trial started, and there was no legitimate interest of the applicant to be protected by injunction.

The position in relation to obtaining oral depositions, or materials after the trial,[92] is different. This may well interfere with the conduct of the English proceedings, be unfair and therefore be restrained.

In *Armstrong v Armstrong*[93] the petitioner for divorce also sought to carry out an oral examination of potential witnesses abroad to see what

---

[89] *Shell International Petroleum Co. Ltd v Coral Oil Co. Ltd* [1999] 2 Lloyd's Rep. 606 at 609 RHC (anti-suit injunction to restrain the pursuit abroad of a claim which was bound to fail and "utterly absurd").

[90] *British Airways Board v Laker Airways Ltd* [1985] A.C. 58 at 81.

[91] [1987] A.C. 24.

[92] An injunction was granted in *Bankers Trust International Plc v P. T. Dharmala Sakti Sejahtera* [1996] C.L.C. 252 in which the application in New York was made after trial but before judgment was delivered, included oral depositions as well as documents, and went well beyond the materials and points considered at the trial.

[93] [1892] P. 98.

they would say. Their depositions could not be put into evidence in the divorce suit. This amounted to interrogating the wife's witnesses before trial. This was restrained because it was "an interference with the proper course of administration of justice" in England.[94] The purpose of the injunction was to protect the integrity of the administration of justice by the English court in the proceedings pending before it.

14.037 It follows that such an application can be made by application notice issued in the proceedings and that the court's jurisdiction to entertain the application for the anti-suit injunction is a consequence of its jurisdiction over the respondent in the pending proceedings. Where the respondent is domiciled in another Member State covered by the Judgments Regulation the injunction is an aspect of the determination of the pending substantive proceedings in England. Another possible justification is that in this particular class of anti-suit case the injunction is a provisional or protective measure within Art.31 of the Regulation in relation to the pending English proceedings. Another possible justification is that the procedure falls outside the scope of the Regulation altogether because the anti-suit injunction is not based on any substantive cause of action and the process is not a civil or commercial matter.

In *Omega Group Holdings v Kozeny*[95] the court restrained an attempt to depose witnesses in the United States under 28 USC s.1782 because the witnesses would be subjected to double cross-examination, the trial would suffer from unnecessary duplication and there was the risk that a witness once deposed in the United States might be discouraged from giving evidence at the trial in England.[96] In contrast, in *Arab Monetary Fund v Hashim*,[97] proceedings had been brought in California against someone who might be a witness but it was not necessary to grant the anti-suit injunction so as to protect the doing of justice in the English proceedings.

14.038 In *Bank of Tokyo Ltd v Karoon*,[98] the subsidiary of the applicant had disclosed confidential information to the applicant which it then used in interpleader proceedings in London. The subsidiary was a New York bank. Its customer who was a party to the interpleader proceedings sued the New York bank in New York for damages for breach of its duty of confidentiality. The subsidiary was not a party to the interpleader proceedings in London. It sought an anti-suit injunction on the ground that English public policy favoured collection of evidence without interference so that the truth could be established by the court. This injunction was refused because the New York action was against the subsidiary which was a separate entity from the parent and so the public policy, even if it did exist, would not protect the New York bank from an action for breach of confidence brought by its customer. That was a matter properly for the

---

[94] *Bank of Tokyo Ltd v Karoon* [1987] A.C. at 60G–H, *per* Robert Goff L.J.
[95] [2002] C.L.C. 132.
[96] See also *Allstate Life Insurance v ANZ Banking Corporation*, 64 F.C.R. 1 at 44, 61 (1996).
[97] *Financial Times*, July 23, 1992.
[98] [1987] A.C. 45.

New York court,[99] and public policy favoured leaving that to the New York court.

(12) Anti-anti-suit injunctions

There has also grown up the use of "anti-anti-suit" injunctions which are **14.039** granted by a court (Court A) because of the threat that an application for an "anti-suit" injunction will be made to another court (Court B) to restrain a party from continuing with ongoing proceedings in Court A. The justification is to protect the jurisdiction of Court A in the ongoing proceedings. An account is given of this in the Laker Airways litigation by Lord Goff in *Airbus Industrie GIE v Patel*.[1]

Where the "anti-anti-suit" injunction is sought in proceedings brought in England for the protection of those proceedings from interference by a foreign court, the application is for a provisional measure enabling the English court to go on hearing and determining the underlying claim. The purpose of the injunction is to protect the integrity of the administration of justice by the English court in the proceedings pending before it; the consequence is that on jurisdiction to entertain an application for such an injunction the position would appear to be the same in principle as discussed at paras 14.029 and 14.037, above.

(13) Restraining arbitration proceedings

An injunction can be granted to restrain the pursuit of arbitration **14.040** proceedings based on a supposed arbitration agreement when the applicant seeks to impeach the validity of that agreement.[2]

---

[99] See also *X, Y and Z v B* [1983] 2 Lloyd's Rep. 535 (also reported under the name *X AG v A Bank* [1983] 2 All E.R. 464) where the English court granted an injunction to a client restraining a branch in London of a bank which had its head office in New York from complying with a subpoena from a United States District Court in New York when to do so would place it in breach of its duty of confidentiality owed to that customer, which was a duty governed by English law, and when if restrained the bank would not be held in contempt of the New York court. Likewise the English court should respect the jurisdiction of the New York court over a New York bank about the confidentiality attaching to an account at a branch in New York; see also *British Nylon Spinners Ltd v Imperial Chemical Industries Ltd* [1953] Ch. 19 at 27 and 28.

[1] [1999] 1 A.C. 119 at 136.

[2] *Kitts v Moore* [1895] 1 Q.B. 253; *Compagnie Nouvelle France Navigation SA v Compagnie Navale Afrique Du Nord (The Oranie and The Tunisie)* [1966] 1 Lloyd's Rep. 477 (alleged that the charterparties were not the effective bargains in proceedings in France). After *Bremer Vulkan Schiffbau v South India Shipping Corporation Ltd* [1981] A.C. 909 at 981, *The Ithaka* (1939) 64 Ll.L.Rep. 141 (injunction refused when agreement being impeached for duress in Turkey) must also be regarded as falling within this category.

Chapter 15

Injunctions affecting letters of credit, performance bonds and bank guarantees payable on demand or their proceeds

(1) Introduction

Sale contracts often provide for payment to be made by irrevocable letter **15.001** of credit. First, the parties will conclude a contract of sale. Secondly, the buyer pursuant to the terms of that contract has to procure a bank to open an irrevocable letter of credit in favour of the seller with payment to be made against documents. The next stage is for the seller to ship the goods and collect together the documents he needs to present under the letter of credit in order to obtain payment. Then he presents the documents to obtain payment. In this situation there are three contracts. First, the contract of sale, secondly, there is the letter of credit between the bank and the beneficiary and, thirdly, there is the contract between the buyer and the bank providing for the opening of the letter of credit and payment of an indemnity and a fee to the bank. The letter of credit is a separate and independent contract—it is autonomous.[1] The bank only deals with documents and looks at the documents presented to it, and even then without going through the small print on the reverse of bills of lading.[2] It is not concerned with whether the contract of sale has been performed.

A letter of credit in relation to a sale transaction is the mechanism for exchanging goods for money with the letter of credit providing both a solvent paymaster and one who will not dispute payment based on alleged defects in the goods.

---

[1] The autonomy principle and the fraud exception have been applied by the Chinese Supreme Court: see "Documentary Credits and Fraud: English and Chinese Law Compared" [2004] J.B.L. 155.
[2] *Homburg Houtimport BV v Agrosin Private Ltd (The Starsin)* [2004] 1 A.C. 715 and [78], *per* Lord Hoffmann referring to *National Bank of Egypt v Hannevig's Bank* (1919) 3 L.D.A.B. 213 at 214, *British Imex Industries Ltd v Midland Bank* [1958] 1 Q.B. 542 at 551–552 and Art.23 of the ICC Uniform Customs and Practice for Commercial Credits (UCP 500).

A performance bond issued by a bank, insurance company or other financial institution, may be used in a variety of different commercial situations. A classic case is in construction projects[3] where the principal requires a contractor who is going to build the works to provide a bond which can be drawn down simply by demand made by the principal based on the principal's belief that there has been a breach of contract. Because of the comparative bargaining powers of the principal and the contractor, it is common on international projects for the principal to require this in return for awarding the contractor the contract. The contractor then performs with the risk that in the event of dissatisfaction the bond will be drawn down and he will face cash flow difficulties as a result. In practice where the bond is drawn down this is likely to be a prelude to difficult negotiations with the principal about remedial work, quantum of compensation for the principal, and repayment of a balance to the contractor who furnished the bond. A performance bond is security for good performance which ensures that the contractor will take a continuing interest in satisfying his customer, and which, in the event of dispute, enables the principal, as long as he does not act fraudulently, to get cash in hand from the bond, leaving any dispute to be resolved with the contractor already out of pocket. A performance bond can be called by a variety of different names, including a demand guarantee or a stand-by letter of credit. It is very different from a guarantee in the sense of an obligation entered into by a guarantor as surety for the contractor's obligations under the underlying transaction[4]; such a guarantee would risk embroiling the guarantor in the underlying dispute. It falls short of an actual cash deposit made by the contractor, but can readily be converted without significant delay into the equivalent of one through an appropriate demand being made by the beneficiary in compliance with the conditions set out in the bank's undertaking. In form it may be a bond payable against a draft,[5] or more usually it requires a demand which has to comply with certain requirements, such as stating there has been a breach of contract and what it is.[6] Its purpose is very different from a letter of credit which is furnished as the mechanism of payment for the sale of goods, and this has led to the suggestion that the courts should distinguish between them when considering whether to restrain a demand by a beneficiary.[7]

15.002   Another situation in which a demand guarantee issued by a bank is used is where payment is to be made in the future of a debt which is accruing due where the creditor requires a first class paymaster and the debtor does not wish to grant security over his own assets to the creditor.

---

[3] "Unconditional Bank Guarantees" [2003] Int. C.L.R. 240 (Julian Bailey) at 240–241.
[4] "Unconditional Bank Guarantees" [2003] Int. C.L.R. 240 (Julian Bailey) at 244–248.
[5] Called in the US a "suicide bond".
[6] The ICC *Uniform Rules For Demand Guarantees* ICC Publication No. 458, article 20, paragraph a.
[7] See "Performance Bonds and Letters of Credit: A Cracked Mirror Image" [1997] J.B.L. 289 at 302–303 (Professor Charles Debattista), where it is argued that because of the difference in purpose the courts should be more ready to protect a contractor who furnishes a performance bond from an unscrupulous beneficiary.

As between the commercial parties to an underlying transaction their rights are governed by the contract between them. It is the interpretation of that contract which will determine in what circumstances the beneficiary has an obligation not to make a demand.[8] As between the bank and the beneficiary of a letter of credit, performance bond or demand guarantee it is the terms of the bank's undertaking which will control what has to be tendered to the bank to trigger the bank's obligation to pay. The bank will not be involved in any dispute on the underlying transaction, and in general has only to concern itself with the documents presented to it.

There are three questions:

(a) When does the bank have a good defence to the seller's action based on dishonour of the letter of credit or performance bond?

(b) When does the bank have a right of indemnity against its customer if it does pay the beneficiary? and

(c) Whether at the interlocutory stage which takes place before or soon after presentation of the documents the court will grant an injunction restraining payment either at the suit of the applicant for the credit or a person having a commercial interest in preventing payment?

(2) Question (a): The bank's defence to the seller's action based on dishonour of the letter of credit or performance bond

(i) The "fraud" of the beneficiary and the "validity" defence available to the bank

Whether the bank had a good defence was the issue in *United City* 15.003 *Merchants (Investments) Ltd v Royal Bank of Canada*.[9] There the question was whether the bank had a good defence when the beneficiary was innocent of any fraud and had presented documents which included a bill of lading with a notation on it which was untruthful about the date of shipment on board the carrying vessel. None of the documents had been forged; a genuine document told a lie. The House of Lords held that the bank had no defence to the sellers' claim because the sellers had genuinely believed that the date of shipment was that stated in the notation.

---

[8] *Sirius Insurance Co. v FAI Insurance Limited* [2003] 1 W.L.R. 2214 at 29–30 (a contractual undertaking not to draw down except in certain events will normally be enforced by injunction); *Bachmann Pty Limited v BHP Power New Zealand Limited* [1999] 1 V.L.R. 420 at 28 citing earlier authorities; *Fletcher Construction Australia Limited v Varnsdorf Pty Limited* [1998] 3 V.L.R. 812 (which regards the question as one going to the allocation of risk between contracting parties in the event of a dispute arising).

[9] [1983] 1 A.C. 168.

Often when there is fraud by the beneficiary in making a demand there will be a lie told by the documents presented to the bank. But the fraud exception should not be limited to cases in which the documents themselves contain a lie, but should extend to where the beneficiary in presenting the documents is acting fraudulently including where the presentation is the means of carrying out a fraud in the underlying transaction.[10] Commercial morality demands, and the honest expectation of the bank and the beneficiary is, that the bank will not pay a beneficiary when it is obvious to the bank at the time of presentation of the documents that the beneficiary is acting dishonestly in presenting the documents and claiming payment under the letter of credit. In these circumstances any payment made by the bank would be outside its mandate from its customer (question (b)).

In *United City Merchants (Investments) Ltd v Royal Bank of Canada*[11] Lord Diplock said:

> "The exception for fraud on the part of the beneficiary seeking to avail himself of the credit is a clear application of the maxim ex turpi causa non oritur actio or, if plain English is to be preferred, 'fraud unravels all'. The courts will not allow their process to be used by a dishonest person to carry out a fraud."

15.004   In *Czarnikow-Rionda Sugar Trading v Standard Bank London Ltd*,[12] Rix J. said of Lord Diplock's words that:

> "It would be less pithy but more accurate to fill out the dictum by saying that fraud unravels the bank's obligation to act on the appearance of documents provided that the bank knows in time of the beneficiary's fraud."

This statement appears immediately after citation of a series of cases[13] all of which were concerned with injunctions, and was made in the course of considering the "balance of convenience" in that case. In answering question (c) the state of the evidence at the time of the determination of the application for the injunction is critical.

However, for the reasons set out below, it is considered that the proviso added by Rix J. is not a correct statement of the defence of fraud of the beneficiary available to a bank sued under the letter of credit for refusing to

---

[10] *Edward Owen v Barclays Bank* [1978] Q.B. 159 at 169 G–H *per* Lord Denning M.R.; *Bank of Nova Scotia v Angelica Whitewear Limited* [1987] 1 S.C.R. 59 at 11–20; and see para.15.009.

[11] [1983] 1 A.C. 168 at 184B.

[12] [1999] 2 Lloyd's Rep. 187 at 199.

[13] *Discount Records Ltd v Barclays Bank* [1975] 1 W.L.R. 315; *Sztejn v J. Henry Schroeder Banking Corporation.* 31 N.Y.S. 2d 631 (1941); *Harbottle v National Westminster Bank* [1978] Q.B. 146; *Edward Owen v Barclays Bank* [1978] Q.B. 159.

pay,[14] *i.e.* question (a). If the beneficiary has acted fraudulently then it does not matter how late the evidence becomes available to the bank. As Sir John Donaldson M.R. said in *Bolivinter Oil SA v Chase Manhattan Bank*:[15]

"... if, as Lord Diplock said, the principle is that 'fraud unravels all' and if the issue is whether payment should now be made, it is nothing to the point that at an earlier stage the fraud was unknown to the payer and so could not begin its unravelling, if fraud is now known to him and has now unravelled his obligations."

The House of Lords in *United City Merchants (Investments) Ltd* placed   **15.005** the defence on the basis of public policy, and not on the basis of an implied term in the letter of credit. The beneficiary is not entitled to rely on his own deceitful conduct in order to ground a cause of action against the bank. Logically public policy would not distinguish between a fraudulent beneficiary who had been uncovered to the knowledge of the bank at the time of presentation and one who had only been unmasked later. In both situations commercial morality and public policy demand that the court give no assistance to the fraudulent claimant who relies on his own fraud as part of his cause of action. The case law on *ex turpi causa* refuses assistance to the claimant who has to found his cause of action on illegality regardless of when the unlawful conduct had been discovered by the defendant.[16] The defence is allowed not for the benefit of the defendant, who may be wholly undeserving, but for the public benefit.[17] It is not enough to show that a reasonable banker would infer fraud at the time of presentation. The defence requires proof of fraud by the beneficiary not merely that a reasonable banker would have inferred fraud.[18] The defence is the fraud and not the evidence of it.

This is also shown by the case of a letter of credit which provides for payment to be made sometime after the presentation of documents, a deferred payment letter of credit. Where there is fraud which the bank discovers after presentation of documents but before the expiry of the period stipulated for deferred payment, then the bank has a complete defence.[19] In principle if the time has expired for payment but the bank has not paid and then discovers the fraud, it has a complete defence because

---

[14] In *Montrod Ltd v Grundkötter Fleischvertriebs GmbH* [2002] 1 W.L.R. 1975 at [41] Rix J.'s statement was quoted and also reference was made to *Group Josi Re v Walbrook Insurance* [1996] 1 W.L.R. 1152 at 1161. But the latter is addressed to where the beneficiary has at no time acted fraudulently and at the time of trial has knowledge that someone else has acted fraudulently. This does not give the bank a defence against the beneficiary.
[15] [1984] 1 Lloyd's Rep. 251 at 256 LHC.
[16] *Bolivinter Oil SA v Chase Manhattan Bank* [1984] 1 Lloyd's Rep. 251 at 256; see also *Simpson v Bloss* (1816) Taunt. 246; *Marles v Philip Trant & Sons Ltd* [1954] 1 Q.B. 29 at 38; *Bedford Insurance Company v Instituto de Resseguros* [1985] Q.B. 966.
[17] *Holman v Johnson* (1775) 1 Cowp. 341.
[18] *Society of Lloyd's v Canadian Imperial Bank of Commerce* [1993] 2 Lloyd's Rep. 579.
[19] *Banco Santander SA v Bayfern Ltd* [1999] Lloyd's Rep. (Bank.) 239 at 245, affirmed [2000] Lloyd's Rep. (Bank.) 165.

the court will not allow its process to be used to enforce alleged rights founded on a fraud. The same is true of a claim to enforce those alleged rights made by an innocent assignee of the fraudster.[20]

15.006 If a bank had paid and then found out that it had paid against documents which were untruthful to the knowledge of the beneficiary at the time of presentation, then at that time all the necessary elements would have been present to constitute the tort of deceit, and the bank would be entitled to damages from the beneficiary equivalent to the amount of its payment under the letter of credit. The bank could also claim against the beneficiary for money paid under a mistake of fact.[21] It would be strange if, at trial, the bank was entitled to get all its money back if it had paid on presentation, but liable to judgment for the full amount of the credit if it had not paid. Furthermore if, as is sometimes the case, the beneficiary's claim is itself properly to be analysed as a claim for damages for breach of the letter of credit by the bank (*e.g.* refusal to accept a draft), then the bank would be entitled to show that if it had honoured the letter of credit, the beneficiary would have been no better off because it would have been liable to refund the amount to the bank as damages for deceit, or money paid by the bank under a mistake of fact. Even if the claim is one for debt these cross-claims would be available as a set-off.[22]

These considerations lead to the conclusion that when the beneficiary sues the bank for non-payment, the bank is entitled to defend itself by proving fraud by the beneficiary at the time of presentation, regardless of whether at that time it was obvious to the bank that the beneficiary was acting fraudulently. Both public policy, and the claims which would have vested in the bank against the beneficiary had payment been made, lead to this conclusion. The result is that fraud of the beneficiary is a good defence if it can be established at trial, or at a summary judgment application,[23] regardless of whether the bank had the evidence to establish it at the time of presentation of documents or when payment would have become due under the letter of credit had there been no fraud.[24] On an injunction application the time at which fraud has to be clearly established to the knowledge of the bank is when the application is decided.[25]

---

[20] *Banco Santander SA v Bayfern Ltd* [2000] Lloyd's Rep. (Bank.) 165 affirming [1999] Lloyd's Rep. (Bank) 239.
[21] *Edward Owen v Barclays Bank* [1978] Q.B. 159 at 169 H–170 A and 172H, referring to *Bank Russo-Iran v Gordon, Woodroffe & Co. Ltd*, unreported, October 3, 1972 (Browne J.); this was common ground in *Bank Tejarat v Hong Kong and Shanghai Banking Corporation (CI) Ltd* [1995] 1 Lloyd's Rep. 239 at 244 and in *Niru Battery Manufacturing Co. v Milestone Trading Ltd* [2003] EWCA Civ 1446 at [143].
[22] *Safa Ltd v Banque du Caire* [2000] 2 Lloyd's Rep. 600 at 607.
[23] *Safa Ltd v Banque du Caire* [2000] 2 Lloyd's Rep. 600 at 607 modifying the earlier analysis made in *Balfour Beatty Civil Engineering Ltd v Technical & General Guarantee* [2000] C.L.C. 252, which was on the position as it stood before the CPR. The facts in *Safa Ltd v Banque du Caire* were "most unusual" and appeared not to be of "a normal commercial transaction"—see [2000] 2 Lloyd's Rep. 600 at 610.
[24] *Mahonia Ltd v J. P. Morgan Chase Bank* [2003] 2 Lloyd's Rep. 911 at [46].
[25] *United Trading v Allied Arab Bank* [1985] 2 Lloyd's Rep. 554 at 560.

If the beneficiary has not acted fraudulently in presenting the documents, **15.007** then this defence does not apply. In *Montrod Ltd v Grundkötter Fleischvertriebs GmbH*[26] a document which purported to be a certificate of inspection issued on behalf of the opener of the credit was presented to the bank. It had in fact been signed by the beneficiary but the beneficiary did not have the authority of the opener of the credit to sign the document on its behalf. The beneficiary had not acted fraudulently. It was held that the bank had been bound to pay,[27] and that in consequence the bank was entitled to an indemnity. This decision proceeded on the basis that the document purported to be a document which complied with the terms of the credit, the beneficiary had not acted in any way dishonestly because it honestly believed that it was entitled to issue the certificate, the document itself was genuine, and the bank could not have refused to pay based on the fraud defence.

In *Montrod Ltd*[28] it was suggested that if the beneficiary had acted "unscrupulously" in presenting the documents, then this might give rise to a defence. This suggests that public policy might intervene even if the beneficiary has acted honestly but without regard to the interests of others. It is considered that public policy will only bar the claim if there is conduct of the beneficiary of such lack of honesty as to justify overriding the contractual bargain. Dishonesty is essential[29] because carelessness or fault of the beneficiary should not result in a refusal to enforce the bank's promise. Commercial men often act carelessly and selfishly, but this is not a ground for refusing them access to the court to enforce their bargains. Furthermore, for the system to be workable, the banks need a clear test to apply; dishonesty meets this requirement whilst unscrupulousness, without further definition, is too vague.

What amounts to dishonesty in this context? The "Robin Hood" test of **15.008** allowing a beneficiary to apply his own subjective standards of honesty would not be sufficient to protect the public interest. This has been consistently rejected as a benchmark by the courts.[30] The choice is between applying a purely objective standard of honesty according to the standards of ordinary commercial men, or a "combined" standard of this, together with proof that the beneficiary realised that what he was doing was contrary to those standards. The latter applies to establishing the liability of a constructive trustee in a case of "dishonest assistance".[31] It allows enforcement of the bank's promise except where the beneficiary has acted consciously knowing that what he did was contrary to the standards of

---

[26] [2002] 1 W.L.R. 1975.
[27] *Montrod Ltd v Grundkötter Fleischvertriebs GmbH* [2002] 1 W.L.R. 1975 at [57–61].
[28] [2002] 1 W.L.R. 1975 at [59].
[29] *Sundance Spas NZ Limited v Sundance Spas Inc.* [2001] 1 N.Z.L.R. 111.
[30] *Twinsectra Ltd v Yardley* [2002] 2 A.C. 164 at [27], *per* Lord Hutton referring to *Walker v Stones* [2001] Q.B. 902 at 939.
[31] See *Royal Brunei Airlines v Tan* [1995] 2 A.C. 378 at 389 and *Twinsectra Ltd v Yardley* [2002] 2 A.C. 164; *cf. Lambias (Importers and Exporters) Co. Pte Ltd v Hong Kong and Shanghai Banking Corporation* [1993] 2 S.L.R. 751 at 765–766.

honesty adopted by the ordinary standards of reasonable and honest commercial men. It is considered that this should be the test in this context. This is an area in which there is a strong public interest in enforcing the bank's undertaking, because of the needs of international commerce and the proper working of the financial system. Denial of access to the courts to enforce the bank's promise should only occur when absolutely necessary. This test achieves that aim.

The bank can also defend a claim by showing that its undertaking to the beneficiary is void or was voidable and has been lawfully avoided,[32] or that it was cancelled by mutual agreement, or that it is not a legally enforceable obligation.

(ii) Documents which are not genuine—the "nullity" defence

15.009 Do the documents tendered have to be genuine documents? In *United City Merchants (Investments) Ltd* the bill of lading had on it a false notation, but it was a genuine bill of lading. All documents relate to matters, things and concepts outside of the document. For example, in relation to a bill of lading there will appear to be a carrier, a vessel and goods shipped on board and the document refers to each of these. On the other hand the general principle is that the bank deals in documents not facts and is not concerned to inquire into facts outside of the documents themselves, and this is part of the terms of the credit. Would a purported bill of lading issued by a fictitious carrier in respect of non-existent goods on a non-existent ship be good tender under a letter of credit? One would have thought that the document was so devoid of any genuine feature that it was not a bill of lading at all, and so would not comply with the description of the document required by a letter of credit, which called for "a bill of lading". In *United City Merchants (Investments) Ltd* the Court of Appeal judgments, which were reversed on other grounds, support this view,[33] and the House of Lords left the point open.[34]

If without negligence the bank paid against such a document it would still be entitled to reimbursement under its indemnity (question (b)) because the risk of this is taken by the opener of the credit and not the bank. This result is not based on any fraud by the beneficiary. It is the consequence of the interpretation of the letter of credit itself and a refusal to interpret it as only calling for any documents which appear to comply with its requirements even though the documents themselves are only waste paper. The fact that the bank is not concerned with outside facts and will only examine the documents to see whether they comply does not

---

[32] *Solo Industries UK Ltd v Canara Bank* [2001] 1 W.L.R. 1800 at [35–40].
[33] [1982] Q.B. 208 at 246F–H and 254D; see also "The Identity of the Fraudulent Party under the Fraud Rule in the Law of Letters of Credit" [2001] U.N.S.W.L.J. 14 at paras 62–70, which helpfully cites a number of judicial observations in support of the proposition that the tendered documents must be "genuine" and "valid".
[34] [1983] 1 A.C. 168 at 188 A–C.

dictate a solution that as between the beneficiary and the bank, the bank has no defence when the beneficiary has honestly tendered waste paper.

(iii) Illegality

Illegality can be a defence to a claim based on a letter of credit,[35] just as **15.010** with any other contract. However, it does not follow that because the underlying contract is affected by illegality that this will necessarily taint the letter of credit and that it will be unenforceable; it is a separate contract and may be valid and enforceable depending on the nature of the alleged illegality, and the circumstances.[36] So if a letter of credit was provided by a reinsurer as the means of payment under a reinsurance contract which was illegal because it was not licensed to carry on business in London, the letter of credit remained valid and enforceable;[37] the illegality concerning the contract of reinsurance did not taint the letter of credit. On the other hand where the letter of credit itself is procured in order to effect a dishonest and fraudulent scheme public policy precludes its enforcement and the court will not allow its process to be used for this purpose.[38]

In *Mahonia Ltd v J. P. Morgan Chase Bank*[39] the claimant was a corporate vehicle used as part of a dishonest scheme to deceive third parties and it was held that there was a strongly arguable case that the letter of credit would not be enforceable. In principle, one would expect the same result when a beneficiary was seeking to obtain payment as the proceeds of a fraud carried out on the opener of the letter of credit. This would be so independently of any defect in the documents presented, as is shown by the example of a letter of credit issued as the means of payment for an illegal arms shipment. The dividing line is between a commercial dispute about performance of the underlying transaction and where the letter of credit is the mechanism for obtaining the proceeds of a dishonest scheme. Even if the bank does have available to it a defence of illegality, it would still be entitled to an indemnity from its customer if, without fault or culpability, it paid under the letter of credit.

(iv) Summary judgment application against the bank

On a summary judgment application the bank will succeed when it can **15.011** show that it has a real prospect of succeeding at trial in establishing fraud,[40] or that the documents tendered do not strictly comply with the requirements of the credit, or impeaching the validity of its own undertaking to

---

[35] *Group Josi Re v Walbrook Insurance Co. Ltd* [1996] 1 W.L.R. 1152 at 1164.
[36] *Mahonia Ltd v J. P. Morgan Chase Bank* [2003] 2 Lloyd's Rep. 911 at [48–62].
[37] *Group Jose Re v Wallbrook Insurance Co. Ltd* [1996] 1 Lloyd's Rep. 345 considered in *Mahonia Ltd v J. P. Morgan Chase Bank* [2003] 2 Lloyd's Rep. 911 at [48–62].
[38] *Mahonia Ltd v J. P. Morgan Chase Bank* [2003] 2 Lloyd's Rep. 911.
[39] [2003] 2 Lloyd's Rep. 911.
[40] *Solo Industries UK Ltd v Canara Bank* [2001] 1 W.L.R. 1800; *Safa Ltd v Banque du Caire* [2000] 2 Lloyd's Rep. 600 at 607 modifying the earlier analysis made in *Balfour Beatty*

the beneficiary.[41] Thus, *e.g.* where a bank has been misled by its customer and the beneficiary into opening a letter of credit, and has avoided it for misrepresentation, this would be a good defence.

In *Solo Industries UK Ltd v Canara Bank*[42] it was said that on a summary judgment application merely showing a real prospect of proving fraud at trial would not be sufficient; it had to be shown by the bank that there was a real prospect of showing at trial that on the material now available "the only realistic inference" was the relevant fraud. This test applies to question (c), concerning injunctions. It also affects question (b) because where that test is satisfied at the time of attempted drawdown the bank is not entitled to an indemnity if the beneficiary has in fact acted fraudulently.[43] On an application for summary judgment against the bank, the question is whether the case should be summarily decided against the bank by way of final decision on the merits. This must be decided by reference to what defences would be available to the bank if a trial were to take place.[44] At trial fraud has to be proved by the bank on the balance of probabilities, taking into account the inherent improbability of such an allegation being true.[45] Where it is proved, then public policy applies to bar the claim regardless of what material the bank had at an earlier stage and regardless of whether fraud is also proved by the bank to be the "only realistic inference". It is considered in *Solo Industries UK Ltd* the test was misstated. The court on the application should first consider the material then available and ask itself whether the bank would have a real prospect of proving fraud, if a trial were to take place. If the answer is yes, then the case should go to trial. If the answer is no, then the court should go on to consider whether, pursuant to CPR r.24.2(b), nevertheless there is some "other compelling reason" for a trial. This view is supported by the decision in *Safa Ltd v Banque du Caire*.[46]

(3) Question (b): The bank's right to an indemnity

15.012 Whether the bank has a right to an indemnity depends upon (1) the true interpretation of the contract of indemnity and (2) the principles of public policy.

Civil Engineering Ltd v Technical & General Guarantee [2000] C.L.C. 252, which was on the position as it stood before the CPR. The facts in *Safa Ltd v Banque du Caire* were "most unusual" and appeared not to be of "a normal commercial transaction"—see [2000] 2 Lloyd's Rep. 600 at 610.

[41] *Solo Industries UK Ltd v Canara Bank* [2001] 1 W.L.R. 1800 at [35–40].

[42] [2001] 1 W.L.R. 1800 at [70], referring to *United Trading v Allied Arab Bank* [1985] 2 Lloyd's Rep. 554.

[43] If the beneficiary has not acted fraudulently the bank has no defence to the beneficiary's claim at trial regardless of what appeared to be "the only realistic inference" at the time of presentation: *Society of Lloyd's v Canadian Imperial Bank of Commerce* [1993] 2 Lloyd's Rep. 579

[44] Before CPR this approach was approved in *Society of Lloyd's v Canadian Imperial Bank of Commerce* [1993] 2 Lloyd's Rep. 579 at 581 RHC.

[45] *Re H (Minors) (Sexual Abuse: Standard of Proof)* [1996] A.C. 563; *Hornal v Neuberger Products* [1957] 1 Q.B. 247.

[46] [2000] 2 Lloyd's Rep. 600 at 607.

If the bank has been obliged to pay and has paid, then it will be entitled to an indemnity. If on the other hand it did not have to pay because (1) in fact the beneficiary was acting fraudulently, and (2) the bank knew this at the time of presentation, then it will not be entitled to an indemnity. This will be the position if at the time of presentation the beneficiary was in fact acting fraudulently and it is obvious to the bank that the beneficiary in presenting the documents was acting fraudulently. In those circumstances the beneficiary had no legally enforceable right to payment under the letter of credit and the bank knew that this was the case.

What about the position where the bank pays without negligence and it subsequently comes to light that the beneficiary was acting fraudulently? The bank has a right of indemnity if, without negligence, it pays against documents which it did not know were fraudulent:[47]

> "In the ordinary case visual inspection of the actual documents presented is all that is called for. The bank is under no duty to take any further steps to investigate the genuineness of a signature which, on the face of it, purports to be the signature of the person named or described in the letter of credit."[48]

It is not for the bank to make inquiries about an allegation of fraud made   **15.013** by one side.[49] Whether it has an indemnity in other situations, falling short of actual knowledge of the fraud, depends upon the interpretation of the indemnity. Where the bank itself has actual knowledge of the fraud at the time of its payment[50] it would be dishonest to seek an indemnity and an indemnity clause would not be interpreted to permit this.[51] In general the bank is only concerned with the sufficiency of the documents based simply upon a physical examination of those documents. In a well-executed fraud the documents will appear satisfactory even though the beneficiary is acting fraudulently and the bank will be entitled to an indemnity.[52]

Where the instructions given to the bank are themselves ambiguous or capable of covering more than one type of document, then the bank is entitled to act upon a reasonable interpretation of that authority.[53]

---

[47] *Gian Singh & Co. Ltd v Banque de L'Indochine* [1974] 1 W.L.R. 1234.
[48] *Gian Singh Ltd v Banque de L'Indochine* [1874] 1 W.L.R. 1234 at 1239A–B.
[49] *Turkiye v Bank of China* [1996] 2 Lloyd's Rep. 611 at 617, rejecting an argument that the bank could have inferred fraud and therefore should not have paid, subsequently upheld [1998] 1 Lloyd's Rep. 250.
[50] Later knowledge will not affect the bank's right to an indemnity provided that it has complied with its mandate: *United Trading v Allied Arab Bank* [1985] 2 Lloyd's Rep. 554 at 560.
[51] *HIH Casualty and General Insurance Ltd v Chase Manhattan Bank* [2003] 2 Lloyd's Rep. 61 at [68], *per* Lord Hoffmann; *GKN Contractors Ltd v Lloyds Bank* (1985) 30 B.L.R. 48 at 63.
[52] *Gian Singh & Co. Ltd v Banque de L'Indochine* [1974] 1 W.L.R. 1234.
[53] *Midland Bank v Seymour* [1955] 2 Lloyd's Rep. 147; *Commercial Banking Co. v Jalsard* [1973] A.C. 279.

(3) Question (c): An injunction restraining a bank from making payment on the application of a person liable to be damaged if payment were made

15.014   If the bank has made payment, it may still be entitled to an indemnity notwithstanding that the beneficiary has acted fraudulently. Indeed the better the fraud, the more likely it is that the bank will be entitled to be indemnified. Where it is entitled to an indemnity, the payment radically affects the buyer's rights. The buyer will have to chase after the beneficiary for the return of the money, which may be an expensive and entirely fruitless exercise.

(i) A "cause of action"

15.015   An injunction can be sought by a person who is not in a contractual relationship with the bank. For example the applicant who had applied to the opening bank to establish a letter of credit can obtain an injunction against the bank who had confirmed that credit from making payment, when if it paid against fraudulent documents, it would be the applicant who would be likely to have to shoulder the loss. The injunction is granted under s.37 of the Supreme Court Act 1981. The cases proceed on the basis that an injunction can be granted on the application of a claimant who will be prejudiced if the money is paid out by the bank; but there has been uncertainty on what is the underlying "cause of action".[54]

The formulation[55] of the need to have a legal or equitable right against the defendant to which an injunction is ancillary has led to the question being asked—what is the cause of action against the bank? The spotlight has naturally focused on the position between the buyer and its bank, instead of the position as between the buyer and the fraudulent seller. In consequence it has been said that the applicant for an injunction faces a dilemma—either the bank is good for damages if it acts wrongly, or there is no cause of action against the bank in respect of which an injunction can be granted.[56] Indeed on this analysis the very fact that the bank is good for damages is itself sufficient for refusal of the injunction.[57] Thus, it has been suggested that the party who has procured the opening of the letter of credit is owed a duty of care in tort by the bank.[58] This is very

---

[54] *Group Josi Re v Walbrook Insurance* [1996] 1 W.L.R. 1152 at 1159. The appeal was against the decision of Phillips J. reported sub. nom. *Deutsche Rückversicherung A.G. v. Wallbrook Insurance Co. Ltd* [1995] 1 W.L.R. 1017.

[55] See *The Siskina* [1979] A.C. 210 at 256 and the authorities cited by Lord Diplock.

[56] *Harbottle v National Westminster Bank* [1978] Q.B. 146 at 155A–D "an insuperable difficulty", *per* Kerr J.; *Czarnikow-Rionda Sugar Trading v Standard Bank London Ltd* [1999] 2 Lloyd's Rep. 187 at 202–203.

[57] *Consolidated Oil v American Express Bank* [2002] C.L.C. 488.

[58] *United Trading v Allied Arab Bank* [1985] 2 Lloyd's Rep. 554 at 560, doubted in *GKN Contractors Ltd v Lloyds Bank Plc* (1985) 30 B.L.R. 48 at 62, and referred to in *Deutsche Rückversicherung v Walbrook Insurance Co.* [1995] 1 W.L.R. 1017 at 1029E–F and *Ermis Skai Radio & Television v Banque Indosuez SA*, unreported, February 24, 1997, Comm Ct (Thomas J.).

questionable[59] given subsequent developments in the law of negligence, including the overruling of *Anns v Merton London Borough Council*[60] by *Murphy v Brentwood District Council*.[61] But this suggested cause of action would not support an injunction restraining payment, because, even if such a duty existed, the bank is good for the damages. The position is the same in those cases in which there is a contract between the applicant for the injunction and the bank to be restrained, and the suggested cause of action is to restrain a threatened breach of contract.

However, the formulation of the jurisdiction to grant injunctions in *The* 15.016 *Siskina* was too narrowly expressed. It does not explain the jurisdiction to grant Mareva relief against non-parties[62] nor certain of the cases of anti-suit injunctions, a point which Lord Diplock accepted in *British Airways Board v Laker*.[63] In *Williams v Marac Australia Ltd*[64] the plaintiff was granted an injunction against the Registrar General from registering an instrument which, if registered, would result in the plaintiff losing his rights as against others. This injunction was not based on a cause of action against the Registrar General but was granted in the interests of justice to preserve the underlying rights of the applicant as against the non-parties and ensure that full relief could be obtained against them.[65]

In the cases about letters of credit, if payment is made by the bank, this will irreversibly affect the position as between the buyer and the seller. Once payment is made the applicant has a cause of action for the wrong done to him by the beneficiary. This wrong could be regarded as an action in deceit which the seller has in respect of a false representation made to the bank as its agent for effecting payment. Or the wrong could be an injurious falsehood being a false statement made to the bank, which was known to be false, acted upon by the bank causing loss to the applicant. In these circumstances the application for an injunction against the bank restraining payment or an injunction against the beneficiary restraining presentation of documents or receipt of payment, can properly be viewed as an injunction sought *quia timet* in support of the applicant's right not to be defrauded by the beneficiary through documents being presented fraudulently,[66] or his right not to be the victim of an injurious falsehood.

---

[59] *Czarnikow-Rionda Sugar Trading v Standard Bank London Ltd* [1999] 2 Lloyd's Rep. 187 at 200.

[60] [1978] A. C. 728.

[61] [1991] 1 A. C. 398.

[62] See Chapter 13.

[63] [1985] A. C. 58 at 81.

[64] (1985) 5 N.S.W.L.R. 529, referred to in *Australian Broadcasting Corporation v Lenah Game Meats Pty Ltd* (2001) 208 C.L.R. 199 at para.285.

[65] See also *Jonray (Sydney) Pty Ltd v Partridge Bros Pty Ltd* (1969) 89 W.N. (Part 1) (N.S.W.) 568; *IAC (Finance) Pty Ltd v Courtenay* (1963) 110 C.L.R. 550; and *Halaga Developments Pty Ltd v Grime* (1986) 5 N.S.W.L.R. 740.

[66] *Bolivinter Oil SA v Chase Manhattan Bank* [1984] 1 Lloyd's Rep. 251 at 254 (the report in Lloyd's Law Reports is a complete one and that in [1984] 1 W.L.R. 392 is a practice note which does not contain this passage); *Turkan Timber v Barclays Bank* [1987] 1 Lloyd's Rep. 171 at 176–177; *Korea Industry v Andoll Ltd* [1990] 2 Lloyd's Rep. 183.

15.017   It might be objected that the actions of deceit and injurious falsehood are claims at common law for damages. There is "no such thing as an equitable action for deceit".[67] It might further be said that, prior to the Judicature Acts, the common law courts had no jurisdiction under the Common Law Procedure Act 1854 to grant an injunction except where a past wrong had been committed for which an action for damages had been brought.[68]

But such an objection would overlook two matters:

(1) The fact that in cases of actual fraud, including fraudulent misrepresentation,[69] the Courts of Chancery and of Common Law exercised a "concurrent jurisdiction from the earliest times".[70] In Chancery the remedies of delivery-up, inquiries and taking of accounts long pre-dated[71] the establishment of the common law action for deceit in *Pasley v Freeman*.[72] The fraud intended to be committed by a dishonest beneficiary of a letter of credit is unusual. Although the opener of the credit is aware of the threat, the bank's promise to the beneficiary leaves the intended victim powerless unless the court intervenes. It is a threatened actual fraud to be carried out on the bank causing loss to the opener of the credit.

(2) Although before the Judicature Acts the Court of Chancery had no jurisdiction to restrain a libel, after those Acts it became established that the High Court had jurisdiction to restrain a libel[73] or a malicious falsehood.[74]

15.018   It is suggested that the jurisdiction to grant an injunction against the beneficiary or the bank can be traced back to equity's concurrent jurisdiction in cases of actual fraud, and also to the jurisdiction recognised after the Judicature Acts to restrain a malicious falsehood. The court's jurisdiction is to act *quia timet* under s.37(1) of the Supreme Court Act 1981.

(ii) Discretion—the general principle

15.019   Whether the injunction is direct against the bank or is against the beneficiary is merely mechanics and cannot affect the substantive principles which are to be applied.[75] An injunction preventing payment by the bank

---

[67] *Derry v Peek* (1889) 14 App. Cas.337 at 360
[68] Compare the analysis in *White v Mellin* [1895] A.C.154 at 163 about trade libels.
[69] *Snell's Equity* (30th ed., 2000) para.38–02.
[70] *Nocton v Lord Ashburton* [1914] A.C. 932 at 951–952; R. P. Meagher, J. D. Heydon and M. J. Leeming, *Meagher Gummow and Lehane's Equity: Doctrines and Remedies* (4th ed., 2002) paras 12–005–12–030.
[71] See *Muchies Management v Belperio* (1989) 84 A.L.R. 700 at 711 and *Demetrios v Gilcas Dry Cleaning Industries* (1991) 22 N.S.W.L.R. 561 at 573.
[72] (1789) 3 T.R. 51.
[73] See Chapter 1, above.
[74] *Thorley's Cattle Food v Massam* (1877) 6 Ch.D. 582.
[75] *Group Josi Re v Walbrook Insurance Co. Ltd* [1996] 1 W.L.R. 1152 at 1161H–1162B; *Czarnikow-Rionda Sugar Trading v Standard Bank London Ltd* [1999] 2 Lloyd's Rep. 187 at 190.

or restraining presentation of documents by the beneficiary interferes with the letter of credit and prevents it from being treated as the equivalent of cash. The following factors affect the answer to question (c):

(1) It is inherent in the provision of a letter of credit that subject to presentation of conforming documents,[76] it is to be the equivalent of cash. Part of its purpose is to implement an agreement between buyer and seller that the seller gets paid and questions of defects in quality and other such disputes are resolved outside of the payment transaction. The buyer has agreed to this and equity will not intervene so as to enable him to go back on what he has agreed.

(2) The bank itself has made a contractual promise as a banker. It is an essential part of its business that it honours its word. The court should not restrain payment when to do so could be to cause the bank to dishonour its engagement undertaken as a banker, and thereby to damage its reputation for contractual and commercial probity.[77]

(3) Letters of credit are relied upon as a means of raising finance. To allow payment to be restrained would threaten the future use of letters of credit as an available mechanism for raising credit to fulfil commercial transactions. Such instruments are regarded as the "lifeblood" of commerce. Merchants rely upon them as being the equivalent of cash.

For these reasons, as a general principle, the court will not grant an injunction interfering with performance by the bank under the banking contract, except where the letter of credit or other banking contract is itself impeached as being invalid, or if prior to payment,[78] it is obvious to the bank that the beneficiary is acting fraudulently. This principle applies whether the applicant for the injunction sues only the bank seeking *quia timet* relief restraining payment, or sues the beneficiary seeking an injunction restraining him from receiving payment under the banking contract after a claim has been made under that contract[79] or sues both of them.[80]

Whether the general principle applies to an undertaking by a bank to **15.020** pay, depends on the interpretation of the commercial instrument, and whether in substance it amounts to an independent undertaking by the

---

[76] Until presentation, the letter of credit is a contingent right to payment: *Chiu Yu Man v HKSAR* (2001) 4 H.K.C.F.A.R. 331.
[77] *Bolivinter Oil SA v Chase Manhattan Bank NA* [1984] 1 W.L.R. 392 at 393D–E.
[78] *United Trading v Allied Arab Bank* [1985] 2 Lloyd's Rep. 554 at 560.
[79] *Group Josi Re v Walbrook Insurance Co. Ltd* [1996] 1 W.L.R. 1152 at 1161; *Howe Richardson Scale Co. Ltd v Polimpex-Cekop* [1978] 1 Lloyd's Rep. 161 (the bank appeared saying that it wished to make payment); *Dong Jin Metal Co. Ltd v Raymet Ltd*, unreported, July 13, 1993, CA, which was followed in *Deutsche Rückversicherung v Walbrook Insurance Co.* [1995] 1 W.L.R. 1017 at 1031G–H (this is the first instance decision in *Group Josi Re v Walbrook Insurance Co. Ltd*).
[80] *Bolivinter Oil SA v Chase Manhattan Bank* [1984] 1 Lloyd's Rep. 251 at 256–257.

bank to pay the beneficiary which is not conditional or dependent on the actual performance of the underlying transaction or whether the beneficiary has in fact suffered loss.[81] Such undertakings are payable against presentation of documents or simply on demand.

The fact that a document is called a performance guarantee does not mean that the obligations of the bank are simply as a surety—its terms may show that it is to be interpreted as an unconditional undertaking by the bank to pay following a written demand by the beneficiary.[82] A performance bond may require something more than just a demand for payment. It may stipulate that the demand is made in a certain form, or in certain terms.[83] What has to be tendered is a question of the wording in the bond, and this may be interpreted as not requiring a particular verbal formula provided that the substance of what is required is set out in the demand.[84]

The ICC Uniform Rules for Demand Guarantees[85] are often used as a basis for the bank guarantee. Under article 20, paragraph a, there has to be in the written demand or accompanying document an express statement that the "Principal is in breach of his obligation(s) under the underlying contract (s) or, in the case of a tender guarantee, the tender conditions. . . ." and ". . . the respect in which the Principal is in breach." These requirements of article 20 are a safeguard in that the beneficiary has to ask himself what breach there has been and whether he would be acting honestly in asserting that breach. Furthermore, instead of there only being an implied representation of honesty by the beneficiary, the demand itself must show what breach is relied upon, and if there were to be dishonesty in making the demand, it would be that much easier for this to be proved, and for a claim to be advanced before the court to restrain an attempted deceit, or for damages for deceit.

With a letter of credit, the beneficiary has to tender particular documents and the requirements are strictly construed so that "there is no room for documents which are almost the same, or which will do just as well. . .".[86] Requirements such as a demand in a particular form or presentation of documents do not result in the bank's undertaking to pay falling outside of this general principle which applies to the granting of an injunction.

---

[81] *Esal (Commodities) Ltd v Oriental Credit* [1985] 2 Lloyd's Rep. 546; *Siporex v Banque Indosuez* [1986] 2 Lloyd's Rep. 146 at 157–158; *Hortico (Australia) v Energy Equipment Co. (Aus)* (1985) 1 N.S.W.L.R. 545 and *Trafalgar House Ltd v General Surety Co.* [1996] A.C. 199.

[82] *Edward Owen v Barclays Bank* [1978] Q.B. 159; *Frans Maas v Habib Bank* [2001] Lloyd's Rep. (Bank). 14.

[83] In *Esal (Commodities) Ltd v Oriental Credit* [1985] 2 Lloyd's Rep. 546, the demand had to recite that there had been a breach of the commercial contract.

[84] *IE Contractors Ltd v Lloyds* [1990] 2 Lloyd's Rep. 496 (see especially at 501: "The degree of compliance required by a performance bond may be strict, or not so strict . . ."); *Ermis Skai Radio & Television v Banque Indosuez SA*, unreported, February 24, 1997, Comm Ct (Thomas J.), in which it was held that the claim failed because the demand referred to a contract made before the bond was issued instead of to a contract concluded afterwards.

[85] ICC Publication No. 458.

[86] *Equitable Trust Co. of New York v Dawson Partners Ltd* (1927) 27 Lloyd's Rep. 49 at 52, *per* Lord Sumner.

In *Esal (Commodities) Ltd v Oriental Credit* there was a performance **15.021**
bond payable on demand, and the Court of Appeal rejected the argument
that on the construction of the bond it required the beneficiary, when
making a demand, to tender evidence of non-performance. In general a
bank will not become involved in evaluating evidence; its business is
dealing in documents, and this factor is part of the "background" to be
taken into account when interpreting the undertaking given by the bank.
There are two exceptions[87] to the general principle:

(1) where the "validity" of the letter of credit or performance bond is
itself impeached; and

(2) when there is a fraud which is obvious to the bank at the time of
payment.

(iii) Exception (1)—"validity" of the letter of credit or performance bond

This exception only applies where the validity of the letter of credit or **15.022**
performance bond is itself impeached in the sense of it being a presently
enforceable legal obligation. It is not enough that there is a dispute about
the underlying transaction between buyer and seller.[88]

(iv) Exception (2)—the fraud exception

In transactions involving the provision of a letter of credit, performance **15.023**
bond, performance guarantee or other similar unconditional undertaking
by a bank, the only implied term is that the beneficiary will not seek to
obtain payment unless he has an honest belief that he is entitled to do so.[89]

---

[87] *Czarnikow-Rionda Sugar Trading v Standard Bank London Ltd* [1999] 2 Lloyd's Rep. 187;
Hamzeh Malas v British Imex Industries Ltd [1958] 2 Q.B. 127; *Discount Records v Barclays
Bank* [1975] 1 W.L.R. 315; *Howe Richardson Scale Co. Ltd v Polimex-Cekop* [1978] 1
Lloyd's Rep. 161; *Harbottle v National Westminster Bank* [1978] Q.B. 159; *Edward Owen
v Barclays Bank* [1978] Q.B. 159; *Intraco v Notis Shipping* [1981] 2 Lloyd's Rep. 256;
UCM v Royal Bank of Canada [1983] 1 A.C. 168 at 182–188; *Bolivinter Oil SA v Chase
Manhattan Bank* [1984] 1 W.L.R. 392; *United Trading v Allied Arab Bank* [1985] 2 Lloyd's
Rep. 554; *Siporex v Banque Indosuez* [1986] 2 Lloyd's Rep. 146; and *Society of Lloyd's v
Canadian Imperial Bank* [1993] 2 Lloyd's Rep. 579. See also *Elian v Matsas* [1966] 2
Lloyd's Rep. 495, in which the Court of Appeal granted an injunction in the absence of an
allegation of fraud. The decision can be regarded as one in which there was a dispute as to
the continuing validity of the bank guarantee given the subsequent conduct of the
beneficiary.
[88] *Bolivinter Oil SA v Chase Manhattan Bank* [1984] 1 W.L.R. 392 at 393E.
[89] *Deutsche Rückversicherung A.G. v Wallbrook Insurance Co Limited* [1995] 1 W.L.R. 1017
at 1030 H–1031 H. *United Trading v Allied Arab Bank* [1985] 2 Lloyd's Rep. 554 following
State Trading Corporation of India v E. D. & F. Man (Sugar) [1981] Com. L. Rep. 235;
Dodsal PVT Ltd v Kingpull Ltd, Court of Appeal (Civ Div) Transcript No.345 of 1985 (July
1, 1985); *Ermis Skai Radio & Television v Banque Indosuez SA*, unreported, February 24,
1997, Comm Ct (Thomas J.), rejecting as an implied term that the beneficiary would not
make a demand under the bond ". . . for sums which he did not honestly believe were due
under [the commercial contract]".

For the fraud exception to apply and an injunction to be granted, the claimant must show clear evidence[90] of fraud by the beneficiary, and show that it is obvious that a fraud is being carried out by the beneficiary to the knowledge of the bank.[91] The uncorroborated evidence of the claimant is not sufficient. The test is whether the claimant has established, with the assistance of strong corroborative evidence, that the only realistic inference is that there has been fraud by the beneficiary. This does not require the claimant to show that there is no possibility whatsoever of the beneficiary's having acted honestly.[92]

15.024 The knowledge of the bank is repeatedly stated as a necessary requirement in the case law.[93] This is because of the need to justify interference with performance by the bank of its banking obligation undertaken to the beneficiary[94] and the interference with the smooth working of the system of commercial credits. It is a requirement which can also be associated with difficulties in analysing the cause of action. If what is being sought is based on a threatened breach of duty by the bank, then it is natural to include this as a necessary ingredient.

A question which has been raised is whether the court is limited to considering the extent of the knowledge of the bank at the date of the issue of the claim form.[95] First, the true nature of the injunction is an injunction sought *quia timet* to restrain a future fraud, which includes, as a necessary ingredient, the obtaining of *payment* by deceit or malicious falsehood. The proof of the threat to commit a fraud is only a matter of evidence—it is not a matter of the vesting in the applicant of an existing cause of action. Secondly, the fraud exception is available as a defence to the bank as against the beneficiary at any time up until when it actually pays,[96] regardless of when payment should have been made under the letter of credit (see question (a) above). So likewise whether the customer is entitled to object to payment being made by the bank is not dependent upon what was the state of the evidence at the date on which under the letter of credit payment ought to have been made. If the bank does not pay and subsequently acquires actual knowledge of the fraud then the bank is not liable under the letter of credit and its customer is entitled to object to

---

[90] *United Trading v Allied Arab Bank* [1985] 2 Lloyd's Rep. 554 at 561 LHC ("The evidence of fraud must be clear, both as to the fact of fraud and as to the bank's knowledge"); *Kvaerner John Brown Ltd v Midland Bank Plc* [1998] C.L.C. 446; *Korea Industry v Andoll Ltd* [1990] 2 Lloyd's Rep. 183 at 188; *Inflatable Toy Co. Pty Ltd v State Bank of NSW* (1994) 34 N.S.W.L.R. 243, Supreme Court of New South Wales.

[91] *Bolivinter Oil SA v Chase Manhattan Bank* [1984] 1 W.L.R. 392.

[92] *United Trading v Allied Arab Bank* [1985] 2 Lloyd's Rep. 554 at 561.

[93] *Bolivinter Oil SA v Chase Manhattan Bank* [1984] 1 Lloyd's Rep. 251 at 255 and 257; *United Trading v Allied Arab Bank* [1985] 2 Lloyd's Rep. 554 at 561 LHC; *Edward Owen Engineering Co. Ltd v Barclays Bank International Ltd* [1978] Q.B. 159 at 169G, 171B, 172H and 175E.

[94] See also *Czarnikow-Rionda Sugar Trading v Standard Bank London Ltd* [1999] 2 Lloyd's Rep. 187 at 203 RHC where this and the availability of Mareva relief against the proceeds were regarded as sufficient to justify a refusal of relief.

[95] *United Trading v Allied Arab Bank* [1985] 2 Lloyd's Rep. 554 at 560.

[96] *Bolivinter Oil SA v Chase Manhattan Bank* [1984] 1 Lloyd's Rep. 251 at 256.

payment being made. In deciding whether to grant an injunction restraining payment by the bank, the court should take into account all the available evidence, regardless of when the bank first had knowledge of it.[97] In any event, the difficulty can be surmounted by the claimant issuing a new claim form on conclusion of the *inter partes* hearing, by which time the bank will have had notice of all the evidence before the court.

If the applicant for the injunction alleges that the letter of credit is **15.025** unenforceable for illegality, this could also have the effect that the documents presented on the attempted drawdown made a false representation to the bank. If so the "fraud exception" could be engaged.

(v) Express or implied promise not to draw down

The general principle does not apply where the beneficiary has entered into **15.026** an express agreement with the applicant not to draw down on the letter of credit or performance bond. In those circumstances the court is free to enforce the negative promise given by the beneficiary by injunction.[98] The fact that the bank if called upon by the beneficiary would be legally obliged to pay under the letter of credit is why an injunction should be granted to the applicant to restrain the beneficiary for demanding or receiving payment.

This situation is different from that in which a letter of credit has been provided under a contract of sale as the means of payment. There the function of the letter of credit as between the buyer and seller is to provide cash to the buyer free of set-off for any counterclaim or dispute as to performance of the contract of sale. There is no room for an implied term that the seller will not use the letter of credit, except an implied term that the seller will not act dishonestly in presenting the documents and claiming on the credit. With a performance bond where the purpose is to enable the beneficiary to have the cash pending resolution of the underlying claim, the only term to be implied in a contract of sale would be that the seller must have an honest belief that he is entitled to claim on the bond.[99] This implied term enables the buyer to apply *quia* timet to restrain a threatened breach of contract but the principles which apply to that application are those set out above for the "fraud" exception.

Whether or not the underlying contract pursuant to which the performance bond was established contains restraints on the beneficiary cashing the bond, and if so what they are, is a matter of interpretation. Part of the exercise in interpretation involves taking into account the terms of the

[97] *Inflatable Toy Co. Pty Ltd v State Bank of NSW* (1994) 34 N.S.W.L.R. 243.
[98] *Sirius Insurance Co. v FAI Insurance Ltd* [2003] 1 W.L.R. 2214 at [29–30]. *Bachmann Pty Ltd v BHP Power New Zealand Ltd* [1999] 1 V.R. 420 at para. 28 citing earlier authorities; *Baulderstone Hornibrook Pty Ltd v Qantas Airways Ltd* [2000] F.C.A. 672 at para. 10.
[99] *United Trading v Allied Arab Bank* [1985] 2 Lloyd's Rep.554 at 559. *Bachmann Pty Ltd v BHP Power New Zealand Ltd* [1999] 1 V.R. 420; *Fletcher Construction Australia Limited v Varnsdorf Pty Limited* [1998] 3 V.L.R. 812.

bond required to be established. If it is an unconditional undertaking by the bank to pay on demand, even if there is a requirement, which in practice is common, that the demand or accompanying document state that there has been a breach of contract and what it is, this is itself indicative that the parties intended to provide the beneficiary with a mechanism under which he could obtain the cash provided that there was a bona fide claim.[1] Why have the parties have contracted for this mechanism? It is a question of identifying the agreed allocation of risk between the contracting parties about what was to happen in the event of a dispute.[2] No question of "unconscionability" arises because it is a matter of identifying what the parties have agreed, and the court giving effect to that agreement.[3]

(vi) Misrepresentation inducing the underlying transaction or failure of consideration

15.027   It has been suggested that the position between buyer and seller could still be that independently of fraud the seller is not entitled to call on a performance bond,[4] *e.g.* if the contract of sale was avoided for misrepresentation or there was a complete failure of consideration. Where a performance bond is furnished under the contract then if, as is laid down in the case law, the common intention to be imputed to the parties is that it is to be equivalent to cash subject only to the fraud exception, then it is this agreement which should bind buyer and seller. This should be so even if there has been a purported avoidance of the contract for misrepresentation.[5] A distinction is to be drawn between the right of the other party to prevent demand being made by the beneficiary on the bond or payment by the bank, and his right as against the beneficiary to any proceeds of that demand. If an injunction is to be granted restraining demand or payment under the bond, it is because of the right of the applicant to object to payment being made by the bank under the bond and receipt of it by the beneficiary, and not simply because if the payment is made the applicant would be entitled as against the beneficiary to the proceeds.

(vii) Unconscionability and drawing down performance bonds

15.028   It has been suggested that because, unlike a credit furnished under a sale transaction, a performance bond does not involve the bank obtaining any assets in return for payment, the courts should be prepared to grant

[1] *Bachmann Pty Ltd v BHP Power New Zealand Ltd* [1999] 1 V.R. 420.
[2] *Fletcher Construction Australia Limited v Varnsdorf Pty Limited* [1998] 3 V.L.R. 812.
[3] *Olex Focas Pty Limited v Skodaexport Co Limited* [1998] 3 V.L.R. 380 at 400.
[4] *Potton Homes Ltd v Coleman Contractors (Overseas) Ltd* (1984) 28 B.L.R. 19, *per* Eveleigh L.J., a dictum not followed in *Guangdong Transport Ltd v Ancora Transport* [1987] H.K.L.R. 923.
[5] Compare *Mackender v Feldia AG* [1967] 2 Q.B. 590 on the effect of an arbitration clause. The performance bond is intended to be available even in the case of a dispute.

injunctions more readily to restrain payment based on a beneficiary having made an "unfair" call on a bond.[6] The courts in Singapore have recognised that a beneficiary can be restrained from drawing down a performance bond in circumstances amounting to unconscionability[7] but falling short of fraud. This is a vague concept. It is also not based on any express or implied term in the underlying contract. Although unconscionability is used by equity as a benchmark in other contexts, *e.g.* for anti-suit injunctions or for an estoppel, there is no general cause of action in equity based on the defendant's unconscionable conduct.[8] The English courts adopt the test of no honest belief in the entitlement to draw down because this test is what would be expected by reasonable commercial men acting honestly. It is also a clear test which is workable simple to apply and enables performance bonds to perform their commercial function. It applies the same test as that which applies as between the bank and the beneficiary at trial of a claim for non-payment (see question (a) above). If there is a contractual[9] or other legally enforceable obligation on the beneficiary owed to the contractor which requires the beneficiary not to draw down on the performance bond, then this can be enforced by the court granting an injunction restraining demand. It also leaves untouched the remedies which may be available once payment has been made by the bank.

(viii) Claim by a third party against the beneficiary

If someone else has a claim against a beneficiary and would like to obtain **15.029** Mareva relief against him, he can seek an injunction in respect of the proceeds of the credit. Payment to the beneficiary by the bank under the letter of credit would not amount to the type of dissipation of assets or removal of assets from the jurisdiction which Mareva relief is intended to prevent, and the court would refuse to interfere with a genuine business transaction.[10]

---

[6] See "Performance Bonds and Letters of Credit: A Cracked Mirror Image"; [1997] J.B.L. 289 at 302–303 (Professor Charles Debattista).

[7] *Dauphin Offshore Engineering & Trading Pte Ltd v The Private Office of HRH Sheik Sultan bin Khalifa bin Sayed Al Nahyan* [2000] 1 S.L.R. 657 at paras 34–41 which cites the earlier authorities in Singapore; *GHL Pte Ltd v Unitrack Building Construction Pte* [1999] 4 S.L.R. 604 at paras 14–25; *Bocotra Construction Pte Ltd v A–G (No.2)* [1995] 2 S.L.R. 733. *Samwoh Asphalt Premix Pte Ltd v Sum Cheong Piling Pte Ltd* [2002] B.L.R. 459 (granting an injunction on appeal restraining drawdown on the ground that the beneficiary was using the demand guarantee as a bargaining tool, for the collateral purpose of seeking to compel the sub-contractor to enter into a new, direct contract, and the demand was "utterly lacking in bona fides"); *McConnell Limited v Sembcorp Ltd* [2002] B.L.R. 450 (distinguishing unconscionability as involving "unfairness" as an element ". . . as distinct from dishonesty or fraud. . ."); "Unconscionability and Bank Guarantees" [2004] L.M.C.L.Q. 148 (Alexia Ganotaki).

[8] *Australian Broadcasting Corporation v Lenah Game Meats Pty Ltd* (2001) 208 C.L.R. 199.

[9] *Sirius Insurance Co. v FAI General Insurance Limited* [2003] 1 W.L.R. 2214 at paras 26–32.

[10] See also *Lewis & Peat (Produce) Ltd v Almatu Properties Ltd* [1993] 2 Bank L.R. 45 at 48, *per* Parker L.J.

(ix) Balance of convenience

15.0030 In cases in which the court has looked for a cause of action against the bank based on a threatened breach of its contract with the customer or negligence, the balance of convenience has been analysed as being either that there is no cause of action against the bank, or the bank is good for the damages.[11] But these cases mistake the nature of the application, which is based on restraining a threatened fraud by the beneficiary which, if committed could result in the bank paying, being entitled to recover on its indemnity, and the applicant being left to bear the loss.

However, the test for obtaining an injunction involves clear proof both of fraud and of the knowledge of the bank of the fraud at the time of determination of the application (see question (c) above), and where this is shown before payment is made, the bank will not be entitled to an indemnity (see question (b) above). In practice so high is this test that it is very difficult to obtain an injunction restraining payment under the letter of credit.

When deciding whether to grant an injunction, whether against the beneficiary restraining him from receiving payment or against a bank restraining it from making payment, after a demand has been made on the bank, it is relevant also to take into account what would be the possible consequences of the injunction for the bank. With a letter of credit or performance guarantee which is issued by a branch which is abroad one relevant consideration is what attitude may be taken by the local court having jurisdiction over that branch. In *United Trading Corporation v Allied Arab Bank*, the performance bonds had been issued by the state bank of Iraq acting on a counter-indemnity from another bank. There was a very real risk that an injunction granted against the Iraqi bank would not be recognised by the courts of Iraq. It would not have been fair to expose the bank to the risk of inconsistent results in the English and Iraqi courts.[12] What this shows is that where the letter of credit or performance bond has been issued by a bank or a branch abroad, the likely attitude of the local court to an injunction is very relevant.

15.031 It is also important to consider whether the applicant would be good for damages on the cross-undertaking in damages.[13]

Another factor which is relevant is whether the position can adequately be dealt with by Mareva relief over the proceeds.[14] Where it can be, no injunction should be granted restraining payment.[15]

---

[11] *Czarnikow-Rionda Sugar Trading v Standard Bank London Ltd* [1999] 2 Lloyd's Rep. 187; *Harbottle v National Westminster Bank* [1978] Q.B. 146 at 155.
[12] *United Trading v Allied Arab Bank* [1985] 2 Lloyd's Rep.554 at 566.
[13] *ibid.*
[14] *Czarnikow-Rionda Sugar Trading v Standard Bank London Ltd* [1999] 2 Lloyd's Rep. 187 at 203.
[15] Contrast *Themehelp Ltd v West* [1996] Q.B. 84.

(4) Mareva relief over the proceeds

A Mareva injunction must not prevent payment by the bank under the 15.032 letter of credit or performance guarantee in accordance with its terms[16]—it is directed to the proceeds of the payment. The jurisdiction to grant Mareva relief is not limited to assets within the jurisdiction and so an injunction can be granted in relation to proceeds which are payable abroad.

If payment is made under a performance bond or guarantee, ordinarily, as a matter of interpretation of the underlying contract providing for provision of the bond or guarantee, the beneficiary will be obliged to account under the commercial contract to the opener for any surplus received over and above that which he is entitled to keep for breach of the commercial contract. This is because the term requiring the bond or guarantee is usually to be interpreted as providing for security[17] for due performance of the contractual obligations under the commercial contract. It is therefore implicit that there will be a mutual accounting, with the beneficiary repaying any excess over any loss caused by failure to perform or breach of contract.[18] The right to a mutual accounting gives rise to a creditor/debtor relationship and not to any proprietary right in the proceeds. The cause of action for the refund will only arise once the beneficiary has been overpaid and this could give rise to a difficulty about the non-availability of Mareva relief prior to the acquisition of an existing cause of action against the beneficiary.[19] In *Siporex Trade SA v Comdel Commodities*[20] the beneficiary had already obtained judgment on the performance bonds[21] and it was expected that the bank would appeal. However, the beneficiary had not received any cash and no request had been made by the defaulting buyer that the beneficiary agreed to return any surplus. In these circumstances Bingham J. held that there was no existing cause of action and set aside the Mareva relief. One would have thought that where the bank is indebted to the beneficiary, then the position would be that the beneficiary has a valuable chose in action, namely the debt owed to it by the bank, and this is sufficient to vest in the other party a

---

[16] *Intraco Ltd v Notis Shipping Corporation (The Bhoja Trader)* [1981] 2 Lloyd's Rep. 256; *Sundance Spas NZ Limited v Sundance Spas Inc.* [2001] 1 N.Z.L.R. 111 (where there was also a refusal to grant Mareva relief over the proceeds of the letter of credit because the plaintiff had no cause of action against the foreign defendant for which the plaintiff could serve proceedings out of the jurisdiction and so in New Zealand the plaintiff could not overcome the lack of jurisdiction to entertain a substantive claim on the merits, following *The Siskina* [1979] A.C. 210). Contrast *Themehelp Ltd v West* [1996] Q.B. 84, which is discussed below.

[17] *Harbottle v National Westminster Bank* [1978] Q.B. 146 at 149B.

[18] *Cargill International SA v Bangladesh Sugar & Food Industries Corporation* [1996] 2 Lloyd's Rep. 524, upheld by the Court of Appeal in [1998] 1 W.L.R. 461; *Comdel Commodities Ltd v Siporex Trade SA* [1997] 1 Lloyd's Rep. 424 at 431.

[19] *Siporex Trade SA v Comdel Commodities* [1986] 2 Lloyd's Rep. 428; *Re Q's Estate* [1999] 1 Lloyd's Rep. 931; and see Chapter 12, above.

[20] [1986] 2 Lloyd's Rep. 428 at 436–437.

[21] *Siporex Trade SA v Banque Indosuez* [1986] 2 Lloyd's Rep. 146.

right to an account and payment of the difference. The applicant for Mareva relief would have to show a good arguable case that this was so. The decision in *Siporex Trade SA v Comdel Commodities* pre-dated the decision in *Cargill International SA v Bangladesh Sugar & Food Industries Corporation*[22] which finally established the right to an account, and the route based on an implied term was not referred to in the judgment.[23]

15.033   A Mareva injunction may be granted to restrain the defendant to restrain dealings with the proceeds after payment has been made[24] or from assigning his right to receive the proceeds of the letter of credit, performance bond, or bank guarantee. There are also cases in which such an injunction has been refused on the grounds that on the facts there was no more than "the usual likelihood of a defendant who is being sued so organising his assets that any judgment . . . [would] be frustrated".[25]

It is also open to the court to appoint a receiver to receive the proceeds.[26] The order would only affect the proceeds and would operate in the same way as a Mareva injunction except that possession of the proceeds would be in the receiver instead of the beneficiary. Since the receiver would only be appointed to receive the proceeds this would not interfere with the bank making payment.

15.034   Even if Mareva relief is granted over the proceeds, there is the risk that it may not be of any assistance to the claimant. It is common practice for a trading organisation to raise finance by assigning its right to receive payment under a letter of credit or bank guarantee to a bank, in return for a loan; such transactions usually take place a long time before the claimant is in a position to challenge the validity of the documents tendered for payment under the letter of credit, or before the claimant discovers that the goods are not what he contracted to buy. The bona fide assignee will have a better right to the assets than the defendant, and he will be entitled to the discharge of the Mareva injunction by producing evidence of the assignment: *Pharaoh's Plywood Co. Ltd v Allied Wood Products.*[27] This is so whether or not notice of the assignment has been given to the bank liable on the letter of credit, performance bond or guarantee. Where there has been a contract for value by the defendant to assign the proceeds to the assignee, then once the proceeds come into existence, the assignor holds them on trust for the assignee. This does not depend on the continued enforceability of the contract by specific performance[28] or even the

---

[22] [1996] 2 Lloyd's Rep. 524, upheld by the Court of Appeal in [1998] 1 W.L.R. 461.
[23] See [1986] 2 Lloyd's Rep. 428 at 436, which refers to acceptance of repudiation or a claim for money had and received.
[24] See *Intraco Ltd v Notis Shipping Corporation (The Bhoja Trader)* [1981] 2 Lloyd's Rep. 256; *Power Curber International Ltd v National Bank of Kuwait SAK* [1981] 1 W.L.R. 1233 at 1241–1242; *Themehelp Ltd v West* [1996] Q.B. 84.
[25] *Hortico (Australia) v Energy Equipment Co.* [1985] 1 N.S.W.L.R. 545; *Dodsal PVT Ltd v Kingpull Ltd,* Court of Appeal (Civ Div) Transcript No.345 of 1985 (July 1, 1985); *Britten Norman Ltd v State Ownership Fund of Romania* [2000] 1 Lloyd's Rep. Bank. 315.
[26] See Chapter 16, below.
[27] Court of Appeal (Civ Div) Transcript No.217 of 1980 (January 18, 1980).
[28] The theory adopted by Sir George Jessel M.R. in *Collyer v Isaacs* (1881) 19 Ch.D. 342 at 351–353.

continued existence of the contract.[29] It depends on the principle that once the proceeds come into existence equity treats the assignor as a trustee of the asset, and will enforce that trust which is thus the subject of an equitable charge in favour of the assignee.[30] The principle applies regardless of whether there is a prohibition of assignment in the letter of credit, performance bond, or other banking contract.[31]

(5) Effect of injunction over the proceeds on whether payment has effectively been made on the underlying transaction

If an injunction is obtained by a buyer in respect of the proceeds of a **15.035** payment made to the seller under a sale contract[32] or through a letter of credit[33] furnished by the claimant as the means of payment, the question may arise whether the claimant, has made a payment which is effective as a payment under a term of the contract. This will depend on interpretation of the terms of the sale contract. Such an injunction does not restrain payment and receipt, but restricts the defendant in the use of the money when received. So the injunction does not in itself prevent the payment being an unconditional payment.[34]

(6) Injunction before presentation of documents or demand being made

In *Themehelp Ltd v West*,[35] there was a bank guarantee which would be **15.036** payable following the giving of a notice by the beneficiary, who was the seller of shares. It was alleged that the underlying contract under which the shares would be sold had been obtained through fraudulent misrepresentation by the beneficiary. An injunction was sought by the opener against the beneficiary from making a claim under the performance guarantee. Such an injunction would not interfere with the bank performing its contract because if an injunction was granted nothing would become due under that contract. However, such an injunction would mean that the performance guarantee could not be turned into cash.

---

[29] *Palette Shoes Pty Ltd v Krohn* (1937) 58 C.L.R. 1 at 27, *per* Dixon J.
[30] *Re Lind: Industrial Finance Syndicate Ltd v Lind* [1915] 2 Ch. 345.
[31] *Re Turcan* (1888) 40 Ch.D. 5; *Linden Garden Trust v Lenesta Sludge Disposals* [1994] 1 A.C. 85 at 106E–H; *Don King Productions Inc. v Warren* [2000] Ch. 291 at 321 and 335, para.26; see Chapter 16, above.
[32] *The P* [1992] 1 Lloyd's Rep. 470.
[33] *Intraco v Notis Shipping Corporation of Liberia (The Bhoja Trader)* [1981] 2 Lloyd's Rep. 256.
[34] *Ateni Maritime Corporation v Great Marine Ltd (The Great Marine No.1)* [1990] 2 Lloyd's Rep. 245.
[35] [1996] Q.B. 84.

Under the commercial contract the beneficiary had stipulated for and been provided with an instrument which he was entitled to regard as being separate from the commercial contract and capable of being turned into cash on his demand, even if there was some dispute with the opener relating to the commercial contract or its performance. Although there was a claim to avoid the underlying contract for fraud that contract remained binding on the parties and there was every prospect that it would remain binding on them.[36]

The majority of the Court of Appeal considered that an injunction was rightly granted. They distinguished the cases on banking contracts on the ground that they all related to a point of time at which the banking contract had been triggered for payment. An injunction at this earlier time would not interfere with performance by the bank of its contract: the bank would not be called upon to pay.

15.037   Evans L.J. was of the opinion that the injunction should be discharged, but would have granted Mareva relief over the proceeds. He pointed out that such relief could have extended to requiring the proceeds to be paid into court.[37]

The court had jurisdiction to grant an injunction against the seller ancillary to the cause of action of the buyer against the seller for fraudulent misrepresentation. But the injunction had to be genuinely ancillary to that cause of action in the sense of forwarding the claim based on that cause of action by promoting the effectiveness of a remedy to be granted in respect of that cause of action. This would include an injunction granted to preserve the situation so that a future judgment would not go unsatisfied.

15.038   The reasons for not granting an injunction restraining the giving of a notice calling upon the merchant bank to pay under its guarantee were:

(1) Given that the underlying transaction would remain binding, then under that transaction the applicant had agreed to the provision of the bank guarantees. Equity would hold both parties to their bargain and would not interfere with performance of the binding contractual bargain agreed upon between the parties.

(2) Given the uncovering of the fraud in inducing the contract, and the affirmation of the sales contract by the buyers, there would be no defence available to the bank justifying non-payment of the guarantee, once notice was given. In the case where a buyer affirms a contract induced by fraudulent misrepresentation the buyer is liable for the price and can be sued for it. Public policy is not engaged and the defence of *ex turpi causa* is not available. Likewise the bank who is the agent for paying the price has no public policy defence. This is a material distinction from the fraud exception cases in which the

---

[36] [1996] Q.B. 84 at 102C–D and 106D–E.
[37] *United Norwest Co-operatives Ltd v Johnstone*, Court of Appeal (Civil Division) Transcript No.1482 of 1994 (December 6, 1994).

relevant fraud would provide a defence to the bank in answer to a claim based on non-payment. In those cases the purpose of the injunction is to prevent a fraud being carried out on the bank and the seller.

(3) Damages for the fraudulent misrepresentation which had induced the contract was the only remedy available to the applicant for the cause of action and this was an adequate and effective remedy given the availability of Mareva relief in respect of the proceeds of the guarantee.

For these reasons no injunction restraining the giving of notice to the bank should have been granted, and it is considered that the reasoning of the majority, which has been questioned in subsequent cases,[38] was wrong.

What is the position where the purpose of an injunction is to operate *quia timet* to prevent the applicant becoming the victim of a fraud carried out on the bank as his agent for payment? Does it make a material difference if the injunction is sought before presentation of documents under the letter of credit or demand is made under a performance bond? If such an injunction were to be granted, then it would not interfere with performance by the bank of its undertaking to the beneficiary; but such an injunction would go against (1) the commercial purpose of the provision of the bank's undertaking by the applicant to the beneficiary and thus would be inconsistent with the underlying bargain under which the seller has assumed the risks associated with the unconditional wording of the guarantee, and (2) the utility of that undertaking as the "lifeblood" of commerce.

These two considerations are powerful reasons in themselves in support **15.039** of the application of the general principle.[39] The majority in *Themehelp Ltd v West* overlooked the fact that at the earlier stage these considerations are still effective.[40] It is considered that at this time the general principle should still apply, subject to the "validity" and "fraud" exceptions. Furthermore the facts in *Themehelp Ltd v West* did not give rise to the present problem because of the uncovering of the fraud, the buyer's election to affirm the contract and the unavailability of the public policy defence in that case.

---

[38] *Sirius Insurance Co. v FAI Insurance Ltd* [2003] 1 W.L.R. 2214 at [31] and [2003] 1 W.L.R. 87 at [16]; *Group Josi Re v Walbrook Insurance Co. Ltd* [1996] 1 W.L.R. 1152 at 1162B (the Court of Appeal decision affirming *Deutsche Rückversicherung A.G. v. Wallbrook Insurance Co. Ltd* [1995] 1 W.L.R. 1017).
[39] See *Harbottle v National Westminster Bank* [1978] Q.B. 146 at 155–156 approved in *Edward Owen v Barclays Bank* [1978] Q.B. 159 at 171.
[40] See [1996] Q.B. 84 at 99A–B, *per* Waite L.J., "it does not seem to me that the slightest threat is involved to the autonomy of the performance guarantee . . ." and at 106F–H, *per* Balcombe L.J., "the same considerations of policy do not apply where the beneficiary has not yet made a demand . . . I see no reason why the ordinary principles for the grant of interlocutory relief should not apply".

(7) Interim specific performance to obtain a complying document signed by the buyer

15.040   The court can grant a mandatory injunction under s.37(1) of the Supreme Court Act 1981 so as to pave the way to a decree of specific performance of a sale contract at the suit of the seller. This relief may be granted in respect of producing a conforming document which can be tendered under a letter of credit where the credit requires a document signed by the buyer.[41] Where the letter of credit is governed by English law and requires a document signed on behalf of the buyer, then if the buyer refuses to sign in breach of a court order the court can direct that the document be signed by a master of the Supreme Court on his behalf[42] and such a document takes effect under English law as if signed on behalf of the buyer. The document signed by the master is good tender under a letter of credit governed by English law[43] provided that the requirement in the letter of credit is not to be interpreted as requiring the actual autograph of a particular person.

---

[41] *Astro Exito Navegacion SA v Chase Manhattan Bank NA (The Messiniaki Tolmi)* [1983] 2 A.C. 787 and see Chapter 7, above.

[42] Under s.39 of the Supreme Court Act 1981.

[43] The notice of readiness so signed was held to be a document conforming to the letter of credit in *Astro Exito Navegacion SA v Chase Manhattan Bank NA (The Messiniaki Tolmi)* [1986] 1 Lloyd's Rep. 455 at 459–460.

Chapter 16

Appointment of a receiver

(1) General principles

(i) Description of the jurisdiction

A receiver is an individual[1] appointed by a court order, which may be made **16.001** prior to commencement of proceedings, or at any time after the commencement of proceedings including after judgment,[2] to receive, and if authorised by the court also to manage, specified assets and to deal with them as authorised under that order. The receiver is an officer of the court, is not an agent of either of the parties,[3] has an equitable "lien" on the assets covered by the order, regardless of whether they are in his possession,[4] for the costs and expenses of the receivership and his own remuneration, which continues even after discharge of the receivership order,[5] and looks to those assets for payment. The court may at any time terminate the appointment or substitute another receiver.[6] The receiver is the "servant or officer of the court" and if any question arises about what is to happen to the assets it is the court which will decide the matter and gives directions accordingly.[7] If appointed by the order to manage a business the receiver has all the powers necessary to carry on that business but depending upon the wording of the order it may well not carry with it a power to sell the business itself.[8]

The appointment of a receiver by the court, whether or not accompanied with powers to manage the property, is necessarily an interlocutory order in the sense that it is a means to an end and not an end in itself.[9] Although it is not listed in CPR r.25.1(1), it is an interim measure, and the fact that it

---

[1] CPR r.69.2(2).
[2] CPR r.69.2(1).
[3] *Gardner v London Chatham and Dover Railway Co.* (1867) L.R. 2 Ch. App.201 at 211–212; *Evans v Clayhope Ltd* [1988] 1 W.L.R. 358 at 362.
[4] *Mellor v Mellor* [1992] 1 W.L.R. 517 at 527G–H.
[5] *Mellor v Mellor* [1992] 1 W.L.R. 517.
[6] CPR r.69.2(3).
[7] *Gardner v London Chatham and Dover Railway Co.* (1867) L.R. 2 Ch. App. 201 at 211–212; *Re P (Restraint Order: Sale of Assets)* [2000] 1 W.L.R. 473 at 482.
[8] *Re P (Restraint Order: Sale of Assets)* [2000] 1 W.L.R. 473 at 483 (pre-trial appointment of receiver and manager of defendant's assets did not have power to sell them).
[9] *Re Newdigate Colliery Ltd* [1912] 1 Ch. 468 at 472.

has not been listed in that sub-paragraph does not affect the power the court has to grant it.[10]

The parties to the proceedings in which the order is made are bound to co-operate in enabling him to obtain possession of the assets. The practice for appointment and terminating the appointment of a receiver is regulated by CPR Pt 69 and the CPR Pt 69 Practice Direction—Court's Power to Appoint a Receiver. The receiver is entitled to remuneration but only in an amount as authorised by the court, and the receiver has to lodge accounts and is responsible for the proper conduct of the receivership.

16.002 Where a receiver is appointed over an asset he has a responsibility to all the interested parties to preserve that asset. The content of the duties owed depend on the circumstances and may include duties to act with due diligence as well as a duty to act in good faith.[11] If appointed over a business it is part of his responsibilities owed to all the interested parties to preserve that business and not to destroy the goodwill, and for this reason the court will not authorise him to repudiate pre-existing contracts entered into as part of the running of that business.[12] The receiver cannot be sued by a party in respect of his conduct as a receiver unless the permission of the court has first been obtained, which should be sought in the proceedings in which the appointment was made.[13]

(ii) The jurisdiction to appoint a receiver and the effect of an order on parties and non-parties

16.003 The jurisdiction of the High Court to appoint a receiver is contained in s.37(1) of the Supreme Court Act 1981, which provides that:

"(1) The High Court may by order (whether interlocutory or final) grant an injunction or appoint a receiver in all cases in which it appears to the court to be just and convenient to do so."

The section also provides the court with jurisdiction to grant relief by way of injunction, including Mareva relief. Section 37(1) is the successor to s.45 of the Supreme Court of Judicature (Consolidation) Act 1925, which in turn replaced s.25(8) of the Judicature Act 1873.

Despite the apparent breadth of the statutory jurisdiction its scope used to be governed by the principles which were applied by the Court of Chancery before the coming into force of the Judicature Act of 1873,[14]

---

[10] CPR r.25.1(3).

[11] *Medforth v Blake* [2000] Ch. 86 at 102E–H.

[12] *Ibid. Re Newdigate Colliery* [1912] Ch. 468.

[13] *Re Maidstone Palace of Varieties Ltd* [1909] 2 Ch. 283 at 286; *McGowan v Chadwick* [2002] EWCA Civ 1758.

[14] *North London Railway & Co. v Great Northern Railway Co.* (1883) 11 Q.B.D. 30; *Holmes v Millage* [1893] 1 Q.B. 551 at 557; *Anglo-Italian Bank v Davies* (1878) 9 Ch.D. 275; *Manchester & Liverpool District Banking Co. v Parkinson* (1888) 22 Q.B.D. 173; *Harris v Beauchamp* [1894] 1 Q.B. 801.

although it was said that "to some extent" the statutory jurisdiction had enlarged the powers of the court.[15] Section 37 of the Supreme Court Act 1981, like its statutory predecessors, has been treated as circumscribed by judicial authority going back for many years.[16] However, the Mareva jurisdiction is now confirmed by s.37(3) of the 1981 Act.

With the emergence of the Mareva jurisdiction, the power of the court **16.004** to appoint a receiver *pre-judgment* by interlocutory order is exercisable whenever it is "right or just" to do so.[17] In particular that power is exercisable even when the claimant does not claim any proprietary interest in the relevant assets or any legal or equitable entitlement to have them dealt with in a particular way.[18] Thus it is sufficient that the claimant has a claim against the defendant, even though that claim is unrelated to the assets sought to be made subject to the appointment of a receiver, provided that in all the circumstances of the case it is "just and convenient" to appoint a receiver. These circumstances could be, *e.g.* that the defendant may deal with the assets so as to frustrate enforcement of an eventual judgment against him. Here the appointment of a receiver may be made either in support of a Mareva injunction or independently of the granting of Mareva relief.

Where the appointment is made pre-trial as preservative Mareva relief the court will seek to preserve the assets; it may still be appropriate for assets to be sold by the receiver as part of the running of a business or because they are perishable or liable to deteriorate, but the court will be mindful of the fact that the assets belong to the defendant and take into account his wishes about whether a sale should take place, and not order a

---

[15] *Cummins v Perkins* [1899] 1 Ch. 16 at 20, *per* Chitty L.J.
[16] *Mercedes Benz AG v Leiduck* [1996] A.C. 284 at 298; *P v Liverpool Daily Post and Echo* [1991] 2 A.C. 370 at 420–421; *South Carolina Co. v Assurantie NV* [1987] A.C. 24 at 40; *British Airways Board v Laker Airways Ltd* [1985] A.C. 58; *Bremer Vulkan Schiffbau und Maschinefabrik v South India Shipping Corporation* [1981] A.C. 909; *The Siskina* [1979] A.C. 210.
[17] *Derby & Co. Ltd v Weldon (Nos 3 and 4)* [1990] Ch. 65; *Bond Brewing Holdings Ltd v National Australia Bank Ltd* [1991] 1 V.L.R. 386, Supreme Court of Victoria, Full Court; see also *sub nom National Australia Bank Ltd v Bond Brewing Holdings Ltd* (1990) 169 C.L.R. 271 at 276–277 (High Court of Australia); *Lee Kuan Yew v Tang Liang Hong (No.2)* [1997] 2 S.L.R. 833 at paras 7–10 (receiver appointed when defendant not obeying disclosure order ancillary to Mareva relief); *Westpac Banking corporation v Lameri* [2000] N.S.W.S.C. 393 (May 3, 2000) at para.7. See also *Ballabil Holdings Pty Ltd v Hospital Products* (1985) 1 N.S.W.L.R. 155, in which a receiver was appointed over assets outside the jurisdiction of the courts of New South Wales, and *Ka Wah International Merchant Finance Ltd v Asean Resources* (1986) 8 I.P.R. 241 in which the High Court in Hong Kong appointed a receiver over shares in a Singapore company so that the receiver could use the voting rights so as to secure the underlying assets.
[18] If there is a contractual or other right for a fund not to be dealt with except in a particular way, this can be enforced by injunction; see 12.012 above. *Cummins v Perkins* [1899] 1 Ch. 16 is not a case of "equitable execution" (as suggested in *Meagher, Gummow and Lehane's Equity: Doctrines and Remedies* (4th ed. 2002) at para. 28–090) because an untaxed order for costs could not be used to found execution before the amount was taxed, see para. 16.011. It is a case in which the costs had to be paid from the separate estate of a married woman, and that estate could be preserved pending taxation and execution.

sale just because the claimant wants to maximise the value of the assets under restraint.[19]

16.005   That it is not necessary for the claimant to claim some interest in or right over or in respect of the assets to justify the appointment of a receiver was put beyond doubt by the decision of the Court of Appeal in *Derby & Co. Ltd v Weldon (Nos 3 and 4)* (above). In that case, the Court of Appeal upheld (with certain variations) an order made by Sir Nicolas Browne-Wilkinson V.-C. appointing a receiver over a corporate defendant's assets wherever situated and requiring disclosure of information about the relevant assets. The receivership applied to assets outside the jurisdiction. The Court of Appeal varied the order made by the Vice-Chancellor by deleting a proviso to the effect that the defendants to the action should become bound to vest the foreign assets in the receiver only if the order was recognised by the Luxembourg courts. It was contemplated that such recognition would be accorded by virtue of Art.25 of the Brussels Convention. The Court of Appeal held that it was inappropriate to insert such a proviso in relation to the effect of the order on the parties to the action.[20] This is because the parties to the proceedings are bound by the order.

This is to be contrasted with the position of non-parties in relation to the appointment of a receiver by the court over assets abroad.[21] There the position is the same as that which applies to Mareva relief in respect of assets abroad.[22] The English court does not exercise an exorbitant jurisdiction over foreigners in relation to their conduct abroad.[23] The proper tribunal to do that is the local court. Furthermore those foreigners should be able to conduct themselves by reference to the laws which would be applied by that local court. The provisos which are set out in paras 19 and 20 of the example freezing injunction should be put into an order appointing a receiver over assets abroad.[24] These provisos apply to a branch of a bank in the foreign jurisdiction irrespective of whether the same legal entity has a presence within the jurisdiction. This is because non-parties, even if having a branch or presence within the jurisdiction thus making them subject to the coercive power of the English court, should not be required to place themselves in a position of double jeopardy,[25] either being potentially held in contempt of the English court, or potentially being subjected to liability in the local jurisdiction as a consequence of complying with the purpose of the English order.

---

[19] *Re P (Restraint Order: Sale of Assets)* [2000] 1 W.L.R. 473 at 481H, *per* Simon Brown L.J.
[20] [1990] Ch. 65 at 80–82.
[21] *Re Maudsley Sons & Field* [1900] 1 Ch. 602.
[22] See paras 19–041–19.047 below; *Derby & Co. Ltd v Weldon (Nos 3 and 4)* [1990] Ch. 65; *Babanaft International Co. SA v Bassatne* [1990] Ch. 13 at 44; *Derby & Co. Ltd v Weldon (No.1)* [1990] Ch. 48.
[23] *Société Eram Shipping Co. Ltd v Compagnie Internationale de Navigation* [2004] 1 A.C. 260; *Mackinnon v Donaldson Lufkin & Jenrette Securities Corporation* [1986] Ch. 482; *Babanaft International Co. SA v Bassatne* [1990] Ch. 13 at 44.
[24] *Bank of China v NBM LLC* [2002] 1 W.L.R. 844; *Baltic Shipping Co. v Translink Shipping Ltd* [1995] 1 Lloyd's Rep. 673; see further Chapter 12, paras 12.45–12.46.
[25] *Bank of China v NBM LLC* [2002] 1 W.L.R. 844 at [11–13].

When the court appoints a receiver over assets abroad, it does not **16.006** automatically put him in possession of foreign assets.[26] The court recognises that, to do this, something more is required to put the receiver into possession under the law of the country where the assets are situated. Accordingly, the court will not hold a non-party, whether or not resident in this country, liable for contempt in refusing to deliver up foreign assets to the receiver or taking steps to obtain those assets for himself. In contrast, parties to the action in which the receiver has been appointed would be liable for contempt if they refused to deliver up the assets to the receiver or if they took steps to prevent the receiver obtaining possession of the assets.

The power of the court to appoint a receiver *pre-judgment* when the claimant does not claim any interest in the relevant assets or any right over or in respect of them has been exercised in a series of landlord and tenant cases.[27] In *Parker v Camden London Borough Council*[28] the question was whether a receiver should be appointed to manage certain housing estates because the local council was not providing various services. The Court of Appeal declined to appoint a receiver on discretionary grounds only, namely that the power of managing the estates had been vested in the council by statute.[29] Sir John Donaldson M.R. expressly rejected the contention that the statutory power to appoint a receiver was only to be exercised in accordance with "the pre-Judicature Act practices of the Court of Chancery or any other court".[30] This line of authority had been criticised on the ground that the plaintiff in each case had "no conceivable claim" to the rents payable to the landlord and no interest in them, and that therefore there was no basis for appointing a receiver.[31] This criticism was founded on the principle that the Judicature Act had not altered the principles which were applied by the Court of Chancery to this jurisdiction.[32] But with the recognition of the existence of the Mareva jurisdiction[33] it is clear that the claimant does not have to show a claim to an

---

[26] *Re Huinac Copper Mines Ltd* [1910] W.N. 218; *Re Maudsley Sons & Field* [1900] 1 Ch. 602 at 611–612.
[27] *Hart v Emelkirk Ltd* [1983] 1 W.L.R. 1289; *Daiches v Bluelake Investments Ltd* (1986) 51 P.&.C.R. 51; *Blawdziewicz v Diadon* [1988] 2 E.G. 52. See also the appointment by the master in *Clayhope Properties v Evans* [1986] 1 W.L.R. 1223 at 1225.
[28] [1986] Ch. 162.
[29] Applying the principle that it is improper for the court to appoint its own officer to exercise powers of management and to discharge duties which have been respectively vested in or imposed upon the council by statute. See also *Gardner v London Chatham and Dover Railway Co. (No.1)* (1867) L.R. 2 Ch. App. 201.
[30] [1986] Ch. 162 at 173.
[31] Muir Hunter, *Kerr on Receivers and Administrators* (17th ed., 1989), pp. 76–77.
[32] See *Holmes v Millage* [1893] 1 Q.B. 551 at 557, *per* Lindley L.J.
[33] That the same principles must be applied to the appointment of receivers as to the granting of injunctions was expressly recognised in *Holmes v Millage* [1893] 1 Q.B. 551 at 557. Both are now dealt with in the same terms in the single statutory subsection and are types of relief which are closely related. The appointment of a receiver is liable to involve greater interference with the status quo, and more expense and complexity than the granting of an injunction, and this falls to be taken into account on the exercise of the discretion.

interest in the rent or right over, or in respect of, the rent to justify the appointment of a receiver under s.37(1) of the Supreme Court Act 1981.[34]

The county court has power to appoint a receiver as a remedy in proceedings under s.38 of the County Courts Act 1984 and in aid of execution under s.107 of that Act.

(iii) Discretion and the Mareva jurisdiction

16.007 The appointment of a receiver is a discretionary remedy, and has the same effect as an interlocutory injunction granted in respect of the assets. When the appointment is over a chose in action the order prevents the defendant from dealing with the asset or receiving its proceeds and it prevents a non-party from discharging the chose in action through dealings with the defendant including payment to him.[35] If the circumstances are such that it would not be just and convenient to grant an injunction, then *a fortiori* a receiver should not be appointed.[36] Thus, *e.g.* Mareva relief pre-judgment will not be granted in a form which has the effect of preventing the defendant from carrying out ordinary transactions in the course of business,[37] and similarly a receiver should not be appointed in these circumstances.

The jurisdiction to appoint a receiver, like the jurisdiction to grant injunctions, is not to be used so as to rewrite the insolvency laws. Mere risk of insolvency without more does not justify appointing a receiver.[38] The court will be astute to avoid appointing a receiver as a means of administering the affairs of an insolvent company, particularly when the company resists that application.[39]

16.008 The nature of the remedy is more intrusive, more expensive, and less reversible than the granting of an injunction. The receiver has to be paid. The defendant no longer has control of the assets. Irreparable damage may be done to the business of the defendant through the publicity.[40] The claimant must show that the appointment is appropriate because other less invasive remedies would be inadequate. If the claimant has contractual or other rights as to how assets may or may not be used (*e.g.* a negative

---

[34] *Bond Brewing Holdings Ltd v National Australia Bank Ltd* [1991] 1 V.L.R. 386, Supreme Court of Victoria, Full Court; see further (1990) 169 C.L.R. 271, High Court of Australia *Derby & Co. Ltd v Weldon (Nos 3 and 4)* [1990] Ch. 65; *Lee Kuan Yew v Tang Liang Hong (No.2)* [1997] 2 S.L.R. 833 at paras 7–10.

[35] *Allied Irish Bank v Ashford Hotels Ltd* [1997] 3 All E.R. 309 at 313–314.

[36] *Bond Brewing Holdings Ltd v National Australia Bank Ltd* [1991] 1 V.L.R. 386.

[37] *Normid Housing Association Ltd v Ralphs and Mansell (No.2)* [1989] 2 Lloyd's Rep. 274; *Avant Petroleum Inc. v Gatoil Overseas Inc.* [1986] 2 Lloyd's Rep. 236; *Iraqi Ministry of Defence v Arcepey Shipping (The Angel Bell)* [1981] Q.B. 65.

[38] *Midas Merchant Bank v Bello*, unreported, October 14, 2002, CA; *Brigitte Lipman v AG Lifestyle Management Pty Ltd* [2001] N.S.W.I.R. Comm. 115 at para.24; *Woodside Hospital Consulting Pty v Stockleton Nominees* [1998] V.S.C. 121 at paras 26–33; *Tranquil Holdings Ltd v Hudson* (1987) 2 P.R.N.Z. 551.

[39] *Bond Brewing Holdings Ltd v National Australia Bank Ltd* [1991] 1 V.L.R. 386.

[40] *Don King Productions Inc. v Warren* [1999] 2 Lloyd's Rep. 392 at 399 RHC third point.

pledge), then before appointing a receiver the court will consider whether damages or an injunction is a sufficient remedy.[41] The court, in exercising its discretion, will take into account the likely costs of the appointment.[42] Ordinarily an unsecured creditor is left to obtain judgment and then to enforce his judgment without the assistance of a receiver.

If (1) assets are liable to be dissipated or are otherwise in jeopardy[43] and (2) cannot satisfactorily be preserved by injunction,[44] then it may be appropriate to appoint a receiver.[45] This arises when the defendant controls a network of overseas trusts or companies and it appears that he has arranged his affairs in such a complicated way that if the step were not to be taken he might be judgment proof. The appointment of a receiver would be effective relief when an injunction, on its own, would not be. The principles enabling relief to be granted against those entities or over assets on the basis of "piercing the corporate veil" are discussed in Chapter 13 at paras 13.007–13.013. Other examples of situation calling for the appointment of a receiver are where the defendants are likely to act in disregard of an injunction or have already done so, or where assets need to be managed and if relief were limited to an injunction their value would not be preserved, *e.g.* a portfolio of share or commodity options, or where the assets need to be exploited in order to realise their true worth, *e.g.* a patent or a business. The court will not shrink from making an appointment in an appropriate case on an application made without notice,[46] however this is a very strong thing to do and will only be done when an injunction may not hold the position satisfactorily and there is imminent peril of substantial irreparable damage if an immediate appointment is not made.

---

[41] *Don King Productions Inc. v Warren* [1999] 2 Lloyd's Rep. 392 (declining to appoint a receiver when the position could be held by accepting undertakings offered to the court which would be policed by an accountant); *Bond Brewing Holdings Ltd v National Australia Bank Ltd* [1991] 1 V.L.R. 386, Supreme Court of Victoria, Full Court; *Wallace Kevin James v Merrill Lynch International Bank Ltd* [1998] 1 S.L.R. 785 (declining to appoint a receiver when injunctions were sufficient relief).

[42] CPR Pt 69, Practice Direction—Court's Power to Appoint a Receiver, para.5(3) which applies to the appointment of a receiver by way of equitable execution. Logically the same consideration must be relevant to appointment prior to judgment; *Beach Petroleum v Johnson* (1992) A.C.S.R. 404, Federal Court of Australia.

[43] *Ninemia Maritime Corporation v Trave Schiffahrtsgesellschaft GmbH (The Niedersachsen)* [1983] 1 W.L.R. 1412; *National Australia Bank Ltd v Bond Brewing Holdings Ltd* (1990) 169 C.L.R. 271 at 277, High Court of Australia, referring to *Jackson v Sterling Industries Ltd* (1987) 162 C.L.R. 612 at 623.

[44] *Don King Productions Inc. v Warren* [1999] 2 Lloyd's Rep. 392 (where undertakings to the court were accepted on the opposed *ex parte* application for the appointment of an interim receiver); *Wallace Kevin James v Merrill Lynch International Bank Ltd* [1998] 1 S.L.R. 785.

[45] *International Credit and Investment Company (Overseas) Ltd v Adham* [1998] B.C.C. 134 (Robert Walker J.), a claim for huge amounts based on allegations of dishonesty found proved at trial in the Cayman Islands, in which a receiver was appointed in respect of assets covered by Mareva relief; *Derby v Weldon (Nos 3 and 4)* [1990] Ch. 65; *Ballabil Holdings Pty Ltd v Hospital Products Ltd* (1985) 1 N.S.W.L.R. 155.

[46] *Don King Productions Inc. v Warren* [1999] 2 Lloyd's Rep. 392 at 399 LHC.

(2) Appointment of a receiver by way of equitable execution

16.009 Before the Judicature Acts 1873–1875, the High Court of Chancery exercised a jurisdiction to enable there to be enforcement of a judgment when execution could not be had at common law. The procedure was by bill in equity seeking the payment of the judgment debt by means of the appointment of a receiver over an asset of the judgment debtor. The practice was for the application for the receiver to be made by interlocutory application before the hearing.[47]

The most common case concerned land.[48] The legal theory was that a judgment creditor who wished to enforce his judgment against land of the debtor, which could not be reached by legal execution, could obtain the assistance of equity to do this. This was not because the judgment gave him an "interest" in the land of the debtor; what he had was a right to be paid on the judgment and a need for the assistance of equity to obtain satisfaction of the judgment. The procedure was available because there was an impediment to execution being had at common law and an asset which could be realised through the appointment of a receiver.

That impediment had to be formally proved.[49] The High Court of Chancery granted equitable relief[50] so as to put the judgment creditor in the same position as if he had been able to proceed with legal execution. Satisfaction of the judgment debt was obtained by means of the appointment of the receiver over the judgment debtor's interest in the property. After the Judicature Acts it was open to the judgment creditor to apply in the action in which he had obtained judgment for the appointment post-judgment of a receiver.[51] This was done under s.25(8) of the Judicature Act 1873.[52] Although called "equitable execution", it was the granting of equitable relief to enable satisfaction of a judgment to be obtained—it was not execution but a substitute for execution.[53]

16.010 The case law about the availability of equitable execution remained dominated by the purpose for which such relief had been granted before the Judicature Acts; namely for providing a remedy when execution could not be had at common law, and when there was some asset which could be realised for the benefit of the judgment creditor through the appointment of the receiver.

---

[47] *Anglo-Italian Bank v Davies* (1878) 9 Ch.D. 275 at 283.
[48] *Harris v Beauchamp Brothers* [1894] 1 Q.B. 801 at 808.
[49] The judgment creditor had to issue a writ of *elegit* and it was essential that he did so even though in itself it could not assist him to get at the judgment debtor's interest in the land: *Neate v Duke of Marlborough* (1838) 3 My & Cr.407.
[50] "Equitable execution" is not a form of execution; it is a substitute for execution. It is equitable relief which enables an asset of the judgment debtor to be realised and the judgment debt paid: *Re Shephard Atkins v Shephard* (1889) 43 Ch.D. 131 at 136, *per* Cotton L.J. and 137, *per* Bowen L.J.
[51] *Smith v Cowell* (1880) 6 Q.B.D. 75.
[52] The statutory predecessor of s.45 of the Supreme Court of Judicature (Consolidation) Act 1925 and s.37 of the Supreme Court Act 1981.
[53] *Re Shephard Atkins v Shephard* (1890) 43 Ch.D. 131.

In *Holmes v Millage*,[54] the judgment creditor sought the appointment of a receiver to receive future salary of the judgment debtor who was a newspaper correspondent residing abroad and paid a weekly salary. No garnishee order could be made because the future salary had not been earned and there was no existing debt to be attached, even one to be paid in the future. The salary would not become payable except in return for personal services to be rendered. The Court of Appeal held that there was no jurisdiction to proceed by way of equitable execution because there was no interest of the judgment debtor in property over which a receiver could be appointed by way of equitable execution.[55] In short, there was no relevant asset[56] owned by the judgment debtor over which a receiver could be appointed.[57]

In *Edwards & Co. v Pickard*,[58] the judgment creditor unsuccessfully sought the appointment of a receiver over a patent, but there was no evidence that it was being exploited or that there were any royalties. There was a hindrance to execution which "even equity could not remove".[59]

Before the emergence of the Mareva jurisdiction: **16.011**

(1) Equitable execution had as its purpose *the enforcement of a judgment* through the receiver collecting the relevant asset, turning it into cash (if it was not already in this form) and paying off the judgment. The procedure was not to provide a convenient means for administering assets,[60] or to be an alternative to legal execution by garnishee proceedings,[61] or to facilitate legal execution.[62] But it

---

[54] [1893] 1 Q.B. 551.

[55] Lindley L.J. said at 555 that "The only cases of [equitable execution] in which Equity ever interfered were cases in which the judgment debtor had an equitable interest in property which could have been reached at law, if he had had the legal interest in it . . .". This was a historical statement about the position before the Judicature Acts in the High Court of Chancery. Equitable execution was also available in other circumstances—see Lindley L.J.'s judgment at 558. In *Maclaine Watson & Co. v International Tin Council* [1988] Ch. 1 at 19H, Millett J. criticised the statement as being too narrowly stated even as a historical proposition; see the cases cited by Davey L.J. in *Harris v Beauchamp Brothers* [1894] 2 Q.B. 801 at 808.

[56] It could be said that there was "an asset" in the sense that future earnings could be assigned, but it was not an asset over which equity would give equitable execution.

[57] The court was being asked to use s.25(8) of the Judicature Act 1873 as a mechanism for introducing execution on earnings of an individual. This would have involved considerations of policy and was not justified by the established practices of the court. Subsequently there was statutory intervention; see the Attachment of Earnings Act 1971. Contrast the explanation of this case in *Soinco v Novokuznetsk Aluminium Plant* [1998] Q.B. 406, which is that equitable execution could not be granted over assets which could not be reached by legal execution. But equitable execution could be had on a debt payable by the Accountant General of the court, or a debt payable out of a fund in court, neither of which could be reached by legal execution—see *Harris v Beauchamp Brothers* [1894] 1 Q.B. 801 at 808. The indemnity cases also fall into this category.

[58] [1909] 2 K.B. 903.

[59] *Maclaine Watson & Co. v International Tin Council* [1988] Ch. 1 at 20G.

[60] *Harris v Beauchamp Brothers* [1894] 1 Q.B. 801.

[61] *Manchester and Liverpool District Banking Co. v Parkinson* (1888) 22 Q.B.D. 173.

[62] *Morgan v Hart* [1914] 2 K.B. 183 (where the judgment debtor's furniture was mixed up with that of others).

could be used to enforce a judgment against debts when it was impossible to proceed by way of garnishee proceedings because of a lack of information which was essential for that mode of procedure and when there was a danger of the foreign judgment debtor collecting the debts and making off with them.[63] It could also be used to enforce a judgment against a legally enforceable contractual right of indemnity, which was in existence and which could be legally enforced.[64] The claim on an indemnity is for damages[65] and not for a debt and for this reason third party debt order (formerly garnishee) proceedings are not available.[66]

(2)   An injunction could be granted to preserve the asset pending equitable execution, when there was a danger of it being dissipated.[67]

(3)   A receiver could also be appointed in order to enforce a charge on an asset[68] or a right to be paid out of a fund.[69] This jurisdiction was exercised so as to give effect to rights or interests in the asset. That asset could be preserved meanwhile by injunction if it was in danger of being dissipated.

(4)   The court exercised jurisdiction under s.25(8) to preserve assets by injunction when those assets were in danger, so that there could be legal execution.[70]

The effect of the emergence of the Mareva jurisdiction has been the recognition of a jurisdiction, available before and after judgment, to grant an injunction or appoint a receiver for the purpose of preserving assets of a defendant. The appointment of a receiver involves the court through its officer, the receiver, taking control of the relevant assets. It is only a short step post-judgment for the court to order the assets controlled by the receiver to be used to satisfy the judgment. A receiver appointed to

---

[63] *Goldschmidt v Oberrheinische Metallwerke* [1906] 1 K.B. 373.
[64] *Bourne v Colodense* [1985] I.C.R. 291; *Maclaine Watson & Co. v International Tin Council* [1988] Ch. 1 at 21; see also the facts in *Allied Irish Bank v Ashford Hotels Ltd* [1997] 3 All E.R. 309.
[65] *Chandris v Agro Insurance Company Ltd* [1963] 2 Lloyd's Rep. 65 at 73–74; *Firma C-Trade SA v Newcastle Protection and Indemnity Association* [1991] 2 A.C. 1 at 35–36 and 40–42.
[66] *Israelson v Dawson (Port of Manchester Insurance Co. Ltd) (Garnishees)* [1933] 1 K.B. 301.
[67] *Lloyd's Bank v Medway Upper Navigation Company* [1905] 2 K.B. 359.
[68] *Holmes v Millage* [1893] 1 Q.B. 551 at 555.
[69] *Cummins v Perkins* [1899] 1 Ch. 16 (this was not a case on equitable execution because the order for costs was untaxed—see *Willis v Cooper* (1900) 44 S.J. 698); *Kearns v Leaf* (1864) 1 M. & M. 681.
[70] *Bullus v Bullus* (1910) 102 L.T. 399, referred to in *Deutsche Schachtbau-und Tiefbohrgesellschaft mbH* [1990] 1 A.C. 295 at 317, *per* Sir John Donaldson M.R., and in *Mercantile Group (Europe) A.C. v Aiyela* [1994] Q.B. 366 at 376, *per* Hoffmann L.J.; *Goldschmidt v Oberrheinische Metallwerke* [1906] 1 K.B. 373, in which a receiver was appointed in part because of the assets being in jeopardy of being removed by the foreign judgment debtor, for the purposes of preserving the assets and enforcing the judgment against them.

preserve assets of the defendant pending judgment in the action may in due course become the means for satisfying the judgment. Similarly, post-judgment, if a receiver is appointed to preserve assets, then in principle the assets which he collects ought to be available to satisfy the judgment.[71]

These considerations show that in deciding whether to appoint a **16.012** receiver post-judgment the court should take into account whether, unless the appointment is made, the relevant assets are liable to be dissipated, and that the limits of "equitable execution" as operated by the former High Court of Chancery are no longer determinative. Instead the court should proceed in each case on the basis that s.37 confers on it a jurisdiction to make the appointment, but there remains a question of discretion, which will be exercised flexibly, taking into account all the circumstances of the case, including practical convenience,[72] avoiding unnecessary delay, cost or expense,[73] and considering whether the appointment is likely to provide the claimant with satisfaction of his judgment.

In *Soinco v Novokuznetsk Aluminium Plant*[74] the judgment debtors had a supply contract with a Guernsey company, which was also a party to the English proceedings. It was expected that from time to time money would become payable to the judgment debtors under the supply contract, if the judgment debtor continued to perform it. Mareva relief had been granted post-judgment against the judgment debtors. That relief operated *in personam* against the judgment debtors to restrain them from dealing with their assets and included an injunction restraining them from receiving payment of debts by the Guernsey company under the supply contract.[75] The effect of the injunction was that if and when a debt came into existence (regardless of when it was payable) there was then an asset of the judgment debtor which was within the scope of the injunction. What the Mareva relief did not do was to stop the judgment debtors arranging matters with the Guernsey company so that debts did not come into existence under the supply contract.[76] Such a collusive arrangement would stop the judgment debtor acquiring assets by way of debts coming into existence in return for supplies made. Garnishee proceedings would have been of no use—there was no debt due or accruing due to be attached. In these circumstances the court appointed a receiver to receive[77] all sums due

---

[71] *Soinco v Novokuznetsk Aluminium Plant* [1998] Q.B. 406.
[72] *Levermore v Levermore* [1979] 1 W.L.R. 1277; *Walter E. Heller Financial Corporation v American General Supply of Canada (1969) Ltd* (1986) 30 D.L.R. (4th) 600 (receiver appointed post-judgment pending appeal when the defendant had ceased doing business and had mixed assets which should have been the subject of security in favour of the plaintiff with other assets).
[73] The former RSC Ord. 51, r.1 enabled there to be an inquiry as to likely costs before the court decided whether an appointment was to be made.
[74] [1998] Q.B. 406.
[75] On the need for this, see Chapter 3, para.3.014, above.
[76] Such an arrangement might be through the Guernsey company lending money to the judgment debtor against which debts for supplies could be offset.
[77] The receiver was not appointed to manage supplies under the supply contract, so whether debts would arise in the future under the contract was a matter which depended upon the judgment debtor. An attachment of earnings order likewise depends for its efficacy on whether the employee chooses to go on working.

or to become due under the supply contract, and made an ancillary order for disclosure of documents relating to performance of the supply contract. This was done notwithstanding that under the former practice "equitable execution" could not be had on a debt which did not yet exist.[78]

16.013   The justification for the order in *Soinco v Novokuznetsk Aluminium Plant* was that it provided a practical, convenient way of collecting in assets as and when they came into existence and using them to satisfy the judgment debt, and that on the facts the garnishee procedure was an inadequate substitute for this. It is true that there was no existing debt due from the Guernsey company to the judgment debtor but if the supply contract was performed by the judgment debtor then there would be. The logic of the case was to apply Mareva principles to the situation and in addition to providing for an injunction to restrain dealings with the debts as and when they came into existence, to appoint a receiver to receive them.

(3) Non-assignable assets or interests

16.014   If a contract has a clause which forbids assignment then an assignment will not be effective as against the other party to the contract.[79] Nevertheless the benefit of the contract is an asset and the party who holds the benefit can still be a trustee of the proceeds, and subject to the liabilities of a trustee.[80] It follows that a receiver can be appointed over the proceeds.

In *Field v Field*,[81] a husband had been ordered to pay a lump sum to his former spouse and had defaulted in making the second payment. The husband's pension scheme had a clause which provided that:

> "No pension annuity or lump sum benefit on retirement shall be capable of being assigned or charged to someone else. If a trustee in bankruptcy is appointed in respect of a Member the Member's Fund and entitlements under the Scheme shall not vest in the trustee in Bankruptcy. If through the operation of this Clause a benefit ceases to be payable, the Trustee with the consent of the Provider may in case of hardship apply all or any part of it for the support and maintenance of the person who would have been the recipient . . . (but in no case shall any payment be made to an assignee or purported assignee)."

---

[78] *Holmes v Millage* [1893] 1 Q.B. 551. The order made in *Goldschmidt v Oberrheinische Metallwerke* [1906] 1 K.B. 373 had been restricted to debts due and was thus limited to debts which existed.

[79] *Linden Garden Trust v Lenesta Sludge Disposals* [1994] 1 A.C. 85 at 106E–H; *Helstan Securities Ltd v Hertfordshire County Council* [1978] 3 All E.R. 262;

[80] *Re Turcan* (1888) 40 Ch.D. 5; *Linden Garden Trust v Lenesta Sludge Disposals* [1994] 1 A.C. 85 at 106E–H; *Don King Productions Inc. v Warren* [2000] Ch. 291 at 321 and 335, para.26.

[81] [2003] 1 F.L.R. 376.

There was no power conferred on the court by legislation to override this. Under the pension scheme the husband had no beneficial interest in any funds held by trustees and so no charging order could be made. The court held that the pension could not be reached through requiring the husband to elect for a lump sum payment and appointing a receiver to receive the proceeds, because the fact that the husband could not assign his entitlement to call for a lump sum or an annuity was fatal.

One reason that non-assignable property cannot be reached by a receiver **16.015** appointed by way of equitable execution is on grounds of public policy. The salary or pay of officers in the army or navy could not be assigned because the public had an interest in the continued fit state of the officer.[82] There the same public policy requires equity not to intervene.

Another situation in which a receiver cannot be appointed is if there is a condition of the acquisition of the property that it is enjoyed personally by the judgment debtor. This is because then the condition would not be satisfied and there would be nothing to receive. The same is true of such a condition which applies to receipt of an annuity. Unless it is satisfied when each instalment is to vest, there is nothing to be received.

In contrast, if cash belongs to a judgment debtor absolutely, then a term which prevented its alienation would be inconsistent with the right in the property and void.[83] So once there are proceeds in the hands of the judgment debtor which belong to him absolutely, a receiver can be appointed over such property.

In *R. v The Judge of the County Court of Lincolnshire and Dixon*[84] the **16.016** trustees of a will were directed to set apart and invest an amount and were authorised at their absolute discretion to pay the judgment debtor, who therefore had no beneficial interest in that amount. The court could not order the trustees to make over the amount to a receiver because it was not property of the judgment debtor and the order would be inconsistent with the trust which gave them a discretion as to its use.

In *Field v Field* the clause prohibited assignment of the right to call for the lump sum or annuity, prohibited assignment of benefits to be paid under the scheme, and provided for consequences if a benefit ceased to be payable. No call could be made by an assignee because under the clause, the rights were not "capable of" assignment. If a trustee in bankruptcy was appointed the rights of the husband would cease, but none had been appointed. The clause did not preclude any transfer of *the fruits* of such a call, whether of a lump sum or an annuity, once they came into existence in the hands of the husband. Those proceeds once received would be bound by an assignment.[85] Furthermore, the clause did not prevent the

---

[82] *Re Miriams* [1891] 1 Q.B. 594 at 595–596; s.203 Army Act 1955 and s.128G Naval Discipline Act 1957.
[83] *Re Nelson* [1928] Ch. 920 at 921.
[84] (1887) 20 Q.B.D. 167.
[85] *Re Smith* [1928] Ch. 915 at 919; *Re Lind* [1915] 2 Ch. 345; *Re Turcan* (1888) 40 Ch.D. 5; *Linden Garden Trust v Lenesta Sludge Disposals* [1994] 1 A.C. 85 at 106E–H; *Don King Productions Inc. v Warren* [2000] Ch. 291 at 335, para.26.

husband making such a call unless he also expected personally to enjoy the proceeds, and therefore it did not invalidate such a call if it was made by the husband under the compulsion of a court order. In these circumstances there was jurisdiction to grant a mandatory order requiring the husband to make the call for a lump sum and an injunction restraining him from dealing with the proceeds when received, pending enforcement of the unsatisfied order against that cash.

16.017   In *Field v Field*, Wilson J. also relied on his earlier decision in *B v B (Injunction: Jurisdiction)*,[86] in support of the proposition that s.37 "could be used as an aid to the court's established procedures for enforcement of a judgment but not as a free-standing enforcement procedure in its own right".

First, that proposition misunderstands the ambit and purpose of s.37. It was part of the function of the Court of Chancery to intervene by injunction in support of legal or equitable rights where there was no remedy at law. That function is now performed by the High Court under s.37. The order for payment of the lump sum by the husband gave rise to a legal right in the wife which could be enforced by injunction.[87] The section empowers the court to grant an injunction, which itself is a remedy, and can be shaped into any of an infinite variety of orders. These include free-standing mandatory orders such as a disclosure order in aid of execution of a judgment.[88] Like a disclosure order a mandatory order requiring the husband to make the election would produce a situation in which the established execution procedures of the court could operate. The fact that but for the section the remedy would not exist is not a justification for refusing it as an injunction.

Secondly, in *B v B (Injunction: Jurisdiction)* the decision was that a husband could not be ordered to remain within the jurisdiction indefinitely until he satisfied an order for costs. That would have been to grant a remedy for enforcing debts which would infringe the liberty of the individual[89] and run counter to the policy underlying the Debtors Act 1869 and abolition of imprisonment for debt.

16.018   Thirdly, *B v B (Injunction: Jurisdiction)* had nothing to do with use of the jurisdiction under s.37 to grant a mandatory injunction requiring the husband to make an election so that cash proceeds of a call would be received by him on which there could then be execution. No one would have any difficulty with that being done under the section by way of

---

[86] [1998] 1 W.L.R. 329 at 334F–335E.
[87] *Mercantile Group AG v Aiyela* [1994] Q.B. 366 at 375H–376C; *Bullus v Bullus* (1910) 102 L.T. 399.
[88] *Maclaine Watson & Co. v International Tin Council (No.2)* [1989] Ch. 286 at 303; *Gidrxslme Shipping Co. Ltd v Tantomar Transportes Maritimos Lda (The Naftilos)* [1995] 1 W.L.R. 299 at 309; see Chapter 22.
[89] *Re B (Child Abduction: Wardship Power to Detain)* [1994] 2 F.L.R. 479 at 488.

enforcement of a contractual promise by the husband to do it,[90] and the same should be the position when enforcement is of the order of the court. For these reasons it is considered that *Field v Field* was wrongly decided.

(4) Effect of appointment of a receiver over assets in England

A receiver is not an agent or trustee for the party on whose application he 16.019 has been appointed or for any of the other parties.[91] If he contracts in his own name he is liable on the contract as principal.[92] Mere performance by him of a pre-existing contract does not make him personally liable on the contract.[93] The receiver does not have any title or interest in the assets by virtue of his appointment.[94] On the other hand, he may, as a result of his appointment, acquire a chose in action which he can enforce personally, *e.g.* if he becomes the holder of a bill of exchange.[95] The order appointing the receiver has effect as an injunction[96] restraining the parties to the action from receiving any part of the property. Commonly[97] the order expressly provides for any party who has possession of a relevant asset to surrender possession to the receiver. If the order is for the appointment of the receiver upon the provision of security, then ordinarily the order will be construed as providing for the appointment to take effect only once the security has been provided.[98] The appointment of a receiver over assets does not create any charge or lien over them.[99] Interference by a party to the action with the performance by the receiver of his duties under the order appointing him will constitute a contempt of court. Furthermore, if a

---

[90] This was the function of the mandatory injunction in *Astro Exito Navegacion SA v Southland Enterprise Co. Ltd (The Messiniaki Tolmi) (No.2)* [1983] 2 A.C. 787 affirming [1982] Q.B. 1248, *i.e.* to provide the key to unlock the letter of credit.
[91] *Boehm v Goodall* [1911] 1 Ch. 155.
[92] *Moss Steamship Co. Ltd v Whinney* [1912] A.C. 254.
[93] *Parsons v Sovereign Bank of Canada* [1913] A.C. 160.
[94] *Vine v Raleigh* (1883) 24 Ch.D. 238 at 243, *per* Chitty J.; *Re Muirhead Ex p. Muirhead* (1876) 2 Ch.D. 22; *Re Sacker Ex p. Sacker* (1888) 22 Q.B.D. 179; *Stevens v Hutchinson* [1953] Ch. 299; *Levermore v Levermore* [1979] 1 W.L.R. 1277 at 1281; *Clayhope Properties Ltd v Evans* [1986] 1 W.L.R. 1223 at 1227–1228.
[95] *Ex p. Harris* (1876) 2 Ch.D. 423, as explained in *Re Sacker* (above).
[96] *Re Sartoris's Estate* [1892] 1 Ch. 11; *Tyrell v Painton* [1895] 1 Q.B. 202; *Re Marquis of Anglesey* [1903] 2 Ch. 727; *Allied Irish Bank v Ashford Hotels Ltd* [1997] 3 All E.R. 309 at 313–314.
[97] When the ground upon which the appointment is made is that the assets are in jeopardy of being dissipated, there will be an express direction in the order requiring the defendant to give up possession of the assets to the officer of the court. In contrast, if the purpose of the appointment is simply to safeguard the interim profits to be made from land in a mortgagee's action for foreclosure or sale, the court might in the exercise of its discretion allow the mortgagor to stay in possession subject to his paying rent to the receiver: *Pratchett v Drew* [1924] 1 Ch. 280 at 286.
[98] *Ridout v Fowler* [1904] 1 Ch. 658 at 662.
[99] *Re Potts* [1893] 1 Q.B. 648; *Stevens v Hutchinson* [1953] Ch. 299 at 305; *Re Whiteheart Ex p. Trustee in Bankruptcy v John A. Clark & Co.* (1971) 116 S.J. 75; *Clayhope Properties v Evans* [1986] 1 W.L.R. 1223 at 1229.

non-party with knowledge of the order and without the leave of the court takes steps which will interfere with the receiver's getting in the assets, or which constitute an interference with the possession by the receiver of the assets, this will constitute a contempt.[1] This is subject to the position of non-parties abroad.[2]

(5) Effect of appointment over assets abroad

16.020   If an order is made appointing a receiver over assets abroad, on the grounds that the defendant may otherwise dissipate the assets, it will ordinarily contain an express provision directed to the defendant to give up possession of the assets to the receiver or his agent.

The court has power under s.37(l) of the Supreme Court Act 1981 to order the defendant to deliver up specified chattels to the receiver or to provide the receiver with particular funds or their proceeds held by the defendant. The court will not, though, make an order under the Mareva jurisdiction the effect of which is to require the defendant to provide the claimant with security for his claim.[3]

An order may be made for the appointment of a receiver over assets abroad even though the defendant is a foreigner with no presence in England and Wales, provided that the defendant can be served with proceedings out of the jurisdiction.[4] That order will be effective against the parties to the action, although non-parties will not be affected unless and until the order is enforced by the courts of the place where the assets are situated.

(6) Appointment of a receiver over a chose in action

16.021   The order appointing a receiver over a chose in action does not vest the chose in action in the receiver.[5] The court may authorise a receiver to take proceedings in the name of particular parties to the proceedings in respect

---

[1] *Allied Irish Bank v Ashford Hotels Ltd* [1997] 3 All E.R. 309 at 313–314; *Re Ling Ex p. Enrobook Pty Ltd* (1996) 142 A.L.R. 87 at 92–93, Federal Court of Australia, referring to *Underhay v Read* (1887) 20 Q.B.D. 209 at 218–219; *Ames v Birkenhead Docks Trustee* (1855) 20 Beav. 332; *Royal Bank of Canada v Canstar Sports Group Inc.* [1989] 1 W.W.R. 662, Manitoba Court of Appeal.

[2] *Bank of China v NBM LLC* [2002] 1 W.L.R. 844; *Baltic Shipping Co. v Translink Shipping Ltd* [995] 1 Lloyd's Rep. 673; see further Chapter 12, paras 12.045–12.046 and 19.041–19.046.

[3] *Jackson v Sterling Industries* (1987) 162 C.L.R. 612, High Court of Australia; *Bond Brewing Holdings Ltd v National Australia Bank Ltd* [1991] 1 V.L.R. 386, Supreme Court of Australia, Full Court and para.3.001 above. For views on introducing a different rule, see A.A.S. Zuckerman "Mareva Injunctions and Security for Judgment in a Framework of Interlocutory Remedies" (1993) 109 L.Q.R. 432; A.A.S Zuckerman, "Interlocutory Remedies in Quest of Procedural Fairness" (1993) 56 M.L.R. 325.

[4] *Duder v Amsterdamsch Trustees Kantoor* [1902] 2 Ch. 132; *Republic of Haiti v Duvalier* [1990] 1 Q.B. 202 at 216 applying *Re Liddell's Settlement Trusts* [1936] Ch. 365 at 374.

[5] *Rodriguez v Speyer Brothers* [1919] A.C. 59 at 112.

of a chose in action over which he has been appointed.[6] Such proceedings will be brought in the name of the party to the action who has title to sue on the chose in action.[7] The court may order the party to assign to the receiver the chose in action so that the receiver can take proceedings in respect of it in his own name. Thus, *e.g.* if a judgment debtor has a right to an indemnity against a third party, or may have such a right, then the court may appoint a receiver over that entitlement and authorise him to make a call or claim on the indemnity in the name of and on behalf of the judgment debtor.[8] Thus, jurisdiction to appoint a receiver before trial could provide an important interlocutory remedy in relation to the preservation of "disappearing assets" (see Chapter 7, above). For example, a receiver could be appointed for the purpose of selling perishable assets and receiving the proceeds of sale. Similarly, a receiver could be authorised to act on behalf of a defendant to protect time limits in relation to that defendant's potential claims against third parties.[9]

(7) Third Parties (Rights Against Insurers) Act 1930

The purpose of this Act was to remedy an injustice relating to liability **16.022** insurance. Prior to the Act, A could successfully sue B who was insured against liabilities to parties such as A, but then find that the proceeds of the policy went not towards paying off the judgment obtained by A against B, but for the benefit of B's creditors, who could prove in a liquidation or bankruptcy.[10] If B becomes insolvent,[11] the Act enables A, when he has obtained judgment against B,[12] to go directly under the policy against the insurers.

Protection and Indemnity Associations commonly have provisions in their cover which make it a condition precedent to their liability to a

---

[6] *Levermore v Levermore* [1979] 1 W.L.R. 1277 at 1283; *Wilton v Commonwealth Trading Bank* [1974] 2 N.S.W.L.R 96 at 99.
[7] *Re Backer* (1888) 22 Q.B.D. 179.
[8] *Bourne v Colodense Ltd* [1985] I.C.R. 291; *Madeline Watson & Co. v ITC* [1988] Ch. 1 at 17, *per* Millett J. (affirmed at [1989] Ch. 253, CA and [1990] 2 A.C. 418, HL).
[9] For example, by giving notice of claim to an insurer—see the facts in *The Vainqueur Jose* [1979] 1 Lloyd's Rep. 557.
[10] *Bradley v Eagle Star Insurance* [1989] 1 A.C. 957 at 967; *Cox v Bankside Members Agency Ltd* [1995] 2 Lloyd's Rep. 437 at 457.
[11] The particular triggering events are defined in s.1 of the Act.
[12] This is because under the standard form of liability policy an insurer only comes under a liability to pay when A has obtained judgment against B: *Bradley v Eagle Star Insurance* above, approving *Post Office v Norwich Union* [1967] 2 Q.B. 363. In *Bradley v Eagle Star Insurance*, B was a company which had already been wound up and dissolved and so there was no means of obtaining judgment against it, and therefore no possibility of any transfer of insurance rights to A. Section 141 of the Companies Act 1989 amended s.651 of the Companies Act 1985 removing the two-year time limit for restoring a company when there is a claim for personal injuries, and on the facts in Bradley this would now enable a judgment to be obtained against the insured company.

member that the member shall first have paid the third party. Before an event of insolvency covered by s.1, this condition precedent continues to apply because the member does not have the money to pay A, and so is not able to satisfy the condition precedent and thereby put himself in a position to obtain payment under the policy. After an event of insolvency, even though there is then a transfer of insurance rights to A, he will not be able to sue the Association because the condition precedent remains unsatisfied by the member.[13]

The jurisdiction to appoint a receiver under s.37 of the Supreme Court Act 1981 can provide a practical solution so as to enable the judgment debt to be satisfied. When A (namely the cargo interests) obtains judgment against B (the member), B has existing contractual rights against the Association under the P & I cover. Those rights exist. They include a contingent right to an indemnity. In principle, the court has jurisdiction to appoint a receiver in respect of those rights. Such a receiver could, for the purpose of realising those rights, agree to sell them to a third party (D). The proceeds would then be applied by the receiver to pay off the judgment debt, thereby paying A's claim. D will be left with the benefit of the contractual rights with the condition precedent satisfied.

16.023   In practice D could be a company formed specially for the purpose of acquiring the rights from the receiver. D will be paying full value to the receiver for the assignment of the contractual rights, but will in turn recoup its outlay from the Association. No question of champerty would arise.[14]

The overall result would be that the judgment debt will be paid, and no one will be any worse off except the Association which will have had to pay an indemnity under the P & I cover.

(8) Remuneration and costs of a receiver

(i) Remuneration

16.024   Prior to CPR the position was that a receiver as an officer of the court and not an agent for the parties, had to look to the court to see that he is paid out of the assets which were the subject of the appointment. If those assets were insufficient, the court, prior to CPR, had no jurisdiction to order any of the parties to the action to pay the remuneration, costs or expenses of the receiver.[15]

---

[13] *Firma C-Trade SA v Newcastle Protection & Indemnity Association* [1991] 2 A.C. 1.
[14] *R. (Factortame Ltd) v Transport Secretary No.8* [2003] Q.B. 381; *Giles v Thompson* [1994] 1 A.C. 142 at 163–164.
[15] *Boehm v Goodall* [1911] 1 Ch. 155; *Evans v Clayhope Ltd* [1988] 1 W.L.R. 358; followed in the cases on receivers appointed over property which may be confiscated as a result of a successful criminal prosecution: *Re Andrews* [1999] 1 W.L.R. 1236 at 1242; *Hughes v Customs & Excise Commissioners* [2003] 1 W.L.R. 177.

Under CPR r.69.7 (2):
" The court may specify—

(a) who is to be responsible for paying the receiver; and
(b) the fund or property from which the receiver is to recover his remuneration."

This provides a jurisdiction to order a person to pay the receiver's remuneration but not costs or expenses of the receivership.

(ii) Costs and expenses of the receivership

The receiver is entitled to an indemnity out of the assets in respect of costs **16.025** and expenses properly incurred by him in performing the functions which he is authorised to perform as receiver under the court order; if he wishes to incur costs which are beyond what has been authorised then he must bring the matter before the court before incurring them.[16]

Those costs and expenses are likely to include items which would have to be paid regardless of whether a receiver had been appointed; *e.g.* the salaries of employees employed in a business. On the other hand, remuneration of the receiver stands on a different footing because if he had not been appointed he would not have had to be remunerated.

The remuneration, costs and expenses of the receiver do not form part of the defendant's costs of the proceedings covered by s.51 of the Supreme Court Act 1981 because they are not "of and incidental to" the proceedings; they are costs of the receivership.[17]

In relation to extra costs and expenses caused by the order appointing a **16.026** receiver these would be potentially covered by a cross-undertaking in damages given by the applicant for the order. That cross-undertaking would also potentially apply to the remuneration, but the court also has power under CPR r.69.7(2) to order who is to be responsible for this.

If an order appointing a receiver has been discharged, the successful defendant may be entitled to an inquiry on the undertaking in damages[18] and, if he can show loss caused by the order because the assets have had to bear the remuneration, costs and expenses of the receiver, then this would fall within the scope of the undertaking. This jurisdiction did not arise in the cases on the legislation providing for the appointment of a receiver when there is a criminal prosecution, because the legislation itself together with the underlying public policy result in no cross-undertaking being provided by the prosecutor and the conclusion that an acquitted defendant is not to be compensated for loss caused by the making of the receivership order.[19]

---

[16] *Re British Power Traction and Lighting Company Ltd* [1906] 1 Ch. 497 at 506.
[17] *Re Andrews* [1999] 1 W.L.R. 1236 at 1244G–1246H and 1248.
[18] See above, paras 11.017–11.021.
[19] *Re Andrews* [1999] 1 W.L.R. 1236; *Hughes v Customs & Excise Commissioners* [2003] 1 W.L.R. 177.

If a fund over which a receiver has been appointed is to be distributed, then the fund will be applied first to meet the costs and expenses of realising the fund, secondly, to pay the receiver his remuneration and expenses and, thirdly, as between the parties to the proceedings.[20] Because the receiver has to look to the assets for his costs and expenses, and also, subject to the power under CPR r.69.7(2) in respect of his remuneration, it is the practice of the court not to make an order for distribution of even a part of those assets without being satisfied that the receiver's position is adequately safeguarded. Thus, if the defendant seeks an order releasing funds to him to pay legal costs or living expenses, the court would not grant the application, if to do so would prejudice the receiver's position.[21]

(9) Receiver appointed over land

16.027　Unlike the position in relation to Mareva injunctions, if an order is made appointing a receiver over land, the appointment will be registrable[22] as a land charge or caution, according to whether or not the land is registered. This is the case even though the order appointing the receiver does not have the effect of giving the applicant an interest in the land, and even though the applicant has no interest in the land over which the appointment has been made.

(10) Recognition of an order appointing a receiver

16.028　Provided an order is made *inter partes*,[23] it will be capable of being enforced in the courts of a Member State under Chap. III, section 2 of Council Regulation 44/2001 (the Judgments Regulation).[24] If a receiver is appointed by a foreign court and the order does not fall within the Regulation, it may still be recognised in this country provided that there is sufficient connection between the defendant whose assets have been made the subject of the appointment and the jurisdiction in which the appointment was made.[25]

(11) Practice and procedure

16.029　Practice and procedure are addressed in CPR Pt 69 and the supplementary Practice Direction. An order appointing a receiver may, in cases of extreme urgency (*e.g.* when assets are in imminent jeopardy), be made on an

---

[20] *Batten v Wedgwood Coal and Iron Co.* (1884) 28 Ch.D. 317.
[21] *Clark Equipment Credit of Australia Ltd v Como Factors* (1988) 14 N.S.W.L.R. 552 at 568, *per* Powell J., New South Wales Supreme Court.
[22] *Clayhope Properties Ltd v Evans* [1986] 1 W.L.R. 1223.
[23] *Denilauler v Snc Couchet Frères* [1980] E.C.R. 1553; *Babanaft International Co. SA v Bassatne* [1990] Ch. 13; *EMI Records Ltd v Modern Music Karl-Ulrich Waltenbach GmbH* [1992] Q.B. 115; see further Chapter 6, paras 6.014–6.015.
[24] See also under Art.25 of the Brussels Convention—*Derby v Weldon (Nos 3 and 4)* [1990] Ch. 65 at 85H.
[25] *Schemmer v Property Resources Ltd* [1975] Ch. 273.

application made without notice.[26] Ordinarily, however, the court will appoint a receiver only upon a hearing of an application made on notice. An injunction may be granted *ex parte* restraining the defendant from dealing with the assets pending the hearing of the application for the appointment.

The application must be supported by written evidence.[27] That written evidence must include the matters set out in para.4 of CPR Pt 69, Practice Direction—Court's Power to Appoint a Receiver. These are:

"Evidence in support of an application—rule 69.3

4.1 The written evidence in support of an application for the appointment of a receiver must—

(1) explain the reasons why the appointment is required;
(2) give details of the property which it is proposed that the receiver should get in or manage, including estimates of—
(a) the value of the property; and
(b) the amount of income it is likely to produce;

(3) if the application is to appoint a receiver by way of equitable execution, give details of—
(a) the judgment which the applicant is seeking to enforce;
(b) the extent to which the debtor has failed to comply with the judgment;
(c) the result of any steps already taken to enforce the judgment; and
(d) why the judgment cannot be enforced by any other method; and

(4) if the applicant is asking the court to allow the receiver to act—
(a) without giving security; or
(b) before he has given security or satisfied the court that he has security in place, explain the reasons why that is necessary.

4.2 In addition, the written evidence should normally identify an individual whom the court is to be asked to appoint as receiver ('the nominee'), and should—

(1) state the name, address and position of the nominee;
(2) include written evidence by a person who knows the nominee, stating that he believes the nominee is a suitable person to be appointed as receiver, and the basis of that belief; and

---

[26] CPR r.69.3(a). It is exceptional to do this and there must be strong reason for such an order to be made: *Bond Brewing Holdings Ltd v National Australia Bank Ltd* [1991] 1 V.L.R. 386, Supreme Court of Victoria, Full Court; *Don King Productions Inc. v Warren* [1999] 2 Lloyd's Rep. 392 (declining to appoint on an opposed *ex parte* application).
[27] CPR r.69.3(b).

(3) be accompanied by written consent, signed by the nominee, to act as receiver if appointed.

4.3　If the applicant does not nominate a person to be appointed as receiver, or if the court decides not to appoint the nominee, the court may—

(1) order that a suitable person be appointed as receiver; and

(2) direct any party to nominate a suitable individual to be appointed.

4.4 A party directed to nominate a person to be appointed as receiver must file written evidence containing the information required by paragraph 4.2 and accompanied by the written consent of the nominee."

16.030　It is often desirable that a receiver appointed to act under the order of the court should be independent of the parties and their solicitors and have no interest in the assets.[28] The receiver should be independent of the solicitors because their function includes monitoring on behalf of their clients the activities and accounts of the receiver. However, there can be reasons for appointing a party to be a receiver, particularly where the affairs of a partnership or business are to be carried on by the receiver,[29] and the party concerned has knowledge of those affairs[30] and can be relied upon to conduct them properly. There is no rule that a receiver will only be authorised to manage a business with a view to its winding up or sale.

The court has a discretion whether or not to require the person appointed to give security. The receiver can at any time request the court to give him directions in connection with his appointment, and may do so informally by letter. A master or a district judge has the power to grant an injunction "in connection with or ancillary to" the appointment of a receiver by way of equitable execution.[31]

If security is not to be required from the receiver before he takes up his appointment, then ordinarily the applicant will be required to furnish an undertaking to the court to be answerable for all the funds or other assets obtained or collected by the receiver. The applicant will in any event be required to furnish an undertaking in damages on an application without notice or *inter partes* before judgment.[32]

(12) Variations

16.031　The principles applying to funds which are the subject of an injunction apply also to an application to permit to be used, for a particular purpose, funds over which a receiver has been appointed. So, *e.g.* the court may

---

[28] *Re Lloyd* (1879) 12 Ch.D. 447.
[29] For an example of a receiver in a case concerning dissolution of a partnership, see *Davy v Scarth* [1906] 1 Ch. 55.
[30] *Sargant v Read* (1876) 1 Ch.D. 600.
[31] CPR Pt 2, second Practice Direction and CPR Pt 69, Practice Direction, para.3.2.
[32] *National Australia Bank Ltd v Bond Brewing Holdings* (1990) 169 C.L.R. 271 at 277, High Court of Australia. See further on the requirement of a cross-undertaking, Chapter 11, paras 11.001–11.002.

order funds to be released to pay the defendant's legal costs; such an order may be made even when the claimant has an arguable claim that he is the owner of the funds.[33] But when an order appointing a receiver has been made, there is a risk that other creditors of the defendant may be induced to believe that the assets are being protected by the court through its officer, the receiver. If there is a risk that the defendant is insolvent, the court may consider it appropriate to require notice of the application to be given to the defendant's creditors, so that they can consider bringing bankruptcy or winding-up proceedings to preserve the assets for all the creditors.[34]

---

[33] *NMB Postbank Groep NV v Naviede (No. 2)* [1993] B.C.L.C. 715.
[34] *NMB Postbank Groep NV v Naviede (No. 1)* [1993] B.C.L.C. 707. The court will not allow the receivership to delay or mislead other creditors; see also *Bond Brewing Holdings Ltd v National Australia Bank Ltd* [1991] 1 V.L.R. 386, Supreme Court of Victoria, Full Court.

Chapter 17

Search orders and Anton Piller Relief

(1) Introduction

A "search order"[1] is an order made on a without notice application which **17.001**
requires permission to be given for certain representatives of the claimant
and the supervising solicitor to enter premises for the purpose of searching
them, and removing articles or documents, or obtaining information (*e.g.*
from computers). It is extreme relief because, if it is complied with, it will
result in the representatives entering premises (*e.g.* a private house) and
searching them and, what is more, doing so before the defendant has put
his side of the case to the court and in circumstances capable of causing
great affront and serious loss of reputation. It has been described as one of
the law's two nuclear weapons,[2] the other being Mareva relief.

The jurisdiction was based by the courts on their inherent jurisdiction,
and was upheld by the Court of Appeal in the *Anton Piller* decision,[3] which
has given its name to this jurisdiction. Following criticisms of the procedure, the Judges' Council appointed a committee to report to it on "the
practical operation of Anton Piller orders". Staughton L.J. was the
chairman of the committee. Its report[4] stated in para.2.3:

> "The overriding principle upon which the grant of these orders ought
> . . . to be based is that of necessity. No such order ought to be made
> unless it is necessary in the interests of justice. No order ought to be
> made in wider terms than is necessary to achieve the legitimate object
> of the order. The safeguards incorporated into the order for the
> protection of the respondent should be as full as would be consistent
> with the achieving of that object."

Part V of the Report of the Staughton Committee recommended the **17.002**
drafting of a form of order for inclusion in the *Supreme Court Practice*,
commenting that a form of order then used in the Chancery Division ". . .

---

[1] Under CPR r.25.1(1)(h) it is described as an order made under s.7 of the Civil Procedure
Act 1997, and in practice this section covers most Anton Piller relief granted by the courts.
[2] *Bank Mellat v Nikpour* [1985] F.S.R. 87 at 92, *per* Donaldson L.J.
[3] *Anton Piller KG v Manufacturing Processes Ltd* [1976] Ch. 55 at 61A. It can also be justified
as an injunction granted under s.37(1) of the Supreme Court Act 1981.
[4] Lord Chancellor's Department, 1992.

would not be readily intelligible to the layman". Standard form orders were provided by Practice Direction,[5] and there is an example search order now given by the Practice Direction—Interim Injunctions which supplements CPR Pt 25.

Section 7 of the Civil Procedure Act 1997 gives a statutory jurisdiction to the High Court to make an order in existing or proposed civil proceedings which will enable entry and search of premises and for various steps to be taken. During consideration of the draft Bill there was concern that the proposed measure might have the effect of cutting down the scope of the jurisdiction exercised by the court under its inherent jurisdiction. However, the section is expressed as an empowering measure and the Lord Chancellor expressly assured peers that:

"The purpose of [the draft clause] is certainly not to limit or reduce the jurisdiction which is currently being exercised under the Anton Piller order but to seek to put it on a secure statutory foundation as recommended some time ago by a working party of the Judges' Council."[6]

17.003   The Lord Chancellor also said that:

"This clause gives power to the court; in other words, it confers jurisdiction to make this order; but it does not exclude any other jurisdiction of the court to make any other order. If the court has jurisdiction to make two orders, there is no reason why we should not have a composite order with two parts in it . . ."[7]

These two assurances are borne out by the wording of the section which contains no abolition of or restriction upon any existing jurisdiction of the court, and which does not in any way limit the power of the court to make an order partly based on s.7 and partly on some other jurisdiction.

Thus, *e.g.* an order can be made[8] directing that:

(1) premises can be searched and certain goods removed (s.7(5) (b) of the Civil Procedure Act 1997 enables property to be removed from the premises "for safe keeping");

and directing that:

(2) any goods removed are to be delivered up to the claimant (this can be done under s.4 of the Torts (Interference with Goods) Act 1977).

---

[5] *Practice Direction (Mareva Injunctions and Anton Piller Orders: Forms)* [1996] 1 W.L.R. 1552 replaced the previous standard form in *Practice Direction (Mareva Injunction and Anton Piller Orders: New Forms)* [1994] 1 All E.R. 52.
[6] *Hansard*, Vol. 575, CWH 30, November 20, 1996 (Committee stage).
[7] *Hansard*, Vol. 575, CWH 38, November 20, 1996 (Committee stage); see also *Hansard*, Vol. 576, col. 898, December 9, 1996.
[8] *Hansard*, Vol. 576, cols 897–898, December 9, 1996, Lord Mackay L.C. referring to advice received from Sir Richard Scott V.-C.

CPR r.25.1(1)(h) states that the court may grant as one of the "interim remedies" available to it:

"(h) an order (referred to as a 'search order') under section 7 of the Civil Procedure Act 1997 (order requiring a party to admit another party to premises for the purpose of preserving evidence, etc.)".

"Anton Piller" relief is available, at least in theory, in respect of **17.004** materials held at premises outside of England and Wales,[9] and thus outside of the confines of s.7, and that section exists alongside and does not abrogate the court's jurisdiction to grant such relief under its inherent jurisdiction or under s.37(1) of the Supreme Court Act 1981.

After CPR, the House of Lords has continued to use the words Anton Piller to describe the jurisdiction,[10] and it is appropriate to bear in mind that the expression "search order" does not cover the full scope of the Anton Piller jurisdiction; it does not cover orders made under s.37(1) of the Supreme Court Act 1981 or the inherent jurisdiction, nor orders which are outside the scope of s.7 of the Civil Procedure Act 1997. For these reasons it remains convenient to refer to the Anton Piller jurisdiction.

The Anton Piller jurisdiction is also established in other common law jurisdictions including Australia,[11] and New Zealand.[12]

(2) Civil Procedure Act 1997, s.7

The section applies to existing or proposed proceedings in the High Court **17.005** and enables orders to be made for the purpose of securing:

"(a) the preservation of evidence, which is or may be relevant, or
(b) the preservation of property, which is or may be the subject-matter of the proceedings or as to which any question arises or may arise in the proceedings."

Section 7(1)(a) is concerned with evidence which is or may be relevant to the proceedings. Section 7(1)(b) would, *e.g.* include property to which the claimant laid claim in the proceedings, property in which the claimant claimed an interest, or in respect of which the claimant claimed a right in the proceedings. Since there is nothing in the section seeking to cut down on the existing inherent jurisdiction or limit its availability and peers were

---

[9] see Chapter 6, para.6.006–6.009 above about extra-territorial relief.
[10] *R. (McCann) v Crown Court at Manchester* [2003] 1 A.C. 787 at [25] (Lord Steyn whose reasons were also adopted by Lord Hobhouse and Lord Scott).
[11] *The Principles of Equity* (Patrick Parkinson ed., 2003) Ch. 19.
[12] *Equity and Trusts in New Zealand* (2003) (A. Butler ed., 2003) Ch. 24.

assured by the Lord Chancellor that there was no intention to do this, and since s.7 is a provision which equips the court with a statutory jurisdiction to do justice, s.7(1) should be given a liberal and generous interpretation.

The Anton Piller jurisdiction based on the inherent jurisdiction of the court can be used to enable documents to be obtained which could be relevant to execution of a judgment, *e.g.* when a claimant seeks information about the nature and whereabouts of the defendant's own assets.[13] In principle this would come within s.7(1)(b) because execution or enforcement of a judgment can be had through steps taken in proceedings in the High Court and a question may arise at some stage in those proceedings as to whether particular assets can be made the subject of an order in those proceedings.[14] In the meantime an order can be made under s.7 for the purpose of securing such property in contemplation that such a question may eventually arise in such proceedings.

17.006   The Anton Piller jurisdiction can also be used to establish the location of information relevant to whether there are persons who should be sued by the claimant and if so who they are and what they have done.[15] For example, the claimant may be concerned that there is unlawful stock produced in breach of copyright which is in the hands of a supplier and the claimant needs to know who is the supplier and where is the stock.[16] If it is proposed to sue the supplier in the High Court, then an order can be made under s.7(1)(a) for the purpose of securing the evidence against the supplier and under s.7(1)(b) for the purpose of securing the unlawful stock.

An order can be sought under the section by a person "who is, or appears to the court likely to be, a party to proceedings in the [High Court] . . .".[17] This applies to defendants as well as claimants.

Section 7(3) provides that an order under the section can:

". . . direct any person to permit any person described in the order, or secure that any person so permitted—

(a) to enter premises[18] in England and Wales, and
(b) while on the premises, to take . . . any of the . . . steps [set out in subs (4)."

17.007   The standard forms of Anton Piller order were of an order made against the defendant. The practice before the first standard form order was published in 1994 was that the order required the defendant, by himself, or

---

[13] *CBS United Kingdom Ltd v Lambert* [1983] Ch. 37 at 44–45 (pre-judgment); *Distributori Automatici v Holford Trading Co* [1985] 1 W.L.R. 1066 (post-judgment).
[14] For example, by way of third party debt proceedings or receiver appointed in aid of execution: *Smith v Cowell* (1880) 6 Q.B.D. 75.
[15] This can be sought under the principle in *Norwich Pharmacal Co. v Customs and Excise Commissioners* [1974] A.C. 133. See paras 22.048–22.050.
[16] See the letter from Laddie J. quoted by Lord Brightman in *Hansard*, Vol. 575, CWH 34, November 20, 1996.
[17] Civil Procedure Act 1997, s.7(2).
[18] "Premises" includes any vehicle: s.7(8).

by any person appearing to be in control of the premises, to give the permission needed for entry on to the premises and for the search to take place.[19] The 1994 standard form order stated in para.1(2) that:

"(2) This order must be complied with either by the defendant himself or by a responsible employee of the defendant or by the person appearing to be in control of the premises."

The 1996 standard form order provided in para.1(2)[20] that:

(2) This order must be complied with either by the defendant himself or by an employee of the defendant or other person appearing to be in control of the premises *and having authority to permit the premises to be entered and the search to proceed.*[21]

The example order given by the CPR Practice Direction provides: **17.008**

"5. This order must be complied with by—

(a) the Respondent;
(b) any director, officer, partner or responsible employee of the Respondent; and
(c) if the Respondent is an individual any other person having responsible control of the premises to be searched."

This wording is to be read together with the rest of the order including the Penal Notice and para.1. The Penal Notice reads:

---

[19] *Manor Electronics v Dickson* [1988] R.F.C. 618; *Bhimji v Chatwani* [1991] 1 W.L.R. 989 at 997C. Contrast the irregular form of order made in *VDU Installations Ltd v Integrated Computer Systems and Cybernetics Ltd* [1989] F.S.R. 378 at 383 which provided that: "the defendant or any person appearing to be in control of the premises hereinafter mentioned do permit". See also M. Dockray and H. Laddie, Piller Problems" (1990) 106 L.Q.R. 601 at 610–612.

[20] See also the terms of the standard form order in para.1(1) which was expressed as requiring "The Defendant" to allow entry and the terms of the "NOTICE TO THE DEFENDANT". This was consistent with the principle that an injunction should be addressed to a party to an action or someone who is about to become a party—see Chapter 13, para.13.001. Contrast the observations of Lord Irvine of Lairg in committee in *Hansard*, Vol. 575, CWH 36, November 20, 1996.

[21] The 1996 Practice Direction added the words in italics, and dropped the word "responsible" before "employee". The purpose of the change was apparently to ensure that entry and search of premises did not take place on the basis of a "consent" given by someone who had no authority to give it. In view of this, para.1(2) of the 1996 standard form order was to be read as not applying to an employee of the defendant who did not have the requisite authority to allow entry and search. The word "responsible" was omitted because (1) under the 1996 wording the employee in any case had to have the authority specified; and (2) if "responsible" had been retained, it might have been interpreted as giving rise to some extra requirement in addition to the requirement that, before there can be entry or search based on the consent of an employee of the defendant, the employee must have the specified authority. The word "responsible" has now reappeared in the example order given under the CPR.

"PENAL NOTICE

IF YOU [   ] DISOBEY THIS ORDER YOU MAY BE HELD IN
CONTEMPT OF COURT AND MAY BE IMPRISONED, FINED
OR HAVE YOUR ASSETS SEIZED.

ANY OTHER PERSON WHO KNOW OF THIS ORDER AND
DOES ANYTHING WHICH HELPS OR PERMITS THE RESPOND-
ENT TO BREACH THE TERMS OF THIS ORDER MAY ALSO BE
HELD TO BE IN CONTEMPT OF COURT AND MAY BE
IMPRISONED, FINED OR HAVE THEIR ASSETS SEIZED."

Paragraph 1 states that the order was made against the respondent. So both
the form of penal notice[22] and para.1 make it clear that the order is only
directed to the respondent: someone who is not the respondent named in
the order is not himself ordered to give the relevant permission. The
example search order is an order *in personam* directed to the named
respondent, who is to comply with its mandatory requirements either
personally or through a person within the categories set out in para.5.[23]
The consequences of this are that first the example order does not itself
authorise entry; it is only if permission is given by the defendant pursuant
to the order that entry can lawfully take place. Secondly, if entry is refused
or not given pursuant to the order, the defendant will be in contempt of
court.

17.009   At the committee stage Lord Irvine of Lairg had observed that "The
execution of an Anton Piller order may . . . be entirely frustrated if the
respondent named in the proceedings or in the order is not actually present
and cannot be reached when the order comes to be served . . .". Section
7(3) of the 1997 Act enables an order to be made against "any person".
The intention was that the court would be empowered by the section to
bring about entry or search of the premises, by making orders directed to
the defendant or to others. Lord Mackay L.C. said at the report stage:[24]

"The main purpose of [the clause] is to dispense with the fiction that
the entry on the premises is with the consent of the owner/respondent
. . . [The clause] will have the effect that in future it is more clearly the
court order which is the basis of the requirement to permit entry, not
the implied consent of the owner. It will no longer be desirable to
imply that the execution of the Anton Piller order is dependent upon
the consent of the owner or a person whom he might have authorised
to give consent on his behalf."

---

[22] If it had been the intention that under the example order given under CPR the practice
would be different from that set out in *Bhimji v Chatwani* [1991] 1 W.L.R. 989 at 997 and
that someone other than the defendant was ordered by the order to give permission for
entry and search, then there should have been a notice at the beginning of the order
explaining this to him, and a different form of penal notice.
[23] See also *Long v Specifier Publications Pty Limited* (1998) 44 N.S.W.L.R. 545 at p. 548 A–B.
[24] *Hansard*, Vol. 576, col. 900, December 19, 1996.

The section gives effect to this intention by authorising the court to make orders which are designed to achieve entry and search regardless of whether consent is in fact forthcoming from the respondent. Thus, *e.g.* the premises in question might be an apartment in a block of flats. The lessee may be away abroad but there are keys with the hall porter who also has the combination number for the burglar alarm. It is feared that the lessee may have also left keys and the combination number with one of his confederates in wrongdoing. Under the section there is jurisdiction to make an order requiring the hall porter to give access to the premises and to deactivate the alarm. In practice, if such an order was to be made, there would have to be amendments to the standard form order which made it crystal clear to the hall porter what he was required to do, and which contained orders addressed to the hall porter setting out those requirements.

Anton Piller relief could be granted against someone against whom the **17.010** claimant did not have a substantive cause of action. Thus, *e.g.* such relief could be granted when there was a right to assistance from a person under the *Norwich Pharmacal* principle, because he had been "mixed up" in wrongdoing whether innocently or not.[25] Alternatively it could be said that as long as there is an existing cause of action against someone an order could be made under s.37(1) of the Supreme Court Act 1981 against a non-party which is ancillary to and for the purpose of prosecution or enforcement of that cause of action.[26]

The section would authorise the making of an order against such a person. The assistance which can be ordered is not limited to obtaining the names of wrongdoers. For example, it can include providing information about what has happened to assets so as to enforce a judgment[27] or assets to which the claimant says he is entitled,[28] or articles which have been made through infringing intellectual property rights.

In using the words "any person", s.7(3) would appear to go further and confer *jurisdiction* to make an order against anyone in respect of any premises in England and Wales. If an applicant sought an order which was in respect of premises owned and occupied by innocent third parties, then in practice this would be very relevant (if not decisive) as to why the order sought should be refused as a matter of discretion.[29]

---

[25] *Mercantile Group (Europe) AG v Aiyela* [1994] Q.B. 366, affirming Hobhouse J. reported at [1993] F.S.R. 745: Mrs Aiyela was said to have information about assets upon which a judgment might be enforced and to have been mixed up in dealings with assets which should have been made available to satisfy the judgment against her husband.

[26] *Yukong Line Ltd v Rendsburg Investments Corporation* [2001] 2 Lloyd's Rep. 113; *TSB Bank International v Chabra* [1992] 1 W.L.R. 231 at 241–242; *Mercantile Group (Europe) AG v Aiyela* [1994] Q.B. 366 at 376D, affirming Hobhouse J. reported at [1993] F.S.R. 745; *C Inc. v L* [2001] 2 Lloyd's Rep. 459 at 474–475, applying *Cardile v LED Builders Pty Ltd* (1999) 198 C.L.R. 380.

[27] *Mercantile Group (Europe) AG v Aiyela* [1994] Q.B. 366.

[28] *Bankers Trust Co. v Shapira* [1980] 1 W.L.R. 1274 at 1280–1281; *Mediterranea Raffineria Siciliana Petroli SpA v Mabanaft*, Court of Appeal (Civ Div) Transcript No.816 of 1978 (December 1, 1978); *Cook Industries v Gallagher* [1979] Ch. 439.

[29] See also *Galaxia Maritime SA v Mineralimport/export* [1982] 1 W.L.R. 539.

17.011   Section 7(3) allows for an order to be made in respect of ". . . premises in England and Wales" and the section does not apply to premises outside England and Wales. The court can grant interlocutory relief requiring a defendant to allow the search of premises abroad,[30] but in practice the court would be most reluctant to make an *ex parte* order requiring a defendant to allow premises abroad to be searched—such an order should usually be sought, if at all, from the local court.

Section 7(3) provides for permission to be given to "any person described in the order . . .". This wording does not require a person to be named in the order or for the order to apply only to specified persons who are capable of being identified at the time of making the order. The person can be described by a form of words and selection of the person concerned may be done after the order has been granted, *e.g.* a solicitor retained for the purpose who is independent of the claimant and of the firm of solicitors acting for him in the action and who has been qualified for a certain length of time. Lord Mackay L.C. said:[31]

> "I understand . . . from [Sir Richard Scott V.-C.] that it is not always the practice that all the persons who are authorised to enter the premises under the order will . . . be named in the order. They will be described in some cases by their function . . . or by reference to the numbers of those who are authorised to enter."

17.012   Section 7(4) and (5) provides what "steps" can be taken on the premises and what assistance may have to be given under the order. The "steps" are to search for something, to inspect it, to take it away for safe keeping, to take copies, photographs or samples of it, or to make or obtain a record. The assistance which can be required is to provide information or "an article described in the order". The Lord Chancellor gave an assurance that the wording was sufficiently wide to allow an order to be made which would enable printouts to be made from a computer or copies to be made on to disks,[32] *e.g.* an order as, *per* para.17 of the example order.

Section 7(5)(a) would also extend to giving information about passwords, which is addressed in para.17 of the example order, and how to obtain electric power for the system, and s.7(4)(a) and (b) enable a computer system to be tested in order to try to retrieve information from it which had been deleted and for a record to be made of the result.

A person could be ordered under s.7(5)(a) to provide electric power so as to enable information to be obtained from a computer, this being incidental to securing that "information". A person could also be restrained from cutting off the electric power. Although electric power is not within the phrase "any information or article", an injunction could be granted as an ancillary order pursuant to s.7(5)(a) because it would operate

---

[30] *Cook v Galliher* [1979] Ch. 439; see Chapter 6, paras 6.006–6.009.
[31] *Hansard*, Vol. 576, col. 899, December 9, 1996.
[32] *Hansard*, Vol. 576, col. 903, December 9, 1996; see also *Gates v Swift* [1982] R.F.C. 339.

in aid of securing that any information on the computer is "provided" as required by the order.[33] An order requiring the delivery-up of keys to the premises would fall within the section because keys are articles.

Section 7 leaves unaffected the right of any person to refuse to do **17.013** anything because of privilege against self-incrimination.

(3) Gagging orders

It may be necessary for an injunction to be granted restraining those served **17.014** with the order or others from informing third parties of the existence of the proceedings or the fact that an order has been made. Paragraph 20 of the example order provides that:

> "Except for the purpose of obtaining legal advice, the Respondent must not directly or indirectly inform anyone of these proceedings or the contents of this Order, or warn anyone that proceedings have been or may be brought against him by the Applicant until 4.30 p.m. on the return date or further order of the court."[34]

This order may be needed so as to give the applicant time to use information obtained through execution of the order so as to secure assets or preserve evidence located elsewhere. It is not a requirement of s.7(1) that the relevant evidence or the particular property to be preserved has to be located on the premises which are to be searched. Thus an order can be made under the section which is to be executed at particular premises in the expectation that as a result further information will become available to the applicant enabling him to preserve evidence or property located elsewhere. An injunction restraining those served with the order from

---

[33] Such an injunction can also be justified as being granted against a defendant under s.37(1) of the Supreme Court Act 1981 ancillary to a substantive right claimed in the action: see generally *Bayer v Winter* [1986] 1 W.L.R. 497. In *Re Oriental Credit* [1988] Ch. 204, Harman J. considered that s.37(1) enabled an injunction to be granted in aid of an order made under a statute (in that case s.561 of the Companies Act 1985) even though it was not in aid of a legal right or protection of an equitable interest—however, this dictum should not be followed: see *Morris v Murjani* [1996] 1 W.L.R. 848 at 852–853.

[34] This is similar to para.6(1) of the standard order provided by the Practice Direction in 1996. In cases involving locating assets and taking steps to freeze them abroad (*e.g. Republic of Haiti v Duvalier* [1990] 1 Q.B. 202) a week for this type of injunction may be very short. The duration depends on what may have to be done whilst secrecy is preserved but should not be longer than is reasonably necessary. Sir Donald Nicholls V.-C. commented in *Universal Thermosensors Ltd v Hibben* [1992] 1 W.L.R. 840 at 860: "In the present case that injunction was expressed to last for a whole week. That is far too long. I suspect something went awry with the drafting of the order in this case." See also *Goldtron Ltd v Most Investment Ltd* [2002] J.L.R. 424 at paras 34 and 35 (requiring the application for a gagging order in support of a post-arbitration award freezing injunction to be drawn specifically to the attention of the court on the *ex parte* application, describing the relief as "exceptional" and requiring "convincing" evidence to justify it. The 14-day gag appears to have been much longer than could reasonably have been justified on the facts of that case).

informing those third parties of the existence of the proceedings or the fact that an order has been made may in certain circumstances be necessary in order to achieve the statutory purpose set out in s.7(1).

The section does not expressly confer on the High Court jurisdiction to make a gagging order. Nevertheless the power to do so is part of and thus inherent in the jurisdiction conferred on the court by s.7(1).[35] This is because the purpose of the gagging order is to preserve evidence or property. The evidence might otherwise be destroyed or the property disposed of or hidden. The gagging order prevents the defendant being alerted to what is afoot. It is a procedural mechanism[36] for achieving the statutory purpose.

17.015   A further basis of jurisdiction can be found in the inherent jurisdiction of the court to ensure that its orders are not rendered futile and ineffective to achieve their purpose. This was the original basis for making Anton Piller orders. Section 7 does not derogate from that jurisdiction. The making of a gagging order is an aspect of the exercise of that jurisdiction.

There can also be jurisdiction to grant a gagging order based on s.37(1) of the Supreme Court Act 1981 in that the injunction is granted against third parties in support of and ancillary to protecting the claimant's substantive claim against the defendant. Thus, *e.g.* in a tracing case or a case in which the claimant is seeking to locate assets on which to enforce a judgment, the injunction is granted in aid of the claimant's substantive right in respect of those assets.

It can also be justified in a case in which the persons served have been mixed up in wrongdoing whether innocently or otherwise as being an order granted under s.37(1) ancillary to obtaining effective assistance from them by way of discovery/information under the *Norwich Pharmacal* principle. For example, the evidence is that a large amount of money has been taken fraudulently. There is reason to believe that part of it has been remitted through a bank in London. The claimant wishes to trace the missing funds and freeze them. An order can be sought against the bank for the purpose of finding out full information[37] about relevant payments, *e.g.* what has been received, from whom and what payments the bank has

---

[35] The jurisdiction to make order for disclosure of assets in support of a Mareva injunction is inherent in s.37(1) of the Supreme Court Act 1981 because it is ancillary to carrying out the Mareva jurisdiction and making it effective (see, *e.g. Bekhor Ltd v Bilton* [1981] Q.B. 923 at 940–942). Likewise the gagging order is ancillary to achieving effective operation of the jurisdiction under s.7 of the Civil Procedure Act 1997.

[36] Parliament legislated in the knowledge that a gagging order was included in the standard form and must have contemplated that this procedure would continue to be used in appropriate cases. See also *Hansard*, Vol. 575, CWH 37, November 20, 1996 (Committee stage), *per* Lord Mackay L.C.: "If one takes the full order this would be a very large section before it were finished. I am anxious to try and keep the statute book reasonably succinct . . .".

[37] *Mercantile Group (Europe) AG v Aiyela* [1994] Q.B. 366 at 374G–H, rejecting the submission that disclosure could only be sought of the identities of those who might be sued. The purpose of the discovery was to trace what had happened to the money: "there would be no point in the plaintiff seeking the information at the trial. By that time the money would be gone . . .", *per* Hoffmann L.J.

made, when, to whom and on whose instructions. But without a gagging order on the bank the purpose of tracing the money would be imperilled, because the bank would be expected to inform its customer of what was happening.[38] In such a case an *ex parte* gagging injunction can be sought against the bank to take effect over the hearing of an application to be made *inter partes* for an order under the *Norwich Pharmacal* principle requiring the bank to disclose the information and for continuation of the gagging order so as to enable the claimant to use the information so as to freeze funds. The gagging order is ancillary to the disclosure order—its purpose is to facilitate successful tracing of the missing money.

17.016 The gagging order in para.6(1) of what was the standard form Anton Piller order under the 1996 Practice Direction restrained both the defendant and "anyone else with knowledge of this order". Those words have been dropped in the example order. Such an order would be an injunction *contra mundum*, whereas the example order is only directed against the respondent. In relation to others with "knowledge of the order", they are alerted to what is the purpose of the court in making the order against the defendant and if such a person were to inform others of the proceedings or the order this could constitute a deliberate interference with the administration of justice and thus constitute a contempt of court.[39]

(4) The requirements to be satisfied for a search order to be granted

17.017 In *Anton Piller KG v Manufacturing Processes Ltd*,[40] Ormrod L.J. specified "three essential pre-conditions" for the making of the order, namely:

(1) there must be "an extremely strong *prima facie* case";

(2) the damage, "potential or actual", must be "very serious" for the applicant;

(3) there must be "clear evidence" that the defendants have in their possession "incriminating documents or things" (which was the

---

[38] The bank may have a legal duty to the customer to use its best endeavours to inform him of the proceedings: *Robertson v Canadian Bank of Commerce* [1994] 1 W.L.R. 1493 at 1499. Gagging orders are an exceptional form of relief and so should only be used where necessary, *e.g.* in cases involving dishonest misappropriation of the claimant's assets: *A Co. v B Co.* [2002] 3 H.K.L.R.D. 111 (in which the court in making the gagging order against the bank contemplated that if the bank was placed in particular difficulties by the gag it could apply to the court for an interim declaration citing *Bank of Scotland v A* [2001] 1 W.L.R. 75. See also paras 2.018–20.019 (bank's obligation of confidentiality).

[39] See Chapter 19, paras 19.028–19.034, below; *Attorney-General v Punch* [2003] 2 W.L.R. 49; *Attorney-General v Times Newspapers* [1992] 1 A.C. 191 at 206–207, 214–215, 224 and 230–232.

[40] [1976] Ch. 55 at 62.

subject-matter sought to be preserved in that case) and that there is a "real possibility"[41] that the defendants may destroy such material before any application *inter partes* can be made.

The Staughton Committee report (para.2.8) added a fourth precondition, namely that "The harm likely to be caused by the execution of the Anton Piller order to the respondent and his business affairs must not be excessive or out of proportion to the legitimate object of the order". In relation to the four preconditions, the Staughton Committee observed (at para.2.9) that:

"If any of these four pre-conditions is absent, the weight of judicial authority should lead to an application for the grant of an Anton Piller order being refused. If each of these pre-conditions appears to be present, an order will not necessarily be justified. The court will still have to weigh in the balance the plaintiff's need for the order against the injustice to the respondent in making the order ex parte without any opportunity for the respondent to be heard. The judge who hears the application for the order should keep in mind that, in as much as audi alteram partem is a requirement of natural justice, the making of an ex parte mandatory order always risks injustice to the absent and unheard respondent. The order should not be made unless it appears that, without the order, the plaintiff will be likely to suffer a greater injustice than that which the court, by making the order, will be inflicting on the respondent (see *Columbia Picture Industries v Robinson* [1987] 1 Ch. at 76 and *Lock International plc v Beswick* [1989] 1 W.L.R. at 1281)."

17.018   Precondition (1) laid down by Ormrod L.J. requires that the applicant make out "an extremely strong *prima facie case*" on the merits of his claim, but it is thought that this should not be viewed as an inflexible requirement. In an intellectual property case the evidence may be clear that the claimant has the rights and that they are being infringed. In a case of alleged dishonesty against a partner the available evidence may be predominantly oral and that is why the documentary material is crucial, the purpose of the order being to preserve evidence which the claimant needs in order to prove the claim. In *Yousif v Salama*,[42] the Court of Appeal granted Anton Piller relief directed to preserving documents on two files and a desk diary which were described by Lord Denning M.R. as "the best possible evidence to prove the plaintiff's case". Although Donaldson L.J. dissented, in the course of his judgment he envisaged the relief as being

---

[41] See also *Booker McConnell v Plasgow* [1985] R.F.C. 425 at 441, *per* Dillon L.J., cited in the Staughton Committee Report at para.2.7; *Channel Islands & International Law Trust Co. Ltd v Scarborough, Warrant Secretaries Ltd and Pett* [1989] J.L.R. 354 and in *Long v Specifier Publications Pty Limited* (1998) 44 N.S.W.L.R. 545 at pp.554–555.

[42] [1980] 1 W.L.R. 1540.

available to preserve evidence even when otherwise the "plaintiff will be left without any evidence to enable him to put forward his claim".[43]

When the purpose of the application for relief is to preserve evidence, this must be of sufficient potential importance to the case to make it necessary in the interests of justice to grant the search order. But it is not a precondition that the evidence is essential or absolutely necessary in the sense that without it there would be a miscarriage of justice.[44] The Staughton Committee report (para.2.5) contrasted precondition (1) as stated by Ormrod L.J. with *suspicion* that there may be a cause of action, which "should not be enough".

It has been pointed out that Anton Piller relief may make serious inroads into what are regarded as ordinary civil liberties,[45] such as the right of a defendant to be heard in his own defence before an order is made against him,[46] the right to be fully protected against unjustified and arbitrary searches and seizures,[47] and the right to privacy in one's own home.[48] Although there are cases in which it is appropriate that the relief should be granted because of the risk that the interests of justice would otherwise be defeated, the possible alternatives to granting the relief and the extent of the risk if it is not granted, must be considered on each application. The principle is that interlocutory relief should be the minimum necessary to achieve justice.[49] This is particularly important in, but is not confined to, cases where there is a strong risk of harm, against which the possibility of an eventual award of damages under the cross-undertaking is unlikely to be an adequate safeguard.

In *Lock International plc v Beswick*, Anton Piller relief had been granted **17.019** to a former employer of the defendant who had gone into competition with him. The order had been made ostensibly for the purpose of protecting trade secrets and other information which was said to be confidential to the employer.[50] Hoffmann J. observed that a lack of particularity in the applicant's evidence about the precise nature of the trade secrets sought to be protected is often "a symptom of an attempt to prevent the employees from making legitimate use of the knowledge and skills gained in the plaintiffs service". He went on to say:[51]

---

[43] *ibid.* at 1543.
[44] *Shoba v Officer Commanding, Temporary Police Camp, Wagendrift Dam* [1995] (4) S.A. 1 at 15–16, disapproving of the more stringent test which had been adopted in *Ex p. Matshini* [1986] (3) S.A. 605.
[45] *Lock International plc v Beswick* [1989] 1 W.L.R. 1268 at 1279.
[46] *Jeffrey Rogers Knitwear Productions Ltd v Vinola (Knitwear) Manufacturing Co.* [1985] F.S.R. 184 at 187; *Columbia Pictures Inc. v Robinson* [1987] Ch. 37 at 73–74.
[47] *Lock International plc v Beswick*, above.
[48] *Columbia Pictures Inc v Robinson*, above, at 73. The family distress and humiliation which would result from a search of a home may result in any search order excluding domestic premises (see also *Petromar Energy Resources Pte Ltd v Glencore AG* [1999] 2 S.L.R. 609 at para.16, where no Anton Piller order should have been made in respect of the manager's home).
[49] *Frigo v Culhaci* [1998] N.S.W.S.C. 393, (NSW Court of Appeal); *Long v Specifier Publications Pty Limited* (1998) 44 N.S.W.L.R. 545 at 548 C.
[50] See generally *Faccenda Chicken Ltd v Fowler* [1987] Ch. 117; *Laming Linde Ltd v Kerr* [1991] 1 W.L.R. 251 at 259.
[51] [1989] 1 W.L.R. 1268 at p 1281; See also *Overholt v Overholt* [1999] 2 H.K.L.R.D. 445.

"Even in cases in which the plaintiff has strong evidence that an employee has taken what is undoubtedly specific confidential information, such as a list of customers, the court must employ a graduated response. To borrow a useful concept from the jurisprudence of the European Community, there must be *proportionality* between the perceived threat to the plaintiff's rights and the remedy granted. The fact that there is overwhelming evidence that the defendant has behaved wrongfully in his commercial relationships does not necessarily justify an *Anton Piller* order. People whose commercial morality allows them to take a list of the customers with whom they were in contact while employed will not necessarily disobey an order of the court requiring them to deliver it up. Not everyone who is misusing confidential information will destroy documents in the face of a court order requiring him to preserve them.

In many cases it will therefore be sufficient to make an order for delivery up of the documents to the claimant's solicitor for copying and then return to the defendant, or an order that the defendant do preserve documents pending further order. The more intrusive orders allowing searches of premises or vehicles require a careful balancing of, on the one hand, the purpose of the order, and, on the other hand, violation of the privacy of a defendant who has had no opportunity to put his side of the case. It is not merely that the defendant may be innocent. The making of an intrusive order *ex parte* even against a guilty defendant is contrary to normal principles of justice and can only be done when there is a paramount need to prevent a denial of justice to the claimant. An order will not be made against persons of good standing who are unlikely to disobey an order of the court.[52] The absolute extremity of the court's powers is to permit a search of a defendant's dwelling house, with the humiliation and family distress which that frequently involves."

17.020   The Staughton Committee's precondition (4) followed this reasoning.[53] The committee mentioned that this "pre-condition is particularly relevant where the seizure of trading stock or the perusal by the plaintiff of

---

[52] *Randolph M. Fields v Watts* (1985) 129 S.J. 67 (a case concerning barristers and barristers' clerks); *Booker McConnell plc v Plasgow* [1985] R.F.C. 425 at 438–439, in relation to the second and third defendants who were "highly reputable public companies"; *Naf Naf SA v Dickens (London) Ltd* [1993] F.S.R. 424 (filed accounts, although out of date, showed substantial assets, and the business was conducted from substantial premises); *Channel Islands & International Law Trust Co. Ltd v Scarborough, Warrant Secretaries Ltd and Pett* [1989] J.L.R. 354 (order refused against professional men). The risk of disobedience may be inferred from clear evidence of dishonesty, see *Dunlop Holdings Ltd v Staravia Ltd* [1982] Com. L.R. 3; *Yousif v Salama* [1980] W.L.R. 1540; and *Capitanescu v Universal Weld Overlays Inc.* [1997] 3 W.W.R. 714 (individual plaintiffs had given an undertaking, so the fact that the corporate plaintiff was a shell company was not material). See Chapter 12, para. 12.040 above for the corresponding position in relation to establishing a real risk of dissipation of assets on an application for Mareva relief.

[53] See also: *Araghchinchi v Araghchinchi* [1997] 2 F.L.R. 142; *Interest Research Bureau Pty v Interest Recount Pty Ltd* (1997) 38 I.P.R. 468 at 473, Supreme Court of Western Australia.

confidential commercial documents will be the effect of execution of the order . . .".[54]

In the case of an *ex parte* Mareva injunction, it is open to the defendant or a third party to apply to discharge or vary the order on short notice or even, in cases of absolute urgency, *ex parte*.[55] Although this is also true of Anton Piller relief, by its nature it is a mandatory order which, unless stayed by the court, must be acted upon within hours, after a short period to allow the defendant to obtain legal advice or to apply immediately to the judge to discharge or stay the order,[56] and the defendant will not have the opportunity to assemble evidence. Even if an urgent application were to be made for discharge of the order or a stay, experience shows that the court is most reluctant to alter its order, at least not without very good reason supported by sworn evidence. Once the order had been acted upon, the claimant's representatives will have had access to the premises in question and will have at least commenced a search. This itself exposes the defendant to stigma, and loss of reputation. Search orders unleash consequences which are irreversible and of great importance to everyone involved. It may at a stroke destroy the defendant's business and replace it with a hope of compensation available only at the end of protracted litigation.

These considerations show that at the *ex parte* stage the applicant must present the application with scrupulous fairness (see Chapter 9). All material facts must be disclosed. The applicant must say what investigations have been made, and with what results; whether or not in the absence of the search order the proposed subject-matter of the order would be done away with,[57] even in the face of an injunction restraining the defendant from so acting; and whether the claimant is likely to be good for damages if these are awarded in due course under the undertaking in damages.[58] The court should not make the order unless satisfied by clear evidence that the interests of justice require that the order be made and implemented before the defendant is afforded a proper opportunity to present his side of the case.[59] For these reasons the jurisdiction is to be regarded as ". . . an extreme remedy for extreme cases."[60]

---

[54] Staughton Committee Report, para.2.8. When an order enabled a plaintiff to conduct a search of all the documents of a competitor, this was described as "most unsatisfactory", per Sir Donald Nicholls V.-C. in *Universal Thermosensors Ltd v Hibben* [1992] 1 W.L.R. 840 at 860–861.

[55] *London City Agency (JCD) Ltd v Lee* [1970] Ch. 597.

[56] Paragraph 10 of the example order.

[57] *Jeffrey Rogers Ltd v Vinola (Knitwear) Manufacturing Co.* [1985] F.S.R. 184; *Columbia Pictures Inc v Robinson* [1987] Ch. 37 at 77–81.

[58] *Manor Electronics v Dickson* [1988] R.F.C. 618; *Jeffrey Rogers Ltd v Vinola (Knitwear) Manufacturing Co.* [1985] F.S.R. 184; *Intercontex v Schmidt* [1988] F.S.R. 575; *Vapormatic Co. v Sparex Ltd* [1976] 1 W.L.R. 939 at 940–941 (where a bond was provided in support of the undertaking in damages).

[59] *Columbia Pictures Inc. v Robinson* [1987] Ch. 37 at 76. Because of the irreversible nature of the relief it has been suggested that the procedure should involve the appointment of an *amicus curiae* to help the judge vet the application: "Anton Piller Orders Revisited" [2000] J.B.L. 387. But this would add delay and further expense to what is already an expensive procedure, making it less accessible to the deserving applicant, and would duplicate the examining function which should normally be capable of being performed by the judge.

[60] *Busby v Thorn EMI Video Programmes Ltd* [1984] 1 N.Z.L.R. 461 at p.467, per Cooke J.

(5) Matrimonial proceedings and Anton Piller relief

17.021 A search order may be made in matrimonial proceedings,[61] but almost invariably as a measure of last resort, after other orders have failed (see Staughton Committee Report, para.1.9). In *Emanuel v Emanuel*,[62] relief was granted in proceedings for ancillary relief brought by a wife following a divorce, when it had been clearly shown that the husband was ready to flout the authority of the court and mislead the court if he considered it in his interests to do so. He had acted in breach of previous court orders, had been committed to prison for six weeks for contempt and there was prima facie evidence that he had previously lied to the court on two occasions. In the course of his judgment Wood J. referred to the relief as being granted "only very rarely". In matrimonial proceedings "family feelings are well known to be very strong at times, and in a family environment suspicion can grow out of all reason",[63] and this may colour the evidence presented to the court, particularly when spouses or former spouses are in contention over financial provision. Strong evidence in support of the *ex parte* application is insisted upon in the context of matrimonial proceedings[64] and it is "a rare weapon for use only in extreme or exceptional cases",[65] and then only when the perceived threat to the applicant's rights is sufficiently grave to justify the relief and its likely consequences.[66]

(6) Naming defendants

17.022 A claimant may find himself confronted with a number of persons who are infringing his rights but whose identities are unknown to him. In *EMI Records Ltd v Kudhail*,[67] the plaintiffs wished to obtain relief against street traders who were dealing in pirated cassette tapes which had been recorded illegally and which were being sold to the public under the name "Oak

---

[61] See also *K v K* (1982) 13 Fam. Law 46; *Kepa v Kepa* (1982) 4 F.L.R. 515.

[62] [1982] 1 W.L.R. 669.

[63] *Yousif v Salama* [1980] 1 W.L.R. 1541 at 1543, *per* Donaldson L.J. (in his dissenting judgment).

[64] *Francis v Francis*, Court of Appeal (Civ Div) Transcript No.197 of 1986.

[65] *Burgess v Burgess* [1996] 2 F.L.R. 34 at 41. See also *Overholt v Overholt* [1999] 2 H.K.L.R.D. 445.

[66] *Araghchinchi v Araghchinchi* [1997] 2 F.L.R. 142, where relief was refused because if the relevant information was suppressed the court could still proceed satisfactorily by drawing adverse inferences against the relevant party. But contrast the facts in *Hellyer v Hellyer* [1996] 2 F.L.R. 579 at 581, where the husband had been hiding assets over a number of years.

[67] [1985] F.S.R. 36.

Records". In Canada, the courts have permitted proceedings to be brought against unnamed defendants (commonly called "John Doe") and have granted relief in those proceedings.[68] In England there used to be a firmly established rule of practice that, save in accordance with special provisions in the rules of court,[69] the defendants must be named in the proceedings, and that even a description of them would not suffice.[70] Nevertheless, the former RSC Ord. 15, r.12 allowed proceedings to be brought against named defendants who represent a class consisting of numerous persons who "have the same interest in any proceedings". In cases falling within the rule the plaintiff was not required to name members of the class other than those who were the representative defendants, and an injunction could be granted against the whole class. Thus in *EMI Records Ltd v Kudhail* injunctive relief was granted by the Court of Appeal against the persons who sold the pirated cassettes,[71] and Anton Piller relief was also granted against certain named individuals.[72]

Under CPR the previous rule of practice has gone. It is open to the court to grant relief, including an injunction, against persons who are only described in the claim form and the order.[73] The description must be sufficiently clear to identify those included and those excluded.

(7) Duty to the court of legal advisers of the applicant

The applicant and his representatives must present all aspects of the application with scrupulous fairness. This includes disclosure of all material facts, and fair presentation of the draft order itself and all circumstances material to whether it should be made.[74] **17.023**

In *Memory v Sidhu (No.2)*[75] the applicant obtained both a search order and a worldwide freezing order. The defendant sought to discharge by

---

[68] See G. Hayhurst, "Ex Parte Anton Piller Orders with John Doe Defendants" [1987] 9 E.I.P.R. 257.
[69] RSC Ord. 113 permits summary proceedings for the possession of land against unnamed defendants.
[70] *Friern Barnet Urban District Council v Adams* [1927] 2 Ch. 25; *Re Wykeham Terrace* [1970] Ch. 204 at 213–214.
[71] Applying *Kennaway v Thompson* [1981] Q.B. 88. See also *M. Michaels (Furriers) Ltd v Askew, The Times*, June 25, 1983.
[72] The headnote at [1985] F.S.R. 36 is misleading on this point. However, in principle it is considered that Anton Piller relief could be granted against the whole class in respect of particular premises.
[73] *Bloomsbury Publishing Group Ltd v News Group Newspapers Ltd* [2003] 1 W.L.R. 1633(publisher of a Harry Potter book obtained a mandatory injunction against the persons who had offered the book to certain newspapers); *Hampshire Waste Services Ltd v Persons as described* [2003] EWHC 1738, ChD.
[74] *Memory v Sidhu (No.2)* [2000] 1 W.L.R. 1443; *Budget Shop Ltd v Bug.Com Ltd* [2001] F.S.R. 383 at [48]; *Re S (A Child) (Family Division: Without Notice Orders)* [2001] 1 All E.R. 362.
[75] [2000] 1 W.L.R. 1443.

orders on the ground that counsel misled the judge by telling him that the draft freezing order was in the form of the standard form provided for under the 1996 Practice Direction. In fact the disclosure order in respect of the defendant's assets provided that if the defendant claimed to be entitled to the privilege against self-incrimination, he still had to provide it to the supervising solicitor ". . . who will hold such information to the order of the court". The idea was that the supervising solicitor would hold the information pending a decision whether it should be returned to the defendant. The problem with this was that once the defendant had been compelled to provide this information there could be no guarantee that the material would not reach the hands of a prosecutor and so the order itself purported to override the privilege against self-incrimination to which the defendant might be entitled. The Court of Appeal had already criticised this form of order as inadequate to safeguard the privilege.[76] The misrepresentation was a serious breach of the duty to present the application fairly, but in the circumstances did not lead to discharge of the order.

In *Booker McConnell plc v Plasgow*,[77] Dillon L.J. observed that there was a responsibility on the plaintiff's advisers to consider seriously whether it is justifiable to seek an Anton Piller order against the particular defendant, and if so the width of the order to be sought. This observation was criticised by Scott J. in *Columbia Pictures Inc. v Robinson*,[78] on the ground that the responsibility for deciding what order is to be made (if any) lies with the judge and not with the legal advisers to the plaintiff.[79]

17.024   If the applicant and its representatives are to discharge the duty of fair presentation they must consider whether it is justifiable to apply for a search order and what are the points for and against the application, and the granting of the proposed order. This will include considering the facts and the law on the privilege against self-incrimination when this may be relevant.

Whilst lawyers act on their instructions, these cannot affect the discharge of their duties to the court.

The advocate is expected to use the current[80] example order as the starting point for drafting the proposed order, not to misrepresent it to the judge,[81] to draw the salient features of the draft to the attention of the judge hearing the *ex parte* application, to draw to the judge's attention any relevant points based on the practice of the court, and to give disclosure of all facts and circumstances relevant to the judge's assessment of whether to grant the application and if so what should be the terms of the order. These include those material to:

(1) the content of undertakings;

---

[76] *Den Norske Bank ASA v Antonatos* [1999] Q.B. 271 at 290B.
[77] [1985] R.F.C. 425.
[78] [1987] Ch. 37 at 78 and 82.
[79] [1987] Ch. 37 at 82.
[80] *Gadget Shop Ltd v Bug.Com Ltd* [2001] F.S.R. 383 at [97–101].
[81] *Memory v Sidhu (No.2)* [2000] 1 W.L.R. 1443.

(2) the standing and experience of the solicitor who is to execute the order (*e.g.* whether he is a partner in the firm);[82]

(3) the standing and experience of the proposed supervising solicitors.[83] The Practice Direction provides:

> "7.2 The Supervising Solicitor must be experienced in the operation of search orders. A Supervising Solicitor may be contacted either through the Law Society or, for the London area, through the London Solicitors Litigation Association.[84]
>
> 7.3 Evidence:
>
> (1) the affidavit must state the name, firm and its address, and experience of the Supervising Solicitor . . .".

(4) the address at which the search is to be carried out, whether it is private or business,[85] and all circumstances relevant to whether a search order for that address ought to be made;

(5) what information is to be provided to the Supervising Solicitor to help him identify items within the scope of the order;[86]

(6) the arrangements to be made for listing and preserving items to be removed from the premises to be searched;

(7) whether a woman is likely to be at the premises which are to be, or may be searched, pursuant to the order,[87] and may be the person who has to deal with the Supervising Solicitor and the search party;

(8) service of the order or its execution.

(7) An order for disclosure of names and addresses and other information

(i) *The Norwich Pharmacal principle*

This principle is discussed in Chapter 22, paras 22.048–22.050 below. It **17.025** applies whether or not the defendant is a wrongdoer provided that there is evidence that he has become "mixed up" in wrongdoing, or participated or

---

[82] *Gadget Shop Ltd v Bug.Com Ltd* [2001] F.S.R. 383 at [87–89].

[83] *Gadget Shop Ltd v Bug.Com Ltd* [2001] F.S.R. 383 at [109].

[84] This is an association of solicitors specialising in litigation, which can be contacted through The Law Society. In *Gadget Shop Ltd v Bug.Com Ltd* the supervising solicitors had no experience of supervising the execution of search orders and the position was misrepresented to the judge. This was one of the factors which led to the order being set aside *inter partes*.

[85] Practice Direction, para.7.3(1).

[86] *Gadget Shop Ltd v Bug. Com Ltd* [2001] F.S.R. 383 at [102–104].

[87] *Gadget Shop Ltd v Bug. Com Ltd* [2001] F.S.R. 383 at [83–86].

became involved in it. In *Norwich Pharmacal v Customs & Excise*,[88] the particular information which was ordered to be disclosed was the names and addresses of the persons who were infringing the patent. As stated by Lord Reid in that case,[89] the principle obliged the Customs and Excise Commissioners to give "full information and disclosing the identity of the wrongdoers" to the person who has been wronged. Whether an order is to be made is discretionary. But the jurisdiction to order disclosure is not limited to ordering identification of wrongdoers.[90] Under the principle an order may be made for disclosure of information in which the claimant has a legitimate interest, provided that the contemplated disclosure does not offend against the "mere witness" rule, namely it is not for the purpose of obtaining pre-trial discovery of what a witness would say if called at the trial, whether as a voluntary witness or under a witness summons.

(ii) Names of customers or suppliers

17.026 A question which may arise, particularly in intellectual property cases, is whether the defendant should be ordered to disclose documents or answer interrogatories relating to the names and addresses of his customers. Such information could result in considerable damage to the defendant's business if customers learn of the claimant's claim, or if the claimant takes any steps in relation to the customers. In these circumstances, even in the context of the usual disclosure procedures of the court, disclosure of the names and addresses of customers involves an exercise of discretion by the court. The court would take into account on the one hand the likely prejudice to the defendant by way of damage to his business, and on the other hand whether the discovery is material for the purpose of enabling the claimant to prove his claim, and not merely the quantum of his damages, which can be assessed in a subsequent inquiry following the trial.[91] It is well established that the court has jurisdiction to require disclosure of names and addresses of customers and other information to enable the claimant to bring proceedings or take other action against the customers concerned.[92] This can be done by interlocutory order.[93] But because the making of such an order is particularly liable to cause damage to a defendant, the jurisdiction to grant relief on an application made without notice should be exercised with great caution, particularly in

---

[88] [1974] A.C. 133.
[89] *ibid.*, at 1758–C.
[90] *Mercantile Group (Europe) AG v Aiyela* [1994] Q.B. 366 at 374G.
[91] *Carver v Pinto Leite* (1871) 7 L.R. Ch. App. 90; *Moore v Craven* (1871) 7 L.R. Ch. App. 94 (note).
[92] *Norwich Pharmacal Co. v Customs and Excise Commissioners* [1974] A.C. 133; *British Steel v Granada* [1981] A.C. 1096; *Lagenes Ltd v It's At (UK) Ltd* [1991] F.S.R. 492 at 505; *CHC Software Care Ltd v Hopkins & Wood* [1993] F.S.R. 241 at 250; *Jade Engineering (Coventry) Ltd v Antiference Window Systems Ltd* [1996] F.S.R. 461.
[93] *RCA Corporation v Reddingtons Rare Records* [1974] 1 W.L.R. 1445; *Loose v Williamson* [1978] 1 W.L.R. 639.

circumstances when the defendant may suffer substantial prejudice in the conduct of his business as a result. In *Sega Enterprises Ltd v Alca Electronics*,[94] an order for disclosure had been granted *ex parte* in conjunction with Anton Piller relief. The defendants hired out video games to public houses, and there was "a serious issue to be tried with regard to copyright".[95] The Court of Appeal held that the order should be discharged. The discovery was not necessary for determining the plaintiff's claim (as opposed to the quantum of damages if the plaintiff succeeded at trial), and in the circumstances of the case it could not be said that there was any serious risk of prejudice to the plaintiff if the discovery was not ordered pending the outcome of the trial on liability. The public houses were apparently responsible third parties, and if the plaintiff succeeded at trial, discovery could be ordered for the purposes of quantifying the damages against the defendant. (See also *Baldock v Addison*[96] on what is now disclosure being limited to the issue of liability when there is a split trial.)

On the other hand, the balance of convenience may be such that immediate disclosure should be ordered *ex parte*. In particular this may be the case if, in the absence of an order made *ex parte*, the defendant may destroy or hide the information, or if the claimant's right can be adequately safeguarded only if he is able to take immediate steps against the third parties concerned, *e.g.* because on the evidence the customers are likely themselves to be "irresponsible wrongdoers who will seek to evade their responsibilities or conceal their activities".[97] But such relief should not be granted simply as part and parcel of a search order without investigation of the circumstances of the case, and the court's "coming to the conclusion that it is necessary for the long-term protection of the [claimant] that such a draconian course should be taken".

17.027 If relief without notice is sought by way of disclosure order or by way of a search order which will have the effect of providing to the claimant names and addresses of customers, and the court is minded to grant the relief, it may be appropriate to require the claimant to furnish an undertaking to the court not to use or act upon the information without the leave of the court.

The same principles apply whenever an applicant seeks disclosure, under *ex parte* relief, of information which will enable him to proceed against third parties in circumstances where, as a result, substantial damage or prejudice maybe unfairly caused to the defendant. In the case of *suppliers* of alleged infringing articles to the defendant, different considerations arise than those applicable to customers. It is one matter to allow a defendant to continue to deal with its customers and not to ruin the goodwill of his business pending trial; it is another matter whether or not the claimant

---

[94] [1982] F.S.R. 516.
[95] *ibid.*, at 521, *per* Lawton J.
[96] [1995] 1 W.L.R. 158.
[97] [1982] F.S.R. 516 at 525, *per* Templeman L.J.

should be informed of the sources of the articles in question so that he can bring proceedings or take other steps against persons directly responsible for putting the articles into circulation.[98] Relief is often granted for this purpose.[99]

(iii) The example order

17.028   The provisions of para.18 of the example order relate to disclosure of information about suppliers, customers and supplies, including offers made by suppliers and to customers. The judge on the without notice application should be asked specifically to consider on the particular facts whether relief should be granted in this form. This is because of the potential for irreversible damage to be caused to the defendant by this form of order. It may well be that if an order is to be made it should go no further than to require the information to be given to the supervising solicitor pending further order of the court to be made on an application made *inter partes*.

(iv) Risk of violence to the defendant

17.029   In *The Coca Cola Company v Gilbey*,[1] the defendant contended that an order requiring him to give information about the activities of third parties would expose him to the risk of violence from those individuals, and asked for the order made as part of Anton Piller relief to be set aside because of this risk. The court declined as a matter of discretion to set aside the order. Simon Brown L.J. considered that save "just possibly, in the very most exceptional circumstances . . . the court ought never to accede to such a submission . . .". The reason is the public interest in the upholding of the rule of law. The risk of violent repercussions might be relevant in the context of mitigating a contempt of court, but the court is bound to approach such a submission with caution and to have regard that the public interest lies in not giving in to violence.[2]

(8) Privilege against self-incrimination

(i) Introduction—relevance of the privilege

17.030   Privilege against self-incrimination is relevant to the the decision whether to make any mandatory order against a person or company requiring that person to furnish documents or information under pain of a penalty for

---

[98] *Jade Engineering (Coventry) Ltd v Antiference Window Systems Lid* [1996] F.S.R. 461.
[99] *Rank Film Ltd v Video Information Centre* [1982] A.C. 380 at 444, *per* Lord Fraser; *EMI Ltd v Sarwar* [1977] F.S.R. 146; *Golf Lynx v Golf Scene* (1984) 59 A.L.R. 343, Supreme Court of South Australia, where an order was made in respect of suppliers, after considering *Sega Enterprises Ltd v Alca Electronics* [1982] F.S.R. 516.
[1] [1996] F.S.R. 23; see also *Levi Strauss & Co. v Barclays Trading Corporation Inc.* [1993] F.S.R. 179 (declining to limit use of information disclosed pursuant to an undertaking).
[2] *R. v Montgomery* [1995] 2 All E.R. 28 at 33h–j.

non-compliance when there is a real risk of self-incrimination. It is therefore of potentially very great relevance to search orders or mandatory orders made ancillary to freezing injunctions or mandatory orders designed to obtain information. It is also the background against which an application to stay civil proceedings may be made on the grounds that there are concurrent criminal proceedings concerning the same subject-matter.

(ii) The privilege under statute and at common law—its content and limits

Under s.14(1) of the Civil Evidence Act 1968 it is provided that: **17.031**

"PRIVILEGE AGAINST INCRIMINATION OF SELF OR SPOUSE

14.—(1) The right of a person in any legal proceedings other than criminal proceedings to refuse to answer any question or produce any document or thing if to do so would tend to expose that person to proceedings for an offence or for the recovery of a penalty—

(a) shall apply only as regards criminal offences under the law of any part of the United Kingdom and penalties provided for by such law; and

(b) shall include a like right to refuse to answer any question or produce any document or thing if to do so would tend to expose the husband or wife of that person to proceedings for any such criminal offence or for the recovery of any such penalty."

It is based on the privilege available at common law,[3] and codifies what has been described as one of the "basic freedoms secured by English law . . .".[4]

It is different from the protection given by Art.6 of the European Convention on Human Rights. That Article applies to compelling the defendant to make statements himself which go into evidence, but not to requiring him to furnish documents or other material which already exist and which have not been created by the defendant as a result of the compulsion.[5] The Article does not apply to non-judicial investigations[6] but it forbids the use of admissions obtained in such investigations in subsequent criminal proceedings.[7]

The privilege at common law and under s.14(1) of the Civil Evidence **17.032** Act 1968 is available to a person compelled on pain of punishment to provide information,[8] or to disclose documents,[9] or to produce "any . . .

---

[3] *Re Westinghouse Uranium Contract* [1978] A.C. 547 at 637, *per Lord* Diplock.
[4] *Hamilton v Naviede (Re: Arrows (No.4))* [1995] 2 A.C. 75.
[5] *R. v Kearns* [2002] 1 W.L.R. 2815 at [53(4)].
[6] *R. v Hertfordshire County Council Ex p. Green* [2000] 2 A.C. 412 at 422.
[7] *Saunders v United Kingdom* (1996) 23 E.H.R.R. 313.
[8] *Sociedade Nacionale de Combustiveis de Angola UEE v Lundqvist* [1991] 2 Q.B. 310.
[9] *Rank Film Ltd v Video Information Centre* [1982] A.C. 380 at 441–444; *Spokes v Grosvenor Hotel Company* [1897] 2 Q.B. 124 (objection can be made to producing documents on discovery which may tend to incriminate the defendant).

thing" if, in the words of s.14(1) "to do so would tend to expose that person to proceedings for an offence or for the recovery of a penalty". It includes an order compelling that person to permit the claimant to enter the defendant's premises to search for and seize incriminating documents:[10] ". . . if a man is entitled to refuse to produce documents, it would be strange if the law permitted an order to be made which forced him to admit others to his house for the purpose of seizing those documents".[11]

The privilege does not apply to service of a defence because that is not compelled on pain of punishment; the defendant can let judgment go against him by default.[12]

In *Istel (A. T. & T.) Ltd v Tully*, Lord Templeman said[13] that the privilege against self-incrimination can be justified on two grounds only, first, that it discourages ill-treatment of a suspect and, secondly, that it discourages the production of dubious confessions. He observed that it is difficult to see any reason why, in civil proceedings, the privilege should be exercisable to enable a litigant to refuse to disclose relevant documents.

17.033   Parliament has intervened in this area to produce a number of exceptions to the application of the privilege. Privilege remains in place, however, and may be invoked in cases outside the statutory exceptions. Of particular practical importance is that it is available in civil proceedings where there is a real possibility of a prosecution in England for conspiracy to defraud: *Sociedade Nacionale de Combustiveis de Angola UEE v Lundqvist*.[14]

In England, the privilege is available to companies: *Triplex Safety Glass Co. Ltd v Lancegauge Safety Glass (1934) Ltd*.[15] In Australia, the courts have held that the privilege is not available to companies; the rationale for the privilege does not apply to them.[16]

The privilege relates to self-incrimination, must be claimed personally (*Downie v Coe, The Times*, November 28, 1997), and does not extend to the incrimination of others, except for a spouse.[17]

17.034   The section enables a party to claim privilege in respect of documents or information which could be used to ground or forward proceedings for contempt of court, including contempt committed in the proceedings in which the disclosure is sought to be compelled.[18] The privilege is not

---

[10] *Tate Access Floors Inc. v Boswell* [1991] Ch. 512 at 529–530.

[11] *Tate Access Floors Inc. v Boswell* [1991] Ch. 512 at 530C.

[12] *V v C* [2001] EWCA Civ 1509.

[13] [1993] A.C. 45 at 53.

[14] [1991] 2 QB 310.

[15] [1939] 2 K.B. 395; *Phelby v Paier* [2003] 2 H.K.L.R.D. 323.

[16] *Environment Protection Authority v Caltex Refining Co. Ltd* (1993) 178 C.L.R. 477, High Court of Australia (privilege against self-incrimination); *Trade Practices Commission v Abbco Ice Works Pty Ltd* (1994) 123 A.L.R. 603 (privilege in relation to exposure to a penalty).

[17] *British Steel Corporation v Granada Television* [1981] A.C. 1096 at 1106; and see *Sociedade Nacionale de Combustiveis de Angola UEE v Lundqvist* [1991] 2 Q.B. 310 at 336 (a company has no privilege not to incriminate its directors, but the directors can invoke the privilege for the company in respect of company documents).

[18] *Memory Corporation v Sidhu* [2000] Ch. 645; *Cobra Golf Inc. v Rata* [1998] Ch. 109; *Bhimji v Chatwani (No.2)* [1992] 1 W.L.R. 1158, not following *Garvin v Domus Publishing Ltd* [1989] Ch. 335. See also *Exagym Pty Ltd v Professional Gymnasium Equipment Pty Ltd (No.2)* [1994] 2 Qd R. 129 (Queensland).

limited by a principle which would prevent a person taking advantage of his own dishonesty or wrongdoing.[19]

For privilege to apply, the risk of incrimination must be real and not remote or insubstantial, and it must be established objectively: *Sociedade Nacionale de Combustiveis de Angola UEE v Lundqvist*, above. Once that risk has been established, "great latitude" should be allowed to the witness to judge for himself the likely effect of a particular question: *R. v Boyes*.[20] The privilege does not, however, apply when the witness is already at risk and the risk would not be increased if he were required to give the information or documents, or comply with what is sought.[21] Just because a defendant has made a statement to the police or someone else that he committed the offence does not remove the risk of self-incrimination from compelling the defendant to repeat that admission on oath in the presence of a judge and his own lawyers.[22] It would make a potentially retractable admission impossible to retract.

Whether the witness is acting is good faith in claiming the privilege is not a relevant consideration. If objectively he has the right it does not matter that he has mixed motives for asserting it or even that he is acting mala fide.[23]

The fact that if there were a prosecution the answers might be excluded **17.035** by the court from being given in evidence is not directly relevant to whether the privilege can be claimed. The relevant risk includes that of exposing a person to prosecution; if he is exposed to greater risk of prosecution, this suffices to justify the claim.[24] It applies to anything that a prosecutor might later deploy against that person, or find useful. This includes information or material which is not itself an admission but which may set in train a process which may lead to incrimination or which may lead to the discovery of evidence which is incriminating.[25] The privilege applies to charges of criminal offences in England and Wales only.[26] Where a voluntary confession is obtained this can be adduced in evidence in a criminal prosecution.

---

[19] *Bishopsgate Investment Management Ltd v Maxwell* [1993] Ch. 1 at 37–38; *Memory Corporation v Sidhu* [2000] Ch. 645 at 659–660.
[20] (1861) 1 B. & S. 311 at 330. The privilege should be taken on a question by question basis and the fact that the witness is taking the privilege on legal advice does not affect the court's function of adjudicating on whether the witness's claim in relation to that question is justified: *R. (CPS) v Bolton Magistrates' Court* [2004] 1 W.L.R. 835 at [25–26].
[21] *Sociedade Nationals de Combustiveis de Angola UEE v Lundqvist*, [1991] 2 Q.B. 310 at 324; *Marcel v Commissioner of Police of the Metropolis* [1992] Ch. 225 at 257.
[22] *Den Norske Bank ASA v Antonatos* [1999] Q.B. 271 at 289B–F; *V v C* [2001] EWCA Civ 1509.
[23] *Den Norske Bank ASA v Antonatos* [1999] Q.B. 271 at 289F–H.
[24] *Renworth Ltd v Stephansen* [1996] 3 All E.R. 244; *Den Norske Bank ASA v Antonatos* [1999] Q.B. 271 at 289A–B.
[25] *Rank Film Ltd v Video Information Centre* [1982] A.C. 380 at 443; see also *Vasil v National Australia Bank* [1999] N.S.W.C.A. 161 at para.37 citing *Sorby v The Commonwealth* (1983) 152 C.L.R. 281 at 294–295 and 310.
[26] *Arab Monetary Fund v Hashim* [1989] 1 W.L.R. 565; *Brannigan v Davison* [1997] A.C. 238; *Crédit Suisse Fides Trust v Cuoghi* [1998] Q.B. 818.

Where the prosecuting authorities have given a binding undertaking not to use the information or documents resulting from compliance with an order for the purposes of a prosecution, then the risk of self-incrimination has been removed, and the claim to privilege will not be upheld.[27] Such an undertaking should not be limited to use of the disclosure made, but should extend to any evidence or information obtained as a direct result of the disclosure.[28] Even if the confession is involuntary and so is inadmissible in criminal proceedings the prosecutor is free to use it as a source of information from which to obtain other evidence which is admissible; in English law there is no doctrine of excluding evidence which is the fruit of the poisonous tree. It is for this reason that the undertaking by the prosecuting authority must be wide enough to prevent derivative use if it is to be effective as removing the risk of self-incrimination.[29] The factual basis for the privilege is not removed by granting injunctions designed to prevent the prosecution from obtaining or using material sought by the claimant.[30]

17.036　In a case in which there is a proprietary or tracing claim, the privilege can be invoked in respect of an order for disclosure of documents or information about what has happened to the assets.[31] It is not defeated by the argument that if the claimant is correct in the action the documents relate to assets which are held on constructive trust for him.[32] However, a search order can be made to enable a claimant to search for and preserve his own property and the privilege will have no application to such an order. The privilege applies to the defendant's own documents or property, not stolen documents or property.[33] Also, prior to CPR, the implied undertaking that discovery would only be used for those proceedings did not apply to an order under which the claimant recovered his own property,[34] and CPR has not changed the position.

There are cases at first instance which support the proposition that the defendant is not entitled to invoke the privilege on the grounds that compliance with an order may tend to show that he has already perjured himself in evidence given in the same proceedings. In *Emanuel v Emanuel*,[35] there was an issue in divorce proceedings as to what assets a husband

---

[27] *Istel Ltd v Tully* [1993] A.C. 45, approving *Re O* [1991] 2 Q.B. 520; *Boden v Inca Gemstones plc*, unreported, January 20, 1994, CA, in which an undertaking given by the prosecuting authorities which covered all real risks of prosecution but did not extend to fanciful risks was held sufficient to overcome the claim to privilege.

[28] *Re C (Restraint Order)* [1995] C.O.D. 263; *The Times*, April 25, 1995. *Cf.* the narrower undertaking accepted in *Re T (Restraint Order: Disclosure of Assets)* [1992] 1 W.L.R. 949.

[29] *HKSAR v Lee Ming Tee* [2001] 4 H.K.C.F.A.R. 133.

[30] *United Norwest Co-operatives Ltd v Johnstone, The Times*, February 24, 1994 (there was no assurance or undertaking given by the Crown Prosecution Service not to use the information disclosed); see also *Istel Ltd v Tully* [1993] A.C. 45 at 68F, *per* Lord Lowry.

[31] *Istel Ltd v Tully* [1993] A.C. 45 at 65.

[32] Where the existence of a trust is not in doubt, then the beneficiary will have a proprietary right to inspect trust documents: *Re Londonderry's Settlement* [1965] Ch. 918.

[33] *Process Development Ltd v Hogg* [1996] F.S.R. 45; *Istel Ltd v Tully* [1992] Q.B. 315 at 324–325, approved at [1993] A.C. 45 at 65.

[34] *Process Development Ltd v Hogg* [1996] F.S.R. 45, in which the plaintiff was allowed to disclose to the police where it had found its property pursuant to execution of the Anton Piller order.

[35] [1982] 1 W.L.R. 669.

owned; this was relevant to the question of what orders should be made in favour of his ex-wife for financial relief ancillary to the divorce. It appeared that the husband might have committed perjury about his assets in the course of the proceedings. Wood J. granted an *ex parte* application for Anton Piller relief which included a mandatory order that the ex-husband produce documents in relation to his assets. The judge considered that there should not be any provision in the order to protect the ex-husband against self-incrimination in relation to perjury. In his view, the privilege would not be available because the perjury would have been in the course of the proceedings themselves. If privilege could be invoked, there would be an inducement to a defendant to commit perjury at an early stage in the proceedings and then seek to hide behind the privilege in an attempt to prevent the court from establishing the true position. The view of Wood J. was adopted by Leggatt J. in *Distributori Automatici v Holford Trading Co.*,[36] in which it appeared that the defendant might have perjured himself in relation to the existence of assets upon which a judgment could be enforced. The judge granted Anton Piller relief (including mandatory orders requiring the defendant to disclose information and documents) notwithstanding the risk of self-incrimination in respect of perjury.[37]

17.037 The rationale for denying the privilege in respect of perjury which may have been committed in the same proceedings is that if it were available it could seriously interfere with the ability of the court to establish the true facts and thus to do justice in those proceedings. The decision in *Memory v Sidhu*[38] that the privilege applies to the risk of being held in contempt, even in the same proceedings, shows that these cases on perjury committed in the same proceedings are out of line with the general principle and that it is doubtful whether they were correctly decided.

The position in relation to restraint orders granted for the purpose of preserving assets to satisfy a confiscation order which may be made in the future, or which has been made, is considered in Chapter 25.

(iii) Statutory exceptions to the privilege

17.038 The privilege was abrogated by Parliament for cases within s.72 of the Supreme Court Act 1981, which concerns intellectual property rights,[39] for cases governed by s.31 of the Theft Act 1968, and for several other situations. These include investigations by company inspectors,[40] examinations by liquidators under s.236 of the Insolvency Act 1986,[41] when documents and information are sought by the official receiver from a

---

[36] [1985] 1 W.L.R. 1066 at 1073.
[37] See also *Cobra Golf Inc. v Rata* [1998] Ch. 109 at 157–158.
[38] [2000] Ch. 645.
[39] See *Istel Ltd v Tully* [1993] A.C. 45; *Universal City Studios Inc. v Hubbard* [1984] Ch. 225; *Charles of the Ritz Group Ltd v Jory* [1986] F.S.R. 14 (the section applies whether or not criminal proceedings have been commenced).
[40] *Re London United Investments plc* [1992] Ch. 578.
[41] *Bishopsgate Investment Management Ltd v Maxwell* [1993] Ch. 1.

bankrupt, and investigations of suspected offences involving serious or complex fraud when the Director of the Serious Fraud Office requires information or documents under s.2 of the Criminal Justice Act 1987, and care proceedings concerning children.[42] A statutory provision which entitled a waste regulation authority to obtain information impliedly excluded the privilege at common law leaving the provider to take his chance on persuading the judge at any criminal trial to exclude it.[43]

Section 72 of the Supreme Court Act 1981 enables Anton Piller relief or mandatory disclosure orders to be granted in cases falling within its ambit. It was enacted after the decision of the House of Lords in *Rank Film Ltd v Video Information Centre*.[44] The complexities of the section are considered in *Cobra Golf Inc. v Rata*.[45]

17.039   Section 31 of the Theft Act 1968[46] removes the privilege only when a person may be incriminated with "an offence under this Act . . .". That does not include a charge of conspiracy either at common law or under the Criminal Law Act 1977: *Sociedade Nacionale de Combustiveis de Angola UEE v Lundqvist*, above. In consequence it may often be important whether, on the facts of a particular case, there is a real risk of a conspiracy charge. If there is no evidence showing a real risk of such a charge, the court may decline to uphold the claim to privilege. The mere claim to privilege coupled with an unsubstantiated assertion of risk will not suffice. The court decides whether there is, objectively, a sufficient factual basis disclosed by the evidence to give rise to a risk, which is real and not merely fanciful, of a charge of conspiracy.[47]

In *Khan v Khan*,[48] it was suggested that the defendants might face a charge of forgery, as well as a charge of theft under the Theft Act 1968. The court held that the defendants were not protected by privilege. It might have been thought that the judgment of Stephenson L.J. supported the proposition that privilege would not be available when the main offence is one of theft under the Theft Act 1968. But the decision has been explained as a case in which a forgery charge was no more than a fanciful possibility.[49]

17.040   In a case in which the person claiming the privilege puts forward a suggested offence for which the privilege has not been removed by statute but also on the facts there may be a prosecution for an offence for which

---

[42] *Re Y & K (Children)* [2003] 2 F.L.R. 273.
[43] *R. v Hertfordshire County Council Ex p. Green* [2000] 2 A.C. 412 at 413C–F.
[44] [1982] A.C. 380.
[45] [1998] Ch. 109 at 159–164.
[46] See Appendix A, para.A3.007.
[47] *Tarasov v Nassif*, Court of Appeal (Civ Div) Transcript No.110 of 1994 (February 11, 1994), applying *Ex p. Reynolds* (1882) 20 Ch. 294 at 300. *Renworth Ltd v Stephansen* [1996] 3 All E.R. 244. *Phelby v Paier* [2003] 2 H.K.L.R.D. 323 (where on the facts a conspiracy to defraud charge was a possibility in addition to theft charges, and so the claim to privilege was upheld).
[48] [1982] 1 W.L.R. 513.
[49] *Renworth Ltd v Stephansen* [1996] 3 All E.R. 244; *Mirror Group Newspapers v Maxwell* [1992] B.C.C. 218; *Tarasov v Nassif*, Court of Appeal (Civ Div) Transcript No.110 of 1994 (February 11, 1994); see also *Sociedade v Lundqvist* [1991] 2 Q.B. 310 at 323, 337.

privilege has been removed (*e.g.* under the Theft Act 1968), then the correct approach is to evaluate the claim by reference to each offence separately. On the offence for which the privilege has not been removed the court will consider whether there is a real risk that the answers sought could expose the person to prosecution for that offence.[50] It may be that, although the answers would be likely to show commission of that offence, the facts are such that in practice a prosecution would only be brought for the Theft Act offence and not the other. If in practice the risk of being prosecuted for the other is therefore non-existent or fanciful, the claim for privilege by reference to the risk of exposure to such a prosecution will fail.[51]

(iv) Inconsistency between the privilege and the proposed order

If an order sought *ex parte* could give rise to a claim of privilege against self-incrimination, the court will consider whether, objectively, there is a risk, and whether the case falls within a statutory exception. If a proposed order is to take effect after a short interval to enable the defendant to take legal advice, and there is the possibility that the defendant might wish to claim privilege, the order should contain an express provision preserving the privilege and requiring the defendant to be informed of his right to take the point if he so chooses.[52] An order which is silent on these matters should not be made.[53] It is not permissible to make a mandatory order for disclosure of the potentially incriminating materials leaving it to the respondent to disobey the order on the ground of self-incrimination.

17.041

If a mandatory order for disclosure is to be made on a without notice application, and potentially it could include material for which the privilege might be available, the order itself must enable the respondent to claim the privilege without that being in breach of the order, and a unqualified mandatory order for disclosure can only be made when there is no possibility of the incriminating material being used by a prosecutor.[54] The order must not provide that notwithstanding the claim to privilege the material must be handed over for safe keeping pending determination of the claim to privilege. This is because if the privilege applies the order for handing over the material would itself be inconsistent with the privilege.[55]

---

[50] See also *Memory v Sidhu* [2000] Ch. 645 at [24].
[51] *Renworth Ltd v Stephansen* [1996] 3 All E.R. 244.
[52] *IBM v Prima Data International* [1994] 1 W.L.R. 719.
[53] *Rank Film Ltd v Video Information Centre* [1982] A.C. 380 at 443; *Tate Access Floors Inc. v Boswell* [1991] Ch. 512 at 530; *Vasil v National Australia Bank* [1999] N.S.W.C.A. 161; *Reid v Howard* (1995) 184 C.L.R. 1.
[54] This was possible in *Istel Ltd v Tully* [1993] A.C. 45, approving *Re O* [1991] 2 Q.B. 520, because of the undertaking given by the prosecuting authorities. In Australia section 128 of the Evidence Act 1995 enables the court to order the defendant's attendance in court to see whether a certificate can be granted which will give the witness statutory protection under the Australian legislation against the material being used in a criminal proceeding: *Bax Global v Evans* [1999] N.S.W.S.C. 815 at paras 24–46.
[55] *Den Norske Bank ASA v Antonatos* [1999] Q.B. 271 at 290A–B; *Vasil v National Australia Bank* [1999] N.S.W.C.A. 161; *Reid v Howard* (1995) 184 C.L.R. 1.

In *Memory v Sidhu (No.2)* the order provided that if the defendant claimed to invoke the privilege he had to provide the information to the supervising solicitor ". . . who will hold such information to the order of the court". The Court of Appeal had already criticised this form of order as inadequate to safeguard the privilege,[56] and the point that this was justifiable was not pursued on the appeal.

17.042   Paragraph 11 of the example order is modelled on para.3(2) of the standard form order[57] provided by the Practice Direction made in 1996.[58] It has not taken into account the case law. It states that:

"11. Before permitting entry to the premises by any person other than the Supervising Solicitor, the Respondent may, for a short time (not to exceed two hours, unless the Supervising Solicitor agrees to a longer period), gather together any documents he believes may be [incriminating or] privileged and hand them to the Supervising Solicitor for him to assess whether they are [incriminating or] privileged as claimed. If the Supervising Solicitor decides that any of the documents may be [incriminating or] privileged documents or is in any doubt as to their status, he will exclude them from the search and retain them in his possession pending further order of the court."

This requires the respondent to hand over to the supervising solicitor (1) documents which both of them consider to be incriminating; and (2) documents of "doubtful status". This mechanism would result in the defendant handing over to the supervising solicitor both clearly incriminating documents and documents of "doubtful status". It is either that, or the respondent must comply with the mandatory provisions for a search and for disclosure. This is unjustifiable. It is like the provision condemned in *Den Norske Bank ASA v Antonatos*. It infringes the privilege.

In *IBM v Prima Data International*,[59] the court upheld an order which expressly provided that the supervising solicitor was to explain to the defendant that he "may be entitled to avail himself of the privilege against self-incrimination", and that various parts of the order were to have effect only in so far as privilege was not claimed. This is consistent with the privilege but not entirely satisfactory.

17.043   First, it imposes on a defendant a short time limit, without the benefit of mature reflection, for deciding, in a highly stressful situation, whether to claim privilege.

Secondly, the rationale for granting Anton Piller relief is that in the absence of an immediate order the defendant might destroy documents or

---

[56] *Den Norske Bank ASA v Antonatos* [1999] Q.B. 271 at 290A–B.
[57] This had only required the handing over of documents of "doubtful status", but infringed the privilege because (1) the question of self-incrimination remained unresolved and at large; and (2) the decision of the supervising solicitor was not a judicial decision arrived at after receiving evidence and argument.
[58] [1996] 1 W.L.R. 1552.
[59] [1994] 1 W.L.R. 719.

evidence or other subject-matter of the order, notwithstanding an injunction restraining him from doing so. If the defendant is entitled, at his choice, to halt implementation of the order, retaining in his possession certain of the materials sought, this removes a corresponding part of the justification for making the order in the first place, and this should be taken into account by the judge on the without notice application, when to consider making the order.

While it is wrong in principle for the court to grant *ex parte* a mandatory order which is inconsistent with maintaining the privilege, this does not preclude the court from considering the relevant evidence and reaching a judgment at the *ex parte* stage as to whether the privilege would be available to be invoked. If the court concludes that the privilege would clearly not be available in the circumstances of the case, then privilege against self-incrimination on the part of the defendant does not preclude the making of the contemplated order. In *Cobra Golf*, Rimer J. considered that an order should *not* be made if there were provisions in it which were "foreseeable as likely to require the defendant to incriminate himself",[60] citing *Tate Access Floors Inc. v Boswell*[61] in which the Vice-Chancellor had stated that an order should not be made "which might in practice" prevent privilege being claimed. No order should destroy the availability of the privilege. On the other hand, the court should not be deflected from making an order because of a far-fetched or fanciful risk that this might happen. If on the evidence on a without notice application there is a real risk (as opposed to a far-fetched or insignificant risk) that if the order is made it will infringe a right to claim privilege against self-incrimination, then the order should not be made. In the *Rank Film* case there was no safeguard at all, and the privilege provided a complete answer to the mandatory orders made.

(v) The drawing of adverse inferences when the privilege is invoked

There have been different judicial observations as to whether it could be   **17.044**
permissible to draw an affirmative inference against a person who invoked the privilege. The better view is that such an inference can be drawn.[62] This is a question of public policy. The present procedure in criminal proceedings is to allow a negative inference to be drawn from invoking the right to silence provided that the correct procedures have been followed and the circumstances are such that such an inference can fairly be drawn. It would be odd if the defendant to civil proceedings were in a better position than in criminal proceedings. Assuming that the defendant has had independent

---

[60] [1998] Ch. 109 at 127G.
[61] [1991] Ch. 512 at 530.
[62] *V v C* [2001] EWCA Civ 1509 at [40]; *Den Norske Bank ASA v Antonatos* [1999] Q.B. 271 at 295H–296C which cites the dicta for and against; *Great Future International Ltd v Sealand Housing Corporation* [2004] EWHC 124 at [30], Ch.

legal advice and has had a fair opportunity to consider what to do then the public policy does not preclude the drawing of a negative inference.

The problem on the *IBM v Prima Data International* form of order is that the safeguard removes much of the practical usefulness of the search order and therefore a corresponding part of the justification for granting it in the first place. In *IBM*, if the defendant had said that he had incriminating materials and that he wished to claim the privilege, the mandatory provisions of the order would have fallen away under the proviso to the order, leaving only an injunction in negative terms preserving what was under the control of the defendant.

(vi) Seeking a stay of civil proceedings pending the outcome of criminal proceedings

17.045   It is open to a defendant to apply for a stay of proceedings pending the outcome of a criminal prosecution on the ground that if the civil proceedings continued that could prejudice the fair trial of the criminal proceedings or that the existence of the criminal proceedings made it unfair for the civil proceedings to continue. However the circumstance that if the civil proceedings continue the defendant will have to reveal his defence has not been treated as sufficient ground to justify such a course, and except when the risk of unfairness is real and unavoidable no stay will be granted.[63] With the prosecution of contempt proceedings when there are criminal proceedings arising out of the same matters, the court seeks to deal with contempt swiftly and effectively and will not ordinarily stay the contempt proceedings pending the outcome of the criminal proceedings.[64]

Incrimination under foreign laws

17.046   Although there is no privilege against self-incrimination available to a person in respect of prosecution abroad,[65] if the court is being asked to make an order compelling disclosure and it has a discretion (*e.g.* whether to make a disclosure order ancillary to Mareva relief or an order to enable missing assets or their proceeds to be traced), then it is relevant to the exercise of that discretion to take into account the possible consequences of making the order, including any possibility that as a result the person compelled[66] or third parties[67] may face prosecution abroad or some other

---

[63] *V v C* [2001] EWCA Civ 1509; *Jefferson Ltd v Bhetcha* [1979] 1 W.L.R. 898; *Re DPR Futures* [1989] 1 W.L.R. 778; *Surrey Oaklands NHS Trust v Hurley*, unreported, May 20, 1999 (Sullivan J.)—in all of which the civil proceedings were allowed to continue because there was no factor which made that unfair to the defendant and fairness to the plaintiff/claimant in each case made it inappropriate to impose a stay.

[64] *Barnet London Borough Council v Hurst* [2003] 1 W.L.R. 722 at [44]. On penalty for contempt when there are contemporaneous criminal proceedings, see para. 19.070.

[65] *Re Westinghouse Uranium Contract* [1978] A.C. 547 at 637, *per* Lord Diplock; *Attorney-General for Gibraltar v May* [1999] 1 W.L.R. 998 at 1003G.

[66] *Crédit Suisse Fides Trust v Cuoghi* [1998] Q.B. 818; *Levi Status & Co. v Barclays Trading Corporation Inc.* [1993] F.S.R. 179.

[67] *Arab Monetary Fund v Hashim* [1989] 1 W.L.R. 565 at 578.

adverse consequence. This is so whether the result will flow from the fact that the person has broken a foreign law requiring information to be kept secret[68] or from the information itself being used. In the latter situation, the court may find a mechanism which will minimise the risk of leakage whilst still enabling the information to be used by the claimant (*e.g.* limiting the scope of the disclosure and the persons to whom it is disclosed). It may also be that a court in civil proceedings has a discretion to excuse a witness from giving evidence of a material matter because of such a risk.[69]

Thus, in cases falling outside the scope of the common law privilege the court may, in the exercise of its discretion, under s.37(1) of the Supreme Court Act 1981, take into account the risk of adverse consequences befalling the defendant or third parties if there is compliance with the relief sought. In *Arab Monetary Fund v Hashim* (above) there was a concern that third parties might be exposed to criminal proceedings in Iraq as a result of disclosure of information. Part of the order was therefore limited to disclosure of information to the solicitors acting for the claimant, and not to the claimant itself. This was an exceptional form of limitation, the general rule being that disclosure will be ordered to be made to the other party to the litigation.

In *Crédit Suisse Fides Trust v Cuoghi*[70] there was no significant risk of prosecution in the United Kingdom and so the common law privilege did not arise. The judge at first instance ordered a further affidavit from the defendant with a view to shaping an order which would avoid granting a mandatory disclosure order which would expose the defendant to the risk of self-incrimination in Switzerland. The Court of Appeal held that the judge had been fully entitled to take this course.

Where the relevant foreign country gives effect to Art.6 of the European **17.047** Convention on Human Rights this is relevant to the exercise of discretion because the question then becomes whether the English court, basing itself on the scope of the privilege at common law, should give a greater measure of protection to the defendant than is afforded by that convention. This point did not arise in *Crédit Suisse Fides Trust v Cuoghi*. There is something unattractive about a court giving a defendant who is at risk of prosecution abroad a lesser protection against self-incrimination than is available to a defendant facing the risk of prosecution in the United Kingdom. On the other hand the common law privilege has been criticised at the highest levels, and if the protection afforded by the foreign criminal procedure meets the European standard and is fair, then the English court could conclude that this is sufficient. In *Attorney-General for Gibraltar v May*[71] the question arose as to release of material by the English court after the disclosure had been given, and so it was too late to invite the court to

---

[68] *Brannigan v Davison* [1997] A.C. 238.
[69] *ibid.*
[70] [1998] Q.B. 818 at 830B–G.
[71] [1999] 1 W.L.R. 998.

shape its disclosure order so as to avoid self-incrimination. The court permitted the release of the material to the prosecuting authority and the defendant was left to rely on his right corresponding to that under Art.6, which was available to him in Gibraltar, and the jurisdiction of the trial judge in Gibraltar to exclude evidence when it would be unfair to admit it.

(9) The example order

17.048 Part V of the Report of the Staughton Committee recommended the drafting of a form of order for inclusion in the *Supreme Court Practice*, commenting that a form of order used in the Chancery Division "would not be readily intelligible to the layman". The *Practice Direction (Mareva and Anton Piller Orders: New Forms)*[72] provided a specimen order, which was drafted taking into account the case law, including in particular the judgment of the Vice-Chancellor in *Universal Thermosensors v Hibben*,[73] and the Staughton Committee Report. This was replaced by the standard form order attached to *Practice Direction (Mareva and Anton Piller: Forms)*,[74] and then by the "example order" annexed to the CPR Practice Direction—Interim Injunctions supplementing CPR Pt 25.

The example order is the starting point from which a draft order should be prepared and also for presenting the without notice application to the judge. Each material respect in which the proposed draft is different from the example order, whether of omission or addition, must be pointed out, and the judge's approval obtained.[75]

Paragraph 11 of the example order is inconsistent with the privilege of self-incrimination. In a case in which that potentially arises, the "listed items",[76] which are the items for which the search is to be made, should exclude any materials which fall within the scope of the privilege. There is therefore no room for the respondent to refuse to permit the search to proceed on the grounds of self-incrimination. If the listed items potentially include self-incriminating materials, then if the respondent is entitled to claim privilege and does so, this extends to refusing to allow the search party to search for such items.[77] Once there are in fact self-incriminating materials within "the listed items", because the claim to privilege does not in fact narrow the definition of the listed items, it is considered that the respondent would be within his rights in refusing to allow the search to proceed.

---

[72] [1994] 4 All E.R. 52.
[73] [1992] 1 W.L.R. 840.
[74] [1996] 1 W.L.R. 1552.
[75] *Memory v Sidhu (No.2)* [2000] 1 W.L.R. 1443; *Gadget Shop Ltd v Bug.Com Ltd* [2001] F.S.R. 383 at [48]; *Re S (A Child) (Family Division: Without Notice Orders)* [2001] 1 All E.R. 362.
[76] See para.6(c) of the example order.
[77] *Tate Access Floors Inc. v Boswell* [1991] Ch. 512 at 529–530.

What about documents which can be the subject of a bona fide claim for **17.049** privilege against self-incrimination but which, at the end of the day might be decided not to have been privileged? The position is entirely different from that when a party gives inspection of documents pursuant to the ordinary procedure for disclosure in the action.[78] There the party has a full opportunity to consider privilege and what to produce. It would not be appropriate to draft an order so that a respondent who makes a bona fide claim which turned out to be unjustified or too wide would find himself in breach of the order and therefore in contempt of court.[79] Whether he would be in contempt depends on breach of the order and not on his intent or whether he acted bona fide.[80] It should not be the purpose of the court to punish a defendant for taking what turns out to be a wrong point on privilege. The order in *IBM v Prima Data International*[81] did not have this effect.

Paragraph 11 also addresses privileged documents. If documents are the subject of legal professional or litigation privilege, this entitlement to confidentiality is a substantive legal right to which the court is bound to give effect. The jurisdiction under s.7 of the Civil Procedure Act 1997 was to confirm by statute a procedure and not to take away the substantive right to confidentiality and privilege from production.[82] The defendant is entitled to refuse to produce them because of his legal right, and it follows that he is entitled by reason of the privilege to refuse to allow the search party to enter his premises in order to search for them and take them into their possession or put them into the possession of the supervising solicitor.[83] Paragraph 11 does not address this problem satisfactorily. Documents which are the subject of litigation or legal professional privilege must be excluded from the scope of the search and the mandatory orders for production.

Paragraph 16 also needs to be adjusted—it cannot be right that the order requires self-incriminating documents to be handed over to the supervising solicitor.[84] It also cannot be right to order documents protected by legal

---

[78] For which see *Guinness Peat Properties Ltd v Fitzroy Robinson Partnership* [1987] 1 W.L.R. 1027 at 1043–1044; *Derby & Co. Ltd v Weldon (No.8)* [1991] 1 W.L.R. 72 at 95–97.
[79] Lord Wilberforce was concerned about this in *Rank Film Distributors Ltd v Video Information Centre* [1982] A.C. 380 at 443G.
[80] *Adam Phones v Goldschmidt* [1999] 4 All E.R. 486 at 492–494 in which *Irtelli v Squatriti* [1993] Q.B. 83 was not followed because it is inconsistent with other case law; *Bird v Hadkinson, The Times*, April 7, 1999.
[81] [1994] 1 W.L.R. 719.
[82] In *R. v Derby Magistrates' Court Ex p. B* [1996] A.C. 487 legal professional privilege was described as "... a fundamental condition on which the administration of justice as a whole rests". In *General Mediterranean Holdings SA v Patel* [2000] 1 W.L.R. 272, what was CPR r.48.7(3) made under s.1 of the Civil Procedure Act 1997, purported to enable the court to override privilege by requiring production to the court, and was held to be *ultra vires*.
[83] For the same reasons as apply to self-incrimination. If a mandatory order cannot properly be made for their production, then it cannot be right to make a mandatory order requiring the respondent to permit someone to come in and search for them so that they can be taken—see *Tate Access Floors Inc. v Boswell* [1991] Ch. 512 at 529–530.
[84] *Den Norske Bank ASA v Antonatos* [1999] Q.B. 271 at 290A–B.

professional privilege or litigation privilege to be delivered up to the supervising solicitor.

17.050 Paragraph 27 requires that if there is to be an application to vary or discharge the order, then the substance of the evidence to be relied upon must be communicated to the applicant's solicitors in advance. Whilst this is desirable, it cannot properly be made a mandatory requirement of any application. The inclusion of it in the example order gives the impression of unfairness. The court has made an order at the limits of its jurisdiction without notice, which is to be executed almost immediately, and the example order allows in paras 10 and 27 for an application to vary or discharge it, but then places a procedural requirement in paras 10(a) and 27, which can only cause delay and interfere with an application made perfectly properly on urgent and pressing grounds.

The Schedule C of the example order does not include the undertaking in favour of non-parties which is standard for freezing injunctions—see example freezing injunction, Schedule B, undertaking (7). This should be included in all search orders.[85]

(10) The supervising solicitor

17.051 In *Anton Piller v Manufacturing Processes Ltd*,[86] Lord Denning M.R. said that on service of the order "the plaintiffs should be attended by their solicitor, who is an officer of the court . . .". It became part of the standard practice of the court to require the order to be served and executed by a qualified solicitor.[87] The Staughton Committee considered whether it should be mandatory for an independent supervisor to be present at the execution of the order. In particular, the adequacy of a requirement that the plaintiff's solicitor be present had been criticised, on the basis that the solicitor, particularly if inexperienced, would be liable to make mistakes, or could give the impression of bias against the defendant. On the other hand, there was concern that a requirement for an independent supervisor could give rise to an unjustified increase in costs. The Staughton Committee recommended[88] that it should be left to the discretion of the judge in each case whether to require an independent supervisor. In *Universal Thermosensors v Hibben*,[89] Sir Donald Nicholls V.-C. said[90] that there should be "serious consideration" in each case of whether to require service of the order and supervision of its execution by a solicitor other than a member

---

[85] see Chapter 11, para.11.008–11.012; *Imutran Ltd v Uncaged Campaigns Ltd* [2002] F.S.R. 20 at [45].

[86] [1976] Ch. 55 at 61C.

[87] *Vaparmatic Co. v Sparex* [1976] 1 W.L.R. 939 at 940; *Protector Alarms Ltd v Maxim Alarms Ltd* [1978] F.S.R. 442 at 444.

[88] At para.3.15.

[89] [1992] 1 W.L.R. 840.

[90] *ibid.*, at 861C–D.

of the firm acting for the plaintiff. The Practice Direction[91] left this to the discretion of the judge, and required that if the judge does not think it appropriate to do so, his reasons should be set out in the order itself. The CPR Practice Direction-Interim Injunctions reproduces this in para.8.2, and provides in para.7.4(1) that the order must be served personally by the supervising solicitor unless the court otherwise orders. In practice the use of a supervising solicitor has become a standard part of the search order procedure.

Paragraph 26 of the example order provides for it to be served by a supervising solicitor, and carried out in his presence and under his supervision. The supervising solicitor should be experienced in the execution of search orders and not be an employee or member of the firm acting for the applicant.[92] The evidence in support of the application must include the identity and experience of the proposed supervising solicitor,[93] and must deal with any matters material to the experience or standing of any member of the proposed search party and whether it is appropriate for that individual to be part of the search party.

If the order is to be executed at premises likely to be occupied by an **17.052** unaccompanied woman and the supervising solicitor is a man, the order should provide that at least one of those present on service of the order should be a woman. In *Universal Thermosensors*, the Vice-Chancellor referred[94] to this requirement in the context of execution at a private house. The Staughton Committee declined to recommend that a woman should always be present at execution of an order, because "it would often be unnecessary".[95] The Practice Direction—Interim Injunctions provides in para.7.4(5):

> "(5) where the Supervising Solicitor is a man and the respondent is likely to be an unaccompanied woman, at least one other person named in the order must be a woman and must accompany the Supervising Solicitor".[96]

Under the Practice Direction—Interim Injunctions para.7.5(11), the supervising solicitor must prepare a report on the carrying out of the order and to provide a copy to the applicant's solicitors, and under para.7.5(12),

---

[91] *Practice Direction (Mareva and Anton Piller Orders: New Forms)* [1994] 4 All E.R. 52; [1994] R.P.C. 604 [1994] 1 W.L.R. 1233 (without the forms).
[92] Practice Direction—Interim Injunctions, para.8.1; *Manor Electronics Ltd v Dickson* [1988] R.P.C. 618.
[93] In *Gadget Shop Ltd v Bug.Com Ltd* [2001] F.S.R. 383 at [94–101] and [109], the supervising solicitor had had no relevant experience of execution of an order involving a supervising solicitor, and the judge on the without notice application had been misled about the previous experience. This was a factor relied upon for discharging the order *inter partes*.
[94] [1992] 1 W.L.R. 840 at 860D–G.
[95] Staughton Committee Report, para.4.15.
[96] See also *Gadget Shop Ltd v Bug.Com Ltd* [2001] F.S.R. 383 at [83–86] (possibility of search of the homes of two women).

as soon as it is received the applicant's solicitors must serve a copy on the respondent and file a copy with the court. This is prepared in part for the protection of the respondent[97] and for this reason the court in the exercise of its discretion may decide not to permit release of it to the police.[98]

(11) Insurance

17.053 The Staughton Committee recommended[99] that in appropriate cases the plaintiff should be required to undertake to insure seized items. The Practice Direction made in 1994 made provision for this in appropriate cases,[1] and this is now provided for in para.7.5(5) of the Practice Direction-Interim Injunctions. The example order has a sample undertaking expressed in general terms providing for insurance (see Schedule C, para.(6)).

(12) The persons to be allowed to enter

17.054 The example order does not adopt a procedure requiring that those who are to be allowed to execute the order are to be individually named in it.[2] But there is a footnote to the order which states that:

"None of these persons should be people who could gain personally or commercially from anything they might read or see on the premises, unless their presence is essential."[3]

(13) The entry and search order

17.055 The example order is directed against the defendant alone. It requires compliance by him either personally or by those described in para.5: "any director, officer, partner or responsible employee of the Respondent . . .", or, "if the Respondent is an individual, any other person having responsible control of the premises . . .".

---

[97] *Taylor Made Golf Co. Inc. v Rata & Rata* [1996] F.S.R. 528 at 535.
[98] *Process Development Ltd v Hogg* [1996] F.S.R. 45.
[99] Staughton Committee Report. para.4.13.
[1] See the former Practice Direction, [1994] 4 All E.R. 52; para.(3)(B)3.
[2] See also *Hansard*, Vol. 576, cols 899–900, December 9, 1996, *per* Lord Mackay L.C.; contrast the suggestion in *Vapormatic Co. Ltd v Sparex Ltd* [1976] 1 W.L.R. 939 at 940.
[3] See the concern expressed in *Universal Thermosensors Ltd v Hibben* [1992] 1 W.L.R. 840 at 861A.

The order is not directed to an employee or other person falling within this description, but such persons, and anyone else who knows of the order, must not deliberately take steps to prevent or interfere with implementation of the order.[4] The example order contains a number of requirements with which the respondent must comply. These are designed to enable those executing the order to go on to premises and obtain access to computers and facilities to copy what is found on them, documents, or other items. A key definition is that of "THE LISTED ITEMS" in Schedule B. This governs what is within and what is outside of the scope of the search and the mandatory disclosure orders.

The example order requires a respondent:

(1) to allow entry on to premises mentioned in Schedule A, any other premises disclosed by the respondent pursuant to a mandatory order requiring him to disclose the location of all "the listed items", and to vehicles on or around these premises;

(2) to deliver up all the listed items except for computers;

(3) to provide information stored on computers;

(4) to give information about where listed items are; and

(5) to give information about suppliers, customers, supplies and offers.

(14) Hours for service of the order

The Staughton Committee recommended that a plaintiff should not be able **17.056** to execute his order outside normal office hours, other than in exceptional cases.[5] In *Universal Thermosensors*, a woman who was alone in a house with her children in bed was brought to the door at 7.15am in her night attire. Paragraph 7.4(6) of the CPR Practice Direction-Interim Injunctions prohibits service of the order other than between 9.30am and 5.30pm on a weekday, unless the court otherwise orders. Once served, the order operates immediately and continues in operation without interruption until completion of the search.

(15) Legal advice and discharge or variation of the order

The Staughton Committee considered that a defendant "should be entitled **17.057** to apply for the discharge or variation of an order before its execution. He should be entitled to make such an application *ex parte*, but, if possible, on notice to the applicant".[6]

---

[4] See Chapter 19, below.
[5] Staughton Committee Report, para.4.11.
[6] *ibid.*, para.4.7.

The Committee drew attention to the need for an order to be clear and said that:[7]

". . . an Anton Piller order ought to be drawn so as to make clear whether the respondent may postpone entry while he takes legal advice or applies for the discharge of the order and, if some delay is permissible, what safeguards to protect the interests of the [claimant] are to be imposed over the period of the delay. Entry but no search might, for example, be a solution. There is, as yet, no clear practice that has emerged.

We consider that this is a problem to which there is no ready solution because of the wide variety of circumstances in which the problem can arise. In some cases the order can provide for a defined period of delay, provided a representative of the [claimant] remains on the defendant's premises to ensure that nothing untoward happens in the meantime with regard to the evidence which is the subject of the order. In other cases no such precision will be possible."

Under para.7.4(4) of the CPR Practice Direction—Interim Injunctions it is provided that:

"the Supervising Solicitor must explain the terms and effect of the order to the respondent in every day language and advise him of his right to—

(a) legal advice, and

(b) apply to vary or discharge the order".

17.058   The respondent is not bound to permit anyone on to the premises until service has been completed, and an explanation given (if the offer to explain is accepted). After this the respondent must allow immediate entry to the premises to the supervising solicitor. Under the example order, the supervising solicitor must be allowed to enter, even if the respondent wishes to seek legal advice or to apply to the court to vary or discharge the order.

Under the example order, if the respondent wishes to take legal advice and to ask the court to discharge or vary the order , then the respondent can ask the supervising solicitor, "to delay starting the search for up to 2 hours or such other longer period as the Supervising Solicitor may permit."[8] There will be some inevitable delay before legal advice is actually received, and this is why the supervising solicitor can extend the two-hour period.[9] If there is genuine difficulty in obtaining advice, then it is to be expected that the supervising solicitor will extend the time.

---

[7] Paragraphs 4.8 and 4.9. See also M. Dockray and H. Laddie, "Piller Problems" (1990) 106 L.Q.R. 601 at 608; *Ng Chun-fai v Tamco Electrical & Electronics (Hong Kong) Ltd* [1994] 1 H.K.L.R. 178, discussed in [1994] 11 J.I.B.L. 480.

[8] Paragraph 10 of the example order.

[9] See also the approach of Scott J. in *Bhimji v Chatwani* [1991] 1 W.L.R. 989 at 1000.

A respondent may wish to apply to vary or discharge the order, but does **17.059** not have time to come before the judge within the two-hour limit allowed under para.10 of the example order. As this is drafted, the respondent would be in breach of the order if he refused to allow the search to start as soon as the two hours have expired, unless that period is extended.[10] The supervising solicitor can extend the period and can make any extension subject to terms for safeguarding the items in the meantime. The supervising solicitor must bear in mind that the judge has made the order because, on the evidence, there is a real risk that the defendant may destroy or hide the relevant items. If an extension is to be allowed, it should be for a short period to enable the matter to be brought before the court, whilst in the meantime taking any appropriate steps to safeguard the situation. The supervising solicitor can do this by granting an extension conditional on compliance with certain terms or further direction by him.

The example order contains, in paras 16 and 17, mandatory orders for delivery of listed items and computer printouts, and for disclosure of information. As para.10 of the example order is drafted, it allows delay before commencing the search but not in complying with paras 16 and 17. However, the judge, on the *ex parte* application, should be invited to consider including a provision to this effect.

(16) Confidentiality

The fact that a search order has been made could in itself be extremely **17.060** damaging to the defendant's business: *Columbia Pictures Inc. v Robinson.*[11] The defendant has an interest in keeping this information confidential. The Staughton Committee recommended[12] that an undertaking of confidentiality should be required from the applicant, to remain in force until after the return date; otherwise information about the proceedings and the order, given to third parties, could seriously prejudice the defendant by undermining the confidence of others, such as investors and customers. The example order contains such an undertaking in Schedule C, undertaking (4).

(17) Undertakings

The example order sets out undertakings to be given to the court on the **17.061** without notice application by the applicant (Schedule C), the applicant's solicitors (Schedule D) and the supervising solicitor (Schedule E).

---

[10] See para. 19.006.
[11] [1987] Ch. 38 at pp 72H–73A.
[12] Staughton Committee Report, para.4.6.

Often, the claimant will not issue the claim form before the search order is executed, so as to preserve secrecy. If this is to be done then a direction should be sought under Para.4.4(1) of the Practice Direction. If so, the claim form should be issued immediately after commencement of execution.[13] The affidavits and exhibits capable of being copied which were relied on in support of the application, the skeleton argument, the claim form or draft claim form, and the application notice in respect of the hearing on the return date should be served on the respondent at the same time as service of the order.[14] The respondent should also be provided with a notice of the hearing held without notice. If information is given to the court which is not in the affidavit or draft affidavit placed before the court, it should be included, either by adding to the draft affidavit or by means of a supplementary affidavit, which is served on the defendant at the time of service of the order.

17.062   It is good practice for the respondent to be handed a general explanatory leaflet, immediately before execution of the order, describing his rights and the various undertakings which have been given, and for the applicant's solicitor to tape record all important conversations to avoid subsequent disputes.[15]

(18) Execution of the order

17.063   No items may be removed from the property until a list of those to be removed has been prepared, and a copy of the list given to the respondent, and he has been given a reasonable opportunity to check the list.[16] The respondent, ought to be allowed a full opportunity to see the items to be removed so that they can check the list as it is being prepared.

The premises can be searched and items removed only if respondent or a person who appears to be a responsible employee of the respondent is present.[17]

The claimant should avoid searching among belongings of members of the defendant's family. The order is directed to the defendant personally and any permission given by the defendant pursuant to the requirements of

---

[13] *VDU Installations Ltd v Integrated Computer Systems and Cybernetics Ltd* [1989] F.S.R. 378.

[14] See Practice Direction, para.5.1(2); see also *Booker McConnell plc v Plasgow* [1985] R.F.C. 425 at 442; *AB v CDE* [1982] R.F.C. 509 at 510; *International Electronics Ltd v Weight Data Ltd* [1980] F.S.R. 423.

[15] Staughton Committee Report, para.4.14.

[16] Practice Direction para.7.5(7) and example order, para.13; Staughton Committee Report, para.4.13; *Columbia Pictures Inc. v Robinson* [1987] Ch. 37 at 76; *Universal Thermosensors v Hibben* [1992] 1 W.L.R. 840 at 860F.

[17] Practice Direction, para.7.5(2) and example order, para.14; see also *Universal Thermosensors Ltd v Hibben* [1992] 1 W.L.R. 840 at 860 and Staughton Committee Report, para.4.14.

the order does not entitle the claimant to interfere with property belonging to third parties, even if it is thought to consist of the proceeds of crime.[18]

17.064 The applicant's solicitors are usually required to furnish an undertaking (example order, Schedule D, undertaking (2)) to the court to answer questions about whether or not documents or other items are said to be within the scope of the order. This includes providing a reasonable justification of why any documents or articles not self-evidently within the scope of the order are said to be so. If the intention is to remove a large number of documents, it will not be reasonable to require the solicitors to give a detailed justification, document by document. But solicitors should usually be prepared, in response to appropriate questions, to say why particular categories or classes of document are considered to be within the order. If a justification cannot be provided, the solicitors should reconsider removing the particular categories or classes. Under para.7.5(1) of the Practice Direction, "no material shall be removed unless clearly covered by the terms of the order".

The applicant's solicitors should not seek agreement from the respondent to the removal of documents or articles additional to those specified in the order. In *Columbia Pictures Inc. v Robinson*,[19] Scott J. said that he would not be prepared to accept that in the circumstances in which Anton Piller orders are "customarily executed (the execution is often aptly called 'a raid')", apparent consent to additional material being removed had been "freely and effectively given unless the respondent's solicitor had been present to confirm and ensure that the consent was a free and informed one". The justification for Anton Piller relief is that the defendant is otherwise liable to destroy or hide away the documents, even in the face of less draconian relief such as an injunction prohibiting destruction, or a mandatory order requiring delivery-up of the documents in question.[20] It is unlikely that such a defendant would voluntarily agree to additional material being removed. But, in any case, it is unfair that the defendant should be both subjected to the pressures of complying with an Anton Piller order, and required to deal with a request for additional material outside the scope of the order. The order ought not to be used as the opportunity to obtain any further advantage from the defendant beyond what is provided for in the order.

---

[18] Staughton Committee Report, para.4.16. The order should be executed with due sensitivity to the privacy of the defendant and others using the premises. So, *e.g.* in a family case where the plaintiff has taken a camera and formed part of the search party this has been strongly criticised: *Overholt v Overholt* [1999] 2 H.K.L.R.D. 445. Damages on the cross-undertaking can be awarded for an improper manner of search: see para.11.030. There is a strong public interest in deterring misconduct in the execution of search orders and in British Columbia this has even resulted in defaulting solicitors being removed from the record: *Grenzservice Speditions GesmbH v Jans* (1995) 129 D.L.R. (4th) 733.

[19] [1987] Ch. 38 at 77; applied in *J C Techforce Pty Ltd v Pearce* (1996) 138 A.L.R. 522 at 526–527. See also *VDU Installations Ltd v Integrated Computer Systems and Cybernetics Ltd* [1989] F.S.R. 378.

[20] A mandatory order requiring delivery-up of articles was made in preference to Anton Piller relief in *Universal Studios v Mukhtar & Sons* [1976] 1 W.L.R. 568, where there was merely suspicion that the defendants were not acting in good faith.

(19) Presence of the police

17.065 A search order is granted in civil litigation, and it is undesirable that the police should be involved[21] save in so far as their presence is necessary to prevent a breach of the peace. If police are present, this may give rise to the impression that they are there to enforce the order of the court, and that the entry and search will take place regardless of whether or not permission is given by the defendant. This is not the effect of the order, and it is not appropriate that such an impression should be given.[22]

The order must not be served and executed so as to coincide with a police raid on the premises.[23] In *ITC Films Distributors Ltd v Video Exchange (No.2)*,[24] an Anton Piller order was executed on premises simultaneously with a police search carried out under a warrant to search for and seize any pornographic video films. The judge on the *ex parte* application had not apparently been informed of any intention to execute the order in this way. The Court of Appeal upheld the original Anton Piller order, but criticised the manner in which it had been implemented, Lawton L.J. observing that it was most undesirable that solicitors executing an Anton Piller order should be "seen to be hangers-on of a squad of police carrying out a warrant". In subsequent proceedings the European Court of Human Rights[25] held that the mode of execution of the order had not resulted in a violation of Art.8 of the European Convention on Human Rights, but agreed with the Court of Appeal's criticisms of the mode of obtaining entry and carrying out the search. If a police officer is present when an Anton Piller order is served, the person served should be told that the officer is present only in case of a breach of the peace.

(20) Alternative method of service

17.066 Under para.7.4(1) of the Practice Direction, the order must be served personally by the supervising solicitor. As a general rule it is highly undesirable that an order for service by an alternative method of service to be made in respect of an Anton Piller order. The nature of the relief requires almost immediate compliance, backed up with the possibility of sanctions for contempt of court. In relation to mandatory orders, RSC Ord. 45, r.7 permits enforcement pursuant to RSC Ord. 45, r.5 only if there has been non-compliance following personal service of the order

---

[21] Staughton Committee Report, para.4.12.
[12] Staughton Committee Report, para.4.6.
[23] Practice Direction, para.8.3.
[24] (1982) 126 S.J. 672.
[25] Case 17/1987/140/194 *Chappell v United Kingdom* (1990) 12 E.H.R.R. 1, also reported at [1989] F.S.R. 617.

endorsed with a penal notice. A defendant is not then able to say that he did not know of the order or that he did not understand the possible consequences of not complying with it. Service by an alternative method should not be employed as a device to strip the defendant of this safeguard. In *Gates v Swift*,[26] an order was made providing that service of the order on "any apparently responsible person appearing to be in charge of the . . . premises shall be deemed good service of this order"; the report does not set out the evidence before the court which resulted in this order. This would not be acceptable under the modern practice.[27]

(21) Ordering the return of documents when an order for compulsory disclosure is set aside *inter partes* or on appeal

What is the position when a search order or an order for almost immediate **17.067** compulsory disclosure[28] is set aside *inter partes* or on appeal? The position appears to be as follows:

(1) An order made *ex parte* is a temporary order which applies until it is set aside or replaced.

(2) An interlocutory order made *inter partes* will itself lay down the machinery for it to be varied or discharged, *e.g.* "until further order", which enables the court to bring it to an end.

(3) An order may be set aside on appeal.

(4) The general rule is that all such orders are binding on the parties and must be obeyed unless and until they are set aside.[29] This includes orders obtained *ex parte* by material non-disclosure or misrepresentation.[30] The reason is one of public policy upholding the authority of the courts as part of the rule of law.

(5) If acts have been done by the other party or by non-parties which are compelled by the order or authorised by it, those acts have been sanctioned by the court and the general principle is that a party cannot acquire a cause of action based on those acts.[31] Actions for

---

[26] [1982] R.F.C. 339.
[27] *Capital Performance International Inc. v Jenkins* [2002] N.S.W.S.C. 797 (September 3, 2002) (applying the text to Mareva relief).
[28] Like the order made in *Adam Phones v Goldschmidt* [1999] 4 All E.R. 486.
[29] *Isaacs v Robertson* [1985] A.C. 97; *Hadkinson v Hadkinson* [1952] P. 285; *Wardle Fabrics Ltd v G. Myristis Ltd* [1984] F.S.R. 263.
[30] In *Williams v Smith* (1863) 14 C.B. N.S. 596 at 622, Erle C.J. expressed the view that such orders were obtained irregularly, but nevertheless the order remains valid unless and until it is set aside as is illustrated by the cases on the jurisdiction not to set aside the order notwithstanding the irregularity (see para.9.015–9.020).
[31] The principle does not necessarily confer an immunity for acts of negligence: *Inland Revenue Commissioners v Hoogstraten* [1985] Q.B. 1077.

malicious arrest or based on abuse of the process of the court are exceptions to this general principle.

(6) Once an order has been set aside it ceases to have effect for the future.

(7) A defendant whose documents have been seized by the other party under a court order which has been set aside, can get them back from that other party based on:

(a) his own title to the documents, or
(b) the jurisdiction of the court to put that party into the position as if the order had not been made.

That is a restorative jurisdiction which gives rise to substantive legal rights as a result of the judgment or order being set aside.[32]

(8) With Anton Piller relief which has been set aside, a successful respondent has to apply to the court (normally the court which set aside the order) to order the claimant to restore the documents and information taken from him, because although the respondent has a substantive right to the documents and the information, there is a discretion whether to grant the relevant remedies of specific restitution and an injunction to protect the information, because that information has been obtained under an order which has been set aside. If the information is confidential information protected by a duty of confidence, then the other party will also be subject to the equitable jurisdiction to protect confidential information.[33]

(9) In practice when Anton Piller relief is discharged *inter partes* or on appeal, prima facie the defendant has the right to have documents and materials restored to him. The point often arises that the documents obtained would in any event have to be disclosed on disclosure and so it is more cost effective and less disruptive not to order the return of the seized documents. When this point is made out, it may be sensible not to order the return of what has been seized particularly since the result of the order being set aside is that the claimant already faces the prospect of an substantial adverse order for costs and potentially an order directing an inquiry as to damages sustained by reason of the order.

(10) The supervising solicitor who has received documents under a search order in the form of the example order is bound by an

---

[32] *Osenton v Johnston* [1942] W.N. 75 (the setting aside by the House of Lords of an order for costs had the effect the money paid under the set-aside order had to be repaid, even though the House of Lords had not expressly directed this); *Rodger v Comptoir d'Escompte* (1871) L.R. 3 P.C. 465 (the setting aside of an order for payment of an amount and interest had the effect that the successful appellant was entitled to repayment of all the sums paid, together with interest).
[33] See para.18.008.

express undertaking given to the court that "The Supervising Solicitor will retain in the safe keeping of his firm all items retained by him as a result of this order until the court directs otherwise".[34] Even where there is no express undertaking, the view has been expressed that the supervising solicitor is under an implied obligation not to do anything with the documents without the consent of the defendant or an order of the court.[35] Also, once the order is set aside, the defendant has title in the documents and, unless an order is made governing documents in the hands of the supervising solicitor, the defendant can assert that title against the supervising solicitor, although what remedy he may obtain is a further question.

(11) It may be that materials have been disclosed because of the immediate pressure of a search order even though the defendant might have claimed legal professional or litigation privilege for them, and retained them notwithstanding the order. The court should still be prepared to grant relief requiring the return of the materials so as to enforce their confidentiality. This is because if the compulsory order was wrongly granted and if it was a consequence of the urgency and pressure of the execution of the wrongly granted order that the disclosure was made in the first place, then this should go in favour of granting equitable relief.[36]

(22) Costs of preparing an application for a search order

The costs of preparing an application to be made in intended proceedings 17.068 for a search order fall within the court's jurisdiction over costs conferred by s.51 of the Supreme Court Act 1981. These costs can include costs incurred before the proceedings were commenced.[37] Once a party has commenced the immediate steps which are to lead to an application to the court for an injunction, the court also has jurisdiction over him to award the other party its costs.[38]

---

[34] Example order, Schedule E, para.(3).
[35] *Gordon v Summers* [2003] F.S.R. 719 at [10].
[36] Contrast the unforced error situation addressed in *Guiness Peat Properties Ltd v Fitzroy Robinson Partnership* [1987] 1 W.L.R. 1027 and *Derby & Co. Ltd v Weldon (No.8)* [1991] 1 W.L.R. 73 at 96–97.
[37] *Admiral Management Services Ltd v Para-Protect Europe Ltd* [2002] 1 W.L.R. 2722; *Pêcheries Ostendaises (SA) v Merchants' Marine Insurance Co.* [1928] 1 K.B. 750; *Re Nossen's Letter Patent* [1969] 1 W.L.R. 638; *Re Gibson's Settlement Trusts* [1981] Ch. 179.
[38] *Associated Newspapers v Impac* [2002] F.S.R. 18.

Chapter 18

Injunctions to preserve privileged information or to prevent lawyers or other professionals from acting

(1) The "cause of action"

The word "privileged" has several different meanings. Legal professional **18.001** privilege is a right not to be required to produce documents or information within its scope. But those materials are also confidential protected by a duty of confidence owed by the lawyer to his client and an enforceable right to confidentiality available against anyone into whose hands the information might come. The justification for the privilege is the due administration of justice and the need for a person to be able to make a clean breast of matters to his lawyers and to obtain legal advice without the fear that he will be prejudiced through this process.[1]

Likewise materials the subject of litigation privilege are confidential materials collected for the purpose of obtaining advice on, or possible use in, anticipated or actual litigation. In principle they are protected by an enforceable duty of confidence. The justification for this privilege is to enable the client to have confidential communications with his lawyers, seek and obtain their advice, and conduct the litigation without any fear that communications could be used against him.[2] It includes reports prepared for the dominant[3] purpose of dealing with anticipated litigation, proofs of evidence whether factual or expert, and communications of the client or his advisers with potential witnesses.

In contrast, the privilege against self-incrimination is a right not to be compelled, under pain of a penalty, to provide documents or information which could incriminate that person or that person's spouse. It does not depend upon the material itself being the subject of an enforceable duty of confidence. Thus, *e.g.* a former employee who has accepted bribes must

---

[1] *Anderson v Bank of British Columbia* (1876) 2 Ch.D. 644 at 648–649.
[2] *Re Barings plc* [1998] Ch. 356 at 366; *Ventouris v Mountain* [1991] 1 W.L.R. 607 at 609–610 (privilege did not apply to an original document which came into existence before any contemplated litigation but which was acquired because of the litigation).
[3] *Waugh v British Railways Board* [1980] A.C. 521 (if there is an equally important purpose of investigating the cause of an accident to prevent repetition, then this is not enough).

account for them to his employer who also has a proprietary right to them.[4] Information about the receipt of the bribes was not covered by an enforceable duty of confidence, and so is not to be protected under the equitable jurisdiction to protect confidential information.[5]

18.002   Material which comes into existence through "without prejudice" negotiations is sometimes called privileged. The "without prejudice" rule is one of exclusion of evidence on the ground of encouraging settlement discussions. Whether that material is to be protected by injunction depends upon finding a justification outside of the rule of evidence. It may be found in an enforceable equitable duty of confidence[6] or through contract.

Just because material is confidential does not make it inadmissible in evidence. Even if it was the subject of legal professional or litigation privilege it is not inadmissible.[7] But it does not follow that because a party has come into possession of another person's confidential material and it is admissible in evidence, therefore he has a right to adduce it in evidence or use it in litigation. There is a confusion here.[8] It may be that the confidentiality of the material can still be protected by injunction thus making it unavailable to be adduced in evidence, by restraining its use and ordering delivery-up of the documents and all copies,[9] or by prohibiting lawyers or other professionals from acting.[10]

There is no general rule preventing parties from contracting that certain evidence is not to be relevant and therefore admissible when determining their substantive rights. For example, this can be done by a conclusive evidence clause in a contract which makes a certificate conclusive about the quality or description of goods supplied.[11] Public policy favours such clauses because they narrow the potential for disputes and litigation between the parties. It is no objection that the clause involves the third party resolving questions of law such as interpretation of a contract. As for whether the clause applies in the particular case, the question is whether the third party certifier has acted within the walls of the clause—adopting a method of determination which differs from that specified in the contract will not do, even though it is just as good as the method agreed or even better than it.[12]

18.003   Another example is when the parties agree in the course of settlement negotiations to bring into existence a report which is to be used to further those negotiations. There they have contracted that such a report is not to

---

[4] *Attorney-General for Hong Kong v Reid* [1994] 1 A.C. 324 in which it was held that *Lister v Stubbs* (1890) 45 Ch.D. 1 was wrongly decided.
[5] *Bell Cablemedia Plc v Simmons* [2002] F.S.R. 551.
[6] *Prudential Insurance Company of America v Prudential Assurance Company Ltd* [2003] EWCA Civ 1154.
[7] *Calcraft v Guest* [1898] 1 Q.B. 759.
[8] *Lord Ashburton v Pape* [1913] 2 Ch. 469 at 475–477.
[9] *Goddard v Nationwide* [1987] Q.B. 670 applying *Lord Ashburton v Pape* [1913] 2 Ch. 469 and distinguishing *Calcraft v Guest* [1898] 1 Q.B. 759.
[10] *Bolkiah v KPMG* [1999] 2 A.C. 222; *Re a Firm of Solicitors* [1997] Ch. 1; *Ablitt v Mills & Reeve, The Times*, October 25, 1995.
[11] *Alfred C. Toepfer v Continental Grain Co.* [1974] 1 Lloyd's Rep. 11.
[12] *Veba Oil Supply & Trading GmbH v Petrotrade Inc.* [2002] 1 Ll. Rep. 295.

be used in evidence and the court will respect that bargain.[13] This is different from the rule that there is no property in a witness whether of fact or expert,[14] because that rule has nothing to do with whether a party is to have access to confidential information or to use it by adducing it in evidence.

(2) Granting relief in respect of self-incriminating materials to which the claimant or the supervising solicitor has had access or taken into their hands under a search order or other mandatory order

A search order can be made, notwithstanding the possibility of the respondent having self-incriminating documents or materials, if it contains a proviso that the mandatory terms shall only come into effect once the respondent has taken legal advice and has waived the privilege against self-incrimination.[15] It is open to a respondent to waive this privilege, but in the circumstances of execution of a search order this is not lightly to be inferred. The respondent may be highly emotional over what has happened. If the respondent has taken independent legal advice, the court will consider whether in all the circumstances there has been effective consent to waive privilege.[16] But leaving this aside, the respondent will not be taken to have given his voluntary consent to waive privilege.[17] An order can only properly be made if it provides for the claim to privilege, and execution of it is only proper if on the facts true consent has been obtained to the voluntary waiver of the privilege. 18.004

Leaving aside the possibility of waiver of the privilege against self-incrimination, the order should not compel production of documents protected by the privilege against self-incrimination. Thus, *e.g.* in a case in which there is a real risk of a prosecution for conspiracy to defraud there is no statutory provisional which removes the risk of self-incrimination or which excludes the availability of the privilege, and no Anton Piller or other mandatory relief will be granted.

If documents which are privileged against self-incrimination are removed by the applicant on execution of the order, can the respondent obtain the return of them?

---

[13] *Rabin v Mendoza & Co.* [1954] 1 W.L.R. 271, approved in *Rush & Tomkins v Greater London Council* [1989] A.C. 1280 at 1303–1304.
[14] *Harmony Shipping SA v Davis* [1979] 1 W.L.R. 1380, in which the handwriting expert previously consulted by the plaintiff was made the subject of a subpoena issued by the defendant, but this did not enable the defendant to adduce the confidential communications between the expert and the plaintiff's lawyer—see [1979] 1 W.L.R. at 1385C–F.
[15] See paras 17.041–17.043 above; *Tate Access Floors Inc. v Boswell* [1991] Ch. 512 at 530 and 532; *IBM v Prima Data International* [1994] 1 W.L.R. 719 at 728–729.
[16] *IBM v Prima Data International* [1994] 1 W.L.R. 719 at 730–731 (the defendant was a businessman of some experience and so this procedure could be used without unfairness).
[17] *Columbia Pictures Inc. v Robinson* [1987] Ch. 38 at 77; *J. C. Techforce Pty Ltd v Pearce* (1996) 138 A.L.R. 522 at 526–527.

18.005   First, this privilege is only a privilege against being forced to produce materials or answer questions compulsorily. In *Bell Cablemedia Plc v Simmons*[18] the defendant was subject to a Mareva injunction and disclosure order in respect of a claim alleging acceptance of bribes. He was asked to return a laptop computer, which he did together with a diskette containing incriminating material. The Court of Appeal refused to order the return of the information or to prevent the plaintiff from relying on the material in evidence, and upheld the summary judgment given against the defendant. The privilege against self-incrimination is only an answer to compulsory production. It does not in itself result in the material being confidential and thus within the scope of the equitable jurisdiction[19] of the court to grant an injunction to protect confidentiality and order the return of confidential materials.[20] In that case information about the receipt of bribes whilst acting in the plaintiff's employment was not confidential to the defendant. Even if the material had been confidential, the defendant would have had no assistance from the court's equitable jurisdiction because the defendant's mistake had been unforced, and equity would not assist a dishonest man from the consequences of mistakenly disclosing evidence of his dishonesty.[21]

Secondly, if the documents are both privileged and confidential, the court can protect the privilege and the confidentiality by injunction.[22] However, this is a discretionary jurisdiction and subject to considerations which include whether it is right to protect someone who is guilty of wrongdoing from the consequences of this.

18.006   In *Universal City Studios v Hubbard*,[23] the defendant sought unsuccessfully to assert that s.72 of the Supreme Court Act 1981 did not apply, and that he had a right to privilege against self-incrimination. At first instance Falconer J. had thought that if s.72 did not apply, then he should have ordered return of the documents, but this conclusion was the subject of "serious doubt" on appeal. In that case, however, the privilege relied upon was solely that against self-incrimination and there was a serious question[24] whether the defendant had any rights of confidentiality in the documents.

Thirdly, where the documents have been obtained compulsorily under a court order, the court has jurisdiction to discharge the search order or to

---

[18] Decided on April 29, 1997 and reported at [2002] F.S.R. 551.
[19] *Lord Ashburton v Pape* [1913] 2 Ch. 469; *Goddard v Nationwide* [1987] Q.B. 670.
[20] *ISTIL Group Inc. v Zahoor* [2003] 2 All E.R. 252; *Webster v James Chapman & Co.* [1989] 3 All E.R. 939; A.L.E. Newbold, "Inadvertent Disclosure in Civil Proceedings" (1991) 107 L.Q.R. 98.
[21] *Bell Cablemedia Plc v Simmons* [2002] F.S.R. 551.
[22] *Naf Naf SA v Dickens (London) Ltd* [1993] F.S.R. 424 at 427–428; *Lord Ashburton v Pape* [1913] 2 Ch. 469; *English & American Insurance Co. Ltd v Herbert Smith* [1988] F.S.R. 232; *Goddard v Nationwide Building Society* [1987] Q.B. 670; *Marcel v Commissioner of Police of the Metropolis* [1992] Ch. 225 at 235–239 (unaffected on this point by the subsequent appeal).
[23] [1984] Ch. 225.
[24] *ibid.*, at 233F–234A.

vary it so as to exclude from its ambit the information and materials. The order may be set aside either because it was wrongly granted or because of its mode of execution. In *Universal City Studios*, no argument appears to have been addressed to the court on its jurisdiction to restore to a party what has been taken from him under an order which is subsequently set aside, and in *Bell Cablemedia Plc v Simmons*[25] that point did not arise.

The court may order restoration of documents pursuant to its jurisdiction to restore to a party what has been taken from him under an order which is set aside.[26]

This is an aspect of the court's powers to reverse the effects of a **18.007** judgment or order which is set aside.[27] It is a jurisdiction available against the party who had the benefit of the order as a restitutionary remedy to restore to him what was taken from him under the order which has been set aside. It also affects third parties who derive their possession of the documents from having acts done under the authority of the discharged order. The defendant having been in possession of the documents has a superior title.

(4) Granting relief in respect of materials protected by legal professional or litigation privilege to which the other party or his advisers have had access

The jurisdiction depends upon an enforceable duty of confidence but its **18.008** application depends upon the way in which the other party has obtained access to the materials.

If counsel's papers are sent by mistake to the other side, it will be obvious to the other side that a mistake has been made and an injunction will be granted[28] which could include preventing the other side's lawyers from acting.[29]

If documents are disclosed on disclosure by mistake; listing the document does not waive the privilege which also applies to production of it. Once the document has been produced and inspected ordinarily the privilege is lost and the court will not interfere to protect the confidentiality of the document. This is because parties and their advisers have to be careful in the steps they take in litigation and the client cannot use

---

[25] [2002] F.S.R. 551.
[26] *Bond Brewing Holdings Ltd v National Australia Bank Ltd (No.2)* [1991] 1 V.L.R. 580, Supreme Court of Victoria, Full Court; see also *Dubai Bank v Goladari* [1990] 1 Lloyd's Rep. 120 at 131–135 (jurisdiction to order return of documents where the order was set aside for non-disclosure); see Chapter 17, para.17.067.
[27] D. M. Gordon, Q.C., "Effect of a Reversal of Judgments on Acts Done between Pronouncement and Reversal" (1958) 74 L.Q.R. 517 and (1959) 75 L.Q.R. 85, which discuss the authorities.
[28] *English & American v Herbert Smith* [1988] F.S.R. 232.
[29] *Ablitt v Mills & Reeve, The Times*, October 25, 1995.

the equitable jurisdiction to relieve himself of an unforced error made in the course of conducting litigation, when the other party has in no way contributed to the mistake by any fraud or dishonesty, and is unaware that an error has been made.[30] If the circumstances are such as to make it obvious to the recipient,[31] putting in the place of the actual recipient a reasonable person having the attributes of that recipient,[32] that a mistake had been made,[33] and this is proved by the applicant for the relief,[34] then equity will intervene[35] unless there are good reasons not to do so. Those include not assisting on a public policy ground such as not suppressing evidence of serious misconduct in the public interest, not intervening because the clock cannot satisfactorily be turned back and the trial court might otherwise be misled,[36] and inordinate delay by the applicant in seeking the relief.[37]

18.009   CPR r.31.20 provides:

"RESTRICTION ON USE OF A PRIVILEGED DOCUMENT INSPECTION OF WHICH HAS BEEN INADVERTENTLY ALLOWED

31.20 Where a party inadvertently allows a privileged document to be inspected, the party who has inspected the document may use it or its contents only with the permission of the court."

This provides machinery for what is to happen when there is disclosure by mistake, but does not affect the governing principles.[38] It requires the receiving party to apply to the court so that the position can be resolved so that he cannot simply deploy the document and thus create a *fait accompli*.

---

[30] *Re Briarmore Manufacturing Ltd* [1986] 1 W.L.R. 1429.
[31] *Pizzey v Ford Motor Co. Ltd* [1994] P.I.Q.R. P15; Court of Appeal (Civ Div) Transcript No.315 of 1993 (the small volume of discovery was consistent with the documents being disclosed intentionally).
[32] *IBM Corporation v Phoenix International (Computers) Ltd* [1995] 1 All E.R. 413 at 422 proposition (6).
[33] *ibid.*, at 423d–f.
[34] *ibid.*, at 422 proposition (6).
[35] *ibid.*, at 422 propositions (5) and (6) (discovery carried out carelessly on the cheap, therefore greater risk of error, and the mistake about production of the legal bills would have been obvious to a reasonable solicitor); *Breeze v John Stacey & Sons Ltd, The Times,* July 8, 1999 (continuously paginated exhibit which included privileged material did not make it obvious that an error had been made); *Derby & Co. Ltd v Weldon (No.8)* [1991] 1 W.L.R. 73 at 96–97; *Guinness Peat Properties Ltd v Fitzroy Robinson Partnership* [1987] 1 W.L.R. 1027.
[36] *ISTIL Group Inc. v Zahoor* [2003] 2 All E.R. 252 at [115].
[37] *Goddard v Nationwide Building Society* [1987] Q.B. 670 at 684–685.
[38] *Al Fayed v Commissioner of Police for the Metropolis* [2002] EWCA Civ. 780, *The Times,* June 17, 2002; *Breeze v John Stacey & Sons Ltd* [2001] N.P.C. 2.

(5) Granting relief in respect of materials protected by legal professional or litigation privilege to which the claimant or the supervising solicitor has had access or taken into their hands under a search order

Materials, which are the subject of legal professional privilege or litigation **18.010** privilege, are confidential and are subject to the court's jurisdiction to protect the confidentiality.[39] They are also privileged from production. That privilege from production can be asserted by the principal, his agent or his successor in title,[40] it cannot be asserted by someone who is a mere witness.[41]

No inference could properly be drawn from a refusal by the respondent to waive these privileges. No mandatory order should be made which infringes the privilege. The court also would not adopt a procedure which had the effect of undermining the practical utility of the privileges. This is because of their fundamental importance to the due administration of justice.

If as a result of the order privileged materials come into the hands of the supervising solicitor or of the applicants or their solicitors, they remain confidential. They are not inadmissible in evidence.[42] But they are subject to the court's equitable jurisdiction to protect confidential information, and relief can be granted so as to ensure that they are not available to be adduced into evidence or to be produced to a third party.

This situation is to be distinguished from those in which a solicitor on **18.011** disclosure, or in the conduct of the proceedings, has made an unforced mistake in disclosing privileged materials to the other side in circumstances where it is not clear that an error has been made. In those circumstances, although the privilege is that of the client, unless the documents have been obtained by misconduct of the other side, or if, with knowledge that the documents are likely to be privileged, the other side or their solicitors read the documents, no injunction will be granted.[43]

Where documents have been obtained by the applicant or the supervising solicitor through a search order the position is different. Here the handing

---

[39] *Bell Cablemedia Plc v Simmons* [2002] F.S.R. 551; *Lord Ashburton v Pape* [1913] 2 Ch. 469; *English & American Insurance Co. Ltd v Herbert Smith* [1988] F.S.R. 232; *Goddard v Nationwide Building Society* [1987] Q.B. 670.

[40] *The Aegis Blaze* [1986] 1 Lloyd's Rep. 203 at 209–210.

[41] *Schneider v Leigh* [1955] 2 Q.B. 195; hence the problem in *Gordon v Summers* [2003] F.S.R. 719, where the supervising solicitor held documents which were the subject of legal professional and litigation privilege and the police had given advance notice of their intention to seek from the Crown Court an order compelling their production.

[42] *Calcraft v Guest* [1898] 1 Q.B. 759.

[43] *IBM Corporation v Phoenix International (Computers) Ltd* [1995] 1 All E.R. 413 at 422 propositions (5) and (6); *Breeze v John Stacey & Sons Ltd*, *The Times*, July 8, 1999; *Derby & Co. Ltd v Weldon (No.8)* [1991] 1 W.L.R. 73 at 96–97; *Guinness Peat Properties Ltd v Fitzroy Robinson Partnership* [1987] 1 W.L.R. 1027.

over or seizure of the documents cannot be compared with the unforced error of a solicitor conducting litigation. In the Anton Piller situation if the documents have been obtained by misconduct of the applicant, or if, with knowledge that the documents are likely to be privileged, the applicant or its solicitors read the documents this provides a strong additional reason for granting the equitable relief.[44]

As for an argument that the use of the privileged material in evidence would facilitate the establishment of the truth, for reasons of public policy the privileges exist notwithstanding this consideration. It follows that there is no balancing exercise to be done weighing up the desirability of getting to the truth as against maintaining the protection of the privileges. That balancing exercise has already been done and public policy favours upholding the privileges.[45]

18.012   If an injunction is not to be granted in support of the privilege this must be because of some other consideration, grounded in public policy or fairness, which precludes protection of the privilege.[46] This might be because of a strong public interest favouring disclosure of serious misconduct, or where the due administration of justice itself requires that the material is put into evidence because otherwise the court might be misled.[47]

If the applicant's solicitors see documents which are covered by legal professional or litigation privilege and, knowing that they are privileged, proceed to read them, then the court may decide not only to grant an injunction preventing use of the information and ordering the return of the documents,[48] but also grant an injunction restraining the solicitors from acting further in the case.[49]

If the materials have been obtained compulsorily under a court order, then the court can set aside that order and the question will then arise about restoring what had been obtained under that order (see para.18.006–18.007, above). The remedy is discretionary and the same considerations arise as apply under the court's equitable jurisdiction to protect confidential information.

(6) Burden of proof

18.013   A solicitor moves firm. He joins the firm instructed by the other side. Can the new firm continue to act? This was the question in *Re a Firm of Solicitors*.[50] The jurisdiction to grant an injunction against the individual

---

[44] *ISTIL Group Inc v Zahoor* [2003] 2 All E.R. 252.

[45] *Derby & Co. Ltd. v Weldon (No.8)* [1991] 1 W.L.R. 73 at 99; *ISTIL Group Inc. v Zahoor* [2003] 2 All E.R. 252.

[46] *ISTIL Group Inc. v Zahoor* [2003] 2 All E.R. 252 at [74] and [89–94].

[47] This was the ground on which relief was refused in *ISTIL Group Inc. v Zahoor* [2003] 2 All E.R. 252 at [115]—it was too late to put back the clock because of the risk that at trial, if the privileged materials were not before it, the court would be misled as to the weighing of other evidence.

[48] *English & American v Herbert Smith* [1988] F.S.R. 232.

[49] *Bolkiah v KPMG* [1999] 2 A.C. 222; *Re a Firm of Solicitors* [1997] Ch. 1; *Ablitt v Mills & Reeve, The Times*, October 25, 1995.

[50] [1997] Ch. 1.

who left and his new firm depend on the equitable jurisdiction to protect confidential information. There is a public interest in not interfering with lawyers changing firms so promoting freedom of competition within the legal profession. But this plays no real part in the question of whether an injunction is to be granted. The client has a right not to have his confidential information used against him, and usually that information will also be the subject of legal professional or litigation privilege. The rule is that the solicitor and the new firm must act scrupulously to ensure that there is no risk that this will happen.[51] It is necessary as an adjunct of the principle that a client must be free to communicate with his lawyers so as to obtain advice, to make decisions about the conduct of the litigation and to assist his lawyers in that conduct.[52] The same public policy as underlies legal professional and litigation privilege shapes the equitable jurisdiction to intervene by injunction.

The first question is whether the solicitor has any confidential information of the client. In *Re a Firm of Solicitors* the solicitor had been a partner in the first firm and so was a party to the contract of retainer. Also there was no doubt that the first firm had much confidential and privileged material of the client. The solicitor had worked at the first firm at the same time as the client's litigation was being conducted. In these circumstances there was the possibility that the solicitor might have learned confidential information at meetings within the firm or at social encounters or just through being in the same location as that from which the litigation was being conducted. It was for the solicitor who had moved to show that he had no confidential information. In that case he succeeded in proving this and so no injunction was granted, and he was at liberty to become involved in advising and acting for the other side. There was no rule that just because the solicitor was a party to the retainer by the client of the first firm therefore he was precluded from being retained by the opponent. That had been established by *Rakusen v Ellis Munday & Clarke*[53] in which the facts were that a two-partner firm had been retained by the client, but the partners carried on what amounted to totally separate practices each with his own clients and without knowledge of what the other partner was doing. One partner had been retained by the client without the knowledge of the other and the retainer had come to an end. The other partner was still free to act for the other side because there was no risk of disclosure of confidential information to that partner.

(7) The information barrier and Chinese walls

In *Bolkiah v KPMG* the question was whether the defendant firm of accountants, who had previously been retained by the prince, had accepted instructions to act against him? The new instructions were from the Brunei

18.014

---

[51] *Bolkiah v KPMG* [1999] 2 A.C. 222.
[52] *ibid.*, at 236F–G.
[53] [1912] 1 Ch. 831.

Investment Authority in respect of litigation against the prince. The accountants had confidential information but could they still act against the prince on the ground that a Chinese wall had been set up inside the firm to preserve the confidentiality of the information? The majority of the Court of Appeal, reversing the judge had held that the duty of the accountants was limited to taking reasonable steps to protect the confidential information and that the prince would not suffer any "real prejudice" if the injunction was refused. This decision was itself reversed by the House of Lords. The test to be applied depended on the risk of use of confidential information against the client. Unless there was "no risk",[54] an injunction would be granted. The position was different from that of auditors where competitors instructed the same auditors and consented to them acting provided that their confidential information was kept confidential.[55] This was like the position of solicitors in relation to litigation. The House of Lords refused to approve any of the various tests expressed in the judgments in *Rakusen v Ellis Munday & Clarke* because they placed an unfair burden on the client who was seeking to protect his confidential information.

In *Bolkiah v KPMG* part of the new retainer was simply what the accountants would have been expected to do as auditors to the Brunei Investment Authority and so within the scope of what the prince must have been taken to have consented because of their relationship as auditors which already existed at the date of their acceptance of instructions from the prince. Had this been the full extent of the new retainer, no injunction would have been granted because of consent by the prince. But it was not, the new retainer went well beyond that and was adverse to the interests of the prince. The Chinese wall which was put in place was not effective to ensure that there was no risk of confidential information being used. It was an ad hoc arrangement within a single department, there were not separate offices in different buildings, there were many personnel involved, and the personnel had a constantly rotating membership making enforcement of confidentiality all the more difficult.

18.015 Once it appears that one or more persons who have confidential information are part of the firm acting against the client the burden is upon that firm to satisfy the court that the arrangements to safeguard the information are effective to eliminate the risk of leakage, including inadvertently or unconsciously. This includes leakage which might arise through social or professional contact including internal meetings. It is a question of fact. The later that arrangements are put in place to create

---

[54] *Bolkiah v KPMG* [1999] 2 A.C. 222 at 237A–B; applying this test it follows that *Re a Firm of Solicitors* [1992] Q.B. 959 was correctly decided by the majority and the judge at first instance because the wall was not impregnable and still gave rise to a real risk of leakage, in particular because of the notoriety of the alleged wrongdoing which was part of the confidential information. The references to the tests in *Rakusen v Ellis Munday & Clarke* and to the Law Society's guide have been overtaken by *Bolkiah v KPMG*.

[55] *Bolkiah v KPMG* [1999] 2 A.C. 222 at 235, referring to the analogous case of estate agents being free to be retained by competing clients—*Kelly v Cooper* [1993] A.C. 205.

information barriers after the situation of potential leakage has arisen, the more difficult it will be for the firm to show that such arrangements are effective, and that information has not already passed within the firm to those who would be acting against the client or to persons to whom they have access. The court will look for arrangements which will work,[56] usually arrangements which include clear and workable undertakings by both those who have the information and other members of the firm, and physical separation of personnel and their places of work.[57] This does not mean that the two groups must have no contact at all whether on a social level or professionally.[58]

In *Koch Shipping Inc. v Richards Butler*[59] two solicitors had moved to the defendant firm at which two solicitors were engaged in the arbitration for the other side. One of those solicitors had acted for the claimant in the arbitration, and the other had acted for the claimant. The Court of Appeal held that given that the undertakings offered, which included an undertaking by the solicitor, who was the only potential discloser of the confidential information which was to be protected, not to talk to anyone about the arbitration, eliminated any risk of disclosure even inadvertently and therefore no injunction should have been granted against the firm continuing to act. It was not necessary to ban her from the defendant's building, and to require her to work from home.[60]

(8) Conflicting Duties

A professional may find himself under one duty to one client and another **18.016** to another which are inconsistent with each other. A solicitor cannot act for both the claimant and the defendant in the same contentious litigation because his duty to do his best for one party is inconsistent with doing his best for the other. A solicitor must not place himself in a position in which there is an actual or potential conflict in fulfilling his obligations to each of two principals. In *Bristol and West Building Society v Mothew*,[61] a solicitor had acted for both the purchasers of a house and the building society which lent them part of the purchase money on mortgage. The solicitor mistakenly informed the building society that the balance of the purchase money was coming from the purchasers' without resort to further borrowing. In fact they did borrow a relatively small sum by way of second charge on the property. This was not a breach of the fiduciary duties of loyalty

[56] *Young v Robson Rhodes* [1999] 3 All E.R. 524 at [42] and [43].
[57] *Halewood International Ltd v Addleshaw Booth & Co.* [2000] P.N.L.R. 788.
[58] *Young v Robson Rhodes* [1999] 3 All E.R. 524 at [42].
[59] [2002] 2 All E.R. (Comm) 957.
[60] See also *In the Matter of a Firm of Solicitors* [2000] 1 Lloyd's Rep.31 where the evidence that the information barrier put in place would work was "most compelling" and an injunction was refused.
[61] [1998] Ch. 1.

and fidelity owed by the solicitor to the building society; it was a negligent mistake. In the course of his judgment Millett L.J. reviewed the class of case in which a fiduciary is placed in breach of his fiduciary duty to one principal because of "the double employment rule", which applies where his duty of loyalty and fidelity may conflict with what he has undertaken for another client. With the exception of cases in which informed consent can properly be obtained and has been obtained from both principals,[62] once the fiduciary places himself in the position of potential conflict in fulfilling the fiduciary duties owed to each client, this is a breach of the duty of loyalty and fidelity owed to each. The fiduciary must also not act when there is an actual conflict in that fulfilling his fiduciary duty owed to one principal would result in actual breach of the fiduciary duty owed to another. This is not confined to same matter conflicts but extends to cases in which there are matters which are related and which may generate conflicting fiduciary duties.[63]

Where a solicitor is threatening to place himself in a position where he cannot, or potentially may not be able, to fulfil his fiduciary duties owed to one client because of what he is proposing to undertake for another this may be restrained by injunction.[64]

---

[62] *Clark Boyce v Mouat [1994]* 1 A.C. 428 at 435–436; *Boulting v Association of Cinematograph, Television and Allied Technicians* [1963] 2 Q.B. 606 at 636.

[63] *Marks and Spencer plc v Freshfields Bruckhaus Deringer* [2004] EWHC 1337 at para.16 (permission to appeal was refused by the Court of Appeal).

[64] *Marks and Spencer plc v Freshfields Bruckhaus Deringer* [2004] EWHC 1337 at paras 23–25 (permission to appeal was refused by the Court of Appeal), where the solicitors were already acting for the claimant on the Davies contract which was also a very important part of the take-over bid which was being launched by Mr. Green.

Chapter 19

Contempt of court: the position of the defendant and non-parties

(1) Introduction: the effects of an injunction

The law of contempt of court is of ancient origin and fundamental **19.001** contemporary importance.[1] It has been described as "the Proteus of the legal world, assuming an almost infinite diversity of forms".[2] Breach of a court order by the party restrained is only one of these forms. This form of disobedience is a civil contempt or "contempt in procedure"[3] and not a criminal contempt.

The general principle is that an injunction is addressed to the party enjoined, who must be a party to the proceedings.[4] There is also a power in the court to grant an injunction *contra mundum*;[5] but this only arises in very particular circumstances, such as in connection with publication of information by the media which if published could damage a ward of court, or lead to a clear and present risk of physical or psychological harm to an individual.

---

[1] N. Lowe and B. Sufrin, *Borrie and Lowe: The Law of Contempt* (3rd ed., 1996), p.2. The present chapter considers the law of contempt in relation to commercial injunctions. For works devoted to the law of contempt, see *Borrie and Lowe* (above); A. Arlidge, Sir David Eady and A.T.H. Smith, *The Law of Contempt* (2nd ed., 1999) and C.J. Miller, *The Law of Contempt* (2000).

[2] J. Moskovitz, "Contempt of Injunctions, Civil and Criminal" (1943) 43 Col. L.R. 780. This statement is referred to in a passage from *Borrie and Lowe: The Law of Contempt* (2nd ed., 1983), cited by Sir John Donaldson M.R., in *Attorney-General v Newspaper Publishing plc* [1988] Ch. 333 at 361–362.

[3] *Hadkinson v Hadkinson* [1952] P. 285 at 295, *per* Denning L.J.

[4] *Marengo v Daily Sketch* [1948] 1 All E.R. 406 at 407; *Iveson v Harris* (1802) 7 Ves. Jun. 251; *Brydges v Brydges* [1909] P. 187; *Attorney-General v Newspaper Publishing plc*; [1988] Ch. 333 *Royal Bank of Canada v Canstar Sports Group Inc.* [1989] 1 W.W.R. 662, Manitoba Court of Appeal. See Chapter 13, para.13.001, above.

[5] *Venables v News Group* [2001] Fam. 430 at [98–100] granting an injunction *contra mundum* in order to protect the claimants against the risk of serious physical injury if their new identities were to be disclosed ; *X, a Woman formerly known as Mary Bell v S and News Group Newspapers* [2003] F.S.R. 850 at [63] and [64] (protecting the identity of Mary Bell); *Attorney-General v H* [2001] 2 F.L.R. 895 (protecting a child from a clear risk of harm from an estranged father); *Re X (A Minor) (Wardship: Injunction)* [1984] 1 W.L.R. 1422; *Attorney-General v Newspaper Publishing plc* [1988] Ch. 333.

Non-parties are not themselves enjoined by an injunction.[6] If a defendant acts in breach of an injunction restraining him, then he will be in contempt of court. But the effect of an injunction is much wider.

19.002   When considering whether a defendant restrained by an injunction is in breach of that order questions can arise about whose conduct is to be treated as that of the defendant. It may be that the conduct of a person is to be treated as conduct of the defendant, so that the conduct will place the defendant in breach of the order. Questions can also arise as to the extent of the responsibility of the defendant to prevent others from carrying out the prohibited acts.

A further question is whether someone other than the defendant is liable for contempt of court. For example an employee can by his conduct put his employer in breach of an injunction and at the same time become personally liable for contempt. This question can arise whether or not the non-party's conduct is to be imputed to the defendant for the purpose of deciding whether the defendant is in contempt. The liability of the non-party for contempt can be based on:

(1) the non-party knowingly aiding and abetting a breach of an injunction.[7] In this situation there has to have been a breach of the injunction by the defendant; or

(2) a non-party with knowledge of the order doing "something which disables the court from conducting the case in the intended manner" and thereby interfering with the due administration of justice.[8] This can arise entirely independently of whether there has been any breach of the injunction. For example, where an injunction has been granted against publication by a defendant so as to keep the information confidential pending trial, a non-party who publishes that information knowing of the injunction will be in contempt of court.

(2) The position of the defendant against whom an injunction has been granted

(i) When the injunction commences

19.003   An injunction takes effect at the moment it is pronounced,[9] unless the court orders that it is to take effect from a later date.[10]

---

[6] *Lord Wellesley v Earl of Mornington* (1848) 11 Beav. 180.

[7] *Lard Wellesley v Earl of Mornington* (1848) 11 Beav. 180; *Lord Wellesley v Earl of Mornington (No.2)* 11 Beav. 181; *Seaward v Paterson* [1897] 1 Ch. 545; *Acrow Automation Ltd v Rex Chainbelt Inc.* [1971] 1 W.L.R. 1676; *Z Ltd v A–Z and AA–LL* [1982] Q.B. 558.

[8] *Attorney-General v Punch* [2003] 1 A.C. 1046; *Attorney-General v Times Newspapers* [1992] 1 A.C. 191 at 206D–H, 214C–215B, 224–225, 231B; *Attorney-General v Newspaper Publishing plc* [1988] Ch. 333; *Harrow London Borough Council v Johnstone* [1997] 1 W.L.R. 459 at 468.

[9] *Z Ltd v A–Z and AA–LL* [1982] Q.B. 558 at 572; CPR r.40.7(1).

[10] Under CPR r.40.7(1) there is power to make the order effective from a later date, but not a power to make an order effective from an earlier date *nunc pro tunc*.

(ii) Mens rea *of the defendant, capacity to understand and minors*

If the defendant has broken the terms of an injunction then he is in contempt of court.[11] There is no need to establish any intent to act contumaciously or any *mens rea*.[12] He must have the limited mental capacity which is required so as to understand what he could not do and the nature of the possible consequences.[13] The fact that a defendant obtained and acted on professional advice provides him with no defence, even if he believed that what he was doing did not infringe the requirements of the injunction.[14] It may or may not, depending on the circumstances,[15] go to mitigation of the penalty. Nor is it a defence for a defendant to contend that a variation to the injunction would have been granted, had one been sought, which would have permitted the act in question (*e.g.* to enable him to pay legal costs).[16] However, the "technicality" of the contempt and the absence of any serious fault will mitigate the position and may lead to no penalty being imposed by the court.

An injunction will not be granted against a minor who has no assets because the court will not commit him to prison for contempt and there is no effective means of enforcement.[17]

19.004

(iii) *Effect of an undertaking given to the court*

An undertaking by a defendant to the court has the same effect as an injunction.[18] A person who has given an undertaking may be held liable

19.005

---

[11] *Miller v Scorey* [1996] 1 W.L.R. 1122 at 1132C–F; *Re the Agreement of the Mileage Conference Group of the Tyre Manufacturers' Conference Ltd* [1966] 1 W.L.R. 1137 at 1162; *Spectravest Inc. v Aperknit Ltd* (1988) 14 F.S.R. 161 at 173–174.

[12] *Adam Phones v Goldschmidt* [1999] 4 All E.R. 486 at 492–494 in which *Irtelli v Squatriti* [1993] Q.B. 83 was not followed because it is inconsistent with other case law; *Bird v Hadkinson, The Times*, April 7, 1999 also declining to follow *Irtelli v Squatriti*, which was inconsistent with a series of earlier cases which laid down a requirement of strict liability .

[13] *P v P (Contempt of Court: Mental Capacity)* [1999] 2 F.L.R. 897; *Wookey v Wookey* [1991] Fam. 121.

[14] *Re the Agreement of the Mileage Conference Group of the Tyre Manufacturers' Conference Ltd* [1966] 1 W.L.R. 1137; *Z Bank v DI* [1994] 1 Lloyd's Rep. 656 at 660; *Spectravest Inc. v Aperknit Ltd* (1988) 14 F.S.R. 161; *C. H. Giles & Co. v Morris* [1972] 1 W.L.R. 307 at 319E–F (where the motion to commit/sequestrate was adjourned to give the contemnors the opportunity of complying with the order); *Summit Holdings Ltd v Business Software Alliance* [1999] 3 S.L.R. 197.

[15] *Parker v Rasalingham, The Times*, July 25, 2000; *Re the Agreement of the Mileage Conference Group of the Tyre Manufacturers' Conference Ltd* [1966] 1 W.L.R. 1137 at 1162; *Summit Holdings Ltd v Business Software Alliance* [1999] 3 S.L.R. 197; *Deputy Commissioner of Taxation v Hickey* [1999] F.C.A. 259 (March 18, 1999) at para.36 (where the solicitors had not applied for a variation, which "any reasonably competent solicitor" ought to have been able to have granted, and which would have authorised the dealings which were in contempt of court, and this was "a very significant mitigating factor").

[16] *TDK Tape Distributor (UK) Ltd v Videochoice Ltd* [1986] 1 W.L.R. 141; *Z Bank v DI* [1994] 1 Lloyd's Rep. 656 at 668. The order remains in force unless and until it is varied, and the fact that an application could have been made successfully to vary the order is no answer to the charge of contempt. See para.19.055, below.

[17] *London Borough of Harrow v G* [2004] EWHC 17, QBD.

[18] *Biba Ltd v Stratford Investments* [1973] Ch. 281 at 287; *Cobra Golf Inc. v Rata* [1998] Ch. 109. If a solicitor acts in breach of an undertaking given by him to the court (*e.g.* as the

in contempt of the undertaking even though it has not been served on him.[19]

(iv) What an injunction prohibits or orders

19.006 Injunctions can be purely negative, prohibiting prescribed conduct, or can be mandatory, requiring the defendant to take certain steps. Whatever the nature of the injunction it must be drafted so as to specify clearly what it requires. The general principle is that the person enjoined and any non-party simply through inspection of the order should be able to understand exactly what is ordered. If the order[20] or undertaking[21] is ambiguous, then the court will not punish for contempt.[22] Every order will refer to persons things and matters outside of the document. But the objective is to produce so far as is possible a free-standing document, which does not refer to other documents,[23] and which is clear and precise. In interpreting the document the court treats it as a free-standing document. So, *e.g.* if an injunction is granted giving effect to and adopting the words of a contractual promise, what matters is what the words mean in the injunction and this may not be the same as what they mean in the contract.[24] The court places itself in the position of the reasonable recipient of the order together with all the background knowledge which is reasonably available to the class consisting of the defendant and non-parties who may be affected by the order.[25]

---

price of obtaining an injunction or search order for his client) then he is in contempt of court; *Long v Specifier Publications Pty Ltd* (1998) 44 N.S.W.L.R. 545. See further on enforcement of an undertaking given to the court, para.24.043 below.

[19] *Hussain v Hussain* [1986] Fam. 134; *D v A & Co.* [1900] 1 Ch. 484.

[20] *Federal Bank of the Middle East v Hadkinson* [2000] 1 W.L.R. 1695 at 1705C–D; *Iberian Trust Ltd v Founders Trust and Investment Co. Ltd* [1932] 2 K.B. 87 at 95; *R. v City of London Magistrates' Court, Ex p. Green* [1997] 3 All E.R. 551 at 558; *R & I Bank of Western Australia Ltd v Anchorage Investments* (1992) 10 W.A.R. 59.

[21] *Redwing Ltd v Redwing Forest Products Ltd* [1947] R.P.C. 67 at 71.

[22] *cf Australian Consolidated Press Ltd v Morgan* (1965) 112 C.L.R. 483 at p.492 *per* Barwick C.J.; *Long v Specifier Publications Pty Ltd* (1998) 44 N.S.W.L.R. 545 at pp. 567–568, which support a narrower view of the scope of this defence, *i.e.* that unless the wording is so unclear it cannot be interpreted, the court must first interpret it finding the correct meaning, and then decide what to do as a matter of discretion in the light of that interpretation, including refusing to make an order holding a party in contempt because the party proceeded against reasonably misinterpreted the words, and was thus prejudiced by the defective state of the undertaking or order (*e.g.* in *Togher v Customs and Excise Commissioners* [2001] EWCA Civ 474 at [53–56], Lightman J. held that there was a good defence because of the ambiguity in the wording of the order, and Mr Togher's state of mind about what he thought the order meant).

[23] *Rudkin-Jones v Trustee of the Property of the Bankrupt* (1965) 109 S.J. 334; *Telesystem International Wireless Incorporated v CVC/Opportunity Equity Partners L.P.* [2002] C.I.L.R. at [46].

[24] *World Wide Fund for Nature v THQ/Jakks Pacific LLC (World Wrestling Federation intervening)* [2004] F.S.R. 10, p.161 at [16] ("Although the injunction was . . . framed with the . . . Agreement in mind, it must stand on its own terms . . .").

[25] *Homburg Houtimport BV v Agrosin Private Ltd (The Starsin)* [2004] 1 A.C. 715 at [73]; *Dairy Containers Ltd v Tasman Orient Line CV (The Tasman Discoverer)* [2004] UKPC 22 at [12].

The order may require the defendant to prevent others from acting in a particular way. What steps the defendant is required to take to bring this about is a matter of interpretation of the order. It may be that the defendant is required to use all reasonable efforts to bring about the desired result.[26] This is a separate point from whose conduct is to be imputed to the defendant as being his conduct for the purpose of contempt proceedings.

A mandatory order necessarily includes a prohibition forbidding the **19.007** defendant from doing anything or permitting anything to occur which would disable him from complying with the mandatory terms of the order. So if an order requires disclosure of documents the defendant is by implication forbidden to destroy them or to give them away, and he must take proper care of them. If after the date of the order the documents are destroyed or lost he will be in breach of the order and liable to be proceeded against for contempt unless the defendant's inability to comply arose despite the exercise of proper care by himself, his servants and agents.[27] In *Re Bramblevale*[28] the former managing director was acquitted of contempt because contempt was not proved beyond reasonable doubt; there were the possibilities that he had destroyed the documents before the order had been made,[29] or that the documents had been lost before that date, or had been lost afterwards without any fault on his part, and therefore were not in his control at the date on which he was ordered to produce them.

Depending on the terms of an interim injunction the court may find itself trying out on a motion for contempt issues which overlap with the issues to be resolved in the underlying action.[30]

For the effect of para.7 of the example order, which is the clause which **19.008** identifies assets which are described as coming "in particular" within the restraint in para.5, see paras 19.038–19–040, below.

(v) The defendant being placed in breach of the order by his servants or agents—imputing conduct of others to the defendant for the purpose of finding contempt

The defendant is personally enjoined by the injunction. He also must not **19.009** do prohibited acts through others including his servants or agents. The principle is also that he who acts through another, carries out the acts himself.

---

[26] *World Wide Fund for Nature v THQ/Jakks Pacific LLC (World Wrestling Federation intervening)* [2004] F.S.R. 10, p.161.
[27] *Re Supply of Ready Mixed Concrete (No.2)* [1992] Q.B. 213, approving *Stancomb v Trowbridge Urban and District Council* [1910] 2 Ch. 190—see para.19.017, below.
[28] [1970] Ch. 128.
[29] *ibid.*, at 138D.
[30] *Spectravest Inc v Aperknit Ltd* [1988] F.S.R. 161; *Chanel Ltd FGM Cosmetics* [1981] F.S.R. 471.

It used to be standard wording to restrain the defendant from doing the relevant acts whether by himself his servants or agents or otherwise. This did not extend the injunction to being an order directly against the servants or agents but was to make it clear to the defendant that he would be in breach of the order whether he broke it himself or through the act of his servant or agent.[31]

In *Yukong Line Ltd v Rendsburg*[32] the third defendant had been found not liable to the plaintiff at the trial but funds had been removed from the first defendant in breach of a freezing injunction. The background to the making of the order had been that money had been removed from the first defendant even though a Mareva injunction against it was in force and, on the findings of the trial judge, the third defendant was the person who controlled the first defendant. The trial judge made an order that "The first defendant do by the third defendant . . . pay [a sum of money] into court . . .". In contempt proceedings against the third defendant, the judge had held that because the money was not paid by the relevant date, the third defendant was in breach of the order. He granted leave to sequestrate the third defendant's assets. The Court of Appeal reversed this decision on the ground that para.1 of the order was directed only to the first defendant and required that defendant to pay money into court through the third defendant. The case illustrates the distinction between the person against whom the order is made and the persons whose conduct may put that person in breach of the order. It also shows that an order is to be interpreted as a free-standing document unaffected by considerations such as what the trial judge may have intended. Freedom of the individual depends upon this principle. It is also a matter going to the integrity of the judicial process. This is because the right of appeal is against the court order.[33] An unclear order itself interferes with the proper working of the appellate process. It would not be fair to hold him in contempt based upon something other than the clear ordinary meaning of the words used in the order.

19.010   The example form of freezing injunction given by the Practice Direction—Interim Injunctions which supplements CPR Pt 25 provides:

"INTERPRETATION OF THIS ORDER

14.   A Respondent who is an individual who is ordered not to do something must not do it himself or in any other way. He must not do it through others acting on his behalf or on his instructions or with his encouragement.

---

[31] *Marengo v Daily Sketch* [1948] 1 All E.R. 406.
[32] [1998] EWCA Civ 2795, which is put into the context of the litigation as a whole in P. Devonshire, "Freezing Orders, Disappearing Assets and the Problem of Enjoined Non-parties" (2002) 118 L.Q.R. 124 at 132–136.
[33] *Cie Noga d'impotation et d'Exportation SA v Australia and New Zealand Banking Group* [2003] 1 W.L.R. 307 at [27].

15. A Respondent which is not an individual which is ordered not to do something must not do it itself or by its directors, officers, partners, employees or agents or in any other way."

Under the formula in the Practice Direction, the defendant must not do the prohibited acts either himself or through others. If a servant or agent commits a prohibited act in the course of his employment or within the scope of his authority, this will place the defendant in breach of the injunction.[34] An agent may have limited authority confined to a particular task, or more general authority to act for his principal. The scope of his authority will depend upon the facts of the case. Provided the acts are done by a servant in the course of his employment, or by an agent in the course of his agency, the principal will be in contempt of court if the acts are in breach of the order.[35] This is so even though the servant or agent has acted carelessly or through neglect.

What if the servant has been expressly forbidden to do the act by his **19.011** employer? If the servant acts contrary to the instructions of his employer but in the course of his employment,[36] then this will still place the employer in breach of the court order and thus in contempt.

What about the case of an agent if the principal has instructed not to do the act but he then acts in disobedience of that instruction? The critical question is whether the agent was acting on behalf of, and within the scope of the authority conferred by the principal.[37] If the authority of the servant or agent to act for the defendant had been revoked before the relevant act was committed so that the act was not that of the defendant,[38] then the defendant is not in contempt.

For the purpose of deciding whether an act of a servant or agent is to be imputed to the defendant and thus place him in contempt[39] there is no additional requirement that the employer or principal ". . . could reasonably have foreseen such acts and failed to take any reasonable steps to prevent them".[40] In *Re Supply of Ready Mixed Concrete (No.2)* the Court of Appeal held that there was not contempt because the employer had

[34] *Re Supply of Ready Mixed Concrete (No.2)* [1992] Q.B. 213.
[35] *Re Supply of Ready Mixed Concrete (No.2)* [1995] 1 A.C. 456, overruling *Re Supply of Ready Mixed Concrete (No.2)* [1992] Q.B. 213. *Hone v Page* [1980] 6 F.S.R. 500, and *Z Bank v DI* [1994] 1 Lloyd's Rep. 656 at 661–662 must be treated as overruled on this point. In *Z Ltd v D1*, the Bulgarian bank was the plaintiff in the English proceedings which it had brought under s.25 of the Civil Jurisdiction and Judgments Act 1982 in support of the Irish proceedings, and had itself been restrained by Mareva injunction granted in support of the claims made by the defendants on the bank's cross-undertaking in damages. In that situation the bank's liability for contempt was that of a party restrained by a court order and not that of a non-party.
[36] *Re Supply of Ready Mixed Concrete (No.2)* [1995] 1 A.C. 456 at 481C.
[37] *ibid.*, at 480B–D and 481A–B.
[38] *Heatons Transport v TGWU* [1973] A.C. 15 at 109H–110C.
[39] *World Wide Fund for Nature v THQ/Jakks Pacific LLC (World Wrestling Federation intervening)* [2004] F.S.R. 10, p.161 at [17].
[40] Requirement (c)(ii) set out in *Hone v Page* [1980] F.S.R. 500 at 507, approved in the Court of Appeal in *Re Supply of Ready Mixed Concrete (No.2)* [1992] Q.B. 213.

taken such steps including giving instructions forbidding the prohibited acts. In the House of Lords this was reversed because the employees were acting in the course of their employment and so the acts were to be imputed to the employer.

19.012   In *World Wide Fund for Nature v THQ/Jakks Pacific LLC (World Wrestling Federation intervening)*[41] the injunction was expressed to be against the defendant company restraining it whether by "its officers, servants, agents, subsidiaries, licensees or sublicensees, its television or other affiliates or otherwise howsoever. . .". These words did not widen the person restrained; the only person restrained was the defendant company. These words were only referring to different ways in which the defendant might commit the prohibited acts. In the absence of clear words, an injunction does not make the defendant strictly liable for the act of a third party, such as an independent contractor.

(vi) A responsibility to take all reasonable steps to prevent the prohibited acts or to achieve the purpose of the order

19.013   The defendant has a responsibility when he can foresee the possibility that a servant or agent might act contrary to the terms of an injunction to take all reasonable steps to prevent them doing so.[42] This is upon the basis that the injunction is intended to prevent the relevant acts and the defendant is bound not only not to do those acts either personally or through others acting on his behalf, but also to take all reasonable steps to ensure that those acts will not be done by others. If those acts would be done on his behalf or by reason of previous instructions or authority given by the defendant, then he must take all reasonable steps to ensure that they do not occur. This responsibility is additional to the responsibility which the defendant has under the imputation principle.

A stranger is bound not to bring about the prohibited acts under the principle that he must not deliberately interfere with the administration of justice by frustrating the purpose of the order. Under this principle, destruction of a document which has been made the subject of a subpoena is a contempt because it interferes with the administration of justice.[43] There can be contempt when a document relevant to litigation is destroyed so as to interfere with the doing of justice, regardless of whether there is an order requiring its production.[44]

19.014   Where the defendant can foresee the possibility that the prohibited acts may be done by someone over whom he has some control or influence but who is not a servant or agent, then where those acts would frustrate the

---

[41] [2004] F.S.R. 10, p.161.

[42] *World Wide Fund for Nature v THQ/Jakks Pacific LLC (World Wrestling Federation intervening)* [2004] F.S.R. 10, p.161 at [18] and 19 referring to *Hone v Page* [1980] F.S.R. 501 at 507.

[43] *Registrar of Supreme Court v McPherson* [1980] 1 N.S.W.L.R. 688; *Mane Market v Temple* [1998] S.A.S.C. 6986.

[44] *British Steel Corporation v Granada Television* [1981] A.C. 1096 at 1127A–E and 1142A.

purpose of the court in making the order, it is considered that the general principle is that he must take all reasonable steps to prevent those acts. This can be viewed as being:

(1) a duty on the defendant, implicit in the order which has been made against him, to take reasonable steps to prevent frustration of the order of the court by others over whom he has a measure of control or influence; or

(2) depending upon the facts, the failure to take such reasonable steps can be regarded as implied consent to the non-party to do those acts on behalf of, or with the approval of, the defendant; silence is consent.

In *World Wide Fund for Nature v THQ/Jakks Pacific LLC (World Wrestling Federation intervening)*, the Federation accepted that they had to take reasonable steps to stop their licensees using the initials "WWF". This was because the Federation had given them a licence to use the initials which resulted in the licensees acting in the prohibited way, and because the Federation still had some control over the licensees by virtue of the licences. The licensees were independent persons but the Federation had a responsibility to try to get them not to act inconsistently with the injunction.

(vii) Corporate defendants and the position of directors

19.015 RSC Ord. 45, rr.5 and 7, which are in the Schedule to the CPR, provide for enforcement against corporate defendants by sequestration, or committal against a director or other officer of the company, provided that the officer in question had been served personally with a copy of the order endorsed with a penal notice,[45] or the court could proceed under RSC Ord. 45, r.7(6) or (7).

This procedure was originally introduced by s.33 of the Common Law Procedure Act 1860. Following breach by the company, penalties can be imposed personally on its directors.[46] Under RSC Ord. 45, r.5(1) the liability of the director to sequestration or committal for contempt depends upon the company being in breach of the order or undertaking—in the case of a mandatory order the company must have refused or neglected to do the required act in time and in the case of a prohibited act the company must have disobeyed the order.

In *Lewis v Pontypridd Caerphilly and Newport Railway Company*,[47] the company had been ordered to build a line connecting with certain premises

---

[45] *Attorney-General for Tuvalu v Philatelic Distribution Corporation Ltd* [1990] 1 W.L.R. 937. See also para.19.051, below.
[46] Compare *Iberian Trust Ltd v Founders Trust and Investment Co. Ltd* [1932] 2 K.B. 87.
[47] (1895) 11 T.L.R. 203.

and had failed to do so. The directors, who were proceeded against personally in respect of the company's failure, contended that the company's inaction was justified because of other pressing reasons for expenditure from the company's limited resources. This was rejected on the facts, but if it had been established that the company had been incapable of complying with the mandatory order, this would have been a good defence for the directors based on what was then RSC Ord. 42, r.31.

19.016   The mere fact that a corporate defendant acts in breach of an injunction does not mean that any director or other officer who has been personally served with an order endorsed with a penal notice is liable for contempt of court. Thus, if no allegation is made against such a director of failure to supervise or investigate, or of wilful blindness, his mere passivity will not amount to contempt (see *Director-General of Fair Trading v Buckland*).[48] It appears that a director will be liable for contempt if he either knowingly participates in the breach of the order (*Re Galvanized Tank Manufacturers' Association Agreement*[49]), or "wilfully" fails to take steps to ensure compliance with the order by the corporation, or is guilty of "culpable conduct".[50] But he is not to be made vicariously liable for the conduct of others. This is to be contrasted with the position of an individual who is personally enjoined by an injunction and will be placed in contempt of court as a result of the conduct of his servants or agents. The director is responsible if he fails to take adequate steps to ensure continuing compliance with the order unless he could reasonably and responsibly leave this task to be performed by others.[51]

If an undertaking is given by a company, a director can be made liable for contempt if he knows of the undertaking and his conduct is culpable (*e.g.* if he failed to take proper steps to ensure that the company complied on a continuing basis with the undertaking, when he had a responsibility to do so).[52]

If a director is proceeded against under these rules any penalty must be dealt with separately from any penalty against the company.[53]

(viii) Acts which are "casual or accidental and unintentional"

19.017   There is an exception from liability to committal or sequestration when the act in question has been "casual or accidental and unintentional". This does not mean that the defendant can only be proceeded against if there

---

[48] [1990] 1 W.L.R. 920.
[49] [1965] 1 W.L.R. 1074 at 1092.
[50] *Attorney-General for Tuvalu v Philatelic Distribution Corporation Ltd* [1990] 1 W.L.R. 926.
[51] For example, if the director in question was a non-executive director who was not part of the "management" of the company responsible for the conduct of its day-to-day affairs: *Director General of Fair Trading v Buckland* [1990] 1 W.L.R. 920 at 925. In contrast, in Hong Kong, Ord. 45 enables contempt proceedings to be brought even where the director is not to blame: *Aqua-Leisure Industries Inc. v Aqua-Splash (No.2)* [2002] H.K.L.R.D. 241 at paras 9–15.
[52] *Attorney-General for Tuvalu v Philatelic Distribution Corp. Ltd* [1990] 1 W.L.R. 926 at 937; *Telesystem International Wireless Incorporated v CVC/Opportunity Equity Partners L.P.* [2002] C.I.L.R. 96 at [48].
[53] *McMillan Graham Printers Ltd v RR (UK) Ltd* [1993] T.L.R. 152.

has been deliberate or wilful contumacy. The exception applies only if the relevant act was itself accidental and unintentional, and occurred despite the exercise of proper care by the defendant and his servants or agents.[54] Originally the rules of court required the conduct in question to have been carried out "wilfully" and it was in that context that Warrington J. in *Stancomb v Trowbridge UDC*[55] referred to this exception, which applies in the context of the present rules even though that word no longer appears. The reason for it is that such acts are not sufficiently serious for committal or sequestration to be justified.[56]

(ix) Personal service of the order and contempt proceedings

There is a difference between when an injunction takes effect and therefore **19.018** from what moment it can be broken and the enforcement of an injunction by contempt proceedings.[57] Contempt proceedings seeking a writ of sequestration or committal pursuant to RSC Ord. 45, r.5, can be taken in respect of disobedience to the injunction provided that the defendant has been served personally with a copy of the injunction endorsed with a penal notice (see para.19–051, below), pursuant to RSC Ord. 45, r.7. This is itself subject to RSC Ord. 45, r.7(6) and (7) which state:

> "(6) An order requiring a person to abstain from doing an act may be enforced under rule 5 notwithstanding that service of a copy of the order has not been effected in accordance with this rule if the court is satisfied that pending such service, the person against whom or against whose property is sought to enforce the order has had notice thereof either—
>
> (a) by being present when the order was made; or
> (b) by being notified of the terms of the order, whether by telephone, telegram or otherwise.
>
> (7) The court may dispense with service of a copy of an order under this rule if it thinks it just to do so."

RSC Ord. 45, r.7(6) only applies to "An order requiring a person to abstain from doing an act", *i.e.* only to a prohibitory injunction such as a

---

[54] *Re Supply of Ready Mixed Concrete (No.2)* [1995] 1 A.C. 456 at pp. 480E–481F; *Heatons Transport v TGWU* [1973] A.C. 15 at 109; *Steiner Products Ltd v Willy Steiner Ltd* [1966] 1 W.L.R. 986; *Re the Agreement of the Mileage Conference Group of the Tyre Manufacturers' Conference Ltd* [1966] 2 All E.R. 849; *Knight v Clifton* [1971] Ch. 700; *VDU Installations Ltd v Integrated Computer and Cybernetics Systems Ltd* [1989] F.S.R. 378; *Miller v Scorey* [1996] 3 All E.R. 18 at 27; *Great Future International Ltd v Sealand Housing Corporation* [2004] EWHC 124, ChD at [32–34].
[55] [1910] 2 Ch. 190 at 194, referring to *Fairclough v Manchester Ship Canal Co.* [1897] W.N. 7 (see also (1897) 41 S.J. 225).
[56] *Heatons Transport v TGWU* [1973] A.C. 15 at 109; *Fairclough & Sons v The Manchester Ship Canal Company* [1897] W.N. 7 (see also (1897) 41 S.J. 225); *Telesystem International Wireless Incorporated v CVC/Opportunity Equity Partners L.P.* [2002] C.I.L.R. 96 at [48].
[57] *Attorney-General v Newspaper Publishing plc* [1988] Ch. 333 at 377C–E.

freezing injunction in the usual form, and not to a mandatory order such as a disclosure order or an Anton Piller order.[58] The negative injunction may be enforced even if it has not been personally served, if the defendant was present when the order was made or has been notified of its terms (*e.g.* by telephone, telex, facsimile or telegram).

It is discretionary whether the court will enforce the injunction pursuant to r.7(6). In *Hill Samuel & Co. v Littaur*,[59] Parker L.J. said that it was to be regarded as applicable only to cases of emergency which arose pending personal service of a copy of the injunction on the defendant. The words "or otherwise" apply to any communication which has the effect of giving notice to the defendant of the existence of the injunction against him and its terms or the gist of them.

19.019   Under the practice of the court after the Judicature Acts a mandatory order had to be served personally on a defendant before proceedings seeking imprisonment for contempt could be brought against him, unless he was evading service. This applied even when the defendant had been in court when the order had been made.[60] This was so that the defendant would have the formal court order and would thus be warned by its formality of the possible consequences of its breach. RSC Ord. 45, r.7(7) alters that position.[61] It allows the court to dispense entirely with personal service of any injunction whether prohibitory or mandatory before seeking to enforce it by committal or sequestration. It must be "just" to dispense with the personal service requirement. This discretion can be exercised before or after the alleged breach of the order, and so can be used to overcome a past failure to effect personal service, and where time for compliance with a mandatory order has expired before service of it. It is a discretion which is "unfettered" and which can be exercised "retrospectively".[62] This can cover any case in which a defendant has knowingly acted in breach of the injunction.[63] This includes the case in which the defendant was present in court when the order was made.[64]

In *Belgolaise SA v Rupchandani*[65] the defendant had attended for cross-examination but it was alleged that he was in contempt in relation to

---

[58] *Belgolaise SA v Rupchandani* [1999] Lloyd's Rep. (Bank) 116 at 121; see also *Dempster v Dempster, The Independent*, November 9, 1990.

[59] Court of Appeal (Civ Div) Transcript No.126 of 1985 (April 3, 1985).

[60] *Re Tuck: Murch v Loosemoore* [1906] 1 Ch. 692, declining to follow the observation of Cotton L.J. in *Hyde v Hyde* (1888) 13 P.D. 166 at 171–172, an observation which is now correct under RSC Ord. 45 r.7(7)—see *Davy International Ltd v Tazzyman* [1997] 1 W.L.R. 1256 at 1262D–1263H.

[61] *Davy International Ltd v Tazzyman* [1997] 1 W.L.R. 1256 at 1262E–1267C.

[62] *Benson v Richards* [2002] EWCA Civ 1402 at [40–41]; *Hill Samuel & Co. v Littaur*, Court of Appeal (Civ Div) Transcript No.126 of 1985 (April 3, 1985).

[63] *Hill Samuel & Co. v Littaur, above; Davy International Ltd v Tazzyman* [1997] 1 W.L.R. 1256; *Irtelli v Squatriti* [1993] Q.B. 83 at 91.

[64] *Davy International Ltd v Tazzyman* [1997] 1 W.L.R. 1256 which followed *Turner v Turner* (1978) 122 S.J. 696. A company can be "present" within RSC Ord.45, r.7(6) through its solicitors representing it in the proceedings: *Telesystem International Wireless Incorporated v CVC/Opportunity Equity Partners L.P.* [2002] C.I.L.R. 96 at [77].

[65] [1999] Lloyd's Rep. (Bank.) 116 at 121.

certain of his answers. The order had not had a penal notice and the defendant had not had present a legal adviser to advise him on the privilege against self-incrimination and the defendant might have been entitled to claim it. The court refused to dispense retrospectively with service of the order with a penal notice because part of the purpose of service was to alert the defendant to the possibility of imprisonment for breach of the order. He could then have made an arrangement to have a legal adviser present so as to advise him about the availability of the privilege.[66]

RSC Ord. 45, r.6 in the Schedule to the CPR provides: **19.020**

"JUDGMENT, ETC. REQUIRING ACT TO BE DONE: ORDER FIXING TIME FOR DOING IT

Rule 6 (1) Notwithstanding that a judgment or order requiring a person to do an act specifies a time within which the act is to be done, the court shall have power to make an order requiring the act to be done within another time, being such time after service of that order, or such other time, as may be specified therein.

(2) Where a judgment or order requiring a person to do an act does not specify a time within which the act is to be done, the court shall have power subsequently to make an order requiring the act to be done within such time after service of that order, or such other time, as may be specified therein.

(3) An application for an order under this rule must be made in accordance with CPR Part 23 and the application notice must, be served on the person required to do the act in question."

This enables the claimant to obtain an order which can be served personally on the defendant prior to expiry of the time allowed by the order for doing the act. It is not the purpose of the rule to create a "minefield" for the claimant,[67] and it does not derogate from the discretion to dispense with the requirement of service retrospectively under RSC Ord. 45, r.7(7).

There is a principle that the court will not use its powers of committal or sequestration when a lesser alternative could more appropriately be adopted. Thus, *e.g.* if a person refused to execute a document the court could, under s.39 of the Supreme Court Act 1981 order that it be signed by someone else on his behalf and the document so signed would have the

---

[66] *ibid.*
[67] *Benson v Richards* [2002] EWCA Civ 1402 at [40–41].

same effect as if executed on behalf of the defendant.[68] Also if the order turns out to be unexpectedly burdensome the court can stay its provisions[69] or can decline to order immediate committal or sequestration or can fix a new time for compliance. In commercial proceedings an application for committal is a "last resort to be used only in cases of flagrant refusal to disclose assets or for the disclosure of documents relevant to the disclosure of assets".[70]

19.021   The former RSC Ord. 48, r.1(3), which applied to examination of a judgment debtor, provided for "any difficulty arising in the course of an examination under this rule . . . including any dispute with respect to the obligation of the person being examined to any question put to him [to] be referred to the Senior Master or Practice Master. . .". This provided a convenient procedure which might well be more appropriate than an immediate application for committal. That provision does not appear in CPR r.71.8. But if a person is being cross-examined about assets and if he refuses to answer a question, consideration should be given to obtaining a ruling from the court about whether that refusal is justified. The question can then be put again once an appropriate ruling has been obtained. This procedure can be adopted before contempt proceedings are considered.

(3) Freezing Injunctions: the position of the defendant

19.022   Upon receiving notice of a freezing injunction, a defendant must take immediate steps to countermand any payment instructions already given which are inconsistent with the order.[71] This is because unless they are countermanded they will be done on his instructions. He would then be liable for contempt based on the imputation principle, or breach of a duty to take all reasonable steps to avoid this occurring. A freezing injunction restrains the defendant from writing cheques addressed to his bank drawn on an account which is in credit, because in consequence one of his assets, the account in question, will be disposed of to the extent of the amount of the cheque. However, a freezing injunction does not prevent the defendant from incurring new liabilities,[72] and accordingly the defendant is free to write cheques to be debited to an account in overdraft, or to use a credit

---

[68] *Danchevsky v Danchevsky* [1975] Fam. 17 at 22 *Astro Exilo Navigation SA v Southland Enterprise Co. Ltd (The "Messinski" Tolmin) (No. 2)* [1983] 2 A.C. 787.

[69] *World Wide Fund for Nature v THQ/Jakks Pacific LLC (World Wrestling Federation intervening)* [2004] F.S.R. 10, p.161.

[70] *Belgolaise SA v Rupchandani* [1999] Lloyd's Rep. (Bank.) 116 at 122 RHC.

[71] *Re Supply of Ready Mixed Concrete (No.2)* [1995] 1 A.C. 456; *Heatons Transport v TGWU* [1973] A.C. 15 at 108–115, *per* Lord Wilberforce delivering the joint opinion of their Lordships.

[72] *Cantor Index Ltd v Lister*, unreported, November 22, 2001 (Neuberger J.); *Deputy Commissioner of Taxation v Hickey* [1999] F.C.A. 259 (March 18, 1999) at para.32 (use of credit card not a breach of the injunction).

card, thereby committing the credit card company to pay the supplier. The position, however, will be different if the bank or credit card company has security over an asset belonging to the defendant; here the consequence of the transaction will be to increase the burden of the encumbrance on the asset in question, thereby diminishing its value to the defendant.

As soon as the defendant is notified of a freezing injunction, he must take immediate steps to ensure that assets covered by the order are preserved and to prevent acts contrary to the terms of the injunction. Thus, *e.g.* the defendant should notify his bank and stop payment of cheques.

It does not affect payment by a bank under a letter of credit or performance guarantee, because the bank is under a personal contractual duty to make payment under such an instrument. Similarly, charge card companies must still pay third parties under credit card transactions. The credit card company undertakes a personal commitment. As between the user of the card and the supplier, acceptance by the supplier of payment by credit card may constitute absolute payment,[73] but whether or not this is the case, the credit card company must still pay.

19.023 The defendant's obligation under a disclosure order ancillary to Mareva relief which requires him to give information about his assets to the claimant, is not only to answer honestly but also to make reasonable inquiries to ensure that his answers are accurate.[74]

Paragraph 9(1) of the example order uses the words "to the best of his ability" and where these words are used this sets the standard of care for what the defendant must do. The words apply to the particular defendant's ability, and so if the defendant is elderly or disabled, allowance should be made for this in deciding whether there has been a breach of the order.

These words do not enlarge the scope of what has to be disclosed; so when information is required to enable the claimant to identify and preserve proceeds of an asset or transaction, careful consideration should be given by the claimant to drafting an order which is both sufficiently precise to enable contempt proceedings to be based on it, and sufficiently wide to cover information relevant to the tracing exercise, even though falling short of revealing where the proceeds are and in what form.[75]

19.024 An order which simply requires a defendant to disclose full particulars of his assets, and which does not specify whether the defendant is simply to do his best on what he has, or whether he has to set out full particulars come what may, is ambiguous on this point.[76] In practice this may not matter if the defendant had the information and did not even do what he could. But if the defendant did what he could, then this ambiguity in the order is a good defence to the proceedings for contempt.[77]

---

[73] *Re Charge Card Services Ltd* [1989] Ch. 497.
[74] *Bird v Hadkinson, The Times*, April 7, 1999.
[75] *Nokia France SA v Interstone Trading Ltd* [2004] EWHC 272 at [30–32], Comm Ct.
[76] *Togher v Customs and Excise Commissioners* [2001] EWCA Civ 474 at [53–55].
[77] *ibid.*, at [53–56].

(4) Search orders: the position of the defendant

19.025 A search order will include both mandatory and prohibitory orders. The order has to be served by the supervising solicitor.

The search order will contain prohibitory orders, an order requiring the defendant to permit entry on to premises and to vehicles, and mandatory orders for co-operation in the search and to provide information.

It is incumbent on the defendant, on receiving notice of the order, to take immediate steps to ensure that the documents or articles specified or described in it are preserved. This is because of the principles set out at paras 19.006–19.017. It is similar to the position of a defendant served with a freezing injunction who should take immediate steps to countermand authority given for payments. If a defendant is contacted by telephone by an employee at the premises in question, the employee having been served with a copy of the order, the defendant ought to instruct the employee to ensure that the subject-matter of the order is preserved. If he fails to do this, and the material is subsequently destroyed or damaged by one of his servants or agents, the defendant will be liable for contempt of the order.

19.026 If, after the service of the order on him, the defendant fails to provide documents or information as ordered, because he had in the meantime with notice of the order, but before service of the order, disabled himself from complying, he will be liable to be proceeded against for contempt of court. This is because, once the defendant knows of the order, he is prohibited implicitly by its terms from doing anything which would prevent him from complying with it. If he does anything which would prevent him, he is in contempt and can be proceeded against by committal or sequestration proceedings unless his inability to do so arose despite the exercise of all proper care by himself, his servants and agents, and so was accidental and unintentional.[78] If a non-party with knowledge of the court order were to destroy the documents so as to frustrate the intended search, he would be guilty of contempt[79] and the defendant is not in any stronger position. If the defendant, knowing of the order, were to cause to be destroyed documents falling within the ambit of the search to be permitted under its terms, this would constitute a contempt of court. Although the search could still proceed, the documents would no longer be there, the defendant having destroyed part of what was intended to be preserved pursuant to the court order.

---

[78] *Re Supply of Ready Mixed Concrete (No.2)* [1995] 1 A.C. 456 at pp.480E–481F, approving *Stancomb v Trowbridge Urban and District Council* [1910] 2 Ch. 190; for a case where the defendant concealed and shredded documents for the purpose of frustrating the search order, whilst the order was being executed see *Nokia France SA v Interstone Trading Ltd,* February 18, 2004 at [41], Comm Ct ("serious contempts").

[79] *Attorney-General v Newspaper Publishing plc* [1988] Ch. 333 at 372 and 379–390; *Attorney-General v Times Newspapers* [1992] 1 A.C. 191.

This is not inconsistent with the principle which enables a party in **19.027** breach of a mandatory order to raise the defence that he was genuinely unable to comply. In proceedings for contempt, it must be proved beyond reasonable doubt that the defendant could have complied with the order.[80] However, disablement or inability caused by the defendant after he knows of the existence of the order takes the case outside of this category. Once the defendant has been personally served with the order, then, subject to its provisions, he will become under an obligation to comply with its mandatory terms. Refusal or failure to do so will constitute contempt. This is so even if he subsequently applies to the court to discharge the order, and even if that application is successful.[81]

(5) Mareva injunction: the position of non-parties

(i) Aiding and abetting a breach and intentionally frustrating the purpose of the order

A non-party can be guilty of contempt if either he knowingly aids and abets **19.028** a breach of the order, or he intentionally frustrates the achievement of the purpose of the order.[82] A person who has been notified of a Mareva injunction is bound not to take any steps which would constitute a breach of the order if done by the defendant. This is regardless of whether the defendant has been served with or knows of the order. Thus, *e.g.* a bank, once served with notice of the order, must not knowingly assist in the disposal of funds by honouring cheques drawn by the defendant. The non-party will be liable in contempt of court, if, with knowledge of the order, he aids and abets a breach by the party enjoined,[83] or he intentionally frustrates the purpose of the order. This is so regardless of whether or not the party enjoined would himself be liable in contempt.

In the example order it is provided:

"PARTIES OTHER THAN THE APPLICANT AND RESPONDENT

16. **Effect of this order**

It is a contempt of court for any person notified of this order knowingly to assist in or permit a breach of this order. Any person doing so may be imprisoned, fined or have their assets seized."

---

[80] *Re Bramblevale Ltd* [1970] Ch. 129.
[81] *Bhimji v Chatwani* [1991] 1 W.L.R. 989 at 1000F–1001H; *Wardle Fabrics Ltd v G. Myristis Ltd* [1984] F.S.R. 263; *Columbia Pictures Inc. v Robinson* [1987] Ch. 38 at 71–72.
[82] *Attorney-General v Punch* [2003] 1 A.C. 1046 at [39–48], [79], [104–105].
[83] *Lord Wellesley v Earl of Mornington (No.2)* (1848) 11 Beav. 181; *Seaward v Paterson* [1897] Ch. 545; *Acrow (Automation) Ltd v Rex Chainbelt Inc.* [1971] 1 W.L.R. 1676; *Z Ltd v A-Z and AA-LL* [1982] Q.B. 558; *Incandescent Gas Light Co. v Sluce* (1900) 17 R.P.C. 173.

The word "knowingly" reflects the need for proof of *mens rea*[84] in order to establish knowing interference with the administration of justice. The word "permit" reflects the fact that the non-party may be in contempt if he allows what would be a breach of the order when he is in a position to stop it. But the drafting does not fully reflect the extent of the potential jeopardy of a person notified of the order. He will be in contempt of court when he deliberately frustrates the purpose of the order, even when there is no conduct of the defendant which could amount to a breach of the order or a contempt of court.

19.029   What is meant by the purpose of the injunction in this context? It is not the purpose of the litigant in obtaining the order. It is the purpose of the court in making the particular order, the aim of that order. How that purpose is formulated is the key to the width of the effect of the injunction on the non-party.

In *Attorney-General v Punch* Lord Hoffmann said the purpose of the order in that case, which concerned preservation of the confidentiality of information, was "no more or less than to do what the order purported to do, namely to restrain the publication, pending trial or further order, of information falling within its terms and not excepted by the provisos . . .",[85] and, "simply to prevent from happening whatever the order said should not happen".[86] This omitted any requirement that the defendant had to be responsible for causing it to happen. This was because what mattered was the preservation of the confidentiality of the information and not the identity of the person who was responsible for destroying it.

19.030   It is not always the case that whether the defendant has caused something is not part of the purpose of the injunction. For example, if an injunction restrained a person from trespassing on the land of another, a trespass on to that land committed by someone else would neither be in breach of the injunction nor inconsistent with the court's purpose in granting it.[87] In *World Wide Fund for Nature v THQ/Jakks Pacific LLC (World Wrestling Federation intervening)*[88] the question arose whether a licensee of the defendant Federation would be acting intentionally to frustrate the purpose of the injunction granted against the defendant by continuing to use the WWF logo. The Court of Appeal held that this conduct would not place the licensee in contempt because it was "an independent party pursuing its own legitimate commercial interests under a licence granted to it well before the order was made".[89] This illustrates that where the non-party is someone at arm's length from the defendant, and is pursuing his own commercial interests which are separate and distinct from those of the defendant, the normal principle ought to be that the claimant

---

[84] *Mens rea* is an essential element: *Attorney-General v Times Newspapers* [1992] 1 A.C. 179 at 224E.
[85] [2003] 1 A.C. 1046 at [70].
[86] *ibid.*, at [76].
[87] *Attorney-General v Times Newspapers* [1992] 1 A.C. 191 at 231.
[88] [2004] F.S.R. 10, p.161
[89] [2004] F.S.R. 10, pp.176–177, paras 40–43.

must proceed against that non-party in order to get an injunction against him. It is suggested that in these circumstances the court will lean towards limiting the "purpose" of an injunction granted against someone else as being limited to that person. But there is no absolute rule; a newspaper is pursuing its own independent commercial interests in publishing news, but it still cannot be allowed to publish confidential information which it is the purpose of the injunction to keep out of the public domain. In those circumstances it is impractical to expect the claimant to proceed against every newspaper and television channel, and the formulation of the "purpose" of the injunction must reflect this.

The errors of the Court of Appeal in *Attorney-General v Punch*, which were corrected by the House of Lords, were (1) to add in a further qualification of the purpose by a requirement that the disclosure be in breach of what was required for national security; and (2) to distinguish between interim and final injunctions.[90] As for (1), this would have emasculated the effect of the injunction on non-parties and undermined the ability of the court to grant effective relief. As for (2), drawing that distinction overlooked the public interest in the court being able to grant relief either interlocutory or final which is effective: "Without sanctions an injunction would be a paper tiger".[91]

In *Harrow London Borough Council v Johnstone*[92] an injunction had **19.031** been granted against a wife which prevented her from excluding or attempting to exclude her husband from the matrimonial home. The aim of the order was to stop the wife from acting violently towards her husband or molesting him. Subsequently the wife wanted to be rehoused by the council and, in accordance with council policy, it was necessary for the wife to give up the existing joint tenancy on the matrimonial home in order to obtain another tenancy elsewhere. Pursuant to the council's request, the wife served notice terminating the periodic tenancy (which would otherwise have continued). It was held that this duly brought the joint tenancy to an end. There was no question of the council being in contempt of court. The husband could no longer go to the matrimonial home because the tenancy had come to an end. The injunction had said nothing about terminating the tenancy. It was not a purpose of the injunction to preserve the tenancy as an asset of the husband and the wife: the purpose was to stop the wife physically molesting the husband. Furthermore, the council had known nothing of the injunction or its purpose. The injunction did not forbid the wife from terminating the tenancy and this was not to be implied into the order. The termination of the tenancy had nothing to do with what the injunction sought to prevent.

For a non-party to be liable for contempt under this principle, it is not sufficient that he has failed to take steps to prevent the destruction of the

---

[90] [2001] Q.B. 1028 at [84], a distinction followed by Gray J. in *Jockey Club v Buffham* [2003] Q.B. 462 at [26] and [27] before the decision of the House of Lords in *Attorney-General v Punch* [2003] 1 A.C. 1046.
[91] *Attorney-General v Punch* [2003] 1 A.C. 1046 at [32], *per* Lord Nicholls.
[92] [1997] 1 W.L.R. 459.

subject-matter of the injunction or the frustration of its objective. The non-party, either himself or through those for whom he is responsible, must have acted in some way which has had this consequence, with knowledge of the injunction.[93]

19.032   Applying the approach of the House of Lords in *Attorney-General v Punch* the purpose of the example freezing injunction is that the defendant's assets are not to be disposed of, dealt with or diminished in value, or removed from the jurisdiction, within the meaning of the corresponding words in the court order, except as permitted by the terms of that order, or with leave of the court. Like an injunction to preserve confidentiality of information, a freezing injunction seeks to preserve intact particular subject-matter, subject to what is permitted by the order. It is the achievement of this which the non-party must not intentionally frustrate through his actions. The purpose of the injunction does not depend upon who has carried out the prohibited acts and so the position is to be distinguished from an injunction stopping a named individual from trespassing. A freezing injunction might restrain a defendant from removing certain specified cargo from the jurisdiction. The shipowners could not allow their ship to proceed out of the jurisdiction with the cargo on board[94] because that would defeat the purpose of the order, even though their motive for doing so was to honour the vessel's next commitment, and even though their ownership of the vessel entitled them to direct where it should go.[95]

The example order for a freezing injunction provides for the defendant to make withdrawals for living expenses and legal costs and contains a provision:

> "**18. Withdrawals by the Respondent**
>
> No bank need enquire as to the application or proposed application of any money withdrawn by the Respondent if the withdrawal appears to be permitted by this order."

The bank has no general duty to the court, either at common law or under the terms of the example order, to police the order. It does not have to check up on the defendant to ensure that the money is spent as permitted by the order.[96] However, the bank does have a responsibility not to connive[97] at a breach of the order or knowingly to frustrate its purpose.[98]

---

[93] *Attorney-General v Observer Ltd* [1988] 1 All E.R. 385.

[94] *Attorney-General v Newspaper Publishing plc* [1988] Ch. 333 at 367, *per* Sir John Donaldson M.R.

[95] See also *Boeing Capital Corporation v Wells Fargo Bank Northwest* [2003] EWHC 1364, Comm Ct where the claimant had judgment for delivery up on its proprietary claim on a Boeing 737, but were not allowed to enforce the order for delivery-up of the aeroplane until after first obtaining a variation to the Mareva injunction obtained by a third party; see paras 3.007 and 20.070.

[96] *Z Ltd v A–Z and AA–LL* [1982] Q.B. 558 at 583.

[97] *Z Ltd v A–Z and AA-LL* [1982] Q.B. 558 at 582F and 583E.

[98] *Attorney-General v Times Newspapers* [1992] 1 A.C. 191.

It will not be sufficient to constitute contempt that a clerk in the bank **19.033** made a payment without knowing of the order, even if another department of the bank did have such knowledge. It is not possible to add together the act of the clerk and the knowledge of the other department to constitute contempt by the bank.[99] If, on the other hand, payment is made because of a deliberate failure on the part of the relevant department to stop transactions, then there would be a contempt, based on the culpability of the person who took that decision. It is not clear whether recklessness as such would suffice. In *Z Ltd v A-Z and AA-LL*, Eveleigh L.J. said the test is whether or not there had been a "deliberate" failure to stop a payment, either when the payment was authorised by the department in question, or "knowing that the payment was likely to be made under a general authority derived from" that department. If a payment is requested which could be consistent with compliance with the injunction, and the bank makes that payment, then this would not amount to a contempt of court by the bank. Eveleigh L.J. said that carelessness "or even recklessness on the part of the banks" would not make them liable for contempt "unless it can be shown that there was indifference to such a degree that was contumacious". The test is whether the bank's employee with knowledge of the order acted in such a way as knowingly to frustrate the purpose of that order.

A freezing injunction in the example form, provides that the defendant must not "in any way dispose of, deal with or diminish the value of any of his assets which are in England and Wales up to the value of £   ". The defendant is not precluded from drawing sums out of his bank.[1] This is under the theory that the money left in the account together with the withdrawal held by the defendant represent the same asset as the credit balance which existed immediately prior to the withdrawal. But if the withdrawal is preparatory to a disposal of that withdrawal which will be in breach of the order, and the bank knew that this was the case, it would have acted in contempt of court.

In *Attorney-General v Newspaper Publishing plc*[2] an injunction had been **19.034** granted against certain newspapers prohibiting them from publishing allegedly confidential information. Other newspapers, which were not enjoined, published extracts from the information. This did not constitute a breach of the injunction. But it resulted in partial frustration of the objective sought to be achieved by the injunction, in that information which was intended to be preserved as confidential had been published. The Court of Appeal held that such conduct by the non-parties was *capable* of constituting a contempt of court, provided that it was done with the requisite intent.[3] In that case the requisite intent fell to be decided in the

---

[99] *Z Ltd v A-Z and AA-LL* [1982] Q.B. 558 at 581–582, *per* Eveleigh L.J.
[1] *Bank Mellat v Kazmi* [1989] Q.B. 541. See further paras 3.012–3.014, above.
[2] [1988] Ch. 333.
[3] Approved in *Attorney-General v Times Newspapers Ltd* [1992] 1 A.C. 191; see also *Harrow London Borough Council v Johnstone* [1997] 1 W.L.R. 459.

context of the Contempt of Court Act 1981, since it involved a publication.[4] The non-party does not have to *desire* to bring about a contempt of court or have this as his motive.[5]

If there were a freezing injunction in the form of the example order against a defendant owner, and a mortgagee took possession and sold the property, it is considered that this would not constitute a contempt of court. This is because what had been done by the mortgagee did not infringe the purpose of the order. The defendant's beneficial interest in the property was an equity in redemption which was itself subject to the mortgagee's rights, and the freezing injunction did not forbid the mortgagee from exercising those rights, even though the effect would be to destroy the equity.[6] It was no part of the purpose of the injunction to preserve the equity of redemption against the lawful exercise of the mortgagee's rights. The duty of the mortgagee is no higher than to act in good faith in the ordinary course of business in relation to the exercise of its rights,[7] without "collusion" with the mortgagor to achieve an unjustifiable dissipation of assets by the mortgagor. If, on the other hand, a third party knowing of a freezing injunction deliberately destroyed the defendant's car so as to spite the claimant, this would be a contempt of court, because part of the purpose of the injunction was to ensure that the car would not be destroyed with this objective.[8]

(ii) Joint accounts

(a) With a freezing injunction which includes the extension in para.6 of the example order

19.035   The example freezing injunction given by the Practice Direction supplementing CPR Pt 25 states:

> "6. Paragraph 5 applies to all the Respondent's assets whether or not they are in his own name and whether they are solely or jointly owned. For the purpose of this order the Respondent's assets include any asset which he has the power, directly or indirectly, to dispose of or deal with as if it were his own. The Respondent is to

---

[4] See also *Attorney-General v News Group Newspapers plc* [1989] Q.B. 110.
[5] *Attorney-General v Newspaper Publishing plc* [1988] Ch. 333 at 375A; *Attorney-General v Newspaper Publishing plc (No.2)* [1989] F.S.R. 457 applying *R. v Moloney* [1985] A.C. 905 at 926. In *Re Lonrho* [1990] 2 A.C. 154, Lord Goff had assumed that the case had been correctly decided, but left the matter open, it being contemplated that an appeal was likely.
[6] *Gangway Ltd v Caledonian Park Investments (Jersey) Ltd* [2001] 2 Lloyd's Rep. 715 at [15] ("where the bank has a security interest in the asset it is entitled to exercise its rights in accordance with its own commercial judgment, provided always that it does nothing inconsistent with the underlying purpose of the injunction . . .")
[7] *Gangway Ltd v Caledonian Park Investments (Jersey) Ltd* [2001] 2 Lloyd's Rep. 715 at [16] and [17].
[8] *Standard Chartered Bank v Walker* [1992] 1 W.L.R. 561.

be regarded as having such power if a third party holds or controls the asset in accordance with his direct or indirect instructions."

An order without para.6 would not apply to a joint account in which the defendant has no beneficial interest.[9] But the second and third sentences in para.6 bring within the scope of the injunction a joint account over which the defendant has power to dispose of or deal with as his own, regardless of whether he has any beneficial interest in it. The effect of para.6 of the example freezing order is to extend the freezing injunction to that account. It is considered that if the other account holder sought to diminish the value of that account, regardless of whether it diminished the value of any beneficial interest of the defendant in the account, and did so knowing of the injunction, this would be a contempt of court, unless the drawing was permitted under a liberty in the freezing injunction.

(b) Independently of the second and third sentences of para.6 of the example order

A freezing injunction may be granted which does not include the second **19.036** and third sentences of para.6, or the account may not fall within those sentences. The freezing injunction may be granted against a defendant, who has a joint account in his name and that of another on which that other account holder is an authorised signatory. Can the other account holder make a payment out of that account to a third party without being in contempt of court?

If the defendant has some beneficial interest in the joint account, his interest in the chose in action represented by the account is part of the "assets" which he owns beneficially. This is an asset of the defendant to which the freezing injunction applies. If the other account holder writes a cheque on the account, then if the cheque is honoured from a credit balance on the account, the overall effect, if the defendant has a percentage share in the account, is that the defendant has the same percentage share, but this is now an asset diminished in value as a result of the payment. The terms of the order have the purpose[10] of preserving the value of the defendant's assets and ensuring that his assets will not be diminished in value, except in accordance with the liberties in the order.

What if the drawing on the account by the other account holder was not permitted by the liberties in the order, would diminish in value the defendant's beneficial interest in the bank account, and the other account holder knew this? It is considered that this would be a contempt of court by the other account holder. In that situation the other account holder would not be free to deal with the account, except in accordance with the exceptions permitted under the order.[11] Like the example of the

---

[9] *Federal Bank of the Middle East v Hadkinson* [2000] 1 W.L.R. 1695.
[10] *Attorney-General v Punch* [2003] 1 A.C. 1046.
[11] Compare the facts in *SCF v Masri* [1985] 1 W.L.R. 876, where the injunction was expressly extended to the wife who was joined as a co-defendant, and see the observations of Lloyd L.J. in *Attorney-General v Newspaper Publishing plc* [1988] Ch. 333 at 378–380.

shipowners, it would not be to the point that in the absence of the order the other account holder's own rights in respect of the account would have entitled him to write the cheque. If this were not the position he could empty the account spending the money in ways which were inconsistent with the purpose of the Mareva jurisdiction. Another way of putting the point is that the mandate is given to the bank by both of the account holders. Under that mandate the defendant has authorised the bank to make payments out of the account on the signature of the other account holder which will diminish the value of the defendant's beneficial interest in the account. That mandate given by the account holders is inconsistent with the terms of the injunction against the defendant. This is because the defendant is no longer permitted to allow dealings with or disposals of his assets which diminish their value. The assets include his beneficial interest in the account. Therefore the bank no longer has authority from the defendant to make payment from the account on an instruction whether signed by either of the account holders. This is because if the defendant authorised such a payment it would be a dealing with or disposal of his asset diminishing it in value, and would be a breach of the injunction by him.[12]

(c) Summary of the position with joint accounts

19.037
(1) The example order contains an extension to the ambit of the freezing injunction to cover assets regardless of any beneficial interest of the defendant in them (para.6).

(2) Where para.6 is included, and the account is within the second and third sentences, then no drawing on the account is allowed except as permitted by the liberties in the injunction. This is so regardless of whether any drawing would diminish the value of any beneficial interest of the defendant in the account.

(3) If para.6 is not included, or the account is not caught by the terms of the second and third sentences of that paragraph because the defendant has no relevant power over the account, then the freezing injunction only affects a joint account in which the defendant has a beneficial interest. If there is such a beneficial interest, dealings on the account by the other account holder which diminish the value of the defendant's beneficial interest in the account are only permitted in so far as they are allowed by the liberties in the injunction.

(iii) The "in particular" clause

19.038 The wording of the injunction in *The Siskina* restrained the defendant shipowners from disposing of any of their assets within the jurisdiction ". . . including in particular the insurance proceeds in respect of their

---

[12] *Z Ltd v A-Z and AA-LL* [1982] Q.B. 558 at 574.

former vessel".[13] A freezing injunction usually refers to particular assets which are to be frozen. It is the practice of the court to grant an injunction which not only refers in general terms to the defendant's assets, but also refers to particular assets of the defendant which are described in the order. Thus, para.7 of the example order adopts this practice by providing that:

"7. This prohibition includes the following assets in particular—

(a) the property known as *[title/address]* or the net sale money after payment of any mortgages if it has been sold;
(b) the property and assets of the Respondent's business [known as *[name]*] [carried on at *[address]*] or the sale money if any of them have been sold; and
(c) any money in the account numbered *[account number]* at *[title/address]*."

What is the effect of this? In the example order the restraint imposed by para.5 is restricted, by the definition in para.6 which states:

"Paragraph 5 applies to all the Respondent's assets whether or not they are in his own name and whether they are solely or jointly owned. For the purpose of this order the Respondent's assets include any asset which he has the power, directly or indirectly, to dispose of or deal with as if it were his own. The Respondent is to be regarded as having such power if a third party holds or controls the asset in accordance with his direct or indirect instructions."

The example freezing injunction applies to assets in which the defendant has a beneficial interest[14] or the extension of this in para.6. The first sentence of para.6 uses the expression "all the Respondent's assets" and an asset will only qualify under this sentence if the respondent has a beneficial interest in it, a bare legal title is not enough. The second and third sentences extend para.5 so as to cater for situations in which the respondent does not have any interest in the asset but has the power "directly or indirectly, to dispose of or deal with as if it were his own".

19.039 The court has been asked to make the assumption that the assets described in para.7 fall within this restraint. Paragraph 7 of the order can only properly refer to assets which are covered by the restraint in para.5. If the order accords with the facts then no difficulty arises, and para.7 merely alerts the reader to particular assets covered by para.5, interpreted with the assistance of para.6.

What if the defendant denies that the assets described in para.7 come within the restraint in para.5? The effect is that the claimant will only

---

[13] [1979] A.C. 210 at 215.
[14] See the first sentence of para.6 and *Federal Bank of the Middle East Ltd v Hadkinson* [2000] 1 W.L.R. 1695.

secure a finding of contempt based on breach of the restraint imposed by para.5 if the assets which have been dealt with allegedly in breach of the order come within para.5 interpreted with the assistance of para.6.

What about a finding of contempt based on a contention that if assets in para.7 are dealt with, this, in itself, deliberately frustrates the purpose of the order, regardless of paras 5 and 6? It is considered that the inclusion of the assets in para.7 shows that the court in making the order was assuming that the assets come within the restraint. If the court had intended to restrain dealings with those assets until a decision had been taken on whether they in fact came within para.5, the wording would have been different. There would have been a separate restraint in relation to the assets designated in para.7 regardless of whether they were assets of the defendant or otherwise came within para.5. This is the consequence of the principle that an order must be clear and unambiguous. It is also in accordance with good civil practice because if, at the without notice application, the court is to be asked to make an order in respect of designated assets when there may be an issue whether they are beneficially owned by the defendant or otherwise come within para.5, then the court should be told this and asked to consider the strength of the evidence on this point.

19.040   It is considered that on the wording of the example order before there can be a finding of contempt made against the defendant or a non-party, based on a dealing with an asset designated in para.7, it must be proved beyond reasonable doubt that the asset falls within the restraint imposed by para.5. Put another way the purpose of the order is to restrain dealings with assets which come within para.5, including the assets identified in para.7 but only on the assumption that they are beneficially owned by the defendant or come within para.5 because of the extension in para.6. The consequences are that:

(1) as against the defendant he will have committed a contempt if he has in fact dealt with assets within paras 5 and 6 in a way inconsistent with the restraint, but not otherwise. There is no requirement to prove *mens rea*.[15]

(2) As against a non-party to the restraint, a case in contempt will fail if either:

(a) the assets which have been dealt with do not come within paras 5 and 6, in which case there is no *actus reus* because there is no interference with the administration of justice, or

(b) the non-party honestly believed that, at the time that he dealt with the assets, they fell outside paras 5 and 6, in which case there is no *mens rea*; the interference with the administration of

---

[15] *Adam Phones v Goldschmidt* [1999] 4 All E.R. 486 at 492–494 in which *Irtelli v Squatriti* [1993] Q.B. 83 was not followed because it is inconsistent with other case law; *Bird v Hadkinson, The Times*, April 7, 1999.

justice was not deliberate. The fact that the assets are listed in para.7 will provide an evidential problem for a defence based solely on absence of *mens rea.*

(6) Extra-territorial Mareva injunctions and non-parties

The fact that a freezing injunction or the appointment of a receiver relates **19.041** to assets abroad makes no difference to a defendant's potential liability for contempt of court. This is also the case in relation to an Anton Piller order in respect of premises abroad. In the context of contempt of court a party to the proceedings can be held in contempt in respect of actions abroad. This is on the principle that where a foreigner is a party to English proceedings he must conduct himself in accordance with the rules that apply to those proceedings.

But the position of non-parties in relation to extra-territorial Mareva injunctions has attracted special attention from the courts. This has resulted in the practice of inserting a "proviso" in the order which restricts its effect on third parties.

The injunction should not affect non-parties who are resident abroad, and who are in no sense subject to the court's territorial jurisdiction. As Nicholls L.J. said in *Babanaft International Co. v Bassatne*:[16]

> "It would be wrong for an English court, by making an order in respect of overseas assets against a defendant amenable to its jurisdiction, to impose or attempt to impose obligations on persons not before the court in respect of acts to be done by them abroad regarding property outside the jurisdiction. That self-evidently would be for an English court to claim an altogether exorbitant, extra-territorial jurisdiction."

The proviso in the example form order was modelled on the *Babanaft* **19.042** proviso as revised in *Derby & Co. Ltd v Weldon (Nos 3 and 4)*[17] It reads as follows:

> "19. PERSONS OUTSIDE ENGLAND AND WALES
>
> (1) Except as provided in paragraph. (2) below, the terms of this order do not affect or concern anyone outside the jurisdiction of this court.
> (2) The terms of this order will affect the following persons in a country or state outside the jurisdiction of this court—

---

[16] [1990] Ch. 13 at 44.
[17] [1990] Ch. 65 at 84C–F.

(a) the Respondent or his officer or agent appointed by power of attorney;

(b) any person who—

    (i) is subject to the jurisdiction of this court;

    (ii) has been given written notice of this order at his residence or place of business within the jurisdiction of this court; and

    (iii) is able to prevent acts or omissions outside the jurisdiction of this court which constitute or assist in a breach of the terms of this order; and

(c) any other person, only to the extent that this order is declared enforceable by or is enforced by a court in that country or state."

This proviso assumed that anyone within the territorial jurisdiction of the court and who was thus amenable to the court's coercive powers should be bound by the court order. In the context of granting a subpoena, or making an order for inspection and taking copies of extracts in a banker's book under s.7 of the Bankers' Books Evidence Act 1879, the court declined as a general rule to exercise jurisdiction to grant such relief against a bank in respect of an account held at a foreign branch.[18] The justified restraint exercised by the court in this area was to be contrasted with the position under this provision.[19] Thus a bank which had a branch in England was required to observe the effect of the injunction in relation to a bank account at a branch abroad.[20]

19.043   The proviso overlooked (1) the difference between jurisdiction over the person and subject-matter jurisdiction,[21] (2) the court's restraint in making orders affecting the conduct of foreigners abroad, and (3) not imposing solutions which were properly a matter for the foreign court which exercised jurisdiction where assets were located. A branch of a bank abroad should be able to govern its actions by reference to what would be decided by the local court or what was provided for in the contract with its customer.

In the end of year statement made by the judge in charge of the Commercial Court list on July 30, 1993, Saville J. stated:

"A problem emerged earlier this year which was of great concern to those banks which are subject to the jurisdiction of both the English

---

[18] *Mackinnon v Donaldson Lufkin and Jenrette* [1986] Ch. 482; *cf. Re Mid East Trading Ltd (No.2), The Times,* December 20, 1997 (ordering production under the Insolvency Act 1986, s.236).

[19] See further L. Collins, "The Territorial Reach of Mareva Injunctions" (1989) 105 L.Q.R. 262 at 281–286.

[20] *Securities and Investments Board v Pantell SA* [1990] Ch. 426 at 432–433.

[21] *Société Eram Shipping Co. Ltd v Compagnie Internationale de Navigation* [2004] 1 A.C. 860; *Mackinnon v Donaldson Lufkin & Jenrette Securities Corporation* [1986] Ch. 482 and see Chapter 6, above.

court and the courts of the country or countries where they may be holding assets of the defendant which are made the subject of a worldwide Mareva. Certain countries may not recognise or give effect to *ex parte* orders made in this jurisdiction and indeed may make inconsistent orders. In such cases third party banks can be put in an impossible position, being required to do something by a court in this country and the opposite by a court abroad. The *Derby v Weldon* proviso does not seem to help as it does not apply to persons who are subject to the jurisdiction, which of course is the case with most major banks. To solve this problem of double jeopardy we would suggest in appropriate cases that something along the lines of the following provision be added to the order. 'Nothing in this Order shall, in respect of assets located outside England and Wales' (and in particular [specify if necessary the foreign country concerned]) prevent [the Bank] or its subsidiaries from complying with:

(1) what it reasonably believes to be its obligations, contractual or otherwise, under the laws and obligations of the country or state in which those assets are situated or under the proper law of the account in question;
(2) any orders of the Courts of that country or state."

In *Baltic Shipping Company v Translink Shipping Ltd,*[22] Clarke J. decided **19.044** that the bank should not have to run the risk that it would be in breach of contract abroad if it refused to pay its customer because of an *ex parte* Mareva order. He modified the proviso suggested by Saville J. to allow the bank to pay, provided that its belief that it was obliged to do so under the foreign law was formed on reasonable grounds. The bank should not be forced into a situation where it faces the risk of litigation from its customer, even against an indemnity from the claimant.[23]

The *Commercial Courts Guide* provides in para. F15.10 that:

"**F15.10** As regards freezing orders in respect of assets outside the jurisdiction, the standard wording in relation to effects on third parties should normally incorporate wording to enable overseas branches of banks or similar institutions which have offices within the jurisdiction to comply with what they reasonably believe to be their obligations under the laws of the country where the assets are located or under the proper law of the relevant banking or other contract relating to such assets."

The proviso has to be updated to reflect the result of the decision in *Bank of China v NBM LLC.*[24]

---

[22] [1995] 1 Lloyd's Rep. 673.
[23] Compare *Galaxia Maritime SA v Mineralimportexport* [1982] 1 W.L.R. 539 at 541F–H.
[24] [2002] 1 W.L.R. 844.

The provisos adopted in *Bank of China v NBM LLC* were:

19.045   "It is further ordered and directed that nothing in this order shall, in respect of assets located outside England and Wales, prevent [a bank or other similar institution] or its subsidiaries from complying with:

(i)   what it reasonably believes to be its obligations, contractual or otherwise under the laws and obligations of the country or state in which those assets are situated or under the proper law of any bank account in question; and

(ii)   any orders of the courts of that country or state provided reasonable notice of any application for such an order by [the bank or other similar institution] or any of its subsidiaries (to the extent such notice is permitted by the criminal law of such country or state) is given to the claimant's solicitors."

The extra-territorial freezing injunction is in the nature of holding relief pending an order of the court having jurisdiction at the place where the account is kept. If the claimant cannot obtain an order from that court, then the bank should be allowed to comply with what it reasonably believes to be its obligations under local law, rather than forced into litigation with its customer. In such cases the claimant must apply promptly to the foreign court to seek relief blocking use of the account and so protect the bank from the possibility of litigation with its customer.

19.046   If the intention is to apply in England for Mareva relief and, once the order has been obtained, to apply in a foreign jurisdiction for equivalent relief ancillary to the claims advanced in England, there will be a gap between the granting of the order in England and the outcome of the application abroad. An order made on a without notice application in England does not attract recognition in cases governed by Regulation 44/2001 (the Judgments Regulation),[25] and so even in that category of case it cannot be assumed that the foreign application will necessarily succeed, or that the order[26] will give the bank any protection abroad.

A claimant should seek to make the applications in England and abroad at the same time or as nearly so as possible.

(7)   A search order and non-parties

19.047   A search order is often served on a person other than the defendant. The example order provides:

"THIS ORDER

---

[25] OJ LO12, January 16, 2001, pp.1–23 (see Chapter 6, paras 6.014–6.015).
[26] With an *inter partes* order the position is different; see Chapter 6, para.6.015 above and *Ghoth v Ghoth* [1992] 2 All E.R. 920 at 923.

1. This is a Search Order made against [   ] ('the Respondent') on [   ] by Mr Justice [   ] on the application of [   ] ('the Applicant'). The Judge read the Affidavits listed in Schedule F and accepted the undertakings set out in Schedules C, D and E at the end of this order.

. . .

5. This order must be complied with by—

   (a) the Respondent;
   (b) any director, officer, partner or responsible employee of the Respondent; and
   (c) if the Respondent is an individual, any other person having responsible control of the premises to be searched."

The example order is an order made against the defendant The practice used to be that the order required the defendant, by himself, or by any person appearing to be in control of the premises, to give the permission needed for entry on to the premises and for the search to take place.[27] The wording of the example order has the same effect as the previous practice. Someone who is not the defendant enjoined under the order is not himself required by the terms of the order to give the relevant permission.

The words in para.5(b) and (c) show what the defendant must do in order to comply with the order. If he personally cannot go to the premises he must still comply with the order through a person falling within these categories.

The principles applicable to the personal position of such an individual **19.048** are set out at paras 19.025–19.027, above. For example, if that individual, knowing of the order, deliberately destroyed documents which fell within the scope of the order, so as to prevent their being found and preserved by the representatives of the claimant, then this would constitute a contempt of court.

But is the individual, on being served with the order, obliged, after an opportunity to take legal advice, to give permission for the entry and the search? If the individual does not have the authority so to act, he is under no obligation personally to purport to give permission. But is such a person then obliged to seek authority from the defendant? Although in practice the individual concerned might well be prepared to contact his principal for instructions, as a general rule he would not be in contempt of court if he chose not to do so. The order is not addressed to him personally. Furthermore, while seeking instructions would tend to progress matters

---

[27] *Manor Electronics v Dickson* [1988] R.F.C. 618; *Bhimji v Chatwani* [1991] 1 W.L.R. 989 at 997C. Contrast the irregular form of order made in *VDU Installations Ltd v Integrated Computer Systems and Cybernetics Ltd* [1989] F.S.R. 378 at 383 which provided that: "the defendant or any person appearing to be in control of the premises hereinafter mentioned do permit". See also M. Dockray and H. Laddie, "Piller Problems" (1990) 106 L.Q.R. 601 at 610–612.

more rapidly, it could not usually be said that the mere failure to seek instructions constituted an intentional interference with the administration of justice.[28] If, however, the individual does seek instructions, he must do nothing to influence the defendant to refuse permission for the entry and search.

19.049   If the individual concerned does have the authority to give permission for the entry and search, what then is the position? Would the failure to give permission constitute a contempt of court? It might be suggested that a mere omission by a third party cannot constitute contempt.[29] Thus, it might be said that the third party can be liable for contempt only if he *actively* participates in a breach of the court order or deliberately *interferes* with the administration of justice. As a general proposition this is no doubt correct. But is a refusal to give permission to be viewed as a mere omission? In *Acrow (Automation) Ltd v Rex Chainbelt Inc.*,[30] the defendant, in breach of an injunction, instructed a third party not to continue to supply certain machinery parts to the plaintiff, and the third party, knowing of the injunction, acted on the instruction and refused to continue to supply the plaintiff. The Court of Appeal held that the third party, by acting on the instruction, had committed a contempt of court, even though on one view of the matter it might have been said that the third party had simply "omitted" to supply the parts.

If the defendant does not yet know of the order, the individual who appears to be in control of the premises would not be aiding or abetting a breach of the order by refusing entry. But if he has authority to give admittance and refuses, has he deliberately interfered with the administration of justice?[31] Ordinarily he has not: *Bhimji v Chatwani*.[32] He can seek the defendant's instructions and meanwhile ensure that nothing is removed from the premises which would frustrate the search which has been ordered. If the individual does knowingly facilitate the removal from the premises of items relevant to the search, or deliberately fails to take steps to prevent the removal of such items knowing that they are about to be removed, then he commits a contempt of court.[33] The individual cannot properly do any acts based on instructions given by the defendant which in themselves constitute a contempt of court by the defendant. If the

---

[28] See also *Eccles & Co. v Louisville and Nashville Railroad Company* [1912] 1 K.B. 135, in which a servant who had been ordered to produce documents which he held for his master was held not to be in contempt when he did not produce them and had not sought permission from his master to produce them.

[29] *Seaward v Paterson* [1897] 1 Ch. 545 at 557; *Thorne Rural District Council v Bunting (No.2)* [1972] 3 All E.R. 1084; *Attorney-General v Observer Ltd* [1988] 1 All E.R. 385 at 399.

[30] [1971] 1 W.L.R. 1676.

[31] *Attorney-General v Times Newspapers* (1992) 1 A.C. 191 at 206D–E, 211H–215B, 281B, 229H–231A.

[32] [1991] 1 W.L.R. 989 at 997B–C.

[33] *Attorney-General v Punch* [2003] 1 A.C. 1046; *Attorney-General v Times Newspapers*, above, at 220D–223B; *Harrow London Borough Council v Johnstone* [1997] 1 W.L.R. 459. This is because he has frustrated the purpose of the order, see *Attorney-General v Times Newspapers*, above, at 206G–H, 222C.

defendant wishes to be present while the search is conducted, and is able to go to the premises promptly to supervise the search, he is entitled to comply with the order in this way. If the defendant tries to block the search or unreasonably to delay it, he will be in contempt. If the person appearing to be in control of the premises has authority to allow the search to proceed, the defendant cannot validly revoke that authority, once he knows of the court order, so as to prevent compliance with the order.[34]

(8) Cross-examination on affidavit

Cross-examination is considered in Chapter 22, paras 22.023–22.026.   **19.050**
    The court will not in the exercise of its discretion order cross-examination for the purpose of seeing whether there has been a contempt of court[35] and thereby furnishing material which can be used in contempt proceedings, and the court will proceed with caution to ensure that this does not happen.
    The defendant also has a privilege against self-incrimination in respect of being found to be in contempt of court.[36]

(9) Service of injunctions and the penal notice

A negative order restraining someone from doing something is effective **19.051** when pronounced and can be enforced by committal or writ of sequestration even though not served on the person provided that the person was in court when the order was made or has been notified of the terms whether by telephone, fax, or otherwise,[37] or if the court decides to dispense with service under RSC Ord. 45, r.7(7). Otherwise the order must have been served personally and endorsed with a penal notice. This is a written warning addressed to the person[38] served that disobedience to the order

---

[34] Such an instruction would be a request to the person in control of the premises to participate in frustrating the search required by the court order and would itself be a contempt of court.
[35] *Phillips v Symes* [2003] EWCA Civ 1769 at [51]; *RAC Ltd v Allsop*, unreported, October 3, 1984, quoted by Rimer J. in *Cobra Golf Inc. v Rata* [1998] Ch. 109; *Bhimji v Chatwani (No.2)* [1992] 1 W.L.R. 1158 at 1166–1169; *Bekhor Ltd v Bilton* [1981] Q.B. 923 at 949, *per* Griffiths L.J. who dissented on the particular facts of the case, but whose judgment on this point appears to be correct; *Bayer v Winter (No.2)* [1986] 1 W.L.R. 540 at 544; *Yau Chiu Wah v Gold Chef Investment Ltd* [2002] 2 H.K.L.R.D. 832; *Exagym Pty Ltd v Professional Gymnasium Equipment Pty Ltd (No.2)* [1994] 2 Od R. 129 (Queensland).
[36] See Chapter 17, paras 17.030–17.037.
[37] RSC Ord.45, r.7(6).
[38] RSC Ord.45, r.7(4); *R. v City of London Magistrates' Court, Ex p. Green* [1997] 3 All E.R. 551, a penal notice addressed to ". . . any officers of the police or serious fraud office" was bad; see, for form of penal notice, Appendix 5, para.A5.019, below.

574 *Contempt of court: the position of the defendant and non-parties*

would be a contempt of court punishable by imprisonment or, in the case of a body corporate, by sequestration of its assets and imprisonment of the person responsible. On the example freezing injunction the warning reads:

"If you [. . .] disobey this order you may be held to be in contempt of court and may be imprisoned, fined, or have your assets seized".

In the case of a mandatory order there must be a time within which the act is to be done, and the order must be served prior to that time endorsed with a penal notice. There is a general power in RSC Ord. 45, r.7(7) to dispense with service of the order which can be exercised before or after the relevant breach,[39] and an order can also be served by an alternative mode of service under CPR r.6.8. However, the general principle is that the court in contempt proceedings will require to be satisfied of personal service prior to time expiring for the doing of the act.

In order to bring a successful contempt proceeding it is essential as a minimum to prove that the defendant knew of the order, which was clear and unambiguous, and broke the terms of the order.[40]

(10) Service of an order to attend for cross-examination about assets: conduct money

19.052   An order to attend for cross-examination about assets can be made post-judgment under CPR Pt 71, or at any time in the proceedings under s.37 of the Supreme Court Act 1981.[41]

There is a rule which covers the tender of conduct money for a person ordered to attend for cross-examination under CPR Pt 71[42] which enables a judgment creditor to obtain information from a judgment debtor:

"TRAVELLING EXPENSES

71.4 (1) A person ordered to attend court may, within 7 days of being served with the order, ask the judgment creditor to pay him a sum reasonably sufficient to cover his travelling expenses to and from court.

(2) The judgment creditor must pay such a sum if requested."

Before CPR there was no express rule requiring tender of conduct money to a person ordered to attend for cross-examination about his assets

---

[39] *Davy International Ltd v Tazzyman* [1997] 1 W.L.R. 1256; and see para.19.019 above.
[40] *R. v City of London Magistrates' Court, Ex p. Green* [1997] 3 All E.R. 551.
[41] Chapter 22, paras 22.023–22.026, below.
[42] See para. 22.033, below.

under s.37 of the Supreme Court Act 1981, or a witness served within the jurisdiction with a subpoena. Section 36(4) of the Supreme Court Act 1981, which requires tender of conduct money, applies only to special subpoenas which run throughout the United Kingdom. But there is a common law rule which applied to them. This originated with an enactment made in the time of Elizabeth I—s.12 of 5 Eliz. c. 9, an enactment which was also the origin of writs of subpoena. The section provided for penalties to be imposed on "any person" served with "any process" to testify who did not appear but only if that person had

". . . tendered unto him . . . according to his Countenance or Calling, such reasonable sums of money for his . . . costs and charges as having regard to the distance of the places is necessary to be allowed in that behalf."

A number of decisions established that the money had to be tendered at **19.053** the time of service of the subpoena and that sufficient had to be tendered at the time of service to cover going to the court and coming back, including lodging. The Divisional Court in *Protector Endowment Co. v Whitlam*[43] held that it was necessary to tender conduct money to a judgment debtor ordered to attend under the predecessor of RSC Ord. 48, r.1 and the rules applicable to subpoenas applied to such an order. The common law rule applied even though:

(1) attendance was compelled before an examiner and not a judge;[44]

(2) attendance was compelled of a party to the proceedings who had solicitors acting for him.[45]

There was some question as to whether what had to be tendered was cash, or whether something else would do. It seemed that provided that what was tendered was the equivalent of cash, this would suffice.[46]

In cases where conduct money had to be tendered, then if there was no tender there could not be proceedings for contempt in respect of the breach of an order requiring attendance to give evidence. This was so even though the person summonsed had enough money of his own to come had he wished.[47]

The position for a witness summons is now regulated by CPR r.34.7 which provides:

---

[43] (1877) 36 L.T. 467.
[44] See the argument in *Townsend v Tawnsend* [1907] P. 239n; *Beeston Shipping v Babanaft* [1985] 1 All E.R. 923 at 928c–e.
[45] *Protector Endowment Co. v Whitlam* (1887) 36 LT 467; *Rendell v Grundy* [1895] 2 Q.B. 16 at 20; *Beeston Shipping Ltd v Babanaft International SA* [1985] 1 All E.R. 923.
[46] *Union Bank of Finland v Lelakis* [1997] C.L.C. 20.
[47] *Townsend v Townsend* [1907] P. 239n reported also at (1905) 21 T.L.R. 657.

"RIGHT OF WITNESS TO TRAVELLING EXPENSES AND COMPENSATION FOR LOSS
OF TIME

34.7 At the time of service of a witness summons the witness must be
offered or paid—

(a) a sum reasonably sufficient to cover his expenses in travelling to
and from the court; and

(b) such sum by way of compensation for loss of time as may be
specified in the relevant practice direction."

19.054   Although CPR r.34.7(a) does not mention hotel or lodging expenses,
such expenses were treated as falling within the words of the statute of
Elizabeth I and it seems that where this would reasonably be a part of the
expenses to be incurred in going to give evidence, then these are to be
treated as included within the words of (a), which appear to correspond
with the reqirement of conduct money. CPR r.34.7(b) is additional to what
was covered by conduct money at common law. The intention of CPR
r.34.7 was to give the witness a reasonable indemnity against his expenses
and loss of remuneration from having to go to court to give evidence.

The position for a compelled attendance for the purpose of being cross-
examined about assets in aid of a freezing injunction appears to be
governed by the equivalent provisions in CPR r.34.8(6) which applies to an
order to examine a person "before the hearing takes place". This provides:

"(6) At the time of service of the order the deponent must be offered
or paid—

(a) a sum reasonably sufficient to cover his expenses in travelling to
and from the place of examination; and

(b) such sum by way of compensation for loss of time as may be
specified in the relevant practice direction."

Like a witness summons this includes a requirement to pay compensation
for loss of time. CPR r.71.4 does not include such a requirement
apparently on the basis that the judgment debtor should have paid the
judgment and therefore it would not be appropriate to require this
additional sum to be paid.

(11) Irregular or unjustified orders

19.055   No one can justify contempt on the grounds that the order should never
have been made, or was irregular. If an order has been made, it must be
obeyed until it is set aside.[48]

---

[48] *Isaacs v Robertson* [1985] A.C. 97; *Hadkinson v Hadkinson* [1952] P. 285; *M v Home
Office* [1992] Q.B. 270 (affirmed on different grounds at [1994] A.C. 377).

(12) Proceedings for contempt

(i) Service of the application and affidavit, giving notice of the grounds on which contempt is alleged

If proceedings are to be taken for contempt it is essential that there is strict **19.056** observance of the procedural requirements. Furthermore, contempt proceedings engage the right to a fair trial under Art.6(1) of the European Convention on Human Rights and the allegation of contempt is the bringing of a criminal charge[49] within the autonomous meaning of this expression in the Convention. This is because although the proceedings are classified as civil proceedings under English domestic law, contempt proceedings can be brought against anyone who commits what is alleged to be contempt, and the outcome of the proceedings may be the imposition of a penalty or punishment which could be up to two years' imprisonment or a fine.[50] The commencement of contempt proceedings moves from enforcement of civil rights by injunction to a different arena. The procedural rules which apply under the CPR, if followed, ensure compliance with these requirements of the Convention.

The consequence is that Art.6(2) and (3) of the Convention apply. These provide:

"2. Everyone charged with a criminal offence shall be presumed innocent until proven guilty according to law.

3. Everyone charged with a criminal offence has the following minimum rights:

(a) to be informed promptly, in a language which he understands and in detail, of the nature and cause of the accusation against him;

(b) to have adequate time and facilities for the preparation of his defence;

(c) to defend himself in person or through legal assistance of his own choosing or, if he has not sufficient means to pay for legal assistance, to be given it free when the interests of justice so require;

(d) to examine or have examined witnesses against him and to obtain the attendance and examination of witnesses on his behalf under the same conditions as witnesses against him;

(e) to have the free assistance of an interpreter if he cannot understand or speak the language used in court."

---

[49] *Kyprianou v Cyprus*, Application No.73797/01, January 27, 2004, at para.31 European Court of Human Rights (Second Section); *Berry Trade v Moussavi* [2002] 1 W.L.R. 1910 at [31].

[50] See *R. (McCann) v Crown Court at Manchester* [2003] 1 A.C. 787 at [28–33], applying the three tests in *Engel v The Netherlands* (No.1) (1976) 1 E.H.R.R. 647 at 678–679, para.82; *Han v Customs and Excise Commissioners* [2001] 1 W.L.R. 2253 at [55–68].

19.057 Committal proceedings are regulated by RSC Ord. 52. Contempt proceedings in connection with breach of an injunction are held in open court before a single judge and are made by claim form or application notice, supported by affidavit, and the procedure must comply with RSC Ord. 52, r.4, which provides:

> "Rule 4 (1) Where an application for an order of committal may be made to a court other than a Divisional Court, the application must be made by claim form or application notice and be supported by an affidavit.
>
> (2) Subject to paragraph (3) the claim form or application notice, stating the grounds of the application and accompanied by a copy of the affidavit in support of the application, must be served personally on the person sought to be committed.
>
> (3) Without prejudice to its powers under Part 6 of the CPR, the court may dispense with service under this rule if it thinks it just to do so."

The claim form or application notice must clearly state the grounds of the application, specify with particulars precisely what the alleged contemnor is said to have done,[51] and be served with a copy of the affidavit in support personally on the alleged contemnor. There is power to dispense with this requirement.[52] An application for leave to issue a writ of sequestration is made by application notice. Under RSC Ord. 46, r.5:

> Rule 5 (1) Notwithstanding anything in rules 2 and 4, an application for permission to issue a writ of sequestration must be made in accordance with CPR Part 23 and be heard by a Judge.
>
> (2) Subject to paragraph (3), the application notice, stating the grounds of the application and accompanied by a copy of the witness statement or affidavit in support of the application, must be served personally on the person against whose property it is sought to issue the writ.
>
> (3) The court may dispense with service of the application notice under this rule if it thinks it just to do so.
>
> (4) The judge hearing an application for permission to issue a writ of sequestration may sit in private in any case in

---

[51] *Attorney-General for Tuvalu v Philatelic Distribution Corporation Ltd* [1990] 1 W.L.R. 926 at 934–935 (where the complainant has not witnessed the acts complained of and must rely on inference, he must "make clear the thrust of the case"). *Chiltern District Council v Keane* [1985] 1 W.L.R. 619; *Churchman v Joint Shop Stewards' Committee* [1972] 1 W.L.R. 1094; *Summit Holding Ltd v Business Software Alliance* [1999] 3 S.L.R. 197.

[52] RSC Ord. 52, r.4(2); *Mansour v Mansour* [1989] 1 F.L.R. 418; *Medina Housing Association Ltd v Connelly*, unreported, . . . July 26, 2002 CA, (no written notice of allegations or evidence but sentence of imprisonment upheld on appeal because there had been a fair trial).

which, if the application were for an order of committal, he would be entitled to do so by virtue of Order 52, rule 6 but, except in such a case, the application shall be heard in public."

The respondent to the application ought to be served personally with **19.058** notice of the date for the hearing of the application and with the date of any adjourned hearing of the application, but failure to do this will not render the contempt proceedings defective if the respondent is in court on the adjourned hearing and is represented by solicitors who have been acting for him throughout the contempt proceedings.[53] Proceedings for contempt of court should be initiated within a reasonable time of a party obtaining knowledge of a breach of a court order or undertaking or of other misconduct and should be prosecuted diligently, otherwise they may be dismissed or struck out as an abuse of the process of the court.[54] In *Berry Trade v Moussavi*[55] the claimant did not want a delay to contempt proceedings whilst the defendant sought legal aid and so offered to fund the defence of the application and resisted an adjournment. The Court of Appeal held that the defendant had the right to seek legal aid which was part of his right to a fair trial under Art.6(1) and that an adjournment had to be granted for this purpose.

At the beginning of any contempt proceedings where there is a risk of imprisonment an unrepresented defendant should be asked by the judge whether he wishes to be represented.[56]

(ii) Burden and standard of proof

Although the proceedings are civil and not criminal, the burden of proof is **19.059** equivalent to the criminal burden.[57]

When proof of contempt involves establishing that the defendant is not telling the truth on affidavit, and the defendant is available so that he could be cross-examined, the applicant should not invite the court to make a finding based on inferences to be drawn from documents unless he has first

---

[53] *Bhimji v Chatwani* [1991] 1 W.L.R. 989. This situation is to be distinguished from the case where the defendant is alleged to have broken a court order requiring his attendance (*e.g.* for cross-examination), and he has not been served personally with the order fixing the date and time when he is to attend: *Beeston Shipping Ltd v Babanaft International SA* [1985] 1 All E.R. 92.

[54] *Taylor v Ribby Hall Leisure Ltd* [1997] 4 All E.R. 887.

[55] [2002] 1 W.L.R. 1910.

[56] *Newman v Modern Bookbinders* [2000] 2 All E.R. 814 at 822; *Togher v Customs and Excise Commissioners* [2001] EWCA Civ 474 at [38] and [52].

[57] *Re Bramblevale* [1970] Ch. 128; *Commissioner of Water Resources v Federated Engine Drivers' and Firemen's Association of Australasia* [1988] 2 Qd R. 385, Supreme Court of Queensland; *Attorney-General for Tuvalu v Philatelic Distribution Corporation Ltd*, [1990] 1 W.L.T. 926 *Attorney-General v Newspaper Publishing plc (No.2)* [1989] F.S.R. 457; *Z Bank v DI* [1994] 1 Lloyd's Rep. 656 at 660; *Cobra Golf. Inc. v Rata* [1998] Ch. 109; *Phillips v Symes* [2003] EWCA Civ 1769 at [51].

sought to cross-examine.[58] This is because such a course is liable to be unsatisfactory and unfair to the respondent.

19.060　　Freezing relief is usually granted subject to a financial limit. In contempt proceedings, the question may arise whether the claimant has the burden of proof to show that the transaction complained of was a breach of the injunction notwithstanding the financial limit. This would create an obstacle for the applicant in almost every case because usually his information about the defendant's assets is limited. In contrast, the defendant knows what he has. In contempt proceedings the court will expect the defendant to adduce evidence about other assets for the purpose of showing that transactions which appear to have been in breach of the injunction were in fact permitted by reason of there being other assets satisfying the financial limit. If no evidence is forthcoming on other assets, the court will be prepared to make a finding of contempt, even though the applicant has not put in evidence negativing the existence of such assets.[59] The principle does not appear to go further than to create an evidential burden upon the defendant[60] of placing material before the court on the basis of which a reasonable doubt is established as to whether he has acted in breach of the injunction. If that threshold is not met then breach will be found. It is considered that this approach is not barred by the presumption of innocence in Art.6(2)[61] because:

(1)　it only operates once the relevant facts showing prima facie breach of the order have been proved by the applicant; and

(2)　it is a reasonable and proportionate presumption in the circumstances securing a legitimate aim,[62] because of the public interest in having a system of freezing injunctions which is effective, the difficulty in enforcement which would arise if the applicant had to prove the value of other assets of the defendant at the time of the alleged breach, and that the evidence ought to be readily available to the alleged contemnor. The presumption of fact is within "reasonable limits".[63]

Unless there was such a presumption it would make it unduly onerous for the applicant to prove contempt in cases based on a freezing injunction

---

[58] *Atlantic Capital Corporation v Sir Cecil Denniston Burney*, Court of Appeal (Civ Div) Transcript No.1142 of 1994 (September 15, 1994), applying *Smith v Fawcett* [1942] 1 Ch. 304 at 308.

[59] *Canadian Imperial Bank of Commerce v Bhattessa*, Court of Appeal (Civ Div) Transcript No.694 of 1993 (April 21, 1993), approving *The Times*, September 10, 1991.

[60] *Great Future International Ltd v Sealand Housing Corporation* [2004] EWHC 124 at [15–16], Ch.D.

[61] *Great Future International Ltd v Sealand Housing Corporation* [2004] EWHC 124 at [19–21] assumes that there was no more than "an evidential burden" and proceeds on the basis that this is compliant with Art.6.

[62] *Brown v Stott* [2003] 1 A.C. 681 at 693–694; *R. v Lambert* [2002] 2 A.C. 545; *R. v Matthews* [2003] 3 W.L.R. 693; *Salabiaku v France* (1988) 13 E.H.R.R. 379.

[63] *R. v Director of Public Prosecutions Ex p. Kebilene* [2000] 2 A.C. 326 at 385.

subject to a financial limit, which is a provision adopted almost universally in freezing injunctions. The defendant has the facts and it is not an unfair burden for him to have.[64]

A standard exception to a freezing order is para.11(2) of the example **19.061** order which provides that the order does not prohibit the defendant from dealing with or disposing of any of his assets "in the ordinary and proper course of business". This is under the heading "EXCEPTIONS TO THIS ORDER". When a question arises as to whether a payment falls within this exclusion the burden of proof remains on the applicant throughout to prove that the relevant payment did not fall within this exclusion.[65]

(iii) Procedure at the application

The alleged contemnor has a right to cross-examine witnesses, and can **19.062** compel by witness summons the attendance of witnesses to testify as part of the defence. The defendant cannot be compelled to give evidence, although if he chooses to do so he can be ordered to be cross-examined,[66] in which case the court will limit cross-examination to the alleged contempt. If he does not submit to cross-examination the court may give little weight to his evidence.[67] Privilege against self-incrimination applies to an allegation or possible allegation of contempt.[68]

Since contempt proceedings, although not in fact criminal proceedings, partake of a criminal nature,[69] the alleged contemnor is permitted to make a submission of no case to answer, without being put to his election whether or not he chooses to call evidence: *Attorney-General for Tuvalu v Philatelic Distribution Corporation Ltd* (above). This is in contrast with the usual position in civil proceedings: *Alexander v Rayson*.[70]

The court will not make a finding of contempt if the relevant part of the **19.063** order or undertaking is vague or imprecise in a material respect[71] or is

---

[64] See also Chapter 4, paras 4.011–4.015.

[65] *Nokia France SA v Interstone Trading Ltd* [2004] EWCH 272, at [54], Comm Ct.

[66] *Great Future International Ltd v Sealand Housing Corporation* [2004] EWHC 124 at [26] points 1 and 2.

[67] *Phillips v Symes* [2003] EWCA Civ 1769 at [51]; *Great Future International Ltd v Sealand Housing Corporation* [2004] EWHC 124 at [26] point 4, and [30]; *Comet Products UK Ltd v Hawkex Plastics* [1971] 2 Q.B.67.

[68] *Memory Corporation v Sidhu* [2000] Ch. 645; *Cobra Golf Inc. v Rata* [1998] Ch. 109; *Bhimji v Chatwani (No.2)* [1992] 1 W.L.R. 1158, not following *Garvin v Domus Publishing Ltd* [1989] Ch. 335; *Great Future International Ltd v Sealand Housing Corporation* [2004] EWHC 124 at [26] at point 5. See also *Exagym Pty Ltd v Professional Gymnasium Equipment Pty Ltd (No.2)* [1994] 2 Qd R. 129 (Queensland).

[69] See also *Irtelli v Squatriti* [1993] Q.B. 83, where it was held before CPR that the rules laid down in *Ladd v Marshall* [1954] 1 W.L.R. 1489 do not apply to adducing evidence on an appeal against a committal order.

[70] [1936] 1 K.B. 169.

[71] *Hussain v Hussain* [1986] Fam. 134 at 142; *Iberian Trust Ltd v Founders Trust and Investment Co. Ltd* [1932] 2 K.B. 87 at 95. *cf Australian Consolidated Press Ltd v Morgan* (1965) 112 C.L.R. 483 at p.492 *per* Barwick C.J. and *Long v Specifier Publications Pty Ltd* (1998) 44 N.S.W.L.R. 545 at pp.567–568.

genuinely ambiguous,[72] in the sense that it is reasonably open to more than one meaning, and that on one view of the order no breach has occurred. An order should be clear on its face and should not require the defendant to cross-refer to other documents to ascertain the full extent of his obligations.[73] The person to whom the order is directed should be able, by reading it and without more, to know at once what it is that he must do or refrain from doing to comply with its terms. For this reason, an order which refers to another document (e.g. a contract, another order of the court or an affidavit) and grants relief by reference to what is set out in that document is defective and contempt proceedings founded upon it may be unsuccessful.[74]

(iv) Formal requirements of an order for committal

19.064   When there is a contempt consisting of failure to comply with a mandatory order requiring something to be delivered up or something to be done by a certain time, the contemnor can only be punished once for that contempt. There is a single offence. There must then be a further order setting a new time limit if there are to be further contempt proceedings.[75]

An order for committal must state on its face for what reason the contemnor has been committed. The reason for this is so that there can be due process of law accorded to the person committed.

Thus by reading the order he knows for what he has been held in contempt in case he wishes to purge it. The court hearing an application to purge can inform itself of the particulars of the contempt. An appeal, if brought, will be against those findings. Neither the person committed nor any court will be in any doubt what contempt has been found.

19.065   However, on appeal the Court of Appeal has jurisdiction to amend or vary a committal order which is defective and will use this power to correct technical defects in the order which have caused no prejudice to the person committed.[76]

RSC Ord.52. r.7(1) enables the court to suspend the execution of an order for committal. Although the court has the jurisdiction to make a suspension of execution which is to remain in effect until further order, the practice is that the court will provide in the order for a time at which the

---

[72] *R & I Bank of Western Australia Ltd v Anchorage Investments* (1992) 10 W.A.R. 59 (concerning the meaning of "assets" when applied to a beneficiary of a discretionary trust which he controlled); *Haddonstone Ltd v Sharp, Court of Appeal* (Civ Div) (January 23, 1996) ("the same" not construed as including "substantially the same" item). M. Dockray and H. Laddie, "Piller Problems" (1990) 106 L.Q.R. 601 at 608.
[73] *Rudkin-Jones v Trustee of the Property of the Bankrupt* (1965) 109 S.J. 334; *Harris v Harris* [2001] 3 F.C.R. 193 at 228; *H. C. Mathews v I. V. Mathews and C. E. Coutanche* [2001] J.L.R. 671 at para.41.
[74] *Commissioner of Water Resources v Federated Engine Drivers' and Firemen's Association of Australasia* [1988] 2 Qd R. 385 at 390.
[75] *Kumari v Jalal* [1997] 1 W.L.R. 97; *Danchevsky v Danchevsky (No.2)* (1977) 121 S.J. 796.
[76] *Nicholls v Nicholls* [1997] 1 W.L.R. 314; *M v P (Contempt of Court: Committal Order)* [1993] Fam. 167; *Oswald v Hyde*, unreported, March 19, 1999.

warrant will expire.[77] Where the execution of the warrant is suspended the order should set out on its face the terms on which it is suspended and the period for which the warrant will remain in force.

(13) Interference with the due administration of justice: deliberate false statements made to the court or in evidence provided to the court

Intentional interference with the due administration of justice by the court **19.066** constitutes contempt of court. The *Commercial Courts Guide* states:

> "F7.4 Proceedings for contempt of court may be brought against a person who makes, or causes to be made, a false statement in a witness statement (or any other document verified by a statement of truth) without an honest belief in its truth: rule 32.14(1)."

In the case of deliberately untruthful statements made in an affidavit required to be made about assets, there will be contempt consisting of non-compliance with the order. With disclosure statements CPR r.31.23 provides:

FALSE DISCLOSURE STATEMENTS

31.23 (1) Proceedings for contempt of court may be brought against a person if he makes, or causes to be made, a false disclosure statement, without an honest belief in its truth.

(2) Proceedings under this rule may be brought only—

(a) by the Attorney General; or
(b) with the permission of the court.

Any deliberate falsehood told to the court made with the intention of misleading the court will constitute contempt.

The mere omission of coming back to court for the purpose of correcting **19.067** material relied upon on a without notice application in order to enable the court to reconsider its order, whilst constituting a breach of duty owed to the court, does not in itself amount to contempt.[78]

---

[77] *Griffin v Griffin* [2000] 2 F.L.R. 44; *Oswald v Hyde*, unreported, March 19, 1999.
[78] *Knox D'Arcy Ltd v Jamieson, Court of Appeal* (Civ Div) Transcript No.1759 of 1995 (December 19, 1995).

(14) Injunctions: conduct which is a contempt independently of breach of the order or frustrating its purpose

(i) Threatening contempt proceedings so as to obtain a settlement

19.069 The threat of contempt proceedings or of continuing contempt proceedings should not be made for any purpose other than securing compliance with the relevant order of the court. To use such a threat to secure a settlement is a gross abuse of the process of the court and itself constitutes a contempt of court. [79]

(ii) Misrepresentation of what has happened in court proceedings or the effect of an order

19.069 In *Gillette Safety Razor v A. W. Gamage Ltd*,[80] the plaintiff was refused an interlocutory injunction on the sole ground of delay, and the defendant misrepresented what had happened to its customers giving the impression that the determination had been on the merits of the underlying case. This was a contempt because the defendant had misrepresented what had happened in the proceedings and therefore the effect of the order, to the prejudice of the plaintiff; it was the misrepresentation which was the vice of the conduct. No issue arose in that case about *mens rea*.

The decision is an illustration of the principle that ". . . any act done or writing published calculated to obstruct or interfere with the due course of justice or the lawful process of the Courts is a contempt of Court".[81] If a person deliberately or recklessly misrepresented the order or the nature of the proceedings to obtain some advantage, then he would be acting deceitfully, and there would be full justification for holding that he has acted in contempt. It is suggested that mere carelessness would not be sufficient. People often make mistakes about what court orders or other documents mean, and it is not necessary to the integrity of the process to hold the negligent interpreter of a court order in contempt of court.

(15) Penalties for contempt

19.070 If the court makes a finding of contempt, the penalty to be imposed will depend on the circumstances of the case. The relevant considerations include the following:

---

[79] *Knox D'Arcy Ltd v Jamieson*, Court of Appeal (Civ Div) Transcript No.1759 of 1995 (December 19, 1995).

[80] (1907) 24 R.P.C. 1, applying the judgment in *Re Read and Huggonson* (1742) 2 Atk. 469 (Lord Hardwicke L.C.). See also *Kabushiki Kaisha Yakult Honsha v Yakudo Group Holdings Ltd (No.3)* [2003] 1 H.K.L.R.D. 391 at paras 13–17 (misreporting is a contempt if it interferes with the due administration of justice).

[81] *Ambard v Attorney-General for Trinidad and Tobago* [1936] A.C. 322 at 344.

(1) Whether the claimant has been prejudiced by virtue of the contempt, and if so whether that prejudice can be rectified and how. For example, if money which ought to have been preserved under a freezing injunction has been paid to a third party, the defendant, or possibly the third party,[82] might be required to reconstitute the fund to purge their contempt,[83] and a penalty may be held in suspense pending the fund being restored.[84] If the defendant has hidden away assets which are the subject of a freezing injunction, the court may decide to use committal to compel the defendant to restore the position.[85]

(2) The extent to which the contemnor has acted under pressure. In the context of a search order, a defendant is liable to act under the pressure of the moment rather than by way of deliberate misconduct. If so, this provides good reason for not making a committal order.[86]

(3) If there has been a deliberate and contumacious breach of a court order, then the court has to bear in mind the public interest in ensuring that court orders are obeyed. Thus a committal order may be fully appropriate when there has been a deliberate breach of a freezing injunction,[87] even if in the meantime the defendant has sought to rectify the prejudice suffered by the claimant. Committal is normally only appropriate for serious contumacious flouting of a court order.[88]

---

[82] The difficulty with this is that the defendant who has acted in contempt and had the benefit of the money should not obtain any benefit from the third party rectifying the position as against the innocent party, see *Customs & Excise v Barclays Bank* [2004] 2 All E.R. 789 at [56], Comm Ct. The answer could be to require the bank to indemnify the applicant against its loss in return for the applicant transferring to the bank a corresponding interest in the underlying claim.

[83] *Great Future International Ltd v Sealand Housing Corporation* [2004] EWHC 124 at [82–84]; *State of Qatar v Al Thani and Al Kuwari* [1996] J.L.R. Notes-13b (return of the money with an apology by the defendants sufficed to purge)

[84] *Z Bank v DI* [1994] 1 Lloyd's Rep. 656 at 668; *Inn Spirit Limited v Burns* [2003] EWHC 2397 (declaration made that the contemnors were in contempt and order to do various acts with a view to remedying the effects of the contempt); see also *Guinness Peat Aviation (Belgium) NV v Hispania Lineas Aereas SA* [1992] 1 Lloyd's Rep. 190 at 196 (see the discussion of this case in Chapter 20, para.20.024.

[85] *Enfield London Borough Council v Mahoney* [1983] 1 W.L.R. 749.

[86] *Bhimji v Chatwani* [1991] 1 W.L.R. 989 at 1001H–1003D; *HPSI Ltd v Thomas and Williams* (1983) 133 N.L.J. 598. Staughton Committee Report on Anton Piller orders, para.4.10.

[87] *Popischil v Philips, The Times*, January 19, 1988; Court of Appeal (Civ Div) Transcript No.31 of 1988; *Golden Portfolio Holidays Ltd v Cordingly*, Court of Appeal (Civ Div) Transcript No.272 of 1992 (March 20, 1992): "There must never be any room for supposing that the game is worth the candle"; *Great Future International Ltd v Sealand Housing Corporation* [2004] EWHC 124 at [85–87].

[88] *Gulf Azov Shipping Co. Ltd v Chief Idisi* [2001] EWCA Civ 21. *Oystertec Plc v Paul Anthony Davidson* [2004] EWHC 627 (Ch) at para.30 (where contemnor had apologised for serious breaches and there was no benefit to be gained from even a suspended committal order).

(4) Whether the contemnor has been placed in breach of the court order by reason of the conduct of others, and if so the extent to which he is personally at fault: *Z Bank v DI* (above).

(5) If the contemnor has refused to restore the position even though he could do so (*e.g.* by restoring funds transferred away in breach of a freezing injunction). The penalty can contain a coercive element[89] designed to persuade the contemnor to co-operate.

(6) Whether the contemnor has acted on mistaken legal advice.

(7) Whether the contemnor now appreciates the seriousness of a deliberate and flagrant breach and whether a custodial sentence is necessary to bring home to him the need in the future to obey court orders or whether the case can be suitably dealt with by a substantial fine.[90]

(8) Whether the contemnor has belatedly co-operated.[91]

The court should apply the criminal burden of proof when deciding whether there are facts which make it appropriate to impose a more serious penalty, *e.g.* whether the contempt was deliberate and contumelious: *Z Bank v DI*.[92] If there are contemporaneous contempt proceedings and criminal proceedings arising out of the same events, the court hearing the contempt proceedings cannot ignore the criminal proceedings and may have to take into account their outcome. Although the contempt proceedings and the criminal proceedings have different purposes, and even if the overlap is not exact, the court which sentences second[93] will ensure that the contemnor is not in effect punished twice for the same offence.[94]

(16) Suspension of a committal order

19.071   Once contempt has been proved, the court may adjourn the question of penalty, or can order the warrant for committal to lie in the office for a period to see whether the contemnor will now comply with the order of the court,[95] or can make an order for committal and suspend it on certain terms.

---

[89] *Burton v Winters* [1993] 1 W.L.R. 1077 at 1080; *Shalson v Russo*, unreported, August 2, 2002 (Neuberger J.); *Raja v Van Hoogstraten* [2002] EWCA 2233 ChD,—fine increasing week by week whilst the contemnor failed to co-operate.
[90] *Taylor Made Golf Co. Inc. v Rata & Rata* [1996] F.S.R. 528 at 536 (£75,000 fine for deliberate breaches of an Anton Piller order).
[91] *Microsoft Corporation v Backslash Distribution Ltd (No.2)*: [1991] Masons C.L.R. 24, ChD.
[92] [1994] 1 Lloyd's Rep. 656 at 667.
[93] *Lomas v Parle* [2004] 1 W.L.R. 1642 at para.48.
[94] *Lomas v Parle* [2004] 1 W.L.R. 1642 at paras 29 and 48; *Hale v Tanner* [2000] 1 W.L.R. 2377 at p.2381F (proposition (9)).
[95] *Dent v Dent* [1962] P. 187.

This power of suspension is a common law power of the court,[96] which is part of its inherent jurisdiction,[97] and is regulated procedurally by RSC Ord. 52, r.7. It enables the court to pass a sentence which through suspension can induce compliance with the order of the court.

Where a committal order has been made for contempt and it is suspended subject to conditions, then if there is an issue whether those conditions have been complied with, and a new allegation of contempt is involved, then the defendant has the benefit of privilege against self-incrimination,[98] and the defendant is entitled to decline to be cross-examined.

It has been decided by the Court of Appeal[99] that if the application is only about compliance or not with the conditions, and does not involve proof of a contempt, then privilege against self-incrimination does not arise. In *Phillips v Symes*,[2] the Court of Appeal said: **19.072**

> "The relevant contempt has already been proved and the only question is the implementation of a sentence already imposed. The right time to worry about whether committal is the right order is when the committal order is made. Thereafter it would not be right to ignore the fact that the committal order has been made and treat any subsequent application in relation to it as a fresh application to commit."

However, if the conditions have been breached it does not automatically follow that the contemnor will be sent to prison. The court has a discretion about what to do.[2] The suspended committal order does not automatically become an unsuspended committal order as a result of the breach.[3] If the breach is proved the consequence of this is to expose the contemnor to in substance what amounts to sentencing for the original contempt, taking into account the existence of the original committal order, the breach and other supervening circumstances.

It is considered that Art.6(2) of the European Convention on Human Rights, which provides for the presumption of innocence, is not engaged in this situation because the contemnor is not charged with a criminal offence.[4] However, the common law privilege against self-incrimination

---

[96] *Lee v Walker* [1985] Q.B. 1191 at 1200A–C; *Morris v Crown Office* [1970] 2 Q.B 114 at p.125A–B.
[97] *Morris v Crown Office* [1970] 2 Q.B. 114 at 122B–D.
[98] *Phillips v Symes* [2003] EWCA Civ 1769 at [51].
[99] *ibid.*, at [61].
[1] *ibid.*, at [51] point iv.
[2] *Re W (B)* [1969] 2 Ch. 50, a decision of a three-judge Court of Appeal deciding not to send the contemnor to prison, reversing Megarry J. who thought that the committal order became activated as a result of the breach and that he had no discretion in the matter ([1969] 2 Ch. 50 at 52G–H), and decided after a two-judge Court of Appeal had split on what was the correct analysis.
[3] *Re W (B)* [1969] 2 Ch. 50 at 56F.
[4] *Phillips v United Kingdom* (2001) 11 B.H.R.C. 280 at [26–36] (holding that Art.6(2) was not engaged on proceedings for a confiscation order under the Drug Trafficking Act 1994); *McIntosh v Lord Advocate* [2003] 1 A.C. 1078 at [25–29] (concluding that confiscation proceedings were proceedings for a penalty but did not involve the making of a criminal charge).

applies to "proceedings for an offence or for the recovery of a penalty",[5] and it is considered that the privilege against self-incrimination at common law applies to the sentencing process following conviction of an offence. It should likewise apply to proceedings where the defendant is at risk of being sentenced for the original contempt, and for this reason one would expect the contemnor to have the benefit of the common law privilege against self-incrimination even though the alleged breach did not involve proof of a new contempt.

19.073   In addition, Art.6(1) of the European Convention on Human Rights applies to such a hearing. Through this Article it is considered that the defendant would have the right not to have compelled admissions used against him for the purpose of sentencing him for the original contempt.[6]

It is considered that in the situation where a committal order has been suspended on terms which require the contemnor to provide information or take other steps which will enable the claimant to trace assets with a view to enforcement of a judgment or order of the court, and questions arise about the contemnor's compliance with those terms, the matter should be approached in stages. If the claimant seeks to activate the committal order this will require him to prove breach of the terms on which it was suspended. Since the substance of the matter is an application which exposes the contemnor to sentencing for the original contempt, the issue of breach, and all matters relied upon as going to penalty, should be resolved requiring the claimant to satisfy a criminal standard of proof and allowing the contemnor privilege against self-incrimination and a right to remain silent.

19.074   Once that stage has been concluded, or the claimant has agreed not to pursue lifting the suspension to the committal order, and the court has consented to this course being adopted, the claimant can then proceed to steps designed to secure effective enforcement of the judgment or order of the court which is unsatisfied. For this purpose issues are to be resolved using the civil standard of proof, and since there is no question of using any information to activate the committal order or impose some penalty, no privilege against self-incrimination arises.

(17) Purging contempt

19.075   A person who is being punished for contempt can apply to the court to purge his contempt. The theory underlying this application is that the contemnor is entitled to seek forgiveness from the court. On the application the court can either dismiss it, or allow it. It cannot substitute a

---

[5] See s.14(1) of the Civil Evidence Act 1968 and Chapter 17, paras 17.030–17.040.
[6] *Phillips v United Kingdom* (2001) 11 B.H.R.C. 280 at [37–47]; *R. v Hertfordshire County Council Ex p. Green* [2000] 2 A.C. 412 at 422 and *Saunders v United Kingdom* (1996) 23 E.H.R.R. 313.

different penalty in the light of changed events. So, *e.g.* if the contemnor has been committed to prison for a particular period and that warrant has been executed there is no power to impose a suspended sentence in place of the contemnor serving out the rest of the sentence.[7] Except for cases of contempt in the face of the court, when there can be a remand pending summary determination of the allegation,[8] there is no power at common law to remand a contemnor in custody pending a hearing deciding whether he is in contempt or a decision on sentence. This has the consequence that, in the absence of a statutory power to remand a contemnor in custody, the court can only send him to prison by imposing an immediate custodial sentence for the contempt albeit with the possibility that the contemnor can subsequently apply to purge his contempt.[9]

(18) Refusal to hear a party in contempt

If a defendant is in contempt of court in respect of compliance with an order, the question may arise whether the court will refuse to hear the party in contempt until after he has purged that contempt. Previously there had been a tendency to articulate a general rule refusing to hear a party in contempt subject to categorised exceptions.[10] This has given way to the exercise of a discretion not to hear based on principle. This discretion has to take into account the right to a fair trial guaranteed under Art.6(1) of the European Convention on Human Rights. The general principles which apply are: **19.076**

(1) Not hearing a party who is in contempt is a strong thing to do which has to be properly justified on the particular facts and which is a proportionate means of securing a legitimate end.

(2) The contemnor is not to be prevented from making applications in other proceedings.[11]

(3) The contemnor is not to be precluded from defending himself in the proceedings (*e.g.* by appearing to resist an interlocutory application made by another party or by himself at the trial).[12]

(4) The contemnor is not to be precluded from making an application or advancing an appeal in the action for the purpose of seeking to

---

[7] *Harris v Harris* [2002] Fam. 253.
[8] *Wilkinson v S* [2003] 2 All E.R. 184 at [15–22].
[9] *Delaney v Delaney* [1996] Q.B. 387.
[10] *Motorola Credit Corporation v Uzan* [2004] W.LR. 113 at [49] referring to Brandon L.J. in *Astro Exito Navegation v Southland Enterprises (The Messiniaki Tolmi)* [1981] 2 Lloyd's Rep. 595 at 602 RHC.
[11] *Hadkinson v Hadkinson* [1952] P. 285 at 296.
[12] *Hadkinson v Hadkinson*, above, at 289–290 and 296; *Parry v Perryman* (MR July 1838) referred to in the notes to *Chuck v Cremer* (1846) 1 Coop. temp. Cott. 205 at p.207; *Midland Bank v Green (No.3)* [1979] Ch. 496 at 506.

set aside the very order in respect of which he is in contempt,[13] or an earlier order on which that order depends.[14] This principle may be overridden if, *e.g.* the contempt, if persisted in, would impede the course of justice[15] and there is no other effective means of securing his compliance: *X Ltd v Morgan-Grampian Ltd.*[16]

This principle applies regardless of whether or not the grounds of the application or appeal contend that the order was itself irregular or was made as a result of irregular proceedings.[17] In the context of a search order it has the effect that a defendant who is in breach of the provisions of the order is not precluded by reason of his contempt from seeking to have the order discharged, either by interlocutory application or at the trial. But he may still be penalised for contempt.[18]

(5) The contemnor is not to be precluded from making an application or advancing an appeal for the purpose of setting aside subsequent proceedings in the action on the grounds that an order has been made without jurisdiction or there has been some other irregularity.[19]

(6) Where a contemnor seeks to make a voluntary application or to advance an appeal in the action which does not fall within (4) or (5) above, then the court has a discretion to refuse to hear the contemnor until he has purged his contempt, recognising that this would be a strong thing to do and which has to be properly justified as proportionate to a legitimate end to be secured. The discretion will be exercised taking into account the nature and apparent strength[20] of the application sought to be made and the circumstances of the case.[21]

Under Art.6(1) of the European Convention on Human Rights there is a right to a fair trial. There is implied a right of access to the courts, but this is not absolute.[22] It may have to give way to an extent for reasons of public

---

[13] *Chuck v Cremer, above; Hadkinson v Hadkinson*, above; *Astro Exito Navegacion SA v Southland Enterprise Co. Ltd* [1981] 2 Lloyd's Rep. 595 at 601–602, *per* Brandon L.J.
[14] *Motorola Credit Corporation v Uzan* [2004] 1 W.L.R. 113 at [51].
[15] For example, by making it more difficult to ascertain the truth or to enforce court orders.
[16] [1991] 1 A.C. 1 at 46.
[17] *Astro Exito Navegacion SA v Southland Enterprise Co. Ltd* [1981] 2 Lloyd's Rep. 595 at 602.
[18] *Wardle Fabrics Ltd v G. Myristis Ltd* [1984] F.S.R. 264; *Columbia Pictures Inc. v Robinson* [1987] Ch. 38 at 71–72.
[19] *Gordon v Gordon* [1904] P. 163.
[20] *Atlantic Capital Corporation v Sir Cecil Denniston Burney*, Court of Appeal (Civ Div) Transcript No.1142 of 1994 (September 15, 1994).
[21] *AMF v Hashim*, Court of Appeal (Civ Div) Transcript No.417 of 1997 (March 21, 1997) (AMF could not find stolen assets because of contempts—substantive appeal struck out) *Hadkinson v Hadkinson* [1952] P. 285; *Garstin v Garstin* (1865) 4 Sw. & Tr. 73; *Cavendish v Cavendish and Rochefoucauld* (1866) 15 W.R. 182; *Jademan (Holdings) Ltd v Wong Chun-loong* [1990] 2 H.K.L.R. 577 (a Mareva case).
[22] *Golder v United Kingdom* (1975) 1 E.H.R.R. 524

interest and to secure a legitimate end in a way which is proportionate.[23] There must be a reasonable relationship of proportionality between the means employed and the end sought to be secured.[24] There cannot be an automatic rule that because the contemnor is in contempt, therefore the court will not hear him.[25]

In *National Bank of Greece v Constantinos Dimitriou*,[26] the defendant, **19.077** who was subject to a Mareva injunction, was in contempt of court in failing to disclose details of his assets and their whereabouts pursuant to a disclosure order against him. The defendant applied to the court for a variation to the injunction to enable him to use assets subject to the injunction to pay his solicitors. The Court of Appeal refused to make the proposed variation, and said that the court would not assist the defendant who was abusing the process of the court and in contempt of court.[27] This case did not involve a refusal to hear the defendant but it did have a consequence which could have interfered with the subsequent representation of the defendant in the proceedings. The Court of Appeal considered that to be a fair consequence in the circumstances.

Under Art.6(1), a party to civil proceedings has no absolute right to legal representation. The position in criminal proceedings is different because of Art.6(3)(c). In civil proceedings, there is the principle of "equality of arms", which is fact sensitive,[28] but there is no general principle that a party to civil proceedings has a right to legal representation.[29]

(19) Ordering a defence to be struck out on the grounds that the defendant is in contempt of court

A different but related question which may arise is whether the court will **19.078** make an order striking out the defence of a contemnor when there has been a breach of a court order granting Anton Piller or Mareva relief. Article 6(1) is engaged with the effect set out at paras 19.076–19.077, above.

The court has jurisdiction to order that a defence be struck out under the inherent jurisdiction of the court to regulate its own proceedings. In *Derby*

---

[23] *Brown v Stott* [2003] 1 A.C. 681 at 694–695.
[24] *Tinnelly & Sons Ltd v United Kingdom* (1998) 27 E.H.R.R. 249 at 288, para.72; *National and Provincial Building Society v United Kingdom* (1997) 25 E.H.R.R. 127 at 178, para.105.
[25] *Motorola Credit Corporation v Uzan* [2004] 1 W.L.R. 113 at [57] and [58].
[26] *The Times*, November 16, 1987. See also 20.056 below.
[27] See also *Fakih Brothers v A. P. Moller (Copenhagen) Ltd* [1994] 1 Lloyd's Rep. 103 at 108.
[28] This can involve a right to legal representation in cases which are of great complexity or emotional or where the individual is incapable of representing himself: *Airey v Ireland* (1979) 2 E.H.R.R. 305.
[29] *Dombo Beheer v Netherlands* (1993) 18 E.H.R.R. 213; *Re Kingsley Healthcare Ltd*, unreported, September 25, 2001 (Neuberger J.).

& Co. Ltd v Weldon (Nos 3 and 4).[30] Lord Donaldson M.R. referred to the possibility that the court could bar a defendant from defending the action if there was a failure to co-operate with the receiver appointed over its assets. Furthermore, in *Richco International Ltd v International Industrial Food Co. SAL*,[31] the plaintiffs had a very strong proprietary claim, advanced in arbitration proceedings, and an order was made by the court under s.12(6)(f) of the Arbitration Act 1950 for payment of the fund in dispute into court, and that in default the contemnor be debarred from defending the arbitration. Hirst J. held that there would have been jurisdiction to debar a defendant from defending High Court proceedings on the merits if an order had been made for the preservation of the fund in those proceedings, and that there was an equivalent jurisdiction to prevent the defendant defending arbitration proceedings in such circumstances.[32] In the course of the judgment the judge said that the sanction was "undoubtedly a severe one", but on the facts of the case there was no other practicable way in which the preservation order could be enforced; and in calculating the sum to be preserved under the order, the court excluded any amount in respect of which the defendants might conceivably have had a viable defence.

19.079   It will be only in extreme circumstances that this inherent jurisdiction can properly be exercised by the court. When a defendant within the jurisdiction was in breach of an order requiring an interim payment to be made, the Court of Appeal set aside an order striking out the defence in the action.[33] Lawton L.J. observed that there were other ways in which the order could be enforced, and that the provisions regulating the making of interim payments orders left "no room" for invoking the inherent jurisdiction of the court. It is considered that the inherent jurisdiction of the court to strike out a defence can only arise when it can be shown that (1) there is no other measure that could reasonably be taken and (2) striking out the defence is necessary in the interests of justice and is reasonably proportionate to deal with the contempt which has occurred. This formulation gives effect to Art.6(1) of the European Convention on Human Rights as enacted by the Human Rights Act 1998. The function of the court is to provide a fair trial of the case. This right to a fair trial will normally give rise to a right to be heard on the merits but this may have to give way when it is necessary so that justice can be done.

In *Hardy v Focus Insurance Co. Ltd*[34] there was an "unless order" made against a defendant requiring the defendant to provide a letter of authority directed to certain banks and companies authorising them to disclose to the

---

[30] [1990] Ch. 65 at 81.
[31] [1989] 2 Lloyd's Rep. 106.
[32] Reasoning by analogy with the power of the court to strike out a claim made in arbitration proceedings when there was a failure to comply with an order for security for costs made under s.12(6)(a) of the Arbitration Act 1950, and applying *The Argenpuma* [1984] 2 Lloyd's Rep. 563.
[33] *H. H. Property Co. Ltd v Rahim* [1987] 1 E.G.L.R. 52.
[34] Privy Council, Appeal No.6 of 1995 (July 13, 1995).

plaintiff documents relating to the defendant's accounts, and to provide a list of assets. The defendant was not present within the jurisdiction and had continually failed to co-operate with the court and had disobeyed orders of the court. His defence was struck out. The defendant's appeal to the Privy Council failed because on the particular facts "it is difficult to see what else the Chief Justice could have done to enforce obedience to the order . . .".

The result of exercising the jurisdiction in any particular case will be to **19.080** confer upon the claimant a judgment in default of defence, or the benefit of an arbitration award obtained in circumstances where the defendant has been prevented from defending himself. The claimant may well have difficulties in seeking to enforce such a judgment or award abroad. If the claimant is entitled to succeed in full on the merits of his claim, invoking the inherent jurisdiction of the court may leave him in a substantially worse position (save in relation to the incurring of legal costs) than would otherwise be the case. This is particularly likely where there is no other way to enforce the court order which the defendant has breached. If, on the other hand, the true position is that the claimant would not succeed in full on his claim on the merits, then it must be seriously open to doubt whether striking out the defence is in accordance with the justice of the case. Furthermore, there is apparent injustice in preventing a defendant from putting forward his defence, when the relevant contempt has not given rise to any real prejudice to the innocent party in relation to advancing the claim on the merits. In *Richco International Ltd v International Industrial Food Co. SAL* (above), Hirst J. sought to negative this apparent injustice by limiting the preservation order to a sum in respect of which the defendants had no conceivable viable defence. But if striking out is to be ordered only in such circumstances, then the threatened sanction is unlikely to achieve the aim of procuring the defendant's compliance with the order of the court. If, on the other hand, striking out is sought when the defendant may have a defence to the claim, the granting of the application may well result in substantial injustice.

(20) Restoring the funds

If a defendant or non-party has acted in contempt of court, the court may **19.081** impose a penalty which will be alleviated or removed altogether if the assets which have been dissipated are restored or replaced.[35] If the assets remain intact, but have been removed or transferred in breach of the order, the court could order that the defendant transfer them back to where they were previously.[36] If the assets have been transferred within the jurisdiction

---

[35] *Z Bank v DI* [1994] 1 Lloyd's Rep. 656 at 668; see also *Burton v Winters* [1993] 1 W.L.R. 1077 at p 1080.
[36] *Derby v Weldon (No.6)* [1990] 1 W.L.R. 1139.

to a non-party who took them knowing of the order and that the transfer was in breach of the order, the non-party has acted in contempt of court,[37] and the non-party can be required by mandatory order to restore the assets. This is because the court has jurisdiction to grant an injunction to restrain a non-party from committing a contempt;[38] if a non-party does commit a contempt, the court has jurisdiction to grant a mandatory injunction requiring him to undo what he has done.[39] Furthermore the court has jurisdiction to grant an injunction against the non-party ancillary to the cause of action against the defendant.[40]

If the assets consisted of money which has been paid to a non-party who is a bona fide purchaser for value, in principle there is no remedy available against him. But what about a non-party who facilitates or assists in such a transfer knowing of the injunction (*e.g.* a bank or a solicitor who pays the money out of injuncted funds)? Such a non-party has acted in contempt of court, and is subject to the jurisdiction of the court to punish the contempt. Solicitors can also be ordered to put back the value of the funds, under the court's jurisdiction over its officers.[41] The claimant may also have a personal right under s.423 of the Insolvency Act 1986 against a non-party who has received the funds and is not a bona fide purchase for value. But this requires showing that the defendant made the transfer for the purpose of prejudicing enforcement of claims against him. If the defendant made the transfer to pay for goods or services provided to him this may well not be possible.

19.082   There is some authority[42] that the claimant might have a cause of action in tort if he has sustained loss by reason of the non-party's contempt of court.

If there is a freezing injunction which applies to certain assets of the defendant only (*e.g.* assets within the jurisdiction), then if there is a contempt of court which results in the depletion of the funds subject to the injunction, the court will ordinarily seek to exercise its jurisdiction so as to restore the funds. In accordance with this principle, the defendant should be required to discharge its liabilities for costs resulting from the contempt proceedings from assets other than those covered by the injunction.[43]

---

[37] *Attorney-General v Times Newspapers* [1992] 1 A.C. 1991.
[38] *Hubbard v Woodfield* (1913) 57 S.J. 729; *TSB Private Bank International SA v Chabra* [1992] 1 W.L.R. 231 at 240.
[39] *Esso Petroleum v Kingswood Motors* [1974] Q.B. 142 at 156; *Acrow v Rex Chainbelt Inc.* [1971] 1 W.L.R. 1676 at 1683C–D.
[40] See Chapter 13, above.
[41] *TDK Tape Distributor v Videochoice* [1986] 1 W.L.R. 141 at 147C–D appears best explained as an exercise of this jurisdiction. The parties were liable under that jurisdiction for the serious misconduct of their employee, even though they themselves were not personally at fault and were held not to have acted in contempt of court: *Myers v Elman* [1940] A.C. 282. In *Lewin Atkins & Co. v Anil Khanna* & Co., Court of Appeal (Civ Div) Transcript No.900 of 1991 (October 4, 1991), the Court of Appeal declined to strike out a claim advanced on this basis against solicitors.
[42] *Parker v Rasalingham, The Times*, July 25, 2000 reviews the authorities and other materials; *Acrow v Rex Chainbelt Inc.* [1971] 1 W.L.R. 1676. It is not every contempt which gives rise to tortious liability; see *Attorney-General v Butterworth* [1963] 1 Q.B. 696.
[43] In subsequent proceedings in *Z Bank v DI*, Colman J. required the contemnor to bring assets within the jurisdiction to meet the liabilities for costs.

(21) Claim for damages

The purpose of the contempt jurisdiction in civil proceedings is to uphold **19.083** the rule of law and to ensure that orders of the court are obeyed. It is not its purpose to give compensation to the claimant for the contempt,[44] but there can be situations in which the conduct is both a contempt and a civil wrong. Where there is a breach of an order made by consent, which may be an order imposing an injunction or in which an undertaking is given to the court, there may be both a remedy for contempt of court and also a remedy for breach of contract, the contract being to settle the matter on the terms of the consent order. In those circumstances on the contempt motion the court can also direct an inquiry into the damages resulting from the breach of contract.[45]

(22) Permission to appeal to the Court of Appeal

Under CPR r.52.3(1)(a) permission to appeal is not required in order to **19.084** appeal against the making of a committal order or a committal order execution of which is suspended.[46] If in contempt proceedings a committal order is not made but some other order, such as ordering the defendant to pay the costs[47] or imposing a fine, then permission to appeal is required.[48] In a second tier appeal from a decision reached on appeal from a committal order, permission to appeal is required because the order under appeal to the Court of Appeal is not itself a committal order.[49]

---

[44] *Johnson v Walton* [1990] 1 F.L.R. 350 at 353.
[45] *Parker v Rasalingham*, *The Times*, July 25, 2000 at [18–26]; *Midland Marts Ltd v Hobday* [1989] 1 W.L.R. 1143.
[46] *Barnet London Borough Council v Hurst* [2003] 1 W.L.R. 722; *Wilkinson v S* [2003] 2 All E.R. 184
[47] *Government of Sierra Leone v Davenport* [2003] EWCA Civ 230.
[48] *Barnet London Borough Council v Hurst* [2003] 1 W.L.R. 722.
[49] *ibid.*

Chapter 20

Freezing injunctions: the effects on non-parties, "maximum sum" orders, variations to permit payments to non-parties, including legal costs

(1) Introduction

(i) Effects of a freezing injunction on non-parties

A freezing injunction affects non-parties. **20.001**

First, the injunction has direct effects on non-parties because they must not aid and abet a breach of the injunction or knowingly frustrate the purpose of the injunction. These effects are the result of the law on contempt of court discussed in Chapter 19, above.

Secondly, a non-party may be affected by the effects of the injunction on the defendant. Thus, *e.g.* the freezing of the defendant's assets may result in a creditor of the defendant not being paid or interference with the defendant's ability to pay expenses in the course of running a business or in the defence of the litigation.

Thirdly, it is often the case that as a result of an injunction a person is left in control of assets subject to the injunction or becomes an asset holder. In such circumstances that person may have responsibilities to the claimant about the assets. Where the assets are held by a warehouse, the warehouse operator who provides a receipt for the assets is a bailee of them, and will have a responsibility as a bailee to a claimant who has a proprietary interest in, or possessory right to, the assets. This is independently of the granting of the injunction.

In the case of a bank, where the claimant does not assert a proprietary **20.002** interest in an account, responsibility will depend on contract and the law of negligence. It is possible for a freezing injunction or other injunction concerning assets, or an undertaking given to the court by a party, to lead to a voluntary assumption of responsibility by the asset holder to the claimant. This could give rise to a claim in tort for negligence if the asset holder carelessly allows the assets to be removed,[1] or damaged.

(ii) Locus standi of non-party to apply to the court for a variation or discharge

20.003   Although the injunction has not been granted against non-parties, because of the potential effects of the injunction upon them, it is just that they should be entitled to be heard on whether the injunction should be discharged or varied. Therefore a non-party, who is affected by the injunction, is entitled to apply to the court to vary or discharge the order, or for directions as to its effect.[2] Such applications are common. The example order provides:

> "VARIATION OR DISCHARGE OF THIS ORDER
>
> 13. Anyone served with or notified of this order may apply to the court at any time to vary or discharge this order (or so much of it as affects that person), but they must first inform the Applicant's solicitors. If any evidence is to be relied upon in support of the application, the substance of it must be communicated in writing to the Applicant's solicitors in advance."

This sets out good practice to be followed on an application to vary or discharge the order, but the court has jurisdiction to hear an application, which is urgent, made without notice and regardless of compliance with these requirements.[3] The *Commercial Courts Guide* provides:

> "F15.9 A provision for the defendant to give notice of any application to discharge or vary the order is usually included as a matter of convenience but it is not proper to attempt to fetter the right of the defendant to apply without notice or on short notice if need be."

The same is true of a non-party.

20.004   Similarly, non-parties can be heard in relation to an order appointing a receiver.[4] If a non-party is aggrieved by what has been done by the court-appointed receiver (*e.g.* if a receiver takes control of assets which belong to

---

[1] *Customs & Excise Commissioners v Barclays Bank Plc* [2004] 2 All E.R. 789, discussed at para.20.015, below; *Al-Kandari v J. R. Brown & Co.* [1988] Q.B. 665 (an undertaking had been given by a husband to his wife that the husband's solicitors would retain the husband's passport. The solicitors were held liable in tort to the wife for negligently releasing the passport to the husband).
[2] *Attorney-General v Newspaper Publishing plc* [1988] Ch. 333 at 375; *Harbottle Ltd v National Westminster Bank* [1978] Q.B. 146 at 157G; *Howe Richardson Scale Ltd v Polimpex-Cekop* [1978] 1 Lloyd's Rep. 161 at 166; *Cretanor Maritime Co. Ltd v Irish Marine Ltd* [1978] 1 W.L.R. 966 at p 978; *Galaxia Maritime v Mineralimportexport* [1982] 1 W.L.R. 539; *Z Ltd v A-Z and AA-LL* [1982] Q.B. 558 at 588, *per* Kerr L.J.
[3] *London City Agency (JCD) Ltd v Lee* [1970] Ch. 597.
[4] See Chapter 16.

the third party) he should apply to the court which appointed the receiver by application in the action in which the receiver was appointed.[5] If a non-party wishes to contend that the effect of the order appointing a receiver is unjust to him, then in principle there is *locus standi* for him to seek discharge or variation of the order by application made in the proceedings. In *Allied Irish Bank v Ashford Hotels Ltd*[6] the court decided that it had *jurisdiction* to require the plaintiff to furnish a cross-undertaking in damages in favour of the third parties who were affected by an order appointing a receiver post-judgment, in aid of execution. Thus, *e.g.* the receiver may have been appointed over an asset which the non-party says belongs to him, and if he is correct he may suffer loss from being deprived of his asset whilst the dispute about ownership is decided. A non-party who wishes to obtain the protection of a cross-undertaking in damages should apply in the proceedings in which the receiver has been appointed.

The court also has an inherent jurisdiction to vary or discharge an injunction granted *ex parte* at any time.[7]

(iii) *Entitlement of non-party to costs*

Provided that the application is made reasonably and is the natural result 20.005 of the injunction being in force, it is the practice to order the claimant to pay the non-party's costs of applying. This can be done under s.51 of the Supreme Court Act 1981 or under the standard undertaking in Schedule B, undertaking (7) of the example freezing injunction which is "to pay the reasonable costs . . . incurred as a result of this order . . .".

Prior to the change to the taxation rules to provide for costs on the "standard basis", the order would provide for such costs to be taxed on an "indemnity basis" but with the burden of proof to show reasonableness on the non-party.[8] These included the costs of applying to the court. The standard basis as set out in CPR r.44.4(2) is now the appropriate basis for the taxation.[9] If the court decides that the non-party should not get the costs under s.51 the reasons for that decision produce the same result under the jurisdiction conferred by the undertaking.[10]

---

[5] *Re Maidstone Palace of Varieties Ltd* [1909] 2 Ch. 283; *Searle v Choat* (1884) 25 Ch.D. 723.
[6] [1997] 3 All E.R. 309.
[7] *Harbottle Ltd v National Westminster Bank* [1978] Q.B. 146 at 158A–G where Kerr J. discharged *ex parte* injunctions which had been granted by him against defendants who had not appeared before the court because of the reasons for discharging injunctions against those who had appeared.
[8] *Project Development Co. Ltd SA v KMK Securities Ltd* [1992] 1 W.L.R. 1470 at 1473.
[9] See the reasoning in *British Racing Drivers' Club v Hextall Erskine & Co.* [1996] 3 All E.R. 667 and Chapter 11, paras 11.033–11.035.
[10] *Imutran Ltd v Uncaged Campaigns Ltd* [2002] F.S.R. 20 at [45].

(2) Effect of notification of the injunction to non-parties

(i) Contempt of court

20.006 The non-party can only be held to have acted in contempt of court[11] if (1) he knows of the injunction and (2) he knowingly aided and abetted breach of it, or he knowingly acted contrary to its purpose. The claimant would have to prove this beyond reasonable doubt in contempt proceedings against the non-party. Unless the claimant tells him of the injunction he may not know of it, or the claimant may not be able to prove that he knew of it.

The effect of para.7 of the example order which identifies particular assets as being within the restraint imposed by para.5 is to alert a non-party to the fact that on the evidence the court has made the assumption that the defendant has a beneficial interest in those assets or that they come within the second and third sentences of para.6.[12]

The defendant has an independent obligation to comply with the terms of the order whether or not those in control of his assets know about it. The claimant by giving prompt notice of the injunction to non-parties (such as banks) whom he believes to be holding assets belonging to the defendant reduces the risk that a defendant who is prepared to break the injunction will succeed in removing his assets. The form of notification usually does not matter; it is quite common for the claimant's solicitor to read the terms of the order to the third party over the telephone. The notification exposes the claimant to greater risk of having liabilities under the undertaking to pay the reasonable costs of anyone other than the person restrained by the injunction which are incurred in finding out whether he holds any assets covered by the order or any loss caused to that person by the injunction. It also increases the risk that a non-party will require a variation of the order and that this will generate legal costs which the claimant will have to pay.

20.007 Once a non-party has been notified of the making of an injunction, he should examine its precise terms and regard himself as bound not to take any steps inconsistent with the preservation of the assets covered by the injunction, subject to the liberties contained within the order (*e.g.* for the defendant to pay his ordinary living expenses). Otherwise, if the non-party assists in the disposal of the assets in question, he may find himself subject to proceedings for contempt of court.

A non-party served with notice of the injunction will usually tell the defendant about it. Indeed, he may be under a contractual obligation to take reasonable steps to do so; *e.g.*, if the non-party is a bank and the injunction prohibits it from honouring cheques drawn on the defendant's account. However, the non-party cannot delay complying with the terms

---

[11] Chapter 19, para.19.028, above.
[12] See Chapter 19, paras 19.038–19.040.

of the injunction pending the receipt of instructions from the defendant. He is bound to obey its terms from the moment he becomes aware of them.

(ii) Provision of a full copy of the order

Under the example order for a freezing injunction the applicant is required **20.008** to give an undertaking (see Schedule B) that:

"[(6) Anyone notified of this order will be given a copy of it by the Applicant's legal representatives.]"

Therefore the claimant undertakes to follow up any such communication by delivery of a copy of the order initialled by the judge or when it has been drawn up, a copy of the order sealed by the court. This is so that the non-party is aware of the exact terms of the injunction.

In the example order there is no undertaking to serve non-parties, who are notified, with copies of the affidavit and exhibits used on the without notice application.[13] If the non-party reasonably requires copies, they should be provided. If there is difficulty the non-party can apply to the court for a direction that the affidavit and exhibits be supplied. Provided that the non-party acts reasonably, he will be entitled to his costs under the standard undertaking in favour of third parties.

(3) Banks notified of a freezing injunction made against a customer

(i) Paying out of an account to a non-party

A bank should not honour a cheque drawn by the defendant in favour of a **20.009** third party or other payment order given to it by its customer, if the effect of honouring it would be to diminish the defendant's credit balance at the bank, or increase the level of indebtedness secured by mortgages or charges over assets covered by the injunction. This applies even if the cheque was issued or payment order given, before the Mareva injunction was granted.[14] The injunction takes effect as soon as it is pronounced and from that moment[15] the customer is bound by it irrespective of notification, which only affects whether he can be proceeded against for contempt of court. The bank has no authority from its customer to pay banker's orders, or cheques, when to make payment would be a breach of the injunction by

---

[13] See also *Guinness Peat Aviation (Belgium) NV v Hispania Lineas Aereas SA* [1992] 1 Lloyd's Rep. 190 at 196.

[14] *Z Ltd v A-Z and AA-LL* [1982] Q.B. 558.

[15] CPR r.40.7(1); *Z Ltd v A-Z and AA-LL* [1982] Q.B. 558 at 572G–H.

the customer.[16] This is because the authority given to the bank does not extend to authorising it to do an act on behalf of the customer which would be in breach of the order of the court and therefore an illegal act. The bank is not prevented from honouring a cheque on an unsecured overdraft because the injunction does not prevent the defendant from increasing its liabilities;[17] it only affects dealings with his assets.

(ii) Paying into an account

20.010 If a non-party has issued a cheque to the defendant, the example form of order does not prevent the bank presenting it for payment, and crediting the proceeds obtained to the defendant.[18] That transaction simply involves obtaining the proceeds of the cheque; although the cheque has been dealt with, the defendant's overall asset position remains the same. However, the bank is not at liberty to credit the proceeds to an account which is in overdraft, unless the bank has a right of set-off in respect of the proceeds, which it is permitted to exercise under the order. Assets received by the bank after the granting of the injunction are part of the defendant's assets and therefore subject to the injunction.[19]

(ii) Withdrawals by the person restrained

20.011 The example form of order does not restrain the defendant from receiving payment of a debt or receiving money.[20] The position of the bank about withdrawals by the customer is considered in Chapter 19, above.

(iii) Set-off by a bank, dealings with future assets and enforcing a bank's own rights of security

20.012 In *Oceanica Castelana Armadora SA v Mineralimportexport*[21] the plaintiffs had obtained Mareva injunctions which applied to two cargoes of coke which had been shipped on vessels within the jurisdiction. The owners of one of the vessels successfully applied to have the injunction affecting their vessel discharged on the ground that it was substantially interfering with the trading of the vessel and the lives of its crew.[22] This had the consequence that the defendant did not have to provide bank guarantees which it was in the course of providing so as to secure the release of its

---

[16] *Z Ltd v A-Z and AA-LL* [1982] Q.B. 558 at 574A–D.
[17] See para.19.022 above; *Cantor Index Ltd v Lister*, unreported, November 22, 2001 (Neuberger J.).
[18] *Bank Mellat v Kazmi* [1989] Q.B. 541.
[19] *Cretanor Maritime Co. Ltd v Irish Marine Management Ltd* [1978] 1 W.L.R. 966 at 973D–E (*cf.* the suggestion made by Kerr L.J. in *Z Ltd v A-Z and AA-LL* [1982] Q.B. 558 at 592D–F which has not been adopted in the example order or its predecessors).
[20] See Chapter 3, paras 3.012–3.014.
[21] [1983] 1 W.L.R. 1294.
[22] *Galaxia Maritime v Mineralimportexport* [1982] 1 W.L.R. 539.

cargoes. The transfer made to Barclays Bank to back those guarantees came from a Roumanian bank which in turn became subject to a Mareva injunction granted in support of a claim against it. It resulted in a credit balance in favour of the Roumanian bank which belonged beneficially to it. Barclays had granted substantial loan facilities to that bank and wished to use its rights under those facilities to deduct from the credit balance which it held. It was argued that the Roumanian bank should only be permitted to use this credit to repay Barclays if it could show that it had no other assets from which to make the repayments.[23]

This argument missed the point. What was in issue was not the right of the Roumanian bank to use the credit balance to repay its trading debt, but the rights of a non-party, Barclays Bank. Those rights included the right to set off repayments due to it against the credit balance. It was no part of the function of the Mareva injunction granted against the Roumanian bank to interfere with the exercise by Barclays Bank of its own substantive rights. Furthermore, it would not be appropriate to require Barclays Bank to apply to the court each time it wished to exercise its rights and so a set off provision was included in the order. Since there was no reason to distinguish the position of Barclays Bank from the position of any other bank which had a right of set off against an account in credit it is the practice of the court to include the provision in Mareva relief. Under the example order:

"17. **Set off by banks**

This injunction does not prevent any bank from exercising any right of set off it may have in respect of any facility which it gave to the respondent before it was notified of this order."

The position would be different for a freezing injunction granted in **20.013** support of a proprietary claim, because if the credit balance belonged beneficially to the claimant, what would be an account held on trust for the claimant could not be taken by the bank to discharge the trustee's personal liabilities.

If a bank is contemplating entering into a new facility with a defendant who is subject to a Mareva injunction, then under the example order the defendant is not entitled to grant the bank a power to set off repayments against an existing credit balance because the transaction would be a dealing with that credit balance within the meaning of the order.

What about granting in the new facility a power to the bank to exercise a set-off against a future credit balance? That would not be a present dealing with an existing asset; it would be a contractual arrangement which would bite as soon as the future asset came into existence. The effect of the grant

---

[23] Relying on *A v C (No.2)* [1981] Q.B. 961.

of the power to the bank by the defendant, and the future asset coming into existence, would be to subject that asset of the defendant to a security interest of the bank. It would be like an equitable assignment of the future asset, which creates an immediate equitable charge upon the property when it comes into existence.[24] The agreement for set-off would be an immediate dealing with that asset by the defendant upon its coming into existence. If the bank then exercised its power of set-off, the defendant, as a result of entering into the new facility, would have disposed of the asset. It is considered that such a transaction would be a dealing with the credit balance once it came into existence and therefore a breach of the Mareva injunction.

It may be that the court would grant a variation to the order to enable these transactions to be done.

20.014   What about security rights of a bank which pre-date notification to it of a freezing injunction but which are by way of mortgage or charge on real property? These are not within the set-off provision in the example form. In *Gangway Ltd v Caledonian Park Investments (Jersey) Ltd*[25] the judge expressed the view that the bank as a non-party had to apply to the court for a variation of the injunction to enable it to exercise its security rights. That dictum relied upon a statement of Lord Denning M.R. in *Z Ltd v A-Z*;[26] but this analysis of the effect of a Mareva injunction has been disapproved.[27] The bank as a non-party[28] could only be liable for contempt if either it knowingly aided and abetted a breach of the injunction by its customer, or it knowingly frustrated the purpose of the injunction. It is considered that in *Gangway Ltd*, whilst the application by the bank was a sensible course for it to take, it would not have been in contempt had it proceeded to exercise its security rights without having obtained a variation. What the case does show is that the court will not under the Mareva jurisdiction place the bank under an order imposing procedures on it which are designed to ensure that it realises the best price for the assets, and that it acts at arm's length from its customer.

(iv) Negligence by the bank allowing assets to be removed

20.015   Where a bank is notified by a claimant of a freezing injunction, the bank has the opportunity to take advantage of the undertaking given by the claimant to the court to pay the reasonable costs of anyone other than the respondent which have been incurred as a result of the order.[29] In *Customs & Excise Commissioners v Barclays Bank Plc*[30] the bank had sent to the

[24] *Industrial Finance Syndicate Ltd v Lind* [1915] 2 Ch. 345.
[25] [2001] 2 Lloyd's Rep. 715 at [717].
[26] [1982] 1 Lloyd's Rep. 240 at 244, the corresponding reference in the official law reports being to [1982] Q.B. 558 at 573–574E.
[27] *The Law Society v Shanks* [1988] 1 F.L.R. 504; this is discussed in Chapter 3, para.3.012.
[28] Contrast the position of the bank in *Z Ltd v D1* [1994] 1 Lloyd's Rep. 656,in which the Bulgarian bank had itself been restrained by Mareva injunction.
[29] See Chapter 11, above.
[30] [2004] 2 All E.R. 789, Comm Ct.

claimant a letter from its legal adviser confirming "the Bank will abide by the terms of the order . . .", referring to its entitlement to reimbursement, and requiring payment of £150. The bank had permitted payments amounting to several million pounds after service of the order. There were two orders and letters involved. In each case the letter had not been received by the claimant before the payments were made. The judge held that the letters were received too late by the claimant to ground a voluntary assumption of responsibility by the bank to use due care not to allow the funds to be withdrawn. This was because voluntary assumption of responsibility depends upon what crosses the line between the claimant and the third party. If however the letter had been received first and then the payments had been made, the judge would have found a duty of care actionable in tort.

In principle a bank could either contract to be responsible to the claimant or could provide services to the claimant for which it voluntarily assumed a responsibility to act carefully. The latter would be the assumption of a duty of care. The fact that the bank insisted upon payment by the claimant for those services would make it all the easier to conclude that the bank were undertaking voluntarily a responsibility to the claimant to act carefully.

At present the undertaking given to the court by an applicant does not **20.016** have any qualification to it providing that it is not to have effect in the case of a particular bank unless the bank writes back to the applicant within a period following service of the order, agreeing to assume responsibility for carefully preserving the assets under its control. In view of the decision in *Customs & Excise Commissioners v Barclays Bank Plc*[31] it is suggested that on the without notice application the court is asked to consider accepting an undertaking qualified in this way so that a bank can choose whether it wants to obtain payment but in return accept a duty of care, or alternatively be left without the benefit of the undertaking. In principle this would also apply to other asset holders who wished to charge the applicant for looking after or preserving the assets caught by an injunction.

(4) Non-parties have no obligation to disclose information about assets unless the court so orders

(i) In the absence of an order for disclosure there is no duty to disclose information to the claimant

The claimant may believe that there are sufficient assets in one bank **20.017** account to satisfy his claim. In those circumstances, he may not wish to risk exposing himself to wider liability under his cross-undertaking by notifying

---

31 [2004] 2 All E.R. 789, Comm Ct.

more banks (and thus potentially widening the damage to the defendant). There is no obligation on a non-party served with notice of a Mareva injunction to tell the claimant how much, if anything, is frozen under the order. Disclosure orders against non-parties are discussed in Chapter 22.

(ii) *Bank's obligation of confidentiality owed to its customer*

20.018   A bank has to comply with the obligation of confidentiality owed to its customer. That obligation is a qualified one. In *Tournier v National Provincial Bank*[32] the customer brought an action for slander and breach of the duty of confidentiality in respect of statements made to a third party by the bank based on the fact that the endorsee of a cheque from its customer was a bookmaker. The Court of Appeal held that this information which had not been acquired as a result of their position as bankers to the plaintiff was nevertheless subject to the duty of confidentiality because it related to the plaintiff and was acquired by the bank in "its character as the plaintiff's banker."[33] The confidentiality attaches not just to information given to the bank by its customer or the state of its account, but extends to all information obtained from any other source by the bank in connection with acting as a banker to its customers, including information obtained by the bank from a third party with a view to deciding how to conduct its business in relation to the customer or how to treat its customer.[34]

Bankes L.J. authoritatively[35] stated the following qualifications to the duty:

(a)   where disclosure is under compulsion of law;

(b)   where there is a duty to the public to disclose;

(c)   where the interests of the bank require disclosure (*e.g.* suing the customer on an overdraft or protecting or enforcing a security interest of the bank);

(d)   where there is express or implied consent of the customer.

20.019   In *Robertson v Canadian Bank of Commerce*[36] the bank's acting manager obeyed a subpoena and gave oral evidence about the account and the customer was held not to be entitled to damages because disclosure was made under compulsion of law, the duty to warn the customer could not

---

[32] [1924] 1 K.B. 461.
[33] *ibid.*, at 474–475.
[34] *ibid.*, at 485, *per* Atkin L.J.
[35] *ibid.*, at 473, cited as "common ground" by the Privy Council in *Robertson v Canadian Bank of Commerce* [1994] 1 W.L.R. 1493 at 1498, and as "not open to doubt" in *Lipkin Gorman v Karpnale Ltd* [1989] 1 W.L.R. 1340 at 1357 and *Turner v Royal Bank of Scotland Plc* [1999] Lloyd's Rep. (Bank.) 231 (where a practice of exchanging credit information between banks was found not to be sufficiently notorious, as far as customers were concerned, as to be impliedly consented to by them).
[36] [1994] 1 W.L.R. 1493.

have been higher than a duty to use best endeavours to do so and there was no proof of breach of duty or any loss.

Where circumstances arise such as:

(1) where the bank's own substantive rights against the customer are in question; or

(2) where its commercial reputation and good name may be called into question, according to how it acts; or

(3) which might result in contempt proceedings being brought against it;

the disclosure by the bank of confidential information for the purpose of an application to the court by the bank for directions would be justified by qualification (c) above as long as such disclosure was made reasonably by the bank in pursuit of this purpose. This is because in each of these situations it is defending its own interests. A bank or third party, which seeks a variation of the Mareva injunction, is under no duty to disclose to the claimant information about the defendant's assets as a precondition of obtaining such relief.[37]

(iii) Disclosure of information by a bank: money laundering inquiries and tipping off

Under the money laundering legislation (including regulations) a bank may 20.020
find itself in a position in which it should not "tip off" its customer about an investigation or give any information to anyone which is likely to prejudice that investigation.[38]

A bank may find itself faced with an application for an order for disclosure of information to the claimant under the principle in *Norwich Pharmacal v Customs & Excise Commissioners*,[39] or an *ex parte* order made against it, which relates to information which it may not be able to give consistently with the provisions in the legislation concerning tipping off and the prejudicing of an investigation. In such a case three important public policies can come into conflict:

(1) The public interest in the successful pursuit of investigations into proceeds of crime and the securing of those proceeds.

(2) The public interest in the open administration of justice.

(3) The public interest in the due administration of justice which includes the principle of hearing both sides, with both sides having

---

[37] *Oceanica Castelana Armadora SA v Mineralimportexport* [1983] 1 W.L.R. 1294.
[38] See also Chapter 25, para.25.065.
[39] [1974] A.C. 1551.

access to all the materials which have been laid before the court which is to determine an application, and the principle that a court should give reasons for its decision which are available to the parties.

20.021   In *C v S (Money Laundering: Discovery of Documents)*[40] the Court of Appeal gave general guidance as to the procedures to be followed:

"1. As soon as a financial institution is aware that a party to legal proceedings intends to apply for or has obtained an order for discovery which might involve the institution having to give disclosure of information which could prejudice an investigation it should inform [the National Criminal Intelligence Services (NCIS)] of the position and the material which it is required to disclose.

2. The NCIS will then have the opportunity to identify the material which it does not wish to be disclosed and indicate any preference which it has as to how an application or order should be handled. In doing this it should be borne in mind that usually it will not be necessary to disclose any document or part of a document which refers to the fact of the investigation since this will not be relevant to the issues with which the applicant for the order is concerned. A case such as the present is likely to cause particular difficulty because the NCIS did not wish the applicant, C, to know that there was an investigation in progress. However there should be cases where the NCIS is not concerned about the applicant knowing about the investigation. Where this is the position it may be sufficient to make the compliance with the order subject to an appropriate undertaking to keep the relevant information confidential.

3. If NCIS has no objection to partial disclosure the applicant may be satisfied by partial disclosure if it is explained that the alternative is for the matter to be considered by the court. Whether an explanation for the partial disclosure can be given will depend on the attitude of NCIS.

4. If the restricted disclosure is unacceptable to the applicant then the directions of the court will have to be sought. The extent to which the applicant can be informed of the reason for the issue being referred to the court will depend on the circumstances. The circumstances will also influence the way in which the matter is brought before the court. The application can be to set aside the order if it was made *ex parte*. Alternatively there can be an application for directions. If the order has not been made the problem can be brought to the attention of the court without the need for a separate application. The court will have to be warned

---

[40] [1999] 1 W.L.R. 1551.

in advance of the difficulties. Where a high degree of confidentiality is required a sealed letter can be written to the judge in
charge of the relevant court setting out the circumstances and that
judge can then put in place the necessary arrangements. In this
case we found the provision of a skeleton argument to the court
alone setting out the background facts and issues and identifying
the problem a very convenient way of ensuring that the court is
sufficiently informed of the situation.

5. On the issue being brought before the court the degree to which
the applicant can be involved and the extent that it is possible for
the issues to be resolved in open court again will depend on the
circumstances, but the general approach must be to comply with
the ordinary principles to the extent that this is possible. If
necessary the stratagems which were deployed in this case will
have to be used. Where these sort of arrangements are necessary
there should always be a transcript prepared and the institution
should be required to provide a copy to the applicant when it is
informed by the NCIS that there is no longer any requirement for
secrecy.

6. In deciding what order should be made the court will have to
decide what evidence it requires. In an obvious case a letter from
NCIS will suffice. In other cases their attendance will be required.
If the court considers this is justified to achieve justice, the NCIS
can be made a party.

7. It will be for the NCIS (or other investigating authority) to
persuade the court that, were disclosure to be made, there would
be a real likelihood of the investigation being prejudiced. If the
NCIS did not cooperate with the institution (and with any
requirements of the court) in advancing such a case, the court
could properly draw the inference that no such prejudice would be
likely to occur and could accordingly make the disclosure order
sought without offending the principle in *Rowell v Pratt* and
without putting the institution at risk of prosecution.

8. Especially when the applicant can not be heard it is important that
the court recognises its responsibility to protect the applicant's
interests. The court must have material on which to act if it is to
deprive an applicant of his normal rights. . . . The court should
bear in mind that a partial order may be better than no order. It
should also consider the desirability of adjourning the issue in
whole or in part since the expiry of a relatively short period of
time may remove any risk of the investigation being prejudiced.
The NCIS will no doubt wish to co-operate with the courts in
achieving speedy progress as this will be the most productive way
of avoiding prejudicing an investigation and protecting the interests of litigants.

   . . . An order such as that which was made in this case is not
subject to any implied limitation excluding the obligation to make

disclosure because to do so would involve committing a criminal offence. Unless the applicant agrees to the order not being complied with in whole or part, it will be necessary for the court to be informed and directions obtained if it considered that the order cannot be obeyed. As a financial institution will normally not be subject to a forthwith order there should be time to make an application but if necessary an ex parte application for a stay will have to be made.

[The Bank] points out that the order is sometimes coupled with an order not to disclose the fact that an order has been made. Such an order should not be regarded as preventing the financial institution from approaching NCIS; seeking the cooperation of the NCIS is a step which is necessary in complying with the requirement to give disclosure. The approach to the NCIS is to be regarded as being impliedly permitted despite the non disclosure requirement."

20.022   What information can properly be given by the bank to the claimant or anyone else under a court order, consistently with the legislation, is a matter concerning criminal liability. It may be that an impasse is reached between the bank and the authorities as to what the bank is free to do and this has to be resolved by the court through the procedure of granting an interim advisory declaration to the bank in proceedings to which the relevant public body is a party about what information can be disclosed.[41] The *Commercial Courts Guide* provides:

"F15.11 Any bank or third party served with, notified of or affected by a freezing order may apply to the court without notice to any party for directions, or notify the court in writing without notice to any party, in the event that the order affects or may affect the position of the bank or third party under legislation, regulations or procedures aimed to prevent money laundering."

This problem is different from those listed below, which arise under the money laundering legislation independently of any order having been made by the court:

(1) whether the bank is contractually obliged to make payment to its customer given the effect of the money laundering rules. This is a matter of the substantive obligations between the bank and its customer;[42] or

(2) whether the bank can make a payment to its customer consistently with the criminal provisions in those rules and without being

[41] *Bank of Scotland v A* [2001] 1 W.L.R. 751; *P v P (Ancillary Relief: Proceeds of Crime)* [2003] 3 W.L.R. 1350 at [68].
[42] *Amalgamated Metal Trading Ltd v City of London Police* [2003] 1 W.L.R. 2711.

prosecuted. This is a matter between the bank and the public authorities and may in a proper case result in an advisory interim declaration being made by the court; or

(3) whether the bank can discharge its own liabilities through paying its customer, given what it sees as a potential liability, as a constructive trustee to a third party for dishonest assistance in a breach of trust, which it may incur through making such a payment.[43] This is a matter between the bank, its customer and the third party. The possible procedures open to a person who may potentially face liability as a constructive trustee are discussed at paras 20.063–20.065 below.

(5) Rights of non-parties to an indemnity from the claimant against costs incurred by them which result from the order or losses caused by the order

(i) *The form of undertaking*

The example form of freezing injunction given by the Practice Direction— 20.023 Interim Injunctions supplementing CPR Pt.25 contains the following undertaking:

> "(7) The Applicant will pay the reasonable costs of anyone other than the Respondent which have been incurred as a result of this order including the costs of finding out whether that person holds any of the Respondent's assets and if the court later finds that this order has caused such person loss, and decides that such person should be compensated for that loss, the Applicant will comply with any order the court may make."

This wording is the same as that in the standard form previously provided by the 1996 Practice Direction.[44]

This form of undertaking is different from the previous standard form of undertaking given in the *Commercial Court Guide* (1990) at Appendix II which read:

> "(6) To pay the reasonable costs and expenses incurred by any third party to whom notice of the terms of this Order has been given, in

---

[43] *United Mizrachi Bank v Doherty* [1998] 1 W.L.R. 435; *Finers v Miro* [1991] 1 W.L.R. 35; *US International Marketing Ltd v National Bank of New Zealand* [2004] 1 N.Z.L.R. 589 (a bank can refuse to make payment on the instructions of its customer, when, if it made payment, this would result in the bank becoming liable to a third party as a constructive trustee, the bank having acted "dishonestly" in the sense used in *Twinsectra v Yardley* [2002] 2 A.C. 164); see paras 20.063–20.065, below.

[44] *Practice Direction (Mareva Injunctions and Anton Piller Orders: Forms)* [1996] 1 W.L.R. 1552.

ascertaining whether any assets to which this Order applies are within their control and in complying with this Order and to indemnify any such person against all liabilities which may flow from such compliance."

That wording only operated in favour of third parties to whom "notice of the terms of this Order has been given . . ." whereas the present wording applies to anyone other than the person restrained. It was based on the theory stated by Lord Denning M.R. in *Z Ltd v A-Z*[45] that where a plaintiff had notified a third party he had by implication requested him to comply with the injunction and thereby assumed an implied promissory obligation to indemnify him against the consequences of his complying with the order.

20.024   In *Guinness Peat Aviation (Belgium) NV v Hispania Lineas Aereas SA*[46] the undertaking was "to indemnify any person . . . to whom notice of this order is given against any costs, expenses, fees or liabilities reasonably incurred in complying or seeking to comply with the terms of this order . . .". This was not materially different from the form of undertaking in the *Commercial Court Guide* (1990). The *ex parte* order restrained the defendant from removing certain aircraft from the jurisdiction and required it to deliver them up to the plaintiff. The non-party was the charterer of one of the aircraft. This had been delivered up to the plaintiff by the defendant before the non-party had knowledge of the order. The charterer suffered loss because of the disruption to its passengers caused by the order. This was not covered by the undertaking because nothing done by the charterer was for the purpose of complying with the order; it had sustained a loss by reason of the making of the order but not through its compliance with the terms.[47]

The plaintiff had also given an undertaking to the court to notify any third parties affected by the order of their right to apply to the court for a variation or discharge. This had been broken and so the plaintiff was in contempt of court. The result of the breach was that the charterer was deprived of the opportunity of applying to the court for discharge or variation of the order so that it could meet its obligations to its passengers. The judge considered that had such an application been made the court would have varied the order unless the undertaking in favour of third parties had been widened so as to apply to any costs, expenses, fees or liabilities, incurred as the result of the making of the order.[48] If there had been contempt proceedings brought before the court it would have sought to impose a penalty which would not take effect if the plaintiff restored the position to what it would have been had the breach of the undertaking not occurred. However, because the charterer had not brought contempt

---

[45] [1982] Q.B. 558 at 575A–D.
[46] [1992] 1 Lloyd's Rep. 190.
[47] *ibid.*, at 194.
[48] *ibid.*, at 196 LHC.

proceedings against the plaintiff for breach of the undertaking, there was
no mechanism enabling the court to do this.[49]

The undertaking in favour of third parties in the example form of order, **20.025**
like the cross-undertaking in damages, is an undertaking given to the court.
It is given as "the price" for the injunction, and the court may refuse to
grant the injunction or discharge it unless the claimant agrees to provide a
suitable undertaking. The width of its terms are based on what is required
so as to protect the legitimate interests of innocent third parties who are
affected by an injunction granted in proceedings between others. That is
why it is not restricted to an indemnity against the consequences of the
third party complying with the order but extends to what is caused by the
making of the order. For the practice about providing the undertaking in
favour of third parties, see Chapter 11, paras 11.008–11.012.

(ii) Recovery from the claimant of costs resulting from the order

An innocent non-party who has been notified of an injunction and has **20.026**
reasonably incurred expense as a result of the order (*e.g.* in taking steps to
comply with its terms) will be able to recover those expenses from the
claimant under the first part of undertaking (7) in the example freezing
order. If the non-party reasonably obtains legal advice in relation to its
position in respect of the order, then in principle the costs of so doing are
recoverable under the first part of the undertaking. For the basis of
assessment of those costs, see para.20.005, above. The wording also covers
costs incurred as a result of the order which are not incurred in complying
with its terms and the costs incurred by the charterer in *Guinness Peat
Aviation (Belgium) NV v Hispania Lineas Aereas SA* would have been
covered by that wording.[50]

Under the first part of the undertaking there is no need for a further
order of the court, exercising a discretion in favour of the non-party. If the
claimant refuses or fails to pay a demand which is within the undertaking,
he breaks the undertaking and he will be in contempt of court. That is not
to say that it is appropriate to apply for committal or to bring sequestration
proceedings.[51] If there is difficulty in obtaining the "costs" from the
claimant, then an application can be made for an order requiring the
claimant to pay a particular sum within a particular time,[52] and this order
in favour of the third party can be enforced by him by the same methods as
if he were a party to the proceedings.[53] These are set out in the Practice
Direction—Enforcement of Judgments and Orders supplementing CPR Pt
70 at para.1.

---

[49] *ibid.*, at 196 RHC.
[50] [1992] 1 Lloyd's Rep. 190 at 193 and 194.
[51] *Belgolaise SA v Rupchandani* [1999] Lloyd's Rep. (Bank.) 116 at 121; and see Chapter 19.
[52] *Carter v Roberts* [1903] 2 Ch. 312. This is analogous to the procedure under RSC Ord. 45,
r.6.
[53] CPR r.70.4.

20.027   Since the court has jurisdiction to release the undertaking,[54] it has full jurisdiction over the undertaking and can give directions to enable any dispute to be resolved, and can release the claimant either conditionally or unconditionally from having to make payment on the undertaking.[55]

(iii) Recovery of losses caused by the order to a non-party

20.028   Undertaking (7) also includes a cross-undertaking as to damages in favour of anyone other than the person restrained (see Chapter 11). The words "such a person" refer back to "anyone other than the Respondent." This includes subsidiary companies of the defendant which sustain losses caused by the injunction. Had this form of undertaking been used in *Guinness Peat Aviation (Belgium) NV v Hispania Lineas Aereas SA*, above, it would have provided the court with jurisdiction to award compensation to the charterer of the aircraft for its own loss.

(iv) The claimant recovering payments made under the undertaking as part of the costs of the proceedings

20.029   If the claimant has to pay such costs under undertaking (7), can he recover them from the defendant as part of the costs of the proceedings under s.51 of the Supreme Court Act 1981? They are "costs" incurred by the claimant during the proceedings. The test for whether they come within s.51 is whether they are "costs of" or "incidental to" the proceedings. Costs and expenses incurred by a receiver in the course of a receivership do not fall within s.51 because those costs include such items as the costs of running a business incurred in order to earn the profits, or the costs of preservation of the subject-matter of the receivership. Those costs are not costs within s.51 because they do not meet this test;[56] they are not an expense of pursuing the litigation before the court.

It is considered that the payments to non-parties are incurred under the undertaking for the purpose of pursuing the litigation against the defendant before the court. They are incurred by the claimant for the purpose of pursuing the case before the court to judgment against the defendant; they are an expense of the litigation itself. Accordingly it is considered that these do fall within the section.[57]

(6) Bailees

(i) Bailees who are incurring costs

20.030   Persons who are looking after the defendant's goods can find that the practical effect of a freezing injunction is to make them liable to keep the assets in question (and maintain them in a reasonable condition) until

---

[54] *Cutler v Wandsworth Stadium Ltd* (1945) 172 L.T. 207.
[55] See para.11.024 above.
[56] *Re Andrews* [1999] 1 W.L.R. 1236 at 1244G–1246H and 1248.
[57] This view is supported by *Searose v Seatrain UK Ltd* [1981] 1 W.L.R. 894 at 896, *per* Robert Goff J.

further order. If the third party wishes to avoid incurring the expenditure involved in looking after the assets for a length of time, he can apply to court for relief. The court may, as the price for continuance of the injunction, require an undertaking from the claimant to pay the storage costs to the third party at a given rate in advance, or it may require the claimant through his solicitors to make arrangements for the assets to be stored. In *Miller Brewing Co. v Mersey Docks and Harbour Company*,[58] the claim was for trade mark infringement and sought delivery-up and destruction of the goods. An injunction was obtained which led to the bailee continuing to incur storage charges in respect of the goods. No undertaking corresponding to undertaking (7) of the example freezing order was provided to the court. The third party bailee did not apply for relief until it was too late to impose an undertaking as the price for the continuance of the interim relief. The result was that the bailee had incurred substantial storage charges which it was unable to recover from the claimant.

(ii) Carriers and freight forwarders

A third party bailee may be under an obligation to deliver the goods 20.031 belonging to the defendant to someone else; *e.g.* he may be a carrier of goods to a purchaser to whom the property has not yet passed, or he may be a freight forwarder who is about to ship them on a vessel or conveyance which is to leave the jurisdiction. Such a situation requires a variation of the original Mareva injunction to enable delivery or the shipment to be made. If the contract of sale is proved, and the transaction appears to be a legitimate business transaction, the practice of the court is to permit it to proceed.

(iii) Court's powers to order a sale

The question might arise as to whether the court has power to order a sale 20.032 of assets caught by a Mareva injunction. CPR r.25.1(c) enables interim relief to be granted by the court in the form of:

"an order—

(i) for the detention, custody or preservation of relevant property;
(ii) for the inspection of relevant property;
(iii) for the taking of a sample of relevant property;
(iv) for the carrying out of an experiment on or with relevant property;
(v) for the sale of relevant property which is of a perishable nature or which for any other good reason it is desirable to sell quickly;
. . . "

---

[58] [2004] F.S.R. 5, p.81. This case is discussed in Chapter 11, para.11.009.

The expression "relevant property" is defined in CPR r.25.1(2):

> "'relevant property' means property (including land) which is the subject of a claim or as to which any question may arise on a claim."

This appears to cover only property which is the actual subject of the litigation, *e.g.* a case in which there is a dispute about ownership of property, or property as to which an issue arises in the litigation itself. So, *e.g.* it would apply where the property is itself the subject of a proprietary claim made in the proceedings, or where the property is itself important evidence in a case (*e.g.* a document relevant to the resolution of the issues in the case). But in a Mareva case the asset is not "the subject of a claim" nor is it relevant as a piece of evidence.

20.033   However, a sale may be ordered by granting a mandatory injunction pursuant to s.37(1) of the Supreme Court Act 1981 requiring the defendant to sell the asset or to consent to a sale arranged by the claimant's solicitors. The case law on the scope of s.37(1) provides ample authority for the court to do this (*Bekhor v Bilton*;[59] *House of Spring Garden Ltd v Waite*;[60] and *Bayer v Winter (No.1)*[61]). Alternatively, the court could appoint a receiver under s.37(1) with power to take possession of the goods and effect a sale even though the goods are not part of the subject-matter of the action.[62] As a matter of discretion, particularly before the claimant has obtained judgment in the action, the courts would be reluctant to make an order requiring assets of the defendant to be sold;[63] thus "the courts must be vigilant to ensure that a Mareva defendant is not treated like a judgment debtor": *Bekhor v Bilton*.[64] The position is entirely different from that which arises when the Admiralty Court decides whether to sell an arrested ship *pendente lite*[65] because in that situation the ship is the subject of the proceedings and stands encumbered with the claimant's claim.

(7) Debtors of the defendant

20.034   Mareva relief in the form of the example order does not prevent third parties from paying their debts to the defendant.[66] If the claimant wishes to obtain an injunction which has this effect, then he will need to seek special

---

[59] [1981] Q.B. 923.
[60] [1985] F.S.R. 173.
[61] [1986] 1 W.L.R. 497.
[62] *Hart v Emelkirk Ltd* [1983] 1 W.L.R. 1289 and see Chapter 16, paras 16.005–16.008.
[63] *Re P (Restraint Order: Sale of Assets)* [2000] 1 W.L.R. 473 at 481H.
[64] [1981] Q.B. 923 at 942.
[65] *The Myrto* [1977] 2 Lloyd's Rep. 243.
[66] *Bank Mellat v Kazmi* [1989] Q.B. 541; *The Law Society v Shanks* [1988] 1 FLR 504; see Chapter 3, paras 3.012–3.014, above.

wording or apply for the appointment of a receiver by the court. Ordinarily, before judgment, the court will not interfere with the way in which the defendant carries on his business, and if he uses one account to receive payments from trade debtors and to pay his trade creditors, that pattern will not be disturbed without very good reason.[67]

If the defendant has a claim against a third party (*e.g.* an insurer) and wishes to enter into a bona fide settlement of that claim, the Mareva injunction will ordinarily be varied so as to enable this to occur.[68] On such an application the court will not be concerned with any investigation of the merits and demerits of any proposed settlement, unless there is clear prima facie evidence that the settlement would be in bad faith or collusive.[69]

(8) The effect of a "maximum sum" order

(i) *The practice of making orders subject to a maximum sum*

The practice is to make a freezing injunction subject to a maximum sum 20.035 limit so that the defendant is not affected more than is justified by the size of the claimant's claim.

In *Z Ltd v A-Z and AA-LL*,[70] Lord Denning M.R. had suggested that in some cases the best course could be for the injunction to omit a maximum sum altogether because of the difficulty it is liable to cause to a bank; the bank should not be expected to monitor what other assets a defendant has within the jurisdiction and the value of those assets. The suggestion made by Kerr L.J. was that the injunction should be subject to a maximum sum and that there should be a special injunction in respect of assets held or controlled by each bank or other third party served with a copy of the order so as to "freeze" the assets held by each third party up to the maximum sum.[71] If an injunction were to be granted in either of these forms, potentially it would cause unfairness to both parties; it would freeze far more than was justified by the amount of the claim, and it would leave the claimant with a greater exposure on his cross-undertaking as to damages.

In practice the courts have granted injunctions in forms limited to a single maximum sum (which makes an allowance for interest and costs[72]), leaving it to banks or other third parties to apply to the court for a variation if there is difficulty in any particular case.

The defendant may have accounts at various banks, but each bank may 20.036 not know how much money the other banks are holding; it may be unaware of the existence of the accounts with other banks. If the bank is

---

[67] *Avant Petroleum Inc. v Gatoil Overseas Inc.* [1986] 2 Lloyd's Rep. 236.
[68] *Normid Housing Association Ltd v Ralphs and Mansell (No.2)* [1989] 1 Lloyd's Rep. 274; see Chapter 3, above.
[69] [1989] 1 Lloyd's Rep. 274 at 279, *per* Slade L.J.
[70] [1982] Q.B. 558 at 576.
[71] *ibid.*, at 589, *per* Kerr L.J.; see also the judgment of Lord Denning M.R. at 576.
[72] See Chapter 12, para.12.004, above.

holding assets which exceed the maximum sum, it will permit the defendant to use anything in excess of the maximum sum. If the bank becomes aware that there are other assets which, together with the assets which it is holding, exceed the maximum sum, then provided that it is satisfied that those assets belong to the defendant and what their value is, it can allow dealings without being in contempt of court.[73]

(ii) The quantification of the maximum sum to be fixed by the order

20.037   In deciding the value of the assets to be subject to the injunction, the courts might have taken the view that it would be appropriate to retain sufficient assets to satisfy the claim (with interest and costs), together with an additional amount to meet the ongoing commitments of the defendant. This approach would have had the merit of preserving extra funds to be available to the defendant to make bona fide payments. However, the courts have refused to allow Mareva injunctions to be used in this way on the grounds that it would in effect involve a rewriting of the established law of insolvency: *K/S A/S Admiral Shipping v Portlink Ferries Ltd*[74] Thus, the maximum sum to be retained under a Mareva injunction is calculated solely by reference to the claim, interest and costs, and the value of the assets of the defendant subject to the injunction at any one time is assessed subject to existing mortgages, but not taking into account liabilities of the defendant. It is true that the assets caught by the Mareva are then subject to reduction (*e.g.* as set-offs arise on a bank account in respect of loan interest on an outstanding overdraft), but this has been said to be "an inevitable consequence of a defendant who is subject to a 'maximum sum' Mareva—and who has no other free assets, being allowed to pay his debts as they fall due".[75]

(iii) What is meant by the words "up to the value" in the order? How is the "value" of an asset to be assessed?

20.038   These questions are relevant to the effects of the injunction both on non-parties, such as banks, and the defendant himself.

Is it necessary to take into account existing rights of set-off against choses in action belonging to the defendant in calculating the value of assets of the defendant subject to the injunction? If the set-off has already been asserted by the third party, then it has already reduced the value of the chose in action.

What is the position if the set-off has not yet been asserted by the third party but is available to it? The wording of the example order for a freezing injunction limited to assets in England and Wales is:

---

[73] *Z Ltd v A-Z* [1982] Q.B. 558 at 583C–G, *per* Eveleigh L.J.
[74] [1984] 2 Lloyd's Rep. 166 at 168.
[75] *Oceanica Castlelana Armadora SA v Mineralimportexport* [1983] 1 W.L.R. 1294 at 1301, *per* Lloyd J.

"5. Until the return date or further order of the court, the Respondent must not remove from England and Wales or in any way dispose of, deal with or diminish the value of any of his assets which are in England and Wales up to the value of £ ."

The first question is whether the debt subject to set off is an 'asset' within the meaning of the phrase 'any of his assets' in the order. On this:

(1) it is a matter for the third party to decide whether or not to exercise a set-off; and

(2) the third party is not obliged to do so,[76] and until he does so, the undiminished chose in action is an asset of the defendant.

The second question is what is the effect of the words "up to the value   **20.039** of . . ."? On the second question the person restrained must not by any of the acts set out in the order reduce the value of his assets caught by the order below the amount set out in the order. This wording is directed to freezing assets regardless of liabilities of the defendant; it is not an injunction directed to requiring the defendant to maintain a quantified net worth of assets over liabilities. On the second question the issue becomes what is the "value" of the asset, namely the undiminished chose in action? The purpose of the order is to safeguard sufficient assets so that a future order of the court will not go unsatisfied. For this purpose what matters is the value which can be realised from the asset on execution or, in the case of a world wide injunction, enforcement of a judgment against assets abroad. This was the context adopted in *Federal Bank of the Middle East v Hadkinson*[77] as relevant to the interpretation of "his assets". It is thought that this also provides the context for the interpretation of the word "value" in the order. Given this context, the word means the value of the assets realisable through the process of execution or enforcement of a future judgment obtained in the proceedings. Thus the fact that an account in credit is a security for liabilities is a matter which goes to its "value" within the meaning of the order. Consequently the "value" of an account in credit is not necessarily the same as the amount by which it is in credit. A credit balance may have been made the subject of an equitable assignment by way of charge as security for a debt. In those circumstances the "value" of the account has to take into account the charge, because the only asset realisable on execution is the net proceeds of the account after taking it into account.[78] A third party debt order would only bind so much of the debt represented by the account as the judgment debtor could "honestly deal with".[79]

---

[76] See *Davis v Hedges* (1871) L.R. 6 Q.B. 687, which was a case on the entitlement of the defendant to abate the price on a building contract at common law; the same principles apply to the entitlement of the third party to assert an equitable set-off.
[77] [2000] 1 W.L.R. 1695 at 1709F–H.
[78] *Holt v Heatherfield Trust Ltd* [1942] 2 K.B. 1.
[79] *Re General Horticultural Company Ex p. Whitehouse* (1886) 32 Ch.D. 512.

Where a debt due to a judgment debtor is subject to a right of the third party to assert an equitable set-off, this affects what can be taken from the third party in execution.[80] So if there is an account at a bank which is subject to a right of set-off by the bank, there can only be taken from the bank in execution the net amount remaining after the exercise of the bank's right of set-off. It is considered that for the purpose of a freezing injunction, in assessing the "value" of that account, it is necessary make a deduction for the right of set-off.

20.040 Do the words in the second and third sentences of para.6 of the example order which extend the meaning of "his assets" in para.5, affect the operation of the maximum sum provision? Paragraph 6 includes as "his assets", assets which are not beneficially owned by the defendant. The purpose of drafting the example order in this way was to extend the grasp of the injunction to assets which were not beneficially owned by the defendant but which in a practical sense were at the disposal of the defendant for use for his own benefit.[81] It is considered that the words "up to the value" in para.5 have the effect that only the value of such assets which are realisable through execution or enforcement of a future judgment obtained in the proceedings count towards the maximum sum.

(9) Notice of more than one injunction: aggregation of maximum sums

20.041 It is often the case that the court has granted a freezing order against the same person in each of two or more different proceedings. Once a freezing order has been obtained by one claimant other claimants apply for the corresponding relief in support of their claims. Each freezing order will have a maximum sum calculated by reference to the claim in those proceedings.

The literal wording of each injunction enjoins dealing with assets only up to the value of its maximum sum. But the reasonable reader knowing of the context that each order has been made in support of the claim in those proceedings, would realise that the maximum sums had to be added to together. So as a matter of interpretation the orders are to be read as applying separately, thus having a cumulative effect. The injunctions should therefore be read as each having effect on the defendant, with the maximum sum provisions becoming relevant only when the "value" of the defendant's assets available for execution, exceeds the aggregate of the maximum sums.

If the claimant knows of another Mareva injunction against the defendant, then prima facie he will be entitled to obtain a Mareva injunction

---

[80] *Hale v Victoria Plumbing Co.* [1966] 2 Q.B. 246.
[81] See Chapter 3, paras 3.009–3.011.

which is cumulative in its effect with the other injunction. In such circumstances it is desirable for the claimant to apply for express words to be inserted into the injuction to the effect that the defendant is restrained from dealing with his assets within the jurisdiction save in so far as these exceed the aggregate of the maximum sum and the sum which the defendant is enjoined from dealing with under the other injunction. For the purposes of any contempt proceedings which might subsequently be taken it is essential to have an injunction which is clear and precise in its terms and effect. These words would be clarification.

(10) Payment of the defendant's creditors and legal costs

(i) Mareva injunctions and payments to creditors of the defendant

The court will always be concerned to ensure that a Mareva injunction 20.042 does not operate oppressively and that a defendant will not be hampered in his ordinary business dealings any more than is absolutely necessary to protect the claimant from the risk of improper dissipation of assets. Since the claimant is not in the position of a secured creditor, and has no proprietary claim to the assets subject to the injunction, there can be no objection in principle to the defendant's dealing in the ordinary way with his business and with his other creditors, even if the effect of such dealings is to render the injunction of no practical value.[82]

A non-party who has security over assets of the defendant which was taken by it prior to notification to it of a freezing injunction is entitled to exercise its security rights bona fide and in the ordinary course of business. The court will not impose fetters on the non-party designed to ensure that it raises the best price for the assets and that it is dealing at arm's length with its client.[83]

Upon the application of the defendant or an interested third party with 20.043 notice of the injunction (usually, but not invariably, a third party creditor or a bank), the court may make an order varying the terms of the injunction enabling payment to be made of bona fide business debts or commitments, or other expenses (*e.g.* living expenses). These may include expenses such as staff salaries, normal office expenses, payments due to trade creditors, and legal fees. The type of expenses in respect of which such a variation will be ordered depends on the circumstances of each case. Such an order has become known as an "Angel Bell" order; a term derived from the leading case, *Iraqi Ministry of Defence v Arcepey Shipping*

---

[82] This paragraph was approved in *Halifax Plc v Chandler* [2001] EWCA Civ 1750 at [19]; *Perczynski v Perczynski* [2001] J.L.R. Note 26 [trustee allowed to pay bona fide debt incurred before injunction imposed).
[83] *Gangway Ltd v Caledonian Park Investments (Jersey) Ltd* [2001] 2 Lloyd's Rep. 715; see the discussion of this case at para.20.014, above.

Company SA (The Angel Bell).[84] A defendant may be well aware of the possibility of rendering a Mareva injunction worthless by obtaining variations and then making sufficient payments out of his funds within the jurisdiction to exhaust them.

20.044   The court does not usually consider whether the business venture is reasonable or whether the particular business expenses are reasonable. Nor does the court balance the defendant's case that he should be able to spend such moneys against the strength of the claimant's case and the effects of allowing the expenditure on the prospects of the defendant satisfying a future judgment.[85]

Where a party seeks a variation to the injunction to enable a payment to be made, he has the burden of persuading the court that the proposed payment from the proposed source would not be in conflict with the principle underlying the Mareva jurisdiction.[86] This is because the claimant by obtaining the injunction has already shown a risk of dissipation of assets and therefore the burden passes to the defendant to show that what he proposes would be just. Where the defendant is seeking the variation, it is usual for him to satisfy this requirement by making a witness statement which includes the amount of the proposed payment, and the reason for making it. If the proposed payment is for a number of items, these should be identified. If the payment concerns a particular transaction between the defendant and the third party, ordinarily the defendant will give some details of that transaction and exhibit any appropriate documents to negative any suggestion that the transaction is other than bona fide.

20.045   In *Avant Petroleum Inc. v Gatoil Overseas Inc.*[87] the Court of Appeal allowed an appeal so that the defendant trading company could continue to use its bank accounts in accordance with an established pattern of commercial dealings. A Mareva injunction should not be used so as to compel a defendant to change his established method of trading. If the defendant wishes to continue to use its bank accounts for making bona fide trading payments of a type which were normally made from those accounts before the injunction, then the injunction should be varied so as to allow them to be made. The court did not inquire into what other assets the defendant might have available for making the payments. This was because it was to be expected in the ordinary course of affairs that such payments would be made from those accounts and therefore the payments were to be regarded as being made bona fide regardless of whether or not other assets might be available to meet the trading debts. The approach in *A v C (No.2)*[88] of requiring evidence about other assets outside of the jurisdiction

---

[84] [1981] Q.B. 65.
[85] *Halifax Plc v Chandler* [2001] EWCA Civ 1750 at [18]; see Chapter 12, para.12.037.
[86] *A v C (No.2)* [1981] Q.B. 961; *A. C. Maugher & Son (Sunwin) Ltd v Victor Hugo Management Ltd* [1989] J.L.R. 295.
[87] [1986] 2 Lloyd's Rep. 236.
[88] [1981] Q.B. 961.

before permitting a variation is not an "inflexible rule"[89] and is "not of universal application".[90]

In *Atlas Maritime SA v Avalon (No.1)*,[91] the defendant had borrowed money from its parent company to use as trading capital to buy a vessel. The defendant applied for a variation to the injunction to allow it to pay back the parent company from the funds caught by the injunction. The Court of Appeal refused to allow this, because in effect the parent company had advanced venture capital to the defendant and it was not proper that the venture capital should be repaid to the parent company from the sole remaining asset of the defendant before the plaintiff's claim had been heard and determined. For the purposes of exercising the discretion the court could take into account the relationship between the parent and the subsidiary,[92] and in the circumstances it would be unfair to allow the parent to leave the subsidiary without any assets prior to resolution of the claim. The intended repayment was not merely a payment in the ordinary course of business. In contrast, where the payment to the parent would be a repayment in the ordinary course of business, it will be permitted.[93]

A question sometimes arises as to whether, as a term of the variation of **20.046** the injunction, the defendant should be required to bring into the jurisdiction future business proceeds. This is a matter for the discretion of the court, and depending on the circumstances such a requirement may be imposed. The defendant should not be permitted to change his established course of business so as to whittle away assets subject to the injunction, without topping them up from time to time in accordance with his established mode of trading from the proceeds of the business: *Polly Peck International v Nadir*.[94]

In general, however, the court should avoid producing an order which is complicated and likely to be onerous for a defendant in its operation. It is not appropriate to place the affairs of the defendant under a form of administration which prevents, or risks interfering with, ordinary trading activities. If the real problem is that of absence of assets to satisfy the claim

---

[89] *Avant Petroleum Inc. v Gatoil Overseas Inc.* [1986] 2 Lloyd's Rep. 236 at 242; *China Merchants Bank v I-China Holdings Ltd (No.2)* [2003] 1 H.K.L.R.D. 299 (where certain of the proposed payments were permitted although there were many unanswered questions about possible other assets and whether full disclosure of assets had been made).

[90] *Campbell Mussells v Thompson, The Times*, May 30, 1984 (and see also the report in (1985) 135 N.L.J. 1012 and Court of Appeal (Civ Div) Transcript No.234 of 1984).

[91] [1991] 1 Lloyd's Rep. 563.

[92] The court did not "pierce the corporate veil", but lifted it so as to take into account all the facts in exercising the discretion; see [1991] 1 Lloyd's Rep. 563 at 571–572, *per* Staughton L.J., and *Atlas Maritime SA v Avalon (No.3)* [1991] 1 W.L.R. 917 at 924. See also *Canadian Pacific (Bermuda) Ltd v Nederhoorn Pte* [1992] 1 S.L.R. 659 (Singapore) where, surprisingly, the court refused to allow the principal shareholder to be repaid a loan, the loan having been made because the injunction had prevented the defendant making a payment which it had to make in the ordinary course of business.

[93] *Hurrell v Fitness Holdings Europe Ltd* unreported, March 15, 2002 (Cooke J.).

[94] Court of Appeal (Civ Div) Transcript No.60 of 1992 (February 3, 1992), referred to by Scott L.J. in *Polly Peck International plc v Nadir (No.2)* [1992] 4 All E.R. 769 at p.775d.

if it is successful, the correct conclusion may well be that an injunction is inappropriate.[95]

20.047   In the case of payment of business debts and expenses, it is often not appropriate or practicable for the defendant to be required to justify to the court each proposed payment. It is more usual for the court to grant a variation of the injunction expressed in general terms to enable business payments to be made subject to the safeguard that the defendant contacts the claimant before making payments and supplies the claimant with sufficient information to enable him to investigate whether the proposed payments are genuine and reasonable in amount. The terms of the Angel Bell variation can be expressed so as to permit the defendant to make payments out of assets caught by the injunction, provided that the claimant has been informed of the intended payment and supplied with supporting documents, and has not within a specified period after notification objected to the proposed payment. In practice, this notification may operate by means of a weekly list supplied by the defendant's solicitors to the claimant's solicitors supported by copy invoices, vouchers and other relevant documentation.

Sometimes, however, the advance notification procedure is too cumbersome and would place the defendant in real business difficulties. If, *e.g.* he is in a business such as insurance, where brokers operate a complex system of set-offs with insurers regarding moneys due in respect of premiums, commission and claims, prior notification to a claimant of every set-off transaction or claim payment would be impracticable. In that situation, the variation may provide instead for subsequent notification of all relevant transactions with sufficient details to enable the claimant to check that they were genuine. The defendant should not be prejudiced in the conduct of his ordinary business affairs by a procedure which would or could work oppressively. The claimant's cross-undertaking is not sufficient ground for inflicting on a defendant a notification procedure which would halt or hinder ordinary business transactions.

20.048   A further safeguard, which is sometimes combined with prior or subsequent notification, is to place a financial limit on the payments which may be made by the defendant during a certain period, so that if he wishes to make larger payments he must apply to the court. The sum may be fixed by reference to the defendant's normal business expenditure each week or month on the basis of affidavit evidence showing a pattern of payments; if an average sum cannot be ascertained, the court may instead decide on an appropriate figure by reference to the size and nature of the defendant's business and turnover.

In *Halifax Plc v Chandler*[96] the defendant wished to spend frozen funds in prosecuting an action against a third party. Whether he was to be

---

[95] *Gold Leaf Investments Inc. v Uniform International*, Court of Appeal (Civ Div) Transcript No.582 of 1990 (June 7, 1990); *Pressurefast Ltd v Hall and Brushett Ltd*, Court of Appeal (Civ Div) Transcript No.336 of 1993 (March 9, 1993); see further *Bond Braving Holdings Ltd v National Australia Bank Ltd* [1991] 1 V.L.R. 386, Supreme Court of Victoria, Full Court and para.12.039 above.
[96] [2001] EWCA Civ 1750.

entitled to do so depended upon the same principles as apply to ordinary business expenses, and he was permitted to do so.

(ii) Illegal transactions

In *Iraqi Ministry of Defence v Arcepey Shipping Co. SA (The Angel Bell)*[97] **20.049** the plaintiffs, who had a substantial claim for unliquidated damages against the defendant one-ship company, sought to oppose an application by the mortgagees that the defendant should be at liberty to use almost all of the insurance proceeds on the vessel to repay the loan secured by a mortgage on the vessel. The plaintiffs alleged that the loan secured by the mortgage was void as a moneylending transaction. The court granted the variation holding that by doing so it was not enforcing the transaction but merely giving the defendant permission to pay the mortgagees.

(iii) Mareva relief and legal costs

The court is in principle anxious to ensure that a defendant is not deprived **20.050** of professional legal representation by reason of a freezing injunction and where there is no proprietary claim this is an important factor to take into account in favour of permitting the expenditure,[98] because the defendant ought to be able to use his own assets to defend himself.

The example order provides:

"EXCEPTIONS TO THIS ORDER

11. (1) This order does not prohibit the Respondent from spending £   a week towards his ordinary living expenses and also £   [or a reasonable sum] on legal advice and representation. [But before spending any money the Respondent must tell the Applicant's legal representatives where the money is to come from.]"

This wording enables money to be spent on legal advice and representation for the person restrained by the injunction but not for someone else, even a relative in related proceedings.[99]

On an application for a variation to permit funds to be released to meet **20.051** legal costs, it is relevant to take into account whether legal costs have in the past been met from other funds or by third parties, and if so whether

---

[97] [1981] Q.B. 65.
[98] *Investors and Pensions Advisory Service v Gray* [1990] B.C.L.C. 38. This is also the position for freezing relief in matrimonial proceedings: *P v P* [2002] J.L.R. Note 18 even though the claim is for what in substance is a share in the assets (see further Chapter 3, para.3.001 and Chapter 7, paras 7.018–7.023).
[99] *Perotti v Watson*, unreported, January 12, 2001, Ch.D. (Lawrence Collins J.).

there is a real risk that if the variation were not permitted, the defendant would be unfairly prejudiced. In *Atlas Maritime SA v Avalon Ltd (No.3)*,[1] the costs of the defendant had been met by its parent company, which had chosen to operate the purse strings so as to leave the defendant with no assets to pay for its defence other than the funds which were subject to the injunction. The Court of Appeal declined to permit the variation when it was to be expected that the parent company would fund the litigation, having previously denuded the defendant of funds for its defence. It did not matter, on the facts of the case, that the subsidiary had no legal right to insist that the parent company fund the defence.[2] In exercising its discretion whether to permit a variation, the court looks to what is likely in fact to occur depending on the order made. So if the court is satisfied that refusal of the variation will not prejudice the defence of the claim because the costs will in practice be funded from elsewhere, the court will take this into account. If this is the position, it is irrelevant whether or not the defendant has a legal right to require a third party to fund the defence. Conversely, it may be right for the court to permit a variation if the defendant has a legal right to require the defence to be paid for, but the third party will not honour its obligations.

Under Art.6(1) of the European Convention on Human Rights there is no specific right in civil proceedings to legal representation.[3]

(iv) Mareva relief: permission to make payments out of assets frozen within the jurisdiction when there may be assets outside the jurisdiction

20.052   In *A v C (No.2)*,[4] Robert Goff J. declined to grant an application by certain defendants for a variation to enable them to make a payment out of frozen assets in respect of legal costs likely to be incurred in the defence of the proceedings. In that case Mareva relief had been granted limited to assets within the jurisdiction and the defendants placed no evidence at all before the court concerning assets other than those covered by the injunction. On the facts of the case, which concerned a substantial claim for fraud, the judge held that the evidence had not satisfied him that the proposed payment would not conflict with the principle underlying the Mareva jurisdiction,[5] which he formulated as:

"to prevent . . . defendants from causing assets to be removed from the jurisdiction in order to avoid the risk of having to satisfy any judgment

---

[1] [1994] 1 W.L.R. 917.
[2] [1994] 1 W.L.R. 917 at 926 applying *Browne v Browne* [1989] 1 F.L.R. 291; *Armco Inc. v Donohue* [1998] J.L.R. Notes–12a, principle 4.
[3] Chapter 19, paras 19.076–19.077.
[4] [1981] Q.B. 961.
[5] See also *Armhouse Lee Ltd v Anthony Chappell*, Court of Appeal (Civ Div) Transcript No.1063 of 1994 (August 9, 1994) where the court inferred that other assets were available.

which may be entered against them in pending proceedings in [England]".

This wording suggested that, in determining whether the defendant should be permitted to use frozen assets to meet legal costs or living expenses, what mattered was the motive of the defendant for wanting to make the payment out of frozen assets, or that to be imputed to him on the evidence.

A note appeared in the Supreme Court Practice which suggested that in every case the defendant would have to adduce evidence about his unfrozen assets outside the jurisdiction before the court would permit him to use assets frozen within the jurisdiction to meet such expenditure. In subsequent cases the Court of Appeal made it clear that this was not a universal rule.[6]

In *Campbell Mussells v Thompson*[7] the defendant was a Nigerian chief 20.053 who was an entrepreneur dealer in arms. He wanted to use his assets within the jurisdiction to discharge living expenses in England for his wives and 19 children, and the legal costs of his defence. In the ordinary course it was to be expected that these would be met from funds within the jurisdiction. There was no evidence from the defendant about the extent and nature of his assets outside the jurisdiction. The court permitted the expenditure to be made by the defendant from his assets within the jurisdiction because it would be usual for those expenses to be paid out of such assets, and consequently the proposed payments did not conflict with the purpose of the Mareva injunction as stated in *A v C (No.2)*. Griffiths L.J. said that the purpose of requiring evidence from the defendant in *A v C (No.2)* was to show that there was "no ulterior motive" for making the payment of legal costs from assets frozen within the jurisdiction.

In *Kea Corporation v Parrott Corporation Ltd*,[8] the question was the same as that considered in *A v C (No.2)*. Mareva relief had been obtained against a foreigner limited to assets within the jurisdiction, and he applied for permission to use those assets to pay his legal expenses in respect of the proceedings brought against him in England. The plaintiffs contended that it was likely that the defendant had assets abroad which could be used to pay his legal costs, and that the English assets should be preserved subject to the injunction so as to be available to pay a future judgment. The Court of Appeal rejected this contention, Sir John Donaldson M.R. observing that on the facts of the case it could not "possibly be said that [the defendant's] purpose [was] to ensure that assets are not available to satisfy a judgment".

---

[6] *Campbell Mussells v Thompson, The Times*, May 30, 1984 (and see also the report in (1985) 135 N.L.J. 1012); *Kea Corporation v Parrott Corporation Ltd*, Court of Appeal (Civ Div) Transcript No.808 of 1986 (September 24, 1986); *Avant Petroleum Inc. v Gatoil Overseas Inc.* [1986] 2 Lloyd's Rep. 236.

[7] *The Times*, May 30, 1984 (and see also the report in (1985) 135 N.L.J. 1012).

[8] Court of Appeal (Civ Div) Transcript No.808 of 1986 (September 24, 1986) which was followed in *Laager v P.Kruger* [1996] C.I.L.R. 361 (mareva relief granted against wife to enforcement of a judgment against her husband, variation so as to allow her to use assets within the jurisdiction to pay legal costs, living expenses and other liabilities.)

He also suggested that the court should consider in relation to the proposed use of frozen assets whether it was "an unnatural thing to do" and "unreasonable": "The real purpose must be to remove assets from the potential clutches of a plaintiff."

These cases looked at the purpose of the defendant in making the payment, including the purpose to be imputed to him on the evidence.

20.054   In exercising the discretion whether or not to grant an application to vary an injunction the court acts in accordance with what is "just and convenient". This is the test laid down in s.37(1) of the Supreme Court Act 1981. On an application for a variation, the claimant has already established a real risk of dissipation and a good arguable case. The principles which apply in considering whether to grant a variation are the same as those which apply when considering whether or not to grant Mareva relief.[9] So the fact that the defendant's purpose in applying for the variation is not deliberately to frustrate enforcement of a judgment does not mean that the variation is to be permitted. Later authorities, including a judgment of Lord Donaldson M.R.[10] (as he had become), show that the test for risk of dissipation is not one depending on the subjective intent of the defendant or his "design", but depends on evidence establishing objectively a real risk of dissipation of assets.[11] Motive for making the proposed payment is not to be equated with the risk of unfair dissipation of assets.

The correct test is to consider objectively the overall justice of allowing the payment to be made including the likely consequences of permitting it on the prospects of a future judgment being left unsatisfied, and bearing in mind that the assets belong to the defendant and that the injunction is not intended to provide the claimant with security for his claim or to create an untouchable pot which will be available to satisfy an eventual judgment.

Therefore, the principle is that a defendant can use his own money which is frozen under a Mareva injunction to fund the defence provided that it is apparent that there are no other funds or source of payment which should as a matter of objective fairness be used to pay for the defence rather than the frozen funds. This may require the defendant to adduce "credible evidence"[12] about his other assets before the court can be

---

[9] See Chapter 12.

[10] *R. v Secretary of State for the Home Department Ex p. Muboyayi* [1992] Q.B. 244 at 257H explaining his observation in *Derby & Co. Ltd v Weldon (Nos 3 and 4)* [1990] Ch. 65 at 76.

[11] *Ketchum International plc v Group Public Relations* [1997] 1 W.L.R. 4 at 13A–D, referring to *Ninemia Maritime Corporation v Trave Schiffahrtsgesellschaft mbH* [1983] 1 W.L.R. 1412 at 1422 and *R. v Secretary of State for the Home Department Ex p. Muboyayi* [1992] Q.B. 244 at 257H; *Felixstowe Dock & Railway Co. v United States Lines Inc.* [1989] Q.B. 360; *Customs and Excise Commissioners v Anchor Foods Ltd* [1999] 1 W.L.R. 1139; *Hurrell v Fitness Holdings Europe Ltd*, March 15, 2002 (Cooke J.) at p.23 of the transcript; see Chapter 12 paras 12.032–12.034.

[12] *Re Kingsley Healthcare Ltd*, unreported, September 25, 2001, Ch.D. (Neuberger J.) referring to *A v C (No.2)* [1981] Q.B. 961;.

satisfied that it is just that he should be able to use the particular frozen assets.[13]

Because a real risk of dissipation has already been established by the **20.055** evidence, judges are entitled to have a "very healthy scepticism"[14] about assertions made by the party against whom the Mareva injunction has been granted, and this should be borne in mind in deciding whether further evidence should be required. If in addition the defendant has been less than frank in his dealings with the court or the claimant over legal or living expenses, this would tend to reinforce the case for putting in place a regime requiring the defendant to adduce evidence showing a complete picture each time he requires further funds, thus enabling the court to police the payments.[15]

If in the circumstances it would be entirely usual for the defendant to make the proposed expenditure out of assets within the jurisdiction, as was the case for the living expenses and legal costs in *Campbell Mussells v Thompson*[16] and the proposed payments in accordance with the established pattern of trading in *Avant Petroleum Inc. v Gatoil Overseas Inc.*,[17] this is also a relevant factor in deciding what is fair and, depending on the facts, can be conclusive. But as the decision in *A v C (No.2)* shows, the fact that it would be usual to make the proposed payment from assets within the jurisdiction, may not be enough on its own to establish the fairness of doing so, without investigating the position about other assets. What is fair depends on the circumstances of the case. When there is reason to believe that the defendant has no assets outside the jurisdiction, then, on an application to vary the injunction to permit payment of legal costs, it would be an empty exercise for the court to insist on production of evidence from the defendant about his assets abroad before deciding whether to permit the payment.[18]

---

[13] *Halifax Plc v Chandler* [2001] EWCA Civ 1750 at [17] principle (3) requires a defendant in a Mareva case to show that he has no other assets which he can use, see also *Zakharov v White* [2003] EWHC 2560 at [47–52], Ch.D. It is considered that this should not be read as a universal or inflexible requirement, see *Campbell Mussells v Thompson, The Times*, May 30, 1984 (and see also the report in (1985) 135 N.L.J. 1012); *Kea Corporation v Parrott Corporation Ltd*, Court of Appeal (Civ Div) Transcript No.808 of 1986 (September 24, 1986); *Avant Petroleum Inc. v Gatoil Overseas Inc.* [1986] 2 Lloyd's Rep. 236; *A. S. Design Ltd v Lam Yiu To Joseph*, October 11, 2001, HKCFI (defendant not required to use his home in mainland China for funding legal costs and permitted to use funds in Hong Kong on undertaking to place title deeds to his home with his solicitors subject to further order of the court).

[14] *Campbell Mussells v Thompson*, above. *Per* Sir John Donaldson M.R., repeated in *Southern Cross v Martin*, Court of Appeal (Civ Div) Transcript No.128 of 1986 (February 11, 1986).

[15] *Zakharov v White* [2003] EWHC 2560 at [47–52], Ch.D. (the defendant had acted with a lack of frankness in taking his own frozen assets to pay legal costs and the judge required the defendant to make specific applications in the future on each occasion that he wanted spend money on legal or living expenses).

[16] *The Times*, May 30, 1984 (and see also the report in (1985) 135 N.L.J. 1012).

[17] [1986] 2 Lloyd's Rep. 236.

[18] *A v C (No.2)* [1981] Q.B. 961 at 963 referring to the facts of *Iraqi Ministry of Defence v Arcepey Shipping Co. SA (The Angel Bell)* [1981] Q.B. 65 (proceeds of insurance of the ship of a one ship company); see also *Clark Equipment Credit of Australia Ltd v Como Factors* (1988) 14 N.S.W.L.R. 552 at 569.

20.056   The same principle of objective fairness applies when an injunction is granted worldwide and the question arises whether the defendant should be at liberty to pay an expense using his English assets or assets safely frozen outside the jurisdiction by a local court, or whether he should be left to make the payment from assets which are not effectively frozen or may not be available for execution or satisfaction of the judgment.

If the evidence indicates that the defendant has already hidden away substantial assets abroad, it would be unjust to permit him to use what is left of the depleted English assets to make such a payment. In *National Bank of Greece v Constantinos Dimitriou*,[19] Mareva relief had been granted against a defendant in respect of assets within the jurisdiction, and a disclosure order had been made in respect of all assets. A variation to the injunction had been granted for legal costs, it having appeared on the evidence that the defendant did not have available assets outside the jurisdiction. Subsequently it emerged that, contrary to the defendant's sworn evidence, there were substantial funds abroad from which the payments could be made. The defendant had given false evidence and was in contempt of court in respect of the disclosure order, and it appeared from the evidence that he was doing everything he could to preserve and keep secret his assets abroad. The Court of Appeal refused to sanction a variation to enable assets subject to the injunction to be used to pay the legal expenses.

(v) Proprietary claims and the release of funds to pay legal costs from an injunction or by a receiver

20.057   What if there is a proprietary claim by the claimant? The purpose of an injunction granted in aid of a proprietary claim is to stop the defendant expending for his own benefit what may be the claimant's property. No one has the right to use someone else's money to pay for their defence and so before there can be any question of allowing a defendant to use funds to which the claimant has a very strong proprietary claim he must show an arguable case for denying that they belong to the claimant.[20] "If he cannot show that there is an arguable claim in his part to the funds, he has no right to use the money . . . No man has a right to use somebody else's money, for the purpose of defending himself against legal proceedings".[21]

Where there are assets which may belong to the claimant, the court will not allow those funds to be used for legal costs until the defendant has

---

[19] *The Times*, November 16, 1987; see also Chapter 19, para.19.077.
[20] *Ostrich Farming Corporation Ltd v Ketchell*, unreported, December 10, 1997, CA; the same principle applies to a defendant resisting an application for an interim injunction to restrain a trespass on land which belongs to the claimant: *Patel v W. H. Smith (Eziot) Ltd* [1987] 1 W.L.R. 853.
[21] *Ostrich Farming Corporation Ltd v Ketchell*, unreported, December 10, 1997, at p.7 of the transcript, *per* Millett L.J.; *Cogent Nominees v Anthony* [2003] N.S.W.S.C. 804 (September 1, 2003) at para.28.

shown by "proper evidence"[22] that he has no other assets which can be used for this purpose.[23] If there are such funds, then the defendant must use these first before any question arises of his having access to funds which are the subject of a proprietary claim.[24] But once it is shown there are no other assets except those subject to a proprietary claim, the court must make a difficult decision in the exercise of its discretion as to what is to be done.[25] If, within the reasonable confines of an interlocutory application, the claimant can demonstrate a strong probability that his proprietary claim to the assets is well founded, this must be taken into account in the court's decision whether, and if so on what terms, any variation is to be permitted.[26] The same principles apply to permitting living expenses out of assets which are subject to a proprietary claim (see below).

In *Xylas v Khanna*[27] there was a strong case that funds were held on trust **20.058** for the plaintiff. The defendant was representing himself and applied, during the trial, for an adjournment and for leave to use the funds to instruct lawyers. The Court of Appeal upheld the decision of the judge to refuse the application, observing that the exercise of the discretion involved balancing the risk of injustice to the defendant in presenting his defence with the risk of injustice to the plaintiff that his own money might be used to fight the litigation against him. The same principles apply whether the defendant is contemplating using all of the assets which are the subject of a proprietary claim or only a small part of them.[28]

The same principles apply when a receiver has been appointed over assets in support of a proprietary claim. As long as it is arguable that the assets may not be trust assets or belong to someone else, then the court may order the release of funds by the receiver to fund the defence.[29]

Where the court is minded to allow the defendant to pay legal costs out of what may be the claimant's money, the court considers whether it can impose safeguards for the claimant so that if his proprietary claim is well founded he may have some protection.[30]

---

[22] *Ostrich Farming Corporation Ltd v Ketchell*, unreported, December 10, 1997, at p.7 of the transcript.

[23] *Fitzgerald v Williams* [1996] Q.B. 657 at p 669G–H; *Armco Inc. v Donohue* [1998] J.L.R. Notes–12a, principle 3; *P v P* [2002] J.L.R. Note 18, principle B.

[24] *PCW (Underwriting Agencies) Ltd v Dixon* [1983] 2 All E.R. 158.

[25] *Fitzgerald v Williams* [1996] Q.B. 657 at 669G–H; *Sundt Wrigley & Co. Ltd v Wrigley*, Court of Appeal (Civ Div) Transcript No.685 of 1993 (June 23, 1993).

[26] *Sundt Wrigley & Co. Ltd v Wrigley*, Court of Appeal (Civ Div) Transcript No.685 of 1993 (June 23, 1993); *NMB Postbank Group v Naviede (No.2)* [1993] B.C.L.C. 715 at 719; *Polly Peck International plc v Nadir (No.2)* [1992] 4 All E.R. 769 at 784; *Armco Inc. v Donohue* [1998] J.L.R Notes–12a, principle 2.

[27] Court of Appeal (Civ Div) Transcript No.1036 of 1992 (November 4, 1992).

[28] *United Mizrahi Bank Ltd v Doherty* [1998] 1 W.L.R. 435 at 438–439 quoting from *Xylas v Khanna*.

[29] *NMB Postbank Groep v Naviede* [1993] B.C.L.C. 707; *NMB Postbank Groep v Naviede (No.2)* [1993] B.C.L.C. 715.

[30] *United Mizrachi Bank v Doherty* [1998] 1 W.L.R. 435 at 439–440, including agreement by the defendant's solicitors that if the claimant is successful he can have their costs taxed; *Armco Inc. v Donohue* [1998] J.L.R. Notes–12a, principle 6 (undertaking by defendant to

20.059   Where the court is acting in support of a foreign court under s.25 of the Civil Jurisdiction and Judgments Act 1982 and the foreign court has made an order about provision for legal costs the English court will follow that order even though a different result would have been reached applying the principles set out above.[31]

(vi) Variations to pay legal costs and quantum

20.060   Where a variation is to be allowed, in a Mareva case the court will not ordinarily concern itself with the quantum of individual items of costs, although it may well fix a limit to the overall amount to be allowed for this purpose pending further application to the court. The court is not concerned with whether the defendant might have gone to cheaper lawyers, or whether the lawyers could have spent less time on the case, and will not act as a form of provisional taxing body for the purpose of scrutinising the defendant's legal fees.[32] In a case concerning a proprietary claim the position is different because part of the exercise of the discretion involves taking into account the risks of injustice to a claimant in having his own money used to litigate against him. There the court will act more cautiously so as to ensure that the funds are not wasted.[33]

(vii) The Chanel v Woolworth principle, abuse of the process and the number of applications for variations so as to pay legal costs

20.061   The principle in *Chanel Ltd v F. W. Woolworth & Co. Ltd*[34] is that if a point was open to the applicant on an earlier interlocutory application and was not pursued, then it is not open to the applicant to take the point in a later application when there has been no material change of circumstances and no new facts.[35] This principle is discussed in Chapter 23, paras 23.014–23.016. It applies when a freezing injunction is continued *inter partes*, or where an undertaking is given in equivalent terms, which is

---

make good out of funds to which the plaintiff had no proprietary claim any sums spent on costs which are subsequently found to have come out of property to which the plaintiff has a good proprietary claim). In *Laager v P. Kruger* [1996] C.I.L.R. 361 the plaintiff obtained mareva relief against a wife based on a judgment against the husband and the allegation that she held assets of the husband or assets transferred with the intention of defeating creditors. The court declined to impose a regime under which the wife would have to use assets first which were "most clearly hers" because this could lead to undesirable mini trials about the status of particular assets).

[31] *State of Brunei Darussalam v Prince Jefri Bolkiah*, *The Times*, September 5, 2000 (Jacob J.; *Kobuleti Shipping Co. Ltd v Dilworth* [2000] M.L.B. 33, pp.60–61 (Isle of Man court following variation permitted in main proceedings in London).

[32] *Cala Cristal SA v Emran Al-Borno*, *The Times*, May 6, 1994; *Armco Inc. v Donohue* [1998] J.L.R. Notes–12a, principle 5.

[33] *NMB Postbank Groep v Naviede (No.2)* [1993] B.C.L.C. 715.

[34] [1981] 1 W.L.R. 485.

[35] *Leadmill Ltd v Omare*, unreported, April 19, 2002, Ch.D. (Hart J.).

expressed to be until trial or further order, and no specific reservation is made before the court by the applicant.[36] It also applies to a decision reached taking into account evidence served late when no adjournment was sought by the applicant.[37] The principle is founded on the basis that the applicant has a responsibility to take a point when it is first reasonably available to him before the court and that it would be an abuse to delay taking it until a subsequent application.

It is an abuse of the process of the court to rely upon a set of facts for obtaining a variation and then to apply again a short time afterwards for different relief based on the same facts or when there has been no material change of circumstances. In *Halifax Plc v Chandler*[38] the defendant applied to the court for a different variation to govern payment of legal costs only five days after the court had already granted a variation but in a lower amount and to be funded from a different source of funds. The Court of Appeal held that it was an abuse of the process of the court to do this and that the defendant should wait until he had exhausted the provision under the first variation before applying again. When an application is made to the court for a variation the defendant should put before the court the full picture and if a different application is made almost immediately afterwards an explanation should be furnished showing a material change in circumstances.

The court will not rehear an application which it has already heard and determined *inter partes*. A party aggrieved by such a determination will have to appeal.

Subject to these limits, there is no restriction laid down as a matter of law or practice to the number of applications which can be made for variations to an injunction. Nevertheless, it is not cost-efficient or desirable for a party to keep on making interlocutory applications to the court for variations for legal costs to cover the next stage of the litigation. Accordingly, the court can give directions which are intended to hold the position until trial and can direct that there should not be a further application until the commencement of the trial. Such a direction does not deprive the court of *jurisdiction* to deal with a further application, but has the consequence that if a further application is to be made then the applicant will have to show a material change in circumstances as foreseen or reasonably foreseeable at the time of the earlier application, otherwise the application will be dismissed as an abuse of the process of the court.[39]

20.062

---

[36] *Re Kingsley Healthcare Ltd*, unreported, September 25, 2001 (Neuberger J.).
[37] *Royal Bank of Scotland Plc v Ezekiel* [1999] EWCA Civ 1398 (May 12, 1999).
[38] [2001] EWCA Civ 1750.
[39] See also *Temsign Pty Ltd v Biscen Pty Ltd* (1996) 68 F.C.R. 1, Federal Court of Australia.

(11) Proprietary claims, legal costs and the potential liability of the defendant's solicitor as a constructive trustee

20.063   A solicitor may be concerned about becoming liable to third parties as a constructive trustee if he receives money subject to a proprietary claim in payment of his legal fees, or if he were to pay over to his client money which is subject to a trust. In *Finers v Miro*[40] the plaintiff solicitors held assets for their client which they suspected belonged a company in liquidation in the United States. The evidence that, although they had acted honestly, their client had consulted them for the purpose of secretly holding assets misappropriated by him was strong enough to reach the conclusion that legal professional privilege would not apply. The Court of Appeal held that the assets held by the solicitors were held on trust for someone and so there was jurisdiction for an administration action to be brought.[41] Directions were given in that action for funds to be released from the assets for legal costs of the defendant client.

In *United Mizrahi Bank Ltd v Doherty*[42] a variation to an injunction was granted permitting funds which were the subject of a proprietary claim to be released from a freezing injunction and spent on funding the defendant's defence. The question arose whether the court should also order that the defendant's solicitors should have immunity from any claim that, if they received the funds and applied them to discharge the defendant's costs, they would become liable as constructive trustees to the plaintiff. The judge refused to grant this relief because the evidence before him did not give him the full picture as to the extent of risk to the solicitor.

In *Bank of Scotland v A*,[43] the Court of Appeal said (obiter) that an administration action could be brought and directions obtained even when it was only arguable that there was a trust.

20.064   Where a solicitor receives money which he applies in discharge of his professional fees and which is the subject of a proprietary claim there is the possibility that the solicitor may afterwards be sued by a claimant alleging liability as a constructive trustee. The issues likely to arise in such a claim are liable to be difficult to resolve.[44] It could be unfair (1) to place the defendant in a position where he has to find a solicitor prepared to take the risk of this; and (2) to require the solicitor, if he is going to continue to act, to take the risk of subsequently being sued.

One possible way of dealing with this pre-emptively would be for the solicitor to seek a pre-emptive costs order in the proceedings directing for payment of the defendant's costs out of the claimed fund. A second way is

---

[40] [1991] 1 W.L.R. 35.
[41] Previously under RSC Ord. 85 and now under CPR Pt 64.
[42] [1998] 1 W.L.R. 435.
[43] [2001] 1 W.L.R. 751.
[44] The case law on constructive trusts is not straight forward; see *Goff and Jones: The Law of Restitution* (6th ed., 2002) at para.33–029.

to bring an administration action and seek interim relief in it like that granted in *Finers v Miro*.[45] A third possibility is for the solicitor to seek negative declaratory relief against the claimant and apply for an interim declaration. The jurisdiction to grant an interim declaration is a new jurisdiction available to the court under CPR 25.1(1)(b).[46] It does not involve a final decision of the substantive rights of the parties. The court can however gives guidance under its advisory jurisdiction, as to what in its opinion ought to happen pending any determination of substantive rights. An interim declaration could be granted stating that on an interim basis it is the opinion of the court that the solicitor can use the money to fund the defence. If the court granted a declaration on an interim basis that in its opinion the solicitor can use certain funds, then this would be relevant to any attempt subsequently by the claimant to hold the solicitor liable as a constructive trustee. This is because the declaration would be relevant to whether the solicitor in subsequently using the funds was acting unconscionably or dishonestly. *United Mizrahi Bank Ltd v Doherty*[47] pre-dated the availability of an interim declaration and refused the solicitor final relief which would have given him complete immunity.

It is considered that there can be circumstances in which the due administration of justice, and fairness to the solicitor, requires that the court protect him from being under the constant pressure of a threatened action to be brought against him by the claimant depending on whether his proprietary claim succeeds. The procedure, should be simple and workable, and the court should reach an informed decision on whether the solicitor ought to act given the source of the funds and taking into account all the available evidence.

Whichever of the possible procedures is adopted the court would need **20.065** to consider (1) the strength of evidence for alleging that the solicitor would become liable as a constructive trustee; and (2) the matters relevant to deciding whether it is just to allow what may be the claimant's assets to be used to fund the defence, including the strength of the case for saying that the assets belonged to the claimant and the strength of the defendant's claim to the assets.

(12) Living expenses of the defendant

(i) *Mareva relief and living expenses*

Mareva relief granted against an individual defendant must always make **20.066** suitable provision for the defendant to pay his ordinary living expenses, unless there is reason to believe that he has other assets to which the

---

[45] [1991] 1 W.L.R. 35.
[46] See para.3.032 above.
[47] [1998] 1 W.L.R. 435.

injunction does not apply and which would be available for that purpose. This is so even in the context of relief granted or continued post-judgment.[48] The same principles apply to whether frozen funds are to be used to pay living expenses as apply to permitting payment out of frozen funds for legal costs incurred in the defence of the case (see above).

Ordinary living expenses have been described as "ordinary recurrent expenses involved in maintaining the subject of the injunction in the style of life to which he is reasonably accustomed. It does not include exceptional expenses like the purchase of a Rolls-Royce or the equivalent in legal terms of the private employment of Queen's Counsel to defend you against a serious criminal charge".[49] This is not intended to be a comprehensive definition and it is considered that, in deciding whether or not an intended payment is such an expense, all the surrounding circumstances concerning the payment and the lifestyle of the individual would fall to be taken into account.[50] Thus, *e.g.* a comparatively modest bill for private medical treatment might be unusual for the particular defendant, but in accordance with his usual lifestyle. The defendant is of course entitled to carry on maintaining his family as well as himself if this was his practice before the granting of the injunction.

20.067   The claimant must make provision for ordinary living expenses, where appropriate, in the draft order on the without notice application. If the figure provided for is not sufficient, the defendant can apply to the court to increase it.[51]

(ii) Proprietary claims and living expenses

20.068   If the relevant assets are subject to a proprietary claim by the claimant, the same principles apply to permitting living expenses as apply to allowing legal costs. The defendant has no right to spend the claimant's money. Where the claim is disputed and there is an argument that the funds do not belong to the claimant he has no absolute entitlement to an injunction, and it is a question of discretion whether or not the injunction will be varied and if so subject to what terms.[52] It may be unjust to prevent the defendant from maintaining his ordinary living standards out of assets which may in fact be his own. Thus, as a matter of discretion, the court may vary the injunction to allow the defendant to use the disputed assets, see *PCW (Underwriting Agencies) Ltd v Dixon*.[53] Nevertheless, the court will require

---

[48] *The Law Society v Shanks* [1988] F.L.R. 504; *Mayo Associates SA v Anagram (Bermuda) Ltd* [1995] J.L.R. 190 at 204; *Baptiste Builders Supply Ltd v F. W. Smith* [1995] J.L.R. Notes–16a.

[49] *TDK Tape Distributor (UK) Ltd v Videochoice Ltd* [1986] 1 W.L.R. 141 at 146, *per* Skinner J.

[50] See also para.12.037, above.

[51] *PCW (Underwriting) Agencies Ltd v Dixon* [1983] 2 Lloyd's Rep. 197; *House of Spring Gardens v Waite* [1984] F.S.R. 173 at 284.

[52] *Fitzgerald v Williams* [1996] Q.B. 657. *Investors and Pensions Advisory Service Ltd v Gray* (1989) 139 N.L.J. 1415 at 1416, *per* Morritt J.

[53] [1983] 2 Lloyd's Rep. 197 (Lloyd J.), and [1983] 2 All E.R. 697, CA.

the defendant to use first what are indisputably his own assets.[54] In the *PCW* case the injunction was varied by the Court of Appeal so as to provide that the defendant was first to draw against any funds which were indisputably his own. Then he could draw against funds which he reasonably believed to be free from any equitable interests, and next against any funds which he did not know to be subject to such an interest. To the extent that funds withdrawn were later held by the court or agreed to be subject to an equitable interest, the defendant was to replace the sums withdrawn out of his own funds. The Court of Appeal ordered that a schedule of assets should be prepared to assist in this task. In a tracing case, the court might well impose, as a term of a variation permitting the defendant to use disputed assets, a requirement that the defendant furnish an undertaking to bring into the jurisdiction assets presently located abroad. Once there has been judgment upholding a proprietary claim, the position is different.[55]

(13) Application by third party creditors for variations

A third party with notice of the Mareva injunction will have liberty to apply on notice to have the order set aside or varied, but it is usual to proceed by issuing an application notice in the proceedings. If the third party is a trade creditor whom the defendant wishes to pay, it is likely that the defendant will make the application for a variation himself, or at least lend his support to an application by the third party, providing evidence to satisfy the court that it is appropriate to grant a variation of the injunction. If the defendant is unsympathetic, the third party may find that, without the assistance of evidence from the defendant, and not being a judgment creditor, he has difficulty in satisfying the court that it is appropriate to vary the injunction. Even if he does succeed, the fact that the defendant has the liberty to make payment without breaching the injunction does not mean that he will do so. He will be in a strong position to obtain the variation if he can show that the debt relates specifically to the frozen assets and that, at the date of the injunction, he had an existing right to payment from that particular source: see generally: *A v B (X intervening)*;[56] *SSAB Oxelasund AB v Xendral Trading Ltd.*[57] The creditor should obtain a variation if he can show that it would be entirely usual for the debt to be paid from assets within the jurisdiction (*e.g.* the debt is an ordinary living expense of a defendant resident within the jurisdiction). **20.069**

---

[54] *Fitzgerald v Williams* [1996] Q.B. 657 at 669G–H.
[55] See Chapter 3, para.3.025, above.
[56] [1983] 2 Lloyd's Rep. 532.
[57] [1992] 1 S.L.R. 600 (Singapore) (agreement regulating distribution of proceeds of hull insurance).

(14) Application by a non-party judgment creditor for a variation

20.070   If a judgment is to be enforced against assets of the defendant which are subject to a Mareva injunction, then normally:

(1) such enforcement would simply be carrying out an order of the court; and

(2) the enforcement would not involve any dealing with the relevant assets by or on behalf of the defendant.

Thus the enforcement of the judgment would not normally involve any breach of the injunction as such by the person restrained[58] because it is not the defendant who is doing anything to produce diminution in the value of his assets. If there was to be any question of contempt it would have to be on the ground that the non-party was defeating the purpose of the injunction.[59]

In so far as any difficulty is encountered by the judgment creditor arising from the existence of the injunction, then it can be said that the court should vary the injunction as a matter of course, because the claimant should not be permitted to use the Mareva injunction so as to give his claim priority, or even to ensure that a reserve is made for his claim from the defendant's assets. As a matter of general principle, once a person has an enforceable judgment, he should be able to proceed to enforce it even though the effect of this may be to leave inadequate assets with the defendant to satisfy some other claim brought against him should that claim succeed.[60] Accordingly, there can be circumstances in which both A and B have claims against C. A obtains Mareva relief subject to a limit calculated by reference to his claim[61] but B obtains judgment first and exhausts the funds of C by enforcing his judgment.

In practice a third party creditor could obtain judgment by default or even simply by formal consent of the defendant. If obtaining a judgment enabled a third party to circumvent a Mareva injunction as a matter of course, this could be open to abuse. In particular, the defendant could incur liabilities, consent to judgment on those liabilities and then leave the third party free to enforce the judgment on assets within the jurisdiction; this could amount to a breach of the injunction. Alternatively, the defendant could simply allow judgment on a claim against him to go by default, and leave it to the third party to decide whether to seek to execute on assets within the jurisdiction.

---

[58] See further Chapter 3, paras 3.005–3.007.
[59] See Chapter 19 above.
[60] *Cox v Bankside Members Agency Ltd* [1995] 2 Lloyd's Rep. 437.
[61] *K/S A/S Admiral Shipping v Portlink Ferries Ltd* [1984] 2 Lloyd's Rep. 166 at 168.

If there was a collusive plan to use the process of the court to obtain a   **20.071**
judgment as a mechanism in order to release assets from the Mareva, this
would in itself constitute a serious abuse of process and a contempt of
court. In particular this would be so if there was a deliberate attempt to
frustrate the purpose of the Mareva injunction.[62] There can also be cases in
which the judgment creditor was acting in good faith but where enforcement of the judgment against the assets might be inconsistent with the
"purpose" of the injunction.

When the third party has obtained a judgment, the question arises as to
how he can enforce it. If the relevant asset of the defendant is a bank
account, the judgment creditor may seek to proceed by way of third party
debt procedure. However, it is a matter of discretion for the court whether
or not a third party debt order should be granted.[63] The court would
decline to grant a third party debt order if satisfied that the granting of the
order would result in the injunction being improperly circumvented;[64] it
would be inequitable for the order to be made absolute. The position
would be the same in relation to an application for a charging order.

There are circumstances in which the judgment creditor can execute the   **20.072**
judgment by way of writ of *fieri facias* without the leave of the court. If the
judgment creditor requires leave in order to execute, the court could grant
a stay of proceedings in the action in which judgment has been obtained.[65]
However, where the judgment creditor has the right to execute on assets as
of right and without some further order of the court, then, where on the
facts the proposed course would be an abuse of the process, the claimant
could still apply either for an injunction against the judgment creditor
executing, or for a stay of execution on the judgment. The claimant who
has obtained Mareva relief against the judgment debtor could support his
application for an injunction against the judgment creditor or a stay of
execution on the judgment by reference to the cause of action which he has
in his action against the judgment debtor.[66] The stay of execution would be
sought under the court's inherent jurisdiction to regulate its own procedures and prevent abuse of them.

In *Atlas Maritime SA v Avalon Ltd (No.3)*,[67] the Court of Appeal declined
to allow the defendant leave to pay its solicitors' fees out of an account
held in the name of the solicitors for the defendant. If the solicitors had
obtained a judgment for their fees against their clients, they could not have
drawn money to satisfy the judgment from the account without the leave

---

[62] See Chapter 19, paras 19.028–19.034, above.
[63] *Roberts Petroleum Ltd v Bernard Kenney Ltd* [1983] 2 A.C. 192.
[64] *Atlas Maritime SA v Avalon Ltd (No.3)* [1991] 1 W.L.R. 917 at 927 and 930 supports this
view.
[65] *Re Artistic Colour Printing Company* (1880) 14 Ch.D. 502; *Wright v Redgrave* (1879) 11
Ch.D. 24; *T. C. Trustees Ltd v J. S. Darwen (Successors)* [1969] 2 Q.B. 295 at 303;
Llewellyn v Carrickford [1970] 1 W.L.R. 1124; the stay would be under the jurisdiction
preserved by s.49(3) of the Supreme Court Act 1981.
[66] See Chapter 13, paras 13.005–13.013.
[67] [1991] 1 W.L.R. 917.

of the court, because the injunction prohibited any dealing with the account by the defendant or on its behalf. Execution would have been by way of charging order on the defendant's beneficial interest in the account or by way of appointing a receiver in aid of execution. Either way, the solicitors, on the facts of the case, could not enforce a judgment against the bank account held in their name for their clients without assistance from the court, and the court had a discretion whether to grant that assistance. If the case had come before the court on an application by the solicitors for a charging order, or for an appointment of a receiver by way of equitable execution, the court would have refused that application for the same reason as that for which it refused the application to vary the injunction to allow the solicitors to be paid their fees. The reason was that, on the facts, it would have been unjust to allow the only asset within the jurisdiction to be used to pay fees which would otherwise have been met by the parent company of the defendant. This was the position whether or not the solicitors went through the procedure of obtaining a judgment for their fees.

20.073   However, the question whether a defendant should be able to use frozen assets for the purpose of discharging legal fees is not the same as whether solicitors who have obtained judgment against him for their fees should be allowed to execute against those assets. In *Abdul-Haq Al-Ani v Shubber*[68] the defendant had not properly responded to a disclosure order, and therefore had not obtained permission to pay his solicitors from assets frozen by the injunction. Those solicitors ceased to act for him, obtained a judgment in default of defence against the defendant for their fees, and were granted a garnishee order and an order varying the injunction so as to permit them to execute. The solicitors were not at fault in relation to the failure to comply with the disclosure order, and there was no reason for the court to interfere with execution of the judgment.

In *Nathan v Orchard*,[69] the claimant had recovered a substantial costs order at the trial of the action against the client of the respondent solicitors, and the trial judge granted a new freezing order over funds which had been paid into court. The solicitors were owed substantial sums by way of fees for acting for their client. They obtained a judgment for their fees and sought a charging order over the funds frozen by the claimant. The claimant in the action subsequently obtained a default costs certificate, and disputed the solicitors' entitlement to a charging order. In that case, no bankruptcy proceedings were threatened, otherwise the matter ought to have been dealt with under the insolvency legislation. Therefore the court had a wide discretion to do what was just under s.1 of the Charging Orders Act 1979 in relation to the fund in court. Pitchers J. observed that the fact that the solicitors had obtained a money judgment against their client before the claimant had done so was the only point in

---

[68] [1999] EWCA Civ 1363 (May 10, 1999).
[69] [2004] EWHC 344 (Q.B.).

the solicitors' favour ". . . but it is not nothing." The judge exercised his discretion so as to apportion the fund in court between the claimant and the solicitors, but deciding that overall the claimant would have the greater share. There was an obvious justice in the claimant, who had substantially won the action against the solicitors' client, and had frozen the relevant fund, being accorded a greater share of that fund, than the solicitors, who had allowed their former client to run up a very large unsecured bill for fees in unsuccessfully defending the underlying proceedings.

To obtain a stay the claimant would need to show some legitimate interest which should be protected by the court: *European Asian Bank AG v Punjab & Sind Bank*.[70] If the claimant claims an interest in the relevant assets, then he would have a legitimate interest in preventing execution.

In the absence of a proprietary claim, if the conduct of the defendant and the third party would, on the facts, allow the Mareva injunction to be unfairly or improperly circumvented, the court could intervene by granting a stay so as to ensure that the Mareva relief was effective; it would be in support of the existing cause of action[71] and ancillary to the Mareva relief so as to ensure that the injunction was effective.

In cases where the defendant is seeking to transfer assets for the purpose **20.074** of defeating his creditors or prejudicing claimants, the claimant may be able to obtain relief preventing enforcement or execution of the judgment, or successfully resist such enforcement or execution by reference to ss.423, 424 and 425 of the Insolvency Act 1986.[72]

In the case of a proprietary claim, and an adverse judgment obtained by a third party judgment creditor against the defendant, the court will not take assets which may well belong to the claimant by way of enforcement or execution of the judgment. That would be to take one man's money to pay another man's debt.[73] In such circumstances, if the judgment creditor wished to enforce his judgment against the assets, the issue of the ownership of the assets as between the judgment creditor and the claimant would have to be tried. The injunction would ordinarily be maintained pending the determination of such an issue.[74]

(15) Variation of the injunction after the claimant has obtained judgment

Once the claimant becomes a judgment creditor, he will be in a much **20.075** stronger position to resist an application by the defendant or a third party for a variation of the injunction to enable the defendant to pay them. The

---

[70] [1982] 2 Lloyd's Rep. 356 at 369.
[71] See Chapter 13, para.13.005 above.
[72] See paras 13.018–13.028, above.
[73] *Harrods Ltd v Tester* (1937) 157 L.T. 7.
[74] *Northwest Airlines Inc. v Shouson Chen* [1989] H.K.L.R. 382 (Hong Kong).

court will take into account the claimant's status as a judgment creditor,[75] and the remedies which are or may be available to him through execution or enforcement of the judgment, or the commencement of bankruptcy or winding-up proceedings. If the claimant could petition to wind up the defendant company and intends to present a winding-up petition, then it would usually be appropriate to restrain the defendant company from disposing of its property except as sanctioned by the Companies Court under s.127 of the Insolvency Act 1986.[76] If the claimant intends to seek a third party debt order or the appointment of a receiver in aid of execution, the court ordinarily will refuse the variation pending the determination of that process.

If a default judgment has been obtained which the defendant intends to seek to set aside, the court may well grant a variation to the injunction pending the hearing of that application, even though such a variation would not have been permitted after final judgment had been obtained at trial or by way of proceedings for summary judgment. It is common for default judgments to be set aside, albeit sometimes, on terms, and the fact that the judgment is only a default judgment will be taken into account.[77] The court hearing the application for a variation is not obliged to deal in detail with the merits of the application to set aside the judgment, but is entitled to take into account the apparent merits or demerits. Often it would be entirely premature to treat such a defendant as being in substantially the same position as if judgment had been obtained after the merits of the claim had been determined.

20.076   In cases involving the enforcement of a foreign judgment by way of registration, CPR r.74.9(1) prohibits enforcement of the judgment until after the expiry of the period allowed to the defendant to make an application to set aside the registration, and if the application is to be made, then until after that application has been finally determined. There is a corresponding prohibition which applies in proceedings to enforce an arbitration award (CPR r.62.18(9)). If an application is made to vary Mareva relief pending the final determination by the High Court of an application to set aside registration of a judgment or foreign award, or an order giving leave to enforce an award in the same manner as a judgment or order, the court will take into account that the claimant has already achieved[78] the status of a judgment creditor. Once the High Court has finally determined the defendant's application then the mandatory stay of execution or enforcement under CPR ceases to have effect.

Even though the claimant has become a judgment creditor, the court will not grant or maintain an injunction over assets which will not or

---

[75] See Chapter 3, paras 3.023–3.027, above; *Soinco v Novokuznetsk Aluminium Plant* [1998] Q.B. 406; *Dillon v Baltic Shipping*, unreported, September 23, 1994, New South Wales Supreme Court (Carruthers J.).

[76] See paras 3.007, 6.002 and 6.065–6.068, above.

[77] *Baptiste Builders Supply Ltd v F. W. Smith* [1995] J.L.R. Notes–16a.

[78] *Deutsche Schachtbau-und Tiefbohrgesellschaft GmbH v R'as Al-Khaimah* [1990] 1 A.C. 295 at 317 (see the judgment of Sir John Donaldson M.R. in the Court of Appeal), and paras 3.024–3.027, above.

should not[79] be available to satisfy the judgment through execution, or through bankruptcy or winding-up proceedings. In *Prekookeanska Plovidba v LNT Lines*[80] the plaintiffs had obtained leave to enforce an arbitration award in the same manner as a judgment or order pursuant to what was then s.26 of the Arbitration Act 1950, and an injunction was granted *ex parte*, which restrained the defendants from dealing with their assets within the jurisdiction, including sums held by their solicitors on client account. Provision was made for the solicitors to be at liberty to exercise any right of set-off for bills already delivered to the defendants for past legal services. The solicitors concerned had funds in their client account over which they had a lien, and on the evidence the plaintiffs had no prospect of obtaining any part of those sums in satisfaction of the amounts due to them. The sums could not be attached by means of garnishee proceedings and the solicitors' rights would prevail over any claim by a liquidator. Accordingly, Hirst J. varied the injunction in relation to the funds held on client account so as to enable the solicitors to obtain payment. In *Deutsche Schachtbau-und Tiefbohrgesellschaft GmbH v R'as Al-Khaimah*,[81] the House of Lords declined to maintain in place an injunction in favour of judgment creditors when garnishee proceedings were dismissed, even though there remained the theoretical possibility of winding-up proceedings. In that case the reasons that made it inequitable to grant a garnishee order likewise made it inequitable to maintain the injunction. In *Camdex International Ltd v Bank of Zambia (No.2)*,[82] the injunction granted in aid of enforcement of a judgment was varied to enable the bank to deal with unissued bank notes which had been printed in England but which had no market value whatever. If the injunction had not been varied, there could have been great hardship to the public in Zambia.

There could be circumstances in which a judgment creditor has taken a **20.077** deliberate decision not to commence bankruptcy or winding-up proceedings and is permitting the judgment debtor to continue to trade in the hope of obtaining satisfaction of the judgment in due course. Here the court might decline to allow proceedings for a third party debt order to be taken against the defendant's solicitors' client account because it would be unfair to deprive the judgment debtor of the benefit of continuing legal advice and representation. The court would also ensure that any injunction granted in aid of execution did not prevent the solicitors paying themselves out of the client account.

---

[79] *Camdex International Ltd v Bank of Zambia (No.2)* [1997] 1 W.L.R. 632.
[80] [1989] 1 W.L.R. 753.
[81] [1990] 1 A.C. 295.
[82] [1997] 1 W.L.R. 632, see further Chapter 3, paras 3.025–3.027, above.

(16) Mareva relief and insolvent defendants

(i) The principles

20.078 If the defendant is a company which is in the process of liquidation, the liquidator will take over the conduct of all of the defendant's affairs, including the conduct of any litigation to which the company is a party. Once a liquidator or provisional liquidator has obtained control of the defendant's assets there will be no justification for continuing the Mareva relief.[83] If a winding-up petition has been presented, the company, or any creditor or contributory, may apply for a stay of court proceedings brought against the company (s.126 of the Insolvency Act 1986). In the event of a winding-up order being made or a provisional liquidator being appointed, no action or proceedings against the company can be commenced or continued without the leave of the court (Insolvency Act 1986, s.130). These provisions also apply in the case of winding-up proceedings against an unregistered company under Pt V of the Insolvency Act 1986 (s.221(1)), in which case they are extended so as to apply also to proceedings brought against a contributory of the company (ss.227 and 228). An unregistered foreign company which has been carrying on business in Great Britain and has ceased to do so may be wound up under Pt V of the 1986 Act notwithstanding that it has been dissolved or has otherwise ceased to exist under the laws of the place of incorporation (s.225).[84] If an action has been brought against a company which has ceased to exist under the laws of the place of its incorporation, any judgment obtained will be a nullity and no process of execution will be permitted.[85]

If bankruptcy proceedings against an individual are pending, or a bankruptcy adjudication has been made, the court may stay proceedings against that individual (s.285). In the event of control of an individual's property being obtained by an interim receiver appointed under s.286 of the Insolvency Act 1986 or by the trustee in bankruptcy, there will be no basis for continuing Mareva relief granted against the defendant, and ordinarily the action will be stayed.[86]

20.079 If the judgment debtor is a company which is the subject of a winding-up order, or an individual who has been adjudged bankrupt, a judgment creditor will not be able to execute or enforce his judgment against the assets of the judgment debtor, nor will the judgment creditor be entitled to retain the benefit of execution or attachment, unless the execution or attachment had been completed before the commencement of the winding-up or bankruptcy proceedings (ss.183 and 346). The claimant or judgment

---

[83] See Chapter 3, para.3.007.
[84] See further on winding up foreign companies, paras 6.065–6.008, above. Section 225 does not limit the jurisdiction to wind up foreign companies, including those which have ceased to exist.
[85] *Lazard Brothers v Midland Bank* [1933] A.C. 289 at 296–297.
[86] See also para.3.007, above.

creditor may, though, be able to justify the continuation of Mareva relief so as to preserve the assets for the benefit of all the creditors[87] in the bankruptcy or liquidation if the assets in question remain within the control of the defendant personally or others closely associated with him.

Under s.1 of the Third Parties (Rights Against Insurers) Act 1930, if there is insurance covering a liability, and the insured becomes bankrupt or makes an arrangement or composition with his creditors, or (in the case of a company) is the subject of a winding-up order, the rights against the insurer are transferred to and vest in the person to whom the insured is liable. The court could make a winding-up order even in respect of a foreign unregistered company which has no assets within the jurisdiction, where as a result of the order the petitioner will acquire rights under the Act. Thus in *Re Eloc Electro-Optiek and Communicate BV*,[88] a foreign company was ordered to be wound up when it had no assets or place of business within the jurisdiction, to enable the petitioning creditors to make an application to the Secretary of State for Employment for payment out of a redundancy fund established under statute, and there was a reasonable possibility of the petitioners obtaining payment out of the fund. A claimant may contemplate in due course being in a position, after obtaining judgment, to bring bankruptcy or winding-up proceedings with a view to obtaining rights under a contract of insurance pursuant to the Act. However, this in itself does not entitle the claimant to obtain an injunction preventing a defendant from settling with the insurers.[89]

(ii) Insolvent foreign company and the claimant has not obtained a judgment

In *Iraqi Ministry of Defence v Arcepey Shipping Co. SA (The Angel Bell)*,[90] **20.080** Robert Goff J. considered that the Mareva jurisdiction was not intended to rewrite the laws of insolvency by giving the plaintiffs, who had not yet obtained a judgment, the right to block payments or require distribution of assets *pari passu*. In that case the plaintiff cargo interests had a claim for US$ 3 million for loss of their cargo when the vessel sank and its insurance proceeds amounted to £240,000 of which the intervening mortgagees sought payment to them of £200,000 when the validity of their security arrangements was contested. The cargo interests had *locus standi* to petition for winding up of the company[91] and might possibly have done so on the "just and equitable" ground or on the ground of alleged insolvency, even though they only had a good arguable case and not a judgment in their favour. The "rule" of insolvency was a rule of practice in winding-up

---

[87] See para.3.007, above.
[88] [1982] Ch. 43.
[89] See paras 3.017–3.019, above.
[90] [1981] Q.B. 65.
[91] *Re a Company* [1973] 1 W.L.R. 1566 at 1571; see the discussion of *The Siskina* [1979] A.C. 210 in Chapter 6, paras 6.001–6.002, above.

proceedings, which had to give way in circumstances where otherwise justice would not be done to alleged creditors of a foreign company, who would otherwise be left with no effective remedy.[92]

(17) Substantial interference with business or other rights of third parties

20.081   The court will protect third parties against exposure to unacceptable interference by an injunction with their business or other activities. It may be possible to do this by modifying the injunction.[93] In *Galaxia Maritime SA v Mineralimportexport*,[94] an injunction had been obtained restraining the defendant cargo owners from removing cargo out of the jurisdiction. The shipowners had been given notice of the injunction and faced possible contempt proceedings if they allowed the vessel to sail.[95] The vessel was on voyage charter to the defendants, and therefore prima facie the shipowners would not be paid extra money by the defendants for the delay. The plaintiffs had given an undertaking to the court to pay the reasonable costs of third parties, such as the shipowners, in complying with the order. The shipowners applied to the judge to discharge the injunction, but he ordered the injunction to be maintained on terms that the plaintiffs provided a first class bank guarantee against the shipowners' loss and expense. However, on appeal the injunction was discharged on the grounds that it constituted too great an interference with the freedom of action of third parties, and the plaintiff had no entitlement or justification to effect a "compulsory purchase" by means of the guarantee.[96] It was also unfair to the crew to require the vessel to be detained subject to the injunction, because it interfered with their personal arrangements. Even if the vessel had been on time charter, so that the defendants had to pay hire during the delay, this would not have materially altered the position. In substance it would merely have affected who had the responsibility to pay the shipowners for the period of the detention, but it would not have lessened the degree of interference with the shipowners' freedom of action or with the crew. Even if a defendant is poised to provide security, an injunction may still be

---

[92] *Re Russian and English Bank* [1932] 1 Ch. 663 at 670 (a foreign company, where the alleged creditor would otherwise be without remedy, and an immediate winding-up order was made leaving the validity of the debt to be dealt with by the liquidator); the authorities after the decision in *Iraqi Ministry of Defence v Arcepey Shipping Co. SA (The Angel Bell)* are: *Re Claybridge Shipping Co. SA* [1981] Com. L.R. 107, Court of Appeal (Civ Div) Transcript No.143 of 1981 (March 9, 1981) now reported at [1997] 1 B.C.L.C. 572; *Alipour v Ary* [1997] 1 W.L.R. 534 at 546A–B.
[93] See also Chapter 2, para.2.042.
[94] [1982] 1 W.L.R. 539.
[95] See Chapter 19, para.19.032 above, and *Attorney-General v Newspaper Publishing plc* [1988] Ch. 333 at 367 and 380.
[96] [1982] 1 W.L.R. 539 at 541, *per* Eveleigh L.J.

discharged.[97] This principle has also resulted in the refusal of Mareva relief in respect of bunkers on board a trading vessel, being bunkers alleged to belong to the defendant charterers of the vessel.[98]

In *Clipper Maritime v Mineralimportexport*,[99] an injunction was granted *ex parte* over cargo and bunkers belonging to the defendants, who were the time charterers of the vessel, which prevented removal of these assets from the jurisdiction. The shipowners in that case did not apparently appear before the court to object to the injunction. This may have been because the vessel was on time charter to the defendants who were presumably still liable for the time charter hire notwithstanding the existence of the injunction.

---

[97] *Zephros Maritime v Mineralimportexport* (1981) 133 N.L.J. 234.
[98] *Unicom Shipping Ltd v Demet Navy Shipping Co. Ltd* [1987] F.T.L.R. 109; *Gilfoyle Shipping v Binosi Pty* [1984] N.Z.L.R. 742.
[99] [1981] 1 W.L.R. 1262.

Chapter 21

The writ *ne exeat regno* and s.6 of the Debtors Act 1869

(1) Introduction

The historical origins of the writ *ne exeat regno* are to be found in the **21.001** exercise by the Crown of its prerogative power to prevent individuals from leaving the realm. It was used from the 13th century by the Crown for "great political objects and purposes of state, for the safety and benefit of the realm".[1] The writ came to be used in cases between individuals. This development started during the reign of Elizabeth I and had become "well established by the reign of James I".[2] In 1820, Lord Eldon L.C. observed:[3]

> "This writ was originally issued in attempts against the safety of the state . . . How it happened that this great prerogative writ, intended by the laws for great political purposes and the safety of the country, came to be applied between subject and subject, I cannot conjecture. Where Courts in this side of the Hall[4] have held debtors to bail by analogy, though it is a very imperfect one, to what is done on the other side, they have said they could give this equitable bail in equitable cases; but they did not grant it where you can arrest at law, except in this particular case,[5] in which being matter of account, they have concurrent jurisdiction."

As a result of dissatisfaction with the process whereby claimants could have defendants imprisoned before obtaining judgment, the Debtors Act 1869 was enacted. It abolished the power of arrest, with certain limited exceptions, one of which was contained in s.6 of the Act.[6] This section as amended is still in force and provides:

---

[1] Story's *Commentaries on Equity Jurisprudence* (3rd English ed.) pp 620–624. See also generally *A Brief View of the Writ Ne Exeat Regno* (1812) by Beames.

[2] *Felton v Callis* [1969] 1 Q.B. 200 at 205; *Ne Exeat Regno* Toth 136.

[3] *Flack v Holm* (1820) 1 Jac. & W. 405 at p 414.

[4] *i.e.* in the High Court of Chancery.

[5] There came to be two recognised exceptions to the general rule that the writ was only available in respect of equitable debts and claims, namely a claim on an account where the debtor admitted some but not all of the claim, and a claim for alimony: *Felton v Callis* [1969] 2 Q.B. 200 at 215, *per* Megarry J.

[6] Subsequently this was amended by s.1 of and Sch.1 to the Statute Law Revision (No.2) Act 1893.

"Where the plaintiff in any action . . . in which . . . the defendant would have been liable to arrest, proves at any time before final judgment by evidence on oath, to the satisfaction of a judge . . . that the plaintiff has good cause of action against the defendant to the amount of £50 or upwards, and that there is probable cause for believing that the defendant is about to quit England unless he is apprehended, and that the absence of the defendant from England will materially prejudice the plaintiff in the prosecution of his action, such judge may . . . order such defendant to be arrested."

21.002   Since the Court of Chancery, in exercising the jurisdiction to issue the writ of *ne exeat regno*, acted by analogy with the procedure for arrest available at common law, a consequence of the enactment of the Debtors Act 1869 was that the courts, by analogy with the statutory provisions, limited the circumstances in which the writ of *ne exeat regno* could be issued.[7]

(2) Debtors Act 1869, s.6

21.003   This section enables an order to be made against a defendant requiring his arrest at "any time before final judgment", when the absence of the defendant would "materially prejudice the plaintiff in the prosecution of his action". Thus in *Yorkshire Engine Co. v Wright*,[8] the Court of Appeal held that once final judgment had been obtained against the defendant, the section did not apply, and security which had been obtained from the defendant in return for his release from arrest under the section had to be returned to him. This is because the purpose of the section was to ensure the presence of the defendant so that the judgment could be obtained. At that stage the section ceased to apply. If the defendant had been under arrest under s.6, then once final judgment had been obtained he would have been entitled to be released, because "the prosecution of the action" within the meaning of the section ended with final judgment.[9] At that stage, s.4 of the 1869 Act, which prohibits arrest or imprisonment, would have been applicable. Section 6 does not apply post-judgment, nor may its power of arrest be invoked for the purpose of assisting a claimant in connection with the contemplated enforcement of a possible future judgment.

Section 6 is also limited by the requirements that:

(1) the claim must be one which, prior to the enactment of the statute, would have rendered the defendant liable to arrest in an action

---

[7] *Drover v Beyer* (1879) 13 Ch.D. 242 at 243, *per* Sir George Jessel M.R.; *Felton v Callis* [1969] 2 Q.B. 200 at 208–210.
[8] (1872) 21 W.R. 15. See also *Felton v Callis* [1969] 1 Q.B. 200 at 212–213.
[9] *Hume v Druyff* (1873) L.R. 8 Exch. 214.

brought in one of the "superior courts of law" (*e.g.* a claim for debt);

(2) the plaintiff has clearly to show a strong claim for at least £50;

(3) the evidence shows "probable cause" for believing that the defendant is about to leave the country;

(4) the plaintiff has an existing cause of action;[10]

(5) as a matter of discretion it is appropriate to make the order.[11]

(3) The writ of *ne exeat regno*

The Debtors Act 1869 severely restricted the jurisdiction of the common **21.004** law courts to order the arrest of a defendant on *mesne* process (*i.e.* in proceedings prior to judgment). Since the courts of equity proceeded by analogy with the common law courts in relation to arrest, the process of *ne exeat regno* could be no wider. Following the passing of the Judicature Acts, common law and equity were administered by the same courts, and the consequence of allowing the writ to issue in circumstances outside the ambit of s.6 would have been to restore the availability of arrest as *mesne* process to what it had been prior to the Debtors Act 1869. In *Drover v Beyer*,[12] Sir George Jessel M.R. held that the availability of the writ of *ne exeat regno* was limited by analogy with s.6 of the Act. In the Court of Appeal it was held that since the claim in question was for a debt due under the mortgage of a ship, it was not an equitable claim but a claim which, prior to the Judicature Acts, would have been dealt with in the common law courts. Accordingly, the case was directly governed by s.6, and the Court of Appeal did not address the question whether by analogy the availability of the writ of *ne exeat regno* was also limited by the requirements of the section. Nevertheless, it subsequently became clear that this was the case.[13]

Prior to 1985, the last successful application for the writ had been in 1893 and subsequently there have been only four applications.[14] In *Yiu Wing Construction Company (Overseas) v Ghosh*,[15] Anthony Evans J. declined to allow the writ to be issued in the circumstances of that case but observed, in the course of a judgment given in chambers, that the writ

---

[10] *Colverson v Bloomfield* (1885) 29 Ch.D. 341 at 342.
[11] *Hasluck v Lehman (1890)* 6 T.L.R. 376; *Felton v Callis* [1969] 1 Q.B. 200 at 211.
[12] (1879) 18 Ch.D. 242.
[13] *Colverson v Bloomfield* (1885) 29 Ch.D. 341; *Felton v Callis* [1969] 1 Q.B. 200 at 208–210; *Allied Bank v Hajjar* [1988] Q.B. 787 at 792.
[14] L.J. Anderson, "Antiquity in Action–Ne Exeat Regno Revived" (1987) 103 L.Q.R. 246 at 249.
[15] February 21, 1985 in Chambers, referred to in *Al Nahkel Trading Ltd v Lowe* [1986] Q.B. 235 at 238–239.

could be issued for the purpose of ensuring that the defendant did not leave the jurisdiction so as to defeat the effect of a Mareva injunction.

21.005   In *Al Nahkel Trading Ltd v Lowe*,[16] an *ex parte* application was made for the issue of the writ against a former employee of the plaintiff. The defendant was suspected by his employers of corruption. He had left Saudi Arabia, where he had been employed, having first travelled to Mecca and collected from third parties considerable sums of money owed to his employers. He had also managed "by an admitted ruse" to recover his passport, which had been held by his employers. At London airport he was met by representatives of the plaintiffs and the police. He surrendered certain cheques which were payable to his employers, but declined to hand over the large sums of cash which he held. The view was apparently taken that the police could not intervene in the matter because the alleged thefts had taken place in Saudi Arabia. The defendant intended to leave the jurisdiction the next day for Manila.

In these circumstances Tudor Price J. granted the application for a writ of *ne exeat regno* and gave his reasons in open court. In *Felton v Callis*,[17] Megarry J. had set out four requirements before an order could be made for the arrest of a defendant pursuant to s.6 of the Debtors Act 1869 as follows:

(1)   the action is one in which the defendant, prior to the coming into force of the 1869 Act, would have been liable to arrest at law;

(2)   a good cause of action for at least £50 is established;

(3)   there is "probable cause" for believing that the defendant is "about to quit England" unless he is arrested; and

(4)   "the absence of the defendant will materially prejudice the plaintiff in the prosecution of the action".

21.006   These were cited by Tudor Price J., and it appears that he considered that these requirements were met in the case before him. The decision has been the subject of criticism.[18] The purpose for which the writ was issued was said to be in aid of Mareva relief, namely to preserve the cash assets held by the defendant. However, this purpose does not satisfy the statutory requirement that the plaintiff must prove "that the absence of the defendant from England will materially prejudice the plaintiff in the prosecution of his action". A clear distinction has been drawn between, on the one hand, prosecuting the action up to final judgment and, on the other hand, the execution of that judgment. It is to enable a claimant to obtain final judgment[19] that arrest can be justified under s.6 of the Act, or in the

---

[16] [1986] Q.B. 235 at 238–239.
[17] [1969] 1 Q.B. 200 at 211.
[18] See the analysis by L.J. Anderson in (1987) 103 L.Q.R. 246 at 257–259.
[19] *Felton v Callis* [1969] 1 Q.B. 200 at 212–214; *Hume v Druyff* (1873) L.R. 8 Exch. 214; *Lipkin Gorman v Cass, The Times*, May 29, 1985; *Allied Bank v Hajjar* [1988] Q.B. 787 at 793.

case of equitable claims[20] or a claim on an account[21] which has been partially but not wholly admitted, that the writ *ne exeat regno* can be issued. The remedies are not available on the ground that the absence of the defendant "may be very embarrassing to the plaintiff in regard to obtaining the fruit of his action".[22] The same criticism is to be made of the decision of Wood J. in *Thaha v Thaha*,[23] when he granted an *ex parte* application to issue the writ in aid of enforcement of a periodic payments order. However, in *Allied Arab Bank v Hajjar*,[24] in a judgment given after a hearing *inter partes*, Leggatt J. held that an *ex parte* order for the writ should be discharged, and directed an inquiry as to damages on the undertaking given by the plaintiff on the *ex parte* application, when the purpose for which the writ had been sought was to enforce Mareva relief and an order for disclosure of information concerning assets. Such a purpose did not fall within s.6 of the Debtors Act 1869 because it was not for advancing "the *prosecution* of the action" as required by the section. This decision is in accordance with the principles laid down in the case law. In an appropriate case this requirement would not preclude the granting of the writ as part of an order which included Anton Piller relief, directed to obtaining discovery of documents or information, designed to assist the claimant in respect of proving his claim and obtaining the appropriate final relief in the action.

The Mareva injunction has now evolved its own ancillary remedy to prevent a defendant from leaving the jurisdiction, based on s.37(1) of the Supreme Court Act 1981.[25] This ancillary remedy is not a free-standing mode of enforcement of an order for payment of money. So it is not available simply as a means of putting pressure on a judgment debtor to pay a money judgment.[26] That would be inconsistent with statutory provisions which, subject to certain exceptions, abolished imprisonment for debt. But an order can be made under s.37 of the Supreme Court Act 1981 in aid of other orders of the court, such as orders requiring the defendant to give information about his assets or to attend court for cross-examination about his assets, and an order can be made in anticipation that such an order may be made at a hearing which is about to take place.[27]

---

[20] *Glover v Walters* (1950) 80 C.L.R. 172 at 173, *per* Dixon J.; *Felton v Callis* [1969] 1 Q.B. 200 at 215–216, *per* Megarry J.; *Drover v Beyer* (1879) 13 Ch.D. 242; 28 W.R. 89 at 110, *per* James L.J.; *Allied Arab Bank v Hajjar* [1988] Q.B. 787 at 794, *per* Leggatt J.

[21] This, historically, was a claim which could be dealt with by the High Court of Chancery or in the common law courts and is therefore referred to as falling within the "concurrent jurisdiction" of equity and common law: [1969] 1 Q.B. 200 at 216.

[22] *Felton v Callis* [1969] 1 Q.B. 200 at 214 citing from the report of the judgment of James L.J. in *Drover v Beyer* at 49 L.J. Ch. 37 at 38.

[23] [1987] 2 F.L.R. 142. The text of the writ issued in that case is set out at pp. 144–145 of the report.

[24] [1988] Q.B. 787.

[25] See Chapter 22, para.22.059, below; *Bayer AG v Winter* [1986] 1 W.L.R. 497; *Re Oriental Credit Ltd* [1988] Ch. 204, explained in *Morris v Mujani* [1996] 1 W.L.R. 848 at 853; *B v B (Injunction: Jurisdiction)* [1998] 1 W.L.R. 329.

[26] *B v B (Injunction: Jurisdiction)* [1998] 1 W.L.R. 329.

[27] *Re S (Financial Provision: Non Resident)* [1996] 1 F.C.R. 148.

21.007   When the justification for such an order is derived from s.37 of the Supreme Court Act 1981, the order can only be made when the claimant has an existing cause of action and the injunction is being granted in support of that cause of action and in aid of an order made or which may soon be made in proceedings based on that cause of action.[28] The injunction restraining the defendant from leaving the jurisdiction can only be justified if and in so far as its purpose is to back up enforcement of an existing order or an order which may be about to be made and the circumstances make it appropriate to make an order restricting individual liberty for this purpose; the order can only be made when it is reasonably proportionate to make it for this purpose. It can also be that there is jurisdiction to make such an ancillary order under the inherent jurisdiction of the court to ensure that there is not what would amount to an abuse of its process.[29]

Claims have been made that the court has an "inherent jurisdiction" to make orders, including orders interfering with the liberty of an individual for the purpose of making its own orders effective; but these claims have been justifiably criticised,[30] and are too wide. There is no "inherent jurisdiction" to detain people or restrict their liberty because the court considers that it would be in the interests of justice.

21.008   In *Re B (Child Abduction)*[31] children had been made wards of court and an order had been made in the wardship proceedings for the father to return the children to the jurisdiction and to give them into the care of the mother. The father had been served with the order but before he had had any opportunity to comply with it he was arrested and kept in custody in a police cell under a bench warrant. The father was not in contempt of court. The judge made an order that the father be detained by the tipstaff until the children were taken to the relevant British Embassy. In wardship proceedings the court has a power to order the arrest of a person so that he can be brought before the court and to order detention of a person in aid of carrying out the court's orders. But even in wardship proceedings the court has no jurisdiction to detain someone simply for the purpose of bringing pressure on a third party (in that case the grandparents abroad) to do something which the court considers ought to be done.

As for the writ of *ne exeat regno*, its availability is defined by the case law,[32] and the restrictions imposed by s.6 of the Debtors Act 1869 apply by analogy. It appears to be available only:

---

[28] *Morris v Murjani* [1996] 1 W.L.R. 848 at 852–853, disapproving of dicta in *Re Oriental Credit* [1988] Ch. 204.

[29] *B v B (Injunction: Jurisdiction)* [1998] 1 W.L.R. 329 at 333; in *Cardile v LED Builders Pty Ltd* (1999) 198 C.L.R. 381 this reasoning as was used to justify Mareva relief in Australia based on the inherent jurisdiction of the court.

[30] M. Dockray, "The Inherent Jurisdiction to Regulate Civil Proceedings" (1997) 113 L.Q.R. 120 at 128–129. See also *B v B (Injunction: Jurisdiction)* [1998] 1 W.L.R. 329, explaining *Re S (Financial Provision: Non Resident)* [1996] 1 F.C.R. 148.

[31] [1994] 2 F.L.R. 479, followed in *B v B (Injunction: Jurisdiction)* [1998] 1 W.L.R. 329.

[32] In *Bayer AG v Winter* [1986] 1 W.L.R. 497 at 501, the plaintiffs accepted that the case was not one in which a writ of *ne exeat regno* could be granted, but nevertheless were granted an injunction restraining the first defendant from leaving the jurisdiction and an order requiring him to deliver up his passports to the person serving the order upon him.

(1) when there is an equitable claim or demand, or a demand in respect of a partially admitted account;[33]

(2) the claim or demand is presently payable,[34] and is not merely a claim or demand in respect of a sum to become due in the future;

(3) a good cause of action for at least £50 is clearly established;

(4) there is probable cause for believing that the defendant is about to leave the jurisdiction;

(5) the absence of the defendant will materially prejudice the claimant in the *prosecution* of the action. Prejudice in relation to obtaining the fruits of a possible future judgment does not qualify under this requirement;

(6) the application is made before judgment. The defendant must be released after judgment is obtained;

(7) as a matter of discretion it is appropriate to issue the writ.

The Final Report of the Committee on Supreme Court Practice and **21.009** Procedure[35] considered the writ[36] and observed that the writ is "useless in its present application". The availability of the writ is limited in the respects set out above, by virtue of the case law, and should not be extended.[37] Thus:

(1) ss.4 and 6 of the Debtors Act 1869 are still in force, and were enacted in pursuance of a deliberate policy to restrict judicial powers of arrest;

(2) the Insolvency Act 1986 contains specific powers of arrest in relation to certain cases in which a person is threatening to abscond.[38] The powers of arrest in the context of civil litigation are pre-eminently a matter to be dealt with by statute, and indeed restricted powers are conferred on the courts by the 1986 Act;

(3) the courts have evolved a separate jurisdiction in aid of Mareva relief for preventing a defendant from leaving the jurisdiction, based on s.37(1) of the Supreme Court Act 1981 by the granting of an injunction.

---

[33] In *Felton v Callis*, Megarry J. doubted when a claim in the nature of *quia timet* proceedings was sufficient.
[34] *Colverson v Bloomfield* (1885) 29 Ch.D. 341.
[35] 1953, Cmd. 8878.
[36] At paras 455 and 456. See also [1969] 1 Q.B. 200 at 213–214.
[37] *Ali v Naseem, The Times*, October 3, 2003.
[38] Section 158 (power to arrest absconding contributory) and s.364 (power of arrest of a debtor to whom a bankruptcy petition relates, an undischarged bankrupt or a discharged bankrupt whose estate is still being administered under the Act).

(4) Procedure

21.010 The application is made on a without notice application, with evidence by affidavit or witness statement.[39] The claimant is required to provide an undertaking in damages. A form of order is set out in Daniell's *Chancery Forms*[40] and this was modified in *Al Nahkel Trading Ltd v Lowe* so that:

> (1) the writ is addressed to the tipstaff and not to the sheriff;
>
> (2) the writ requires the tipstaff to bring the defendant before the judge forthwith or as soon as possible, so that he can make the appropriate order.

The order made in *Thaha v Thaha*[41] is set out in full in the report and follows the modified form adopted in *Al Nahkel Trading Ltd v Lowe*. The writ is marked with a specified sum which the defendant may pay in order to avoid arrest pursuant to the order.

---

[39] The requirement in para.3.1 of the Practice Direction-Interim Injunctions supplementing CPR Pt 25 for evidence by affidavit applies to an application for a freezing injunction or a search order.

[40] 7th ed., 1932, at pp. 756–758.

[41] [1987] 2 F.L.R. 142 at 144–145.

Chapter 22

Disclosure orders, *Norwich Pharmacal* relief and orders ancillary to injunctions

(1) Introduction

With the emergence of the Mareva jurisdiction the courts have found **22.001** justification in s.37(1) of the Supreme Court Act 1981, not merely for granting Mareva relief itself, but also for granting other relief ancillary to an injunction to ensure that it is effective.[1] This ancillary jurisdiction under s.37(1) includes power to make orders:

(1) requiring the defendant to give disclosure of documents[2] or provide information about his assets,[3] wherever situated;[4]

(2) requiring the defendant not to leave the jurisdiction and to deliver up his passport;[5]

(3) requiring the defendant to attend court for immediate cross-examination about his assets;[6]

(4) requiring the defendant to deliver up forthwith certain of his assets into the custody of the claimant's solicitors;[7]

---

[1] *A. J. Bekhor v Bilton* [1981] Q.B. 923.
[2] This can be ordered under s.37(1) of the Supreme Court Act 1981, or, in the case of disclosure by a party, under CPR r.31.12 (specific disclosure of documents or classes of documents).
[3] *Maclaine Watson & Co. Ltd v International Tin Council (No.2)* [1989] Ch. 286; *A v C* [1981] Q.B. 956; *Bekhor Ltd v Bilton* [1981] Q.B. 923; *CBS United Kingdom Ltd v Lambert* [1983] Ch. 37 at 42–43.
[4] *Babanaft International Co. SA v Bassatne* [1990] Ch. 13; *Republic of Haiti v Duvalier* [1990] 1 Q.B. 202; *Derby & Co. Ltd v Weldon (No.1)* [1990] Ch. 48.
[5] *Bayer AG v Winter* [1986] 1 W.L.R. 497; *Morris v Murjani* [1996] 1 W.L.R. 848 and *Re Oriental Credit* [1988] Ch. 204 (relief granted in aid of an order made for the private examination of a person in connection with the affairs of a company in liquidation).
[6] *House of Spring Gardens Ltd v Waite* [1985] F.S.R. 173; *Bayer AG v Winter (No.2)* [1986] 1 W.L.R. 540.
[7] *CBS United Kingdom Ltd v Lambert* [1983] Ch. 37; *Johnson v L. & A. Philatelics Ltd* [1981] F.S.R. 286.

(5) requiring the defendant to sign a document directing his bank to disclose information to the claimant.[8] If the defendant fails to comply with the order, the court could nominate a person to sign the necessary document in the name of the defendant pursuant to s.39 of the Supreme Court Act 1981. The bank would then be bound to treat the document for all purposes as if it had been signed by the defendant;[9]

(6) by way of Anton Piller relief in aid of the injunction.[10]

These orders can be made as mandatory injunctions[11] granted under s.37(1) of the Supreme Court Act 1981, and, if so, the order can be "freestanding" in the sense that there need be no injunction in place to which the order is ancillary. In *Bayer AG v Winter* (above), Fox L.J. said in relation to s.37(1):

> "Bearing in mind we are exercising a jurisdiction which is statutory, and which is expressed in terms of considerable width, it seems to me that the court should not shrink, if it is of opinion that an injunction is necessary for the proper protection of a party to the action, from granting relief, notwithstanding it may, in its terms, be of a novel character."

22.002   Thus a free-standing disclosure order can be made purely for the purpose of enabling a judgment or award to be enforced.[12] In the case of worldwide Mareva relief, the intention is that the Mareva relief holds the position pending orders being made by foreign courts. The disclosure order enables the claimant to obtain information which can be used so as to apply for relief preserving assets in the foreign jurisdiction. In such a case the Mareva relief could be described as ancillary to the disclosure order[13] because it is the disclosure order which will be of the greater importance to the claimant.

CPR r.25.1(g) provides an interim remedy, which is:

---

[8] *Bank of Crete v Koskotas* [1991] 2 Lloyd's Rep. 587 at 589; *Bayer AG v Winter (No.3)* reported *sub nom Bayer AG v Winter (No.2)* [1986] F.S.R. 357 at 365. Hoffmann J's view that disclosure orders should not be limited to assets within the jurisdiction was rejected in *Ashtiani v Kashi* [1987] Q.B. 888 at 898, but was approved by Kerr L.J. in *Babanaft Co. SA v Bassatne*, above.

[9] *Astro Exito Navegacion SA v Chase Manhattan Bank* [1983] 2 A.C. 787 at 802.

[10] *Distributori Automatici Italia SpA v Holford General Trading Co. Ltd* [1985] 1 W.L.R. 1066; *Emanuel v Emanuel* [1982] 1 W.L.R. 669; *CBS United Kingdom Ltd v Lambert* [1983] Ch. 37.

[11] *Maclaine Watson & Co. v International Tin Council (No.2)* [1989] Ch. 286 at 303; *Gidrxslme Shipping Co. Ltd v Tantomar Transportes Maritimos Lda (The Naftilos)* [1995] 1 W.L.R. 299 at 309.

[12] *Gidrxslme Shipping Co. Ltd v Tantomar Transportes Maritimos Lda* [1995] 1 W.L.R. 299.

[13] *Grupo Torras v Sheik Al-Sabah*, Court of Appeal (Civ Div) Transcript No.159 of 1994 (February 16, 1994), *per* Steyn L.J. referring to L. Collins, "The Territorial Reach of Mareva Injunctions" (1989) 105 L.Q.R. 262.

"an order directing a party to provide information about the location of relevant property or assets or to provide information about relevant property or assets which are or may be the subject of an application for a freezing injunction".

The words "relevant property" are defined by CPR r.25.1(2) as "property (including land) which is the subject of a claim or as to which any question may arise on a claim". However, the words "or assets" extend the ambit of the rule to cover assets which are or may be the subject of a freezing injunction which grants Mareva relief.

In *Field v Field*[14] the judge considered that s.37 could only be used in aid of the court's established procedures for enforcement of a judgment and not as "a free-standing procedure in its own right". An injunction granted under s.37 is itself a remedy. The content of injunctions is infinite; they can be shaped according to the justice of the case whether as a negative order preserving assets, or as a mandatory one such as an order requiring disclosure of their existence, or active steps to be taken to realise them or otherwise make them available so that an order of the court can be satisfied. This decision is discussed in Chapter 16, paras 16.014–16.018 and for the reasons given there it is considered that the case was wrongly decided.

(2) Ancillary orders in aid of a freezing injunction to obtain disclosure of documents or information by a defendant concerning his assets

(i) *The legitimate purposes of the order*

An order can be made if the purpose is to identify and preserve assets of 22.003 the defendant which might otherwise be dissipated notwithstanding the injunction.[15] This will include obtaining the information so that notice of the injunction can be given to third parties who will then become bound not to commit a contempt of court (see Chapter 19), or so that an order can be obtained from a foreign court freezing the assets there, or so that, if necessary, an order can be made for delivery-up of specified assets.

Other reasons for needing a disclosure order were given by Robert Goff J. in *A v C*:[16]

---

[14] [2003] 1 F.L.R. 376.

[15] *House of Spring Gardens v Waite* [1985] F.S.R. 173 at 181 and 183; *Yau Chiu Wah v Gold Chief Investment Ltd* [2002] 2 H.K.L.R.D. 832.

[16] [1981] Q.B. 956 at 959. In *Petromar Energy Resources Pte Ltd v Glencore AG* [1999] 2 S.L.R. 609 the disclosure order was held to be too wide because it was not confined to identifying existing assets (*e.g.* it enabled investigation of past movements on a bank account); see also *Wallace Kevin James v Merrill Lynch International Bank Ltd* [1998] 1 S.L.R. 785 at para.34 (for the same reason the order was too wide because it required the defendant to consent in writing to a bank providing any information).

"The defendant may have more than one asset within the jurisdiction—for example, he may have a number of bank accounts. The plaintiff does not know how much, if anything, is in any of them; nor does each of the defendant's bankers know what is in the other accounts. Without information about the state of each account it is difficult, if not impossible, to operate the Mareva injunction properly: for example, if each banker prevents any drawing from his account to the limit of the sum claimed, the defendant will be treated oppressively, and the plaintiff may be held liable on his undertaking in damages. Again, there may be a single claim against a number of defendants; in that event the same difficulties may arise. Furthermore, the very generality of the order creates difficulties for the defendant's bankers, who may for example be unaware of the existence of other assets of the defendant within the jurisdiction; indeed, if a more specific order is possible, it may give much-needed protection for the defendant's bankers, who are after all simply the innocent holders of one form of the defendant's assets."

22.004   In *Parker v CS Structured Credit Fund Ltd*[17] the claimant sought an order for disclosure in relation to a transaction or proposed transaction which he asserted on evidence which did not detail its sources, was to be carried out at an undervalue. The application was made under CPR r.25.1(g) and it was argued that under the rule an order could be made otherwise than as part of an application for a freezing injunction or in order to make the injunction effective or assist in the formulation of its terms or a decision about them. Reliance was placed on the words in that rule "relevant property or assets which . . . may be the subject of an application for a freezing injunction" and it was suggested that the order could be granted with a view to providing the applicant with information which might lead to an application being made for a freezing injunction. This proposition was rejected because the intended use was too remote; it involved "fishing" for material which might justify an application for freezing relief. The position was the same under s.37(1); the claimant did not have a judgment so the jurisdiction to act in aid of the enforcement of a judgment by making a disclosure order[18] did not arise.

Normally a disclosure order is made as part of an order granting or continuing freezing relief, but there are also situations in which the court makes such an order to obtain information which will enable it to decide whether to continue freezing relief, and if so on what terms.[19] For example, there may be some evidence that the defendant had assets within the jurisdiction at some time in the past, but it is uncertain whether those

[17] [2003] 1 W.L.R. 1680.
[18] *Maclaine Watson & Co. v International Tin Council (No.2)* [1989] Ch. 286 at 303; *Gidrxslme Shipping Co. Ltd v Tantomar Transportes Maritimos Lda (The Naftilos)* [1995] 1 W.L.R. 299 at 309.
[19] *A v C* [1981] Q.B. 956 at 959.

assets or their proceeds are in the jurisdiction. In that situation the court could grant a temporary freezing injunction and a disclosure order with a view to reviewing the position once disclosure has been given. One could also envisage a situation in which, unusually, the court would order disclosure to enable it to resolve a pending application for freezing relief. However, the more remote the purpose is from the freezing injunction, the more that the applicant runs up against the position that (1) before any judgment has been obtained information about the defendant's assets is confidential, and (2) a defendant is not to be treated in the same way as a judgment debtor. In *Smith v Hegard*[20] an order was not granted when it was sought so as to show past dealings with assets within the jurisdiction in order to justify restoration of a Mareva injunction which had already been discharged.

In *Derby & Co. Ltd v Weldon (Nos 3 and 4)*,[21] the Court of Appeal left 22.005 open the question whether a disclosure order can have a wider ambit than the Mareva relief. When the Mareva jurisdiction had been regarded as limited to assets situated within the jurisdiction, it had been decided that a disclosure order should not be granted with wider ambit than the Mareva relief to which it was ancillary.[22] But once it became accepted that relief can be granted under s.37(1) of the Supreme Court Act 1981 in relation to assets abroad for the purpose of preserving them, it became a question of machinery whether this is done by Mareva relief combined with a disclosure order, or a disclosure order which is intended to be in aid of steps taken abroad to preserve those assets.[23] It is proper to seek information for the purpose of initiating proceedings abroad to preserve assets there[24] or to enforce the judgment.[25] Although a disclosure order can be made simply as a measure ancillary to Mareva relief, it may be made with the objective of enabling proceedings to be initiated abroad to preserve assets, or to facilitate the conduct of those proceedings, and accordingly a disclosure order can be made for this purpose, regardless of whether or not Mareva relief is granted, or is of narrower ambit. In *Gidrxslme Shipping v Tantomar Transportes*,[26] Colman J. concluded that this view is correct post-judgment or award when the disclosure order is made in aid of execution or enforcement.

The practice of the court is not to make an order for the purpose of investigating whether an injunction has been broken and (if so) to supply material for contempt proceedings.[27]

---

[20] Court of Appeal (Civ Div) Transcript No.603 of 1980 (August 7, 1980).
[21] [1990] Ch. 65 at 86 and 94–95.
[22] *Ashtiani v Kashi* [1987] Q.B. 888; *Reilly v Fryer* (1988) 138 N.L.J. 134.
[23] See also *Grupo Torras v Sheik Al-Sabah*, above and Chapter 6, para.6.011.
[24] *Babanaft International Co. SA v Bassatne*, [1990] Ch. 13; *Republic of Haiti v Duvalier* [1990] 1 Q.B. 202; *Derby & Co. Ltd v Weldon (No.1)* [1990] Ch. 48; *Bayer AG v Winter (No.3)* reported *sub nom Bayer AG v Winter (No.2)* [1986] F.S.R. 357.
[25] *Interpool Ltd v Galani* [1988] Q.B. 738 at 742.
[26] [1995] 1 W.L.R. 299.
[27] *Bhimji v Chatwani (No.2)* [1992] 1 W.L.R. 1158 at 1166–1169; *Bekhor Ltd v Bilton* [1981] Q.B. 923 at 949, *per* Griffiths L.J. who dissented on the particular facts of the case, but

(ii) Disclosure to see whether the defendant has assets which make it worthwhile for the claimant to pursue proceedings to judgment: s.37(1) and CPR r.3.1(m)

22.006   In *Nigel Upchurch Associates v Aldridge Estates International Co. Ltd*,[28] there was a counterclaim for damages against an architect, who had made an individual voluntary arrangement with his creditors. The counter-claimant wished to find out whether the architect had insurance cover, and, if so, its details. The trial had been estimated to last 12–20 weeks and so the costs of pursuing the counterclaim would have been substantial. The application for disclosure of the information was made under s.2 of the Third Parties (Rights Against Insurers) Act 1930. It was refused on the incorrect ground that the court had no jurisdiction under that section because no rights under a liability contract of insurance had yet been transferred to the counterclaimant.[29] The decision on s.2 has been over-ruled.[30] The rights are transferred once an event of insolvency within section 1 has occurred and information has to be provided under s.2 regardless of whether liability has been established by the claimant against the assured; the rights transferred may be inchoate until liability is established, but this does not remove the obligation to give information under s.2.[31]

In the *Upchurch* case it was argued that such an order could have been made under s.37(1) of the Supreme Court Act 1981 regardless of the position under s.2 of the Act. The counterclaimant had a cause of action against the architect. If the architect had been threatening to dissipate his assets, Mareva relief could have been granted against him, and a disclosure order made in relation to his assets, including any insurance policy. This would have been for the purpose of preserving the assets. But the jurisdiction to make a disclosure order under s.37(1) is not dependent on the granting of Mareva relief, and the ground for exercising the jurisdiction post-judgment does not depend on showing a risk of dissipation of assets.[32] The jurisdiction depends on whether it is "just and convenient" to make a disclosure order in aid of the rights claimed.[33] If there was a risk of the substantive rights being abandoned unless an order was made, then there was jurisdiction to make a disclosure order under s.37(1).

A disclosure order invades a defendant's privacy. Before judgment, a defendant is normally entitled to keep his financial affairs confidential. But

---

whose judgment on this point appears to be correct; *Bayer v Winter (No.2)* [1986] 1 W.L.R. 540 at 544; *Yau Chiu Wah v Gold Chief Investment Ltd* [2002] 2 H.K.L.R.D. 832 *Exagym Pty Ltd v Professional Gymnasium Equipment Pty Ltd (No.2)* [1994] 2 Qd R. 129 (Queensland).

[28] [1993] 1 Lloyd's Rep. 535.

[29] Following *Bradley v Eagle Star Insurance* [1989] 1 A.C. 957.

[30] In the matter of Computers Limited, *First National Tricity Finance Limited v OT Computers Limited* [2004] EWCA Civ 653 at para.42.

[31] In the matter of Computers Limited, *First National Tricity Finance Limited v OT Computers Limited* [2004] EWCA Civ 653.

[32] *Machine Watson & Co. v ITC (No.2)* [1989] Ch. 286; *Gidrxslme Shipping v Tantomar Transportes* [1995] 1 W.L.R. 299.

[33] *House of Spring Gardens v Waits* [1985] F.S.R. 173; *Smith v Peters* (1875) L.R. 20 Eq. 511.

this confidentiality may be overridden. Disclosure may be required if the information is relevant to the resolution of the issues in the case, or if it is needed to make Mareva relief effective. Confidentiality may have to give way to the doing of justice between the parties or to the advancement of the public interest.

On the facts of the *Upchurch* case there would have been an argument **22.007** for overriding confidentiality and ordering disclosure, had an application been made under s.37(1).

If the insolvent architect did not have effective insurance and this was disclosed, the counterclaimant could have avoided throwing away further substantial costs on a pointless trial leading to a useless judgment; valuable court time would have been saved and the public interest would have been served.

On the other hand, if the architect had had effective insurance cover and this had been disclosed, the counterclaimant would have been relieved from pressure to abandon his claim or settle it on unfair terms because of the fear of incurring substantial further costs. If the counterclaimant had pursued the matter to trial and recovered judgment, he would have been entitled to the benefit of the insurance policy under s.1 of the Third Parties (Rights against Insurers) Act 1930. It would be an injustice to the counterclaimant if the insurers and the architect could bring about abandonment of the counterclaim, or an unfair settlement, because the counterclaimant did not know the true position.

The *Upchurch* case pre-dated the CPR. Under CPR r.3.1(m) the court **22.008** can "take any other step or make any other order for the purpose of managing the case and furthering the overriding objective". That objective includes:

"(b) saving expense;
 (c) dealing with the case in ways which are proportionate—

   (i) to the amount of money involved;
   . . .
   (iv) to the financial position of each party".

It seems that the court has jurisdiction either under this rule or under CPR r.31.12 (specific disclosure of documents from a party) or under s.37(1) to make a disclosure order so that in an appropriate case the claimant can make a sensible decision whether to pursue his claim before the court taking into account information about the defendant's assets or means of satisfying a judgment. Although the court would have to bear in mind the principle that prior to judgment information about the defendant's assets is confidential and that he is not to be treated as a judgment debtor, the interests of justice could require this to be overridden and that a disclosure order be made. The exercise of the jurisdiction under s.37(1) should take into account the policy objectives of the CPR.

(iii) Privilege against self-incrimination

22.009 There may be circumstances in which the claimant has a justifiable concern that assets are at risk of dissipation, or assets which are the subject of a proprietary claim are in jeopardy, and there is a legitimate purpose for ordering disclosure ancillary to the effective working of the injunction. However, the privilege against self-incrimination may be available to the defendant either because of the underlying allegations in the proceedings,[34] or even in relation to a potential allegation of contempt arising from breach of the freezing injunction.[35] This privilege must be taken into account both in deciding whether to make a disclosure order and in the provision of machinery in the order enabling the defendant to invoke the privilege.

In *Den Norske Bank ASA v Antonatos*[36] the claimant bank had a powerful case of dishonesty against the defendant, who was a former manager, for allegedly receiving bribes and had justifiable concerns about what had happened to the proceeds. Mareva and Anton Piller relief was granted *ex parte* which included both a disclosure order in relation to his assets and also requiring to say whether he had taken bribes and what had happened to the proceeds. That order required him, if he claimed the privilege to provide the information to the supervising solicitor. This mechanism exposed the defendant to the risk that he would be compelled to incriminate himself and the information would come into the hands of a prosecutor. Therefore the order should not have been made.[37]

22.010 The scope of the privilege against self-incrimination is considered in Chapter 17, para.17.030 and following and the question of what form of order can legitimately be made, on an application made without notice or on notice, consistently with the privilege against self-incrimination, is considered at para.17.041 and following. Even with a disclosure order made in the form in the example freezing order there can be a question of self-incrimination, *e.g.* employees on a modest salary who disclose substantial unexplained assets could be incriminating themselves on a charge of conspiracy to defraud.

(iv) Disclosure by a defendant of what bribes he has received or what money he has stolen

22.011 A claimant who can show a strong case that a defendant has taken some bribes or stolen some money may want to obtain disclosure from the defendant about the full extent of his wrongdoing. The evidence the claimant has produced may show a dishonest course of conduct. From the claimant's point of view this is a perfectly reasonable request so that he can

---

[34] As in *Den Norske Bank ASA v Antonatos* [1999] Q.B. 271.
[35] *Memory v Sidhu* [2000] Ch. 645.
[36] [1999] Q.B. 271.
[37] See also *Memory v Sidhu (No.2)* [2000] 1 W.L.R. 1443.

obtain full redress from the defendant, who on this theory is holding assets which belong to the claimant.[38]

The problem of the privilege against self-incrimination exists in these circumstances. This was fatal to the orders made in *Den Norske Bank ASA v Antonatos*[39] and *Memory v Sidhu (No.2)*[40] because no machinery was included in the order which enabled the privilege to be respected.

In *International Fund for Agricultural Development v Jazayeri*[41] the claimant had shown a good arguable case that the defendant had been taking bribes and wanted to find out whether he had taken any other bribes. The judge refused to make a disclosure order requiring him to answer this, on the ground that it related to whether the claimant had other claims against the defendant and was not ancillary to the claims which were before the court.

22.012 Disclosure could have been required for this purpose under the equitable jurisdiction to protect trust money.[42] Once a course of conduct was shown on the evidence, or was to be inferred, the questions became how much had been taken and where was it? Also CPR r.31.16 (pre-action disclosure of documents) could have applied. This provision enables the applicant to obtain disclosure of documents before proceedings are started in respect of other bribes or thefts, and it is not necessary to show that it is probable that proceedings would be taken in respect of other bribes or thefts.[43]

The objection might be taken that English law requires allegations of dishonesty to be properly based[44] and adequately formulated[45] and that historically the court has not allowed discovery in relation to allegations of dishonesty which were not pleaded; the court would not allow a plaintiff to fish for material on which to make an allegation of dishonesty because the civil process was accusatory and not inquisitorial.[46]

22.013 But this fails to distinguish between a case in which no allegation of dishonesty has been advanced and one in which the dishonesty is alleged, and is based on evidence. That each bribe or each theft gives rise to a separate cause of action is descriptive of the legal mechanics, but it conceals that the real question is about the full extent of the dishonesty, which has been alleged, and quantum. It also overlooks the need for urgency in preserving dishonestly acquired assets; the process there is inquisitorial. Subject to the question of self-incrimination of the defendant,

---

[38] In the case of bribes the employer has a proprietary claim to the bribe: *Attorney-General for Hong Kong v Reid* [1994] 1 A.C. 324 disapproving of *Lister & Co. v Stubbs* (1890) 45 Ch.D. 1. *Daraydon Holdings Limited v Solland International Limited* [2004] EWHC 622 (Ch) at paras 79–86 (declining to follow *Lister v Stubbs*); *Corporacion Nacional del Cobre de Chile v Interglobal Inc* (2002–03) 5 I.T.E.L.R. 744 (Cayman Islands).

[39] [1999] Q.B. 271; see Chapter 17, para.17.041.

[40] [2000] 1 W.L.R. 1443.

[41] March 8, 2001 (Morison J).

[42] See para.22.053 and following below.

[43] *Black v Sumitomo Corporation* [2002] 1 W.L.R. 1562 at [68] and [73].

[44] *Medcalf v Mardell* [2003] 1 A.C. 120.

[45] *Black v Sumitomo Corporation* [2002] 1 W.L.R. 1562 at [57].

[46] *ibid.*, at [55–57].

it would not be consistent with the doing of justice to allow the thief to keep a part of his ill-gotten gains, and to deny the victim an effective and full remedy. It is considered that for these reasons the view of the judge in *International Fund for Agricultural Development v Jazayeri* was mistaken. Self-incrimination can be relevant:

(1) On the facts does the privilege against self-incrimination at common law and under s.14(1) of the Civil Evidence Act 1968 arise? If it does, then no order should be made which is inconsistent with either the defendant claiming the privilege, or, if he does, with the defendant declining to provide information which could incriminate him.

(2) Is there is a risk of self-incrimination in relation to a prosecution abroad? If there is, this can be relevant to the exercise of discretion by the court. This is discussed in Chapter 17, para.17.046.

(v) Form of disclosure order and what has to be done in order to comply with it

22.014 It has become the usual practice of the court to order disclosure of information about assets as an ancillary order in aid of a freezing injunction, and this is reflected in the example order. The justification for this is that once the claimant has shown a real risk of dissipation of assets it will usually be appropriate to grant relief to assist the claimant make the injunction effective.

The example order provides:

"PROVISION OF INFORMATION

9. (1) Unless paragraph (2) applies, the Respondent must [immediately] [within   hours of service of this order] and to the best of his ability inform the Applicant's solicitors of all his assets [in England and Wales] [worldwide] [exceeding £   in value] whether in his own name or not and whether solely or jointly owned, giving the value, location and details of all such assets.

(2) If the provision of any of this information is likely to incriminate the Respondent, he may be entitled to refuse to provide it, but is recommended to take legal advice before refusing to provide the information. Wrongful refusal to provide the information is contempt of court and may render the Respondent liable to be imprisoned, fined or have his assets seized.

10. Within [   ] working days after being served with this order, the Respondent must swear and serve on the Applicant's solicitors an affidavit setting out the above information."

The standard form orders provided under the 1996 Practice Direction[47] **22.015** required the defendant to give the information in writing to the plaintiff "at once". This form of disclosure order was criticised by the Court of Appeal as unduly draconian.[48] An order which imposes an unrealistic time limit for compliance should not be made because it will place a party in breach of it even when he wishes to obey it.[49] The disclosure order ought to have a reasonable time limit in it. The requirement that a defendant disclose all his assets immediately will almost inevitably result in the defendant being in breach of it.

The previous standard form order had required disclosure in writing but this is no longer a requirement under the example order, although in practice one would expect the disclosure to be in writing in view of the importance of having a reliable record of it.

The previous form had applied to all assets regardless of value. Depending on the size of the claim and the defendant's circumstances it may be more appropriate and fair to provide for a minimum value for assets which have to be disclosed.[50] This point is reflected by the words "[exceeding £   in value]" in the form of disclosure order in the example order (see para.9(1)).

The example order states "giving the value, location and details of all **22.016** such assets". If an order is to be made for disclosure of information about bank accounts, it is desirable that it should require the defendant to specify, in relation to each account, the name or names in which the account is held, the number of the account, the branch of the bank at which the account is held, and the balance.[51] In New South Wales it has been held that a disclosure order expressed in general terms in relation to bank accounts requires these particulars to be furnished.[52]

---

[47] *Practice Direction (Mareva Injunctions and Anton Piller Orders: Forms)* [1996] 1 W.L.R. 1552.

[48] *S. & T. Bautrading v Nordling*, Court of Appeal (Civ Div) Transcript No.1005 of 1996 (July 5, 1996). See also *Tamco Electrical & Electronics v Ng Chun-fai* [1994] 1 H.K.L.R. 178 criticising an order made for disclosure "forthwith" when the defendant was entitled to an opportunity to take legal advice. An order should give the defendant a proper opportunity to instruct a lawyer and obtain advice; this need not take more than a matter of hours during the working day, and the liberty to do so should be spelt out in clear terms in the order.

[49] *Oystertec Plc v Paul Anthony Davidson* [2004] EWHC 627 (Ch) at para.11 *per* Patten J.: ". . . judges who are asked to make orders of this kind, particularly where they are made (as in most cases) on a without notice basis, need, . . . to have firmly in mind what is a realistic timetable for compliance, having regard to the scope of the information and the range of documents which the respondent is required to produce. It is not satisfactory to impose an almost impossible deadline simply on the basis that the respondent, if in difficulties, can always apply to the Court for a variation of the order. Some respondents may not have immediate access to legal advice, and a failure to appreciate the implications of not complying within the time limits prescribed by the order may have extremely serious consequences."

[50] T. Willoughby and S. Connal, "The Mareva Injunction: A Cruel Tyranny?" (1997) 8 E.I.P.R. 479 at 482.

[51] See A5.030, below.

[52] *Ausbro Forex Pty Ltd v Mare* (1986) 4 N.S.W.L.R. 419.

The example restraint order for applications under the Drug Trafficking Act 1994 and the Criminal Justice Act 1988,[53] which is provided under para.2 of the Practice Direction supplementing RSC Ord. 115, has a more detailed form of disclosure order in para.10. The sub-paragraph which relates to gifts made by the defendant is for the purpose of identifying gifts caught by that legislation and is not applicable in other cases.

The example order requires disclosure of "all his assets" "giving the value, location and details of all such assets". The words "all his assets" include all assets in which the defendant has a beneficial interest and the assets as set out in para.6 of the example order. The ambit of this is considered in Chapter 3, para.3.009–3.011. The question of how the value of an asset is to be assessed is considered in Chapter 20, para.20.038–20.039.

22.017   To what point of time does the disclosed information have to relate? It is considered that the example form of order requires the information required to be accurate at the time it is provided. The word "giving" is in the present tense and in the context there would be no purpose in requiring out-of-date information. The order also requires the defendant to "swear and serve on the Applicant's solicitors an affidavit setting out the above information". The words "the above information" refer back to the words "giving the value, location and details of all such assets". It is considered that, as with the earlier disclosure, what has to be disclosed is up-to-date information; if there has been a material change in the position after the initial disclosure but prior to service of the affidavit, this should be disclosed in the affidavit.

The example order requires the information to be given to "the best of [the defendant's] ability". It is not enough to give an honest answer—the defendant has to make all reasonable inquiries[54] and provide information accordingly.

(vi) Undertakings given by the applicant to the court about the use of information obtained under the disclosure order

22.018   The example order provides (see Schedule B, Undertakings):

[(9)   The Applicant will not without the permission of the court use any information obtained as a result of this order for the purpose of any civil or criminal proceedings, either in England and Wales or in any other jurisdiction, other than this claim.]

[(10)   The Applicant will not without the permission of the court seek to enforce this order in any country outside England and Wales [or seek an order of a similar nature including orders conferring a charge or other security against the Respondent or the Respondent's assets].]"

---

[53] See Chapter 25.
[54] *Bird v Hadkinson, The Times*, April 7, 1999.

Undertaking (9) enables the court to retain control over information obtained under the disclosure order by restricting the use of the information to the proceedings in which the disclosure order has been made. The purpose of this undertaking is to avoid the use of the information for an improper purpose.[55] The purpose of an order for disclosure of assets ancillary to a freezing injunction is to aid in the effective working of the freezing injunction and so one would expect the disclosure could only be used for this limited purpose. However, undertaking (9) as set out in the example order is not so narrowly limited. It gives rise to the same difficulty as CPR r.34.12 which limits the permitted use to "the purpose of the proceedings in which the order was made"; this is discussed at para.22.027 and following.

In addition to undertaking (9) there is the restriction on use of documents disclosed in the proceedings imposed by CPR r.31.22.[56]

In *Attorney-General for Gibraltar v May*,[57] an implied undertaking had **22.019** been given by the plaintiff in civil proceedings brought in England against a former civil servant. The defendant had no privilege against self-incrimination because he was to be prosecuted in Gibraltar. The plaintiff was also the prosecuting authority in Gibraltar. The information given under the disclosure order revealed what the plaintiff alleged to be significantly greater assets than could be explained by the defendant's salary. The court in Gibraltar had power to exclude the evidence and could give "full weight" to the aspect of self-incrimination because it had incorporated the European Convention on Human Rights into its domestic law. The English court released the implied undertaking so that the criminal court in Gibraltar could decide whether the material should be used, the view being taken that the criminal court in Gibraltar would be in a much better position than the English court to decide whether as a matter of human rights or fairness to the defendant the material should be excluded from the criminal trial.

The Human Rights Act 1998 was not in force at the date of the decision in this appeal. Would that have made any difference to the result? There are two distinct rights relating to self-incrimination. The first is that which arises under the Convention,[58] and the second is that at common law. The immunity which arose under Art.6 of the Convention did not bar the making of the disclosure order or release of the material to the prosecutor; it only barred the use of material obtained under compulsion in the subsequent criminal proceedings themselves.[59] Compliance with Art.6, and the fairness of the criminal proceedings in Gibraltar, were matters for the Gibraltar criminal court; the release of the material to the prosecutor did not in itself constitute an infringement of the defendant's human rights

---

[55] *Derby & Co. Ltd v Weldon (No.1)* [1990] Ch. 48 at 57.
[56] This is discussed in Chapter 24.
[57] [1999] 1 W.L.R. 998.
[58] See Chapter 17, para.17.031.
[59] *R. v Hertfordshire County Council Ex p. Green* [2000] 2 A.C. 412 at 422.

under the Convention. As for the privilege at common law, this did not directly arise because it does not apply to prosecutions abroad, and there was no reason for it to affect the exercise of the discretion because of the safeguards which would be applied by the Gibraltar court.

22.020   If undertaking (9) was left out of a mandatory order requiring disclosure of information to be made orally, and this was not the deliberate decision of the judge, then either the order would fall to be corrected under the slip rule,[60] or it is considered that there would be an implied undertaking given by the applicant to the court, not to use the material except for the purpose of the proceedings in which the order was made.[61]

Undertaking (10) enables the court to retain control over foreign proceedings taken to enforce the freezing injunction or to obtain similar asset-preserving relief abroad including the imposition of a security interest over such assets or the arrest of assets. It follows the wording of certain of the undertakings given by the plaintiff in *Derby & Co. Ltd v Weldon (No.1)* which were set out in *Re Bank of Credit and Commerce International SA.*[62] The words "[or seek an order of a similar nature including orders conferring a charge or other security against the Respondent or the Respondent's assets]" are a "minor embellishment"[63] to the earlier part of the undertaking added on for the purpose of clarification of its ambit.

If a freezing injunction or disclosure order is to be made in relation to assets abroad, the court will require the claimant to furnish this undertaking so that the English court will retain a measure of control over the bringing of foreign proceedings against the defendant. This is for the purpose of avoiding oppression of the defendant through multiplicity of suits.[64]

22.021   Leaving aside use of information obtained under a disclosure order, which is dealt with by undertaking (9), in the example order there is no undertaking which interferes with bringing criminal proceedings abroad or communicating with the foreign criminal authorities. In *Re Bank of Credit and Commerce International SA* it was regarded as "highly undesirable"[65] that the mere fact that the applicant has obtained freezing relief should interfere in any way with the pursuit of criminal proceedings abroad in respect of alleged wrongdoings by the defendants. The undertaking may have to be narrowed in relation to civil proceedings, depending on the circumstances of the particular case.[66]

---

[60] See the discussion in Chapter 11, para.11.013.
[61] *Attorney-General for Gibraltar v May* [1999] 1 W.L.R. 998 at 1005D–1008A. If the disclosure had to be made in writing then CPR r.31.22(1) would apply, see para.22.030 and following, below.
[62] [1994] 1 W.L.R. 708 at 714D.
[63] *Re Bank of Credit and Commerce International SA* [1994] 1 W.L.R. 708 at 714H.
[64] *Re Bank of Credit and Commerce International SA* [1994] 1 W.L.R. 708 at 713 and 717–718; *Derby & Co. Ltd v Weldon (No.1)* [1990] Ch. 48 at 55 and 59. See also L. Collins, "The Territorial Reach of Mareva Injunctions" (1989) 105 L.Q.R. 262 at 286–288.
[65] *Re Bank of Credit and Commerce International SA* [1994] 1 W.L.R. 708 at 715D–E.
[66] *Re Bank of Credit and Commerce International SA* [1994] 1 W.L.R. 708 at 713–714 and 717–718.

When the purpose of the foreign proceedings is to safeguard assets which should be preserved so as to be available to satisfy a possible future English judgment, the undertakings should be released to enable this to be done.[67]

In *Bates v Microstar Ltd*[68] there was an undertaking not to commence any proceedings abroad against the defendants, or to use in civil or criminal proceedings abroad information obtained from asset disclosure orders. The claimant obtained certain shares as a result of an order made in the English proceedings. The undertaking was released by the court to enable the claimant to bring a minority shareholder's action in Jersey to get back into the relevant company assets said to have been stripped from it by the second defendant. This purpose was in effect part of obtaining for the claimant the fruits which he should have had from succeeding on his claim in England.

(vii) Disclosure orders for a proprietary claim

When the claimant asserts a proprietary claim to assets there are other jurisdictions to order disclosure of what has happened to the assets or their proceeds. These are: 22.022

(1) An order requiring disclosure of information including documents based on the equitable jurisdiction of the court to safeguard trust assets; this is discussed at para.22.053, below.

(2) An order based on the principle in *Norwich Pharmacal v Customs & Excise Commissioners*;[69] this is discussed at para.22.048 and following, below.

(3) An order giving an interim remedy under CPR r.25.1(1) to which a disclosure order could be granted as ancillary under s.37(1) of the Supreme Court Act 1981. The relevant provisions are CPR r.25.1(1)(c), (d)(i)[70] and (l). CPR 25.1(c) provides a range of orders applicable to property which is the subject of a claim or as to which any question may arise on a claim, including orders for the preservation,[71] custody detention or sale of such property. CPR r.25.1(d) allows them to be implemented through an order permitting a person to enter land or a building in the possession of the defendant. CPR r.25.1(1)(l) applies to a fund to which the claimant makes a claim in the proceedings, and is discussed in Chapter 12, para.12.013.

---

[67] *Bayer v Winter (No.2)* [1986] F.S.R. 357; see also *Cobra Golf Inc. v Rata* [1996] F.S.R. 819 at 828 (Laddie J.).
[68] [2003] EWHC 661, Ch.D.
[69] [1974] A.C. 133 at 175.
[70] See Chapter 12, para.12.012.
[71] This can apply, *e.g.* where real property which is the subject of a vendor's action for specific performance is in the possession of the defendant who is allowing it to become flooded: *Strelley v Pearson* (1880) 15 Ch.D. 113.

(4) An order made for pre-action disclosure of documents under CPR r.31.16 and s.33(2) of the Supreme Court Act 1981.

(3) Cross-examination of a defendant about his assets

(i) *Ancillary order in support of the injunction*

22.023   The claimant can apply for cross-examination of the defendant about his assets.[72] The order may be made even if the defendant has not yet been ordered to make an affidavit or has not made an affidavit as to his assets,[73] but normally would only be contemplated if the defendant has already made an affidavit, and there are serious justifiable concerns about the disclosure made. It is often the case that a claimant will be suspicious that a defendant has not been truthful in an affidavit served in compliance with a court requiring the giving of information; it is exceptional to allow cross-examination.[74] This is because it entails an invasion of the defendant's privacy, the use of court time and the expenditure of costs. This is difficult to justify before judgment. The usual time for this is post-judgment.[75]

The order is made in aid of the Mareva injunction for the purpose of getting further information about the location, value, or details of assets.

It will not be permitted for the purpose of uncovering whether the defendant has acted in contempt of court or furnishing material for contempt proceedings to be brought.[76] In *Bayer v Winter (No.2)*,[77] the plaintiff applied for an order for cross-examination to establish whether the defendant had complied properly with a mandatory order for disclosure of information. In the course of dismissing the application Scott J. said:

> "Star Chamber interrogatory procedure has formed no part of judicial process in this country for several centuries. The proper function of a judge in civil litigation is to decide issues between parties. It is not, in my opinion, to preside over an interrogation. The police, charged with upholding of the public law, cannot subject a citizen to cross-examination before a judge in order to discover the truth about the

---

[72] *Yukong Line Ltd v Rendsburg Investments Corporation. The Times*, October 22, 1996; *Den Norske Bank ASA v Antonatos* [1999] Q.B. 271 at 290B–C; *Maclaine Watson & Co. v International Tin Council (No.2)* [1989] Ch. 286 at 305–306; *House of Spring Gardens v Waite* [1985] F.S.R. 173; *A. J. Bekhor v Bilton* [1981] Q.B. 923.

[73] *House of Spring Gardens Ltd v Waite* [1985] F.S.R. 173.

[74] *Yukong Line Ltd v Rendsburg Investments Corporation, The Times*, October 22, 1996; *Mayo Associates SA v Anagram (Bermuda) Ltd* [1994] J.L.R. Notes-10c.

[75] *Yau Chiu Wah v Gold Chief Investment Ltd* [2002] 2 H.K.L.R.D. 832; *Junestar Investment Corporation v Boldwin Construction Co. Ltd* [2004] 1 H.K.L.R.D. 32 at para.15; *Phillips v Symes* [2003] EWHC 117, Ch.D., quoted in the judgment of the Court of Appeal at [2003] EWCA Civ 1769 at [50(4)].

[76] See Chapter 19, para.19.050.

[77] [1986] 1 W.L.R. 540.

citizen's misdeeds. How then, as a matter of discretion, can it be right in a civil case, in aid of rights which, however important, are merely private rights, to subject a citizen to such a cross-examination? *A fortiori* it cannot be right to do so in a case where the plaintiff seeking cross-examination of the defendant is holding itself free to use the defendant's answers for the purpose of an application to commit him to prison for contempt."

In *House of Spring Gardens Ltd v Waite*,[78] the Court of Appeal was **22.024** concerned with the existence of jurisdiction in the court to order cross-examination of the defendant, and not directly with the question of how any discretion should be exercised. At first instance, Scott J. (whose judgment was summarised by Slade L.J. at 178) had held that cross-examination could not take place *in vacuo*, *i.e.* unless it was directed towards the decision of particular issues between the parties. However, the Court of Appeal rejected this view, and held that cross-examination could be ordered even though it would be purely interrogatory in nature and not directly relevant to the determination of any issues between the parties; the procedure under CPR Pt 71 (examination of a judgment debtor, see below) is another example of purely interrogatory proceedings not directed to the determination of issues between the parties.

In view of the decision of the Court of Appeal in *House of Spring Gardens Ltd v Waite* and later authorities, the part of Scott J.'s reasoning in *Bayer v Winter (No.2)* which proceeds on the grounds that there was no relevant issue pending for determination by the court to which the cross-examination would be directed cannot be supported. However, the other part of the reasoning is cogent.

Once the defendant is in danger of proceedings for contempt the privilege against self-incrimination applies to contempt of court.[79]

Because of the privilege against self-incrimination in respect of allega- **22.025** tions of contempt and the right to remain silent on such an allegation, it is not right to "blend together" a cross-examination for the purpose of enabling there to be effective enforcement of a court order, with a cross-examination directed to uncovering whether the defendant has broken undertakings given to the court.[80] In such circumstances the defendant's right to silence on the question of contempt must be respected and a procedure should be drawn up which enables that to be done. This would involve hearing and determining any allegations of contempt before going on to any cross-examination designed to bring about compliance with a court order or making that order effective.[81]

---

[78] [1985] F.S.R. 173.

[79] *Memory Corporation v Sidhu* [2000] Ch. 645; *Cobra Golf Inc. v Rata* [1998] Ch. 109; *Bhimji v Chatwani (No.2)* [1992] 1 W.L.R. 1158, not following *Garvin v Domus Publishing Ltd* [1989] Ch. 335; *Phillips v Symes* [2003] EWCA Civ 1769 at [54(iv)] (conceded by the applicant). See also *Exagym Pty Ltd v Professional Gymnasium Equipment Pty Ltd (No.2)* [1994] 2 Qd R. 129 (Queensland).

[80] *Phillips v Symes* [2003] EWCA Civ 1769 at [64–65].

[81] *ibid.*, at [64–69].

The court will not allow cross-examination for the purpose of furnishing evidence on the issues to be resolved at trial. This would give the claimant an unfair procedural advantage.[82] The proper purpose of such a cross-examination is to reveal further information about assets so that they can be located and preserved. Unless the claimant discharges the burden of showing there is some real prospect of achieving this by cross-examination, the court should decline to make an order. If there are already sufficient assets revealed, to meet the financial limit in a Mareva injunction and which will be available to satisfy a judgment,[83] the court will not order cross-examination to see if there are further assets.[84]

22.026   The court should not allow cross-examination to be unnecessarily protracted, and should be reluctant to allow questions about dealings which are not recent and which are therefore less likely to lead to undisclosed assets being revealed. An application for cross-examination should be made promptly.

Under the Practice Direction which supplements CPR Pt 34 (Depositions and court attendance by witnesses), cross-examination may be ordered before a judge, an examiner of the court or such other person as the court may appoint. This is the position under CPR Pt 34. Practice Direction, para.4.1 that superseded the former RSC Ord. 29, r.1A, which had required the cross-examination to be before a judge or a master, or if the master so ordered before an examiner, and which did not permit an examination before a "court officer".[85] It therefore follows that where there is an examination to be carried out before a court officer under CPR r.71.6(2) that person can also be appointed to hear a cross-examination about assets ordered as ancillary to a freezing injunction.

(ii) The effect of CPR r.34.12 and the confidentiality of information obtained in the examination

22.027   Under the former RSC Ord. 29, r.1A(3) no transcript or other record of the cross-examination on an affidavit about assets could be used by any person, other than the person being cross-examined, for any purpose "other than the purpose of the proceedings in which the order for the

---

[82] *Yukong Line Ltd v Rendsburg Investments Corporation*, *The Times*, October 22, 1996; *Den Norske Bank ASA v Antonatos* [1999] Q.B. 271 at 290G–291D; *Yau Chiu Wah v Gold Chief Investment Ltd* [2002] 2 H.K.L.R.D. 832 (including cross-examination which could be used as going to credit if the defendant gives evidence at the trial). See also chapter 14, paras 14.033–14.034 on the granting of an anti-suit injunction to restrain deposition abroad of witnesses who would be called at the trial in England of the substantive case.

[83] *Motorola Credit Corporation v Uzan* [2004] 1 W.L.R. 113 at [143–147].

[84] *DFC of Taxation v Hickey* (1996) 33 A.T.R. 453; 96 A.T.C. 4892 (Western Australia), where the injunction was confined to assets in Western Australia and cross-examination about assets was refused because there were already sufficient assets uncovered to meet the financial limit in the Mareva injunction.

[85] *Belgolaise SA v Rupchandani* [1999] Lloyd's Rep. (Bank.) 116 at 119.

cross-examination was made . . .." except with consent of the party being cross-examined or the leave of the court. This is now reproduced with no material alteration in CPR r.34.12 which provides:

> "34.12 (1) Where the court orders a party to be examined about his or any other assets for the purpose of any hearing except the trial, the deposition may be used only for the purpose of the proceedings in which the order was made.
> (2) However, it may be used for some other purpose—
>
> (a) by the party who was examined;
> (b) if the party who was examined agrees; or
> (c) if the court gives permission."

This contains a restriction on the use of the cross-examination. However, there would need to be a further undertaking given by the claimant as the price for an order being made under that rule in order to avoid material becoming available to be used in contempt proceedings. This is because the bar on use of such material is not wide enough to prevent material coming out in a cross-examination of a defendant about his assets being used for the purpose of contempt proceedings brought in the same action. The further undertaking would be that the information obtained at such a cross-examination and any further information or evidence obtained in consequence of the cross-examination would not be used without the further leave of the court. At such a cross-examination it may be that the defendant would not be able to claim privilege against self-incrimination for perjury committed in the same proceedings because of the case law, which is somewhat questionable, to this effect.[86] But if there has been perjury in that the defendant has lied about his assets it is likely that this would be dealt with in contempt proceedings rather than solely by criminal prosecution for perjury, and the risk of contempt proceedings would itself be sufficient to engage the protection of the privilege.

The "deposition" under CPR r.34.12 includes the oral answers given in the course of the examination, the transcript made of them, and any other record including counsel's or solicitors' notes, or a tape recording of the cross-examination.

In *Yukong Line Ltd v Rendsburg Investments Corporation*[87] there were **22.028** observations which proceeded on the basis that RSC Ord. 29, r.1A(3) itself prohibited use of information obtained by the cross-examination at the trial of the action, unless the court gave leave. But the trial is part of "the proceedings" in which the cross-examination took place, and therefore use of the transcript or other record at the trial was not in itself prohibited by the rule. Nor did the implied undertaking which applied to information obtained by compulsion through an order of the court prevent use of the information in the same proceedings.

---

[86] Chapter 17, paras 17.036–17.037, above.
[87] *The Times*, October 22, 1996.

The cross-examination may include questions which are also relevant to the merits of the underlying substantive claim,[88] but where there is a risk of this, the court should be asked to require an undertaking from the claimant, as the price of making the order, that he will not, without permission of the court, use any information obtained save for the purpose of preserving assets. This is because it is most undesirable that the claimant should be able to use such a cross-examination in order to build up his case on the substantive merits. It would be an abuse of the process if a party intended to use the cross-examination for this purpose, and formulated questions to achieve this objective.

(iii) Use by the claimant of documents handed over by the defendant during the course of the cross-examination

22.029   If documents are produced at the cross-examination, it is considered that they are a part of the "deposition" ordered by the court and are therefore protected by CPR r.34.12.

(iv) Use by the claimant of documents produced by the defendant before the deposition

22.030   Is protection given by the CPR to documents produced by the defendant before the deposition but in connection with it?

The compulsion principle which applied before CPR has not been preserved under CPR r.31.22 and r.32.12; this is discussed in Chapter 24, below.

If the court makes an order for disclosure, CPR Pt 31 provides provisions which are consequential on that order being made. For example if the court orders standard disclosure then the consequences of this are specified in the rule. CPR r.31.22 provides:

"SUBSEQUENT USE OF DISCLOSED DOCUMENTS

31.22 (1) A party to whom a document has been disclosed may use the document only for the purpose of the proceedings in which it is disclosed, except where—

(a) the document has been read to or by the court, or referred to, at a hearing which has been held in public;
(b) the court gives permission; or
(c) the party who disclosed the document and the person to whom the document belongs agree.

---

[88] *Yukong Line Ltd v Rendsburg Investments Corporation, The Times*, October 22, 1996.

(2) The court may make an order restricting or prohibiting the use of a document which has been disclosed, even where the document has been read to or by the court, or referred to, at a hearing which has been held in public.

(3) An application for such an order may be made—

(a) by a party; or
(b) by any person to whom the document belongs."

This rule applies to "disclosed documents". If documents are disclosed **22.031** as a result of an order of the court, then this is a consequence. The rule does not specify that the document must have been disclosed by compulsion under a court order in order to be protected. Under the former Rules of the Supreme Court, protection of the confidentiality of documents disclosed under a court order was achieved through the protection of an implied undertaking given to the court by the party who was to receive disclosure under that order. The reason was to limit the invasion of that confidentiality to the purpose for which the order for disclosure had been made by the court.

Likewise, as is apparent from its opening words "Where the court orders a party to be examined about his or any other assets . . .", CPR r.34.12 regulates the consequence of the court ordering a party to be examined about his or any other assets.

In view of these provisions of the CPR there does not appear to be any room for an implied undertaking by the other parties not to use the information for any purposes other than those of the proceedings in which it was disclosed, because this is dealt with in the express prohibition in the rules.

It is considered that documents produced by the defendant for the **22.032** purpose of assisting the claimant in taking the deposition, but not under the compulsion of an order, would be "disclosed" documents falling within CPR r.31.22.

If an order for the deposition was made as an ancillary order to the disclosure provisions in a freezing injunction then undertakings (9) and (10) in that form of order would also continue to be applicable.

(v) *CPR Pt 71: examination of a judgment debtor*

An order for cross-examination may also be made in aid of execution of a **22.033** judgment. In cases falling within CPR Pt 71, an examination of a judgment debtor is not limited to assets (including debts owed to him) within the jurisdiction,[89] and can include questions directed to obtaining information which will enable the judgment in question to be enforced abroad. Under CPR r.71.2(1) the rule only applies to a judgment debtor who is an

---

[89] *Interpool Ltd v Galani* [1988] Q.B. 738.

individual, a company or a corporation. There is also jurisdiction under s.37(1) of the Supreme Court Act 1981 to order such an examination, which is not limited by this rule.[90] An examination under CPR Pt 71 is concerned with the questions whether debts are owed to the judgment debtor, and whether the judgment debtor has any and if so what property or other means of satisfying the judgment. If the judgment debtor is a company, the order can be for an officer of the company to attend. The purpose of the examination is to ascertain the "means" of the judgment debtor and any other matter relevant to enforcement.[91] The examination is not limited to present assets (*e.g.* the defendant can be asked about future salary). An examination under this rule should not, though, be used as a vehicle for pre-action discovery for contemplated proceedings to set aside transfers in intended bankruptcy or winding-up proceedings.[92] The procedure under CPR Pt 71 cannot be used to examine third parties or to obtain documents from them.[93] For the position on tender of conduct money, see 19.052–19.054, above.

(vi) Cross-examination on a witness statement or affidavit in interlocutory proceedings

22.034   The claimant may make such an application in relation to a witness statement or an affidavit which has been made by the defendant in support of a pending application for a variation of the Mareva injunction under *Angel Bell* principles. The application is made pursuant to CPR r.32.7, which provides:

> "ORDER FOR CROSS-EXAMINATION
>
> 32.7 (1) Where, at a hearing other than the trial, evidence is given in writing, any party may apply to the court for permission to cross-examine the person giving the evidence.
>
> (2) If the court gives permission under paragraph (1) but the person in question does not attend as required by the order, his evidence may not be used unless the court gives permission."

Whether the application is to be granted is a matter of discretion, but in general the court is reluctant to allow cross-examination unless it is

---

[90] *Madeline Watson & Co. Ltd v International Tin Council (No.2)* [1989] Ch. 286 at 305–306.
[91] CPR r.71.2(1).
[92] *Watkins v Ross* (1893) 68 L.T. 423; *McCormack v National Australian Bank* (1992) 106 A.L.R. 647.
[93] *Hood & Barrs v Herriott Ex p. Blythe* [1896] 2 Q.B. 338 (subpoena); *D. B. Deniz Nakliyati Tas v Yugopetrol* [1992] 1 W.L.R. 437 (Bankers' Books Evidence Act 1879, s.7).

necessary in order to do justice between the parties.[94] The court will not usually order cross-examination on an affidavit in support of an application to discharge or vary Mareva relief, because this would tend to turn such an application into a mini-trial involving unnecessary costs and excessive use of court time. Exceptionally, the court might order certain defined discovery for the purpose of testing factual assertions made in such an affidavit.[95]

In the context of subsisting contempt proceedings, the claimant may wish to cross-examine on an affidavit (which may or may not have been served in relation to the particular contempt motion) so as to prove contempt of court. The question whether an order should be made for the cross-examination of the defendant is a matter of discretion. In exercising that discretion the court will take into account the proposed width of the cross-examination. Thus, *e.g.* in *Comet Products v Hawkex Plastics*,[96] the defendant in a passing-off action filed an affidavit in relation to the plaintiff's motion to commit the defendant to prison for contempt of court. The plaintiff wished to conduct a wide-ranging cross-examination going beyond the particular events relied upon as constituting contempt, and including previous events said to be relevant to the defendant's state of mind. The Court of Appeal refused to grant the application as a matter of discretion. However, the judgments recognised that cross-examination could be ordered on a contempt motion even though the defendant is liable to be asked questions the answers to which could prejudice him.[97] Privilege against self-incrimination extends to affording protection to a person who is at risk of prejudicing himself in relation to contempt proceedings,[98] whether or not those proceedings have been commenced.

(4) An order for the delivery-up of the defendant's assets

The power of the court to make ancillary orders in aid of a freezing injunction extends to making orders for the delivery-up of assets belonging to the defendant, and their safe preservation pending trial. The power to order the delivery-up of assets where it is "just and convenient" to do so, in order to enforce or make effective an injunction, may be exercised even where the claimant has no proprietary claim in respect of the assets.   **22.035**

---

[94] Contrast *Comet Products v Hawkex Plastics* [1971] 2 Q.B. 67 at 76 and 77.
[95] *Bank of Crete v Koskotas* [1991] 2 Lloyd's Rep. 587 at 588.
[96] [1971] 2 Q.B. 67.
[97] See also *Bekhor Ltd v Bilton* [1981] Q.B. 923 at 946 (*per* Ackner L.J.) and at 955 (*per* Stephenson L.J.), and the dicta of Scott J. at first instance in *House of Spring Gardens Ltd v Waits* [1985] F.S.R. 173 referred to by Slade L.J. at 178 and Cumming-Bruce L.J. at 182 without disapproval on this point.
[98] *Cobra Golf Inc. v Rata* [1998] Ch. 109; *Bhimji v Chatwani (No.2)* [1992] 1 W.L.R. 1158 at 1170–1175, not following *Garvin v Domus Publishing Ltd* [1989] Ch. 335. On privilege against self-incrimination, see paras 17.030 and following above.

In CBS *United Kingdom Ltd v Lambert*,[99] it was alleged that certain assets (motor cars) had been purchased by the defendants with the proceeds of sale of "pirated" cassettes infringing the plaintiffs' copyright. The Court of Appeal made an order for discovery, directing the defendants to disclose the full value and whereabouts of their assets, and an order for the delivery-up of the motor cars into the custody of the plaintiffs' solicitors. Lawton L.J., who delivered the judgment of the court, considered the principles governing the exercise of the court's power to order delivery-up of assets. He pointed out that such an order would cause a defendant extreme hardship if the assets were used in his business:

> "Even if a plaintiff has good reason for thinking that a defendant intends to dispose of assets so as to deprive him of his anticipated judgment, the court must always remember that rogues have to live and that all orders, particularly interlocutory ones, should as far as possible do justice to all parties."

22.036   The nature of the assets (which were disposable) and the fact that they were not used in the defendants' business were factors which significantly influenced the decision of the Court of Appeal in that case. The practice which applies is as follows:

(1) The claimant must show, by clear evidence, that the defendant is likely, unless restrained by order, to dispose of or otherwise deal with his assets so as to deprive the claimant of the fruits of any judgment he may obtain.

(2) The court should be slow to order the delivery-up of property belonging to the defendant unless there is some evidence or inference that the property was acquired by the defendant as a result of his alleged wrongdoing.

(3) No order should be made for the delivery-up of a defendant's wearing apparel, bedding, furnishing, tools of his trade, farm implements, livestock or any machines (including motor vehicles) or other goods such as materials or stock in trade, which it is likely he uses for the purposes of lawful business. (However, if there is strong evidence that the defendant has purchased antique furniture or valuable paintings for the purposes of frustrating judgment creditors, these may be included in the order, notwithstanding the fact that they might fall within the broad description "furnishings".)

(4) The order should specify as clearly as possible what chattels or classes of chattels are to be delivered up. (If the claimant is unable to identify the chattels which he wishes to be delivered up, or to

---

[99] [1983] Ch. 37 followed in *Dunbar Sloane Ltd v Gill* [1996] 3 N.Z.L.R. 252 (delivering up of clearly specified chattels which had been bought using mainly the plaintiff's money).

state clearly his reasons for the application, the court should refuse
to make the order.)

(5) Section 37(1) of the Supreme Court Act 1981 does not empower
the court to authorise the claimant to enter on the defendant's
premises or to seize the defendant's property save by permission of
the defendant. In the case of an order made under CPR r.25.1(c) the
court itself can by CPR r.25.1(d) authorise a person to enter any
land or building in the possession of a party to the proceedings. But
this only applies to relevant property as defined in CPR r.25.1(2),
namely "property (including land) which is the subject of a claim or
as to which any question may arise on a claim". Except in that
situation any order made for the purpose of enabling someone to go
on to someone else's land to obtain assets, would be a search order.[1]

(6) No order should be made for delivery-up to anyone other than the
claimant's solicitor or a receiver appointed by the High Court. The
court should appoint a receiver unless it is satisfied that the
claimant's solicitors have, or can arrange, suitable safe custody for
what is delivered to him.

(7) The order must make provision for protecting the interests of
innocent non-parties. This is discussed in Chapter 20.

(8) Provision should always be made for liberty to apply to stay, vary or
discharge the order.

If the defendant has cash, the court may order delivery-up of that cash **22.037**
for safe keeping. Although there is jurisdiction to order payment of funds
into a blocked account or into court,[2] this is a jurisdiction which is
sparingly exercised. Ordinarily, a defendant will be expected to observe the
terms of an injunction restraining dealings with his assets. But there can be
circumstances in which the defendant should not be left in control of the
assets subject to an injunction because there remains a serious risk that he
will dissipate the assets notwithstanding the injunction. One possibility may
be to appoint a receiver to take control of the assets.[3] Another possibility is
to grant a mandatory order for the funds to be paid into a blocked account
or into court. Such an order may be justifiable provided that it is proved
that there is a specific fund which can be clearly identified and which can
be made the subject of the order: *United Norwest Co-operatives Ltd v
Johnstone (No.2)*.[4] Such an order can then be enforced if necessary by
proceedings for contempt.

---

[1] See Chapter 17 above.
[2] See Chapter 4, para.4.019, above.
[3] See Chapter 16, para.16.004, above.
[4] Court of Appeal (Civ Div) Transcript No.1482 of 1994 (December 6, 1994); *Dunbar
Sloane Ltd v Gill* [1996] 3 N.Z.L.R. 252 at p.255 (proposition (3), specifying as clearly as
possible what chattels were to be delivered up and to whom); see also chapter 4 paras
4.001 and following on the need for certainty and precision before an order can properly
be made.

(5) Orders against non-parties leading to the disclosure of information about assets

22.038   A non-party may have information about assets of a defendant. What jurisdictions does the court have for ordering a non-party to give disclosure? A distinction must be drawn between cases in which a claimant is asserting a proprietary claim and those in which he is not:

> Case (1): A case not involving a proprietary claim prejudgment; the information is potentially relevant to the granting of interim remedies in respect of someone else's property in anticipation of obtaining an eventual judgment.
>
> Case (2): A case involving a proprietary claim.
>
> Case (3): A case after judgment based on a non-proprietary claim; the information is potentially relevant to actual execution or enforcement of the judgment.

The nature of the claimant's rights is different, the purposes for which the information is required is different and the available procedures are different.

The potential procedures which might be relevant are:

(1)   witness summons under CPR r.34.2;

(2)   disclosure by a non-party under CPR r.31.17;

(3)   pre-action disclosure under CPR r.31.16;

(4)   an order made against a bank under s.7 of the Bankers' Books Evidence Act 1879;

(5)   an order giving an interim remedy under CPR r.25.1 to which a disclosure order would be ancillary;

(6)   an injunction granted under s.37(1) of the Supreme Court Act 1981 against the non-party, requiring him to disclose information about assets, based on the cause of action against the defendant;

(7)   an order based on the principle in *Norwich Pharmacal v Customs & Excise Commissioners*;[5]

(8)   in case (2) only, an order requiring disclosure based on the equitable jurisdiction of the court to safeguard trust assets;

(9)   in Case (3) only, an order made ancillary to execution or enforcement of a judgment.

---

[5] [1974] A.C. 133 at 175.

(6) Case (1): a case not involving a proprietary claim pre-judgment

(i) *Case (1): purposes for which the information may be needed*

In cases not based on a proprietary claim it is unusual for the claimant to 22.039 seek information from third parties for the purpose of the court proceedings concerning the granting or continuation of Mareva relief. However, such situations can occur; *e.g.* there may be an issue as to whether certain assets belong beneficially to the defendant, and therefore should be subject to a Mareva injunction,[6] or information may be needed to enable the court to formulate injunctions against several defendants in appropriate terms, as in *A v C*,[7] or to make a Mareva injunction fully effective (*e.g.* by enabling the court to specify particular assets in the order which can then be notified to non-parties holding the defendant's assets). It may be that information is needed because the defendant cannot be relied upon to obey the court order and it is necessary to take steps to preserve the assets in the hands of non-parties.

(ii) *Case (1): witness summons and other procedures under CPR*

If the claimant needs to obtain information for the purpose of the court 22.040 proceedings by way of an order directed to a non-party, can the claimant seek permission to issue a witness summons under CPR r.34.2 and r.34.3, returnable on an application to continue a freezing injunction?

Under CPR r.34.2 a witness summons applies both to oral evidence and the production of documents. Permission is required if a witness summons is to be returnable for a hearing other than the trial. Under CPR r.34.2(5):

> "(5) The only documents that a summons under this rule can require a person to produce before a hearing are documents which that person could be required to produce at the hearing."

This rule appears to have in mind the procedure developed before CPR under which a *subpoena ad testificandum* could be made returnable at a date prior to the commencement of the main part of a trial so that the parties would have the opportunity of reading and considering the documents beforehand.[8] CPR r.34.2(5) is saying that the court cannot

---

[6] See Chapter 13.
[7] [1981] Q.B. 956.
[8] *BNP Paribas v Deloitte & Touche LLP* [2003] EWHC 2874 at para.12 (referring to s.43(4) Arbitration Act 1996); *Khanna v Lovell White Durrant* [1995] 1 W.L.R. 121, which distinguished between the commencement of the trial and the commencement of the main part of the trial.

require documents under the rule which could not be required at "the hearing", but it does not tell the reader what documents can be ordered for production then.

In particular, can the court order production of documents which are not relevant to the underlying issues but which are relevant to a freezing injunction?

22.041 What is meant by "the hearing" in the rule? It may be that this is referring to whatever hearing there is to be before the court to which the documents are relevant. So, *e.g.* if there was an application made by application notice pursuant to RSC Ord. 46, r.4(1) for permission to issue a writ of sequestration based on alleged contempt then "the hearing" would be the hearing of that application. With a freezing injunction "the hearing" would be the hearing of the application to continue the relief or for directions to be given so as to ensure that the relief was effective. On this view the words "the hearing" are to be read as meaning that hearing for which the documents are required. If this is the correct reading of the rule then CPR r.34.2(5) only affects timing for production and not what can be ordered for the hearing of an interlocutory application in the proceedings.

A narrower interpretation is that "the hearing" is referring to the trial of the proceedings. Significantly for disclosure by a non-party under CPR r.31.17, CPR r.31.17(3) provides:

> "The court may make an order under this rule only where—
>
> (a) the documents of which disclosure is sought are likely to support the case of the applicant or adversely affect the case of one of the other parties to the proceedings; and
>
> (b) disclosure is necessary in order to dispose fairly of the claim or to save costs."

This is potentially applicable when the claim is proprietary because then the claimant's claim, and his case founded on that claim, may involve investigation of issues to which the information held by the non-party is relevant. But it would not be satisfied by a non-proprietary claim.

22.042 It is considered that CPR r.34.2 can be used to obtain information relevant to the granting of freezing relief or ensuring that such relief is effective. It is considered that the wider interpretation of the hearing in CPR r.34.2(5) is to be preferred. This is because:

(1) If CPR r.34.2 had been intended to be limited in a way similar to CPR r.31.7, then one would have expected similar words to have been used.

(2) The former RSC Ord. 38, r.13 allowed the court to make an order for production by "any person" of documents "necessary for the purpose of that proceeding", which were wide enough to apply to documents required in connection with Mareva relief granted in

that proceeding. If a more limited jurisdiction was to be in place under the CPR it was to be expected that the formulators of the rule would have used words clearly intended to have this effect.

(3) Unless the wider interpretation of "the hearing" were correct there would be no procedure for a witness summons on an application made by application notice pursuant to RSC Ord. 46, r.4(1) for permission to issue a writ of sequestration based on alleged contempt, or on a committal application commenced by application notice under RSC Ord. 52, r.4(1).

Even on the narrower meaning of "the hearing", an order could be made because:

(1) CPR r.34.2(5) would then only exclude documents or evidence which could not be relevant at the trial of the proceedings.

(2) The trial includes the period following the handing down of the judgment and the working out and finalisation of the order of the court. When there is a freezing injunction granted pre-judgment, matters concerning that freezing relief will arise at the trial. It is considered that this would be part of the trial and the court could obtain documents from a non-party which were relevant to the just determination of that part of "the hearing". On this interpretation CPR r.34.2(5) would have as its purpose ruling out a witness summons covering documents or evidence which could not be relevant to anything which would arise at the trial, as opposed to ruling out anything other than what is relevant to the determination of the substantive issues.

A *subpoena duces tecum* had to be specific in identifying what documents **22.043** are to be produced, although there was no absolute rule which forbade a requirement expressed in terms of the production of a file.[9] This was so as not to place an unreasonable and oppressive burden on the witness. It is to be expected that the same principle would be applied to a witness summons.

CPR r.25.1(g) only applies to orders against "a party" to proceedings. Accordingly this would not apply to production sought from a non-party.

CPR r.25.1(c) is limited by the definition of "relevant property" in CPR r.25.1(2),[10] and CPR r.25.1(l) only applies to securing a fund claimed by the claimant.[11]

(iii) Case (1): Bankers' Books Evidence Act 1879

The Bankers' Books Evidence Act 1879 applies to "bankers' books" which **22.044** are defined in s.9[12] as including "ledgers, day books, cash books, account books, and all other books used in the ordinary business of the bank,

---

[9] *Wakefield v Outhwaite* [1990] 2 Lloyd's Rep. 157.
[10] See Chapter 20, para.20.032.
[11] See Chapter 12, para.12.012.
[12] As amended by s.51(1) of the Banking Act 1979.

whether those records are in written form or are kept on microfilm, magnetic tape or any other form of mechanical or electronic data retrieval mechanism". It was enacted so as to avoid having to bring these records to court. Section 7 of the Bankers' Books Evidence Act 1879 provides as follows:

> "On the application of any party to a legal proceeding a court or judge may order that such party be at liberty to inspect and take copies of any entries in a banker's book for any of the purposes of such proceedings. An order under this section may be made either with or without summoning the bank or any other party, and shall be served on the bank three clear days before the same is to be obeyed, unless the court or a judge otherwise directs."

This applies to "entries" in a book and so does not extend to unsorted cheques or paying in slips held by a bank;[13] nor does the section apply to notes of meetings (*e.g.* between the bank and its customer[14]). Records of banking transactions kept on microfilm or other electronic form do qualify.[15] Whether copies of correspondence kept sorted on a file qualifies depends on whether the correspondence is in substance a record of one or more transactions done by the bank in the course of its banking business for the customer.[16]

In *A v C*[17] Robert Goff J. referred to the power of the court under s.7 as follows:

> "In order to establish his right to relief at all the plaintiff has at least to give grounds for believing that the defendant has assets here, but having established that, it may be necessary for the exercise of the jurisdiction that the defendant should be required to give discovery, or provide information, about a particular asset—though obviously, if the asset is worth more than the plaintiff's claim, he need do no more than establish that fact. But if the asset is a bank balance, the court, if it holds that the plaintiff is entitled to discovery in respect of that balance, may exercise its powers under s.7 of the Bankers' Books Evidence Act 1879."

In the immediately preceding part of his judgment he had referred to the power of the court to order discovery from the defendant about his assets under the statutory jurisdiction to grant an injunction.

---

[13] *Williams v Williams* [1988] Q.B. 161.
[14] *Re Howglen Ltd* [2001] 1 All E.R. 376; [2001] 2 B.C.L.C. 695.
[15] *Barker v Wilson* [1980] 1 W.L.R. 884.
[16] Contrast *R. v Dadson* (1983) 77 Cr.App.Rep. 91 at 93 (correspondence not a "book") with *Wee Soon Kim Anthony v UBS AG* [2003] 5 L.R.C. 171 (Singapore). It is considered that an English court would be likely to follow *R. v Dadson*, unless a letter contained a record of one or more transactions carried out in the ordinary course of banking.
[17] [1981] Q.B. 956 at 960.

Section 7 of the Act was passed to relieve bankers from the inconvenience   22.045
of producing their books in court under subpoena.[18] If the defendant could
be ordered to disclose the information,[19] then in principle s.7 is applicable to
an entry in the bank's records as stated by Robert Goff J. and an order can
be made that the claimant be at liberty to inspect and take copies of entries
in those books. An order was made in chambers under s.7 against Williams
& Glyn's Bank by Kerr J. in *H. & H. Brothers v Astro-Naviero (The Calliope
L)*,[20] when the question arose as to whether a Mareva injunction should be
continued until trial and if so in what form, and it was not known whether
or not the defendants had any credit balance at the bank. This information
could have been ordered to be disclosed by the defendant under what was
then s.45 of the Supreme Court of Judicature (Consolidation) Act 1925 and
so in principle s.7 was available to be used by Kerr J. so as to require
disclosure by the defendant's bank.

Furthermore if, as appears to be the case, CPR r.34.2 is applicable in
principle to a non-party in relation to information relevant to the granting
or enforcement of freezing relief, then one would expect there to be a
corresponding procedure available against banks under s.7 of the Act. The
alternative would be that CPR r.34.2 would apply and the bank would not
have the advantages of the section.

The courts have refused to allow s.7 to be used as a vehicle for obtaining
discovery from bankers of information about the affairs of persons who are
not parties to the proceedings. This is so both before and after judgment.[21]
This requirement is met when the disclosure is required so as to reveal the
affairs of the defendant; he is not a non-party.

As a matter of practice it is only in exceptional circumstances that any   22.046
order will be made in respect of an account which is not in the name of the
defendant.[22] Such an order can be made if there is evidence that the
defendant has been using for his own purposes an account in the name of a
third party.[23] Even post-judgment, an order will not be made for the
purpose of enabling a claimant to find out if documents relating to an
account might contain evidence of the judgment debtor's assets.[24] An order
may be made when it is virtually certain that an account is an account of
the defendant.

An order under s.7 can be made at any stage of the proceedings.
Although a court might make an order on an application made without
notice,[25] the normal procedure is to apply with notice to the bank. In *A v*

---

[18] *Pollock v Garle* [1898] 1 Ch. 1; *Douglas v Pindling* [1996] A.C. 890 at 900–901.
[19] If the material would be privileged from disclosure in the hands of the defendant on
grounds of self-incrimination, then the court should not make an order against his bank:
Waterhouse v Barker [1924] 2 K.B. 759
[20] Unreported, November 30, 1976.
[21] *Hill Samuel Bank v Nicholas Soutos*, unreported, October 23, 1996 (Langley J.).
[22] *D. B. Deniz Nakliyati v Yugopetrol* [1992] 1 W.L.R. 437.
[23] *Ironmonger & Co. v Dyne* (1928) 44 T.L.R. 579; see further *Mercantile Group (Europe) v
Aiyela* [1994] Q.B. 366.
[24] *Hill Samuel Bank Ltd v Nicholas Soutos*, above, where an order was refused because it was
sought in order to try to find assets of the defendant.
[25] *Arnott v Hayes* (1887) 36 Ch.D. 731.

C,[26] Robert Goff J. granted relief which included an order under s.7 directed to a bank (which had been joined as sixth defendant) on the grounds that such an order was required for the proper exercise of the injunction jurisdiction in that case.

Before CPR, if an order was made under s.7, the claimant gave an implied undertaking to the court not to use the documents except for the purpose for which the order was made.[27] The position appears now to be governed by CPR r.31.22 (see paras 24.015–24.016, below).

(iv) An injunction granted under the Supreme Court Act 1981, s.37(1) against the non-party, requiring him to disclose information about assets, based on the cause of action against the defendant

22.047   The jurisdiction under the section can be exercised so as to grant an injunction against a non-party based on the cause of action against the defendant. This is discussed in Chapter 13. Provided that the order for disclosure is genuinely ancillary to Mareva relief granted against the defendant, then the court has jurisdiction under s.37(1) to grant an injunction against the non-party requiring production of the information.

(v) The Norwich Pharmacal principle

22.048   Disclosure can in certain circumstances be obtained under the principle applied by the House of Lords in *Norwich Pharmacal v Customs & Excise Commissioners*,[28] which is derived from the discovery which can be ordered by a court of equity:

(1) The principle is that if a person, through no fault of his own, gets "mixed up" in the tortious acts of others so as to facilitate their wrongdoing, he may not incur any personal liability, but he comes under an obligation to assist the person wronged by giving him "full information" and disclosing the identity of the wrongdoers, *per* Lord Reid in *Norwich Pharmacal v Customs & Excise Commissioners*.[29] Thus, *e.g.* information has been ordered to enable the person wronged to identify a mole within the organisation,[30] to

---

[26] [1981] Q.B. 956 at 961.
[27] *Bhimji v Chatwani (No.2)* [1991] 1 W.L.R. 1158 (where the plaintiff had improperly disclosed them to the police).
[28] [1974] A.C. 133 at 175.
[29] *ibid.* The principle does not operate so as to enable the prosecuting authorities to find out who has committed a crime so that the individual can be prosecuted by them or can be proceeded against by them for contempt of court: *Secretary for Justice v Apple Daily Ltd* [2000] 2 H.K.L.R.D. 704 (procedure invoked unsuccessfully against a newspaper to find out the name of a journalist who had misreported a murder trial in apparent contempt of court).
[30] *British Steel Corporation v Granada Television* [1981] A.C. 1096; *X v Morgan Grampian* [1991] 1 A.C. 1.

trace assets which have been taken without the alleged fraudsters being alerted,[31] to locate assets upon which a judgment could be enforced,[32] to enable third parties to be identified who had themselves done nothing wrong but who had received letters containing allegedly false statements,[33] and to obtain information which is central to a contemplated claim, and which will show whether the applicant does have a good cause of action against a named person.[34]

(2) It does not apply to a bystander who has written down the details of a hit and run driver who caused an accident because he has not "participated" or been "involved" or become "mixed up" in the wrong.[35]

(3) It applies irrespective of whether the third party has himself committed a tort or a breach of contract or another wrong.[36]

(4) It can be invoked whatever the nature of the wrong which the claimant has suffered including a wrong actionable in civil proceedings, an alleged breach of contract,[37] and a crime of which the claimant is a victim.[38]

(5) The principle applies when the applicant is not able to identify the cause of action without discovery, but when it appears that some wrong has been committed.[39]

(6) There may only be evidence that a wrong has been committed and the assistance is needed to see whether an actionable tort or wrong has been committed.[40] Thus the principle has been used to enable a

---

[31] *Bankers Trust v Shapira* [1980] 1 W.L.R. 1274. *A Co. v B Co.* [2002] 3 H.K.L.R.D. 111 (it is not necessary to have sufficient information to establish a tracing claim). For the use of a gagging order so as to prevent a potential defendant to a tracing claim being alerted, see Chapter 17, para.17.014 and following.

[32] *Mercantile Group (Europe) AG v Aiyela* [1994] Q.B. 366.

[33] *CHC Software Care Ltd v Hopkins & Wood* [1993] F.S.R. 241; see also *Jade Engineering Ltd v Antiference Window Systems* [1996] F.S.R. 461 at 466.

[34] *Carlton Film Distributors Ltd v VCI Plc* [2003] F.S.R. 47, following the observation of Morritt L.J. in *Ara Equity & Law Life Assurance Society Plc v National Westminister Bank* [1998] C.L.C. 1177, which affirmed the first instance decision at [1998] P.N.L.R. 433.

[35] *Ashworth Hospital Authority v MGN Ltd* [2002] 1 W.L.R. 2033 at 25–36; *Norwich Pharmacal v Customs & Excise Commissioners* [1974] A.C. 133 at 174.

[36] *Ashworth Hospital Authority v MGN Ltd* [2002] 1 W.L.R. 2033; *British Steel Corporation v Granada Television* [1981] A.C. 1096 at 1171F.

[37] *Carlton Film Distributors Ltd v VCI Plc* [2003] F.S.R. 47, Ch.D. (disclosure ordered from a third party to see whether applicant had good cause of action for breach of contract against a contemplated defendant).

[38] *Ashworth Hospital Authority v MGN Ltd* [2002] 1 W.L.R. 2033 at [53–56] disapproving contrary dicta in *Financial Times Ltd v Interbrew SA* [2002] 2 Lloyd's Rep. 229.

[39] *P v T Ltd* [1997] 1 W.L.R. 1309; *Ashworth Hospital Authority v MGN Ltd* [2002] 1 W.L.R. 2033 at [57].

[40] *P v T Ltd* [1997] 1 W.L.R. 1309; *Murphy v Murphy* [1999] 1 W.L.R. 282 at 291F–H; *Arsenal Football Club Plc v Elite Sports Distribution* [2003] F.S.R. 450 at [46] and [48].

third party to be identified whom the applicant *might* decide to sue[41] and regardless of whether he is in England.[42] Usually it will be clear to the court on the evidence that some wrongdoing has been committed. However, even when it is questionable whether some wrongdoing has occurred, the circumstances may be such that unless disclosure is ordered the applicant will not be able to investigate what has occurred and if appropriate bring proceedings against those responsible. In those circumstances the court has power to order disclosure under the principle.[43]

(7) It follows that the principle is available when there is only evidence that the respondent may have been mixed up, participated or become involved in a wrong.

(8) The principle can arise independently of a tracing claim, *e.g.* where the claimant has been wronged and needs to find out the identity of the wrongdoer so that he can take steps against him.

(9) In principle, the contemplated steps should be effective to redress the wrong, and the information is not restricted to identifying the wrongdoer but can extend to "full information" required for this purpose, including information about what the wrongdoer has done with his assets.[44]

(10) The key to the jurisdiction is that it enables the claimant to obtain legitimate redress for a wrong which otherwise would not be available to him. This may not be through court proceedings. So, *e.g.* an employer can be assisted in identifying his employee who has acted in breach of confidence so that he can dismiss him.[45]

(11) The "mere witness" rule excludes ordering discovery against a person who would in due course be compellable to give that

---

[41] *Crédit Suisse Fides Trust SA v Cuoghi*, Court of Appeal (Civ Div) Transcript No.1623 of 1995 (December 14, 1995), following *British Steel Corporation v Granada Television* [1981] A.C. 1096.

[42] *Smith Kline and French Laboratories Ltd v Global Pharmaceutical Ltd* [1986] F.S.R. 394; *Jade Engineering Ltd v Antiference Window Systems* [1996] F.S.R. 461. In principle, the fact that the applicant would have to take proceedings abroad should not be a bar to relief; *e.g.* the information might be required to enable a tracing claim to proceed in relation to assets which have been transferred abroad, *cf. Manufacturer's Life Insurance Co. of Canada v Harvest Hero International Ltd* [2001] 2 H.K.L.R.D. 248. However, the jurisdiction should not be used as a means for bypassing the procedures which are in place for regulating the obtaining of evidence to be used in foreign proceedings.

[43] *P v T* [1997] 1 W.L.R. 1309 (disclosure ordered in contemplation that there might be proceedings for libel or malicious falsehood against third parties who had brought about the applicant's dismissal from his employment).

[44] *Mercantile Group AG v Aiyela* [1994] Q.B. 366 at 374G–H.

[45] *British Steel Corporation v Granada Television* [1981] A.C. 1096; *Ashworth Hospital Authority v MGN Ltd* [2002] 1 W.L.R. 2033.

information as a witness at the trial or under a *subpoena duces tecum*.[46] Therefore the *Norwich Pharmacal* principle cannot, *e.g.* be used to obtain a pre-trial deposition from a potential witness.[47]

(12) But the "mere witness" rule will not prevent an order being made when the information is needed pre-trial, to give the claimant effective redress against the wrongdoers,[48] albeit that the information will also be available to be used at trial.

(13) When the third party is a company or corporation its servants or agents can be ordered to give the information on its behalf.[49]

(14) The jurisdiction is discretionary and will be exercised taking into account what would be reasonable and proportionate in the circumstances.[50]

(15) The jurisdiction will not be exercised against a journalist requiring him to reveal his source unless there is a pressing overriding public interest.[51]

(16) The width of the order and whether it is limited to specific documents is itself part of the exercise of the discretion. It may not be appropriate in certain situations to impose any greater burden on a third party than requiring specific documents as can be imposed on a third party by a witness summons,[52] in others the disclosure can be required as a class of documents.[53]

(17) Normally, if the person giving the disclosure is not himself a wrongdoer, the claimant will have to indemnify him against his costs incurred in assisting him.[54] Those costs may be recoverable in due course as damages against the wrongdoer,[55] or as legal costs

---

[46] *Mercantile Group AG v Aiyela* [1994] Q.B. 366 at 374B–375C; *Axa Equity & Law Life Assurance Society Plc v National Westminster Bank* [1998] P.N.L.R. 433 at paras 19 and 23.
[47] *Axa Equity & Law Life Assurance Society Plc v National Westminster Bank* [1998] P.N.L.R. 433.
[48] *Bankers Trust Co. v Shapira* [1980] 1 W.L.R. 1274 (tracing stolen money at the commencement of proceedings); *Arab Monetary Fund v Hashim (No.5)* [1992] 2 All E.R. 911 (jurisdiction applies to trust property which might be dissipated before the trial); *Axa Equity & Law Life Assurance Society Plc v National Westminster Bank* [1998] P.N.L.R. 433 at para.23.
[49] *Harrington v North London Polytechnic* [1984] 1 W.L.R. 1293.
[50] *Ashworth Hospital Authority v MGN Ltd* [2002] 1 W.L.R. 2033 at [36].
[51] *Goodwin v United Kingdom* (1996) 22 E.H.R.R. 123 at 143, para.39 on the effect of Art.10 of the European Convention on Human Rights; *Mersey Care NHS Trust v Ackroyd* [2003] F.S.R. 820 in which the journalist successfully resisted a claim for summary judgment for information about his source (this case is the sequel to *Ashworth Hospital Authority v MGN Ltd* [2002] 1 W.L.R. 2033).
[52] *Arab Monetary Fund v Hashim (No.5)* [1992] 2 All E.R. 911 at 919H considered in *Marc Rich & Co. Holding GmbH v Krasner* [1999] EWCA Civ 581 (January 15, 1999).
[53] *Marc Rich & Co. Holding GmbH v Krasner*, above.
[54] *Totalise Plc v The Motley Fool Ltd* [2002] E.M.L.R. 20, p.358, at para.30; *Norwich Pharmacal v Customs & Excise Commissioners* [1974] A.C. 133 at 175.
[55] *Totalise Plc v The Motley Fool Ltd* [2002] E.M.L.R. 20, p. 358; *Morton-Norwich Products v Intercen Ltd (No.2)* [1981] 1 F.S.R. 337 at 341, 347–350.

under s.51 of the Supreme Court Act 1981. In *Totalise Plc v The Motley Fool Ltd*,[56] Aldous L.J. said:

"29. . . . Norwich Pharmacal applications are not ordinary adversarial proceedings, where the general rule is that the unsuccessful party pays the costs of the successful party. They are akin to proceedings for pre-action disclosure where costs are governed by Part 48.3 CPR. That rule . . . reflects the just outcome and is consistent with the views of Lord Reid and Lord Cross in the *Norwich Pharmacal* case. In general, the costs incurred should be recovered from the wrongdoer rather than from an innocent party. That should be the result, even if such a party writes a letter to the applicant asking him to draw to the court's attention matters which might influence a court to refuse the application. Of course such a letter would need to be drawn to the attention of the court. Each case will depend on its facts and in some cases it may be appropriate for the party from whom disclosure is sought to appear in court to assist. In such a case he should not be prejudiced by being ordered to pay costs.

30. The Court when considering its order as to costs, after a successful *Norwich Pharmacal* application should consider all the circumstances. In a normal case the applicant should be ordered to pay the costs of the party making the disclosure including the costs of making the disclosure. There may be cases where the circumstances require a different order, but we do not believe they include cases where:

(a) the party required to make the disclosure had a genuine doubt that the person seeking the disclosure was entitled to it;

(b) the party was under an appropriate legal obligation not to reveal the information, or where the legal position was not clear, or the party had a reasonable doubt as to the obligations; or

(c) the party could be subject to proceedings if disclosure was voluntary; or

(d) the party would or might suffer damage by voluntarily giving the disclosure; or

(e) the disclosure would or might infringe a legitimate interest of another.

31. That does not mean that a party who supports or is implicated in a crime or tort or seeks to obstruct justice being done should believe that the Court will do other than require that party to bear its costs and, if appropriate, pay the other party's costs."

---

[56] [2002] E.M.L.R. 20, p.358.

The principle can apply where the defendant has set out deliberately to **22.049** make himself judgment proof so as to deny the claimant an effective remedy for his claim, and the third party has facilitated or been involved in this, even if this has been done by him innocently. This could give rise to claims under s.423 of the Insolvency Act 1986[57] and is a "wrong". The jurisdiction is exercisable after judgment has been obtained.[58] Can it be exercised pre-judgment? The objection might be made that pre-judgment the jurisdiction is barred by the "mere witness" exclusionary rule. The exclusionary rule did not apply on the facts in *Norwich Pharmacal* because without the discovery there would not be a trial. *Bankers Trust Co. v Shapira*[59] was a tracing case, in which immediate steps were needed to find out what had happened to stolen money; an order was made in part based on the *Norwich Pharmacal* principle. Unless the information became available it would have been pointless having a trial.

The objection to exercising the jurisdiction pre-judgment overlooks the point that the information is not required for the purpose of establishing the claimant's substantive rights by evidence at the trial, but is required for the wholly different purpose. This is to obtain effective Mareva relief, so that the claimant will have an effective remedy in respect of the wrongdoing which the third party has facilitated. Without the disclosure the claimant would be left without redress for the wrong which the third party had facilitated.

Accordingly, where the non-party has become mixed up in an attempt by **22.050** the defendant to make himself judgment-proof and to defraud his creditors, the third party comes under an obligation to disclose to the claimant "full information"[60] about the relevant assets so as to assist the claimant in the enforcement of his rights against the defendant.[61] An order for disclosure can apply to assets whether in the name of the defendant or the third party[62] and can be made before the claimant has obtained a judgment against the wrongdoer. Application of the *Norwich Pharmacal* principle does not depend upon there being a proprietary claim. It could apply where the defendant has set about concealing or transferring assets so as to deny the claimant a remedy, because this is a "wrong", and the jurisdiction can be exercised irrespective of whether the third party has acted innocently or whether any remedy would on the facts be available against him based on s.423 of the Insolvency Act 1986.

---

[57] See Chapter 13, paras 13.018 and following.
[58] *Mercantile Group AG v Aiyela* [1994] Q.B. 366 (post-judgment in aid of enforcement of a judgment)
[59] [1980] 1 W.L.R. 1274; see also *Arab Monetary Fund v Hashim (No.5)* [1992] 2 All E.R. 911 (jurisdiction applies to trust property which might be dissipated before the trial); *Axa Equity & Law Life Assurance Society Plc v National Westminster Bank* [1998] P.N.L.R. 433 at para.23.
[60] *Norwich Pharmacal v Customs & Excise* [1974] A.C. 133 at 175; *Bankers Trust Co. v Shapira* [1980] 1 W.L.R. 1274; *Arab Monetary Fund v Hashim (No.5)* [1992] 2 All E.R. 911.
[61] *Mercantile Group (Europe) v Aiyela* [1994] Q.B. 366, affirming [1993] F.S.R. 745.
[62] [1993] F.S.R. 745 at 752, *per* Hobhouse J.

(7) Case (2): orders for disclosure of information by third parties in tracing actions

(i) Purposes for which the information may be required

22.051   The information is potentially relevant to (a) who to sue; (b) proof of the cause of action; (c) the granting of interim remedies in respect of the assets or their proceeds which are the subject of the claim; (d) the formulation of final relief in substantive proceedings based on the substantive cause of action of the claimant in respect of his property; and (e) the enforcement of a future judgment.

(ii) Case (2): available remedies

22.052   The remedies available against a third party are:

(1)   Witness summons under CPR r.34.2—see paras 22.040 and following, above.

(2)   Disclosure by a non-party under CPR r.31.17. Disclosure under CPR r.31.17 is available because CPR r.31.17(3) is satisfied. The purpose of the rule is to enable disclosure from a third party for the same purposes as disclosure between the parties to the proceedings.[63] This includes resolution at the trial of the substantive rights of the parties, including the question of what substantive relief is to be granted and in what terms.

(3)   Pre-action disclosure under CPR r.31.16. This could be relevant in a potential tracing claim when the applicant is considering a substantive claim against the respondent and wants to obtain information to see whether this should be done. The applicant does not have to show that the commencement of such proceedings is itself likely.[64]

(4)   An order made against a bank under s.7 of the Bankers' Books Evidence Act 1879. This is discussed at paras 22.044 and following. *A v C*[65] was a tracing claim.

(5)   An order giving an interim remedy under CPR r.25.1 to which a disclosure order would be ancillary. Where a non-party holds the assets claimed by the claimant, he can be joined as a defendant in the proceedings and an interim remedy can be granted directly against him. The interim remedies in CPR r.25.1(1)(c) and (l) apply to proprietary claims where the assets or their value need to be

---

[63] For the requirements to be satisfied under CPR r.31.17, see *Three Rivers District Council v Governor and Company of the Bank of England (No.4)* [2003] 1 W.L.R. 210.

[64] *Black v Sumitomo Corporation* [2002] 1 W.L.R. 1562.

[65] [1981] Q.B. 956 at 960.

preserved pending determination of the case, leaving the substantive rights of the parties unaffected.[66]

(6) An order under CPR r.31.16 for pre-action disclosure under s.33(2) of the Supreme Court Act 1981.

(7) An injunction granted under s.37(1) of the Supreme Court Act 1981 against the non-party, requiring him to disclose information about assets, based on the cause of action against the defendant. The jurisdiction against non-parties is discussed in Chapter 13. In addition where a non-party holds the assets claimed by the claimant, he can be joined as a defendant to a claim for substantive relief.

(8) An order based on the principle in *Norwich Pharmacal v Customs & Excise Commissioners.*[67]

(9) An order requiring disclosure based on the equitable jurisdiction of the court to safeguard trust assets.

(iii) *Case (2): the equitable jurisdiction of the court to safeguard trust assets and* Norwich Pharmacal

The court has an equitable jurisdiction to find out what has happened to **22.053** missing trust funds:

> "A court of equity has never hesitated to use the strongest powers to protect and preserve a trust fund in interlocutory proceedings on the basis that, if the trust fund disappears by the time the action comes to trial, equity will have been invoked in vain".[68]

This is a separate[69] principle from the Norwich Pharmacal principle and has a different purpose. It enables orders to be made against a defendant and against innocent third parties[70] for the purpose of protecting the claimant's substantive rights to the fund.

The courts have adopted this principle in tracing actions for justifying interlocutory orders made at any stage of the proceedings requiring those

---

[66] *On Demand Information Ltd v Michael Gerson (Finance) Plc* [2003] 1 A.C. 368 and see Chapter 23, paras 23.005–23.007.
[67] [1974] A.C. 133 at 175.
[68] *Mediterranea Raffineria Siciliana Petroli SpA v Mabanaft GmbH*, Court of Appeal (Civ Div) Transcript No.816 of 1978 (December 1, 1978), *per* Templeman L.J. cited in *Bankers Trust Co. v Shapira* [1980] 1 W.L.R. 1274 at 1280H–1281D, *per* Lord Denning M.R.
[69] *Murphy v Murphy* [1999] 1 W.L.R. 282 at 288–289; *Aoot Kalmneft v Denton Wilde Sapte* [2002] 1 Lloyd's Rep. 417.
[70] See generally *Mediterranea Raffineria Siciliana Petroli SpA v Mabanaft GmbH*, Court of Appeal (Civ Div) Transcript No.816 of 1978 (December 1, 1978); *A v C* [1981] Q.B. 956; *Bankers Trust Co. v Shapira* [1980] 1 W.L.R. 1274; *Mackinnon v Donaldson Lufkin and Jenrette Corporation* [1986] Ch. 482; and also *London & Counties Securities Ltd (In Liquidation) v Caplan*, unreported, May 26, 1978 (Templeman J.), which is referred to in the other cases.

who may have information (including documents) about what has happened to particular assets, and who have been involved in their disposal, to provide that information to the claimant. This has included orders made against banks for disclosure of information about assets. When the claimant has the right to shares in a company and the assets in the company have gone missing, the court can disregard the corporate veil and grant orders designed to reveal what has happened to the company's assets or their proceeds.[71]

There is also the *Norwich Pharmacal* principle (see paras 22.048 and following, above). In a case in which trust assets have been transferred and are missing, both principles can apply.

22.054   The relief can be granted on an application made without notice and may take the form of a search order, but more usually is granted as against the third party on an application made with notice. Although it is not essential, the person from whom information is sought is usually joined as a defendant in the action.[72]

The person from whom information is sought may be restrained from communicating with the defendant or other third parties (except for the purpose of seeking legal advice) about what is afoot.[73] An example of a "gagging order" is the order granted by Walton J. set out in *Rank Film Ltd v Video Information Centre*.[74]

When it is necessary to obtain a gagging order, the claimant should consider first obtaining such an injunction without notice over a hearing to take place *inter partes* against the third party at which an application will be made to continue the gag and for an order requiring the information to be furnished. This procedure stops the third party communicating with others about the proceedings whilst at the same time allowing the matter to be dealt with at an *inter partes* hearing at which the third party can be represented. If a gagging order is granted, this would as a matter of English law override any duty which the third party has to communicate with the defendant (*e.g.* a contractual duty of a bank to do its best to communicate with its customer).[75] Unless the gagging order clearly stipulates to the contrary it would impliedly permit the bank to communicate with the authorities in relation to money laundering.[76] It is upon the principle that so far as is possible an injunction should not be interpreted as requiring a person to do an illegal act.

22.055   The jurisdiction is directed to uncovering the location of assets so that they can be preserved, and any application for an order pursuant to this jurisdiction should be honed so as to pursue this purpose. An order should

---

[71] *Omar v Omar* [1995] 1 W.L.R. 1428 at 1431.
[72] *A v C* [1981] Q.B. 956 at 958 and 959.
[73] See further Chapter 17, paras 17.014 and following.
[74] [1982] A.C. 380 at 385.
[75] See Chapter 20, paras 20.018–20.019.
[76] *C v S (Money Laundering: Discovery of Documents)* [1999] 1 W.L.R. 1551 at 1557A–B. See also Chapter 20, paras 20.020–20.022.

not be made unless there is a real prospect[77] that as a result assets can be located and preserved. If the relevant transactions go back several years, this may make it unlikely that an order would advance the purpose of the jurisdiction.

The order should not be too general or wide. It should, so far as possible,[78] be specific, and directed to uncovering the particular assets which are to be traced: *Arab Monetary Fund v Hashim (No.5)*.[79]

The court should also consider whether the case merits any invasion of privacy or confidentiality involved in requiring the third party to disclose the information sought. The court must balance the interests of the claimant in seeking the order and the possible detriment to the third party if the order is made: *Arab Monetary Fund v Hashim (No.5)*, above.[80]

If an order is to be made against a bank or other third party, the **22.056** claimant is required to furnish an undertaking in damages, and must pay the expenses of the innocent third party in complying with the order. The documents or information obtained can be used only for tracing the assets or their proceeds.[81]

(8) Case (3): orders for disclosure of information by third parties post-judgment

The court has in addition to the remedies available to it pre-judgment the **22.057** jurisdiction to grant an injunction in aid of enforcement or execution of a judgment. This can take the form of an injunction granted directly against a third party with an ancillary disclosure order.[82] The fact that a final judgment has been obtained weighs with the court in exercising any discretion.

(9) Information from a bank relating to an account at a branch abroad

The claimant might wish to seek information from a bank about an account **22.058** held abroad, either in the context of a tracing claim or simply to preserve assets of the defendant either pre-judgment or in aid of execution of a judgment. The plaintiff may seek the information in the following ways:

---

[77] *Arab Monetary Fund v Hashim (No.5)* [1992] 2 All E.R. 911 at 918; *Dubai Bank v Galadari, The Times*, October 14, 1992; Sir Leonard Hoffmann, "Changing Perspectives on Civil Litigation" [1993] M.L.R 297 at 304.
[78] *Marc Rich & Co. Holding GmbH v Krasner* [1999] EWCA Civ 581 (January 15, 1999).
[79] [1992] 2 All E.R. 911 at 919.
[80] *ibid.*
[81] *Bankers Trust Co. v Shapira* [1980] 1 W.L.R. 1274 at 1282.
[82] See Chapter 13.

(1) Under CPR r.34.13 a letter of request can be issued to the judicial authorities of a foreign country to obtain the evidence. The rule is not limited to obtaining evidence directed to the determination of the substantive claim on the merits. If there is a tracing claim, information about assets subject to the claim may well be relevant evidence in the substantive proceedings. In the context of a non-tracing claim, the information may still be relevant evidence for the purpose of proceedings concerning Mareva relief, or an injunction granted in aid of execution of the judgment.

(2) An application may be made directly to the foreign court to order disclosure of the information. Such an application would ordinarily be entirely appropriate, and would be viewed by the English court as entirely proper. There can be no objection in principle to the claimant obtaining information under a court order made by a court abroad which can be used to preserve the relevant assets either abroad or within the jurisdiction. Thus, in the converse position in *Republic of Haiti v Duvalier*,[83] the English court itself made orders directed to obtaining information about assets, when the proceedings on the merits were in France, and did so whether or not the claim on the merits was properly to be regarded as the equivalent of a tracing or proprietary claim.[84] The English court would restrain the application to the foreign court for information only if, in the circumstances, it would be "unconscionable" for the claimant to make the application.[85]

(3) The claimant might seek to serve a witness summons issued under CPR r.34.2 on the English branch of the bank, or might seek an order from the court under s.7 of the Bankers' Books Evidence Act 1879. The courts have laid down the principle that in general the foreign branch should be subject to the orders of the foreign court, and that the English court should not seek information from the foreign branch by means of process served on the English branch. Although there is territorial jurisdiction to uphold the witness summons or to make an order under s.7, the English court, as a matter of restraint, will, as a general rule, refrain from requiring disclosure of documents or information from the English branch in relation to an account at the foreign branch.[86] In *Mackinnon v Donaldson, Lufkin and Jenrette Securities*, a subpoena had been

---

[83] [1990] 1 Q.B. 202.

[84] *Ibid.*, at 214–215.

[85] *South Carolina Co. v Assurantie NV* [1987] A.C. 24 at 41; see Chapter 14, paras 14.033–14.035.

[86] *Mackinnon v Donaldson, Lufkin and Jenrette Securities Corporation* [1986] Ch. 482; *Société Eram Shipping Co. Ltd v Compagnie Internationale de Navigation* [2004] 1 A.C. 260 at [22–23] and [67]; *R. v Grossman* (1981) 73 Cr. App. R. 302; *Power Curber v National Bank of Kuwait* [1981] 1 W.L.R. 1233 at 1241. Contrast the position under the Insolvency Act 1986, s.236: *Re Mid East Trading (No.2)*, [1998] 1 All E.R. 577.

served, and an order obtained *ex parte* under s.7, which had the effect of requiring the production by a non-party of documents outside the jurisdiction, concerning business which it had transacted outside the jurisdiction. Hoffmann J. set aside both the subpoena and the order, and said:[87]

> "In principle and on authority it seems to me that the court should not, save in exceptional circumstances, impose such a requirement upon a foreigner, and in particular, upon a foreign bank. The principle is that a state should refrain from demanding obedience to its sovereign authority by foreigners in respect of their conduct outside the jurisdiction."

This is a question of subject-matter jurisdiction; it does not follow from the fact that the bank is subject to the coercive power of the English court that an order can properly be made against it in respect of a matter which should be regulated by the local court which has jurisdiction over its foreign branch.[88] In the converse situation, where a foreign court seeks to serve process on a branch abroad compelling disclosure of information concerning transactions or an account at an English branch, the court may grant an injunction to prevent the bank complying with the foreign court order.[89]

(4) In the context of a tracing claim, the claimant might seek to obtain relief against the bank under the *Norwich Pharmacal* principle or the equitable jurisdiction to order disclosure for the purpose of protecting a trust fund.[90] However, this route is subject to precisely the same discretionary constraints as applied in the case of a *subpoena duces tecum* and now apply under a witness summons, or the exercise of the jurisdiction under s.7 of the Bankers' Books Evidence Act 1879.[91] The fact that under this route disclosure is sought by way of enforcement of the bank's duty to give assistance to the claimant does not affect the self-imposed restraint which the English court will exercise.

(10) Orders affecting the liberty of the defendant

The court has jurisdiction under s.37(1) to grant in support of a claim an injunction which prevents the defendant from leaving the jurisdiction and requires him to surrender his passport. This is an interference with the   **22.059**

---

[87] [1986] Ch. 482 at 493. See further *Grupo Torras v Sheik Fahad Al-Sabah*, Court of Appeal (Civ Div) Transcript No.159 of 1994 (February 16, 1994), *per* Steyn L.J.
[88] See Chapter 19, paras 19.041–19.046.
[89] *X, Y and Z v B* [1983] 2 Lloyd's Rep. 535.
[90] *Bankers Trust Co. v Shapira* [1980] 1 W.L.R. 1274 at 1281–1282; *Norwich Pharmacal Co. v Customs and Excise Commissioners* [1974] A.C. 133 at 175, *per* Lord Reid.
[91] *Mackinnon v Donaldson, Lufkin and Jenrette Corporation* [1986] Ch. 482 at 497–499.

defendant's liberty and so will not be ordered unless it is reasonable and proportionate to do so and will remain in force for no longer than is necessary to accomplish its legitimate purpose.[92] In *Bayer AG v Winter*,[93] relief granted against the defendants included mandatory orders for the disclosure of documents and information concerning both the substantive claim on the merits and the defendants' assets, and an Anton Piller order covering both premises and vehicles. The plaintiffs claimed that the defendants were engaged in marketing counterfeit insecticides, which appeared as if they had been manufactured by the plaintiffs. It was hoped that the information and documents would enable the plaintiffs to identify other parties involved in supplying or purchasing the goods. The first defendant appeared to have no permanent residence within the jurisdiction, and it was feared that he might leave the jurisdiction and thus frustrate subsequent enforcement of the orders of the court (*e.g.* by means of an order for cross-examination). The Court of Appeal, sitting *in camera*, granted an injunction of short duration restraining him from leaving the jurisdiction and ordering him to deliver up his passports. If hardship was caused to the defendant, he could apply forthwith to the High Court to vary or discharge the order.

The jurisdiction to grant this relief is derived from s.37(1) of the Supreme Court Act 1981.[94] It is separate from and not subject to the limitations of the procedure by way of the writ *ne exeat regno*.[95] Since this relief constitutes an interference with the liberty of the subject, it should be in force for no longer than is strictly necessary to achieve its purpose,[96] namely to ensure that the orders of the court can be enforced. In *B v B (Injunction: Jurisdiction*[97] an order was sought by a wife against her husband so as to enforce an unpaid order for costs. The order was refused because this would have introduced a new remedy for enforcement of an unpaid debt.[98]

22.060   If the circumstances are appropriate for seeking such an order, it will usually be essential to keep secret the existence of the proceedings and the order prior to service. Unless some precaution is taken, the defendant may acquire information about what is afoot from the court file[99] or from the fact that a claim form has been issued against him. In the case of the court file, the court appears to have inherent jurisdiction to give directions about access to it, and can make an order for the file to be sealed up, and marked

---

[92] *Bayer AG v Winter* [1986] 1 W.L.R. 497; *Ali v Naseem, The Times*, October 3, 2003; *Robinson v Robinson*, [2004] 1 P. & C.R. D7 (Richards J.) (to enable enforcement of an order for disclosure of assets whilst the defendant to counterclaim was kept subject to the coercive powers of the court).
[93] [1986] 1 W.L.R. 497.
[94] *Morris v Murjani* [1996] 1 W.L.R. 848 at 852–853, disapproving of dicta in *Re Oriental Credit* [1988] Ch. 203; *Maclaine Watson & Co. v International Tin Council (No.2)* [1989] Ch. 286 at 305–306.
[95] See Chapter 21, above.
[96] *Allied Arab Bank Ltd v Hajjar* [1988] Q.B. 787 at 795–796.
[97] [1998] 1 W.L.R. 329 at 334F–335E.
[98] This case is discussed in Chapter 16, at paras 16.014–16.018, in connection with the decision in *Field v Field* [2003] 1 F.L.R. 376.
[99] CPR r.5.4(1).

with a reference number and a direction that it is not to be inspected save with the leave of the court. In the case of the claim form, the court can direct that information relating to the issuing of the claim form is similarly to be kept confidential by the court pending further direction. The basis for this jurisdiction lies in the court's inherent jurisdiction to control its own process so as to prevent its orders being rendered useless.

(11) Gagging orders

It may be necessary to prevent anyone informing others of the existence of 22.061 proceedings or orders made in those proceedings. For example, a claimant who has lost assets may want to trace those assets and freeze them before the wrongdoers are alerted to what is happening. The example search order contains the following prohibitions:

"PROHIBITED ACTS

20. Except for the purpose of obtaining legal advice, the Respondent must not directly or indirectly inform anyone of these proceedings or of the contents of this order, or warn anyone that proceedings have been or may be brought against him by the Applicant until 4.30 p.m. on the return date or further order of the court."

Gagging orders are discussed at paras 17.014–17.016, above.

(12) Disclosure by a solicitor of names and addresses of third party intervenors

The court can order a solicitor who has acted for persons who have 22.062 intervened in proceedings in respect of an interlocutory order made under s.37(1), but who have not become parties, to disclose the names and addresses of those for whom he had acted. Such an order can be made under s.37(1), as being incidental to the exercise of jurisdiction under that section, or under the inherent jurisdiction of the court to regulate its own proceedings.[1]

---

[1] *International Credit & Investment Company (Overseas) v Adham*, Court of Appeal Transcript No.1740 of 1997 (October 28, 1997).

Chapter 23

Expiry of an injunction, discharge, variations and appeals

(1) Expiry of the injunction

CPR Pt 25, Practice Direction—Interim Injunctions para.5.2 provides:

> "5.2 An order for an injunction made in the presence of all parties to **23.001** be bound by it or made at a hearing of which they have had notice, may state that it is effective until trial or further order."

In the Commercial Court it was common to use the expression "until trial or further order". That expression is ambiguous because it does not say whether the injunction is to expire at the beginning or at the end of the trial.[1] In practice, if an injunction had been granted until trial or further order, a formal application was usually made at the commencement of the trial to continue the injunction until after judgment had been given in the action. The practice changed so that normally a Mareva injunction granted without a return date or *inter partes* would be "until judgment or further order". In the 1996 standard forms for Mareva injunctions,[2] provision was made for alternatives:

> Alternative A was for the injunction to last up until the return date inserted in the order unless previously varied or discharged.
> Alternative B was for the injunction to last up until judgment in the action unless previously varied or discharged.

These alternatives do not appear in the example form of freezing injunction obtained on a without notice application, because of para.5.1(3) of the Practice Direction, which provides that unless the court orders otherwise there is to be a return date. The *Chancery Guide* in para.5.20 states:

> "When an application for an injunction is heard without notice, and the Judge decides that an injunction should be granted, it will

---

[1] *Yamabuta v Tay (No.2)* (1995) 16 W.A.R. 262—"until trial" included the giving of judgment.
[2] [1996] 1 W.L.R. 1552.

normally be granted for a limited period only—usually not more than seven days. The same applies to an interim order appointing a receiver. The applicant will be required to give the respondent notice of his or her intention to apply to the court at the expiration of that period for the order to be continued. In the meantime the respondent will be entitled to apply, though generally only after giving notice to the applicant, for the order to be varied or discharged."[3]

23.002   The practice now in the Commercial Court is that a return date will be provided for in the order unless the judge otherwise orders[4] and that the initial return date will be a Friday or the date of a case management conference if one has already been fixed.[5] In the case of an injunction which is expressed to last until a specified date which is the return date, then the injunction lasts for that date,[6] and expires at midnight at the end of that day. This is because the purpose of the order is to hold the position until the injunction can be reconsidered on the specified date and the words are to be interpreted in that context.

The *Admiralty and Commercial Courts Guide* at para.F.16 provides that the phrase "until judgment or further order" covers the period up until the delivery of a final judgment. The purpose of this wording is to hold the position until the injunction can be considered by the court following the handing down of judgment and so the injunction does not expire until the end of the hearing at which the judgment is formally handed down by the court to the parties. At para.K1.1(b) the Guide states:

> "If a party wishes to continue a freezing order after trial or judgment, care should be taken to ensure that the application is made before the existing freezing order has expired."

23.003   If an injunction is granted "until further order", then it continues until it is expressly or by necessary implication discharged by an order of the court. In *Cantor Index v Lister*[7] the entry by consent of a final judgment did not amount to such a "further order", nor did an order for payment into court for the credit of the action, which was not by way of security for the judgment.

If the claimant succeeds in the action, he may apply for an extension of the injunction in aid of execution.

---

[3] See also *Queen's Bench Guide*, para.7.13.2.

[4] *Admiralty and Commercial Courts Guide*, para.F.8(a) and CPR Pt 25 Practice Direction, para.5.1(3).

[5] If more than 15 minutes is required for the hearing it is necessary to inform listing. *Admiralty and Commercial Courts Guide*, para.F.8(b).

[6] *Medina Housing Association Ltd v Connolly*, unreported, July 26, 2002, CA.

[7] Unreported, November 22, 2001 (Neuberger J.); see also *Telesystem International Wireless Incorporated v CVC/Opportunity Equity Partners L.P.* [2002] C.I.L.R. 96 at paras. 37–42 (Interim injunction prohibiting any use of a document superseded by limited use prohibition as soon as pronounced orally at trial).

The granting of an injunction pending appeal is discussed in para.23.036 and following, below, and paras 3.025–3.026, above.

(2) Discharge of Mareva relief on settlement

If the claimant wishes to conclude a settlement of the claim, the cause of **23.004** action itself may become extinguished, being superseded by the rights under the settlement agreement. Notwithstanding the settlement, an injunction until judgment or further order will continue until formally discharged by the court,[8] but discharge would be granted as a matter of course because the claimant no longer has the cause of action to which the injunction was ancillary. This is because if the settlement agreement results in an immediate compromise of the cause of action and provides for the defendant to perform certain obligations in due course, the *Siskina* rule will have the consequence that Mareva relief can only be granted once a new cause of action is acquired by the claimant; ordinarily this would be on default by the defendant under the settlement.

If it is desired to continue the Mareva injunction pending payment, the options are:

(1) A settlement agreement which leaves intact the claimant's underlying cause of action and the injunction until payment has been made.

(2) A settlement agreement with the defendant providing to the court an undertaking in terms corresponding to those of the Mareva injunction, to support performance by him of the settlement agreement. The undertaking should be expressed to continue until after payment under the settlement. The undertaking given to the court can be enforced by contempt proceedings.[9] If made in the form of a Tomlin order, the rights under the settlement agreement, which are only contractual rights and do not have the effect of a judgment, can be enforced by the court in the existing proceedings.[10]

(3) An agreement providing for the defendant to comply with the freezing injunction pending payment and that the injunction should remain in force. The injunction is then based on the negative promise given by the defendant as part of the settlement agreement.

(4) The defendant submits to judgment, with the injunction being continued in aid of execution.

8 *Isaacs v Robertson* [1985] A.C. 97; *Hadkinson v Hadkinson* [1952] P. 285 at 288.
9 *Macteldir Pty Ltd v Dimovski* (2003) 202 Q.L.R. 83.
10 *E. F. Philips & Sons Ltd v Clarke* [1970] Ch. 322.

If the defendant has submitted to judgment for the full amount of a claim based on allegations of dishonesty, this may provide a good reason for granting an injunction in aid of execution.[11]

(3) Discharge of an injunction by an alternative arrangement or an interim order made by the court

(i) Interim orders and agreements

23.005   It is often the case that in proceedings an order is made granting an interim remedy, or an arrangement is worked out by agreement of the parties, and then the question arises as to whether that interim remedy or voluntary arrangement has changed the substantive rights of the parties.

In *On Demand Information Ltd v Michael Gerson (Finance) Plc*[12] there was a claim for relief from forfeiture by the lessees of equipment, and an interlocutory order was made for the sale of that equipment as the subject-matter of the action under what was then RSC Ord. 29, r.4.[13] The equipment was the subject-matter of the claim in the proceedings for relief from forfeiture. Once the goods had been sold there was no longer a subject for relief from forfeiture. The House of Lords decided that the order for the sale was not intended by the court to affect the parties' substantive rights. The sale only affected the remedy. The consequence was that the court had to make equivalent orders in relation to the proceeds of sale as if the equipment had not been sold. Often a voluntary, interim arrangement is intended by the parties to be a substitution for the interim remedy, which may be an interim injunction or one granted on a without notice application, but is not intended by them to affect the parties' substantive rights as against each other, as they were prior to the conclusion of the arangement.

A freezing injunction does not create any security for the claimant.[14] The example freezing injunction provides in para.11(4):

"(4) The order will cease to have effect if the Respondent—

(a) provides security by paying the sum of £   into court, to be held to the order of the court; or

(b) makes provision for security in that sum by another method agreed with the Applicant's legal representatives."

This provides a facility for the defendant so that the injunction immediately ceases to have effect once the defendant has provided security. If

---

[11] *Snap-On UK Holdings Ltd v S Winkles*, unreported, November 26, 2002 (Judge Rich, Q.C.) see Chapter 12, para.12.040.
[12] [2003] 1 A.C. 368.
[13] Under the CPR the jurisdiction is listed in CPR r.25.1(1)(c)(v).
[14] See Chapter 3 para.3.001.

the defendant does provide security under this paragraph the position of the claimant will be improved because his claim will be transformed from one that is unsecured to one which is secured.

More usually the parties negotiate an agreement for an interim **23.006** arrangement which is to stand in place of the freezing order. Often the arrangement provides a fund over which the claimant has no security interest but which is frozen and held in safe custody pending determination of the proceedings. The effect of the agreement is a question of construction which depends on the words of the interim agreement interpreted against the background. Likewise when an interim order is made by the court its effect is a question of construction. The fact that the injunction conferred no security interest is part of that background. When the object of the voluntary agreement or interim order is restricted to preserving the asset position pending determination of the substantive rights, then it is a natural conclusion that the parties' rights in respect of the fund mirror the pre-existing position.

In *Flightline Ltd v Edwards*[15] a freezing injunction had been made against a company in the Swissair group. It did not have para.11(4). The company applied to discharge the injunction. When the application was pending, a sum of money became available to the company which by agreement was paid into a joint account established by the two firms of solicitors and an amount equivalent to the maximum sum of the freezing injunction was paid into it. Subsequently the company compromised the interlocutory dispute on terms where the freezing injunction was discharged and a smaller amount remained in the joint account subject to an undertaking by the company "Not to withdraw or in any way dispose of or deal with or encumber its interest in the moneys in the [joint account] up to [an agreed limit] pending further order of the court or the written consent of [the two firms of solicitors]". The question was whether the claimant had acquired a security interest over the joint account. The Court of Appeal held that it did not because although it restricted use of the fund it did not provide that a judgment had to be paid out of that fund. Before there could be an equitable charge there had not only to be a restraint of use of the fund, which would have been sufficient to justify intervention by injunction,[16] but also a legal obligation in favour of the creditor to pay him out of that fund.[17] The words of the undertaking only froze the fund and did not subject it to a contractual promise to pay the creditor out of the fund.[18]

In *Halvanon Co. Ltd v Central Reinsurance Corporation*[19] money had **23.007** been placed in a joint account in the names of the parties' then solicitors, as a result of an order for conditional leave to defend an action. Part of

---

[15] [2003] 1 W.L.R. 1200.
[16] See Chapter 12, paras 12.012–12.013.
[17] Applying *Palmer v Carey* [1926] A.C. 703 at 706–707, *per* Lord Wrenbury, and *Swiss Bank Corporation v Lloyds Bank Ltd* [1982] A.C. 584 at 613A–E, *per* Lord Wilberforce.
[18] See also *Celtic Contractors Ltd v Infinite Environmental Services*, April 15, 2003, CA.
[19] [1988] 1 W.L.R. 1122 at 1128.

the purpose of such an order when it requires a payment into court, is to lead to constitution of a fund over which the claimant had a security interest.[20] The establishment of a joint account was machinery for the constitution of the fund, and the effect was to create a security interest over that fund for the plaintiff's claim.

Where the arrangement is in substitution for Mareva relief, and only freezes the fund, without creating a security interest in it for the claimant, the question arises as to in what circumstances the defendant is to be allowed access to it. This depends on the following:

(1) The interpretation of the agreement: What is the scope of the negative contractual promise given by the defendant in relation to the fund? Has the defendant expressly or impliedly promised not to touch the fund until after the proceedings are over and any judgment has been satisfied?

(2) If there is such a promise as part of an agreement, the court will respect that agreement, and will not assist the defendant to unfreeze the fund even though the defendant is the beneficial owner of it. A similar problem arises when a court declines to give effect to the claimant's ownership in land when the defendant has a contractual licence to remain. The analysis is that where the defendant seeks to go back on his contract a court of equity can grant an injunction to restrain a breach of the negative covenant not to touch the fund, and normally would do so.[21] The corollary is that the court will not grant any relief to the defendant to rescue his fund or any part of it based upon his ownership of it, whilst the negative promise not to touch it would be enforced by injunction.

In addition, "Equity will not assist a man to break his contract".[22] If in breach of his contract with the claimant, the defendant seeks discretionary assistance from the court to release the claimant's grip on the fund, the court will not grant it.[23] The rule is not an absolute one as is shown by the cases on exercising the discretion to grant leave to serve a foreigner out of the jurisdiction in the face of an exclusive jurisdiction clause in favour of a foreign court.[24] There the applicant requires the discretionary assistance of the court to assist him in acting in breach of his contract and the court will not assist him without very strong reason to do so.

(3) Assuming that the answer is that the fund is frozen, but the promise not to touch it is subject to the discretion of the court to

---

[20] *W. A. Sherratt Ltd v John Bromley (Church Stretton) Ltd* [1985] Q.B. 1038; see further, para.23.008, below.

[21] See Chapter 2, paras 2.010–2.012 and Chapter 12, para.12.012.

[22] *Hounslow London Borough Council v Twickenham Garden Developments Ltd* [1971] Ch. 233 at 248E.

[23] *ibid.*, at 254E proposition (4).

[24] *Evans Marshall & Co. v Bertola SA* [1973] 1 W.L.R. 349 at 362.

release amounts to the defendant, when will the court be prepared to release an amount to the defendant? In Re *Kingsley Healthcare Ltd*[25] an undertaking was given by consent not to dispose of or deal with a particular interest in land given in return for discharging a freezing injunction. The first question was whether the consent order was to be interpreted as not preventing the defendant from applying to the court for a variation to allow legal costs of the defence to come out of the asset. The second question was whether there had been a material change of circumstances since the undertaking had been given or whether the principle in *Chanel v F. W.Woolworth & Co. Ltd*[26] applied. The third question was how to exercise the discretion. As regards discretion, it was relevant to take into account the advantage which the defendant had obtained through the undertaking in relation to dealing with his other assets free from the freezing injunction and so the court refused to release anything from the fund frozen by agreement unless and until the defendant showed that there were no other funds from which to meet the expenditure and that it was just that the expenditure be allowed.

(ii) *The effect of a payment into court or payment to the defendant's solicitor to be held subject to the order of the court*

Under CPR r.37.1:   23.008

"(2) Money paid into court under a court order may not be paid out without the court's permission except where—

(a) the defendant treats the money as a Part 36 payment under rule 37.2; and
(b) the claimant accepts the Part 36 payment without needing the permission of the court."

This rule envisages that the money paid into court by the defendant under a court order remains available to the defendant to settle the claimant's claim. Assuming that to be the case, then the defendant can use the fund to make an offer under CPR Pt 36.

Money in court is subject to the control of the court. Where it is money belonging to the defendant which has been paid into court, it remains his property. Whether a charge has been created over it for the claimant's claim and what the circumstances are in which the court will release it to the claimant or the defendant depend upon the circumstances

[25] Unreported, September 25, 2001, Ch.D. (Neuberger J.).
[26] [1981] 1 W.L.R. 485; para.20.016.

in which the payment into court has been made. The rules controlling payments into court have changed with CPR, but the basic principle remains the same, namely that the court retains physical custody of the fund and that the effect of the payment into court depends on the circumstances in which the payment into court has been made:

(1) When payment is made into court in the proceedings as the price of obtaining permission to defend in an application for summary judgment, the effect is to subject the money to the claimant's claim and therefore the claimant has a secured claim.[27] The reason is that the purpose of the order is to put the claimant in no worse a position than if he had obtained final judgment and had been able to execute on the defendant's assets.

(2) The same is true of a voluntary payment into court made by a defendant[28] in order to get the claimant to settle and to protect the defendant's position on costs pursuant to CPR Pt 36.

(3) Likewise an order made for the purchaser of land who has gone into possession to pay the purchase money into court creates a security interest in the vendor over the amount paid into court.[29]

(4) If there is a freezing injunction limited to a maximum sum, payment by the defendant of an amount into court from his assets will go towards the maximum sum, and therefore produce a corresponding reduction in the effect of the injunction in relation to the defendant's other assets.

(5) Where the payment into court is made under a court order everything depends on what was the purpose of the order; this is a question of construction of the order.[30] Not every payment into court under a court order creates security for the claim.

(6) A payment into court may be made under an order the intent of which is to put the money into safe custody and not to subject it to the claimant's claim. For example, this would be so of a payment into court made under a mandatory injunction granted under the Mareva jurisdiction made to safeguard the assets. In that case the court's jurisdiction to order release of the funds to the defendant would be exercised on the basis of the principles set out in Chapter 20.

---

[27] *W. A. Sherratt Ltd v John Bromley (Church Stretton) Ltd* [1985] Q.B. 1038; *Halvanon Insurance Co. Ltd v Central Reinsurance Corporation* [1988] 1 W.L.R. 1122 at 1133F; *Re Ford Ex p. The Trustee* [1900] 2 Q.B. 211 at 213.
[28] *Re Gordon* [1897] 2 Q.B. 516 at 519; *W. A. Sherratt Ltd v John Bromley (Church Stretton) Ltd* [1985] Q.B. 1038.
[29] *Pearlberg v May* [1951] Ch. 699.
[30] *On Demand Information Ltd v Michael Gerson (Finance) Plc* [2003] 1 A.C. 368 at [8], [33] and [46].

(7) The payment into court may be made pursuant to an order made by consent in which case the court will give effect to the underlying agreement as set out at paras 23.005 and following, above. If that agreement leaves it open to the court to release funds to the defendant consistently with what he has agreed, the question will arise as to whether there has been a material change of circumstances or whether the principle in *Chanel v F. W. Woolworth & Co. Ltd*[31] applies. This question arises regardless of whether the interim agreement was given effect to by provision of an undertaking or by consent order. Then there is an exercise of discretion to be made taking into account the history, the purpose of the consent order and whether it would be just to allow the release.[32]

When the court has ordered that a fund be held by the defendant's **23.009** solicitor to the order of the court, the same principles apply. Whether the fund is held to the order of the court through payment into court or through the court's officer is mechanics and does not control the effect of the order. For example, such an order may be made under CPR r.3.1(2)(m) in order to provide the other party with security for costs, or under s.37(2) of the Matrimonial Causes Act 1973 for a party to provide security for the claim.[33] When the purpose of the order for the fund to be held by the court's officer was to produce security for the claimant, then as soon as the fund is constituted the claimant will have a security interest in it.[34]

When there is a tracing claim but the effect of the order is only to "ear mark" a fund to be set aside pending the outcome of the claim[35] but without any requirement that it be constituted by the defendant as security for that claim, then the claimant will not have, as a result of the order, a security interest in that fund.[36] If the claimant has pre-existing rights to trace into that fund, those rights will continue.

If the claimant's claim is proprietary and concerns a misappropriated trust fund, and an order is made for the defendant to create a new fund from his own assets, the possibilities are that either (a) the fund is only available as assets of the defendant to meet a future judgment, or (b) the overall effect is to reconstitute the missing trust fund. It is a matter of construction of the order requiring the fund to be put in place as to whether the fund remains the absolute property of the defendant or whether it is a reconstituted trust fund.

---

[31] [1981] 1 W.L.R. 485.
[32] *Cantor Index Ltd v Lister*, unreported, November 22, 2001 (Neuberger J.).
[33] *Re Mordant; Mordant v Hills* [1996] 1 F.L.R. 334.
[34] *ibid.*
[35] See the order made in *Polly Peck International plc v Nadir (No.2)* [1992] 4 All E.R. 769.
[36] *Millenium Federation Pty Ltd v Bigjig Pty* [2000] 1 Qd Rep. 275.

(iii) Provision of security by interim agreement in place of an injunction

23.010 The defendant may incur expenses in providing security (*e.g.* bank charges), but the claimant's cross-undertaking in damages will not protect the defendant unless it is specially extended for that purpose. This is because the charges are not regarded as having been incurred by reason of the granting of the injunction. In such circumstances, the defendant should ask the claimant to agree to furnish a further undertaking to the court to abide by any order which the court may make as to costs, expenses, loss or damage suffered by the defendant by reason of the provision of security. Such an undertaking could then be incorporated in an order of the court discharging the injunction upon the giving of security by the defendant in a designated form. If the claimant declined to proffer the further undertaking, it would be open to the defendant to apply to discharge the Mareva injunction, unless such an undertaking was provided.

The effect of giving security will be to release the funds from the Mareva obtained by the particular claimant. But those funds may be made subject to a Mareva injunction obtained by some other claimant and it is therefore sensible when drafting replacement security by way of guarantee for the defendant's legal advisers to consider having wording which makes the guarantee only come into effect after the funds caught by the Mareva have been released from the Mareva and are not frozen by some other injunction. If the defendant wishes to replace the funds frozen with an equivalent guarantee which will be available to all the claimants who put forward claims arising from a particular casualty such as the sinking of a ship, the guarantee should be expressed with an aggregate limit which will be reduced as and when claims are paid.

The provision of a guarantee to a claimant will usually be on terms that the claimant promises not to take any steps to freeze or place any restraint on any assets of the defendant until after judgment. Such a promise can itself be enforced by injunction and in principle if it is broken, the defendant can claim damages for breach of contract.[37]

(4) Discharge of a freezing injunction by the provision of an undertaking

23.011 The defendant may prefer to replace the freezing injunction by providing to the court an undertaking in terms corresponding to those of the injunction. Such an undertaking has the same effect as an injunction, and if it is broken by the defendant, he will be in contempt of court. It has a similar effect as regards third parties who have knowledge of its terms.[38]

---

[37] *Mantovani v Carapelli* [1980] 1 Lloyd's Rep. 375, see paras 6.030–6.032, 14.014 and 14.019 above.
[38] *Biba Ltd v Stratford Investments* [1973] Ch. 281 at 287.

When the defendant proffers an undertaking in lieu of the injunction he should ask the claimant to give a cross-undertaking as to damages should the defendant suffer any damage, by reason of giving the undertaking, which the claimant ought to pay. It has been the practice since 1904 in the Chancery Division to require the claimant to furnish such a cross-undertaking,[39] and unless the claimant agrees to furnish the further undertaking, the court may discharge the injunction. The *Chancery Guide* provides:

"IMPLIED CROSS-UNDERTAKINGS IN DAMAGES WHERE UNDERTAKINGS ARE GIVEN TO THE COURT

> 5.22 Often the party against whom an injunction is sought gives to the court an undertaking which avoids the need for the court to grant the injunction. In these cases, there is an implied undertaking in damages by the party applying for the injunction in favour of the other. The position is less clear where the party applying for the injunction also gives an undertaking to the court. The parties should consider and, if necessary, raise with the Judge whether the party in whose favour the undertaking is given must give a cross-undertaking in damages in those circumstances."

Where the defendant obtains discharge of a freezing injunction by providing a guarantee or other security, the defendant may not be able to recover under the original cross-undertaking as to damages, which was given to the court by the claimant as the price for that injunction, costs, fees or losses resulting from the furnishing of the security. This is because they result from the voluntary provision of the security and not from the granting of the order for the injunction.[40] Consideration should be given by the defendant to stipulating for a cross-undertaking to cover expressly costs, fees and losses which are caused by the provision of the security. **23.012**

(5) Application for variation or discharge based on a point available to be taken at an earlier *inter partes* hearing: abuse of the process

This is also discussed in Chapter 20, para.20.061.   **23.013**

(i) *Where an undertaking has been furnished*

If an undertaking is furnished, the question may arise whether the defendant can subsequently apply to have it discharged or modified before the trial and, if so, whether the defendant's application will fall to   **23.014**

---

[39] Practice Note [1904] W.N. 203 at 208.
[40] See the reasoning of Evans J. in *Barclays Bank v Rosenberg*, *Financial Times*, June 12, 1985, in regard to the undertaking furnished by Mr Rosenberg on August 11, 1981.

be dealt with in the same way as if he were applying to discharge the original injunction.

If an undertaking is expressed to be "until further order", this necessarily contemplates that it may be discharged by a further order of the court.[41] Even if the order was "by consent", the undertaking itself contains provision for it to be discharged or modified.

However, a distinction is to be drawn between an undertaking which is given with the intention that it should be binding until trial, and an undertaking given when it is in contemplation that there will or may be a further interlocutory hearing in relation to the subject-matter of the undertaking. If an undertaking is expressed to be "until trial or further order" and is furnished as part of a consent order which also stands over the interlocutory motion to be dealt with at the trial, then it is contemplated that the undertaking will be binding until trial. The court will discharge or modify it prior to trial only if there are good grounds for doing so, such as a significant change of circumstances[42] or new facts. A change of heart prompted by recent case law will not be sufficient.[43] In *Pet Plan Ltd v Protect-A-Pet Ltd*,[44] an undertaking given at an *ex parte* application was expressed to be "until trial or further order", and was embodied in a consent order which included an express liberty to apply to discharge or vary the order on 48 hours' notice. The defendant in the consent order had agreed to comply with various positive obligations to be performed for some time ahead. In the circumstances the Court of Appeal ruled that this was not a case in which the undertaking had been provided as a short-term holding operation until there could be an interlocutory hearing. Accordingly, the defendant had to show good reason to discharge the undertaking.[45]

23.015 In contrast, in *Butt v Butt*,[46] an undertaking had been given as part of an order adjourning generally the relevant interlocutory hearing. Furthermore, there had been an express intimation that the defendant was contemplating an application to discharge once his evidence was in order. In these circumstances, the defendant was not faced with the burden of showing good reason for reopening the matter before the trial.

Accordingly, if the defendant wishes to preserve an unfettered right to apply to discharge or modify an undertaking, prior to the trial, he should expressly reserve the right to make such an application, orally before the judge,[47] or by express wording in the undertaking.

---

[41] *Chanel Ltd v Woolworth & Co.* [1981] 1 W.L.R. 485.
[42] *Chanel Ltd v Woolworth & Co.* [1981] 1 W.L.R. 485; *Re Kingsley Healthcare Ltd*, unreported, September 25, 2001, Ch.D. (Neuberger J.).
[43] *Chanel Ltd v Woolworth & Co.* [1981] 1 W.L.R. 485.
[44] [1988] F.S.R. 34.
[45] See also: *Esal Commodities Ltd v Pujara* [1989] 2 Lloyd's Rep. 479 at 484, *per* Slade L.J.; *Levi Strauss & Co. v Barclays Trading Corporation Inc.* [1993] F.S.R. 179 at 183.
[46] [1987] 1 W.L.R. 1351.
[47] In *OMV Supply & Trading AG v Nicholas Clarke*, unreported, January 14, 1999, Ch.D. (counsel had expressly reserved the position orally to apply to discharge the order when providing an undertaking to the court in place of the injunction and so the subsequent application to discharge for non-disclosure on the *ex parte* application went ahead on the merits); see also *Gantenbrink v British Broadcasting Corporation* [1995] F.S.R. 162.

There is jurisdiction in the court to release an undertaking given to it even when it has been furnished as part of a final order intended to dispose of the litigation.[48] When such an undertaking has been furnished as part of a contractual settlement, the court will require to be satisfied that it is appropriate to release it notwithstanding that it was given pursuant to a contract; *e.g.* because the other party has itself broken the contract and it is no longer just to hold the provider of the undertaking bound by the contract.

(ii) Previous interlocutory hearing at which the point was available to be taken, no material change in circumstances and abuse of the process of the court

The same principle applies when there has been a consent order for **23.016** continuance of an injunction,[49] even if it includes an express liberty to apply to discharge or vary the order,[50] or a contested *inter partes* application for an injunction or for a variation or discharge, and the defendant wishes to take a new point which was available to him at the time of the original application.[51] The reason is that the defendant must take his point at the earlier hearing, if it was available to be taken by him at that hearing, and he cannot be allowed to delay taking it until later unless the point was expressly reserved by him.

(6) Submission to the merits jurisdiction of the court and an application to discharge or vary an injunction

(i) What constitutes a submission to the merits jurisdiction

CPR r.11.1 lays down the procedure for the defendant to challenge the **23.017** jurisdiction of the court to entertain the merits. If it is followed,[52] the taking of these steps will not be a voluntary submission to the jurisdiction until the defendant lodges his second acknowledgment of service. However, submission to the court's jurisdiction to hear the merits can

---

[48] *Kensington Housing Trust v Oliver*, Court of Appeal Transcript No.1341 of 1997 (July 24, 1997).

[49] *Esal (Commodities) Ltd v Pujara* [1989] 2 Lloyd's Rep. 479 at 484; *Ryan v Friction Dynamics, The Times*, June 14, 2000, which related to a consent order for an injunction granted under s.25 of the Civil Jurisdiction and Judgments Act 1982 until disposal of the US proceedings or further order.

[50] *Chanel Ltd v Woolworth & Co.* [1981] 1 W.L.R. 485 at 492; *Esal (Commodities) Ltd v Pujara* [1989] 2 Lloyd's Rep. 479 at 484.

[51] *Leadmill Ltd v Omare*, unreported, April 19, 2002, Ch.D. (Hart J); see Chapter 20, para.20.061.

[52] An application for a stay on grounds of *forum non conveniens* is not an application within CPR r.11.1(1): *Astro Exito Navegacion SA v Hsu (The Messiniaki Tolmi)* [1984] 1 Lloyd's Rep. 266.

occur independently of that rule. This is because the conduct of the defendant in the particular circumstances has had this consequence. That conduct may have this effect because:

(1) the defendant's conduct, viewed objectively by the reasonable observer,[53] unequivocally recognises the jurisdiction of the court to decide the merits; or

(2) of an agreement made with the claimant to confer jurisdiction on the court;

(3) of an estoppel which precludes the defendant from denying that he has submitted as in (1) or made an agreement as in (2), or

(4) were the defendant to contest jurisdiction this would in the circumstances be an abuse of the process of the court.

Analysis (1) does not depend upon any contract between the parties; it depends upon the unilateral conduct of the defendant and an unequivocal recognition by the defendant of the court's jurisdiction to decide the merits. Analyses (2) and (3) look to the rights as between the claimant and the defendant. Analysis (4) concludes that given the defendant's conduct it would be an abuse of the process to allow the defendant to challenge the court's jurisdiction.

For analysis (1) to apply the conduct of the defendant which has this consequence must be "wholly unequivocal"[54] in the sense that the defendant has given up his right to challenge the jurisdiction. Whether this is so depends on the circumstances. So, *e.g.* an application to strike out the claim may or may not amount to a submission.[55] Seeking or participating in the obtaining of directions for pleadings and disclosure leading to a trial can be a submission to the jurisdiction if no oral reservation is made before the court.[56]

(ii) Submission to the jurisdiction by a defendant against whom an injunction has been granted

23.018 A defendant outside the jurisdiction who is made subject to a freezing injunction, in proceedings in which permission has been granted to the claimant to serve the claim form on the defendant out of the jurisdiction under CPR r.6.20, or in which the claim form has been served without permission under CPR r.6.19, may combine an application for discharge

---

[53] *Esal (Commodities) Ltd v Pujara* [1989] 2 Lloyd's Rep. 479 at 483 RHC.
[54] *SMAY Investments Ltd v Sachdev* [2003] 1 W.L.R. 1973 at [41].
[55] *Astro Exito Navegacion SA. v Hsu (The Messiniaki Tolmi)* [1984] 1 Lloyd's Rep. 266; *Eagle Star Insurance Co. Ltd v Yuval Insurance Co. Ltd* [1978] 1 Lloyd's Rep. 357 (strike out application not a step in the action so as to preclude application for a stay for the case to go to arbitration).
[56] *Spargos Mining NL v Atlantic Capital Corporation, The Times.* December 11, 1995.

of the injunction with an application challenging the jurisdiction of the court to entertain the merits (see CPR r.11.1(6)(c)). If he does so, then this in itself will not be a submission.

But it is not essential for the defendant to adopt this course. The injunction is effective as soon as it is granted and fairness requires that the defendant is able to apply to discharge or vary it without having to give up his entitlement to challenge the merits jurisdiction of the court. If a defendant seeks to oppose renewal of an injunction granted on a without notice application, this will not in itself amount to a submission to the jurisdiction so as to preclude him from challenging the jurisdiction under the procedure laid down in CPR r.11.1.[57] Logically the defendant is also entitled to seek discharge or variation of the injunction, pending the determination of his application challenging the jurisdiction, without thereby submitting to the jurisdiction. It is prudent for a defendant to make it clear that he is seeking only a variation of the injunction, pending the determination of his application to challenge the jurisdiction of the court and to discharge the injunction. In such circumstances, the application for variation does not involve the court in making any assumption that it has jurisdiction to determine *the merits* of the claimant's claim in the action.[58] On the application, the defendant in order to protect his position would be well advised if he invited the court to maintain the varied injunction only until after the determination of his application to challenge the jurisdiction of the court over the merits, or further order; the injunction can then be extended at that stage.

If the defendant agrees to an injunction until judgment or further **23.019** order, he can thereby submit to the jurisdiction. In *Esal (Commodities) Ltd v Pujara,*[59] prior to service of the statement of claim, the defendant consented to Mareva relief in "far reaching terms" expressed to be "until after judgment in this action or further order", and which provided for the opening of a deposit account in which moneys were "to abide the outcome of these proceedings" and reserved the costs of the motion "to the trial". There was an express liberty to apply to discharge or vary the order on 24 hours' notice. On these facts, the Court of Appeal held that the defendant had unequivocally submitted to the jurisdiction.

A defendant does not submit to the jurisdiction on the merits by providing information about his assets under an order made ancillary to a freezing injunction. Nor does he do so by obtaining an extension of time within which to provide information about assets upon the representation that he intends to provide the information ordered.[60]

---

[57] See *Obikoga v Silvernorth Ltd, The Times,* July 6, 1983 (Parker J.), which was a decision under the former RSC Ord. 12, r.8(1), and which was cited in *Esal (Commodities) Ltd v Pujara* [1989] 2 Lloyd's Rep. 479 at 485.
[58] *William & Glyn's Bank plc v Astro Dinamico Compania Naviera SA* [1984] 1 W.L.R. 438.
[59] [1989] 2 Lloyd's Rep. 479.
[60] *Qingdao Ocean Shipping Co. v Grace Shipping Establishment* [1995] 2 Lloyd's Rep. 15 at 20–21.

(7) Discharge or variation of an injunction by the court

(i) Application to the court of first instance

23.020 If the defendant wishes to set aside an injunction obtained without notice by the claimant, he must apply to the judge; he should not try to appeal to the Court of Appeal without having first been before the court at first instance for reconsideration of the without notice order.[61]

If the defendant wishes to apply to have the order set aside or varied, he should make his application promptly.

The court has jurisdiction to grant an application made without notice by a defendant to discharge or vary the Mareva injunction, but this power will be exercised only in cases of great urgency.[62]

23.021 The example order provides for a return date and the Practice Direction—Interim Injunctions supplementing CPR Pt 25 provides in para.5.1(3) that there is to be a return date unless the court otherwise orders. Whichever form of order is adopted it is open to the defendant to apply by application notice to discharge or vary the injunction, or to give informal notice of such an application.

Where the defendant, or a non-party, is seeking to vary the injunction and there are a number of interested parties, it is sensible to proceed by application notice. The terms of the variation can then be set out in the application notice and this may facilitate reaching an agreement.

The application to discharge the injunction takes the form of a complete rehearing of the matter, with each party being at liberty to put in evidence. Thus, *e.g.* the defendant may seek to persuade the court that on all the evidence there is insufficient risk of a judgment being unsatisfied to justify the granting of Mareva relief. The court decides the application on all the evidence before the court.[63] This includes evidence of matters which have occurred since the without notice application, so for example it would include evidence resulting from execution of a

---

[61] *WEA Records Ltd v Visions Channel 4 Ltd* [1983] 1 W.L.R. 721.

[62] *London City Agency (J. C. D.) Ltd v Lee* [1970] Ch. 597. The right to apply to discharge or vary the order cannot be fettered by a provision in the order made *ex parte: Tamco Electrical & Electronics v Ng Chun-fai* [1994] 1 H.K.L.R. 178 at 196 criticising a provision requiring 24 hours prior notice. Paragraph 13 of the example order allows an application "at any time" and directs that if evidence is to be relied upon the substance is to be communicated in writing to the applicant's solicitors "in advance". This is because the evidence in any event would have to be seen by the applicant before the court would rule on it: *WEA Records Ltd v Visions Channel 4 Ltd* [1983] 1 W.L.R. 721, except in the very rare case in which the application to discharge or vary can itself properly be made *ex parte*.

[63] *Ninemia Maritime Corporation v Trave Schiffahrtsgesellschaft GmbH (The Niedersachsen)* [1983] 1 W.L.R. 1412 at 1425–1426; in *Société Libanaise pour L'Industrie du bois "Libanbois" Sal v Fama Shipping Ltd*, Court of Appeal (Civ Div) Transcript No.651 of 1991 (June 13, 1991), the judge had refused Mareva relief by reference only to the affidavit evidence of the plaintiff, but this decision was reversed on appeal when the Court of Appeal took into account the defendant's own affidavit in deciding that there was a good arguable case based on fraudulent misrepresentation; *D. B. Baverstock Ltd v Haycock* [1986] 1 N.Z.L.R. 342 at p.344 (. . . on the basis of all the evidence . . .").

search order or how the defendant has acted in relation to an order for disclosure of information and the information obtained.[64] The court has power under CPR 32.7 to order that there be cross-examination of a person giving evidence in writing, with the possibility of excluding the evidence if the person does not attend. In practice the court is most reluctant to allow cross-examination on a discharge application because this is may turn it into a lengthy, costly, and unnecessary mini-trial.[65]

(ii) An order for disclosure or production of documents in connection with a challenge to the jurisdiction

An order for disclosure, in connection with the resolution of factual matters relevant to jurisdiction,[66] can be made against a defendant when that defendant is challenging the jurisdiction of the court. Such an order can be made under CPR r.31.12. Non-parties can be ordered to produce documents under the witness summons procedure in CPR r.34.2(1)(b).[67] In practice the power to order disclosure or production of documents is rarely exercised so as to avoid a challenge to the jurisdiction becoming a mini-trial. **23.022**

(iii) Disclosure of documents or information by the defendant or non-party in connection with resolving the issues arising on an application to discharge or vary an injunction

A freezing injunction may be the subject of an application to discharge it made at the same time as an application challenging the jurisdiction of the court in the action. The court has jurisdiction to order disclosure by a defendant[68] in connection with the issues arising on an application to discharge or vary a freezing injunction. However, in practice the power is rarely exercised because of the court's policy of not allowing interlocutory hearings to become unnecessarily complicated and protracted. The jurisdictions to order production of documents or information by a non-party are discussed in Chapter 22, para.22.038 and following. **23.023**

The court will not usually stay a disclosure of assets order made ancillary to a freezing injunction pending the outcome of a challenge to the jurisdiction of the court to hear the proceedings; this is discussed in Chapter 6, paras 6.011–6.012.

---

[64] Para.23.006; *Bradford & Bingley Plc v Holden* [2002] EWHC 2445 (taking into account defendant lied about possession of listed items when served with the search order).
[65] *Donelly v Karess Properties Ltd* [1998] C.I.L.R. Notes-13 referring to *Re Bank of Credit and Commerce International S.A. (No. 6)* [1994] 1 B.C.L.C. 450.
[66] *Rome v Punjab Bank* [1989] 2 Lloyd's Rep. 424.
[67] *Canada Trust Co. v Stolzenberg* [1997] 1 W.L.R. 1582.
[68] *Bank of Crete v Koskotas* [1991] 2 Lloyd's Rep. 587 at 588.

(8) Discharge by the court of a search order

23.024   A search order is intended to be implemented forthwith after there has been an opportunity to take legal advice. A defendant who has been served with a search order and refuses to comply with its terms is at risk of being penalised for contempt of court, even if he makes a speedy and successful application to have the order set aside. The fact that a search order is subsequently set aside does not prevent any disobedience of that order, while it was in force, from being a contempt of court.[69] In *Hallmark Cards Inc. v Image Arts Ltd.* Buckley L.J. stated[70] that while a defendant who refuses access to his premises pending an application to have the Anton Piller order set aside is technically in contempt of court, he could not conceive of the defendant being liable to any penalties for that contempt if the order was set aside. This approach was approved by Sir John Donaldson M.R. in *WEA Records Ltd v Visions Channel 4 Ltd.*[71] But in *Wardle Fabrics Ltd v G. Myristis Ltd* (above), a case in which an Anton Piller order was set aside for non-disclosure, Goulding J. penalised the successful defendants by ordering them to pay the costs of the plaintiff's motion for contempt on an indemnity basis.

   The court has a discretion to suspend the operation of a search order pending an application by the defendant to have it set aside, but that discretion should be exercised only on production of evidence and not simply on the basis of what is said by counsel on behalf of the defendant: *Hallmark Cards Inc. v Image Arts Ltd* (above). The discretion to suspend is unlikely to be exercised save in special cases. As Scott J. pointed out in *Columbia Picture Industries v Robinson*:[72]

> "if respondents to Anton Piller orders were to be allowed to delay their execution while applications to apply to discharge were being made, the purpose of Anton Piller orders and procedure would be largely lost. Ample time would then be available to those disposed to destroy evidence or to secrete away master tapes to do so."

23.025   Under para.10 of the example order the defendant must allow immediate entry to the supervising solicitor and then he is allowed a period not exceeding two hours, unless extended by the supervising solicitor, to seek legal advice, to apply to set aside the order and to gather up incriminating or privileged documents.[73] The defendant will be in breach of the order if, after the two hours and any extension granted by the supervising

---

[69] *Wardle Fabrics Ltd v G. Myristis Ltd* [1983] F.S.R. 263; *Tamco Electrical & Electronics v Ng Chun-Fai* [1994] I H.K.L.R. 178 at 197.
[70] [1977] F.S.R. 150 at 153.
[71] [1983] 1 W.L.R. 721.
[72] [1987] Ch. 37 at 72.
[73] See para.11 of the example order.

solicitor have expired, he refuses to allow entry and the search.[74] The supervising solicitor's function is to ensure that the order which has been made is fairly and properly implemented. The judge has decided that there is a real risk that items may be destroyed or hidden unless the order is made without notice, and speedily implemented. The supervising solicitor may allow a short time extension if it is reasonable to do so, bearing in mind the length of the extension, the circumstances at the premises, and whether steps are taken to preserve the items.[75]

If an application to discharge the search order is not made until after the order has been fully executed, a question which is likely to arise is whether such an application should be stood over until the trial. This question arises particularly in the context of applications to discharge for non-disclosure, and it is considered in Chapter 9, above.[76] The same principles apply even if the grounds for discharge do not include, or are not limited to, allegations of non-disclosure. The court has jurisdiction to determine, at an interlocutory hearing, an application to discharge a fully executed search order, but may in its discretion adjourn the matter to be dealt with at the trial, depending on the issues involved and whether it would be appropriate to adjourn.[77] The fact that it has to be decided what is to happen to certain of the materials obtained during the search, or whether to continue an injunction when that gives rise to points overlapping with the discharge application, are reasons for deciding at an interlocutory stage the merits of the application to discharge the search order.[78]

The court considers an application to discharge a search order taking **23.026** into account all the evidence available on the hearing of the discharge application, including the results of the execution of order.[79]

With a fully executed order where the only purpose of the application to discharge is to obtain damages on the cross-undertaking, and the only grounds for discharge are that the judge on the *ex parte* application did not have enough material at that time to justify making the order, the court will adjourn the matter to be dealt with at trial, taking into account

---

[74] See also *Bhimji v Chatwani* [1991] 1 W.L.R. 989 at 1000–1001.
[75] The Staughton Committee Report referred to the absence of any practice governing whether, and if so on what terms, time should be extended for compliance pending an immediate application to the court to discharge or vary the order; see para.4.8.
[76] See paras 9.025 and following.
[77] *Gadget Shop Ltd v Bug.Com Ltd* [2001] F.S.R. 383 at [44–45]; *Booker McConnell Plc v Plasgow* [1985] R.P.C. 425 at 443, *per* Dillon L.J. (contrast the view of Kerr L.J. at 435 that this should be exceptional); *Tate Access Floors Inc. v Boswell* [1991] Ch. 512 at 533.
[78] *Gadget Shop Ltd v Bug.Com Ltd* [2001] F.S.R. 383 at [44–45].
[79] *Hoechst UK Ltd v Chemiculture Ltd* [1993] F.S.R. 270 at 279; *WEA Records Ltd v Visions Channel 4 Ltd* [1983] 1 W.L.R. 721 at 727–728; *Fujitsu General New Zealand v Melco New Zealand Ltd* (2002) 16 P.R.N.Z. 395; [2002] N.Z.C.A. 91 (May 8, 2002) at para.8; *Interest Research Bureau Pty v Interest Recount Pty Ltd* (1997) 38 I.P.R. 468 at 473, Supreme Court of Western Australia.

the full picture of the case, including the fruits of the search.[80] This is because the real issue of substance is whether to enforce the cross-undertaking and it is appropriate to adjourn the application for discharge to be dealt with together with the application to enforce the undertaking which, in this situation, should be decided at the trial on the basis of all the evidence then available.[81]

(9) Discharge of an injunction or a search order for failure to comply with an undertaking to commence proceedings forthwith or some other undertaking given to the court by the claimant

23.027   Under CPR r.25.2(1) an order for an interim remedy, which under CPR r.25.1 includes an interim injunction or search order, can be made at any time, including before proceedings are commenced and after judgment has been given. The issue of the claim form is the commencement of the proceedings. The court can, however, make an order in advance of the commencement of proceedings but only on the basis that a claim form will be issued in the immediate future. It is common for a freezing injunction or search order to be granted on an application made without notice before the claim form is issued, the claimant providing an undertaking to the court to issue it. Under para.5.1 of the Practice Direction—Interim Injunctions, unless the court otherwise orders, on any order for an injunction made before issue of a claim form, there must be an undertaking to issue the claim form, and pay the appropriate fee, on the same or the next working day, or directions given for the commencement of the claim. On the without notice application the judge's attention should be drawn to the need to make provision in the order for the issuing of the claim form and this paragraph in the Practice Direction. In the case of a search order, the claimant often does not issue the claim form until the search order itself has been served;[82] the delay in the issue of the claim form is to keep the matter secret until service—surprise being part of what is needed for the remedy to be effective.

---

[80] *Fujitsu General New Zealand v Melco New Zealand Ltd* (2002) 16 P.R.N.Z. 395; [2002] N.Z.C.A 91 (May 8, 2002) at para.8, citing *WEA Records Ltd v Visions Channel 4 Ltd* [1983] 1 W.L.R. 721 at 727–728: "The courts are concerned with the administration of justice, not with playing a game of snakes and ladders. If it were now clear that the defendants had suffered any injustice by the making of the order, taking account of all relevant evidence including the affidavits of the personal defendants and the fruits of the search, the defendants would have their remedy in the counter-undertaking as to damages."
[81] See Chapter 11, paras 11.017 and following *Cheltenham & Gloucester Building Society v Ricketts* [1993] 1 W.L.R. 1545 (where the order for an inquiry made at an interlocutory hearing was set aside on appeal).
[82] *VDU Installations Ltd v Integrated Computer Systems and Cybernetics Ltd* [1989] F.S.R. 378.

Unless the undertaking is complied with, the court may discharge the without notice order, regardless of whose fault it was that the undertaking was not performed, and regardless of whether or not the defendant has been prejudiced by the irregularity.[83] The irregularity, being a breach of an undertaking, is a contempt of court.[84] There is a clear duty on the solicitor personally to ensure that an undertaking given on behalf of his client to the court is complied with. If, as is usually the case, the applicant has given the general conduct of the proceedings to the solicitor, the solicitor will be in breach of his duties both to the court and to his own client if he fails.

The client is usually held to be legally responsible for his lawyer's default in the conduct of the litigation; the general principle is that the court declines to distinguish between the fault of the litigant and the fault of his adviser. One of the reasons for this is that, in matters of discipline in the conduct of proceedings, it is undesirable to create a charter for incompetent lawyers.[85] But there are other means of penalising the solicitors, and it is just that the court should not penalise a litigant, who is innocent,[86] for the error of his solicitor.[87] **23.028**

Undertakings given to the court on without notice applications are binding as soon as they are given irrespective of whether or not the order is then drawn up. Delay in complying with them is not justified by delay in drawing up the order.[88] If there is any difficulty in complying with them timeously, an application must be made to the court so that the court can reconsider the matter.[89] When an undertaking is given to the court to do something within a certain time there must be strict compliance with this; time is of the essence.[90]

The same principles apply if the claimant fails to comply with an undertaking other than one relating to the commencement of proceedings, such as an undertaking to serve a copy of the evidence on the

---

[83] An example of a case in which the originating process was not issued for some two months and the injunction was discharged is *Siporex Trade SA v Comdel Commodities Ltd* [1986] 2 Lloyd's Rep. 428.

[84] *Refson v Saggers* [1984] 1 W.L.R. 1025; *Spanish General Agency Corporation v Spanish Corporation Ltd* (1890) 64 L.T. 161.

[85] *Hytec Ltd v Coventry City Council* [1997] 1 W.L.R. 1666 at 1675H.

[86] In *Hytec Ltd v Coventry City Council* [1997] 1 W.L.R. 1666 the defendant bore a measure of personal responsibility for what had happened (see at 1679C) and so was not entirely innocent.

[87] This approach was adopted by Potter J. in *Sabani v Economakis, The Times*, June 17, 1988 when there had been failure to comply with undertakings concerning notification to the defendant of the terms of the order and his right to apply for its discharge, and to serve on the defendant the affidavit relied upon *ex parte*; see also the position on non-disclosure considered in *Eastglen International Corporation v Monpare* (1987) 137 N.J. 56, a case which was highly exceptional, see *Lloyd's Bowmaker Ltd v Britannia Arrow* [1988] 1 W.L.R. 1337 at 1347; *Behbehani v Salem* [1989] 1 W.L.R. 723 at 729.

[88] *Banque Indosuez v Euro Canadian Securities*, Court of Appeal (Civ Div) Transcript No.152 of 1991 (February 28, 1991).

[89] *Re S (A Child) (Family Division: Without Notice Orders)* [2001] 1 All E.R. 362.

[90] *ibid.*, at 373h.

defendant within a certain time,[91] or to inform the defendant or a third party of his right to apply to discharge or vary the order.[92]

(10) Delay by the claimant in progressing the proceedings after obtaining an injunction or other interim remedy

(i) The principles
The general principles are that:

23.029
(1) A claimant who has obtained an injunction, search order or other interim remedy is bound to get on with his action as rapidly as he can.

(2) He is not entitled to retain the relief except on the basis that the proceedings are progressed promptly and without unnecessary delay.

(3) If there is delay, the relief may be discharged.

(4) In deciding whether to discharge the relief and not to regrant it the court is exercising a wide discretion taking into account all the circumstances and bearing in mind the need to deter other litigants from delaying pursuit of proceedings in which an injunction has been granted. Therefore the exercise of the jurisdiction also has a disciplinary aspect.

(ii) The application of the principles[93]
23.030
Search order procedure should not be used to enable a claimant to find out whether allegations or charges can be made against the defendant and if so how they might be formulated. Accordingly, it is no justification or excuse for a claimant who has obtained a search order, but has failed to serve his particulars of claim in accordance with the time limits laid down by the rules of court, or any court order extending that time, to say that more time was required to consider the material which became available under the search order order, so that the pleading could be drafted.[94]

---

[91] *Flightwise Travel Service Ltd v Gill* [2003] EWHC 3082; *The Times*, December 5, 2003 (Neuberger J.); evidence served late in breach of an undertaking.
[92] *Sabani v Economakis*, above.
[93] The discussion of the relevant considerations in the 4th edn of this book was referred to with approval by the Privy Council in *Jeanette Walsh v Deloitte & Touche Inc.* [2002] L.R.C. 545 at [26], and in *Sakellarios Mavros v AA Constructions Pty Ltd* [1995] N.T.S.C. 19 (February 21, 1995) at para.67 where the delay by the liquidator was fatal to the continuation of the injunction. See also *China Merchants Bank v I-China Holdings Ltd* [2003] 1 H.K.L.R.D. 271 at para.11 (the fact that the defendant has a counterclaim and has not taken steps to prosecute it can be relevant to whether the court ought to discharge the relief because the defendant may be considered to have acquiesced in the delay).
[94] *Hytrac Conveyors Ltd v Conveyors International Ltd* [1983] 1 W.L.R. 44 (where the action was struck out on the grounds of inordinate delay).

Similarly, when a claimant has obtained a freezing injunction, he is bound to prosecute the action to trial, not simply to "rest content with the injunction".[95] If an injunction is granted pending the hearing of an application to continue the relief, the claimant is under a duty to press on with that hearing.[96] Accordingly, if there is unjustified delay, the injunction may be discharged. The same principles apply to a case in which the defendant is applying to discharge an existing injunction on the grounds of delay,[97] and where the court has already decided to discharge the injunction for some other reason (*e.g.* non-disclosure) and is considering whether or not to grant a new injunction, notwithstanding the delay.[98]

Whether or not any injunction is to be discharged (or not regranted) is **23.031** a matter of discretion but in principle the court will not permit a claimant to obtain an injunction and then to rest content with that relief and not prosecute the proceedings. In *Town and Country Building Society v Daisystar*[99] the plaintiff had obtained Mareva relief against an individual defendant in respect of a claim for fraud, but had taken the view that the defendant did not have sufficient assets for it to be worthwhile pursuing the proceedings. After a long delay, the defendant applied to discharge the injunction, and the Court of Appeal (allowing an appeal from the decision of the judge) discharged the Mareva relief, on the grounds that it was an abuse of the jurisdiction for a plaintiff to obtain Mareva relief but then leave the proceedings in abeyance. Farquharson L.J. observed that it was the duty of the plaintiff to press on with the claim so that the defendant was subjected to the Mareva injunction for as little time as possible, and that if the plaintiff wished not to proceed with the claim expeditiously, even temporarily, then it was his duty to apply to the court to discharge the injunction. The duty is to prosecute with expedition,[1] the claimant being "under an obligation to press on with the action as rapidly as he can".[2]

---

[95] *Lloyd's Bowmaker Ltd v Britannia Arrow Ltd* [1988] 1 W.L.R. 1337 at 1349–1350, *per* Dillon L.J.; *Comdel Commodities Ltd v Siporex Trade SA* [1997] 1 Lloyd's Rep. 424 (injunction discharged for delay in proceeding with arbitration).

[96] *Hong Kong Toy Centre v Tomy UK*, The Times, January 14, 1994 (Aldous J.); *Intercontex v Schmidt* [1988] F.S.R. 575.

[97] *Town and Country Building Society v Daisystar Ltd*, The Times, October 16, 1989. *Francesca Black v Mohammed Al Mereikhi*, unreported, judgment delivered October 20, 1989 (Mr Anthony Colman, Q.C. sitting as a Deputy Judge of the High Court).

[98] This was the position in *Lloyd's Bowmaker Ltd v Britannia Arrow Ltd* [1988] 1 W.L.R. 1337.

[99] The Times, October 16, 1989.

[1] *Anago Inc. v Fox*, Court of Appeal (Civ Div) Transcript No.1018 of 1993 (July 23, 1993).

[2] *Lloyd's Bowmaker Ltd v Britannia Arrow Ltd* [1988] 1 W.L.R. 1337 at 1347 and 1349; *A/S D/S Svendborg v Awada* [1999] 2 Lloyd's Rep. 244 at 245 LHC ("to press on with his action as rapidly as is practical . . ."); *Newsgroup Newspapers Ltd v Mirror Group Newspapers (1986) Ltd* [1991] F.S.R. 487; *Mellor v Mellor* [1992] 1 W.L.R. 517 at 528–529; *Fox v Fontana Holdings*, Court of Appeal (Civ Div) Transcript No.216 of 1991 (March 5, 1991); *Banque Indosuez v Euro Canadian Securities*, Court of Appeal (Civ Div) Transcript No.152 of 1991 (February 28, 1991; *Tay Long Kee Impex Pte Ltd v Tan Beng Huwah (t/a Sin Kwang Wah)* [2000] 2 S.L.R. 750 at para.38 (where an application for a

However, the court will not always discharge the injunction where there has been delay, even though the delay has been substantial.[3] The court will take into account all the circumstances of the case,[4] including the following:

(1) whether the delay was the result of a deliberate decision on the part of the claimant;[5]

(2) the length of the delay, and any explanations put forward by the claimant (*e.g.* the pursuit of settlement negotiations,[6] or difficulties in funding the pursuit of the proceedings);

(3) the degree of prejudice liable to be caused to the claimant if the injunction is discharged;[7]

(4) whether the claimant sought to rectify the position and proceed with the action or whether the delay is still continuing at the time of the hearing;

(5) the degree of prejudice caused to the defendant as a result of the delay. This should be shown by evidence and not merely based on the assertions of counsel;[8]

(6) whether the defendant has through his conduct either caused the delay or contributed to it.

In the *Francesca Black* case, there had been a failure to prosecute proceedings for eight months, followed by a further delay attributable to the plaintiff's lack of means while she changed solicitors and successfully applied for legal aid. If the injunction were to have been discharged, the prospect of the plaintiff recovering anything from the defendant would have been "very substantially diminished". The fund subject to the injunction had been earning interest on deposit. In these circumstances the judge decided not to discharge the injunction. But even though the effect of discharging the injunction may very well be to make it not worthwhile to pursue the claim because of the likely difficulties of enforcement, this factor may be outweighed by very long delay.[9] The

---

second interlocutory injunction was refused where there had been culpable non-disclosure and the plaintiff had not diligently pursued the case to trial). *Re Cayman Capital Trust Company* [1992–1993] C.I.L.R. Notes-17 (plaintiff must not refrain from proceeding while attempting to gather evidence.

[3] The injunction was not discharged in *Francesca Black v Mohammed Al Mereikhi*, above; see also *Jeanette Walsh v Deloitte & Touche Inc.* [2002] L.R.C. 545 which concerned a delay of several years but there had not yet been disclosure under the disclosure order and so the material for exercising the discretion was not complete.

[4] *A/S D/S Svendborg v Awada* [1999] 2 Lloyd's Rep. 244 at 245.

[5] *ibid.*, at 247.

[6] *ibid.*, at 247.

[7] *ibid.*, at 248 RHC.

[8] *Comdel Commodities Ltd v Siporex Trade SA* [1997] 1 Lloyd's Rep. 424 at 434.

[9] *Comdel Commodities Ltd v Siporex Trade SA* [1997] 1 Lloyd's Rep. 424 (injunction discharged when the claim was stale and the delay very long).

Town and Country Building Society case is one in which the plaintiff had deliberately decided not to continue to prosecute the proceedings, and the injunction was discharged.

Information obtained from a defendant under an asset disclosure order 23.032
can be relevant. In *Jeanette Walsh v Deloitte & Touche Inc.*[10] the estate of Mr Walsh had not yet complied with the order for disclosure of assets and this was capable of affecting the discretion whether to continue the injunction against that estate notwithstanding a delay of several years in prosecuting the substantive claim.

If an injunction is discharged because of delay in prosecuting the proceedings, a subsequent application for an injunction pre-judgment may be an abuse of the process of the court, because the discharge of the injunction is a penalty for misusing the court's process and there is a policy of deterring other litigants from acting in this way. It is similar to the discretion which falls to be exercised once material non-disclosure is shown to have occurred on a without notice application in that whether to discharge the injunction and not to regrant it takes into account the deterrent effect on other litigants who can see that material non-disclosure can result in the claimant being left with no remedy.

(11) Appeals

(i) *The jurisdiction of the Court of Appeal*

Under the former rules of court which applied to the Court of Appeal the 23.033
procedure was that if an application made *ex parte* for an injunction or search order had been refused in whole or in part, then the applicant could renew the application *ex parte* to the Court of Appeal under what was formerly RSC Ord. 59, r.14(3). The renewed application had to be made within seven days of the refusal, and was not an application for leave to appeal.[11] If an order was granted *ex parte* by the Court of Appeal, any application to discharge the order had to be made to the court of first instance.[12] The position has changed: in CPR r.52.3 the requirement for obtaining permission to appeal applies to a "decision" of a judge. This is an almost[13] universal requirement and operates as a filtering process for appeals without merit. The word "decision" includes when the first instance judge announced his determination orally[14] even though the formal order has not been drawn up.

---

[10] [2002] L.R.C. 545.
[11] *Araghchinchi v Araghchinchi* [1997] 2 F.L.R. 142.
[12] *Ocean Software v Kay* [1992] Q.B. 583; *Hon Hing Enterprises Ltd v Skai Import Export Ltd* [1994] 1 H.K.L.R. 248 at 257.
[13] It does not apply for example to appeals against a committal order—see CPR r.52.3(1)(a)(i).
[14] CPR r.52.3(2)(a).

The jurisdiction of the Court of Appeal is statutory. Under s.16(1) of the Supreme Court Act 1981 the Court of Appeal is to ". . . hear and determine appeals from any judgment or order of the High Court". When a judge decides to refuse part or all of the relief sought he makes a decision capable of being put into a formal order. The jurisdiction of the Court of Appeal to hear an appeal does not depend upon whether that formal order has been drawn up or whether physically there is an order on a piece of paper.[15] A defendant subject to a Mareva injunction, or a third party affected by such an injunction, can appeal to the Court of Appeal against a refusal to discharge or modify the injunction.

23.034   The Court of Appeal has said that it is an abuse of the process of the court for a defendant to seek to challenge Anton Piller relief granted *ex parte* by way of an appeal direct to that court.[16] If relief granted *ex parte* is to be challenged, this should be by way of application to the High Court to discharge or vary the order, and then by way of appeal, which in general should be brought only against a refusal to discharge or vary the order made on an application when the relevant evidence is complete.[17]

If an application to discharge or vary an injunction has been dismissed on its merits, with the relief being granted or left in place to continue "until judgment or further order", the first instance court still has jurisdiction to entertain a further application to discharge or modify the injunction.[18] As a general rule, however, the court will require good reason for discharging or varying the injunction notwithstanding the previous decision of the court; *e.g.* that there has been a significant change of circumstances, or new evidence has come to light.[19] In such circumstances, the application to discharge or vary the injunction should be made to the court of first instance, and not by way of an application for permission to appeal out of time against the previous decision of the court.

(ii) Hearing in private of an appeal from a decision made on a without notice application for a search order or an injunction

23.035   Before CPR there was a Practice Note issued in 1982[20] on the procedure to be followed if the applicant desired to make what was then an *ex parte* application to the Court to Appeal *in camera* for Anton Piller relief. The court also heard other applications *in camera*, including *ex parte* applications for Mareva relief, if it was necessary to do so.[21] The position is

---

[15] *Re B (A Minor) (Split Hearings: Jurisdiction)* [2000] 1 W.L.R. 790; *Compagnie Noga SA v Australian and New Zealand Banking Group* [2003] 1 W.L.R. 307.
[16] *WEA Ltd v Visions Channel 4 Ltd* [1983] 1 W.L.R. 721.
[17] *Hunters & Partners v Wettings & Partners* [1987] F.S.R. 83.
[18] This is so even if the injunction has been granted or continued by consent, see *Chanel Ltd v Woolworth & Co.* [1981] 1 W.L.R. 485 at 492.
[19] Discussed at paras 23.013–23.016 above.
[20] [1982] 1 W.L.R. 1420.
[21] This was done, *e.g.* in *Republic of Haiti v Duvalier; Re an application by Mr Turner and Mr Martin*, Court of Appeal (Civ Div) Transcript No.490 of 1988 (June 7, 1988).

now governed by CPR r.39.2(3) which enables a hearing to be heard "in private" if (*inter alia*) publicity would defeat the purpose of the hearing, it is an application made without notice and publicity would be unjust to the respondent, or if this is necessary in the interests of justice.

(iii) The jurisdiction to grant an injunction pending appeal to an applicant who has lost at first instance or pending a further appeal

If an applicant wishes to appeal against a decision declining to grant or continue an injunction, he may apply for an injunction pending appeal.[22] **23.036**

The High Court may refuse to grant an injunction at an *inter partes* application made either before the trial[23] or at the end of the trial,[24] but still grant an injunction pending an appeal. Ordinarily an application for relief pending appeal must be made in the first instance to the judge who refused the relief, although another judge of the court of first instance does have jurisdiction to deal with the application.[25] Even if the court of first instance is not minded to grant the injunction pending an appeal, the court will normally maintain the status quo pending the hearing of an application to the single judge or the Court of Appeal (as the case may be).

The Court of Appeal's jurisdiction to grant an injunction pending appeal is an original jurisdiction which is concurrent to that of the High Court.[26] In a case in which the relief is sought to hold the position pending a determination of an appeal, the Court of Appeal's jurisdiction is "incidental" to the appeal and therefore can be dealt with by a single judge of the Court of Appeal under s.58 of the Supreme Court Act 1981. If the decision of the single judge is made without a hearing then a party can request a hearing for that decision to be reconsidered.[27] In addition a single judge may refer any matter for a decision by a court consisting of two or more judges.[28] It may be that a single judge reaches a decision on an injunction at on oral hearing but it seems that under CPR r.52.16(7) he could still refer the matter to a court of two or more judges. It is thought that s.58 of the Supreme Court Act 1981 and CPR r.52.16(7) would still apply and so the single judge could still refer the matter of the

---

[22] *Ketchum International plc v Group Public Relations Holdings* [1997] 1 W.L.R. 4; *Erinford Properties v Cheshire County Council* [1974] Ch. 261.
[23] *Erinford Properties Ltd v Cheshire County Council* [1974] Ch. 261. See also *Williams v Minister for the Environment and Heritage* (2003) 199 A.L.R. 352.
[24] *Ketchum plc v Group Public Relations Ltd* [1997] 1 W.L.R. 4; *Orion Property Trust Ltd v Du Cane Court Ltd* [1962] 1 W.L.R. 1085.
[25] This is the ordinary principle: *Warren v T. Kilroe & Sons* [1988] 1 W.L.R. 516 (a case on s.18(1)(h) of the Supreme Court Act 1981, which has now been repealed, and the former RSC Ord. 59, r.14(4)).
[26] As is the jurisdiction to grant a stay of execution pending appeal.
[27] CPR r.52.16(6).
[28] CPR r.52.16(7).

injunction to a court of two or more judges. This is because CPR r.52.16(7) is not qualified by a requirement that the referral take place before the single judge has made a decision.

In *Paringa Mining & Exploration Co Plc v North Flinders Mines Limited (No.2)*[29] the plaintiff had been refused an interim injunction at first instance in an urgent case, and the appeal court to which an appeal lay could not expedite the appeal or hear an application for an injunction pending appeal because of pressure of other business. Instead it was left to the first instance judge to decide on the question of granting an injunction pending appeal. The High Court of Australia held that it was inappropriate to leave the appeal court's concurrent jurisdiction to be exercised by the judge at first instance who had refused to grant an interim injunction, and itself granted an injunction pending appeal.

23.037   The Court of Appeal can grant an injunction to hold the position pending the determination by the House of Lords of a petition for leave to appeal or an appeal,[30] and the House of Lords can grant an injunction pending the outcome of an appeal. The Privy Council can grant an injunction pending the outcome of an appeal.[31] Whether a court from which an appeal lies to the Privy Council can grant an injunction pending application to the Privy Council depends on[32] its jurisdiction under statute including the rules governing the right of appeal, and the inherent jurisdiction of that court. It is not the case that because there is to be an appeal to the Privy Council that there is necessarily an inherent jurisdiction in the lower court to grant the relief.

(iv) The principle to be applied to granting an injunction pending appeal

23.038   The general principle is that the court will seek to preserve the status quo so that the appeal, if successful, is not rendered nugatory.[33]

Applied to the Mareva jurisdiction where the applicant is the unsuccessful claimant for substantive relief, the principle is that ". . . justice requires that the court should be able to take steps to ensure that its judgments are not rendered valueless by an unjustifiable disposal of assets";[34] the questions are (1) whether the applicant has a good arguable

---

[29] (1988) 165 C.L.R. 452 (High Court of Australia).
[30] *Wilson v Church No.2* (1879) 12 Ch.D. 454; *Polini v Gray* (1879) 12 Ch.D. 438; *Belize Alliance of Conservation Non-Governmental Organisations v Department of Environment and Belize Electricity Company* [2003] 1 W.L.R. 2839 at [32]. See also *Secretary for Justice v To Kan Chi* (2000) 3 H.K.C.F.A.R. 264 (inherent jurisdiction to grant a stay pending appeal outside statutory power of stay of the Hong Kong Court of Final Appeal).
[31] *Belize Alliance of Conservation Non-Governmental Organisations v Department of Environment and Belize Electricity Company* [2003] 1 W.L.R. 2839
[32] *Prior v Parshelf 45 Ltd* [1999] N.Z.C.A. 259 (November 10, 1999), holding that although there was a power to grant relief over the subject-matter of the proceedings, there was not power to grant Mareva relief.
[33] *Erinford Properties Ltd v Cheshire County Council* [1974] Ch.261; *Paringa Mining and Exploration Company plc v North Flinders Mines Ltd (No.2)* (1988) 165 C.L.R. 452.
[34] *Ketchum plc v Group Public Relations Ltd* [1997] 1 W.L.R. 4 at 10.

appeal and (2) whether there is a real risk of dissipation of assets such that an eventual judgment may not be satisfied. The overlap between this jurisdiction and the jurisdiction to grant a stay of execution pending appeal is discussed in Chapter 3, para.3.025.

If a party pays money to another party pending appeal, then until the appeal is heard and determined he may have no existing cause of action against the payee for the money. Thus, *e.g.* if a judgment has been entered against the paying party which he has paid, the right to get back the money, together with interest,[35] is a right in restitution[36] which will arise once the judgment is set aside on appeal. This is the position regardless of whether the payer has waited for execution or has paid voluntarily before execution but in anticipation of execution. In the former situation payment by mistake does not arise; he has paid by compulsion of law. In the latter it would be difficult for him to establish that he has paid by mistake, whether of fact or of law; this is because he has paid because of the judgment. The inference is likely to be that he would still have paid to avoid execution, even if he had realised that the judgment would be reversed on appeal.

It is also the position when a declaration has been granted that he owes **23.039** the money and he has paid against a promise to repay if and when the appeal is successful. The *Siskina* rule will apply to prevent Mareva relief in relation to the repayment because the payer has no subsisting cause of action against the payee. In the case where there is a promise to repay there is also no mistake; the parties have struck a bargain about what is to happen and when the cause of action for repayment is to accrue.

If the payer has paid to avoid being made bankrupt based on a statutory demand and is seeking to set aside that demand on appeal the only *lis* between the parties on the appeal is the legality of the statutory demand; whether the money has to be returned is not directly in issue in the appeal and no order will be made about that on the appeal if successful. In these circumstances an application for Mareva relief to provide for a refund is premature because of the *Siskina* rule, and because the relief sought is not incidental to the appeal.[37]

(v) Imposing terms on a successful applicant for an injunction when the respondent wishes to appeal

Terms can be imposed on a successful applicant for an injunction pending **23.040** an appeal by the unsuccessful respondent. This can be done through use of the stay jurisdiction and imposing the terms as a condition of not staying the injunction pending appeal. Thus, *e.g.* where a claimant has succeeded at trial and been granted an injunction without being required

---

[35] *Rodger v Comptoir D'Escompte de Paris* (1871) 3 L.R.P.C. 465.
[36] *Lissenden v C. A. V. Bosch Ltd* [1940] A.C. 412 at 430.
[37] *Aspermont Ltd v Lechmere Financial Corporation* [2002] W.A.S.C.A. 52 (March 15, 2002).

to provide a cross-undertaking in damages, terms can be imposed on the claimant requiring him to give a cross-undertaking, failing which the injunction will be stayed.[38]

(vi) Interfering on appeal with an exercise of discretion concerning an injunction

23.041   The principles upon which an appellate court will interfere with the decision of a judge in granting or discharging an interlocutory injunction are stated in *Hadmor Productions Ltd v Hamilton*[39] (and see *Garden Cottage Foods Ltd v Milk Marketing Board*[40]; *G v G (Minors: Custody Appeal)*,[41] and *The Niedersachsen*[42]). The appellate court will not interfere with the exercise by the judge of his discretion merely on the grounds that the members of the appellate court would have exercised their discretion differently. However, it may conclude that the judge exercised his discretion wrongly, by reason of a misunderstanding of the law or the evidence before him, by taking into account irrelevant factors or failing to take into account relevant ones,[43] because fresh evidence which has become available since the hearing at first instance shows an inference drawn by the judge to have been wrong, although it may have appeared to be correct at the time of the hearing. The Court of Appeal has emphasised that in general appeals in Mareva cases should be "rare" and confined to matters of principle.[44]

(vii) Applications in relation to an interim injunction granted by the Court of Appeal on appeal

23.042   If an interim injunction is granted by the Court of Appeal, any applications by either party in relation to that relief should be made at first instance, except for applications for amendment of the order made by the

---

[38] *Minnesota Mining and Manufacturing v Johnson & Johnson Ltd* [1976] R.F.C. 671. The first instance court and the Court of Appeal (CPR r.52.7 and r.52.10(1)) have concurrent jurisdictions to suspend an injunction pending appeal, and this can be done subject to terms imposed on the enjoined party such as the provision of a fortified cross-undertaking in damages for losses caused by the suspension: *Pacific Islands Shipbuilding Co. Ltd v Don the Beachcomber Ltd (No.2)* [1963] H.K.L.R. 447.

[39] [1983] 1 A.C. 191.

[40] [1984] A.C. 130.

[41] [1985] 1 W.L.R. 647 at pp.652B-653G (rejecting a test of whether no reasonable judge could have reached the decision in question).

[42] [1983] 1 W.L.R. 1412 at 1421.

[43] If an important matter is not referred to expressly in the judgment, it may still be inferred that, given the arguments before him, the judge must have considered it: *Topline Ltd v Viall*, Court of Appeal (Civ Div) Transcript No.194 of 1990 (March, 5, 1990) (no reference to risk of dissipation of assets).

[44] *Derby & Co. Ltd v Weldon* [1990] Ch.48; *Allied Trust Bank v Shukri, Financial Times,* November 14, 1989; *Dubai Bank v Galadari* [1990] 1 Lloyd's Rep. 120 at 125 ("It is easy to show that on very many of the questions . . . the Judge could legitimately have taken a different view. But that falls miles short of showing that it was not open to the Judge to take the view he did . . . The relevant discretion is that of the Judge . . .", *per* Dillon L.J.).

Court of Appeal or for minor variations to that order, namely applications which are for an order which can be regarded as ancillary[45] to the determination of the appeal.

(12) Costs of an application to continue, discharge or vary an interim injunction or a search order

Under s.51 (1) of the Supreme Court Act 1981, the court has "full power **23.043** to determine by whom and to what extent . . . costs are to be paid."

Under CPR Pt 44 it is now common practice to make orders for costs which are immediately payable in contested interlocutory proceedings and for the court to make an order for interim payment pending a detailed assessment. It is also open to the court to make costs orders based on who has won on which issue and to reflect culpable conduct by a party in the course of the proceedings, or misconduct which has led to the justifiable need to seek a search order[46] or to pursue other expensive proceedings for an injunction or other interim remedy.

Even prior to CPR costs orders were made taking into account culpability of a party or those for whom he was responsible. CPR encourages such an approach. If a claimant has made inadequate inquiries before seeking a search order or a freezing injunction, this can result in his being deprived of costs relating to the obtaining of such relief where otherwise the costs might have been awarded to him.[47] Where relief is obtained without notice on the basis of false evidence relied upon by the claimant, the court may order the defendant's costs to be paid by the claimant on an indemnity basis regardless of whether or not the false evidence had been fabricated by a third party without the knowledge of the claimant.[48] The court may also order the claimant to pay costs on an indemnity basis if there has been an abuse of the process of the court,[49] or breach of a duty owed to the court, either in obtaining the order or in the manner in which it has been implemented. The fact that an application for a search order was unjustified may become apparent from (*inter alia*) the absence of material becoming available in consequence of execution of the order;[50] if an application was not justified this can readily lead to an adverse costs order against the applicant made on an indemnity basis.

---

[45] *Ocean Software Ltd v Kay* [1992] 1 Q.B. 583 applying *WEA Records Ltd v Visions Channel 4 Ltd* [1983] 1 W.L.R. 721 at 727.

[46] *Taylor Made Golf Company Inc. v Rata & Rata* [1996] F.S.R. 528 at 536–537 (Laddie J.).

[47] *Systematica Ltd v London Computer Centre* [1983] F.S.R. 313.

[48] *Bir v Sharma, The Times*, December 7, 1988.

[49] *Granvias Oceanicas Armadora v Jibsen Trading Co.* [1977] 2 Lloyd's Rep. 344 at 353. See also *NZ Michalos v Food Corporation of India* [1983] 1 Lloyd's Rep. 409 at 416.

[50] *Burgess v Burgess* [1996] 2 F.L.R. 34 at 41 where at the final hearing there had been a total lack of evidence to justify the allegations of concealment or suppression of documents; *John Siddall Holdings v Simmonds*, unreported, July 14, 1997 (Lloyd J.).

23.044   Although material non-disclosure on the *ex parte* application is a breach of the claimant's duty to the court, there is no general practice of the court that where there has been non-disclosure, and costs are to be awarded against the claimant, they ought to be on an indemnity basis.[51] However, the fact that there has been material non-disclosure is plainly a relevant factor to be taken into account on the question of costs and is capable of justifying an award on this basis, and such an order will usually be made if the non-disclosure was deliberate or seriously culpable.[52]

If an innocent non-party affected by a freezing injunction reasonably applies to the court to discharge or vary the injunction so as to protect his interests, he ought as a general rule to be awarded his costs.[53]

Once an intended application for an injunction has passed from negotiation to being almost at the door of the court, there is an inherent jurisdiction to award costs to the intended respondent when the application does not proceed, and that application can be made by a claim form issued under CPR Pt 8.[54]

23.045   If an interim injunction is continued pending an expedited trial on the ground of balance of convenience, and where matters at trial will shed further light on who is right on the underlying dispute, then the respondent is not a losing party within CPR r.44.3(2) and it is unjust for the court to make such an order against him on the ground that he lost on the injunction issue.[55]

---

[51] For example, see *Thermax v Schott Industrial Glass* [1981] F.S.R. 289 at 298; *Lloyd's Bowmaker Ltd v Britannia Arrow plc* [1988] 1 W.L.R. 1337 at 1350; *Bank Mellat v Nikpour* [1985] F.S.R. 87 at 93.

[52] For example, *Naf Naf SA v Dickens (London) Ltd* [1993] F.S.R. 424 at 430; *John Siddall Holdings v Simmonds*, unreported, July 14, 1997 (Lloyd J.); indemnity costs ordered when Anton Piller order and Mareva relief obtained by "misconduct of the plaintiffs consisting of . . . misrepresentations and non-disclosures."

[53] This is discussed at Chapter 20, para.20.005.

[54] *Associated Newspaper Ltd v Impac* [2002] F.S.R. 293.

[55] *Desquenne et Giral UK Ltd v Richardson* [2001] F.S.R. 1 (employee restrained from working for a competitor pending the court investigating the underlying merits at a speedy trial: the Court of Appeal set aside costs order made in any event against the former employee).

Chapter 24

Restrictions on the use which may be made of documents or information

(1) Introduction

This chapter is about the restrictions on use of documents or information **24.001** under the CPR, or an undertaking given to the court, a contractual undertaking and the scope of privacy which applies to arbitration proceedings. Questions may arise about the uses to which documents or information acquired in the course of legal proceedings may be put, *e.g.*, if the claimant is considering commencing new proceedings and making an application in those proceedings supported by documents or information obtained in other proceedings. If the claimant obtained documents or information as a result of an order made ancillary to a freezing injunction or a search order, what use may he make of the documents or information? What is the position if documents and information are supplied by the defendant voluntarily in support of an application to vary an injunction? What use can be made of information obtained under an order made on the *Norwich Pharmacal* principle[1] or under an asset disclosure order made ancillary to a freezing injunction?

In civil proceedings information is revealed to a party as a product of the litigation process. The questions which arise are:

(1) When are documents or information subject to restrictions about their use?

(2) What is the scope of the restrictions?

(3) When do they come to an end?

(4) When can the restrictions be terminated or modified by a court, and when will the court do so?

---

[1] See Chapter 22, para.22.038.

(2) The restrictions on use before the Civil Procedure Rules

(i) The former Rules of the Supreme Court

24.002   The former rules of the Supreme Court did not have a rule restricting the use of documents or information obtained under discovery or through compulsion or threat of compulsion by court order. The rule was that documents and information obtained by a party under compulsion[2] of a court order were subject to an implied undertaking given to the court by the recipient restricting their use.

In *Home Office v Harman*,[3] confidential documents had been provided by the Home Office on discovery, and were read out by counsel in open court. The solicitor acting for the party to whom discovery had been given subsequently allowed a journalist to have access to the documents, which he used for the purpose of writing a newspaper article highly critical of Home Office ministers and civil servants. The House of Lords held by a majority of three to two that the solicitor had acted in breach of the implied undertaking given on discovery and was in contempt of court. The undertaking did not come to an end when the documents were read out in court. Subsequently there was a "friendly settlement" between the solicitor (Ms Harman) and the United Kingdom of an application made by Ms Harman against the United Kingdom before the European Commission of Human Rights[4] which resulted in a change of the law. This change took the form of a new rule of court,[5] RSC Ord. 24, r.14A:

> "14A Any undertaking, whether express or implied, not to use a document for any purposes other than those of the proceedings in which it is disclosed shall cease to apply to such document after it has been read to or by the court, or referred to, in open court, unless the court for special reasons has otherwise ordered on the application of a party or of a person to whom the document belongs."

24.003   The rule related to question (3) above. It applied to the implied undertaking and also applied when an undertaking restricting the use of a document or information in it had been obtained expressly. Otherwise the purpose of the change, which was to promote freedom of speech and free availability of information in relation to matters which had entered the public domain, would have been undermined.

There was a debate in the case law about the width of the release achieved by this rule; did it go so far as enabling a person to commence

---

[2] *Prudential Assurance v Fountain Page* [1991] 1 W.L.R. 757; *Derby & Co. Ltd v Weldon (No.2), Independent*, November 2, 1988; *The Times* October 20, 1988.

[3] [1983] 1 A.C. 280.

[4] The text of the settlement is set out in *Bibby Bulk Carriers v Consulex Ltd* [1989] Q.B. 155 at 159.

[5] The history is set out in *SmithKline Beecham Biologicals SA v Connaught Laboratories* [1999] 4 All E.R. 498.

new proceedings based upon the previously protected information? Ought it to be operated by the court to allow this to be done? In *Taylor v Director of the Serious Fraud Office*[6] defamation proceedings were brought based upon materials which had to be disclosed to a defendant in criminal proceedings. Those materials were generated as part of the process of investigating the alleged criminal offence. The House of Lords, reversing the Court of Appeal and overruling *Mahon v Rahn*,[7] held that there was an implied undertaking by the defendant to the criminal proceedings not to use those materials except for the purpose of the defence. The suggestion that once the materials were used in open court they could be freely used by a non-party to bring defamation proceedings against the investigators threatened to chill the proper investigation of crime. Lord Hoffmann observed that there was much force in the view that RSC Ord. 24, r.14A had been too widely drawn.

So the former rules of court provided some assistance on question (3), **24.004** but otherwise the matter was regulated outside of the rules, through the machinery of an implied undertaking given to the court and non-parties being in no better position to use the materials disclosed than the party who gave the undertaking.

(ii) The implied undertaking

The theory of the implied undertaking was that because the discovery was **24.005** compelled by the court order for a limited purpose, the documents were subject to an implied undertaking not to use them for another purpose.

The implied undertaking also applied to documents revealed for the purpose of a taxation of costs.[8] But this was not because disclosure had been compelled by court order but because the party revealing them had to do so if he was to prove his costs before the taxing master. If the taxing master required to see the documents in order to assess the costs he made an offer to the party seeking payment of costs which he could not refuse without losing his right to recover them.

In the first edition of *Bray on Discovery*,[9] the principle was stated:

> "A party who has obtained access to his adversary's documents under an order for production has no right to make their contents public or communicate them to any stranger to the suit: . . . nor to use them or copies of them for any collateral object . . . If necessary an undertaking to that effect will be made a condition of granting an order."

Such an undertaking was implied.[10] A party who obtained discovery in proceedings did so on condition that he would make use of the documents

---

[6] [1999] 2 A.C. 177.
[7] [1998] Q.B. 424.
[8] *Bourns v Raychem No.2* [1999] 1 All E.R. 908 at [19] and [20] and [1999] 3 All E.R. 154 at 170.
[9] 1st ed., 1885, p.238.
[10] *Harman v Home Office* [1983] 1 A.C. 280; *Riddick v Thames Board Mills* [1977] Q.B. 881; *Crest Homes plc v Marks* [1987] A.C. 829; *Alterskye v Scott* [1948] 1 All E.R. 469 at 470.

only for the purposes of that action.[11] This was to encourage and ensure full and unreserved disclosure of documents,[12] and because the documents belong to the party disclosing them, and use of the documents for some purpose collateral to the action by the other party was an infringement of the disclosing party's rights in them.[13]

24.006   The implied undertaking prevented the use of the documents in another action, even though it was based on the same cause of action.[14] They could, though, be used to obtain further discovery or disclosure of information for use in the action even if this is done by means of a second set of proceedings brought for the purpose.[15] This was because the disclosed documents were still being used solely for the purpose of prosecuting the first action.

The implied undertaking took effect in respect of any documents disclosed as a result of an order of the court, including documents obtained by a party pursuant to Anton Piller relief.[16] It applied so as to prevent the use of the documents in question in a second set of proceedings between the same parties, even when the subject-matter of the second set of proceedings was closely related to that of the proceedings in which the discovery has been obtained.[17]

24.007   The use to which the plaintiff could have put the documents consistently with the implied undertaking depended on the purpose for which the court ordered disclosure. It did not include any "collateral" or "ulterior" purpose, even in the same action as that in which disclosure was ordered. So when documents were disclosed under a discovery order made in aid of Mareva relief to enable the plaintiff to identify and preserve assets, the plaintiff could not disclose the documents to another defendant in the same action to enable that defendant to consider them in deciding whether to seek contribution in respect of the claimant's claim against the defendant who was ordered to disclose them.[18] Nor could the documents

---

[11] *Miller v Scorey* [1996] 1 W.L.R. 1122; *Riddick v Thomas Board Mills* [1977] Q.B. 881 at 896, 901–902 and 910; *Crest Homes plc v Marks* [1987] A.C. 829 at 853; *Sybron Corporation v Barclays Bank* [1985] Ch. 299 at 319–321, *per* Scott J.

[12] *Home Office v Harman* [1983] 1 A.C. 280 at 306, 308 and 321–322.

[13] *Halcon International Inc. v Shell Transport and Trading Co.* [1979] RFC 97 at 121, *per* Megaw L.J.

[14] *Cobra Golf Inc. v Rata* [1997] 2 W.L.R. 629; *Sybron Corporation v Barclays Bank* [1985] Ch. 299.

[15] *Wilden Pump v Fusfeld* [1985] F.S.R. 581.

[16] *Crest Homes plc v Marks* [1987] A.C. 829; *Customs and Excise Commissioners v A. E. Hamlin & Co* [1984] 1 W.L.R. 509 at 517–518; *VDU Installations Ltd v Integrated Computer Systems and Cybernetics Ltd* [1989] F.S.R. 378 at 395–396.

[17] *Cobra Golf Inc. v Rata* [1998] Ch. 109; *Halcon International Inc. v Shell Transport and Trading Co.* [1979] R.F.C. 97 (discovery by the defendants in English proceedings brought by the plaintiffs to restrain alleged infringements of UK letters patent could not be used in Dutch proceedings between the same parties concerning applications made by the plaintiffs for patents in The Netherlands); *Riddick v Thames Board Mills* [1977] Q.B. 881 (memorandum obtained on discovery in the first action could not be used to launch libel proceedings).

[18] *Savings & Investment Bank Ltd v Gray*, Court of Appeal (Civ Div) Transcript No.702 of 1990 (August 8, 1990).

disclosed in discovery given in an action be used to plead a counterclaim in that action which was not connected with the claim: *Derek Joseph Parry v Bentley*.[19]

In *Milano Assicurazioni SpA v Walbrook Insurance Co. Ltd*,[20] the plaintiff sought leave to amend a statement of claim which had been specially endorsed on the writ in the action. The proposed amendments were based on information derived from discovery in the action given by the defendant. On the facts the plaintiff had an ulterior purpose in carrying out the amendment by way of amending the writ. This was so that the document as amended would be available to third parties to inspect and thereby to obtain information which they could use for bringing proceedings. In these circumstances leave was given to make the amendments in a separate document which would not be available to third parties. By this means the plaintiff would be able to use the discovery in the action but would not be able to reveal the protected information to third parties, which was a purpose which was inconsistent with the implied undertaking. The formulation of the implied undertaking in *Bray on Discovery* prevented the use of the documents for "any collateral object . . .". This covered any case in which the party has an intention to use the documents to achieve a particular purpose which was other than solely to take steps in the proceedings, and which was thus "collateral" or "ulterior".[21] If documents were properly used for the purpose of the proceedings and the effect of what was done by a party was unintentionally to reveal information to third parties, then there was no breach of the implied undertaking by the relevant party.

Under the implied undertaking if documents were referred to in an **24.008** affidavit put in on an interlocutory application otherwise than to disclose information under compulsion of a court order, then the information was given voluntarily and not under compulsion. The implied undertaking did not apply. So, *e.g.* if the defendant provided information in evidence served in support of an application to discharge or vary an injunction, then that information was not protected. In the context of Mareva relief, if the defendant applied for a variation to the injunction in order to make a payment in the ordinary course of business or for some other justifiable purpose (*e.g.* payment of legal costs), and relied on evidence which included details of his assets and affairs, that evidence was adduced by the defendant voluntarily in the sense that he was not compelled by an order of the court to disclose it to the plaintiff. Hence the information comprised in that evidence was not protected by an implied undertaking. Similarly if the defendant was ordered to produce the documents as documents referred to in an affidavit even though production was compelled by court order or under the rules of court, the implied undertaking would not apply because the original reference to the documents had been made voluntarily

---

[19] [1994] 1 H.K.L.R. 265.
[20] [1994] 1 W.L.R. 977.
[21] *Milano Assicurazioni SpA v Walbrook Insurance Co. Ltd* [1994] 1 W.L.R. 977 at 983.

and production was only the consequence of that voluntary conduct.[22] The same rule applied to documents voluntarily referred to in a pleading,[23] and information about assets supplied voluntarily in correspondence when this did not have to be supplied under a disclosure order granted ancillary to a Mareva injunction.[24]

In *Derby & Co. Ltd v Weldon (No.2)*,[25] the defendants had provided affidavits and exhibits about their assets pursuant to an order of the court. Sir Nicolas Browne-Wilkinson V.-C. held that the affidavits and exhibits were obtained subject to the implied undertaking.[26] In principle this was true of any document prepared and served under a court order[27] requiring disclosure of information (*e.g.* information given in a letter). In consequence, the implied undertaking, while it continued to apply, prohibited the plaintiffs from producing these affidavits in response to a subpoena served on them by a third party in New York. The defendants had also sworn and served affidavits with exhibits in order to challenge Mareva relief which had been granted against them. The defendants by their own voluntary act had destroyed the privacy in the documents. The affidavits also referred to other documents which were not exhibited, but which had to be produced pursuant to an order of the court. The Vice-Chancellor held that by swearing the affidavit referring to the documents, the documents were voluntarily relied upon and therefore were not subject to any implied undertaking. In effect the court order was merely perfecting the previous voluntary disclosure. The defendants must have known that they could not rely on the documents without being liable to produce them if required.[28] So also witness statements and experts' reports were not protected by any implied undertaking.

(iii) Release of the implied undertaking

24.009   In the context of Anton Piller orders the courts did not regard the fact that the documents may evidence criminal offences as in itself providing good reason for releasing the undertaking.[29]

---

[22] *Derby & Co. Ltd v Weldon (No.2)*, *Independent*, November 2, 1988; *The Times*, October 20, 1988; *Cassidy v Hawcroft*, unreported, July 27, 2000 at [17–18].

[23] *Eagle Star Insurance v Arab Bank*, unreported, February 25, 1991 (Hobhouse J.) referred to in C. Hollander, *Documentary Evidence* (8th ed., 2003), p.311.

[24] *White v Biddulph*, unreported, May 22, 1998 (Hart J.).

[25] *Independent*, November 2, 1988; *The Times*, October 20, 1988; extracts of the case are set out in *SmithKline Beecham Biologicals SA v Connaught Laboratories* [1999] 4 All E.R. 498 at 507–508.

[26] Referred to in *Prudential Assurance Co. v Fountain Page Ltd* [1991] 1 W.L.R. 756 at 765–768.

[27] Including an order made under s.7 of the Bankers' Books Evidence Act 1879 (*Bhimji v Chatwani (No.2)* [1992] 1 W.L.R. 1158), or a subpoena (*Sybron Corporation v Barclays Bank* [1985] Ch. 299; *Welfare v Bidon Sands Pty Ltd* (1997) 149 A.L.R. 378, Federal Court of Australia).

[28] cf. *Bhimji v Chatwani (No.2)* [1992] 1 W.L.R. 1158 at 1163.

[29] *EMI Records Ltd v Spillane* [1986] 1 W.L.R. 967 at 977, where Sir Nicolas Browne-Wilkinson V.-C. disagreed with the view of Falconer J. in *Customs and Excise Commissioners v A. E. Hamlin & Co.* [1984] 1 W.L.R. 509. See also *General Nutrition Ltd v Pattni* [1984] F.S.R. 403.

The courts were willing to allow documents obtained on discovery to be used for the purposes of contempt proceedings in the same action as that in which contempt proceedings are to be brought.[30]

However, when documents were disclosed in one action and the contempt proceedings were to be brought in another action, then the implied undertaking prevented use of the documents in the contempt proceedings without permission of the court. In *Crest Homes v Marks* it was only because of a technicality that there were two actions. In substance the two actions comprised a single piece of litigation and because of this leave was given.[31] In contrast in *Cobra Golf Inc. v Rata*[32] the plaintiff sued in the first action to a final consent order, and then brought a second action based on infringements of the plaintiff's rights allegedly committed after the consent order in the first action. The purpose of the Anton Piller order granted in the second action was to preserve evidence for use in the second action. Leave to use this material in contempt proceedings in the first action was refused. It was a use which was collateral to the purpose for which the Anton Piller order had been made and there was no technicality in having two sets of proceedings.[33] Furthermore, the plaintiff had already been refused Anton Piller relief in the first action for the purpose of obtaining material on which to launch contempt proceedings and the proposed use of the material obtained in the second action for the purpose of advancing contempt proceedings in the first action would be inconsistent with this refusal.

When substantial assets have been misappropriated there will often be **24.010** criminal inquiries going on at the same time as civil proceedings, which are being pursued in order to find out what has happened to the assets or their proceeds and to obtain redress. There is no privilege against self-incrimination available to a defendant in respect of the risk of prosecution abroad.[34] Funds misappropriated abroad may be transferred through banks or other institutions in England and Wales, and this may result in the court granting relief enabling the funds or their proceeds to be traced, but subject to undertakings restricting the use of the information. In *Bank of Crete v Koskotas (No.2)*,[35] leave was sought by the plaintiff bank to use information obtained under orders of the English court from banks in London about its missing funds. Leave was granted in order to enable the plaintiff to comply properly with its obligations under Greek law to compile audit reports about its foreign exchange transactions, which would in due course go to the Bank of Greece and an examining magistrate.

A party who was subject to an undertaking (express or implied) to keep disclosed documents confidential and not to use them except for certain

---

[30] *Crest Homes plc v Marks* [1987] A.C. 829 at 860; *Re Barlow Clowes Ltd* [1992] Ch. 208; but not on the facts in *Bourns v Raychem No.2* [1999] 3 All E.R. 154.
[31] See also *Omar v Omar* [1995] 1 W.L.R. 1428 at 1436; *Cobra Golf Inc. v Rata* [1996] F.S.R. 819 at 829 (Laddie J.).
[32] [1998] Ch. 109 (Rimer J.).
[33] See also *Cobra Golf Inc. v Rata* [1996] F.S.R. 819 (Laddie J.).
[34] See Chapter 17, para.17.046, above.
[35] [1992] 1 W.L.R. 919.

purposes (*e.g.* the purposes of the action) could find himself being required to disclose the information to the foreign authorities, who are pursuing the criminal inquiries, under threat of a penalty if he does not comply. In such circumstances the court would give leave for the information to be disclosed to the foreign authorities because it would be a grave injustice for a person who has been granted relief to redress the wrong done to him to find himself compelled to choose between breaking the undertaking or breaking the law where he resides or carries on business and suffering a penalty abroad because of this.[36] Furthermore, disclosure would further international co-operation in combating fraud.

In *Bank of Crete v Koskotas (No.2)*, leave had already been granted to enable the information to be used so as to prevent a serious miscarriage of justice occurring in Greece, namely the conviction of an innocent man based on untrue evidence.[37] The public interest could justify release of the implied undertaking.[38]

24.011   It could also be the case that substantive proceedings on the merits of a claim have been commenced in England and the claimant wished to use documents disclosed under compulsion of a court order in those proceedings to assist in proceedings abroad taken for the purpose of preserving assets to satisfy an eventual judgment in England. The contemplated foreign proceedings were then merely ancillary to the English action and in *Bayer v Winter (No.2)*[39] Hoffmann J. gave leave allowing the discovery to be used in the foreign proceedings.

In *Cobra Golf Inc. v Rata*,[40] Laddie J. summarised the principles about release of the implied undertaking as follows:

> "1. Documents may not be used for a collateral purpose without leave of the court or the party from whom they came.
> 2. That restriction on collateral use covers not only the documents themselves but also copies of them and the information they contain.
> 3. In this context collateral purpose means some purpose not reasonably necessary for the proper conduct of the action in which the discovery was given.
> 4. Strictly speaking, asking for release of the documents for use outside the proceedings in which they were disclosed is itself a collateral use, since it is a use of knowledge of the contents of the documents for a purpose collateral to those proceedings. However, this must be taken to be a necessary exception to the otherwise all-embracing effect of the undertaking.
> 5. The unsanctioned collateral use constitutes an abuse of process or contempt of court. Whether it gives rise to a civil cause of action is not clear.

---

[36] *Bank of Crete v Koskotas (No.2)* [1992] 1 W.L.R. 919 at 926.
[37] *ibid.*
[38] *A v A (Ancillary Relief); B v B (Ancillary Relief)* [2000] 1 F.L.R. 701 (disclosure to the Revenue of tax evasion).
[39] [1986] F.S.R. 357; see also *Cobra Golf Inc. v Rata* [1996] F.S.R. 819 at 828 (Laddie J.).
[40] [1996] F.S.R. 819 at 830–832, referred to in *SmithKline Beecham Plc v Generics (UK) Ltd* [2003] 4 All E.R. 1302 at [37].

6. The existence of the implied undertaking means that an application to release the party from restraint must be made before there is collateral use.

7. Normally the application will be made first to the other party and only after refusal will it be made to the court.

8. In exceptional cases, such as ones in which notice to the party of the intended use to which the documents may be put are likely to defeat the ends of justice, the application for release from the undertakings may be made *ex parte*.

9. When made *ex parte*, the court should normally impose an *inter partes* return date in the near future when the affected party will be able if he so wishes to argue that the documents should not be used (see *Naf Naf SA v. Dickens (London) Ltd* [1993] F.S.R. 424).

10. On any application to relax the undertaking, the court has a discretion which must be exercised to achieve justice on the basis of all the circumstances of the case.

11. The circumstances which may be taken into account include the following:

   (a) The extent to which relaxation of the undertaking will cause injustice to the party which provided the discovery.

   (b) Whether the proposed collateral use is in court proceedings or outside litigation (*e.g.* for disclosure to the press as in *Harman*). Prima facie if it is for use outside litigation, it is not the court's function to release for that purpose.

   (c) Whether, if the collateral use is in aid of criminal or civil proceedings, those proceedings are in this country or abroad.

   (d) In so far as the satellite proceedings are in this country:

      (i) If they are criminal proceedings, the court must take into account the possibility of the application being a method of bypassing the privilege against self-incrimination.

      (ii) If the collateral use is for civil proceedings, the court should take into account:

         (a) whether the hub proceedings and the satellite proceedings are similar in character;

         (b) whether the parties in the two sets of proceedings are the same;

         (c) the extent to which the party seeking relaxation of the undertaking would be able to obtain discovery by another route and, if so, which route is likely to be cheaper or quicker;

         (d) whether the effect of the relaxation of the undertaking will have the effect of generating new proceedings or whether it will merely help in pursuing a claim or defence which already exists or could be run anyway;

         (e) prima facie it is not in the interests of justice to hinder a party from advancing a good claim or defence in other proceedings;

(f) prima facie it is not in the interests of justice to allow discovery in the hub action to be released for the purpose of supporting the initiation of contempt proceedings in the satellite action, at least if the two proceedings are 'unrelated'.

(iii) In so far as the documents are to be used in proceedings abroad,

(a) Whether those proceedings are criminal or civil.

(b) If the satellite proceedings are criminal, the court here should be wary of doing anything in this country which may subject the disclosing party to an unfair disadvantage in those proceedings.

(c) If the satellite proceedings are civil, the court should take into account whether the disclosure would put the disclosing party at a significant disadvantage in those proceedings—for example by forcing it to produce in the public domain documents which, under the local procedure, would not otherwise be made public.

(e) There does not appear to be any reason in principle why documents properly obtained as a result of an *Anton Piller* order should be treated differently to any other discovery documents. Once disclosed they are no more nor less protected by the implied undertaking."

24.012   The decided cases on whether or not leave was to be granted to release the implied undertaking were simply illustrations of the application of the same general principle that "the court will not release or modify the implied undertaking given on discovery save in special circumstances and where the release or modification will not occasion injustice to the person giving discovery".[41] If the new use was to be permitted, the applicant had to demonstrate "cogent and persuasive reasons".[42]

(iv) The effect of the former RSC Ord.24, r.14A

24.013   This rule came into force on October 1, 1987 and was not retrospective.[43] It is not part of the CPR. It had the effect of limiting the duration for which an express or implied undertaking had effect, subject to the power of the court "for special reasons" to order to the contrary. For example, if documents which contained confidential information as to a secret invention or process were disclosed,[44] then this would be capable of giving rise

---

[41] *Crest Homes plc v Marks* [1987] A.C. 829 at 860.

[42] *Crest Homes plc v Marks* [1987] A.C. 829 at 859, *per* Lord Oliver; *Bibby Bulk Carriers v Consulex Ltd* [1989] Q.B. 155 at 161; *Savings & Investment Bank Ltd v Gray*, Court of Appeal (Civ Div) Transcript No.702 of 1990 (August 10, 1990).

[43] *Bibby Bulk Carriers v Consulex Ltd* [1989] Q.B. 135.

[44] *Lubrizol Corporation v Esso Petroleum Co. Ltd (No.2)* [1993] F.S.R. 53; *Attorney-General v Newspaper Publishing plc* [1988] Ch. 333 at 389; *Warner-Lambert Co. v Glaxo Laboratories Ltd* [1975] R.F.C. 354; *Arab Monetary Fund v Hashim* [1989] 1 W.L.R. 565 at 577 (the need to keep confidential industrial secrets of this nature could justify the making of an order for discovery limited to a party's lawyers and experts only).

to "special reasons" for keeping the documents confidential. The rule applied to "a document" which was subject to an express or implied undertaking. Thus, *e.g.*, if an order was made requiring a party to make and serve an affidavit containing certain information, the affidavit disclosed under that order was subject to the implied undertaking, as were the exhibits. This rule also applied to the affidavit and the exhibits.

When did the rule operate so as to cause the undertaking to cease? In *Derby & Co. Ltd v Weldon (No.2)*,[45] the affidavits and exhibits relating to assets within the jurisdiction had been included in the bundle of documents before the Court of Appeal in *Derby & Co. Ltd v Weldon (No.1)*.[46] The affidavits had been referred to in the skeleton argument lodged by the plaintiffs with the Court of Appeal, and the judgment of Parker L.J. in the Court of Appeal had referred to those assets as being "wholly insufficient to afford protection". In these circumstances, Sir Nicolas Browne-Wilkinson V.-C. held that the implied undertaking had ceased to apply by reason of RSC Ord. 24, r.14A. The affidavits had been "read to or by the court, or referred to, in open court". The rule was not confined to releasing the implied undertaking once a document has been read out in open court, but it applied even to documents which were read silently by the judge, or documents which were "referred to", although not read out, in open court. The reference could have been by means of a skeleton argument lodged with the court which subsequently formed part of counsel's submission in open court.[47]

Prior to the making of the new rule of court it had been decided in *Sybron Corporation v Barclays Bank plc*[48] that documents obtained by subpoena and which were referred to in a judgment given in open court were still subject to an implied undertaking. In cases governed by RSC Ord. 24, r.14A, in such circumstances the implied undertaking did not apply.

RSC Ord. 24, r.14A had the effect that unless the court has made an **24.014** order on the application of a party or the person to whom the document belongs, the undertaking not to use the document except in the proceedings ceased to apply.

The rule had to be applied on a document by document basis. The inclusion of a document in the bundle before a court for the purposes of a hearing in open court was insufficient in itself to cause the undertaking to cease. But once the document had been read to the court or by the court, or had been referred to "in open court", the undertaking ceased to apply to it. The words "referred to" had the effect that even though none of the contents of a document were exposed in the course of the hearing in open court, nevertheless the document as a whole became public if reference was made to it "in open court". When a judge in a short hearing in open court referred compendiously to the documents lodged with the court, then the

---

[45] *The Times*, October 20, 1988.
[46] [1990] Ch. 48.
[47] *Derby & Co. Ltd v Weldon (No.2)*, *The Times*, October 20, 1988.
[48] [1985] Ch. 299.

implied undertaking ceased to apply.[49] The same would include to any compendious reference made in open court and whether made orally or in a skeleton argument.

In *Singh (Tejendra) v Christie*,[50] Drake J. held that notwithstanding the width of the wording of the rule, libel proceedings could not be brought based on a document which had been disclosed and read in open court. Leave to appeal against this decision was refused by the Court of Appeal.[51] However, the correctness of this decision was doubtful.[52] The better view was that unless there was a contrary order of the court, the undertaking completely ceased to apply once a disclosed document had been read to the court or by the court, or had been referred to in open court. Such a document became a public document.

(3) The position under CPR

(i) CPR r.31.22

24.015   CPR r.31.22 provides:

"SUBSEQUENT USE OF DISCLOSED DOCUMENTS

31.22 (1) A party to whom a document has been disclosed may use the document only for the purpose of the proceedings in which it is disclosed, except where—

(a)   the document has been read to or by the court, or referred to, at a hearing which has been held in public;

(b)   the court gives permission; or

(c)   the party who disclosed the document and the person to whom the document belongs agree.

(2) The court may make an order restricting or prohibiting the use of a document which has been disclosed, even where the document has been read to or by the court, or referred to, at a hearing which has been held in public.

(3) An application for such an order may be made–

(a)   by a party; or

(b)   by any person to whom the document belongs.

CPR r.31.2 provides:

---

[49] *SmithKline Beecham Biologicals SA v Connaught Laboratories* [1999] 4 All E.R. 498.
[50] *The Times*, November 11, 1993.
[51] *Sub nom Tejendrasingh v Metsons* [1997] E.M.L.R. 597.
[52] The division in the authorities is described in *Cassidy v Hawcroft* [2001] C.P. Rep. 49 (July 27, 2000) at [14], CA.

"MEANING OF DISCLOSURE

31.2   A party discloses a document by stating that the document exists or has existed."

The following points arise on CPR r.31.22:   24.016

(1)   The rule applies to disclosure to a party but has no requirement that the disclosure be given by a party. In principle it applies to disclosure in the proceedings given by anyone, including non-parties.[53]

(2)   The rule applies to disclosure of the existence of a document in a witness statement, an affidavit, an expert's report, or a pleading, or as a result of third party disclosure, or a witness summons,[54] or any other way in the course of the proceedings.

(3)   Disclosure under the CPR can be done by voluntary agreement between the parties or between a party and a non-party, rather than through a court order. The same restriction on use applies regardless of how the document has come to be "disclosed" in the proceedings. Thus the rule applies to a document which "has been disclosed" and does not have a requirement in it that the disclosure is pursuant to a court order. That this is a deliberate change is also supported by CPR r.32.12, which does not depend upon the witness statement being supplied under compulsion of a court order. In addition the Practice Direction on pre-action protocols provides:

> "4.8 Documents disclosed by either party in accordance with this practice direction may not be used for any purpose other than resolving the dispute, unless the other party agrees."

Again this does not operate on the basis that restriction in use depends upon the material being required by compulsion. The old system that there could only be a restriction by an implied undertaking when material was obtained by compulsion under a court order, or perhaps under threat of compulsion by a court order, has gone. There is no limitation in CPR r.31.22 that on how the document has come to be "disclosed" in the proceedings.

(4)   CPR r.31.22 takes account of the "friendly settlement" between the United Kingdom and Ms Harman. It refers to hearings held in

---

[53] *SmithKline Beecham Plc v Generics (UK) Ltd* [2004] 1 W.L.R. 1479 at [29].
[54] *SmithKline Beecham Plc v Generics (UK) Ltd* [2004] 1 W.L.R. 1479 at [29] *cf.* the contrary view expressed obiter in *Marlwood Commercial Incorporated v Viktor Kozeny* [2004] EWHC 189 (February 9, 2004) at [32] (Moore-Bick J.) which apparently proceeded on the basis that the words "to whom a document has been disclosed . . ." only applied to disclosure to a party by another party to the proceedings.

public and provides for that to affect the restriction. It does so whilst retaining the court's jurisdiction to rule to the contrary.

(5) It would be pointless to protect the documents disclosed without also protecting the information in them. The implied undertaking applied both to the documents themselves and the information derived from the documents.[55] CPR r.31.22 has to be read in the same way.[56]

(6) An obligation of confidentiality can exist independently of the restriction in CPR r.31.22. It could be contractual or non-contractual. This obligation can be enforced by injunction.

(7) The word "use" in CPR r.31.22 extends to use by that party or allowing the document or a copy to be used for any collateral or ulterior purpose, or allowing any third party to have access to the document for such a purpose.[57]

(ii) Witness statements: CPR r.32.12

24.017   CPR r.32.12 imposes a restriction on the use of witness statements. Previously witness statements produced voluntarily in the course of litigation were not protected by any implied undertaking.[58] Witness statements produced for use at the trial were protected under the former RSC Ord. 38, r.2A.

CPR r.32.12 provides:

"Use of witness statements for other purposes

32.12 (1) Except as provided by this rule, a witness statement may be used only for the purpose of the proceedings in which it is served.
(2) Paragraph (1) does not apply if and to the extent that—
(a) the witness gives consent in writing to some other use of it;
(b) the court gives permission for some other use; or
(c) the witness statement has been put in evidence at a hearing held in public."

The following points arise:

24.018   (1) The rule is to be read as imposing a restriction on the use of the document and the information in it.

---

[55] *Sybron Corporation v Barclays Bank* [1985] Ch. 299 at 318; *Cobra Golf Inc. v Rata* [1996] F.S.R. 819 at 830 (Laddie J.).
[56] *Marlwood Commercial Incorporated v Viktor Kozeny* [2004] EWHC 189 (February 9, 2004) at [32] (Moore-Bick J.).
[57] *Marlwood Commercial Incorporated v Viktor Kozeny* [2004] EWHC 189 (February 9, 2004) at [34] (Moore-Bick J.), following *Harman v Home Office* [1983] 1 A.C. 280 at 304.
[58] *Prudential Assurance v Fountain Page* [1991] 1 W.L.R. 757 at 769.

(2) It applies whoever has placed the witness statement before the court, whether a party or a non-party.

(3) CPR r.32.12 provides a restriction regardless of whether the witness statement has been produced by compulsion under a court order or, voluntarily, but under the exigencies of the litigation or in order to obtain some advantage in the litigation.

(4) The witness statement includes its exhibits. These are part of the witness statement just as much as if they had been copied out in full in the text of the witness statement.[59] These will also be documents "disclosed" and so subject to CPR r.31.22 which provides an equivalent restriction on use to that in CPR r.32.12.

(5) Like CPR r.31.22 it refers to a hearing in public so as to limit the restriction.

(iii) Affidavits and expert reports served on a party

24.019 An affidavit is different from a witness statement.[60] CPR r.32.12 does not apply to an affidavit. Is an affidavit served as evidence on a party to the proceedings within CPR r.31.22? In *SmithKline Beecham Plc v Generics (UK) Ltd*[61] test results on samples given to a party were treated as a document "disclosed" to that party under the rule; thus the rule is capable of applying to documents which have come into existence for the purpose of use in the proceedings as evidence. One would expect the same regime to apply to an affidavit which was used to provide evidence to the court as applies to a witness statement; they both serve the same function and only differ in their formal requirements.[62] The CPR rules have to be read as a free-standing, complete code, and the word "disclosed" is not to be read as limited to situations in which before the CPR an undertaking was to be implied.[63] An affidavit sworn in the proceedings and served on the other party, and its exhibits, would each appear to be a document "disclosed" to a party in those proceedings within CPR r.31.22, and the same reasoning would apply to an expert's report and its appendices served in proceedings on a party.[64] The rule would also appear to apply to documents referred to

---

[59] *Re Hinchcliffe* [1895] 1 Ch. 117; *Barings Plc v Coopers & Lybrand* [2000] 1 W.L.R. 2353 at [44–48].
[60] CPR r.32.15.
[61] [2003] 4 All E.R. 1302.
[62] The differences can be seen in Practice Direction—Written Evidence which supplements CPR Pt 32.
[63] *SmithKline Beecham Plc v Generics (UK) Ltd* [2004] 1 W.L.R. 1479 at [29] rejecting the argument for a narrow meaning of "disclosed" in CPR r.31.22 which was summarised at paras 23–26 and depended on the old law about implied undertakings.
[64] A contrary view is taken by Charles Hollander, Q.C. in *Documentary Evidence* (8th ed., 2003), pp.319–320, where he places reliance ((h) at p.319) on the "compulsion" principle, which justified the implied undertaking analysis, and reads this as colouring the meaning of "disclosed" in CPR r.31.22.

by an affidavit or expert's report served on a party in the course of the proceedings because the existence of those documents is disclosed to that party by service of the affidavit or expert's report.

It might be suggested that the court should imply an undertaking equivalent to the restriction in CPR r.32.12 when an affidavit is used, or alternatively has to be used (*e.g.* on an application for a freezing injunction or search order under para.3.1 of the Practice Direction—Interim Injunctions which supplements Pt 25), instead of a witness statement. This is a less elegant solution, and it is considered that it should be rejected because CPR r.31.22 applies, the restrictions on use in CPR appear to have been intended as a complete express code, which could be safely relied upon by the ordinary litigant, and the law about an implied undertaking cannot co-exist with the express provisions of that code. Another route to a restriction on use is that if the affidavit contains confidential information the court can protect that information by injunction on the basis that the confidentiality remains intact except that the information can be used for the purpose of the proceedings in which the affidavit is served.

(iv) Information obtained under the example freezing injunction: undertakings (9) and (10)

24.020 Undertaking (9), given expressly under the example form of freezing injunction, limits the use of any information "obtained as a result of this order" to "this claim". Undertakings (9) and (10) of the example order are considered in Chapter 22, from para.22.018. These undertakings apply both to documents and to oral disclosure made under the order. In these circumstances it is likely to be academic whether CPR r.31.22 would apply to documents disclosed in compliance with such an order including an affidavit of assets or documents relating to assets. It is considered that the rule does apply because these are documents "disclosed" to a party.[65]

(v) Use of information obtained as a result of a search order

24.021 There was no implied undertaking in an Anton Piller order to the effect that whatever the representatives happen to see on the premises in the course of a search permitted pursuant to the order, would be kept confidential. Thus, in *L. T. Piver Sàrl v S. & J. Perfume Co. Ltd*,[66] a representative saw an article on the premises which he thought infringed the rights of a third party and it was held that he was at liberty to report this to the third party concerned.

The 1996 standard form order included, in Schedule 3, para.6, an undertaking by the plaintiff:

---

[65] *SmithKline Beecham Plc v Generics (UK) Ltd* [2004] 1 W.L.R. 1479 at [29], *cf.* the contrary view expressed obiter in *Marlwood Commercial Incorporated v Viktor Kozeny*, [2004] EWHC 189, February 9, 2004, at [32] (Moore-Bicle J.).

[66] [1987] F.S.R. 159.

"(6) Not, without the leave of the Court, to use any information or documents obtained as a result of carrying out this Order nor to inform anyone else of these proceedings except for the purposes of these proceedings (including adding further Defendants) or commencing civil proceedings in relation to the same or related subject matter to these proceedings until after the Return Date."

Undertaking (4) of the example search order follows this model:

(4) The Applicant will not, without the permission of the court, use any information or documents obtained as a result of carrying out this order nor inform anyone else of these proceedings except for the purposes of these proceedings (including adding further Respondents) or commencing civil proceedings in relation to the same or related subject matter to these proceedings until after the return date.

This undertaking applies to information or documents "obtained as a result of carrying out this order . . ." and so applies to information obtained as a result of the search. If a representative, as a result of being admitted to the premises, came across a trade secret, then he is bound not to disclose that secret. This is so under undertaking (4) to the example search order, and also because of the ordinary legal rules concerning the preservation of confidential information.

It is considered that undertaking (4) of the example search order, and **24.022** undertaking (9) in the example freezing injunction, would apply to information required to be given orally under the order. The implied undertaking in an Anton Piller order applied to information which had to be disclosed orally under the order,[67] and these express undertakings both in the words used and their purpose, also apply to information given orally. Each undertaking would also apply to the written disclosure made pursuant to the relevant order.

The uses permitted by undertaking (4) of the example search order include commencing new civil proceedings "in relation to the same or related subject-matter to these proceedings". This form of wording assumes that a purpose of the search order is to enable this to be done; this would be so for an order made under the *Norwich Pharmacal* jurisdiction (para.22.048), or in order to safeguard trust assets (paras 22–053 *et seq*).

(vi) The jurisdiction to safeguard trust assets and the Norwich Pharmacal *principle*
These are discussed in Chapter 22, paras 22.053 *et seq*.   **24.023**

---

[67] *Rank Film Ltd v Video Information Centre* [1982] A.C. 380 at 447, *per* Lord Fraser; *VDU Installations Ltd v Integrated Computer Systems and Cybernetics Ltd* [1989] F.S.R. 378 at 395–396.

If disclosure is ordered by the court under the principle that the defendant, by virtue of having become innocently mixed up in the wrongdoings of others, is under a duty to give the claimant full information concerning the wrongdoing,[68] the purpose for which the disclosure is ordered is to enable the claimant to identify and to sue the wrongdoers, or to obtain some form of redress. *Norwich Pharmacal* relief has a different purpose from disclosure given in an action to help resolve the issues in that action. In a case in which assets have been taken, redress includes full information (not necessarily confined merely to identifying wrongdoers)[69] to enable the assets or their proceeds to be traced, preserved and made over to the claimant. It will include obtaining compensation from the wrongdoers.

The reason for *Norwich Pharmacal* relief is to dictate the purposes that information obtained in consequence of it can be used. So, in principle, in a tracing claim the claimant can use the information obtained to preserve assets, to identify wrongdoers, and to sue them successfully both on proprietary claims and personal claims, including proving the case against them at trial.[70]

In such circumstances there is no implied undertaking by the claimant which precludes him from using the documents or other information obtained for the purpose of suing the third parties whether they are in England or abroad, and there should be no express undertaking prohibiting this.[71]

24.024   In the context of a tracing claim, if disclosure of documents or information is ordered to be given by a bank so as to enable the claimant to trace assets,[72] there will be no implied undertaking by the claimant preventing him from using the documents or information to preserve the relevant assets or their proceeds, or to sue third parties: *Omar v Omar.*[73] Nor should there be an express undertaking prohibiting this. But the information cannot be used for the purpose of pointing out to a third party some wrongdoing on the part of the defendant, because this is not within the purpose of the order or part of the process of conducting the proceedings.[74]

For the purpose of CPR r.31.22 it is considered that where an order is made by the court under either jurisdiction, then in the absence of an

---

[68] *i.e.* under the principle referred to by Lord Reid in *Norwich Pharmacal v Customs and Excise Commissioners* [1974] A.C. 133 at 175. See further Chapter 22, para.22.048.

[69] *Mercantile Group (Europe) AG v Aiyela* [1994] Q.B. 366 at 374.

[70] *Omar v Omar* [1995] 1 W.L.R. 1428.

[71] *Jade Engineering (Coventry) Ltd v Antiference Window Systems Ltd* [1996] F.S.R. 461 at 464; *Sony Corporation v Anand* [1981] F.S.R. 398; *Rank Film Ltd v Video Information Centre* [1982] A.C. 380 at 447; *Levi Strauss & Co. v Barclays Trading Corporation Inc.* [1993] F.S.R. 179.

[72] For example, as in *Bankers Trust Co. v Shapira* [1980] 1 W.L.R. 1274.

[73] [1995] 1 W.L.R. 1428.

[74] *VDU Installations Ltd v Integrated Computer Systems and Cybernetics Ltd* [1989] F.S.R. 378 *Bhimji v Chatwani (No.2)* [1992] 1 W.L.R. 1158 (documents improperly disclosed to the police).

express undertaking restricting use of the information obtained as a result of the order, the court is to be regarded as having consented to a use of the information within the scope of the purpose which the court had in making the order.

(vii) CPR r.34.12, protection of the "deposition": cross-examination about assets
CPR r.34.12 is considered in Chapter 22, para.22.027.   24.025

(viii) An implied undertaking to protect information disclosed under compulsion of a court order
Normally it is to be expected that a court making a mandatory order for 24.026 disclosure of information will provide for what is the permitted use of that information by way of requiring an express undertaking by the applicant controlling use. This is the mechanism used in the example orders and what undertaking should be given is a matter which should be raised with the judge on an application made without notice. The restriction imposed by CPR r.31.22 operates on information in documents which are "disclosed";[75] it does not apply to oral disclosure required under a search order, freezing injunction or other mandatory order made by the court. It may also be too wide in the use permitted because it allows use for the purpose of the proceedings in which the disclosure is given. It is considered that in a case in which the question of an express undertaking has not been raised, then the court can imply that an undertaking was given only to use the information for the purpose for which the information was ordered to be disclosed.

(ix) Protection of confidential information by injunction
If information acquired by the claimant is confidential, the court can grant 24.027 an injunction preserving the confidentiality. For example, this power can be exercised in relation to confidential information in witness statements or exhibits,[76] or obtained through a search conducted under a search order, or to enforce the privacy of arbitration proceedings (see below).

(4) Entry into the public domain: public hearings and the position under the CPR

(i) CPR r.31.22
CPR r.31.22(a) follows the wording in the former RSC Ord. 24, r.14A and 24.028 so the restriction in the rule will cease even for a compendious reference to documents in open court. There is a practice for documents to be read in

---

[75] *SmithKline Beecham Plc v Generics (UK) Ltd* [2004] 1 W.L.R. 1479 at [29]. *cf. Marlwood Commercial Incorporated v Viktor Kozeny* [2004] EWHC 189 (February 9, 2004) at [34] (Moore-Bick J.).
[76] *Lubrizol Corporation v Esso Petroleum Company Ltd (No.2)* [1993] F.S.R. 53.

advance by the court. Once a document is in the bundles for a public hearing and that hearing goes ahead on the merits, then the burden passes to the person claiming that it was not read by the judge in advance to prove that it was not read and to do so without calling the judge to give evidence.[77] If the public hearing does not go ahead on the merits (*e.g.* the application or the claim is dismissed by consent) then whether the document was read in advance by the judge does not matter because none of his pre-hearing reading was relevant in any way to understanding what happened in court in public. The fact that documents are read in advance or out of court cannot cut down on the principle that the public should be able to understand what has happened at a public hearing. This does not give the right to a member of the public to demand production of a document by the court or a party; it causes the termination of the restriction on use of the document.

Under CPR r.32.22(2) the court has power to continue the restriction even after the document has already been read in court or referred to in court in the course of a hearing held in public, but this will only be done if sufficiently good reason is shown for overriding the general principle that once a document has entered the public domain the protection will cease. For example, this can be shown through the fact that the document contains sensitive confidential information which it would be unfair to disseminate and which is not needed in order to understand what happened at the public hearing.[78]

Under CPR r.31.22(3) for the restriction to continue the applicant must be a party or someone to whom the document belongs. An example of where this could arise is a non-party required to produce confidential documents under a witness summons. The witness summons if not set aside would override his rights of confidentiality for the purpose of production of documents to the court.[79] But if he would be producing a document which was his own then he could apply to the court under this provision.

(ii) Application by a non-party who is not an owner of the document for an injunction maintaining confidentiality of material to be used in evidence

24.029   CPR r.31.22(3) proceeds on the basis that CPR r.31.22(2) is only concerned with the restriction imposed by r.31.22(1) and leaves unaffected any substantive rights a non-party may have in relation to the continued confidentiality of the information in the document.

A non-party, who is not an owner of the document itself, can apply to the court to enforce those rights by injunction. He may be met with the defence that by virtue of the public hearing the documents will pass into

---

[77] *Lily Icos LLC v Pfizer* [2002] 1 W.L.R. 2253 at [8].
[78] *SmithKline Beecham Plc v Generics (UK) Ltd* [2004] 1 W.L.R. 1479 at [30–33].
[79] *Marcel v Commissioner of Police of the Metropolis* [1992] Ch. 225.

the "public domain". But it does not necessarily follow that an injunction will be refused; the court can decide to hold part of the hearing in private (see below), or could impose a procedure under CPR r.3.1(2)(m) (an order for the purpose of managing the case) to be adopted in public calculated so far as possible to maintain the confidentiality of that material. This could include imposing a requirement that a party who wishes to have access to the material must give an undertaking designed to preserve its confidentiality. The court could also grant injunctions designed to preserve the confidentiality. Procedurally the court could also add the person applying for the injunction as a party to the proceedings so that he could also apply for an order under CPR r.31.22(2).

(iii) Application by a non-party who is not an owner of the document for an injunction maintaining confidentiality of material used at a public hearing

Once there has been a public hearing, as long as the information has not **24.030** been disseminated publicly and the court could still grant an effective injunction to preserve the confidentiality, then an injunction could still be granted for this purpose. Factors to be taken into account would be any delay in applying for the relief and whether in the circumstances where an public hearing has already taken place an injunction should be granted. This would include taking into account the public interest in being able to understand what has taken place in the public hearing and Art.10 of the European Convention on Human Rights.

(iv) CPR r.32.12

Under CPR r.32.12(c) the restriction ceases to apply when "the witness **24.031** statement has been put in evidence at a public hearing". These words do not require that the statement has been read or referred to at a public hearing, once it has gone into evidence the restriction ceases to apply.[80]

(v) CPR r.34.12

This restriction does not have a public hearing exception, but the court can **24.032** give permission for the restriction not to apply. It is to be expected that once material comes into the public domain as a result of a public hearing, permission would be granted unless there was sufficiently good reason to preserve the confidentiality.

---

[80] See also *Barings Plc v Coopers & Lybrand* [2000] 1 W.L.R. 2353 at [53] which was concerned with transcripts exhibited in disqualification proceedings. These were treated by the Court of Appeal in the same way as one would expect a witness statement to be treated under CPR r.32.12.

(vi) Undertaking (9) to the example freezing injunction, undertaking (4) to the example search order or other undertaking given to the court

24.033   These can be released by the court, and would be released once the material had entered the public domain through a public hearing, subject to the power to retain confidentiality if sufficiently good reason were shown.

(vi) Part of the hearing in private

24.034   The general principle is that the administration of justice is done in public. However, under CPR r.39.2(3), a hearing or part of a hearing can be held in private if the hearing "involves confidential information (including information relating to personal financial matters) and publicity would damage that confidentiality". This power if exercised would have the consequence that the public hearing provisions of CPR r.31.22 and r.32.12 would not apply and the information could continue to be safeguarded as confidential information. In practice the court may be able to hold the entire hearing in public subject to a procedure designed to safeguard that confidentiality.

(5) Release of a restriction imposed by the CPR or an undertaking

(i) Jurisdiction to permit another use

24.035   Each of CPR rr.31.22, 32.12 and 34.12 contains a provision enabling the court to permit another use for the material. The express undertakings can all be released either wholly or in part by the court and this is also true of any implied undertaking which might exist (*e.g.* to protect information provided orally under compulsion of a court order when there is no express undertaking in place).

(ii) The principles

24.036   The position is very different according to whether or not the material has already entered the public domain through a hearing in public. If it has, the burden is upon the person applying for the continuation of confidentiality to justify it. This must be done through submissions and evidence.[81] It must be sufficient to override the need for open justice, the interests of freedom of speech, and the recipient's rights under Art.10 of the European Convention on Human Rights.[82] The exercise is one of discretion, balancing the various interests concerned and the consequences of releasing the restrictions and those if the restrictions are not released.

---

[81] *Lily Icos LLC v Pfizer* [2002] 1 W.L.R. 2253.
[82] *SmithKline Beecham Biologicals SA v Connaught Laboratories* [1999] 4 All E.R. 498 at 510g.

The court may decide to maintain the restriction whilst allowing use of the material in other related litigation, whether or not concerning the same parties, subject to arrangements designed to protect confidentiality. The fact that an order could be obtained for third party disclosure under CPR r.31.17 in those other proceedings is a very relevant factor.[83] If there is a material risk to the proper administration of justice in the other proceedings unless the documents are released solely to be used in those proceedings, this is a very powerful reason in favour of release. In principle this factor applies regardless of whether the other proceedings are in England or abroad.

If a public hearing has not already taken place, then the burden is upon **24.037** the person applying to lift the confidentiality to justify doing so. At that stage there has been no public hearing and therefore no legitimate interest of the public in understanding exactly what has happened at the public hearing. The authorities on the position before the CPR remain relevant,[84] but not in any way determinative.[85] The general principle is that the documents or information obtained should only be used for a purpose for which the documents or information was disclosed, and that if some further use is to be permitted this must be justified.

The decision whether or not to lift a restriction is a matter of discretion, taking into account the purpose for which the document or information is now sought to be used, and the likely consequences of releasing or not releasing the recipient from the undertaking or the restriction in the rules, including any possible prejudice which might be suffered by the party who provided the disclosure, and taking into account the public interest.

(6) Release of an undertaking of confidentiality given as part of a contract entered into with another party, or given to the court, or both

There are occasions in which a party enters into an express undertaking to **24.038** maintain confidentiality. This may be an undertaking given to the court or a contractual undertaking given to the other party or both. The question may arise what powers the court has in respect of such an undertaking. The position appears to be as follows:

(1) If a contractual undertaking has been given to the other party it may be that on its true construction it allows the court to modify what

---

[83] *SmithKline Beecham Plc v Generics (UK) Ltd* [2004] 1 W.L.R. 1479 at [34–43].
[84] *Marlwood Commercial Incorporated v Viktor Kozeny* [2004] EWHC 189 (February 9, 2004) at [15–21] (Moore-Bick J.), where the restriction in CPR r.31.22 was lifted to enable the Director of the Serious Fraud Office to have access to disclosed documents, which had been demanded by the Director under notices issued under s.2 of the Criminal Justice Act 1987, for the purpose of investigating a possible fraud, upheld at [2004] EWCA Civ 798.
[85] *SmithKline Beecham Plc v Generics (UK) Ltd* [2004] 1 W.L.R. 1479 at [37] is an example of this approach.

has to be done to comply with the contractual undertaking.[86] Thus, *e.g.* if a confidentiality undertaking is entered into relating to use of documents disclosed in the proceedings, then it may be that the contractual promises allow the court to modify or release them. If the contract requires an undertaking to be given to the court, it must be taken to have been entered into with knowledge of the power of the court to release the undertaking given to it; it is a short step to hold that the contractual promise made to the other party is co-extensive, and so likewise is subject to the power of the court to release it. The power of the court to modify the contractual promise must be found through interpretation of the contract.

(2) Even if the contractual promise on its true construction is not subject to court modification, the question of remedy will arise. The court can decline to enforce performance through a discretionary remedy, such as by injunction, of the contractual undertaking given to the other party, leaving the promisee to his remedy in damages which may or may not be of any use to him.

(3) The court has jurisdiction to release an undertaking given to it including an undertaking provided to it pursuant to a contract between the parties. However, the fact that it was provided pursuant to a contract is itself a relevant consideration in deciding whether wholly or in part to release the undertaking. If the release would run counter to the purpose for which the contract was entered into, then the court requires special circumstances before it will do so.[87] This reflects the general principle that the court will hold a party to his bargain and will not exercise a discretion so as to assist a party to go back on a binding contractual promise.[88]

(7) Ordering production to a non-party of documents used in proceedings

24.039 Whether to order production to a non-party of documents used in the course of proceedings so that he can understand what has happened at a public hearing, is a different question to what restrictions may apply, or be released, in respect of the use of documents by a party to the proceedings.

Under CPR r.32.13 during a trial a witness statement which stands as evidence in chief is open for inspection by anyone. Under CPR r.5.4(2)

---

[86] *Ropac Ltd v Intreprenneur Pub Co. (CPC) Ltd, The Times*, June 21, 2000, referred to in *Placito v Slater* [2004] 1 W.L.R. 1605.

[87] *Placito v Slater* [2004] 1 W.L.R. 1605; *Eronat v Tabbah* [2002] EWCA Civ 950 ("special circumstances" test led to refusal of the court to release undertaking of confidentiality given as part of price for a settlement of proceedings)

[88] See the discussion in Chapter 23, para.23.007.

anyone can obtain from court records a copy of the claim form and a judgment or order made in public. The court can also give permission for any other document to be released from the court records under that rule. The court also has an inherent jurisdiction to order that documents necessary for a full understanding of what has happened at a public hearing, such as pleadings, skeleton arguments or written openings, are made available to anyone interested, which may be someone interested in using them in other litigation.[89] The court's interest is to put such a person in the same position as if the proceedings in public had in fact been conducted openly, instead of with the use of written materials which are conducive to speed and economy but, if unexposed, would conceal from an observer what had been happening at the hearing.

(8) Confidentiality of arbitration proceedings

Arbitration proceedings are private proceedings. As between the parties to an arbitration agreement or arbitration proceedings it is impliedly agreed **24.040** that the proceedings and what is generated by the proceedings, such as pleadings, proofs of evidence, written submissions, transcripts and the award, are to remain private.[90] This has been analysed as an implied term of an arbitration agreement which is implied as a matter of law as a consequence of having agreed private resolution of a dispute through arbitration, which has been said to create an obligation of confidentiality subject to exceptions.[91] However, in *Associated Electric and Gas Insurance Services Ltd v European Reinsurance Co.*,[92] the Privy Council criticised this approach as eliding privacy and confidentiality, failing to distinguish between the status of different types of documents or their purpose, and relying by analogy on the position pertaining to a banker's duty of confidentiality owed to his customer, when *Tournier v National Provincial and Union Bank of England*,[93] which is the leading case,[94] had neither been cited nor referred to in the judgment.

In *London & Leeds Estates Ltd v Paribas (No.2)*[95] a subpoena was issued to see whether an expert was giving evidence inconsistent with what had

---

[89] *GIO Personal Investment Services Ltd v Liverpool and London Steamship Protection and Indemnity Association (FAI General Insurance Co. Ltd Intervening)* [1999] 1 W.L.R. 984 at 996 (skeleton argument or written opening to be made available under the inherent jurisdiction on application made in the course of the trial); *Law Debenture Trust v Lexington Insurance Company* [2003] EWHC 2297, Comm Ct (pleadings and written openings, but excluding parts devoted to unpleaded points, made available after the case had settled to enable non-party to consider making allegations of fraud).
[90] *Dolling-Baker v Merrett* [1990] 1 W.L.R. 1205 at 1213E–G
[91] *Ali Shipping Corporation v Shipyard Trogir* [1999] 1 W.L.R. 314 at 326C–H.
[92] [2003] 1 W.L.R. 1041.
[93] [1924] 1 K.B. 461.
[94] This is discussed in Chapter 20, para.20.018.
[95] [1995] 1 E.G.L.R. 102.

previously been said by him in an arbitration. Once the subpoena was issued the party was compelled to give disclosure by order of the court; this was therefore an example of where the court was prepared to use its coercive power so as to ensure that justice was done. The court would also presumably have refused an injunction to prevent the material being used for this purpose on the ground that the public interest, which includes the proper administration of justice, required that no injunction be granted.

24.041   In *Ali Shipping Corporation v Shipyard Trogir*[96] an injunction was granted restraining a party to arbitration proceedings from using certain materials from the arbitration in support of a plea of issue estoppel in a second arbitration which was not between the same parties.[97] The party seeking to use that material was unable to make good the proposition that the material was "reasonably necessary for the establishment or protection of an arbitrating party's legal rights . . ."[98] whether in founding a cause of action against a non-party or providing a defence to a claim of a non-party. The decision in the case appears to have been correct because the shipyard, which was trying to use the materials, had no basis which could be objectively justified for invading the privacy of the first arbitration.

In *Kruger (Service) Gibraltar v In-Town Developments Ltd*[99] the applicant for Mareva relief (Kruger) used on an *ex parte* application an interim award from arbitration proceedings between the defendant (In-Town) and another party (the Government of Gibraltar) which the applicant had been allowed to attend but only for the specific purpose of assisting In-Town in relation to its case in that arbitration. Kruger had had to give a confidentiality undertaking to the Government, but not to In-Town, in return for being allowed to attend. As against In-Town it was a stranger to those proceedings who had been permitted to attend them for a limited purpose. Kruger was not seeking to enforce its own rights under the award; it was not a party to that arbitration and had no rights under the award to enforce. In these circumstances the Court of Appeal of Gibraltar declined to grant Mareva relief to Kruger based on evidence introduced by it in breach of the obligation to respect the privacy which applied to the interim award.

24.042   In *Associated Electric and Gas Insurance Services Ltd v European Reinsurance Co.*,[1] the two sets of arbitration proceedings were between the same parties, and the successful party in the earlier proceedings wanted to rely on the award in those proceedings for the purpose of supporting a plea of issue estoppel in the second set of proceedings. The Privy Council refused to grant an injunction restraining it from doing so. The procedural

---

[96] [1999] 1 W.L.R. 314.
[97] [1999] 1 W.L.R. 314 at 330E–F considering *Hassneh Insurance Company of Israel v Mew* [1993] 2 Lloyd's Rep. 243 at 249.
[98] *Ali Shipping Corporation v Shipyard Trogir* [1999] 1 W.L.R. 314 at 327 referring to *Hassneh Insurance Company of Israel v Mew* [1993] 2 Lloyd's Rep. 243, and considering *Insurance Co. v Lloyd's Syndicate* [1995] 1 Lloyd's Rep. 272.
[99] Civil Appeal No.18 of 1999 (Gibraltar).
[1] [2003] 1 W.L.R. 1041.

directions containing the confidentiality provision in the earlier arbitration were not to be interpreted as precluding the winner from enforcing its rights or enabling the loser not to recognise or respect the rights arising from the first award; in fact the loser was seeking the discretionary remedy of an injunction for the purpose of enabling it to throw over its contractual obligations owed to the winner under the award. The proposed purpose did not involve revealing the material to a non-party who might have interests adverse to the other party to the arbitration.

It seems that:

(1) There is a well-established right of privacy of a party in respect of arbitration proceedings. This right arises from the arbitration agreement and is a contractual right based on an express, or an implied,[2] term. The scope of the term, and the exceptions to the contractual right to privacy, are matters of construction of the arbitration agreement or the agreed terms of reference in the arbitration. Public policy can also affect the enforceability of the contractual term and thus create an exception.

(2) This is not to be confused with protection of confidential information. For example, information may be given in arbitration proceedings which is already widely available to the public and is not confidential information, but the arbitration proceedings are private and the fact that it has been used in the arbitration proceedings is confidential. If confidential information is used in arbitration proceedings, then (1) the information itself will remain confidential; and (2) the fact that it was used in the arbitration is confidential information because the proceedings are private.

(3) These rights can affect different documents differently.

(4) The rights potentially affect any documents generated by the arbitration proceedings for use in them including pleadings, proofs of evidence, witness statements, skeleton arguments, written submissions, transcripts.[3] They also can affect an award.[4]

(5) The rights do not prevent the winner enforcing his rights under an award or allow the loser to avoid performing his obligations under an award.[5]

(6) These rights and the corresponding obligations apply between the parties to the arbitration proceedings. The obligations arising from the privacy of the proceedings can be released in whole or in part by agreement of both parties to the arbitration.

---

[2] *Dolling-Baker v Merrett* [1990] 1 W.L.R. 1205 at 1212.
[3] *Ali Shipping Corporation v Shipyard Trogir* [1999] 1 W.L.R. 314.
[4] *Kruger (Service) Gibraltar v In-Town Developments Ltd*, Civil Appeal No.18 of 1999 (Gibraltar).
[5] *Associated Electric and Gas Insurance Services Ltd v European Reinsurance Co.* [2003] 1 W.L.R. 1041.

(7) A non-party will be bound to respect those rights.[6] His obligations arising from the privacy of the proceedings can be released by agreement of both parties to the arbitration.

(8) The rights to privacy and in confidential information can be enforced by injunction.

(9) The privacy also affects court proceedings relating to the arbitration proceedings or an award. Court proceedings are affected by the need to administer justice in public and for justice to be seen to be done, for a judgment to be given in public (Art.6(1) of the ECHR), and for decisions on important points of law to be generally available. Under CPR 62.10, the court may order any arbitration claim to be heard in private or in public; each case and each stage in that case has to be considered separately in deciding whether that stage should be private. CPR 62.10(3) distinguishes between (1) the determination of a preliminary point of law or an appeal on a question of law, and (2) other arbitration claims. For the former the starting point is that the hearing be in public, and for the latter it is for the hearing to be in private. In *Department of Economics, Policy and Development of the City of Moscow v Bankers Trust Co*[7] the Court of Appeal upheld the judge's decision declining as a matter of discretion to make public the reasoned judgments given by him dismissing the challenges made by the banks to an arbitration award. The judge had decided that the judgments were not to be available to the public, because they contained confidential information, and this was not outweighed in the circumstances of that case by other considerations including the need for open administration of justice and the public interest in points of law of general application decided by the court to be freely available to the public and practitioners.[8] The court is more ready to hold that the oral hearing is to be in private, than to restrict publication of the judgment. This is because, as is shown by the requirement in art.6(1) ECHR that a judgment must be pronounced publicly, there is a substantial public interest in the publication of judgments so that the system of administration of justice remains transparent. Also judges can formulate their judgments so as to avoid unnecessary disclosure of sensitive material and to make anonymous details which might otherwise be sensitive. The court is least amenable to restrict publication of the order. This is because the order is the least likely to contain any confidential information;

---

[6] *Kruger (Service) Gibraltar v In-Town Developments Ltd*, Civil Appeal No.18 of 1999 (Gibraltar).

[7] [2004] EWCA Civ 504, *The Times*, April 15, 2004 affirming [2003] 1 W.L.R. 2885, except allowing publication of a Lawtel report which did not disclose any confidential information.

[8] *Department of Economics, Policy and Development of the City of Moscow v Bankers Trust Co* [2004] EWCA Civ 504 at [39]; [2003] 1 W.L.R. 2885 at para.30.

(10) If a non-party seeks to use material generated by arbitration proceedings, without the permission of both parties, to obtain an injunction on a without notice application against a party to the arbitration, he may be refused the relief, or the injunction may be discharged *inter partes* as having been obtained through the improper use of confidential material.[9]

(11) The court can override those rights by granting a mandatory order such as a witness summons[10] or an order under CPR r.31.17 for disclosure by a non-party, or by not granting a discretionary remedy enforcing these rights such as an injunction, when disclosure is required for the purpose of the due administration of justice;[11] so materials from an arbitration may be ordered to be produced so that justice can be done in other proceedings, whether or not involving a party to the arbitration.

(9) Remedies and sanctions

(i) Undertaking given to the court

24.043 An undertaking given by a person to the court has the same effect as an injunction granted against that person.[12] Breach of an undertaking given to the court is a contempt of court. This is so regardless of whether the relevant party acted bona fide.[13]

If proceedings are commenced in breach of an undertaking given to the court,[14] or using material in breach of such an undertaking,[15] they can be struck out as an abuse of the process of the court.

The fact that the undertaking might have been released had this been sought in advance for the use to which the documents have been put, does not excuse the contempt. In *Miller v Scorey* (above) the new action was struck out notwithstanding that leave, had it been sought in advance, might have been granted, and notwithstanding that the defendant could in consequence raise a limitation defence in relation to any further attempt to introduce the new claim. The fact that the defendant had not sought release from the undertaking prior to the accrual of the limitation defence was fatal.

---

[9] *Kruger (Service) Gibraltar v In-Town Developments Ltd*, Civil Appeal No.18 of 1999 (Gibraltar).
[10] *London & Leeds Estates Ltd v Paribas (No.2)* [1995] 1 E.G.L.R. 102.
[11] *Science Research Council v Nassé* [1980] A.C. 1028 at 1065E–G; *Ali Shipping Corporation v Shipyard Trogir* [1999] 1 W.L.R. 314 at 327–328.
[12] See Chapter 19, para.19.005.
[13] *Watkins v A. J. Wright (Electrical) Ltd* [1996] 3 All E.R. 31; *Miller v Scorey* [1996] 1 W.L.R. 1122.
[14] *Placito v Slater* [2003] EWCA Civ 1863.
[15] *Miller v Scorey* [1996] 1 W.L.R. 1122.

24.044   If there is an imminent threat to break the undertaking, this can be restrained by injunction. For example, an injunction can be granted restraining the party who gave the undertaking, or received confidential information under compulsion of a court order, from using the material in other proceedings before the court.[16] It is considered that this is justified:

(1)   as being a remedy to enforce compliance with the binding promise given to the court; or

(2)   on the ground that the court has an inherent jurisdiction to grant an injunction restraining a threatened contempt of court;[17]

(3)   on the ground that the injunction restrains what would otherwise be an abuse of the process of the court which the court has power to control as part of its inherent jurisdiction;[18]

(4)   the information disclosed under compulsion of the court order remained confidential in the hands of the recipient, and an injunction can be granted to preserve that confidentiality.[19]

The court may also grant relief designed to find out what use has been made of the documents with a view to enabling remedial steps to be taken if necessary against third parties in order to recover the documents or copies, and to preserve the confidentiality of the information.[20] Because the effect of compliance with such relief may be to expose the defaulting party to contempt proceedings, the court may grant the relief on terms which will prevent the material obtained being used for this purpose.

(ii) Breach of the restrictions in CPR rr.31.22, 32.12 and 34.12

24.045   The restriction in CPR r.31.22 replaces what previously had been done through the implied undertaking. The fact that the restriction is contained expressly in the CPR as opposed to being in a formal order made by the court is a matter of form and not substance. One would expect that breach of the restriction by a party to the proceedings would have the same consequences as breach of an order made in the proceedings against that

---

[16] *Medway v Doublelock Ltd* [1978] 1 W.L.R. 710, which is surprisingly criticised in *Meagher, Gummow and Lehane's* Equity: *Doctrines and Remedies* (4th ed., 2002), at para.21–020 as a mistaken revival of the jurisdiction to restrain a defendant from setting up an inequitable defence, whereas it was a means of enforcing the confidentiality of the information which had been disclosed under compulsion.

[17] *Hubbard v Woodfield* (1913) 57 S.J. 729; *Elliot v Klinger* [1967] 1 W.L.R. 1165 at 1166 citing Oswald's *Contempt of Court* (3rd ed., 1910), p.16 (an injunction would now be granted under the principles discussed in Chapter 13 against a non-party who threatened to assist in disposing of assets frozen under an undertaking given to the court).

[18] This is the reasoning in *Cardile v LED Builders Pty Ltd* (1999) 198 C.L.R. 381 and *Jackson v Sterling Industries Ltd* (1987) 162 C.L.R. 61.

[19] *Medway v Doublelock Ltd* [1978] 1 W.L.R. 710 at p.714 D–E appears to proceed on the ground of protecting confidentiality.

[20] *Bhimji v Chatwani (No.2)* [1992] 1 W.L.R. 1158.

party. A further consideration is that for the restriction to be effective it must be backed by a sufficient sanction in the event of breach. Unless breach of the restriction was a contempt of court then, depending upon the circumstances, the restriction would be without teeth. This would threaten the effectiveness of the rule.

The same remedies are available in relation to a threatened breach of the restriction or an actual breach as apply in relation to an undertaking given to the court. For example, an injunction can be granted against a party or non-party[21] enforcing the restriction on use, on the ground of restraining a threatened contempt of court or under the inherent jurisdiction to prevent an abuse of the process of the court. If there is a breach of the restriction by a party there can be contempt proceedings against him. If a non-party aids and abets a breach by a party or knowingly destroys the confidentiality protected by the restriction, he is in contempt of court.[22]

The same reasoning applies to the restrictions in CPR rr.32.12 and 34.12.

(iii) Breach of a contractual undertaking

If an attempt is made to adduce the material into evidence or otherwise use **24.046** it in other proceedings the court can grant an injunction restraining such use.[23] If proceedings are brought using material in breach of a contractual undertaking, the court can strike out those proceedings, stay them, or refuse to grant discretionary relief in those proceedings.

---

[21] *S v S (Judgment in Chambers: Disclosure)* [1997] 1 W.L.R. 1621 at 1626C–D enforcing a restriction in the Family Proceedings Rules 1991 by injunction requiring delivery-up of copies in the hands of a non-party.
[22] See Chapter 19, paras 19.028 *et seq.*
[23] See Chapter 18, para.18.003.

Chapter 25

Criminal Marevas, restraint orders and receivers

(1) Introduction

At common law a constable has the right to seize goods which he **25.001** reasonably believes to have been stolen.[1] This right is sufficient to enable Mareva relief to be granted to the police in respect of property which they believe on reasonable grounds to have been obtained dishonestly.

Alongside the common law jurisdiction, there is statutory jurisdiction for the courts to grant restraint orders or appoint receivers over property for the purpose of preserving or realising that property so that it will be available to satisfy confiscation orders made by a criminal court. This is all a part of preventing criminals benefiting from crime.

This statutory jurisdiction commenced with the Drug Trafficking Offences Act 1986 (DTOA). This was followed by the Criminal Justice Act 1988 (CJA), which extended preservation and confiscation to indictable offences and certain summary offences where the benefits of crime were likely to be high. The legislation relating to drug trafficking and certain provisions of the Criminal Justice (International Co-operation) Act 1990 were consolidated in the Drug Trafficking Act 1994 (DTA). Both the CJA and the DTA involve proceedings in the High Court for restraint orders, receivership orders, and realisation of property. These are subject to RSC Ord.115. Likewise the statutory jurisdiction under Sch.4 to the Terrorism Act 2000.

The Proceeds of Crime Act 2002 (POCA) received Royal Assent on July **25.002** 24, 2002 and came into force on March 24, 2003. This is an important date for the purpose of deciding which statutory regime applies to a particular case. The legislation has been drafted so as to avoid retrospective provisions. The consequence is to have various different statutory regimes in force contemporaneously with the DTA and CJA regimes fading away in importance as more and more cases come into the POCA regime, which applies to drug trafficking and other offences, and which provides for the

---

[1] *Chief Constable of Kent v V* [1983] Q.B. 34 at 46, *per* Donaldson L.J.; *Chic Fashions (West Wales) Ltd v Jones* [1968] 2 Q.B. 299.

Crown Court to have the jurisdiction for restraint, receivership and realisation of property. Where the POCA applies it does so regardless of whether there are criminal proceedings commenced or about to be commenced. Under the POCA a new agency has been established called the Asset Recovery Agency (ARA) which has an important role in investigating cases, obtaining appropriate preservation orders and realising property.

This statutory jurisdiction under the DTA is analogous to the Mareva jurisdiction[2] in certain respects, and involves similar procedures and concepts. Under that Act there are provisions for confiscating the proceeds of drug trafficking and granting relief by the High Court both before and after the criminal trial so as to preserve or realise property. In Pt VI of CJA there are provisions which have wide application.

This chapter reviews both the role of the ordinary Mareva jurisdiction and the statutory jurisdiction.

(2) The common law Mareva jurisdiction

25.003 The civil courts could have developed a general common law jurisdiction based on s.37(1) of the Supreme Court Act 1981 to act in aid of proceedings or possible proceedings before the criminal courts. However, in the enforcement of private rights the rule is that Mareva relief will not be granted unless the applicant has some existing cause of action. In *Chief Constable of Kent v V*,[3] the defendant was alleged to have stolen blank cheques and to have forged the victim's signature. He had apparently cashed the forged cheques and the proceeds were mixed with money of his own. Neither the victim nor her bank brought proceedings to restrain the defendant from dealing with money in his bank accounts, but the Chief Constable sought and was granted relief by the majority of the Court of Appeal. In his judgment Lord Denning M.R. said that s.37(1) was not subject to a limitation that the applicant must have some legal or equitable right to be protected, and he distinguished the wording of the section from its predecessors. He considered that the correct test was whether the applicant had "a sufficient interest".[4] However, this approach was rejected by both the other members of the court, was not subsequently followed[5] and has been disapproved by the House of Lords.[6] Accordingly, it is became established that the police could obtain Mareva relief only when the applicant claimed a civil right to seize or preserve the property which

---

[2] *Re Peters* [1988] Q.B. 871.
[3] [1983] Q.B. 34.
[4] *ibid.*, at 42.
[5] *Chief Constable of Hampshire v A Ltd* [1985] Q.B. 132; *Chief Constable of Leicestershire v M* [1989] 1 W.L.R. 20 at 22–23, *per* Hoffmann J.
[6] *P v Liverpool Daily Post* [1991] 2 A.C. 370 at 420–421; see also *Mercedes Benz AG v Leiduck* [1996] A.C. 284 at 298.

was the subject of the application. Thus in *Chief Constable of Kent v V*, Donaldson L.J. (who together with Lord Denning M.R. formed the majority) held that at common law the police had the right to "detain" money which they reasonably believed had been taken from a victim in breach of the criminal law. This right enabled Mareva relief to be granted in respect of money in the form of bank notes or a credit balance at a bank (i.e. in the form of a chose in action). Therefore, Donaldson L.J. held that in the circumstances an injunction could be granted under s.37(1) of the Supreme Court Act 1981, but only "if and to the extent that [the moneys in the bank accounts] can be shown to have been obtained from another in breach of the criminal law". Donaldson L.J. left open the point whether the common law right of seizure or detention would apply to money which was the proceeds of realisation of stolen goods and which had been paid into a bank account.[7]

In *West Mercia Constabulary v Wagner*,[8] the defendant had been charged with fraudulently obtaining cheques from members of the public which he had paid into his bank. Forbes J. granted relief limited to the proceeds of the improperly obtained cheques, and found justification for granting the relief in the former RSC Ord.29, r.2. But that rule enabled property to be detained or preserved only when it was the subject-matter of an action.[9] It was an ancillary power to be exercised when there are substantive proceedings on the merits before the High Court. The reasoning of Forbes J. was rejected by Donaldson L.J. in *Chief Constable of Kent v V*, because it failed to address the question whether the applicant had a substantive cause of action against the defendant. Nevertheless, with the extension of the common law right to include money taken from a victim and paid into a bank account, the decision of Forbes J. can be justified, because the applicants did have a substantive cause of action against the defendant.

If a defendant is alleged to have benefited from crime, this does not itself **25.004** confer a private law cause of action on the police so as to enable them to obtain Mareva relief over either the proceeds of crime or the defendant's assets. Thus, in *Chief Constable of Hampshire v A Ltd*,[10] the defendants were alleged to have carried on a fraudulent business involving selling motor cars with false mileometer readings. The profits of the business had been used to repay bank loans which had been taken out to purchase properties. The police wished to obtain Mareva relief over the proceeds of sale of the properties, but their application was dismissed. The police had not succeeded in identifying any asset which was itself property which had been stolen or obtained by fraud, or the proceeds of such property. Similarly, if a defendant is alleged to have made substantial profits as a

---

[7] It seems that the right would so extend: *Chief Constable of Hampshire v A Ltd*, above, at 136, *per* Waller L.J. and at 137, *per* Slade L.J.
[8] [1982] 1 W.L.R. 127.
[9] Likewise under CPR r.25.1(1) (c) (i) and CPR r.25.1(2), which defines "relevant property" as "property . . . which is the subject of a claim or as to which any question may arise on a claim".
[10] [1985] Q.B. 132.

result of obtaining mortgage advances by fraud and investing the money in properties which have substantially increased in value, the police have no common law right to detain the profits.[11] The police have no general common law right of detention over property held by an accused unless it is property which is the subject-matter of a charge.[12] With the advent of statutory intervention in this field, it has been held by Hoffmann J. that "the courts should not indulge in parallel creativity by the extension of common law principles".[13]

In *Chief Constable of Leicestershire v M*,[14] the purpose of seeking the relief was to ensure that the profits made by M as the result of the alleged frauds would be available to meet a fine or an order for costs in the criminal proceedings. But the Chief Constable had no private law cause of action against M. Any fine lay in the future. There was no existing order for costs. In *R. v Consolidated Fastfrate Inc.*,[15] the Court of Appeal for Ontario held that civil courts have power to stop accused persons from disposing of assets which might otherwise be used to pay future fines. This was on the basis that the civil courts are acting in aid of the criminal courts. But in England there has to be an existing justiciable right capable of enforcement in the civil courts in order for there to be jurisdiction to grant an injunction or appoint a receiver under s.37(1) of the Supreme Court Act 1981.[16]

25.005 In *Broadmoor Special Hospital Authority v Robinson*[17] Lord Woolf M.R. put the decision in *Chief Constable of Kent v V* on a different basis. Instead of looking at the case for a private right of the Chief Constable, he looked at the matter as being in the sphere of the enforcement of public rights and responsibilities. Since the police had a public responsibility to preserve the assets pending the outcome of the criminal trial, the applicant had standing to apply for an injunction to assist in the discharge of that public responsibility, and the court would grant an injunction when it was just and convenient to do so. Lord Woolf M.R. distinguished the actual decision in *Chief Constable of Kent v V* on the ground that it involved no statute.

But there is no common law right to confiscate the earnings of criminals or anyone else, and in view of the extensive intervention in this area by statute, the House of Lords in *Attorney-General v Blake*[18] subsequently

---

[11] *Chief Constable of Leicestershire v M* [1989] 1 W.L.R. 20.

[12] *Malone v Metropolitan Police Commissioner* [1980] Q.B. 49.

[13] *Chief Constable of Leicestershire v M* [1989] 1 W.L.R. 20 at 23 and see also *Chief Constable of Surrey v A, Daily Telegraph*, November 11, 1988. *Worcestershire CC v Tongue* [2004] EWCA Civ 140 (where the court declined to grant an injunction permitting the local authority to go onto land belonging to the defendant in order to remove cattle kept there, when the criminal legislation did not go this far).

[14] [1989] 1 W.L.R. 20.

[15] (1995) 24 O.R. (3rd) 564.

[16] See further Chapter 12, above. In *Attorney-General v Blake, The Times*, December 22, 1997 an injunction was granted based on the public law right of the Attorney-General to enforce the criminal law.

[17] [2000] Q.B. 775.

[18] [2001] 1 A.C. 268 at 289, 292–293 and 296.

decided that it would be inappropriate for the courts to extend the injunction jurisdiction through developing a common law right to take, confiscate or detain property held by a criminal. The position is now regulated by statute including the Proceeds of Crime Act 2002.[19]

(3) Drug Trafficking Act 1994

(i) The "confiscation" jurisdiction

The Drug Trafficking Act 1994 (DTA) consolidates provisions formerly in **25.006** the Drug Trafficking Offences Act 1986 and the Criminal Justice (International Co-operation) Act 1990 relating to drug trafficking. Section 1 of DTA defines "drug trafficking" (whether in England and Wales or elsewhere) and a "drug trafficking offence". Section 2 empowers the Crown Court to make a "confiscation order" when a defendant convicted of one or more "drug trafficking offences"[20] appears before it for sentence. The purpose of the confiscation order is to "confiscate" (a misuse of the word because the order is for payment of a sum of money to be satisfied out of the defendant's resources or those of a donee who has received a gift caught by the Act) from the convicted defendant an amount equivalent to the benefit obtained by him from "drug trafficking", which is defined in wide terms in s.1(1) and (2). The Crown Court has to decide whether he has benefited from drug trafficking and, if so, assess the value of the proceeds of drug trafficking. The confiscation order is to be for the value of the proceeds as assessed by the Crown Court unless the court is satisfied that the amount "that might be realised . . . is less", in which case the confiscation order is limited to what can be realised or a nominal amount.[21]

A confiscation order is an order of the court requiring the defendant to pay an amount assessed in accordance with s.5. The amount to be paid depends on the extent to which the defendant has "benefited from drug trafficking" and, by s.5(3), is limited by how much the court is satisfied "might be realised at the time the confiscation order is made . . .".

Under s.2(8) the standard of proof for issues relating to whether the **25.007** defendant has benefited from drug trafficking and the quantification of a confiscation order is balance of probabilities.

(ii) The purpose of a restraint order, a charging order and the appointment of a receiver

Under ss.25–29 of DTA, powers are conferred on the High Court to grant **25.008** relief in the form of a restraint order, a charging order, and the appointment of a receiver. The purpose of a restraint order is to preserve

---

[19] See, *e.g.* the powers to seize "cash" in s.294 of POCA.
[20] Listed in s.1(3) of DTA.
[21] DTA, s.5(3).

assets, which may be needed or are needed to satisfy a future or existing confiscation order. It does not create any charge over assets.

The purpose of a charging order is to impose a charge over particular assets in favour of the Crown for payment of a confiscation order or future order. This gives the Crown a proprietary, security right in the asset.

A receiver can be appointed under s.26(7) where a restraint order has been made. This is a form of interim receivership which can enable the court to provide for management of the asset or sale of it or any other activities in relation to the asset (*e.g.* renting out the asset or repairing or maintaining it.) Where the defendant has not been convicted the primary purpose of the receivership is preservative rather than realisation to obtain maximum value for a prospective confiscation order.[22]

25.009 A receiver can be appointed after a confiscation order has been made which is not subject to appeal and which has not been satisfied, for the purpose of realising an asset.

A receiver can also be appointed by the court in aid of enforcement of a charge imposed on an asset by a charging order.[23]

A restraint order and a charging order are alternatives because a restraint order may not be made in respect of property subject to a charging order.[24]

25.010 It is a feature of all these various orders that they can be made before conviction and the making of a confiscation order, or afterwards and that they can be made for the purpose of preserving assets pending the outcome of the criminal proceedings against a defendant or any appeal, or as part of the process of enforcing a confiscation order which is not subject to appeal. Often orders are sought after conviction of a defendant, but they can be made at any stage of the criminal proceedings or in contemplation that criminal proceedings will be brought.[25]

(iii) "Realisable property"

25.011 What might be realised depends on what assets the defendant or a relevant donee holds, which includes property in which he has an interest.[26] In addition, the DTA has provisions catching gifts of property which were received by the defendant in connection with drug trafficking or its proceeds.[27] Realisable property is not limited to assets derived from crime or which represent the proceeds of crime. Thus the defendant's ordinary assets acquired entirely lawfully and independently of any crime are assets which are available to satisfy a confiscation order. Likewise, the entire assets of a donee of a gift caught by s.8 of DTA, are "realisable property".

---

[22] *Re P (Restraint Order: Sale of Assets)* [2000] 1 W.L.R. 473 at 482.
[23] See DTA, s.29(3).
[24] DTA, s.26(3) and CJA, s.77(4); *Re a Defendant, The Times*, April 7, 1987.
[25] DTA, s.25(3); the orders may subsequently be discharged if proceedings are not instituted within a reasonable time: DTA, s.25(5).
[26] DTA, s.62(5).
[27] DTA, s.8.

This includes a gratuitous transfer made since the commencement of a six-year period before criminal proceedings were "instituted",[28] or a transfer at an undervalue,[29] made out of the proceeds of drug trafficking. The purpose of the charging order jurisdiction is to enable a charge to be imposed on whatever beneficial interest the defendant or donee may have in the underlying property.[30]

(iv) Freezing, charging, managing and realisation, not confined to orders binding the named defendant in the criminal proceedings

Under s.26(1) of DTA, the court may make a restraint order which binds **25.012** "any person" and restrains that person from dealing with "realisable property" as defined in s.6(2). Under s.26(1) the court has jurisdiction to freeze "realisable property" by making an order against any third parties,[31] *e.g.* a wife or child of the alleged drug trafficker, or a business associate who holds or controls such property.

Under s.26(7) of DTA the court also has the power, when a restraint order has been made, to appoint a receiver to take possession of the property and to "manage or otherwise deal with" it. If a third party holds the property, he can be required by an order of the court to give possession of it to the receiver. If the drug trafficker is convicted and a confiscation order made against him, which is not subject to appeal, the court may appoint a receiver over the property for the purpose of realising it (s.29). Again, provision is made for any third party who holds "realisable" property to give possession of it to the receiver.

Thus under DTA, the High Court exercises jurisdiction to preserve or realise "realisable property" not only as against an alleged or convicted drug trafficker, but also directly against any third parties who hold "realisable property", including but not limited to, third parties who have received a "gift" caught by the Act. Through the High Court proceedings, property which belongs to a third party may be subject to a restraint or charging order, and may be used to satisfy a confiscation order made by the Crown Court against a convicted drug trafficker. Thus, *e.g.* the credit balance in a wife's or child's bank account may be subject to a restraint order and can be taken in due course by a receiver under s.29(5) and dealt with by him pursuant to s.30(1).

Similarly, if a matrimonial home has been bought with money derived by **25.013** a husband from drug trafficking, and his wife has been given an interest in the home, this may be made the subject of a charging order imposed under DTA, s.27(1). Under s.26(2) a restraint order can be made in respect of

---

[28] See DTA s.41(2) for the definition of this.
[29] DTA, s.8.
[30] See s.27(4) for the scope of the power to charge, and *Re Norris* [2001] 1 W.L.R. 1388 at [15].
[31] *Re D (Restraint Order), The Times*, January 26, 1995.

property held at the date of the order or property which is subsequently received by the person specified in the order. Thus if, *e.g.* an arrangement had been made for a drug trafficker to receive a future payment, a restraint order can be made which catches that payment when made and subjects it to the terms of the order. This mirrors the position in relation to a Mareva injunction which, while in force, restrains a defendant from dealing with assets, regardless of whether a particular asset has come into being or has been acquired only since the date of the order.[32]

It may be that an alleged drug trafficker has only a limited interest in certain property. For example, he may have a joint bank account with his wife. There is express provision in s.62(5)(a) of DTA to the effect that "property is held by any person if he holds any interest in it". This has the consequence that restraint and charging orders may be imposed over any property in which a drug trafficker has an interest, even though it is only a limited interest. Thus a restraint order could be made preventing any dealings with the joint account.[33]

25.014   Section 29(8) provides for a reasonable opportunity for persons holding an interest in any property to make representations to the court before the powers to realise that property are exercised. The purpose of this is so that third parties' rights relating to or connected with the property are safeguarded by the High Court.[34] The Crown Court has jurisdiction over the defendant and the confiscation proceedings whilst the High Court is the jurisdiction for deciding the rights of third parties.[35] The High Court proceedings are in nature civil proceedings even though they are supportive of a confiscation order made or contemplated in criminal proceedings in the Crown Court, and so appeal from the High Court lies to the Court of Appeal (Civil Division).[36]

(v) Assets outside of the jurisdiction

25.015   Under s.62(2) of DTA, the Act applies to "property whether it is situated in England and Wales or elsewhere", and under s.6(2) the definition of "realisable property" is formulated as extending to "any property" within its ambit. Section 102(3) of CJA applies to property "wherever situated". Thus the powers of the court are exercisable in relation to property wherever situated. This is also the case with Mareva relief, or relief granted under s.37(2) of the Matrimonial Causes Act 1973.[37] In *Derby & Co. Ltd v Weldon (No.6)*,[38] however, Staughton L.J. observed that Parliament had

---

[32] *Soinco SACI v Novokuznetsk Aluminium Plant* [1998] Q.B. 406 at p.422B–E; *TDK Tape Distributor v Videochoice Ltd* [1986] 1 W.L.R. 141 at 145; *Cretanor Maritime Co. Ltd v Irish Marine Ltd* [1978] 1 W.L.R. 966 at 973.
[33] *Re a Defendant, The Times*, April 7, 1987.
[34] *Re Norris* [2001] 1 W.L.R. 1388.
[35] *Re Norris* [2001] 1 W.L.R. 1388 (wife entitled to be heard by the High Court on her claim to an interest in her home).
[36] *Government of USA v Montgomery* [2001] 1 W.L.R. 196
[37] See *Hamlin v Hamlin* [1986] Fam. 11, and para.7.022, above.
[38] [1990] 1 W.L.R. 1139 at 1154.

"deliberately abstained from asserting a worldwide jurisdiction" for restraint orders, referring to s.8(7) of the Drug Trafficking Offences Act 1986 (now see s.26(8)(b) of DTA in support of that view.[39] But s.26(8)(b) is concerned with what constitutes "dealing" with any realisable property. In the context of Mareva relief a defendant does not "deal" with his assets by receiving payment of a debt.[40] Section 26(8)(a) makes it clear that a restraint order can prohibit a person from receiving payment of a debt, and s.26(8)(b) makes it clear that a restraint order can bar a defendant from taking property out of Great Britain, even though he is not disposing of it. This observation of Staughton L.J. on the scope of the jurisdiction to grant restraint orders cannot be supported.

The powers of the court include an inherent power to make a restraint or charging order, or appointment of a receiver, effective. This includes ordering repatriation of assets abroad.[41]

(vi) RSC Ord.115 procedure

These powers are exercisable in civil proceedings brought before the High Court in accordance with the provisions of RSC Ord.115 which is in the Schedule to the CPR, and the Practice Direction which supplements RSC Ord.115, and constitute a jurisdiction exercised by a judge in chambers for granting interim relief in aid of a confiscation order which may be made or which has been made in criminal proceedings. The proceedings should be issued out of the Administrative Court office and be heard by a judge of the Queen's Bench Division unless the judge directs the matter to be heard by a judge of the Chancery Division.   **25.016**

The High Court proceedings are commenced by claim form (RSC Ord.115, r.3(1)) which is entitled "In the matter of" the defendant (naming him) and in the matter of the Act (RSC Ord.115, r.2A). The initial application for relief is ordinarily made without notice by the prosecutor[42] (RSC Ord.115, r.3(1)) to the judge, on the basis of a witness statement or affidavit (RSC Ord.115, r.3(2)). The claim form should be a CPR Pt 8 claim form.[43]

There is jurisdiction to grant permission for service out of the jurisdiction of the claim form, pursuant to CPR r.6.20(18) and CPR Pt 6, Practice Direction—Service Out of the Jurisdiction, para.5.2(4). This enables the claim form to be served on a party outside the jurisdiction[44] and because of

---

[39] Section 9 of the Drug Trafficking Offences Act 1986, which concerned charging orders, had an ambit similar to that of s.2 of the Charging Orders Act 1979.

[40] See Chapter 3, para.3.012.

[41] *DPP v Scarlett* [2000] 1 W.L.R. 515.

[42] Only the prosecutor has *locus standi* to apply for a restraint order; see s.8(4)(a). In *Re M (Restraint Order)* [1992] Q.B. 377, Otton J. held that only the prosecutor could apply for the appointment of a receiver, and that the defendant had no *locus standi* to make such an application.

[43] See CPR Pt 8, Practice Direction, Pt 8, section B, Table 2 (these refer to the DTA but are also applicable to the CJA because of RSC Ord. 115, r.23.)

[44] There is an equivalent power for claims made under Pt VI of CJA under para.5.2(7) of the Practice Direction.

the definitions in CPR r.6.18(h) and (i),[45] this provision also enables service out of the jurisdiction of an application notice for relief under the legislation.

(vii) Confiscation order made by a foreign court

25.017   Section 39 of DTA enables Orders in Council to be made for the purpose of applying the provisions of the Act to confiscation orders made by a court in a "designated country" and to proceedings which have been or are to be instituted in such a country and which may result in a confiscation order being made there. The purpose of the section is to empower the making of delegated legislation for the purpose of providing machinery for the English court to act in aid of proceedings abroad. Provision is made in DTA for enforcement or registration of confiscation orders made abroad by a court of a country or territory designated by Order in Council (ss.39 and 40).

In *Re S-L*,[46] there were bank accounts in London which were said to contain the proceeds of drug trafficking which had been carried out in the United States of America. There were proceedings in New York nominally brought against the bank accounts themselves in which confiscation was sought of the accounts. There was no prosecution pending in the United States or elsewhere and no person was named as a defendant in the New York proceedings. The alleged drug trafficker was outside the jurisdiction of the United States courts, probably in Colombia.

25.018   The question arose whether under the Drug Trafficking Offences Act 1986, as modified by the Drug Trafficking Offences Act 1986 (Designated Countries and Territories) Order 1990, there was power in England to grant a restraint order in respect of the London bank accounts. The Court of Appeal held that there was such a power and upheld the restraint order. There was no need for a prosecution or proceedings in the United States against an individual. In s.39(2) of DTA an "external confiscation order" is defined as "an order made by a court in a designated country for the purpose of recovering . . . payments or other rewards received in connection with drug trafficking". An order confiscating particular property, because it has been received in connection with drug trafficking, is itself an "external confiscation order" and as such comes within the definition in s.39(2).

(viii) Insolvency

25.019   Section 32 of DTA concerns insolvency. If a restraint order is made before an order adjudging the defendant bankrupt, then under s.32(1)(a) property covered by the restraint order is excluded from the bankrupt's estate for

---

[45] *C Inc. v L* [2001] 2 Lloyd's Rep.459 at 477, footnote 117.
[46] [1996] Q.B. 272.

the purposes of Pt IX of the Insolvency Act 1986. There is similar protection in s.32(1)(b) for property in the hands of a receiver prior to the adjudication of bankruptcy. This enables a confiscation order to be satisfied out of assets which are excluded from the bankruptcy (s.31(2)).

If the restraint order is subsequently discharged, then the assets covered by the order would form part of the bankrupt's estate.[47] A voluntary arrangement does not affect the court's powers to make a restraint order or appoint a receiver.[48] Thus, under ss.32 and 34 of DTA, the making of a restraint order will result in the assets covered by the order, while it is in force, being excluded from a subsequent bankruptcy or liquidation. Those assets are available to satisfy a confiscation order, whether made before or after the bankruptcy or liquidation. Similarly, a charging order is not affected by a subsequent bankruptcy or liquidation, and the proceeds of property realised under DTA which are in the hands of a receiver are unaffected. This contrasts with the position where there is a bankruptcy adjudication or winding-up order and Mareva relief has been granted. A Mareva injunction should not be allowed to interfere with assets being dealt with as part of a bankrupt's estate or by a liquidator.[49]

If the adjudication of bankruptcy of the defendant is prior to any restraint order being made or proceeds of property coming into the hands of a receiver, then the bankruptcy takes priority.[50]

(ix) Ancillary relief granted by the court in relation to divorce

The court has statutory power in divorce proceedings to order one spouse **25.020** to transfer property to another. The DTA does not take "priority" over this power. Where there are statutory powers relating to the same property conferred on the court which are discretionary the court decides how to exercise those powers in the circumstances of the case.[51] This puts a potential premium on one spouse divorcing the other so that the innocent spouse can preserve her home, when the guilty spouse has a beneficial interest in it.[52]

(4) "Realisable property"

(i) The statutory definition

Section 26 of DTA empowers the High Court to grant a restraint order **25.021** prohibiting "any person from dealing with any realisable property". Under s.26(7) a receiver can be appointed to take possession of "any realisable

---

[47] There are equivalent exclusion provisions for a company which is ordered to be wound up; see s.34.
[48] See *Re M (Restraint Order)* [1992] Q.B. 377.
[49] See Chapter 3, para.3.007, above.
[50] DTA, s.32(2); this was one of the reasons for the appeal being moot in *Crown Prosecution Service v Compton* [2002] EWCA Civ 1720.
[51] *Customs & Excise Commissioners v A* [2003] Fam. 55.
[52] Compare *Crown Prosecution Service v Malik* [2003] EWHC 660 at [38] where there was no potentially competing statutory discretion to avail the sister of the convicted defendant who gave her the home before he came under investigation for trafficking in drugs (see at [16]).

property". The term "realisable property" is defined in s.6(2) as property "held" by the defendant or a person to whom the defendant has directly or indirectly made a gift caught by the Act.[53] The word "property" is defined in wide terms in s.62 and under that section property is "held" by a person if he holds any interest in it or has any right in respect of it.

(ii) The relevance of "realisable property"

25.022   Under the statutory schemes, what is "realisable property" is relevant to:

(1)   what property can be made subject to a restraint order, a charging order, or an order appointing a receiver for the purpose of preserving that property by way of interim order. This is a matter for the High Court in the civil proceedings brought under RSC Ord.115;

(2)   what property is to be taken into account for the purpose of deciding the amount which might be realised at the time a confiscation order is made. This is a matter for the Crown Court applying the standard of proof required in civil proceedings;[54]

(3)   what property can be taken to satisfy a confiscation order. This is a matter for the High Court in the civil proceedings. It will include legitimately acquired property[55] of the defendant or a donee caught by the Act.

However, if at stage (2) before the Crown Court the prosecutor has conceded that certain property should not be treated as "realisable property", it may be an abuse of the process of the court for the prosecutor subsequently to apply to the High Court for that property to be treated as "realisable property" and for it to be taken to satisfy a confiscation order. In *Crown Prosecution Service v Cruddas*[56] the CPS sought to treat a home occupied by the wife of the defendant as realisable property to be taken to satisfy a confiscation order which had been made under the CJA and applied for relief to do this. Because of a concession made previously by the prosecution in the Crown Court at stage (2) it was held that, albeit the court retained jurisdiction to grant the relief, the application was an abuse of the process of the court and it was dismissed.

(iii) "Piercing the corporate veil" and interim orders

25.023   An alleged drug trafficker may have dealt through companies. A shareholder in a company has no interest in the property of the company. If the company is prosecuted, then no difficulty arises. But what if only the

---

[53] *Re Norris* [2001] 1 W.L.R. 1388 at [13].
[54] DTA, s.2(8); CJA, s.71(7A).
[55] *R. v Chrastny (No.2)* [1991] 1 W.L.R. 1385 at 1395E.
[56] Court of Appeal (Civ Div) Transcript No.92 of 1997 (January 24, 1997).

individual is prosecuted? Can a restraint order be made in respect of the company's property? This is particularly important where the company has been used as a money launderer or to assist in the carrying out of the offence.

In the context of civil claims based on private rights, the expression "piercing the corporate veil" and different situations contemplated by that expression are considered in Chapter 13, para.13.011.

In the field of drug trafficking or the CJA, for the purpose of making interim orders to hold the position, the courts are ready to pierce the veil on the ground that a company is being used as a vehicle to carry on criminal activities or receive the proceeds of crime.

In *Re H (Restraint Order: Realisable Property)*[57] companies had been **25.024** allegedly used by the defendants for the purpose of carrying out fraudulent evasion of excise duty. No prosecution was brought against the companies. A receiver was appointed over property of the companies. The Court of Appeal held that the jurisdiction to appoint a receiver under s.77(8) of CJA (which is in terms corresponding to s.26(7) of DTA) did not extend to appointing a receiver over the property of the companies, but that on the particular facts it was right to disregard the corporate veils and treat the property as property of the defendants. In substance on the facts as alleged the individuals had used the companies for the purpose of carrying out fraudulent evasion of excise duty and profiting thereby, and it was pointless to prosecute the companies simply for the purpose of securing their assets.

In *Crown Prosecution Service v Compton*,[58] an individual (RC) had pleaded guilty to possession of heroin and cannabis with intent to supply and sentenced to seven years' imprisonment. Stanley Burnton J. refused to make a restraint order and receivership order against a small family company which had apparently been used to receive proceeds of drug dealing. The judge had thought that *prima facie* the proceeds were a loan to the company (as shown in its accounts) and that the corporate veil was not to be pierced. Subsequently the Crown Court judge after hearing evidence from RC concluded that the accounts of a small family company were used by RC to receive proceeds of drug trafficking. The appeal from the refusal by Stanley Burnton J. was moot for two reasons: (1) s.32(2) of DTA applied because the relevant bankruptcy had preceded the making of any restraint order; and (2) the decisions on the interim applications had been overtaken by the making of the confiscation order; this meant that the High Court should now proceed to a final determination of the rights.

The difficulty in that case arose because the company was a separate **25.025** legal entity from RC and, if the drug proceeds were a loan to the company, then the money became beneficially owned by the company and there was

---

[57] [1996] 2 All E.R. 391 (also called *Customs and Excise v Hare* [1996] 2 B.C.L.C. 500); applied by the High Court in Northern Ireland in *Re Morgan and Morgan*, March 20, 1996, referred to in R.E. Bell, "Restraint Orders" (1997) 48 N.I.L.Q. 128 at 132.

[58] [2002] EWCA Civ 1720.

difficulty in saying that the proceeds were a "gift" to that company. If, on the other hand, the proceeds were simply held by the company for RC, no difficulty arose. On an interim basis there was in any event a proper case for preserving the position. Once there was a good arguable case for regarding particular assets as "realisable property", an interim order could properly be made.[59] That view should have been reached either because the defendant had a beneficial interest in them or on the ground that the company's assets were to be regarded as those of the defendant. The position is analogous to that of freezing the assets of non-parties, which is considered in Chapter 13.

(5) The without notice application

25.026 An application is made often without notice to the judge in chambers by the prosecutor. Since the application is without notice, the prosecutor is under a duty to make full and frank disclosure to the court of all matters which are material to the application.[60] Even if there is material non-disclosure, the court would hesitate to discharge an order on that ground alone: this is so because of the public interest in the prevention of crime and confiscation of its proceeds. Instead, the court may make an order for costs.

The witness statement or affidavit in support of the application must set out the information required under RSC Ord.115, r.3(2), which includes the grounds for believing that the defendant has benefited from drug trafficking, details about the assets which are said to be "realisable property" and who holds the assets, and details about the criminal proceedings, whether intended or already instituted. Under RSC Ord.115, r.3(3) there is a provision corresponding to para.18.2 of the Practice Direction—Written Evidence supplementing CPR Pt 32 and the former RSC Ord.41, r.5(2), which permitted "statements of information or belief with the sources and grounds thereof" to be contained in the affidavit. In *Re a Defendant* (above), the affidavit had been made by an investigating officer. He had obtained the information from a named officer, who in turn had received information from members of the drug squad who had kept watch on certain premises but who were not identified by name in the affidavit. Webster J. held that, at least on the *ex parte* application, the reference in the affidavit to the unnamed members of the drug squad was sufficient compliance with the rule.

---

[59] *Crown Prosecution Service v Crompton* [2002] EWCA Civ 1720 at [38]; *Crown Prosecution Service v Malik* [2003] EWHC 660 at [23]; the "good arguable case" test is used in s.246(5) of POCA in relation to applying for an interim receiving order in aid of proceedings for a recovery order.

[60] *Re a Defendant, The Times*, April 7, 1987; *Re AJ and DJ*, Court of Appeal (Civ Div) Transcript No.1295 of 1992 (December 9, 1992), a case under CJA, Pt VI. This is a continuing duty: *Re JL*, March 18, 1994, referred to in R.E. Bell, "Restraint Orders" (1997) 48 N.I.L.Q. 128 at 131, cp. Chapter 9, paras 9.021–9.024, above.

On an application for a restraint order the prosecutor must show that **25.027**
there is a risk of dissipation of assets: *Re AJ and DJ*.[61] In a case under the
DTA the evidence supporting the charge may itself readily lead the court to
be satisfied of this. Similarly this evidence will support the conclusion that
the defendant has benefited from "drug trafficking" and thus to satisfy the
requirement in s.25(1)(c).

It is envisaged by RSC Ord.115, r.4 that the defendant to the proceedings in the High Court will be the alleged drug trafficker who is to be
prosecuted or is being prosecuted. Under RSC Ord.115, r.4(3) provision is
made for service of a copy of the restraint order and of the affidavit relied
on in support of the application, on the defendant "and on all other named
persons restrained by the order and [the prosecutor] shall notify all other
persons or bodies affected by the order of its terms".[62]

In contrast to the position under the ordinary Mareva jurisdiction where
the principle is that an injunction will be directed to a defendant only,[63] a
restraint order can prohibit "any person from dealing with realisable
property" (DTA, s.26(1)), and under RSC Ord.115 persons other than the
defendant to the proceedings may be named in the restraint order.

An example form of restraint order is given by the Practice Direction **25.028**
supplementing RSC Ord.115, which is in the Schedule to the CPR.

The Practice Direction supplementing RSC Ord.115 provides:

"RESTRAINT ORDERS AGAINST THIRD PARTIES

5.1 Where a restraint order applies to property held in the name of a
person other than the defendant—
(1) the order must be addressed to that person in addition to the
defendant; and
(2) in applying for the order, the prosecutor must consider the
guidance given in the matter of G (restraint order) [2001]
EWHC Admin 606.

5.2 Examples of additional persons to whom an order must, where
appropriate, be addressed include—
(1) a person who has a joint bank account with the defendant;
(2) in proceedings under the 1988 Act or the 1994 Act, a person
to whom the defendant is alleged to have made a gift which
may be treated as realisable property of the defendant under
the provisions of the relevant Act; or
(3) a company, where the prosecutor alleges that assets apparently
belonging to the company are in reality those of the
defendant.

---

[61] Court of Appeal (Civ Div) Transcript No.1295 of 1992 (December 9, 1992).
[62] There is a similar provision in relation to charging orders in RSC Ord. 115, r.4(4).
[63] See Chapter 13, paras 13.001 *et seq.*, above.

5.3   However, an order should not normally be addressed—
(1) to a bank with whom a defendant has an account; or
(2) to the business name of a defendant who carries on an unincorporated business (such business not being a separate legal entity from the defendant)."

25.029   In *Re G*,[64] Stanley Burnton J. was considering a draft restraint order submitted by Customs and Excise which had a number of defects. It related to evasion of duty and VAT on hydrocarbon oil and was an application under the CJA. The intended restraint applied to a joint bank account with the defendant's wife, and the assets of a company. In the case of the wife the restraint was justified on the basis that either the joint account was "realisable property" or on the ground that the wife had received a gift caught by the Act. In these circumstances the judge held that the wife should be both a defendant to the proceedings and a respondent to the application for the restraint order. He also held that provision should be made in the order for living expenses for the wife and for payment for her separate legal advice and representation.

As for the company, the judge held that the order should be addressed to the company and should make provision for payment for its separate legal advice and representation. There was also the question of allowing it to deal with its assets in the ordinary course of business.

If the order is intended to apply to assets held by a person which that person is likely to consider to be assets which he is free to use as his own, then normally that person should be named as a co-defendant in the claim form, as a co-respondent in the application for a restraint order, and in the order as an addressee of the order, and careful consideration should be given as to what qualifications should be inserted so that living and legal expenses can be met and there is not unnecessary interference with the carrying on of a legitimate business or trade.

25.030   Under RSC Ord.115, r.5(1) anyone served with a restraint or charging order, or notified of the order, can apply to discharge or vary it. This corresponds to the position of third parties under Mareva relief. The position is also dealt with in ss.26(6) and 27(8) of DTA. These sections expressly enable any person affected by a restraint order or a charging order to apply for a discharge or variation of the order.[65]

Once a receiver has been appointed under s.26(7) of DTA over property of a defendant, third party mortgagees should not seek to go into possession of the property or to sell it. Instead they should apply to the High Court for relief in the proceedings in which the receiver has been appointed.[66]

A restraint order made *ex parte* will be made only up to a return date for the application *inter partes* (RSC Ord.115, r.4(2)) unless the court otherwise directs. In practice orders are often made "until further order" leaving

---

[64] [2001] EWHC Admin 606; [2002] S.T.C. 391.
[65] *Re Norris* [2001] 1 W.L.R. 1388.
[66] *Re M, The Times*, May 20, 1991.

it up to the defendant or anyone affected by the order to apply for discharge or variation.

The *ex parte* restraint order, besides being expressed to be in force until **25.031** after the hearing on the return date, should include an express provision giving the defendant liberty to apply to discharge the order: *Re C.*[67] Similarly, a charging order made *ex parte* will be an order "to show cause, imposing the charge until such day".[68]

A restraint order will also usually provide for an indemnity to be given by the prosecutor to third parties in respect of expenses incurred in complying with the order (RSC Ord.115, r.4(1)). This is done by way of an undertaking given by the prosecutor to the court.

(6) The legislative steer on the exercise of discretion under the Drug Trafficking Act 1994 and the Criminal Justice Act 1988

(i) The legislative steer on the judicial exercise of discretion

Section 31 of DTA contains what was called in argument in *Re Peters*[69] a **25.032** "legislative steer" as to how the court is to exercise its powers over assets which are the subject of a restraint or charging order or an order appointing a receiver. Section 31(2) of DTA (formerly s.13 of DTOA) provides:

> "the powers . . . shall be exercised with a view to making available for satisfying . . . any confiscation order that may be made in the defendant's case the value for the time being of realisable property held by any person, by means of the realisation of such property".

Under s.31 (4) of DTA it is provided that the powers conferred on the High Court by ss.26–30 are to be exercised "with a view to allowing any person other than the defendant or the recipient of any . . . gift [caught by the Act] to retain or recover the value of any property held by him".

Thus, if another person has an interest in the property, and that person has not received a gift caught by the Act, then that person should be allowed to retain his interest or recover its value. If, on the other hand, the other person has received a gift caught by the Act, then, regardless of whether his interest in the property was derived from the gift, the property is liable to be dealt with under the Act pursuant to s.31(3) ". . .with a view to realising no more than the value for the time being of the gift". Accordingly, if, *e.g.* a wife has an interest in the matrimonial home which she owns together with her husband who is an alleged drug trafficker, the

---

[67] [1990] 1 H.K.L.R. 127.
[68] See RSC Ord.115, r.4(2).
[69] [1988] Q.B. 871.

court has jurisdiction to make a charging order over the matrimonial home, regardless of whether or not the wife's interest was itself acquired with money which belonged to her and was not in any way derived from drug trafficking.

25.033   If the husband is convicted and a confiscation order is made, the extent of the court's powers over the matrimonial home and how they should be exercised may fall to be considered. Once the confiscation order is no longer subject to appeal, the court has jurisdiction under s.29(2) to appoint a receiver over the home for the purpose of selling it. If the wife has not received a gift caught by the Act, then if the home is sold she should be paid the full value of her interest. If, on the other hand, she has received a gift caught by the Act from her husband, this is to be taken into account under s.31(3) of DTA in assessing how much she should be paid (if anything) in respect of her interest in the home.

(ii) Living expenses and legal costs

25.034   A restraint order will almost inevitably make provision for living expenses and legal expenses of the defendant.[70] These are referred to expressly in RSC Ord.115, r.4(1). It may also make provision for other payments by the defendant, such as a child's school fees. In exercising the discretion to qualify the order to allow a particular payment, the court is directed to exercise the powers conferred by ss.26–30 in accordance with the objectives set out in s.31. The statutory intent is that property subject to a restraint order should, so far as is reasonably possible, be made available to satisfy a confiscation order or any future confiscation order which may be made. Paragraph 4 of the Practice Direction supplementing RSC Ord.115 provides:

LIVING EXPENSES AND LEGAL FEES

4. A restraint order will normally, unless it is clear that a person restrained has sufficient assets which are not subject to the order, include an exception to the order permitting that person to spend assets—

(1) in the case of an individual, for reasonable living expenses; and
(2) in the case of either an individual or a company, to pay reasonable legal fees so that they may take advice in relation to the order and if so advised apply for its variation or discharge."

In *Re Peters*,[71] the Court of Appeal set aside an order permitting a drug trafficker[72] to make a capital payment to his son for future school fees.

---

[70] *Re G* [2001] EWHC Admin 606; [2002] S.T.C. 391.
[71] [1988] Q.B. 871.
[72] The defendant was convicted between the hearing at first instance and the appeal.

While proceedings were at the stage that an alleged drug trafficker was facing prosecution and the court did not know whether he would be convicted, it was right that he should be able to pay for his living expenses, his legal costs, and interim expenses reasonably incurred before it was known whether or not he had been convicted including, *e.g.* school fees and medical expenses. In relation to his son's education, the defendant, while he was an unconvicted person, was entitled not to have his son's education interrupted. But that did not justify making a lump sum payment to cover future school fees which were expected to arise only after the alleged drug trafficker had been convicted or acquitted. The jurisdiction to make or vary restraint orders were described as being "closely analogous"[73] to the jurisdiction to grant Mareva relief, in the sense that it involved striking a balance between, on the one hand, preserving assets to satisfy a confiscation order if one was made, and, on the other hand, meeting "the reasonable requirements of their owner in the meantime".[74]

The court will not sanction payments for the purpose of enabling the **25.035** defendant to pursue a "Rolls Royce lifestyle until his guilt or innocence is established".[75]

Ordinarily a restraint order will make provision for payment of the legal expenses of the defendant pursuant to RSC Ord.115, r.4(1). But in a case involving substantial costs, the prosecutor may be concerned to preserve as much as possible intact under the restraint order. In principle, the defendant should be free to choose his own lawyers and how much to pay, provided that he is not patently over-extravagant. The defendant is entitled to defend himself and s.31(2) should not be taken as cutting down that entitlement. Nor should the court become involved, at the stage of deciding whether to vary the restraint order, in questions of taxation. On the other hand, the court can provide for legal costs to be taxed after the verdict, as between the solicitor and client, so as to ensure that the funds removed from the restraint order are limited to what is proper for the conduct of the defence. In *Re P and W*,[76] the Court of Appeal upheld an order which allowed the defendants to grant a charge in favour of their solicitors for their costs over property subject to a restraint order, with a provision that, after verdict, the amount should be taxed.

In a taxation as between solicitor and own client there are presumptions **25.036** which are made in favour of the solicitor under CPR r.48.8(2) which apply where there has been express or implied approval from the client. However, it would be inconsistent with the statutory scheme if the amount which would be available to satisfy a confiscation order could be reduced because of unreasonable conduct by a defendant. Also, solicitors should not

---

[73] [1988] Q.B. 871 at 879, *per* Lord Donaldson M.R. and at 880, *per* Nourse L.J.
[74] *ibid.*, at 880, *per* Nourse L.J.
[75] *Re D and D*, unreported, October 28, 1992 (Hutchinson J.); see also Chapter 20, para.20.066, and the reference on legal expenses to the equivalent of a "Rolls Royce" in *TDK Tape Distributor (UK) Ltd v Videochoice Ltd* ob1986] 1 W.L.R. 141 at 146.
[76] *The Times*, April 11, 1990.

expect to be paid costs which are unreasonable out of funds subject to a restraint order. Because of these considerations, costs may be allowed on an "indemnity" basis as between solicitor and own client, but without the solicitor having the benefit of the presumptions which would otherwise be made in his favour under CPR r.48.8(2).[77]

In *R. (Dechert Solicitors) v Southwark Crown Court*,[78] a restraint order had been made under which provision was made for legal costs in the criminal proceedings. The proviso to the order allowed the serious fraud office to object to the costs claimed and if so then 65 per cent was to be allowed and the costs would be taxed, on a solicitor and own client basis. The defendant was convicted in the criminal proceedings and the question then arose of a confiscation order in the Crown Court proceedings. The Crown Court judge purported to order an investigation by a costs judge into the solicitors' fees. This was quashed on judicial review because the question of taxation or not was a matter for the civil proceedings concerning the restraint order before the High Court and the Serious Fraud Office did not challenge the fees claimed, so the High Court would not order taxation.

The position is different where the POCA applies because of s.41 of POCA: see para.25.063, below.

(iii) Creditors

25.037　In *Re W*,[79] a bona fide judgment creditor of the defendant applied to vary a restraint order made under Pt VI of the CJA, which is in similar terms to those of the scheme laid down by the DTA. Buckley J. declined to do so, relying on s.82 of CJA, which corresponds to s.31 of DTA. In particular the judgment relied on s.82(2) and (6) which correspond to s.31(2) and (5) of DTA, and it was held that priority was to be given to satisfying a confiscation order if one was made.

The reasoning for this decision is difficult to support. First, the wording of s.82(6) of CJA, and s.31(5) of DTA, does not lead to this conclusion. The words appear to relate solely to the situation which arises after a confiscation order has been made. This is because[80] the section refers only to "the confiscation order" and, unlike s.82(2) of CJA, and s.31(2) of DTA, not also to "any confiscation order that may be made."

Secondly, there is a balance to be struck between two competing considerations, which were referred to in *Re P (Restraint Order: Sale of Assets)*.[81] This was in relation to an interim order made before trial and s.31(2) of DTA. After referring to the judgments in *Re Peters*,[82] Simon Brown L.J., with whom the other members of the court agreed, said:

---

[77] *Re L (Restraint Order), The Times*, July 10, 1996.
[78] [2001] EWHC Admin 477.
[79] *The Times*, November 15, 1990.
[80] *Re Peters* [1988] Q.B. 871 at 879B.
[81] [2000] 1 W.L.R. 473 at 481.
[82] [1988] Q.B. 871.

"a balance has to be struck between, on the one hand, preserving the worth of the defendant's realisable property against the possibility that he may be convicted and a confiscation order made against him, and on the other hand allowing him meantime to continue the ordinary course of his life . . .".

25.038 *Re W*[83] was cited, but not mentioned in the judgment. What is to be made of this? It is suggested that the same principle of striking a balance must be applied to deciding whether to permit discharge of a bona fide judgment debt. The fact that a judgment has been obtained cannot be conclusive, but a fair balance is to be struck. Before the making of a confiscation order, the restraint order is to be operated as a preservative order[84] which, normally, is not to be operated so as to force into bankruptcy a defendant who has not been tried.[85]

(iv) Use of proposed exhibit of cash to make payments

25.039 The fact that the Crown intended to exhibit cash found in the control of the defendant at the criminal trial does not prevent the court directing that the cash be used to pay living expenses or legal costs. In an unreported decision,[86] Laws J. considered that the evidence could equally well be presented to a jury by photographic evidence.

(v) Post-confiscation order

25.040 Section 31(5) of DTA is applicable once a confiscation order has been made. If a convicted drug trafficker is subject to a confiscation order which has not been satisfied, then he will not be allowed to use his property to satisfy other obligations. To do so would reduce the amount available to be paid towards satisfaction of the confiscation order, leaving it unsatisfied. To pay the other obligations would, in the words of s.31(5), "conflict with the obligation to satisfy the confiscation order". Thus, provision would preclude payment of school fees when payment would conflict with a convicted drug trafficker's obligation to pay a confiscation order. It did not apply in *Re Peters*, because although there had been a conviction, the Crown Court had not dealt with the question of whether a confiscation order was to be made. Section 31(5) also applies to the property of a person who had received a "gift" caught by the Act from the convicted drug trafficker, and whose property is therefore liable to be taken towards satisfaction of the confiscation order. That property is liable to be taken

---

[83] *The Times*, November 15, 1990.
[84] *Re P (Restraint Order: Sale of Assets)* [2000] 1 W.L.R. 473 at 482 referring to the effect of appointment of a receiver before a defendant has been convicted.
[85] *Re Peters* [1988] Q.B. 871 at 879H, 880H–881A, 881D–E; *cp.* Chapter 20, para.20.070 *et seq.*; see also RSC Ord.115, r.4(1).
[86] *Re C*, 1993.

"with a view to realising no more than the value for the time being of the gift" (s.31(3)). So, *e.g.*, if the recipient had property worth more than "the value for the time being of the gift", he should be permitted freely to use the excess.

An analogy can be drawn between s.31(5) and the exercise of the jurisdiction to vary an injunction once the claimant has obtained judgment.[87] At that stage the injunction is in aid of execution of the judgment, and not merely a Mareva injunction granted for the purpose of preserving assets in contemplation of a possible future judgment. Similarly, once a confiscation order has been made it would be wrong in principle to allow the drug trafficker to use property otherwise than in connection with satisfying the confiscation order.

25.041   Even after a confiscation order has been made, however, if the defendant wishes to appeal, the court may allow him to spend money subject to a restraint order on the legal costs of an appeal. In *Customs & Excise Commissioners v Norris*,[88] the defendant had been granted leave to appeal against his conviction. He was subject to a confiscation order for a very large sum, and had been sentenced to a long period of imprisonment together with a further long term in default of compliance with the confiscation order. All the defendant's property was needed to meet the confiscation order and it was argued that no variation should be made to the restraint order on the grounds that s.13(2) of DTOA (corresponding to s.31(2) of DTA) showed that Parliament intended that the property subject to the restraint order should be used to pay off the confiscation order. The Court of Appeal allowed access to funds caught by the restraint order. It was wrong in principle to force the defendant to rely on his family or on legal aid, when there was a real appeal against conviction.[89]

(7) No undertaking in damages and compensation for loss

(i) *Compensation under s.18 of the Drug Trafficking Act 1994*

25.042   No undertaking in damages is given on an application under the DTA,[90] but there is a right under s.18 for compensation to be awarded in certain limited circumstances. Section 89 of CJA provides a corresponding right under that legislation.

The application for compensation is made by application under CPR Pt 23.[91]

The circumstances in which compensation may be ordered under s.18 are narrower than would be the case if the person suffering the loss had the benefit of an undertaking in damages.

---

[87] See para.3.024, above.
[88] [1991] 2 Q.B. 293.
[89] See also R.E. Bell, "Restraint Orders" (1997) 48 N.I.L.Q. 128 at 135–136.
[90] See RSC Ord.115 r.4(1).
[91] RSC Ord. 115, r.10.

First, there has to have been "some serious default" by a person 25.043
"concerned in the investigation or prosecution" of the offence, who was a
police officer, a member of the Crown Prosecution Service or acting on its
behalf, or a Customs officer, or a member of the Serious Fraud Office or an
officer of the Inland Revenue.[92]

Secondly, the "serious default" has itself to be causative of the criminal
proceedings being instituted or continued. Once the "serious default" has
been shown then, on the wording of s.18(3), the legal burden of proof
appears to be on the respondent to the compensation application to show
that the criminal proceedings would have been instituted and continued
regardless of the occurrence of the default.

Thirdly, the applicant can be the defendant to the criminal proceedings
or anyone else but must have held property which was "realisable
property".[93] Property may be frozen by interim order on the basis that
there is a good arguable case that it is "realisable property";[94] but s.18(1)
only permits an application for compensation by someone who did hold
"realisable property".

Fourthly, there is a bar on compensation unless the court is satisfied that 25.044
"the applicant has suffered loss in consequence of anything done in
relation to the property" by or in pursuance of an order under ss.26–29 of
DTA (*e.g.* a restraint order or an order appointing a receiver).[95] It is
suggested that the words of s.18(2)(b) "anything done in relation to the
property" are referring back to property which was "realisable property"
and not just property which was arguably realisable property. That
something might be done by a receiver to property on the mistaken
assumption that it was realisable property is contemplated in s.30(1) of
DTA which provides an immunity for loss except for that caused by his
negligence. This shows that it was within the contemplation of the
legislature that loss might be caused to a person by what was done under a
restraint order in relation to property which was not in fact realisable
property, but s.18 does not appear to cover this.

The requirements are that (1) the order has caused something to be done
in relation to the property; (2) the applicant has suffered "loss" as a result.
For example, if the property was sold under an order of the court at the
bottom of the market, then it is suggested that this would come within
these words.

Fifthly, s.18(4) provides that the compensation such be such as the court 25.045
thinks is just. It is suggested that the compensation should be limited to the
"loss" which enables the applicant to make the application. This seems to
be an appropriate limitation to be read into s.18(4) because if the applicant
only has standing to pursue a compensation application if he has sustained

---

[92] CJA, s.89(4) and DTA, s.18(5).
[93] DTA, s.18(1).
[94] *Crown Prosecution Service v Crompton* [2002] EWCA Civ 1720 at [38]; *Crown Prosecution Service v Malik* [2003] EWHC 660 at [23].
[95] DTA, s.18(2)(b).

such a "loss", then logically the purpose of the jurisdiction is to give compensation for that "loss". The wide wording of s.18(4) shows that the court may still limit the compensation by reference to considerations of remoteness and whether it is fair in the circumstances that the applicant should obtain full compensation for that "loss".[96]

(ii) Compensation outside of s.18 of the Drug Trafficking Act 1994

25.046   It might be suggested that, independently of s.18, a claim could be brought in tort for loss caused by relief granted by the court under the Act, if the claimant could either show a case of malicious prosecution[97] of the proceedings brought under RSC Ord.115, or that there had been some tortious abuse of the process of the court.[98] A claim for malicious prosecution would require the claimant to show, *inter alia*, that the applicant was actuated by malice and that there had been no reasonable and probable cause for bringing the proceedings. A claim for tortious abuse of the process would require the claimant to show that at least the predominant purpose of the applicant had been deliberately to use the proceedings to achieve some objective not within the jurisdiction's intended purposes.

Leaving aside the remote possibility of a claim in tort, the general rule is that if loss is caused by an order of the court, the party damaged has no claim against the person who obtained the order. That is why, in the context of an interim injunction, the claimant is required to furnish an undertaking in damages.[99] The court has no power to award compensation to the defendant or a third party who has been caused loss by a restraint order by "implying" a cross-undertaking on the part of the prosecutor, or treating the case as if such a cross-undertaking had been given: *Re R (Restraint Order).*[1]

(8) Disclosure of information and privilege against self-incrimination

(i) Disclosure by the defendant

25.047   In proceedings under RSC Ord.115, the court can order disclosure to be made by the defendant for the purposes of the civil proceedings. The object is to identify the defendant's assets and make the order effective by

---

[96] Compare Chapter 11, para.11.028 *et seq.*
[97] *Metall und Rohstoff v Donaldson Inc.* [1990] 1 Q.B. 391.
[98] *Speed Seal Products Ltd v Paddington* [1985] 1 W.L.R. 1327; *Metall und Rohstoff v Donaldson Inc.* [1990] 1 Q.B. 391 at 469–472; *Grainger v Hill* (1838) 4 Bing. N.C. 212.
[99] *Bond Brewing Holdings Ltd v National Australia Bank Ltd (No.2)* [1991] 1 V.L.R. 580, Supreme Court of Victoria, Full Court; *Chisholm v Rieff* (1953) 2 F.L.R. 211, Supreme Court of the Northern Territory of Australia; *Digital Equipment Corporation v Darkcrest Ltd* [1984] Ch. 512.
[1] [1990] 2 Q.B. 307 at 312–313.

enabling the prosecutor to give notice of it to relevant third parties, or to take other steps to preserve the assets, *e.g.* by applying for the appointment of a receiver. The jurisdiction to order such disclosure can be based on s.37(1) of the Supreme Court Act 1981 or it is conferred on the court by implication[2] in the statute enpowering the court to make the restraint order or charging order, or appoint a receiver. The decision in *Re O (Restraint Order: Disclosure of Assets)*[3] was in relation to the CJA; the same is the position under the DTA.[4]

(ii) Privilege against self-incrimination

The example restraint order given by the Practice Direction supplementing 25.048 RSC Ord.115 contains a disclosure order (paras 10 and 11) and prohibitions on the use of that information (para.11).

In contrast to the position on orders in aid of Mareva relief or a proprietary injunction, or on Anton Piller relief, the prosecutor can give an undertaking not to use the information obtained in the criminal proceedings, and this serves to negative the invoking by the defendant of privilege against self-incrimination.[5] The undertaking prevents any risk of self-incrimination as a result of compliance with the order, because it is binding on the prosecution. In the example order the matter is dealt with by para.11 which operates as a restraint of the use of the disclosure which is binding on the prosecutor.

In *Re C (Restraint Order)*[6] it was held that the undertaking to be given by a prosecutor should be sufficient in itself to eliminate any risk of self-incrimination and that it was not good enough to have an undertaking which provided partial protection, leaving it to the judge at a criminal trial to exclude any other evidence not covered by the undertaking, but which had been obtained as a result of disclosure made by a defendant. It was insufficient protection for the defendant to have an undertaking that no disclosure made in compliance with the order would be used in evidence, because this did not cover evidence which resulted from the disclosure made by the defendant. Instead the prosecutor was required to undertake that "no use shall be made in any such prosecution against the defendant or his spouse of evidence obtained as a direct result of such disclosure."

In *R. v Martin and White*[7] the Court of Appeal held that use of the 25.049 information for cross-examination of the defendant on credit was not in breach of the particular undertaking given by the prosecutor to the High Court because it had not been used as "evidence in the prosecution". This

[2] *Re O (Restraint Order: Disclosure of Assets)* [1991] 2 Q.B. 520 at 528, applying the reasoning in *A. J. Bekhor & Co. Ltd v Bilton* [1981] Q.B. 923 to Pt VI of CJA.
[3] [1991] 2 Q.B. 520.
[4] *Re T (Restraint Order: Disclosure of Assets)* [1992] 1 W.L.R. 949.
[5] *Re O* [1991] 2 Q.B. 520 (CJA), approved in *Istel (A. T. & T.) Ltd v Tully* [1993] A.C. 45; *Re T* [1992] 1 W.L.R. 949 (DTOA); *Re a Defendant, The Times*, April 7, 1987.
[6] [1995] C.O.D. 263; *The Times*, April 21, 1995.
[7] (1998) 2 Cr.App.R. 385.

decision indicated that the width of the undertaking approved in *Re O*[8] was not sufficiently wide to safeguard the full width of the defendant's entitlement not to incriminate himself.

The incorporation into English law of the European Convention on Human Rights by the Human Rights Act 1998, has brought with it a separate form of privilege against self-incrimination. The common law privilege and that under Art.6[9] are considered in Chapter 17, para.17.031. The protection to be given by the prosecutor must satisfy the scope of each privilege or right. In the case of the common law privilege it will only be effective if claimed in the civil restraint proceedings and can only be circumvented with a sufficiently wide undertaking given by the prosecutor or restraint binding upon him. In the case of the right to a fair trial under Art.6(1) this depends upon what happens in the criminal trial and the fairness of that trial, and does not protect the defendant in relation to providing information for regulatory purposes or extra-judicial inquiries, which are not part of the criminal proceedings.[10] Paragraph 11 of the example order adopts wording approved by Collins J. in *Re C (Restraint Order: Disclosure)*.[11] The restraint on use of information does not apply to the confiscation proceedings because these are civil proceedings which are not part of the penalty to be imposed for a criminal offence.[12]

(iii) Disclosure by a person other than the defendant

25.050 Disclosure may be ordered against a person who holds "realisable property" even though he is not a defendant to the criminal proceedings: *Re D (Restraint Order)*.[13] This is because the statutory scheme enables the High Court to grant relief preserving "realisable property" regardless of who has control of that property or in whose name such property is held. It suffices if the defendant to the criminal proceedings or someone to whom he has made a gift caught by the legislation has an interest in the property or a right in respect of it. The property which can be made the subject of a restraint is not limited to the proceeds of crime. It is inherent in the statutory scheme that the High Court has power to make ancillary orders to ensure the effective operation of the statutory jurisdiction. This extends to ordering third parties to disclose information about property which is or may be "realisable property". In appropriate circumstances para.11 of the example restraint order will have to be modified to protect the third party against self-incrimination.

---

[8] [1991] 2 Q.B. 520.
[9] See *Saunders v United Kingdom* (1996) 23 E.H.R.R. 313; *R. v Hertfordshire County Council Ex p. Green* [2000] 2 A.C. 412 at 422–423.
[10] *R. v Hertfordshire County Council Ex p. Green* [2000] 2 A.C. 412 at 422–423.
[11] Unreported, September 4, 2000.
[12] See also *Re E; Re H*, unreported, May 24, 2001 (Henriques J.).
[13] *The Times*, January 26, 1995.

(9) Effect of a restraint order

A restraint order prevents any dealing (DTA, s.26(1)) with the property **25.051** subject to the order, by the defendant or by any person specified in the order, either by themselves, their servants or agents or otherwise. This precludes payment by a third party debtor to the person restrained (DTA, s.26(8)(a)).[14] It also prohibits, in the case of property within Great Britain, its removal from Great Britain (DTA, s.26(8)(6)).

A restraint order does not prevent a third party forfeiting a lease held by the alleged drug trafficker,[15] nor does it prevent a bank from exercising existing rights of set-off or combination of accounts in respect of an overdraft which had been granted and drawn down prior to any restraint order being made.[16]

If contempt proceedings are to be brought for breach of a restraint order, they are properly brought before a single judge of the High Court pursuant to RSC Ord.52, r.1.[17] An appeal against a restraint order or charging order, or the appointment of a receiver, or an order for discovery in aid of these preservative orders, is an appeal in a civil matter and lies from the High Court to the Court of Appeal (Civil Division).[18]

If the powers under the Act are sought to be exercised in relation to the **25.052** property of a third party who is said to have received a "gift" caught by the Act, it will be open to the third party to put in issue whether or not there has been such a "gift" and, if so, its amount. Such an issue falls to be resolved in the High Court proceedings.[19]

In relation to placing a financial limit on a restraint order the prosecutor is often not in a position on the interim application to assess accurately what may be the quantum of any eventual confiscation order and so the court does the best it can, given the information available on the application, with the prosecutor being allowed some latitude.[20] The Practice Direction supplementing RSC Ord.115 provides:

"AMOUNT UNDER RESTRAINT

3.1 A restraint order may, where appropriate, apply to—

(1) all of the defendant's realisable property;

---

[14] Contrast, in relation to Mareva relief, *Bank Mellat v Kazmi* [1989] Q.B. 541, and paras 3.012–3.014, above.
[15] *Re R* [1990] 2 Q.B. 307.
[16] *Re K* [1990] 2 Q.B. 298.
[17] *Re H, The Times*, April 1, 1988. For examples of penalties imposed for contempt, see R. E. Bell, "Restraint Orders" (1997) 48 N.I.L.Q. 128 at 139–141.
[18] *Re O* [1991] 2 Q.B. 520; see also *Government of USA v Montgomery* [2001] 1 W.L.R. 196.
[19] *Crown Prosecution Service v Malik* [2003] EWHC 660; *Re Norris* [2001] 1 W.L.R. 1388.
[20] *Re K, The Times*, September 30, 1990.

> (2) the defendant's realisable property up to a specified value; or
> (3) one or more particular specified assets.
>
> 3.2 Where—
>
> > (1) a confiscation order or forfeiture order has already been made against the defendant in a particular amount; or
> > (2) the prosecutor is able to make a reasonably accurate estimate of the amount of any confiscation order or forfeiture order that might be made against him,
>
> and, in either case, it is clear that the defendant's realisable property is greater in value than the amount or estimated amount of that order, the court will normally limit the application of the restraint order in accordance with paragraph 3.1(2) or (3).
>
> 3.3 In such cases the prosecutor's draft order should normally either include an appropriate financial limit or specify the particular assets to which the order should apply."

(10) Payment of the receiver's remuneration and expenses

(i) Before a confiscation order is made

25.053   A receiver appointed by the court looks to the assets over which he has been appointed for the costs of the receivership and for his remuneration and expenses.[21] This is the usual position at common law[22] and the CJA and the DTA are not inconsistent with this, and so the same regime applies. Where these assets are insufficient, if criminal proceedings are not instituted, the person who applied for the receiver to be appointed, is responsible.

There is a power for the court to make an order under CPR r.69.7(2)(a) about who is to be responsible for payment of the receiver's remuneration, and RSC Ord.115, r.8(1) provides for CPR Pt 69 to apply to an appointment of a receiver under the DTA. CPR r.69.7(2)(a) is different from the former RSC Ord.30, r.3 which applied in *Hughes v Customs and Excise*,[23] and gives jurisdiction for the court to order a person to bear the remuneration of the receiver, as opposed to leaving that remuneration to be paid from the assets.

(ii) After a confiscation order

25.054   After a confiscation order has been made everything under the hands of the receiver goes towards payment of the confiscation order and then the receiver is reimbursed his remuneration and expenses under s.30(6) of

---

[21] *Hughes v Customs and Excise* [2003] 1 W.L.R. 177.
[22] See Chapter 16, paras 16.024–16.026.
[23] [2003] 1 W.L.R. 177 at [61] and [70].

DTA. Thus the general principle is that if the receiver has obtained money available to be paid towards satisfaction of the confiscation order, then he is to be paid his remuneration and expenses out of these funds after they have been paid over in satisfaction of the confiscation order.

If that mode of reimbursement proves insufficient then the prosecutor is responsible to pay the balance under s.36(2).

(11) Information from third parties

There are wide powers under the DTA to obtain information from third **25.055** parties for the purposes of an investigation. These powers are sufficiently wide to enable information to be obtained about realisable property" so that it can be preserved. Thus, *e.g.* under s.55 a circuit judge has power to make an order against a bank to disclose information about a suspected drug trafficker's affairs. Where the bank complies with such an order, it will not be in breach of contract with its customer and cannot be successfully sued for breach of its duty of confidentiality, because the order overrides the duty of confidentiality owed to the customer.[24] It is also considered that a bank is not ordinarily under any duty to its customer to seek to oppose the making of an order or to apply for its discharge.[25] Furthermore, a bank would usually be well advised not to inform its customer about the making of an order, in view of s.58 of DTA, which makes it a criminal offence to make "any disclosure which is likely to prejudice the investigation."

(12) Costs

If the defendant is acquitted, then ordinarily the prosecutor will be ordered **25.056** to pay the costs of the civil proceedings brought under RSC Ord.115: *Re W (Drug Trafficking) (Restraint Order: Costs).*[26] This is because the usual order is that costs follow the event.[27] But this is not an invariable rule. In *Re Mason*[28] the defendants had been acquitted, but the trial judge had refused them costs of the criminal proceedings in view of their conduct and because of this they were refused their costs of the restraint proceedings. A third party who had intervened in the proceedings was awarded her costs out of central funds, but that was subsequently held not to be justified.[29] A

---

[24] See Chapter 20, paras 20.018–20.019.
[25] See *Barclays Sank v Taylor* [1989] 1 W.L.R. 1066, in relation to the position on an order made under s.9 and Sch.1 to the Police and Criminal Evidence Act 1984.
[26] *The Times,* October 13, 1994.
[27] The former RSC Ord.62, r.3(3) and CPR 44.3(2)(a).
[28] [1993] 1 W.L.R. 824.
[29] *Holden & Co. v CPS (No.2)* [1994] 1 A.C. 22.

third party intervenor ought ordinarily to be awarded costs against one or other of the parties to the proceedings. If the intervention is before verdict in the criminal proceedings, the costs can be awarded against the prosecutor and then, if the prosecutor is successful, he can seek an indemnity against those costs in an award of costs against the defendant which includes the costs the prosecutor has to pay to the intervenor.

(13) Criminal Justice Act 1988

25.057 Part VI of CJA contains a scheme for making restraint orders, charging orders and orders appointing a receiver similar to that contained in the DTA. Under s.71 the Crown Court has power to make confiscation orders in connection with any indictable offence of which the defendant is convicted, and the magistrates' court has power in relation to offences listed in Sch.4 to CJA. The defendant must have benefited from the offence. A person who has received a "gift" caught by the CJA (defined in s.74(1)) is liable to have his property made subject to orders made under Pt VI, the intention being that his property can be applied towards satisfying a confiscation order to the extent of "the value for the time being of the gift" (s.82(3)). RSC Ord.115, r.23 applies with certain modification the rules applicable to proceedings under the DTA to regulate proceedings brought under Pt VI of CJA.

Under s.76(1)(c)(ii), except where (i) applies, the court has to be satisfied that there is "reasonable cause to believe" that:

(1) the criminal proceedings have resulted in or may result in a relevant conviction; and

(2) the defendant may be, or has been, shown to have benefited from that offence.

In a case under the CJA the amount of benefit derived from the offence or offences is relevant to the amount of a confiscation order,[30] and to the financial limit to be placed on a restraint order.

25.058 Under s.71(4), where the defendant has received property as the result of an offence the relevant "benefit" obtained by him is the value of the property received. In *Re K*[31] the defendant had been charged with offences of mortgage fraud. The judge decided that the "property" obtained by the defendant in a case of mortgage fraud was the house, and not the equity of redemption, or the funds advanced by the lender, and so the relevant

---

[30] CJA, s.71(6).
[31] *The Times*, September 30, 1990, subsequently approved in *R. v Layode*, unreported, March 12, 1994, CA.

"benefit" under s.71(4) was the value of the house. Thus "benefit" is not restricted to the profit made by the defendant from his crime.

The prosecutor should disclose on the *ex parte* application matters relevant to the assessment of the net benefit made by a defendant from the alleged offence.[32]

(14) Reports of proceedings

Section 4(2) of the Contempt of Court Act 1981 provides: 25.059

> "(2) In any such proceedings the court may, where it appears to be necessary for avoiding a substantial risk of prejudice to the administration of justice in those proceedings, or in any other proceedings pending or imminent, order that the publication of any report of the proceedings, or any part of the proceedings, be postponed for such period as the court thinks necessary for that purpose."

Under this provision, the court has power to postpone reporting the civil proceedings brought under RSC Ord.115 to avoid any substantial risk of prejudicing the fair trial of "pending or imminent" criminal proceedings. This power has been exercised by the Court of Appeal to prevent publication of any details which might identify the defendants so that the jury will not know what had happened in the proceedings for a restraint order and the evidence disclosed in those proceedings: *Re AJ and DJ*, above. Whether it is to be exercised in a particular case depends on the circumstances, and is a matter for the discretion of the court.[33]

(15) Repatriation orders

Restraint orders under the DTA or Pt VI of the CJA can apply to assets 25.060 outside the jurisdiction. The court has jurisdiction under both Acts to require repatriation of assets to England.[34] First, the power to appoint a receiver includes power to require that assets be transferred into the name of the receiver. A repatriation order does not go as far as requiring assets to be transferred to a receiver, which is a form of order authorised by s.26(7) of DTA and s.77(8) of CJA. This indicates that Parliament intended the

---

[32] *Re AJ and DJ*, Court of Appeal (Civ Div) Transcript No.1295 of 1992 (December 9, 1992).
[33] *Ex p. Telegraph Group Plc* [2002] E.M.L.R. 10, p.169; *MGN Pension Trustees Ltd v Bank of America, The Times*, December 21, 1994.
[34] *DPP v Scarlett* [2000] 1 W.L.R. 515. The decision to this effect, of Brooke J., is referred to in *Re WJT*, Court of Appeal (Civ Div) Transcript No.1286 of 1994 (September 13, 1994); see also R.E. Bell, "Restraint Orders" (1997) 48 N.I.L.Q. 128 at 134–135.

court to have a lesser power (*i.e.* to require a change of location of assets) as well as a larger power (*i.e.* to require a change of location and a change of possession).

Secondly, the power to order repatriation can be viewed as an ancillary power, to make the restraint order fully effective in preserving the assets. As such, the power to make the ancillary order is inherent[35] in the power to impose a restraint order.

25.061   Thirdly, the power can be viewed as preliminary to considering the appointment of a receiver over the assets transferred, and thus ancillary to the power to appoint a receiver. It is a power impliedly conferred on the court by the statute to enable the court to preserve assets with a view to operating, either immediately or in due course, the jurisdiction to appoint a receiver.

(16) Proceeds of Crime Act 2002

(i) Introduction

25.062   This Proceeds of Crime Act 2002 (POCA) came into force on March 24, 2003 and it applies only in cases where the offences to which proceedings relate are committed after that date. Offences committed prior to that date continue to be governed by the DTA and the CJA, and the jurisdiction over civil proceedings relating to them continues to be vested in the High Court.

POCA applies to drug trafficking and other criminal offences. Instead of splitting the jurisdiction between criminal proceedings in the Crown Court and civil proceedings in the High Court, the jurisdiction to make restraint orders and to appoint a receiver is vested in the Crown Court. Restraint orders affecting land can be protected by registration.[36] The jurisdiction to grant charging orders under the DTA and CJA was seldom used and there is no corresponding jurisdiction under the POCA.

Restraint orders may be made under the POCA as soon as a "criminal investigation"[37] has commenced in England and Wales for an offence where there are reasonable grounds to believe that the defendant has benefited from his criminal conduct. The Act creates a statutory agency called the Asset Recovery Agency (ARA) headed by a director.

(ii) Restraint orders under the Proceeds of Crime Act 2002

25.063   Section 41 enpowers the Crown Court to grant a restraint order over "realisable property",[38] which includes any "free"[39] property held by the defendant or a recipient of a tainted gift, in each of the situations covered

---

[35] *DPP v Scarlett* [2000] 1 W.L.R. 515; see also *Re O* [1991] 2 Q.B. 520 at 528.
[36] POCA, s.47.
[37] Defined in s.88(2) as an investigation which the police or someone else is under a duty to conduct to ascertain whether someone should be charged.
[38] POCA, s.83.
[39] See POCA, s.82.

by s.40, on the application of the prosecutor, the director of the ARA, or an "accredited financial investigator".[40] Under s.41(4) there is not to be an exception made for legal expenses for the defendant or a donee of a "tainted gift" which relate to an offence within s.41(5); this includes legal expenses for the defence of the associated criminal proceedings. The assumption is that this will be dealt with through legal aid. There is provision for exceptions for living expenses, or legal expenses outside of s.41(4), and for carrying on a trade, business, profession, or occupation.[41] Third parties "affected" by a restraint order granted by the Crown Court can apply to that court to discharge or vary the order.[42] Appeals are then to the Court of Appeal and the House of Lords.[43] A receiver can be appointed by the Crown Court over any property subject to a restraint order.

(iii) The statutory steer in the Proceeds of Crime Act 2002

Section 69 of POCA provides: **25.064**

"POWERS OF COURT AND RECEIVER

69—(1) This section applies to—

    (a) the powers conferred on a court by sections 41 to 60 and sections 62 to 67;

    (b) the powers of a receiver appointed under section 48, 50 or 52.

(2) The powers—

    (a) must be exercised with a view to the value for the time being of realisable property being made available (by the property's realisation) for satisfying any confiscation order that has been or may be made against the defendant;

    (b) must be exercised, in a case where a confiscation order has not been made, with a view to securing that there is no diminution in the value of realisable property;

    (c) must be exercised without taking account of any obligation of the defendant or a recipient of a tainted gift if the obligation conflicts with the object of satisfying any confiscation order that has been or may be made against the defendant;

---

[40] See POCA, s.3(5).
[41] POCA, s.41(3).
[42] POCA, s.42(3).
[43] POCA, ss.43 and 44.

> (d) may be exercised in respect of a debt owed by the Crown.
>
> (3) Subsection (2) has effect subject to the following rules—
>
>   (a) the powers must be exercised with a view to allowing a person other than the defendant or a recipient of a tainted gift to retain or recover the value of any interest held by him;
>
>   (b) in the case of realisable property held by a recipient of a tainted gift, the powers must be exercised with a view to realising no more than the value for the time being of the gift;
>
>   (c) in a case where a confiscation order has not been made against the defendant, property must not be sold if the court so orders under subsection (4).
>
> (4) If on an application by the defendant, or by the recipient of a tainted gift, the court decides that property cannot be replaced it may order that it must not be sold.
>
> (5) An order under subsection (4) may be revoked or varied."

These provisions give a different "statutory steer" from that under the CJA and the DTA.

First, the decision in *Re P (Restraint Order: Sale of Assets)*[44] has been in effect reversed. The court will sell assets by interim order so as to maximise the eventual proceeds which will available to satisfy a confiscation order if and when one is made.

Secondly, this principle is modified in the case of property which "cannot be replaced" so as to provide that the court has a discretion to order that it must not be sold. Thus, if the property under restraint included a valuable unique work of art, this power could be exercised. So could it be exercised to order that a home not be sold.

(iii) Money laundering under Pt 7 of the Proceeds of Crime Act 2002 and "tipping off" under s.342

25.065 POCA creates a series of criminal offences in connection with "criminal property".[45] The idea is that no one should be involved with facilitating the retention or use of property which he knows or suspects to be derived from crime. Such a person can protect his position by making a "disclosure" to the authorities but even then must not prejudice the position by tipping off a suspected criminal; see s.342(2)(a). Legal advisers can find themselves in a position where substantial assets which are the subject of

---

[44] [2000] 1 W.L.R. 473.
[45] Defined in POCA, s.340.

litigation appear to be derived from crime. Guidance as to how to proceed was given in *P v P (Ancillary Relief: Proceeds of Crime)*,[46] and guidance was issued by the Money Laundering Working Party of the General Council of the Bar in December 2003.[47] The court can regulate the position by, in appropriate cases, granting an interim declaration which binds the relevant authority.[48]

---

[46] [2003] 3 W.L.R. 1350.
[47] The position of a bank is discussed in Chapter 20, paras 20.020–20.022.
[48] *Bank of Scotland v A* [2001] 1 W.L.R. 751; *P v P (Ancillary Relief: Proceeds of Crime)* [2003] 3 W.L.R. 1350 at [68].

Appendix 1

Obtaining Mareva-type provisional relief in New York state and federal courts

*Jonathan Greenblatt and A. Benjamin Spencer**

This Appendix will discuss the availability of Mareva-type relief in the federal **A1.001** courts throughout the United States and the state courts in New York.[1] In general, such relief is largely unavailable—strictly speaking—in either court system. However, there are some conditions under which this type of relief can be obtained and there are also various alternative measures that can provide similar degrees of protection, provided the right circumstances exist. Below, after a discussion of federal and New York law rejecting Mareva injunctions, we review the approaches that practitioners may use in their efforts to secure assets for the satisfaction of prospective money judgments.

---

* Jonathan Greenblatt is a Litigation Partner with Shearman & Sterling LLP, a New York-based global law firm, who specialises in complex commercial litigation in the areas of antitrust, banking, and international cross-border disputes and has extensive experience in international arbitration. A. Benjamin Spencer is an Assistant Professor of Law at the University of Richmond School of Law, specialising in Civil Procedure and Administrative Law, formerly a Litigation Associate with Shearman & Sterling LLP, formerly law clerk to the Honorable Judith W. Rogers, Circuit Judge, US Court of Appeals for the D.C. Circuit and a former Editor of the *Harvard Law Review*. Inquiries may be directed to Mr Greenblatt at 801 Pennsylvania Avenue, N.W., Suite 900, Washington, D.C. 20004, USA and to Mr Spencer at University of Richmond, School of Law, Richmond VA 23173.
[1] This Appendix does not touch on the availability of Anton Piller relief in New York state or federal courts because there is no counterpart to such relief in the United States. Plaintiffs under no circumstances are entitled to have a defendant's premises searched in order to find and seize items or documents that might become evidence in a later civil action filed by the plaintiff. See, *e.g.*, *Luciano v Marshall*, 593 P.2d 751, 752 (Nev. 1979) ("Even could a statutory basis for the procedure have been found, the search of petitioner's residence, and wholesale seizure of his personal property therein, in aid of civil process, would have been precluded by the constitutional prohibitions against unreasonable searches and seizures found in the United States and Nevada constitutions."). Such searches and seizures can only occur within the context of a criminal action, and then are executable only by officers of the relevant governmental authority, not by private parties. See US Const., Amendments IV, V, XIV; Kern Alexander, "The Mareva Injunction and Anton Piller Order: The Nuclear Weapons of English Commercial Litigation", 11 Fla. J. Int'l L. 487, 512 (1997) ("[T]here is no counterpart in U.S. civil procedure to the Anton Piller order. The nearest equivalent of an Anton Piller order under U.S. law is the use of a criminal warrant issued by a judge on an *ex parte* basis so that law enforcement authorities may seize important evidence before it is destroyed.").

(1) PROVISIONAL RELIEF IN AN AMERICAN CONTEXT: UNDERSTANDING THE FEDERAL SYSTEM

A1.002   The United States is organized as a federal system, with the several states each having their own governments and judicial systems that are separate and independent from the Government and judiciary of the United States itself. In general, disputes arising under a state's law are taken up in the courts of that state, and disputes arising under federal law (federal question), or disputes between litigants from different states (diversity) may be taken up in federal court, although these disputes can be heard in state court as well.[2] Disputes between a litigant from a state and a non-US litigant (referred to as subjects of foreign states or "aliens") may also be heard in federal courts; however, there is no provision for federal diversity jurisdiction in disputes between aliens.[3] Thus, when faced with a dispute within the State of New York, a prospective litigant potentially may bring suit in either the courts of New York or the federal courts located within that state, depending upon whether the jurisdictional requisites for having the case heard in federal court are satisfied.

When diversity cases are heard in the federal courts, the applicable substantive law will typically be the law of the state in which the federal court sits (or the otherwise applicable state law), while the governing procedural law generally will be that of the federal system.[4] The authority of the federal trial courts in New York to grant provisional relief is largely governed by the Federal Rules of Civil Procedure (FRCP), the precedent established by the US Supreme Court, and then the precedents of the US Court of Appeals for the Second Circuit, to the extent not contradicted or overruled by the Supreme Court; however, the authority to order state provisional remedies, which is granted to federal courts through FRCP Rule 64, is governed by the forum state's law. In the state courts of New York the authority to extend provisional relief is governed mostly by the New York Civil Practice Law and Rules (CPLR) (although provisional relief is also available through other New York statutes), the decisions of New York's highest court, the New York Court of Appeals, and the decisions of the Appellate Divisions of New York, again to the extent not contradicted or overruled by the Court of Appeals.

The practical import of the state/federal distinction is diminished in the context of the availability of Mareva-type relief in New York because, as will be seen below, neither the federal nor the New York state courts recognize their ability to grant such relief, under federal or state law. However, the courts or the legislatures of the two separate jurisdictions could conceivably strike divergent paths going forward, with the authorities in one determining that such relief is available while the other holds fast to its denial of such relief. For now, however, the outcome in the federal and New York state courts will be the same: Mareva-type relief is unavailable, but the full panoply of provisional and injunctive remedies under New York state law is available in both court systems.

---

[2] Although disputes under state law between litigants from different states or between an alien and a US litigant can be heard in state court, as can disputes involving federal questions, the defendants in such cases have the right to remove the case to federal court. See 28 U.S.C. § 1441.

[3] See 28 U.S.C. § 1332.

[4] See *Erie R. R. Co. v. Tompkins*, 304 U.S. 64 (1938).

(2) FEDERAL EQUITY JURISDICTION: MAREVA RELIEF UNAVAILABLE UNDER FEDERAL LAW

The perspective of the American federal courts on Mareva-type relief is governed **A1.003** by the case of *Grupo Mexicano de Desarrollo, SA v Alliance Bond Fund, Inc.*[5] In that case, the Supreme Court faced the question of "whether, in an action for money damages, a United States District Court has the power to issue a preliminary injunction preventing the defendant from transferring assets in which no lien or equitable interest is claimed".[6]

This question arose out of a dispute between a Mexican holding company (GMD) issuing unsecured, guaranteed[7] notes to finance its operations and several investment funds (the "respondents") that had purchased $75 million in notes from GMD.[8] GMD fell into serious financial trouble as the Mexican economy worsened and as difficulties on a toll road construction programme GMD had invested in mounted.[9] These financial difficulties cast doubt on whether GMD could continue as a going concern and resulted in GMD being unable to make an interest payment on the notes issued to the respondent investment funds.[10] Efforts to restructure the debt with the respondents failed, and they brought suit on the notes in the US District Court for the Southern District of New York.[11] The respondents sought a preliminary injunction pursuant to Rule 65 of the Federal Rules of Civil Procedure[12] restraining GMD from transferring its only substantial asset—rights to millions of dollars in toll road notes from the Mexican Government—to others for the satisfaction of other debts and obligations.[13]

The district court granted the injunction and the US Court of Appeals for the Second Circuit affirmed. The district court reasoned that GMD's risk of insolvency and its use of the toll road notes to satisfy its Mexican creditors to the exclusion of the respondents meant that any judgment the respondents obtained in the action would be frustrated; thus, the injunction was warranted.[14]

---

[5] 527 U.S. 308 (1999).
[6] *ibid.* at 310.
[7] The Notes were guaranteed by four subsidiaries of GMD. See *ibid.*
[8] *ibid.*
[9] *ibid.*, at 311.
[10] *ibid.*
[11] *ibid.*, at 312.
[12] Rule 65 provides federal courts with the authority to issue preliminary injunctions and temporary restraining orders.
[13] 527 U.S. 308 at 312 (1999).
[14] *ibid.*, at 312–313. Although the respondents had also alleged in their complaint that the assignments of the rights to receive the Toll Road Notes violated the negative pledge clause of the note instrument, the district court's order was not entered on those grounds. Rather, the district court's order was entered "to protect its judgment before the judgment was rendered". *ibid.*, at 315 n.2. Thus on appeal the Supreme Court was not faced with the issue of whether an injunction prohibiting a violation of the negative pledge would have been proper.

Had the propriety of an injunction based on the negative pledge been before the court, it probably would have held that a court cannot enjoin specific performance of a negative pledge where monetary damages would adequately compensate any breach. See, *e.g. Lewis v Rahman*, 147 F. Supp. 2d 225, 238 (S.D.N.Y. 2001) (denying injunctive relief to single-fight boxing promoter where the boxer's breach of his negative covenant obligations was "compensable in money").

A1.004   In an opinion by Justice Scalia, the Supreme Court reversed. Referring to the grant of equity jurisdiction made in the Judiciary Act of 1789,[15] the court emphasised that under this grant, federal courts only have authority to administer in equity suits the principles of the system of judicial remedies that had been devised and were being administered by the English Court of Chancery at the time of the separation of the United States from Great Britain.[16] The court further noted, "[T]he substantive prerequisites for obtaining an equitable remedy as well as the general availability of injunctive relief are not altered by Rule 65 and depend on traditional principles of equity jurisdiction."[17] The question then became, as the court styled it, "whether the relief respondents requested here was traditionally accorded by courts of equity".[18]

After reviewing the relief obtained in the English equitable action known as a "creditor's bill" during the Revolutionary period, the court determined that such relief was not analogous to the relief granted by the lower courts in this case. As the court noted, "a creditor's bill could be brought only by a creditor who had already obtained a judgment establishing the debt".[19] This rule was the product of two equally important principles that remain fundamental ideals in American equity jurisprudence: (1) "the procedural requirement that remedies at law had to be exhausted before equitable remedies could be pursued" and (2) "the substantive rule that a general creditor had no cognizable interest, either at law or in equity, in the property of his debtor, and therefore could not interfere with the debtor's use of that property".[20]

A1.005   The court found that no such relief as fashioned by the district court then existed in England and held that the rule that a judgment establishing the debt was necessary before a court could interfere with the debtor's use of his property governed.[21] Rejecting Justice Ginsburg's suggestion in her dissent that "the grand aims of equity" could accommodate such relief as the respondents sought in this case, the court looked to the words of the English jurist, Justice Blackstone, who wrote:

---

[15] Commentators have suggested that the court should have undertaken an inquiry into whether the All Writs Act, 28 U.S.C. § 1651(a), which provides, "the Supreme Court and all courts established by Act of Congress may issue all writs necessary or appropriate in aid of their respective jurisdictions and agreeable to the usages and principles of law," could serve as the basis for authorising the type of injunctive relief granted by the district court in *Grupo Mexicano*. See, *e.g.* Elizabeth K. Cheung, Note, "Congressmen, the Ball Is in Your Court: *Grupo Mexicano de Desarrollo v Alliance Bond Fund*", 26 J. Legis. 147, 155–156 (2000). The court claims to have engaged in such an analysis by indicating that the determination of the powers granted under the All Writs Act and its predecessor, the Judiciary Act of 1789, are one and the same, that is, the determination of the injunctive authority conferred under both is limited by "what is the usage, and what are the principles of equity applicable in such a case". *Grupo Mexicano*, 527 U.S. at 326 n.8 (quoting *DeBeers Consol. Mines, Ltd v United States*, 325 U.S. 212, 219 (1945)).

[16] *Grupo Mexicano*, 527 U.S. at 318.

[17] *ibid.* at 318–319.

[18] *ibid.* at 319.

[19] *ibid.*

[20] *ibid.*, at 319–20.

[21] *ibid.*, at 321. The court considered, but rejected, two potential exceptions to this principle. The first was the suggested exception in cases of the debtor's insolvency. The court concluded, "that particular exception does not exist". *Ibid.*, at 320 n.4, citing *Pusey & Jones Co. v Hanssen*, 261 U.S. 491, 495–97 (1926). The second potential exception— where the debt was admitted or confessed—was not endorsed by the court, and the court disposed of it by determining that even if such an exception existed, it was inapplicable to the case before it. *Ibid.*, at 320 n.5. The United States as *amicus curiae* argued that there were additional exceptions to this general rule, but the court declined "to speculate upon the existence or applicability to this case of any exceptions". *Ibid.*, at 321.

"It is said, that it is the business of a Court of Equity, in England, to abate the rigor of the common law. But no such power is contended for. Hard was the case of bond creditors, whose debtor devised away his real estate. . . . But a Court of Equity can give no relief . . ."[22]

Thus, while the court agreed that equity is flexible, it determined that such flexibility "is confined within the broad boundaries of traditional equitable relief", which, as its review of extant English approaches revealed, would not permit the restraint of a debtor's assets to secure a money judgment where no lien or equitable interest in the assets were claimed.[23] If the federal courts are to provide such relief, the court wrote, it is up to the US Congress to expand the courts' authority to embrace such power.[24]

The court was bolstered in its view that English courts did not provide the type of relief sought in this case at the time of the First Congress by the fact that the English Court of Chancery itself did not provide such injunctive relief until 1975 in *Nippon Yusen Kaisha v Karageorgis*,[25] "in which Lord Denning recognized the prior practice of not granting such injunctions, but stated that 'the time has come when we should revise our practice.'"[26] The court went on to note that this practice was solidified by the Court of Appeal in *Mareva Compania Naviera SA v International Bulkcarriers SA*,[27] and later by statute.[28] The acknowledgment by Lord Denning and commentators that "the adoption of *Mareva* injunctions was a dramatic departure from prior practice" buttressed the court's argument that American federal courts lacked such authority, which was still bound by the traditional limits of equity from which the English courts had departed.[29]

In the end, it was the court's determination that English Courts of Chancery did **A1.006** not exercise authority to grant Mareva injunctions at the time America was formed that undergirded the court's decision, and thus the courts were not in any position to expand their authority to the abrogation of the core principle that "equity will not, as a general matter, interfere with the debtor's disposition of his property at the instance of a nonjudgment creditor".[30] The court was unwilling itself to

---

[22] 527 U.S. at 321, quoting Joseph Story, 1 Commentaries on Equity Jurisprudence § 12, pp.14–15 (1836).

[23] 527 U.S. at 322. The court made reference to its earlier case of *De Beers Consol. Mines, Ltd v United States*, 325 U.S. 212, 65 S.Ct. 1130 (1945), for statements it made rejecting this type of relief:

"To sustain the challenged order would create a precedent of sweeping effect. This suit, as we have said, is not to be distinguished from any other suit in equity. What applies to it applies to all such. Every suitor who resorts to chancery for any sort of relief by injunction may, on a mere statement of belief that the defendant can easily make away with or transport his money or goods, impose an injunction on him, indefinite in duration, disabling him to use so much of his funds or property as the court deems necessary for security or compliance with its possible decree. And, if so, it is difficult to see why a plaintiff in any action for a personal judgment in tort or contract may not, also, apply to the chancellor for a so-called injunction sequestrating his opponent's assets pending recovery and satisfaction of a judgment in such a law action. No relief of this character has been thought justified in the long history of equity jurisprudence."

Grupo Mexicano, 527 U.S. at 327 (quoting *De Beers*, 325 U.S. at 222–223).

[24] 527 U.S. at 322.

[25] [1975] 2 Lloyd's Rep. 137, CA.

[26] *Grupo Mexicano*, 527 U.S. at 328, n.9 (quoting *Nippon Yusen*, n.25 above, at 138).

[27] [1975] 2 Lloyd's Rep. 509.

[28] See *Grupo Mexicano*, 527 U.S. at 328 (citing Supreme Court Act of 1981, § 37, 11 Halsbury's Statutes 966, 1001 (1991 reissue)).

[29] *Grupo Mexicano*, 527 U.S. at 328.

[30] *ibid.*, at 329.

eliminate "this significant protection for debtors" and work an expansion of courts' equitable powers, choosing instead to "leave[] any substantial expansion of past practice to Congress".[31]

The limits of the court's holding in *Grupo Mexicano* should be enunciated. *Grupo Mexicano* stands for the proposition that the federal courts do not have the power to issue preliminary injunctions freezing a defendant's own *unrelated* assets in order to protect a potential *money judgment*. This holding only prevents general unsecured creditors from gaining any right in a defendant's property before obtaining a final judgment. Creditors possessing a lien or some type of equitable interest in the funds or property at issue remain able to obtain preliminary freezing orders within the federal system.[32] As the *Grupo Mexicano* court emphasized, its statement in *De Beers Consol. Mines, Ltd v United States*[33] remains true: 'A preliminary injunction is always appropriate to grant intermediate relief of the same character as that which may be granted finally.'[34] What this means is that litigants who assert an equitable or lien interest in the assets sought to be frozen are in no way prevented from obtaining a preliminary restraint on those assets under *Grupo Mexicano*.[35]

A1.007   Additionally, the *Grupo Mexicano* decision should not be viewed as paring back federal courts' ability to grant Mareva-type equitable relief where there are statutory bases for doing so. Justice Scalia, writing for the court, indicated the

---

[31] *ibid.*, One commentator remarked on the propriety of deferring consideration of a rule granting federal courts Mareva-type injunctions to the legislative and executive branches of government by stating:

"[T]he likelihood that the proposed rule would have bite in, and perhaps chiefly in, cases involving internationally foreign parties should give pause, prompting further inquiry. If that inquiry revealed either that the matter implicated an existing treaty or that exercises of power under it could, in a predictable class of cases, adversely affect the foreign relations of the United States, the judiciary should abandon the effort as rulemaking and recommend the desired rule as legislation . . . Both the Congress and the President should be involved in making policy choices where the foreign relations implications of procedure are direct and obvious."

Stephen B. Burbank, "The Bitter with the Sweet: Tradition, History, and Limitations on Federal Judicial Power—A Case Study", 75 Notre Dame L.R. 1291, 1337–1338 (2000). Burbank also noted the impact of the Brussels Convention on Britain's ability to support Mareva relief impacting foreign assets: "[T]he United Kingdom is a party to the Brussels Convention, which regulates provisional remedies to some extent and which therefore provides a shared framework, judicial review, and diplomatic cover for the application of such remedies to assets located in other signatory states." *ibid.*, at 1341. To the extent the United States lacks similar treaty commitments the expansion of judicial authority to embrace extraterritorial restraints will be difficult for the judiciary to undertake on its own.
[32] See paras A1.011–A1.013, below.
[33] 325 U.S. 212 (1945).
[34] *Grupo Mexicano*, 527 U.S. at 326 (quoting *De Beers*, 325 U.S. at 220). See also *Rahman v Oncology Assoc. P.C.*, 198 F.3d 489, 496 (4th Cir. 1999) ("[W]hen the plaintiff creditor asserts a cognizable claim to specific assets of the defendant, or seeks a remedy involving those assets, a court may in the interim invoke equity to preserve the status quo pending judgment where the legal remedy might prove inadequate and the preliminary relief furthers the court's ability to grant the final relief requested.").
[35] See, *e.g. Wishnatzki & Nathel, Inc. v H.P. Island-Wide, Inc.*, 2000 WL 1610790, at *1 (S.D.N.Y. Oct. 27, 2000) ("[C]ourts have held that where the particular funds sought to be frozen are also the funds at issue in the suit, a preliminary injunction is proper."); *III Finance Ltd v The Aegis Consumer Funding Grp., Inc.*, No.99 Civ. 2579 (DC), 1999 WL 461808, at *4 n.1 (S.D.N.Y. July 2, 1999) (holding that a creditor seeking to stop the dissipation of its alleged collateral could obtain a preliminary injunction consistent with *Grupo Mexicano*).

authority of Congress to grant the federal courts additional equitable powers through statutes, and noted that they have done so in other contexts such as the tax code and bankruptcy law.[36] Thus, in at least the bankruptcy context, there is statutory authority permitting a court to enter such orders as are necessary during the reorganisation or liquidation of the debtor that remains in place undisturbed by *Grupo Mexicano* and to which litigants may continue to resort as support for such relief, although strictly speaking such authority may not be as broad as *Mareva* relief.[37] More generally, however, because Congress retains the authority to grant courts expanded equitable authority, statutes may grant and courts may exercise such authority unimpaired by the prohibition of *Grupo Mexicano*.[38]

(3) FEDERAL EQUITY JURISDICTION: OBTAINING PROVISIONAL RELIEF IN THE FACE OF *GRUPO MEXICANO*

The *Grupo Mexicano* decision leaves federal court litigants in a difficult position if **A1.008** they are interested in securing an eventual money judgment by freezing the defendant's assets.[39] Although the Supreme Court has foreclosed the availability of such relief in most cases involving money judgments, there are various ways litigants in federal courts can obtain similar relief notwithstanding *Grupo Mexicano*, under certain circumstances.

(i) State law provisional remedies are available via Federal Rule of Civil Procedure 64

Grupo Mexicano involved a determination of the federal courts' authority to issue **A1.009** Mareva-type relief under FRCP Rule 65. That rule governs the authority of federal courts under federal law to fashion preliminary or temporary injunctive relief. A

---

[36] See *Grupo Mexicano*, 527 U.S. at 322 ("Congress is in a much better position than we . . . to design the appropriate remedy . . . The law of fraudulent conveyances and bankruptcy was developed to prevent such conduct . . ."); 527 U.S. at 326 (distinguishing the authority to grant Mareva-type relief in the form of tax injunctions under the Internal Revenue Code from the lack of such authority under the courts' general equitable powers as conferred by the Judiciary Act of 1789; see also, *e.g. Re Stone & Webster, Inc.*, 286 B.R. 532, 538–539 (Bankr. D. Del. 2002) (distinguishing the availability of equitable relief available under the Bankruptcy Code from the general equitable powers of the courts addressed in *Grupo Mexicano*).

[37] See *Adelphia Communications Corp. v Rigas*, Nos 02 Civ. 8495, 02–41729, 2003 WL 21297258, at *4 (S.D.N.Y. July 4, 2003) ("[D]efendants contend that this case involves a substantial and material conflict between non-bankruptcy federal law and Title 11, in that the bankruptcy court's authority to issue a pre-judgment order freezing assets under 11 U.S.C. § 105 conflicts with the United States Supreme Court's decision in *Grupo Mexicano*. This argument has no merit . . . *Grupo Mexicano*'s holding specifically applied to the district courts, and therefore is inapplicable in the bankruptcy context."). Such authority exists in the tax context as well; however, because the plaintiff in such cases will generally be the US Government as the enforcer of federal tax law, this injunctive provision is of little use to ordinary litigants.

[38] See para.A1.015, below for a fuller discussion of this issue.

[39] See, *e.g. Enron Corp. Sec. Lit.*, Nos Civ. A. G-02–0084, H-01–3624, 01–CV-3645, 2002 WL 1001058, at *3 (S.D. Tex. May 16, 2002) (refusing to grant a preliminary injunction restraining "the transfer, release or assignment of Andersen assets to foreign Andersen affiliates" in an effort to preserve the availability of those assets for the satisfaction of a prospective money judgment).

separate rule, Rule 64, gives federal courts the power, in suits seeking monetary damages, to grant any provisional (pre-judgment) relief that is available under the law of the state in which the federal court is located, whether the court's jurisdiction is based on diversity, federal question, or other subject-matter jurisdictional bases.[40] For example, New York Law would govern the grant of provisional remedies such as pre-trial attachment by any of the federal courts located in the state of New York.[41] Thus, if the law of the forum state permits injunctions restraining defendants from dealing with or dissipating unrelated assets pending resolution on the merits in a money judgment action—in other words, Mareva-type relief—then presumably the federal court would be able to provide such relief.[42]

Although Rule 64 would appear to provide a way around the holding of *Grupo Mexicano*—which determined federal courts' authority under Rule 65—there is a major difficulty that virtually eliminates any opportunity that Rule 64 might have presented to obtain Mareva-type relief in New York. The difficulty is that New York law does not permit Mareva relief.[43] As will be discussed further below, although there are specific factual circumstances where a court can grant similar (or superior) relief, in the circumstance of a foreign defendant with no assets within the court's jurisdiction, a New York court does not have the means for restraining that defendant's dealings with its non-New York property wholly unrelated to the action where money damages are being sought. As much was recognized by the federal appeals court ruling reversed by the Supreme Court in *Grupo Mexicano*:

> "All parties acknowledge that [the district court] could not have enjoined the use of the Toll Road Notes under Rule 64 (and New York's injunction statute) because the Investors sought only monetary damages. Under New York law, "a preliminary injunction is . . . unavailable in an action for a sum of money

---

[40] Fed.R.Civ.P. 64. Rule 64 reads, in relevant part:

> "At the commencement of and during the course of an action, all remedies providing for seizure of person or property for the purpose of securing satisfaction of the judgment ultimately to be entered in the action are available under the circumstances and in the manner provided by the law of the state in which the district court is held, existing at the time the remedy is sought . . ."

[41] *Bank Leumi Trust Co. of New York v Istim*, Inc., 892 F. Supp. 478, 481 (S.D.N.Y. 1995) ("New York law governs orders of attachment issued by this Court.") (citing Fed.R.Civ.P. 64).

[42] The Second Circuit has recognized that injunctive relief may be granted under Rule 64 in federal courts if authorized by the applicable state law. See *Alliance Bond Fund, Inc. v Grupo Mexicano*, 143 F.3d 688, 692 (2d Cir. 1998), *rev'd on other grounds*, 527 U.S. 308 (1999); *Inter-Regional Fin. Group, Inc. v Hashemi*, 562 F.2d 152, 154–5 (2d Cir. 1977) (holding that Rule 64 includes Connecticut's pre-judgment remedy of attachment as well as injunctions in aid of attachment). Other circuits have concurred in this view of Rule 64. See *United States v Oncology Associates*, 198 F.3d 489, 500 (4th Cir. 1999) ("The scope of Federal Rule of Civil Procedure 64 incorporates state procedures authorizing any meaningful interference with property to secure satisfaction of a judgment, including any state-authorized injunctive relief for freezing assets to aid in satisfying the ultimate judgment in a case."); *FDIC v Antonio*, 843 F.2d 1311, 1313–1314 (10th Cir. 1988) (utilizing Rule 64 in applying Colorado state law that authorised pre-judgment injunctive relief); *Lechman v Ashkenazy Enterprises, Inc.*, 712 F.2d 327, 330 (7th Cir. 1983) (affirming the grant of a temporary restraining order under Rule 64 because it approximated an attachment and clearly was issued "for the purpose of securing satisfaction of the judgment ultimately to be entered"). However, the ability of the federal courts to grant Mareva-type relief if provided for under the law of the forum state assumes that the Supreme Court will not extend its decision in *Grupo Mexicano* to prohibit federal courts from granting such relief under Rule 64.

[43] See *Credit Agricole Indosuez v Rossiyskiy Kredit Bank*, 708 N.Y.S.2d 26 (2000). See paras A1.017–A1.021, below for a full discussion of this issue.

only." N.Y. C.P.L.R. 6301, Practice Commentaries (McKinney 1980) (Joseph M. McLaughlin) (citing *Campbell v Ernest*, 19 N.Y.S. 123 (1892)). Furthermore, the use of New York's attachment statute would be unavailing because the Toll Road Notes are not located in New York State."[44]

If New York law does not permit Mareva-type relief just as federal law does not, **A1.010** then of what use is Rule 64? The utility of Rule 64 lies solely in its exemption from the harsh prohibition of the *Grupo Mexicano* court; that is, the *Grupo Mexicano* decision was based on an interpretation of the injunctive authority of federal courts under Rule 65. Litigants are thus encouraged to explore fully what state law provisional remedies are available under state law because recourse to those may be had through Rule 64. Although state law may not provide the precise form of relief desired, there is potential for finding provisional relief among state statutes. At paras A1.022 *et seq.*, below, we will explore the relevant provisional remedies available under New York law that may be accessed in the federal system via Rule 64.

(ii) Causes of action pursuing equitable claims may qualify for preliminary injunctive relief

The decision of the court in *Grupo Mexicano* was limited to holding that in the **A1.011** federal system, a general unsecured creditor seeking a money judgment may not preliminarily restrain a defendant from dealing with or dissipating its assets in which no lien or equitable interest is claimed.[45] Thus, in the context of an action involving monetary assets, to the extent that an equitable interest can be claimed in the assets, the *Grupo Mexicano* decision will not impede a court's ability to grant a plaintiff an order enjoining the defendant's disposition of those assets.

An example of a claim that asserts an equitable interest in a specific fund of assets can be found in *Deckert v Independence Shares Corp.*,[46] which was cited approvingly by the court in *Grupo Mexicano*. In *Deckert*, the preliminary injunction restraining the defendant's disposition of its assets was appropriate because the plaintiff stated "a cause of action for the equitable remedies of rescission of the contracts and restitution of the consideration paid . . . Such a bill states a cause of action for equitable relief".[47] Rescission of contract is an equitable action that seeks to render a contract "void in its inception and to put an end to it as though it never were".[48] The remedy of rescission is available when a party is entitled to be relieved of its obligations under a contract on grounds including, but not limited to, fraud in the inducement, mutual mistake, and impossibility.[49] Once the contract is declared void, the claimant may demand repayment of funds paid on account of the contract as further relief; such relief is distinct from an award of damages.[50] Because seeking

---

[44] *Alliance Bond Fund*, 143 F.3d at 693 (citation omitted).
[45] *Grupo Mexicano*, 527 U.S. at 322.
[46] 311 U.S. 282 (1940).
[47] *Grupo Mexicano*, 527 U.S. at 325.
[48] Black's Law Dictionary, 1306 (6th ed., 1990).
[49] See *ibid.*; *Deckert*, 311 U.S. at 289 (holding that a suit to rescind a contract induced by fraud may be maintained in equity); *Hadden v Consolidated Edison Co.*, 356 N.Y.S.2d 249, 257 (N.Y. 1974) (holding that an agreement may be rescinded if it was induced by fraudulent misrepresentation); *Classic Office Supplies, Inc. v Classic Commercial Office Prods, Inc.*, 657 N.Y.S.2d 7, 7 (N.Y. App. Div. 1997) (holding that rescission is proper where the plaintiff relied upon a material misrepresentation in entering the contract).
[50] See *Classic Office Supplies*, 657 N.Y.S.2d at 7.

a return of one's own funds paid in consideration for a voided contract comprises a claim asserting an equitable interest in the funds sought, *Group Mexicano* imposes no barrier to the provisional restraint of such funds pending resolution of the dispute. As the *Grupo Mexicano* court pointed out, "A preliminary injunction is always appropriate to grant intermediate relief of the same character as that which may be granted finally."[51]

A1.012   Similar results should obtain where a plaintiff claims an equitable lien over the assets to be frozen; where the creditor asserts some sort of "equitable lien on the property" an injunction against its dissipation may be appropriate.[52] "An equitable lien is a right to charge specific property or its proceeds with the payment of a particular debt",[53] and arises when a party's efforts or resources have rendered an uncompensated benefit to the property in question such that the holder of that property would be unjustly enriched if restitution were not ordered.[54] When a party seeks to impose an equitable lien over certain property, consistent with *Grupo Mexicano*, dealings with that property can be preliminarily enjoined because an equitable interest is asserted in property to which the plaintiff claims some entitlement.[55]

An action to impose a constructive trust over certain assets is yet another example of an action for equitable relief laying claim to specific assets; as such, the *Grupo Mexicano* decision would not stand in the way of obtaining such relief.[56] A constructive trust can be an appropriate remedy in cases where "property has been acquired in such circumstances such that the holder of the legal title may not in good conscience retain the beneficial interest."[57] More specifically, in order to impose a constructive trust in New York four elements ordinarily must be present: "(1) a confidential or fiduciary relationship, (2) a promise, express or implied, (3) a transfer in reliance thereon, and (4) unjust enrichment."[58] Further, it is generally

---

[51] 527 U.S. at 326 (quoting *De Beers*, 325 U.S. at 220). See also *Rahman v Oncology Assoc. P.C.*, 198 F.3d 489, 496 (4th Cir. 1999) ("[W]hen the plaintiff creditor asserts a cognizable claim to specific assets of the defendant, or seeks a remedy involving those assets, a court may in the interim invoke equity to preserve the status quo pending judgment where the legal remedy might prove inadequate and the preliminary relief furthers the court's ability to grant the final relief requested.").

[52] *Grupo Mexicano*, 527 U.S. at 326.

[53] *Reisner v Stoller*, 51 F. Supp. 2d 430, 453 (S.D.N.Y. 1999) (holding that a woman who paid the initial down payment and all mortgage payments on a property pursuant to a confidential agreement with her paramour who retained title to the property was entitled to an equitable lien against the property in the full amount of her expenditures).

[54] See *ibid.*; Restatement (First) of Restitution § 161 comment a (1936).

[55] *Grupo Mexicano*, 527 U.S. at 326 (distinguishing a claimant asserting an equitable lien from a general unsecured creditor).

[56] See, *e.g. Comcast of Illinois X, LLC v Till*, 293 F. Supp. 2d 936, 942 n.6 (E.D. Wis. 2003) ("A district court is not authorized to freeze a defendant's assets solely to preserve a party's right to recover damages. However, a court may order an asset freeze to preserve a party's right to equitable relief. In the present case, plaintiff requests equitable relief in the form of an accounting and constructive trust.") (citing *Grupo Mexicano*).

[57] *Simonds v Simonds*, 408 N.Y.S.2d 359, 363 (N.Y. 1978). See also Restatement of Law—Restitution 160 (1937) ("Where a person holding title to property is subject to an equitable duty to convey it to another on the ground that he would be unjustly enriched if he were permitted to retain it, a constructive trust arises.").

[58] *Urdang v Kaufman*, 758 N.Y.S.2d 125, 126 (N.Y. App. Div. 2003) (imposing constructive trust over decedent's assets because her son relied on the decedent's promise to bequeath her estate to him if he agreed to forego other professional opportunities). See also *Koslowski v Koslowski*, 747 N.Y.S.2d 583, 585 (N.Y. App. Div. 2002) (stating the constructive trust standard). These four factors are meant to be useful guidelines, not rigid absolutes; the New York Court of Appeals has indicated that such rigidity is inappropriate for courts of equity and that a constructive trust may be imposed "even in the absence of a

necessary to be able to trace one's claimed equitable interest to identifiable property in the hands of the purported constructive trustee.[59] If the property allegedly subject to a constructive trust is not fairly identified as or traceable to the property of the party seeking to impose a constructive trust, courts will decline to recognise such a trust over the property in question.[60]

An example of a situation where a constructive trust could be imposed is where a **A1.013** fiduciary misuses funds belonging to another to purchase a house for himself; the owner of the misused funds can seek to impose a constructive trust on the house to the extent of the misused funds so long as the owner can trace its funds to the funds used to purchase the home.[61]

The only challenge in using a constructive trust theory to assert an equitable interest over specific funds is that a constructive trust ordinarily may not be imposed where only an action for money damages is pleaded because an adequate remedy exists at law.[62] Notwithstanding this general rule, courts have imposed constructive trusts over funds where those funds are traceable to funds in which a plaintiff asserts an equitable interest. For example, in *Simonds v Simonds*,[63] the decedent's first wife had an entitlement, by virtue of a separation agreement, to be named as the beneficiary of the decedent's life insurance policies to the extent of $7,000. When, upon his death, the decedent's policies did not name his first wife as a beneficiary, the court affirmed the imposition of a constructive trust over the insurance proceeds that were paid out to the decedent's second wife and daughter, notwithstanding that they had legal title to the proceeds by operation of the policies.[64]

In light of *Simonds*, although a damages remedy might be available, where the plaintiff can assert an equitable interest in the very funds over which it seeks to impose a constructive trust, courts should be willing to impose a constructive trust because the plaintiff is stating, in effect, "those funds belong to me" rather than "those funds should be held to compensate me for unrelated debts or damages".

---

confidential or fiduciary relation, a promise by the trustee, and a transfer in reliance". *Simonds v Simonds*, 408 N.Y.S.2d at 363 (N.Y. 1978). "A court of equity in decreeing a constructive trust is bound by no unyielding formula." *Ibid.*, at 365.

[59] See *United States v Peoples Benefit Life Ins. Co.*, 271 F.3d 411, 416 (2d Cir. 2001). Although commingling of funds can complicate an effort to trace assets to certain property, such does not prevent tracing by the courts. See *Drexel Burnham Lambert Grp., Inc.*, 142 B.R. 633, 637 (Bankr. S.D.N.Y. 1992). However, once funds dwindle below the purported trust amount, those funds are deemed dissipated and any new funds deposited into a commingled account will not be used to account for any wrongfully held but now dissipated trust assets. See *ibid.* Equity can permit this requirement to be relaxed in limited situations. See *Rogers v Rogers*, 483 N.Y.S.2d 976, 977 (N.Y. 1984). For example, where one has a right to proceeds of an insurance policy that lapses and is replaced by a new insurance policy, the equitable right to proceeds of the original policy will not be defeated merely because that right is not traceable to the new policy. See *ibid.* at 978 (explaining that the "inability to trace plaintiff's equitable rights precisely should not require that they not be recognized") (citation omitted).

[60] See *Peoples Benefit*, 271 F.3d at 416.

[61] *Mid-Valley Produce Corp. v 4-XXX Produce Corp.*, 833 F. Supp 193, 196 (E.D.N.Y. 1993).

[62] See Restatement of Law—Restitution 160, comment e ("[W]here money is paid by one person to another as a result of a mistake of such a character that the payor is entitled to restitution, he is ordinarily not entitled to maintain a suit in equity for the specific recovery of the money."). The Restatement recognises an exception to this general rule in the case of an insolvent constructive trustee. See *ibid.*, comment f.

[63] 408 N.Y.S.2d 359.

[64] *ibid.*, at 361.

(iii) Preliminary freezing orders are available when asserting a fraudulent conveyance

A1.014 One of the strongest exceptions to the prohibition of *Grupo Mexicano* lies in the area of fraudulent conveyances.[65] Fraudulent conveyances is an area that the *Grupo Mexicano* court expressly indicated was outside of its holding; indeed, the court indicated that it was rejecting the requested injunctive authority in part because of the existence of the law of fraudulent conveyances as the appropriate source of such relief.[66]

The fraudulent conveyances exception to the prohibition of *Grupo Mexicano* was specifically addressed in *Trafalgar Power, Inc. v Aetna Life Ins. Co.*[67] There, the creditor filed a claim to collect on notes serving as collateral for a debt. Then, in a separate action, the creditor sought to set aside as fraudulent a transfer—occurring during the pendency of the first claim—of a tort judgment that the debtor obtained against third parties.[68] The creditor sought a preliminary injunction freezing the debtor's assets pending adjudication of the fraudulent conveyance claims and the court granted the injunction.[69] In upholding the magistrate judge's grant of the injunction, the district court held that such injunctive relief was available notwith-standing *Grupo Mexicano*. Finding that case to be clearly distinguishable, the court noted that a fraudulent conveyance claim seeks equitable relief, *i.e.* to "restrain the defendant from disposing of his property".[70] Because the "request for preliminary injunctive relief is thus rooted in the ultimate equitable relief to which [the creditor] is entitled under Debtor and Creditor Law 279," the court was empowered to grant such preliminary relief under FRCP Rule 65.[71]

The federal rules explicitly permit the joining of a claim for money damages and a claim to set aside a fraudulent conveyance "without having first obtained a judgment establishing the claim for money".[72] Creditors asserting fraudulent conveyance claims thus are in a strong position—once an actual conveyance is made—to curtail the further dissipation of assets and to bring transferred assets back within the reach of an eventual money judgment.[73] Fraudulent conveyances under New York law will be discussed in greater detail below.

(iv) Some federal statutes provide courts with expanded injunctive powers

A1.015 *Grupo Mexicano* addressed federal courts' authority to grant injunctions pursuant to the general equitable powers of federal courts under the Judiciary Act of 1789.[74] The court indicated that Congress has the ability to give federal courts expanded

---

[65] A fraudulent conveyance claim permits a creditor to seek to reverse a conveyance of a debtor deemed to be fraudulent under the relevant state law. Creditors who bring such actions typically may obtain an order restraining the debtor's further transfer of assets and seek to avoid (reverse) those transfers that have already occurred. The topic of fraudulent conveyances under New York Law is more fully discussed at para.A1.028, below.

[66] See *Grupo Mexicano*, 527 U.S. at 322 ("The law of fraudulent conveyances and bankruptcy was developed to prevent such conduct; an equitable power to restrict a debtor's use of his unencumbered property before judgment was not.").

[67] 131 F. Supp. 2d 341 (N.D.N.Y. 2001).

[68] *ibid.*, at 343.

[69] *ibid.*, at 344.

[70] *ibid.*, at 350.

[71] *ibid.*

[72] Fed. R. Civ. P. 18.

[73] However, if the transferees cannot be brought within the jurisdiction of the court, those transfers that have already occurred may be unavoidable. See, *e.g. Koehler v Bank of Bermuda, Ltd*, 2002 WL 1766444, at *5 (S.D.N.Y. July 31, 2002). This makes it critical to catch any transfers early on to prevent the assets from getting out of reach.

[74] See *Grupo Mexicano*, 527 U.S. at 318.

equitable powers and has done so in several instances, including in the areas of bankruptcy and federal income taxation (and possibly in the securities law area).[75] Thus, where a litigant's cause of action arises under a federal statute, the provisions of that statute should be consulted for language giving expanded equitable authority to the court.

The two statutes alluded to by the court that provide expanded equitable authority—the injunction provisions of the Bankruptcy Code and the Internal Revenue Code—illustrate the type of language litigants should look for as providing expanded equitable authority. The bankruptcy provision provides, "The court may issue *any* order, process, or judgment that is necessary or appropriate to carry out the provisions of this title."[76] This language has been interpreted to give bankruptcy courts much greater equitable powers than have been traditionally accorded to federal courts in general.[77] Similarly, the injunction provision in the Internal Revenue Code provides a clear grant of expanded equitable powers:

"The district courts . . . shall have such jurisdiction to make and issue . . . writs and orders of injunction . . . and such other orders and processes . . . as may be necessary or appropriate for the enforcement of the internal revenue laws. The remedies hereby provided are *in addition to* and not exclusive of any and all other remedies of the United States in such courts or otherwise to enforce such laws."[78]

Whether a given provision is meant to be a Congressional grant of expanded **A1.016** injunctive powers will depend primarily on the statute's language and case law and secondarily on the legislative history. Provided the courts have not previously interpreted whether a particular injunctive provision in a federal statute provides expanded injunctive authority, litigants are encouraged to look to whatever federal statute is at issue in their case for possible authority for obtaining Mareva-type relief.[79]

---

[75] *ibid.* at 322, 325, 326; see also *United States v First Nat. City Bank*, 379 U.S. 378 (1965) (upholding a tax injunction issued under the Internal Revenue Code); *Deckert v Independence Shares Corp.*, 311 U.S. 282 (1940) (upholding injunction issued under the Securities Act).

[76] 11 U.S.C. 105 (emphasis added).

[77] See, *e.g. Adelphia Communications Corp. v Rigas*, Nos 02 Civ. 8495, 02–41729, 2003 WL 21297258, at *4 (S.D.N.Y. July 4, 2003) ("Section 105 of Title 11 provides the bankruptcy courts with a broad range of equitable powers over cases within its jurisdiction . . . The bankruptcy court, therefore, may issue a pre-judgment order preventing a party from disposing of assets."); *Re Stone & Webster, Inc.*, 286 B.R. 532, 538–539 (Bankr. D. Del. 2002) (distinguishing the availability of equitable relief available under the Bankruptcy Code from the general equitable powers of the courts addressed in *Grupo Mexicano*).

[78] 26 U.S.C. § 7402 (emphasis added).

[79] Arguing that a particular federal statute other than the two alluded to by the Supreme Court embodies a grant of expanded injunctive authority will be quite difficult because most injunctive provisions in federal statutes only grant courts jurisdiction to grant injunctions, "according to the principles of equity". See, *e.g.* 15 U.S.C. § 1116(a) (trade mark statute); 35 U.S.C. § 283 (patent statute). The Supreme Court in *Grupo Mexicano* undertook to define the parameters of the principles of equity, and determined that they do not include the power of general unsecured creditors to restrain a debtor's assets pre-judgment. See *Grupo Mexicano*, 527 U.S. at 322 (stating that in the federal system "the broad boundaries of traditional equitable relief" serve as a limit to courts' equitable powers); *ibid.*, at 326 n.8 (noting that the inquiry the court is engaging in involves a consideration of "what are the principles of equity").

(4) PROVISIONAL REMEDIES IN NEW YORK STATE COURTS: MAREVA RELIEF
UNAVAILABLE UNDER NEW YORK STATE LAW

A1.017   The New York Court of Appeals did not hesitate in the wake of *Grupo Mexicano* to
re-emphasise that the sort of provisional relief rejected by the Supreme Court in
that case was similarly unavailable under New York state law. In *Credit Agricole
Indosuez v Rossiyskiy Kredit Bank*[80] the Court of Appeals affirmed the notion that in
New York, unsecured creditors have no right to interfere with defendants' property
through use of a preliminary injunction when they are seeking money damages.

The plaintiffs in *Credit Agricole* were three foreign banking institutions suing on
unsecured debts totaling $30 million of defendant Rossiyskiy Kredit Bank, a
Russian banking institution.[81] Due to financial difficulties, Rossiyskiy defaulted on
an interest payment, which prompted the plaintiffs to exercise their right to
accelerate the entire principal and interest on the debt securities.[82] In bringing suit,
the plaintiffs set forth two causes of action on the debts and a separate cause of
action alleging that Rossiyskiy, as an insolvent company,[83] owed a fiduciary duty to
preserve assets for the benefit of general creditors and that Rossiyskiy had breached
that duty by transferring its principal assets to another Russian bank, Impexbank.[84]
The plaintiffs moved for an order of attachment and a preliminary injunction
against Rossiyskiy's further transfer of assets.[85]

The trial court granted the plaintiffs both provisional remedies, with the
preliminary injunction prohibiting defendants from "(1) dissipating, transferring,
conveying or otherwise encumbering their assets and (2) taking steps in furtherance
of [Rossiyskiy's] alliance with Impexbank."[86] The Appellate Division affirmed the
provisional remedy in all respects.[87]

A1.018   The New York Court of Appeals reversed the order affirming the grant of the
preliminary injunction. Beginning with the language of the statute governing the
grant of preliminary injunctions, the court quoted CPLR 6301—the New York
statutory provision governing the grant of injunctions—as stating,

"A preliminary injunction may be granted in any action where it appears that
the defendant threatens or is about to do, or is doing . . . an act in violation
of the plaintiff's rights respecting the *subject of the action*, and tending to
render the judgment ineffectual, or in any action where the plaintiff has
demanded and would be entitled to a judgment restraining the defendant from
the commission or continuance of an act, which, if committed or continued
during the pendency of the action, would produce injury to the plaintiff."[88]

The subject of the action in this instance was deemed to be the debt sued upon,
with plaintiffs standing as "unsecured contract creditors, whose ultimate objective is

---

[80] 708 N.Y.S.2d 26 (N.Y. 2000).
[81] *ibid.*, at 27.
[82] *ibid.*
[83] Although insolvent, Rossiyskiy was apparently not at that time subject to bankruptcy
protection. Had Rossiyskiy enjoyed such protection, a stay might have been issued pursuant
to the bankruptcy which would likely have protected it against the attachment sought.
[84] *ibid.*
[85] See *ibid.* In New York, an order of attachment is a provisional remedy granted under
certain limited circumstances in civil actions that freezes a defendant's New York assets, up
to the amount sought by the plaintiff, pending litigation of the case. See CPLR § 6201; see
para.A1.023, below.
[86] 708 N.Y.S.2d at 27.
[87] See *Credit Agricole Indosuez v Rossiyskiy Kredit Bank*, 697 N.Y.S.2d 273, 274 (N.Y. App.
Div. 1999).
[88] *Credit Agricole*, 708 N.Y.S.2d at 28 (quoting N.Y. C.P.L.R. § 6301) (emphasis supplied by
the court).

attaining an enforceable money judgment".[89] Dismissing the plaintiffs' third cause of action seeking injunctive relief on a fiduciary duty theory, the court described that action as merely "incidental to and in aid of the monetary relief [the plaintiffs] seek".[90] So construed, the court had no difficulty enunciating and adhering to its "consistent[] refus[al] to grant general creditors a preliminary injunction to restrain a debtor's asset transfers that allegedly would defeat satisfaction of any anticipated judgment."[91]

In articulating this principle, the Court of Appeals discussed earlier cases in which **A1.019** this rule took its early shape. Starting with the early case of *Campbell v Ernest*,[92] the *Credit Agricole* court pointed out that in *Campbell* the plaintiffs were concerned that the defendant would dispose of his property during the pendency of the action and sought injunctive relief under CPLR 6301's predecessor, § 604(2) of the Code of Civil Procedure to enjoin any such disposition. The *Campbell* court held that s.604(2) did not apply "to an action of this character, where a moneyed judgment only is sought".[93] As the *Campbell* court explained.

> "In no proper or legal sense can a defendant do or permit any act in violation of the plaintiff's rights respecting the subject of the action, in an action on contract for the recovery of money only. The plaintiff in such an action has no rights as against the property of the defendant until he obtains a judgment, and until then he has no legal right to interfere with the defendant in the use and sale of the same."[94]

The *Credit Agricole* court then noted that the US Supreme Court had recently reached the same conclusion in *Grupo Mexicano*, wherein Justice Scalia writing for the court cited early New York authority—*Wiggins v Armstrong*—for support for the rule: "The reason of the rule seems to be, that until the creditor has established his title, he has no right to interfere, and it would lead to an unnecessary, and, perhaps, a fruitless and oppressive interruption of the exercise of the debtor's rights."[95] The *Credit Agricole* court also cited a long line of New York cases since *Wiggins* that uniformly followed the precept of *Campbell v Ernest*, both before and after the enactment of the CPLR.[96]

The plaintiffs' effort to avoid the application of the *Campbell* rule through the **A1.020** pleading of an equitable claim was rejected outright by the *Credit Agricole* court as too contrived. The court reiterated its position that the third cause of action was purely for the purposes of enforcement of the primary relief sought, a money judgment. If an exception were made in such an instance, the court wrote, there "would be too facile a way to avoid and undermine the settled proscription against preliminary injunctions merely to preserve a fund for eventual execution of judgment in suits for money damages".[97] Next, because the plaintiffs were general unsecured creditors, the court noted that they had no rights in the debtor's unencumbered property, and thus the debtor's disposal of such property could not

[89] 708 N.Y.S.2d 6 at 28.
[90] *ibid.*
[91] *ibid.*
[92] 19 N.Y.S. 123 (N.Y. Gen. Term 1896).
[93] *ibid.*, at 125.
[94] *ibid.*
[95] *Grupo Mexicano*, 527 U.S. at 320 (quoting *Wiggins v Armstrong*, 2 Johns Ch. 144, 145–146).
[96] See *Credit Agricole*, 708 N.Y.S.2d at 29 (citing *Eastern Rock Prods. v Natanson*, 269 N.Y.S. 435 (1933); *Babho Realty Co. v Feffer*, 245 N.Y.S. 118 (1930); *First Natl. Bank v Highland Hardwoods*, 471 N.Y.S.2d 360 (1983); *Fair Sky Int'l Cable Ride Corp.*, 257 N.Y.S.2d 351 (1965)).
[97] *Credit Agricole*, 708 N.Y.S.2d at 30.

produce any cognizable injury to the plaintiffs such that could support a temporary injunction.[98] Finally, the court stated that the plaintiffs' reliance on the so-called "trust fund doctrine" by which fiduciaries of an insolvent corporation are said to hold the corporate assets in trust for the benefit of its general creditors was misplaced because that doctrine "does not automatically create an actual lien or other equitable interest as such in corporate assets upon insolvency".[99] The court went on to state that general contract creditors may not invoke the doctrine until they have "exhausted legal remedies by obtaining judgment on the debt and having execution returned unsatisfied".[1]

As a final point, the *Credit Agricole* court echoed Justice Scalia's comments regarding the appropriate entity empowered to alter the landscape of equitable rules to accommodate the type of relief that plaintiffs sought by stating that the New York state legislature, rather than the Court of Appeals, would have to act to achieve such an innovation of "far-reaching impact on the existing balance between debtors' and creditors' rights".[2]

A1.021   As with the court in *Grupo Mexicano*, the *Credit Agricole* court refused to give ground on the notion that a general unsecured creditor has no rights in the unencumbered property of a debtor prior to obtaining a judgment. Such rights can be granted by statute, as has been done in the context of CPLR 6201, which creates the attachment remedy for use against New York assets,[3] in certain circumstances discussed below, in support of an action for money damages. Indeed, the court in *Credit Agricole* left undisturbed the lower court's affirmance of the attachment order obtained by the plaintiffs.[4] Of course, the attachment order was limited in its reach to New York assets and thus was of no utility in restraining the Russian defendants from dissipating foreign assets. Such an outcome is not disturbing to the New York Court of Appeals; because it has long been held that a general unsecured creditor has no rights in a debtor's assets prior to obtaining a judgment, there is no perceived or actual harm to the rights of such creditors when their debtors dissipate their assets.[5] It is of no moment that the creditor's judgment may be meaningless as it faces the absence of debtor resources upon which to execute; New York courts and the US Supreme Court have determined that the balance of power between debtors and creditors would be unduly disturbed in favour of unsecured creditors if they were permitted to tie up debtors' resources on a mere preliminary showing of a right to money damages.

What must be understood, then, is the near absolute prohibition against the issuance of preliminary injunctive relief in the circumstances covered by a Mareva injunction in England: where a general unsecured creditor seeks money damages through litigation[6] and asserts no equitable interest in the debtor's property, that creditor may not obtain a preliminary injunction restraining the defendant from dealing with or dissipating its assets.[7]

---

[98] *ibid.*

[99] *ibid.*, at 31.

[1] *ibid.*

[2] *ibid.*, at 32.

[3] See para.A1.025, below for a discussion of what constitutes New York property.

[4] The Appellate Division's affirmance of the attachment order was not appealed. See 708 N.Y.S.2d at 27.

[5] *ibid.* at 30.

[6] As will be discussed below, parties pursuing arbitration may have access to Mareva-type relief from New York courts pending *arbitration* (see para.A1.031, below).

[7] It should be noted that although the New York Court of Appeals rejects the authority of New York state courts to grant Mareva injunctions, New York courts do not find them so offensive that they would refuse to recognise an English money judgment that had been previously secured by a Mareva injunction. See *CIBC Mellon Trust Co. v Mora Hotel Corp.*

(5) New York provisional remedies approximating Mareva-type relief

Having determined that New York law does not afford general unsecured creditors **A1.022** the ability to obtain injunctive relief against defendants preventing them from dissipating unrelated assets prior to judgment, it becomes important to consider the provisional remedies that New York courts are authorised to dispense, with the aim of mapping out where New York may provide relief that is tantamount in its effect to Mareva-type relief and where the law of New York leaves some gaps in that regard.

(i) Pre-judgment attachment

Attachment, provided for under Art.62 of the CPLR, comes to mind as the most **A1.023** analogous form of relief offered by New York courts that achieves virtually the same ends as a Mareva injunction, with several important limitations. As David Siegel, the pre-eminent exponent of New York state civil practice and procedure, defines it, "Attachment seizes the defendant's property and prevents the defendant from using it during the pendency of a money action unless the defendant discharges the attachment with a bond."[8] More specifically, to be eligible for an attachment, a litigant must be pursuing a money judgment action and satisfy one of the five subdivisions of CPLR 6201. The three principal subdivisions pertaining to provisional relief in civil actions are as follows:

> "1. the defendant is a nondomiciliary residing without the state, or is a foreign corporation not qualified to do business in the state; or
> 2. the defendant resides or is domiciled in the state and cannot be personally served despite diligent efforts to do so; or
> 3. the defendant, with intent to defraud his creditors or frustrate the enforcement of a judgment that might be rendered in plaintiff's favor, has assigned, disposed of, encumbered or secreted property, or removed it from the state or is about to do any of these acts;"[9]

NV, 762 N.Y.S.2d 5, 10 (N.Y. 2003) (enforcing an English money judgment where Mareva injunctions had been issued during the pendency of the proceedings in England). This position results from the fact that New York courts will uphold foreign orders issued within a system of law that comports with "the requirements of due process of law", see N.Y. CPLR 5304(a)(1), which unquestionably includes the English system, "considering that our own jurisprudence is based on England's", *CIBC Mellon*, 762 N.Y.S.2d at 10. The enforcement of foreign country money judgments in New York is governed by Art.53 of the New York CPLR. It appears, however, that US federal and state courts may not be in a position to enforce a Mareva injunction issued by an English court because "[t]he violation of the *Mareva* Injunction . . . is an offense against the issuing court that is punishable with contempt and sanctions rather than an act that gives rise to an independent cause of action . . . ": *Citadel Management, Inc. v Telesis Trust, Inc.*, 123 F. Supp. 2d 133, 153 (S.D.N.Y. 2000).
[8] David D. Siegel, N.Y. Prac. 306 (3d ed., 1999). It should be noted that in matrimonial actions, the remedy of sequestration rather than attachment is available to serve the same purpose as an attachment. N.Y. Domestic Relations Law 233. Indeed, sequestration has become synonymous with attachment in that the body of law applying to one has been deemed to apply to both. See *Chapman v Chapman*, 339 N.Y.S.2d 404, 407 (N.Y. Fam. Ct. 1972) ("[T]he separate bodies of law applying to sequestration and attachment respectively have been held to apply to both, thus rendering, at least in judicial reasoning, both remedies to be synonymous.").
[9] N.Y. CPLR 6201. Subdivision 4 of § 6201 provides for an attachment remedy for plaintiffs representing victims of crime pursuing money damages against persons convicted of those crimes; subdivision 5 provides for an attachment where a judgment creditor seeks to enforce a foreign money judgment in New York.

Under subdivision 1 a plaintiff need only demonstrate that the defendant is a non-domiciliary of New York or an unregistered non-New York corporation in order to qualify for an attachment order; no demonstration of intent to defraud need be shown. Subdivision 2 concerns defendants who are New York residents, but who cannot be personally served; plaintiffs have to demonstrate, generally through an affidavit, that diligent efforts were made to effect service in order to qualify for an attachment under this subdivision.[10]

Under subdivision 3 of § 6201, which also concerns New York residents, a plaintiff must demonstrate that a fraudulent intent to avoid the effect of a judgment actually exists in the defendant's mind.[11] Mere suspicion of an intent to defraud is not enough.[12] Similarly insufficient is a showing of the actual removal or assignment or other disposition of property in the absence of a showing with respect to the defendant's intent.[13]

A1.024   Once one of these provisions is satisfied, to obtain an attachment order the applicant will have to demonstrate a likelihood of success on the merits of the underlying cause of action and will have to post a bond to secure the defendant against any damages arising from a wrongful attachment.[14] Practitioners should note that there is no right to a grant of attachment; the granting of an attachment under CPLR 6201 is discretionary, meaning that the court may still deny an attachment even if the grounds for granting it exist.[15] Although strictly speaking there is no requirement of demonstrating irreparable harm, because the granting of an attachment order is viewed as a harsh remedy and it is within the court's discretion to grant or deny an attachment, a plaintiff should seek to convince the court that the attachment is needed for security.[16]

The seizure of a defendant's property subject to an attachment is effected by levy, whereby the sheriff of the county where the property is located takes constructive or sometimes actual possession of the property under the terms of the attachment order.[17] While the order is in effect, the defendant is deprived of all use of any property seized.

An attachment thus can provide some level of security, insuring the availability of assets for satisfaction of an eventual money judgment. Attachment not only serves a security function, but it can have a jurisdictional function as well; attachment can

---

[10] See, *e.g. Executive House Realty v Hagen*, 438 N.Y.S.2d 174, 177 (N.Y. Sup. Ct. 1981) ("The affidavits and other exhibits demonstrate that Ronald Hagen could not be personally served despite diligent efforts.").

[11] See *Computer Strategies, Inc. v Commodore Business Machines, Inc.*, 483 N.Y.S.2d 716, 721 (N.Y. App. Div. 1984).

[12] *ibid.*

[13] *ibid.*

[14] See N.Y. CPLR § 6212.

[15] See N.Y. CPLR § 6201 ("An order of attachment *may* be granted") (emphasis supplied); See *Elliott Associates v Republic of Peru*, 948 F. Supp. 1203, 1211 (S.D.N.Y. 1996) ("The granting of prejudgment attachments pursuant to CPLR §§ 6201 and 6212 is discretionary with the district courts, and even when the statutory requisites are met, the order may be denied.") (citations omitted); *Sartwell v Field*, 68 N.Y. 341, 342 (1877) (indicating that whether an attachment should be ordered rests within the discretion of the court hearing the motion). Such discretion may be exercised if the court determines there is an insufficient need for the attachment, see, e.g. Elliott Associates, 948 F. Supp. at 1212, or if the equities suggest that the party seeking attachment is not deserving of such an order, see *Drexel Burnham Lambert Inc. v Ruebsamen*, 525 N.Y.S.2d 184, 185 (N.Y. Sup. Ct. 1988) (applying doctrine of unclean hands) *Interpol Bermuda Ltd v Trinidad and Tobago Oil Co. Ltd*, 513 N.Y.S.2d 598, 604–605 (N.Y. Sup. Ct. 1987) (citing plaintiff's lack of diligence in pursuing the action).

[16] See, *e.g. General Textile Printing & Processing Corp. v Expromtorg Int'l Corp.*, 862 F. Supp. 1070, 1073–1074 (S.D.N.Y. 1994).

[17] N.Y. CPLR §§ 6214, 6215, 6216.

be used, under limited circumstances, in New York to secure quasi *in rem* jurisdiction[18] against a defendant in a money action.[19]

At first glance, the attachment remedy appears to mirror the relief that a Mareva **A1.025** injunction delivers. However, there is an important limitation to an attachment: it can only operate against property of the defendant located within the state's territory.[20] This is because to be attachable, property must be within the jurisdiction of New York courts, and property sited outside of New York lies beyond the jurisdiction of New York state courts.[21] Within this limitation, attachable property of the defendant includes all property, personal or real, tangible or intangible, that could be assigned or transferred, "whether it consists of a present or future right or interest and whether or not it is vested, unless it is exempt from application to the satisfaction of the [eventual] judgment".[22] Debts owed to the defendant are also attachable, provided the debt is due as a certainty either on demand or eventually resulting from the passage of time.[23]

Although the New York situs of real property may be readily ascertained, the situs of property consisting of deposited funds, debts, and intangible property has required determination by the courts. Regarding deposited bank funds, New York

---

[18] Quasi *in rem* jurisdiction refers to personal jurisdiction obtained over the defendant personally on the basis of, and only to the extent of, property of that defendant located within the jurisdiction of the court. See *Black's Law Dictionary*, 1245 (6th ed., 1990). Per *Shaffer v Heitner*, 433 U.S. 186 (1977), there must be a connection between the property and the subject-matter of the action. See *ibid.*, at 207.

[19] Siegel, above, n.8, para.A1–023, above, at § 306.

[20] See *ABKCO Indus., Inc. v Apple Films, Inc.*, 385 N.Y.S.2d 511, 512 (1976); *Re Nat'l Life Ins. Co. of Pittsburgh v Advanced Employment Concepts, Inc.*, 703 N.Y.S.2d 3, 4 (N.Y. App. Div. 2002). Professor Siegel suggests based on *Starbare II Partners, L.P. v Sloan*, 629 N.Y.S.2d 23 (N.Y. App. Div. 1995), which held that a judgment debtor within the personal jurisdiction of New York courts could be ordered to deliver out-of-state property to the sheriff, that so long as the property is in the control of someone in New York, it is attachable no matter where it may be found because, as he states, "the same property that is applicable to a judgment [is] applicable as well to a prejudgment attachment". David D. Siegel, 95 *Siegel's Practice Review*, p.1 (May 2000). Professor Siegel's analysis may not be followed by New York courts for two reasons. First, the attachment statute does not make all property that is applicable to a judgment applicable to a pre-judgment attachment. CPLR 6202 only incorporates CPLR 5201 and thereby limits attachable property to property and debts described therein (CPLR 5201 delineates the debt or property subject to enforcement of a money judgment in New York). In *Starbare*, the ability to reach the property in question was based on CPLR 5225, which is not incorporated by CPLR 6202 (CPLR 5225 provides for orders against judgment debtors to deliver property in their possession for the satisfaction of judgments). Secondly, the apparent reasoning of *Starbare* was that because the judgment debtor was within the jurisdiction of New York courts, he could be ordered to deliver property he owned regardless of location, an order which is more in the nature of an injunction rather than an attachment. That is, such an order operated against the person of the judgment debtor, not his property; an attachment operates against property and is not capable of compelling the delivery of non-New York property. Indeed, any attempt to transform the type of post-judgment order condoned in *Starbare* to a provisional order against a defendant would be to create the very sort of order prohibited by *Credit Agricole* and *Grupo Mexicano*.

[21] See *Shaffer v Heitner*, 433 U.S. 186, 197 (1977) ("'[N]o State can exercise direct jurisdiction and authority over persons or property without its territory.'") (quoting *Pennoyer v Neff*, 95 U.S. 714, 722 (1878)).

[22] N.Y. CPLR §§ 5201(b), 6202.

[23] N.Y. CPLR 6202, 5201(a). Where a debt does not meet the requirements of 5201(a), it may be possible to view the debt as property under § 5201(b). The right to receive payment under a contract is considered property rather than debt where the duty to pay is conditioned upon contractual contingencies. See *Glassman v Hyder*, 296 N.Y.S.2d 783, 786 (N.Y. 1968); *ABKCO Indus.*, 385 N.Y.S.2d at 513.

adheres to the so-called separate entity rule, which holds that each bank branch is a separate entity and thus in order to reach a particular bank account, the branch of the bank where the account is maintained must be served.[24] Thus, funds are sited in the location of the branch where the account is maintained, meaning that if a non-New York bank happens to have a branch in New York, funds maintained in the bank's non-New York branches are not attachable in New York.[25] Debt owed to a defendant is located where the debtor may be found.[26] Where a defendant has interests arising under a contract, the situs of such intangible property is determined by the location of the other party to the agreement upon whom rests the obligation of performance.[27]

A1.026   If an attachment order is granted a plaintiff may obtain a court order requiring the defendant to disclose the location or extent of its assets, or whether such assets exist. This order to disclose in aid of attachment is authorised under CPLR § 6220, which makes available to the court any disclosure device contained in Art.31 of the CPLR, "if the court finds the device appropriate or helpful to reveal the nature or whereabouts of the defendant's property".[28]

Attachment orders may be sought and obtained *ex parte*. If an attachment is granted, then within five days (within 10 if granted under subdivision 1) after execution of the attachment order the plaintiff must seek confirmation of the order from the court, with notice and an opportunity to be heard being given to the defendant.[29]

With these aspects of the remedy in full view, the utility of the attachment order to the litigant seeking Mareva-type relief becomes clear. Where a defendant has significant assets located within New York, a plaintiff may freeze those assets pending litigation provided the plaintiff can demonstrate satisfaction of one of the subdivisions of CPLR 6201. Under such circumstances, the plaintiff can obtain relief that is virtually identical to a Mareva injunction. Unfortunately, there will be many situations where a plaintiff either cannot satisfy one of the subdivisions of CPLR 6201 or more likely where the defendant will not have significant New York

---

[24] See *McCloskey v Chase Manhattan Bank*, 228 N.Y.S.2d 825, 825 (N.Y. 1967); *Therm-X Chem. & Oil Corp. v Extebank*, 444 N.Y.S.2d 26, 27 (N.Y. App. Div. 1981).

[25] *Nat'l Union Fire*, 703 N.Y.S.2d at 4. Courts have recognised a minor exception to the separate entity rule, holding that service upon a bank's main branch will suffice to attach funds deposited at another branch of the bank provided the main office and branch where the account is maintained are within the same jurisdiction (New York) and the bank branches are connected to the main office by high-speed computers and are under its centralised control. See *ibid*. (citing *Limonium Maritime, SA v Mizushima Marinera, S.A*, 961 F. Supp. 600, 607 (S.D.N.Y. 1997).

[26] *Harris v Balk*, 198 U.S. 215 (1905), *overruled on other grounds, Shaffer v Heitner*, 433 U.S. 186 (1977); *Lenchyshyn v Pelko Elec. Inc.*, 723 N.Y.S.2d 285, 291 (N.Y. App. Div. 2001); Siegel, above n.8, para.A1.023, at § 104.

[27] ABKCO Indus., 385 N.Y.S.2d at 513.

[28] Siegel, above, n.8, para.A.023, at § 324.

[29] See N.Y. CPLR § 6211(b). A prompt post-attachment hearing is one of the safeguards that can render an *ex parte* attachment procedure in compliance with the Due Process Clause of the Fourteenth Amendment to the US Constitution. See *North Georgia Finishing, Inc. v Di-Chem, Inc.*, 419 U.S. 601, 607 (1975); *Mitchell v W. T. Grant Co.*, 416 U.S. 600, 618 (1974). Such a hearing is merely one component of protecting due process; in the absence of other procedural safeguards such as the requirement to show extraordinary circumstances or the posting of a bond, a post-attachment hearing will not save an attachment statute from running afoul of the requisites of due process. See *Connecticut v Doehr*, 501 U.S. 1, 4 (1991).

sited assets. Where that is the case, the attachment remedy is of little use[30] and other strategies will have to be pursued to secure the defendant's assets against dissipation.

Indeed, it should be noted that attachment is a disfavoured remedy, in derogation **A1.027** of the common law, and thus it is not readily given to qualifying plaintiffs as a matter of course. To the contrary, courts heavily scrutinise attachment requests and deny them if plaintiffs fail to make sufficient showing of need.

The difficulty of obtaining an attachment is illustrated by *Computer Strategies, Inc. v Commodore Bus. Machines, Inc.*[31] In *Computer Strategies*, Commodore claimed as collateral to a distributorship agreement the inventory that its distributor, Computer Strategies, had in its possession. When Computer Strategies defaulted on its payment obligations under the agreement, Commodore initiated an action on the debt and obtained an *ex parte* order of attachment on the grounds that Computer Strategies, a company under the jurisdiction of New York, was removing its inventory in an effort to deprive Commodore of recourse to it for satisfaction of any eventual judgment in violation of subdivision 3 of the attachment statute. When Computer Strategies moved to vacate the *ex parte* order, the court granted the motion and vacated the attachment. The appellate division upheld the vacatur of the attachment order because Commodore had failed to provide sufficient evidentiary support for its claims regarding Computer Strategies' fraudulent intentions *and* because Commodore had failed to demonstrate a probability of success on the merits of its claim.[32] Commodore's evidence of fraud was insufficient because it had submitted affidavits alleging only a suspicion of fraud without proffering evidence that a fraudulent intent actually existed on the part of Computer Strategies. Commodore failed to demonstrate its likelihood of success on the merits because Computer Strategies had asserted an equally meritorious counterclaim that could wholly defeat Commodore's claim.

(ii) Preliminary restraint in aid of a fraudulent conveyance claim

A fraudulent conveyance claim permits a creditor to seek to reverse a conveyance **A1.028** of a debtor deemed to be fraudulent under New York's Debtor and Creditor Law.[33] Under New York law, a plaintiff does not have to reduce its claim to a judgment to stand as a creditor who may avail itself of the right to set aside a

---

[30] One commentator encapsulated this situation aptly by writing:

> "[A]n attachment applies only within New York. Thus, a plaintiff might be able to attach the defendant's New York assets, but has little relief with respect to assets that are located outside of New York. Short of bringing multiple actions in different jurisdictions, such a plaintiff can well find that by the time the judgment is entered on the underlying claim in New York, the defendant's assets outside of New York have been transferred away. New York provisional remedies appear to be of little help to prevent such a result."

Paul H. Aloe, "1999–2000 Survey of New York Law: Civil Practice", 51 Syracuse L.R. 247, 269 (2001) (footnote omitted).
[31] 483 N.Y.S.2d 716 (N.Y. App. Div. 1984).
[32] *ibid.* at 721.
[33] The provisions of New York's Debtor and Creditor Law are based upon, and also referred to as, the Uniform Fraudulent Conveyance Act. See *Shelly v Doe*, 671 N.Y.S.2d 803, 806 (N.Y. App. Div. 1998); *State v First Investors Corp.*, 592 N.Y.S.2d 561, 568 (N.Y. Supr. 1992).

conveyance as fraudulent. Thus, a plaintiff can proceed with a fraudulent conveyance claim solely on the strength of its status as a plaintiff in its main cause of action.[34]

The importance of the ability to bring a fraudulent conveyance claim lies in the array of provisional remedies that may be obtained in aid of such a claim. These remedies are as follows:

1. a preliminary injunction preventing the defendants from further disposing of their property;

2. the appointment of a receiver to take charge of the property;

3. a court order setting aside those transfers that have already occurred; or

4. any other relief that the circumstances of the case may require.[35]

The first of these remedies turns out to be tantamount to Mareva relief, rendering it a truly powerful tool for the plaintiff once available. Because New York law expressly provides for fraudulent conveyance claims and the attendant provisional remedies, *Credit Agricole* serves as no barrier to obtaining this extraordinary relief.

To make a fraudulent conveyance claim a transfer undertaken by the defendant must be shown to be fraudulent,[36] which generally requires demonstrating "actual intent" to "to hinder, delay, or defraud either present or future creditors".[37] However, because actual intent is difficult to prove by direct evidence, the creditor in a fraudulent conveyance action is allowed to rely on "badges of fraud" to support its claim for actual fraud, *i.e.* circumstances so commonly associated with fraudulent transfers that their presence gives rise to an inference of intent.[38] Among such circumstances are:

1. a close relationship between the parties to the alleged fraudulent transaction;

2. a questionable transfer not in the usual course of business;

3. inadequacy of the consideration;

4. the transferor's knowledge of the creditor's claim and the inability to pay it;

5. retention of control of the property by the transferor after the conveyance.[39]

A1.029   Also, there are circumstances in which a transfer is deemed to be fraudulent without need for an actual fraudulent intent including (1) if the transferor is made insolvent or left undercapitalised by the transfer, and the conveyance is made without fair consideration, it is considered fraudulent under the statute without regard to intent;[40] and (2) no fraudulent intent need be shown after a judgment is

---

[34] See *Cablevision Systems Dev. Co. v Annasonic Elec. Supply*, No. CV-83–5159, 1984 WL 254933, at *3 (E.D.N.Y. June 24, 1984); *Bernheim v Burden*, 1 N.Y.S.2d 689, 690 (N.Y. App. Div. 1938).

[35] N.Y. Debtor and Creditor Law § 279.

[36] *Ibid.*; see *Greene v East Side Ominbus Corp.*, 84 N.Y.S.2d 484, 485 (N.Y. App. Div. 1948).

[37] N.Y. Debtor and Creditor Law 276. Plaintiffs prevailing on fraudulent conveyance claims who demonstrate actual fraudulent intent are entitled to attorneys' fees. See *Heimbinder v Berkovitz*, 670 N.Y.S.2d 301, 306 (N.Y. Supr. 1998) (citing *Polkowski v Mela*, 532 N.Y.S.2d 159, 161 (N.Y. App. Div. 1988)).

[38] *Wall Street Associates v Brodsky*, 684 N.Y.S.2d 244, 247 (N.Y. App. Div. 1999); *Shelly*, 671 N.Y.S.2d at 806.

[39] 684 N.Y.S.2d 244, at 248.

[40] N.Y. Debtor and Creditor Law §§ 273, 274.

entered and returns unsatisfied.[41] Although there is no requirement that the intent to defraud be the sole or primary purpose of a transfer in order to be deemed fraudulent, courts will consider the defendant's evidence of alternative legitimate explanations for why the transfer occurred.[42]

In order to obtain a preliminary order restraining a defendant from disposing of its property during the pendency of the prosecution of a fraudulent conveyance claim a plaintiff would have to demonstrate (1) irreparable harm in the event that an injunction is not granted and (2) either (a) a likelihood of success on the merits or (b) sufficiently serious questions going to the merits to make them a fair ground for litigation and a balance of hardships tilting in favour of the plaintiff.[43] Importantly, the likelihood of success on the merits showing relates to the merits of the fraudulent conveyance claim rather than the merits of any principal cause of action that a plaintiff may be pursuing.[44] That is, if a fraudulent conveyance claim is brought by a plaintiff in an existing action in order to challenge the wrongful dissipation of assets pending the first action, the merits inquiry in the fraudulent conveyance case only touches on whether a fraudulent conveyance occurred, not whether the merits of the principal case favour the plaintiff. Thus, whereas such a merits showing might be difficult with regard to the principal cause of action, making a showing of likelihood of success respecting a fraudulent conveyance is a less onerous task, particularly if it is clear that the defendant is attempting to render itself judgment-proof.

Although a litigant may not initially be able to get a Mareva-type injunction or an **A1.030** attachment order, in the event that asset transfers occur during the litigation, the fraudulent conveyance action and its accompanying set of provisional remedies enable a plaintiff to prevent future transfers and undo those that have already occurred. Indeed, it is difficult to demonstrate that a given transfer is fraudulent, particularly if the defendant is sophisticated in its methods; however, if a convincing argument demonstrating fraud can be made, the ability to obtain what is in effect a Mareva injunction is quite powerful.

In sum, although this approach requires awaiting an initial transfer on the part of a defendant, the power of asserting a fraudulent conveyance lies in the ability to get wide-sweeping injunctive relief akin to a Mareva injunction. Once an initial fraudulent transfer takes place, the potential restraint on a defendant's further dealings with its assets is complete and extends to all of its assets wherever they are located. Litigants desirous of obtaining a preliminary restraint on their adversary's assets but who are unable to qualify for other provisional relief should focus attention on identifying any transfers that do occur as fraudulent.

(iii) Injunctive relief in aid of arbitration

Both federal and New York state law adopt a policy of promoting the arbitration of **A1.031** disputes where the parties have agreed to submit their disputes to arbitration. Under the Federal Arbitration Act and the New York CPLR parties can move courts to stay any judicial proceedings concerning disputes that are subject to an agreement to arbitrate.[45] In the context of arbitration, the question becomes the

---

[41] N.Y. Debtor and Creditor Law § 273-a.
[42] See, *e.g. First Fidelity Bank, NA v Manzo*, 673 N.Y.S.2d 196, 197 (N.Y. App. Div. 1998) (considering, and rejecting, defendant's claims that there was in fact consideration for the transfer at issue).
[43] *Pashaian v Eccelston Properties, Ltd*, 88 F.3d 77, 85 (2d Cir. 1996); *Blum v Schlegel*, 18 F.3d 1005, 1010 (2d Cir. 1994).
[44] See, *e.g. Daley v Related Companies, Inc.*, 581 N.Y.S.2d 758, 761–2 (N.Y. App. Div. 1992).
[45] See 9 U.S.C. 3 (Federal Arbitration Act); N.Y. SPLR 7503(a).

extent to which provisional relief is available—either from the courts or from the arbitrators—and whether the scope of relief available differs in any respect from that ordinarily available to parties within a traditional litigation context.

Depending upon the body of rules that parties adopt in the event that they arbitrate their disputes, provisional relief pending the arbitration of a matter may be available from the arbitration panel itself. The rules of both the American Arbitration Association[46] and the International Court of Arbitration of the International Chamber of Commerce[47] provide arbitrators with the authority to grant "interim measures" of any kind deemed appropriate. Federal courts recognise this authority and treat arbitrators' orders granting interim relief as final awards subject to judicial review and confirmation.[48] It is less clear whether New York state courts treat the interim awards of arbitrators as final and confirmable although there is some indication that they might.[49] The availability of judicial review of provisional remedies issued by arbitrators—at least in federal courts and perhaps in New York courts—strengthens their effect because once such orders are confirmed by a court, a judgment is entered which is enforceable in the same manner as other judgments of the courts.

CPLR § 7502(c) authorises courts themselves to order the provisional remedies of attachment or a preliminary injunction in connection with an arbitrable

---

[46] The American Arbitration Association's rules provide:

"(a) The arbitrator may take whatever interim measures he or she deems necessary, including injunctive relief and measures for the protection or conservation of property and disposition of perishable goods.

(b) Such interim measures may take the form of an interim award, and the arbitrator may require security for the costs of such measures.

(c) A request for interim measures addressed by a party to a judicial authority shall not be deemed incompatible with the agreement to arbitrate or a waiver of the right to arbitrate."

American Arbitration Association, Commercial Arbitration Rules and Mediation Procedures, Rule R-34.

[47] The International Court of Arbitration's rules provide:

"Unless the parties have otherwise agreed, as soon as the file has been transmitted to it, the Arbitral Tribunal may, at the request of a party, order any interim or conservatory measure it deems appropriate. The Arbitral Tribunal may make the granting of any such measure subject to appropriate security being furnished by the requesting party. Any such measure shall take the form of an order, giving reasons, or of an Award, as the Arbitral Tribunal considers appropriate."

International Court of Arbitration, Rules of Arbitration, Art.23.1.

[48] See *Yonir Technologies, Inc. v Duration Sys., Ltd.* 244 F. Supp. 2d 195, 204 (S.D.N.Y. 2002) ("[E]quitable awards involving the preservation of assets related to the subject of arbitration are generally considered 'final' arbitral awards subject to judicial review."). Federal courts will only have jurisdiction over arbitrable disputes between citizens of the United States that otherwise could be heard in the federal courts on the basis of an independent grant of jurisdiction or where the dispute concerns property located outside of the United States or has some other reasonable relation with foreign states. See 9 U.S.C. §§ 4, 202; see also para.A1.002, above (brief discussion of the bases for federal court jurisdiction). Federal courts may hear actions on arbitration agreements not between citizens of the United States. See 9 U.S.C. §§ 204, 205.

[49] Compare *Kings Park Classroom Teachers Ass'n v Kings Park Central Sch. Dist.*, 474 N.Y.S.2d 816, 817 (N.Y. App. Div. 1984) (indicating a confirmation of an interim arbitration award by the N.Y. trial court, but reversing the judgment on the ground that the arbitrator exceeded its power), with *Condell v Shanker*, 542 N.Y.S.2d 387, 388 (N.Y. App. Div. 1989) (indicating that the N.Y. trial court denied an application to confirm an arbitration award "on the ground that it was an interim award and, therefore, not final").

controversy.[50] This provision applies only to domestic arbitrations–that is, arbitrations not subjects to an international convention arbitrated in the United States.[51] Under the terms of the statute, "the sole ground for the granting of the remedy shall be as stated above", which refers to the statement that an application for attachment or injunction may be entertained "only upon the ground that the award to which the applicant may be entitled may be rendered ineffectual without such provisional relief".[52]

The major question presented by this language is whether the general equitable **A1.032** criteria for the granting of injunctive relief—*i.e.* showing a likelihood of success, irreparable harm, and a balance of the equities in the applicant's favour—apply to determinations of whether to grant provisional relief in the arbitration context, notwithstanding that the statute seems to suggest that the only consideration should be the effectiveness of the award.

There is a split of authority on this question.[53] Although some decisions have indicated that this language precludes reference to the equitable standards of likelihood of success and irreparable harm embodied in CPLR Art.63,[54] other cases have determined that New York courts "apply the general criteria governing the

---

[50] See N.Y. CPLR § 7502(c). The text of the provision reads as follows:

"The supreme court in the county in which an arbitration is pending, or, if not yet commenced, in a county specified in subdivision (a), may entertain an application for an order of attachment or for a preliminary injunction in connection with an arbitrable controversy, but only upon the ground that the award to which the applicant may be entitled may be rendered ineffectual without such provisional relief. The provisions of articles 62 and 63 of this chapter shall apply to the application, including those relating to undertakings and to the time for commencement of an action (arbitration shall be deemed an action for this purpose) if the application is made before commencement, except that the sole ground for the granting of the remedy shall be stated above. The form of the application shall be as provided in subdivision (a)."

[51] See *Contichem LPG v Parsons Shipping Co., Ltd*, 229 F.3d 426, 432 (2d Cir. 2000) ("Rule 7502(c) . . . is limited to domestic arbitrations.").

[52] See N.Y. CPLR § 7502(c).

[53] See Robert L. Haig, 2 N.Y. Prac., Commercial Litigation in New York State Courts § 14.5 (2002) ("New York case law continues to be ambivalent regarding the issue of whether a party seeking a preliminary injunction under CPLR § 7502 must satisfy the traditional three-prong test for preliminary injunctive relief."); James M. Wicks and Jennifer M. Mone, "Courts Differ on Standard Applicable When Parties in Arbitration Cases Seek Provisional Remedies", 72 N.Y. St. B.J. 35 (September 2000) ("When courts in New York are asked to authorize provisional remedies in aid of arbitration, some apply a traditional three-prong test . . . Others, however, consider only whether the ultimate arbitration award may not be effective if the remedy is not granted.").

[54] See, *e.g.* *H.I.G. Capital Management, Inc. v Ligator*, 650 N.Y.S.2d 124, 125 (N.Y. App. Div. 1996) (holding that the standard articulated in § 7502 "is the sole applicable standard"); *Guarini v Severini*, 650 N.Y.S.2d 4–5 (N.Y. App. Div. 1996) ("[U]nder CPLR 7502(c), the only consideration in deciding whether to grant a preliminary injunction is whether the award to which the applicant may be entitled may be rendered ineffectual without such provisional relief."); *Nat'l Telecommunications Ass'n, Ltd v Nat'l Telecommunications Ass'n, Inc.* 592 N.Y.S.2d 591, 591 (N.Y. App. Div. 1993) ("In arguing that petitioner has failed to demonstrate irreparable harm and a probability of success on the merits, respondent would have this Court adopt an inappropriate standard for deciding whether relief should be granted under CPLR 7502(c)."); *County Natwest Sec. Corp. USA v. Jesup Josephthal & Co.*, 579 N.Y.S.2d 376, 376–377 (N.Y. App. Div. 1992); *Int'l Union of Operating Eng'rs, Local No. 463 v City of Niagara Falls*, 743 N.Y.S.2d 236, 239 (N.Y. Sup. Ct. 2002).

issuance of injunctive relief to an application for a preliminary injunction under CPLR 7502(c)".[55]

The latter position incorporating the general equitable criteria appears to be the slightly more accepted view in New York, because the most recent decision of the First Department of the Appellate Division has adopted this view. Also, commentators support this view, arguing that while the ineffectiveness of the arbitration award may be the sole ground for supporting relief, that is distinct from and does not limit "the procedural conditions that may apply when such ground is established", such conditions being the traditional equitable considerations.[56] Indeed, the United States Court of Appeals for the Second Circuit has adopted this position with respect to New York law, holding that § 7502(c) incorporates the equitable criteria traditionally required for granting of preliminary injunctive relief and even suggested that due process required as much.[57] This decision of the Second Circuit along with the fact that the federal rules govern procedure in the federal courts means that the traditional equitable criteria will need to be satisfied in order to obtain provisional relief in aid of arbitration in federal court in New York.[58]

A1.033   To the extent that the balance of viewpoints tips toward the idea that the traditional equitable standards of likelihood of success and irreparable harm are embodied in § 7502(c), parties pursuing arbitration will face challenges as they attempt to restrain their opponents' dealings with their assets pending arbitration. Were the contrary and more lenient[59] interpretation of § 7502(c) more prevalent— that is, the view that the only criterion for obtaining an injunction in aid of arbitration is that any arbitration award would be "rendered ineffectual without such provisional relief"—parties would be able to obtain injunctions freezing the assets of their adversaries, *i.e.* Mareva-type relief, during the pendency of the arbitration proceedings, provided they could show that absent such a freeze they would not be able to collect on any future arbitration award.

This is precisely what occurred in *H. I. G. Capital Mgmt, Inc. v Ligator.*[60] In *H.I.G. Capital* the applicant sought to enjoin the dissipation of its adversary's assets in an effort to thwart collection upon any potential arbitration award. The trial court granted the injunction, restraining the respondent from transferring assets in the amount of $7,000,000.[61] The appellate court held that the imposition of the restraint was proper, reasoning that "[t]he uncontrolled disposal of respondents' assets . . . might render an award ineffectual".[62] Because, as noted above, the court

---

[55] *Cullman Ventures, Inc. v Conk*, 682 N.Y.S.2d 391, 396 (N.Y. App. Div. 1998). See also *Erber v Catalyst Trading*, LLC, 754 N.Y.S.2d 885, 885 (N.Y. App. Div. 2003) ("Contrary to petitioner's argument, the criteria for provisional relief set forth in CPLR articles 62 and 63 are not relaxed when such relief is sought in aid of arbitration pursuant to CPLR 7502(c).").

[56] Vincent C. Alexander, Practice Commentaries, McKinney's Cons Laws of NY, C.P.L.R. C7502:6 [1998].

[57] *SG Cowen Sec. Corp. v Messih*, 224 F.3d 79, 83 (2d Cir. 2000). Prior to *SG Cowen*, one New York federal court took the contrary view, that "under N.Y. CPLR 7502(c) . . . the standards generally applicable to attachments under CPLR articles 62 and 63 do not apply". Kidder, *Peabody & Co. Inc. v Int'l Acceptance Grp.*, 94 Civ. 4725 (CSH), 1999 U.S. Dist. LEXIS 132, at * 6 (S.D.N.Y. Jan. 13, 1999).

[58] See *AIM Int'l Trading, LLC v Valcucine SpA.*, 188 F. Supp. 2d 384, 386 n.4 (S.D.N.Y. 2002).

[59] The authors of one article noted, "[r]equiring applicants in an arbitration context to show only that an arbitration award could be rendered ineffectual without the remedy is a far more lenient test". Wicks and Mone, above, n.53, para.A1.032 at 35.

[60] 650 N.Y.S.2d 124 (N.Y. App. Div. 1996).

[61] *ibid.*, at 125.

[62] *ibid.*

viewed the potential ineffectiveness of an arbitration award as the "sole applicable standard" for granting injunctive relief in aid of arbitration, the court had no difficulty concluding that the restraint against the dissipation of assets was appropriate.[63]

H. I. G. Capital has not been repudiated by the New York Court of Appeals, **A1.034** notwithstanding contrary interpretations of § 7502(c) by the same Department (First) of the Appellate Division subsequently in *Cullman Ventures, Inc. v Conk*[64] and other decisions.[65] Indeed, the issue apparently has not been presented for resolution to the Court of Appeals because the lower courts supporting the minority view tend to issue their holdings on alternative grounds in the event that the traditional equitable standards are determined to apply.[66] The issue is likely to remain unresolved until a party seeks and obtains an injunction in aid of arbitration solely on the ground that the award would otherwise be ineffectual, without reference to the traditional equitable criteria for the grant of injunctive relief.

In the meantime, until the Court of Appeals or the New York State legislature decides the matter, parties remain free—at least in New York State courts—to argue that the traditional equitable standards do not apply to applications for provisional relief in aid of arbitration.[67]

(6) Conclusion

This Appendix makes it clear that although both federal and state courts in New **A1.035** York are prohibited from granting Mareva relief, there is a range of approaches within both court systems that in many instances can be undertaken to obtain similar levels of security.

In the federal system, the critical avenues for circumventing the prohibition of *Grupo Mexicano* include the use of state provisional remedies through FRCP Rule 64; the casting of one's claim in equitable as opposed to legal terms; the assertion of a fraudulent conveyance claim in the event the defendant begins to dissipate its assets; and the use of injunctive provisions in certain federal statutes potentially providing expanded equitable authority to federal courts. Within New York state courts, the key provisional remedies are attachment and the preliminary restraint that can accompany a fraudulent conveyance claim. Additionally, subject to the legal uncertainty discussed above, parties pursing arbitration in the United States will also have access to preliminary injunctive relief that could restrain their adversary's assets pending arbitration.

Each of these approaches in both systems is highly dependent on the facts of each individual case and whether the court will view artful equitable pleading of what is

---

[63] *ibid.* (but the court stated that even if the CPLR, Art.63 standard was applicable, the relief granted was within the court's discretion), *cf. County Natwest Sec. Corp. USA v Jesup Josephthal & Co.*, 579 N.Y.S.2d 376, 376–377 (N.Y. App. Div. 1992) (permitting attachment of opponent's New York assets under § 7502(c) without reference to the standards of CPLR 6201).

[64] 682 N.Y.S.2d 391, 396 (N.Y. App. Div. 1998).

[65] See, *e.g. Erber v Catalyst Trading, LLC*, 754 N.Y.S.2d 885, 885 (N.Y. App. Div. 2003).

[66] See, *e.g. Int'l Union of Operating Eng'rs, Local No. 463 v City of Niagara Falls*, 743 N.Y.S.2d 236, 239 (N.Y. Sup. Ct. 2002) (after granting a preliminary injunction in aid of arbitration by stating "the only issue is whether an arbitration award would be 'rendered ineffectual' but for the preliminary injunction", the court also found that "even if the traditional equity requirements are applicable to the injunctive relief under article 75" the injunctive relief would still be appropriate). *cf. H.I.G. Capital Mgmt, Inc.*, 650 N.Y.S. 2d at 125.

[67] See, *e.g.* 217 *Second Avenue LLC v J. P. Friedman & Associates, Inc.*, N.Y. Law Journal, April 17, 2000, p.26, col. 6 (Sup. Ct. N.Y. County; Figueroa, J.).

in effect a money damages claim as too contrived. Indeed, the most solid ground for obtaining Mareva relief appears to be the restraint in aid of a fraudulent conveyance claim. This is because once fraud is shown, the permissible restraint on a defendant's dealings with its assets mirrors Mareva relief in virtually all respects. Beyond this area, litigants will face greater challenges as they attempt the other strategies discussed above. An attachment presents challenges because it is limited to New York assets and is quite difficult to obtain. Casting a money damages claim as an equitable one is often impossible to do and can be seen through by courts. Arguing that a particular federal statute provides expanded equitable powers will generally be unsuccessful as most injunctive provisions tie relief to traditional equitable principles, which are arguably what the *Grupo Mexicano* Court determined prohibited federal courts from granting Mareva relief.

A1.036   In the end, it will behoove litigants to think creatively if they are committed to obtaining some provisional restraint on their adversary's assets. Much can be done under the right circumstances.

Saisie conservatoire—historical perspective

French civil procedure was codified in 1806. The Napoleonic Code of Civil **A2.001** Procedure was to a great extent based on pre-revolutionary laws. These did not have any procedure of general application for dealing with the risk that a defendant might dispose of his assets before the claimant could obtain judgment and proceed to execution. There was therefore a serious lacuna in the *Ancien Code.*

Certain conservatory procedures of limited application did exist, however, prior to the Revolution. Pothier's works draw together numerous diverse sources of law and procedure in France before the Revolution, including customary laws of different localities, ordinances and case law. His writings were to have a profound influence on the Napoleonic codes.

Volume 3 of Pothier's *Oeuvres Posthumes* (1778) describes the various *saisies* and modes of execution available at that time. A *saisie-exécution* allowed a creditor to seize the debtor's moveables in order to sell them and pay himself out of the proceeds. A *saisie-arrêt* was meant to prevent dissipation of assets (which Pothier called *détournements)* and enabled a creditor to compel a third party indebted to the debtor to pay the creditor instead. A simple *arrêt* was a notification freezing the debtor's assets in the hands of the debtor or of a third party indebted to the debtor (see pp. 167, 195–196, 202–203).

Pothier also observed (p.195) that under Art.144 of the Statutory Ordinance of **A2.002** Orleans, a claimant was able to obtain permission from a judge to effect a *saisie arrêt* even though the claim was based on a simple promise in dispute.This procedure was a form of pre-judgment attachment. If granted, the *saisie* was at the risk of the claimant—Pothier said it was "aux risque, péril et fortune du créancier" (at the risk, peril and fortune of the claimant creditor).

The customs of Orleans are described in a publication of 1635 by Charles Du Moulin,[1] updating an earlier work of 1568. Under the customs of Orleans there was an *ex parte* procedure of foreign attachment available to residents in the Orleans area against foreigners and travellers who were said to be liable under a contract or promise.[2] Pothier referred to this (at p.203) in his section on simple *arrêts.* The procedure available in Orleans was similar to the procedure of foreign attachment available by custom in the City of London.

Before 1955, a variety of particular *saisies* was available in France under specific **A2.003** articles of the *Ancien Code* of Civil Procedure. These included certain *saisies* which could be obtained *ex parte.* Whilst there were specific types of *saisies-conservatoires,* there was no general regime for conserving a debtor's assets before judgment.

---

[1] *Customs of France*, Vol. I, p.974.
[2] The relevant section number of the customs of the Duchy of Orleans was 442 (shown in the text as ccccxlii).

In Alsace Lorraine, which had its own local code of civil procedure, the position was different. Article 917 provided for a general form of *saisie-conservatoire* when it was feared that unless the relief was granted execution of a judgment might be hindered or made impossible.

In July 1950 reform of conservatory measures in France was discussed at a meeting of lawyers at Chambéry, and a proposed law was subsequently put forward to the National Assembly by M. Maurice Grimaud. This led to the enactment of the Law n° 55–1475 of November 12, 1955 which introduced *Mesures Conservatoires* into the *Ancien Code* of Civil Procedure. These were regulated by Arts 48–57 which were inserted into the Code.[3]

A2.004   Three conservatory procedures were introduced:

(1) *Saisie-conservatoire of general application.* A creditor with a claim that appeared to be grounded could, in case of emergency, ask the court to be authorised to freeze the assets of his debtor temporarily. Then, within a time specified in the order, the creditor had to obtain a judgment in order to convert this *saisie-conservatoire* into an execution of the frozen assets.

(2) *L'inscription de nantissement sur le fonds de commerce du débiteur* (Art.53). This was a temporary lien, authorised by the court, registered against a business of the defendant if the defendant was a merchant registered in the Commercial Register. This temporary lien had to be converted into a definitive registration within a specified time, on the basis of a judgment against the debtor.

(3) *L'inscription d'hypothèque judiciaire sur les immeubles du débiteur* (Art.54). This was a form of temporary lien registered on land, authorised by the court, and also had to be converted into a definitive registration within a specified time.

Despite these improvements, the law of modes of execution still needed a broad reform. This was, to a large extent, achieved with the Law n° 91–650 of July 9, 1991 which aimed to modernise further the modes of execution. It sought to establish a proper balance between the rights of creditors and the legitimate interests of defendants. The Law came into effect on January 1, 1993. By Art.94–2, Arts 48–57 of the *Ancien Code* of Civil Procedure were replaced.

The modernisation was completed by a Decree n° 92–755 of July 31, 1992 which put in place new rules for the application of the principles set out in the Law.

A2.005   A creditor whose debt remains unpaid can now make use of two kinds of procedure: the *mesures d'exécution* and the *mesures conservatoires*. The main distinction between them lies in whether or not a creditor has a "titre executoire".

The *saisies d'exécution* enable a creditor who has an executory title recording "une créance liquide et exigible"—a liquid and exigible debt—to execute on the debtor's assets.

Eight *saisies d'exécution were* introduced into the *Nouveau Code* of Civil Procedure in 1991.

A2.006   The *saisie-attribution* replaced the former *saisie-arrêt,* under which it had not mattered whether the creditor had had a *titre exécutoire.* The new *saisie-attribution* can only be used by a creditor who has a *titre exécutoire* and enables him to compel a third party who is indebted to the debtor to pay the creditor instead. Immediate payment has to be made by the third party directly to the creditor.

Saisie-vente replaced what was formerly accomplished by *saisie- exécution* and, in part, by *saisie-arrêt.* The creditor can seize the debtor's moveables in order to sell them and pay himself out of the proceeds.

---

[3] These numbers in the Code had become vacant in 1949.

The *saisies-appréhension* and *revendication* created by the new Law allow a claimant to recover his property held by the debtor.

Other *saisies d'exécution* apply to specific types of assets. For example, the *saisie des* **A2.007** *rémunérations* enables execution on sums owed to a wage-earner by his employer under a contract of employment, and the *saisie des droits incorporels* applies to intangible assets, such as shares in companies.

A claimant who does not have an executory title recording *une créance liquide et exigible* cannot use the *saisies d'exécution*. But he can ask the court for a *mesure conservatoire*. This can take the form of a *saisie-conservatoire* or a *sûrêté judiciaire* (Arts 67–79 of the new Law and Arts 210–265 of the Decree).

The *sûrêtés judiciaires* are similar to the former *inscription provisoire de nantissement sur le fonds de commerce* and *inscription provisoire d'hypothèque judiciaire sur les immeubles,* and can also be granted over company shares. They are regulated by Arts 77–79 of the new Law and Arts 250–265 of the Decree.

The *saisie-conservatoire* is similar to the *saisie-conservatoire* of the 1955 Law, but **A2.008** the procedure is simplified. It is dealt with in Arts 74–76 of the new Law and Arts 220–249 of the Decree. Article 74 provides that the procedure can be invoked in relation to any moveable property whether tangible or intangible belonging to the defendant, and the order, if made, will prevent dissipation of the assets. It can be granted for any type of debt or claim; *e.g.* for a debt which is not presently due, which is not for a sum certain, or which is disputed and might not succeed. But the creditor must establish a claim which is at least good in principle (*fondée en son principe*[4]), and a risk under (*une menace*) that without the saisie the claim will not be satisfied. There is no requirement of urgency.

The application must be made to the *juge de l'exécution* for authorisation to commence the procedure. The *saisie-conservatoire* has to be successfully enforced within three months of the court order, otherwise it lapses. Also, within one month of enforcement the claimant has to commence substantive proceedings in order to obtain a *titre exécutoire*.

Lord Denning M.R. discussed foreign attachment in his judgment *Rasu Maritima SA v Perusahaan*.[5] That judgment referred to Serjeant Pulling, who wrote of foreign attachments according to the custom in the City of London. Pulling described the custom as being in the form of *saisie-arrêt*. He also referred to Pothier in a footnote on *saisie-arrêts*. However, *saisie-arrêt* was not a procedure limited to foreign defendants or travellers. In fact, foreign attachment in London is more precisely related to the procedure in pre-Revolution France allowed under the customs of Orleans on claims (whether disputed or not) against foreigners or travellers based on a contract or promise.

Lord Denning M.R., in his judgment in the *Pertamina* case, also referred to the **A2.009** decision of the Supreme Court of the United States in *Ownby v Morgan*.[6] The judgment in that case referred to "non resident or absconding debtors . . .", *i.e.* a procedure not of general application but involving a concept similar to that of foreign attachment in the City of London or in accordance with the customs of Orleans.

The historical antecedents which inspired the Mareva procedure have their roots in the customary law of England, France and elsewhere. The need for a procedure to conserve assets pre-judgment led in 1955 to the introduction of *saisie-conservatoire* in France, and 20 years later to the emergence of the Mareva procedure.

---

[4] This can be compared with the requirement in England that there must be a "good arguable case".

[5] [1978] Q.B. 644 at 658 (the *Pertamina* case).

[6] 256 U.S. 94 (1921).

Appendix 3

Statutory materials

Contents

(1) Statutory materials relating to the powers of the court to grant injunctions, appoint receivers, grant a search order and other interim orders in respect of property

Supreme Court Act 1981

Powers of High Court before commencement of action

33.—(1) On the application of any person in accordance with rules of court, the **A3.001** High Court shall, in such circumstances as may be specified in the rules, have power to make an order providing for any one or more of the following matters, that is to say—

    (a) the inspection, photographing, preservation, custody and detention of property which appears to the court to be property which may become the subject-matter of subsequent proceedings in the High Court, or as to which any question may arise in any such proceedings; and

    (b) the taking of samples of any such property as is mentioned in paragraph (a), and the carrying out of any experiment on or with any such property.

Powers of High Court to order disclosure of documents, inspection of documents, etc. in proceedings for personal injuries or death

34. . . .

           A3.002

(3) On the application, in accordance with rules of court, of a party to any proceedings, the High Court shall, in such circumstances as may be specified in the rules, have power to make an order providing for any one or more of the following matters, that is to say—

(a) the inspection, photographing, preservation, custody and detention of property which is not the property of, or in the possession of, any party to the proceedings but which is the subject-matter of the proceedings or as to which any question arises in the proceedings;

(b) the taking of samples of any such property as is mentioned in paragraph (a) and the carrying out of any experiment on or with any such property.

(4) The preceding provisions of this section are without prejudice to the exercise by the High Court of any power to make orders which is exercisable apart from those provisions.

Provisions supplementary to ss.33 and 34

A3.003   35.—(1) The High Court shall not make an order under section 33 or 34 if it considers that compliance with the order, if made, would be likely to be injurious to the public interest.

(2) Rules of court may make provision as to the circumstances in which an order under section 33 or 34 can be made; and any rules making such provision may include such incidental, supplementary and consequential provisions as the rule-making authority may consider necessary or expedient.

(3) Without prejudice to the generality of subsection (2), rules of court shall be made for the purpose of ensuring that the costs of and incidental to proceedings for an order under section 33(2) or 34 incurred by the person against whom the order is sought shall be awarded to that person unless the court otherwise directs.

(4) Sections 33(2) and 34 and this section bind the Crown; and section 33(1) binds the Crown so far as it relates to property as to which it appears to the court that it may become the subject-matter of subsequent proceedings involving a claim in respect of personal injuries to a person or in respect of a person's death.

In this subsection references to the Crown do not include references to Her Majesty in Her private capacity or to Her Majesty in right of Her Duchy of Lancaster or to the Duke of Cornwall.

(5) In sections 33 and 34 and this section—

"*property*" includes any land, chattel or other corporeal property of any description;

"*personal injuries*" includes any disease and any impairment of a person's physical or mental condition.

Powers of High Court with respect to injunctions and receivers

A3.004   37.—(1) The High Court may by order (whether interlocutory or final) grant an injunction or appoint a receiver in all cases in which it appears to the court to be just and convenient to do so.

(2) Any such order may be made either unconditionally or on such terms and conditions as the court thinks just.

(3) The power of the High Court under subsection (1) to grant an interlocutory injunction restraining a party to any proceedings from removing from the jurisdiction of the High Court, or otherwise dealing with assets located within that jurisdiction shall be exercisable in cases where that party is, as well as in cases where he is not, domiciled, resident or present within that jurisdiction.

(4) The power of the High Court to appoint a receiver by way of equitable execution shall operate in relation to all legal estates and interests in land; and that power—

(a) may be exercised in relation to an estate or interest in land whether or not a charge has been imposed on that land under section 1 of the Charging

Orders Act 1979 for the purpose of enforcing the judgment, order or award in question; and
  (b) shall be in addition to, and not in derogation of, any power of any court to appoint a receiver in proceedings for enforcing such a charge.
(5) Where an order under the said section 1 imposing a charge for the purpose of enforcing a judgment, order or award has been, or has effect as if, registered under section 6 of the Land Charges Act 1972, subsection (4) of the said section 6 (effect of non-registration of writs and orders registrable under that section) shall not apply to an order appointing a receiver made either—
  (a) in proceedings for enforcing the charge; or
  (b) by way of equitable execution of the judgment, order or award or, as the case may be, of so much of it as requires payment of moneys secured by the charge.

Withdrawal of privilege against incrimination of self or spouse in certain proceedings

72.—(1) In any proceeding to which this subsection applies a person shall not be **A3.005** excused, by reason that to do so would tend to expose that person, or his or her spouse, to proceedings for a related offence or for the recovery of a related penalty—
  (a) from answering any question put to that person in the first-mentioned proceedings; or
  (b) from complying with any order made in those proceedings.
(2) Subsection (1) applies to the following civil proceedings in the High Court, namely—
  (a) proceedings for infringement of rights pertaining to any intellectual property or for passing off;
  (b) proceedings brought to obtain disclosure of information relating to any infringement of such rights or to any passing off; and
  (c) proceedings brought to prevent any apprehended infringement of such rights or any apprehended passing off.
(3) Subject to subsection (4), no statement or admission made by a person—
  (a) in answering a question put to him in any proceedings to which subsection (1) applies; or
  (b) in complying with any order made in any such proceedings,
shall, in proceedings for any related offence or for the recovery of any related penalty, be admissible in evidence against that person or (unless they married after the making of the statement or admission) against the spouse of that person.
(4) Nothing in subsection (3) shall render any statement or admission made by a person as there mentioned inadmissible in evidence against that person in proceedings for perjury or contempt of court.
(5) In this section—
"*intellectual property*" means any patent, trade mark, copyright, registered design, technical or commercial information or other intellectual property;
"*related offence*", in relation to any proceedings to which subsection (1) applies, means—
  (a) in the case of proceedings within subsection (2) (a) or (b)—
    (i) any offence committed by or in the course of the infringement or passing off to which those proceedings relate; or
    (ii) any offence not within sub-paragraph (i) committed in connection with that infringement or passing off, being an offence involving fraud or dishonesty;
  (b) in the case of proceedings within subsection (2) (e), any offence revealed by the facts on which the plaintiff relies in those proceedings;

"*related penalty*", in relation to any proceedings to which subsection (1) applies, means—

(a) in the case of any proceedings within subsection (2)(a) or (b), any penalty incurred in respect of anything done or omitted in connection with the infringement or passing off to which those proceedings relate;

(b) in the case of proceedings within subsection (2) (c), any penalty incurred in respect of any act or omission revealed by the facts on which the plaintiff relies in those proceedings.

(6) Any reference in this section to civil proceedings in the High Court of any description includes a reference to proceedings on appeal arising out of civil proceedings in the High Court of that description.

CIVIL PROCEDURE ACT 1997

Power of courts to make orders for preserving evidence, etc

A3.006   7.—(1) The court may make an order under this section for the purpose of securing, in the case of any existing or proposed proceedings in the court—

(a) the preservation of evidence which is or may be relevant, or

(b) the preservation of property which is or maybe the subject-matter of the proceedings or as to which any question arises or may arise in the proceedings.

(2) A person who is, or appears to the court likely to be, a party to proceedings in the court may make an application for such an order.

(3) Such an order may direct any person to permit any person described in the order, or secure that any person so described is permitted—

(a) to enter premises in England and Wales, and

(b) while on the premises, to take in accordance with the terms of the order any of the following steps.

(4) Those steps are—

(a) to carry out a search for or inspection of anything described in the order, and

(b) to make or obtain a copy, photograph, sample or other record of anything so described.

(5) The order may also direct the person concerned—

(a) to provide any person described in the order, or secure that any person so described is provided, with any information or article described in the order, and

(b) to allow any person described in the order, or secure that any person so described is allowed, to retain for safe keeping anything described in the order.

(6) An order under this section is to have effect subject to such conditions as are specified in the order.

(7) This section does not affect any right of a person to refuse to do anything on the ground that to do so might tend to expose him or his spouse to proceedings for an offence or for the recovery of a penalty.

(8) In this section—

"*court*" means the High Court, and

"*premises*" includes any vehicle;

and an order under this section may describe anything generally, whether by reference to a class or otherwise.

(2) Statutory materials relating to privilege against self-incrimination

THEFT ACT 1968

Effect on civil proceedings and rights.

31.—(1) A person shall not be excused, by reason that to do so may incriminate **A3.007** that person or the wife or husband of that person of an offence under this Act—

    (a) from answering any question put to that person in proceedings for the recovery or administration of any property, for the execution of any trust or for an account of any property or dealings with property; or

    (b) from complying with any order made in any such proceedings;

but no statement or admission made by a person in answering a question put or complying with an order made as aforesaid shall, in proceedings for an offence under this Act, be admissible in evidence against that person or (unless they married after the making of the statement or admission) against the wife or husband of that person.

(2) Notwithstanding any enactment to the contrary, where property has been stolen or obtained by fraud or other wrongful means, the title to that or any other property shall not be affected by reason only of the conviction of the offender.

THEFT ACT 1978

Supplementary

5.—. . .   **A3.008**

(2) Sections 30(1) (husband and wife), 31(1) (effect on civil proceedings) and 34 (interpretation) of the Theft Act 1968, so far as they are applicable in relation to this Act, shall apply as they apply in relation to that Act.

(3) Bankers' Books Evidence Act Materials

BANKERS' BOOKS EVIDENCE ACT, 1879

Court or judge may order inspection, &c.

7. On the application of any party to a legal proceeding a court or judge may **A3.009** order that such party be at liberty to inspect and take copies of any entries in a banker's book for any of the purposes of such proceedings. An order under this section may be made either with or without summoning the bank or any other party, and shall be served on the bank three clear days before the same is to be obeyed, unless the court or judge otherwise directs.

BANKING ACT 1979

Section 51(1)   SCHEDULE 6

CONSEQUENTIAL AMENDMENTS

PART I

ENACTMENTS AMENDED

The Bankers' Books Evidence Act 1879 (c.11)

1. For section 9 of the Bankers' Books Evidence Act 1879 (meaning of "bank", **A3.010** "banker", and "bankers' books" for the purposes of that Act) there shall be substituted the following section:—

"Interpretation of "bank" "banker", and "bankers' books"".

9.—(1) In this Act the expressions "bank" and "banker" mean—
  (a) a recognised bank, licensed institution or municipal hank, within the meaning of the Banking Act 1979;
  (b) a trustee savings bank within the meaning of section 3 of the Trustee Savings Banks Act 1969;
  (c) the National Savings Bank; and
  (d) the Post Office, in the exercise of its powers to provide banking services.

(2) Expressions in this Act relating to "bankers' books" include ledgers, day books, cash books, account books and other records used in the ordinary business of the bank, whether those records are in written form or are kept on microfilm, magnetic tape or any other form of mechanical or electronic data retrieval mechanism."

(4) Statutory materials relating to the Brussels Convention, Lugano Convention and the Judgments Regulation and for free standing interim relief in support of other jurisdictions

CIVIL JURISDICTION AND JUDGMENTS ACT 1982

Interim relief and protective measures in cases of doubtful jurisdiction

A3.011   24.—. . .

(1) Any power of a court in England and Wales or Northern Ireland to grant interim relief pending trial or pending the determination of an appeal shall extend to a case where—
  (a) the issue to be tried, or which is the subject of the appeal, relates to the jurisdiction of the court to entertain the proceedings; or
  (b) the proceedings involve the reference of any matter to the European Court under the 1971 Protocol.

(2) [*Applies to Scotland only.*]

(3) Subsections (1) and (2) shall not be construed as restricting any power to grant interim relief or protective measures which a court may have apart from this section.

Interim relief in England and Wales and Northern Ireland in the absence of substantive proceedings

A3.012   25.—(1) The High Court in England and Wales or Northern Ireland shall have power to grant interim relief where—
  (a) proceedings have been or are to be commenced in a Contracting State other than the United Kingdom or in a part of the United Kingdom other than that in which the High Court in question exercises jurisdiction; and
  (b) they are or will be proceedings whose subject-matter is within the scope of the 1968 Convention as determined by Article 1 (whether or not the Convention has effect in relation to the proceedings).

(2) On an application for any interim relief under subsection (1) the court may refuse to grant that relief if, in the opinion of the court, the fact that the court has no jurisdiction apart from this section in relation to the subject-matter of the proceedings in question makes it inexpedient for the court to grant it.

(3) Her Majesty may by Order in Council extend the power to grant interim relief conferred by subsection (1) so as to make it exercisable in relation to proceedings of any of the following descriptions, namely—
  (a) proceedings commenced or to be commenced otherwise than in a Contracting State;
  (b) proceedings whose subject-matter is not within the scope of the 1968 Convention as determined by Article 1;
  (c) [*repealed.*]
(4) An Order in Council under subsection (3)—
  (a) may confer power to grant only specified descriptions of interim relief;
  (b) may make different provision for different classes of proceedings, for proceedings pending in different countries or courts outside the United Kingdom or in different parts of the United Kingdom, and for other different circumstances; and
  (c) may impose conditions or restrictions on the exercise of any power conferred by the Order.
(5) [*Repealed.*]
(6) Any Order in Council under subsection (3) shall be subject to annulment in pursuance of a resolution of either House of Parliament.
(7) In this section "interim relief", in relation to the High Court in England and Wales or Northern Ireland, means interim relief of any kind which that court has power to grant in proceedings relating to matters within its jurisdiction, other than—
  (a) a warrant for the arrest of property; or
  (b) provision for obtaining evidence.

Security in Admiralty proceedings in England and Wales or Northern Ireland in case of stay, etc

26.—(1) Where in England and Wales or Northern Ireland a court stays or **A3.013** dismisses Admiralty proceedings on the ground that the dispute in question should be submitted to the determination of the courts of another part of the United Kingdom or of an overseas country, the court may, if in those proceedings property has been arrested or bail or other security has been given to prevent or obtain release from arrest—
  (a) order that the property arrested be retained as security for the satisfaction of any award or judgment which—
    (i) is given in respect of the dispute in the legal proceedings in favour of which those proceedings are stayed or dismissed; and
    (ii) is enforceable in England and Wales or, as the case may be, in Northern Ireland; or
  (b) order that the stay or dismissal of those proceedings be conditional on the provision of equivalent security for the satisfaction of any such award or judgment.
(2) Where a court makes an order under subsection (1), it may attach such conditions to the order as it thinks fit, in particular conditions with respect to the institution or prosecution of the relevant legal proceedings.
(3) Subject to any provision made by rules of court and to any necessary modifications, the same law and practice shall apply in relation to property retained in pursuance of an order made by a court under subsection (1) as would apply if it were held for the purposes of proceedings in that court.

SCHEDULE 1

TEXT OF 1968 CONVENTION, AS AMENDED

Article 1

A3.014   This Convention shall apply in civil and commercial matters whatever the nature of the court or tribunal. It shall not extend, in particular, to revenue, customs or administrative matters.

The Convention shall not apply to:

(1)   The status or legal capacity of natural persons, rights in property arising out of a matrimonial relationship, wills and succession;

(2)   Bankruptcy, proceedings relating to the winding-up of insolvent companies or other legal persons, judicial arrangements, compositions and analogous proceedings;

(3)   Social security;

(4)   Arbitration.

TITLE II

. . .

SECTION 9

PROVISIONAL, INCLUDING PROTECTIVE, MEASURES

Article 24

A3.015   Application may be made to the courts of a Contracting State for such provisional, including protective, measures as may be available under the law of that State, even if, under this Convention, the courts of another Contracting State have jurisdiction as to the substance of the matter.

TITLE III

RECOGNITION AND ENFORCEMENT

Article 25

A3.016   For the purposes of this Convention 'judgment' means any judgment given by a court or tribunal of a Contracting State, whatever the judgment may be called, including a decree, order, decision or writ of execution, as well as the determination of costs or expenses by an officer of the court.

SECTION 1

RECOGNITION

Article 26

A3.017   A judgment given in a Contracting State shall be recognised in the other Contracting States without any special procedure being required.

Any interested party who raises the recognition of a judgment as the principal issue in a dispute may, in accordance with the procedures provided for in Sections 2 and 3 of this Title, apply for a decision that the judgment be recognised.

If the outcome of proceedings in a court of a Contracting State depends on the determination of an incidental question of recognition that court shall have jurisdiction over that question.

Article 27

A judgment shall not be recognised: **A3.018**
  1. if such recognition is contrary to public policy in the State in which recognition is sought;
  2. where it was given in default of appearance, if the defendant was not duly served with the document which instituted the proceedings or with an equivalent document in sufficient time to enable him to arrange for his defence;
  3. if the judgment is irreconcilable with a judgment given in a dispute between the same parties in the State in which recognition is sought;
  4. if the court of the State of origin, in order to arrive at its judgment, has decided a preliminary question concerning the status or legal capacity of natural persons, rights in property arising out of a matrimonial relationship, wills or succession in a way that conflicts with a rule of the private international law of the State in which the recognition is sought, unless the same result would have been reached by the application of the rules of private international law of that State;
  5. if the judgment is irreconcilable with an earlier judgment given in a non-Contracting State involving the same cause of action and between the same parties, provided that this latter judgment fulfils the conditions necessary for its recognition in the State addressed.

Article 28

Moreover, a judgment shall not be recognised if it conflicts with the provisions of **A3.019** Sections 3, 4 or 5 of Title II, or in a case provided for in Article 59.
  In its examination of the grounds of jurisdiction referred to in the foregoing paragraph, the court or authority applied to shall be bound by the findings of fact on which the court of the State of origin based its jurisdiction.
  Subject to the provisions of the first paragraph, the jurisdiction of the court of the State of origin may not be reviewed; the test of public policy referred to in point 1 of Article 27 may not be applied to the rules relating to jurisdiction.

  [*In the Lugano Convention an additional paragraph is inserted between the second and third paragraphs of this article, which reads: "A judgment may furthermore be refused recognition in any case provided for in Article 54B(3) or 57(4)".*]

Article 29

Under no circumstances may a foreign judgment be reviewed as to its substance.   **A3.020**

Article 30

A court of a Contracting State in which recognition is sought of a judgment given in **A3.021** another Contracting State may stay the proceedings if an ordinary appeal against the judgment has been lodged.
  A court of a Contracting State in which recognition is sought of a judgment given in Ireland or the United Kingdom may stay the proceedings if enforcement is suspended in the State of origin, by reason of an appeal.

SECTION 2

ENFORCEMENT

Article 31

A judgment given in a Contracting State and enforceable in that State shall be **A3.022** enforced in another Contracting State when, on the application of any interested party, it has been declared enforceable there.

However, in the United Kingdom, such a judgment shall be enforced in England and Wales, in Scotland, or in Northern Ireland when, on the application of any interested party, it has been registered for enforcement in that part of the United Kingdom.

CIVIL JURISDICTION AND JUDGMENTS ACT 1982 (INTERIM RELIEF) ORDER 1997

(SI 1997/302)

A3.023   1. This Order may be cited as the Civil Jurisdiction and Judgments Act 1982 (Interim Relief) Order 1997 and shall come into force on 1st April 1997.

A3.024   2. The High Court in England and Wales or Northern Ireland shall have power to grant interim relief under section 25(1) of the Civil Jurisdiction and Judgments Act 1982 in relation to proceedings of the following descriptions, namely—
   (a) proceedings commenced or to be commenced otherwise than in a Brussels or Lugano Contracting State or Regulation State;
   (b) proceedings whose subject-matter is not within the scope of the Regulation as determined by Article 1 of the Regulation.

[*This order came into force on April 1, 1997, and has been amended by the Civil Jurisdiction and Judgments Order 2001, SI 2001/3929.*]

COUNCIL REGULATION NO 44/2001

CHAPTER II—JURISDICTION

SECTION 10—PROVISIONAL, INCLUDING PROTECTIVE, MEASURES

Article 31

a3.025   aPPLIcation may be made to the courts of a Member State for such provisional, including protective, measures as may be available under the law of that State, even if, under this Regulation, the courts of another Member State have jurisdiction as to the substance of the matter.

CHAPTER III—RECOGNITION AND ENFORCEMENT

Article 32

A3.026   For the purposes of this Regulation, "judgment" means any judgment given by a court or tribunal of a Member State, whatever the judgment may be called, including a decree, order, decision or writ of execution, as well as the determination of costs or expenses by an officer of the court.

SECTION 1—RECOGNITION

Article 33

A3.027   1. A judgment given in a Member State shall be recognised in the other Member States without any special procedure being required.

2. Any interested party who raises the recognition of a judgment as the principal issue in a dispute may, in accordance with the procedures provided for in Sections 2 and 3 of this Chapter, apply for a decision that the judgment be recognised.

3. If the outcome of proceedings in a court of a Member State depends on the determination of an incidental question of recognition that court shall have jurisdiction over that question.

Article 34

A judgment shall not be recognised:

A3.028

1. if such recognition is manifestly contrary to public policy in the Member State in which recognition is sought;
2. where it was given in default of appearance, if the defendant was not served with the document which instituted the proceedings or with an equivalent document in sufficient time and in such a way as to enable him to arrange for his defence, unless the defendant failed to commence proceedings to challenge the judgment when it was possible for him to do so;
3. if it is irreconcilable with a judgment given in a dispute between the same parties in the Member State in which recognition is sought;
4. if it is irreconcilable with an earlier judgment given in another Member State or in a third State involving the same cause of action and between the same parties, provided that the earlier judgment fulfils the conditions necessary for its recognition in the Member State addressed.

Article 35

1. Moreover, a judgment shall not be recognised if it conflicts with Sections 3, 4 **A3.029** or 6 of Chapter II, or in a case provided for in Article 72.
2. In its examination of the grounds of jurisdiction referred to in the foregoing paragraph, the court or authority applied to shall be bound by the findings of fact on which the court of the Member State of origin based its jurisdiction.
3. Subject to the paragraph 1, the jurisdiction of the court of the Member State of origin may not be reviewed. The test of public policy referred to in point 1 of Article 34 may not be applied to the rules relating to jurisdiction.

Article 36

Under no circumstances may a foreign judgment be reviewed as to its substance. **A3.030**

Article 37

1. A court of a Member State in which recognition is sought of a judgment given **A3.031** in another Member State may stay the proceedings if an ordinary appeal against the judgment has been lodged.
2. A court of a Member State in which recognition is sought of a judgment given in Ireland or the United Kingdom may stay the proceedings if enforcement is suspended in the State of origin, by reason of an appeal.

(5) Statutory materials relating to transactions defrauding creditors

Insolvency Act 1986

Transactions defrauding creditors

423.—(1) This section relates to transactions entered into at an undervalue; and **A3.032** a person enters into such a transaction with another person if—

    (a) he makes a gift to the other person or he otherwise enters into a transaction with the other on terms that provide for him to receive no consideration;

    (b) he enters into a transaction with the other in consideration of marriage; or

    (c) he enters into a transaction with the other for a consideration the value of which, in money or money's worth, is significantly less than the value, in money or money's worth, of the consideration provided by himself.

(2) Where a person has entered into such a transaction, the court may, if satisfied under the next subsection, make such order as it thinks fit for—

    (a) restoring the position to what it would have been if the transaction had not been entered into, and

    (b) protecting the interests of persons who are victims of the transaction.

(3) In the case of a person entering into such a transaction, an order shall only be made if the court is satisfied that it was entered into by him for the purpose—

    (a) of putting assets beyond the reach of a person who is making, or may at some time make, a claim against him, or

    (b) of otherwise prejudicing the interests of such a person in relation to the claim which he is making or may make.

(4) In this section 'the court' means the High Court or—

    (a) if the person entering into the transaction is an individual, any other court which would have jurisdiction in relation to a bankruptcy petition relating to him;

    (b) if that person is a body capable of being wound up under Part IV or V of this Act, any other court having jurisdiction to wind it up.

(5) In relation to a transaction at an undervalue, references here and below to a victim of the transaction are to a person who is, or is capable of being, prejudiced by it; and in the following two sections the person entering into the transaction is referred to as "the debtor".

Those who may apply for an order under s.423

A3.033   **424.**—(1) An application for an order under section 423 shall not be made in relation to a transaction except—

    (a) in a case where the debtor has been adjudged bankrupt or is a body corporate which is being wound up or in relation to which an administration order is in force, by the official receiver, by the trustee of the bankrupt's estate or the liquidator or administrator of the body corporate or (with the leave of the court) by a victim of the transaction;

    (b) in a case where a victim of the transaction is bound by a voluntary arrangement approved under Part I or Part VIII of this Act, by the supervisor of the voluntary arrangement or by any person who (whether or not so bound) is such a victim; or

    (c) in any other case, by a victim of the transaction.

(2) An application made under any of the paragraphs of subsection (1) is to be treated as made on behalf of every victim of the transaction.

Provision which may be made by order under s.423

A3.034   **425.**—(1) Without prejudice to the generality of section 423, an order made under that section with respect to a transaction may (subject as follows)—

    (a) require any property transferred as part of the transaction to be vested in any person, either absolutely or for the benefit of all the persons on whose behalf the application for the order is treated as made;

    (b) require any property to be so vested if it represents, in any person's hands, the application either of the proceeds of sale of property so transferred or of money so transferred;

    (c) release or discharge (in whole or in part) any security given by the debtor;

(d) require any person to pay to any other person in respect of benefits received from the debtor such sums as the court may direct;

(e) provide for any surety or guarantor whose obligations to any person were released or discharged (in whole or in part) under the transaction to be under such new or revived obligations as the court thinks appropriate;

(f) provide for security to be provided for the discharge of any obligation imposed by or arising under the order, for such an obligation to be charged on any property and for such security or charge to have the same priority as a security or charge released or discharged (in whole or in part) under the transaction.

(2) An order under section 423 may affect the property of, or impose any obligation on, any person whether or not he is the person with whom the debtor entered into the transaction; but such an order—

(a) shall not prejudice any interest in property which was acquired from a person other than the debtor and was acquired in good faith, for value and without notice of the relevant circumstances, or prejudice any interest deriving from such an interest, and

(b) shall not require a person who received a benefit from the transaction in good faith, for value and without notice of the relevant circumstances to pay any sum unless he was a party to the transaction.

(3) For the purposes of this section the relevant circumstances in relation to a transaction are the circumstances by virtue of which an order under section 423 may be made in respect of the transaction.

(4) In this section *"security"* means any mortgage, charge, lien or other security.

Expressions used generally

436. In this Act, except in so far as the context otherwise requires (and subject to Parts VII and XI)— **A3.035**

. . .

"property" includes money, goods, things in action, land and every description of property wherever situated and also obligations and every description of interest, whether present or future or vested or contingent, arising out of, or incidental to, property;

. . .

"transaction" includes a gift, agreement or arrangement, and references to entering into a transaction shall be construed accordingly.

(6) Statutory materials relating to arbitrations

ARBITRATION ACT 1950

Conduct of proceedings, witnesses, &c

12.—(1) Unless a contrary intention is expressed therein, every arbitration **A3.036** agreement shall, where such a provision is applicable to the reference, be deemed to contain a provision that the parties to the reference, and all persons claiming through them respectively, shall, subject to any legal objection, submit to be examined by the arbitrator or umpire, on oath or affirmation, in relation to the matters in dispute, and shall, subject as aforesaid, produce before the arbitrator or umpire all documents within their possession or power respectively which may be required or called for, and do all other things which during the proceedings on the reference the arbitrator or umpire may require.

(2) Unless a contrary intention is expressed therein, every arbitration shall, where such a provision is applicable to the reference, be deemed to contain a provision that the witness on the reference shall, if the arbitrator or umpire thinks fit, be examined on oath or affirmation.

(3) An arbitrator or umpire shall, unless a contrary intention is expressed in the arbitration agreement, have power to administer oaths to, or take the affirmations of, the parties to and witnesses on a reference under the agreement.

(4) Any party to a reference under an arbitration agreement may sue out a writ of subpoena ad testificandum or a writ of subpoena duces tecum, but no person shall be compelled under any such writ to produce any document which he could not be compelled to produce on the trial of an action, and the High Court or a judge thereof may order that a writ of subpoena ad testificandum or a subpoena duces tecum shall issue to compel the attendance before an arbitrator or umpire of a witness wherever he may be within the United Kingdom.

(5) The High Court or a judge thereof may also order that a writ of habeas corpus ad testificandum shall issue to bring up a prisoner for examination before an arbitrator or umpire.

(6) The High Court shall have, for the purpose of and in relation to a reference, the same power, of making orders in respect of—

(a) security for costs;
(b) [*repealed by s 103 of the Courts and Legal Services Act 1990.*]
(c) the giving of evidence by affidavit;
(d) examination on oath of any witness before an officer of the High Court or any other person, and the issue of a commission or request for the examination of a witness out of the jurisdiction;
(e) the preservation, interim custody or sale of any goods which are the subject matter of the reference;
(f) securing the amount in dispute in the reference;
(g) the detention, preservation or inspection of any property or thing which is the subject of the reference or as to which any question may arise therein, and authorising for any of the purposes aforesaid any persons to enter upon or into any land or building in the possession of any party to the reference, or authorising any samples to be taken or any observation to be made or experiment to be tried which may be necessary or expedient for the purpose of obtaining full information or evidence; and
(h) interim injunctions or the appointment of a receiver;

as it has for the purpose of and in relation to an action or matter in the High Court:

Provided that nothing in this subsection shall be taken to prejudice any power which may be vested in an arbitrator or umpire of making orders with respect to any of the matters aforesaid.

[*This section was repealed by the Arbitration Act 1996, Sch.4, para.1, but continues to apply to arbitral proceedings commenced before January 31, 1997 (see Arbitration Act 1996, s.109(2) and the Arbitration Act 1996 (Commencement No.1) Order 1996, SI 1996/3146).*]

ARBITRATION ACT 1996

Scope of application of provisions

A3.037   2.—(1) The provisions of this Part apply where the seat of the arbitration is in England and Wales or Northern Ireland.

(2) The following sections apply even if the seat of the arbitration is outside England and Wales or Northern Ireland or no seat has been designated or determined—

(a) sections 9 to 11 (stay of legal proceedings, &c), and
(b) section 66 (enforcement of arbitral awards).
(3) The powers conferred by the following sections apply even if the seat of the arbitration is outside England and Wales or Northern Ireland or no seat has been designated or determined—
(a) section 43 (securing the attendance of witnesses), and
(b) section 44 (court powers exercisable in support of arbitral proceedings);
but the court may refuse to exercise any such power if, in the opinion of the court, the fact that the seat of the arbitration is outside England and Wales or Northern Ireland, or that when designated or determined the seat is likely to be outside England and Wales or Northern Ireland, makes it inappropriate to do so.
(4) The court may exercise a power conferred by any provision of this Part not mentioned in subsection (2) or (3) for the purpose of supporting the arbitral process where—
(a) no seat of the arbitration has been designated or determined, and
(b) by reason of a connection with England and Wales or Northern Ireland the court is satisfied that it is appropriate to do so.
(5) Section 7 (separability of arbitration agreement) and section 8 (death of a party) apply where the law applicable to the arbitration agreement is the law of England and Wales or Northern Ireland even if the seat of the arbitration is outside England and Wales or Northern Ireland or has not been designated or determined.

The seat of the arbitration

3. In this Part 'the seat of the arbitration' means the juridical seat of the **A3.038** arbitration designated—
(a) by the parties to the arbitration agreement, or
(b) by any arbitral or other institution or person vested by the parties with powers in that regard, or
(c) by the arbitral tribunal if so authorised by the parties,
or determined, in the absence of any such designation, having regard to the parties' agreement and all the relevant circumstances.

Mandatory and non-mandatory provisions

4.—(1) The mandatory provisions of this Part are listed in Schedule 1 and have **A3.039** effect notwithstanding any agreement to the contrary.
(2) The other provisions of this Part (the "non-mandatory provisions") allow the parties to make their own arrangements by agreement but provide rules which apply in the absence of such agreement.
(3) The parties may make such arrangements by agreeing to the application of institutional rules or providing any other means by which a matter may be decided.
(4) It is immaterial whether or not the law applicable to the parties' agreement is the law of England and Wales or, as the case may be, Northern Ireland.
(5) The choice of a law other than the law of England and Wales or Northern Ireland as the applicable law in respect of a matter provided for by a non-mandatory provision of this Part is equivalent to an agreement making provision about that matter.
For this purpose an applicable law determined in accordance with the parties' agreement, or which is objectively determined in the absence of any express or implied choice, shall be treated as chosen by the parties.

General powers exercisable by the tribunal

38.—(1) The parties are free to agree on the powers exercisable by the arbitral **A3.040** tribunal for the purposes of and in relation to the proceedings.

(2) Unless otherwise agreed by the parties the tribunal has the following powers.

(3) The tribunal may order a claimant to provide security for the costs of the arbitration.

This power shall not be exercised on the ground that the claimant is—

(a) an individual ordinarily resident outside the United Kingdom, or

(b) a corporation or association incorporated or formed under the law of a country outside the United Kingdom, or whose central management and control is exercised outside the United Kingdom.

(4) The tribunal may give directions in relation to any property which is the subject of the proceedings or as to which any question arises in the proceedings, and which is owned by or is in the possession of a party to the proceedings—

(a) for the inspection, photographing, preservation, custody or detention of the property by the tribunal, an expert or a party, or

(b) ordering that samples be taken from, or any observation be made of or experiment conducted upon, the property.

(5) The tribunal may direct that a party or witness shall be examined on oath or affirmation, and may for that purpose administer any necessary oath or take any necessary affirmation.

(6) The tribunal may give directions to a party for the preservation for the purposes of the proceedings of any evidence in his custody or control.

Court powers exercisable in support of arbitral proceedings

A3.041
44.—(1) Unless otherwise agreed by the parties, the court has for the purposes of and in relation to arbitral proceedings the same power of making orders about the matters listed below as it has for the purposes of and in relation to legal proceedings.

(2) Those matters are—

(a) the taking of the evidence of witnesses;

(b) the preservation of evidence;

(c) making orders relating to property which is the subject of the proceedings or as to which any question arises in the proceedings—

(i) for the inspection, photographing, preservation, custody or detention of the property, or

(ii) ordering that samples be taken from, or any observation be made of or experiment conducted upon, the property;

and for that purpose authorising any person to enter any premises in the possession or control of a party to the arbitration;

(d) the sale of any goods the subject of the proceedings;

(e) the granting of an interim injunction or the appointment of a receiver.

(3) If the case is one of urgency, the court may, on the application of a party or proposed party to the arbitral proceedings, make such orders as it thinks necessary for the purpose of preserving evidence or assets.

(4) If the case is not one of urgency, the court shall act only on the application of a party to the arbitral proceedings (upon notice to the other parties and to the tribunal) made with the permission of the tribunal or the agreement in writing of the other parties.

(5) In any case the court shall act only if or to the extent that the arbitral tribunal, and any arbitral or other institution or person vested by the parties with power in that regard, has no power or is unable for the time being to act effectively.

(6) If the court so orders, an order made by it under this section shall cease to have effect in whole or in part on the order of the tribunal or of any such arbitral or other institution or person having power to act in relation to the subject-matter of the order.

(7) The leave of the court is required for any appeal from a decision of the court under this section.

(7) Statutory materials relating to restraint orders in connection with Crime

DRUG TRAFFICKING ACT 1994

PART I

CONFISCATION ORDERS

Exercise of powers for the realisation of property

Exercise by High Court, county court or receiver of powers for the realisation of property

31.—(1) The following provisions apply to the powers conferred— **A3.042**
   (a) on the High Court or a county court by sections 26 to 30 of this Act; or
   (b) on a receiver appointed under section 26 or 29 of this Act or in pursuance of a charging order.
(2) Subject to the following provisions of this section, the powers shall be exercised with a view to making available for satisfying the confiscation order or, as the case may be, any confiscation order that may be made in the defendant's case, the value for the time being of realisable property held by any person, by means of the realisation of such property.
(3) In the case of realisable property held by a person to whom the defendant has directly or indirectly made a gift caught by this Act, the powers shall be exercised with a view to realising no more than the value for the time being of the gift.
(4) The powers shall be exercised with a view to allowing any person other than the defendant or the recipient of any such gift to retain or recover the value of any property held by him.
(5) In exercising the powers, no account shall be taken of any obligations of the defendant or of the recipient of any such gift which conflict with the obligation to satisfy the confiscation order.
(6) An order may be made or other action taken in respect of a debt owed by the Crown.

[*This section was repealed by the Proceeds of Crime Act 2002, Sch.12 : see Chapter 25. This is the "statutory steer" given to powers to be exercised by the court including those in respect of restraint orders.*]

PROCEEDS OF CRIME ACT 2002

Conditions for exercise of powers

40.—(1) The Crown Court may exercise the powers conferred by section 41 if **A3.043**
any of the following conditions is satisfied.
(2) The first condition is that—
   (a) a criminal investigation has been started in England and Wales with regard to an offence, and
   (b) there is reasonable cause to believe that the alleged offender has benefited from his criminal conduct.
(3) The second condition is that—

(a) proceedings for an offence have been started in England and Wales and not concluded, and

(b) there is reasonable cause to believe that the defendant has benefited from his criminal conduct.

(4) The third condition is that—

(a) an application by the prosecutor or the Director has been made under section 19, 20, 27 or 28 and not concluded, or the court believes that such an application is to be made, and

(b) there is reasonable cause to believe that the defendant has benefited from his criminal conduct.

(5) The fourth condition is that—

(a) an application by the prosecutor or the Director has been made under section 21 and not concluded, or the court believes that such an application is to be made, and

(b) there is reasonable cause to believe that the court will decide under that section that the amount found under the new calculation of the defendant's benefit exceeds the relevant amount (as defined in that section).

(6) The fifth condition is that—

(a) an application by the prosecutor or the Director has been made under section 22 and not concluded, or the court believes that such an application is to be made, and

(b) there is reasonable cause to believe that the court will decide under that section that the amount found under the new calculation of the available amount exceeds the relevant amount (as defined in that section).

(7) The second condition is not satisfied if the court believes that—

(a) there has been undue delay in continuing the proceedings, or

(b) the prosecutor does not intend to proceed.

(8) If an application mentioned in the third, fourth or fifth condition has been made the condition is not satisfied if the court believes that—

(a) there has been undue delay in continuing the application, or

(b) the prosecutor or the Director (as the case may be) does not intend to proceed.

(9) If the first condition is satisfied—

(a) references in this Part to the defendant are to the alleged offender;

(b) references in this Part to the prosecutor are to the person the court believes is to have conduct of any proceedings for the offence;

(c) section 77(9) has effect as if proceedings for the offence had been started against the defendant when the investigation was started.

Restraint orders

A3.044   **41.**—(1) If any condition set out in section 40 is satisfied the Crown Court may make an order (a restraint order) prohibiting any specified person from dealing with any realisable property held by him.

(2) A restraint order may provide that it applies—

(a) to all realisable property held by the specified person whether or not the property is described in the order;

(b) to realisable property transferred to the specified person after the order is made.

(3) A restraint order may be made subject to exceptions, and an exception may in particular—

(a) make provision for reasonable living expenses and reasonable legal expenses;

(b) make provision for the purpose of enabling any person to carry on any trade, business, profession or occupation;

(c) be made subject to conditions.

(4) But an exception to a restraint order must not make provision for any legal expenses which—

(a) relate to an offence which falls within subsection (5), and

(b) are incurred by the defendant or by a recipient of a tainted gift.

(5) These offences fall within this subsection—

(a) the offence mentioned in section 40(2) or (3), if the first or second condition (as the case may be) is satisfied;

(b) the offence (or any of the offences) concerned, if the third, fourth or fifth condition is satisfied.

(6) Subsection (7) applies if—

(a) a court makes a restraint order, and

(b) the applicant for the order applies to the court to proceed under subsection (7) (whether as part of the application for the restraint order or at any time afterwards).

(7) The court may make such order as it believes is appropriate for the purpose of ensuring that the restraint order is effective.

(8) A restraint order does not affect property for the time being subject to a charge under any of these provisions—

(a) section 9 of the Drug Trafficking Offences Act 1986 (c. 32);

(b) section 78 of the Criminal Justice Act 1988 (c. 33);

(c) Article 14 of the Criminal Justice (Confiscation) (Northern Ireland) Order 1990 (S.I. 1990/2588 (N.I. 17));

(d) section 27 of the Drug Trafficking Act 1994 (c. 37);

(e) Article 32 of the Proceeds of Crime (Northern Ireland) Order 1996 (S.I. 1996/1299 (N.I. 9)).

(9) Dealing with property includes removing it from England and Wales.

PART 2

CONFISCATION: ENGLAND AND WALES

Exercise of powers

Powers of court and receiver

A3.045

69.—(1) This section applies to—

(a) the powers conferred on a court by sections 41 to 60 and sections 62 to 67;

(b) the powers of a receiver appointed under section 48, 50 or 52.

(2) The powers—

(a) must be exercised with a view to the value for the time being of realisable property being made available (by the property's realisation) for satisfying any confiscation order that has been or may be made against the defendant;

(b) must be exercised, in a case where a confiscation order has not been made, with a view to securing that there is no diminution in the value of realisable property;

(c) must be exercised without taking account of any obligation of the defendant or a recipient of a tainted gift if the obligation conflicts with the object of satisfying any confiscation order that has been or may be made against the defendant;

(d) may be exercised in respect of a debt owed by the Crown.

(3) Subsection (2) has effect subject to the following rules—

(a) the powers must be exercised with a view to allowing a person other than the defendant or a recipient of a tainted gift to retain or recover the value of any interest held by him;

(b) in the case of realisable property held by a recipient of a tainted gift, the powers must be exercised with a view to realising no more than the value for the time being of the gift;

(c) in a case where a confiscation order has not been made against the defendant, property must not be sold if the court so orders under subsection (4).

(4) If on an application by the defendant, or by the recipient of a tainted gift, the court decides that property cannot be replaced it may order that it must not be sold.

(5) An order under subsection (4) may be revoked or varied.

[*This is the "statutory steer" given to powers to be exercised by the court under the Proceeds of Crime Act 2002 including those in respect of restraint orders made by the Crown Court under s.41(1) of the Act and includes in s.41(4) release of funds for legal expenses in the circumstances set out in the subsection.*]

Civil Procedure Rules materials

CPR Part 25

I Interim Remedies

Orders for interim remedies

25.1 (1) The court may grant the following interim remedies— **A4.001**
  (a) an interim injunction;
  (b) an interim declaration;
  (c) an order—
      (i) for the detention, custody or preservation of relevant property;
      (ii) for the inspection of relevant property;
      (iii) for the taking of a sample of relevant property;
      (iv) for the carrying out of an experiment on or with relevant property;
      (v) for the sale of relevant property which is of a perishable nature or which for any other good reason it is desirable to sell quickly; and
      (vi) for the payment of income from relevant property until a claim is decided;
  (d) an order authorising a person to enter any land or building in the possession of a party to the proceedings for the purposes of carrying out an order under sub-paragraph (c);
  (e) an order under section 4 of the Torts (Interference with Goods) Act 1977 to deliver up goods;
  (f) an order (referred to as a "freezing injunction")—
      (i) restraining a party from removing from the jurisdiction assets located there; or
      (ii) restraining a party from dealing with any assets whether located within the jurisdiction or not;
  (g) an order directing a party to provide information about the location of relevant property or assets or to provide information about relevant property or assets which are or may be the subject of an application for a freezing injunction;
  (h) an order (referred to as a "search order") under section 7 of the Civil Procedure Act 1997 (order requiring a party to admit another party to premises for the purpose of preserving evidence etc.);
  (i) an order under section 33 of the Supreme Court Act 1981 or section 52 of the County Courts Act 1984 (order for disclosure of documents or inspection of property before a claim has been made);
  (j) an order under section 34 of the Supreme Court Act 1981 or section 53 of the County Courts Act 1984 (order in certain proceedings for

disclosure of documents or inspection of property against a non-party);

   (k) an order (referred to as an order for interim payment) under rule 25.6 for payment by a defendant on account of any damages, debt or other sum (except costs) which the court may hold the defendant liable to pay;

   (l) an order for a specified fund to be paid into court or otherwise secured, where there is a dispute over a party's right to the fund;

  (m) an order permitting a party seeking to recover personal property to pay money into court pending the outcome of the proceedings and directing that, if he does so, the property shall be given up to him;

  (n) an order directing a party to prepare and file accounts relating to the dispute;

  (o) an order directing any account to be taken or inquiry to be made by the court.

(Rule 34.2 provides for the court to issue a witness summons requiring a witness to produce documents to the court at the hearing or on such date as the court may direct)

(2) In paragraph (1)(c) and (g), "relevant property" means property (including land) which is the subject of a claim or as to which any question may arise on a claim.

(3) The fact that a particular kind of interim remedy is not listed in paragraph (1) does not affect any power that the court may have to grant that remedy.

(4) The court may grant an interim remedy whether or not there has been a claim for a final remedy of that kind.

Time when an order for an interim remedy may be made

A4.002 25.2 (1) An order for an interim remedy may be made at any time, including—

   (a) before proceedings are started; and

   (b) after judgment has been given.

(Rule 7.2 provides that proceedings are started when the court issues a claim form)

(2) However—

   (a) paragraph (1) is subject to any rule, practice direction or other enactment which provides otherwise;

   (b) the court may grant an interim remedy before a claim has been made only if—

     (i) the matter is urgent; or

     (ii) it is otherwise desirable to do so in the interests of justice; and

   (c) unless the court otherwise orders, a defendant may not apply for any of the orders listed in rule 25.1(1) before he has filed either an acknowledgment of service or a defence.

(Part 10 provides for filing an acknowledgment of service and Part 15 for filing a defence)

(3) Where the court grants an interim remedy before a claim has been commenced, it may give directions requiring a claim to be commenced.

(4) In particular, the court need not direct that a claim be commenced where the application is made under section 33 of the Supreme Court Act 1981 or section 52 of the County Courts Act 1984 (order for disclosure, inspection etc. before commencement of a claim).

How to apply for an interim remedy

A4.003 25.3 (1) The court may grant an interim remedy on an application made without notice if it appears to the court that there are good reasons for not giving notice.

(2) An application for an interim remedy must be supported by evidence, unless the court orders otherwise.

(3) If the applicant makes an application without giving notice, the evidence in support of the application must state the reasons why notice has not been given.

(Part 3 lists general powers of the court)

(Part 23 contains general rules about making an application)

Application for an interim remedy where there is no related claim

25.4 (1) This rule applies where a party wishes to apply for an interim remedy **A4.004** but—

    (a) the remedy is sought in relation to proceedings which are taking place, or will take place, outside the jurisdiction; or

    (b) the application is made under section 33 of the Supreme Court Act 1981 or section 52 of the County Courts Act 1984 (order for disclosure, inspection etc. before commencement) before a claim has been commenced.

(2) An application under this rule must be made in accordance with the general rules about applications contained in Part 23.

(The following provisions are also relevant—

- Rule 25.5 (inspection of property before commencement or against a non-party)
- Rule 31.16 (orders for disclosure of documents before proceedings start)
- Rule 31.17 (orders for disclosure of documents against a person not a party))

Inspection of property before commencement or against a non-party

25.5 (1) This rule applies where a person makes an application under— **A4.005**

    (a) section 33(1) of the Supreme Court Act 1981 or section 52(1) of the County Courts Act 1984 (inspection etc. of property before commencement);

    (b) section 34(3) of the Supreme Court Act 1981 or section 53(3) of the County Courts Act 1984 (inspection etc. of property against a non-party).

(2) The evidence in support of such an application must show, if practicable by reference to any statement of case prepared in relation to the proceedings or anticipated proceedings, that the property—

    (a) is or may become the subject matter of such proceedings; or

    (b) is relevant to the issues that will arise in relation to such proceedings.

(3) A copy of the application notice and a copy of the evidence in support must be served on—

    (a) the person against whom the order is sought; and

    (b) in relation to an application under section 34(3) of the Supreme Court Act 1981 or section 53(3) of the County Courts Act 1984, every party to the proceedings other than the applicant.

. . .

Interim injunction to cease if claim is stayed

25.10 If— **A4.006**

    (a) the court has granted an interim injunction other than a freezing injunction; and

    (b) the claim is stayed other than by agreement between the parties,

the interim injunctionshall be set asideunless the court orders that it should continue to have effect even though the claim is stayed.

Interim injunction to cease after 14 days if claim struck out

A4.007 25.11 (1) If—

    (a) the court has granted an interim injunction; and

    (b) the claim is struck out under rule 3.7 (sanctions for non-payment of certain fees),

the interim injunction shall cease to have effect 14 days after the date that the claim is struck out unless paragraph (2) applies.

    (2) If the claimant applies to reinstate the claim before the interim injunction ceases to have effect under paragraph (1), the injunction shall continue until the hearing of the application unless the court orders otherwise.

PRACTICE DIRECTION—INTERIM INJUNCTIONS

THIS PRACTICE DIRECTION SUPPLEMENTS CPR PART 25

Contents of this Practice Direction

Jurisdiction

A4.008 1.1 High Court Judges and any other Judge duly authorised may grant "search orders"[1] and "freezing injunctions".[2]

    1.2 In a case in the High Court, Masters and district judges have the power to grant injunctions:

    (1) by consent,

    (2) in connection with charging orders and appointments of receivers,

    (3) in aid of execution of judgments.

    1.3 In any other case any judge who has jurisdiction to conduct the trial of the action has the power to grant an injunction in that action.

    1.4 A Master or district judge has the power to vary or discharge an injunction granted by any Judge with the consent of all the parties.

Making an application

A4.009 2.1 The application notice must state:

    (1) the order sought, and

    (2) the date, time and place of the hearing.

    2.2 The application notice and evidence in support must be served as soon as practicable after issue and in any event not less than 3 days before the court is due to hear the application.[3]

    2.3 Where the court is to serve, sufficient copies of the application notice and evidence in support for the court and for each respondent should be filed for issue and service.

2.4   Whenever possible a draft of the order sought should be filed with the application notice and a disk containing the draft should also be available to the court in a format compatible with the word processing software used by the court. This will enable the court officer to arrange for any amendments to be incorporated and for the speedy preparation and sealing of the order.

Evidence

3.1   Applications for search orders and freezing injunctions must be supported by **A4.010** affidavit evidence.

3.2   Applications for other interim injunctions must be supported by evidence set out in either:
(1) a witness statement, or
(2) a statement of case provided that it is verified by a statement of truth,[4] or
(3) the application provided that it is verified by a statement of truth,
unless the court, an Act, a rule or a practice direction requires evidence by affidavit.

3.3   The evidence must set out the facts on which the applicant relies for the claim being made against the respondent, including all material facts of which the court should be made aware.

3.4   Where an application is made without notice to the respondent, the evidence must also set out why notice was not given.
(See Part 32 and the practice direction that supplements it for information about evidence.)

Urgent applications and applications without notice

4.1   These fall into two categories: **A4.011**
(1) applications where a claim form has already been issued, and
(2) applications where a claim form has not yet been issued,
and, in both cases, where notice of the application has not been given to the respondent.

4.2   These applications are normally dealt with at a court hearing but cases of extreme urgency may be dealt with by telephone.

4.3   Applications dealt with at a court hearing after issue of a claim form:
(1) the application notice, evidence in support and a draft order (as in 2.4 above) should be filed with the court two hours before the hearing wherever possible,
(2) if an application is made before the application notice has been issued, a draft order (as in 2.4 above) should be provided at the hearing, and the application notice and evidence in support must be filed with the court on the same or next working day or as ordered by the court, and
(3) except in cases where secrecy is essential, the applicant should take steps to notify the respondent informally of the application.

4.4   Applications made before the issue of a claim form:
(1) in addition to the provisions set out at 4.3 above, unless the court orders otherwise, either the applicant must undertake to the court to issue a claim form immediately or the court will give directions for the commencement of the claim,[5]
(2) where possible the claim form should be served with the order for the injunction,
(3) an order made before the issue of a claim form should state in the title after the names of the applicant and respondent 'the Claimant and Defendant in an Intended Action'.

4.5   Applications made by telephone:
(1) where it is not possible to arrange a hearing, application can be made between 10.00 a.m. and 5.00 p.m. weekdays by telephoning the Royal

Courts of Justice on 020 7947 6000 and asking to be put in contact with a High Court Judge of the appropriate Division available to deal with an emergency application in a High Court matter. The appropriate district registry may also be contacted by telephone. In county court proceedings, the appropriate county court should be contacted,

(2) where an application is made outside those hours the applicant should either—

    (a) telephone the Royal Courts of Justice on 020 7947 6000 where he will be put in contact with the clerk to the appropriate duty judge in the High Court (or the appropriate area Circuit Judge where known), or

    (b) the Urgent Court Business Officer of the appropriate Circuit who will contact the local duty judge,

(3) where the facility is available it is likely that the judge will require a draft order to be faxed to him,

(4) the application notice and evidence in support must be filed with the court on the same or next working day or as ordered, together with two copies of the order for sealing,

(5) injunctions will be heard by telephone only where the applicant is acting by counsel or solicitors.

Orders for injunctions

A4.012 5.1 Any order for an injunction, unless the court orders otherwise, must contain:

(1) an undertaking by the applicant to the court to pay any damages which the respondent(s) (or any other party served with or notified of the order) sustain which the court considers the applicant should pay,

(2) if made without notice to any other party, an undertaking by the applicant to the court to serve on the respondent the application notice, evidence in support and any order made as soon as practicable,

(3) if made without notice to any other party, a return date for a further hearing at which the other party can be present,

(4) if made before filing the application notice, an undertaking to file and pay the appropriate fee on the same or next working day, and

(5) if made before issue of a claim form—

    (a) an undertaking to issue and pay the appropriate fee on the same or next working day, or

    (b) directions for the commencement of the claim.

5.2 An order for an injunction made in the presence of all parties to be bound by it or made at a hearing of which they have had notice, may state that it is effective until trial or further order.

5.3 Any order for an injunction must set out clearly what the respondent must do or not do.

FREEZING INJUNCTIONS

Orders to restrain disposal of assets worldwide and within England and Wales

A4.013 6.1 An example of a Freezing Injunction is annexed to this practice direction.

6.2 This example may be modified as appropriate in any particular case. In particular, the court may, if it considers it appropriate, require the applicant's solicitors, as well as the applicant, to give undertakings.

SEARCH ORDERS

Orders for the preservation of evidence and property

7.1 The following provisions apply to search orders in addition to those listed **A4.014**
above.

The Supervising Solicitor

7.2 The Supervising Solicitor must be experienced in the operation of search orders. A Supervising Solicitor may be contacted either through the Law Society or, for the London area, through the London Solicitors Litigation Association.

7.3 Evidence:

(1) the affidavit must state the name, firm and its address, and experience of the Supervising Solicitor, also the address of the premises and whether it is a private or business address, and

(2) the affidavit must disclose very fully the reason the order is sought, including the probability that relevant material would disappear if the order were not made.

7.4 Service:

(1) the order must be served personally by the Supervising Solicitor, unless the court otherwise orders, and must be accompanied by the evidence in support and any documents capable of being copied,

(2) confidential exhibits need not be served but they must be made available for inspection by the respondent in the presence of the applicant's solicitors while the order is carried out and afterwards be retained by the respondent's solicitors on their undertaking not to permit the respondent—

(a) to see them or copies of them except in their presence, and

(b) to make or take away any note or record of them,

(3) the Supervising Solicitor may be accompanied only by the persons mentioned in the order,

(4) the Supervising Solicitor must explain the terms and effect of the order to the respondent in everyday language and advise him of his right to—

(a) legal advice, and

(b) apply to vary or discharge the order,

(5) where the Supervising Solicitor is a man and the respondent is likely to be an unaccompanied woman, at least one other person named in the order must be a woman and must accompany the Supervising Solicitor, and

(6) the order may only be served between 9.30 a.m. and 5.30 p.m. Monday to Friday unless the court otherwise orders.

7.5 Search and custody of materials:

(1) no material shall be removed unless clearly covered by the terms of the order,

(2) the premises must not be searched and no items shall be removed from them except in the presence of the respondent or a person who appears to be a responsible employee of the respondent,

(3) where copies of documents are sought, the documents should be retained for no more than 2 days before return to the owner,

(4) where material in dispute is removed pending trial, the applicant's solicitors should place it in the custody of the respondent's solicitors on their undertaking to retain it in safekeeping and to produce it to the court when required,

(5) in appropriate cases the applicant should insure the material retained in the respondent's solicitors' custody,

(6) the Supervising Solicitor must make a list of all material removed from the premises and supply a copy of the list to the respondent,

(7) no material shall be removed from the premises until the respondent has had reasonable time to check the list,

(8) if any of the listed items exists only in computer readable form, the respondent must immediately give the applicant's solicitors effective access to the computers, with all necessary passwords, to enable them to be searched, and cause the listed items to be printed out,

(9) the applicant must take all reasonable steps to ensure that no damage is done to any computer or data,

(10) the applicant and his representatives may not themselves search the respondent's computers unless they have sufficient expertise to do so without damaging the respondent's system,

(11) the Supervising Solicitor shall provide a report on the carrying out of the order to the applicant's solicitors,

(12) as soon as the report is received the applicant's solicitors shall—
(a) serve a copy of it on the respondent, and
(b) file a copy of it with the court, and

(13) where the Supervising Solicitor is satisfied that full compliance with paragraph 7.5(7) and (8) above is impracticable, he may permit the search to proceed and items to be removed without compliance with the impracticable requirements.

General

A4.015 8.1 The Supervising Solicitor must not be an employee or member of the applicant's firm of solicitors.

8.2 If the court orders that the order need not be served by the Supervising Solicitor, the reason for so ordering must be set out in the order.

8.3 The search order must not be carried out at the same time as a police search warrant.

8.4 There is no privilege against self incrimination in Intellectual Property cases (see the Supreme Court Act 1981, section 72) therefore in those cases any references to incrimination in the Search Order should be removed.

8.5 Applications in intellectual property cases should be made in the Chancery Division.

8.6 An example of a Search Order is annexed to this Practice Direction. This example may be modified as appropriate in any particular case.

ANNEX

FREEZING INJUNCTION   IN THE HIGH COURT OF JUSTICE   **A4.016**
                                                 [   ] DIVISION

Before the Honourable Mr Justice   [   ]

Claim No.

Dated

Applicant

Seal

Respondent

Name, address and reference of Respopndent

PENAL NOTICE

IF YOU [   ][1] DISOBEY THIS ORDER YOU MAY BE HELD TO BE IN CONTEMPT OF COURT AND MAY BE IMPRISONED, FINED OR HAVE YOU ASSETS SEIZED.

ANY OTHER PERSON WHO KNOWS OF THIS ORDER AND DOES ANYTHING WHICH HELPS OR PERMITS THE RESPONDENT TO BREACH THE TERMS OF THIS ORDER MAY ALSO BE HELD TO BE IN CONTEMPT OF COURT AND MAY BE IMPRISONED, FINED OR HAVE THEIR ASSETS SEIZED.

[1] Insert name of respondent.

THIS ORDER

A4.017 1. This is a Freezing Injunction made against [   ] ("the Respondent") on [   ] by Mr Justice [   ] on the application of [   ] ("the Applicant"). The Judge read the Affidavits listed in Schedule A and accepted the undertakings set out in Schedule B at the end of this Order.
2. This order was made at a hearing without notice to the Respondent. The Respondent has a right to apply to the court to vary or discharge the order— see paragraph 13 below.
3. There will be a further hearing in respect of this order on [   ] ("the return date").
4. If there is more than one Respondent—
   (a) unless otherwise stated, references in this order to "the Respondent" mean both or all of them; and
   (b) this order is effective against any Respondent on whom it is served or who is given notice of it.

FREEZING INJUNCTION

[For injunction limited to assets in England and Wales]

A4.018 5. Until the return date or further order of the court, the Respondent must not remove from England and Wales or in any way dispose of, deal with or diminish the value of any of his assets which are in England and Wales up to the value of £   .

[For worldwide injunction]

5. Until the return date or further order of the court, the Respondent must not—
   (1) remove from England and Wales any of his assets which are in England and Wales up to the value of £   ; or
   (2) in any way dispose of, deal with or diminish the value of any of his assets whether they are in or outside England and Wales up to the same value.

[For either form of injunction

6. Paragraph 5 applies to all the Respondent's assets whether or not they are in his own name and whether they are solely or jointly owned. For the purpose of this order the Respondent's assets include any asset which he has the power, directly or indirectly, to dispose of or deal with as if it were his own. The Respondent is to be regarded as having such power if a third party holds or controls the asset in accordance with his direct or indirect instructions.
7. This prohibition includes the following assets in particular—
   (a) the property known as *[title/address]* or the net sale money after payment of any mortgages if it has been sold;
   (b) the property and assets of the Respondent's business [known as *[name]*] [carried on at *[address]*] or the sale money if any of them have been sold; and
   (c) any money in the account numbered *[account number]* at *[title/address]*.

[For injunction limited to assets in England and Wales]

8. If the total value free of charges or other securities ("unencumbered value") of the Respondent's assets in England and Wales exceeds £   , the Respondent may remove any of those assets from England and Wales or may dispose of or deal with them so long as the total unencumbered value of his assets still in England and Wales remains above £   .

[For worldwide injunction]

8. (1) If the total value free of charges or other securities ("unencumbered value") of the Respondent's assets in England and Wales exceeds £   , the Respondent may remove any of those assets from England and Wales or may dispose of or deal with them so long as the total unencumbered value of the Respondent's assets still in England and Wales remains above £   .

(2) If the total unencumbered value of the Respondent's assets in England and Wales does not exceed £   , the Respondent must not remove any of those assets from England and Wales and must not dispose of or deal with any of them. If the Respondent has other assets outside England and Wales, he may dispose of or deal with those assets outside England and Wales so long as the total unencumbered value of all his assets whether in or outside England and Wales remains above £   .

PROVISION OF INFORMATION

9. (1) Unless paragraph (2) applies, the Respondent must [immediately] [within   A4.019 hours of service of this order] and to the best of his ability inform the Applicant's solicitors of all his assets [in England and Wales] [worldwide] [exceeding £   in value] whether in his own name or not and whether solely or jointly owned, giving the value, location and details of all such assets.

(2) If the provision of any of this information is likely to incriminate the Respondent, he may be entitled to refuse to provide it, but is recommended to take legal advice before refusing to provide the information. Wrongful refusal to provide the information is contempt of court and may render the Respondent liable to be imprisoned, fined or have his assets seized.

10. Within [   ] working days after being served with this order, the Respondent must swear and serve on the Applicant's solicitors an affidavit setting out the above information.

EXCEPTIONS TO THIS ORDER

11. (1) This order does not prohibit the Respondent from spending £   a week   A4.020 towards his ordinary living expenses and also £   [*or* A reasonable sum] on legal advice and representation. [But before spending any money the Respondent must tell the Applicant's legal representatives where the money is to come from.]

([2] This order does not prohibit the Respondent from dealing with or disposing of any of his assets in the ordinary and proper course of business.]

(3) The Respondent may agree with the Applicant's legal representatives that the above spending limits should be increased or that this order should be varied in any other respect, but any agreement must be in writing.

(4) The order will cease to have effect if the Respondent—
 (a) provides security by paying the sum of £   into court, to be held to the order of the court; or
 (b) makes provision for security in that sum by another method agreed with the Applicant's legal representatives.

COSTS

12. The costs of this application are reserved to the judge hearing the application   A4.021 on the return date.

VARIATION OR DISCHARGE OF THIS ORDER

A4.022   13.   Anyone served with or notified of this order may apply to the court at any time to vary or discharge this order (or so much of it as affects that person), but they must first inform the Applicant's solicitors. If any evidence is to be relied upon in support of the application, the substance of it must be communicated in writing to the Applicant's solicitors in advance.

INTERPRETATION OF THIS ORDER

A4.023   14.   A Respondent who is an individual who is ordered not to do something must not do it himself or in any other way. He must not do it through others acting on his behalf or on his instructions or with his encouragement.

15.   A Respondent which is not an individual which is ordered not to do something must not do it itself or by its directors, officers, partners, employees or agents or in any other way.

PARTIES OTHER THAN THE APPLICANT AND RESPONDENT

16.   **Effect of this order**

A4.024   It is a contempt of court for any person notified of this order knowingly to assist in or permit a breach of this order. Any person doing so may be imprisoned, fined or have their assets seized.

17.   **Set off by banks**

A4.025   This injunction does not prevent any bank from exercising any right of set off it may have in respect of any facility which it gave to the respondent before it was notified of this order.

18.   **Withdrawals by the Respondent**

A4.026   No bank need enquire as to the application or proposed application of any money withdrawn by the Respondent if the withdrawal appears to be permitted by this order.

[For worldwide injunction]

19.   **Persons outside England and Wales**

A4.027   (1)   Except as provided in paragraph (2) below, the terms of this order do not affect or concern anyone outside the jurisdiction of this court.

(2)   The terms of this order will affect the following persons in a country or state outside the jurisdiction of this court—

(a)   the Respondent or his officer or agent appointed by power of attorney;

(b)   any person who—

(i)   is subject to the jurisdiction of this court;

(ii)   has been given written notice of this order at his residence or place of business within the jurisdiction of this court; and

(iii)   is able to prevent acts or omissions outside the jurisdiction of this court which constitute or assist in a breach of the terms of this order; and

(c)   any other person, only to the extent that this order is declared enforceable by or is enforced by a court in that country or state.

[For worldwide injunction]

20. Assets located outside England and Wales

Nothing in this order shall, in respect of assets located outside England and **A4.028** Wales, prevent any third party from complying with—

(1) what it reasonably believes to be its obligations, contractual or otherwise, under the laws and obligations of the country or state in which those assets are situated or under the proper law of any contract between itself and the Respondent; and

(2) any orders of the courts of that country or state, provided that reasonable notice of any application for such an order is given to the Applicant's solicitors.

COMMUNICATIONS WITH THE COURT

All communications to the court about this order should be sent to— **A4.029**

[Insert the address and telephone number of the appropriate Court Office]

If the order is made at the Royal Courts of Justice, communications should be addressed as follows—

Where the order is made in the Chancery Division
Room TM 505, Royal Courts of Justice, Strand, London WC2A 2LL quoting the case number. The telephone number is 0207 947 6754.

Where the order is made in the Queen's Bench Division
Room WG034, Royal Courts of Justice, Strand, London WC2A 2LL quoting the case number. The telephone number is 0207 947 6009.

Where the order is made in the Commercial Court
Room E201, Royal Courts of Justice, Strand, London WC2A 2LL quoting the case number. The telephone number is 0207 947 6826.

The offices are open between 10 a.m. and 4.30 p.m. Monday to Friday.

SCHEDULE A

AFFIDAVITS

The Applicant relied on the following affidavits— **A4.030**
[name] [number of affidavit] [date sworn] [filed on behalf of]

(1)
(2)

SCHEDULE B

UNDERTAKINGS GIVEN TO THE COURT BY THE APPLICANT

(1) If the court later finds that this order has caused loss to the Respondent, and **A4.031** decides that the Respondent should be compensated for that loss, the Applicant will comply with any order the court may make.

[(2) The Applicant will—
   (a) on or before *[date]* cause a written guarantee in the sum of £   to be issued from a bank with a place of business within England or Wales, in respect of any order the court may make pursuant to paragraph (1) above; and
   (b) immediately upon issue of the guarantee, cause a copy of it to be served on the Respondent.]

(3) As soon as practicable the Applicant will issue and serve a claim form [in the form of the draft produced to the court] [claiming the appropriate relief].

(4) The Applicant will [swear and file an affidavit] [cause an affidavit to be sworn and filed] [substantially in the terms of the draft affidavit produced to the court] [confirming the substance of what was said to the court by the Applicant's counsel/solicitors].

(5) The Applicant will serve upon the Respondent [together with this order] [as soon as practicable]—

   (i) copies of the affidavits and exhibits containing the evidence relied upon by the Applicant, and any other documents provided to the court on the making of the application;

   (ii) the claim form; and

  (iii) an application notice for continuation of the order.

[(6) Anyone notified of this order will be given a copy of it by the Applicant's legal representatives.]

(7) The Applicant will pay the reasonable costs of anyone other than the Respondent which have been incurred as a result of this order including the costs of finding out whether that person holds any of the Respondent's assets and if the court later finds that this order has caused such person loss, and decides that such person should be compensated for that loss, the Applicant will comply with any order the court may make.

(8) If this order ceases to have effect (for example, if the Respondent provides security or the Applicant does not provide a bank guarantee as provided for above) the Applicant will immediately take all reasonable steps to inform in writing anyone to whom he has given notice of this order, or who he has reasonable grounds for supposing may act upon this order, that it has ceased to have effect.

[(9) The Applicant will not without the permission of the court use any information obtained as a result of this order for the purpose of any civil or criminal proceedings, either in England and Wales or in any other jurisdiction, other than this claim.]

[(10) The Applicant will not without the permission of the court seek to enforce this order in any country outside England and Wales [or seek an order of a similar nature including orders conferring a charge or other security against the Respondent or the Respondent's assets].]

NAME AND ADDRESS OF APPLICANT'S LEGAL REPRESENTATIVES

A4.032   The Applicant's legal representatives are—

[Name, address, reference, fax and telephone numbers both in and out of office hours and e-mail]

ANNEX

SEARCH ORDER

Before the Honourable Mr Justice

IN THE HIGH COURT OF JUSTICE   A4.033
[   ] DIVISION
[   ]

Claim No.

Dated

Applicant

Seal

Respondent

Name, address and reference of Respondent

PENAL NOTICE

IF YOU [ ]¹ DISOBEY THIS ORDER YOU MAY BE HELD TO BE IN CONTEMPT OF COURT AND MAY BE IMPRISONED, FINED OR HAVE YOUR ASSETS SEIZED.

ANY OTHER PERSON WHO KNOWS OF THIS ORDER AND DOES ANYTHING WHICH HELPS OR PERMITS THE RESPONDENT TO BREACH THE TERMS OF THIS ORDER MAY ALSO BE HELD TO BE IN CONTEMPT OF COURT AND MAY BE IMPRISONED, FINED OR HAVE THEIR ASSETS SEIZED.

---

¹ Insert name of respondent.

THIS ORDER

A4.034 1. This is a Search Order made against [   ] ("the Respondent") on [   ] by Mr Justice [   ] on the application of [   ] ("the Applicant"). The Judge read the Affidavits listed in Schedule F and accepted the undertakings set out in Schedules C, D and E at the end of this order.

2. This order was made at a hearing without notice to the Respondent. The Respondent has a right to apply to the court to vary or discharge the order—see paragraph 27 below.

3. There will be a further hearing in respect of this order on [   ] ("the return date").

4. If there is more than one Respondent—
    (a) unless otherwise stated, references in this order to "the Respondent" mean both or all of them; and
    (b) this order is effective against any Respondent on whom it is served or who is given notice of it.

5. This order must be complied with by—
    (a) the Respondent;
    (b) any director, officer, partner or responsible employee of the Respondent; and
    (c) if the Respondent is an individual, any other person having responsible control of the premises to be searched.

THE SEARCH

A4.035 6. The Respondent must permit the following persons[6]—
    (a) [   ] ("the Supervising Solicitor");
    (b) [   ], a solicitor in the firm of [   ], the Applicant's solicitors; and
    (c) up to [   ] other persons[7] being *[their identity or capacity]* accompanying them,
    (together "the search party"), to enter the premises mentioned in Schedule A to this order and any other premises of the Respondent disclosed under paragraph 18 below and any vehicles under the Respondent's control on or around the premises ("the premises") so that they can search for, inspect, photograph or photocopy, and deliver into the safekeeping of the Applicant's solicitors all the documents and articles which are listed in Schedule B to this order ("the listed items").

7. Having permitted the search party to enter the premises, the Respondent must allow the search party to remain on the premises until the search is complete. In the event that it becomes necessary for any of those persons to leave the premises before the search is complete, the Respondent must allow them to re-enter the premises immediately upon their seeking re-entry on the same or the following day in order to complete the search.

RESTRICTIONS ON SEARCH

A4.036 8. This order may not be carried out at the same time as a police search warrant.

9. Before the Respondent allows anybody onto the premises to carry out this order, he is entitled to have the Supervising Solicitor explain to him what it means in everyday language.

10. The Respondent is entitled to seek legal advice and to ask the court to vary or discharge this order. Whilst doing so, he may ask the Supervising Solicitor to delay starting the search for up to 2 hours or such other longer period as the Supervising Solicitor may permit. However, the Respondent must—

(a) comply with the terms of paragraph 27 below;
(b) not disturb or remove any listed items; and
(c) permit the Supervising Solicitor to enter, but not start to search.

11. Before permitting entry to the premises by any person other than the Supervising Solicitor, the Respondent may, for a short time (not to exceed two hours, unless the Supervising Solicitor agrees to a longer period), gather together any documents he believes may be [incriminating or][8] privileged and hand them to the Supervising Solicitor for him to assess whether they are [incriminating or] privileged as claimed. If the Supervising Solicitor decides that any of the documents may be [incriminating or] privileged or is in any doubt as to their status, he will exclude them from the search and retain them in his possession pending further order of the court.

12. If the Respondent wishes to take legal advice and gather documents as permitted, he must first inform the Supervising Solicitor and keep him informed of the steps being taken.

13. No item may be removed from the premises until a list of the items to be removed has been prepared, and a copy of the list has been supplied to the Respondent, and he has been given a reasonable opportunity to check the list.

14. The premises must not be searched, and items must not be removed from them, except in the presence of the Respondent.

15. If the Supervising Solicitor is satisfied that full compliance with paragraphs 13 or 14 is not practicable, he may permit the search to proceed and items to be removed without fully complying with them.

DELIVERY UP OF ARTICLES/DOCUMENTS

16. The Respondent must immediately hand over to the Applicant's solicitors any **A4.037** of the listed items, which are in his possession or under his control, save for any computer or hard disk integral to any computer. Any items the subject of a dispute as to whether they are listed items must immediately be handed over to the Supervising Solicitor for safe keeping pending resolution of the dispute or further order of the court.

17. The Respondent must immediately give the search party effective access to the computers on the premises, with all necessary passwords, to enable the computers to be searched. If they contain any listed items the Respondent must cause the listed items to be displayed so that they can be read and copied.[9] The Respondent must provide the Applicant's Solicitors with copies of all listed items contained in the computers. All reasonable steps shall be taken by the Applicant and the Applicant's solicitors to ensure that no damage is done to any computer or data. The Applicant and his representatives may not themselves search the Respondent's computers unless they have sufficient expertise to do so without damaging the Respondent's system.

PROVISION OF INFORMATION

18. The Respondent must immediately inform the Applicant's Solicitors (in the **A4.038** presence of the Supervising Solicitor) so far as he is aware—
    (a) where all the listed items are;
    (b) the name and address of everyone who has supplied him, or offered to supply him, with listed items;
    (c) the name and address of everyone to whom he has supplied, or offered to supply, listed items; and
    (d) full details of the dates and quantities of every such supply and offer.

19. Within [   ] working days after being served with this order the Respondent must swear and serve an affidavit setting out the above information.[10]

PROHIBITED ACTS

A4.039 20. Except for the purpose of obtaining legal advice, the Respondent must not directly or indirectly inform anyone of these proceedings or of the contents of this order, or warn anyone that proceedings have been or may be brought against him by the Applicant until 4.30pm on the return date or further order of the court.
21. Until 4.30pm on the return date the Respondent must not destroy, tamper with, cancel or part with possession, power, custody or control of the listed items otherwise than in accordance with the terms of this order.
22. *[Insert any negative injunctions]*
23. *[Insert any further order]*

COSTS

A4.040 24. The costs of this application are reserved to the judge hearing the application on the return date.

RESTRICTIONS ON SERVICE

A4.041 25. This order may only be served between [   ] am/pm and [   ] am/ pm [and on a weekday].[11]
26. This order must be served by the Supervising Solicitor, and paragraph 6 of the order must be carried out in his presence and under his supervision.

VARIATION AND DISCHARGE OF THIS ORDER

A4.042 27. Anyone served with or notified of this order may apply to the court at any time to vary or discharge this order (or so much of it as affects that person), but they must first inform the Applicant's solicitors. If any evidence is to be relied upon in support of the application, the substance of it must be communicated in writing to the Applicant's solicitors in advance.

INTERPRETATION OF THIS ORDER

A4.043 28. Any requirement that something shall be done to or in the presence of the Respondent means—
(a) if there is more than one Respondent, to or in the presence of any one of them; and
(b) if a Respondent is not an individual, to or in the presence of a director, officer, partner or responsible employee.
29. A Respondent who is an individual who is ordered not to do something must not do it himself or in any other way. He must not do it through others acting on his behalf or on his instructions or with his encouragement.
30. A Respondent which is not an individual which is ordered not to do something must not do it itself or by its directors, officers, partners, employees or agents or in any other way.

COMMUNICATIONS WITH THE COURT

A4.044 All communications to the court about this order should be sent to—
[Insert the address and telephone number of the appropriate Court Office]

If the order is made at the Royal Courts of Justice, communications should be addressed as follows—
Where the order is made in the Chancery Division
Room TM 505, Royal Courts of Justice, Strand, London WC2A 2LL quoting the case number. The telephone number is 0207 947 6754.
Where the order is made in the Queen's Bench Division
Room WG034, Royal Courts of Justice, Strand, London WC2A 2LL quoting the case number. The telephone number is 0207 947 6009.
Where the order is made in the Commercial Court
Room E201, Royal Courts of Justice, Strand, London WC2A 2LL quoting the case number. The telephone number is 0207 947 6826.
The offices are open between 10am and 4.30pm Monday to Friday.

SCHEDULE A

THE PREMISES **A4.045**

SCHEDULE B

THE LISTED ITEMS **A4.046**

SCHEDULE C

UNDERTAKINGS GIVEN TO THE COURT BY THE APPLICANT

(1) If the court later finds that this order or carrying it out has caused loss to the **A4.047** Respondent, and decides that the Respondent should be compensated for that loss, the Applicant will comply with any order the court may make. Further if the carrying out of this order has been in breach of the terms of this order or otherwise in a manner inconsistent with the Applicant's solicitors' duties as officers of the court, the Applicant will comply with any order for damages the court may make.
[(2) As soon as practicable the Applicant will issue a claim form [in the form of the draft produced to the court] [claiming the appropriate relief].]
(3) The Applicant will [swear and file an affidavit] [cause an affidavit to be sworn and filed] [substantially in the terms of the draft affidavit produced to the court] [confirming the substance of what was said to the court by the Applicant's counsel/solicitors].
(4) The Applicant will not, without the permission of the court, use any information or documents obtained as a result of carrying out this order nor inform anyone else of these proceedings except for the purposes of these proceedings (including adding further Respondents) or commencing civil proceedings in relation to the same or related subject matter to these proceedings until after the return date.
[(5) The Applicant will maintain pending further order the sum of £ [   ] in an account controlled by the Applicant's solicitors.]
[(6) The Applicant will insure the items removed from the premises.]

SCHEDULE D

UNDERTAKINGS GIVEN BY THE APPLICANT'S SOLICITORS

(1) The Applicant's solicitors will provide to the Supervising Solicitor for service on **A4.048** the Respondent—

     (i) a service copy of this order;

    (ii) the claim form (with defendant's response pack) or, if not issued, the draft produced to the court;

   (iii) an application for hearing on the return date;

   (iv) copies of the affidavits *[or draft affidavits]* and exhibits capable of being wcopied containing the evidence relied upon by the applicant;

    (v) a note of any allegation of fact made orally to the court where such allegation is not contained in the affidavits or draft affidavits read by the judge; and

   (vi) a copy of the skeleton argument produced to the court by the Applicant's [counsel/solicitors].

(2) The Applicants' solicitors will answer at once to the best of their ability any question whether a particular item is a listed item.

(3) Subject as provided below the Applicant's solicitors will retain in their own safe keeping all items obtained as a result of this order until the court directs otherwise.

(4) The Applicant's solicitors will return the originals of all documents obtained as a result of this order (except original documents which belong to the Applicant) as soon as possible and in any event within [two] working days of their removal.

SCHEDULE E

UNDERTAKINGS GIVEN BY THE SUPERVISING SOLICITOR

A4.049 (1) The Supervising Solicitor will use his best endeavours to serve this order upon the Respondent and at the same time to serve upon the Respondent the other documents required to be served and referred to in paragraph (1) of Schedule D.

(2) The Supervising Solicitor will offer to explain to the person served with the order its meaning and effect fairly and in everyday language, and to inform him of his right to take legal advice (such advice to include an explanation that the Respondent may be entitled to avail himself of [the privilege against self-incrimination or] [legal professional privilege]) and to apply to vary or discharge this order as mentioned in paragraph 27 above.

(3) The Supervising Solicitor will retain in the safe keeping of his firm all items retained by him as a result of this order until the court directs otherwise.

(4) Within [48] hours of completion of the search the Supervising Solicitor will make and provide to the Applicant's solicitors, the Respondent or his solicitors and to the judge who made this order (for the purposes of the court file) a written report on the carrying out of the order.

SCHEDULE F

AFFIDAVITS

A4.050 The Applicant relied on the following affidavits—

[name] [number of affidavit] [date sworn] [filed on behalf of]
(1)
(2)

NAME AND ADDRESS OF APPLICANT'S SOLICITORS

A4.051 The Applicant's solicitors are—

[*Name, address, reference, fax and telephone numbers both in and out of office hours.*]

FOOTNOTES

1 Rule 25.1(1)(h).
2 Rule 25.1(1)(f).
3 Rule 23.7(1) and (2) and see rule 23.7(4) (short service).
4 See Part 22.
5 Rule 25.2(3).
6 Where the premises are likely to be occupied by an unaccompanied woman and the Supervising Solicitor is a man, at least one of the persons accompanying him should be a woman.
7 None of these persons should be people who could gain personally or commercially from anything they might read or see on the premises, unless their presence is essential.
8 References to incriminating documents should be omitted from orders made in intellectual property proceedings, where the privilege against self-incrimination does not apply—see paragraph 8.4 of the practice direction.
9 If it is envisaged that the Respondent's computers are to be imaged (*i.e.* the hard drives are to be copied wholesale, thereby reproducing listed items and other items indiscriminately), special provision needs to be made and independent computer specialists need to be appointed, who should be required to give undertakings to the court.
10 The period should ordinarily be longer than the period in paragraph (2) of Schedule D, if any of the information is likely to be included in listed items taken away of which the Respondent does not have copies.
11 Normally, the order should be served in the morning (not before 9.30 a.m.) and on a weekday to enable the Respondent more readily to obtain legal advice.

RSC ORDER 45—ENFORCEMENT OF JUDGMENTS AND ORDERS: GENERAL

Contents of this Order

INTERPRETATION

Rule 1A   In this Order, and in RSC Orders 46 and 47—   A4.052
  (a) "enforcement officer" means an individual who is authorised to act as an enforcement officer under the Courts Act 2003; and
  (b) "relevant enforcement officer" means—
    (i) in relation to a writ of execution which is directed to an single enforcement officer, that officer;
    (ii) in relation to a writ of execution which is directed to two or more enforcement officers, the officer to whom the writ is allocated.

ENFORCEMENT OF JUDGMENT, ETC., FOR PAYMENT OF MONEY

A4.053 Rule 1   (4) In this order references to any writ shall be construed as including references to any further writ in aid of the first mentioned writ.

NOTICE OF SEIZURE

A4.054 Rule 2   When first executing a writ of fieri facias, the Sheriff or his officer or the relevant enforcement officer shall deliver to the debtor or leave at each place where execution is levied a notice in Form No. 55 in the relevant Practice Direction informing the debtor of the execution.

ENFORCEMENT OF JUDGMENT FOR POSSESSION OF LAND

A4.055 Rule 3   (1) Subject to the provisions of these rules, a judgment or order for the giving of possession of land may be enforced by one or more of the following means, that is to say—
(a) writ of possession;
(b) in a case in which rule 5 applies, an order of committal;
(c) in such a case, writ of sequestration.
(2) A writ of possession to enforce a judgment or order for the giving of possession of any land shall not be issued without the permission of the court except where the judgment or order was given or made in proceedings by a mortgagee or mortgagor or by any person having the right to foreclose or redeem any mortgage, being proceedings in which there is a claim for—
(a) payment of moneys secured by the mortgage;
(b) sale of the mortgaged property;
(c) foreclosure;
(d) delivery of possession (whether before or after foreclosure or without foreclosure) to the mortgagee by the mortgagor or by any person who is alleged to be in possession of the property;
(e) redemption;
(f) reconveyance of the land or its release from the security; or
(g) delivery of possession by the mortgagee.
(2A) In paragraph (2) "mortgage" includes a legal or equitable mortgage and a legal or equitable charge, and reference to a mortgagor, a mortgagee and mortgaged land is to be interpreted accordingly.
(3) Such permission as is referred to in paragraph (2) shall not be granted unless it is shown—
(a) that every person in actual possession of the whole or any part of the land has received such notice of the proceedings as appears to the court sufficient to enable him to apply to the court for any relief to which he may be entitled; and
(b) if the operation of the judgment or order is suspended by subsection (2) of section 16 of the Landlord and Tenant Act, 1954,[1] that the applicant has not received notice in writing from the tenant that he desires that the provisions of paragraphs (a) and (b) of that subsection shall have effect.
(4) A writ of possession may include provision for enforcing the payment of any money adjudged or ordered to be paid by the judgment or order which is to be enforced by the writ.

ENFORCEMENT OF JUDGMENT FOR DELIVERY OF GOODS

A4.056 Rule 4   (1) Subject to the provisions of these rules, a judgment or order for the delivery of any goods which does not give a person against whom the judgment is given or order made the alternative of paying the assessed value of the goods may be enforced by one or more of the following means, that is to say—

(a) writ of delivery to recover the goods without alternative provision for recovery of the assessed value thereof (hereafter in this rule referred to as a "writ of specific delivery");

(b) in a case in which rule 5 applies, an order of committal;

(c) in such a case, writ of sequestration.

(2) Subject to the provisions of these rules, a judgment or order for the delivery of any goods or payment of their assessed value may be enforced by one or more of the following means, that is to say—

(a) writ of delivery to recover the goods or their assessed value;

(b) by order of the court, writ of specific delivery;

(c) in a case in which rule 5 applies, writ of sequestration.

An application for an order under sub-paragraph (b) shall be made in accordance with CPR Part 23, which must be served on the defendant against whom the judgment or order sought to be enforced was given or made.

(3) A writ of specific delivery, and a writ of delivery to recover any goods or their assessed value, may include provision for enforcing the payment of any money adjudged or ordered to be paid by the judgment or order which is to be enforced by the writ.

(4) A judgment or order for the payment of the assessed value of any goods may be enforced by the same means as any other judgment or order for the payment of money.

ENFORCEMENT OF JUDGMENT TO DO OR ABSTAIN FROM DOING ANY ACT

A4.057

Rule 5 (1) Where—

(a) a person required by a judgment or order to do an act within a time specified in the judgment or order refuses or neglects to do it within that time or, as the case may be, within that time as extended or abridged under a court order or CPR rule 2.11; or

(b) a person disobeys a judgment or order requiring him to abstain from doing an act,

then, subject to the provisions of these rules, the judgment or order may be enforced by one or more of the following means, that is to say—

(i) with the permission of the court, a writ of sequestration against the property of that person;

(ii) where that person is a body corporate, with the permission of the court, a writ of sequestration against the property of any director or other officer of the body;

(iii) subject to the provisions of the Debtors Act 1869 and 1878,[2] an order of committal against that person or, where that person is a body corporate, against any such officer.

(2) Where a judgment or order requires a person to do an act within a time therein specified and an order is subsequently made under rule 6 requiring the act to be done within some other time, references in paragraph (1) of this rule to a judgment or order shall be construed as references to the order made under rule 6.

(3) Where under any judgment or order requiring the delivery of any goods the person liable to execution has the alternative of paying the assessed value of the goods, the judgment or order shall not be enforceable by order of committal under paragraph (1), but the court may, on the application of the person entitled to enforce the judgment

or order, make an order requiring the first mentioned person to deliver the goods to the applicant within a time specified in the order, and that order may be so enforced.

JUDGMENT, ETC. REQUIRING ACT TO BE DONE: ORDER FIXING TIME FOR DOING IT

A4.058   Rule 6   (1) Notwithstanding that a judgment or order requiring a person to do an act specifies a time within which the act is to be done, the court shall have power to make an order requiring the act to be done within another time, being such time after service of that order, or such other time, as may be specified therein.

(2) Where a judgment or order requiring a person to do an act does not specify a time within which the act is to be done, the court shall have power subsequently to make an order requiring the act to be done within such time after service of that order, or such other time, as may be specified therein.

(3) An application for an order under this rule must be made in accordance with CPR Part 23 and the application notice must, be served on the person required to do the act in question.

SERVICE OF COPY OF JUDGMENT, ETC., PREREQUISITE TO ENFORCEMENT UNDER RULE 5

A4.059   Rule 7   (1) In this rule references to an order shall be construed as including references to a judgment.

(2) Subject to paragraphs (6) and (7) of this rule, an order shall not be enforced under rule 5 unless—

(a) a copy of the order has been served personally on the person required to do or abstain from doing the act in question; and

(b) in the case of an order requiring a person to do an act, the copy has been so served before the expiration of the time within which he was required to do the act.

(3) Subject as aforesaid, an order requiring a body corporate to do or abstain from doing an act shall not be enforced as mentioned in rule 5(1)(b)(ii) or (iii) unless—

(a) a copy of the order has also been served personally on the officer against whose property permission is sought to issue a writ of sequestration or against whom an order of committal is sought; and

(b) in the case of an order requiring the body corporate to do an act, the copy has been so served before the expiration of the time within which the body was required to do the act.

(4) There must be prominently displayed on the front of the copy of an order served under this rule a warning to the person on whom the copy is served that disobedience to the order would be a contempt of court punishable by imprisonment, or (in the case of an order requiring a body corporate to do or abstain from doing an act) punishable by sequestration of the assets of the body corporate and by imprisonment of any individual responsible.

(5) With the copy of an order required to be served under this rule, being an order requiring a person to do an act, there must also be served a copy of any order or agreement under CPR rule 2.11 extending or abridging the time for doing the act and, where the first-mentioned order was made under rule 5(3) or 6 of this order, a copy of the previous order requiring the act to be done.

(6) An order requiring a person to abstain from doing an act may be enforced under rule 5 notwithstanding that service of a copy of the order has not been effected in accordance with this rule if the court is satisfied that pending such service, the person against whom or against whose property is sought to enforce the order has had notice thereof either—

(a) by being present when the order was made; or

(b) by being notified of the terms of the order, whether by telephone, telegram or otherwise.

(7) The court may dispense with service of a copy of an order under this rule if it thinks it just to do so.

COURT MAY ORDER ACT TO BE DONE AT EXPENSE OF DISOBEDIENT PARTY

Rule 8   If a mandatory order, an injunction or a judgment or order for the specific **A4.060** performance of a contract is not complied with, then, without prejudice to its powers under section 39 of the Act and its powers to punish the disobedient party for contempt, the court may direct that the act required to be done may, so far as practicable, be done by the party by whom the order or judgment was obtained or some other person appointed by the court, at the cost of the disobedient party, and upon the act being done the expenses incurred may be ascertained in such manner as the court may direct and execution may issue against the disobedient party for the amount so ascertained and for costs.

MATTERS OCCURRING AFTER JUDGMENT: STAY OF EXECUTION, ETC.

Rule 11   Without prejudice to Order 47, rule 1, a party against whom a judgment **A4.061** has been given or an order made may apply to the court for a stay of execution of the judgment or order or other relief on the ground of matters which have occurred since the date of the judgment or order, and the court may by order grant such relief, and on such terms, as it thinks just.

FORMS OF WRITS

Rule 12   (1) A writ of fieri facias must be in such of the Forms Nos. 53 to 63 in the **A4.062** relevant practice direction as is appropriate in the particular case.

(2) A writ of delivery must be in Form No. 64 or 65 in the relevant practice direction, whichever is appropriate.

(3) A writ of possession must be in Form No. 66 or 66A in the relevant practice direction, whichever is appropriate.

(4) A writ of sequestration must be in Form No. 67 in the relevant practice direction.

FOOTNOTES
[1] 1954 c.56.
[2] 1869 c.62; 1878 c.54.

RSC ORDER 52—COMMITTAL

Contents of this Order

COMMITTAL FOR CONTEMPT OF COURT

A4.063 Rule 1 (1) The power of the High Court or Court of Appeal to punish for contempt of court may be exercised by an order of committal.

(2) Where contempt of court—

(a) is committed in connection with—

(i) any proceedings before a Divisional Court of the Queen's Bench Division; or

(ii) criminal proceedings, except where the contempt is committed in the face of the court or consists of disobedience to an order of the court or a breach of an undertaking to the court; or

(iii) proceedings in an inferior court; or

(b) is committed otherwise than in connection with any proceedings,

then, subject to paragraph (4), an order of committal may be made only by a Divisional Court of the Queen's Bench Division.

This paragraph shall not apply in relation to contempt of the Court of Appeal.

(3) Where contempt of court is committed in connection with any proceedings in the High Court, then, subject to paragraph (2), an order of committal may be made by a single judge of the Queen's Bench Division except where the proceedings were assigned or subsequently transferred to some other Division, in which case the order may be made only by a single judge of that other Division.

The reference in this paragraph to a single judge of the Queen's Bench Division shall, in relation to proceedings in any court the judge or judges of which are, when exercising the jurisdiction of that court, deemed by virtue of any enactment to constitute a court of the High Court, be construed as a reference to a judge of that court.

(4) Where by virtue of any enactment the High Court has power to punish or take steps for the punishment of any person charged with having done anything in relation to a court, tribunal or person which would, if it had been done in relation to the High Court, have been a contempt of that court, an order of committal may be made—

(a) on an application under section 88 of the Charities Act 1993[1], by a single judge of the Chancery Division; and

(b) in any other case, by a single judge of the Queen's Bench Division.

APPLICATION TO DIVISIONAL COURT

A4.064 Rule 2 (1) No application to a Divisional Court for an order of committal against any person may be made unless permission to make such an application has been granted in accordance with this rule.

(2) An application for such permission must be made without notice to a Divisional Court, except in vacation when it may be made to a judge in chambers and must be supported by a statement setting out the name and description of the applicant, the name, description and address of the person sought to be committed and the grounds on which his committal is sought, and by an affidavit, to be filed before the application is made, verifying the facts relied on.

(3) The applicant must give notice of the application for permission not later than the preceding day to the Crown Office and must at the same time lodge in that office copies of the statement and affidavit.

(4) Where an application for permission under this rule is refused by a judge in chambers, the applicant may make a fresh application for such permission to a Divisional Court.

(5) An application made to a Divisional Court by virtue of paragraph (4) must be made within 8 days after the judge's refusal to give permission or, if a Divisional Court does not sit within that period, on the first day on which it sits thereafter.

APPLICATION FOR ORDER AFTER LEAVE TO APPLY GRANTED

Rule 3   (1) When permission has been granted under rule 2 to apply for an order   **A4.065** of committal, the application for the order must be made to a Divisional Court and, unless the court or judge granting permission has otherwise directed, there must be at least 14 clear days between the service of the claim form and the day named therein for the hearing.

(2) Unless within 14 days after such permission was granted, the claim form is issued the permission shall lapse.

(3) Subject to paragraph 4, the claim form, accompanied by a copy of the statement and affidavit in support of the application for permission, must be served personally on the person sought to be committed.

(4) Without prejudice to the powers of the court or judge under Part 6 of the CPR, the court or judge may dispense with service under this rule if it or he thinks it just to do so.

APPLICATION TO COURT OTHER THAN DIVISIONAL COURT

Rule 4   (1) Where an application for an order of committal may be made to a   **A4.066** court other than a Divisional Court, the application must be made by claim form or application notice and be supported by an affidavit.

(2) Subject to paragraph (3) the claim form or application notice, stating the grounds of the application and accompanied by a copy of the affidavit in support of the application, must be served personally on the person sought to be committed.

(3) Without prejudice to its powers under Part 6 of the CPR, the court may dispense with service under this rule if it thinks it just to do so.

(4) This rule does not apply to committal applications which under rules 1(2) and 3(1) should be made to a Divisional Court but which, in vacation, have been properly made to a single judge in accordance with RSC Order 64, rule 4.

SAVING FOR POWER TO COMMIT WITHOUT APPLICATION FOR PURPOSE

Rule 5   Nothing in the foregoing provisions of this order shall be taken as   **A4.067** affecting the power of the High Court or Court of Appeal to make an order of committal of its own initiative against a person guilty of contempt of court.

PROVISIONS AS TO HEARING

A4.068   Rule 6   (1) Subject to paragraph (2), the court hearing an application for an order of committal may sit in private in the following cases, that is to say—

      (a) where the application arises out of proceedings relating to the wardship or adoption of an infant or wholly or mainly to the guardianship, custody, maintenance or upbringing of an infant, or rights of access to an infant;

      (b) where the application arises out of proceedings relating to a person suffering or appearing to be suffering from mental disorder within the meaning of the Mental Health Act 1983[2];

      (c) where the application arises out of proceedings in which a secret process, discovery or invention was in issue;

      (d) where it appears to the court that in the interests of the administration of justice or for reasons of national security the application should be heard in private;

    but, except as aforesaid, the application shall be heard in public.

    (2) If the court hearing an application in private by virtue of paragraph (1) decides to make an order of committal against the person sought to be committed, it shall in public state—

      (a) the name of that person;

      (b) in general terms the nature of the contempt of court in respect of which the order of committal is being made; and

      (c) the length of the period for which he is being committed.

    (3) Except with the permission of the court hearing an application for an order of committal, no grounds shall be relied upon at the hearing except the grounds set out in the statement under rule 2 or, as the case may be, in the claim form or application notice under rule 4.

    (4) If on the hearing of the application the person sought to be committed expresses a wish to give oral evidence on his own behalf, he shall be entitled to do so.

POWER TO SUSPEND EXECUTION OF COMMITTAL ORDER

A4.069   Rule 7   (1) The court by whom an order of committal is made may by order direct that the execution of the order of committal shall be suspended for such period or on such terms or conditions as it may specify.

    (2) Where execution of an order of committal is suspended by an order under paragraph (1), the applicant for the order of committal must, unless the court otherwise directs, serve on the person against whom it was made a notice informing him of the making and terms of the order under that paragraph.

WARRANT FOR ARREST

A4.070   Rule 7A   A warrant for the arrest of a person against whom an order of committal has been made shall not, without further order of the court, be enforced more than 2 years after the date on which the warrant is issued.

DISCHARGE OF PERSON COMMITTED

A4.071   Rule 8   (1) The court may, on the application of any person committed to prison for any contempt of court, discharge him.

    (2) Where a person has been committed for failing to comply with a judgment or order requiring him to deliver any thing to some other

person or to deposit it in court or elsewhere, and a writ of sequestration has also been issued to enforce that judgment or order, then, if the thing is in the custody or power of the person committed, the commissioners appointed by the writ of sequestration may take possession of it as if it were the property of that person and, without prejudice to the generality of paragraph (1), the court may discharge the person committed and may give such directions for dealing with the thing taken by the commissioners as it thinks fit.

(RSC Order 46, rule 5 contains rules relating to writs of sequestration)

SAVING FOR OTHER POWERS

Rule 9   Nothing in the foregoing provisions of this order shall be taken as **A4.072** affecting the power of the court to make an order requiring a person guilty of contempt of court, or a person punishable by virtue of any enactment in like manner as if he had been guilty of contempt of the High Court, to pay a fine or to give security for his good behaviour, and those provisions, so far as applicable, and with the necessary modifications, shall apply in relation to an application for such an order as they apply in relation to an application for an order of committal.

FOOTNOTES

[1] 1993 c.10.
[2] 1983 c.20.

Precedents

PRECEDENTS 1: PRECEDENT FOR PROPRIETARY INJUNCTION, MAREVA INJUNCTION
AND DISCLOSURE ORDERS IN AN ACTION BROUGHT BY ABC LIMITED FOLLOWING
NOTICE OF RESCISSION AVOIDING AN AGREEMENT

IN THE HIGH COURT OF JUSTICE   A5.001
QUEEN'S BENCH DIVISION
COMMERCIAL COURT
The Hon. Mr Justice . . . . . . (hearing in private)

B E T W E E N:

ABC LIMITED

Claimant

- and -

(1) DEF LIMITED
(2) GHI LIMITED
(3) X
(4) Y
(5) Z

Defendants

ORDER

THIS ORDER

To: DEF Limited . . . . . . whose registered office is at . . . . ("DEF");

     GHI Limited . . . . . . whose registered office is at . . . . ("GHI");

     X of . . . . ("X");

     Y of . . . . ("Y"); and

     Z of . . . .

PENAL NOTICE

IF YOU DEF, GHI, X, Y OR Z DISOBEY THIS ORDER YOU MAY BE HELD TO BE IN CONTEMPT OF COURT AND MAY BE IMPRISONED, FINED OR HAVE YOUR ASSETS SEIZED.

IF YOU DEF, OR GHI, DISOBEY THIS ORDER THEN YOU, R, AS DIRECTOR OF DEF, AND YOU, S AND T, AS DIRECTORS OF GHI, MAY BE HELD TO BE IN CONTEMPT OF COURT AND MAY BE IMPRISONED, FINED OR HAVE YOUR ASSETS SEIZED.

ANY OTHER PERSON WHO KNOWS OF THIS ORDER AND DOES ANY-THING WHICH HELPS OR PERMITS ANY OF THE RESPONDENTS TO BREACH THE TERMS OF THIS ORDER MAY ALSO BE HELD TO BE IN CONTEMPT OF COURT AND MAY BE IMPRISONED, FINED OR HAVE THEIR ASSETS SEIZED.

THIS ORDER

A5.002   1   This is a Freezing Injunction made against DEF, GHI, X, Y and Z ("the Respondents") on . . . . by the Hon. Mr Justice . . . . on the application of ABC Limited ("the Applicant"). The Judge read the Affidavits listed in Schedule A and accepted the undertakings set out in Schedule B at the end of this Order, and the undertaking given by the Applicant's Solicitors which is at the end of Schedule B.

2   This order was made at a hearing without notice to the Respondent. The Respondent has a right to apply to the court to vary or discharge the order—see paragraph 18 below.

3   There will be a further hearing in respect of this order on . . . . (the "return date").

4   If there is more than one Respondent—
   (i) unless otherwise stated, references in this order to "the Respondents" or "the Respondent" mean all and each of them; and
   (ii) this order is effective against any Respondent on whom it is served or who is given notice of it.

PERMISSION TO SERVE THE CLAIM FORM AND AN APPLICATION NOTICE OUT OF THE JURISDICTION

A5.003   5   The Applicant has permission to issue a claim form for service out of the jurisdiction on the First Defendant ("DEF"), Second Defendant ("GHI") and Third Defendant ("X") pursuant to CPR 6.20 [*set out each provision on which the judge granted permission*] and to serve the same, the particulars of claim, an application notice seeking interim relief against each of them in these proceedings, a copy of this order, and copies of the affidavits and exhibits containing the evidence relied upon by the Applicant and any other documents provided to the court on the making of the application upon each of them out of the jurisdiction:
   (i) in the case of DEF at . . . ., or elsewhere in [insert foreign jurisdiction], or on R Limited as a director of DEF at . . . .
   (ii) in the case of GHI at . . . . or elsewhere within . . . . or on S or T at . . . . or elsewhere within . . . .
   (iii) in the case of X personally in [foreign jurisdiction], and at . . . .

6   Time for acknowledgment of service of the claim form by the First and Second and Third Respondents shall be [*insert time for acknowledgment as calculated in accordance with CPR r.6.22*] days after service of the particulars

of claim. Time to file an acknowledgment of service or serve an admission by the First, Second and Third Respondents shall be [*insert time for acknowledgment as calculated in accordance with CPR r.6.22*]. Time for filing a defence by the First, Second and Third Respondents shall be [*insert time for acknowledgment as calculated in accordance with CPR r.6.22*] after service of the particulars of claim, or [*insert time for acknowledgment as calculated in accordance with CPR r.6.22*] after service of the particulars of claim where the Respondent has acknowledged service.

PROPRIETARY INJUNCTION

7   Until after the return date or further order of the court, each respondent must **A5.004** not, without the prior consent in writing of the Applicant's solicitors—
   (i) remove from England and Wales if they are located in England and Wales; or
   (ii) in any way dispose of, deal with or diminish the value of the purchase money paid by or on behalf of the Applicant under the written agreement dated [*identify agreement*] paid into [*identify account*], or its fruits or proceeds, including any interest earned or other income received or derived from the said purchase money.

PROVISION OF INFORMATION ABOUT THE ASSETS FROZEN BY THE PROPRIETARY INJUNCTION

8.1 Unless paragraph 8.2 applies, each Respondent within three clear days of **A5.005** service of a copy of this order upon him and to the best of his ability and after making all reasonable inquiries, and in any event within the said time limit, must inform the Applicant's solicitors in writing of the location nature and value of all assets which represent in whole or in part or are derived from the proceeds or fruits including any interest earned of the purchase money paid by or on behalf of the claimant under the written agreement [*insert details*], regardless of whether or not such proceeds are in the Respondent's own name and whether they are solely or jointly owned. Without prejudice to the generality of the foregoing each Respondent is to inform the Applicant's solicitors:
   (i) the name and address of all persons including financial institutions holding any such assets;
   (ii) the names and numbers of all accounts holding any such assets together with the name and address where such account is held, in whose name and the amount in such account;
   (iii) the details of all trusts which have received any of such assets including the names and addresses of the trustees.
8.2 If the provision of any of this information is likely to incriminate the Respondent, he may be entitled to refuse to provide it, but is recommended to take legal advice before refusing to provide the information. Wrongful refusal to provide the information is contempt of court and may render the Respondent liable to be imprisoned, fined or have his assets seized.
9   Within six clear days after being served with a copy of this order, the Respondent must swear and serve on the Applicant's solicitors an affidavit setting out the above information.

FREEZING INJUNCTION (RESPONDENT'S ASSETS)

10   Until after the return date or further order of the court, except with the prior **A5.006** consent in writing given by the Applicant's solicitors, each Respondent must not—

(i) remove from England and Wales any of his assets which are in England and Wales up to the value of [*insert maximum sum fixed by the court*].

(ii) in any way dispose of, deal with or diminish the value of any of his assets whether they are in or outside England and Wales up to the same value.

11 Paragraph 10 applies to all the Respondent's assets whether or not they are in his own name and whether they are solely or jointly owned. For the purpose of this order the Respondent's assets include any asset which he has the power, directly or indirectly, to dispose of or deal with as if it were his own. The Respondent is to be regarded as having such power if a third party holds or controls the asset in accordance with his direct or indirect instructions.

12 This prohibition includes, in particular, the assets set out in Schedule C hereto.

13.1 If the total value free of charges or other encumbrances ("unencumbered value") of the Respondent's assets in England and Wales exceeds [*the maximum sum fixed by the court*] the Respondent may remove any of those assets from England and Wales or may dispose of or deal with them so long as the total unencumbered value of the Respondent's assets still in England and Wales remains at least equal to [*the maximum sum*].

13.2 If the total unencumbered value of a Respondent's assets in England and Wales does not exceed [*the maximum sum fixed by the court*] that Respondent must not remove any of those assets from England and Wales and must not dispose of or deal with any of them. If the Respondent has other assets outside England and Wales, he may dispose of or deal with those assets outside England and Wales so long as the total unencumbered value of all his assets whether in or outside England and Wales remains above [*the maximum sum fixed by the court*].

PROVISION OF INFORMATION (RESPONDENT'S ASSETS)

A5.007 14.1 Unless paragraph 14.3 applies, the Fourth and Fifth Respondents must inform the Applicant's solicitors in writing within six hours (time to run only between 9.30am and 6.00pm Monday to Friday) after service of a copy of this order of all his respective assets worldwide exceeding £100,000 (one hundred thousand pounds) in value whether in his own name or not and whether solely or jointly owned with another, giving the value, location and details of all such assets.

14.2 Unless paragraph 14.3 applies, the Respondent (which, for the avoidance of doubt, shall include the Fourth and Fifth Respondents) within three clear days of service of a copy of this order upon him, and to the best of his ability after making all reasonable inquiries, but in any case within the said time limit, inform the Applicant's solicitors in writing of all his assets worldwide exceeding £ 2,000 in value whether in his own name or not and whether solely or jointly owned, giving the value, location and details of all such assets.

14.3 If the provision of any of this information is likely to incriminate the Respondent, he may be entitled to refuse to provide it, but is recommended to take legal advice before refusing to provide the information. Wrongful refusal to provide the information is contempt of court and may render the Respondent liable to be imprisoned, fined or have his assets seized.

15 Within six clear days after the Respondent has been served with this order, he must swear an affidavit setting out the above information and serve a copy on the Applicant's solicitors.

EXCEPTIONS TO THIS ORDER

A5.008 16.1 This order does not prohibit the Respondent from spending £1,000 per week towards his ordinary living expenses and also reasonable sums on legal advice and representation. But before spending any money the Respondent must tell the Applicant's legal representatives where the money is to come from, and any amount must be taken from the Respondent's assets and not from the purchase moneys paid by or on behalf of the Applicant under the written agreement [*insert details*] being [*set out details of amounts paid into what account(s)*], or their fruits or proceeds including any interest earned or other income received or derived from the said purchase moneys.

16.2 This order does not prohibit the Respondent from dealing with or disposing of any of his assets in the ordinary and proper course of business. This does not apply to the purchase money paid by or on behalf of the Applicant under the written agreement [*insert details*] being [*set out details of amounts paid into what account(s)*], or its fruits or proceeds, including any interest earned or other income received or derived from the said purchase moneys.

16.3 The Respondent may agree with the Applicant's legal representatives that the above spending limits should be increased or that this order should be varied in any other respect, but any agreement must be in writing.

16.4 The order, except for the permission to serve outside of the jurisdiction, will cease to have effect if the Respondent—
   (i) provides security by paying the sum of [*the maximum sum fixed by the court*] into court, to be held to the order of the court; or
   (ii) makes provision for security in that sum by another method agreed with the Applicant's legal representatives.

COSTS

17   The costs of this application are reserved to the judge hearing the application on the return date. **A5.009**

VARIATION OR DISCHARGE OF THIS ORDER

18   Anyone served with or notified of this order may apply to the court at any time to vary or discharge this order or so much of it as affects that person, but they must first inform the Applicant's solicitors. If any evidence is to be relied upon in support of the application, the substance of it must be communicated in writing to the Applicant's solicitors in advance. **A5.010**

INTERPRETATION OF THIS ORDER

19   A Respondent who is an individual who is ordered not to do something must not do it himself or in any other way. He must not do it through others acting on his behalf or on his instructions or with his encouragement. **A5.011**

20   A Respondent which is not an individual which is ordered not to do something must not do it itself or by its directors, officers, partners, employees or agents or in any other way.

PARTIES OTHER THAN THE APPLICANT AND RESPONDENT

21   *Effect of this order* **A5.012**
It is a contempt of court for any person notified of this order knowingly to assist in or permit a breach of this order. Any person doing so may be imprisoned, fined or have their assets seized.

22   *Set-off by banks*
This injunction does not prevent any bank from exercising any right of set-off it may have in respect of any facility which it gave to the respondent before it was notified of this order.

23   *Withdrawals by the Respondent*
No bank need inquire as to the application or proposed application of any money withdrawn by the Respondent if the withdrawal appears to be permitted by this order.

24   Persons outside England and Wales

24.1 Except as provided in paragraph (2) below, the terms of this order do not affect or concern anyone outside the jurisdiction of this court.

24.2 The terms of this order will affect the following persons in a country or state outside the jurisdiction of this court—

(i) the Respondent or his officer or agent appointed by power of attorney;

(ii) any person who—

(a) is subject to the jurisdiction of this court;

(b) has been given written notice of this order at his residence or place of business within the jurisdiction of this court; and

(c) is able to prevent acts or omissions outside the jurisdiction of this court which constitute or assist in a breach of the terms of this order; and

(iii) any other person, only to the extent that this order is declared enforceable by or is enforced by a court in that country or state.

25   *Assets located outside England and Wales*

Nothing in this order shall, in respect of assets located outside England and Wales, prevent any third party from complying with—

(i) what it reasonably believes to be its obligations, contractual or otherwise, under the laws and obligations of the country or state in which those assets are situated or under the proper law of any contract between itself and the Respondent; and

(ii) any orders of the courts of that country or state, provided that reasonable notice of any application for such an order is given to the Applicant's solicitors.

COMMUNICATIONS WITH THE COURT

A5.013   All communications to the court about this order should be sent to—

Room E201, Royal Courts of Justice, Strand, London WC2A 2LL quoting the case number. The telephone number is 0207 947 6826.

The offices are open between 10am and 4.30pm Monday to Friday.

SCHEDULE A

Affidavits

A5.014   The Applicant relied on the following affidavits—

[*Name*]	[*Number of affidavit*]	[*Date sworn*]	[*Filed on behalf of*]

SCHEDULE B

Undertakings Given to The Court by the Applicant

A5.015   1   If the court later finds that this order has caused loss to the Respondent, and decides that one or more of the Respondents should be compensated for that loss, the Applicant will comply with any order the court may make.

2   The Applicant has placed a sum of £....... with the Applicant's solicitors to be held in their client account for the Applicant, and undertakes to the court that the said sum is to be held as security to meet any award of compensation made under paragraph 1 above and/or as security for the costs of the Respondents, or any of them, in these proceedings, as may be directed by the court, and that the Applicant will not seek to deal in any way whatsoever with the said sum held in the said client account without prior permission of the court.

3   As soon as practicable the Applicant will issue and serve a claim form in the form of the draft produced to the court together with particulars of claim in the same or substantially the same form as produced before the court.

4   The Applicant will cause the affidavits relied upon in the course of the without notice application to be sworn and filed.

5   The Applicant will serve upon each of the Respondents as soon as practicable
    (i)   copies of the affidavits and exhibits containing the evidence relied upon by the Applicant, and any other documents provided to the court on the making of the application;
    (ii) the claim form when issued; and
    (iii) an application notice for continuation of the order.
    In the case of item (i) above the Applicant will serve the same by leaving copies for:
    DEF at its registered office which is at ....;
    GHI at its registered office at ....;
    X by leaving the same at ....;
    Y by leaving the same at ....; and
    Z by leaving the same at ....

6   Anyone notified of this order will be given a copy of it by the Applicant's legal representatives.

7   The Applicant will pay the reasonable costs of anyone other than a Respondent which have been incurred as a result of this order including the costs of finding out whether that person holds any of a Respondent's assets and if the court later finds that this order has caused such person loss, and decides that such person should be compensated for that loss, the Applicant will comply with any order the court may make.

8   If this order ceases to have effect (for example, if a Respondent provides security) the Applicant will immediately take all reasonable steps to inform in writing anyone to whom he has given notice of this order, or who he has reasonable grounds for supposing may act upon this order, that it has ceased to have effect.

9   The Applicant will not without the permission of the court use any information obtained as a result of this order for the purpose of any civil or criminal proceedings, either in England and Wales or in any other jurisdiction except [*insert details*], other than this claim.

10 The Applicant will not without the permission of the court seek to enforce this order in any country outside England and Wales or seek an order of a similar nature including orders conferring a charge or other security against the Respondent or the Respondent's assets save in relation to proceedings in [*insert details*].

11 The Applicant will serve copies of the affidavits and exhibits containing the evidence relied upon by the Applicant and any other documents provided to the court on the making of the application at any address within this jurisdiction, which is nominated for such purpose by any Respondent served with this order outside of this jurisdiction.

12 The Applicant will procure that the Affidavit of [   ] will be sworn forthwith, and, in any event, within 48 hours of the making of this Order.

UNDERTAKING GIVEN TO THE COURT BY THE APPLICANT'S SOLICITORS

A5.016 The Applicant's solicitors, [insert details], hereby undertake to the court that they hold the said sum amounting to £....... in client account, which has been paid to them for the applicant and which under this order is to stand as security as aforesaid, and that they will abide by any order of the court made directed to them in relation to that sum held in their client account.

SCHEDULE C

ASSETS

A5.017 (i) DEF:

Jurisdiction   Assets

(ii) GHI:

Jurisdiction   Assets

(iii) X

Jurisdiction   Assets

(iv) Y

Jurisdiction   Assets

	Bank and Branch	Nature of Account	Account Number	Account Holder

(v) Z

Jurisdiction   Assets

The Applicant's legal representatives are—   A5.018

[*Insert details including telephone and fax numbers*]

Out of office hours

[*Insert details*]

IN THE HIGH COURT OF JUSTICE   A5.019
QUEEN'S BENCH DIVISION
COMMERCIAL COURT
The Hon. Mr Justice . . . . . . (hearing in private)

B E T W E E N:

ABC LIMITED
                                                                        Claimant

- and -

(1) DEF LIMITED
(2) GHI LIMITED
(3) X
(4) Y
(5) Z
                                                                        Defendants

---

ORDER

PENAL NOTICE

IF YOU DEF, GHI, X, Y OR Z DISOBEY THIS ORDER YOU MAY BE HELD
TO BE IN CONTEMPT OF COURT AND MAY BE IMPRISONED, FINED OR
HAVE YOUR ASSETS SEIZED.

IF YOU DEF, OR GHI, DISOBEY THIS ORDER THEN YOU, R, AS DIRECTOR
OF DEF, AND YOU, S AND T, AS DIRECTORS OF GHI, MAY BE HELD TO
BE IN CONTEMPT OF COURT AND MAY BE IMPRISONED, FINED OR
HAVE YOUR ASSETS SEIZED.

ANY OTHER PERSON WHO KNOWS OF THIS ORDER AND DOES ANY-
THING WHICH HELPS OR PERMITS ANY OF THE RESPONDENTS TO
BREACH THE TERMS OF THIS ORDER MAY ALSO BE HELD TO BE IN
CONTEMPT OF COURT AND MAY BE IMPRISONED, FINED OR HAVE
THEIR ASSETS SEIZED.

[*Solicitors' details*]

Notes to Precedent 1

A5.020   1.   Schedule C contains details of assets known to the applicant which the applicant claims fall within the "in particular" clause of the freezing injunction. There should be evidence before the court showing why each asset listed is said to come within that clause. As drafted the clause only applies to assets within the words in para.11.

2.   The Precedent includes in para.14.1 a disclosure order to be complied with within six hours of service of the order. The six hours is intended to allow the respondent to obtain legal advice on privilege against self-incrimination and whether he is obliged to provide the information. This length of time limit is only suitable for a respondent who has ready access to English legal advice. It is assumed that this is a case in which the judge will have formed the clear view on the without notice application that privilege against self-incrimination will not apply, and that therefore the six-hour period is fair in the circumstances.

3.   The example order of freezing injunction uses drafting which makes refusal to give the disclosure even when based on a mistaken invoking privilege against self incrimination, a contempt of court. In a case in which the judge forms the clear view that the privilege against self-incrimination will not apply, this is a fair order to make. In cases which are likely to raise a problem of some complexity about the privilege, and where the respondent could make a bona fide claim to privilege against self-incrimination, careful consideration needs to be given about how long the respondent should be allowed for taking legal advice. Also it is considered that normally an order should provide that if the respondent makes the claim to privilege the mandatory disclosure order falls away.[1] This is so that the respondent is not placed in contempt of court by a bona fide, albeit mistaken, claim to the privilege: see Chapter 22, paras 22.009 *et seq.*

4.   Under CPR 2.9:

"Dates for compliance to be calendar dates and to include time of day

2.9   (1) Where the court gives a judgment, order or direction which imposes a time limit for doing any act, the last date for compliance must, wherever practicable—
(a) be expressed as a calendar date; and
(b) include the time of day by which the act must be done.
(2) Where the date by which an act must be done is inserted in any document, the date must, wherever practicable, be expressed as a calendar date."

Accordingly wherever possible disclosure orders should be fixed with a specified time on an identified day.

5.   However, in paras 8.1, 9, 14.2 and 16 it is assumed that it is not "practicable" to fix a particular time on an identified day because of uncertainties about when personal service will be successfully effected on each respondent. Instead the drafting uses the expression "clear day" which is defined in CPR r.2.8, and which for a period of five days of less excludes Saturdays, Sundays, Bank Holidays, Good Friday and Christmas Day.

6.   Paragraph 2 of the Schedule B undertakings is drafted so as to constitute the fund of £200,000 as security in favour of the respondents.

---

[1] *IBM v Prima Data International* [1994] 1 W.L.R. 719.

PRECEDENT 2: EXAMPLE LIST OF TOPICS TO BE DEALT WITH IN A SKELETON
ARGUMENT TO BE DRAFTED FOR USE ON A WITHOUT NOTICE APPLICATION FOR AN
INJUNCTION AS IN PRECEDENT 1

1. Identify bundles [*each bundle should be numbered and have an index of the* **A5.021**
   *contents both on the front and on the inside of the front cover, so that it can be
   read when the bundle is open*], and affidavits before the court, giving the
   bundle reference to each affidavit and identifying any which have not been
   sworn but which have been approved by the intended deponent.
2. Explain who is who and annex *dramatis personae.*
3. Explain essence of case [*e.g. if the case is about fraudulent misrepresentation
   explain what representation was allegedly made by whom to whom, when and
   how, and the respects in which it was false and why it is said that the
   misrepresentation was made fraudulently*].
4. Refer to draft particulars of claim and explain which causes of action there are
   against each intended defendant [*e.g. if there is a proprietary claim the basis for
   it and its relevance to the application should be addressed. Has notice of
   rescission been served?*].
5. Set out any relevant provisions of a contract giving the terms of them in the **A5.022**
   body of the skeleton. Explain the applicant's case on them and the possible
   position(s) of the defendants in relation to them [*e.g. set out an entire
   agreement clause and explain what may be said by the defendants about it and
   why, in the claimant's submission, it does not bar the claim*].
6. Address possible defences of each defendant to the claims advanced against
   him. [*On a complicated application there should be a separate law bundle
   which contains copies of statutory materials and cases.*]
7. Chronology: there should be a chronology annexed to the skeleton which is
   cross-referenced to the bundles before the court.
8. When did claimant discover he had a claim, when was evidence available to
   make freezing application? Has there been unreasonable delay by applicant in
   making the application?
9. Risk of dissipation: the "solid evidence" relied upon should be identified and
   grounds for risk of dissipation given.
10. Give details as to why the applicant is proceeding on a without notice **A5.023**
    application.
11. Quantum of claims and how calculated: explain legal measure of damages or
    restitution, refer to any accountants' report.
12. Where are each of the defendants to be found?
13. What is known about the assets of each defendant?
14. Disclosure of material facts or matters: identify any particular facts or matters
    which need to be disclosed to the judge and where the detail about them can
    be found in the body of the affidavits giving references to pages in the
    bundles. [*Disclosure has to be undertaken by specifically drawing the judge's
    attention to particular matters, in the skeleton and/or the body of (as opposed
    to the exhibits to) the affidavits.*]
15. Permission to serve out of jurisdiction: explain who can be served without
    permission and in relation to each such person the ground(s) which enable
    service without permission [*e.g. a defendant is within the jurisdiction, or can
    be served under CPR r.6.19, listing the ground(s)*]. Comply with CPR 6.21 in
    relation to each defendant for whom permission is sought to serve the claim
    form and other documents outside of the jurisdiction. If there is a jurisdiction
    clause or arbitration agreement this should be set out in the skeleton and its
    effect addressed.
16. Identify draft order in the documents before the court and draw attention to **A5.024**
    each change from example freezing injunction. Explain calculation of max-
    imum sum.

17. Explain how it is intended to serve each defendant, when and where.
18. Are any applications intended to be made to foreign courts for freezing or other interim relief?
19. Privilege against self-incrimination: deal with this in relation to each defendant. How does the draft order address the possibility that the privilege may be claimed?
20. Claimant's assets and liabilities, dealing with whether the claimant is likely to be good for damages on the cross-undertaking or liabilities under the undertakings tendered by it to the court. If security is to be offered, explain quantum and precisely how it is to be given.

PRECEDENT 3: SPECIMEN LETTER OF GUARANTEE PROVIDING FORTIFICATION OF THE CLAIMANT'S CROSS-UNDERTAKING IN DAMAGES

A5.025   Barclays Private Bank
49, Grosvenor Street,
London W1
Tel 0207–487–2000

[*Date*]
Our reference: [HJM/1]

Aggregate Limit of Liability: [*insert limit*]
To: [*Names and addresses of defendants*]

WHEREAS

(1) an action ("the action") is being or has been commenced in the High Court of Justice, Queen's Bench Division, Commercial Court ("the Court") by [*name of claimant*] (hereinafter called "the claimant") against [*insert names of defendants*] (hereinafter called "the defendants") in respect of claims arising from [*insert brief description of claims*];

(2) a cross-undertaking ("the undertaking") as to damages is being given or has been given to the Court by the claimant in favour of the defendants in connection with the granting of an order against the defendants in the action;

(3) the claimant has requested us, Barclays Private Bank ("the Bank"), to give this letter of guarantee in support of the undertaking;

A5.026   NOW in consideration of the sum of £1.00 (one pound sterling, GBP) receipt of which is hereby acknowledged and other consideration:

1. Subject always to the terms set out below including the limit of liability, the Bank guarantees to the defendants and each of them payment of any order which may be made by the Court in the action against the claimant which requires payment of damages under the undertaking, or interest thereon or costs in connection with the enforcement of the undertaking as to damages given by the claimant to the court in the action.

2. The Bank's total liability under this letter of guarantee is not to exceed the sum of [*insert amount of limit*] in all. Upon payment by the Bank of an amount of, or amounts totalling [*insert limit*] under this guarantee, all liability of the Bank will cease, and the defendants must deliver up this letter of guarantee to the Bank.

3. Payment under this guarantee will be made on first demand in writing by the defendants or any of them in London at our counters at 49, Grosvenor

Street, London W1 in sterling, against presentation of an order of the Court in the action requiring payment of a quantified amount by the claimant and which is an order guaranteed by the Bank under this letter of guarantee.

4. Payment up to the aggregate limit of [insert limit] will be made by the Bank in respect of orders as and when presented, and the orders will rank for payment hereunder in order of receipt at the Bank's counters at 49, Grosvenor Street, London W1.

5. An order enforcement of which is stayed by the Court and an untaxed order **A5.027** for costs (whilst the costs remain untaxed and unagreed with the claimant) do not qualify for payment under this guarantee.

6. Payment will be made under this letter of guarantee of an order which has not been stayed even though an appeal is to be brought or has been brought against the order.

7. This guarantee is governed by English law and is subject to the exclusive jurisdiction of the High Court of Justice in London.

8. This letter of guarantee will remain in force for the period of one year from the date hereof and will be renewed by the Bank for a further period of one year on terms including this clause on written demand made prior to the expiry of the year by the defendants or any of them, except where the Court has made an order releasing the claimant from the undertaking. In the event of such an order being made this guarantee will cease with immediate effect.

Signed for and on behalf of Barclays Private Bank,

[H. J. Maizels]
Director

PRECEDENT 4: ADDITIONAL INJUNCTION TO PREVENT A DEFENDANT RECEIVING PAYMENT OF A DEBT EXCEPT INTO A DESIGNATED ACCOUNT WITHIN THE JURISDICTION

Collection of debts

1) The defendant must not receive payment of any amount due or becoming due to **A5.028** him from [set out name of debtor] except into a bank account in England and Wales, opened specially for the purpose of receiving payment, and which is not subject to any right of set-off by the bank. Before receiving any credit to the account the defendant must give the claimant's solicitors 48 hours' notice, with details of where the bank account has been opened, the name of the account holder and the number of the account.

2) If the total unencumbered value of the defendant's assets in England and Wales exceeds the [amount fixed by the court as the maximum sum] the defendant may receive payment of any amounts due or becoming due to him from anyone so long as after payment the unencumbered value of his assets in England and Wales still remains above the amount stated.

PRECEDENT 5: ADDITIONAL INJUNCTION TO PREVENT A DEFENDANT FROM CUTTING HIMSELF OUT FROM BENEFITING FROM A TRUST

Trusts

The Respondent must not make any arrangement or take any steps which may **A5.029** prevent him from benefiting from any trust.

Modify the wording of the order requiring disclosure of information (see para.9(1) of the example freezing injunction) by adding:

The Respondent must also inform the claimant in writing at once of any trust of which he is a beneficiary or in respect of which he or he in association with others can make the defendant a beneficiary, giving the names and addresses of the trustees, details of his relationship to the trust, and the value, location and details of the trust assets.

Precedent 6: Disclosure order for disclosure of information about assets worldwide

A5.030   Substitute the following for para.9(1) of the example freezing injunction provided by the Practice Direction supplementing CPR Pt 25:

Provision of information

(1) Unless paragraph (2) applies, the Respondent must inform the claimant in writing [by 4.30pm on [*insert date*] [by 4.30pm on the day after the date on which service of this order is effected upon him] of all his assets whether in or outside England and Wales and whether in his own name or not, and whether solely or jointly owned, giving information up to date at the time of giving the information about the value, location and details of all such assets, including in respect of any bank account, the name and address of the branch, the name of the account holder and the number of the account and the amount of the credit balance.

Note: for the time by which the information must be provided see CPR r.2.9 on the desirability of fixing a time and a date by which the information must be provided. The words "immediately" and "at once", which appears to mean "as soon as is reasonably practicable",[2] fail to comply with CPR r.2.9 and are normally too draconian, and fail to provide for a period within which to take legal advice, which ordinarily ought to be permitted before the respondent becomes in contempt of court.

Precedent 7: Wording for order to be sought by application notice seeking discharge or variation of Mareva injunction and disclosure order

A5.031   1. The order made on [*date*] by the Hon Mr Justice [*insert name*] be discharged on the grounds that:

(1) in all the circumstances of the case it is just and convenient that the order be discharged on the grounds that (*e.g. the claimant has not shown that there is a real risk of dissipation of assets based on solid evidence*);

(2) there was material non-disclosure and/or misrepresentation on the without notice application to the Hon Mr Justice [*insert name*] [*insert particulars of non-disclosure/misrepresentation, e.g. failure to disclose the defences available to the claim*].

---

[2] See Chapter 22, para.22.015; *Wallace Kevin James v Merrill Lynch International Bank Ltd* [1998] 1 S.L.R. 785 at para.31.

2. Alternatively to paragraph 1, the order made by the Hon. Mr Justice [*insert name*] be varied [*set out nature of variation sought, e.g. for increased living expenses, and ground on which it is sought*].
3. Alternatively to paragraph 1, the claimant do fortify the undertakings given by him to the court with security by bank guarantee or payment into court.
4. In the event of the said order being discharged the court do enforce the undertaking in damages in the exercise of its discretion, and do direct an inquiry on causation and amount of damage, or do assess the damages summarily and direct immediate payment by the claimant.
5. The claimant do pay the costs of this application.

PRECEDENT 8: PARTICULARS OF CLAIM IN AN INQUIRY AS TO DAMAGES

CASE No:

IN THE HIGH COURT OF JUSTICE   A5.032
QUEEN'S BENCH DIVISION
COMMERCIAL COURT

BETWEEN:

XYZ

Claimant in the Inquiry
(Defendant in the action)

-and-

ABC

Defendant in the Inquiry
(Claimant in the action)

Particulars of Claim in the Inquiry
as to Damages ordered by the Hon. Mr Justice ..... on .....

1. On [*insert date*] an Order was made by the Hon. Mr Justice [   ] which **A5.033**
included the granting of an injunction against the claimant in this inquiry.
2. These particulars of claim are served in the inquiry as to damages directed by
the Hon Mr Justice [   ] on [*insert date*] on the undertaking as to damages
given to the court by the defendant to this inquiry.
3. The Order prevented the claimant from [*e.g.* conducting his business ....
4. The claimant has suffered loss and damage by reason of the Order referred to
in paragraph 1 as set out below.

PARTICULARS

[*Set out particulars*]

5. Further or alternatively, the claimant seeks general damages for loss to his
business and damage to his reputation caused by the Order.
6. The claimant seeks interest under s.35A of the Supreme Court Act 1981.

AND the claimant in the inquiry seeks: **A5.034**

(1) assessment of the damages to be paid to the respondent to the inquiry;

(2) an award of interest thereon under s.35A of the Supreme Court Act 1981;

(3) costs.

Served [*etc.*]

PRECEDENT 9: SEARCH ORDER PERMITTING THE RESPONDENTS TO EXCLUDE FROM THE SEARCH ITEMS FOR WHICH THEY CLAIM PRIVILEGE, AND ORDERING A THIRD PARTY TO ALLOW ACCESS TO A PARTICULAR PROPERTY

A5.035   IN THE HIGH COURT OF JUSTICE
QUEEN'S BENCH DIVISION
COMMERCIAL COURT
Before the Hon. Mr Justice [   ] (hearing in private)

Claim No.
Dated

BETWEEN:

ABC Limited

Applicant/ Claimant

-and-

(1) X Limited
(2) Y & Co
(3) Z

Respondents/ Defendants

ORDER

PENAL NOTICE

IF YOU [   ] DISOBEY THIS ORDER YOU MAY BE HELD TO BE IN CONTEMPT OF COURT AND MAY BE IMPRISONED, FINED OR HAVE YOUR ASSETS SEIZED.

ANY OTHER PERSON WHO KNOWS OF THIS ORDER AND DOES ANYTHING WHICH HELPS OR PERMITS THE RESPONDENT TO BREACH THE TERMS OF THIS ORDER MAY ALSO BE HELD TO BE IN CONTEMPT OF COURT AND MAY BE IMPRISONED, FINED OR HAVE THEIR ASSETS SEIZED.

THIS ORDER

A5.036   1.   (1) This is a Search Order made against X Limited , Y & Co , and Z ("the Respondents") on [   ] by Mr Hon. Justice [   ] on the application of ABC Limited] ("the Applicant"). The Judge read the Affidavits listed in Schedule F and accepted the undertakings set out in Schedules C, D and E at the end of this order.

(2) This Order is also made against MNO Limited as a person having control over entry to the premises at [*insert address*] for the purpose of directing

MNO Limited to permit or secure that the search party shall have entry to those premises in accordance with the terms of this order for the purpose of acting pursuant to this order.

2. This order was made at a hearing without notice to the Respondents. The Respondent has a right to apply to the court to vary or discharge the order— see paragraph 27 below.

3. There will be a further hearing in respect of this order on [   ] ("the return date").

4. In this Order—
   (a) unless otherwise stated, references in this order to "the Respondent" mean all of them; and
   (b) this order is effective against any Respondent on whom it is served or who is given notice of it.

5. This order must be complied with by each Respondent and MNO Limited, who may comply with it either personally or through a representative, including—
   (a) In the case of X Limited and MNO Limited, any director, officer, or responsible employee of X Limited; and
   (b) In the case of Y & Co, any partner in the firm or responsible employee;
   (c) In the case of Z, any person having responsible control of the premises to be searched.

THE SEARCH

6. MNO Limited in the case only of the premises at [   ], and the **A5.037** Respondent in the case of all of the following premises and vehicles, must permit the following persons—
   (a) [   ] ("the Supervising Solicitor");
   (b) [   ], a solicitor in the firm of [   ], the Applicant's solicitors; and
   (c) up to [   ] other persons being [their identity or capacity] accompanying them,
   (together "the search party"), to enter the premises mentioned in Schedule A to this order and any other premises of the Respondent disclosed under paragraph 18 below and any vehicles under the Respondent's control on or around the premises ("the premises") so that they can search for, inspect, photograph or photocopy, and deliver into the safekeeping of the Applicant's solicitors all the documents and articles which are listed in Schedule B to this order ("the listed items").

7. Having permitted the search party to enter the premises, the Respondent and MNO Limited must allow the search party to remain on the premises until the search is complete. In the event that it becomes necessary for any of those persons to leave the premises before the search is complete, the Respondent must allow them to re-enter the premises immediately upon their seeking re-entry on the same or the following day in order to complete the search.

RESTRICTIONS ON SEARCH

8. This order may not be carried out at the same time as a police search warrant. **A5.038**

9. Before the Respondent or MNO Limited allows anybody onto the premises to carry out this order, he is entitled to have the Supervising Solicitor explain to him what it means in everyday language.

10. (1) If entry to the premises at [   ] is obtained through MNO Limited, then the search is not to begin until after the Supervising Solicitor is satisfied that reasonable attempts have been made to contact each of the Respondents.

   (2) The Respondent is entitled to seek legal advice and to ask the court to vary or discharge this order. Whilst doing so, he may ask the Supervising Solicitor to delay starting the search for up to two hours or such other longer period as the Supervising Solicitor may permit. However, the Respondent must—

   (a) comply with the terms of paragraph 27 below;

   (b) not disturb or remove any listed items, except for the purpose of making a claim to privilege as set out in paragraph 11 below; and

   (c) permit the Supervising Solicitor to enter, but not start to search.

11. Before permitting entry to the premises by any person other than the Supervising Solicitor, the Respondent may, for a short time (not to exceed two hours, unless the Supervising Solicitor agrees to a longer period), gather together any listed items which he believes may be [incriminating or otherwise] privileged, preserve them on the premises, and inform the Supervising Solicitor that he is claiming privilege for them.

   In respect of any documents or other items for which the Respondent claims privilege, they shall be excluded from the search, but, except with the prior written permission of the Supervising Solicitor or the applicant's solicitors, the Respondent is to preserve them intact on the premises pending the conclusion of the hearing which is intended to take place on the Return Date, including during any adjournment of that hearing.

12. If the Respondent wishes to take legal advice and act as permitted by paragraph 11, he must first inform the Supervising Solicitor and keep him informed of the steps being taken.

13. No item may be removed from the premises by the Applicant until a list of the items to be removed has been prepared, and a copy of the list has been supplied to the Respondent, and he has been given a reasonable opportunity to check the list.

14. The premises must not be searched, and items must not be removed from them, except in the presence of the Respondent.

15. If the Supervising Solicitor is satisfied that full compliance with paragraphs 13 or 14 is not practicable, he may permit the search to proceed and items to be removed without fully complying with them.

DELIVERY UP OF ARTICLES/DOCUMENTS

A5.039 16. Except as provided for in paragraph 11:

   (1) The Respondent must immediately hand over to the Applicant's solicitors any of the listed items, which are in his possession or under his control, save for any computer or hard disk integral to any computer.

   (2) Any items the subject of a dispute as to whether they are listed items must immediately be handed over to the Supervising Solicitor for safe keeping pending resolution of the dispute or further order of the court.

17. Except as provided for in paragraph 11, the Respondent must

   (1) immediately give the search party effective access to the computers on the premises, with all necessary passwords, to enable the computers to be searched. If they contain any listed items the Respondent must cause the listed items to be displayed so that they can be read and copied; and

   (2) provide the Applicant's Solicitors with copies of all listed items contained in the computers.

   All reasonable steps shall be taken by the Applicant and the Applicant's solicitors to ensure that no damage is done to any computer or data. The Applicant and his representatives may not themselves search the Respondent's computers unless they have sufficient expertise to do so without damaging the Respondent's system.

PROVISION OF INFORMATION

18. Except as provided for in paragraph 11, the Respondent must immediately **A5.040** inform the Applicant's Solicitors (in the presence of the Supervising Solicitor) so far as he is aware—
    (a) where all the listed items are;
    (b) the name and address of everyone who has supplied him, or offered to supply him, with listed items;
    (c) [the name and address of everyone to whom he has supplied, or offered to supply, listed items]; and
    (d) [full details of the dates and quantities of every such supply and offer].
19. Within [   ] working days after being served with this order the Respondent must swear and serve on the applicant's solicitors a copy of an affidavit setting out the above information, and, if a claim to privilege has been made the grounds upon which the privilege is claimed and in respect of what items or documents.

PROHIBITED ACTS

20. Except for the purpose of obtaining legal advice, or preparing for, or making **A5.041** arrangements in connection with, the hearing scheduled for the return date, the Respondent must not directly or indirectly inform anyone of these proceedings or of the contents of this order, or warn anyone that proceedings have been or may be brought against him by the Applicant until 4.30pm on the return date or further order of the court.
21. Until 4.30pm on the return date the Respondent must not destroy, tamper with, cancel or part with possession, power, custody or control of the listed items otherwise than in accordance with the terms of this order.
22. [*Insert any negative injunctions*]
23. [*Insert any further order*]

COSTS

24. The costs of this application are reserved to the judge hearing the application **A5.042** on the return date.

RESTRICTIONS ON SERVICE

25. This order may only be served between [   ]am/pm and [   ]am/pm [and **A5.043** on a weekday].
26. This order must be served by the Supervising Solicitor, and paragraph 6 of the order must be carried out in his presence and under his supervision.

VARIATION AND DISCHARGE OF THIS ORDER

27. Anyone served with or notified of this order may apply to the court at any **A5.044** time to vary or discharge this order (or so much of it as affects that person), but they must first inform the Applicant's solicitors. If any evidence is to be relied upon in support of the application, the substance of it must be communicated in writing to the Applicant's solicitors in advance.

INTERPRETATION OF THIS ORDER

A5.045 28. Any requirement that something shall be done to or in the presence of the Respondent means—
(a) if there is more than one Respondent, to or in the presence of any one of them; and
(b) if a Respondent is not an individual, to or in the presence of a director, officer, partner or responsible employee.

29. A Respondent who is an individual who is ordered not to do something must not do it himself or in any other way. He must not do it through others acting on his behalf or on his instructions or with his encouragement.

30. A Respondent which is not an individual which is ordered not to do something must not do it itself or by its directors, officers, partners, employees or agents or in any other way.

COMMUNICATIONS WITH THE COURT

A5.046 All communications to the court about this order should be sent to—

[*Insert the address and telephone number of the appropriate Court Office*]

If the order is made at the Royal Courts of Justice, communications should be addressed as follows—
Where the order is made in the Chancery Division
Room TM 505, Royal Courts of Justice, Strand, London WC2A 2LL quoting the case number. The telephone number is 0207 947 6754.
Where the order is made in the Queen's Bench Division
Room WG034, Royal Courts of Justice, Strand, London WC2A 2LL quoting the case number. The telephone number is 0207 947 6009.
Where the order is made in the Commercial Court
Room E201, Royal Courts of Justice, Strand, London WC2A 2LL quoting the case number. The telephone number is 0207 947 6826.
The offices are open between 10am and 4.30pm Monday to Friday.

SCHEDULE A

A5.047   The Premises

SCHEDULE B

A5.048   The Listed Items

SCHEDULE C

Undertakings Given to the Court by the Applicant

A5.049 (1) (a) If the court later finds that this order or carrying it out has caused loss to the Respondent or MNO Limited, and decides that the Respondent or MNO Limited should be compensated for that loss, the Applicant will comply with any order the court may make.

(b) If the carrying out of this order has been in breach of the terms of this order or otherwise in a manner inconsistent with the Applicant's solicitors' duties as officers of the court, the Applicant will comply with any order for damages the court may make.

(c) The Applicant will pay any costs or expenses incurred by MNO Limited in taking legal advice in connection with this Order or in relation to complying with this Order.

[(2) As soon as practicable the Applicant will issue a claim form [in the form of the draft produced to the court] [claiming the appropriate relief].]

(3) The Applicant will [swear and file an affidavit] [cause an affidavit to be sworn and filed] [substantially in the terms of the draft affidavit produced to the court] [confirming the substance of what was said to the court by the Applicant's counsel/solicitors].

(4) The Applicant will not, without the permission of the court, use any information or documents obtained as a result of carrying out this order nor inform anyone else of these proceedings except for the purposes of these proceedings (including adding further Respondents) or commencing civil proceedings in relation to the same or related subject-matter to these proceedings until after the return date.

[(5) The Applicant will maintain pending further order the sum of £ [   ] in an account controlled by the Applicant's solicitors.]

[(6) The Applicant will insure the items removed from the premises.]

SCHEDULE D

Undertakings Given by the Applicant's Solicitors

(1) The Applicant's solicitors will provide to the Supervising Solicitor for service **A5.050** on the Respondent—
   (i) a service copy of this order;
   (ii) the claim form (with defendant's response pack) or, if not issued, the draft produced to the court;
   (iii) an application for hearing on the return date;
   (iv) copies of the affidavits [*or draft affidavits*] and exhibits capable of being copied containing the evidence relied upon by the Applicant;
   (v) a note of any allegation of fact made orally to the court where such allegation is not contained in the affidavits or draft affidavits read by the judge; and
   (vi) a copy of the Applicant's skeleton argument.

(2) The Applicant's solicitors will answer at once to the best of their ability any question whether a particular item is a listed item.

(3) Subject as provided below the Applicant's solicitors will retain in their own safe keeping all items obtained as a result of this order until the court directs otherwise.

(4) The Applicant's solicitors will return the originals of all documents obtained as a result of this order (except original documents which belong to the Applicant) as soon as possible and in any event within [two] working days of their removal.

SCHEDULE E

Undertakings Given by the Supervising Solicitor

(1) The Supervising Solicitor will use his best endeavours to serve this order upon **A5.051** the Respondent and at the same time to serve upon the Respondent the other documents required to be served and referred to in paragraph (1) of Schedule D.

(2) The Supervising Solicitor will offer to explain to the person served with the order its meaning and effect fairly and in everyday language, and to inform him of his right to take legal advice (such advice to include an explanation

that the Respondent may be entitled to avail himself of [the privilege against self-incrimination or] [legal professional privilege]) and to apply to vary or discharge this order as mentioned in paragraph 27 above.

(3) The Supervising Solicitor will retain in the safe keeping of his firm all items retained by him as a result of this order until the court directs otherwise.

(4) Within [48] hours of completion of the search the Supervising Solicitor will make and provide to the Applicant's solicitors, the Respondent or his solicitors and to the judge who made this order (for the purposes of the court file) a written report on the carrying out of the order.

SCHEDULE F

AFFIDAVITS

A5.052 The Applicant relied on the following affidavits—

[Name]	[Number of affidavit]	[Date sworn]	[Filed on behalf of]
(1)			
(2)			

NAME AND ADDRESS OF APPLICANT'S SOLICITORS

A5.053 The Applicant's solicitors are—
[Name, address, reference, fax and telephone numbers both in and out of office hours]

Index